McDougal Littell

CLASSZONE

Visit **classzone.com** and get connected.

ClassZone resources provide instruction, practice and learning support for students and parents.

Literature and Reading Center

- Selection-specific content includes vocabulary practice, research links, and extension activities for writing and critical thinking

- Author Online provides information about each author, as well as in-depth author studies on selected writers

- English Learner support for a variety of languages includes audio summaries of selections and a Multi-Language Academic Glossary

Vocabulary Center

- Vocabulary practice and games reinforce skills

Writing and Grammar Center

- Quick-Fix Editing Machine provides grammar help in a student-friendly format

- Writing Templates and graphic organizers promote clear, orderly communication

Media Center

- Media Analysis Guides encourage critical thinking skills

- Project Ideas, Storyboards, and Production Templates inspire creative media projects

Access the online version of your textbook at **classzone.com**

Your complete text is available for immediate use!

McDougal Littell
Where Great Lessons Begin

OHIO

McDougal Littell
LITERATURE

ACKNOWLEDGMENTS

INTRODUCTORY UNIT

Naomi Shihab Nye: "Making a Fist," from *Hugging the Jukebox* by Naomi Shihab Nye. Copyright © 1982 by Naomi Shihab Nye. Reprinted by permission of the author.

International Creative Management: Excerpt from "Twelve Angry Men," from *Six Television Plays* by Reginald Rose. Published by Simon & Schuster, Inc. Copyright © 1956 by Reginald Rose. Reprinted by permission of International Creative Management, Inc.

Scribner: Excerpt from *Kaffir Boy* by Mark Mathabane. Copyright © 1986 by Mark Mathabane. Reprinted with the permission of Scribner, an imprint of Simon & Schuster Adult Publishing Group.

Scholastic: From "South Africa's Decade of Freedom" by Michael Wines. Published in *The New York Times Upfront,* September 6, 2004. Copyright © 2004 by Scholastic Inc. and the New York Times Company. Reprinted by permission of Scholastic Inc.

HarperCollins Publishers: Excerpt from "Where Is Here?," from *Where Is Here?: Stories* by Joyce Carol Oates. Copyright © 1992 by The Ontario Review, Inc. All rights reserved. Reprinted by permission of HarperCollins Publishers.

Continued on page R155

ART CREDITS

COVER, TITLE PAGE

Detail of *Steppingstones from the Imperial Carriage Stop to the Gepparo (Moon-Wave Pavilion)* (1954), Yasuhiro Ishimoto. Katsura Villa. Photograph © Yasuhiro Ishimoto.

Continued on page R161

ISBN 13: 978-0-618-94486-6   ISBN 10: 0-618-94486-9

Printed in the United States of America.

2 3 4 5 6   0914   13 12 11 10 09

OHIO

McDougal Littell
LITERATURE

Janet Allen

Arthur N. Applebee

Jim Burke

Douglas Carnine

Yvette Jackson

Robert T. Jiménez

Judith A. Langer

Robert J. Marzano

Donna M. Ogle

Carol Booth Olson

Carol Ann Tomlinson

Mary Lou McCloskey

Lydia Stack

Sunset, Cleveland, Ohio © Jeremy Woodhouse/Getty Images

McDougal Littell

EVANSTON, ILLINOIS • BOSTON • DALLAS

SENIOR PROGRAM CONSULTANTS

 **JANET ALLEN** Reading and Literacy Specialist; creator of the popular "It's Never Too Late"/"Reading for Life" Institutes. Dr. Allen is an internationally known consultant who specializes in literacy work with at-risk students. Her publications include *Tools for Content Literacy; It's Never Too Late: Leading Adolescents to Lifelong Learning; Yellow Brick Roads: Shared and Guided Paths to Independent Reading; Words, Words, Words: Teaching Vocabulary in Grades 4–12;* and *Testing 1, 2, 3 . . . Bridging Best Practice and High-Stakes Assessments.* Dr. Allen was a high school reading and English teacher for more than 20 years and has taught courses in both subjects at the University of Central Florida. She directed the Central Florida Writing Project and received the Milken Foundation National Educator Award.

 **ARTHUR N. APPLEBEE** Leading Professor, School of Education at the University at Albany, State University of New York; Director of the Center on English Learning and Achievement. During his varied career, Dr. Applebee has been both a researcher and a teacher, working in institutional settings with children with severe learning problems, in public schools, as a staff member of the National Council of Teachers of English, and in professional education. Among his many books are *Curriculum as Conversation: Transforming Traditions of Teaching and Learning; Literature in the Secondary School: Studies of Curriculum and Instruction in the United States;* and *Tradition and Reform in the Teaching of English: A History.* He was elected to the International Reading Hall of Fame and has received, among other honors, the David H. Russell Award for Distinguished Research in the Teaching of English.

 **JIM BURKE** Lecturer and Author; Teacher of English at Burlingame High School, Burlingame, California. Mr. Burke is a popular presenter at educational conferences across the country and is the author of numerous books for teachers, including *School Smarts: The Four Cs of Academic Success; The English Teacher's Companion; Reading Reminders; Writing Reminders;* and *ACCESSing School: Teaching Struggling Readers to Achieve Academic and Personal Success.* He is the recipient of NCTE's Exemplary English Leadership Award and was inducted into the California Reading Association's Hall of Fame.

 **DOUGLAS CARNINE** Professor of Education at the University of Oregon; Director of the Western Region Reading First Technical Assistance Center. Dr. Carnine is nationally known for his focus on research-based practices in education, especially curriculum designs that prepare instructors of K-12 students. He has received the Lifetime Achievement Award from the Council for Exceptional Children and the Ersted Award for outstanding teaching at the University of Oregon. Dr. Carnine frequently consults on educational policy with government groups, businesses, communities, and teacher unions.

 YVETTE JACKSON Executive Director of the National Urban Alliance for Effective Education. Nationally recognized for her work in assessing the learning potential of underachieving urban students, Dr. Jackson is also a presenter for the Harvard Principal Center and is a member of the Differentiation Faculty of the Association for Supervision and Curriculum Development. Dr. Jackson's research focuses on literacy, gifted education, and cognitive mediation theory. She designed the Comprehensive Education Plan for the New York City Public Schools and has served as their Director of Gifted Programs and Executive Director of Instruction and Professional Development.

 **ROBERT T. JIMÉNEZ** Professor of Language, Literacy, and Culture at Vanderbilt University. Dr. Jiménez's research focuses on the language and literacy practices of Latino students. A former bilingual education teacher, he is now conducting research on how written language is thought about and used in contemporary Mexico. Dr. Jiménez has received several research and teaching honors, including two Fulbright awards from the Council for the International Exchange of Scholars and the Albert J. Harris Award from the International Reading Association. His published work has appeared in the *American Educational Research Journal, Reading Research Quarterly, The Reading Teacher, Journal of Adolescent and Adult Literacy,* and *Lectura y Vida.*

JUDITH A. LANGER Distinguished Professor at the University at Albany, State University of New York; Director of the Center on English Learning and Achievement; Director of the Albany Institute for Research in Education. An internationally known scholar in English language arts education, Dr. Langer specializes in developing teaching approaches that can enrich and improve what gets done on a daily basis in classrooms. Her publications include *Getting to Excellent: How to Create Better Schools* and *Effective Literacy Instruction: Building Successful Reading and Writing Programs*. She was inducted into the International Reading Hall of Fame and has received many other notable awards, including an honorary doctorate from the University of Uppsala, Sweden, for her research on literacy education.

ROBERT J. MARZANO Senior Scholar at Mid-Continent Research for Education and Learning (McREL); Associate Professor at Cardinal Stritch University in Milwaukee, Wisconsin; President of Marzano & Associates. An internationally known researcher, trainer, and speaker, Dr. Marzano has developed programs that translate research and theory into practical tools for K-12 teachers and administrators. He has written extensively on such topics as reading and writing instruction, thinking skills, school effectiveness, assessment, and standards implementation. His books include *Building Background Knowledge for Academic Achievement; Classroom Management That Works: Research-Based Strategies for Every Teacher;* and *What Works in Schools: Translating Research Into Action*.

DONNA M. OGLE Professor of Reading and Language at National-Louis University in Chicago, Illinois; Past President of the International Reading Association. Creator of the well-known KWL strategy, Dr. Ogle has directed many staff development projects translating theory and research into school practice in middle and secondary schools throughout the United States and has served as a consultant on literacy projects worldwide. Her extensive international experience includes coordinating the Reading and Writing for Critical Thinking Project in Eastern Europe, developing integrated curriculum for a USAID Afghan Education Project, and speaking and consulting on projects in several Latin American countries and in Asia. Her books include *Coming Together as Readers; Reading Comprehension: Strategies for Independent Learners; All Children Read;* and *Literacy for a Democratic Society*.

CAROL BOOTH OLSON Senior Lecturer in the Department of Education at the University of California, Irvine; Director of the UCI site of the National Writing Project. Dr. Olson writes and lectures extensively on the reading/writing connection, critical thinking through writing, interactive strategies for teaching writing, and the use of multicultural literature with students of culturally diverse backgrounds. She has received many awards, including the California Association of Teachers of English Award of Merit, the Outstanding California Education Research Award, and the UC Irvine Excellence in Teaching Award. Dr. Olson's books include *Reading, Thinking, and Writing About Multicultural Literature* and *The Reading/Writing Connection: Strategies for Teaching and Learning in the Secondary Classroom*.

CAROL ANN TOMLINSON Professor of Educational Research, Foundations, and Policy at the University of Virginia; Co-Director of the University's Institutes on Academic Diversity. An internationally known expert on differentiated instruction, Dr. Tomlinson helps teachers and administrators develop effective methods of teaching academically diverse learners. She was a teacher of middle and high school English for 22 years prior to teaching at the University of Virginia. Her books on differentiated instruction have been translated into eight languages. Among her many publications are *How to Differentiate Instruction in Mixed-Ability Classrooms* and *The Differentiated Classroom: Responding to the Needs of All Learners*.

ENGLISH LEARNER SPECIALISTS

MARY LOU McCLOSKEY Past President of Teachers of English to Speakers of Other Languages (TESOL); Director of Teacher Development and Curriculum Design for Educo in Atlanta, Georgia. Dr. McCloskey is a former teacher in multilingual and multicultural classrooms. She has worked with teachers, teacher educators, and departments of education around the world on teaching English as a second and foreign language. She is author of *On Our Way to English, Voices in Literature, Integrating English,* and *Visions: Language, Literature, Content.* Her awards include the Le Moyne College Ignatian Award for Professional Achievement and the TESOL D. Scott Enright Service Award.

LYDIA STACK International ESL consultant. Her areas of expertise are English language teaching strategies, ESL standards for students and teachers, and curriculum writing. Her teaching experience includes 25 years as an elementary and high school ESL teacher. She is a past president of TESOL. Her awards include the James E. Alatis Award for Service to TESOL (2003) and the San Francisco STAR Teacher Award (1989). Her publications include *On Our Way to English; Wordways: Games for Language Learning;* and *Visions: Language, Literature, Content.*

CURRICULUM SPECIALIST

WILLIAM L. McBRIDE Curriculum Specialist. Dr. McBride is a nationally known speaker, educator, and author who now trains teachers in instructional methodologies. A former reading specialist, English teacher, and social studies teacher, he holds a Masters in Reading and a Ph.D. in Curriculum and Instruction from the University of North Carolina at Chapel Hill. Dr. McBride has contributed to the development of textbook series in language arts, social studies, science, and vocabulary. He is also known for his novel *Entertaining an Elephant,* which tells the story of a burned-out teacher who becomes re-inspired with both his profession and his life.

MEDIA SPECIALISTS

DAVID M. CONSIDINE Professor of Instructional Technology and Media Studies at Appalachian State University in North Carolina. Dr. Considine has served as a media literacy consultant to the U.S. government and to the media industry, including Discovery Communications and Cable in the Classroom. He has also conducted media literacy workshops and training for county and state health departments across the United States. Among his many publications are *Visual Messages: Integrating Imagery into Instruction,* and *Imagine That: Developing Critical Viewing and Thinking Through Children's Literature.*

LARKIN PAULUZZI Teacher and Media Specialist; trainer for the New Jersey Writing Project. Ms. Pauluzzi puts her extensive classroom experience to use in developing teacher-friendly curriculum materials and workshops in many different areas, including media literacy. She has led media literacy training workshops in several districts throughout Texas, guiding teachers in the meaningful and practical uses of media in the classroom. Ms. Pauluzzi has taught students at all levels, from Title I Reading to AP English IV. She also spearheads a technology club at her school, working with students to produce media and technology to serve both the school and the community.

LISA K. SCHEFFLER Teacher and Media Specialist. Ms. Scheffler has designed and taught media literacy and video production curriculum, in addition to teaching language arts and speech. Using her knowledge of mass communication theory, coupled with real classroom experience, she has developed ready-to-use materials that help teachers incorporate media literacy into their curricula. She has taught film and television studies at the University of North Texas and has served as a contributing writer for the Texas Education Agency's statewide viewing and representing curriculum.

OHIO HIGH SCHOOL LITERATURE TEXTBOOK REVIEWERS

Phyllis Allen
Colonial White High School
Dayton, OH

Dorothy Batson
Toledo Public Schools
Toledo, OH

Angela M. Brill
Mt. Healthy High School
Cincinnati, OH

Sylvia Bower
Hilliard Darby High School
Hilliard, OH

Christine Galvin
Bellafontaine City Schools
Bellafontaine, OH

Michelle M. Lytle
Olentangy Liberty High School
Powell, OH

Cindy G. O'Janpa
West Geauga High School
Chesterland, OH

Linda Spisak
Heights High School
Cleveland Heights, OH

Meg Uhims
Piqua High School
Piqua, OH

NATIONAL TEACHER ADVISORS

These are some of the many educators from across the country who played a crucial role in the development of the tables of contents, the lesson design, and other key components of this program:

Virginia L. Alford
MacArthur High School
San Antonio, Texas

Yvonne L. Allen
Shaker Heights High School
Shaker Heights, Ohio

Dave T. Anderson
Hinsdale South High School
Darien, Illinois

Kacy Colleen Anglim
Portland Public Schools District
Portland, Oregon

Beverly Scott Bass
Arlington Heights High School
Fort Worth, Texas

Jordana Benone
North High School
Torrance, California

Patricia Blood
Howell High School
Farmingdale, New Jersey

Marjorie Bloom
Eau Gallie High School
Melbourne, Florida

Edward J. Blotzer
Wilkinsburg Junior/Senior
High School
Wilkinsburg, Pennsylvania

Stephen D. Bournes
Evanston Township High School
Evanston, Illinois

Barbara M. Bowling
Mt. Tabor High School
Winston-Salem, North Carolina

Kiala Boykin-Givehand
Duval County Public Schools
Jacksonville, Florida

Laura L. Brown
Adlai Stevenson High School
Lincolnshire, Illinois

Cynthia Burke
Yavneh Academy
Dallas, Texas

Hoppy Chandler
San Diego City Schools
San Diego, California

Gary Chmielewski
St. Benedict High School
Chicago, Illinois

Delorse Cole-Stewart
Milwaukee Public Schools
Milwaukee, Wisconsin

L. Calvin Dillon
Gaither High School
Tampa, Florida

Dori Dolata
Rufus King High School
Milwaukee, Wisconsin

Jon Epstein
Marietta High School
Marietta, Georgia

Helen Ervin
Fort Bend Independent
School District
Sugarland, Texas

Sue Friedman
Buffalo Grove High School
Buffalo Grove, Illinois

Chris Gee
Bel Air High School
El Paso, Texas

Paula Grasel
The Horizon Center
Gainesville, Georgia

Christopher Guarraia
Centreville High School
Clifton, Virginia

Rochelle L. Greene-Brady
Kenwood Academy
Chicago, Illinois

Michele M. Hettinger
Niles West High School
Skokie, Illinois

Elizabeth Holcomb
Forest Hill High School
Jackson, Mississippi

Jim Horan
Hinsdale Central High School
Hinsdale, Illinois

James Paul Hunter
Oak Park-River Forest
High School
Oak Park, Illinois

Susan P. Kelly
Director of Curriculum
Island Trees School District
Levittown, New York

Beverley A. Lanier
Varina High School
Richmond, Virginia

Pat Laws
Charlotte-Mecklenburg Schools
Charlotte, North Carolina

Diana R. Martinez
Treviño School of
Communications & Fine Arts
Laredo, Texas

Natalie Martinez
Stephen F. Austin High School
Houston, Texas

Elizabeth Matarazzo
Ysleta High School
El Paso, Texas

Carol M. McDonald
J. Frank Dobie High School
Houston, Texas

Amy Millikan
Consultant
Chicago, Illinois

Terri Morgan
Caprock High School
Amarillo, Texas

Eileen Murphy
Walter Payton Preparatory
High School
Chicago, Illinois

Lisa Omark
New Haven Public Schools
New Haven, Connecticut

Kaine Osburn
Wheeling High School
Wheeling, Illinois

Andrea J. Phillips
Terry Sanford High School
Fayetteville, North Carolina

Cathy Reilly
Sayreville Public Schools
Sayreville, New Jersey

Mark D. Simon
Neuqua Valley High School
Naperville, Illinois

Scott Snow
Sequin High School
Arlington, Texas

Jane W. Speidel
Brevard County Schools
Viera, Florida

Cheryl E. Sullivan
Lisle Community
School District
Lisle, Illinois

Anita Usmiani
Hamilton Township
Public Schools
Hamilton Square, New Jersey

Linda Valdez
Oxnard Union High
School District
Oxnard, California

Nancy Walker
Longview High School
Longview, Texas

Kurt Weiler
New Trier High School
Winnetka, Illinois

Elizabeth Whittaker
Larkin High School
Elgin, Illinois

Linda S. Williams
Woodlawn High School
Baltimore, Maryland

John R. Williamson
Fort Thomas
Independent Schools
Fort Thomas, Kentucky

Anna N. Winters
Simeon High School
Chicago, Illinois

Tonora D. Wyckoff
North Shore Senior High School
Houston, Texas

Karen Zajac
Glenbard South High School
Glen Ellyn, Illinois

Cynthia Zimmerman
Mose Vines Preparatory
High School
Chicago, Illinois

Lynda Zimmerman
El Camino High School
South San Francisco, California

Ruth E. Zurich
Brown Deer High School
Brown Deer, Wisconsin

OHIO

OVERVIEW
Ohio Student's Edition

LESSONS WITH EMBEDDED STANDARDS INSTRUCTION

 Look for the Ohio symbol throughout the book. It highlights grade-level indicators to help you succeed on your test.

OHIO CONTENTS

Sunset, Cleveland, Ohio © Jeremy Woodhouse/Getty Images

OHIO CONTENTS IN BRIEF

Online LITERATURE
CLASSZONE.COM

LITERATURE AND READING CENTER
• Author Biographies
• Additional Selection Background
• Literary Analysis Frames
• Power Thinking Activities

WRITING AND GRAMMAR CENTER
• Writing Templates and Graphic Organizers
• Publishing Options
• Quick-Fix Editing Machine

VOCABULARY CENTER
• Vocabulary Strategies and Practice
• Multi-Language Academic Vocabulary Glossary
• Vocabulary Flash Cards

MEDIA CENTER
• Production Templates
• Analysis Guides

RESEARCH CENTER
• Web Research Guide
• Citation Guide

 ASSESSMENT CENTER
• OGT Practice and Test-Taking Tips
• SAT/ACT Practice and Tips

MORE TECHNOLOGY

eEdition
• Interactive Selections
• Audio Summaries

WriteSmart
• Writing Prompts and Templates
• Interactive Student Models
• Interactive Graphic Organizers
• Interactive Revision Lessons
• Rubric Generator

MediaSmart DVD
• Media Lessons
• Interactive Media Studies

The World of a Story
PLOT, SETTING, AND MOOD

• IN FICTION • IN NONFICTION • IN MEDIA • IN POETRY

VOCABULARY STRATEGIES

Greek roots: *syn, p. 42*

Latin prefixes: *re-, p. 58*

Latin prefixes: *dis-, p. 72*

Connotation and denotation, *p. 93*

Specialized vocabulary, *p. 128*

Word Portraits
CHARACTER DEVELOPMENT

- IN FICTION • IN NONFICTION • IN POETRY • IN DRAMA • IN MEDIA

OHIO STANDARDS

Character Traits, Round and Flat Characters, Character Motivation, Static and Dynamic Characters

Character Traits, Connect

Character Motivation, Make Inferences

Character and Plot, Predict

Characterization in Nonfiction, Author's Purpose

VOCABULARY STRATEGIES

Connotation and denotation, *p. 200*   Latin roots: *contra, p. 258*
Latin roots: *sol, p. 220*

UNIT **3**

OHIO

A Writer's Choice
NARRATIVE DEVICES

- IN FICTION • IN NONFICTION

VOCABULARY STRATEGIES

Latin roots: *man, p. 315*   Latin roots: *plac, p. 358*
Latin roots: *sen, p. 350*

4

OHIO

Message and Meaning
THEME

• IN FICTION • IN POETRY • IN NONFICTION • ACROSS GENRES

OHIO STANDARDS

VOCABULARY STRATEGIES

Connotation, *p. 404*   Prefixes: *im-, p. 440*
Analogies, *p. 418*

UNIT 5
OHIO

Why Write?
AUTHOR'S PURPOSE

• IN NONFICTION • IN MEDIA • IN FICTION • IN POETRY

OHIO STANDARDS

Author's Purpose and Perspective, Text Features, Patterns of Organization

Tone and Diction, Recognize Classification

Author's Purpose, Analyze Cause and Effect

Interpret Graphic Aids

Narrative Nonfiction, Take Notes

Credibility in News Reports

VOCABULARY STRATEGIES
Metaphors and similes, *p. 502*   Latin roots: *fort, p. 541*
Analogies, *p. 522*

Making a Case
ARGUMENT AND PERSUASION

● IN NONFICTION ● IN FICTION ● ACROSS GENRES ● IN MEDIA

OHIO STANDARDS

Analysis of an Argument, Persuasive Techniques, Rhetorical Devices

Argument, Distinguish Fact from Opinion

Evidence, Analyze Deductive Reasoning

Rhetorical Devices, Analyze Inductive Reasoning

Persuasive Techniques, Summarize

Counterarguments, Monitor

> **VOCABULARY STRATEGIES**
>
> Etymology, *p. 584*   Connotation, *p. 626*
> Specialized vocabulary, *p. 601*   Using a thesaurus, *p. 642*
> Analogies, *p. 616*   Similes and metaphors, *p.664*

UNIT 7
OHIO

Sound and Sense
THE LANGUAGE OF POETRY

OHIO
STANDARDS

Form, Poetic Elements, Sound Devices, Imagery, Figurative Language

Sound Devices, Reading Poetry

Lyric Poetry, Figurative Language

Free Verse, Imagery

UNIT 8
OHIO

Signatures
AUTHOR'S STYLE AND VOICE

- IN 19TH-CENTURY WRITING • IN 20TH-CENTURY WRITING

VOCABULARY STRATEGIES

Metaphors and similes, *p. 790*   Etymology, *p. 823*

UNIT 9 OHIO

Product of the Times
HISTORY, CULTURE, AND THE AUTHOR

● IN NONFICTION ● IN FICTION ● IN POETRY ● IN MEDIA

OHIO STANDARDS

Writer's Background, Historical and Cultural Influences

VOCABULARY STRATEGIES

Connotation and denotation, *p. 862*
Prefixes: *in-, p. 878*
Suffixes: *-ion, p. 891*

Greek roots: *cosm, p. 905*
Using a dictionary, *p. 928*

UNIT 10
OHIO

Upholding Honor
GREEK TRAGEDY AND MEDIEVAL ROMANCE
• IN DRAMA • IN FICTION • ACROSS GENRES

VOCABULARY STRATEGIES

Etymology, *p. 1008*   Connotation, *p. 1042*
Analogies, *p. 1029*   Metaphors and similes, *p. 1062*

UNIT 11 OHIO

Shakespearean Drama
THE TRAGEDY OF JULIUS CAESAR
● IN DRAMA ● IN MEDIA

OHIO STANDARDS

Characteristics of Shakespearean Tragedy, The Language of Shakespeare

Tragedy, Tragic Hero, Soliloquy, Aside, Blank Verse, Dramatic Irony, Rhetorical Devices, Reading Shakespearean Drama

Analyze a Theater Review

Investigation and Discovery
THE POWER OF RESEARCH

OHIO STANDARDS

Use Reference Materials and Technology, Evaluate Sources

Research, Synthesis

Student Resource Bank

Selections by Genre

Features

 LITERATURE CENTER at ClassZone.com

MEDIA CENTER at ClassZone.com

 WriteSmart

 MediaSmart DVD

VOCABULARY STRATEGIES

pages 42, 58, 72, 93, 128, 200, 220, 258, 315, 350, 358, 404, 418, 440, 502, 522, 541, 584, 601, 616, 626, 642, 664, 790, 823, 862, 878, 891, 905, 928, 1008, 1029, 1042, 1062

GRAMMAR AND STYLE

pages 43, 59, 73, 110, 129, 184, 201, 221, 259, 303, 351, 359, 405, 419, 441, 503, 523, 585, 602, 617, 627, 643, 703, 711, 791, 807, 863, 879, 906, 929, 1009, 1043, 1185

OHIO

STUDENT GUIDE TO OGT SUCCESS

OGT SUCCESS

Sunset, Cleveland, Ohio © Jeremy Woodhouse/Getty Images

Understanding the Ohio Academic Content Standards

What are the Ohio Academic Content Standards?

The Ohio Academic Content Standards outline what you should know and be able to do at each grade level. They will aid you in taking tests like the Ohio Graduation Tests (OGT) in Reading and Writing and will also help prepare you for everyday life and the workplace. Your teacher uses the standards to create a course of instruction that will help you develop the skills and knowledge you are expected to have by the end of grade 10.

How will I learn the Ohio Academic Content Standards?

Your textbook is closely aligned to the Ohio Academic Content Standards for English language arts, so that every time you learn new information or practice a skill, you are mastering one of the standards. Each unit, each selection, and each workshop in your textbook connects to a standard, which is listed on the opening page of the section.

For a complete listing of Ohio Academic Content Standards, see page S1.

Ohio's Academic Content Standards in English language arts are made up of nine standards:

1. Acquisition of Vocabulary
2. Reading Process: Concepts of Print, Comprehension Strategies and Self-Monitoring Strategies
3. Reading Applications: Informational, Technical and Persuasive Text
4. Reading Applications: Literary Text
5. Writing Processes
6. Writing Applications
7. Writing Conventions
8. Research
9. Communication: Oral and Visual

These nine standards are divided into grade-level indicators. These indicators describe what you must learn to master each standard. Ohio uses a special code to identify the standard and grade-level indicator.

OHIO STANDARD DECODER

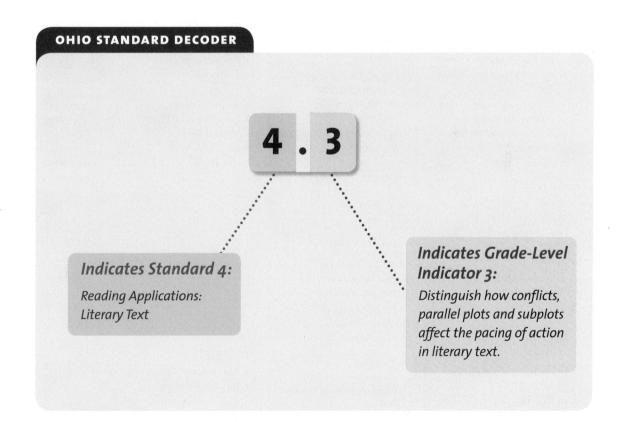

4 . 3

Indicates Standard 4:
Reading Applications: Literary Text

Indicates Grade-Level Indicator 3:
Distinguish how conflicts, parallel plots and subplots affect the pacing of action in literary text.

Embedded Assessment Practice

Each unit has a formatted practice test that covers specific standards-based skills.

Preparing for the OGT

What is the OGT?

OGT stands for Ohio Graduation Tests. All students finishing grade 10 will take the OGT in Reading and Writing. The OGT measure your understanding of the Ohio Academic Content Standards for English language arts. The tests consist of multiple-choice, short-answer, and extended-response items, as well as a writing prompt.

How can I be successful on the OGT?

You can use the passages and questions on the following pages to prepare for the OGT. This section will familiarize you with the format of the test items. The tips and strategies in blue will guide you as you read the passages and answer the questions.

- Read the passages carefully, as well as the tips in the margins. The tips help you focus on important ideas and details in the reading so that you will be better prepared to answer the questions that follow.

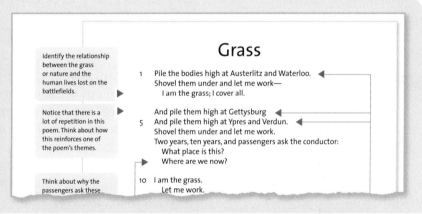

- Each item tests a particular grade-level indicator. There are also strategies for answering the types of questions you will encounter on the OGT.

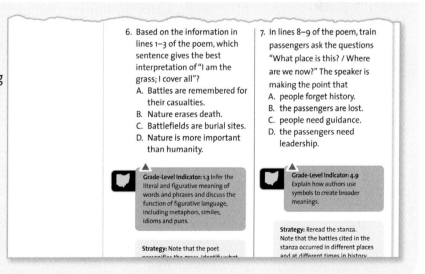

OGT Strategies and Preparation

The following section introduces you to the Ohio Graduation Tests (OGT) and the kinds of questions you may encounter within them. Look for tips and strategies in blue boxes throughout this section.

READING TEST

Directions: Read each passage then answer the questions that follow. You may refer to the passages as often as necessary.

Excerpt from *Narrative of the Life of Frederick Douglass, An American Slave*

Authors provide readers with context clues, such as synonyms or antonyms, to help them define unfamiliar words. What does *chattel* mean in this sentence? Look for context clues to help you figure out its meaning.

As you read through this excerpt, identify how slavery injures the mistress. Note the transformations that occur in her character after the author comes to live with her.

1 My mistress was, as I have said, a kind and tender-hearted woman; and in the simplicity of her soul she commenced, when I first went to live with her, to treat me as she supposed one human being ought to treat another. In entering upon the duties of a slaveholder, she did not seem to perceive that I sustained to her the relation of a mere chattel, and that for her to treat me as a human being was not only wrong, but dangerously so. Slavery proved as injurious to her as it did to me. When I went there, she was a pious, warm, and tender-hearted woman. There was no sorrow or suffering for which she had not a tear. She had bread for the hungry, clothes for the naked, and comfort for every mourner that came within her reach. Slavery soon proved its ability to divest her of these heavenly qualities. Under its influence, the tender heart became stone, and the lamb-like disposition gave way to one of tiger-like fierceness. The first step in her downward course was her ceasing to instruct me. She now commenced to practice her husband's precepts. She finally became more violent in her opposition than her husband himself. She was not satisfied with simply doing as well as he had commanded; she seemed anxious to do better. Nothing seemed to make her more angry than to see me with a newspaper. She seemed to think that here lay the danger. I have had her rush at me with a face made up all of fury, and snatch from me a newspaper, in a manner that fully revealed her apprehension. She was an apt woman; and a little experience soon demonstrated, to her satisfaction, that education and slavery were incompatible with each other.

Reading means something more to the author than the ability to decipher words on a page. In teaching the author to read, what has his mistress really given him? What is the author stepping toward?

2   From this time I was most narrowly watched. If I was in a separate room any considerable length of time, I was sure to be suspected of having a book, and was at once called to give an account of myself. All this, however, was too late. The first step had been taken. Mistress, in teaching me the alphabet, had given me the "inch," and no precaution could prevent me from taking the "ell."

The expression "be given an inch, take an ell" means that once someone gets a small amount of something, he or she will demand more. Where would you look if you wanted to find out where this expression comes from?

1. The author uses the metaphor "the tender heart became stone" in order to describe the

    A. change in the mistress's disposition.
    B. physical expense of slavery.
    C. appearance of the husband.
    D. simplicity of learning to read.

Grade-Level Indicator: 1.3 Infer the literal and figurative meaning of words and phrases and discuss the function of figurative language, including metaphors, similes, idioms and puns.

Strategy: Reread the sentence in the passage that contains the metaphor. Identify that the author is describing how slavery changed his mistress. *A* is a good answer choice because the word *disposition* appears in the original sentence. Slavery demands an emotional cost from the mistress but not a physical one, so you can eliminate *B*. The metaphor does not describe the husband or the act of reading, so you can also eliminate *C* and *D*; therefore, *A* is the best answer choice.

2. Which word means the same as <u>chattel</u> does in this sentence from paragraph 1: "... that I sustained to her the relation of a mere <u>chattel</u> ..."?
   A. spirit
   B. property
   C. human
   D. person

Grade-Level Indicator: 1.1 Define unknown words through context clues and the author's use of comparison, contrast and cause and effect.

Strategy: Reread the sentence that contains the word *chattel* and look for context clues. The author says that his mistress did not perceive him as chattel and that she treated him as a human being. *Chattel* must have an opposite meaning than *human being*. "Spirit," "human," and "person" all support the idea that the mistress treated the author as a human being; therefore, you can eliminate *A, C,* and *D. Property* is a good antonym for *human being* in this context; *B* is the best answer choice.

3. Which statement best describes the author's reasons for reading?
   A. Reading is a way for the author to anger his mistress and her husband.
   B. Reading provides the author with a means of escape from slavery.
   C. Reading is a way for the author to pass his free time.
   D. Reading provides the author with a sense of independence.

Grade-Level Indicator: 3.5 Analyze an author's implicit and explicit argument, perspective or viewpoint in text.

Strategy: Reread the conclusion of the passage. The author says that his mistress is "too late" to stop his reading. She gave him an "inch," so he will take the "ell." What does this passage suggest about the power the mistress has over the author? The author might anger his mistress by reading, but reading means something much more to the author, so you can eliminate *A*. The passage does not indicate that reading allows the author to escape from slavery; eliminate *B*. The author may pass his free time reading, but reading is more than just a way to pass free time to the author, so you can eliminate *C*. Reading provides the author with a sense of independence, providing one aspect of his life over which his mistress has no control. Therefore, *D* is the best answer choice.

4. Explain what the author means when he says, "The first step had been taken." Give at least one detail or example from the passage to support your idea. (2 points)

Sample response for Item 4 (Short Answer):

The response should be similar but not limited to the following:

The author is enslaved by a mistress and her husband. By teaching the author to read, the mistress unwittingly allows the author to take his first step toward freedom.

Scoring Guidelines for Item 4:

Score Point	Description
2 points	The response identifies what the author means by the statement, provides a reasonable explanation of what the author means, and cites at least one appropriate detail or example from the passage in support.
1 point	The response identifies what the author means by the statement, provides a reasonable explanation of what the author means, but does not cite appropriate details or examples from the passage in support.
0 points	The response does not provide sufficient evidence of understanding the task.

Grade-Level Indicator: 4.11 Explain ways in which an author develops a point of view and style (e.g., figurative language, sentence structure and tone), and cite specific examples from the text.

Strategy: In questions like this, the best strategy is to use the author's line as a way to start your response: *The first step had been taken toward* _____. Make sure you cite details or examples from the passage to explain and support your response.

5. Explain how the point of view affects the mood and tone of the passage. Use three details or examples from the passage to support your answer. (4 points)

Sample response for Item 5 (Extended Response):

The response should be similar but not limited to the following:

- The first-person point of view gives the piece an intimate tone. We are not just being told about the conditions of slavery, but we are being told by a person who experienced the conditions first-hand.
- The tone remains matter-of-fact despite the first-person point of view. Although the woman was abusive, Douglass describes his situation in mild terms, as though he has gained some perspective and distance from the situation. The tone is also slightly defiant, such as in the last sentences.

Scoring Guidelines for Item 5:

Score Point	Description
4 points	The response offers a reasonable explanation that is supported by three appropriate details or examples from the passage.
3 points	The response offers a reasonable explanation that is supported by two appropriate details or examples from the passage.
2 points	The response offers a reasonable explanation that is supported by one appropriate detail or example from the passage.
1 point	The response offers a reasonable explanation, but it is not supported by any details or examples from the passage.
0 points	The response does not illustrate an understanding of the prompt.

Grade-Level Indicator: 4.8
Analyze the author's use of point of view, mood and tone.

Strategy: A good strategy for answering this type of question is to first determine the point of view. The passage is autobiographical and is written from a first-person point of view. Then identify the tone and mood of the passage and find at least three examples from the passage that support your statement. Next consider how the point of view contributes to the tone and mood of the passage and how they might be different if the passage were written from a different perspective. Remember to write in complete sentences and support your ideas with examples from the text.

Grass

Identify the relationship between the grass or nature and the human lives lost on the battlefields.

Notice that there is a lot of repetition in this poem. Think about how this reinforces one of the poem's themes.

Think about why the passengers ask these questions. What causes their confusion? What can they no longer see at these locations?

1   Pile the bodies high at Austerlitz and Waterloo.
     Shovel them under and let me work—
         I am the grass; I cover all.

     And pile them high at Gettysburg
5   And pile them high at Ypres and Verdun.
     Shovel them under and let me work.
     Two years, ten years, and passengers ask the conductor:
         What place is this?
         Where are we now?

10   I am the grass.
         Let me work.

"Grass," by Carl Sandburg.

These are names of famous battlefields all over the world and throughout history. You will likely recognize some, if not all, of these locations. This poem is not targeting one specific war, but speaking more generally about war.

6. Based on the information in lines 1–3 of the poem, which sentence gives the best interpretation of "I am the grass; I cover all"?

A. Battles are remembered for their casualties.

B. Nature erases death.

C. Battlefields are burial sites.

D. Nature is more important than humanity.

Grade-Level Indicator: 1.3 Infer the literal and figurative meaning of words and phrases and discuss the function of figurative language, including metaphors, similes, idioms and puns.

Strategy: Note that the poet personifies the grass. Identify what the grass covers: the bodies of the dead at famous battle sites. The grass makes an assertion about itself, not about the battles or battlefields, so you can eliminate A and C. The grass covers the dead bodies, erasing them from the landscape. Therefore, B is the best answer choice. The grass states its job, but it doesn't assert that the job is more important than humanity, so you can also eliminate D.

7. In lines 8–9 of the poem, train passengers ask the questions "What place is this? / Where are we now?" The speaker is making the point that

A. people forget history.

B. the passengers are lost.

C. people need guidance.

D. the passengers need leadership.

Grade-Level Indicator: 4.9 Explain how authors use symbols to create broader meanings.

Strategy: Reread the stanza. Note that the battles cited in the stanza occurred in different places and at different times in history. The passengers on the train are symbolic of those who live in the years after the battles, and the train is a symbol of the passage of time. The passengers' questions suggest that they have no memory of the battles. Therefore, A is a good answer choice. The passengers are not actually lost, they are just curious as to what they are seeing, so you can eliminate B. C is incorrect because although people may need guidance at times, that is not what these questioning train passengers represent in the poem, and that is not the point that the speaker is trying to make. D is incorrect for similar reasons. The passengers are not symbolic of people in need of leadership. A is the best answer choice.

8. Explain how the poet's style or word choice reflects the expression "history repeats itself." Use information from the poem to support your response. (2 points)

Sample information for Item 8 (Short Answer):

The response should be similar but not limited to the following:

- The poet uses repetition of words, phrases, and sentence structures.
- The poet makes a point to list the names of battle sites.
- The poet emphasizes the passage of time.

Scoring Guidelines for Item 8:

Score Point	Description
2 points	The response identifies elements of the author's style or word choice, logically relates the style or word choice elements to the expression, and cites appropriate details or examples from the poem in support.
1 point	The response identifies elements of the author's style or word choice, logically relates the style or word choice elements to the expression, but does not cite appropriate details or examples from the poem in support.
0 points	The response does not provide sufficient evidence of understanding the task.

Grade-Level Indicator: 4.11 Explain ways in which an author develops a point of view and style (e.g., figurative language, sentence structure and tone), and cite specific examples from the text.

Strategy: Identify elements of the author's style or word choice. These may include the repetition of the word *pile*; listing battle sites (Austerlitz, Waterloo, Gettysburg, and so on); emphasizing the passage of time: "two years, ten years"; or the repetition of lines such as "I am the grass" and "let me work." After answering the multiple-choice questions that precede this question, you should have a better understanding of the poem. Use that insight to help you here. Explain how one or two of these elements illustrate the expression "history repeats itself." You can use the question itself to start your first sentence: *The expression "history repeats itself" is reflected in the poem "Grass."* Make sure to cite details or examples from the poem in your response, and write in complete sentences.

The Wily Soybean

Notice the headers. Think about their purpose in the passage, and consider how they connect to the information in each paragraph.

1 Tofu, a soybean product, is one of the most interesting foods in the world. It is a great source of protein. It is low in fats and carbohydrates. Some have called it the perfect food.

A Useful Plant

Authors offer context clues to help readers determine the meaning of unfamiliar words. A context clue may be placed within a sentence or in its surrounding sentences and may take the form of a synonym, an antonym, or an example. Look for clues regarding the meaning of the word *versatile*.

2 Tofu is made from soybean, or *Glycine max*, a crop cultivated throughout the world. The soybean is a remarkably versatile crop. Its oil is used in industry in paints, glues, and other modern products, from fertilizer to insect repellents. As a high-protein meat substitute, it also feeds much of the world, both in the form of soybean paste and as tofu. Its versatility holds out promise for the eventual solution to world hunger.

A "Made" Crop

3 The soybean does not exist in the wild. It was created by human beings somewhere in ancient China. A vine still found in Asia, *Glycine ussuriensis*, is considered to be its wild ancestor. Other similar plants are found throughout Asia, Africa, and Australia.

History of the Soybean

4 The development and cultivation of the soybean began in China before recorded history. Considered in Chinese civilization to be one of the five sacred grains (along with rice, barley, wheat, and millet), the soybean found its way into almost all aspects of East Asian cooking, from soy sauce to the versatile tofu, made from the coagulated curd of soy milk.

Authors must support their claims with evidence. Here the author makes a claim that the soybean may end world hunger. What evidence does he or she offer to support this claim?

Soybeans Across the Globe

5 The soybean traveled from China to the United States in the hands of immigrants. First introduced in 1804, it wasn't until the late nineteenth century that the U.S. Department of Agriculture took notice of the soybean. The USDA began to study the crop and encourage the growth of different varieties of soybeans. Through careful breeding in the 1930s, stronger and healthier varieties of the soybean were created. These new plants were completely different from the ones that originated in Asia. Today, the United States leads the world in production of soybeans. American varieties have been introduced into Asia and have also traveled to Africa and Latin America.

This passage is informational. The author's purpose is to inform readers about the soybean. For the author to achieve this, readers must find the information believable. One strategy authors use is to offer multiple examples.

Note that the author lists many products that are made from soybeans. Think about whether the impact of this information would be greater if the author had presented it in a diagram rather than in a paragraph.

9. Which technique does the author use to make the information presented in the article credible?

A. The author struggles to explain the origin of the soybean.

B. The author explains how to breed soybeans.

C. The author discusses soybean production in different areas of the world.

D. The author expresses hope that the soybean will end world hunger.

Grade-Level Indicator: 3.4 Assess the adequacy, accuracy and appropriateness of an author's details, identifying persuasive techniques (e.g., transfer, glittering generalities, bait and switch) and examples of propaganda, bias and stereotyping.

Strategy: Good researchers cite multiple examples in support of their thesis so readers know the information is credible. Skim the passage. Note that the author discusses soybean production in Asia, Africa, Australia, Latin America, and the United States. The author does not struggle to explain the origin of the soybean; the explanation is clear. Therefore, you can eliminate *A*. The author does not explain how to breed soybeans; this topic is not the author's main focus. You can eliminate *B*. The author discusses the history of soybean production in different areas of the world, so *C* is a good answer choice. The author also states that the soybean holds the promise of ending world hunger, but this is not the main strategy for giving his article credibility, so you can eliminate *D*. *C* is the best answer choice.

10. How do readers know that East Asians highly value the soybean?

A. The soybean is a great source of protein.

B. The soybean is an important part of East Asian cooking.

C. The soybean was first developed and cultivated in China.

D. The soybean may eventually end world hunger.

Grade-Level Indicator: 2.2 Answer literal, inferential, evaluative and synthesizing questions to demonstrate comprehension of grade-appropriate print texts and electronic and visual media.

Strategy: This question asks you to make an inference. The best strategy is to combine textual information with your own knowledge and experiences. The text says that East Asians use the soybean in almost all aspects of their cooking. Based on this information, *B* is a good answer choice. Answer choices *A* and *D* are not specifically about East Asians, so you can eliminate them. Although *C* is true, it does not reflect how the people of the region value the soybean now. *B* is the best answer choice.

11. In the passage, what evidence supports the idea that the soybean may eventually end world hunger?

   A. The development and cultivation of the soybean began in China.
   B. The soybean is one of the most interesting foods in the world.
   C. The soybean has improved through careful breeding.
   D. The soybean is versatile and can be cultivated throughout the world.

Grade-Level Indicator: 3.4 Assess the adequacy, accuracy and appropriateness of an author's details, identifying persuasive techniques (e.g., transfer, glittering generalities, bait and switch) and examples of propaganda, bias and stereotyping.

Strategy: The first step is to review the passage and locate the claim being asked about in the question. Then locate details that support the statement. The second paragraph contains the claim that tofu could be a solution to world hunger. Look at the answer choices. *A* is not correct because that detail has to do with the history of the soybean, not its usefulness. *B* is an opinion about soybeans that does not quite support the statement that the soybean might end world hunger, so *B* is not correct. *C* is not correct. The soybean may have been improved, but this is not the strongest support for the statement in the question. *D* is the best answer choice. In paragraph 2, the author says that the soybean is cultivated throughout the world, is versatile, and is high in protein. This information supports the claim that the soybean may end world hunger.

12. Which word means the same as versatile does in this sentence from paragraph 2:

"The soybean is a remarkably versatile crop"?

   A. adaptable
   B. limited
   C. hard to grow
   D. imperfect

Grade-Level Indicator: 1.1 Define unknown words through context clues and the author's use of comparison, contrast and cause and effect.

Strategy: Read the sentence that follows the one cited in the question. The sentence that follows provides a clue about the meaning of *versatile*. It says that the soybean is used to make many different products, including paint, glue, fertilizer, insect repellent, and food. Now replace the word *versatile* with each of the answer choices and determine which word maintains the meaning of these sentences. *A* is a good answer choice. Answer choices *B, C,* and *D* change the meaning of the sentences, so you can eliminate them. *A* is the best answer choice.

13. Describe how the headers in the passage help organize the information. Give two specific examples from the passage that support your answer. (2 points)

Sample Response for Item 13 (Short Answer):

The response should be similar but not limited to the following:

- The headers give a clue as to what each paragraph is about. A reader can skim the headers to quickly see how the information in the passage is organized.
- "A Useful Plant" describes the various ways in which soybeans are useful, from industrial uses to food.
- Soybeans Across the Globe" tells of the arrival of the soybean in the United States and its impact there. It also explains that soybeans traveled to other parts of the world.

Scoring Guidelines for Item 13:

Score Point	Description
2 points	The response describes how the headers help to organize the information in the passage and cites two specific examples from the passage in support.
1 point	The response describes how the headers help to organize the information in the passage and cites one specific example from the passage in support.
0 points	The response does not illustrate understanding of the prompt.

Grade-Level Indicator: 3.7 Analyze the effectiveness of the features (e.g. format, graphics, sequence, headers) used in various consumer documents (e.g., warranties, product information, instructional materials), functional or workplace documents (e.g., job-related materials, memoranda, instructions) and public documents (e.g., speeches or newspaper editorials).

Strategy: Note that there is a header before each paragraph of the passage. Notice also that the headers state the key idea of each paragraph. Describe how these headers help organize the information in the passage. How are they useful? Make sure to write in complete sentences and cite two supporting examples from the passage in your response.

WRITING TEST

DIRECTIONS: This part of the test will consist of multiple-choice questions, one short-answer question, and one writing prompt. For multiple-choice questions, most of the questions are associated with a brief paragraph or a sentence. Some of the questions are clustered together; others stand alone. After reading the paragraph or sentence and the question, choose the correct answer.

Read the draft paragraph and answer questions 1–4.

1. Do you know anyone named Cooper? **2.** The chances are that long ago someone in his or her family was a cooper, or a maker of casks. **3.** Wooden casks or barrels were essential for transporting goods by ship. **4.** Since the ships had a tendency to take on a little water in choppy seas, the casks, or the voyage would be for naught.

5. Nowadays, we tend to use cardboard or plastic for packaging. **6.** But cooperage is not a lost art. **7.** Well-made casks are critical to the wine industry; and fortunately for the vintners, some people still practice the skill.

8. A good cooper knows his wood. **9.** It must be durable, malleable, and appropriate for the wine that will be stored in it. **10.** The wood has been selected. **11.** Then it must be aged outside for at least five years. **12.** This process takes away tannins and sap, which could harm the wine. **13.** The wood is then moved indoors and dried thoroughly. **14.** At that point, the cask building begins.

Your eyes should hesitate for a moment when you read this sentence. Something is missing. Remember that a clause must contain a subject and an action. Is the clause that begins "the casks" complete?

Writers can form a compound sentence by joining two independent clauses with a comma and a conjunction. If you wrote this passage, would you have done that here?

Short sentences sometimes break the flow of a paragraph. If you wrote this passage, would you have used sentence-combining techniques to improve its fluency?

Remember that you are not just looking at this passage for grammar and sentence structure. Make sure to identify the main idea of the text by asking yourself, "What is this text mostly about?" and "Which details support this main idea?"

1. In the context of the paragraph, what is the correct way to revise sentence 4?
   A. Since the ships had a tendency to take on a little water in choppy seas, the casks had to be watertight, or the voyage would be for naught.
   B. The voyage would be for naught since the ships had a tendency to take on a little water in choppy seas.
   C. Since the ships had a tendency to take on a little water in choppy seas, the casks would be for naught.
   D. The casks and the voyage would be for naught since the ships had a tendency to take on a little water in choppy seas.

Grade-Level Indicator: 5.15 Proofread writing, edit to improve conventions (e.g., grammar, spelling, punctuation and capitalization), identify and correct fragments and run-ons and eliminate inappropriate slang or informal language.

Strategy: Read the original sentence and identify the problem: no action follows the subject *casks*. *A* is a good answer choice because it completes the clause by offering an action for the subject. *B*, *C*, and *D* change the meaning of the original sentence, so you can eliminate them. *A* is the best answer choice.

2. In the context of the paragraph, what is the correct way to revise sentences 5 and 6?
   A. Nowadays, we tend to use cardboard or plastic, but cooperage is not a lost art, for packaging.
   B. But cooperage is not a lost art; nowadays, we tend to use cardboard or plastic for packaging.
   C. But cooperage, nowadays, is not a lost art; we tend to use cardboard or plastic for packaging.
   D. Nowadays, we tend to use cardboard or plastic for packaging; but cooperage is not a lost art.

Grade-Level Indicator: 5.7 Use a variety of sentence structures and lengths (e.g., simple, compound and complex sentences; parallel or repetitive sentence structure).

Strategy: Read the original sentences and identify the problem. *But* is a conjunction that should join two independent clauses, forming a compound sentence. It should not begin a sentence. You can eliminate answer choice *A* because it doesn't make sense. You can eliminate answer choices *B* and *C* because the conjunction *but* begins the sentences. *D* is a correct compound sentence and is therefore the best answer choice.

3. In the context of the paragraph, what is the correct way to revise sentences 10 and 11?

   A. The wood has been selected; but first, it must be aged outside for at least five years.

   B. After the wood has been selected, it must be aged outside for at least five years.

   C. For at least five years, the wood must be aged outside after it has been selected.

   D. The wood has been selected; then, it must be aged outside for at least five years.

 Grade-Level Indicator: 5.15 Proofread writing, edit to improve conventions (e.g., grammar, spelling, punctuation and capitalization), identify and correct fragments and run-ons and eliminate inappropriate slang or informal language.

Strategy: Read the original sentences and identify the problem. Sentence 10 is short and breaks the flow of the paragraph. It should be combined with sentence 11 to form a compound sentence. Eliminate *A* because it changes the chronology of events. According to the passage, the wood is aged outside *after* it has been selected. According to *A*, the wood is aged outside *before* being selected. *B* is a good answer choice because the short sentence becomes an introductory clause in a compound sentence. You can eliminate *C* because it is awkward and not the best way to order the events. *D* does not improve the flow of the paragraph; *has been* is the present perfect, which does not entirely make sense in this sentence. So *D* is not correct. *B* is the best answer choice.

4. Which would not be appropriate to include when expanding on ideas in the text?

   A. how to build a cask

   B. wood types appropriate for cask making

   C. uses for cardboard or plastic packaging

   D. where to get training in cooperage

 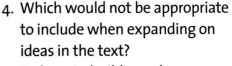 **Grade-Level Indicator: 5.12** Add and delete information and details to better elaborate on a stated central idea and more effectively accomplish purpose.

Strategy: You should first identify the main idea and supporting details of the text. The text discusses cask building, wood, and cooperage. Answer choices *A*, *B*, and *D* might be appropriate additions to expand on this main idea. Although the text mentions cardboard and plastic packaging, this subject is not the focus of the text. More details about it would detract from the main idea of the passage. Therefore, *C* is the best answer choice.

5. Read the sentence. Choose the correct way to revise and/or edit the sentence without changing the meaning.

In your bedroom the night light will be left on so you can get up in the dark without tripping over the furniture.

A. The night light will be left on in your bedroom so you can get up in the dark without tripping over the furniture.

B. In the dark you can get up without tripping over the furniture if the night light is left on.

C. In the dark, in your bedroom, you can get up without tripping over the furniture, if the night light is left on.

D. In the dark, if the night light is left on, you can get up without tripping over the furniture.

Grade-Level Indicator: 5.13 Rearrange words, sentences and paragraphs and add transitional words and phrases to clarify meaning and maintain consistent style, tone and voice.

Strategy: Carefully read each answer choice twice. Think about which choice is grammatically correct *and* maintains the meaning of the original sentence. *A* is a good answer choice because it rearranges the ideas of the original sentence into a clearer sentence without losing any of the original meaning. You can eliminate *B* because it is missing a comma after the introductory phrase. You can also eliminate *C* and *D* due to an overuse of commas. *A* is the best answer choice.

6. Select the correct revision to the underlined portion of the sentence.

Ray Bradbury, <u>the author of *fahrenheit 451*</u>, is a widely regarded science-fiction writer whose works warn readers of a dark future.

A. the Author of *Fahrenheit 451*,

B. The Author Of *Fahrenheit 451*,

C. the author of *FahrenHeit 451*,

D. the author of *Fahrenheit 451*,

Grade-Level Indicator: 7.2 Use correct capitalization and punctuation.

Strategy: Read the underlined portion of the sentence and identify the problem. Titles should be capitalized. *Author* does not need to be capitalized, so you can eliminate *A*. All of the words do not need capital letters, so you can also eliminate *B*. Capital letters do not belong in the middle of words; eliminate *C*. *D* reflects the correct capitalization of the title. Therefore it is the best answer choice.

Use the information below to find the correct answer for question 7.

1. A <u>simple sentence</u> has a subject and a predicate. *(The girl kicked the soccer ball.)*

2. A <u>compound sentence</u> features two independent clauses connected by a comma and a conjunction. *(The girl kicked the soccer ball, and she scored a goal.)*

3. A <u>complex sentence</u> features an independent clause and one or more dependent clauses. *(After the girl kicked the soccer ball, she scored a goal.)*

7. Which is a correct complex sentence?
   A. The boy scrambled by one defender and shot the basketball.
   B. The boy shot the basketball, and another defender blocked the shot.
   C. The girl rebounded the basketball, but the referee blew the whistle.
   D. After the referee made the call, the girl shot a free throw.

 Grade-Level Indicator: 5.7 Use a variety of sentence structures and lengths (e.g., simple, compound and complex sentences; parallel or repetitive sentence structure).

Strategy: Review the explanations of each type of sentence and then examine each answer choice. *A* is a simple sentence. *B* and *C* are compound sentences because the independent clauses are joined by commas and conjunctions. *D* is a complex sentence because it contains an independent clause and a dependent clause. Therefore, *D* is correct.

8. Which topic fits with this graphic organizer?

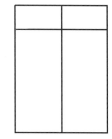

   A. explaining requirements for college entrance
   B. illustrating causes of successful and unsuccessful college graduation
   C. assessing the pros and cons of attending one particular college
   D. comparing and contrasting two colleges

 Grade-Level Indicator: 8.4 Evaluate and systematically organize important information, and select appropriate sources to support central ideas, concepts and themes.

Strategy: A T-chart can be used to assess different aspects of one topic. You would probably use a bulleted list to explain the requirements for college entrance, so you can eliminate *A*. You would probably use boxes connected by arrows to note causes and effects, so you can also eliminate *B*. You might use a T-chart to list pros and cons, so *C* seems like a good answer choice. You would probably use a Venn diagram to compare and contrast, so eliminate *D*. *C* is the best answer choice.

9. You are planning to write a paper recommending that your school adopt a year-round class schedule.

   Which of the following would be the best source of information for your paper?
   A. the director of your school's sports program
   B. the director of a local summer camp
   C. the principal of your school
   D. the principal of a year-round school

Grade-Level Indicator: 8.2 Identify appropriate sources and gather relevant information from multiple sources (e.g., school library catalogs, online databases, electronic resources and Internet-based resources).

Strategy: The first step in writing a persuasive paper is to determine the position of the paper and deciding what sources you should use. While the director of your school's sports program might have some useful insights, he or she would probably not be the best source of information, so *A* is not correct. *B* is not correct, either; the director of a local summer camp would not be the best source of information on year-round schools. The principal of your school, answer choice *C*, might be knowledgeable on the subject, but the principal of a year-round school would have first-hand knowledge of the pros and cons of a year-round class schedule. Therefore, *D* is the best answer choice.

10. Which sentence would be an appropriate opening sentence for an essay?
    A. After examining the research, the administration should consider adopting a year-round schedule.
    B. John Doe, a teacher at Deere Park High School in Tulip, Indiana, says the year-round schedule helps students retain information.
    C. Teresa Taylor, principal of North High School in Rose, Georgia, says the year-round schedule allows for smaller class sizes.
    D. In order to prepare students to compete in an international marketplace, schools must consider new ways of training students.

Grade-Level Indicator: 6.4.c Write informational essays or reports, including research that: create an organizing structure appropriate to the purpose, audience and context.

Strategy: Remember that an opening sentence should introduce the topic. *A* belongs in the conclusion because it suggests that research has already been considered; you can eliminate it. *B* and *C* belong in the body of the essay as supporting details, so you can also eliminate them. *D* introduces the topic of a change in the school schedule; therefore, it is the best answer choice.

11. Ohio is considering raising the minimum age requirement to obtain a driver's license. The proposed minimum age requirement to begin the licensing process is 18 years of age. You are planning to write a letter to a state legislator. Write two arguments you would use to support or oppose raising the age requirement. (2 points)

Sample response for Item 11 (Short Answer):

The response should be similar but not limited to the following:

Opposing: (1) I oppose raising the minimum age to obtain a driver's license. (2) Teenagers work to earn money to support future plans, and they need to be able to drive to their jobs. (3) Teenagers help support their families by running errands.

Supporting: (1) I support raising the minimum age to obtain a driver's license. (2) Teenagers are too easily distracted by cell phones and stereos to be responsible drivers. (3) Teenagers can get rides from family or older friends, or they can take public transportation or ride bicycles, so they do not need to drive.

Scoring Guidelines for Item 11:

Score Point	Description
2 points	Response uses two arguments appropriate to the target audience (state legislator) supporting or opposing raising the age requirement.
1 point	Response uses one argument appropriate to the target audience (state legislator) either supporting or opposing raising the age requirement.
0 points	Response indicates no understanding of the task.

Grade-Level Indicator: 5.4 Determine a purpose and audience and plan strategies (e.g., adapting focus, content structure, and point of view) to address purpose and audience.

Strategy: To answer this question completely, you must first decide whether you support or oppose raising the age requirement for obtaining a driver's license. Then, you must list two reasons for your opinion, in complete sentences. For each reason, write a fact, example, or anecdote that explains that reason. Make sure your response is clear and follows the rules of standard written English.

12. *Our Time,* a national magazine, is developing an issue about the top 100 developments of the last 100 years. In your lifetime, you have witnessed many developments in technology—cell phones, digital music, medical devices, and automotive features, for example. Which new technology do you think is the most important or most useful?

Write a letter to the editor of *Our Time* magazine in which you describe the technology and why you think it is the most important technological development in your lifetime. (18 points)

Strategy: First, develop a thesis statement that states your opinion on this topic. Use this sentence frame: *The most important technological development in my lifetime is _____ because _____.* Then describe the technology. Next, list three reasons for your opinion. For each reason, write a fact, example, or anecdote that explains the reason. Use the description, reasons, and explanations to develop the body of the letter. When you conclude, summarize your main points and leave the readers with a final thought. Make sure to use the appropriate letter format, including the salutation *Dear Editor:* and ending with *Sincerely,* and your name.

The Holistic Rubric for the Ohio Graduation Test in Writing on the next page is a set of guidelines that provide a way to evaluate your composition. The rubric outlines how well your writing demonstrates your ability to develop ideas, organize information logically, make appropriate word choices, and exhibit a unique style. Your writing will be scored appropriately.

Holistic Rubric for the Ohio Graduation Test in Writing

6 This is a superior piece of writing. The prompt is directly addressed, and the response is effectively adapted to audience and purpose. It is exceptionally developed, containing compelling ideas, examples, and details. The response, using a clearly evident organizational plan, actively engages the reader with a unified and coherent sequence and structure of ideas. The response consistently uses a variety of sentence structures, effective word choices and an engaging style.

5 This is an excellent piece of writing. The prompt is directly addressed and the response is clearly adapted to audience and purpose. It is very well developed, containing strong ideas, examples, and details. The response, using a clearly evident organizational plan, engages the reader with a unified and coherent sequence and structure of ideas. The response typically uses a variety of sentence structures, effective word choices and an engaging style.

4 This is an effective piece of writing. While the prompt is addressed and the response adapts to audience and purpose, there are occasional inconsistencies in the response's overall plan. The response is well developed, containing effective ideas, examples and details. The response, using a good organizational plan, presents the reader with a generally unified and coherent sequence and structure of ideas. The response often uses a variety of sentence structures, appropriate word choices and an effective style.

3 This is an adequate piece of writing. While the prompt is generally addressed and the response shows an awareness of audience and purpose, there are inconsistencies in the response's overall plan. Although the response contains ideas, examples and details, they are repetitive, unevenly developed and occasionally inappropriate. The response, using an acceptable organizational plan, presents the reader with a generally unified and coherent sequence and structure of ideas. The response occasionally uses a variety of sentence structures, appropriate word choices and an effective style.

2 This is a marginal piece of writing. While an attempt is made to address the prompt, the response shows at best an inconsistent awareness of audience and purpose. When ideas, examples and details are present, they are frequently repetitive, unevenly developed and occasionally inappropriate. The response, using a limited organizational plan, does not present the reader with a generally unified and coherent sequence and structure of ideas. The response is exemplified by noticeable lapses in sentence structure, use of appropriate word choices and a clear, readable style.

1 This is an inadequate piece of writing. There is a weak attempt made to address the prompt. The response shows little or no awareness of audience and purpose. There is little or no development of ideas, or the response is limited to paraphrasing the prompt. There is little or no evidence of organizational structure. The response is exemplified by severe lapses in sentence structure, use of appropriate word choices and a clear, readable style.

0 The following are categories of papers that cannot be scored: off task, completely illegible, in a language other than English, or no response.

Conventions Rubric for the Ohio Graduation Test in Writing

3 The written response is free from errors that impair a reader's understanding and comprehension. Few errors, if any, are present in capitalization, punctuation and spelling. The writing displays a consistent understanding of grammatical conventions.

2 Occasional errors may impair a reader's understanding of the written response. Some capitalization, punctuation and spelling errors are present. The writing displays some understanding of grammatical conventions.

1 Errors are frequent and impair a reader's understanding of the written response. Numerous errors in capitalization, punctuation and spelling are present. The writing displays a minimal understanding of grammatical conventions.

0 The following are categories of papers that cannot be scored: off task, completely illegible, in a language other than English, or no response.
OR
The length and complexity of the response are insufficient to demonstrate the writer has control over standard English conventions.

The Power of Ideas

INTRODUCING THE ESSENTIALS

- Literary Genres Workshop
- Reading Strategies Workshop
- Writing Process Workshop

What Are Life's Big Questions?

Dignity, progress, justice—ideas like these resonate with all of us because they speak to the shared experiences that make us human. They also serve as the foundation for the big questions we all ask about the world. Consider the questions shown. How can your own experiences help you answer them? Through reading, discussing, and writing about literature, you can discover the answers that others have arrived at and gain new insights of your own.

Does love require SACRIFICE?

Our love for others—family, friends, significant others—can affect us in inexplicable, surprising ways. We might begin to put the needs of someone we love before our own, or we might make sacrifices that we never dreamed we'd make. Works such as W. D. Wetherell's "The Bass, the River, and Sheila Mant" and Chinua Achebe's "Marriage Is a Private Affair" will help you explore this question.

What is the price of FREEDOM?

In the 1960s, Martin Luther King Jr. led millions of African Americans in a fight for freedom. Along the way, his followers had to deal with violence, discrimination, and the assassination of Dr. King himself. From civil rights protesters to refugees fleeing their native countries, people of all times and cultures have faced oppression and injustice. Yet people often continue to fight for freedom in spite of the costs. What is the price of freedom? Is it ever too high?

How does heritage
SHAPE US?

We are all the products of our experiences. In other words, who we are depends on such factors as when and where we grew up, the values that have been instilled in us, and the cultural and religious traditions that have been handed down from the previous generation. In this book, you will consider how your own heritage has shaped you as you read works by such authors as Rudolfo Anaya and Alice Walker.

When is ambition
DANGEROUS?

Ambition is a powerful force that drives us to pursue personal goals and realize our dreams. But even the most well-intentioned person can be blinded by ambition. What happens when someone's pursuit of a goal becomes relentless, or when he or she betrays those who offered support along the way? You will consider this question as you read William Shakespeare's *The Tragedy of Julius Caesar*.

Exploring Ideas in Literature

If you've thought about questions like the ones on the preceding pages, you may have more in common with Shakespeare, Sophocles, and Gwendolyn Brooks than you realize. Throughout history, authors have searched for answers to thought-provoking questions and have shared their ideas through writing. By discussing and analyzing ideas in all forms of literature, you can learn how others see the world and arrive at your own deeply personal answers to the big questions in life.

OHIO STANDARDS

READING & WRITING STANDARDS
2.1 Apply reading comprehension strategies
4.5 Analyze how choice of genre affects theme or topic
5.6 Organize writing to create a coherent whole

The Genres

By now you are familiar with the genres of literature—fiction, poetry, drama, and nonfiction—and many of their forms. In addition to traditional genres, this book contains other types of "texts," including movies, advertisements, and online news sites. These texts are worth reading and analyzing because they communicate many of the messages and ideas that you are exposed to daily.

Regardless of the genre, all texts can acquaint you with unfamiliar times and cultures and help you explore such key ideas as loss or progress. Before you begin reading the selections in this book, review the characteristics of each genre.

GENRES AT A GLANCE

FICTION
Fiction is narrative writing that springs from an author's imagination. It includes many subgenres, such as mystery and romance.
- novels
- short stories
- novellas

POETRY
Poetry is a type of literature in which words are chosen and arranged to create certain effects and to evoke emotional responses in readers.
- ballads
- sonnets
- narrative poems
- lyric poems

DRAMA
Drama is literature that is intended to be performed.
- comedies
- tragedies
- farces

NONFICTION
Nonfiction is writing about real people, events, and places.
- essays
- autobiographies
- news articles
- speeches
- biographies
- feature articles

TYPES OF MEDIA

Media are forms of communication that reach large numbers of people.
- TV shows
- news media
- advertising

FICTION

Truth is stranger than fiction, as the old saying goes. Actually, the line between them is not always easy to define. At the heart of fiction is **narrative,** or the telling of a story. That story can be a work of pure imagination (science fiction, for example) or have roots in reality (such as historical fiction based on real people and events). Regardless of what inspired its creation, a work of fiction is usually one of three types.

- A **short story** is a brief work of fiction that can usually be read in one sitting. It often focuses on a single event or incident and develops only a few characters in depth.

- A **novel** is an extended work of fiction. Many novels have sweeping story lines that span long periods of time, involve intricate subplots, and develop a wide range of characters.

- A **novella** is longer than a short story but shorter than a novel. Most novellas take place over a short period of time and involve a limited number of characters.

Read the Model Set against the backdrop of the French Revolution, Charles Dickens's novel *A Tale of Two Cities* portrays characters who are swept along by the forces of history. Here, a French character named Lucie Manette receives some earthshattering personal news from the man who, years earlier, brought her to England. As you read, notice the elements of fiction that the author uses to communicate the **key idea** of revelation.

---

from A Tale OF *Two Cities*

Novel by **Charles Dickens**

"Miss Manette, . . . when she [your mother] died—I believe broken-hearted—having never slackened her unavailing search for your father, she left you, at two years old, to grow to be blooming, beautiful, and happy, without the dark cloud upon you of living in uncertainty whether your father soon
5   wore his heart out in prison, or wasted there through many lingering years."

As he said the words he looked down, with admiring pity, on the flowing golden hair; as if he pictured to himself that it might have been already tinged with gray.

"You know that your parents had no great possession, and that what they
10   had was secured to your mother and to you. There has been no new discovery, of money, or of any other property; but—"

He felt his wrist held closer, and he stopped. The expression in the forehead, which had so particularly attracted his notice, and which was now immovable, had deepened into one of pain and horror.
15   "But he has been—been found. He is alive."

Close Read

1. Using terms from the Academic Vocabulary list, describe what is happening in this scene.

2. **Key Idea: Revelation** The discovery of a long-lost family member is a heart-stopping revelation that deeply affects Miss Manette. What other kinds of **revelations**— both good and bad—can change people's lives?

POETRY

Technically, poetry involves the artful selection and arrangement of words on a page. Poet Lucille Clifton, however, reminds readers that "poetry is a matter of life, not just a matter of language." A poem derives its power from the way its elements—language, form, and sounds—work together to communicate meaning and emotion.

You already know that poems are composed of short **lines** that are often grouped into **stanzas**. Some poets choose to craft traditional, highly structured poems, such as sonnets or haiku. Other poets, like Clifton, break with convention, often inventing unique forms that suit their subjects.

Poetry is meant to be heard, not just read. For that reason, a poem's sounds—for example, its jarring **rhythms** or singsong **rhymes**—are an essential part of its impact. Language also creates powerful effects. Through the use of **imagery** and **figurative language,** poets tap into our senses and prompt us to think about subjects in ways we might never have before.

Read the Model Here, a speaker reflects on a moment from her childhood that is still imprinted on her memory. As you read this poem, notice its form as well as its use of sound devices and imagery. How does the speaker's recollection of her feelings help you understand the **key idea** of reassurance?

ACADEMIC VOCABULARY FOR POETRY

- form
- line
- stanza
- speaker
- rhyme
- rhythm
- meter
- sound devices
- figurative language
- imagery

Making **a Fist**

Poem by **Naomi Shihab Nye**

For the first time, on the road north of Tampico,
I felt the life sliding out of me,
a drum in the desert, harder and harder to hear.
I was seven, I lay in the car
5   watching palm trees swirl a sickening pattern past the glass.
My stomach was a melon split wide inside my skin.

"How do you know if you are going to die?"
I begged my mother.
We had been traveling for days.
10   With strange confidence she answered,
"When you can no longer make a fist."

Years later I smile to think of that journey,
the borders we must cross separately,
stamped with our unanswerable woes.
15   I who did not die, who am still living,
still lying in the backseat behind all my questions,
clenching and opening one small hand.

Close Read

1. Describe three poetic elements in "Making a Fist." Refer to the Academic Vocabulary list for specific elements.

2. **Key Idea: Reassurance** Like the speaker, many of us turn to others for **reassurance** in moments of uncertainty. In your opinion, do words have the power to reassure us in such moments?

DRAMA

Drama is broadly defined as any story that is performed by actors for an audience. A drama can be a live stage production, a movie, a television, or a radio play. In a drama—whether it's a Shakespearean tragedy, a contemporary musical, or an experimental one-person show—the plot and the characters are developed primarily through **dialogue** and action.

While there's nothing quite as captivating as watching a performance unfold on stage or screen, a drama can also make good reading. By paying attention to the **stage directions**—the writer's instructions for the actors, the director, and the others working on the play—readers can visualize a performance in their minds. Stage directions often describe the characters' appearances, movements, and reactions, as well as the setting, scenery, and props. Such directions are usually set off from the dialogue in italics and parentheses.

Read the Model *Twelve Angry Men* is a television screenplay that was made into a movie in 1957 and again in 1997. In the drama, 12 jurors must decide the fate of a young man accused of murder. Here, the jurors have just heard the case and must now reach a verdict. Use the stage directions and dialogue to help you visualize the jurors' deliberations and consider the key idea of **justice**.

> *from*
>
> # TWELVE Angry Men
>
> Drama by **Reginald Rose**
>
> *from* Act 1
>
> **Foreman.** Anybody doesn't want to vote? (*He looks around the table. There is no answer.*) Okay, all those voting guilty raise your hands. (*Seven or eight hands go up immediately. Several others go up more slowly. Everyone looks around the table. There are two hands not raised, No. 9's and No. 8's. No. 9's hand goes up slowly*
> 5 *now as the foreman counts.*)
>
> **Foreman.** . . . Nine . . . ten . . . eleven . . . That's eleven for guilty. Okay. Not guilty? (*No. 8's hand is raised*) One. Right. Okay. Eleven to one, guilty. Now we know where we are.
>
> **No. 3.** Somebody's in left field. (*To No. 8*) You think he's not guilty?
>
> 10 **No. 8.** (*Quietly*). I don't know.
>
> **No. 3.** I never saw a guiltier man in my life. You sat right in court and heard the same thing I did. The man's a dangerous killer. You could see it.
>
> **No. 8.** He's nineteen years old.
>
> **No. 3.** That's old enough. He knifed his own father. Four inches into the chest.
> 15 An innocent little nineteen-year-old kid. They proved it a dozen different ways.

ACADEMIC VOCABULARY FOR DRAMA

- plot
- character
- act/scene
- stage directions
- monologue
- dialogue
- aside
- soliloquy

Close Read

1. Are all the jurors confident of their opinions? How can you tell?

2. **Key Idea: Justice** In our justice system, juries composed of 12 ordinary citizens must arrive at impartial and **just** verdicts. What qualities are essential for jurors to have in such high-stakes deliberations?

NONFICTION AND INFORMATIONAL TEXT

You are probably used to seeing certain kinds of nonfiction in literature books. Works of **literary nonfiction,** including autobiographies and speeches, have long been studied for their historical significance and lyrical prose. Nonfiction also includes **informational texts,** such as news articles and instruction manuals that provide factual information. Since such texts are critical sources of information, you should learn how to read them with a careful and critical eye.

TYPE OF NONFICTION	CHARACTERISTICS	
AUTOBIOGRAPHY/BIOGRAPHY The true story of a person's life, told by that person (autobiography) or by another person (biography)	• Reveals details about significant events, people, and experiences in a person's life • Is told from the first-person point of view (autobiography) or from the third-person point of view (biography) • Presents the writer's own interpretations of his or her life (autobiography) or information gleaned from many sources (biography)	
ESSAY A short work that focuses on a single subject. Common types include reflective, persuasive, and descriptive essays.	• May have the following purposes: to express feelings, to inform, to entertain, or to persuade • May be **formal,** with an organized structure and an impersonal style • May be **informal,** with a conversational style	A Celebration of Grandfathers *Essay by Rudolfo A. Anaya*
SPEECH An oral presentation of the ideas, beliefs, or proposals of a speaker	• May be intended to express the speaker's feelings, or to educate, entertain, persuade, or inspire an audience • Achieves its power through effective language, as well as through the vocal variations and gestures of the speaker	
NEWS/FEATURE ARTICLES Informative writing in newspapers and magazines. News articles report on recent events. Feature articles focus on human-interest topics.	• Are primarily intended to inform or entertain • Convey information through headlines, photographs, quotations from sources, statistics, and examples • Aim to be objective and accurate	**WORLD EVENTS** **Girl, Trapped in Wat for 55 Hours, Die Despite Rescue Atter**
FUNCTIONAL DOCUMENTS Writing that serves a practical purpose. Types include consumer documents, such as warranties, and workplace documents, such as résumés.	• Are written for a specific audience (for example, business clients or users of a product) • Often use charts, diagrams, and graphics to illustrate and clarify ideas • May include specialized jargon	

MODEL 1: AUTOBIOGRAPHY

Kaffir Boy is the autobiography of the black author Mark Mathabane, who grew up under the system of apartheid, or racial segregation, in South Africa. Here, he recalls a time in his childhood when the police raided the ghetto in which his family lived, intending to rid the neighborhood of people they considered "undesirable." Notice how Mathabane vividly illustrates the **key idea** of fear.

from

Kaffir Boy   Autobiography by **Mark Mathabane**

. . . The darkness was impregnable, ominous; the more I stared into it, the blacker and blacker it became. I felt dizzy. I wanted to scream but my voice was paralyzed. Suddenly flashlights flared through the uncurtained window. Glass shattered somewhere nearby. I yearned to become invisible, to have the ground

5 beneath me open and swallow me until it was all over.

"OPEN UP!" a voice bellowed by the window. "WE KNOW YOU'RE IN THERE!"

I succeeded in reaching the bedroom door, fear all over me.

Close Read

1. How can you tell that this is an autobiographical—rather than a biographical—account?

2. **Key Idea: Fear** Think about the intense **fear** that Mathabane experienced as a child. What are the physical and emotional effects of fear? Support your answer with details.

MODEL 2: FEATURE ARTICLE

This article was published on September 6, 2004, ten years after apartheid was abolished in South Africa. As you read, consider the **key idea** of progress.

SEPTEMBER 6, 2004

South Africa's Decade Of Freedom

by Michael Wines

JOHANNESBURG—"See this yard?" Tom Shiburi waves his hand toward a sprawling field of weeds in the township of Diepkloof (DEEP-kloof), close to

5 downtown Johannesburg. "We used to have some shacks here," he says. "Five thousand shacks—our last count came to something like 10,000 people. They've been relocated, all of them."

10 Shiburi is talking about the changes in the decade since South Africa abolished apartheid and embraced democracy. Under apartheid (the government-run system that forcibly

15 segregated blacks from whites and denied blacks basic rights), South Africa's white rulers herded millions of blacks into townships like Diepkloof, where they lived in tiny houses or in iron

20 shacks, many without electricity or water.

But since South Africa's black majority came to power in 1994, the government has built and given 1.5 million homes to former shanty

25 dwellers—evidence of the transformation that has swept this nation in a blink of history's eye.

Close Read

1. How are the kinds of details in this article different from those in Mathabane's autobiography?

2. **Key Idea: Progress** Consider what both excerpts reveal about life in South Africa before and after apartheid. What **progress** has been made in South Africa?

TYPES OF MEDIA

Subtle product placement in movies, exclusive stories on the nightly news, political campaign sites on the Web—media messages like these are pervasive today. For that reason, being literate now involves the ability to "read" media messages. To become **media literate,** you need to learn how to critically analyze such messages, as well as understand how they are shaping your perceptions of the world.

TYPE OF MEDIA	CHARACTERISTICS	
FEATURE FILMS Motion pictures that use narrative elements to tell a story	• Are intended to entertain and to generate profit • Create gripping narratives through cinematography, music, sets, and actors • Are at least one hour long	
NEWS MEDIA Accounts of current events as presented in newspapers and magazines and on TV, radio, and the Web	• Are meant to inform and to create viewer or reader loyalty • Medium (TV, Web, print) dictates the presentation and delivery of information • May be biased or inaccurate, so must be examined carefully	
TV SHOWS Programs broadcast on TV, including dramas, sitcoms, talk shows, and documentaries	• Are usually intended to entertain or inform • Are financed by sponsors who pay to air ads during the programs • Use visuals and sound effects to create compelling programming • Are typically 30–60 minutes in length	
ADVERTISING Paid promotion of products, services, candidates, or public service messages, using print and broadcast media	• Is designed to persuade a target audience to take action, buy a product or service, or support a candidate • Uses persuasive techniques, visuals, and sounds to sway an audience • Is strategically presented where and when it will have maximum exposure to the target audience	
WEB SITES Collections of "pages" on the Web. From a home page, users can navigate to other pages by clicking menus or hyperlinks.	• Can be accessed at any time by anyone with a computer and an Internet connection • Must be evaluated for reliability (because anyone can publish on the Web) • Convey information through text, graphics, audio, video, and animation	

Strategies That Work: Literature

❶ Ask the Right Questions

Analyzing literature is largely a matter of developing your ability to ask pointed, probing questions, such as the kinds described in the chart.

Kinds of Questions	Where to Look
Big questions about key ideas	▶ **Before Reading** pages (preceding every selection)
Questions that focus on literary analysis and evaluation	▶ Side notes (alongside most selections) and **After Reading** pages (following every lesson)
Guided questions for analyzing specific genres	▶ **Analysis Frames (Literature Center** at ClassZone.com)

❷ Make Connections

To get the most out of literature, you have to make connections to your life, to other selections, and to the world at large. Try the following approaches:

- **Big Questions and Key Ideas** The selections in this book are tied to big questions and key ideas that affect all of our lives. Consider how the situations and experiences you read about relate to those in your own life.

- **Discussion/Writing** Share your insights with others or jot down your impressions in a journal. You might discuss or record

  - conflicts or events that you can personally relate to
  - characters who remind you of people you know
  - quotations that resonate with you
  - similar themes in other works

❸ Record Your Reactions

Keep track of your questions, observations, and reactions in a **Reader's Notebook.** Experiment with a variety of formats.

TWO-COLUMN NOTES

Jot down quotations and information from the selection in one column and your comments in the other.

Details in *Kaffir Boy*	My Impressions
"I yearned to become invisible, to have the ground beneath me open and swallow me." (lines 4–5)	Emphasizes the intense fear that paralyzed Mathabane; no wonder this experience has stayed with him after so many years.

GRAPHIC ORGANIZER

Use a variety of charts, diagrams, or other graphic organizers to help you interpret events, analyze characters, and draw conclusions.

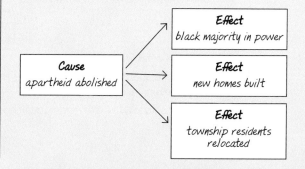

Cause: apartheid abolished
Effect: black majority in power
Effect: new homes built
Effect: township residents relocated

Becoming an Active Reader

To explore life's big questions through literature, you need to be actively engaged in what you're reading. That means you should be picking up on essential details, questioning why events are unfolding as they are, and making connections between situations in the text and those in your life. When you are absorbed in a riveting television show or reading a review of a new CD, you are using these skills and strategies—without consciously thinking about them. Throughout this book, you will apply the following skills and strategies to the literature you read.

SKILLS AND STRATEGIES FOR ACTIVE READING

Preview
Get a sense of a text before you start to read.
- Look for clues in the title, graphics, and subheadings.
- Skim opening paragraphs before you dive in.

Set a Purpose
Decide *why* you are reading a particular text.
- Ask: Am I reading for my own enjoyment, to learn about a topic, or for another reason?
- Think about how your purpose might affect the way you approach a text. Should you read slowly and analytically, or simply settle back and enjoy?

Connect
Relate personally to what you are reading.
- Consider whether you've encountered people or situations like the ones described.
- Ask: If I were in this situation, how would I react?

Use Prior Knowledge
Call to mind what you already know about a topic.
- Before reading, jot down any relevant information or experiences that you bring to the text.
- As you are reading, use your notes to help you connect what you know to what you are learning.

Predict
Try to guess what will happen next.
- Note details about characters and events that hint at possible plot developments.
- Read on to discover whether your predictions were on target.

Visualize
Try to picture what is being described.
- Note descriptive details about characters, settings, and events.
- Use these details to help you "see" a scene unfolding as a movie in your mind.

Monitor
Check your own understanding as you read.
- **Question** what is happening and why. For example, ask: What just happened? Why is the character acting this way?
- **Clarify** your understanding by rereading difficult parts or asking for help.
- **Evaluate** yourself as a reader. Ask: How well am I understanding the text?

Make Inferences
Use evidence in the text and what you know from experience to help you "read between the lines."
- Record details about characters, settings, and plot developments.
- Ask: How can common sense and my own experiences deepen my understanding of what's happening? (The chart below shows how one student made an inference about a character in the story on the next page.)

Details in "Where Is Here?"	What I Know	My Inference
The stranger remembers the room being "Dark by day, dark by night." (line 5)	During the day, houses are usually lit up.	There's something unusual or different about the stranger or his family.

In the story "Where Is Here?" by Joyce Carol Oates, a stranger revisits his childhood home. The current residents—a mother and a father—follow the stranger through their house as he recalls his memories of living there. As you read this excerpt from the story, use the **Close Read** questions to help you to make sense of the mysterious situation.

from *Where Is Here?*

Short story by **Joyce Carol Oates**

Finally, as if remembering the presence of his hosts, and the necessity for some display of civility, the stranger expressed his admiration for the attractiveness of the room, and its coziness. He'd remembered it as cavernous, with a ceiling twice as high. "And dark most of the time," he said wonderingly.

5 "Dark by day, dark by night." The mother turned the lights of the little brass chandelier to their fullest: shadows were dispersed like ragged ghosts and the cut-glass fruit bowl at the center of the table glowed like an exquisite multifaceted jewel. The stranger exclaimed in surprise. He'd extracted a handkerchief from his pocket and was dabbing carefully at his face, where

10 beads of perspiration shone. He said, as if thinking aloud, still wonderingly, "My father was a unique man. Everyone who knew him admired him. He sat *here*," he said, gingerly touching the chair that was in fact the father's chair, at one end of the table. "And Mother sat *there*," he said, merely pointing. "I don't recall my own place or my sister's but I suppose it doesn't matter. . . . I see you

15 have four place settings, Mrs. . . . ? Two children, I suppose?" "A boy eleven, and a girl thirteen," the mother said. The stranger stared not at her but at the table, smiling. "And so too *we* were—I mean, there were two of us: my sister and me."

The mother said, as if not knowing what else to say, "Are you—close?"

20 The stranger shrugged, distractedly rather than rudely, and moved on to the living room.

This room, cozily lit as well, was the most carefully furnished room in the house. Deep-piled wall-to-wall carpeting in hunter green, cheerful chintz drapes, a sofa and matching chairs in nubby heather green, framed reproductions of

25 classic works of art, a gleaming gilt-framed mirror over the fireplace: wasn't the living room impressive as a display in a furniture store? But the stranger said nothing at first. Indeed, his eyes narrowed sharply as if he were confronted with a disagreeable spectacle. He whispered, "Here too! Here too!"

Close Read

1. **Connect** Think of a time when you returned to a place from your childhood, such as an old school or a previous home. In what ways was it different from how you remembered it?

2. **Visualize** What impression do you have of the stranger so far? Cite details about his behavior that helped you to form a mental image.

He went to the fireplace, walking, now, with a decided limp; he drew his
30 fingers with excruciating slowness along the mantel as if testing its materiality.
For some time he merely stood, and stared, and listened. He tapped a section
of wall with his knuckles—"There used to be a large water stain here, like a
shadow."

"Was there?" murmured the father out of politeness, and "Was there!"
35 murmured the mother. Of course, neither had ever seen a water stain there.

Then, noticing the window seat, the stranger uttered a soft surprised cry,
and went to sit in it. He appeared delighted: hugging his knees like a child
trying to make himself smaller. "This was one of my happy places! At least
when Father wasn't home. I'd hide away here for hours, reading, daydreaming,
40 staring out the window! Sometimes Mother would join me, if she was in
the mood, and we'd plot together—oh, all sorts of fantastical things!" The
stranger remained sitting in the window seat for so long, tears shining in his
eyes, that the father and mother almost feared he'd forgotten them. He was
stroking the velvet fabric of the cushioned seat, gropingly touching the leaded
45 windowpanes. Wordlessly, the father and mother exchanged a glance: who was
this man, and how could they tactfully get rid of him? The father made a face
signaling impatience and the mother shook her head without seeming to move
it. For they couldn't be rude to a guest in their house.

The stranger was saying in a slow, dazed voice, "It all comes back to me
50 now. How could I have forgotten! Mother used to read to me, and tell me
stories, and ask me riddles I couldn't answer. 'What creature walks on four legs
in the morning, two legs at midday, three legs in the evening?' 'What is round,
and flat, measuring mere inches in one direction, and infinity in the other?'
'Out of what does our life arise? Out of what does our consciousness arise?
55 Why are we here? Where *is* here?'"

The father and mother were perplexed by these strange words and hardly
knew how to respond. The mother said uncertainly, "Our daughter used to
like to sit here too, when she was younger. It *is* a lovely place." The father said
with surprising passion, "I hate riddles—they're moronic some of the time and
60 obscure the rest of the time." He spoke with such uncharacteristic rudeness,
the mother looked at him in surprise.

Hurriedly she said, "Is your mother still living, Mr. . . . ?" "Oh no. Not at
all," the stranger said, rising abruptly from the window seat, and looking at
the mother as if she had said something mildly preposterous. "I'm sorry," the
65 mother said. "Please don't be," the stranger said, "We've all been dead—*they've*
all been dead—a long time. " . . .

Close Read

3. **Make Inferences** Reread
the boxed text. What
can you infer about the
stranger's relationship
with his parents?

4. **Monitor** How do the
father and the mother feel
about the stranger? Cite
details from lines 45–48
to support your answer.

5. **Use Prior Knowledge**
Reread lines 49–55. How
do these riddles compare
with ones you know?
Consider whether these
riddles seem like ones
that most parents would
tell their children.

6. **Predict** What will the
mother and the father
find out about this
stranger? Give reasons to
support your prediction.

Strategies That Work: Reading

❶ Read Independently

The best way to become a better reader is to make reading a daily habit. Try all kinds of texts, from news Web sites to classic novels.

What Should I Read?	How Will I Benefit?
Novels	Pure enjoyment aside, novels can give you new insights into big questions and key ideas.
Autobiographies and biographies	You'll find out about the struggles and triumphs of influential figures, as well as get a glimpse inside their minds.
Magazines, newspapers, and Web sites	You'll learn about the world and develop your critical thinking skills.

❷ Use Graphic Organizers

Graphic organizers, such as character webs, charts, and timelines, can help you understand characters and track twists and turns in a plot.

What the Stranger Sees	How the Stranger Reacts
Cozy well-lit dining room	• Remembers the room being much darker • Starts perspiring • Recalls his family at the table
Well-furnished, nicely decorated living room	• Looks disturbed at first • Murmurs "Here too!" • Remembers a large water stain
A window seat	• Remembers this as a "happy place" • Starts acting like an overexcited child • Recalls crazy "riddles" his mother told him

❸ Build Your Vocabulary

Creating a personal word list can help you both build your vocabulary and become a better reader. Start a list in your **Reader's Notebook,** adding words as you encounter them.

- **Choose your words.** Consider recording vocabulary words from the selections in this book. You might also include words that you encounter while reading newspapers and Web sites, such as unfamiliar terms connected to innovations or new technologies.
- **Go beyond the definitions.** Write synonyms, antonyms, and sentences to help you remember the words and their meanings.
- **Use the words often.** Studies have shown that you have to use a word multiple times to really learn it. Try to incorporate new words into your writing and discussions.

Word	Meaning
materiality (n.) "Where Is Here?" line 30	**Definition:** being made of physical substance **Synonyms:** solidity, substantiality **Antonyms:** illusion, shadow **Sentence:** The knife sliced right through the vegetables, as if they had no <u>materiality</u>.

Expressing Ideas in Writing

The author E. L. Doctorow once said, "Writing is an exploration. You start from nothing and learn as you go." The journey from an unformed idea to a polished final draft proves that writing is indeed an exploration. Along the way, you can learn more about your own opinions and even enlighten, influence, or inspire others.

Consider Your Options

You might want to describe a memorable experience in colorful detail, take a stand on a controversial issue, analyze the theme of a novel, or apply for a summer job. No matter what you decide to write about, you should start by considering three essential elements—your **purpose,** your **audience,** and the **format** of your writing.

PURPOSE	**AUDIENCE**	**FORMAT**
Why am I writing?	**Who are my readers?**	**Which format will best suit my purpose and audience?**
• to entertain	• other classmates	• essay • short story
• to inform or explain	• teacher	• letter • speech
• to persuade	• friends	• poem • review
• to describe	• community members	• research • journal
• to express thoughts and feelings	• potential employer	paper entry
• to inspire	• customer service department	• script • news article
	• college admissions office	• editorial • Web site
	• Web community	• summary
		• power presentation

Continue with the Process

Every writer follows a unique process for writing. Some writers, for example, dive right into drafting, letting their ideas develop as they go. Others revise their work countless times, generating one improved draft after another. As you tackle the **Writing Workshop** assignments in this book, you will start to adapt the following process to suit your own working style.

THE WRITING PROCESS

What Should I Do?

PREWRITING
Explore your ideas and decide what you want to write about. Once you've defined your purpose, audience, and format, develop and focus your ideas by using prewriting strategies, such as **freewriting** or **brainstorming** with others. Find additional strategies on page 19.

DRAFTING
Transform your ideas into a rough draft, without worrying about errors. If you are writing an informal piece, such as a journal entry or a personal narrative, you might **draft to discover**— start writing with no set plan. If you are writing a formal essay, however, **draft from an outline.**

REVISING AND EDITING
Critically evaluate your draft, looking for ways to improve its content, structure, and style.
- Review the **rubric** on page 18.
- Enlist the help of a **peer reader.**
- **Proofread** for errors in grammar, usage, and mechanics.

PUBLISHING
Get your writing out where others can read it. Where you publish, of course, depends on your **purpose, audience,** and **format.** Visit the **Writing Center** at **ClassZone.com** for publishing options.

What Does It Look Like?

FREEWRITING

Twelve Angry Men
Serving on a jury would be an exciting experience. Deciding someone's fate is a big responsibility, though. The eighth juror seemed to be the only one who took that responsibility to heart. Maybe I could write about the character of Juror No. 8.

OUTLINE

I. Juror No. 8 has all the qualities that a responsible juror should have.
   A. Is impartial (evidence is important, not feelings)
   B. Stands up for his opinion even after other jurors ridicule him for being "in left field" (line 9)

PEER SUGGESTIONS

In Reginald Rose's Twelve Angry Men, Jurer No. 8 is the only one to understand ~~what it means to be a good jurer.~~ this weighty responsibility.

Suggestion: May want to grab readers with a creative statement. Try: "The jury has reached a verdict—one that will seal the fate of the defendant."

PUBLISHING OPTIONS

Do a Self-Check

Whether you're analyzing *Julius Caesar* or posting a movie review on the Web, considering the key traits of effective writing can keep you from getting sidetracked. Use this rubric to evaluate your draft at any point in the process.

KEY TRAITS RUBRIC

	Strong	Average	Weak
Ideas	• centers around a clear, focused topic • is supported by vivid, well-chosen details	• has a topic, but it needs to be developed more • contains general statements with some details	• has no clear topic • omits important details or includes unclear ones
Organization	• opens in an engaging way and wraps up with a satisfying conclusion • flows in a logical manner	• has both an introduction and a conclusion, but they are uninteresting • lacks some transitions	• has no real introduction or conclusion • contains a confusing jumble of ideas
Voice	• conveys a strong sense of individual style • uses a tone that is well-suited to the purpose and audience	• sounds flat in some places • lapses into an inappropriate tone at times	• has little or no life • continuously uses an inappropriate tone for the intended purpose and audience
Word Choice	• uses words that are precise and colorful • conveys meaning in a powerful, yet natural-sounding manner	• uses words that are correct, but ordinary • gets meaning across, but is not memorable	• uses words that are vague or incorrect • fails to convey meaning clearly
Sentence Fluency	• includes sentences of varied lengths and structures • creates a pleasing flow from one idea to the next	• has some sentence variety, but not enough • lacks flow in some places	• includes mostly short or rambling sentences • is awkward or repetitious
Conventions	• shows a strong grasp of grammar and usage • has few problems with mechanics (spelling, capitalization, and punctuation)	• has minor grammar and usage problems • contains some mechanical errors	• has such poor grammar and usage that meaning is unclear • contains so many mechanical errors that the writing is hard to read

Strategies That Work: Writing

❶ Use Prewriting Strategies

The first step in any process is often the hardest—and that can be especially true of writing. Here are some strategies to help you get a strong start:

- **Freewrite.** Write continuously for ten minutes, jotting down the ideas that pop into your head.
- **Chart your course.** Capture your ideas in a graphic organizer, such as a spider map or an observation chart.
- **Search for inspiration.** Look for quotations, photographs, headlines, and other sources of inspiration.
- **Brainstorm with others.** Hear what others have to say about your ideas.
- **Write from a prompt.** Visit the **Writing Center** at **ClassZone.com** for prompts and ideas for writing.

❷ Get Feedback from Peers

Often, peer readers can spot problems that you've overlooked. Consider the following guidelines.

When You're the Writer	When You're the Reader
• Make readers feel comfortable about responding honestly by listening respectfully to what they have to say. • Clarify what kind of feedback you want. Should your readers focus on content, structure, or both? • Think about readers' comments and then make your own decisions about what to change.	• Remember that you could be in the writer's position—so be truthful but tactful. • Be as specific as you can be. Offer detailed explanations to support your reactions and comments. • Respect the writer's right to accept or reject your suggestions and to revise the work in his or her own way.

❸ Read, Read, Read

If you really want to develop and improve your own style, then you should read other people's writing. Consider these sources:

LITERATURE
Take a closer look at some of the fiction, nonfiction, poetry, and drama in this book. Also, don't overlook novels, magazines, and newspapers that interest you.

WRITING COMMUNITY
Form a writing group with other students to share each other's writing processes and products.

CLASSZONE
McDougal Littell

ONLINE RESOURCES
Check out the **Writing Center** at ClassZone.com for interactive models of student writing, as well as links to publication sites on the Web.

The World of a Story

PLOT, SETTING, AND MOOD

- In Fiction
- In Nonfiction
- In Media
- In Poetry

Share What You Know

Which stories are
WORTH *reading?*

So many activities compete for your time and attention. You can spend your leisure time watching television, playing video games, or surfing the Internet. If you decide to invest your time reading a book, you want **value** for that investment. You want to be sure the story is worth reading, making you laugh, cry, or gasp in surprise.

ACTIVITY Which stories made you glad you had read them? What qualities made these stories so good? Create a list of your criteria for a "great read." Think about the following:

- Do you care more about the characters or the events that happen to them?

- Does suspense play a role in the stories you like?

- Are there certain places you like to read about?

- What emotions do you like to feel as you read?

An alien on his own planet....
Complete and Unabridged
H. G. WELLS
THE TIME MACHINE

OHIO STANDARDS

Preview Unit Goals

LITERARY ANALYSIS
- Identify and analyze conflict and its complications
- Analyze setting and its influence on mood and conflict
- Analyze mood and suspense

READING
- Use reading strategies, including monitoring and predicting
- Make inferences and draw conclusions
- Analyze text features and patterns of organization
- Evaluate information against criteria
- Analyze chronological order

WRITING AND GRAMMAR
- Write an interpretive essay
- Support key points with evidence from the text
- Use descriptive details and improve sentence flow

SPEAKING, LISTENING, AND VIEWING
- Present an oral response to literature
- Analyze film techniques that create suspense

VOCABULARY
- Understand connotations and denotations of words
- Understand and use specialized/technical vocabulary
- Use word roots and prefixes to help unlock meaning

ACADEMIC VOCABULARY
- conflict
- connotation and denotation
- inferences and conclusions
- mood
- patterns of organization
- setting
- storyboard
- text features

Plot, Setting, and Mood

Every story transports you to a fictional world. You might be swept away by a love story set during the Civil War or mesmerized by a science fiction adventure that takes place on an uninhabited planet. No matter where and when they unfold, good stories allow you to experience times, places, and conflicts that are outside your everyday life. To understand why a story affects you as it does, you have to analyze the elements—plot, setting, and mood—that make up its world.

OHIO STANDARDS

READING STANDARDS
4.3 Distinguish how conflicts, parallel plots and subplots affect the text
4.8 Analyze the author's use of mood

Part 1: Setting and Mood

Almost every story happens in a particular time and place—for example, "long ago, in a galaxy far, far away," in a modern city, or during the Great Depression. The time and place of the story is its **setting.** Writers create setting through the following:

- details that suggest the time of day, year, season, or historical period
- descriptions of characters, clothing, buildings, weather, and landscapes

Another element that contributes to the world of a story is the **mood,** the feeling or atmosphere that a writer creates for readers. Whether it is ominous or uplifting, a mood is developed through a writer's use of imagery and choice of words and details. Setting details, in particular, help to establish a mood.

In Jack London's "To Build a Fire" (page 74), the setting affects the mood and other elements. The bleak story takes place on a wilderness trail in the Yukon Territory, a region in far northwestern Canada.

SETTING IN

TO BUILD A FIRE

Creates Conflicts
Can the man build a fire to warm his frozen limbs? He faces conflicts like this one as he struggles to survive.

Serves as a Symbol
The man's frozen surroundings symbolize death and the indifference of nature to what people want.

Influences Character
Overconfident and inexperienced in the cold, the man learns a life-or-death lesson.

Helps Create Mood
The setting creates a mood of alienation and fear in the face of a natural world that is indifferent.

MODEL: SETTING AND MOOD

At the beginning of the novel *Ethan Frome*, the narrator hears townspeople allude to a tragedy that ruined the life of the title character, Ethan. When a snowstorm hits the town, the narrator must spend the night at Ethan's, where he finally hears the entire tragic story. This excerpt begins as the storm is approaching.

from

Ethan Frome

Novel by **Edith Wharton**

. . . We set out for Starkfield with a good chance of getting there for supper. But at sunset the clouds gathered again, bringing an earlier night, and the snow began to fall straight and steadily from a sky without wind, in a soft universal diffusion more confusing than the gusts and eddies of the morning. It seemed
5 to be a part of the thickening darkness, to be the winter night itself descending on us layer by layer.

   The small ray of Frome's lantern was soon lost in this smothering medium, in which even his sense of direction, and the bay's homing instinct, finally ceased to serve us. Two or three times some ghostly landmark sprang up to
10 warn us that we were astray, and then was sucked back into the mist; and when we finally regained our road the old horse began to show signs of exhaustion. I felt myself to blame for having accepted Frome's offer, and after a short discussion I persuaded him to let me get out of the sleigh and walk along through the snow at the bay's side. In this way we struggled on for another
15 mile or two, and at last reached a point where Frome, peering into what seemed to me formless night, said: "That's my gate down yonder." . . .

   "Look here, Frome," I began, "there's no earthly use in your going any farther—" but he interrupted me: "Nor you neither. There's been about enough of this for anybody."

20   I understood that he was offering me a night's shelter at the farm, and without answering I turned into the gate at his side, and followed him to the barn, where I helped him to unharness and bed down the tired horse. When this was done he unhooked the lantern from the sleigh, stepped out again into the night, and called to me over his shoulder: "This way."

25   Far off above us a square of light trembled through the screen of snow. Staggering along in Frome's wake I floundered toward it, and in the darkness almost fell into one of the deep drifts against the front of the house. Frome scrambled up the slippery steps of the porch, digging a way through the snow with his heavily booted foot. Then he lifted his lantern, found the latch, and
30 led the way into the house. I went after him into a low unlit passage, at the back of which a ladder-like staircase rose into obscurity.

Close Read

1. Where and when does this story takes place? Describe the setting as completely as you can.

2. Reread lines 1–11. What mood do the setting details help to create? Support your answer.

3. What conflicts does the setting create for Ethan and the narrator?

4. Identify two setting details that may hint at the tragic story that the narrator will soon hear. Explain your choices. One detail has been boxed.

Part 2: Plot and Story Analysis

A story is much more than the world in which the action unfolds. The real power of a story comes from *what happens* in that world. Most stories follow a **plot,** a chain of events that traces a **conflict,** or struggle between opposing forces. The conflict can be **internal,** taking place within the mind of a character, or it can be an **external** conflict between a character and an outside force, such as another character, society, or nature.

Plot is usually talked about in terms of the following stages. Keep in mind, however, that not every story follows this exact structure.

STAGES OF A TYPICAL PLOT	QUESTIONS FOR ANALYSIS
EXPOSITION This part of a plot introduces the setting and characters and establishes a mood. It may also reveal the conflict or set the stage for it.	• What details help to establish the setting and create a mood? • What kind of person is the main character? • What, if anything, is revealed about the conflict?
RISING ACTION Complications arise as the main character struggles to resolve the conflict. "The plot thickens" as suspense builds.	• What is the central conflict? • How do the characters respond to the conflict? • How does the conflict become more complicated?
CLIMAX The climax is a turning point in the story and the moment of greatest suspense. Often the main character makes a decision or takes an action that makes the outcome of the conflict clear.	• What decision or action has the main character made or taken? • What impact might this decision or action have on the characters and the conflict? • How might the conflict be resolved?
FALLING ACTION This stage shows the results of the decision or action that happened at the climax. Tension eases as the conflict is resolved.	• What is the outcome of the main character's decision or action? • What steps does the main character take to resolve the conflict?
RESOLUTION The resolution reveals the final outcome of the story and ties up any loose ends.	• How have the events and conflicts affected or changed the characters? • Through the resolution, what message might the writer be suggesting?

Part 3: Analyze the Literature

In this story, a lovestruck teenager is faced with a difficult choice. As you read, use what you've learned about setting, mood, and plot to analyze the story.

THE BASS, THE RIVER, AND SHEILA MANT

Short story by **W. D. Wetherell**

There was a summer in my life when the only creature that seemed lovelier to me than a largemouth bass was Sheila Mant. I was fourteen. The Mants had rented the cottage next to ours on the river; with their parties, their frantic games of softball, their constant comings and goings, they appeared to me denizens of a
5 brilliant existence. "Too noisy by half," my mother quickly decided, but I would have given anything to be invited to one of their parties, and when my parents went to bed I would sneak through the woods to their hedge and stare enchanted at the candlelit swirl of white dresses and bright, paisley skirts.

Sheila was the middle daughter—at seventeen, all but out of reach. She
10 would spend her days sunbathing on a float my Uncle Sierbert had moored in their cove, and before July was over I had learned all her moods. If she lay flat on the diving board with her hand trailing idly in the water, she was pensive, not to be disturbed. On her side, her head propped up by her arm, she was observant, considering those around her with a look that seemed queenly
15 and severe. Sitting up, arms tucked around her long, suntanned legs, she was approachable, but barely, and it was only in those glorious moments when she stretched herself prior to entering the water that her various suitors found the courage to come near.

These were many. The Dartmouth heavyweight crew would scull by her
20 house on their way upriver, and I think all eight of them must have been in love with her at various times during the summer; the coxswain would curse at them through his megaphone but without effect—there was always a pause in their pace when they passed Sheila's float. I suppose to these jaded twenty-year-olds she seemed the incarnation of innocence and youth, while to me
25 she appeared unutterably suave, the epitome of sophistication. I was on the swim team at school, and to win her attention would do endless laps between my house and the Vermont shore, hoping she would notice the beauty of my flutter kick, the power of my crawl. Finishing, I would boost myself up onto our dock and glance casually over toward her, but she was never watching, and
30 the miraculous day she was, I immediately climbed the diving board and did my best tuck and a half for her, and continued diving until she had left and the sun went down and my longing was like a madness and I couldn't stop.

Close Read

1. The exposition transports you into the world of the story. What do you learn about the setting in lines 1–8? Describe the mood that the setting details help to create.

2. What does the boxed text reveal about the narrator's personality?

3. Consider the description of Sheila in lines 9–18 and the narrator's eagerness to impress her. What do you think the main conflict will be about?

t was late August by the time I got up the nerve to ask her out. The tortured will-I's, won't-I's, the agonized indecision over what to say, the false starts toward her house and embarrassed retreats—the details of these have been seared from my memory, and the only part I remember clearly is emerging from the woods toward dusk while they were playing softball on their lawn, as bashful and frightened as a unicorn.

Sheila was stationed halfway between first and second, well outside the infield. She didn't seem surprised to see me—as a matter of fact, she didn't seem to see me at all.

"If you're playing second base, you should move closer," I said.

She turned—I took the full brunt of her long red hair and well-spaced freckles.

"I'm playing outfield," she said, "I don't like the responsibility of having a base."

"Yeah, I can understand that," I said, though I couldn't. "There's a band in Dixford tomorrow night at nine. Want to go?"

One of her brothers sent the ball sailing over the leftfielder's head; she stood and watched it disappear toward the river.

"You have a car?" she said, without looking up.

I played my master stroke. "We'll go by canoe."

I spent all of the following day polishing it. I turned it upside down on our lawn and rubbed every inch with Brillo, hosing off the dirt, wiping it with chamois until it gleamed as bright as aluminum ever gleamed. About five, I slid it into the water, arranging cushions near the bow so Sheila could lean on them if she was in one of her pensive moods, propping up my father's transistor radio by the middle thwart so we could have music when we came back. Automatically, without thinking about it, I mounted my Mitchell reel on my Pfleuger spinning rod and stuck it in the stern.

I say automatically, because I never went anywhere that summer without a fishing rod. When I wasn't swimming laps to impress Sheila, I was back in our driveway practicing casts, and when I wasn't practicing casts, I was tying the line to Tosca, our springer spaniel, to test the reel's drag, and when I wasn't doing any of those things, I was fishing the river for bass.

Too nervous to sit at home, I got in the canoe early and started paddling in a huge circle that would get me to Sheila's dock around eight. As automatically as I brought along my rod, I tied on a big Rapala plug, let it down into the water, let out some line and immediately forgot all about it.

It was already dark by the time I glided up to the Mants' dock. Even by day the river was quiet, most of the summer people preferring Sunapee or one of the other nearby lakes, and at night it was a solitude difficult to believe, a corridor of hidden life that ran between banks like a tunnel. Even the stars were part of it. They weren't as sharp anywhere else; they seemed to have chosen the river as a guide on their slow wheel toward morning, and in the course of the summer's fishing, I had learned all their names.

I was there ten minutes before Sheila appeared. I heard the slam of their screen door first, then saw her in the spotlight as she came slowly down the path. As beautiful as she was on the float, she was even lovelier now—her

Close Read

4. In lines 33–48, the narrator makes a decision that sets the rising action in motion. Explain what his decision is. How does it make the story more compelling?

5. Reread lines 53–65. What more do you learn about the narrator and the kind of person he is?

6. Compare the description of the setting in the boxed text with that in the first paragraph of the story. How has the mood changed?

80 white dress went perfectly with her hair, and complimented her figure even
more than her swimsuit.

It was her face that bothered me. It had on its delightful fullness a very
dubious expression.

"Look," she said. "I can get Dad's car."

85 "It's faster this way," I lied. "Parking's tense up there. Hey, it's safe. I won't
tip it or anything."

She let herself down reluctantly into the bow. I was glad she wasn't facing me.
When her eyes were on me, I felt like diving in the river again from agony and joy.

I pried the canoe away from the dock and started paddling upstream. There

90 was an extra paddle in the bow, but Sheila made no move to pick it up. She
took her shoes off, and dangled her feet over the side.

Ten minutes went by.

"What kind of band?" she said.

"It's sort of like folk music. You'll like it."

95 "Eric Caswell's going to be there. He strokes number four."

"No kidding?" I said. I had no idea who she meant.

"What's that sound?" she said, pointing toward shore.

"Bass. That splashing sound?"

"Over there."

100 "Yeah, bass. They come into the shallows at night to chase frogs and moths
and things. Big largemouths. *Micropetrus salmonides,*" I added, showing off.

"I think fishing's dumb," she said, making a face. "I mean, it's boring and
all. Definitely dumb."

Now I have spent a great deal of time in the years since wondering why
Sheila Mant should come down so hard on fishing. Was her father a
fisherman? Her antipathy toward fishing nothing more than normal
filial rebellion? Had she tried it once? A messy encounter with worms? It
doesn't matter. What does, is that at that fragile moment in time I would have
given anything not to appear dumb in Sheila's severe and unforgiving eyes.

110 She hadn't seen my equipment yet. What I *should* have done, of course,
was push the canoe in closer to shore and carefully slide the rod into some
branches where I could pick it up again in the morning. Failing that, I could
have surreptitiously dumped the whole outfit overboard, written off the forty
or so dollars as love's tribute. What I actually *did* do was gently lean forward,

115 and slowly, ever so slowly, push the rod back through my legs toward the stern
where it would be less conspicuous.

It must have been just exactly what the bass was waiting for. Fish will trail
a lure sometimes, trying to make up their mind whether or not to attack, and
the slight pause in the plug's speed caused by my adjustment was tantalizing

120 enough to overcome the bass's inhibitions. My rod, safely out of sight at last,
bent double. The line, tightly coiled, peeled off the spool with the shrill,
tearing zip of a high-speed drill.

Close Read

7. Describe Sheila's personality. In what ways does her attitude create conflicts for the narrator?

Four things occurred to me at once. One, that it was a bass. Two, that it was a big bass. Three, that it was the biggest bass I had ever hooked. Four, that
125 Sheila Mant must not know.

"What was that?" she said, half turning around.

"Uh, what was what?"

"That buzzing noise."

"Bats."

130 She shuddered, quickly drew her feet back into the canoe. Every instinct I had told me to pick up the rod and strike back at the bass, but there was no need to—it was already solidly hooked. Downstream, an awesome distance downstream, it jumped clear of the water, landing with a concussion heavy enough to ripple the entire river. For a moment, I thought it was gone, but then
135 the rod was bending again, the tip dancing into the water. Slowly, not making any motion that might alert Sheila, I reached down to tighten the drag.

While all this was going on, Sheila had begun talking and it was a few minutes before I was able to catch up with her train of thought.

"I went to a party there. These fraternity men. Katherine says I could get
140 in there if I wanted. I'm thinking more of UVM or Bennington. Somewhere I can ski."

The bass was slanting toward the rocks on the New Hampshire side by the ruins of Donaldson's boathouse. It had to be an old bass—a young one probably wouldn't have known the rocks were there. I brought the canoe back
145 out into the middle of the river, hoping to head it off.

"That's neat," I mumbled. "Skiing. Yeah, I can see that."

"Eric said I have the figure to model, but I thought I should get an education first. I mean, it might be a while before I get started and all. I was thinking of getting my hair styled, more swept back? I mean, Ann-Margret?
150 Like hers, only shorter."

She hesitated. "Are we going backwards?"

We were. I had managed to keep the bass in the middle of the river away from the rocks, but it had plenty of room there, and for the first time a chance to exert its full strength. I quickly computed the weight necessary to draw a
155 fully loaded canoe backwards—the thought of it made me feel faint.

"It's just the current," I said hoarsely. "No sweat or anything."

I dug in deeper with my paddle. Reassured, Sheila began talking about something else, but all my attention was taken up now with the fish. I could feel its desperation as the water grew shallower. I could sense the extra strain
160 on the line, the frantic way it cut back and forth in the water. I could visualize what it looked like—the gape of its mouth, the flared gills and thick, vertical tail. The bass couldn't have encountered many forces in its long life that it wasn't capable of handling, and the unrelenting tug at its mouth must have been a source of great puzzlement and mounting panic.

165 Me, I had problems of my own. To get to Dixford, I had to paddle up a sluggish stream that came into the river beneath a covered bridge. There was a shallow sandbar at the mouth of this stream—weeds on one side, rocks on the other. Without doubt, this is where I would lose the fish.

Close Read

8. In lines 123–125, the main conflict comes into sharp focus. What is the narrator's conflict?

9. In the rising action, the story cuts back and forth between the narrator's struggle with the fish and Sheila's incessant talking. How does this heighten the suspense?

10. Reread lines 165–168. What conflicts are created by the setting?

"I have to be careful with my complexion. I tan, but in segments. I can't
170 figure out if it's even worth it. I wouldn't even do it probably. I saw Jackie
Kennedy in Boston and she wasn't tan at all."

Taking a deep breath, I paddled as hard as I could for the middle, deepest
part of the bar. I could have threaded the eye of a needle with the canoe, but
the pull on the stern threw me off and I overcompensated—the canoe veered
175 left and scraped bottom. I pushed the paddle down and shoved. A moment of
hesitation . . . a moment more. . . . The canoe shot clear into the deeper water
of the stream. I immediately looked down at the rod. It was bent in the same,
tight arc—miraculously, the bass was still on.

The moon was out now. It was low and full enough that its beam shone
180 directly on Sheila there ahead of me in the canoe, washing her in a
creamy, luminous glow. I could see the lithe, easy shape of her figure. I
could see the way her hair curled down off her shoulders, the proud, alert
tilt of her head, and all these things were as a tug on my heart. Not just Sheila,
but the aura she carried about her of parties and casual touchings and grace.
185 Behind me, I could feel the strain of the bass, steadier now, growing weaker,
and this was another tug on my heart, not just the bass but the beat of the river
and the slant of the stars and the smell of the night, until finally it seemed I
would be torn apart between longings, split in half. Twenty yards ahead of us
was the road, and once I pulled the canoe up on shore, the bass would be gone,
190 irretrievably gone. If instead I stood up, grabbed the rod and started pumping,
I would have it—as tired as the bass was, there was no chance it could get away.
I reached down for the rod, hesitated, looked up to where Sheila was stretching
herself lazily toward the sky, her small breasts rising beneath the soft fabric of
her dress, and the tug was too much for me, and quicker than it takes to write
195 down, I pulled a penknife from my pocket and cut the line in half.

With a sick, nauseous feeling in my stomach, I saw the rod unbend.

"My legs are sore," Sheila whined. "Are we there yet?"

Through a superhuman effort of self-control, I was able to beach the canoe and
help Sheila off. The rest of the night is much foggier. We walked to the fair—there
200 was the smell of popcorn, the sound of guitars. I may have danced once or twice
with her, but all I really remember is her coming over to me once the music was
done to explain that she would be going home in Eric Caswell's Corvette.

"Okay," I mumbled.

For the first time that night she looked at me, really looked at me.
205 "You're a funny kid, you know that?"

Funny. Different. Dreamy. Odd. How many times was I to hear that in the
years to come, all spoken with the same quizzical, half-accusatory tone Sheila
used then. Poor Sheila! Before the month was over, the spell she cast over me
was gone, but the memory of that lost bass haunted me all summer and haunts
210 me still. There would be other Sheila Mants in my life, other fish, and though
I came close once or twice, it was these secret, hidden tuggings in the night
that claimed me, and I never made the same mistake again.

Close Read

11. Lines 179–195 mark the story's climax. Explain what the narrator finally chooses to do. Given his earlier thoughts and actions, did you expect this outcome? Explain.

12. The falling action (lines 196–205) shows what happens after the narrator makes his choice. What are the effects of his decision?

13. In the resolution (lines 206–212), the narrator, now older, reflects on his actions. What lesson has he learned from his experience?

Harrison Bergeron

Short Story by Kurt Vonnegut Jr.

What if everyone were THE SAME?

OHIO STANDARDS

READING STANDARDS
2.1 Draw conclusions
4.3 Distinguish how conflicts, parallel plots and subplots affect the text

KEY IDEA What would the world be like if everyone were the same—**average** in intelligence, talents, appearance, and strength—and no one was better than anyone else? How do you think people would feel and act toward each other? Would they be happy and satisfied?

BRAINSTORM With your class, brainstorm possible advantages and disadvantages of a world where everyone is the same—exactly average. Try to generate as many ideas as possible.

Advantages	Disadvantages
no more jealousy	nothing to live up to

LITERARY ANALYSIS: PLOT AND CONFLICT

The plot of a story is driven by a **conflict,** or struggle between opposing forces. In some stories, the conflict is between the main character and society. In "Harrison Bergeron," for example, the title character struggles with U.S. society in the year 2081. As you read, notice ways in which Harrison and the government oppose each other. Follow events to see who prevails.

READING SKILL: DRAW CONCLUSIONS

When you **draw conclusions,** you make judgments based on story details and your own prior knowledge. Use the following strategies to draw conclusions about the society depicted in "Harrison Bergeron":

- Note what results from the society's practices and laws.
- Apply your own knowledge to speculate about the motives of its officials.

As you read "Harrison Bergeron," use a chart like the one shown to make notes about the society. Also include your own thoughts or reactions about the information.

Details About Society	My Reactions
Constitutional amendments make everyone equal in every way.	It would be hard to enforce equality.
My Overall Conclusions	

▲ VOCABULARY IN CONTEXT

Vonnegut uses the following words in relating his futuristic tale. To see how many words you already know, substitute a different word or phrase for each boldfaced term.

1. **vigilance** with the children crossing the street
2. **wince** in pain after the injection
3. filled with **consternation** at the thought
4. **cower** in the corner
5. **synchronize** our watches
6. **neutralizing** the impact

Author Onine

Serious Humor Kurt Vonnegut Jr. was one of the most acclaimed satiric writers in America. After working briefly as a journalist, he began writing short stories in the late 1940s and continued writing stories, novels, dramas, and essays for more than 50 years. His fiction

Kurt Vonnegut Jr.
1922–2007

deals with sobering topics—war, brutality, and fear of technology. But Vonnegut writes with dark humor and elements of fantasy and even absurdity, which have given his writing lasting appeal.

Voice of Experience During World War II, Vonnegut was held as a prisoner of war in Dresden, Germany. The city was leveled by a fierce firebombing, and the destruction and horror of that event became the focus of his most famous novel, *Slaughterhouse Five.* Vonnegut wrote in a preface to the novel that it was about "the inhumanity of many of man's inventions to man." Vonnegut's early work was not well received by critics, but since the 1970s he has been regarded as a major American writer.

MORE ABOUT THE AUTHOR
For more on Kurt Vonnegut Jr., visit the **Literature Center** at ClassZone.com.

Background

What's Your Handicap? If you have ever run a footrace or played golf, you might know the sports term *handicap.* It refers to a way to even up a game so that good, average, and poor players can compete as equals. In a footrace, for example, faster runners might handicap themselves by giving slower runners a head start. In "Harrison Bergeron," people are given handicaps in daily life so that no one will be any stronger, smarter, or better looking than anyone else.

HARRISON BERGERON

KURT VONNEGUT JR.

The year was 2081, and everybody was finally equal. They weren't only equal before God and the law. They were equal every which way. Nobody was smarter than anybody else. Nobody was better looking than anybody else. Nobody was stronger or quicker than anybody else. All this equality was due to the 211th, 212th, and 213th Amendments to the Constitution, and to the unceasing **vigilance** of agents of the United States Handicapper General.

Some things about living still weren't quite right, though. April, for instance, still drove people crazy by not being springtime. And it was in that clammy month that the H-G men took George and Hazel Bergeron's fourteen-year-old 10 son, Harrison, away.

It was tragic, all right, but George and Hazel couldn't think about it very hard. Hazel had a perfectly average intelligence, which meant she couldn't think about anything except in short bursts. And George, while his intelligence was way above normal, had a little mental handicap radio in his ear. He was required by law to wear it at all times. It was tuned to a government transmitter.[1] Every twenty seconds or so, the transmitter would send out some sharp noise to keep people like George from taking unfair advantage of their brains. **A**

George and Hazel were watching television. There were tears on Hazel's cheeks, but she'd forgotten for the moment what they were about.

20 On the television screen were ballerinas.

A buzzer sounded in George's head. His thoughts fled in panic, like bandits from a burglar alarm.

"That was a real pretty dance, that dance they just did," said Hazel.

"Huh?" said George.

"That dance—it was nice," said Hazel.

"Yup," said George. He tried to think a little about the ballerinas. They weren't really very good—no better than anybody else would have been, anyway. They were burdened with sashweights[2] and bags of birdshot,[3] and

vigilance (vĭj'ə-ləns)
n. alert attention, watchfulness

A DRAW CONCLUSIONS
Reread lines 1–17. Cite specific details that describe society in 2081. What is your opinion of the society so far?

ANALYZE VISUALS
Examine the image of the television announcer and the picture behind him. What does this painting suggest about television?

---

1. **transmitter:** an electronic device for broadcasting radio signals.

2. **sashweights:** lead weights used in some kinds of windows to keep them from falling shut when raised.

3. **birdshot:** tiny lead pellets made to be loaded in shotgun shells.

TVTime-Announcer (2002), Charles Foster-Hall. Acrylic on canvas, 16″ × 20″. © Charles Foster-Hall.

their faces were masked, so that no one, seeing a free and graceful gesture or a
30 pretty face, would feel like something the cat drug in. George was toying with
the vague notion that maybe dancers shouldn't be handicapped. But he didn't
get very far with it before another noise in his ear radio scattered his thoughts.

George winced. So did two out of the eight ballerinas.

Hazel saw him **wince.** Having no mental handicap herself, she had to ask
George what the latest sound had been.

"Sounded like somebody hitting a milk bottle with a ball peen hammer,"[4]
said George.

"I'd think it would be real interesting, hearing all the different sounds," said
Hazel, a little envious. "All the things they think up."

40 "Um," said George. **B**

"Only, if I was Handicapper General, you know what I would do?" said
Hazel. Hazel, as a matter of fact, bore a strong resemblance to the Handicapper
General, a woman named Diana Moon Glampers. "If I was Diana Moon
Glampers," said Hazel, "I'd have chimes on Sunday—just chimes. Kind of in
honor of religion."

"I could think, if it was just chimes," said George.

"Well—maybe make 'em real loud," said Hazel. "I think I'd make a good
Handicapper General."

"Good as anybody else," said George.

50 "Who knows better'n I do what normal is?" said Hazel.

"Right," said George. He began to think glimmeringly about his abnormal
son who was now in jail, about Harrison, but a twenty-one-gun salute in his
head stopped that. **C**

"Boy!" said Hazel, "that was a doozy, wasn't it?"

It was such a doozy that George was white and trembling, and tears stood
on the rims of his red eyes. Two of the eight ballerinas had collapsed to the
studio floor and were holding their temples.

"All of a sudden you look so tired," said Hazel. "Why don't you stretch out
on the sofa, so's you can rest your handicap bag on the pillows, honeybunch."

60 She was referring to the forty-seven pounds of birdshot in a canvas bag, which
was padlocked around George's neck. "Go on and rest the bag for a little
while," she said. "I don't care if you're not equal to me for a while."

George weighed the bag with his hands. "I don't mind it," he said. "I don't
notice it any more. It's just a part of me."

"You been so tired lately—kind of wore out," said Hazel. "If there was just
some way we could make a little hole in the bottom of the bag, and just take
out a few of them lead balls. Just a few."

"Two years in prison and two thousand dollars fine for every ball I took
out," said George. "I don't call that a bargain."

B DRAW CONCLUSIONS
How does the society
affect the thoughts and
reactions of the people?
How does it influence
their job performance?

C PLOT AND CONFLICT
George's thoughts reveal
more about the conflict
between Harrison and
the society. On the basis
of what you've read so
far, what behavior do you
think might be viewed as
abnormal and illegal?

wince (wĭns) v. to shrink
or flinch involuntarily,
especially in pain

---

4. **ball peen hammer:** a hammer with a head having one flat side and one rounded side.

70   "If you could just take a few out when you came home from work," said Hazel. "I mean—you don't compete with anybody around here. You just set around."

    "If I tried to get away with it," said George, "then other people'd get away with it—and pretty soon we'd be right back to the dark ages again, with everybody competing against everybody else. You wouldn't like that, would you?"

    "I'd hate it," said Hazel.

    "There you are," said George. "The minute people start cheating on laws, what do you think happens to society?"

80   If Hazel hadn't been able to come up with an answer to this question, George couldn't have supplied one. A siren was going off in his head.

    "Reckon it'd fall all apart," said Hazel.

    "What would?" said George blankly.

    "Society," said Hazel uncertainly. "Wasn't that what you just said?"

    "Who knows?" said George. **D**

    The television program was suddenly interrupted for a news bulletin. It wasn't clear at first as to what the bulletin was about, since the announcer, like all announcers, had a serious speech impediment.[5] For about half a minute, and in a state of high excitement, the announcer tried to say, "Ladies and
90 gentlemen—"

    He finally gave up, handed the bulletin to a ballerina to read.

    "That's all right—" Hazel said of the announcer, "he tried. That's the big thing. He tried to do the best he could with what God gave him. He should get a nice raise for trying so hard."

    "Ladies and gentlemen—" said the ballerina, reading the bulletin. She must have been extraordinarily beautiful, because the mask she wore was hideous. And it was easy to see that she was the strongest and most graceful of all the dancers, for her handicap bags were as big as those worn by two-hundred-pound men.

100   And she had to apologize at once for her voice, which was a very unfair voice for a woman to use. Her voice was a warm, luminous, timeless melody. "Excuse me—" she said, and she began again, making her voice absolutely uncompetitive.

    "Harrison Bergeron, age fourteen," she said in a grackle[6] squawk, "has just escaped from jail, where he was held on suspicion of plotting to overthrow the government. He is a genius and an athlete, is under-handicapped, and should be regarded as extremely dangerous." **E**

    A police photograph of Harrison Bergeron was flashed on the screen— upside down, then sideways, upside down again, then right side up. The

D DRAW CONCLUSIONS
Reread lines 68–85. What do you think of George's reasons for not lightening his handicap bag?

E PLOT AND CONFLICT
Here the **rising action** begins. What more do you learn about the conflict between Harrison and the society?

---

5. **speech impediment** (ĭm-pĕd′ə-mənt): a physical defect that prevents a person from speaking normally.

6. **grackle:** a blackbird with a harsh, unpleasant call.

TVTime 2 (2002), Charles Foster-Hall. Acrylic on canvas, 16″ × 28″. © Charles Foster-Hall.

110 picture showed the full length of Harrison against a background calibrated in feet and inches. He was exactly seven feet tall.

The rest of Harrison's appearance was Halloween and hardware. Nobody had ever born heavier handicaps. He had outgrown hindrances faster than the H-G men could think them up. Instead of a little ear radio for a mental handicap, he wore a tremendous pair of earphones, and spectacles with thick wavy lenses. The spectacles were intended to make him not only half blind, but to give him whanging headaches besides.

Scrap metal was hung all over him. Ordinarily, there was a certain symmetry, a military neatness to the handicaps issued to strong people, but 120 Harrison looked like a walking junkyard. In the race of life, Harrison carried three hundred pounds.

And to offset his good looks, the H-G men required that he wear at all times a red rubber ball for a nose, keep his eyebrows shaved off, and cover his even white teeth with black caps at snaggle-tooth random. **F**

"If you see this boy," said the ballerina, "do not—I repeat, do not—try to reason with him."

There was the shriek of a door being torn from its hinges.

Screams and barking cries of **consternation** came from the television set. The photograph of Harrison Bergeron on the screen jumped again and again, 130 as though dancing to the tune of an earthquake.

ANALYZE VISUALS
How would you describe the figures watching television? How well do they represent George and Hazel?

F PLOT AND CONFLICT
Why has Harrison been so handicapped by the government?

consternation
(kŏn′stər-nā′shən)
n. confused amazement or fear

George Bergeron correctly identified the earthquake, and well he might have—for many was the time his own home had danced to the same crashing tune. "My God—" said George, "that must be Harrison!"

The realization was blasted from his mind instantly by the sound of an automobile collision in his head.

When George could open his eyes again, the photograph of Harrison was gone. A living, breathing Harrison filled the screen.

Clanking, clownish, and huge, Harrison stood in the center of the studio. **G** The knob of the uprooted studio door was still in his hand. Ballerinas,
140 technicians, musicians, and announcers **cowered** on their knees before him, expecting to die.

"I am the Emperor!" cried Harrison. "Do you hear? I am the Emperor! Everybody must do what I say at once!" He stamped his foot and the studio shook.

"Even as I stand here—" he bellowed, "crippled, hobbled, sickened—I am a greater ruler than any man who ever lived! Now watch me become what I *can* become!"

Harrison tore the straps of his handicap harness like wet tissue paper, tore straps guaranteed to support five thousand pounds.
150 Harrison's scrap-iron handicaps crashed to the floor.

Harrison thrust his thumbs under the bar of the padlock that secured his head harness. The bar snapped like celery. Harrison smashed his headphones and spectacles against the wall.

He flung away his rubber-ball nose, revealed a man that would have awed Thor, the god of thunder.

"I shall now select my Empress!" he said, looking down on the cowering people. "Let the first woman who dares rise to her feet claim her mate and her throne!" **H**

A moment passed, and then a ballerina arose, swaying like a willow.
160 Harrison plucked the mental handicap from her ear, snapped off her physical handicaps with marvelous delicacy. Last of all, he removed her mask.

She was blindingly beautiful.

"Now—" said Harrison, taking her hand, "shall we show the people the meaning of the word dance? Music!" he commanded.

The musicians scrambled back into their chairs, and Harrison stripped them of their handicaps, too. "Play your best," he told them, "and I'll make you barons and dukes and earls."

The music began. It was normal at first—cheap, silly, false. But Harrison snatched two musicians from their chairs, waved them like batons as he sang
170 the music as he wanted it played. He slammed them back into their chairs.

The music began again and was much improved.

G GRAMMAR AND STYLE
Reread line 138. Notice how Vonnegut uses the **precise adjectives** *clanking, clownish,* and *huge* to create a vivid image of Harrison's appearance.

cower (kou´ər) *v.* to crouch down in fear

H PLOT AND CONFLICT
Reread lines 142–158. Notice how Harrison views himself in relation to other people. How do his views put him in conflict with the government?

Harrison and his Empress merely listened to the music for a while—listened gravely, as though **synchronizing** their heartbeats with it.

They shifted their weights to their toes.

Harrison placed his big hands on the girl's tiny waist, letting her sense the weightlessness that would soon be hers.

And then, in an explosion of joy and grace, into the air they sprang!

Not only were the laws of the land abandoned, but the law of gravity and the laws of motion as well.

180 They reeled, whirled, swiveled, flounced, capered, gamboled, and spun.

They leaped like deer on the moon.

The studio ceiling was thirty feet high, but each leap brought the dancers nearer to it.

It became their obvious intention to kiss the ceiling.

They kissed it.

And then, **neutralizing** gravity with love and pure will, they remained suspended in air inches below the ceiling, and they kissed each other for a long, long time. **I**

It was then that Diana Moon Glampers, the Handicapper General, came 190 into the studio with a double-barreled ten-gauge shotgun. She fired twice, and the Emperor and the Empress were dead before they hit the floor.

Diana Moon Glampers loaded the gun again. She aimed it at the musicians and told them they had ten seconds to get their handicaps back on.

It was then that the Bergerons' television tube burned out. **J**

Hazel turned to comment about the blackout to George. But George had gone out into the kitchen for a can of beer.

George came back in with the beer, paused while a handicap signal shook him up. And then he sat down again. "You been crying?" he said to Hazel.

"Yup," she said.

200 "What about?" he said.

"I forget," she said. "Something real sad on television."

"What was it?" he said.

"It's all kind of mixed up in my mind," said Hazel.

"Forget sad things," said George.

"I always do," said Hazel.

"That's my girl," said George. He winced. There was the sound of a riveting gun[7] in his head.

"Gee—I could tell that one was a doozy," said Hazel.

"You can say that again," said George.

210 "Gee—" said Hazel, "I could tell that one was a doozy." ◈ **K**

---

7. **riveting** (rĭv′ĭ-tĭng) **gun:** a power tool used to hammer bolts (called rivets) that are used in construction work and manufacturing to fasten metal beams or plates together.

Comprehension

1. **Recall** Why does the government handicap George but not Hazel?

2. **Recall** Why is the government looking for Harrison?

3. **Recall** What does the Handicapper General do to Harrison?

4. **Clarify** Why don't Harrison's parents respond with more feeling to what they have seen?

OHIO STANDARDS

READING STANDARD
4.3 Distinguish how conflicts, parallel plots and subplots affect the text

Literary Analysis

5. **Analyze Plot and Conflict** Summarize the main conflict in "Harrison Bergeron." How is this conflict resolved?

6. **Recognize Climax** Recall that the climax, or turning point, is the high point of interest and tension in a story. What is the climax of this story?

7. **Draw Conclusions** Look back at the chart you created as you read. What overall conclusions can you draw about the society depicted in the story? Consider how people must function and what has become "normal."

8. **Interpret Theme** What is Vonnegut saying about improving society by making everyone **average?** Support your opinion with evidence from the story.

9. **Evaluate** Would society have been better off if Harrison, instead of Diana Moon Glampers, had been in charge? Using a chart like the one shown, predict the effects of Harrison's becoming emperor.

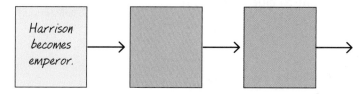

10. **Synthesize** Think about the criticisms of society made in "Harrison Bergeron." What aspects of today's society seem open to Vonnegut's criticisms?

Literary Criticism

11. **Critical Interpretation** One critic has argued that Vonnegut portrays television as "a kind of desensitizing, numbing, and clearly thought-stifling, rather than thought-provoking, medium" that is partly responsible for the state of society. Do you agree or disagree that television is partly to blame for the society portrayed in the story? Support your opinion.

Vocabulary in Context

VOCABULARY PRACTICE

Write the letter of the word that is most different in meaning from the others.

1. (a) vigilance, (b) attention, (c) alertness, (d) laziness
2. (a) grin, (b) flinch, (c) wince, (d) shrink
3. (a) joy, (b) consternation, (c) happiness, (d) elation
4. (a) tower, (b) crouch, (c) cower, (d) cringe
5. (a) time, (b) synchronize, (c) set, (d) separate
6. (a) neutralize, (b) worsen, (c) lessen, (d) decrease

VOCABULARY IN WRITING

Using three or more vocabulary words, describe a situation in which you were fearful as a child. Here is an example of how you could start.

> **EXAMPLE SENTENCE**
>
> I would **cower** under the bedcovers at night as . . .

VOCABULARY STRATEGY: THE GREEK ROOT *syn*

The vocabulary word *synchronize* contains the Greek word root *syn*, which means "together" or "similar." This root is found in a number of English words. To understand the meaning of words with *syn*, use context clues as well as your knowledge of the root.

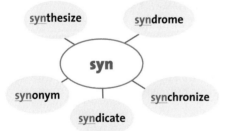

OHIO STANDARDS

VOCABULARY STANDARD
1.5 Use knowledge of Greek roots, prefixes and suffixes to understand words

PRACTICE Write the word from the word web that best completes each sentence. Use context clues to help you or, if necessary, consult a dictionary.

1. A _____ is a group of symptoms that together indicate a disease.
2. A _____ is a word that has the same or a similar meaning to another word.
3. A _____ is a company that is made up of different parts, such as a newspaper, a magazine, and a TV network.
4. Swimmers often _____ their movements in an underwater ballet.
5. To _____ something is to combine separate elements to form a whole.

VOCABULARY PRACTICE
For more practice, go to the **Vocabulary Center** at ClassZone.com.

Reading-Writing Connection

Increase your understanding of "Harrison Bergeron" by responding to these prompts. Then use **Revision: Grammar and Style** to improve your writing.

WRITING PROMPTS	SELF-CHECK
A. Short Response: Describe Plot and Conflict Imagine that a film version of "Harrison Bergeron" is being released and you have been assigned to write a blurb, or brief description, for a local newspaper. In **one or two paragraphs,** describe the plot and conflict in a way that makes people want to see the movie.	***A successful blurb will . . .*** • clearly identify the main characters and the conflict • create suspense about the outcome but not give away the story's ending
B. Extended Response: Interpret Theme What social tendencies is Vonnegut warning against in "Harrison Bergeron"? In **three to five paragraphs,** analyze the flaws of the society he depicts and discuss what he seems to be recommending.	***An effective response will . . .*** • give examples of problems created by Vonnegut's fictional society • apply the story to real-life society

REVISION: GRAMMAR AND STYLE

USE PRECISE LANGUAGE Review the **Grammar and Style** note on page 39. Vonnegut creates effective images, such as the image of Harrison in the TV studio, by using **precise adjectives.** When describing people, places, and events in your own writing, choose adjectives that allow readers to easily visualize them. Avoid using such adjectives as *good* and *nice,* which are too general to give readers a true sense of what is described.

Here are two examples of Vonnegut's use of precise adjectives:

> *She must have been extraordinarily beautiful, because the mask she wore was hideous.* (lines 95–96)

> *Her voice was a warm, luminous, timeless melody.* (line 101)

Notice how the revisions in red make this first draft more descriptive. Revise your responses to the prompts by using more precise adjectives.

 OHIO STANDARDS

WRITING STANDARD
5.9 Use sensory details

> **STUDENT MODEL**
>
>   *difficult*   *smarter, stronger, and more attractive*
> Harrison Bergeron has a ~~big~~ problem. He's ~~better~~ than everyone else, and the
>   *illegal*
> government says that's ~~bad~~.

 **WRITING TOOLS**
For prewriting, revision, and editing tools, visit the **Writing Center** at ClassZone.com.

Everyday Use
Short Story by Alice Walker

What makes something
VALUABLE?

KEY IDEA The word *value* means different things to different people. For example, an old vase might have high monetary value or high sentimental value. To some, it might have great historical, cultural, or artistic value. But others might think it's a useless piece of junk. Often people disagree over the value they assign to an object. Or they may agree that it is **valuable,** but not for the same reason.

QUICKWRITE If you could save only one precious possession of yours from being destroyed or left behind, what would you save? Write a short paragraph identifying the item and telling why it is valuable to you.

● LITERARY ANALYSIS: CONFLICT AND CHARACTER

A story's plot progresses because of a **conflict,** or struggle between opposing forces. In "Everyday Use," the main conflict centers around two sisters, Dee and Maggie, and their mother, who narrates the story. Although the main conflict between these characters is worked out in the **resolution** of the story, some other conflicts linger unresolved.

As you read, pay attention to the conflicts and whether they are resolved. Also think about the differences in the characters' values and priorities.

Review: **Plot**

● READING SKILL: MAKE INFERENCES

Because writers don't always tell you everything you need to know about a character, you must **make inferences,** or logical guesses, based on story details and your own experiences. For example, you might infer that the mother in this story prefers the outdoors from her comment "A yard like this is more comfortable than most people know. . . . It is like an extended living room." As you read, notice what the characters' words and actions tell you about their personalities and attitudes. Take notes on a chart like the one shown.

	Story Details	Inferences
Dee	thinks orchids are tacky flowers	is pretentious
Mama		
Maggie		

▲ VOCABULARY IN CONTEXT

Figure out the meaning of each boldfaced word from the context. Write a sentence that shows your understanding of each word.

1. sneaky, **furtive** behavior
2. need time to **recompose** after your outburst
3. accept the club's **doctrine**
4. remember your **heritage** when you leave home

Author Online

Alice Walker
born 1944

A Humble Start
Alice Walker, one of America's most distinguished authors, comes from humble beginnings. She was the last of eight children born to sharecroppers Willie Lee and Minnie Tallulah Walker. Though money was scarce and life was hard, Walker loved the Georgia countryside where she grew up. Walker's childhood was shattered by a shooting accident when she was eight. She lost sight in one eye and had a disfiguring scar that left her intensely self-conscious. For years afterward, she felt like an outcast.

Travel, Activism, and Fame Walker took comfort in reading and in writing poetry. With her mother's encouragement, she developed her talent for writing and did well in school. She graduated at the head of her high school class and received a college scholarship. During college, she became involved in the civil rights movement and traveled to Africa as an exchange student. After college, she devoted herself to writing and social activism. She has written more than 20 books, including *The Color Purple*, which won a Pulitzer Prize in 1983.

 MORE ABOUT THE AUTHOR
For more on Alice Walker, visit the **Literature Center** at ClassZone.com.

Background

Black Pride "Everyday Use" takes place during the 1960s, when many African Americans were discovering their heritage. The "black pride" movement, which grew out of civil rights campaigns, called upon African Americans to celebrate their African roots and affirm their cultural identity. Many adopted African clothing, hairstyles, and names; some studied African languages.

EVERYDAY USE

ALICE WALKER

I will wait for her in the yard that Maggie and I made so clean and wavy yesterday afternoon. A yard like this is more comfortable than most people know. It is not just a yard. It is like an extended living room. When the hard clay is swept clean as a floor and the fine sand around the edges lined with tiny, irregular grooves, anyone can come and sit and look up into the elm tree and wait for the breezes that never come inside the house.

Maggie will be nervous until after her sister goes: she will stand hopelessly in corners, homely and ashamed of the burn scars down her arms and legs, eying her sister with a mixture of envy and awe. She thinks her sister has held life always in the palm of one hand, that "no" is a word the world never learned to say to her. **A**

You've no doubt seen those TV shows where the child who has "made it" is confronted, as a surprise, by her own mother and father, tottering in weakly from backstage. (A pleasant surprise, of course: What would they do if parent and child came on the show only to curse out and insult each other?) On TV mother and child embrace and smile into each other's faces. Sometimes the mother and father weep, the child wraps them in her arms and leans across the table to tell how she would not have made it without their help. I have seen these programs.

Sometimes I dream a dream in which Dee and I are suddenly brought together on a TV program of this sort. Out of a dark and soft-seated limousine I am ushered into a bright room filled with many people. There I meet a smiling, gray, sporty man like Johnny Carson who shakes my hand and tells me what a fine girl I have. Then we are on the stage and Dee is embracing me with tears in her eyes. She pins on my dress a large orchid, even though she has told me once that she thinks orchids are tacky flowers.

In real life I am a large, big-boned woman with rough, man-working hands. In the winter I wear flannel nightgowns to bed and overalls during the day. I can kill and clean a hog as mercilessly as a man. My fat keeps me hot in zero weather. I can work outside all day, breaking ice to get water for washing; I can eat pork liver cooked over the open fire minutes after it comes steaming from the hog. One winter I knocked a bull calf straight in the brain between the

ANALYZE VISUALS
What qualities do you associate with the woman in the painting? How closely does she match the story's **narrator?**

A **MAKE INFERENCES**
Reread lines 7–10. What can you infer about Maggie and her sister from this description? Which details led to your inference?

Home Chores (1945), Jacob Lawrence. Gouache and graphite on paper, 29$^1/_2$″ × 21$^1/_{16}$″. Anonymous gift. The Nelson-Atkins Museum of Art, Kansas City, Missouri. F69-6. Photo by Jamison Miller © 2008 The Jacob and Gwendolyn Lawrence Foundation, Seattle/Artists Rights Society (ARS), New York.

eyes with a sledge hammer and had the meat hung up to chill before nightfall. But of course all this does not show on television. I am the way my daughter would want me to be: a hundred pounds lighter, my skin like an uncooked barley pancake. My hair glistens in the hot bright lights. Johnny Carson has much to do to keep up with my quick and witty tongue.

But that is a mistake. I know even before I wake up. Who ever knew a Johnson with a quick tongue? Who can even imagine me looking a strange white man in the eye? It seems to me I have talked to them always with one foot raised in flight, with my head turned in whichever way is farthest from them. Dee, though. She would always look anyone in the eye. Hesitation was no part of her nature. **B**

"How do I look, Mama?" Maggie says, showing just enough of her thin body enveloped in pink skirt and red blouse for me to know she's there, almost hidden by the door.

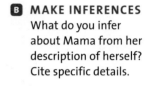

B MAKE INFERENCES
What do you infer about Mama from her description of herself? Cite specific details.

Little Sweet (1944), William H. Johnson. Oil on paperboard, 28″ × 22″. Smithsonian American Art Museum, Washington, D.C. Photo © Smithsonian American Art Museum, Washington, D.C./Art Resource, New York.

"Come out into the yard," I say.

Have you ever seen a lame animal, perhaps a dog run over by some careless person rich enough to own a car, sidle up to someone who is ignorant enough to be kind to him? That is the way my Maggie walks. She has been like this, chin on chest, eyes on ground, feet in shuffle, ever since the fire that burned the other house to the ground.

Dee is lighter than Maggie, with nicer hair and a fuller figure. She's a woman now, though sometimes I forget. How long ago was it that the other house burned? Ten, twelve years? Sometimes I can still hear the flames and feel Maggie's arms sticking to me, her hair smoking and her dress falling off her in little black papery flakes. Her eyes seemed stretched open, blazed open by the flames reflected in them. And Dee. I see her standing off under the sweet gum tree she used to dig gum out of; a look of concentration on her face as she watched the last dingy gray board of the house fall in toward the red-hot brick chimney. Why don't you do a dance around the ashes? I'd wanted to ask her. She had hated the house that much.

I used to think she hated Maggie, too. But that was before we raised the money, the church and me, to send her to Augusta[1] to school. She used to read to us without pity; forcing words, lies, other folks' habits, whole lives upon us two, sitting trapped and ignorant underneath her voice. She washed us in a river of make-believe, burned us with a lot of knowledge we didn't necessarily need to know. Pressed us to her with the serious way she read, to shove us away at just the moment, like dimwits, we seemed about to understand.

Dee wanted nice things. A yellow organdy dress to wear to her graduation from high school; black pumps to match a green suit she'd made from an old suit somebody gave me. She was determined to stare down any disaster in her efforts. Her eyelids would not flicker for minutes at a time. Often I fought off the temptation to shake her. At sixteen she had a style of her own: and knew what style was. **C**

I never had an education myself. After second grade the school was closed down. Don't ask me why: in 1927 colored asked fewer questions than they do now. Sometimes Maggie reads to me. She stumbles along good-naturedly but can't see well. She knows she is not bright. Like good looks and money, quickness passed her by. She will marry John Thomas (who has mossy teeth in an earnest face) and then I'll be free to sit here and I guess just sing church songs to myself. Although I never was a good singer. Never could carry a tune. I was always better at a man's job. I used to love to milk till I was hooked in the side in '49. Cows are soothing and slow and don't bother you, unless you try to milk them the wrong way.

I have deliberately turned my back on the house. It is three rooms, just like the one that burned, except the roof is tin; they don't make shingle roofs any more. There are no real windows, just some holes cut in the sides, like the portholes in a ship, but not round and not square, with rawhide holding the

C CONFLICT
Reread lines 52–74. What conflicts exist between Dee and her mother and sister?

---

1. **Augusta:** a city in Georgia.

shutters up on the outside. This house is in a pasture, too, like the other one.
90 No doubt when Dee sees it she will want to tear it down. She wrote me once
that no matter where we "choose" to live, she will manage to come see us. But
she will never bring her friends. Maggie and I thought about this and Maggie
asked me, "Mama, when did Dee ever *have* any friends?"

She had a few. **Furtive** boys in pink shirts hanging about on washday after
school. Nervous girls who never laughed. Impressed with her they worshiped
the well-turned phrase, the cute shape, the scalding humor that erupted like
bubbles in lye. She read to them.

When she was courting Jimmy T she didn't have much time to pay to us, but
turned all her faultfinding power on him. He *flew* to marry a cheap city girl from
100 a family of ignorant flashy people. She hardly had time to **recompose** herself. **D**

When she comes I will meet—but there they are!

Maggie attempts to make a dash for the house, in her shuffling way, but I
stay her with my hand. "Come back here," I say. And she stops and tries to dig
a well in the sand with her toe.

It is hard to see them clearly through the strong sun. But even the first
glimpse of leg out of the car tells me it is Dee. Her feet were always neat-
looking, as if God himself had shaped them with a certain style. From the
other side of the car comes a short, stocky man. Hair is all over his head a foot
long and hanging from his chin like a kinky mule tail. I hear Maggie suck in
110 her breath. "Uhnnnh," is what it sounds like. Like when you see the wriggling
end of a snake just in front of your foot on the road. "Uhnnnh."

Dee next. A dress down to the ground, in this hot weather. A dress so loud
it hurts my eyes. There are yellows and oranges enough to throw back the light
of the sun. I feel my whole face warming from the heat waves it throws out.
Earrings gold, too, and hanging down to her shoulders. Bracelets dangling and
making noises when she moves her arm up to shake the folds of the dress out
of her armpits. The dress is loose and flows, and as she walks closer, I like it.
I hear Maggie go "Uhnnnh" again. It is her sister's hair. It stands straight up
like the wool on a sheep. It is black as night and around the edges are two long
120 pigtails that rope about like small lizards disappearing behind her ears.

"Wa-su-zo-Tean-o!" she says, coming on in that gliding way the dress makes
her move. The short stocky fellow with the hair to his navel is all grinning
and he follows up with "Asalamalakim,[2] my mother and sister!" He moves to
hug Maggie but she falls back, right up against the back of my chair. I feel her
trembling there and when I look up I see the perspiration falling off her chin.

"Don't get up," says Dee. Since I am stout it takes something of a push.
You can see me trying to move a second or two before I make it. She turns,
showing white heels through her sandals, and goes back to the car. Out she
peeks next with a Polaroid. She stoops down quickly and lines up picture after
130 picture of me sitting there in front of the house with Maggie cowering behind
me. She never takes a shot without making sure the house is included. When

---

2. **Wa-su-zo-Tean-o!** (wä-soo'zō-tē'nō)...**Asalamalakim!** (ə-săl'ə-mə-lăk'əm): African and Arabic greetings.

furtive (fûr′tĭv) *adj.*
sneaky, secretive

recompose (rē′kəm-pōz′)
v. to restore to calm, to
settle again

D **MAKE INFERENCES**
What do you learn about
Dee from the way others
respond to her?

ANALYZE VISUALS
Contrast the style and
subject of this painting
with those of the one
on page 48. Does the
contrast reflect the
differences between
the sisters in the story?
Explain.

*Portrait of a woman with golden
headscarf* (1900's), Attributed to
Lo Babacar. Pikine, Senegal. Glass
painting. Inv.:A.94.4.33 Musée
des Arts d'Afrique et d'Oceanie,
Paris. Photo © Arnaudet/
Réunion des Musées Nationaux/
Art Resource, New York.

a cow comes nibbling around the edge of the yard she snaps it and me and
Maggie *and* the house. Then she puts the Polaroid in the back seat of the car,
and comes up and kisses me on the forehead. **E**

Meanwhile Asalamalakim is going through motions with Maggie's hand.
Maggie's hand is as limp as a fish, and probably as cold, despite the sweat, and
she keeps trying to pull it back. It looks like Asalamalakim wants to shake
hands but wants to do it fancy. Or maybe he don't know how people shake
hands. Anyhow, he soon gives up on Maggie.

140   "Well," I say. "Dee."

"No, Mama," she says. "Not 'Dee,' Wangero Leewanika Kemanjo!"[3]

"What happened to 'Dee'?" I wanted to know.

"She's dead," Wangero said. "I couldn't bear it any longer, being named after
the people who oppress me."

"You know as well as me you was named after your aunt Dicie," I said. Dicie
is my sister. She named Dee. We called her "Big Dee" after Dee was born.

"But who was *she* named after?" asked Wangero.

"I guess after Grandma Dee," I said.

"And who was she named after?" asked Wangero.

E **GRAMMAR AND STYLE**
Reread lines 131–134.
Notice how Walker
adds descriptive details
through the use of
prepositional phrases like
"around the edge of the
yard," "in the back seat
of the car," and "on the
forehead."

---

3. **Wangero Leewanika Kemanjo** (wän-gâr′ō lē-wä-nē′kə kĕ-män′jō).

150   "Her mother," I said, and saw Wangero was getting tired. "That's about as far back as I can trace it," I said. Though, in fact, I probably could have carried it back beyond the Civil War through the branches. **F**

"Well," said Asalamalakim, "there you are."

"Uhnnnh," I heard Maggie say.

"There I was not," I said, "before 'Dicie' cropped up in our family, so why should I try to trace it that far back?"

He just stood there grinning, looking down on me like somebody inspecting a Model A[4] car. Every once in a while he and Wangero sent eye signals over my head. **G**

160   "How do you pronounce this name?" I asked.

"You don't have to call me by it if you don't want to," said Wangero.

"Why shouldn't I?" I asked. "If that's what you want us to call you, we'll call you."

"I know it might sound awkward at first," said Wangero.

"I'll get used to it," I said. "Ream it out again."

Well, soon we got the name out of the way. Asalamalakim had a name twice as long and three times as hard. After I tripped over it two or three times he told me to just call him Hakim-a-barber.[5] I wanted to ask him was he a barber, but I didn't really think he was, so I didn't ask.

170   "You must belong to those beef-cattle peoples down the road," I said. They said "Asalamalakim" when they met you, too, but they didn't shake hands. Always too busy: feeding the cattle, fixing the fences, putting up salt-lick shelters, throwing down hay. When the white folks poisoned some of the herd the men stayed up all night with rifles in their hands. I walked a mile and a half just to see the sight.

Hakim-a-barber said, "I accept some of their **doctrines,** but farming and raising cattle is not my style." (They didn't tell me, and I didn't ask, whether Wangero (Dee) had really gone and married him.)

We sat down to eat and right away he said he didn't eat collards and pork was unclean. Wangero, though, went on through the chitlins and corn bread, the greens and everything else. She talked a blue streak over the sweet potatoes. Everything delighted her. Even the fact that we still used the benches her daddy made for the table when we couldn't afford to buy chairs.

"Oh, Mama!" she cried. Then turned to Hakim-a-barber. "I never knew how lovely these benches are. You can feel the rump prints," she said, running her hands underneath her and along the bench. Then she gave a sigh and her hand closed over Grandma Dee's butter dish. "That's it!" she said. "I knew there was something I wanted to ask you if I could have." She jumped up from the table and went over in the corner where the churn stood, the milk in it
190 clabber[6] by now. She looked at the churn and looked at it.

F CONFLICT
What is causing tension between Dee and Mama?

G MAKE INFERENCES
How do Dee and her companion view Mama?

doctrine (dŏkʹtrĭn) *n.* a set of rules, beliefs, or values held by a group

---

4. **Model A:** an automobile manufactured by Ford from 1927 to 1931.

5. **Hakim-a-barber** (hä-kēʹmə-bärʹbər).

6. **clabber:** curdled milk.

"This churn top is what I need," she said. "Didn't Uncle Buddy whittle it out of a tree you all used to have?"

"Yes," I said.

"Uh huh," she said happily. "And I want the dasher,[7] too."

"Uncle Buddy whittle that, too?" asked the barber.

Dee (Wangero) looked up at me.

"Aunt Dee's first husband whittled the dash," said Maggie so low you almost couldn't hear her. "His name was Henry, but they called him Stash."

"Maggie's brain is like an elephant's," Wangero said, laughing. "I can use the
200 churn top as a centerpiece for the alcove table," she said, sliding a plate over the churn, "and I'll think of something artistic to do with the dasher." **H**

When she finished wrapping the dasher the handle stuck out. I took it for a moment in my hands. You didn't even have to look close to see where hands pushing the dasher up and down to make butter had left a kind of sink in the wood. In fact, there were a lot of small sinks; you could see where thumbs and fingers had sunk into the wood. It was beautiful light yellow wood, from a tree that grew in the yard where Big Dee and Stash had lived.

After dinner Dee (Wangero) went to the trunk at the foot of my bed and started rifling through it. Maggie hung back in the kitchen over the dishpan.
210 Out came Wangero with two quilts. They had been pieced by Grandma Dee and then Big Dee and me had hung them on the quilt frames on the front porch and quilted them. One was in the Lone Star pattern. The other was Walk Around the Mountain. In both of them were scraps of dresses Grandma Dee had worn fifty and more years ago. Bits and pieces of Grandpa Jarrell's Paisley shirts. And one teeny faded blue piece, about the size of a penny matchbox, that was from Great Grandpa Ezra's uniform that he wore in the Civil War.

"Mama," Wangero said sweet as a bird. "Can I have these old quilts?"

I heard something fall in the kitchen, and a minute later the kitchen door
220 slammed. **I**

"Why don't you take one or two of the others?" I asked. "These old things was just done by me and Big Dee from some tops your grandma pieced before she died."

"No," said Wangero. "I don't want those. They are stitched around the borders by machine."

"That'll make them last better," I said.

"That's not the point," said Wangero. "These are all pieces of dresses Grandma used to wear. She did all this stitching by hand. Imagine!" She held the quilts securely in her arms, stroking them.
230 "Some of the pieces, like those lavender ones, come from old clothes her mother handed down to her," I said, moving up to touch the quilts. Dee (Wangero) moved back just enough so that I couldn't reach the quilts. They already belonged to her.

"Imagine!" she breathed again, clutching them closely to her bosom.

---

7. **dasher:** the plunger of a churn, a device formerly used to stir cream or milk to produce butter.

H MAKE INFERENCES
Reread lines 191–201. What do you learn about Dee and Maggie in these lines?

I MAKE INFERENCES
What might these noises mean?

Crazy Quilt (1883-1893), Victoriene Parsons Mitchell. Textile. 195.6 cm x 163.2 cm. © Indianapolis Museum of Art/ Bridgeman Art Library.

"The truth is," I said, "I promised to give them quilts to Maggie, for when she marries John Thomas."

She gasped like a bee had stung her.

"Maggie can't appreciate these quilts!" she said. "She'd probably be backward enough to put them to everyday use."

240 "I reckon she would," I said. "God knows I been saving 'em for long enough with nobody using 'em. I hope she will!" I didn't want to bring up how I had offered Dee (Wangero) a quilt when she went away to college. Then she had told me they were old-fashioned, out of style.

"But they're *priceless*!" she was saying now, furiously; for she has a temper. "Maggie would put them on the bed and in five years they'd be in rags. Less than that!"

"She can always make some more," I said. "Maggie knows how to quilt."

Dee (Wangero) looked at me with hatred. "You just will not understand. The point is *these* quilts, these quilts!"

250   "Well," I said, stumped. "What would *you* do with them?"

"Hang them," she said. As if that was the only thing you *could* do with quilts. ❶

Maggie by now was standing in the door. I could almost hear the sound her feet made as they scraped over each other.

"She can have them, Mama," she said, like somebody used to never winning anything, or having anything reserved for her. "I can 'member Grandma Dee without the quilts."

I looked at her hard. She had filled her bottom lip with checkerberry snuff and it gave her face a kind of dopey, hangdog look. It was Grandma Dee and
260 Big Dee who taught her how to quilt herself. She stood there with her scarred hands hidden in the folds of her skirt. She looked at her sister with something like fear but she wasn't mad at her. This was Maggie's portion. This was the way she knew God to work.

When I looked at her like that something hit me in the top of my head and ran down to the soles of my feet. Just like when I'm in church and the spirit of God touches me and I get happy and shout. I did something I never had done before: hugged Maggie to me, then dragged her on into the room, snatched the quilts out of Miss Wangero's hands and dumped them into Maggie's lap. Maggie just sat there on my bed with her mouth open. ❶

270   "Take one or two of the others," I said to Dee.

But she turned without a word and went out to Hakim-a-barber.

"You just don't understand," she said, as Maggie and I came out to the car.

"What don't I understand?" I wanted to know.

"Your **heritage**," she said. And then she turned to Maggie, kissed her, and said, "You ought to try to make something of yourself, too, Maggie. It's really a new day for us. But from the way you and Mama still live you'd never know it." ❶

She put on some sunglasses that hide everything above the tip of her nose and her chin.

280   Maggie smiled; maybe at the sunglasses. But a real smile, not scared. After we watched the car dust settle I asked Maggie to bring me a dip of snuff. And then the two of us sat there just enjoying, until it was time to go in the house and go to bed. ❧

❶ **CONFLICT**
Reread lines 238–252. Why doesn't Dee want Maggie to have the quilts?

❶ **PLOT**
This point is the **climax** of the story. How is the main conflict resolved?

heritage (hĕr′ĭ-tĭj) *n.* something passed down through generations, such as tradition, values, property

❶ **CONFLICT**
How does Dee view her mother and sister?

Reading for Information

INTERVIEW   Excerpted is a 1992 interview Walker gave to Roland R. Freeman for his book *A Communion of the Spirits: African-American Quilters, Preservers, and Their Stories.*

Alice Walker} *on Quilting*

Well, my mother was a quilter, and I remember many, many afternoons of my mother and the neighborhood women sitting on the porch around the quilting frame, quilting and talking, you know; getting up to stir something on the stove and coming back and sitting down. My mother also had a frame inside the house. Sometimes during the winter she would quilt and she often pieced quilts. Piecing . . . I'm really more of a piecer, actually, than I am a quilter, because I can get as far as piecing all of the little squares or sections together, and sometimes putting them together into big blocks, but then I always have to call in help—spreading it out on the frame, or spreading it out on the floor and putting the batting in and doing the actual quilting.

Alice Walker among her many quilts

[The first quilt] I worked on [was] the In Love and Trouble quilt. And I did that one when I was living in Mississippi. It was during a period when we were wearing African-inspired dresses. So all of the pieces are from dresses that I actually wore.

This yellow and black fabric I bought when I was in Uganda, and I had a beautiful dress made of it that I wore and wore and wore and eventually I couldn't wear it any more; partly I had worn it out and also I was pregnant, so it didn't fit, and I used that and I used the red and white and black, which was a long, floor-length dress that I had when I was pregnant with my daughter, Rebecca, who is now twenty-three. I took these things apart or I used scraps. I put them together in this quilt, because it just seemed perfect. Mississippi was full of political and social struggle, and regular quilts were all African American with emphasis on being here in the United States. But because of the African consciousness that was being raised and the way that we were all wearing our hair in naturals and wearing all of these African dresses, I felt the need to blend these two traditions. So it's a quilt of great memory and importance to me. I use it a lot and that's why it's so worn.

Comprehension

OHIO
STANDARDS

READING STANDARD
2.1 Make inferences

1. **Recall** How has Dee changed when she arrives to see her family?

2. **Recall** Why does Dee want the quilts?

3. **Recall** Who gets the quilts at the end of the story?

4. **Summarize** Why does Dee think Mama and Maggie don't understand their heritage?

Literary Analysis

5. **Make Inferences** Review the notes you took as you read. What positive and negative traits does each character have?

6. **Compare and Contrast** What makes the quilts **valuable** to Dee, and what makes them **valuable** to Maggie? Cite evidence.

7. **Analyze Plot** Reread lines 264–269. Explain why Mama makes the choice she does at the **climax** of the story. How does she feel about her choice?

8. **Analyze Conflict** Use the chart shown to explore the various ways that Dee is in conflict with her family. Which conflicts are resolved and which are not?

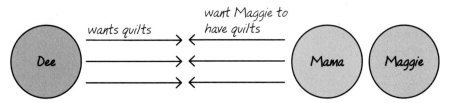

9. **Interpret Theme** What do you think Alice Walker is saying in "Everyday Use" about the nature of heritage? Support your answer.

10. **Synthesize** How do Walker's comments about quilting on page 56 affect your understanding of "Everyday Use"?

Literary Criticism

11. **Historical Context** The story takes place in the late 1960s, a time of growing cultural awareness for African Americans. If the story were set in the present, would the conflicts within the family be different? Explain your answer.

Vocabulary in Context

VOCABULARY PRACTICE

Write *True* or *False* for each statement.

1. Sneaking around is an example of **furtive** behavior.
2. When you **recompose** after a traffic accident, you become more agitated.
3. To believe in a certain group's **doctrine** is to follow their set rules.
4. If you deny your **heritage,** you refuse to acknowledge your cultural history.

VOCABULARY IN WRITING

Create four questions you might ask Dee about herself or her family. Use all four vocabulary words. Here is a sample question.

> **EXAMPLE SENTENCE**
>
> Do you think your sister Maggie appreciates her **heritage**?

VOCABULARY STRATEGY: THE PREFIX *re-*

The vocabulary word *recompose* contains the Latin prefix *re-*, which means "again" or "back." This prefix is found in a number of English words. To understand the meaning of words with *re-*, use your knowledge of the base word as well as your knowledge of the prefix.

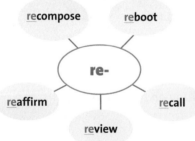

PRACTICE Write the word from the word web that best completes each sentence. Use context clues to help you or, if necessary, consult a dictionary.

1. To celebrate their anniversary, the couple decided to _____ their marriage vows.
2. She tried to _____ herself after her harsh scolding.
3. You need to _____ the computer after installing new software.
4. The toy company issued a _____ on a toy truck with dangerous parts.
5. Be sure to _____ your paper for spelling mistakes before submitting it.

OHIO STANDARDS

VOCABULARY STANDARD
1.5 Use knowledge of Latin roots, prefixes and suffixes to understand words

VOCABULARY PRACTICE
For more practice, go to the **Vocabulary Center** at **ClassZone.com.**

Reading-Writing Connection

Deepen your understanding of "Everyday Use" by responding to these prompts. Then use **Revision: Grammar and Style** to improve your writing.

WRITING PROMPTS	SELF-CHECK

A. Short Response: Analyze Conflict

Maggie and Dee have opposing views of themselves, their family, and the **valuable** quilts made by their grandmother. Write **one or two paragraphs** analyzing the conflicts between the two sisters. Support your analysis with examples from the story.

A strong analysis will . . .
- identify how Maggie's and Dee's views are in opposition
- give specific examples from the story

B. Extended Response: Write a Story Sequel

Imagine that Dee visits the family again ten years after the events in "Everyday Use." Write **one page** showing what she, Mama, and Maggie are now like and how they interact. What conflicts between them are still unresolved?

An effective sequel will . . .
- present characters consistent with those in the story
- present a conflict that was unresolved in the story

REVISION: GRAMMAR AND STYLE

ADD DESCRIPTIVE DETAILS Review the **Grammar and Style** note on page 51. By incorporating **prepositional phrases** into your writing, as Alice Walker does, you can add important details that show *what, when, where,* and *how* events are taking place. Here is an example from the story.

OHIO STANDARDS

WRITING STANDARD
7.3 Use clauses and phrases

> *After dinner Dee (Wangero) went to the trunk at the foot of my bed and started rifling through it. Maggie hung back in the kitchen over the dishpan. Out came Wangero with two quilts. They had been pieced by Grandma Dee and then Big Dee and me had hung them on the quilt frames on the front porch and quilted them.* (lines 208–212)

See how the revisions in red add important descriptive details to this first draft. Revise your response to Prompt B by using these techniques.

> 🔸 **WRITING TOOLS**
> For prewriting, revision, and editing tools, visit the **Writing Center** at ClassZone.com.

STUDENT MODEL

Mama walks over to Dee and gives her a kiss. Dee frowns and [*on the cheek*] [*at Mama*]
wipes off the kiss. [*with a handkerchief*] She crosses the room and sits down heavily. [*on the bench*]

Searching for Summer
Short Story by Joan Aiken

What do you take for
GRANTED?

OHIO STANDARDS

READING STANDARDS
2.3 Monitor comprehension
4.8 Analyze point of view, mood and tone

KEY IDEA There are many things in life that we assume will always be there. Air and water are two. But what if they disappeared? You've probably heard the saying "You never miss the water until the well runs dry." That means that we don't have **appreciation** for certain things until they're gone or scarce. "Searching for Summer" is set in a world that is missing something else we all take for granted.

DISCUSS Conduct an informal class survey, asking each person to name an everyday thing that is taken for granted. Choose the item mentioned most often, and as a class, discuss what you would do if this thing were suddenly gone or in short supply.

> Things We Take for Granted
> 1. Air
> 2. Water

LITERARY ELEMENTS: SETTING AND MOOD

A story may have more than one **setting,** and each setting may convey a different **mood,** or atmosphere. Imagine, for example, the emotional atmosphere in a gym packed with students watching their team winning an important game. Shouts, cheers, upbeat music, exciting plays—all these sights and sounds would create a mood of excitement and joyous anticipation. Now imagine how the mood would change if a character walked out of the gym into a long, dark, deserted hallway. To understand the relationship between the setting and the mood in a story, think about

- the descriptive details that tell what a place is like
- the feelings conveyed by those descriptive details

In "Searching for Summer," you'll encounter two very different settings. As you read, notice the descriptions of each setting and think about the mood those details convey.

Review: **Conflict**

● READING STRATEGY: MONITOR

When you **monitor,** you check to make sure you understand what you are reading. If you don't understand a story, you may have to read more slowly, reread passages, or read aloud. Jot down any questions you have about the story's setting, characters, and events, and then answer them as your reading proceeds. Use a chart like the one shown. Additional monitoring questions are provided to help you clarify your understanding.

My Questions	My Answers
Why were the bombs banned?	probably because they caused too much destruction

▲ VOCABULARY IN CONTEXT

Classify the vocabulary words into three categories: "Words I Know Well," "Words I Think I Know," and "Words I Don't Know at All." Write a short definition for words in the first two categories. After you read "Searching for Summer," correct your definitions if necessary and define the new words you learn.

1. unavailing
2. disengage
3. rudimentary
4. wizened
5. voluble
6. commiserate
7. savoring
8. indomitable

Author Online

Literary Fathers
Joan Aiken (ā′kən) grew up in England in a literary household. Her father, Conrad Aiken, was an American poet, and her stepfather, Martin Armstrong, was a fiction writer. At an early age, she decided to follow in their footsteps.

Joan Aiken
1924–2004

A Writer's Life In 1945 Aiken met and married journalist Ronald Brown. That same year, she began publishing poems and stories in magazines. Her first book for young adults, *All You've Ever Wanted and Other Stories,* appeared in 1953. About two years later, her husband died. To support herself and her two children, she worked as an editor for *Argosy,* a short story magazine, but continued to write at home. Her 1962 children's novel *The Wolves of Willoughby Chase* was a hit with critics and readers alike, enabling her to become a full-time writer. Aiken followed up with many other successful novels, including *Black Hearts in Battersea* and *The Whispering Mountain.* Though she is most often remembered as an author for young people, readers of all ages enjoy her stories.

 MORE ABOUT THE AUTHOR
For more on Joan Aiken, visit the **Literature Center** at **ClassZone.com.**

Background

Nuclear Anxiety Aiken wrote "Searching for Summer" in the 1950s, setting the story in a future "eighties"—perhaps the 1980s or 2080s. When the story was published, nuclear disaster was an ever-present threat. New nuclear weapons were being tested, and radioactive fallout rained down from the sky, polluting the environment.

Searching for Summer

JOAN AIKEN

ANALYZE VISUALS
How would you describe the **mood** of this painting? What qualities contribute to the mood?

Lily wore yellow on her wedding day. In the eighties people put a lot of faith in omens and believed that if a bride's dress was yellow her married life would be blessed with a bit of sunshine.

It was years since the bombs had been banned, but still the cloud never lifted. Whitish gray, day after day, sometimes darkening to a weeping slate color or, at the end of an evening, turning to smoky copper, the sky endlessly, secretively brooded.

Old people began their stories with the classic, fairy-tale opening: "Long, long ago, when I was a liddle un, in the days when the sky was blue …" and
10 children, listening, chuckled among themselves at the absurd thought, because, *blue,* imagine it! How could the sky ever have been *blue?* You might as well say, "In the days when the grass was pink."

Stars, rainbows, and all other such heavenly sideshows had been permanently withdrawn, and if the radio announced that there was a blink of sunshine in such and such a place, where the cloud belt had thinned for half an hour, cars and buses would pour in that direction for days in an **unavailing** search for warmth and light. **A**

unavailing (ŭn′ə-vā′lĭng) *adj.* useless, ineffective

A MONITOR
Reread lines 8–17. How have the sky and climate changed, and why?

After the wedding, when all the relations were standing on the church porch, with Lily shivering prettily in her buttercup nylon, her father prodded
20 the dour and withered grass on a grave—although it was August, the leaves were hardly out yet—and said, "Well, Tom, what are you aiming to do now, eh?"

"Going to find a bit of sun and have our honeymoon in it," said Tom. There was a general laugh from the wedding party.

"Don't get sunburned," shrilled Aunt Nancy.

"Better start off Bournemouth[1] way. Paper said they had a half-hour of sun last Wednesday week," Uncle Arthur weighed in heavily.

---

1. **Bournemouth** (bôrn′məth): a British seaside resort.

Old Willow Lane 2, Mary Iverson.
Oil on canvas, 11″ × 8″. © Mary Iverson/Corbis.

"We'll come back brown as—as this grass," said Tom, and ignoring the good-natured teasing from their respective families, the two young people
30 mounted on their scooter, which stood ready at the churchyard wall, and chugged away in a shower of golden confetti. When they were out of sight, and the yellow paper had subsided on the gray and gritty road, the Whitemores and the Hoskinses strolled off, sighing, to eat wedding cake and drink currant[2] wine, and old Mrs. Hoskins spoiled everyone's pleasure by bursting into tears as she thought of her own wedding day when everything was so different.

Meanwhile Tom and Lily buzzed on hopefully across the gray countryside, with Lily's veil like a gilt banner floating behind. It was chilly going for her in her wedding things, but the sight of a bride was supposed to bring good luck, and so she stuck it out, although her fingers were blue to the knuckles.
40 Every now and then they switched on their portable radio and listened to the forecast. Inverness had seen the sun for ten minutes yesterday, and Southend[3] for five minutes this morning, but that was all. **B**

"Both those places are a long way from here," said Tom cheerfully. "All the more reason we'd find a nice bit of sunshine in these parts somewhere. We'll keep on going south. Keep your eyes peeled, Lil, and tell me if you see a blink of sun on those hills ahead."

But they came to the hills and passed them, and a new range shouldered up ahead and then slid away behind, and still there was no flicker or patch of sunshine to be seen anywhere in the gray, winter-ridden landscape. Lily began
50 to get discouraged, so they stopped for a cup of tea at a drive-in.

"Seen the sun lately, mate?" Tom asked the proprietor.

He laughed shortly. "Notice any buses or trucks around here? Last time I saw the sun was two years ago September; came out just in time for the wife's birthday." **C**

"It's stars I'd like to see," Lily said, looking wistfully at her dust-colored tea. "Ever so pretty they must be."

"Well, better be getting on I suppose," said Tom, but he had lost some of his bounce and confidence. Every place they passed through looked nastier than the last, partly on account of the dismal light, partly because people had given up
60 bothering to take a pride in their boroughs.[4] And then, just as they were entering a village called Molesworth, the dimmest, drabbest, most insignificant huddle of houses they had come to yet, the engine coughed and died on them. **D**

"Can't see what's wrong," said Tom, after a prolonged and gloomy survey.

"Oh, Tom!" Lily was almost crying. "What'll we do?"

"Have to stop here for the night, s'pose." Tom was short-tempered with frustration. "Look, there's a garage just up the road. We can push the bike there, and they'll tell us if there's a pub[5] where we can stay. It's nearly six anyway."

---

2. **currant:** a berry used to make jams, jellies, and wines.

3. **Inverness . . . Southend:** resort towns in the north and south of the British Isles.

4. **boroughs:** towns or districts.

5. **pub:** a British term for a tavern. Pubs in small towns sometimes serve meals and rent rooms to travelers.

64 UNIT 1: PLOT, SETTING, AND MOOD

B **SETTING AND MOOD**
Reread lines 28–42. Note how the countryside looks and feels. What mood is created by this description?

C **MONITOR**
Why are buses and trucks a sign that sunshine has been spotted in the area?

D **SETTING AND MOOD**
Reread lines 58–62. Picture what Molesworth looks like. What feeling do you get from that image?

They had taken the bike to the garage, and the man there was just telling them that the only pub in the village was the Rising Sun, where Mr. Noakes
70 might be able to give them a bed, when a bus pulled up in front of the petrol[6] pumps.

"Look," the garage owner said, "there's Mr. Noakes just getting out of the bus now. Sid!" he called.

But Mr. Noakes was not able to come to them at once. Two old people were climbing slowly out of the bus ahead of him: a blind man with a white stick, and a withered, frail old lady in a black satin dress and hat. "Careful now, George," she was saying, "mind ee be careful with my son William."

"I'm being careful, Mrs. Hatching," the conductor said patiently, as he almost lifted the unsteady old pair off the bus platform. The driver
80 had stopped his engine, and everyone on the bus was taking a mild and sympathetic interest, except for Mr. Noakes just behind who was cursing irritably at the delay. When the two old people were on the narrow pavement, the conductor saw that they were going to have trouble with a bicycle that was propped against the curb just ahead of them; he picked it up and stood holding it until they had passed the line of petrol pumps and were going slowly off along a path across the fields. Then, grinning, he put it back, jumped hurriedly into the bus, and rang his bell.

"Old nuisances," Mr. Noakes said furiously. "Wasting public time. Every week that palaver[7] goes on, taking the old man to Midwick Hospital
90 Outpatients and back again. I know what *I'd* do with 'em. Put to sleep, that sort ought to be." **E**

Mr. Noakes was a repulsive-looking individual, but when he heard that Tom and Lily wanted a room for the night, he changed completely and gave them a leer that was full of false goodwill. He was a big, red-faced man with wet, full lips, bulging pale-gray bloodshot eyes, and a crop of stiff greasy black hair. He wore tennis shoes.

"Honeymooners, eh?" he said, looking sentimentally at Lily's pale prettiness. "Want a bed for the night, eh?" and he laughed a disgusting laugh that sounded like thick oil coming out of a bottle, heh-heh-heh-heh, and gave Lily
100 a tremendous pinch on her arm. **Disengaging** herself as politely as she could, she stooped and picked up something from the pavement. They followed Mr. Noakes glumly up the street to the Rising Sun.

While they were eating their baked beans, Mr. Noakes stood over their table grimacing at them. Lily unwisely confided to him that they were looking for a bit of sunshine. Mr. Noakes's laughter nearly shook down the ramshackle building.

"Sunshine! Oh my gawd! That's a good 'un! Hear that, Mother?" he bawled to his wife. "They're looking for a bit of sunshine. Heh-heh-heh-heh-heh-heh!

E **CONFLICT**
How does Mr. Noakes's response to the Hatchings differ from everyone else's?

disengage (dĭs'ĕn-gāj')
v. to detach or remove oneself

---

6. **petrol:** a British term for gasoline.

7. **palaver** (pə-lăv'ər): useless chatter.

Entrance to Erchless (1900s), Victoria Crowe. Oil on canvas, 96.5 cm × 111.7 cm. The Fleming-Wyfold Art Foundation. Photo © The Bridgeman Art Library.

Why," he said, banging on the table till the baked beans leaped about,
110 "if I could find a bit of sunshine near here, permanent bit that is, dja know
what I'd do?"

The young people looked at him inquiringly across the bread and
margarine.

"Lido,[8] trailer site, country club, holiday camp—you wouldn't know the
place. Land around here is dirt cheap; I'd buy up the lot. Nothing but woods.
I'd advertise—I'd have people flocking to this little dump from all over the
country. But what a hope, what a hope, eh? Well, feeling better? Enjoyed your
tea? Ready for bed? Heh-heh-heh-heh, bed's ready for you."

Avoiding one another's eyes, Tom and Lily stood up.
120 "I—I'd like to go for a bit of a walk first, Tom," Lily said in a small voice.
"Look, I picked up that old lady's bag on the pavement; I didn't notice it till
we'd done talking to Mr. Noakes, and by then she was out of sight. Should
we take it back to her?"

"Good idea," said Tom, pouncing on the suggestion with relief. "Do you
know where she lives, Mr. Noakes?"

"Who, old Ma Hatching? Sure I know. She lives in the wood. But you don't
want to go taking her bag back, not this time o' the evening you don't. Let her
worry. She'll come asking for it in the morning."

"She walked so slowly," said Lily, holding the bag gently in her hands. It
130 was very old, made of black velvet on two ring handles, and embroidered with
beaded roses. "I think we ought to take it to her, don't you, Tom?"

F GRAMMAR AND STYLE
Reread lines 107–118.
Notice how Aiken
incorporates **sentence
fragments, contractions,**
and **interjections** into her
dialogue to make it sound
realistic.

---

8. **lido** (lī′dō): a British term for a public outdoor swimming pool.

"Oh, very well, very well, have it your own way," Mr. Noakes said, winking at Tom. "Take that path by the garage; you can't go wrong. I've never been there meself, but they live somewhere in that wood back o' the village; you'll find it soon enough."

They found the path soon enough, but not the cottage. Under the lowering sky they walked forward endlessly among trees that carried only tiny and **rudimentary** leaves, **wizened** and poverty-stricken. Lily was still wearing her wedding sandals, which had begun to blister her. She held onto Tom's arm,
140 biting her lip with the pain, and he looked down miserably at her bent brown head; everything had turned out so differently from what he had planned. **G**

By the time they reached the cottage Lily could hardly bear to put her left foot to the ground, and Tom was gentling her along: "It can't be much farther now, and they'll be sure to have a bandage. I'll tie it up, and you can have a sit-down. Maybe they'll give us a cup of tea. We could borrow an old pair of socks or something. . . ." Hardly noticing the cottage garden, beyond a vague impression of rows of runner beans, they made for the clematis-grown[9] porch and knocked. There was a brass lion's head on the door, carefully polished.

"Eh, me dear!" It was the old lady, old Mrs. Hatching, who opened
150 the door, and her exclamation was a long-drawn gasp of pleasure and astonishment. "Eh, me dear! 'Tis the pretty bride. See'd ye s'arternoon when we was coming home from hospital."

"Who be?" shouted a voice from inside.

"Come in, come in, me dears. My son William'll be glad to hear company; he can't see, poor soul, nor has this thirty year, ah, and a pretty sight he's losing this minute—"

"We brought back your bag," Tom said, putting it in her hands, "and we wondered if you'd have a bit of plaster[10] you could kindly let us have. My wife's hurt her foot—"

160 My wife. Even in the midst of Mrs. Hatching's **voluble** welcome the strangeness of these words struck the two young people, and they fell quiet, each of them, pondering, while Mrs. Hatching thanked and **commiserated,** all in a breath, and asked them to take a seat on the sofa and fetched a basin of water from the scullery,[11] and William from his seat in the chimney corner demanded to know what it was all about.

"Wot be doing? Wot be doing, Mother?"

" 'Tis a bride, all in's finery," she shrilled back at him, "an's blistered her foot, poor heart." Keeping up a running commentary for William's benefit she bound up the foot, every now and then exclaiming to herself in wonder over
170 the fineness of Lily's wedding dress, which lay in yellow nylon swathes around the chair. "There, me dear. Now us'll have a cup of tea, eh? Proper thirsty you'm fare to be, walking all the way to here this hot day."

Hot day? Tom and Lily stared at each other and then around the room.

---

9. **clematis-grown:** covered with clematis, a flowering vine.

10. **plaster:** a British term for an adhesive bandage.

11. **scullery:** a small room in which dishwashing and other kitchen chores are done.

rudimentary
(roō′də-měn′tə-rē)
adj. very basic, in the beginning stages

wizened (wĭz′ənd)
adj. withered and dry

G **SETTING AND MOOD**
Reread lines 136–141. What mood does the description of the woods convey to you?

voluble (vŏl′yə-bəl) *adj.* especially talkative, fluent with words

commiserate
(kə-mĭz′ə-rāt′) *v.* to express sorrow or pity for another's troubles

Then it was true, it was not their imagination, that a great dusty golden square of sunshine lay on the fireplace wall, where the brass pendulum of the clock at every swing blinked into sudden brilliance? That the blazing geraniums on the windowsill housed a drove of murmuring bees? That, through the window, the gleam of linen hung in the sun to whiten suddenly dazzled their eyes?

"The sun? Is it really the sun?" Tom said, almost doubtfully.

180 "And why not?" Mrs. Hatching demanded. "How else'll beans set, tell me that? Fine thing if sun were to stop shining." Chuckling to herself she set out a Crown Derby tea set, gorgeously colored in red and gold, and a baking of saffron[12] buns. Then she sat down and, drinking her own tea, began to question the two of them about where they had come from, where they were going. The tea was tawny and hot and sweet; the clock's tick was like a bird chirping; every now and then a log settled in the grate; Lily looked sleepily around the little room, so rich and peaceful, and thought, I wish we were staying here. I wish we needn't go back to that horrible pub. . . . She leaned against Tom's comforting arm.

190 "Look at the sky," she whispered to him. "Out there between the geraniums. Blue!" **H**

"And ee'll come up and see my spare bedroom, won't ee now?" Mrs. Hatching said, breaking off the thread of her questions—which indeed was not a thread, but merely a **savoring** of her pleasure and astonishment at this unlooked-for visit—"Bide here, why don't ee? Mid as well. The lil un's fair wore out. Us'll do for ee better 'n rangy old Noakes; proper old scoundrel 'e be. Won't us, William?" **I**

"Ah," William said appreciatively. "I'll sing ee some o' my songs."

A sight of the spare room settled any doubts. The great white bed, huge as 200 a prairie, built up with layer upon solid layer of mattress, blanket, and quilt, almost filled the little shadowy room in which it stood. Brass rails shone in the green dimness. "Isn't it quiet," Lily whispered. Mrs. Hatching, silent for the moment, stood looking at them proudly, her bright eyes slowly moving from face to face. Once her hand fondled, as if it might have been a baby's downy head, the yellow brass knob.

And so, almost without any words, the matter was decided.

Three days later they remembered that they must go to the village and collect the scooter which must, surely, be mended by now.

They had been helping old William pick a basketful of beans. Tom had 210 taken his shirt off, and the sun gleamed on his brown back; Lily was wearing an old cotton print which Mrs. Hatching, with much chuckling, had shortened to fit her.

It was amazing how deftly, in spite of his blindness, William moved among the beans, feeling through the rough, rustling leaves for the stiffness of concealed pods. He found twice as many as Tom and Lily, but then they, even on the third day, were still stopping every other minute to exclaim

H **SETTING AND MOOD**
Reread lines 174–191. Notice that the new setting conveys a different mood. How would you describe that mood?

savoring (sā′vər-ĭng) *n.* a full appreciation and enjoyment **savor** *v.*

I **MONITOR**
Reread lines 192–197. What is Mrs. Hatching saying? Try to clarify by reading her words aloud, then putting her statements in your own words.

---

12. **saffron:** a cooking spice that imparts an orange-yellow color to foods.

Yellow Dress (2003), Jeffrey T. Larson. Oil on linen, 12″ × 16″. © Daylight Fine Art.

ANALYZE VISUALS
How does the use of color affect the **mood** of this painting? Contrast the mood wih that of the painting on page 63.

over the blueness of the sky. At night they sat on the back doorstep while Mrs. Hatching clucked inside as she dished the supper, "Starstruck ee'll be! Come along in, do-ee, before soup's cold; stars niver run away yet as I do

220 know."

"Can we get anything for you in the village?" Lily asked, but Mrs. Hatching shook her head.

"Baker's bread and suchlike's no use but to cripple thee's innardses wi' colic.[13] I been living here these eighty year wi'out troubling doctors, and I'm not faring to begin now." She waved to them and stood watching as they walked into the wood, thin and frail beyond belief, but wiry, **<u>indomitable,</u>** her

indomitable
(ĭn-dŏm′ĭ-tə-bəl) *adj.*
not easily discouraged or defeated

---

13. **cripple . . . colic** (kŏl′ĭk): give yourself a bad case of indigestion.

black eyes full of zest. Then she turned to scream menacingly at a couple of pullets[14] who had strayed and were scratching among the potatoes.

Almost at once they noticed, as they followed the path, that the sky was
230 clouded over.

"It *is* only there on that one spot," Lily said in wonder. "All the time. And they've never even noticed that the sun doesn't shine in other places."

"That's how it must have been all over the world, once," Tom said.

At the garage they found their scooter ready and waiting. They were about to start back when they ran into Mr. Noakes.

"Well, well, well, well, *well!*" he shouted, glaring at them with ferocious good humor. "How many wells make a river, eh? And where did you slip off to? Here's me and the missus was just going to tell the police to have the rivers dragged. But hullo, hul*lo*, what's this? Brown, eh? Suntan? Scrumptious,"
240 he said, looking meltingly at Lily and giving her another tremendous pinch. "Where'd you get it, eh? That wasn't all got in half an hour, *I* know. Come on, this means money to you and me; tell us the big secret. Remember what I said; land around these parts is dirt cheap."

Tom and Lily looked at each other in horror. They thought of the cottage, the bees humming among the runner beans, the sunlight glinting in the red-and-gold teacups. At night, when they had lain in the huge sagging bed, stars had shone through the window, and the whole wood was as quiet as the inside of a shell. **J**

"Oh, we've been miles from here," Tom lied hurriedly. "We ran into a
250 friend, and he took us right away beyond Brinsley." And as Mr. Noakes still looked suspicious and unsatisfied, he did the only thing possible. "We're going back there now," he said. "The sunbathing's grand." And opening the throttle, he let the scooter go. They waved at Mr. Noakes and chugged off toward the gray hills that lay to the north. **K**

"My wedding dress," Lily said sadly. "It's on our bed."

They wondered how long Mrs. Hatching would keep tea hot for them, who would eat all the pasties.[15]

"Never mind, you won't need it again," Tom comforted her.

At least, he thought, they had left the golden place undisturbed. Mr. Noakes
260 never went into the wood. And they had done what they intended; they had found the sun. Now they, too, would be able to tell their grandchildren, when beginning a story, "Long, long ago, when we were young, in the days when the sky was blue . . ." ❧

J CONFLICT
Why do Mr. Noakes's statements fill Tom and Lily with horror?

K MONITOR
What do Tom and Lily decide to do?

---

14. **pullets:** young hens.

15. **pasties** (păs´tēz): a British term for meat pies.

Comprehension

OHIO STANDARDS

READING STANDARD
2.3 Monitor comprehension

1. **Recall** Why are Tom and Lily riding around on their scooter at the beginning of the story?

2. **Recall** Why do Tom and Lily decide to visit the Hatchings?

3. **Recall** What do they find when they get to the cottage?

4. **Clarify** Why don't Tom and Lily go back to the Hatchings' after picking up their scooter?

Literary Analysis

5. **Monitor** Review the questions and answers you wrote while reading. What further insights did you gain into the setting, characters, and events?

6. **Analyze Stages of Plot** Create a list of the events in "Searching for Summer." Then **classify** the events according to the stages of plot: exposition, rising action, climax, falling action, resolution.

7. **Interpret** Why does the sun shine only over the Hatchings' cottage?

8. **Contrast Setting and Mood** Contrast the Hatchings' cottage and yard with the rest of England "since the bombs." What differing moods are created by the descriptions of these settings?

9. **Examine Conflicts** How would you describe the important conflicts in this story? Consider characters who are at odds and desires that are frustrated. Summarize the conflicts in a chart like the one shown.

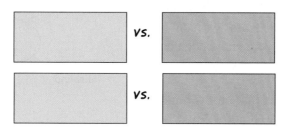

10. **Evaluate Actions** Do Tom and Lily do the right thing in not going back to the cottage? Explain your opinion.

11. **Draw Conclusions About Theme** What does the story suggest to you about the things people don't **appreciate?** Support your answer.

Literary Criticism

12. **Author's Style** Many critics have commented on Aiken's ability to write stories that seem like folk tales. What elements of "Searching for Summer" remind you of "once upon a time" stories you read or heard as a child? Cite evidence from the story.

Vocabulary in Context

VOCABULARY PRACTICE

Identify the word that is not related in meaning to the other words in the set.

1. indomitable, unconquerable, feeble, powerful
2. disengage, detach, remove, connect
3. withered, blooming, shrunken, wizened
4. sympathize, commiserate, pity, accuse
5. complex, rudimentary, basic, preliminary
6. voluble, talkative, fluent, silent
7. distaste, savoring, relishing, enjoyment
8. unavailing, useless, effective, futile

VOCABULARY IN WRITING

Using at least four vocabulary words, describe an encounter with a very chatty person. Here is an example of how you could start.

> **EXAMPLE SENTENCE**
>
> *It is an **unavailing** effort to try and get a word in edgewise with . . .*

OHIO STANDARDS

VOCABULARY STANDARD
1.5 Use knowledge of Latin roots, prefixes and suffixes to understand words

VOCABULARY STRATEGY: THE PREFIX *dis-*

The vocabulary word *disengage* contains the Latin prefix *dis-*, which means "in different directions." This prefix is found in a number of English words. To understand the meaning of words with *dis-*, use your knowledge of the base word as well as your knowledge of the prefix.

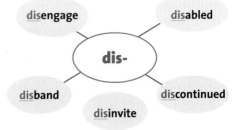

PRACTICE Write the word from the word web that best completes each sentence. Use context clues to help you. If necessary, consult a dictionary.

1. The crab tried to _____ itself from the fisherman's net.
2. After their argument, she decided to _____ her friend to the party.
3. There's a _____ vehicle on the road that needs to be removed.
4. The music group will _____ this month.
5. The store has _____ this brand of clothing.

VOCABULARY PRACTICE
For more practice, go to the **Vocabulary Center** at **ClassZone.com**.

Reading-Writing Connection

Explore your understanding of "Searching for Summer" by responding to these prompts. Then use **Revision: Grammar and Style** to improve your writing.

WRITING PROMPTS	SELF-CHECK
A. Short Response: Describe a Setting Imagine that Mr. Noakes has turned the woods into a vacation spot. What would he say in a presentation to make people want to visit? Write **one or two paragraphs** describing the Rising Sun Resort.	*A successful description will . . .* • use vivid, colorful language to describe the setting • convey a mood that makes people want to visit
B. Extended Response: Analyze Theme What different themes does Aiken's story suggest to you? For instance, what else does it convey besides the importance of **appreciating** sunlight? Write **three to five paragraphs** in response.	*An effective response will . . .* • clearly state one or more themes of the story • use details from the story to support your analysis

REVISION: GRAMMAR AND STYLE

OHIO STANDARDS

READING STANDARD
5.7 Use a variety of sentence structures and lengths

USE REALISTIC DIALOGUE Review the **Grammar and Style** note on page 66. Aiken uses realistic dialogue to help shape her characters and bring them to life. When writing dialogue, follow her example by enlisting these techniques:

1. **Use contractions and interjections.** Contractions—such as *doesn't, we're,* and *they'll*—combine and shorten words, while interjections—such as *well, oh,* and *hey*—express emotion. You can incorporate both into your dialogue to make it sound more like everyday speech.

2. **Form sentence fragments.** Although sentence fragments should be avoided in formal writing, they are often used in dialogue. Here is an example from the story that highlights Aiken's use of these techniques.

   > *"Can't see what's wrong," said Tom, after a prolonged and gloomy survey.*
   > *"Oh, Tom!" Lily was almost crying. "What'll we do?"* (lines 63–64)

Notice how the revisions in red make this first draft's dialogue sound more like real speech. Revise your response to Prompt A by making similar changes.

STUDENT MODEL

"Who wants to be the first to visit the new Rising Sun Resort? I ~~am~~ telling
Not anywhere.
you, you ~~will~~ never find a place like this. ~~The sun is bright, and the sky is blue.~~
Oh,
~~And~~ did I mention the camp for the kids? What more could you want?"

WRITING TOOLS
For prewriting, revision, and editing tools, visit the **Writing Center** at ClassZone.com.

To Build a Fire

Short Story by Jack London

Should you trust your INSTINCTS?

OHIO STANDARDS

READING STANDARDS
2.1 Make predictions
4.2 Analyze setting

KEY IDEA An **instinct** is unlearned, automatic behavior shown by all members of a species, such as birds building a nest. Do people, like animals, have instincts? If they do, when are they likely to use them? Are a person's instincts as good as, say, a dog's? The story "To Build a Fire" attempts to answer such questions.

DISCUSS With a partner, try to answer the questions posed in the previous paragraph. Come up with a definition of human instincts and some examples. Record ideas from your conversation on a word web like the one shown.

Human Instincts

● LITERARY ANALYSIS: SETTING AND CONFLICT

In some stories, the **setting** can create the conflict a character faces. It can even act as the **antagonist,** or opponent, of the main character. In "To Build a Fire," the setting is the Yukon wilderness, and the main character must battle the crippling cold to survive. The setting challenges him in other ways as well. As you read, notice details about this harsh setting and think about the choices the setting forces the character to make.

Review: **Mood**

● READING STRATEGY: PREDICT

When you **predict,** you use text clues to guess what will happen next in a story. Predicting helps you become actively involved in what you are reading and gives you reasons to read on. To make sound predictions about what will happen in "To Build a Fire," use the following strategies:

- Think about the personality, actions, and thoughts of the main character when predicting how he will respond to his situation.

- Note passages of **foreshadowing,** or hints and clues about future plot events.

As you read, jot down at least three predictions and the clues you used to make them. Use a chart like the one shown.

Predictions	Text Clues
The man will . . .	

Review: **Draw Conclusions**

▲ VOCABULARY IN CONTEXT

Jack London uses the following boldfaced vocabulary words in his suspenseful tale. To see how many vocabulary words you know, substitute a different word or phrase for each boldfaced term.

1. **intangible** fear
2. **conjectural** answer
3. baseless **apprehension**
4. **reiterate** the command
5. **smite** in anger
6. **imperative** action
7. forest **conflagration**
8. **peremptorily** dismiss

Author Online

**Jack London
1876–1916**

Teen Adventurer
Born to an indifferent mother and an absentee father, Jack London grew up in a poor neighborhood in Oakland, California. As a boy, his escape from poverty and loneliness was reading books. As a teenager, his escape was the sea. When he was 15, he borrowed money, bought a boat, and became an oyster pirate on the San Francisco Bay. At 17, he worked aboard a schooner that sailed the North Pacific. When he returned home, the only work he could find was low-paying manual labor. Fascinated by rags-to-riches stories he heard about people mining for gold in Canada's Yukon Territory, he sailed north at age 21.

Striking It Rich London did not find gold in the Yukon, but he did find something valuable. Holed up during the fiercely cold Yukon winter, he read widely and listened to other gold prospectors tell stories about life in the frozen northland. Inspired by their tales and his own experiences, London returned to Oakland and began to write. In 1899, magazines began publishing his stories, and his writing career was on its way. His novels *The Call of the Wild, The Sea-Wolf,* and *White Fang* made him one of America's most popular, and financially successful, writers. Almost a century after his death, readers are still captivated by his stark, suspenseful stories.

 MORE ABOUT THE AUTHOR
For more on Jack London, visit the **Literature Center** at **ClassZone.com.**

TO BUILD A FIRE

JACK LONDON

ANALYZE VISUALS
How do you think
it would feel to be
in the **setting** of the
photograph?

Day had broken cold and gray, exceedingly cold and gray, when the man
turned aside from the main Yukon trail and climbed the high earth-bank,
where a dim and little-travelled trail led eastward through the fat spruce
timberland.\It was a steep bank, and he paused for breath at the top, excusing
the act to himself by looking at his watch. It was nine o'clock. There was no
sun nor hint of sun, though there was not a cloud in the sky. It was a clear
day, and yet there seemed an **intangible** pall over the face of things, a subtle
gloom that made the day dark, and that was due to the absence of sun. This
fact did not worry the man. He was used to the lack of sun. It had been days
10 since he had seen the sun, and he knew that a few more days must pass before
that cheerful orb, due south, would just peep above the sky line and dip
immediately from view.

intangible (ĭn-tăn′jə-bəl)
adj. unable to be perceived
with the senses

   The man flung a look back along the way he had come. The Yukon lay a
mile wide and hidden under three feet of ice. On top of this ice were as many
feet of snow. It was all pure white, rolling in gentle undulations where the ice
jams of the freeze-up had formed. North and south, as far as his eye could see,
it was unbroken white, save for a dark hairline that curved and twisted from
around the spruce-covered island to the south, and that curved and twisted
away into the north, where it disappeared behind another spruce-covered
20 island. This dark hairline was the trail—the main trail—that led south five
hundred miles to the Chilcoot Pass, Dyea, and salt water; and that led north
seventy miles to Dawson, and still on to the north a thousand miles to
Nulato, and finally to St. Michael, on Bering Sea, a thousand miles and half a
thousand more. **A**

A MOOD
Reread lines 1–24. What
mood is created by the
description of the **setting?**

But all this—this mysterious, far-reaching hairline trail, the absence of sun from the sky, the tremendous cold, and the strangeness and weirdness of it all—made no impression on the man. It was not because he was long used to it. He was a newcomer in the land, a *chechaquo*, and this was his first winter. The trouble with him was that he was without imagination. He was quick and alert in the things of life, but only in the things, and not in the significances. Fifty degrees below zero meant eighty-odd degrees of frost. Such fact impressed him as being cold and uncomfortable, and that was all. It did not lead him to meditate upon his frailty as a creature of temperature, and upon man's frailty in general, able only to live within certain narrow limits of heat and cold; and from there on it did not lead him to the **conjectural** field of immortality and man's place in the universe. Fifty degrees below zero stood for a bite of frost that hurt and that must be guarded against by the use of mittens, ear flaps, warm moccasins, and thick socks. Fifty degrees below zero was to him just precisely fifty degrees below zero. That there should be anything more to it than that was a thought that never entered his head. **B**

As he turned to go, he spat speculatively. There was a sharp, explosive crackle that startled him. He spat again. And again, in the air, before it could fall to the snow, the spittle crackled. He knew that at fifty below spittle crackled on the snow, but this spittle had crackled in the air. Undoubtedly it was colder than fifty below—how much colder he did not know. But the temperature did not matter. He was bound for the old claim[1] on the left fork of Henderson Creek, where the boys were already. They had come over across the divide from the Indian Creek country, while he had come the roundabout way to take a look at the possibilities of getting out logs in the spring from the islands in the Yukon. He would be in to camp by six o'clock; a bit after dark, it was true, but the boys would be there, a fire would be going, and a hot supper would be ready. As for lunch, he pressed his hand against the protruding bundle under his jacket. It was also under his shirt, wrapped up in a handkerchief and lying against the naked skin. It was the only way to keep the biscuits from freezing. He smiled agreeably to himself as he thought of those biscuits, each cut open and sopped in bacon grease, and each enclosing a generous slice of fried bacon.

He plunged in among the big spruce trees. The trail was faint. A foot of snow had fallen since the last sled had passed over, and he was glad he was without a sled, travelling light. In fact, he carried nothing but the lunch wrapped in the handkerchief. He was surprised, however, at the cold. It certainly was cold, he concluded, as he rubbed his numb nose and cheekbones with his mittened hand. He was a warm-whiskered man, but the hair on his face did not protect the high cheek-bones and the eager nose that thrust itself aggressively into the frosty air. **C**

conjectural
(kən-jĕk′chər-əl) *adj.*
involving guesswork

B DRAW CONCLUSIONS
Based on the description in lines 25–40, what can you conclude about the man's personality?

C SETTING AND CONFLICT
What conflict does the setting create for the man?

---

1. **claim:** a tract of public land claimed by a homesteader or, as in this case, a miner.

At the man's heels trotted a dog, a big native husky, the proper wolf dog, gray-coated and without any visible or temperamental difference from its brother, the wild wolf. The animal was depressed by the tremendous cold. It knew that it was no time for travelling. Its instinct told it a truer tale than was
70 told to the man by the man's judgment. In reality, it was not merely colder than fifty below zero; it was colder than sixty below, than seventy below. It was seventy-five below zero. Since the freezing point is thirty-two above zero, it meant that one hundred and seven degrees of frost obtained.[2] The dog did not know anything about thermometers. Possibly in its brain there was no sharp consciousness of a condition of very cold such as was in the man's brain. But the brute had its instinct. It experienced a vague but menacing **apprehension** that subdued it and made it slink along at the man's heels, and that made it question eagerly every unwonted movement of the man as if expecting him to go into camp or to seek shelter somewhere and build a fire. The dog had
80 learned fire, and it wanted fire, or else to burrow under the snow and cuddle its warmth away from the air. **D**

apprehension
(ăp′rĭ-hĕn′shən) *n.* fear and worry for the future

D PREDICT
What do you think the man and dog will do? Why?

---

2. **obtained:** existed.

The frozen moisture of its breathing had settled on its fur in a fine powder of frost, and especially were its jowls, muzzle and eyelashes whitened by its crystalled breath. The man's red beard and mustache were likewise frosted, but more solidly, the deposit taking the form of ice and increasing with every warm, moist breath he exhaled. Also, the man was chewing tobacco, and the muzzle of ice held his lips so rigidly that he was unable to clear his chin when he expelled the juice. The result was that a crystal beard of the color and solidity of amber was increasing its length on his chin. If he fell down it 90 would shatter itself, like glass, into brittle fragments. But he did not mind the appendage. It was the penalty all tobacco chewers paid in that country, and he had been out before in two cold snaps. They had not been so cold as this, but by the spirit thermometer[3] at Sixty Mile he knew that they had been registered at fifty below and at fifty-five.

He held on through the level stretch of woods for several miles, crossed a wide flat . . . and dropped down a bank to the frozen bed of a small stream. This was Henderson Creek, and he knew he was ten miles from the forks. He looked at his watch. It was ten o'clock. He was making four miles an hour, and he calculated that he would arrive at the forks at half-past twelve. He decided 100 to celebrate that event by eating his lunch there.

The dog dropped in again at his heels, with a tail drooping discouragement, as the man swung along the creek bed. The furrow of the old sled trail was plainly visible, but a dozen inches of snow covered the marks of the last runners. In a month no man had come up or down that silent creek. The man held steadily on. He was not much given to thinking, and just then particularly he had nothing to think about save that he would eat lunch at the forks and that at six o'clock he would be in camp with the boys. There was nobody to talk to; and, had there been, speech would have been impossible because of the ice muzzle on his mouth. So he continued monotonously to chew tobacco and 110 to increase the length of his amber beard.

Once in a while the thought **reiterated** itself that it was very cold and that he had never experienced such cold. As he walked along he rubbed his cheekbones and nose with the back of his mittened hand. He did this automatically, now and again changing hands. But, rub as he would, the instant he stopped his cheekbones went numb, and the following instant the end of his nose went numb. He was sure to frost his cheeks; he knew that, and experienced a pang of regret that he had not devised a nose strap of the sort Bud wore in cold snaps. Such a strap passed across the cheeks, as well, and saved them. But it didn't matter much, after all. What were frosted cheeks? A 120 bit painful, that was all; they were never serious. **E**

Empty as the man's mind was of thoughts, he was keenly observant, and he noticed the changes in the creek, the curves and bends and timber jams,[4] and

reiterate (rē-ĭt′ə-rāt′) v. to repeat

E SETTING AND CONFLICT
Notice the new problem created for the man. How does he view this problem?

---

3. **spirit thermometer:** a thermometer in which temperature is indicated by the height of a column of colored alcohol.

4. **timber jams:** piled-up masses of floating logs and branches.

always he sharply noted where he placed his feet. Once, coming around a bend he shied abruptly, like a startled horse, curved away from the place where he had been walking, and retreated several paces back along the trail. The creek he knew was frozen clear to the bottom—no creek could contain water in that arctic winter—but he knew also that there were springs that bubbled out from the hillsides and ran along under the snow and on top the ice of the creek. He knew that the coldest snaps never froze these springs, and he knew likewise
130 their danger. They were traps. They hid pools of water under the snow that might be three inches deep, or three feet. Sometimes a skin of ice half an inch thick covered them, and in turn was covered by the snow. Sometimes there were alternate layers of water and ice skin, so that when one broke through he kept on breaking through for a while, sometimes wetting himself to the waist.

That was why he had shied in such panic.

He had felt the give under his feet and heard the crackle of a snow-hidden ice skin. And to get his feet wet in such a temperature meant trouble and danger. At the very least it meant delay, for he would be forced to stop and build a fire, and under its protection to bare his feet while he dried his socks
140 and moccasins. He stood and studied the creek bed and its banks, and decided that the flow of water came from his right. He reflected awhile, rubbing his nose and cheeks, then skirted to the left, stepping gingerly and testing the footing for each step. Once clear of the danger, he took a fresh chew of tobacco and swung along at his four-mile gait.[5] **F**

F PREDICT
What do you think will happen? Why?

In the course of the next two hours he came upon several similar traps. Usually the snow above the hidden pools had a sunken, candied appearance that advertised the danger. Once again, however, he had a close call; and once, suspecting danger, he compelled the dog to go on in front. The dog did not want to go. It hung back until the man shoved it forward, and then it
150 went quickly across the white, unbroken surface. Suddenly it broke through, floundered to one side, and got away to firmer footing. It had wet its forefeet and legs, and almost immediately the water that clung to it turned to ice. It made quick efforts to lick the ice off its legs, then dropped down in the snow and began to bite out the ice that had formed between the toes. This was a matter of instinct. To permit the ice to remain would mean sore feet. It did not know this. It merely obeyed the mysterious prompting that arose from the deep crypts of its being. But the man knew, having achieved a judgment on the subject, and he removed the mitten from his right hand and helped tear out the ice particles. He did not expose his fingers more than a minute, and was
160 astonished at the swift numbness that **smote** them. It certainly was cold. He pulled on the mitten hastily, and beat the hand savagely across his chest.

smite (smīt) *v.* to inflict a heavy blow on; *past tense*—**smote** (smōt)

---

5. **four-mile gait:** walking pace of four miles per hour.

At twelve o'clock the day was at its brightest. Yet the sun was too far south on its winter journey to clear the horizon. The bulge of the earth intervened between it and Henderson Creek, where the man walked under a clear sky at noon and cast no shadow. At half-past twelve, to the minute, he arrived at the forks of the creek. He was pleased at the speed he had made. If he kept it up, he would certainly be with the boys by six. He unbuttoned his jacket and shirt and drew forth his lunch. The action consumed no more than a quarter of a minute, yet in that brief moment the numbness laid hold of the exposed
170 fingers. He did not put the mitten on, but, instead, struck the fingers a dozen sharp smashes against his leg. Then he sat down on a snow-covered log to eat. The sting that followed upon the striking of his fingers against his leg ceased so quickly that he was startled. He had had no chance to take a bite of biscuit. He struck the fingers repeatedly and returned them to the mitten, baring the other hand for the purpose of eating. He tried to take a mouthful, but the ice muzzle prevented. He had forgotten to build a fire and thaw out. He chuckled at his foolishness, and as he chuckled he noted the numbness creeping into the exposed fingers. Also, he noted that the stinging which had first come to his toes when he sat down was already passing away. He wondered whether the
180 toes were warm or numb. He moved them inside the moccasins and decided that they were numb. **G**

G **SETTING AND CONFLICT**
Reread lines 162–181. How has the man's situation become more challenging? Cite details.

He pulled the mitten on hurriedly and stood up. He was a bit frightened. He stamped up and down until the stinging returned into the feet. It certainly was cold, was his thought. That man from Sulphur Creek had spoken the truth when telling how cold it sometimes got in the country. And he had laughed at him at the time! That showed one must not be too sure of things. There was no mistake about it, it *was* cold. He strode up and down, stamping his feet and threshing his arms, until reassured by the returning warmth. Then he got out matches and proceeded to make a fire. From the under-growth, where high
190 water of the previous spring had lodged a supply of seasoned twigs, he got his firewood. Working carefully from a small beginning, he soon had a roaring fire, over which he thawed the ice from his face and in the protection of which he ate his biscuits. For the moment the cold of space was outwitted. The dog took satisfaction in the fire, stretching out close enough for warmth and far enough away to escape being singed.

When the man had finished, he filled his pipe and took his comfortable time over a smoke, then he pulled on his mittens, settled the ear flaps of his cap firmly about his ears, and took the creek trail up the left fork. The dog was disappointed and yearned back towards the fire. This man did not know cold.
200 Possibly all the generations of his ancestry had been ignorant of cold, of real cold, of cold one hundred and seven degrees below freezing point. But the dog knew; all its ancestry knew, and it had inherited the knowledge. And it knew that it was not good to walk abroad in such fearful cold. It was the time to lie snug in a hole in the snow and wait for a curtain of cloud to be drawn across the face of outer space whence this cold came. On the other hand, there was no keen intimacy between the dog and the man. The one was the toil slave[6] of the other, and the only caresses it had ever received were the caresses of the whip lash and of harsh and menacing throat sounds that threatened the whip lash. So the dog made no effort to communicate its apprehension to the man. It was not
210 concerned in the welfare of the man; it was for its own sake that it yearned back toward the fire. But the man whistled, and spoke to it with the sound of whip lashes, and the dog swung in at the man's heels and followed after. **H**

The man took a chew of tobacco and proceeded to start a new amber beard. Also, his moist breath quickly powdered with white his mustache, eyebrows, and lashes. There did not seem to be so many springs on the left fork of the Henderson, and for half an hour the man saw no signs of any. And then it happened. At a place where there were no signs, where the soft, unbroken snow seemed to advertise solidity beneath, the man broke through. It was not deep. He wet himself halfway to the knees before he floundered out to the firm
220 crust. He was angry, and cursed his luck aloud. He had hoped to get into camp with the boys at six o'clock, and this would delay him an hour, for he would have to build a fire and dry out his footgear. This was **imperative** at that low temperature—he knew that much; and he turned aside to the bank, which he climbed. On top, tangled in the underbrush about the trunks of several small

H DRAW CONCLUSIONS
Who seems more know-ledgeable about what to do—the man or the dog? Support your answer.

imperative (ĭm-pĕr′ə-tĭv)
adj. urgently necessary

---

6. **toil slave:** a slave who performs hard labor.

spruce trees, was a high-water deposit[7] of dry firewood—sticks and twigs, principally, but also larger portions of seasoned branches and fine, dry, last year's grasses. He threw down several large pieces on top of the snow. This served for a foundation and prevented the young flame from drowning itself in the snow it otherwise would melt. The flame he got by touching a match to a small shred of birch bark that he took from his pocket. This burned even more readily than paper. Placing it on the foundation, he fed the young flame with wisps of dry grass and with the tiniest dry twigs.

    He worked slowly and carefully, keenly aware of his danger. Gradually, as the flame grew stronger, he increased the size of the twigs with which he fed it. He squatted in the snow, pulling the twigs out from their entanglement in the brush and feeding directly to the flame. He knew there must be no failure. When it is seventy-five below zero, a man must not fail in his first attempt to build a fire—that is, if his feet are wet. If his feet are dry, and he fails, he can run along the trail for half a mile and restore his circulation. But the circulation of wet and freezing feet cannot be restored by running when it is seventy-five below. No matter how fast he runs, the wet feet will freeze the harder.

    All this the man knew. The old-timer on Sulphur Creek had told him about it the previous fall, and now he was appreciating the advice. Already all sensation had gone out of his feet. To build the fire he had been forced to remove his mittens, and the fingers had quickly gone numb. His pace of four miles an hour had kept his heart pumping blood to the surface of his body and to all the extremities. But the instant he stopped, the action of the pump eased down. The cold of space smote the unprotected tip of the planet, and he, being on that unprotected tip, received the full force of the blow. The blood of his body recoiled before it. The blood was alive, like the dog, and like the dog it wanted to hide away and cover itself up from the fearful cold. So long as he walked four miles an hour, he pumped the blood, willy-nilly, to the surface; but now it ebbed away and sank down into the recesses of his body. The extremities were the first to feel its absence. His wet feet froze the faster, and his exposed fingers numbed the faster, though they had not yet begun to freeze. Nose and cheeks were already freezing, while the skin of all his body chilled as it lost its blood. ❶

❶ **SETTING AND CONFLICT**
Reread lines 216–258. What new conflict with the setting is the man experiencing?

But he was safe. Toes and nose and cheeks would be only touched by the frost, for the fire was beginning to burn with strength. He was feeding it with twigs the size of his finger. In another minute he would be able to feed it with branches the size of his wrist, and then he could remove his wet footgear, and, while it dried, he could keep his naked feet warm by the fire, rubbing them at first, of course, with snow. The fire was a success. He was safe. He

---

7. **high-water deposit:** debris left on the bank of a stream as the water recedes from its highest level.

remembered the advice of the old-timer on Sulphur Creek, and smiled. The old-timer had been very serious in laying down the law that no man must travel alone in the Klondike after fifty below. Well, here he was; he had had the accident; he was alone; and he had saved himself. Those old-timers were rather womanish, some of them, he thought. All a man had to do was to keep his head, and he was all right. Any man who was a man could travel alone. But it was surprising, the rapidity with which his cheeks and nose were freezing. And he had not thought his fingers could go lifeless in so short a time. Lifeless they were, for he could scarcely make them move together to grip a twig, and they seemed remote from his body and from him. When he touched a twig, he had to look and see whether or not he had hold of it. The wires were pretty well down between him and his finger ends. **J**

All of which counted for little. There was the fire, snapping and crackling and promising life with every dancing flame. He started to untie his moccasins. They were coated with ice; the thick German socks were like sheaths of iron halfway to the knees; and the moccasin strings were like rods of steel all twisted and knotted as by some **conflagration.** For a moment he tugged with his numb fingers, then, realizing the folly of it, he drew his sheath knife.

But before he could cut the strings, it happened. It was his own fault or, rather, his mistake. He should not have built the fire under the spruce tree. He should have built it in the open. But it had been easier to pull the twigs from the brush and drop them directly on the fire. Now the tree under which he had done this carried a weight of snow on its boughs. No wind had blown for weeks, and each bough was full freighted. Each time he had pulled a twig he had communicated a slight agitation to the tree—an imperceptible agitation, so far as he was concerned, but an agitation sufficient to bring about the disaster. High up in the tree one bough capsized its load of snow. This fell on the boughs beneath, capsizing them. This process continued, spreading out and involving the whole tree. It grew like an avalanche, and it descended upon the man and the fire, and the fire was blotted out! Where it had burned was a mantle of fresh and disordered snow.

The man was shocked. It was as though he had just heard his own sentence of death. For a moment he sat and stared at the spot where the fire had been. Then he grew very calm. Perhaps the old-timer on Sulphur Creek was right. If he had only had a trail mate he would have been in no danger now. The trail mate could have built the fire. Well, it was up to him to build the fire over again, and this second time there must be no failure. Even if he succeeded, he would most likely lose some toes. His feet must be badly frozen by now, and there would be some time before the second fire was ready. **K**

Such were his thoughts, but he did not sit and think them. He was busy all the time they were passing through his mind. He made a new foundation for a fire, this time in the open, where no treacherous tree could blot it out. Next he gathered dry grasses and tiny twigs from the high-water flotsam. He could not

J DRAW CONCLUSIONS
Reread lines 259–276. What pattern can you see in the man's attitude and behavior?

conflagration
(kŏn′flə-grā′shən) *n.* a large, destructive fire

K PREDICT
Do you think the man will be able to build a fire quickly enough to save his feet?

bring his fingers together to pull them out, but he was able to gather them by the handful. In this way he got many rotten twigs and bits of green moss that were undesirable, but it was the best he could do. He worked methodically, even collecting an armful of the larger branches to be used later when the fire gathered strength. And all the while the dog sat and watched him, a certain wistfulness in its eyes, for it looked upon him as the fire provider, and the fire was slow in coming.

When all was ready, the man reached in his pocket for a second piece of birch bark. He knew the bark was there, and though he could not feel it with his fingers, he could hear its crisp rustling as he fumbled for it. Try as he would, he could not clutch hold of it. And all the time, in his consciousness, was the knowledge that each instant his feet were freezing. This thought tended to put him in a panic, but he fought against it and kept calm. He pulled on his mittens with his teeth, and threshed his arms back and forth, beating his hands with all his might against his sides. He did this sitting down, and he stood up to do it; and all the while the dog sat in the snow, its wolf brush of a tail curled around warmly over its forefeet, its sharp wolf ears pricked forward intently as it watched the man. And the man, as he beat and threshed with his arms and hands, felt a great surge of envy as he regarded the creature that was warm and secure in its natural covering.

After a time he was aware of the first faraway signals of sensations in his beaten fingers. The faint tingling grew stronger till it evolved into a stinging ache that was excruciating, but which the man hailed with satisfaction. He stripped the mitten from his right hand and fetched forth the birch bark. The exposed fingers were quickly going numb again. Next he brought out his bunch of sulphur matches. But the tremendous cold had already driven the life out of his fingers. In his effort to separate one match from the others, the whole bunch fell into the snow. He tried to pick it out of the snow, but failed. The dead fingers could neither clutch nor touch. He was very careful. He drove the thought of his freezing feet, and nose, and cheeks, out of his mind, devoting his whole soul to the matches. He watched, using the sense of vision in place of that of touch, and when he saw his fingers on each side the bunch, he closed them—that is, he willed to close them, for the wires were down, and the fingers did not obey. He pulled the mitten on the right hand, and beat it fiercely against his knee. Then, with both mittened hands, he scooped the bunch of matches, along with much snow, into his lap. Yet he was no better off. ❶

After some manipulation he managed to get the bunch between the heels of his mittened hands. In this fashion he carried it to his mouth. The ice crackled and snapped when by a violent effort he opened his mouth. He drew the lower jaw in, curled the upper lip out of the way and scraped the bunch with his upper teeth in order to separate a match. He succeeded in getting one, which he dropped on his lap. He was no better off. He could not pick it up. Then he

❶ SETTING AND CONFLICT
Why is the man no better off despite his best efforts?

devised a way. He picked it up in his teeth and scratched it on his leg. Twenty times he scratched before he succeeded in lighting it. As it flamed he held it with his teeth to the birch bark. But the burning brimstone[8] went up his nostrils and into his lungs, causing him to cough spasmodically. The match fell into the snow and went out.

The old-timer on Sulphur Creek was right, he thought in the moment of controlled despair that ensued: after fifty below, a man should travel with a partner. He beat his hands, but failed in exciting any sensation. Suddenly he bared both hands, removing the mittens with his teeth. He caught the whole 360 bunch between the heels of his hands. His arm muscles not being frozen enabled him to press the hand heels tightly against the matches. Then he scratched the bunch along his leg. It flared into flame, seventy sulphur matches at once! There was no wind to blow them out. He kept his head to one side to escape the strangling fumes, and held the blazing bunch to the birch bark. As he so held it, he became aware of sensation in his hand. His flesh was burning. He could smell it. Deep down below the surface he could feel it. The sensation developed into pain that grew acute. And still he endured it, holding the flame

ANALYZE VISUALS
What effect is achieved by placing these two images together?

---

8. **brimstone:** sulfur, a chemical used in match heads.

of the matches clumsily to the bark that would not light readily because his own burning hands were in the way, absorbing most of the flame. **M**

370   At last, when he could endure no more, he jerked his hands apart. The blazing matches fell sizzling into the snow, but the birch bark was alight. He began laying dry grasses and the tiniest twigs on the flame. He could not pick and choose, for he had to lift the fuel between the heels of his hands. Small pieces of rotten wood and green moss clung to the twigs, and he bit them off as well as he could with his teeth. He cherished[9] the flame carefully and awkwardly. It meant life, and it must not perish. The withdrawal of blood from the surface of his body now made him begin to shiver, and he grew more awkward. A large piece of green moss fell squarely on the little fire. He tried to poke it out with his fingers, but his shivering frame made him poke too far, and

380 he disrupted the nucleus of the little fire, the burning grasses and the tiny twigs separating and scattering. He tried to poke them together again, but in spite of the tenseness of the effort, his shivering got away with him, and the twigs were hopelessly scattered. Each twig gushed a puff of smoke and went out. The fire provider had failed. As he looked apathetically about him, his eyes chanced on the dog, sitting across the ruins of the fire from him, in the snow, making restless, hunching movements, slightly lifting one forefoot and then the other, shifting its weight back and forth on them with wistful eagerness.

        The sight of the dog put a wild idea into his head. He remembered the tale of the man, caught in a blizzard, who killed a steer and crawled inside the

390 carcass, and so was saved. He would kill the dog and bury his hands in the warm body until the numbness went out of them. Then he could build another fire. He spoke to the dog, calling it to him; but in his voice was a strange note of fear that frightened the animal, who had never known the man to speak in such a way before. Something was the matter, and its suspicious nature sensed danger—it knew not what danger, but somewhere, somehow, in its brain arose an apprehension of the man. It flattened its ears down at the sound of the man's voice, and its restless, hunching movements and the liftings and shiftings of its forefeet became more pronounced; but it would not come to the man. He got on his hands and knees and crawled toward the dog. This unusual posture again

400 excited suspicion, and the animal sidled mincingly away. **N**

        The man sat up in the snow for a moment and struggled for calmness. Then he pulled on his mittens, by means of his teeth, and got upon his feet. He glanced down at first in order to assure himself that he was really standing up, for the absence of sensation in his feet left him unrelated to the earth. His erect position in itself started to drive the webs of suspicion from the dog's mind; and when he spoke **peremptorily,** with the sound of whip lashes in his voice, the dog rendered its customary allegiance and came to him. As it came within reaching distance, the man lost his control. His arms flashed out to the dog, and he experienced genuine surprise when he discovered that his hands

410 could not clutch, that there was neither bend nor feeling in his fingers. He had

M PREDICT
Given his current difficulties, what do you predict will happen to the man? Why?

N PREDICT
Do you think the man will succeed in tricking the dog?

peremptorily
(pə-rĕmp′tə-rə-lē) *adv.* in a commanding way that does not allow for refusal or contradiction

---

9. **cherished:** tended; guarded.

forgotten for the moment that they were frozen and that they were freezing more and more. All this happened quickly, and before the animal could get away, he encircled its body with his arms. He sat down in the snow, and in this fashion held the dog, while it snarled and whined and struggled.

But it was all he could do, hold its body encircled in his arms and sit there. He realized that he could not kill the dog. There was no way to do it. With his helpless hands he could neither draw nor hold his sheath knife nor throttle the animal. He released it, and it plunged wildly away, with tail between its legs, and still snarling. It halted forty feet away and surveyed him curiously, with
420 ears sharply pricked forward.

The man looked down at his hands in order to locate them, and found them hanging on the ends of his arms. It struck him as curious that one should have to use his eyes in order to find out where his hands were. He began threshing his arms back and forth, beating the mittened hands against his sides. He did this for five minutes, violently, and his heart pumped enough blood up to the surface to put a stop to his shivering. But no sensation was aroused in the hands. He had an impression that they hung like weights on the ends of his arms, but when he tried to run the impression down, he could not find it.

A certain fear of death, dull and oppressive, came to him. This fear quickly
430 became poignant as he realized that it was no longer a mere matter of freezing his fingers and toes, or of losing his hands and feet, but that it was a matter of life and death with the chances against him. This threw him into a panic, and he turned and ran along the old, dim trail. The dog joined in behind and kept up with him. He ran blindly, without intention, in fear such as he had never known in his life. Slowly, as he plowed and floundered through the snow, he began to see things again—the banks of the creek, the old timber jams, the leafless aspens, and the sky. The running made him feel better. He did not shiver. Maybe, if he ran on, his feet would thaw out; and, anyway, if he ran far enough, he would reach camp and the boys. Without doubt he would lose some
440 fingers and toes and some of his face; but the boys would take care of him, and save the rest of him when he got there. And at the same time there was another thought in his mind that said he would never get to the camp and the boys; that he would soon be stiff and dead. This thought he kept in the background and refused to consider. Sometimes it pushed itself forward and demanded to be heard, but he thrust it back and strove to think of other things. ◗

It struck him as curious that he could run at all on feet so frozen that he could not feel them when they struck the earth and took the weight of his body. He seemed to himself to skim along above the surface, and to have no

◗ **SETTING AND CONFLICT**
What has the man's struggle now become?

connection with the earth. Somewhere he had once seen a winged Mercury,[10] and he wondered if Mercury felt as he felt when skimming over the earth.

His theory of running until he reached camp and the boys had one flaw in it: he lacked the endurance. Several times he stumbled, and finally he tottered, crumpled up, and fell. When he tried to rise, he failed. He must sit and rest, he decided, and next time he would merely walk and keep on going. As he sat and regained his breath, he noted that he was feeling quite warm and comfortable. He was not shivering, and it even seemed that a warm glow had come to his chest and trunk. And yet, when he touched his nose or cheeks, there was no sensation. Running would not thaw them out. Nor would it thaw out his hands and feet. Then the thought came to him that the frozen portions of his body must be extending. He tried to keep this thought down, to forget it, to think of something else; he was aware of the panicky feeling that it caused, and he was afraid of the panic. But the thought asserted itself, and persisted, until it produced a vision of his body totally frozen. This was too much, and he made another wild run along the trail. Once he slowed down to a walk, but the thought of the freezing extending itself made him run again.

And all the time the dog ran with him, at his heels. When he fell down a second time, it curled its tail over its forefeet and sat in front of him, facing him, curiously eager and intent. The warmth and security of the animal angered him, and he cursed it till it flattened down its ears appeasingly. This time the shivering came more quickly upon the man. He was losing in his battle with the frost. It was creeping into his body from all sides. The thought of it drove him on, but he ran no more than a hundred feet, when he staggered and pitched headlong. It was his last panic. When he had recovered his breath and control, he sat up and entertained in his mind the conception of meeting death with dignity. However, the conception did not come to him in such terms. His idea of it was that he had been making a fool of himself, running around like a chicken with its head cut off—such was the simile that occurred to him. Well, he was bound to freeze anyway, and he might as well take it decently. With this newfound peace of mind came the first glimmerings of drowsiness. A good idea, he thought, to sleep off to death. It was like taking an anesthetic. Freezing was not so bad as people thought. There were lots worse ways to die. **P**

He pictured the boys finding his body the next day. Suddenly he found himself with them, coming along the trail and looking for himself. And, still with them, he came around a turn in the trail and found himself lying in the snow. He did not belong with himself any more, for even then he was out of himself, standing with the boys and looking at himself in the snow. It certainly was cold, was his thought. When he got back to the States he could tell the folks what real cold was. He drifted on from this to a vision of the old-timer

P DRAW CONCLUSIONS
Reread lines 473–482. What has the man decided to do? What does his decision tell you about his character?

10. **Mercury:** the messenger of the gods in Roman mythology, who flew about by means of wings on his helmet and sandals.

490 on Sulphur Creek. He could see him quite clearly, warm and comfortable, and smoking a pipe.

"You were right, old hoss;[11] you were right," the man mumbled to the old-timer of Sulphur Creek.

Then the man drowsed off into what seemed to him the most comfortable and satisfying sleep he had ever known. The dog sat facing him and waiting. The brief day drew to a close in a long, slow twilight. There were no signs of a fire to be made, and, besides, never in the dog's experience had it known a man to sit like that in the snow and make no fire. As the twilight drew on, its eager yearning for the fire mastered it, and with a great lifting and shifting of 500 forefeet, it whined softly, then flattened its ears down in anticipation of being chidden by the man. But the man remained silent. Later the dog whined loudly. And still later it crept close to the man and caught the scent of death. This made the animal bristle and back away. A little longer it delayed, howling under the stars that leaped and danced and shone brightly in the cold sky. Then it turned and trotted up the trail in the direction of the camp it knew, where there were other food providers and fire providers. ❧ Q

Q PREDICT
Will the dog meet the same fate as the man? Why?

---

11. **old hoss:** old horse—here used as an affectionate term of address.

Comprehension

OHIO STANDARDS

READING STANDARD
4.2 Analyze setting

1. **Recall** Why must the man stop and build a second fire?

2. **Recall** What causes his second fire to go out?

3. **Recall** Why does the man have difficulty rebuilding the second fire?

4. **Clarify** What ultimately happens to the man and the dog?

Literary Analysis

5. **Predict** Look at the chart you created as you read. What predictions did you make about events in the story? Tell what clues helped you guess correctly— or misled you.

6. **Analyze Setting and Conflict** In what ways does the setting act as an **antagonist,** or opponent, of the man? Cite evidence from the story.

7. **Evaluate Behavior** Identify at least three mistakes that the man makes. What traits or qualities within him cause him to make those mistakes? Record your ideas on a chart like the one shown.

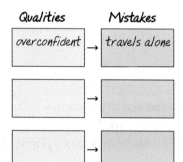

8. **Contrast Characters** Point out differences between the man and the dog. What message about **instincts** do you get from these contrasts?

9. **Analyze Mood** Describe the mood, or atmosphere, of the story. How does the description of setting contribute to the mood?

10. **Make Judgments** What do you blame most for the man's fate? Support your answer.

Literary Criticism

11. **Philosophical Context** Two principles of the philosophy of **naturalism** are that (1) the universe is indifferent to human beings and (2) people are at the mercy of forces over which they have little control. How are these principles illustrated in "To Build a Fire"? Use examples from the story to support your answer.

Vocabulary in Context

VOCABULARY PRACTICE

Decide whether each pair of words contains synonyms or antonyms.

1. intangible/touchable
2. conjectural/theorized
3. apprehension/anxiety
4. reiterate/restate
5. smite/caress
6. imperative/needless
7. conflagration/blaze
8. peremptorily/hesitantly

WORD LIST

apprehension
conflagration
conjectural
imperative
intangible
peremptorily
reiterate
smite

VOCABULARY IN WRITING

Write three or more sentences about a dangerous setting. Use at least three vocabulary words. Here is an example sentence.

> **EXAMPLE SENTENCE**
>
> As I climbed the dark staircase, I was filled with **apprehension**.

VOCABULARY STRATEGY: CONNOTATION AND DENOTATION

A word's **denotation** is its basic dictionary meaning; its **connotation** is the overtones of meaning the word has taken on. For example, the vocabulary word *conflagration* means "a large fire," but it has negative connotations of total destruction, unlike the more neutral word *flame*. When you choose a word in writing, consider whether its connotation fits the context.

PRACTICE Choose the word that works best in each sentence.

1. The queen (assertively/peremptorily) ordered her attendants to stand.
2. The melody would (reiterate/echo) in his ears.
3. The excited children felt (anticipation/apprehension) as they entered the circus tent.
4. Examinations were (imperative/compulsory) for admission to the school.
5. There was an (intangible/unsubstantial) feeling of loss in the community.

OHIO STANDARDS

VOCABULARY STANDARD
1.2 Analyze the relationships of pairs of words

VOCABULARY PRACTICE
For more practice, go to the **Vocabulary Center** at **ClassZone.com**.

from **Deep Survival**

Nonfiction Trade Book

Use with "To Build a Fire," page 76.

What's the Connection?

In "To Build a Fire" you read about a man who is unable to save himself in a desperate situation. But what exactly does he do wrong? Could his fate have been different? In the following selection you'll learn what real people in desperate situations have done to save their lives.

Skill Focus: Use Text Features

Text features are design elements that highlight the organization of information and key ideas in a text. Like numbered steps in a recipe, they make a text easy to follow. For example, in the selection from *Deep Survival*, the following text features point out its key ideas:

- The **title** usually reveals the main topic of the piece.
- **Numbers** make the order of sequential information obvious or establish order of importance.
- **Subheadings**—boldfaced headings in the text—signal the start of new topics or sections and tell what they will be about.
- **Text in parentheses** explains whatever came just before it.

As you read the selection, use these features for help in finding and recording key ideas in the order the writer presents them. Record the writer's subheadings on a chart like the one shown, but then use the examples he gives as a basis for restating the key ideas in your own words.

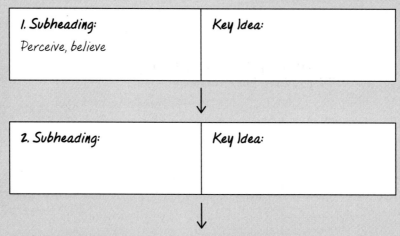

Review: **Summarize**

DEEP SURVIVAL

by LAURENCE GONZALES

A USE TEXT FEATURES
Speculate about the meaning of the **title**. What topic do you predict the writer will discuss?

Lauren Elder, sole survivor of a plane crash

I've been reading accident reports of various kinds for thirty or more years. Call me callous, but to me they're like silent comedy movies. People do the strangest things and get themselves into the most amazing predicaments. You want to go wake up Tolstoy and Dostoevsky and say: Hey, you think your characters are crazy. . . .

In reading about cases in which people survived seemingly impossible circumstances, however, I found an eerie uniformity. Decades and sometimes even centuries apart, separated by culture, geography, race, language, and tradition, they all went through the 10 same patterns of thought and behavior. I eventually distilled those observations down to twelve points that seemed to stand out concerning how survivors think and behave in the clutch of mortal danger. Some are the same as the steps for staying out of trouble. Here's what survivors do:

1. Perceive, believe (look, see, believe). 🅑 Even in the initial crisis, survivors' perceptions and cognitive functions keep working. They notice the details and may even find some humorous or beautiful. If there is any denial, it is counterbalanced by a solid belief in the clear evidence of their senses. They immediately begin to recognize, acknowledge, and even accept the 20 reality of their situation. "I've broken my leg, that's it. I'm dead," as Joe Simpson [who survived a mountain-climbing accident in Peru] put it. They may initially blame forces outside themselves, too; but very quickly they dismiss that tactic and recognize that everything, good and bad, emanates from within. They see opportunity, even good, in their situation. They move through denial, anger, bargaining, depression, and acceptance very rapidly. They "go inside." Bear in mind, though, that many people, such as Debbie Kiley [who survived being lost at sea for five days without water], may have to struggle for a time before they get there.

2. Stay calm (use humor, use fear to focus). In the initial crisis, 30 survivors are making use of fear, not being ruled by it. Their fear often feels like and turns into anger, and that motivates them and makes them sharper. They understand at a deep level about being cool and are ever on guard against the mutiny of too much emotion. They keep their sense of humor and therefore keep calm.

3. Think/analyze/plan (get organized; set up small, manageable tasks). Survivors quickly organize, set up routines, and institute discipline. In successful group survival situations, a leader emerges often from the least likely candidate. They push away thoughts that their situation is hopeless. A rational voice emerges and is often actually heard,

🅑 **USE TEXT FEATURES**
Scan the boldfaced **subheadings** to get an overview of the points Gonzales makes. How would you characterize these points about survival? How many are there?

Joe Simpson, survivor of a mountain-climbing accident

40 which takes control of the situation. Survivors perceive that experience as being split into two people and they "obey" the rational one. It begins with the paradox of seeing reality—how hopeless it would seem to an outside observer—but acting with the expectation of success.

4. Take correct, decisive action (be bold and cautious while carrying out tasks). Survivors are able to transform thought into action. They are willing to take risks to save themselves and others. They are able to break down very large jobs into small, manageable tasks. They set attainable goals and develop short-term plans to reach them. They are meticulous about doing those tasks well. They deal with what is within their power from 50 moment to moment, hour to hour, day to day. They leave the rest behind.

5. Celebrate your successes (take joy in completing tasks). Survivors take great joy from even their smallest successes. That is an important step in creating an ongoing feeling of motivation and preventing the descent into hopelessness. It also provides relief from the unspeakable stress of a true survival situation.

6. Count your blessings (be grateful—you're alive). This is how survivors become rescuers instead of victims. There is always someone else they are helping more than themselves, even if that someone is not present. One survivor I spoke to, Yossi Ghinsberg, who was lost for weeks in the 60 Bolivian jungle, hallucinated about a beautiful companion. . . . Everything he did, he did for her.

7. Play (sing, play mind games, recite poetry, count anything, do mathematical problems in your head). **C** Since the brain and its wiring appear to be the determining factor in survival, this is an argument for expanding and refining it. The more you have learned and experienced of art, music, poetry, literature, philosophy, mathematics, and so on, the more resources you will have to fall back on. Just as survivors use patterns and rhythm to move forward in the survival voyage, they use the deeper activities of intellect to stimulate, calm, and entertain the mind. Counting becomes 70 important, too, and reciting poetry or even a mantra can calm the frantic mind. Movement becomes dance. One survivor who had to walk a long way counted his steps, one hundred at a time, and dedicated each hundred to another person he cared about. . . . Survivors often cling to talismans. They search for meaning and the more you know already, the deeper the meaning. They engage the crisis almost as a game. They discover the flow of the expert performer, in whom emotion and thought balance each other in producing action. "Careful, careful," they say. But they act joyfully and decisively. Playing also leads to invention, and invention may lead to a new technique, strategy, or a piece of equipment that could save you.

C **USE TEXT FEATURES** Notice how the material in **parentheses** helps you understand point 7, **Play.** Read the rest of the section. Then explain in your own words how survivors "play."

80 8. See the beauty (remember: it's a vision quest). Survivors are attuned to the wonder of the world. The appreciation of beauty, the feeling of awe, opens the senses. When you see something beautiful, your pupils actually dilate. This appreciation not only relieves stress and creates strong motivation, but it allows you to take in new information more effectively.

9. Believe that you will succeed (develop a deep conviction that you'll live). All of the practices just described lead to this point: Survivors consolidate their personalities and fix their determination. Survivors admonish themselves to make no more mistakes, to be very careful, and to 90 do their very best. They become convinced that they will prevail if they do those things.

10. Surrender (let go of your fear of dying; "put away the pain"). Survivors manage pain well. Lauren Elder, who walked out of the Sierra Nevada after surviving a plane crash, wrote that she "stored away the information: My arm is broken." That sort of thinking is what John Leach calls "resignation without giving up. It is survival by surrender." Joe Simpson recognized that he would probably die. But it had ceased to bother him, and so he went ahead and crawled off the mountain anyway. **D**

11. Do whatever is necessary (be determined; have the will 100 and the skill). Survivors have meta-knowledge: They know their abilities and do not over- or underestimate them. They believe that anything is possible and act accordingly. Play leads to invention, which leads to trying something that might have seemed impossible. When the plane in which Lauren Elder was flying hit the top of a ridge above 12,000 feet, it would have seemed impossible that she could get off alive. She did it anyway, including having to down-climb vertical rock faces with a broken arm. Survivors don't expect or even hope to be rescued. They are coldly rational about using the world, obtaining what they need, doing what they have to do.

12. Never give up (let nothing break your spirit). E There is 110 always one more thing that you can do. Survivors are not easily frustrated. They are not discouraged by setbacks. They accept that the environment (or the business climate or their health) is constantly changing. They pick themselves up and start the entire process over again, breaking it down into manageable bits. Survivors always have a clear reason for going on. They keep their spirits up by developing an alternate world made up of rich memories to which they can escape. They mine their memory for whatever will keep them occupied. They come to embrace the world in which they find themselves and see opportunity in adversity. In the aftermath, survivors learn from and are grateful for the experiences they've had.

D SUMMARIZE
In a sentence, summarize point 10, **Surrender.**

E USE TEXT FEATURES
Why do you think Gonzales placed this point last?

Comprehension

1. **Recall** What kinds of accidents happened to the people in *Deep Survival?*

2. **Paraphrase** What does it mean to "Perceive, believe"?

Critical Analysis

3. **Analyze Text Features** Review the subheadings you jotted down as you read this selection. What is similar about the way in which they are stated? Why might Gonzales have chosen to phrase them this way?

4. **Make Generalizations** What general attitude do survivors seem to have?

5. **Apply** In what ways can you apply the 12 points to crises other than those involving physical survival in the outdoors?

Read for Information: Evaluate

OHIO STANDARDS

READING STANDARDS
2.3 Take notes and summarize
3.7 Analyze the effectiveness of the features of text

WRITING PROMPT

Use Gonzales's principles for survival to evaluate the performance of the man in "To Build a Fire." How does he demonstrate effective survival behavior? What does he fail to do that survivors tend to do?

To answer this prompt you will need to do the following:

1. Create a checklist of effective survival behaviors based on the 12 principles in *Deep Survival.*

2. Reread "To Build a Fire," rating the man's survival skills based on your checklist.

3. Summarize what you've discovered in a short paragraph. Then support your evaluation with evidence from the story and your checklist.

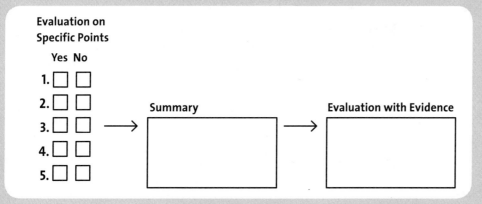

from **The Johnstown Flood**

Historical Narrative by David McCullough

Is SURVIVAL
a matter of chance?

OHIO STANDARDS

READING STANDARDS
3.1 Identify and understand organizational patterns

4.8 Analyze mood

KEY IDEA If you listen to survivors' stories after a disaster, you are bound to hear phrases such as "If I hadn't turned back when I did . . ." or "It missed me by just inches. . . ." Is **survival** determined by pure luck? Or do some survivors make their own luck by thinking quickly and seeing opportunities for escape? Read this account of a little girl who survived one of the deadliest floods in U.S. history, and decide what accounts for her rescue.

QUICKWRITE With your class, discuss survival stories you have read or heard about. In each case, would you attribute survival to luck or other causes?

● LITERARY ANALYSIS: MOOD

The Johnstown Flood is a **historical narrative,** a story about real events that occurred in the past. To tell the story of the horrifying events that occurred in Johnstown, Pennsylvania, in 1889, writer David McCullough creates a mood of tension and impending doom. **Mood** is the feeling or atmosphere that the writer creates for the reader. For example, think about the following description:

In the last few seconds, fighting the current around him that kept getting deeper and faster every second, he reached the hillside just as the wave pounded by below.

To understand how mood is created, notice the following as you read:

- descriptive words and phrases
- details of setting
- imagery

As you read, look for descriptions of what Johnstown was like on the day of the flood and what Gertrude Quinn and her family saw, heard, and said.

Review: **Conflict**

● READING SKILL: ANALYZE CHRONOLOGICAL ORDER

To help readers follow the chaotic events that took place during and after the Johnstown flood, McCullough presents them in **chronological** order, or the order in which the events actually occurred in time. He also includes many **time-order signal words,** such as *before, after, then,* and *meanwhile.*

As you read, look for such signal words and use them to record major events in the order that they occurred on a timeline like the one shown.

Mr. Quinn moves store goods to higher levels.	Mr. Quinn returns for dinner and shares his worries about the rising water.	

Author Online

A Passion for the Past

To many Americans, David McCullough (mə-kŭl′ə) has a familiar face—and voice. He has hosted the PBS series *Smithsonian World* and *The American Experience* and has narrated many TV documentaries. First and foremost, however, McCullough

David McCullough born 1933

is an award-winning writer of histories and biographies. His passion for writing about the past began in the 1960s when he saw old photographs of a tragic flood that had occurred about 70 years before in his native Pennsylvania. Unable to find well-written books about the tragedy, he decided to write one himself. The result was *The Johnstown Flood.* A master storyteller, McCullough has the gift of making the past come alive. "You scratch the surface of the supposedly dead past," he says, "and what you find is life."

> **MORE ABOUT THE AUTHOR**
> For more on David McCullough, visit the **Literature Center** at ClassZone.com.

Background

Dark Day in Johnstown The facts about the Johnstown flood are well documented. A heavy downpour that began on May 30, 1889, caused a man-made lake high in the hills above Johnstown to overflow its banks. The surging water put tremendous pressure on the South Fork dam, and faulty repairs made to it in the past began to buckle. On the afternoon of May 31, the dam collapsed, releasing the entire contents of the lake. About 20 million tons of water rushed down the hills, smashing Johnstown with a wave of water three stories high. Minutes later, more than 2,000 people were dead, and the city lay in ruins.

The Johnstown Flood

David McCullough

On the morning of the 31st, James Quinn had gone to the store early to supervise the moving of goods to higher levels. Before leaving home he had told everyone to stay inside. One of his children, Marie, was already sick with measles, and he did not want the others out in the rain catching cold. He did, however, allow young Vincent to come along with him downtown to lend a hand.

At noon, when he had returned for dinner, the water had been up to his curbstone. He had been restless and worried through the meal, talking about the water rising in the streets and his lack of confidence in the South
10 Fork dam. **A**

A few days before, he and his wife and the infant, Tom, and Lalia had gone to Scottdale for a christening, and Mrs. Quinn and the two children had stayed on to visit with her sister. Now Aunt Abbie and Libby Hipp were more or less running things, and he was doing his best to make sure they understood the seriousness of the situation.

"James, you are too anxious," his sister-in-law said. "This big house could never go."

In recalling the day years afterward, Gertrude felt sure that her father was so worried that he would have moved them all to the hill that morning, even
20 though he had no special place to take them, if it had not been for Marie. He was afraid of the effect the light might have on her eyes.

After dinner he had gone back to the store, and Gertrude slipped out onto the front porch where she began dangling her feet in the water, which, by now, covered the yard just deep enough for the ducks to sport about among the flowers. Everyone who survived the flood would carry some especially vivid mental picture of how things had looked just before the great wave struck; for this child it would be the sight of those ducks, and purple pansies floating face up, like lily pads, in the yellow water. **B**

ANALYZE VISUALS
What does the photograph convey to you about the destructive force of the Johnstown flood?

A **CHRONOLOGICAL ORDER**
What signal words in lines 1–10 tell you when the events took place?

B **MOOD**
Reread lines 22–28. What mood do these unusual details create?

Shortly before four Gertrude's father suddenly appeared in front of her. He
took her with one hand, with the other gave her a couple of quick spanks for
disobeying his order to stay inside, and hurried her through the door.

"Then he gave me a lecture on obedience, wet feet, and our perilous
position; he said he had come to take us to the hill and that we were delayed
because my shoes and stockings had to be changed again. He was smoking a
cigar while the nurse was changing my clothes. Then he went to the door to
toss off the ashes."

It was then that he saw the dark mist and heard the sound of the wave
coming. He rushed back inside, shouting, "Run for your lives. Follow me
straight to the hill."

Someone screamed to him about the baby with the measles. He leaped up
the stairs and in no more than a minute was back down with Marie wrapped
in a blanket, his face white and terrified-looking.

"Follow me," he said. "Don't go back for anything. Don't go back for
anything." Everyone started out the door except Vincent. Just where he was no
one knew. Helen and Rosemary ran on either side of their father, holding on
to his elbows as he carried the baby. When they got to the street the water was
nearly to Rosemary's chin, but she kept going, and kept trying to balance the
umbrella she had somehow managed to bring along. The hill was at most only
a hundred yards away. All they had to do was get two short blocks to the end
of Main and they would be safe. **C**

James Quinn started running, confident that everyone was with him. But
Aunt Abbie, who was carrying her baby, and Libby Hipp, who had Gertrude
in her arms, had turned back.

When she reached the top of the steps that led from the yard down to the
street, Aunt Abbie had had second thoughts.

"I don't like to put my feet in that dirty water," Gertrude would remember
her saying. Libby said she would do whatever Aunt Abbie thought best, so they
started back into the house.

"Well, I kicked and scratched and bit her, and gave her a terrible time,
because I wanted to be with my father," Gertrude said later. How the two
women, each with a child, ever got to the third floor as fast as they did was
something she was never quite able to figure out. Once there, they went to the
front window, opened it, and looked down into the street. Gertrude describe
the scene as looking "like the Day of Judgment I had seen as a little girl in
Bible histories," with crowds of people running, screaming, dragging children,
struggling to keep their feet in the water.

Her father meanwhile had reached dry land on the hill, and turning around
saw no signs of the rest of his family among the faces pushing past him. He
grabbed hold of a big butcher boy named Kurtz, gave him Marie, told him to
watch out for the other two girls, and started back to the house. **D**

C MOOD
Reread lines 37–50. What
details help create a
mood of terror?

D CHRONOLOGICAL
ORDER
Notice the signal word
meanwhile. What two
sets of actions occur at
the same time?

But he had gone only a short way when he saw the wave, almost on top of him, demolishing everything, and he knew he could never make it. There was a split second of indecision, then he turned back to the hill, running with all his might as the water surged along the street after him. In the last few seconds, fighting the current around him that kept getting deeper and faster every second, he reached the hillside just as the wave pounded by below. **E**

Looking behind he saw his house rock back and forth, then lunge sideways, topple over, and disappear.

Gertrude never saw the wave. The sight of the crowds jamming through the
80 street had so terrified her aunt and Libby Hipp that they had pulled back from the window, horrified, dragging her with them into an open cupboard.

"Libby, this is the end of the world, we will all die together," Aunt Abbie sobbed, and dropped to her knees and began praying hysterically, "Jesus, Mary, and Joseph, Have mercy on us, oh, God . . ."

Gertrude started screaming and jumping up and down, calling "Papa, Papa, Papa," as fast as she could get it out.

The cupboard was in what was the dining room of an elaborate playhouse built across the entire front end of the third floor. There was nothing like it anywhere else in town, the whole place having been fitted out and furnished
90 by Quinn's store. There was a long center hall and a beautifully furnished parlor at one end and little bedrooms with doll beds, bureaus, washstands, and ingrain carpets on the floors. The dining room had a painted table, chairs, sideboard with tiny dishes, hand-hemmed tablecloths, napkins, and silverware.

From where she crouched in the back of the cupboard, Gertrude could see across the dining room into a miniature kitchen with its own table and chairs, handmade iron stove, and, on one wall, a whole set of iron cooking utensils hanging on little hooks. Libby Hipp was holding her close, crying and trembling.

Then the big house gave a violent shudder. Gertrude saw the tiny pots and
100 pans begin to sway and dance. Suddenly plaster dust came down. The walls began to break up. Then, at her aunt's feet, she saw the floor boards burst open and up gushed a fountain of yellow water.

"And these boards were jagged . . . and I looked at my aunt, and they didn't say a word then. All the praying stopped, and they gasped, and looked down like this, and were gone, immediately gone."

She felt herself falling and reaching out for something to grab on to and trying as best she could to stay afloat.

"I kept paddling and grabbing and spitting and spitting and trying to keep the sticks and dirt and this horrible water out of my mouth."
110 Somehow she managed to crawl out of a hole in the roof or wall, she never knew which. All she saw was a glimmer of light, and she scrambled with all her strength to get to it, up what must have been the lath[1] on part of the house

E GRAMMAR AND STYLE
Reread lines 71–76. Notice how McCullough makes the scene's action come to life through the use of **strong verbs** and verb forms, such as *demolishing, surged,* and *pounded.*

---

1. **lath:** a narrow strip of wood used to support plaster or tiles.

A bridge washed away by the Johnstown Flood

ANALYZE VISUALS
What does the drawing communicate about the flood that the photo on page 103 does not?

underneath one of the gables.² She got through the opening, never knowing what had become of her aunt, Libby, or her baby cousin. Within seconds the whole house was gone and everyone in it.

The next thing she knew, Gertrude was whirling about on top of a muddy mattress that was being buoyed up by debris but that kept tilting back and forth as she struggled to get her balance. She screamed for help. Then a dead horse slammed against her raft, pitching one end of it up into the air and
120 nearly knocking her off. She hung on for dear life, until a tree swung by, snagging the horse in its branches before it plunged off with the current in another direction, the dead animal bobbing up and down, up and down, in and out of the water, like a gigantic, gruesome rocking horse. **F**

Weak and shivering with cold, she lay down on the mattress, realizing for the first time that all her clothes had been torn off except for her underwear. Night was coming on and she was terribly frightened. She started praying in German, which was the only way she had been taught to pray.

A small white house went sailing by, almost running her down. She called out to the one man who was riding on top, straddling the peak of the roof and
130 hugging the chimney with both arms. But he ignored her, or perhaps never heard her, and passed right by.

"You terrible man," she shouted after him. "I'll never help you."

Then a long roof, which may have been what was left of the Arcade Building, came plowing toward her, looking as big as a steamboat and loaded down with perhaps twenty people. She called out to them, begging someone to

F MOOD
What do the details about the dead horse contribute to the mood of the passage?

---

2. **gable:** a triangular portion of a roof.

save her. One man started up, but the others seemed determined to stop him. They held on to him and there was an endless moment of talk back and forth between them as he kept pulling to get free.

Then he pushed loose and jumped into the current. His head bobbed
140 up, then went under again. Several times more he came up and went under. Gertrude kept screaming for him to swim to her. Then he was heaving himself over the side of her raft, and the two of them headed off downstream, Gertrude nearly strangling him as she clung to his neck.

The big roof in the meantime had gone careening on until it hit what must have been a whirlpool in the current and began spinning round and round. Then, quite suddenly, it struck something and went down, carrying at least half its passengers with it. **G**

Gertrude's new companion was a powerful, square-jawed millworker named Maxwell McAchren, who looked like John L. Sullivan.[3] How far she had
150 traveled by the time he climbed aboard the mattress, she was never able to figure out for certain. But later on she would describe seeing many flags at one point along the way, which suggests that she went as far up the Stony Creek as Sandy Vale Cemetery, where the Memorial Day flags could have been visible floating about in the water. Sandy Vale is roughly two miles from where the Quinn house had been, and when Maxwell McAchren joined her, she had come all the way back down again and was drifting with the tide near Bedford Street in the direction of the stone bridge.

On a hillside, close by to the right, two men were leaning out of the window of a small white building, using long poles to carry on their own rescue
160 operation. They tried to reach out to the raft, but the distance was too great. Then one of them called out, "Throw that baby over here."

McAchren shouted back, "Do you think you can catch her?"

"We can try," they answered.

The child came flying through the air across about ten to fifteen feet of water and landed in the arms of Mr. Henry Koch, proprietor of Koch House, a small hotel and saloon (mostly saloon) on Bedford Street. The other man in the room with him was George Skinner, a Negro porter, who had been holding Koch by the legs when he made the catch. The men stripped Gertrude of her wet underclothes, wrapped her in a blanket, and put her on a cot. Later she
170 was picked up and carried to the hill, so bundled up in the warm blanket that she could not see out, nor could anyone see in very well. **H**

Every so often she could hear someone saying, "What have you got there?" And the answer came back, "A little girl we rescued." Then she could hear people gathering around and saying, "Let's have a look." Off would come part of the blanket in front of her face and she would look out at big, close-up faces looking in. Heads would shake. "Don't know her," they would say, and again the blanket would come over her face and on they would climb.

---

3. **John L. Sullivan:** a boxing champion in the late 1800s.

G CHRONOLOGICAL ORDER
Reread lines 128–147. Notice that several events take place in a short amount of time. Briefly summarize what happened, in order.

H CONFLICT
How is the conflict resolved? What builds suspense just before this resolution?

Survivors of the Johnstown flood take shelter in a cave.

Gertrude never found out who it was that carried her up the hill, but he eventually deposited her with a family named Metz, who lived in a frame
180 tenement also occupied by five other families. The place looked like paradise to her, but she was still so terrified that she was unable to say a word as the Metz children, neighbors, and people in off the street jammed into the kitchen to look at her as she lay wrapped now in a pair of red-flannel underwear with Mason jars full of hot water packed all around her.

Later, she was put to bed upstairs, but exhausted as she was she was unable to sleep. In the room with her were three other refugees from the disaster, grown women by the name of Bowser, who kept getting up and going to the window, where she could hear them gasping and whispering among themselves. After a while Gertrude slipped quietly out of bed and across the
190 dark room. Outside the window, down below where the city had been, she could now see only firelight reflecting on the water. It looked, as she said later, for all the world like ships burning at sea. ∾ ❶

❶ **MOOD**
How has the mood changed at the end of the selection? What atmosphere does the last image create?

Comprehension

OHIO STANDARDS

READING STANDARD
4.8 Analyze mood

1. **Recall** Where did Mr. Quinn order everyone to go when he heard the wave coming?

2. **Recall** Why didn't Gertrude go with Mr. Quinn?

3. **Recall** What happened to the Quinns' house?

4. **Clarify** How was Gertrude finally rescued?

Literary Analysis

5. **Understand Chronological Order** Use the timeline you created as you read to summarize the story, adding details as necessary.

6. **Identify Cause and Effect** What most accounts for Gertrude's miraculous **survival**—sheer luck, Gertrude's own actions, or others' actions? Give evidence from the narrative to support your answer.

7. **Analyze Mood** Describe the overall mood McCullough creates in his account of the Johnstown flood. Which passages are most effective in creating this mood?

8. **Compare and Contrast Settings** Both the excerpt from *The Johnstown Flood* and the story "To Build a Fire" are about people trying to survive in dangerous settings. Compare and contrast the settings and the roles they play in the selections. Record your ideas on a Venn diagram like the one shown.

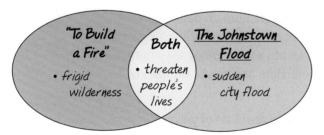

Literary Criticism

9. **Critical Interpretations** David McCullough has said that in his writing he tries to make history "as interesting and human as it really was." Do you think he succeeds in doing so in the selection from *The Johnstown Flood*? Explain, giving examples from the narrative to support your opinion.

Reading-Writing Connection

Increase your understanding of the selection from *The Johnstown Flood* by responding to these prompts. Then use **Revision: Grammar and Style** to improve your writing.

WRITING PROMPTS	SELF-CHECK
A. Short Response: Write a Newspaper Article In the selection, McCullough describes how three men joined forces to rescue Gertrude from her makeshift raft. Using facts and details from the narrative, write a **one- or two-paragraph newspaper article** about the dramatic rescue.	**A well-written newspaper article will . . .** • have an attention-getting headline that sums up the main idea • address the questions *who, what, where, when, why, how*
B. Extended Response: Write Across Texts The story of Amber Colvin, on the next page, tells of a modern child who, like Gertrude Quinn, survived a deadly flood. What do the two stories suggest to you about **survival** in a disaster? What insights into human behavior do they give you? Write **three to five paragraphs** in response.	**A strong interpretation will . . .** • make clear statements about what aids or hinders survival in a disaster • use details from the two stories to support the statements

REVISION: GRAMMAR AND STYLE

EMPHASIZE ACTION Review the **Grammar and Style** note on page 105. Like McCullough, you can create exciting action sequences by incorporating **strong verbs** into your writing. Choose verbs that create a vivid image for your reader. Avoid those that are too general or overused. Here are some examples of McCullough's use of strong verbs.

> . . . *the floor boards burst open and up gushed a fountain of yellow water.* (lines 101–102)

> . . . *a dead horse slammed against her raft . . .* (lines 118–119)

Notice how the revisions in red use strong verbs to emphasize the action in this first draft. Revise your response to Prompt A by using similar techniques.

OHIO STANDARDS

WRITING STANDARD
5.9 Use action verbs

STUDENT MODEL

            flung
McAchren ~~passed~~ Gertrude across the water to the waiting arms of Mr. Koch,
    grasped ∧
who ~~took~~ the child, saving her from drowning.
   ∧

WRITING TOOLS
For prewriting, revision, and editing tools, visit the **Writing Center** at ClassZone.com.

MAGAZINE ARTICLE Though technology can help us predict natural disasters and often reduce the extent of their destructiveness, nature still has a mind of its own.

MICHAEL NEILL AND KEN MYERS

Nine-year-old Amber Colvin Rides Out a Killer Flood in Ohio

About 9:30 on the night of June 14, 1990, a flash flood hit the small town of Shadyside, Ohio, leaving death and destruction in its wake. Before the rain started, Dennis and Karen Colvin had driven to a nearby town to do errands and left their daughter, 9-year-old Amber, playing at home with her friend, 12-year-old Kerri Polivka. Suddenly the flood was in full force, and Amber and Kerri were on their own, fighting for their lives.

The Colvins' basement was inundated, and soon the girls were ankle-deep in water in the living room. At Kerri's suggestion, they got into the bathtub for protection, but within minutes the surging waters broke down the bathroom door and swept the tub from the floor. "It took me so far up I bumped my head on the ceiling," Amber recalls. . . .

When the two girls pressed their hands against the ceiling, it gave way, and they were flung out into the full fury of raging Wegee Creek. . . . As the tub splintered into pieces, Kerri was hit on the head—and was lost. "I tried to save her," says Amber, . . . "I saw her hair and tried to grab it. I pulled it up, then I had to let go." Amber then lunged out, grabbed a floating log—and clung to it all the way down the Wegee and into the Ohio River, 1 1/2 miles away.

"I went under twice," she says, "once when the house went and the second time when I tried to save Kerri. . . . I was thinking there was no hope for me to live." Once she survived the millrace ride to the calmer Ohio, though, Amber realized she had a chance. She floated for seven miles more, at times dozing briefly as she gripped the log for eight hours, until it drifted ashore around 6:30 A.M. near Route 7. Amber managed to flag down Randy and Mitzie Ramsey of Bellaire. . . . "Amber was cold—but real alert and talkative," says Mitzie. . . .

When Dennis and Karen had tried to drive home the night before, they had been stopped at a police roadblock. The Colvins then walked down a hill untouched by the flood that stood behind their rented two-bedroom home, only to find the house had vanished, torn away by Wegee's waters. "Denny and I just held each other," says Karen. "Right there, I thought, there's no way. I thought she was dead," says Dennis. "Somebody was looking out for her, that's for sure."

Amber Colvin and her parents

The Race to Save *Apollo 13*
Nonfiction by Michael Useem

How can we achieve the IMPOSSIBLE?

OHIO STANDARDS

READING STANDARDS
2.3 Take notes and summarize
4.3 Distinguish how conflicts, parallel plots and subplots affect the story

KEY IDEA Some situations may seem hopeless at first. But when lives are at stake, people often find a way to achieve the **impossible.** In "The Race to Save *Apollo 13*," Michael Useem describes the extraordinary efforts of NASA employees to rescue astronauts aboard a damaged spacecraft.

DISCUSS With a small group, discuss strategies that can help people deal with an emergency. Share your list of strategies with the class.

Emergency Strategies
1. Stay calm.
2. Share information.
3.
4.
5.

● LITERARY ANALYSIS: SUSPENSE IN NONFICTION

To draw the reader into a story, writers often create **suspense**— a feeling of excitement or tension about what will happen next. In nonfiction, a writer may create suspense by raising questions about the outcome of a situation or by emphasizing the risks involved. For example, in "The Race to Save *Apollo 13*," Michael Useem lets the reader know how much is at stake in the situation faced by the flight director.

He understood as well that his actions in the hours ahead might determine whether the U.S. space program experienced or avoided its biggest disaster.

As you read, notice the details that Useem included to increase the suspense of the narrative.

● READING STRATEGY: TAKE NOTES

"The Race to Save *Apollo 13*" contains many details about equipment and procedures used in the space mission. When you read this type of information-rich text, take notes to help you understand and remember important information. Your notes may include

- key words and phrases from the text
- ideas rephrased in your own words
- diagrams

As you read "The Race to Save *Apollo 13*," use the **Take Notes** questions in the side column as prompts to help you fill in a chart like the one shown.

Problem	Solution
The fuel cells that provided electricity to <u>Odyssey</u> were losing pressure.	The astronauts shut down all power in <u>Odyssey</u> and moved into the LEM.

▲ VOCABULARY IN CONTEXT

Michael Useem used the following boldfaced words to describe NASA procedures. To see how many you know, substitute a different word or phrase for each boldfaced term.

1. **replenish** our supplies
2. the ball's **trajectory** in the air
3. a **mandate** from my boss
4. her **innovative** approach
5. a **respite** from our labor
6. **collaborative** employees

Author On|ine

Deciding Moments

Michael Useem (yōo-sēm') is a University of Pennsylvania professor who specializes in issues of leadership. "The Race to Save *Apollo 13*" is taken from his book *The Leadership Moment: Nine True Stories of Triumph and Disaster and Their Lessons for Us All*, which relates how leaders from various walks of life have made extremely difficult decisions during emergencies. Useem believes that their experiences illustrate what to do—and what not to do—in times of crisis.

Michael Useem
born 1942

Background

Space Race In May 1961, President John F. Kennedy issued a challenge in a speech to Congress, stating that the United States should become the first nation to land astronauts on the moon and return them home safely. Kennedy believed this goal was necessary because the Soviet Union had recently sent a human into space.

The Apollo Program Although Kennedy did not live to see it, the U.S. National Aeronautics and Space Administration (NASA) achieved his goal. In July 1969, NASA's Apollo program successfully landed astronauts on the moon, and about 700 million television viewers around the world watched the historic moment. But after the mission ended, it was difficult to keep up this level of excitement. The launch of *Apollo 13* in April 1970 stirred little public interest. That changed when an oxygen tank exploded aboard the *Apollo 13* spacecraft *Odyssey*. In just moments, a seemingly routine mission became a full-blown crisis.

BUILDING BACKGROUND
To learn more about *Apollo 13*, visit the **Literature Center** at **ClassZone.com**.

THE RACE TO SAVE *APOLLO 13*

MICHAEL USEEM

*"What do you think we've got in
the spacecraft that's good?"*

"Hey, we've got a problem here."

The day was April 13, 1970. The voice was that of astronaut Jack Swigert, speaking from aboard the spacecraft Odyssey.

Almost immediately, NASA's Mission Control queried back: "This is Houston. Say again, please."

Astronaut and mission commander James Lovell responded this time: "Houston, we've had a problem."

For flight director Eugene Kranz, the message from *Apollo 13* presaged the test of a lifetime.

10   Only nine months earlier, on July 20, 1969, *Apollo 11* had landed Neil Armstrong and Buzz Aldrin in the Sea of Tranquillity,[1] fulfilling John F. Kennedy's promise to place a man on the moon before the end of the decade. Five months earlier, *Apollo 12* had placed Pete Conrad and Alan Bean in the Ocean of Storms. Just fifty-five hours earlier, at 1:13 P.M. on Saturday, April 11, 1970, *Apollo 13* had lifted up from the Kennedy Space Center on what to this moment had seemed a flawless trip to the moon's ridges of Fra Mauro.[2] Now, suddenly, the bottom was falling out.

---

1. **Sea of Tranquillity:** many areas of the moon are called seas or oceans, although the moon has no liquid water.
2. **Fra Mauro:** the area on the moon where *Apollo 13* was supposed to land.

NASA flight director Eugene Kranz at his console

ANALYZE VISUALS
What can you **infer** from the expression on Eugene Kranz's face in the photograph?

NASA technician George Bliss was both transfixed and horrified by what he saw on his computer console[3] in a Houston back room. "We got more than a problem," he warned colleague Sy Liebergot. The video screen told why: One of *Odyssey's* two oxygen tanks had broken down. The pressure in two of its three fuel cells, devices that use oxygen to generate electricity, was plummeting.

As Gene Kranz sifted through damage reports, the picture was distressing. The astronauts and their protective shell were unscathed, but it was evident that some kind of explosion had ripped through vital equipment. Two days into the flight, three quarters of the way to the moon, the astronauts were hurtling away from Earth at 2,000 miles per hour. The only practical way they could return was to round the moon and depend on its gravity to fire them back like a slingshot. But this would require more than three days and demand more oxygen and electricity than Lovell and his crew had left. **A**

As flight director for *Apollo 13,* Kranz was the responsible official, and he was watching his mission spin out of control: his crew would consume their oxygen and power long before they neared Earth. Even if they survived to reenter the Earth's atmosphere, they would have no way to control their capsule's fiery plunge. Kranz could neither retrieve the astronauts nor **replenish** their supplies. He knew what options were out, yet he also knew he must somehow engineer a safe return. He understood as well that his

A SUSPENSE
What facts in lines 24–31 help generate suspense?

replenish (rĭ-plĕn′ĭsh)
v. to fill again

---

3. **computer console:** a computer's monitor and keyboard.

actions in the hours ahead might determine whether the U.S. space program
40 experienced or avoided its biggest disaster.

The Explosion's Wake

Hundreds of officials and engineers confronted the singular task of bringing
the astronauts back alive. Four rotating flight teams—dubbed White,
Black, Gold, and Maroon—were scheduled to spell one another during the
mission's long days ahead. A backup crew for *Apollo 13* was on call to lend
its expertise. Dozens of space program contractors were ready to assist.

Yet no one on the ground bore the burden that Eugene Kranz carried that
evening and would continue to carry over the next four days. NASA's policy
was unflinchingly clear: the flight director had the final call on all decisions.
Moreover, "The flight director can do anything he feels is necessary for the
50 safety of the crew and the conduct of the flight regardless of the mission rules."

As Sy Liebergot, the frontline electrical official, gazed at his console in the
minutes just after the explosion, he allowed himself to hope that the ominous
screen displays might reflect sensor failure rather than a genuine problem.
During NASA's countless simulations[4] of the flight, he had often seen disastrous
instrument readings that had later proved inaccurate. The astronauts themselves
were reporting that their oxygen tanks seemed fine, lending momentary
support to Liebergot's hopeful search for instrumental error.

But Kranz was already learning from other flight officials that the
problems were indeed real. The guidance officer reported that an onboard
60 computer was signaling a major glitch. The communications officer
reported that the craft had mysteriously switched antennas. (As would be
learned later, one had been hit by the explosion's debris.) And the astronauts
themselves soon reported that one oxygen tank had emptied, two of the
three fuel cells were generating no electricity, and two panels supplying
power to the entire spacecraft were losing voltage. Lovell added even more
distressing news: "We are venting[5] something into space." A glowing cloud
was hovering outside *Odyssey*, suggesting rupture of its oxygen tanks.

"OK," called Kranz, sensing signs of panic in Mission Control. "Let's
everybody keep cool. Let's make sure we don't do anything that's going to
70 blow our electrical power or cause us to lose fuel cell number two." Then
he addressed what would have to be done. "Let's solve the problem." And
finally he moved on to self-discipline: "Let's not make it any worse by
guessing." **B**

By now, more bad news from *Odyssey*. Though a moon landing had
been eliminated by the loss of the first oxygen tank and fuel cell, the

B TAKE NOTES
What problems did
Kranz want to prevent
at Mission Control?

---

4. **simulations:** here, mock space flights used to test procedures and train astronauts.

5. **venting:** discharging.

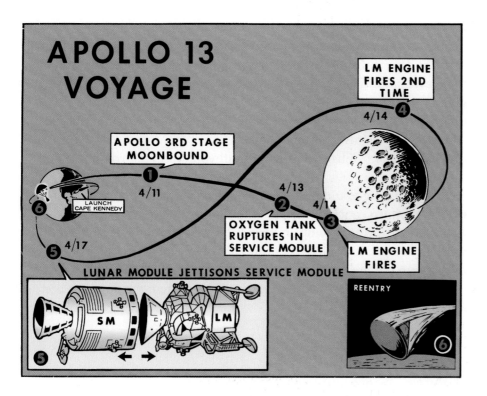

APOLLO 13 VOYAGE

LM ENGINE FIRES 2ND TIME

4/14 ④

APOLLO 3RD STAGE MOONBOUND

① 4/11

4/13

LAUNCH CAPE KENNEDY

⑥

② 4/14 ③

OXYGEN TANK RUPTURES IN SERVICE MODULE

LM ENGINE FIRES

⑤ 4/17

LUNAR MODULE JETTISONS SERVICE MODULE

SM   LM

⑤

REENTRY

⑥

ANALYZE VISUALS
This diagram was created on April 15, 1970, to illustrate the plan for saving the *Apollo 13* voyage. What information does a graphic aid of this sort help clarify?

second system should still carry the astronauts safely home. Lovell noticed, however, that the pressure needle for the second tank was falling as well, and Liebergot was discovering the same thing. Normally the tank should register 860 pounds per square inch (psi); now it was approaching 300. The

80 explosion had come at 9:07 P.M., and the clock was now just past 10 P.M. At that rate of loss, the spaceship would exhaust all of its electricity and air sometime between midnight and 3 A.M.

Kranz telephoned the home of Chris Kraft—the former flight director and his onetime mentor, and now deputy director of the Manned Spacecraft Center. Kraft's wife pulled him out of the shower, and he heard Kranz urging, "Chris, you'd better get over here now. We've got a hell of a problem. We've lost oxygen pressure, we've lost a bus [an electrical power distribution system], we're losing fuel cells. It seems there's been an explosion." Kranz, age thirty-six, had worked with NASA for a decade, overseeing all Apollo

90 missions since taking over from Kraft when the prior Gemini series had come to an end. He was an experienced hand who sounded no undue alarm, solicited no unneeded counsel. Kraft raced to the space center, just ten miles away. When he arrived, Kranz brought his former mentor up to speed. . . .

With the oxygen for *Odyssey's* life support systems in rapid decline, Kranz barked rapid-fire demands for information and support to attack the problems.

To the telemetry and electrical officer: "Will you take a look at the prelaunch data[6] and see if there's anything that may have started the venting?"

To the technicians running NASA's fast, on-site computers: "Bring up another computer . . . will you?"

100　*To the guidance and navigation officer:* "Give me a gross amount of the thruster propellants[7] consumed so far."

To Sy Liebergot: "What does the status of your buses tell you now?"

Off line, Liebergot and his backup engineer, George Bliss, were reaching even more forlorn conclusions: The single remaining oxygen tank was below 300 psi of pressure and losing another 1.7 psi each minute. If tank pressure fell below 100 psi, it would have insufficient force to move its precious contents into the fuel cells for power generation, and that point was just 116 minutes away. They made several attempts to stem the flow, but none succeeded.

110　*Liebergot:* "George, it looks grim."

Bliss: "Yes, it does."

Liebergot: "We're going down. We're losing it."

Bliss: "Yes, we are."

6.　**prelaunch data:** information collected before launch of a spacecraft.

7.　**thruster propellants:** fuel for rockets used to maneuver spacecraft.

Apollo 13 control room

Now Liebergot was back on line with Kranz, arguing that the astronauts must move immediately into the attached lunar excursion module (LEM). Dubbed *Aquarius* on this mission, the LEM had been designed to set two astronauts on the moon and sustain life for several days. For three astronauts, *Aquarius* would be overcrowded, the power system would not work for long, and it would vaporize on reentry. But for the moment

120 it would have to do. The dying command module would support the astronauts for a matter of minutes; the LEM at least offered hours. Kranz again sought instant analysis. "I want you guys figuring our minimum power needed in the LEM to sustain life," he instructed a LEM technical group, which had anticipated no real action until the planned moon landing two days later. "And I want LEM manning around the clock."

The oxygen loss from *Odyssey* was accelerating to 3 psi per minute, and Bliss now estimated that they had eighteen minutes left before total power shutdown. A few moments later, he revised that down to seven minutes. And then, a moment later, to four. **C**

130 The Black Team had just taken over from White, and Glynn Lunney, who would spell Kranz at the director's console while the White Team stood down, sent up an urgent command: "Get 'em going in the LEM!" Lovell and Haise moved through the connecting hatch, and while Swigert stayed behind to wind down *Odyssey,* they powered up *Aquarius.* They worked frantically to transfer irreplaceable guidance data from the command module into the LEM computer in the seconds before everything was lost. Finally, Lovell radioed Houston, *"Aquarius* is up, and *Odyssey* is completely powered down."

There was a momentary relief, but with days to go, they had bought only

140 a little time. "OK, everybody," counseled Lunney, "we've got a lot of long-range problems to deal with."

Oxygen and Power

Among the mission's first long-range problems was that the return **trajectory** would miss the Earth by some forty thousand miles. The astronauts would need to fire the LEM's rocket in just five hours to close the gap. Producing the precision adjustment, however, would require immediate, massive recalibrations of instruments. By now the teams in Houston were humming, and they delivered the requisite data to Jim Lovell and his crew with an hour to spare.

While Glynn Lunney staffed the director's console, Kranz remained only

150 feet away, his mind turning over what to do next. He had already passed word that as soon as Houston had the fuel burn plan set, he would meet

C SUSPENSE
How do the references to time in lines 126–129 increase suspense?

trajectory
(trə-jĕk′tə-rē) *n.* the path of a moving body through space

mandate
(măn'dāt') *n.*
a command or
instruction

with his entire White Team in a nearby room. As it gathered, Kranz laid down his new **mandate:** "For the rest of this mission, I am pulling you men off console. The people out in that room will be running the flight from moment to moment, but it's the people in this room who will be coming up with the protocols they're going to be executing. From now on, what I want from every one of you is simple: options, and plenty of them." Their new name would be the Tiger Team, and for the remainder of the flight they would work and live in Room 210.

160   A mere twenty feet by twenty feet and windowless, Room 210 was bare except for several overhead TVs and tables along the walls, but its location was good: adjacent to the operations room and just a floor below the control room. Above all, it permitted the team to assemble all past and current data in one place. Now, Kranz believed, they could determine what had happened and was happening, essential for deciding what should happen next. **D**

Kranz pressed them to focus on solutions. He sought to build, he later reported, "a positive frame of mind that is necessary to work problems in a time-critical and true emergency environment." And he wanted quick answers to specific questions:

170   "How long can you keep the systems in the LEM running at full power?"

"Where do we stand on water? What about battery power? What about oxygen?"

"In three or four days we're going to have to use the command module **again**. I want to know how we can get that bird powered up and running from a cold stop . . . and do it all on just the power we've got left in the reentry batteries."

"I also want to know how we plan to align this ship if we can't use a star alignment. Can we use sun checks? Can we use moon checks? What about Earth checks?"

180   "I want options on . . . burns and midcourse corrections from now to entry."

"What ocean does it put us in?"

Once again, Kranz insisted on strategies and solutions without guesswork: "For the next few days we're going to be coming up with techniques and maneuvers we've never tried before," he concluded. "And I want to make sure we know what we're doing."

Kranz left his men to do their work and returned to the control room. Glynn Lunney of the Black Team had focused everybody on the forthcoming course correction, and minutes later Lovell and his colleagues

D TAKE NOTES
Why did Kranz create a
new team that would
work in a separate
room?

190 executed a flawless blast of the LEM's engines. In one of the first bits of good news since disaster struck, they had corrected their path perfectly.

Good news, though, was still in terribly short supply. The new course required nearly four days for return, and *Aquarius* was provisioned for less than two. The LEM's oxygen supply was not a problem since enough had been placed on board for several moon walks, yet its supply of lithium hydroxide was another story. This chemical was carried to remove carbon dioxide accumulating in the cabin, but its LEM capacity was for two men for two days, not for three men for twice that long. The available electricity would last for even less time if *Aquarius* remained fully powered. Water, too,
200 was in desperately short supply. **E**

Kranz decided he wanted more seasoned talent crunching the numbers. He sent the Tiger Team's electrical specialist back to the consoles on Tuesday morning and in his place recruited Bill Peters from the Gold Team. Other flight directors had sometimes found Peters slow to react and explain. But Kranz had constructed a relationship with him, and he knew that he brought exceptional experience: Peters had worked every space mission since *Gemini 3* in 1965. "Peters was utterly brilliant," Kranz recalled, but he could not explain himself well and one had to work with him to "bring out the pieces."

210 After consulting with Kranz and the lead engineer for Grumman Aerospace, the LEM maker, Peters was heartened by his preliminary calculations: He could find ways to cut *Aquarius's* electrical flow from 55 amperes to 12, though this would require draconian[8] measures on board: no computer, no guidance system, no heater, no panel display. Communications would stay up, a fan would stir the air, and a little coolant would circulate. Otherwise, all systems would be off.

Kranz also recruited another outsider, John Aaron, the Maroon Team's twenty-seven-year-old electrical specialist. He understood power better than anyone else, he was **innovative,** and he was unflappable—"Mr. Cool under
220 pressure" in Kranz's phrase. Kranz charged Aaron with a similar task for conserving *Odyssey's* power, and together they took a first cut at the figures. Their numbers were encouraging, and Aaron designed the plan. He believed he could find the power to rev up the command module for reentry—but only if almost all engineering corners were cut.

Aaron patiently presented his plan to a skeptical Tiger Team, reporting that the powering up, normally a full day's affair, could take no more than two hours. Bill Strahle, a guidance and navigation officer, interjected, "John, you can't do it in that time." Aaron responded, "Well, now, that's what *I*

E SUSPENSE
What details in lines 192–200 raise questions about the outcome of the mission?

innovative
(ĭn′ə-vā′tĭv)
adj. able to create new, original ideas

---

8. **draconian:** extremely harsh.

thought, Bill. But I think if we're willing to take a few shortcuts, we just
230 might be able to pull it off."

Late on the evening of Tuesday, April 14, nearly twenty-four hours after the accident, Lovell and crew rounded the moon and were scheduled to fire the LEM's rocket to accelerate their return to Earth. The engine burn, like virtually all other maneuvers of the past day, would be crucial, but this one would be especially so. The smallest error of alignment or duration would send the ship in a wrong direction with virtually no fuel remaining for any correction. Though the Gold Team was still on duty as the time of the scheduled firing approached, Kranz decided to install his own Tiger Team at the controls. His men quietly walked into Mission Control, muttered
240 apologies to their sitting counterparts, and took over the consoles. Under Kranz's direction, the "big burn" worked. Another essential milestone for the journey home had been reached, and the room erupted with cheers.

The moment's glow had barely passed when three men made their way from different directions to Kranz's workstation. Chris Kraft was one; Deke Slayton, astronaut and director of flight crew operations, the second. Max Faget, engineering director for the entire Manned Spacecraft Center, trailed slightly behind. "So what's our next step here, Gene?" opened Slayton, one of the original seven Mercury astronauts.

Kranz: "Well, Deke, we're gonna work on that."
250 *Slayton:* "I'm not sure how much there is to work on. We're going to put the crew to bed, right?"
Kranz: "Eventually, sure."
Slayton: "Eventually may not do it, Gene. Their last scheduled sleep period was twenty-four hours ago. They're going to need some rest."

Now Kraft jumped in.

Kraft: "How do we stand with that power-down problem, Gene?"
Kranz: "It's coming along, Chris."
Kraft: "We ready to execute it?"
Kranz: "We're ready, but it's a long procedure and Deke thinks we ought
260 to get the crew ready to sleep first."
Kraft: "Sleep? A sleep period's six hours! Take the crew off stream that long before powering down, and you're wasting six hours of juice you don't need to waste."

Slayton: "But if you keep them up and have them execute a complicated power-down when they're barely awake, someone's bound to screw something up. I'd rather spend a little extra power now than risk another disaster later."

Max Faget appeared, and Kranz drew him into the discussion.

Kranz: "Max, Deke and Chris were just telling me what they think our
270   next step ought to be."
Faget: "Passive thermal control,[9] right?"
Slayton, alarmed: "PTC?"
Faget: "Sure. That ship's had one side pointing to the sun and one pointing out to space for hours. If we don't get some kind of barbeque roll going on soon, we're going to freeze half our systems and cook the other half."
Slayton: "Do you have any idea what kind of pressure it's going to put on the crew to ask them to execute a PTC roll now?"
Kraft: "Or what kind of pressure it's going to put on the available power? I'm not sure we can afford to try something like that at the moment."
280   *Faget:* "I'm not sure we can afford not to."

The three-way argument escalated for several minutes, with each point and counterpoint more fiercely asserted than the last. Kranz said little throughout, mainly listening to what his three superiors had to say. Finally, he held up his hand, and they stopped speaking.

"Gentlemen," Kranz said, "I thank you
290   for your input." The discussion was over, his decision made: "The next job for this crew will be to execute a thermal roll. After that, they will power down their spacecraft. And finally, they will get some sleep. A tired crew can get over their fatigue, but if we damage this ship any further, we're not going to get over that." **F**

With the decision made, Kranz turned to his console, and Slayton and Faget turned to leave. Kraft lingered, considered objecting, but then quietly moved off as well. His protégé was in control, and he had ruled firmly. The

The Latin phrase on this insignia means "From the Moon, Knowledge."

F TAKE NOTES
Reread lines 249–295. What problems did Kranz have to consider before reaching his decision about how to proceed?

---

9. **passive thermal control:** any method of controlling temperature on a spacecraft without using electricity.

astronauts spent the next two hours performing their assigned tasks and
300 finally began a long-overdue slumber.

The Return

With the trajectory successfully fixed for the return to Earth, Kranz and
his Tiger Team resumed their calculations and planning in Room 210. The
biggest challenge: restarting the moribund command module. *Aquarius* had
been life-sustaining, but the LEM would disintegrate on reentry. *Odyssey*
would be life-returning: the command module came with a heat shield to
endure reentry's 5,000 degrees Fahrenheit. For that, though, *Odyssey* would
have to be coaxed back from dormancy—with a defunct regular electric
supply and a mere two hours of power remaining in its auxiliary batteries.

It was now late Wednesday evening, and the Tiger Team had been
310 working relentlessly since Monday evening, struggling to surmount problem
after problem if reentry were to succeed. Most of the team members had
worked nonstop for more than forty-eight hours, and Kranz finally ordered
a six-hour **respite.** Yes, they needed their sleep, but even more compelling
was the fact that the most critical troubleshooting might finally be behind
them. John Aaron, the electrical officer borrowed from the Maroon Team,
had evidently found a way around *Odyssey*'s repowering problem. **G**

It was a **collaborative** solution. One of the command module's chief
engineers, Arnie Aldrich, had worked with Aaron to ensure that the switches
for the various systems would be thrown in a workable sequence so that
320 early systems would be ready for later ones as needed. Kranz himself had
examined each step, and astronaut Ken Mattingly had tested everything
in a nearby command module simulator. Mattingly had been scheduled to
serve as the command module pilot for *Apollo 13,* but after he had been
exposed to German measles, NASA had replaced him with Swigert. Severely
disappointed at first, Mattingly now applied his insider's knowledge to
testing and refining Aaron's scheme. Ultimately, it worked—at least on the
simulator. **H**

To add to the tension, the fate of *Apollo 13* had become a global drama.
The Soviet Union volunteered rescue vessels. Religious groups across
330 America and around the world prayed for the astronauts' safe deliverance.
The Chicago Board of Trade added its own supplication, briefly suspending
trading at 11 a.m. on Thursday "for a moment of tribute to the courage and
gallantry of America's astronauts and a prayer for their safe return to Earth."

By Thursday evening, just eighteen hours before splashdown, the list
of procedures to restart *Odyssey* was finalized and ready for transmission.
Kranz, Aaron, and Aldrich pushed their way through the rows of consoles

respite (rĕs'pĭt) *n.* a
period of rest or relief

collaborative
(kə-lăb'ə-rə'tĭv) *adj.*
done in cooperation
with others

G GRAMMAR AND
STYLE
Reread lines 311–315.
Rather than writing
a series of short
sentences, Useem
uses the **coordinating
conjunctions** *and* and
but to join two sets of
independent clauses.

H TAKE NOTES
How did Ken Mattingly
help solve the problem
of repowering the
command module?

The command module is recovered from the Pacific Ocean after splashdown.

in Mission Control to deliver the list. Mission Control would require nearly two hours to radio the start-up sequence, line by line, to Jack Swigert, who would have to copy each of the hundreds of technical instructions by hand.

340   Swigert and crew successfully followed the start-up protocol, moved back into *Odyssey,* and jettisoned *Aquarius.* By mid-Friday, the command module was approaching Earth's outer atmosphere at 25,000 miles per hour, and Kranz took the director's console for the final time. With four minutes to go before *Odyssey* hit the atmosphere's upper layers, Kranz stood and asked each of the system officers if they were ready. "Let's go around the horn once more before entry," he said. Each officer declared his readiness. Kranz gave the mission communicator, astronaut Joe Kerwin, the green light: "You can tell the crew they're go for reentry."

    Soon all radio contact with the crew was lost as intense heat enveloped
350 the plunging craft. Four minutes of anxious silence passed on the ground until the fiery spray around the capsule subsided; then Kranz instructed Kerwin to resume contact. *"Odyssey,"* Kerwin called. "Houston standing by,

over." No response. Kranz: "Try again." Kerwin did, again and again, to no avail, and another minute passed, more blackout time than experienced on any other mission. ❶

❶ **SUSPENSE**
How did the writer build suspense in lines 349–355?

Then, faintly, came the scratchy but unmistakable voice of astronaut Jack Swigert: "OK, Joe." Moments later Jim Lovell, Jack Swigert, and Fred Haise were floating down on three parachutes for a soft landing in the Pacific. Eugene Kranz punched the air.

360 Sy Liebergot faced weeks of recurrent nightmares about undervoltages. Jim Lovell declared the mission a failure, but, he added, "I like to think it was a successful failure." And Grumman Aerospace, maker of the LEM, sent a mock bill for more than $312,421 to North American Rockwell, producer of the command module, for a "battery charge, road call," and "towing fee" for returning *Odyssey* home.

Eugene Kranz, James Lovell, and their crews matched wits with a technology failure, and they won. They orchestrated thousands of actions— many minute, some momentous—to fix what seemed unfixable. In the end, they triumphed over one of NASA's worst nightmares.

Astronauts Fred Haise, James Lovell, and John Swigert after their return to Earth

OHIO STANDARDS

READING STANDARD
2.3 Take notes and summarize

Comprehension

1. **Recall** What was the original goal of *Apollo 13*?

2. **Recall** Why did NASA have to cancel the mission?

3. **Summarize** What were the main steps taken to save the astronauts?

Literary Analysis

4. **Make Inferences** Why did astronaut James Lovell declare the *Apollo 13* mission "a successful failure"?

5. **Analyze Decisions** What skills, knowledge, and traits did Eugene Kranz look for when choosing members of the Tiger Team? Use a graphic organizer like the one shown to record your answer.

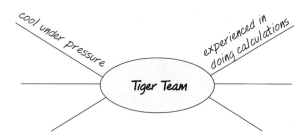

6. **Analyze Notes** Review the chart you created as you read. Which of the problems provided the biggest test of Kranz's leadership? Cite evidence to support your conclusion.

7. **Draw Conclusions** Why might the author have chosen to focus on the employees at Mission Control rather than on the astronauts in space? Support your answer.

8. **Interpret Main Idea** Reread lines 366–369. What idea does the writer express about the ways in which Kranz and his colleagues achieved the **impossible?**

9. **Make Judgments** Do you agree with NASA's policy of giving the flight director final authority on all decisions during the mission? Cite evidence to support your opinion.

10. **Predict** How might the space program have been affected if NASA had failed to rescue the astronauts aboard *Apollo 13*?

11. **Evaluate Suspense** Michael Useem included extensive technical information in his account of *Apollo 13*. How well did he balance the need to explain with the need to tell a suspenseful story? Find examples to support your answer.

Vocabulary in Context

VOCABULARY PRACTICE

Identify the word that is most different in meaning from the others.

1. remove, empty, replenish, discard
2. path, course, trajectory, perimeter
3. command, question, decree, mandate
4. standard, innovative, boring, unoriginal
5. rest, stillness, action, respite
6. oppositional, collaborative, solitary, dividing

WORD LIST
collaborative
innovative
mandate
replenish
respite
trajectory

VOCABULARY IN WRITING

Describe the *Apollo 13* near disaster from the point of view of the astronauts on board. Use at least four vocabulary words. Here is an example of how you might begin.

> **EXAMPLE SENTENCE**
>
> With all the stress we felt, what we needed most was a brief **respite**.

VOCABULARY STRATEGY: SPECIALIZED VOCABULARY

The astronauts, scientists, and engineers who work at NASA have their own specialized vocabulary. This vocabulary includes terms such as *return trajectory*, which is the path of a spacecraft on its return to Earth. It is often possible to figure out the special meanings of words from the context. Otherwise, check a dictionary and look for labels—such as *space flight* and *computer science*—that may precede definitions and indicate special uses of a word.

OHIO STANDARDS

VOCABULARY STANDARD
1.6 Determine unknown words by using dictionaries

PRACTICE Write the space flight term that matches each definition. If you need to, check a dictionary.

> vent   protocols   bus   satellite   transponder

1. an electrical power distribution system
2. a small body that orbits a larger one
3. data transmissions between computers
4. an electronic device that combines a transmitter and a receiver
5. to release or discharge

VOCABULARY PRACTICE
For more practice, go to the **Vocabulary Center** at **ClassZone.com**.

Reading-Writing Connection

Increase your understanding of "The Race to Save *Apollo 13*" by responding to these prompts. Then use **Revision: Grammar and Style** to improve your writing.

WRITING PROMPTS	SELF-CHECK

A. Short Response: Write a Press Release
Imagine that you are working for NASA at the time of the *Apollo 13* crisis. Using information from the selection, write a **one- or two-paragraph press release** in which you describe events in the first hour after the explosion.

A well-written press release will . . .
- summarize the information available to NASA
- describe the initial steps NASA is taking to rescue the astronauts

B. Extended Response: Give Leadership Advice
What lessons in leadership can be learned from Eugene Kranz's management during the *Apollo 13* crisis? Use details from the selection to write a **three-to-five-paragraph response** in which you discuss three strategies that Kranz used effectively to help achieve the **impossible**.

A strong response will . . .
- begin with an introduction that makes the purpose and audience of the essay clear
- end with a conclusion that states the benefits of following your advice

REVISION: GRAMMAR AND STYLE

IMPROVE SENTENCE FLOW Review the **Grammar and Style** note on page 124. Writing flows more smoothly when it doesn't merely consist of short, choppy sentences. Follow Michael Useem's example by inserting a **coordinating conjunction** (such as *and, but, for, or, so,* or *yet*) between two independent clauses to form a longer sentence and to clarify the relationship between ideas. Remember to use a comma before a coordinating conjunction that joins two independent clauses. Here are two examples from the selection.

OHIO
STANDARDS

WRITING STANDARD
5.7 Use a variety of sentence structures and lengths

> *The astronauts and their protective shell were unscathed, but it was evident that some kind of explosion had ripped through vital equipment.*
> (lines 25–26)

> *He knew what options were out, yet he also knew he must somehow engineer a safe return.* (lines 37–38)

Notice how the revisions in red use a coordinating conjunction to make the sentences flow more smoothly. Revise your responses to the prompts by using similar techniques.

WRITING TOOLS
For prewriting, revision, and editing tools, visit the **Writing Center** at ClassZone.com.

STUDENT MODEL

A small explosion has occurred aboard the <u>Odyssey.</u> Some vital equipment

was damaged, *but* The astronauts were not harmed.

from **Apollo 13**

Film Clip on ⊙ **MediaSmart** DVD

What keeps you on the EDGE *of your seat?*

KEY IDEA What type of movie do you prefer? Do you like the relentless **tension** created by nonstop action, or do you prefer the shock of a surprise ending? The scene you are about to view re-creates the tense moments that kept viewers glued to their television sets in 1970, waiting to see if the real *Apollo 13* crew would return home safely.

Background

Unlucky 13 Some people believe that the number 13 is unlucky, but those at the National Aeronautics and Space Administration (NASA) dismissed the superstitious belief. According to NASA, the flight of *Apollo 13* would be a routine mission. After all, *Apollo 11* and *Apollo 12* had already landed on the moon. What could possibly go wrong? The mission was to begin at 1:13 P.M. on April 11. In military time, that time is written as 13:13. *Apollo 13* was supposed to orbit the moon on April 13. Instead, an explosion weakened the ship's oxygen supply and battery life. The crew and the world were about to weather a major crisis.

The *Apollo 13* movie, based on the book *Lost Moon* by astronaut Jim Lovell with writer Jeffrey Kluger, recounts the nerve-racking events of the actual mission. Director Ron Howard captures every detail of NASA's race against time.

Media Literacy: Creating Suspense on Film

In telling a suspenseful story, both writers and filmmakers aim to seize an audience's attention, making it anxious to learn the ultimate outcome. Writers ratchet up the tension primarily through the words that form the complications of the rising action or the vivid descriptions of characters' struggles. Filmmakers deliver suspense through a careful combination of visual and sound techniques.

How do directors keep viewers in suspense when the audience already knows the real-life ending? The secret, according to film director Ron Howard, is "simply storytelling." A director can use **camera shots, editing,** and **music** to tell a well-known story and still raise the level of suspense.

FILM TECHNIQUES	STRATEGIES FOR VIEWING	
Camera shots can build suspense by tracking the emotions of characters as they face certain struggles.	• Consider the effect of a **close-up shot** versus a **long shot.** The first conveys characters' emotions or thoughts, while the second shows characters in relation to their surroundings. Ask yourself: How do close-up shots help viewers sympathize with characters? • Watch for **point-of-view shots,** which show what a character sees. These shots give viewers an opportunity to experience what is happening from a character's point of view.	
Suspenseful scenes can be **edited** in a number of ways. Directors manipulate time, which can affect the flow of a scene.	• Notice how **parallel editing,** which is an editing technique that cuts from one shot to another, shows simultaneous action—often in different locations. Ask yourself: How do sudden shifts to different settings heighten the suspense? • Be aware that suspenseful scenes often rely on a **high-stakes deadline** or a race against time. Directors manipulate time to create suspense or increase viewers' anticipation. They can shorten time, turning minutes to seconds, or they can extend it, stretching a moment to a nail-biting extreme.	
Music can be a key element in a suspenseful scene. It can signal dramatic events, tense moments, or triumphant resolutions.	• Consider how **music** signals major events. You can often predict when something good or bad is about to happen through musical cues. • Notice how your emotions change when music is used. Ask yourself: What effect does the music have on me?	

MediaSmart DVD

- **Film Clip:** *Apollo 13*
- **Director:** Ron Howard
- **Rating:** PG
- **Genre:** Drama
- **Running Time:** 7.5 minutes

Viewing Guide for
Apollo 13

As you watch this scene, keep in mind that it occurs near the climax of *Apollo 13*. The astronauts are in the *Odyssey* command module. This is the only part of the spacecraft that has any chance to reenter Earth's atmosphere. At Mission Control, NASA workers stand by. Family members and others watch and wait.

Plan on viewing the scene several times. To help you analyze suspense, refer to the questions that follow.

NOW VIEW

FIRST VIEWING: Comprehension

1. **Recall** When does NASA expect to regain communication with Lovell, Haise, and Swigert?

2. **Clarify** Where does NASA expect the *Odyssey* command module will land?

CLOSE VIEWING: Media Literacy

3. **Make Inferences** What emotions are revealed through the **close-up shots** of family and friends? What effect do you think these shots have on viewers?

4. **Analyze Parallel Editing** The director uses parallel editing to show how people are waiting at different locations for the reentry of the command module. Describe two of the locations and explain why you think the director chose them.

5. **Analyze Sound** What kinds of sounds contribute to the realism of the event?

6. **Interpret Techniques** How would you describe the **music** soon after the command module goes into blackout?

7. **Evaluate Suspense** The director of *Apollo 13* uses several techniques to build suspense, including **close-up shots, long shots, music, absence of sound, voice-over,** and a **high-stakes deadline.** Which techniques kept you on the edge of your seat? Explain.

Write or Discuss

Evaluate the Film When it seems that hope is fading at Mission Control, the flight coordinator proudly states, "With all due respect, sir, I believe this is gonna be our finest hour." Many film critics consider the movie *Apollo 13* to be one of director Ron Howard's "finest hours." Based on the scene you've viewed, do you agree with the critics? Evaluate the director's effectiveness at portraying a suspenseful situation. Use evidence from the scene. To prepare, think about

- the film techniques used to create suspense
- the emotions you think the director is trying to create in viewers
- your reactions to the clip

Produce Your Own Media

Create a Storyboard A **storyboard** is a device that is used to plan the shooting of a film. It consists of a sequence of sketches showing what will appear in the film's shots. Storyboards help directors create a vision of the finished product. Using the student model as a guide, create a storyboard that depicts an event that is driven by a high-stakes deadline.

HERE'S HOW Think of your storyboard as a rough sketch of a scene. Here are some tips to get you started:

- Be sure to include between eight and ten shots.
- Use close-up shots to show characters' emotions and to create tension.
- Vary shots to show different images or different actions taking place.
- Show how time is a critical factor.

MEDIA TOOLS

For help with creating a storyboard, visit the **Media Center** at ClassZone.com.

Tech Tip

If a video camera is available, film the scene.

STUDENT MODEL

Shot 1
The fans cheer for their team.

Shot 2
Player focuses on hoop.

Shot 3
Time is running out.

Shot 4
Opponent is ready to block shot.

Shot 5
The coach can't watch.

Shot 6
The fans wait for a miracle.

Shot 7
The fans aren't hopeful.

Shot 8
Will he make the shot?

Exile
Poem by Julia Alvarez

Crossing the Border
Poem by Joy Harjo

What makes you feel like an OUTSIDER?

OHIO STANDARDS

READING STANDARDS
2.3 Adjusting speed to fit the purpose
4.5 Analyze how choice of genre affects theme or topic

KEY IDEA Have you ever felt separate from others, like you did not belong? A sense of **alienation** can come from having a different ethnic background, being dressed differently, having different values, or other causes. Almost everyone has had such feelings at one time or another.

QUICKWRITE Write a brief journal entry about a time when you felt alienated. Where were you, and what made you feel different from others? Did the others intend to make you uncomfortable? What thoughts ran through your mind, and what did you end up doing? Exploring your own experience may help you understand the speakers in the two following poems.

I felt alienated when . . .
_____

LITERARY ANALYSIS: NARRATIVE POETRY

A **narrative poem** is a poem that tells a story. Like a short story, it contains characters, setting, and a plot driven by conflict. However, the narrative in a poem is much more condensed. The speaker begins to relate events immediately, without introducing himself or herself as a short story's narrator might. The story is developed through compact images instead of lengthy description or passages of dialogue. Time may shift abruptly, without clear transitions.

As you read "Exile" and "Crossing the Border," prepare to summarize the stories told in the poems. Ask these questions:

- Who are the characters?
- What are the settings?
- What conflicts do the characters face?
- How are the conflicts resolved?

READING STRATEGY: READING POETRY

The following strategies can help you unlock the meaning of the two poems in this lesson, in addition to that of other poetry you'll read in this book.

- You must read a poem slowly, line by line. Notice how the lines are grouped in **stanzas,** comparable to that of other paragraphs in prose. Visualize the images in each stanza.

- It is especially important to interpret **figurative language** in poetry. Often, words in poems communicate ideas beyond their literal meaning. The speaker in "Exile," for example, refers to herself as swimming but is not physically doing so. The key to understanding the poem is seeing what she compares to swimming.

- You must work to identify the **speaker** of a poem, often without many clues. Make inferences about gender, age, ethnicity, and attitudes. Reading the poem aloud may help you hear the speaker's voice. Using a graphic like the one shown, take notes about the speaker in each poem.

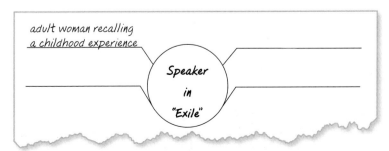

adult woman recalling
a childhood experience

Speaker
in
"Exile"

Author On|ine

Julia Alvarez: American-Born Immigrant
Julia Alvarez was born in New York City but lived in the Dominican Republic until she was ten. Her Dominican parents had previously emigrated to the United States, but shortly after Julia's birth they returned

Julia Alvarez born 1950

to their homeland. At that time, it was ruled by Rafael Trujillo, a cruel dictator. The family was forced to flee in 1960 after Julia's father's participation in a failed plot to overthrow Trujillo. They returned to New York, where Alvarez had to adjust to a new language and way of life. "A lot of what I have worked through," she says, "has had to do with coming to this country and losing a homeland and a culture."

Joy Harjo: Word Artist
Joy Harjo was born in Tulsa, Oklahoma. Her mother was part Cherokee, and her father was a full-blooded Muskogee, or Creek. Growing up, Harjo expected to become a visual artist but later decided to devote herself to poetry. Harjo often writes about the clash

Joy Harjo born 1951

between Native American culture and the culture of mainstream America. She has noted that native women "constantly bump up against images of Indians that have nothing or nearly nothing to do with our lives."

MORE ABOUT THE AUTHOR
For more on Julia Alvarez and Joy Harjo, visit the **Literature Center** at **ClassZone.com.**

Exile

JULIA ALVAREZ

Ciudad Trujillo,[1] **New York City, 1960**

The night we fled the country, Papi,
you told me we were going to the beach,
hurried me to get dressed along with the others,
while posted at a window, you looked out

5 at a curfew-darkened Ciudad Trujillo,
speaking in worried whispers to your brothers,
which car to take, who'd be willing to drive it,
what explanation to give should we be discovered . . .

On the way to the beach, you added, eyeing me.
10 The uncles fell in, chuckling phony chuckles,
What a good time she'll have learning to swim!
Back in my sisters' room Mami was packing

a hurried bag, allowing one toy apiece,
her red eyes belying her explanation:
15 *a week at the beach so Papi can get some rest.*
She dressed us in our best dresses, party shoes. **A**

Something was off, I knew, but I was young
and didn't think adult things could go wrong.
So as we quietly filed out of the house
20 we wouldn't see again for another decade,

I let myself lie back in the deep waters,
my arms out like Jesus' on His cross,
and instead of sinking down as I'd always done,
magically, that night, I could stay up, **B**

---

1. **Ciudad Trujillo:** the name of the capital of the Dominican Republic from 1936–1961, which the dictator Trujillo renamed after himself.

ANALYZE VISUALS
How do you interpret this surrealistic painting, titled *Utopie* [Utopia]? What connections can you make between it and the poem "Exile"?

A **NARRATIVE POETRY**
Notice the place and time of events. Who are the people mentioned and what **conflicts** do they face?

B **READING POETRY**
The speaker is not literally floating in water. What is she actually doing?

Utopie (1999), Bob Lescaux. Oil on canvas, 81 cm × 65 cm. Private Collection. Photo © The Bridgeman Art Library.

25 floating out, past the driveway, past the gates,
    in the black Ford, Papi grim at the wheel,
    winding through back roads, stroke by difficult stroke,
    out on the highway, heading toward the coast.

    Past the checkpoint, we raced towards the airport,
30 my sisters crying when we turned before
    the family beach house, Mami consoling,
    there was a better surprise in store for us!

    She couldn't tell, though, until . . . until we were there.
    But I had already swum ahead and guessed
35 some loss much larger than I understood,
    more danger than the deep end of the pool. **C**

C NARRATIVE POETRY
What new **conflict** does
the speaker recognize?

At the dark, deserted airport we waited.
All night in a fitful sleep, I swam.
At dawn the plane arrived, and as we boarded,
40 Papi, you turned, your eyes scanned the horizon

as if you were trying to sight a distant swimmer,
your hand frantically waving her back in,
for you knew as we stepped inside the cabin
that a part of both of us had been set adrift. **D**

45 Weeks later, wandering our new city, hand in hand,
you tried to explain the wonders: escalators
as moving belts; elevators: pulleys and ropes;
blond hair and blue eyes: a genetic code.

We stopped before a summery display window
50 at Macy's, *The World's Largest Department Store,*
to admire a family outfitted for the beach:
the handsome father, slim and sure of himself,

so unlike you, Papi, with your thick mustache,
your three-piece suit, your fedora hat, your accent.
55 And by his side a girl who looked like Heidi
in my storybook waded in colored plastic. **E**

We stood awhile, marveling at America,
both of us trying hard to feel luckier
than we felt, both of us pointing out
60 the beach pails, the shovels, the sandcastles

no wave would ever topple, the red and blue boats.
And when we backed away, we saw our reflections
superimposed, big-eyed, dressed too formally
with all due respect as visitors to this country.

65 Or like, Papi, two swimmers looking down
at the quiet surface of our island waters,
seeing their faces right before plunging in,
eager, afraid, not yet sure of the outcome. **F**

D READING POETRY
In what sense have the speaker and her father been "set adrift"?

E NARRATIVE POETRY
Notice that the setting has changed. What new conflict does it present?

F READING POETRY
What ideas does this comparison to swimmers bring to mind?

CROSSING THE BORDER

JOY HARJO

We looked the part. **G**
It was past midnight, well into
the weekend. Coming out of Detroit
into the Canada side, border guards
5 and checks. We are asked, "Who are you Indians
and which side are you from?"
Barney answers in a broken English.
He talks this way to white people
not to us. "Our kids."
10 My children are wrapped
and sleeping in the backseat.
He points with his lips to half-eyed
Richard in the front.
"That one, too."
15 But Richard looks like he belongs
to no one, just sits there wild-haired
like a Menominee would.
"And my wife. . . ." Not true.
But hidden under the windshield
20 at the edge of this country
we feel immediately suspicious.
These questions and we don't look
like we belong to either side.

"Any liquor or firearms?"
25 He should have asked that years ago
and we can't help but laugh.
Kids stir around in the backseat
but it is the border guard who is anxious.
He is looking for crimes, stray horses
30 for which he has no apparent evidence. **H**

G READING POETRY
Read the first stanza aloud. What do you learn about the speaker in the poem?

H NARRATIVE POETRY
What is the **conflict** between the border guard and the Indians?

"Where are you going?"
Indians in an Indian car, trying
to find a Delaware powwow
that was barely mentioned in Milwaukee.
35 Northern singing in the northern sky.
Moon in a colder air.
Not sure of the place but knowing the name
we ask, "Moravian Town?"

The border guard thinks he might have
40 the evidence. It pleases him.
Past midnight.
Stars out clear into Canada
and he knows only to ask,
"Is it a bar?"

45 Crossing the border into Canada,
we are silent. Lights and businesses
we drive toward could be America, too,
following us into the north. ▮

▮ READING POETRY
What aspects of America
might follow the Indians
into the north?

Sports Utility Vehicle in Moonlight. Todd Davidson. © Todd
Davidson/Getty Images.

Comprehension

OHIO STANDARDS

READING STANDARD
4.5 Analyze how choice of genre affects theme or topic

1. **Recall** In "Exile," where do the adults tell the speaker that the family is going?

2. **Clarify** Where does the family actually go?

3. **Recall** In "Crossing the Border," what border is the speaker trying to cross?

4. **Clarify** Why do the speaker and the others in the car want to cross the border?

Literary Analysis

5. **Analyze Narrative Poetry** Using the following chart, analyze the narrative elements present in "Exile" and "Crossing the Border." Describe each element in the appropriate box.

Characters	Setting
Conflicts	Resolution (?)

6. **Interpret Figurative Language** Think about the experience Alvarez compares with swimming in "Exile." How fitting is the comparison?

7. **Make Inferences** In "Crossing the Border," how does the speaker feel after crossing into Canada? Explain how you know.

8. **Compare Speakers** Use the graphics you created as you read to describe the speaker in each poem. How do the speakers differ? How do they both express **alienation?**

9. **Evaluate Poetry** Which poem more effectively tells a story? Which poem is more successful at creating a **mood?** Support your answers with evidence.

Reading-Writing Connection

WRITING PROMPT	**SELF-CHECK**
Write a Story Passage How does a narrative poem differ from a short story? Write **three to five paragraphs** of a short story based on one of the poems. Then, in two or three sentences, comment on what is lost in the translation to prose.	*A successful rewrite will . . .* • keep the poem's speaker as the story's narrator • express the same ideas as the poem

Writing Workshop

Interpretive Essay

When you read a work of literature, you want to make sense of what the writer has shown you. In this workshop, you will write an interpretive essay—one that looks closely at a particular story and finds the meaning in it.

WRITER'S ROAD MAP

Interpretive Essay

WRITING PROMPT 1

Writing from Literature When you have closely examined a piece of literature, you are able to **interpret** it—to figure out meanings that are not obvious at first glance. Write an essay that interprets a literary work and helps readers find new meaning or significance in it.

Topics to Consider

- how conflict in "Harrison Bergeron" helps get the author's message across
- how setting and mood in "Searching for Summer" affect the meaning of the story

WRITING PROMPT 2

Writing from the Real World Choose a memorable story from a movie or book that you recently viewed or read. Write an essay that briefly summarizes the story and examines its deeper meaning or overall message.

Places to Look

- movies that have strong characters, such as *Spider-Man* or *Whale Rider*
- television shows that use a particular setting, such as a courtroom or a hospital

 WRITING TOOLS
For prewriting, revision, and editing tools, visit the **Writing Center** at ClassZone.com.

KEY TRAITS

1. IDEAS
- Includes a **thesis statement** that gives the key points of the discussion
- Uses **evidence** from the source to support each key point

2. ORGANIZATION
- Compelling **introduction** includes the title and author of the work being interpreted
- **Organizational pattern** is consistent and includes **transitions**
- Provides **background information** about the work so readers can understand the interpretation
- Summarizes ideas and draws broader **conclusions** about the work

3. VOICE
- **Tone** is appropriate for purpose and audience

4. WORD CHOICE
- Uses **precise language** to interpret the work

5. SENTENCE FLUENCY
- Includes a variety of **sentence structures** to keep the essay from becoming too choppy or bland

6. CONVENTIONS
- Employs **correct grammar and usage**

Part 1: Analyze a Student Model

WRITING STANDARD
6.2 Write responses to literature

Lydia Rodriguez
Eisenhower College Prep

Heritage and "Everyday Use"

At first glance, Alice Walker's story "Everyday Use" seems to be about minor conflicts. However, an analysis of the story shows that the author uses these conflicts to describe her beliefs about a major issue. Three conflicts—over a family's home, a daughter's name, and some heirloom 5 quilts—make the reader think about a larger question: How should people honor and remember their heritage?

At the beginning of the story, the mother describes her bare-dirt yard as "so clean and wavy . . . more comfortable than most people know." When the family home burned down years before, her daughter 10 Dee showed no emotion. The mother believes Dee will feel the same way about the rebuilt house, saying, "No doubt when Dee sees it she will want to tear it down." Dee now lives in a city, and when she comes to visit, she poses her mother and sister in front of their house and snaps Polaroids of them as though she were a tourist and they 15 were picturesque natives. The mother loves the home she has lived in for many years; it is part of her heritage. But Dee sees it only as the backdrop for a photograph.

Another important conflict between Dee and her mother has to do with names. Dee tells her family that she has given herself an African 20 name, Wangero Leewanika Kemanjo. She tells her mother that "Dee" is "dead," saying, "I couldn't bear it any longer, being named after the people who oppress me." Dee's mother replies, "You know as well as me you was named after your aunt Dicie." The mother can trace the name back at least three generations, and perhaps even to before the Civil War.

KEY TRAITS IN ACTION

Identifies the literary work and engages the reader by suggesting an important message will be revealed.

Thesis statement lists the three key points of this essay and gives the reader a question to think about.

Organization is logical. Each body paragraph covers a key point from the thesis.

Tone is serious and sincere. A variety of **sentence structures** helps keep the essay lively.

Includes **background information** about Dee's name change. Uses quotations as **evidence** to support key points.

25 But her daughter rejects the name, preferring to forget all the Dees who came before her.

The last and most important confrontation between Dee and her mother comes when Dee asks for two quilts that Grandma Dee, Aunt Dicie, and the mother had made. Dee wants to hang the quilts in her
30 home as decorations. Her mother had offered her a quilt when she went away to school, but Dee had rejected them as "old-fashioned, out of style." Now, she tells her mother, they are *"priceless!"* When the mother tells Dee that she promised the quilts to the younger daughter as a wedding gift, Dee reacts furiously: "Maggie can't appreciate these quilts.
35 She'd probably be backward enough to put them to everyday use!" Dee can't see that "everyday use" is exactly why the quilts were made. She is more interested in owning a quilt that was intricately hand sewn than in remembering and appreciating the people who sewed it.

As Dee storms out of the house, she tells her mother, "You just don't
40 understand . . . your heritage." The fact is, the mother and Maggie understand their heritage in ways that Dee never will. To the mother, heritage lies in the work of her ancestors; in the humble house that shelters her; in the memories of Grandma Dee, Stash, and Dicie; and in the lovingly pieced quilts that will keep Maggie and her husband warm.
45 The author uses a series of conflicts between the mother and Dee to show that a family's heritage is not something "priceless" to be hung on a wall as a piece of art. Instead, it should be part of people's daily lives—for "everyday use."

Transitional words and phrases make the flow of ideas easy to follow.

Strong, precise words give the essay punch and power.

Ends with an **effective conclusion** that not only summarizes key points but also gives the reader something to think about.

2

WRITING STANDARD
5.1 Generate writing ideas

Part 2: Apply the Writing Process

PREWRITING

What Should I Do?	**What Does It Look Like?**

1. Revisit the work you will interpret.
A second or third reading (or viewing) of the work will likely reveal important details you may have missed. Record thoughts and questions in a reading log or a viewing log.

▶

Text	My Thoughts
"so clean and wavy"	It's a bare-dirt yard, but she makes it sound wonderful.
"She never takes a shot without making sure the house is included."	This is Dee's own family, but she's acting like a tourist. That's insensitive.

2. Try freewriting to find the big idea.
Can't figure out what to write about? Freewriting can help. Ask yourself: What makes a certain character so interesting? Which line of dialogue means more than what it seems to say at first glance?

▶

family is poor
Dee wanted "nice things"—fancy dress
Dee is beautiful and smart but doesn't seem to care about mother and sister
Dee says "You just don't understand ... your heritage," but Maggie is the one who can quilt, who remembers grandma + Stash

3. Zero in on your focus and write a thesis.
Ask yourself: What is the author's message, and how did I figure that out? Write a **working thesis** that explains your main idea. Then list key points from the story that prove your thesis.

▶

The author is saying that understanding and remembering your heritage is important.
Three key conflicts:
 1. family home
 2. Dee's name
 3. quilts

4. Gather evidence to support each key point.
Use details and quotations to lend support to your interpretation.

TIP If you're having trouble finding supporting evidence for a key point, you might have to revise your thesis statement.

▶

2. Conflict over Dee's name
• Dee rejects her name.
• adopts African name—Wangero Leewanika Kemanjo
• Mother: "You know as well as me you was named after your aunt Dicie."

What Should I Do?	What Does It Look Like?

1. Get organized.

You might organize your essay by telling the reader what the story seems to be about at first glance and then explaining what deeper meanings can be understood after several more readings or viewings. This writer chose to state her opinion of the story's significance in a thesis statement and then offer supporting evidence for her key ideas.

TIP Which of your key ideas is strongest? You can emphasize that point by discussing it either first or last.

▶

Introduction

Thesis: *Author uses three conflicts to make the reader think about valuing heritage.*

A. Conflict over home

1. *Mother loves it.*
2. *Dee uses it as backdrop for photograph.*

B. Conflict over name

1. *Dee named for many ancestors.*
2. *She feels she was named for oppressors.*

C. Conflict over quilts

1. *Mother plans to give them to Maggie as a wedding gift.*
2. *Dee wants to hang quilts as art.*

Conclusion

2. Support key ideas with strong evidence from the text.

Solid supporting evidence from the story will make your interpretation much more compelling. As you draft, think about how well each detail supports each key idea.

▶

Another important conflict between Dee and her mother has to do with names. — Key idea

Dee tells her family she has given herself an African name, Wangero Leewanika Kemanjo. She tells her mother that "Dee" is "dead". — Supporting evidence

3. Close with more than just a summary.

A well-crafted conclusion not only summarizes your key points but also includes a statement about their overall meaning.

TIP Before revising, study the **key traits** on page 142 and the **rubric** and **peer-reader questions** on page 148.

▶

The author uses a series of conflicts between the mother and Dee to show that a family's heritage is not something "priceless" to be hung on a wall as a piece of art. — Summary

Instead, it should be part of people's daily lives—for "everyday use." — Meaning

REVISING AND EDITING

What Should I Do?	**What Does It Look Like?**

1. Start smartly.
- Draw a box around your thesis statement.
- If your thesis seems boring or obvious, consider ways to make it more specific.

▶ ~~The author believes that understanding and remembering your heritage is important.~~

Walker describes three conflicts—over a family's home, a daughter's name, and some heirloom quilts—to make the reader think about a larger question: How should people honor and remember their heritage?

2. Check transitions.
- Underline transitional words and phrases.
- If your essay lacks underlines, add words and phrases that signal to the reader how your essay is organized.

▶ At the beginning of the story,
The mother describes her bare-dirt yard as "so clean and wavy ... more comfortable than most people know."

The last and most important confrontation between Dee and her mother comes when
Dee asks for two quilts ...

3. Consider your tone.
- Ask a peer reader to place [brackets] around parts of your essay that seem casual or slangy.
- Rewrite the bracketed parts so that their tone is appropriate for the topic.

▶ The mother can trace the name back at least three generations. But her daughter [~~could care less.~~] rejects the name, preferring to forget all the Dees who came before her.

4. Use strong, precise verbs.
- Circle the verbs in your essay.
- Think about replacing overused verbs such as *is, was, has, does,* and *goes* with more vivid verb choices.
- You don't have to replace every verb in your essay, but consider replacing any verb that appears several times within a few paragraphs.

▶ storms
As Dee ~~goes~~ out of the house, she ...

When the mother tells Dee she promised the quilt to the younger daughter as a wedding gift, Dee ~~is furious,~~ reacts furiously.

Preparing to Publish

Interpretive Essay

Apply the Rubric

A strong interpretive essay . . .

- ☑ identifies and briefly describes the work
- ☑ includes a clear thesis statement that gives the writer's interpretation
- ☑ supports the key points with evidence from the text
- ☑ is logically organized
- ☑ uses precise language and an appropriate tone
- ☑ varies sentence structures to add interest and sophistication
- ☑ concludes by summarizing the writer's interpretation and explaining its importance to understanding the work

Ask a Peer Reader

- What are my key ideas?
- Do any of my key ideas need more support? If so, which ones?
- Could someone who hasn't read the story understand my interpretation?

Check Your Grammar

- Remember that **subjects** and **verbs** must **agree in number.** A singular subject takes a singular verb.

  > But Dee sees it only as the backdrop for . . .

- Plural subjects take plural verbs.

  > Three conflicts—over a family's home, a daughter's name, and some heirloom quilts— make the reader think about a larger question.

- Be sure that **pronouns agree in number with their antecedents.** A singular antecedent requires a singular pronoun.

  > As Dee storms out of the house, she tells . . .

- A plural antecedent requires a plural pronoun.

  > "Maggie can't appreciate these quilts. She'd probably be backward enough to put them to everyday use!"

- A compound antecedent takes a plural pronoun.

  > The fact is, the mother and Maggie understand their heritage in ways that Dee never will.

See page R52: Using Pronouns

Writing Online

PUBLISHING OPTIONS
For publishing options, visit the **Writing Center** at ClassZone.com.

ASSESSMENT PREPARATION
For writing and grammar assessment practice, go to the **Assessment Center** at ClassZone.com.

Presenting an Oral Response to Literature

Here's how to share your interpretive skills and sharpen your skills as a public speaker.

Planning the Response

1. **Break down the essay into its key ideas.** You might put brackets around the sentence that introduces each idea, and number the supporting evidence.

2. **Enrich your background knowledge.** Do some research about the author, the time when the story likely took place, and any important places or objects in the story. You may want to bring in some photographs to enhance your presentation.

3. **Create a script.** Write an engaging introduction. Be sure to write down quotations just as they appear in the story. If possible, practice your presentation in front of friends or family members.

> Dee tells her mother, "You just don't understand . . . your heritage." But it is Dee who does not understand it. The mother knows that her heritage is all around her * in her house, in her family memories, and in her beautiful quilts.
>
> Alice Walker uses a series of conflicts to show that heritage is part of people's daily lives * that it is for "everyday use."
>
> Green = Slow down.
> Blue = Emphasize this.
> * = Pause.

Presenting the Response

1. **Address your audience directly.** Look at different audience members as you talk. If you're using visuals, refer to them at the appropriate times.

2. **Take questions.** At the end of your presentation, ask the audience if they have any questions for you or if anything in your presentation needs clarification. When someone asks a question, repeat it to make sure that everyone in the audience has heard it and that you understand exactly what you're being asked.

   See page R81: Evaluate an Oral Response to Literature

Reading Comprehension

DIRECTIONS *Read the following selection and then answer the questions.*

from The Grapes of Wrath

John Steinbeck

When the first rain started, the migrant people huddled in their tents, saying, It'll soon be over, and asking, How long's it likely to go on?

And when the puddles formed, the men went out in the rain with shovels and built little dikes around the tents. The beating rain worked at the canvas until it penetrated and sent streams down. And then the little dikes washed out and the water came inside, and the streams wet the beds and the blankets. The people sat in wet clothes. They set up boxes and put planks on the boxes. Then, day and night, they sat on the planks.

Beside the tents the old cars stood, and water fouled the ignition wires and water fouled the carburetors. The little gray tents stood in lakes. And at last the people had to move. Then the cars wouldn't start because the wires were shorted; and if the engines would run, deep mud engulfed the wheels. And the people waded away, carrying their wet blankets in their arms. They splashed along, carrying the children, carrying the very old, in their arms. And if a barn stood on high ground, it was filled with people, shivering and hopeless.

Then some went to the relief offices, and they came sadly back to their own people.

They's rules—you got to be here a year before you can git relief. They say the gov'ment is gonna help. They don't know when.

And gradually the greatest terror of all came along.

They ain't gonna be no kinda work for three months.

In the barns, the people sat huddled together; and the terror came over them, and their faces were gray with terror. The children cried with hunger, and there was no food.

Then the sickness came, pneumonia, and measles that went to the eyes and to the mastoids.[1]

And the rain fell steadily, and the water flowed over the highways, for the culverts[2] could not carry the water.

---

1. **mastoids:** parts of the skull that project behind the ears and contain air pockets that can become infected.
2. **culverts:** drains crossing beneath roads.

Then from the tents, from the crowded barns, groups of sodden men went
30 out, their clothes slopping rags, their shoes muddy pulp. They splashed out
through the water, to the towns, to the country stores, to the relief offices, to
beg for food, to cringe and beg for food, to beg for relief, to try to steal, to
lie. And under the begging, and under the cringing, a hopeless anger began
to smolder. And in the little towns pity for the sodden men changed to
anger, and anger at the hungry people changed to fear of them. Then sheriffs
swore in deputies in droves, and orders were rushed for rifles, for tear gas, for
ammunition. Then the hungry men crowded the alleys behind the stores to
beg for bread, to beg for rotting vegetables, to steal when they could.

Frantic men pounded on the doors of the doctors; and the doctors were
40 busy. And sad men left word at country stores for the coroner[3] to send a car.
The coroners were not too busy. The coroners' wagons backed up through the
mud and took out the dead.

And the rain pattered relentlessly down, and the streams broke their banks
and spread out over the country.

Huddled under sheds, lying in wet hay, the hunger and the fear bred anger.
Then boys went out, not to beg, but to steal; and men went out weakly, to try
to steal.

The sheriffs swore in new deputies and ordered new rifles; and the
comfortable people in tight houses felt pity at first, and then distaste, and
50 finally hatred for the migrant people.

---

3. **coroner** (kôr′ə-nər): an official whose job is to investigate deaths
in order to determine their causes.

Comprehension

DIRECTIONS *Answer the following questions about the selection.*

1. Which is the most accurate description of the setting in lines 1–8?

   A. a group of tents that are dry inside

   B. a group of tents alongside a stream

   C. a group of tents being flooded by heavy rains

   D. a group of tents used by workers building dikes

2. The conflict described in lines 1–8 is between the migrant people and

   A. the relief agency

   B. their old cars

   C. the force of nature

   D. their children

3. Events in lines 1–14 are organized in

   A. chronological order

   B. classification order

   C. compare-and-contrast order

   D. least- to most-important order

4. In the description in lines 9–19, the author creates a mood that is

   A. sinister

   B. cheerful

   C. despairing

   D. comforting

5. What is the "greatest terror" faced by the migrant people in lines 20–23?

   A. more rain

   B. lack of work

   C. homelessness

   D. sickness

6. Which word used in lines 25–30 expresses the passage of time and helps to build a mood of hopelessness?

   A. their

   B. then

   C. from

   D. water

7. What new conflict develops when the setting changes to the towns in lines 29–38?

   A. The townspeople become angry at the migrants.

   B. The migrants do not have enough food.

   C. The migrant people can't find work.

   D. The weather gets worse.

8. In lines 29–38, the townspeople change their feelings toward the migrant people in what order?

   A. anger to pity to fear

   B. pity to fear to anger

   C. anger to fear to pity

   D. pity to anger to fear

9. What can you infer from the phrase "and the doctors were busy" in lines 39–40?

   A. The doctors were waiting for the coroner.

   B. The doctors refused to see the people.

   C. The townspeople were sick too.

   D. The doctors were on strike.

10. Which words help you follow the order of events in lines 48–50?

   A. sheriffs, deputies, people

   B. at first, then, finally

   C. new, comfortable, tight

   D. pity, distaste, hatred

11. Which of the following can you infer about how the migrant people act as a group?

   A. They cooperate with each other in their struggle to survive.

   B. They try to become a part of the town's social structure.

   C. They do whatever the government tells them to do.

   D. They rely on the women to keep the group together.

12. What mood is created by the phrases "pattered relentlessly down" and "spread out over the country" in lines 43–44?

   A. anticipation

   B. happiness

   C. desolation

   D. alarm

13. Which inference can you make about the migrant people in this selection?

   A. They had lived in the area for a short time.

   B. They wanted to make trouble for the sheriffs.

   C. They were happy to move to the barns.

   D. They could get jobs if they wanted them.

Written Response

SHORT ANSWER
Write three or four sentences to answer each question.

14. Give at least two reasons why the author may have used the phrase "tight houses" when referring to the "comfortable people" in line 49.

15. List five descriptive details or words that the writer uses to create a particular mood in the excerpt from *The Grapes of Wrath*.

EXTENDED RESPONSE
Write two or three paragraphs to answer the following questions.

16. Summarize, in chronological order, what happens in the excerpt. Use time-order signal words, such as *first* and *finally*, to show when events take place.

17. Compare the two settings described in lines 45–50. Name a conflict that arises from these different settings. Support your answer with details from the excerpt.

Vocabulary

DIRECTIONS *Use context in the excerpt from* The Grapes of Wrath *to help you answer the following questions about specialized vocabulary words.*

1. The word *ignition* in line 9 refers to
   A. an outdoor camp stove for cooking
   B. a portable heating system for tents
   C. the system for firing up an engine
   D. the exhaust system in an automobile

2. Which phrase in lines 9–12 gives the best clue to the meaning of *shorted?*
   A. old cars
   B. gray tents
   C. wouldn't start
   D. engulfed the wheels

3. Which word in lines 16–19 gives the best clue to the meaning of *relief?*
   A. offices
   B. rules
   C. people
   D. help

4. If the word *carburet* means "to combine or mix to increase available fuel energy," the word *carburetors* in line 10 most likely refers to
   A. keys that operate a machine
   B. jumbles of automobile parts
   C. gas used to create power
   D. devices used in an engine

DIRECTIONS *Use your knowledge of connotation and denotation to answer the following questions. The line numbers will help you find the words in the excerpt from* The Grapes of Wrath.

5. What connotation does the word *cringe* have in line 32?
   A. shyness
   B. respect
   C. shame
   D. pride

6. What connotation does the word *frantic* have in line 39?
   A. tension
   B. confusion
   C. desperation
   D. nervousness

7. Choose the word that has the same connotation as the word *smolder* in line 34.
   A. seethe
   B. exist
   C. explode
   D. boil

8. Choose the word that has the same connotation as the word *fouled* in lines 9–10.
   A. tangled
   B. stained
   C. dishonored
   D. contaminated

Writing & Grammar

DIRECTIONS *Read the passage and answer the following questions.*

(1) After the 1929 stock market crash, the country plunged into an economic depression. (2) Farmers plowed under grasslands to plant wheat and earn more money. (3) They didn't realize the plowed land would just blow away. (4) There was no soil, and there were no jobs. (5) About 200,000 people left the Plains states for California. (6) There were no jobs there. (7) Although California had nice weather and fertile soil, it was not the solution the migrants sought.

1. Choose the best way to rewrite sentence 1 using a coordinating conjunction.

   A. The stock market crashed in 1929, and the country plunged into an economic depression.

   B. The stock market crashed in 1929, yet the country plunged into an economic depression.

   C. The stock market crashed in 1929; however, the country plunged into an economic depression.

   D. The stock market crashed in 1929, but the country plunged into an economic depression.

2. Choose the correct way to rewrite sentence 3 by using a prepositional phrase.

   A. What they didn't realize was that the plowed land would just blow away.

   B. They didn't realize the land they had just plowed would blow away.

   C. They didn't realize the plowed land would just blow away in dust storms.

   D. Unfortunately, they didn't realize the plowed land would just blow away.

3. Choose the best way to combine sentences 5 and 6 by using a coordinating conjunction.

   A. Although 200,000 people left the Plains states for California, there were no jobs there.

   B. About 200,000 people left the Plains states for California, but there were no jobs there.

   C. The 200,000 people who left the Plains states couldn't find jobs in California.

   D. About 200,000 people left the Plains states for California, and there were no jobs there.

4. Choose the correct way to rewrite sentence 7 by using a prepositional phrase.

   A. Although California had nice weather and fertile soil, it was not the land that offered the migrants a solution.

   B. Although California had nice weather and good soil, it was not the solution the migrants sought.

   C. Although California had nice weather and fertile soil for crops, it was not the solution the migrants sought.

   D. Although California had nice weather all the time and fertile soil, it was not the solution the migrants sought.

STOP

Ideas for Independent Reading

Which of the questions in Unit 1 intrigued you most?
Continue exploring them with these additional works.

What if everyone were the same?

1984
by George Orwell

This novel is set in a bleak future world where citizens are constantly watched by the government, known as Big Brother. Individuality is forbidden, free thought is suppressed, and words never mean what they say.

Bless the Beasts and Children
by Glendon Swarthout

The heroes of this book are boys who are misfits at a summer camp. They're different from the popular, athletic boys, and working together they plot to free a pen of buffaloes that are to be slaughtered.

Colors of the Mountain
by Da Chen

The author of this memoir grew up in China during the Cultural Revolution, a time of great repression and conformity. Persecuted because of his family's former wealth, he endured and made it to college.

What makes something valuable?

The Piano Lesson
by August Wilson

In this play, an African-American brother and sister clash over their family's legacy—a piano carved in designs by an enslaved ancestor. The brother wants to sell it to buy land; the sister wants to keep it.

Crazy in the Kitchen
by Louise DeSalvo

Several generations of Italian-American women battle in the kitchen over different ways of cooking. The author realizes that food represents a wealth of different values in the lives of her family members.

Brick Lane
by Monica Ali

Nazneen, born in Bangladesh, is sent to England at age 18 to marry a Bengali immigrant twice her age. Eventually she begins to ask what she wants from life, what she finds of value.

Is survival a matter of chance?

The Perfect Storm
by Sebastian Junger

In October 1991, one of the worst storms in history occurred off the coast of New England. This true account describes the sinking of the fishing boat *Andrea Gail* and the dramatic attempts to rescue other vessels.

Left for Dead
by Beck Weathers

He was left for dead on the slopes of Mount Everest. His companions thought he had frozen. But his commitment to his wife and family woke Beck Weathers up in time to save his life, though not all of his fingers.

Isaac's Storm
by Erik Larson

In 1900, a hurricane destroyed much of Galveston, Texas. Over six thousand died. The book tells us why, and also how those who survived did so.

Word Portraits

CHARACTER DEVELOPMENT

- In Fiction
- In Nonfiction
- In Poetry
- In Drama
- In Media

What makes a
CHARACTER *live?*

We can all remember reading about someone—real or fictitious—who seemed to come to life on the page. We can imagine what that **character** might say or do and can probably describe what he or she looks like. We can even imagine meeting that person and having a conversation.

ACTIVITY With a group of classmates, think of several memorable characters from books and movies. Describe each one, including details about appearance and personality. Then consider the following questions:

- Why does this character stand out in your memory?
- How do other people feel about this character?
- What do you know about how this person thinks and acts?

OHIO
STANDARDS

Preview Unit Goals

LITERARY ANALYSIS
- Analyze character traits and motivation
- Identify and analyze different types of characters
- Understand the methods writers use to develop characters
- Analyze the relationship between plot and character

READING
- Use reading strategies, including connecting and predicting
- Make inferences and generalizations
- Identify main ideas and supporting details
- Identify an author's perspective

WRITING AND GRAMMAR
- Write an autobiographical narrative
- Understand and use varied sentence types
- Use precise verbs and modifiers
- Use concrete and abstract nouns

SPEAKING, LISTENING, AND VIEWING
- Identify and analyze characterization and stereotypes in film
- Present an oral history
- Conduct an interview

VOCABULARY
- Understand connotations and denotations of words
- Use word roots to help unlock meaning

ACADEMIC VOCABULARY
- character traits and motivation
- connotation and denotation
- generalizations and inferences
- characterization
- author's perspective

Analyzing Characters

Slovenly manners, a magnetic personality, a competitive streak—these are the kinds of qualities that can shape your impressions of other people. For example, an egomaniac is probably not someone you would want as a friend. But finding out *why* that person behaves the way he or she does might change your opinion. Characters in literature can be just as complicated as real people. By closely analyzing characters, you can get more out of the stories you read and gain insights into human nature.

OHIO STANDARDS

READING STANDARDS
2.1 Apply reading comprehension strategies
4.1 Compare and contrast an author's use of direct and indirect characterization

Part 1: Character Development

Writers use many techniques to create their characters. Sometimes, the narrator of a story will tell you directly about a character, as in this example: "Enrique's active imagination often got him into trouble." More often, though, you will find out about characters indirectly. The writer may describe

- a character's physical appearance
- a character's actions, thoughts, and speech
- other characters' reactions to and comments about the character

By examining these characterization techniques, you can infer a character's **traits,** or qualities, such as insecurity or bravery. For example, what can you infer about this character from the following sentences? "Elena eyed her teammates critically. Am I the *only* one who knows how to play this game? she thought."

The extent to which a writer develops a character depends on the character's role in a story. Complex, highly developed characters, known as **round characters,** take center stage and seem the most lifelike. **Flat characters,** on the other hand, are one-sided.

ROUND CHARACTERS	FLAT CHARACTERS
Characteristics • are complex; exhibit a variety of traits • show a range of emotions • display strengths and weaknesses • often change over the course of a story	**Characteristics** • are defined by only one or two traits • show only a few emotions • may be stereotypes or stock characters • don't grow or change
Role in the Story • to serve as main characters who make a story rich and interesting • to help define the theme	**Role in the Story** • to serve as minor characters who advance the plot or provide information • to reveal something about the main characters

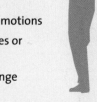

MODEL 1: CHARACTER TRAITS

How do Mrs. Wilson's thoughts about her daughter affect your impression not only of the daughter but also of Mrs. Wilson herself?

from The Opportunity

Short story by **John Cheever**

Mrs. Wilson sometimes thought that her daughter Elise was dumb. Elise was her only daughter, her only child, but Mrs. Wilson was not so blinded by love that the idea that Elise might be stupid did not occasionally cross her mind. The girl's father had died when she was eight, Mrs. Wilson had never
5   remarried, and the girl and her mother lived affectionately and closely. When Elise was a child, she had been responsive and lively, but as she grew into adolescence, as her body matured, her disposition changed, and some of the wonderful clarity of her spirit was lost. At sixteen she seemed indolent, and to have developed a stubborn indifference to the hazards and rewards of life.

Close Read

1. Based on Mrs. Wilson's thoughts about her daughter, how would you describe Elise?

2. What do Mrs. Wilson's thoughts reveal about the kind of mother she is? Cite details to support your answer.

MODEL 2: ROUND AND FLAT CHARACTERS

Here, a man named César reflects on the unfortunate turn his life has taken. As you read, pay attention to César's thoughts about his son.

from A Place Where the Sea Remembers

Novel by **Sandra Benítez**

When he was twenty-one, he had married Concha Ojeda. It was she who had allowed him to turn himself over to the sea. But now Concha was gone and in the months since the accident, the boy had gone mute and was clearly in decline. The boy needed a mother's love, he needed a father's strength, and
5   there was none of one and little left of the other. César thought of Concha's sister, who lived in Oaxaca. She had asked for the boy. She would raise him with her own, she had said at the wake. Since that time, César Burgos had agonized over his sister-in-law's offer and there were moments when he thought he would have to let the boy go.
10   He turned to his son, who sat at the table. . . .
"Why don't you speak?" Cesar cried, heat surging up his neck and into his cheeks.

Close Read

1. Is César a round or flat character? Cite details to support your answer.

2. Reread the boxed text. What do you learn about César from his thoughts about his sister-in-law's offer?

Part 2: Character Behavior

Once you understand *who* the characters are, the next questions concern *why* they act a certain way and *how* they change. Attempting to answer these questions not only takes you deeper into the story but also brings you closer to understanding the complexity of human behavior, including your own.

CHARACTER MOTIVATION

What prompted the man to steal a large sum of money? A character's **motivation**—the reasons behind his or her actions—can affect your perception of that character. For instance, the man might steal money to feed his family or to achieve a lifelong dream of wealth. How do these reasons affect your opinion of him?

Sometimes a character's motivation is stated directly in a story. Usually, though, you need to look for clues and details to try to figure out the motivation. As you read, pay attention to

- the narrator's direct comments about a character's motivation
- the character's actions, thoughts, and values
- your own insights into human behavior

Possible Motives

Character

Resulting Action

STATIC AND DYNAMIC CHARACTERS

In addition to knowing why a character acts a certain way, it is important to analyze how a character changes as a result of the events in a story. A character might grow emotionally, learn a lesson, or alter his or her behavior. Characters who change and grow as the plot develops are **dynamic characters.** In contrast, characters who remain the same are **static characters.**

STRATEGIES FOR ANALYZING CHARACTER CHANGE

First examine the change:		Then analyze the meaning:
• Compare how a character was at the beginning of the story with how he or she is at the end.	▶	• What lesson does the character learn, or what insight does he or she gain?
• Is the change **external,** such as in appearance or circumstance? Is it an **internal** change of attitude or belief?	▶	• Does the change show personal growth, or does it lead to the character's downfall?
• What factors, events, or characters contributed to or caused the change?	▶	• Would the character be motivated to change without the contributing factors?

MODEL 1: CHARACTER MOTIVATION

These two excerpts come from a story about a girl's initiation into a sorority. Why does Millicent want to join the exclusive club?

from **INITIATION**

Short story by **Sylvia Plath**

What girl would not want to be one of the elect, no matter if it did mean five days of initiation before and after school, ending in the climax of Rat Court on Friday night when they made the new girls members? Even Tracy had been wistful when she heard that Millicent had been one of the five girls to
5   receive an invitation.

"It won't be any different with us, Tracy," Millicent had told her. "We'll still go around together like we always have, and next year you'll surely get in."

"I know, but even so," Tracy had said quietly, "you'll change, whether you think you will or not. Nothing ever stays the same."

10   And nothing does, Millicent had thought. How horrible it would be if one never changed . . . if she were condemned to be the plain, shy Millicent of a few years back for the rest of her life.

Close Read

1. The boxed text reveals how difficult it is to get into the sorority. Find another place that explains Millicent's more personal reason for wanting to belong.

2. What does Millicent's desire to join the sorority reveal about her?

MODEL 2: CHARACTER CHANGE

Now read to see how Millicent changes by the end of the story.

As part of her initiation, Millicent has had to ask strangers on a bus what they had for breakfast. One man answered cheerfully, "Heather birds' eyebrows on toast." His unusual response helped Millicent put the experience in perspective.

Outside, the sparrows were still chirping, and as she lay in bed Millicent visualized them, pale gray-brown birds in a flock, one like the other, all exactly alike.

And then, for some reason, Millicent thought of the heather birds. Swooping
5   carefree over the moors, they would go singing and crying out across the great spaces of air, dipping and darting, strong and proud in their freedom and their sometime loneliness. It was then that she made her decision.

Seated now on the woodpile in Betsy Johnson's cellar, Millicent knew that she had come triumphant through the trial of fire, the searing period of the ego
10   which could end in two kinds of victory for her. The easiest of which would be her coronation as a princess, labeling her conclusively as one of the select flock.

The other victory would be much harder, but she knew that it was what she wanted. It was not that she was being noble or anything. It was just that she had learned there were other ways of getting into the great hall, blazing with
15   lights, of people and of life.

Close Read

1. How has Millicent changed since the beginning of the story? Explain whether her change is external or internal.

2. What insight does Millicent gain? Cite details to support your answer.

Part 3: Analyze the Literature

The following excerpts are from a story set on a farm in Ireland. Two characters, husband and wife, are bickering over something that they have clearly argued about many times before. As you read, analyze the characters' traits, motivations, and changes.

from **Brigid**

Short story by **Mary Lavin**

"I see there's no use in talking about it," said the woman. "All I can say is God help the girls, with you, their own father, putting a drag on them so that no man will have anything to do with them after hearing about Brigid."

"What do you mean by that? This is something new. I thought it was
5 only the bit of bread and tea she got that you grudged the poor thing. This is something new. What is this?"

"You oughtn't to need to be told, a man like you that saw the world, a man that traveled like you did, a man that was in England and London."

"I don't know what you're talking about." He took up his hat and felt it to
10 see if the side he had placed near the fire was dry. He turned the other side toward the fire. "What are you trying to say?" he said. "Speak plain!"

> "Is any man going to marry a girl when he hears her aunt is a poor half-witted creature, soft in the head, and living in a poke of a hut, doing nothing all day but sitting looking into the fire?"

15 "What has that got to do with anybody but the poor creature herself? Isn't it her own trouble?"

"Men don't like marrying into a family that has the like of her in it."

"Is that so? I didn't notice that you were put off marrying me, and you knew all about poor Brigid. You used to bring her bunches of primroses. And
20 one day I remember you pulling the flowers off your hat and giving them to her when she started crying over nothing. You used to say she was a harmless poor thing. You used to say you'd look after her."

"And didn't I? Nobody can say I didn't look after her. Didn't I do my best to have her taken into a home, where she'd get the proper care? You can't deny
25 that."

"I'm not denying it. You never gave me peace or ease since the day we were married. But I wouldn't give in. I wouldn't give in then, and I won't give in now, either. I won't let it be said that I had a hand or part in letting my own sister be put away."

30 "But it's for her own good."

Close Read

1. What do you learn about the wife's personality from the things she says to her husband? Cite specific statements to support your answer.

2. The boxed sentence gives one reason why the wife wants to put Brigid in a "home." What other motivation is revealed in this excerpt?

3. Reread lines 18–22 and 26–29. What do you learn about the husband's traits from the way he responds to his wife?

Later in the story, a sudden tragedy prompts the wife to reflect on her relationship with her husband and their argument over Brigid's care.

After their argument, the husband goes to visit Brigid at her tiny cottage within walking distance of the house. When he doesn't return by dark, his wife gets worried and goes to look for him. She finds his body at the cottage, his head badly burned by the hearth fire where he had fallen, while Brigid sits uncomprehending nearby.

I t was dark at the pump, but she could hear people running the way she had pointed. Then when they had reached the cottage, there was no more running, but great talking and shouting. She sat down at the side of the pump, but there was a smell off her hands and desperately she bent forward and began to
5 wash them under the pump, but when she saw there was hair stuck to her fingers she wanted to scream again, but there was a great pain gathering in her heart, not yet the pain of loss, but the pain of having failed; failed in some terrible way.

I failed him always, she thought, from the very start. I never loved him like he loved me; not even then, long ago, the time I took the flowers off my hat. It
10 wasn't for Brigid, like he thought. I was only making myself out to be what he imagined I was. I didn't know enough about loving to change myself for him. I didn't even know enough about it to keep him loving me. He had to give it all to Brigid in the end.

He gave it all to Brigid; to a poor daft thing that didn't know enough to
15 pull him back from the fire or call someone when he fell down in a stroke. If it was anyone else was with him, he might have had a chance.

Oh, how had it happened? How could love be wasted and go to loss like that? . . .

Suddenly she thought of the heavy feet of the neighbors tramping the
20 boards of the cottage up in the fields behind her, and rising up, she ran back up the boreen.[1]

"Here's the poor woman now," someone said, as she thrust past the crowd around the door.

They began to make a way for her to where, on the settle bed, they had
25 laid her husband. But instead she parted a way through the people and went toward the door of the room off the kitchen.

"It's Brigid I'm thinking about," she said. "Where is she?"

"Something will have to be done about her now all right," someone said.

"It will," she said, decisively, and her voice was as true as a bell.
30 She had reached the door of the room.

"That's why I came back," she said, looking around her defiantly. "She'll need proper minding now. To think she hadn't the strength to run for help or pull him back a bit from the fire." She opened a door.

Sitting on the side of the bed, all alone, she saw Brigid.
35 "Get your hat and coat, Brigid," she said. "You're coming with me."

---

1. **boreen:** a narrow country lane.

Close Read

1. Reread the boxed text. What motivated the wife to be kind to Brigid initially?

2. How does the wife change during the story? Explain the lesson she has learned by the end.

3. Do you think the wife would have changed had her husband not died? Support your opinion with evidence.

4. "Brigid" is the title of this story, yet Brigid herself never speaks. Is she a flat or round character? Support your answer.

Shoofly Pie

Short Story by Naomi Shihab Nye

Is there a cure for
GRIEF?

**OHIO
STANDARDS**

READING STANDARDS
2.1 Apply reading comprehension strategies
4.1 Compare and contrast an author's use of direct and indirect characterization

KEY IDEA The death of a loved one can be overwhelming. Yet people who experience such losses must eventually get on with their lives. In "Shoofly Pie," employees at a restaurant give new meaning to the term *comfort food* when they find a way to deal with **grief.**

QUICKWRITE With a small group, make a list of strategies that can help a person overcome grief. You may use the list that is shown to get started. Then write a short paragraph explaining which strategy or strategies might be most helpful to you or someone you know.

Ways of Dealing
with Grief
1. Talk to friends.
2. Keep busy.
3.
4.
5.

● LITERARY ANALYSIS: CHARACTER TRAITS

Characters often have consistent qualities, or **character traits,** that readers learn about over the course of a story. A trait may be a physical quality, such as clumsiness, or an aspect of the character's personality. In "Shoofly Pie," Nye sometimes directly describes a character trait. For example, we find out that the main character's boss is a good mentor in the following statement by the narrator:

That was the greatest thing about Riyad—he never made anyone feel stupid for not knowing something.

Instead of directly describing a character's traits, writers often let the reader draw conclusions about them. Your conclusions may be based on

- the character's words, thoughts, and actions
- what other characters say or think about the character

As you read "Shoofly Pie," note the traits of the main characters.

Review: **Static and Dynamic Characters**

● READING SKILL: CONNECT

You can enhance your understanding and enjoyment of a story when you **connect** to it, or relate the content to your own experiences and knowledge. For example, you might connect your own experience of grief with the main character's grief in "Shoofly Pie." Ask the following questions to help make connections:

- Does a character remind me of myself or of someone I know?
- What do I know about the time, place, event, or situation described in the story?
- How is the story similar to other works I have read?

As you read "Shoofly Pie," record connections you make in a chart like the one shown.

Episode in the Story	My Connection
Mattie grieves over her mother's death.	When my uncle died, I stayed in my room all weekend.

Review: **Compare and Contrast**

Author On|ine

Bicultural Upbringing
Like the character of Mattie, Naomi Shihab Nye (nī) is of Arab descent. She was raised in a bicultural household by her American mother and Palestinian father. As a teenager she spent a year in the Middle East and got to know her Palestinian grandmother, who

**Naomi Shihab Nye
born 1952**

became an important inspiration to her. Nye started writing poetry at age six, taking as subject matter her neighborhood's cats, squirrels, and trees.

In Praise of Diversity Today, Nye is an award-winning poet and fiction writer. She still loves to write about familiar sights and sounds, but she also seeks to promote peace and cross-cultural understanding through her work. Nye believes that connections between people from different backgrounds enrich society as a whole: "I've never understood the impulse to be with people only like ourselves. How dull that would be."

 MORE ABOUT THE AUTHOR
For more on Naomi Shihab Nye, visit the **Literature Center** at **ClassZone.com.**

Background

A Restaurant Remembered Nye's inspiration for the Good for You Restaurant in "Shoofly Pie" came from her own memories. While attending college, she worked as a cook at a natural foods restaurant called the Greenwood Grocery. The experience left a lasting impression. Nye says that she has made several attempts in her writing to memorialize the "characters, flavors, and fragrances" of a place that has since passed out of existence.

SHOOFLY PIE

Naomi Shihab Nye

On our way somewhere we sat at this table—
wood clear-varnished, a design to hold the days:
two people talking toward the center;
candlelight on each face . . .
                                    —William Stafford [1]

Mattie couldn't believe she dropped the giant honey jar on the floor the
moment the boss entered the kitchen after his overseas trip. Have you ever
watched a gallon of honey ooze into a slow-motion golden dance around a
mound of broken glass?

It might have looked glorious if she hadn't been the one who dropped it.

The boss stared at her with his deep eyes, his mouth wide open. "And
you . . . must be . . . ?" he asked.

A secret voice in her head replied, *The idiot. The donkey.* But her real voice
said, "The person they hired while you were out of town." Then she said, "I'm
so sorry—I'm also very sorry about your father," and knelt down.

You couldn't exactly use a *broom* on honey. A shovel maybe? She had a weird
desire to stick both her hands into it.

Or, she might faint. Having never fainted before, she always imagined it
as a way to escape a difficult scene. That, or going to the bathroom. "Excuse
me," she'd said, many other times in her life. "I'll be right back." At her own
mother's funeral recently, she'd spent a lot of time in the bathroom with her

1. **William Stafford (1914–1993):** an American poet who wrote about the daily concerns of people.

ANALYZE VISUALS
Examine the photograph.
What details help you
form a mental image
of the story's **setting?**

forehead pressed against the cool tiles. She felt safe, removed from the grief of what was waiting for her back in the world. **A**

In this case, a huge mess to clean up, and twelve sprouty salads to make, 20 *pronto.*[2] A bouquet of orders hung clipped to the silver line strung over the window between the kitchen and the dining room. She could peek out into the happier part of the restaurant, the eating domain, where regular people with purses and backpacks and boyfriends were waiting for their lunches.

How had she gotten into this?

Long ago, before her mother was diagnosed with cancer, when she still thought she just had migraine headaches, Mattie offered to make dinner by herself. She was twelve. During the whirl of washing lettuce, hulling fresh peas, stirring spaghetti sauce, and lighting the oven to heat the bread, she'd managed to pull down from the wall the giant shelf over the stove that held 30 matchbooks, tea, boxes, spice jars, recipes, birthday candles, half-empty sacks of Arabic coffee, yellowed grocery lists, vitamins, and her mother's favorite cabbage teapot with a china rabbit for a lid. One ear broke off the rabbit and chips of china fell into the spaghetti pot. Her mother came into the kitchen with a wet rag over her head to see what was happening.

Mattie should have known she was destined for disaster.

Today the boss squatted beside her. She felt comfortable to be in the presence of another American-of-Arab-descent, but it didn't seem the right moment to mention it. She'd seen his name on the mail that came in his absence. Despite her clumsiness, he was smiling and mild. "Thank you," he 40 said. "My father was a good man. As for the honey, I think I'll get one of those big scoops we use in the cooler and take care of it myself. Why don't you go back to what you were doing? Don't worry about it!" **B**

She stared after him. What a nice voice! Relieved, she turned back to the counter to sprinkle sunflower seeds and shaved cheese over the bowls of lettuce . . . and there was the empty honey bear sitting with its hat off, waiting for her to refill it for the waitress who had shoved it at her—Mattie would suggest the waitresses take care of such details themselves from now on.

Two weeks ago she'd never even thought about being a cook in a restaurant and now she was ready to help run the place.

50 The boss could have fired her. Some bosses were mean. She'd heard about them from her parents over the years. But suddenly she wanted this job very much. She needed it.

She needed the money, but even more, she needed distraction. It was too hard to be home by herself for the summer since her mother had died the first week of June. Her father was at work all day long until suppertime. Three days after the funeral, she'd gotten on a bus to ride downtown to the library and, in her distraction, had gotten off too early. She saw the *Good for You Restaurant* staring her in the face. **C**

That's what she needed. Something that was good for her.

60 So she stepped inside for a late lunch. After ordering an avocado sandwich

---

2. *pronto* (prŏn'tō): promptly.

A CONNECT
Reread lines 1–18. Based on your experiences, do you find Mattie's reaction to her accident believable? Why or why not?

B CHARACTER TRAITS
What words would you use to describe Mattie's boss?

C CONNECT
Recall a time when you did something to distract yourself from painful thoughts. Why might a restaurant job be a good distraction for Mattie?

with cheese, she'd asked the waitress, "Do you like working here?" It was a cozy environment. Large, abstract paintings, mismatched chairs, real flowers in ceramic vases on each table. Ceiling fans, soft jazz playing.

The waitress sighed and shrugged.

Mattie asked, "Do you get to eat for free?"

"Sure. But who needs food? I'm not hungry. You get sick of food when you haul it around all day." She whispered, "Anyway, I'm too in love to think about food."

"With who?" (Mattie wondered why, when someone else whispered, you
70 whispered back.)

"The guy who washes dishes. Augie. If you go to the restroom, you can see him through the doorway. He has long blond hair and an earring."

Who didn't have an earring, these days? Even men who looked like Mattie's father had an earring.

So she walked back to the restroom just to see the love interest of a person she didn't even know, to distract herself from her own thoughts. The dishwasher looked bubbly and clean in his white apron. As if he washed himself between dishes. Slicked up and soapy. He grinned at Mattie when he caught her glance.
80 "He's cute," Mattie whispered to the waitress, upon her return. She ordered a bowl of fresh peach cobbler. She'd barely eaten in days.

"The problem with working here right now," the waitress said, "is—we're so shorthanded. Johnny's the main cook, but his grandpa died in Alabama, and he went over to help his grandma out two weeks ago. Plus, our boss Riyad was called to Beirut suddenly for his father's funeral—everyone is dying! Riyad's great, he helps out in the kitchen when he's here. But without them both, it's a nightmare! Riyad thought we needed an extra cook even before everybody left. Do you know anybody who'd like to be a cook?"

Fueled by her cobbler, Mattie was a danger to society. Plus, if everyone was
90 bereaved in this place, she'd fit right in. "I would."

"Do you have experience?"

"Of course!" Who didn't? She'd been inventing sandwiches and slicing elegant strips of celery for years. She made quick stir-frys for her parents and super-French-toast on the weekends. She'd often made her mother's sack lunches as well as her own—her mother had taught at a Montessori school where she had to heat up twenty little orange containers in the microwave at lunchtime every day. None of her students ate peanut butter anymore, she said—they ate curries, casseroles, and tortilla soup.

Mattie even read cookbooks for relaxation sometimes. While her mother
100 was dying, she couldn't concentrate very well on novels and found herself fixating on women's magazine recipes describing how to make cakes in the shapes of baby lambs and chicks.

"How do I apply?" The waitress dragged Sergio, temporary cook-in-command, to Mattie's table. He had a frantic glaze in his eyes, but asked a few questions and wrote her phone number down. Then he told her to show up to work the next day. That was it. No application form, no interview. Mattie did not say, "I want to cook here because my mother just died." By the next day she'd applied for a health card, her backpack was stashed under the cash register, and her own white apron was tied around her neck.

110   Augie, the dishwasher, came out wiping his hands to welcome her.

Examining the menu closely from her new perspective, Mattie tried to memorize it on the spot, while Sergio juggled salad-making with the spreading of mayonnaise on homemade bread. His large hands looked awkward sprinkling wispy curls of carrot among lettuce and arugula leaves in the line-up of bowls.

Looking down onto the top of Mattie's head, he said, "Would you wash those flats of strawberries and mushrooms that just arrived—if we don't get this mushroom soup on for dinner soon . . . " which was how Mattie became his goon.

120   She wasn't sure "goon" was the right word, but that's what she felt like.

Do this, do that. He never said "please." He gave her the most tedious jobs and quoted Johnny as if Johnny were the god of cuisine.

ANALYZE VISUALS
Which of Mattie's childhood experiences does this photograph remind you of?

Sergio didn't know the easiest way to peel raw tomatoes—dunk them into boiling water for three minutes, then pluck them out. That was one of the million little things she'd learned from her mother. Would she be remembering them forever? She could hear her mother's voice steering her among the giant spoons and chopping blocks—a hum of kindness, a *you-can-do-it* familiar tone.

Here in this place her mother had never been, it seemed easier to think about her. Easier than at home where every curtain, dusty corner, and wilting
130 plant seemed lonesome right now. The shoes poking out from her mother's side of the bed. The calendar with its blank squares for the last two months. "You know," her mother had said, when there were just a few days left in her life, "this is the last thing in the world I ever wanted to do to you." It was easier right now to be in a madly swirling kitchen her mother had never seen.

"**W**ell, I don't *know* Johnny, okay?" Mattie said to Sergio on the fifth day of heavy labor, after she'd just chopped a line of cucumbers for the daily *gazpacho.*[3] "So he's not such a big deal to me, okay?"

"He will be when he gets back," Sergio said.

He was mixing fresh herb dressings. Mattie had snipped the basil up for
140 him with shiny shears. She peeled fifty cloves of garlic in a row. Even her bed at home would smell like garlic soon. She'd fallen immediately in love with the giant shiny pans, families of knives, containers of grated cheese and chopped scallions lined up to top the splendid House Vegetarian Chili. **D**

And she liked the view through the kitchen window into the dining room. She started guessing what a customer would order before the order had been turned in.

Every day the same young woman with short dark hair came in, sat alone under a cosmic painting (blue planets spinning in outer space), and ordered a vegeburger and a Healthy Waldorf Salad on the side. She wore dangling
150 earrings made of polished stones and glass. By the end of each meal she was patting her teary cheeks with a napkin.

Was it something she was reading?

Mattie had noticed her as she stood next to Sergio mixing up their Date/Nut/Cream Cheese Delight in a huge bowl. It didn't take many brains to do that. So she could observe their crowd of eaters—bodybuilders, marathon-runners, practitioners of yoga, religion professors, and students.

"Do you know that girl?" She poked Sergio's side so he almost cut himself. "Watch it! Who?"

"The crying one."
160 "Huh?"

Men didn't notice anything.

"The beautiful one who comes in here every day, orders exactly the same thing, and starts crying."

D CHARACTER TRAITS
What impression do you get of Mattie's character from reading lines 135–143?

---

3. ***gazpacho*** (gə-spä′chō): a Spanish vegetable soup served cold.

He stared disinterestedly through the window. "Actually she does look vaguely familiar."

Mattie speculated, "Maybe she hates our food, but she's obsessive-compulsive and can't go to any other restaurant. Maybe she's in love with Augie, too."

Mattie asked Riyad if she could ring the crying customer out.

170 "Sure. Do you know how to use the cash register?"

"No."

He showed her. That was the greatest thing about Riyad—he never made anyone feel stupid for not knowing something.

Mattie took the girl's bill and rang it up, whispering, "Is there anything we can do to make you feel better?"

The girl looked shocked. "Who *are* you?" she asked.

"I'm the person who puts dressing on your salad and makes your sandwich. I've noticed you through the window. Right there—see that little window we have? I started working here a few weeks ago. And you seem—upset. I

180 wondered if you could use—someone to talk to or anything." **E**

The girl looked suspicious. "Do you know Johnny? The cook who runs this place?"

Him again. Mattie said, "He's on a trip. I've never seen his face."

"Just wait," the girl whispered. "It's the most amazing face you'll ever see." She shook her head "God! He drives me crazy."

"Me, too," Mattie said. She stepped away from the cash register so Riyad could ring up someone else.

The girl looked confused "But I thought you said . . . "

"I was just kidding, sorry. I don't know him. Is he your boyfriend?"

190 "Well, we were dating before he went to help his grandma. But right before he left, he said we were finished—well, he didn't say that *word* exactly, because I don't think he believes in beginnings and endings, but he said—we needed to follow different paths. God, I love him! I guess that's why I've been coming in so often. I'm hoping he'll be back and will have changed his mind." Her eyes filled up again.

Mattie handed her a Kleenex. "Has he called you since he's been gone? Has he written you at all?"

"Nothing. I've called him maybe four times. His grandma always answers and says Johnny's not there. She must be lying! But you see, Johnny hates to

200 talk on the phone. He doesn't believe in it. It makes him feel—disembodied. So I don't know if he's really not there or if he's simply—sticking to his principles."

"Sorry, but he sounds like a nutcase. How old is he, by the way?" **F**

Her face sobered. "Twenty-one," she said. "But he says he's ageless."

Sergio suddenly stood behind Mattie with a ladle in one hand and a wire whisk in the other. "Are you taking a vacation? Or is this a coffee break I wasn't told about? If you're going to work here, you'll have to carry your weight."

It was his favorite dopey phrase.

Johnny returned the next day.

E CHARACTER TRAITS
What do Mattie's words and actions toward the girl reveal about Mattie? Cite specific words or phrases to support your answer.

F COMPARE AND CONTRAST
How does Mattie's impression of Johnny compare with the girl's description of him?

Sergio was sick and didn't come in.

210   Riyad had to take his wife and babies to the doctor, too. Even with the *Good for You Restaurant*'s wholesome cuisine bolstering them, they'd all managed to get the flu.

So it was Johnny and Mattie on their own, with one lovesick waitress, another waitress with a sprained ankle, and Augie poking his sudsy head around the corner now and then to see if they needed plates.

Amazing face? Mattie couldn't see it. She thought he had an exaggerated square jaw, like Popeye[4] in a cartoon. Huge muscles under rolled-up white shirtsleeves. Deep, dangerous tan. Hadn't he heard about skin cancer? Explosive brown curls circled his head. He had great hair, yes. He also wore an

220 incredibly tight pair of faded jeans. Mattie couldn't imagine he felt very good inside them. **G**

"I'm sorry about your grandpa," she said.

Johnny stared at her hard. "I didn't realize you knew him."

That was mean. No way she would mention her mama when he was as mean as that. She hadn't even told Riyad or Sergio about her mother yet. Immediately Johnny started moving everything around. All the implements and condiments she'd rearranged to make them more available in a rush, all the innovative new placements of towels, tubs, cinnamon—*whoosh!*—he wanted to put things back exactly where they had been when he left.

230   And he was muttering. *Rub, rub, rub,* how dare anyone juggle the balance of his precious sphere? "Here!" he roared, lion-like, as he pulled a giant knife out from the lower shelf where Mattie had hidden it, finding it too large to be very useful. "Here is the sword of the goddess! My favorite sweet saber! And what is this pie on the Specials Board that I've never heard of in my life—*Shoofly?* Where did that come from?"

"Well, first from the Amish[5] communities in Pennsylvania. *Americana,*[6] you know? And now, from me." Mattie had suggested the recipe her second week, since it happened to be her personal favorite pie, and they'd sold out of it every day.

240   "*You?*"

He could make the simplest word sound like an insult. You didn't even want to be "you" anymore. "And who *are* you?"

She brandished her blender cap. "I'm the new—chef."

"Chef? I'm the chef around here. You're the cook, okay? Do you know the difference between the words?"

"I know the difference between lots of words. Between RUDE and NICE, for example." She stalked back to the dishwashing closet.

"Augie, break a plate over his head, will you?"

Augie looked shocked. "Johnny? Johnny's like—the mastermind! He

250 knows—everything! Did you know he even built the tables in this place?"

---

4. **Popeye:** a cartoon character with a prominent jaw.

5. **Amish:** a religious group valuing humility, family, and the simple life.

6. ***Americana:*** things distinctly American.

"I don't care. He doesn't know *me*."

She served nine pieces of Shoofly Pie that day. Arranging generous slices on yellow dessert plates, Mattie savored the sight of their crumbled toppings over the rich and creamy molasses interiors. Her mother used to love this pie.

That day no one ordered buttermilk pie, which apparently had been Johnny's specialty before he went away. His pie was still languishing in its full dish when Mattie wiped the counter at three P.M.

"What's *in* that pie of yours?" he asked her.

"Niceness."

260   During the lunch rush, Johnny had ordered Mattie around more rudely than Sergio ever did. But now she knew where Sergio learned it. Johnny snapped commands. *"Sauté! Stir!"* He kept insisting there were granules of raw sugar on the floor under his feet and making Mattie sweep when he had food all laid out.

"That's very unsanitary, Johnny, to sweep in the presence of food. Didn't your mama ever tell you?" Her words seemed to throw him into a funk.

When his weepy ex-girlfriend materialized, pressing her face up close to the kitchen window for what she hoped might be a welcome-home kiss, he tapped her forehead with his fingertips and busied himself. "Any chance we could

270 spend some time together?" she asked wistfully.

"Sharon, you know what I told you."

Tears welled up in her syrupy eyes.

She said, "Johnny, I think I can make you happy," as he slapped dill sauce around a grilled portabello mushroom on polenta. Ouch.

CHARACTER TRAITS
What traits does Mattie reveal in this incident?

The waitress and Augie had been found wrapped in a bubbly embrace in the broom closet that morning when Mattie whipped open the door looking for the mop.

Sergio now had a crush on a buff bodybuilder who came in every morning for a peach smoothie, dressed in a leopard-printed tank top. Even the Hell's 280 Angel who appeared only on Saturdays had slipped Mattie a note that said, "Good muffin, baby," drawn inside a heart.

Only Riyad, dear Riyad, seemed able to focus on food and the work right in front of him. One day after work Mattie had told him about her own Syrian heritage and her mom's death coinciding with his dad's. Did she only imagine it, or did tears well up in his eyes, too?

After that they both threw Arabic words into their talk. *"Yallah!"* Speed it up. *"Khallas!"* Enough already.

Some days Riyad refilled the bins of flour and apricots and sunflower seeds in the grocery section with careful attention. Some days he polished the front 290 window glass till it glittered. Lots of bosses might never lift a finger. One day Mattie found him down on his knees on a prayer rug in the cooler chanting in Arabic. She respected his devotion to service. He told her he had dreamed of owning a restaurant ever since he was a little boy who loved to eat, wandering the streets of Beirut. Only the ten-year war had made him leave his country. Mattie admitted she had trouble with Johnny's attitude. Riyad whispered, "Listen to this: When he first came to work here, he was our baker, not our chef. He asked me, 'Do I get paid while the bread's rising?'"

"Have you been in the service or what?" Mattie asked Johnny, on her forty-fourth day at work. It was truly summer now, each day swelled full of ninety-300 eight-degree heat. Midsummer in Texas, people forget what a cool breeze ever felt like.

"Why do you ask?"

"You act like a general. I think you'd like me to salute you."

"Well, you're full of it, too." ❶

He was furious that she had started revising the soup list. Today she was making a spicy peanut stew from Eritrea[7] with green beans and sweet potatoes.

"Where is Eritrea?" he asked her. "And what makes you think our customers will know of it if I don't?"

"East Africa. The whole world is tired of your black bean soup, Commander. 310 It's time to BRANCH OUT."

Johnny always stared at her as if he needed an interpreter.

Riyad went wild when he smelled that peanut stew cooking. "I want some! When will it be done?"

Mattie told Johnny the customers were also tired of his boring bouquet of alfalfa sprouts on top of his little salads, too. "Let's try lentil sprouts for a change.

❶ **CHARACTER TRAITS**
What trait is Johnny suggesting that Mattie possesses?

---

7. **Eritrea** (ĕr′ĭ-trē′ə): a country in northeast Africa.

Or nasturtiums.[8] Come on." Basically she was weary of watering them. She wanted to witness some different curls of life sprouting in the jars under the counters. Anyhow, an East Indian professor on the other side of town had just gotten E. coli[9] that was traced to alfalfa sprouts, and she felt nervous about them.

320   An anonymous food critic from the newspaper had eaten at the restaurant recently and written a glowing review. "Happy to say the *Good for You* menu offers new sparkle and a delectable, mysterious dessert called Shoofly Pie. Not to be missed." Mattie made three extras that day and they all sold out. A lady bought a whole one for her book club.

    On the tenth of August, Johnny asked Mattie to sit down after work for a cup of mint tea with him.

    "You think you're really clever, don't you?" he said, tapping his spoon on his cup.

    "Not at all," she said, startled. "I certainly don't. In fact, I usually think I'm
330 pretty dumb. It's just that you were used to making all the decisions around here and it's been really hard for you to share them. I don't know why. I certainly wouldn't want to make all the decisions."

    "You wouldn't?"

    "No way. I think sharing them is better."

    "You do, do you?"

    He was staring at the top of her head as if she had two horns erupting.

---

8. **nasturtiums** (nə-stûr′shəmz): a kind of edible flower.

9. **E. coli** (ē kō′lī): bacteria, certain strains of which can cause sickness.

Then he said, "Would you like to go to a movie with me?" and she almost fell over backwards out of her chair. Late afternoon sunlight had suspended in the air. She could smell the warm sweetness of molasses from the pies just out
340 of the oven. ◆ J

"Um—I'm sorry—I can't. It's not a good idea to mix business—and pleasure." She really wasn't much of a dater—now and then she went out with friends in groups, like migrating monarch butterflies, or ducks—but she simply could not imagine going around with this troublesome—chef.

He looked thunderstruck. "Are you serious?"

"Very."

He shrugged. "It was a good movie, too."

"Which one?"

"I'll never tell." Then he hissed, "What—do you just stick around home
350 with your mama after work and learn new recipes?"

Tears rose up in Mattie's eyes. He stared at her.

"My mother," she said, "died right before I started working here. For your information."

"Why didn't you tell me?"

"You weren't here. Plus, when you got back, you weren't very friendly."

One thing about loss—you decided whom to share it with. You could go around day after day and never give anyone a clue about what had been taken from you. You could hold it inside, a precious nugget of pain. Or you could say it out loud. When you trusted enough. When you felt like it. ◆ K
360 "I didn't feel like it."

You could place it on the table.

Johnny spoke softly now. "I'm sorry. But didn't you know I'd just been at my grandpa's funeral myself?"

"Yes."

"And he was like a daddy to me? He raised me when my own daddy took off? And my mama was already gone?"

Now tears shone in Johnny's eyes. It was a restaurant where every single person ended up crying at one time or another. "Well, I didn't know that," Mattie said. "That must have been really—hard."
370 She found herself with her hand on his arm.

"I'm sorry, too," she said. "I know you really loved your grandpa a lot."

He looked up sharply. "You do? How do you know that?"

"Trust me."

So many times during the days he'd mentioned little things his grandpa used to tell him. How to sharpen a knife. How to "swab the decks"—what Johnny called cleaning a counter.

Now he said, "Let me tell you about my grandpa's favorite corn bread," and he described it so deliciously, with raw pieces of fresh corn tucked into it, that Mattie had the idea they should concoct a meal based on beautiful things his
380 grandpa used to cook for him when he was growing up. Greens, corn bread, quick-fried okra, sweet potato casserole, vinegar coleslaw, pecan pie, and, since

◆ GRAMMAR AND STYLE
Reread lines 337–340.
Note how Nye chooses **adjectives** and **verbs** that appeal to the senses of sight, smell, and touch.

◆ CONNECT
Think about the times when you shared grief with others. Why would Mattie only want to share grief with someone she trusts?

their restaurant didn't serve meat, a special vegeburger seasoned with sage, his grandpa's favorite spice. They could do it In Memoriam (privately), but on the board they'd just call it "From Johnny's Grandpa's Special Recipes." **L**

They could even put white daisies on every table because they were his grandpa's favorite flowers.

The menu was so popular, they kept it up there three whole days. As customers were paying, they said, "Johnny, tell your grandpa we loved his food." No one told them he was dead.

390 Then Mattie said, "Okay, Riyad, what did YOUR daddy eat? Your turn."

For three days they served lentil soup, *baba-ghanouj*,[10] okra with rice, and falafel[11] sandwiches.

They played Arabic music in the restaurant.

Riyad seemed deeply emotional about it. He placed his father's dashing young photograph on the register. He gave Johnny and Mattie raises.

Sergio had left them by that time. He'd gone to sell boring used cars over on San Pedro, because he could make three times as much money over there. "But it won't taste as good," Mattie told him. They'd hired a grandmother, Lucy, to take his place. Lucy loved their new recipes as well as their old ones. She said,

400 "Did you know the name 'Shoofly' came about because the Amish people would shoo away the flies that came to land on their cooling pies when they took them out of the oven?"

Johnny said, "We don't have any flies in here. Mattie catches them in her fists the minute she sees them."

Then they did Mattie's mother's recipes. Mattie had a very hard time deciding which ones to do. Her mother had been a great cook, once upon a time, way back in the other world where things were still normal.

The menu board featured a special green salad with oranges and pecans, fragrant vegetable cous-cous with raisins, buttermilk biscuits, and of course,

410 Shoofly Pie for dessert. "I think your mother had a sweet tooth," Riyad said, staring dreamily at the full plates lined up on the counter.

"That she did," said Mattie, swallowing hard. Her mother had had everything: the best singing voice, the kindest heart, the kookiest wardrobe— she never felt shy about combining checks and stripes and wild colors.

Mattie brought in a tape of her mother's favorite blues singer, Lonnie Johnson, to play while they served her food. Mattie's father came over from his office to eat with them.

"This is kind of like that Anne Tyler book, *Dinner at the Homesick Restaurant*," he said. Mattie sat with him. He put his hand over her hand.

420 "What a rough summer, baby."

Mattie said, "It's also like our own private Days of the Dead." On November 2, people in South Texas made shrines to their beloved deceased family members or friends, arranging offerings of their favorite foods among the lit candles and incense.

---

10. *baba-ghanouj* (bä'bə gə-nōōsh'): Middle Eastern eggplant appetizer.

11. *falafel* (fə-lä'fəl): a Middle Eastern dish of fried, pureed chickpeas.

L CONNECT
Think of a favorite dish that a relative or friend has prepared for you. Why might Johnny have chosen to describe his grandfather's corn bread to Mattie at this moment?

"So who's homesick for Shoofly Pie?" asked a diner seated at the next table. "It's great!"

"Everybody," Mattie said. "Everybody who never lived a simple life." In some ways, you could choose what you remembered and what you did with it. Memories you chose to treasure would never fly away. They were like an adhesive stuck to the underside of your heart. Maybe they kept your heart in your body.

Riyad had an idea that they could offer their In Memoriam menus to the general public, too—letting people bring in groups of recipes belonging to someone they had loved who was gone now, and the *Good for You* staff would revise the recipes to become healthier, then serve special meals designated "Camille's Favorite Ratatouille Feast" or "Jim's Special Birthday Dinner" . . . what a thought.

"Is it creepy?" Johnny wondered out loud. "Will people feel like they eat here, then they die?"

"No," Mattie and Riyad said at once. "It's comforting. TRUST US."

"**H**ow do you think an omelette looks better, folded over or simply flipped? Should we slice the small strawberries in the fruit bowls or leave them whole?" Suddenly Johnny was so full of questions, Mattie could barely answer them all. He seemed to have softened somehow, like beans left to soak. **M**

Sometimes when Mattie came in to work, she'd stop for a moment inside the door of the restaurant as if she were frozen. She'd stare all around the room—the tables, the chairs, the paintings, the vege-salt shakers—trying to remember how the place had looked to her before she'd known it from the inside out.

Now she had the recipes memorized, the arrangements of provisions on silver shelves inside the cooler, the little tubs the blueberries lived in. Even in the dreams she could hear the steady *clip-clip* of their best silver knife against the cutting board.

One day she told Johnny she admired his speed when he had ten things to do at once. He grinned at her so he *almost* looked handsome. He said, "Do you ever think how we'll all remember different things when we're old? When this restaurant feels like a far-away shadowy den we once inhabited together—I might remember the glint of the soup tureen in the afternoon light or the scent of comino, and you might remember—the gleam of my ravishing hair?"

"You wish." But she liked him now. She had to admit it. She really liked him.

One day Riyad said, "Everything is changing!" He gave Mattie a poem by Rumi[12] that read, "The mountains are trembling. Their map and compass are the lines in your palm." The first cold norther had swept down from the skies and everyone was wearing sweaters.

M CHARACTER TRAITS
How has Johnny's character softened? Cite details.

---

12. **Rumi** (rōō′mē): a 13th-century Persian mystic and poet.

That was the day she resigned. She had too much work to do at school now to keep on working here. Plus, she was feeling steadier. The restaurant had been Good for Her in all the ways it needed to be, and she could move on. She could cook better dinners for her father at home, with all her new experience. She could have dinner parties for his friends.

470   It shocked her how Johnny responded to the news of her departure. He shook his head and said, "No, no, no, baby," as if she were a little dog at his feet.

"What do you mean, no no no? Yes yes yes! I have homework piling up on me. I have a major paper to do that I haven't even started! My dad and I haven't even cleaned our house since my mom died. I'll miss this place terribly, but hey, I'll still come in and eat! And maybe you'll go to another movie someday and let me tag along, what do you say?"

Johnny stared at her. He'd been making Shoofly Pie on his own lately—good thing, because everyone still ordered it. Riyad and his wife presented Mattie with a mixed bunch of happy-looking flowers and a card: "This is your
480   home now, too!!! We love and appreciate you—free lunch any time!" Johnny kissed her, first time ever, on the top of her right ear. Her mother used to kiss her there. ❧

N STATIC AND DYNAMIC CHARACTERS
Dynamic characters undergo some sort of change as a story unfolds. In what ways has Johnny changed over the course of the story? Cite specific words or details to show this change.

Comprehension

1. **Recall** Why is Mattie grieving?

2. **Recall** Why does Mattie decide to work at the restaurant?

3. **Recall** How does Johnny react when he first meets Mattie?

4. **Summarize** How do Mattie's and Johnny's feelings toward each other change over the course of the story?

OHIO STANDARDS

READING STANDARD
4.1 Compare and contrast an author's use of direct and indirect characterization

Literary Analysis

5. **Compare and Contrast Characters** What character traits do Mattie and Johnny have in common? In what ways are they different? Use a graphic organizer like the one shown to record your answers.

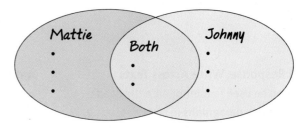

6. **Analyze Characters** A **foil** is a character who provides a striking contrast to another character. How does Riyad serve as a foil to Johnny's character?

7. **Connect** Review the chart you created as you read. How did the connections you made help you understand the effect of **grief** on one or more of the characters? Discuss specific examples in the story.

8. **Analyze Conflict** What incident in the story leads to a resolution of the **conflict,** or struggle, between Mattie and Johnny? Explain your answer.

9. **Draw Conclusions** Reread lines 465–482. Has Mattie gotten over her grief by the end of the story? Cite evidence to support your conclusion.

10. **Evaluate Characterization** Is Mattie a believable character? In your response, consider whether she acts and speaks the way a real person would and whether her relationships and interactions are believable.

Literary Criticism

11. **Author's Style** Nye says she started writing things down in notebooks because she "wanted to remember everything. The quilt, the cherry tree, the creek. The neat whop of a baseball rammed perfectly with a bat." Using examples, explain how Nye's keen eye for detail brings the **setting** and **characters** to life in "Shoofly Pie."

Reading-Writing Connection

Increase your understanding of "Shoofly Pie" by responding to these prompts. Then use **Revision: Grammar and Style** to improve your writing.

WRITING PROMPTS	SELF-CHECK
A. Short Response: Describe Characters Mattie and Johnny often have different approaches to cooking. Write a **one- or two-paragraph description** of them cooking a meal together.	**An evocative description will ...** • use words and phrases that appeal to the readers' senses • include details that suggest character traits
B. Extended Response: Write Across Texts How can food be used to memorialize the dead? Write **three to five paragraphs** in response, using examples from "Shoofly Pie," "A Mexican Feast for Bodies and Souls" (page 185), and your own experiences, if relevant.	**A successful response will ...** • clearly explain how food can honor the dead and comfort the living • provide examples from the story, the article, and relevant experiences

REVISION: GRAMMAR AND STYLE

ADD SENSORY DETAILS Review the **Grammar and Style** note on page 179. You can appeal to your readers' senses, as Nye does, by carefully choosing **adjectives** and **verbs** that reflect what the characters see, hear, smell, touch, and taste. Here are two examples from the story.

> *Have you ever watched a gallon of honey ooze into a slow-motion golden dance around a mound of broken glass?* (lines 2–4)

> *Arranging generous slices on yellow dessert plates, Mattie savored the sight of their crumbled toppings over the rich and creamy molasses interiors.* (lines 252–254)

Notice how the revisions in red create stronger sensory images in this first draft. Revise your responses to the prompts by using similar techniques.

 OHIO STANDARDS

WRITING STANDARD
5.9 Use sensory details

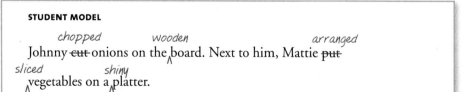

STUDENT MODEL

      chopped   *wooden*   *arranged*

Johnny ~~cut~~ onions on the board. Next to him, Mattie ~~put~~

sliced   *shiny*

vegetables on a platter.

WRITING TOOLS

For prewriting, revision, and editing tools, visit the **Writing Center** at **ClassZone.com**.

NEWSPAPER ARTICLE In "Shoofly Pie," characters base menus on the favorite dishes of deceased loved ones. Connecting with the dead through food is an old Mexican tradition observed during the Day of the Dead holiday.

A Mexican Feast for Bodies and Souls

Dave Roos

Pan de muertos

Sometimes the smell of a steaming, freshly corn-husked tamale is enticing enough to wake the dead.

This time of year, in the mountainous Lake Pátzcuaro region of the Mexican state of Michoacán, villagers prepare a feast for their deceased as part of the annual Day of the Dead celebrations. From the end of October through early November, families dedicate ofrendas (home altars) to the recently departed, setting a lavishly adorned table with the loved one's favorite foods.

In this part of central Mexico, the table is crowded with indigenous classics like corundas, pyramidal tamales filled with salty cheese and poblano pepper; and churipo, a slow-simmered meat and vegetable stew in a ruddy broth of blended chilies, as well as more modern dishes like the regional staple sopa tarasca and the ubiquitous Day of the Dead treat, pan de muertos.

People here believe that the dead are guided by the alluring odors of their favorite foods during the long journey back from the world beyond. Once they arrive, they will share a meal with the living during an all-night vigil in the town cemetery.

The Day of the Dead is not Mexico's answer to Halloween, nor is it a Latin-American interpretation of All Saints' Day. Like Mexican food, itself a complex blend of indigenous and Spanish influences, the Day of the Dead is an inextricable mix of pre-Hispanic spiritualism and post-conquest Roman Catholicism. . . .

The ancient, soul-satisfying taste of slow-steamed corn tamale is the flavor of Pátzcuaro, and the best tamales are prepared by the Purhépecha peasants who commute daily from outlying villages to stock the town's bustling food market and sell handmade crafts in street-side stalls. . . .

If there is one food associated exclusively with the Day of the Dead—not only in Pátzcuaro, but all over Mexico—it is pan de muertos, a moist, eggy cake-bread generously coated with butter and sugar.

Alejandro Rivera Torres, the owner of RivePan bakery in Pátzcuaro, said he bakes and sells thousands of loaves of pan de muertos every season, in the traditional round shape with decorative "bones" or in the form of muertitos, little dead people flecked with pink sugar.

On a chilly November night in the pine mountains of Michoacán, a sweet slice of pan de muertos and a steaming cup of atole—a corn masa drink flavored with cinnamon, vanilla, or many types of fruit—do wonders to warm the souls of the living as they huddle all night in the cemetery sharing favorite traditional foods and fond memories with the spirits of their ancestors. . . .

The Possibility of Evil
Short Story by Shirley Jackson

How good are you at
JUDGING *people?*

OHIO STANDARDS

READING STANDARDS
2.1 Make inferences

4.1 Compare and contrast an author's use of direct and indirect characterization

KEY IDEA The main character in "The Possibility of Evil" believes she can read into the hearts of those around her. Do you think it is so easy to judge people? Are you confident that you would recognize **evil** if you came face to face with it?

DISCUSS With a group, fill in a description wheel for the word *evil*. Then use the ideas you have brainstormed to create a definition of the word.

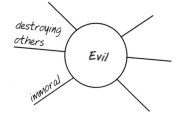

LITERARY ANALYSIS: CHARACTER MOTIVATION

One way of learning about a character is to consider his or her **motivation**—the reasons behind the character's actions. For example, a father in "The Possibility of Evil" forbids a boy to visit his daughter because he believes the boy is immoral. Writers usually do not directly state a character's motivation. Instead, readers often must figure out motivation by thinking about

- the character's words, thoughts, and actions
- how other characters react to him or her

As you read "The Possibility of Evil," think about what motivates Miss Strangeworth's behavior.

READING SKILL: MAKE INFERENCES

When you **make inferences** about a character, you apply your knowledge of human behavior to clues provided in the text. For example, if a character crosses to the other side of the street as another character approaches, you may infer that he or she doesn't like the other character.

As you read "The Possibility of Evil," note details that help you make inferences about the thoughts and feelings of characters. Use a diagram like the one shown here.

Details from Story	Inferences
After Tommy began working at the grocery, Miss Strangeworth called him Mr. Lewis.	She no longer thinks of Mr. Lewis as her friend or equal.

Review: **Evaluate, Predict**

▲ VOCABULARY IN CONTEXT

Figure out the meaning of each boldfaced word from the context provided. Write a sentence that shows your understanding of each word.

1. **infatuated** with the hero of the novel
2. stared with **rapt** attention
3. a decision that isn't **negotiable**
4. **degraded** by trouble-seeking friends
5. could almost see through the **translucent** bowl
6. a **reprehensible** act that deserves punishment

Author Online

Shirley Jackson
1919–1965

Horrifying Debut
Shirley Jackson established her reputation with her story "The Lottery," a chilling tale set in a quiet New England town. After the story was published in the *New Yorker* in 1948, outraged readers bombarded the magazine with letters and requests to cancel their subscriptions. Today, the story is considered a classic of gothic horror. The story's central premise, that ordinary humans are capable of great evil, became a recurring theme in Jackson's writing.

Sinister Small Towns "The Possibility of Evil" and many of Jackson's other stories are set in small American towns that seem peaceful and friendly until their darker sides are revealed. Jackson herself experienced hostility in the small town where she lived, especially after she began publishing fiction. Her biographer, Judy Oppenheimer, wrote that "the idea of people talking about her, judging her, not just her work, made her extremely anxious. Shirley liked her privacy. She wanted to live anonymously in a small town, sending out her fearful disturbing messages to the rest of the world, without consequences."

Fear as a Tool Jackson frequently suffered from panic attacks. Writing was one means of combating this condition. She once said, "I have always loved to use fear. To take it and make it work."

 MORE ABOUT THE AUTHOR
For more on Shirley Jackson, visit the **Literature Center** at ClassZone.com.

THE POSSIBILITY

of

Evil

SHIRLEY JACKSON

Miss Adela Strangeworth stepped daintily along Main Street on her way to the grocery. The sun was shining, the air was fresh and clear after the night's heavy rain, and everything in Miss Strangeworth's little town looked washed and bright. Miss Strangeworth took deep breaths, and thought that there was nothing in the world like a fragrant summer day.

She knew everyone in town, of course; she was fond of telling strangers—tourists who sometimes passed through the town and stopped to admire Miss Strangeworth's roses—that she had never spent more than a day outside this town in all her long life. She was seventy-one, Miss Strangeworth told the
10 tourists, with a pretty little dimple showing by her lip, and she sometimes found herself thinking that the town belonged to her. "My grandfather built the first house on Pleasant Street," she would say, opening her blue eyes wide with the wonder of it. "This house, right here. My family has lived here for better than a hundred years. My grandmother planted these roses, and my mother tended them, just as I do. I've watched my town grow; I can remember when Mr. Lewis, Senior, opened the grocery store, and the year the river flooded out the shanties[1] on the low road, and the excitement when some young folks wanted to move the park over to the space in front of where the new post office is today. They wanted to put up a statue of Ethan Allen"[2]—
20 Miss Strangeworth would frown a little and sound stern—"but it should have been a statue of my grandfather. There wouldn't have been a town here at all if it hadn't been for my grandfather and the lumber mill." **A**

ANALYZE VISUALS
Examine the portrait. What impression do you have of the woman shown? Which **details** helped you form this impression?

A MAKE INFERENCES
How does Miss Strangeworth feel about the contribution her family has made to the town?

---

1. **shanties** (shăn'tēz): roughly built cabins; shacks.
2. **Ethan Allen:** a Revolutionary War hero who led a group of soldiers, called the Green Mountain Boys, from what is now Vermont.

Michele Warner/Illustration Works/
Getty Images.

Miss Strangeworth never gave away any of her roses, although the tourists often asked her. The roses belonged on Pleasant Street, and it bothered Miss Strangeworth to think of people wanting to carry them away, to take them into strange towns and down strange streets. When the new minister came, and the ladies were gathering flowers to decorate the church, Miss Strangeworth sent over a great basket of gladioli; when she picked the roses at all, she set them in bowls and vases around the inside of the house her grandfather had built.

30   Walking down Main Street on a summer morning, Miss Strangeworth had to stop every minute or so to say good morning to someone or to ask after someone's health. When she came into the grocery, half a dozen people turned away from the shelves and the counters to wave at her or call out good morning. **B**

    "And good morning to you, too, Mr. Lewis," Miss Strangeworth said at last. The Lewis family had been in the town almost as long as the Strangeworths; but the day young Lewis left high school and went to work in the grocery, Miss Strangeworth had stopped calling him Tommy and started calling him Mr. Lewis, and he had stopped calling her Addie and started calling her Miss
40 Strangeworth. They had been in high school together, and had gone to picnics together, and to high school dances and basketball games; but now Mr. Lewis was behind the counter in the grocery, and Miss Strangeworth was living alone in the Strangeworth house on Pleasant Street.

    "Good morning," Mr. Lewis said, and added politely, "lovely day."

    "It is a very nice day," Miss Strangeworth said as though she had only just decided that it would do after all. "I would like a chop, please, Mr. Lewis, a small, lean veal chop. Are those strawberries from Arthur Parker's garden? They're early this year."

    "He brought them in this morning," Mr. Lewis said.

50   "I shall have a box," Miss Strangeworth said. Mr. Lewis looked worried, she thought, and for a minute she hesitated, but then she decided that he surely could not be worried over the strawberries. He looked very tired indeed. He was usually so chipper, Miss Strangeworth thought, and almost commented, but it was far too personal a subject to be introduced to Mr. Lewis, the grocer, so she only said, "And a can of cat food and, I think, a tomato."

    Silently, Mr. Lewis assembled her order on the counter and waited. Miss Strangeworth looked at him curiously and then said, "It's Tuesday, Mr. Lewis. You forgot to remind me."

    "Did I? Sorry."

60   "Imagine your forgetting that I always buy my tea on Tuesday," Miss Strangeworth said gently. "A quarter pound of tea, please, Mr. Lewis."

    "Is that all, Miss Strangeworth?"

    "Yes thank you, Mr. Lewis. Such a lovely day, isn't it?"

    "Lovely," Mr. Lewis said.

    Miss Strangeworth moved slightly to make room for Mrs. Harper at the counter. "Morning, Adela," Mrs. Harper said, and Miss Strangeworth said, "Good morning, Martha."

B CHARACTER MOTIVATION
Why does Miss Strangeworth take time to greet so many people?

"Lovely day," Mrs. Harper said, and Miss Strangeworth said, "Yes, lovely," and Mr. Lewis, under Mrs. Harper's glance, nodded.

70   "Ran out of sugar for my cake frosting," Mrs. Harper explained. Her hand shook slightly as she opened her pocketbook. Miss Strangeworth wondered, glancing at her quickly, if she had been taking proper care of herself. Martha Harper was not as young as she used to be, Miss Strangeworth thought. She probably could use a good, strong tonic.[3]

    "Martha," she said, "you don't look well."

    "I'm perfectly all right," Mrs. Harper said shortly. She handed her money to Mr. Lewis, took her change and her sugar, and went out without speaking again. Looking after her, Miss Strangeworth shook her head slightly. Martha definitely did *not* look well. **C**

80   Carrying her little bag of groceries, Miss Strangeworth came out of the store into the bright sunlight and stopped to smile down on the Crane baby. Don and Helen Crane were really the two most **infatuated** young parents she had ever known, she thought indulgently, looking at the delicately embroidered baby cap and the lace-edged carriage cover.

    "That little girl is going to grow up expecting luxury all her life," she said to Helen Crane.

C MAKE INFERENCES
What can you infer from the way Mrs. Harper reacts to Miss Strangeworth's comment?

infatuated
(ĭn-făch′ōō-ā′tĭd) *adj.*
intensely fond

---

3. **tonic:** a medicine for restoring and energizing the body.

Helen laughed. "That's the way we want her to feel," she said. "Like a princess."

"A princess can be a lot of trouble sometimes," Miss Strangeworth said
90 dryly. "How old is her highness now?"

"Six months next Tuesday," Helen Crane said, looking down with **rapt** wonder at her child. "I've been worrying, though, about her. Don't you think she ought to move around more? Try to sit up, for instance?"

"For plain and fancy⁴ worrying," Miss Strangeworth said, amused, "give me a new mother every time."

"She just seems—slow," Helen Crane said.

"Nonsense. All babies are different. Some of them develop much more quickly than others."

"That's what my mother says." Helen Crane laughed, looking a little bit
100 ashamed.

"I suppose you've got young Don all upset about the fact that his daughter is already six months old and hasn't yet begun to learn to dance?"

"I haven't mentioned it to him. I suppose she's just so precious that I worry about her all the time."

"Well, apologize to her right now," Miss Strangeworth said. "*She* is probably worrying about why you keep jumping around all the time." Smiling to herself and shaking her old head, she went on down the sunny street, stopping once to ask little Billy Moore why he wasn't out riding in his daddy's shiny new car, and talking for a few minutes outside the library with Miss Chandler,
110 the librarian, about the new novels to be ordered, and paid for by the annual library appropriation. Miss Chandler seemed absentminded and very much as though she were thinking about something else. Miss Strangeworth noticed that Miss Chandler had not taken much trouble with her hair that morning, and sighed. Miss Strangeworth hated sloppiness. **D**

Many people seemed disturbed recently, Miss Strangeworth thought. Only yesterday the Stewarts' fifteen-year-old Linda had run crying down her own front walk and all the way to school, not caring who saw her. People around town thought she might have had a fight with the Harris boy, but they showed up together at the soda shop after school as usual, both of them looking grim
120 and bleak. Trouble at home, people concluded, and sighed over the problems of trying to raise kids right these days.

From halfway down the block Miss Strangeworth could catch the heavy scent of her roses, and she moved a little more quickly. The perfume of roses meant home, and home meant the Strangeworth House on Pleasant Street. Miss Strangeworth stopped at her own front gate, as she always did, and looked with deep pleasure at her house, with the red and pink and white roses massed along the narrow lawn, and the rambler⁵ going up along the porch; and the neat, the unbelievably trim lines of the house itself, with its slimness and its washed white look. Every window sparkled, every curtain hung stiff

---

4. **plain and fancy:** every kind of.
5. **rambler:** a rose plant that grows upward like a vine, by clinging to a support.

rapt (răpt) *adj.* fully absorbed; entranced

D EVALUATE
Reread lines 90–114. Does Miss Strangeworth seem like a reasonable person? Explain your answer.

130 and straight, and even the stones of the front walk were swept and clear. ◆Ⓔ

People around town wondered how old Miss Strangeworth managed to keep the house looking the way it did, and there was a legend about a tourist once mistaking it for the local museum and going all through the place without finding out about his mistake. But the town was proud of Miss Strangeworth and her roses and her house. They had all grown together.

Miss Strangeworth went up her front steps, unlocked her front door with her key, and went into the kitchen to put away her groceries. She debated having a cup of tea and then decided that it was too close to midday dinnertime; she would not have the appetite for her little chop if she had tea 140 now. Instead she went into the light, lovely sitting room, which still glowed from the hands of her mother and her grandmother, who had covered the chairs with bright chintz[6] and hung the curtains. All the furniture was spare and shining, and the round hooked rugs on the floor had been the work of Miss Strangeworth's grandmother and her mother. Miss Strangeworth had put a bowl of her red roses on the low table before the window, and the room was full of their scent.

Miss Strangeworth went to the narrow desk in the corner, and unlocked it with her key. She never knew when she might feel like writing letters, so she kept her notepaper inside, and the desk locked. Miss Strangeworth's 150 usual stationery was heavy and cream-colored, with "Strangeworth House"

---

6. **chintz:** a colorful printed cotton fabric.

Ⓔ GRAMMAR AND STYLE
Reread lines 125–130. Notice how the author uses **modifiers** such as *red, pink,* and *white* and *unbelievably trim* to vividly describe the house and its surroundings.

ANALYZE VISUALS
Which details in this painting fit Jackson's description of the story's **setting?**

The House with Roses (1936), Henri Le Sidaner. Oil on canvas. Private Collection. Photo © Visual Arts Library/Art Resource, New York.

engraved across the top, but, when she felt like writing her other letters, Miss Strangeworth used a pad of various-colored paper, bought from the local newspaper shop. It was almost a town joke, that colored paper, layered in pink and green and blue and yellow; everyone in town bought it and used it for odd, informal notes and shopping lists. It was usual to remark, upon receiving a note written on a blue page, that so-and-so would be needing a new pad soon—here she was, down to the blue already. Everyone used the matching envelopes for tucking away recipes, or keeping odd little things in, or even to hold cookies in the school lunch boxes. Mr. Lewis sometimes gave them to
160 the children for carrying home penny candy.

Although Miss Strangeworth's desk held a trimmed quill pen, which had belonged to her grandfather, and a gold-frost fountain pen, which had belonged to her father, Miss Strangeworth always used a dull stub of pencil when she wrote her letters, and she printed them in a childish block print. After thinking for a minute, although she had been phrasing the letter in the back of her mind all the way home, she wrote on a pink sheet: DIDN'T YOU EVER SEE AN IDIOT CHILD BEFORE? SOME PEOPLE JUST SHOULDN'T HAVE CHILDREN, SHOULD THEY?

She was pleased with the letter. She was fond of doing things exactly right.
170 When she made a mistake, as she sometimes did, or when the letters were not spaced nicely on the page, she had to take the discarded page to the kitchen stove and burn it at once. Miss Strangeworth never delayed when things had to be done.

After thinking for a minute, she decided that she would like to write another letter, perhaps to go to Mrs. Harper, to follow up the ones she had already mailed. She selected a green sheet this time and wrote quickly: HAVE YOU FOUND OUT YET WHAT THEY WERE ALL LAUGHING ABOUT AFTER YOU LEFT THE BRIDGE CLUB ON THURSDAY? OR IS THE WIFE REALLY ALWAYS THE LAST ONE TO KNOW? **F**

180 Miss Strangeworth never concerned herself with facts; her letters all dealt with the more **negotiable** stuff of suspicion. Mr. Lewis would never have imagined for a minute that his grandson might be lifting petty cash[7] from the store register if he had not had one of Miss Strangeworth's letters. Miss Chandler, the librarian, and Linda Stewart's parents would have gone unsuspectingly ahead with their lives, never aware of possible evil lurking nearby, if Miss Strangeworth had not sent letters to open their eyes. Miss Strangeworth would have been genuinely shocked if there *had* been anything between Linda Stewart and the Harris boy, but, as long as evil existed unchecked in the world, it was Miss Strangeworth's duty to keep her town
190 alert to it. It was far more sensible for Miss Chandler to wonder what Mr. Shelley's first wife had really died of than to take a chance on not knowing. There were so many wicked people in the world and only one Strangeworth left in town. Besides, Miss Strangeworth liked writing her letters. **G**

F MAKE INFERENCES
What is Miss Strangeworth suggesting in this letter to Mrs. Harper?

negotiable
(nĭ-gō'shə-bəl) *adj.* able to be bargained with

G CHARACTER MOTIVATION
What two motives for writing the letters are revealed in lines 180–193?

---

7. **petty cash:** a small fund of money kept handy for miscellaneous expenses.

She addressed an envelope to Don Crane after a moment's thought, wondering curiously if he would show the letter to his wife, and using a pink envelope to match the pink paper. Then she addressed a second envelope, green, to Mrs. Harper. Then an idea came to her and she selected a blue sheet and wrote: YOU NEVER KNOW ABOUT DOCTORS. REMEMBER THEY'RE ONLY HUMAN AND NEED MONEY LIKE THE REST
200 OF US. SUPPOSE THE KNIFE SLIPPED ACCIDENTALLY. WOULD DOCTOR BURNS GET HIS FEE AND A LITTLE EXTRA FROM THAT NEPHEW OF YOURS?

She addressed the blue envelope to old Mrs. Foster, who was having an operation next month. She had thought of writing one more letter, to the head of the school board, asking how a chemistry teacher like Billy Moore's father could afford a new convertible, but all at once she was tired of writing letters. The three she had done would do for one day. She could write more tomorrow; it was not as though they all had to be done at once.

She had been writing her letters—sometimes two or three every day for a
210 week, sometimes no more than one in a month—for the past year. She never got any answers, of course, because she never signed her name. If she had been asked, she would have said that her name, Adela Strangeworth, a name honored in the town for so many years, did not belong on such trash. The town where she lived had to be kept clean and sweet, but people everywhere were lustful and evil and **degraded,** and needed to be watched; the world was so large, and there was only one Strangeworth left in it. Miss Strangeworth sighed, locked her desk, and put the letters into her big, black leather pocketbook, to be mailed when she took her evening walk.

degraded (dǐ-grā′dǐd) *adj.* corrupted, depraved

Mailboxes & Cosmos, Carl Schmalz, W.H.S. Watercolor. Courtesy of the artist.

She broiled her little chop nicely, and had a sliced tomato and good cup of
220 tea ready when she sat down to her midday dinner at the table in her dining
room, which could be opened to seat twenty-two, with a second table, if
necessary, in the hall. Sitting in the warm sunlight that came through the tall
windows of the dining room, seeing her roses massed outside, handling the
heavy, old silverware and the fine, **translucent** china, Miss Strangeworth was
pleased; she would not have cared to be doing anything else. People must live
graciously, after all, she thought, and sipped her tea. Afterward, when her
plate and cup and saucer were washed and dried and put back onto the shelves
where they belonged, and her silverware was back in the mahogany silver chest,
Miss Strangeworth went up the graceful staircase and into her bedroom, which
230 was the front room overlooking the
roses, and had been her mother's
and her grandmother's. Their
Crown Derby dresser set[8] and furs
had been kept here, their fans and
silver-backed brushes and their own
bowls of roses; Miss Strangeworth
kept a bowl of white roses on the
bed table.

    She drew the shades, took the
240 rose-satin spread from the bed,
slipped out of her dress and her
shoes, and lay down tiredly. She
knew that no doorbell or phone
would ring; no one in town would
dare to disturb Miss Strangeworth
during her afternoon nap. She slept,
deep in the rich smell of roses.

    After her nap she worked in her garden for a little while, sparing herself
because of the heat; then she came in to her supper. She ate asparagus from
250 her own garden, with sweet-butter sauce, and a soft-boiled egg, and, while
she had her supper, she listened to a late-evening news broadcast and then
to a program of classical music on her small radio. After her dishes were
done and her kitchen set in order, she took up her hat—Miss Strangeworth's
hats were proverbial in the town; people believed that she had inherited
them from her mother and her grandmother—and, locking the front door
of her house behind her, set off on her evening walk, pocketbook under her
arm. She nodded to Linda Stewart's father, who was washing his car in the
pleasantly cool evening. She thought that he looked troubled. **H**

    There was only one place in town where she could mail her letters, and
260 that was the new post office, shiny with red brick and silver letters. Although
Miss Strangeworth had never given the matter any particular thought, she had

translucent
(trăns-lōō′sənt) *adj.*
allowing light to shine
through

H MAKE INFERENCES
Why would Miss
Strangeworth be
interested in whether
Linda Stewart's father
looked troubled?

---

8. **Crown Derby dresser set:** a hairbrush, comb, and hand mirror made of fine china.

always made a point of mailing her letters very secretly; it would, of course, not have been wise to let anyone see her mail them. Consequently, she timed her walk so she could reach the post office just as darkness was starting to dim the outlines of the trees and the shapes of people's faces, although no one could ever mistake Miss Strangeworth, with her dainty walk and her rustling skirts.

There was always a group of young people around the post office, the very youngest roller-skating upon its driveway, which went all the way around the building and was the only smooth road in town; and the slightly older
270 ones already knowing how to gather in small groups and chatter and laugh and make great, excited plans for going across the street to the soda shop in a minute or two. Miss Strangeworth had never had any self-consciousness before the children. She did not feel that any of them were staring at her unduly or longing to laugh at her; it would have been most **reprehensible** for their parents to permit their children to mock Miss Strangeworth of Pleasant Street. Most of the children stood back respectfully as Miss Strangeworth passed, silenced briefly in her presence, and some of the older children greeted her, saying soberly, "Hello, Miss Strangeworth."

Miss Strangeworth smiled at them and quickly went on. It had been a long
280 time since she had known the name of every child in town. The mail slot was in the door of the post office. The children stood away as Miss Strangeworth approached it, seemingly surprised that anyone should want to use the post office after it had been officially closed up for the night and turned over to the children. Miss Strangeworth stood by the door, opening her black pocketbook to take out the letters, and heard a voice which she knew at once to be Linda Stewart's. Poor little Linda was crying again, and Miss Strangeworth listened carefully. This was, after all, her town, and these were her people; if one of them was in trouble, she ought to know about it.

"I can't tell you, Dave," Linda was saying—so she *was* talking to the Harris
290 boy, as Miss Strangeworth had supposed—"I just *can't*. It's just *nasty*."

"But why won't your father let me come around anymore? What on earth did I do?"

"I can't tell you. I just wouldn't tell you for *any*thing. You've got to have a dirty dirty mind for things like that."

"But something's happened. You've been crying and crying, and your father is all upset. Why can't *I* know about it, too? Aren't I like one of the family?"

"Not anymore, Dave, not anymore. You're not to come near our house again; my father said so. He said he'd horsewhip you. That's all I can tell you: You're not to come near our house anymore."
300 "But I didn't *do* anything."

"Just the same, my father said . . ."

Miss Strangeworth sighed and turned away. There was so much evil in people. Even in a charming little town like this one, there was still so much evil in people. ❶

She slipped her letters into the slot, and two of them fell inside. The third caught on the edge and fell outside, onto the ground at Miss Strangeworth's

reprehensible
(rĕp′rĭ-hĕn′sə-bəl) *adj.* deserving blame and criticism

❶ MAKE INFERENCES
How does Miss Strangeworth feel about the trouble she has caused Linda and Dave? Explain your answer.

feet. She did not notice it because she was wondering whether a letter to the Harris boy's father might not be of some service in wiping out this potential badness. Wearily Miss Strangeworth turned to go home to her quiet bed in her lovely house, and never heard the Harris boy calling to her to say that she had dropped something. **J**

J PREDICT
What do you predict will happen because Miss Strangeworth failed to notice that she dropped the letter?

"Old lady Strangeworth's getting deaf," he said, looking after her and holding in his hand the letter he had picked up.

"Well, who cares?" Linda said. "Who cares anymore, anyway?"

"It's for Don Crane," the Harris boy said, "this letter. She dropped a letter addressed to Don Crane. Might as well take it on over. We pass his house anyway." He laughed. "Maybe it's got a check or something in it and he'd be just as glad to get it tonight instead of tomorrow."

"Catch old lady Strangeworth sending anybody a check," Linda said. "Throw it in the post office. Why do anyone a favor?" She sniffed. "Doesn't seem to me anybody around here cares about us," she said. "Why should we care about them?"

"I'll take it over, anyway," the Harris boy said. "Maybe it's good news for them. Maybe they need something happy tonight, too. Like us."

Sadly, holding hands, they wandered off down the dark street, the Harris boy carrying Miss Strangeworth's pink envelope in his hand.

Miss Strangeworth awakened the next morning with a feeling of intense happiness and, for a minute, wondered why, and then remembered that this morning three people would open her letters. Harsh, perhaps, at first, but wickedness was never easily banished, and a clean heart was a scoured heart. She washed her soft, old face and brushed her teeth, still sound in spite of her seventy-one years, and dressed herself carefully in her sweet, soft clothes and buttoned shoes. Then, going downstairs, reflecting that perhaps a little waffle would be agreeable for breakfast in the sunny dining room, she found the mail on the hall floor, and bent to pick it up. A bill, the morning paper, a letter in a green envelope that looked oddly familiar. Miss Strangeworth stood perfectly still for a minute, looking down at the green envelope with the penciled printing, and thought: It looks like one of my letters. Was one of my letters sent back? No, because no one would know where to send it. How did this get here?

Miss Strangeworth was a Strangeworth of Pleasant Street. Her hand did not shake as she opened the envelope and unfolded the sheet of green paper inside. She began to cry silently for the wickedness of the world when she read the words: LOOK OUT AT WHAT USED TO BE YOUR ROSES. ❧

Comprehension

1. **Recall** What is Miss Strangeworth's reputation in town?

2. **Recall** How does she secretly warn people of "possible evil"?

3. **Recall** How is her secret activity discovered?

4. **Paraphrase** What is Miss Strangeworth's view of human nature?

Literary Analysis

5. **Make Inferences** Review the chart you created as you read. Does Miss Strangeworth seem to understand the harm she is causing? Cite evidence to support your answer.

6. **Analyze Irony** Reread lines 219–238. Explain the irony, or the contrast between appearance and reality, in Miss Strangeworth's insistence upon living "graciously."

7. **Draw Conclusions About Motivation** The narrator offers more than one reason for Miss Strangeworth's secret activity. What would you conclude is her main motivation for writing the letters? Use a graphic organizer like the one shown to record your answer.

Evidence from Text	My Own Knowledge and Experience	Conclusion

8. **Evaluate** Is the punishment that Miss Strangeworth receives at the end of the story appropriate? Explain why or why not.

9. **Predict** How will Miss Strangeworth's life in the town be different after her secret is discovered?

10. **Make Judgments About a Character** Review the definition you created for the word *evil* on page 186. Is Miss Strangeworth an evil person? Support your opinion with evidence from the text.

Literary Criticism

11. **Social Context** Shirley Jackson's husband, the literary critic Stanley Edgar Hyman, said that her dark tales are not just expressions of her private fears but are "fitting symbols for our distressing world." What social or political issues are reflected in "The Possibility of Evil"? Use examples from the story in your response.

OHIO STANDARDS

READING STANDARD
4.1 Compare and contrast an author's use of direct and indirect characterization

Vocabulary in Context

VOCABULARY PRACTICE

Choose the letter of the word that is most different in meaning from the others.

1. (a) disinterested, (b) infatuated, (c) lovesick, (d) smitten
2. (a) rapt, (b) inattentive, (c) absorbed, (d) immersed
3. (a) negotiable, (b) certain, (c) indisputable, (d) inarguable
4. (a) uplifted, (b) elevated, (c) honored, (d) degraded
5. (a) clear, (b) translucent, (c) dense, (d) transparent
6. (a) reprehensible, (b) admirable, (c) respectable, (d) praiseworthy

WORD LIST
degraded
infatuated
negotiable
rapt
reprehensible
translucent

VOCABULARY IN WRITING

Using at least three vocabulary words, write a newspaper editorial about Miss Strangeworth's secret letters. Here is a sample sentence:

> **EXAMPLE SENTENCE**
>
> *Our town was so **infatuated** with Miss Strangeworth's distinguished heritage that we failed to see her true nature.*

VOCABULARY STRATEGY: CONNOTATION AND DENOTATION

A word's **denotation** is its basic dictionary meaning; its **connotation** is the overtones of meaning that it may take on. For example, the vocabulary word *infatuated* means "intensely fond," but it has connotations of an almost foolish obsession that *adoring* does not have. When you choose words in writing, be sure to consider whether their connotations fit the context.

PRACTICE Choose the word that works best in each sentence.

1. The (infatuated/adoring) fans devoted their entire lives to their favorite movie star.
2. Pay (close/rapt) attention to what I am saying!
3. A (reprehensible/blameworthy) crime should be swiftly punished.
4. This issue is not a (negotiable/bargainable) one.
5. The politicians became (degraded/corrupted) by greed.

OHIO STANDARDS

VOCABULARY STANDARD
1.2 Analyze the relationships of pairs of words

VOCABULARY PRACTICE
For more practice, go to the **Vocabulary Center** at ClassZone.com.

Reading-Writing Connection

Enhance your understanding of "The Possibility of Evil" by responding to these prompts. Then use **Revision: Grammar and Style** to improve your writing.

WRITING PROMPTS	SELF-CHECK
A. Short Response: Analyze Characters Has Miss Strangeworth lost her sanity? Is she truly **evil?** Using evidence from the text, write **one or two paragraphs** in response to these questions.	*A strong analysis will . . .* • clearly state an opinion • provide evidence from the story to support your conclusion
B. Extended Response: Write a Scene Write a **three-to-five-paragraph scene** in which Miss Strangeworth goes out into her garden and sees what happened to her roses at the end of the story.	*An effective scene will . . .* • vividly describe the setting • show Miss Strangeworth's emotional response to the destruction

REVISION: GRAMMAR AND STYLE

SET THE SCENE Review the **Grammar and Style** note on page 193. Shirley Jackson uses **modifiers,** words or groups of words that change or limit the meaning of other words, to precisely depict the details of a scene. Adjectives and adverbs, along with phrases and clauses, are examples of modifiers. Use modifiers to add descriptive details that draw the reader into a scene, as Jackson does in the following example:

> *Sitting in the warm sunlight that came through the tall windows of the dining room, seeing her roses massed outside, handling the heavy, old silverware and the fine, translucent china, Miss Strangeworth was pleased. . . .* (lines 222–225)

Notice how the revisions in red help describe a scene more precisely. Revise your draft of Prompt B by adding modifiers.

OHIO STANDARDS

WRITING STANDARD
5.9 Use colorful modifiers

STUDENT MODEL

Miss Strangeworth held her breath as she _{slowly} opened the _{front} door. When she looked at her _{cherished} garden, she saw a row of _{headless, thorny} stems sticking up from the ground. She cried out _{fiercely}.

WRITING TOOLS

For prewriting, revision, and editing tools, visit the **Writing Center** at ClassZone.com.

Like the Sun

Short Story by R. K. Narayan

How important is telling the TRUTH?

OHIO STANDARDS

READING STANDARDS
2.1 Make predictions

4.3 Distinguish how conflicts, parallel plots and subplots affect the story

KEY IDEA We all know that honesty is the best policy. But sometimes the **truth** hurts people's feelings. In "Like the Sun," a schoolteacher is determined to be honest, even if it puts a strain on his relationships.

QUICKWRITE In a brief letter to an advice columnist, describe a situation in which telling the truth would have painful consequences. Then exchange letters with a partner and write a response to your partner's letter.

● LITERARY ANALYSIS: CHARACTER AND PLOT

Although you may focus only on **character** or **plot** when analyzing fiction, these two literary elements are closely related. As characters interact with each other, conflict develops and the plot moves forward. The conflict may occur because the characters have different goals or because their traits are incompatible. To understand the relationship between character and plot, think about

- how the traits and goals of one character can lead to conflicting with another character
- what conflict reveals about characters

In "Like the Sun," the main character decides that for one day he will only tell the truth. As you read, notice how his decision creates conflict as he interacts with other characters.

● READING STRATEGY: PREDICT

While reading a story, have you ever **predicted** that it would have a happy ending or that a character would get into trouble? When you make predictions, you guess what will happen in a story by using text clues and your own knowledge and experience. Even if your guesses turn out to be wrong, the process of making predictions can help you pay attention to important details.

As you read "Like the Sun," make predictions about the consequences of the main character's decision to always tell the truth. Use a chart like the one shown.

Event	Prediction	Outcome
Sekhar's wife serves him breakfast.	He will criticize her cooking and hurt her feelings.	She winces after he says the food isn't good.

Author Online

R. K. Narayan
1906–2001

Love of English Born in southern India, R. K. Narayan (nä-rä′yän) is widely considered one of his country's greatest authors. As a young man, Narayan tried his hand at several professions, including teaching. When he decided to become a fiction writer in the 1930s, he chose to write in English, which was unusual for Indian writers at the time. In an interview Narayan noted, "I was never aware that I was using a different, a foreign, language when I wrote in English, because it came to me very easily. . . . And it's so transparent it can take on the tint of any country."

One Setting Fits All Narayan set most of his novels and short stories in the fictional town of Malgudi, which was based in part on the place where he grew up. He created Malgudi for his first novel, *Swami and Friends* (1935). "As I sat in a room nibbling my pen and wondering what to write," he recalled, "Malgudi with its little railroad station swam into view."

Background

School Life in India Sekhar, the main character in "Like the Sun," is a teacher in India, where schools are modeled on the British educational system. A headmaster, rather than a principal, is in charge of a school. Students progress through forms, which are the equivalent of grades in the United States. Sekhar teaches the third form, or ninth grade.

MORE ABOUT THE AUTHOR
For more on R. K. Narayan, visit the **Literature Center** at **ClassZone.com**.

Like THE Sun

R. K. NARAYAN

ANALYZE VISUALS
Examine the painting. What details suggest the **setting** of the story?

Truth, Sekhar reflected, is like the sun. I suppose no human being can ever look it straight in the face without blinking or being dazed. He realized that, morning till night, the essence of human relationships consisted in tempering truth so that it might not shock. This day he set apart as a unique day—at least one day in the year we must give and take absolute Truth whatever may happen. Otherwise life is not worth living. The day ahead seemed to him full of possibilities. He told no one of his experiment. It was a quiet resolve, a secret pact between him and eternity.

The very first test came while his wife served him his morning meal. He
10 showed hesitation over a titbit, which she had thought was her culinary[1] masterpiece. She asked, "Why, isn't it good?" At other times he would have said, considering her feelings in the matter, "I feel full up, that's all." But today he said, "It isn't good. I'm unable to swallow it." He saw her wince and said to himself, Can't be helped. Truth is like the sun. **A**

His next trial was in the common room when one of his colleagues came up and said, "Did you hear of the death of so-and-so? Don't you think it a pity?"

"No," Sekhar answered. "He was such a fine man—" the other began. But Sekhar cut him short with: "Far from it. He always struck me as a mean and selfish brute."

20 During the last period when he was teaching geography for Third Form A, Sekhar received a note from the headmaster: "Please see me before you go home." Sekhar said to himself: It must be about these horrible test papers. A hundred papers in the boys' scrawls; he had shirked this work for weeks, feeling all the time as if a sword were hanging over his head.

The bell rang, and the boys burst out of the class.

Sekhar paused for a moment outside the headmaster's room to button up his coat; that was another subject the headmaster always sermonized about.

He stepped in with a very polite "Good evening, sir."

A PREDICT
How do you predict Sekhar's wife will behave in their next encounter?

---

1. **culinary** (kyōō′lə-něr′ē): having to do with cooking or the kitchen.

Detail of *The Dance of Krishna* (about 1650). Mewar, Rajasthan, India. From a manuscript of the Sur-Sagar. Opaque watercolor on paper, 11″ × 8¹/₈″. Collection Gopi Krishna, Patna, India.

The headmaster looked up at him in a very friendly manner and asked,
30 "Are you free this evening?"

Sekhar replied, "Just some outing which I have promised the children
at home—"

"Well, you can take them out another day. Come home with me now."

"Oh . . . yes, sir, certainly . . ." And then he added timidly, "Anything
special, sir?"

"Yes," replied the headmaster, smiling to himself . . . "You didn't know my
weakness for music?"

"Oh, yes, sir . . ."

"I've been learning and practicing secretly, and now I want you to hear me
40 this evening. I've engaged a drummer and a violinist to accompany me—this
is the first time I'm doing it full-dress,[2] and I want your opinion. I know it will
be valuable."

Sekhar's taste in music was well-known. He was one of the most dreaded
music critics in the town. But he never anticipated his musical inclinations
would lead him to this trial. . . . "Rather a surprise for you, isn't it?" asked the
headmaster. "I've spent a fortune on it behind closed doors. . . ." They started
for the headmaster's house. "God hasn't given me a child, but at least let him
not deny me the consolation of music," the headmaster said, pathetically, as
they walked. He incessantly chattered about music: how he began one day out
50 of sheer boredom; how his teacher at first laughed at him and then gave him
hope; how his ambition in life was to forget himself in music. **B**

At home the headmaster proved very ingratiating. He sat Sekhar on a red
silk carpet, set before him several dishes of delicacies, and fussed over him as if
he were a son-in-law of the house. He even said, "Well, you must listen with a
free mind. Don't worry about these test papers." He added half humorously,
"I will give you a week's time."

"Make it ten days, sir," Sekhar pleaded.

"All right, granted," the headmaster said generously. Sekhar felt really
relieved now—he would attack them at the rate of ten a day and get rid of
60 the nuisance.

The headmaster lighted incense sticks. "Just to create the right atmosphere,"
he explained. A drummer and a violinist, already seated on a Rangoon mat, were
waiting for him. The headmaster sat down between them like a professional
at a concert, cleared his throat, and began an alapana,[3] and paused to ask,
"Isn't it good Kalyani?"[4] Sekhar pretended not to have heard the question. The
headmaster went on to sing a full song composed by Thyagaraja[5] and followed
it with two more. All the time the headmaster was singing, Sekhar went on
commenting within himself, He croaks like a dozen frogs. He is bellowing like
a buffalo. Now he sounds like loose window shutters in a storm. **C**

---

2. **full-dress:** complete in every respect.

3. **alapana:** improvisational Indian music in the classical style.

4. **Kalyani:** traditional Indian folk songs.

5. **Thyagaraja:** a famous Indian composer (1767–1847).

B CHARACTER AND PLOT
Reread lines 29–51.
Which details suggest
that **conflict** might
develop between Sekhar
and the headmaster?

C PREDICT
What will happen
if Sekhar expresses
his opinion of the
headmaster's singing?

70 The incense sticks burnt low. Sekhar's head throbbed with the medley of sounds that had assailed his eardrums for a couple of hours now. He felt half stupefied. The headmaster had gone nearly hoarse, when he paused to ask, "Shall I go on?" Sekhar replied, "Please don't, sir; I think this will do. . . ." The headmaster looked stunned. His face was beaded with perspiration. Sekhar felt the greatest pity for him. But he felt he could not help it. No judge delivering a sentence felt more pained and helpless. Sekhar noticed that the headmaster's wife peeped in from the kitchen, with eager curiosity. The drummer and the violinist put away their burdens with an air of relief. The headmaster removed his spectacles, mopped his brow, and asked, "Now, come out with your

80 opinion."

"Can't I give it tomorrow, sir?" Sekhar asked tentatively.

"No. I want it immediately—your frank opinion. Was it good?"

"No, sir . . ." Sekhar replied.

"Oh! . . . Is there any use continuing my lessons?"

"Absolutely none, sir . . ." Sekhar said with his voice trembling. He felt very unhappy that he could not speak more soothingly. Truth, he reflected, required as much strength to give as to receive.

All the way home he felt worried. He felt that his official life was not going to be smooth sailing hereafter. There were questions of increment and

90 confirmation[6] and so on, all depending upon the headmaster's goodwill.

All kinds of worries seemed to be in store for him. . . . Did not Harischandra[7] lose his throne, wife, child, because he would speak nothing less than the absolute Truth whatever happened?

At home his wife served him with a sullen face. He knew she was still angry with him for his remark of the morning. Two casualties for today, Sekhar said to himself. If I practice it for a week, I don't think I shall have a single friend left.

He received a call from the headmaster in his classroom next day. He went up apprehensively.

100 "Your suggestion was useful. I have paid off the music master. No one would tell me the truth about my music all these days. Why such antics at my age! Thank you. By the way, what about those test papers?"

"You gave me ten days, sir, for correcting them."

"Oh, I've reconsidered it. I must positively have them here tomorrow. . . ." A hundred papers in a day! That meant all night's sitting up! "Give me a couple of days, sir . . ."

"No. I must have them tomorrow morning. And remember, every paper must be thoroughly scrutinized." **D**

"Yes, sir," Sekhar said, feeling that sitting up all night with a hundred test

110 papers was a small price to pay for the luxury of practicing Truth. ◐

D CHARACTER AND PLOT
How has Sekhar's truthfulness affected his relationship with the headmaster?

---

6. **increment and confirmation:** salary increases and job security.

7. **Harischandra:** a legendary Hindu king and the subject of many Indian stories. His name has come to symbolize truth and integrity.

Tell all the Truth but tell it slant—
Emily Dickinson

Tell all the Truth but tell it slant—
Success in Circuit lies
Too bright for our infirm Delight
The Truth's superb surprise
5 As Lightning to the Children eased
With explanation kind
The Truth must dazzle gradually
Or every man be blind—

Comprehension

1. **Recall** What does Sekhar decide to do for one day?

2. **Recall** How is Sekhar tested during the day?

3. **Summarize** What negative consequences result from Sekhar's decision?

OHIO STANDARDS

READING STANDARD
4.3 Distinguish how conflicts, parallel plots and subplots affect the story

Literary Analysis

4. **Analyze Character and Plot** Which of Sekhar's character traits most directly influence the story's plot? Explain your answer.

5. **Make Inferences** Reread lines 98–108. Do you think the headmaster is sincere when he thanks Sekhar for his honesty? Why or why not?

6. **Draw Conclusions About Plot** How might the outcome of the story have been different if Sekhar had not told the headmaster how he really felt?

7. **Predict** Look back at the predictions you recorded as you read. How close were the predictions to what actually happened? Cite specific clues that influenced your predictions.

8. **Interpret Characters** A **round character** has a variety of traits and different sides to his or her personality. A **flat character** is one-sided and usually displays only one main trait. Decide whether each character in the story is a round or flat character.

9. **Evaluate** How successful was Sekhar's experiment in telling the absolute truth? Use evidence from the story to support your opinion.

10. **Compare Literary Works** "Like the Sun" and "Tell all the Truth but tell it slant—" both address the difficulty of telling the **truth.** Compare and contrast Sekhar's attitude toward truth with the attitude of the speaker in Dickinson's poem. Fill in a chart like the one shown to record your answer.

	Sekhar	Poem's Speaker
What the truth is like		
How you should tell the truth		

Literary Criticism

11. **Critical Interpretations** When asked why the problems of characters are often left unresolved at the end of his stories, Narayan responded, "Life is like that. We cannot manipulate life to suit fictional needs." Do you consider the ending of "Like the Sun" to be realistic? Cite evidence to support your opinion.

The Teacher Who Changed My Life
Essay by Nicholas Gage

Who has made you a BETTER *person?*

OHIO
STANDARDS

READING STANDARDS
3.1 Identify and understand author's purpose
4.1 Compare and contrast an author's use of direct and indirect characterization

KEY IDEA Sometimes one person can have a powerful effect on your life. When you look back, you realize how much you benefited from his or her **influence.** In "The Teacher Who Changed My Life," Nicholas Gage fondly recalls how he was challenged by his seventh-grade teacher, Miss Hurd.

QUICKWRITE Think of a person, such as a teacher, coach, neighbor, or relative, who has inspired you to be your best. Write a paragraph explaining how he or she influenced you.

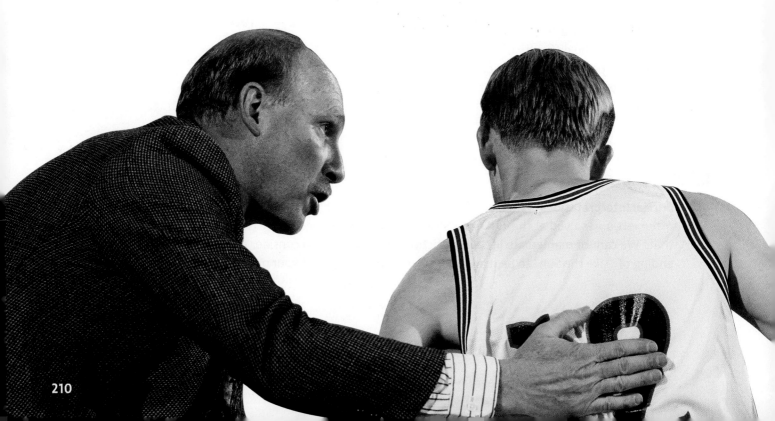

LITERARY ANALYSIS: CHARACTERIZATION IN NONFICTION

Because writers of nonfiction portray real people rather than characters, they are limited in certain ways. A writer cannot make up facts about a real person. However, writers can shape the reader's attitude toward the person by using the same basic methods of **characterization** used in fiction. These are

- making direct comments about the person's nature
- describing the person's appearance
- quoting the person or describing his or her actions
- reporting what other people say or think about the person

As you read "The Teacher Who Changed My Life," notice how Gage uses different methods of characterization to shape your attitude toward Miss Hurd.

READING SKILL: AUTHOR'S PURPOSE

An **author's purpose** is what the writer hopes to achieve in a particular work. For example, the title of Gage's essay suggests that he wants to inform you about how a teacher influenced his life. In addition to providing information, writers may seek to persuade, to express ideas or emotions, or to entertain. A complex piece of writing often has more than one purpose.

As you read, notice how Gage's purposes affect the tone of his writing and his choice of details and words. Use a chart like the one shown in recording your analysis.

Purpose	How Purpose Affects Writing
To show influence of Miss Hurd	Narrates how she pushed him to write about his experiences

▲ VOCABULARY IN CONTEXT

To see how many vocabulary words you know, substitute a different word or phrase for each boldfaced term.

1. The defeat left him lonely and **isolated.**
2. I've learned a lot from my **mentor.**
3. He participated willingly and **avidly.**
4. She **emphatically** endorsed the candidate.
5. We need a **catalyst** to send us in a new direction.
6. They handled the awkward situation with great **tact.**

Background

A Tireless Investigator As an investigative reporter for the *New York Times* and the *Wall Street Journal,* Nicholas Gage reported on important issues such as organized crime and drug trafficking. But ever since childhood, he wanted to cover a more personal story. In 1980, Gage began researching a book about his mother's fate in the Greek civil war. His investigations led him to one of the judges who ordered Eleni's execution. Gage actually considered killing the judge, but he realized that if he took revenge he would "become like him, purging myself as he did of all humanity or compassion." Gage's award-winning book, *Eleni,* was published in 1983.

The Teacher Who Changed My Life

Nicholas Gage

ANALYZE VISUALS
What does this photograph suggest about the relationship between Nicholas Gage and Miss Hurd after he became an adult?

The person who set the course of my life in the new land I entered as a young war refugee—who, in fact, nearly dragged me onto the path that would bring all the blessings I've received in America—was a salty-tongued, no-nonsense schoolteacher named Marjorie Hurd. When I entered her classroom in 1953, I had been to six schools in five years, starting in the Greek village where I was born in 1939.

When I stepped off a ship in New York Harbor on a gray March day in 1949, I was an undersized 9-year-old in short pants who had lost his mother and was coming to live with the father he didn't know. My mother, Eleni
10 Gatzoyiannis,[1] had been imprisoned, tortured and shot by Communist guerrillas for sending me and three of my four sisters to freedom. She died so that her children could go to their father in the United States.

The portly, bald, well-dressed man who met me and my sisters seemed a foreign, authoritarian figure. I secretly resented him for not getting the whole family out of Greece early enough to save my mother. Ultimately, I would grow to love him and appreciate how he dealt with becoming a single parent at the age of 56, but at first our relationship was prickly, full of hostility. **Ⓐ**

As Father drove us to our new home—a tenement in Worcester, Mass.—and pointed out the huge brick building that would be our first school in America,
20 I clutched my Greek notebooks from the refugee camp, hoping that my few years of schooling would impress my teachers in this cold, crowded country. They didn't. When my father led me and my 11-year-old sister to Greendale Elementary School, the grim-faced Yankee principal put the two of us in a

Ⓐ CHARACTERIZATION IN NONFICTION
What methods of characterization does Gage use to explain his initial impression of his father?

---

1. **Eleni Gatzoyiannis** (ĕ-lĕ′nē gät′zô-yän′ĭs).

Nicholas Gage and his family at the harbor in Piraeus, Greece, ready to set out for the United States

class for the mentally retarded. There was no facility in those days for non-English-speaking children.

By the time I met Marjorie Hurd four years later, I had learned English, been placed in a normal, graded class and had even been chosen for the college preparatory track in the Worcester public school system. I was 13 years old when our father moved us yet again, and I entered Chandler Junior High
30 shortly after the beginning of seventh grade. I found myself surrounded by richer, smarter and better-dressed classmates, who looked askance at my strange clothes and heavy accent. Shortly after I arrived, we were told to select a hobby to pursue during "club hour" on Fridays. The idea of hobbies and clubs made no sense to my immigrant ears, but I decided to follow the prettiest girl in my class—the blue-eyed daughter of the local Lutheran minister. She led me through the door marked "Newspaper Club" and into the presence of Miss Hurd, the newspaper adviser and English teacher who would become my **mentor** and my muse.

A formidable, solidly built woman with salt-and-pepper hair, a steely eye
40 and a flat Boston accent, Miss Hurd had no patience with layabouts. "What are all you goof-offs doing here?" she bellowed at the would-be journalists. "This is the Newspaper Club! We're going to put out a *newspaper*. So if there's anybody in this room who doesn't like work, I suggest you go across to the Glee Club now, because you're going to work your tails off here!" **B**

mentor (mĕn′tôr′) *n.*
a wise and trusted
counselor or teacher

B **CHARACTERIZATION
IN NONFICTION**
Why might Gage have
chosen to quote Miss
Hurd's actual words in
this paragraph?

I was soon under Miss Hurd's spell. She did indeed teach us to put out a newspaper, skills I honed during my next 25 years as a journalist. Soon I asked the principal to transfer me to her English class as well. There, she drilled us on grammar until I finally began to understand the logic and structure of the English language. She assigned stories for us to read and discuss; not

50 tales of heroes, like the Greek myths I knew, but stories of underdogs—poor people, even immigrants, who seemed ordinary until a crisis drove them to do something extraordinary. She also introduced us to the literary wealth of Greece—giving me a new perspective on my war-ravaged, impoverished homeland. I began to be proud of my origins. **C**

One day, after discussing how writers should write about what they know, she assigned us to compose an essay from our own experience. Fixing me with a stern look, she added, "Nick, I want you to write about what happened to your family in Greece." I had been trying to put those painful memories behind me and left the assignment until the last moment. Then, on a warm

60 spring afternoon, I sat in my room with a yellow pad and pencil and stared out the window at the buds on the trees. I wrote that the coming of spring always reminded me of the last time I said goodbye to my mother on a green and gold day in 1948.

C **AUTHOR'S PURPOSE**
Reread lines 45–54. Which **details** support Gage's purpose of explaining Miss Hurd's influence on him?

Nicholas Gage (top row, center) with his third-grade class

I kept writing, one line after another, telling how the Communist guerrillas occupied our village, took our home and food, how my mother started planning our escape when she learned that the children were to be sent to re-education camps[2] behind the Iron Curtain[3] and how, at the last moment, she couldn't escape with us because the guerrillas sent her with a group of women to thresh wheat in a distant village. She promised she would try to
70 get away on her own, she told me to be brave and hung a silver cross around my neck, and then she kissed me. I watched the line of women being led down into the ravine and up the other side, until they disappeared around the bend—my mother a tiny brown figure at the end who stopped for an instant to raise her hand in one last farewell.

I wrote about our nighttime escape down the mountain, across the minefields and into the lines of the Nationalist soldiers, who sent us to a refugee camp. It was there that we learned of our mother's execution. I felt very lucky to have come to America, I concluded, but every year, the coming of spring made me feel sad because it reminded me of the last time I saw my mother.

80 I handed in the essay, hoping never to see it again, but Miss Hurd had it published in the school paper. This mortified me at first, until I saw that my classmates reacted with sympathy and **tact** to my family's story. Without telling me, Miss Hurd also submitted the essay to a contest sponsored by the Freedoms Foundation at Valley Forge, Pa., and it won a medal. The Worcester paper wrote about the award and quoted my essay at length. My father, by then a "five-and-dime-store chef," as the paper described him, was ecstatic with pride, and the Worcester Greek community celebrated the honor to one of its own. ⓓ

For the first time I began to understand the power of the written word. A
90 secret ambition took root in me. One day, I vowed, I would go back to Greece, find out the details of my mother's death and write about her life, so her grandchildren would know of her courage. Perhaps I would even track down the men who killed her and write of their crimes. Fulfilling that ambition would take me 30 years.

Meanwhile, I followed the literary path that Miss Hurd had so forcefully set me on. After junior high, I became the editor of my school paper at Classical High School and got a part-time job at the Worcester *Telegram and Gazette*. Although my father could only give me $50 and encouragement toward a college education, I managed to finance four years at Boston University with
100 scholarships and part-time jobs in journalism. During my last year of college, an article I wrote about a friend who had died in the Philippines—the first person to lose his life working for the Peace Corps—led to my winning the Hearst Award for College Journalism. And the plaque was given to me in the White House by President John F. Kennedy.

tact (tăkt) *n.* an understanding of the proper thing to do or say around others

ⓓ **GRAMMAR AND STYLE**
Reread lines 82–88. Notice how Gage uses the **concrete noun** *medal* and **abstract nouns** such as *pride* and *honor* to describe responses to his essay.

---

2. **re-education camps:** camps where people were forced to go to be indoctrinated with Communist ideas and beliefs.

3. **behind the Iron Curtain:** on the Communist side of the imaginary divide between the democracies of Western Europe and the Communist dictatorships of Eastern Europe; in this case, the camps were in Albania.

For a refugee who had never seen a motorized vehicle or indoor plumbing until he was 9, this was an unimaginable honor. When the Worcester paper ran a picture of me standing next to President Kennedy, my father rushed out to buy a new suit in order to be properly dressed to receive the congratulations of the Worcester Greeks. He clipped out the photograph, had it laminated
110 in plastic and carried it in his breast pocket for the rest of his life to show everyone he met. I found the much-worn photo in his pocket on the day he died 20 years later. **E**

In our **isolated** Greek village, my mother had bribed a cousin to teach her to read, for girls were not supposed to attend school beyond a certain age. She had always dreamed of her children receiving an education. She couldn't be there when I graduated from Boston University, but the person who came with my father and shared our joy was my former teacher, Marjorie Hurd. We celebrated not only my bachelor's degree but also the scholarships that paid my way to Columbia's Graduate School of Journalism. There, I met the woman
120 who would eventually become my wife. At our wedding and at the baptisms of our three children, Marjorie Hurd was always there, dancing alongside the Greeks.

By then, she was Mrs. Rabidou, for she had married a widower when she was in her early 40s. That didn't distract her from her vocation of introducing young minds to English literature, however. She taught for a total of 41 years

E CHARACTERIZATION IN NONFICTION
What do the father's **actions** tell you about his feelings for his son?

isolated (ī′sə-lā′tĭd) *adj.* separated from others

Nicholas Gage (left) receiving the Hearst Award from President Kennedy in 1963

and continually would make a "project" of some balky student in whom she spied a spark of potential. Often these were students from the most troubled homes, yet she would alternately bully and charm each one with her own special brand of tough love until the spark caught fire. She retired in 1981 at the age of 62 but still **avidly** follows the lives and careers of former students while overseeing her adult stepchildren and driving her husband on camping trips to New Hampshire. **F**

Miss Hurd was one of the first to call me on Dec. 10, 1987, when President Reagan, in his television address after the summit meeting with Gorbachev,[4] told the nation that Eleni Gatzoyiannis's dying cry, "My children!" had helped inspire him to seek an arms agreement "for all the children of the world."

"I can't imagine a better monument for your mother," Miss Hurd said with an uncharacteristic catch in her voice.

Although a bad hip makes it impossible for her to join in the Greek dancing, Marjorie Hurd Rabidou is still an honored and enthusiastic guest at all our family celebrations, including my 50th birthday picnic last summer, where the shish kebab was cooked on spits, clarinets and *bouzoukis*[5] wailed, and costumed dancers led the guests in a serpentine line around our Colonial farmhouse, only 20 minutes from my first home in Worcester.

My sisters and I felt an aching void because my father was not there to lead the line, balancing a glass of wine on his head while he danced, the way he did at every celebration during his 92 years. But Miss Hurd was there, surveying the scene with quiet satisfaction. Although my parents are gone, her presence was a consolation, because I owe her so much. **G**

This is truly the land of opportunity, and I would have enjoyed its bounty even if I hadn't walked into Miss Hurd's classroom in 1953. But she was the one who directed my grief and pain into writing, and if it weren't for her, I wouldn't have become an investigative reporter and foreign correspondent, recorded the story of my mother's life and death in *Eleni* and now my father's story in *A Place for Us*, which is also a testament to the country that took us in. She was the **catalyst** that sent me into journalism and indirectly caused all the good things that came after. But Miss Hurd would probably deny this **emphatically.**

A few years ago, I answered the telephone and heard my former teacher's voice telling me, in that won't-take-no-for-an-answer tone of hers, that she had decided I was to write and deliver the eulogy at her funeral. I agreed (she didn't leave me any choice), but that's one assignment I never want to do. I hope, Miss Hurd, that you'll accept this remembrance instead. ∾

avidly (ăv'ĭd-lē) *adv.* with great eagerness and enthusiasm

F AUTHOR'S PURPOSE
Reread lines 123–132. What **words** and **details** in this paragraph help Gage pay tribute to Miss Hurd?

G AUTHOR'S PURPOSE
Reread lines 145–149. What purpose is suggested by Gage's **tone** in this paragraph?

catalyst (kăt'l-ĭst) *n.* something or someone that brings about change

emphatically (ĕm-făt'ĭk-lē) *adv.* with strong emphasis

---

4. **summit meeting with Gorbachev** (gôr'bə-chôf'): a high-level meeting between U.S. president Ronald Reagan and Mikhail Gorbachev, the last president of the Soviet Union.

5. ***bouzoukis*** (bōō-zōō'kēz): traditional Greek stringed instruments resembling mandolins.

Comprehension

1. **Recall** Why did Nicholas Gage come to the United States?

2. **Recall** What did Miss Hurd encourage him to write about?

3. **Recall** How did people react to Gage's essay?

4. **Paraphrase** According to Gage, what **influence** did Miss Hurd have on his career?

OHIO STANDARDS

READING STANDARD
3.1 Identify and understand author's purpose

Literary Analysis

5. **Analyze Characterization** For each method of characterization in the chart, give an example of how Gage uses it to convey Miss Hurd's personality. Which method gives you the most vivid impression of Miss Hurd? Explain your answer.

	Words and Actions	Physical Appearances	Gage's Comments
Example from text			
What it reveals about Miss Hurd			

6. **Make Inferences** What led Miss Hurd to take a special interest in Gage when he was her student?

7. **Draw Conclusions About Character** Does Gage offer a realistic or an idealized portrait of Miss Hurd in this essay? Support your conclusion with evidence from the text.

8. **Compare and Contrast Characters** Compare Miss Hurd with Sekhar in "Like the Sun" on page 204. What are the similarities and differences between these two teachers?

9. **Examine Author's Purpose** Review the chart you created as you read. What is the main purpose of Gage's essay? Use evidence from the text to support your answer.

10. **Evaluate Actions** The essay that Gage wrote for Miss Hurd in the seventh grade was about a traumatic event in his life. Should a teacher publish such writing without the student's permission? Why or why not?

Literary Criticism

11. **Author's Style** Some critics have complained that Nicholas Gage includes too many details in works such as *Eleni,* which is almost 500 pages long. Consider the kinds of details Gage included in "The Teacher Who Changed My Life." Would you say they are excessive, or do they serve an important function in conveying his message? Cite evidence in support of your opinion.

Vocabulary in Context

VOCABULARY PRACTICE

Decide whether the words in each pair are synonyms or antonyms.

1. mentor/advisor
2. tact/insensitivity
3. isolated/united
4. avidly/enthusiastically
5. catalyst/observer
6. emphatically/wearily

VOCABULARY IN WRITING

Using at least three vocabulary words, write about someone who had a positive influence on your life. Here is how you might begin:

> **EXAMPLE SENTENCE**
>
> I felt **isolated** in school before I met my best friend.

VOCABULARY STRATEGY: THE LATIN ROOT *sol*

The word *isolated* contains the root *sol,* from the Latin word *solus,* which means "alone." This root is found in a number of English words. To understand the meaning of words with *sol,* use context clues as well as your knowledge of the root.

PRACTICE Write the word from the word web that best completes each sentence. Use context clues to help you, or consult a dictionary if necessary.

1. Accidentally _____ from his family, the young boy asked the police officer for help.
2. In the play, Hamlet performs a _____ in which he talks to himself.
3. Enjoying time alone, she engages in _____ pursuits such as reading and drawing.
4. They enjoyed the quiet _____ of a picnic on an empty stretch of beach.
5. The conductor quiets the rest of the orchestra so that the violinist can perform her _____ .

WORD LIST

avidly

catalyst

emphatically

isolated

mentor

tact

OHIO STANDARDS

VOCABULARY STANDARD
1.5 Use knowledge of Latin roots, prefixes and suffixes to understand words

isolated   soliloquy

sol

solo

solitude   solitary

VOCABULARY PRACTICE
For more practice, go to the **Vocabulary Center** at **ClassZone.com**.

Reading-Writing Connection

Broaden your understanding of "The Teacher Who Changed My Life" by responding to these prompts. Then use **Revision: Grammar and Style** to improve your writing.

WRITING PROMPTS	SELF-CHECK

A. Short Response: Analyze Character Traits
What set Miss Hurd apart from Gage's other teachers? Using examples from the essay, write **one or two paragraphs** describing the character traits that made Miss Hurd an outstanding, **influential** teacher.

A sound analysis will . . .
- provide three examples of Miss Hurd's character traits
- cite ways in which the traits motivated Gage and other students

B. Extended Response: Write a Speech
Imagine that you are the author's father. Write a **three-to-five-paragraph speech** describing your son's life and your feelings for him.

A successful speech will . . .
- have a clear thesis statement
- provide examples that support the statement

REVISION: GRAMMAR AND STYLE

ELABORATE WITH EXAMPLES Review the **Grammar and Style** note on page 216. Illustrating your ideas with examples, as Gage does, can strengthen your message to readers. Note that Gage uses both concrete and abstract nouns in his examples to fully describe events and people's reactions to them. A **concrete noun** names an object that can be seen, heard, smelled, touched, or tasted (such as *sky, whistle, flower, book,* and *lemon*). An **abstract noun** names an idea, quality, or state (such as *democracy, independence, security, comfort,* and *sadness*).

> . . . *she told me to be brave and hung a silver cross around my neck.* . . .
> (lines 70–71)

> . . . *my classmates reacted with* *sympathy and tact* . . . . (line 82)

Notice how the revisions in red use examples to strengthen the main points of this first draft. Use a similar method to revise your responses to the prompts.

OHIO STANDARDS

WRITING STANDARD
6.3.c Include facts and details

WRITING TOOLS
For prewriting, revision, and editing tools, visit the **Writing Center** at ClassZone.com.

STUDENT MODEL

Nick arrived in the United States when he was only nine years
His mother had just died, and he struggled to learn English.
old. It was a difficult time for him. But he eventually succeeded.
His courage and determination led him to write a prize-winning essay at age thirteen.

A Celebration of Grandfathers
Essay by Rudolfo A. Anaya

Are OLD WAYS
the best ways?

OHIO STANDARDS

READING STANDARDS
3.5 Analyze an author's perspective or viewpoint

4.1 Compare and contrast an author's use of direct and indirect characterization

KEY IDEA In "A Celebration of Grandfathers," Rudolfo Anaya pays tribute to the customs and values of his elders. Today most people live in a society very different from the one he describes. Some still cherish **tradition**, but others embrace change.

DEBATE How much should tradition influence your life? With a group, stage a mini-debate about whether old ways are still the best ways.

LITERARY ANALYSIS: CHARACTER TRAITS IN NONFICTION

Some types of nonfiction, such as memoirs and biographies, offer you a glimpse into people's lives. When you read such works, you get to know the **character traits,** or qualities, of individuals. Writers may focus on particular traits to help express ideas about life or provide insight into a time and place. For example, in "A Celebration of Grandfathers," Anaya describes what was special about his grandfather's generation in rural New Mexico.

They shared good times and hard times. They helped each other through the epidemics and the personal tragedies, and they shared what little they had. . . .

As you read, notice what Anaya reveals about his grandfather's traits.

READING SKILL: IDENTIFY AUTHOR'S PERSPECTIVE

People often look at a subject from different viewpoints. For example, a person who loves to ski will probably react to a snowstorm differently than someone who is concerned about getting to work on time would. The combination of beliefs, values, and feelings that influence how a writer looks at a subject is called the **author's perspective.** To determine the author's perspective in a personal essay, readers should examine clues such as the following:

- statements of opinion
- details the writer chooses to include
- the writer's tone, or attitude (such as a humorous or formal tone)

As you read "A Celebration of Grandfathers," use a chart like the one shown to identify how Anaya's perspective is revealed in his statements, details, and tone.

Statement, Detail, or Tone	What It Reveals About Perspective
For me [the farm] was a magical place.	Rural life has a special value.

Author Online

Storyteller's Gift Rudolfo A. Anaya lives in New Mexico, where he was born and raised. He grew up listening to *cuentos* (stories and legends) that are part of the Hispanic oral tradition. Anaya has remarked that listening to his elders tell *cuentos* helped him hone his writing skills, noting that "the storyteller's gift is my inheritance."

Rudolfo A. Anaya
born 1937

A Breakthrough Novel Anaya is best known for his first novel, *Bless Me, Ultima* (1972), the story of a boy in a small New Mexican village who struggles to find his identity. One of the first novels to represent the Mexican-American experience, it helped launch a vibrant Hispanic literary movement in the United States. Anaya's novels, plays, stories, and essays have earned him many literary awards, including the 2001 National Medal of Arts.

MORE ABOUT THE AUTHOR
For more on Rudolfo A. Anaya, visit the **Literature Center** at **ClassZone.com.**

Background

Pride of Place The landscape, culture, and history of New Mexico are important elements in Anaya's writing. During the first part of the 20th century, New Mexico still had a traditional agricultural economy. Its population consisted mainly of Native Americans and descendants of Spanish settlers, who first arrived there in the 1500s. Anaya's grandfather worked land along the Pecos River in the eastern part of the state, using methods that were probably not much different than those of his ancestors. By the late 1940s, however, this way of life was coming to an end. Many young people had moved into cities, depriving villages of the next generation of farmers.

A Celebration of Grandfathers

Rudolfo A. Anaya

"Buenos días le de Dios, abuelo." God give you a good day, grandfather. This is how I was taught as a child to greet my grandfather, or any grown person. It was a greeting of respect, a cultural value to be passed on from generation to generation, this respect for the old ones.

The old people I remember from my childhood were strong in their beliefs, and as we lived daily with them, we learned a wise path of life to follow. They had something important to share with the young, and when they spoke, the young listened. These old *abuelos* and *abuelitas*[1] had worked the earth all their lives, and so they knew the value of nurturing, they knew the sensitivity of the
10 earth. . . . They knew the rhythms and cycles of time, from the preparation of the earth in the spring to the digging of the *acequias*[2] that brought the water to the dance of harvest in the fall. They shared good times and hard times. They helped each other through the epidemics and the personal tragedies, and they shared what little they had when the hot winds burned the land and no rain came. They learned that to survive one had to share in the process of life. . . . **A**

ANALYZE VISUALS
What way of life does the painting depict? Identify details that led you to this conclusion.

A **IDENTIFY AUTHOR'S PERSPECTIVE**
What does Anaya's description of the old people reveal about his perspective?

---

1. **abuelos** (ä-bwĕ′lôs) . . . **abuelitas** (ä-bwĕ-lē′täs) *Spanish:* grandfathers . . . grannies.

2. **acequias** (ä-sĕ′kyäs) *Spanish:* irrigation ditches.

Campesino (1938), Diego Rivera. Watercolor with black ink on rice paper, 38.7 cm × 27.7 cm. Private collection. Photo © The Bridgeman Art Library.

Diego Rivera. 1938

Peasants (1947), Diego Rivera. Museu de Arte, Sao Paulo, Brazil. © Banco de Mexico Trust. Photo © Giraudon/Art Resource, New York.

My grandfather was a plain man, a farmer from the valley called Puerto de Luna on the Pecos River. He was probably a descendant of those people who spilled over the mountain from Taos, following the Pecos River in search of farmland. There in that river valley he settled and raised a large family.

20 Bearded and walrus-mustached, he stood five feet tall, but to me as a child he was a giant. I remember him most for his silence. In the summers my parents sent me to live with him on his farm, for I was to learn the ways of a farmer. My uncles also lived in that valley, there where only the flow of the river and the whispering of the wind marked time. For me it was a magical place.

I remember once, while out hoeing the fields, I came upon an anthill, and before I knew it I was badly bitten. After he had covered my welts with the cool mud from the irrigation ditch, my grandfather calmly said: "Know where you stand." That is the way he spoke, in short phrases, to the point. **B**

30 One very dry summer, the river dried to a trickle; there was no water for the fields. The young plants withered and died. In my sadness and with the impulse of youth I said, "I wish it would rain!" My grandfather touched me, looked up into the sky and whispered, "Pray for rain." In his language there was a difference. He felt connected to the cycles that brought the rain or kept

ANALYZE VISUALS
How does the **style** of this painting reflect the relationship between the land and the people Anaya describes?

B CHARACTER TRAITS
Reread lines 16–29. What do you learn about the grandfather's traits in this passage?

it from us. His prayer was a meaningful action, because he was a participant with the forces that filled our world; he was not a bystander.

A young man died at the village one summer. A very tragic death. He was dragged by his horse. When he was found, I cried, for the boy was my friend. I did not understand why death had come to one so young. My grandfather
40 took me aside and said: "Think of the death of the trees and the fields in the fall. The leaves fall, and everything rests, as if dead. But they bloom again in the spring. Death is only this small transformation in life." **C**

These are the things I remember, these fleeting images, few words.

I remember him driving his horse-drawn wagon into Santa Rosa in the fall when he brought his harvest produce to sell in the town. What a tower of strength seemed to come in that small man huddled on the seat of the giant wagon. One click of his tongue and the horses obeyed, stopped or turned as he wished. He never raised his whip. How unlike today, when so much teaching is done with loud words and threatening hands.
50 I would run to greet the wagon, and the wagon would stop. "*Buenos días le de Dios, abuelo,*" I would say. . . . "*Buenos días te de Dios, mi hijo,*"[3] he would answer and smile, and then I could jump up on the wagon and sit at his side. Then I, too, became a king as I rode next to the old man who smelled of earth and sweat and the other deep aromas from the orchards and fields of Puerto de Luna.

We were all sons and daughters to him. But today the sons and daughters are breaking with the past, putting aside *los abuelitos.* The old values are threatened, and threatened most where it comes to these relationships with the old people. If we don't take the time to watch and feel the years of their final
60 transformation, a part of our humanity will be lessened.

I grew up speaking Spanish, and oh! how difficult it was to learn English. Sometimes I would give up and cry out that I couldn't learn. Then he would say, "*Ten paciencia.*" Have patience. *Paciencia,* a word with the strength of centuries, a word that said that someday we would overcome. . . . "You have to learn the language of the Americanos," he said. "Me, I will live my last days in my valley. You will live in a new time."

A new time did come; a new time is here. How will we form it so it is fruitful? We need to know where we stand. We need to speak softly and respect others, and to share what we have. We need to pray not for material gain,
70 but for rain for the fields, for the sun to nurture growth, for nights in which we can sleep in peace, and for a harvest in which everyone can share. Simple lessons from a simple man. These lessons he learned from his past, which was as deep and strong as the currents of the river of life. **D**

He was a man; he died. Not in his valley but nevertheless cared for by his sons and daughters and flocks of grandchildren. At the end, I would enter his

C CHARACTER TRAITS
What can you **infer** about Anaya's grandfather from this incident?

D IDENTIFY AUTHOR'S PERSPECTIVE
Based on lines 67–73, what would you say Anaya values?

---

3. *mi hijo* (mē ē′hô) *Spanish:* my son.

room, which carried the smell of medications and Vicks. Gone were the aroma of the fields, the strength of his young manhood. Gone also was his patience in the face of crippling old age. Small things bothered him; he shouted or turned sour when his expectations were not met. It was because he could not care
80 for himself, because he was returning to that state of childhood, and all those wishes and desires were now wrapped in a crumbling, old body. **E**

"*Ten paciencia*," I once said to him, and he smiled. "I didn't know I would grow this old," he said. . . .

I would sit and look at him and remember what was said of him when he was a young man. He could mount a wild horse and break it, and he could ride as far as any man. He could dance all night at a dance, then work the *acequia* the following day. He helped the neighbors; they helped him. He married, raised children. Small legends, the kind that make up every man's life.

He was ninety-four when he died. Family, neighbors, and friends gathered;
90 they all agreed he had led a rich life. I remembered the last years, the years he spent in bed. And as I remember now, I am reminded that it is too easy to romanticize[4] old age. Sometimes we forget the pain of the transformation into old age, we forget the natural breaking down of the body. . . . My grandfather pointed to the leaves falling from the tree. So time brings with its transformation the often painful wearing-down process. Vision blurs, health wanes; even the act of walking carries with it the painful reminder of the autumn of life. But this process is something to be faced, not something to be hidden away by false images. Yes, the old can be young at heart, but in their own way, with their own dignity. They do not have to copy the always-young
100 image of the Hollywood star. . . .

I returned to Puerto de Luna last summer to join the community in a celebration of the founding of the church. I drove by my grandfather's home, my uncles' ranches, the neglected adobe washing down into the earth from whence it came. And I wondered, how might the values of my grandfather's generation live in our own? What can we retain to see us through these hard times? I was to become a farmer, and I became a writer. As I plow and plant my words, do I nurture as my grandfather did in his fields and orchards? The answers are not simple.

"They don't make men like that anymore," is a phrase we hear when one
110 does honor to a man. I am glad I knew my grandfather. I am glad there are still times when I can see him in my dreams, hear him in my reverie. Sometimes I think I catch a whiff of that earthy aroma that was his smell. Then I smile. How strong these people were to leave such a lasting impression.

So, as I would greet my abuelo long ago, it would help us all to greet the old ones we know with this kind and respectful greeting: "*Buenos días le de Dios.*" ❧

E CHARACTER TRAITS
How did the grandfather change toward the end of his life?

---

4. **romanticize:** to view in an unrealistic or sentimental way.

Comprehension

1. **Recall** What did Anaya's grandfather do for a living?

2. **Recall** Why did Anaya visit his grandfather each summer?

3. **Recall** What **tradition** from his past does Anaya want people to practice today?

4. **Summarize** What important lessons did Anaya learn from his grandfather?

Literary Analysis

5. **Analyze Imagery** Anaya uses imagery—words and phrases that appeal to the reader's senses—to describe his grandfather. How do the images describing his childhood impressions of his grandfather contrast with the images describing the grandfather as he actually was?

6. **Examine Setting** Anaya's essay describes life in a rural community in eastern New Mexico. What influence did this setting have on his grandfather's values?

7. **Make Inferences** Anaya observed changes in his grandfather's **character traits** as he grew old. How did these changes affect his relationship with his grandfather? Cite evidence from the essay to support your inference.

8. **Analyze Author's Perspective** Review the chart that you created as you read. What beliefs, values, and feelings influence the way Anaya looks at "the pain of the transformation into old age"? Cite evidence.

9. **Interpret** Anaya poses the question "As I plow and plant my words, do I nurture as my grandfather did in his fields and orchards?" Why might Anaya consider his writing an attempt to "nurture"?

10. **Evaluate Author** Anaya cautions his readers not to "romanticize old age." Does Anaya romanticize, or view in an unrealistic way, his experiences with his grandfather? Support your opinion with examples from the essay.

Literary Criticism

11. **Biographical Context** "A Celebration of Grandfathers" was published in 1983. Fifteen years later, Anaya made the following statement in an interview: "The communal traditions of one generation are changed by the next, and we have to accept it and learn how the changes happen, and what is good or bad about that change. Sometimes you have to break free of family and community to find a new level of awareness for yourself." Compare this statement with the views that Anaya expresses in "A Celebration of Grandfathers."

Simply Grand: Generational Ties Matter

Magazine Article

Use with "A Celebration of Grandfathers," page 224.

OHIO STANDARDS

READING STANDARDS
2.1 Apply reading comprehension strategies
2.2 Answer questions to demonstrate comprehension

What's the Connection?

In "A Celebration of Grandfathers," Rudolfo Anaya recalls the deep bond he formed with his grandfather during the 1940s and expresses concern that children are no longer absorbing the traditions and values of their elders. In "Simply Grand: Generational Ties Matter," you will read about the efforts that grandparents make to maintain ties with their grandchildren in today's changing society.

Skill Focus: Identify Main Idea and Supporting Details

In nonfiction, the **main idea** is the most important idea, message, or opinion that the writer wants to communicate to the reader. A writer may state the main idea directly in the title or in a thesis statement or may only imply the idea, allowing the reader to infer it.

Writers develop a main idea through the use of **supporting details,** which appear throughout the body of an article or essay. References to supporting details may also appear in topic sentences or in subheadings. Supporting details can be

- facts or statistics
- examples
- statements from experts
- anecdotes

The chart below shows how the main idea was developed in "A Celebration of Grandfathers." Using a similar chart, record the main ideas and supporting details in "Simply Grand."

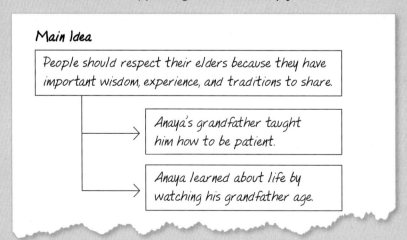

Main Idea

People should respect their elders because they have important wisdom, experience, and traditions to share.

Anaya's grandfather taught him how to be patient.

Anaya learned about life by watching his grandfather age.

SIMPLY GRAND:
Generational Ties Matter

by Megan Rutherford

There is a magical moment in the latter half of life when adults have a chance to reinvent themselves. They take on new names: Nana, Grandma, Bubbeh, Poppy, Grandpa, Zayde. They cast themselves in new roles: caregiver, mentor, pal, pamperer. They are filled with powerful new emotions that make them feel alive and vital. They become
10 grandparents.

"Every time a child is born, a grand-parent is born too," says grand-parenting guru and retired child psychologist Arthur Kornhaber. The bond between grandchild and grand-parent is second only to the attachment between parent and child. Kornhaber calls it "clear love" because it has no strings attached. "There's always some
20 conditional element to parents' love. Grandparents are just glad to have you, and the child can feel that."

That love may be the emotional equivalent of superglue, but it needs points of contact in order to stick. And today, like other family institutions, grandparenthood is being buffeted by sea changes. Working against the free exchange of
30 love are high divorce and remarriage rates, job stresses of dual-career parents (and grandparents), a global economy that puts vast distances between family members, and a pervasive bias against age spawned by the American obsession with youthfulness.

These impediments, however, are counterbalanced by innovations in travel, telecommunications, social
40 understanding, health, and life expectancy. Savvy parents and grandparents are harnessing these to strengthen intergenerational ties. "We have to reinvent ourselves as we go along, but we have more time to get it right," says Lillian Carson, a psychotherapist in Santa Barbara, California. . . . **A**

According to researchers, the better
50 the relationship between parent and grandparent, the greater the contact and closeness between grandparent and grandchild. "It's up to the parents to make the grandparents feel welcome and to send the message to their children that they're really integral," says Sally Newman, executive director of Generations Together at the

A MAIN IDEA AND SUPPORTING DETAILS
What main idea can you **infer** from the first four paragraphs of this article?

University of Pittsburgh. "The parents
60 should encourage frequent visits and
not make the grandparents feel
intrusive." And spending time together
is essential, says Yaffa Schlesinger, who
teaches sociology of the family at New
York City's Hunter College. "If
relationships are to be meaningful, they
have to be deep in time. You cannot be
friends with someone you met
yesterday." . . .

70   No child can have too much love
and attention. But that's not all
grandparents have to offer. "Kids learn
stuff from older people that they can't
get from anybody else," says Newman.
"Wisdom, patience, looking at things
from many perspectives, tolerance, and
hope. Older adults have lived through
wars, losses, economic deprivations,
and they give kids the security of
80 knowing that horrendous things can be
survived." For the older generation, the
relationship is equally precious.
"Having grandchildren is the
vindication of everything one has done
as a parent. When we see our children
passing on our values to another
generation, we know we have been
successful," says Margy-Ruth Davis, a
new grandmother in New York City.

90   Keeping the gates open need not be
expensive or arduous. Kathy Hersh, a
Miami writer who is the mother of
Katie, 11, and David, 7, sends a
weekly packet of their photocopied
poems, essays, teachers' notes, and
report cards to their maternal
grandparents in Indiana and their
paternal grandmother, a widow, in
Arizona. The grandparents respond in
100 kind. Kathy's mother sends homemade
jam, cookies, fudge—and lots and lots
of books. "It's not the value of the
contents," says Kathy. "It's that
the children have been thought of."

The value of that is beyond measure.
"I know my grandmother is always
going to love me and think everything
I do is wonderful," Katie told her
mother recently.

TECHNOLOGICAL AIDS

110 Other grandparents are discovering
the miracles of the technological
revolution. Margy-Ruth and Perry
Davis are heartsick that they cannot
be part of their granddaughter's daily
life in Toronto. But she is already part
of theirs, because the Davises have
equipped their daughter with a digital
camera, and every day she e-mails
them a fresh picture of baby Tiferet.
120 "It's hard for every visit to be a state
occasion, and it's hard not to be able to
pop over and just look in for half an
hour," says Margy-Ruth, "but at least
this way I can watch the baby change
day by day." . . .

The Davises are not alone in
cultivating electronic intimacy. Indeed,
anecdotal evidence suggests that
keeping in touch with grandchildren
130 may be one of the main computer uses
for seniors. Julia Sneden, a retired
North Carolina kindergarten teacher,
began e-mailing five-year-old Gina,
her stepgranddaughter in California,
several months before meeting her in
person. When they finally set eyes on
each other, they were already fast
friends. . . .

Jacquie Golden of Salinas,
140 California, finds that e-mail has an
unexpected advantage over the
telephone when communicating with
her teenage grandson Timothy Haines,
a student at the University of Nebraska.
"On the phone, he'll say everything is
fine, his life is fine, his mother's fine, his
friends are fine. With e-mail he opens
up. He tells me how he's really doing,

how rotten his last football game was,
150 and how school sucks. He gets down."

Many far-flung families have discovered a wonderful Web freebie: create-your-own family sites, where relatives equipped with passwords can post messages, share family anecdotes, keep track of birthdays, scan in snapshots—and see what the rest of their extended family has been up to.
Valerie Juleson lives in Wilton,
160 Connecticut. Her 12 adult children—11 foster kids and one biological child—are spread out all over the United States and Europe, and her two grandchildren live in Florida. She keeps up with everyone through a website. **B**

MULTICULTURAL CHALLENGES

Meera Ananthaswamy has a double challenge in uniting her children and parents: distance and culture. After
170 emigrating with her parents from India to Canada in 1962, she moved with her husband and two daughters to Dallas three years ago. To maintain the closeness they felt when they all lived near one another in Hamilton, Ontario, the three generations try to get together at least twice a year. In addition, the two girls spend summers with their grandparents. Between visits, they
180 stay in touch through weekly phone calls. Perumal Rajaram tells his granddaughters stories from Hindu mythology, instructs them in Indian philosophy and takes them to the Hindu temple in Hamilton for additional prayers. "It gives them history and a sense of where they've come from," says Meera.

But sometimes Suma, 16, and
190 Usha, 13, find their grandparents' sense of tradition onerous. The girls like to wear jeans and shorts, which Rajaram abhors. Then Meera steps in as interpreter. "I tell them, 'Your grandparents' definition of pretty is someone in a sari and not someone in short shorts. You've got to remember where your grandparents come from.'" . . .

200 Good communication and . . . [a] spirit of compromise have helped keep Meera's family close. That's not always the case in modern multicultural America, says sociology professor Schlesinger. The tragic irony is that many immigrants come to the U.S. in search of a better life for their children and grandchildren. But in order to achieve the goal set by their elders, the
210 younger generation must assimilate, and when they do, they become strangers who speak a different language and live by an alien code. "The grandparent has achieved his American Dream," says Schlesinger, "but at a terrible cost." . . .

FAMILY RITUALS

Even grandparents who have no physical or cultural divides separating them from their grandchildren may
220 yearn for ways to get closer. David Stearman and his wife Bernice are lucky enough to have all six grandkids living within a 25-minute drive of their home in Chevy Chase, Maryland. Nonetheless, the Stearmans are always looking for ways to enhance their togetherness. So Bernice has made a habit of taking the kids to "M&Ms"—movies and malls. David does
230 something a little more adventurous. For the past 10 summers, he has gone to camp with one—sometimes two—of his grandchildren. "The food is terrible, the beds are bad, there are no televisions or radios, but, man, you just feel good!" Stearman says. . . .

B MAIN IDEA AND SUPPORTING DETAILS
What supporting details appear in the discussion of technological aids?

Many families create and maintain their own rituals. That's what Beverly Zarin, a retired reading consultant, and her husband Sol have done. For the past 20 years, the Zarins, who live in Connecticut, have vacationed together with their two sons and their sons' families for two weeks every summer in a bungalow colony in Maine. "That's been a tradition, a wonderful way to really get to know one another," she says. In November everyone heads for St. Louis, Missouri, for Thanksgiving with the Zarins' son Larry and his family. At Passover the whole clan gathers at Beverly's house. "So we spend a good time together at least three times a year," says Beverly.

Other grandparents try to share the turning points of their own lives with their grandchildren. Forty years ago, Dorris Alcott of Timonium, Maryland took her first trip abroad, and her exposure to new people and places forever changed the way she viewed the world. This summer she decided to give her granddaughter Sylviane, 16, the same experience. "I felt having this at her age would be far more memorable than any little bit of money I could leave her—plus I'd have her to myself for three weeks!" Sylviane was moved by the experience of traveling with her grandmother. "I realized it was probably the last time I was ever going to spend that much time with her," she says, "and the first time too." As a result of the trip, Sylviane says, "I have more respect for my grandmother." . . .

CARING FOR CHILDREN

In a world with a shortage of good day care and an abundance of single-parent and two-career households, grandparents willing to care for their grandchildren are highly prized. In the old days, such care was generally rendered by Grandma. Today the social forces that produced the stay-at-home dad have introduced the caregiver grandad. Peter Gross, a retired law professor, picks up grandsons Paul, 3, and Mark, 18 months, every weekday morning at 8:15 and cares for them in his San Francisco home until 6 P.M. "It's a very close, intense relationship that's at the center of my life," says Gross. "What a relief to retire from the hurly-burly of the adult institutions of our world, where . . . politics and limitations tend to dominate, and move into this place of love and truth and nurturing and connection." **C**

Gross has a deep, everyday relationship with his grandchildren that many grandparents would move halfway around the world to enjoy. In fact, that's just about what Judith Hendra did. This summer Hendra quit her job as a fund raiser for Beth Israel Medical Center in New York City, sold her loft, and moved with her husband, a free-lance photographer, and her German shepherd to Los Angeles to be near her 18-month-old granddaughter Julia. "I reckon I have a window of opportunity of about 10 years before she turns into a California preteen, and then it'll be over," jokes Hendra. In the meantime Hendra, who plans to work part-time as a consultant, is looking forward to indulging a modest-sounding ambition: "I'd like to be a person who's taken for granted, who picks Julia up from school and does ordinary things that are actually very important for kids. I don't want to be a special event." Now that's something special.

C MAIN IDEA AND SUPPORTING DETAILS
How does the information in lines 276–298 support the writer's main idea?

Comprehension

1. **Recall** Name two factors that can make it difficult for grandparents and grandchildren to develop a close relationship.

2. **Summarize** How do grandchildren benefit from having a close relationship with their grandparents?

Critical Analysis

3. **Analyze Supporting Details** Review the supporting details in the chart you created and identify the kind of supporting detail (such as examples or anecdotes) that the writer used most often. Why might the writer have chosen to use this kind of supporting detail?

4. **Compare and Contrast** In "A Celebration of Grandfathers" and "Simply Grand," Rudolfo A. Anaya and Megan Rutherford discuss how families are affected by changes in society. Compare and contrast their views on this topic.

Read for Information: Make Generalizations

READING STANDARDS
2.1 Apply reading comprehension strategies
2.2 Answer questions to demonstrate comprehension

WRITING PROMPT
After reading "A Celebration of Grandfathers" and "Simply Grand," what general statements can you make about the grandparent-grandchild relationship? Write an **editorial** in which you make three generalizations about this relationship. Use information from both selections and your own experience to support your response.

To answer this prompt, you will need to make generalizations. A **generalization** is an idea or statement that summarizes the general characteristics rather than the specific details of a subject. To make a generalization, follow these steps.

1. Gather evidence—facts, anecdotes, and observations—about the grandparent-grandchild relationship.

2. Look for patterns or connections among the pieces of evidence.

3. Make a general statement that characterizes the patterns or connections.

4. Review the evidence to make sure your generalizations are well supported and fair. Revise them if necessary.

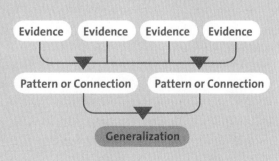

The Gift
Poem by Li-Young Lee

Those Winter Sundays
Poem by Robert Hayden

How do you show you CARE?

OHIO STANDARDS

READING STANDARDS
2.1 Make inferences and draw conclusions

4.1 Compare and contrast an author's use of direct and indirect characterization

KEY IDEA Sometimes the most vivid memories are of ordinary events—for example, a relative tying your shoelaces when you were a child or cooking a favorite meal. What makes such moments special are the feelings you associate with them. In "The Gift" and "Those Winter Sundays," the speakers recall how their fathers showed love through simple acts of **caring.**

QUICKWRITE Make a list of ordinary events or routines that you remember from childhood. Then write a paragraph about one item on the list, explaining why the memory is meaningful to you.

Childhood Memories
1. *Visiting grandparents*
2. *Setting the dinner table*
3.
4.
5.

LITERARY ANALYSIS: CHARACTERS IN POETRY

Characters in poetry are often created with **imagery**—words and phrases that appeal to the reader's senses. By using imagery, poets can create a vivid character in just a few words. For example, in "Those Winter Sundays," the speaker offers the following image of his father:

... cracked hands that ached
from labor in the weekday weather ...

This phrase not only suggests the father's physical appearance but also hints at his personality and the hardship he endures.

As you read the two poems, notice the imagery each poet uses to create a character. Look for words that describe the character's

- appearance
- actions or behavior
- feelings or thoughts
- character traits

READING SKILL: MAKE INFERENCES ABOUT THE SPEAKER

To learn more about the speaker of a poem, readers can **make inferences,** or logical guesses based on clues in the text. For example, in "The Gift" the speaker describes how he reacted when his father began to remove a splinter from his palm.

To pull the metal splinter from my palm
my father recited a story in a low voice.
I watched his lovely face and not the blade.

You may infer from details in these lines that the speaker trusts his father and that they have a loving relationship.

As you read each poem, use a diagram like the one shown to help you organize inferences about the speaker.

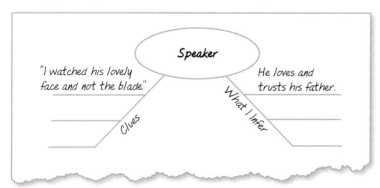

Author Online

Li-Young Lee: A Search for Identity
Li-Young Lee (lē-yŭng lē) was born in Indonesia, where his parents took refuge after fleeing from China. The Indonesian government imprisoned Lee's father in 1958 during a period of anti-Chinese persecution.

Li-Young Lee born 1957

After his release, the family lived in several Asian countries before settling in the United States when Lee was seven years old. Lee's childhood experiences have a strong influence on his poetry. He often writes about immigrants and examines the role that family and memory play in shaping identity.

Robert Hayden: Poetry as Refuge
Robert Hayden grew up in a poor neighborhood in Detroit, Michigan. He was raised by neighbors from an early age after his biological parents separated. Although Hayden's foster parents made sacrifices for his education, their troubled marriage fueled

Robert Hayden 1913–1980

spells of depression in him. Hayden sought escape from his "dark nights of the soul" by reading and writing poetry. His first collection came out in 1940 to little fanfare. However, by 1962, when "Those Winter Sundays" was published in the volume *A Ballad of Remembrance,* Hayden was on his way to becoming a prominent poet.

MORE ABOUT THE AUTHOR
For more on Li-Young Lee and Robert Hayden, visit the **Literature Center** at ClassZone.com.

The Gift

Li-Young Lee

ANALYZE VISUALS
How does this painting reflect the **mood** of the poem?

To pull the metal splinter from my palm
my father recited a story in a low voice.
I watched his lovely face and not the blade.
Before the story ended, he'd removed
5 the iron sliver I thought I'd die from.

I can't remember the tale,
but hear his voice still, a well
of dark water, a prayer.
And I recall his hands,
10 two measures of tenderness
he laid against my face,
the flames of discipline
he raised above my head. **A**

Had you entered that afternoon
15 you would have thought you saw a man
planting something in a boy's palm,
a silver tear, a tiny flame.
Had you followed that boy
you would have arrived here,
20 where I bend over my wife's right hand.

Look how I shave her thumbnail down
so carefully she feels no pain.
Watch as I lift the splinter out.
I was seven when my father
25 took my hand like this,
and I did not hold that shard
between my fingers and think,
Metal that will bury me,
christen it Little Assassin,
30 Ore Going Deep for My Heart.
And I did not lift up my wound and cry,
Death visited here!
I did what a child does
when he's given something to keep.
35 I kissed my father. **B**

A CHARACTERS IN POETRY
What do you learn about the father from **images** in this stanza?

B MAKE INFERENCES
Reread lines 24–35. What can you infer about the feelings of the **speaker** after his father removes the splinter?

Interwoven Hands. Todd Davidson. © Images.com/Corbis.

Those Winter Sundays

Robert Hayden

Vigour, Martine Levy. Musée d'Art Moderne, Troyes, France. Photo © Gerard Blot/
Réunion des Musées Nationaux/Art Resource, New York.

Sundays too my father got up early
and put his clothes on in the blueblack cold,
then with cracked hands that ached
from labor in the weekday weather made
5 banked fires blaze. No one ever thanked him.

I'd wake and hear the cold splintering, breaking.
When the rooms were warm, he'd call,
and slowly I would rise and dress,
fearing the chronic angers of that house, **C**

10 Speaking indifferently to him,
who had driven out the cold
and polished my good shoes as well.
What did I know, what did I know
of love's austere and lonely offices?

C MAKE INFERENCES
What can you infer about
the **speaker's** attitude
toward his family from
clues in lines 1–9? Which
details did you use to
make this inference?

Comprehension

1. **Recall** What two incidents are described in "The Gift"?

2. **Recall** What does the speaker recall his father doing in "Those Winter Sundays"?

3. **Summarize** How does each speaker react to his father's act of **caring?**

Literary Analysis

4. **Examine Characters in Poetry** Fill in a chart like the one shown with details that suggest the traits of the father in each poem. Then write a sentence describing each of these characters.

Father's Traits	"The Gift"	"Those Winter Sundays"
Physical traits		
Personality traits		

5. **Analyze Title** Why might Li-Young Lee have chosen to call his poem "The Gift"?

6. **Interpret** Reread the last two lines of "Those Winter Sundays." What does the speaker mean when he refers to "love's austere and lonely offices"?

7. **Make Inferences** Review the charts you created as you read. Based on your inferences, how would you characterize the father-son relationship in each poem?

8. **Compare and Contrast Speakers** Compare and contrast the attitudes of the speakers toward the experiences they describe in the poems.

9. **Analyze Author's Perspective** Both of the speakers are adults who look back on experiences from their childhood. How does this perspective influence the way each speaker views his experience?

Literary Criticism

10. **Critical Interpretations** The poet Gerald Stern has spoken of "the large vision, the deep seriousness and the almost heroic ideal" in Li-Young Lee's poetry. How well does this phrase describe Lee's poem "The Gift"? Cite evidence from the text to support your opinion.

A Marriage Proposal
Drama by Anton Chekhov

Why do people argue over SILLY THINGS?

OHIO STANDARDS

READING STANDARDS
4.1 Compare and contrast an author's use of direct and indirect characterization
4.5 Analyze how choice of genre affects theme or topic

KEY IDEA When two stubborn people have different opinions about something unimportant, a silly argument is likely to erupt. Such **pettiness** is displayed by the characters in *A Marriage Proposal*, who can't seem to agree on anything, even when they share the same goal.

ROLE-PLAY With a partner, brainstorm a scenario in which you have a difference of opinion about something of little importance. Then role-play an argument. Afterward, discuss any patterns that you noticed during the argument.

● LITERARY ANALYSIS: CHARACTERS IN A FARCE

A **farce** is a humorous play that provokes laughter through ridiculous situations and dialogue. Characters in a farce are usually comical stereotypes who conform to a fixed pattern or are defined by a single trait. Notice in this speech from *A Marriage Proposal* how a character's trait is exaggerated for comic effect:

I have a weak heart, continual palpitation, and I am very sensitive and always getting excited.

As you read the play, create a chart for each character. Record details that help you identify the character's main trait or pattern of behavior.

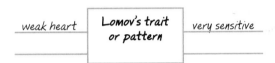

weak heart — Lomov's trait or pattern — very sensitive

● READING SKILL: READING A PLAY

To understand a play, you will need to read **stage directions** that describe the scenery and props, the actions of characters, or the tone in which dialogue should be delivered. Sometimes a stage direction will indicate one of the following:

- an **aside**—a short speech directed to the audience or a character but not heard by the other characters onstage

- a **monologue**—a long speech that is usually delivered by a character who is alone onstage

Asides and monologues can be used to reveal a character's private thoughts and feelings. As you read *A Marriage Proposal*, notice what each stage direction tells you about the characters' words and actions.

▲ VOCABULARY IN CONTEXT

Complete each sentence with a word from the list.

WORD LIST	contrary	glutton	meditate	usurper

1. The scheming _____ tried to seize the king's throne.
2. I need to _____ on this issue awhile before deciding.
3. You insist on being _____ just to be different.
4. Please don't be a _____ at the dinner table.

Author **Online**

Literary Detour
Anton Chekhov (chĕk'ôf) was a master of the short story as well as one of the most important modern playwrights. Born in southern Russia, he moved to Moscow as a young man and planned to become a doctor. While in medical school, he published many literary

Anton Chekhov
1860–1904

sketches to support his family. Although he received his medical degree in 1884, he never practiced medicine on a regular basis. Instead, he chose to pursue a writing career.

Early Success Chekhov quickly won fame for his comical stories and farces, such as *A Marriage Proposal*. He considered humor to be an essential ingredient in all his work, but his writing grew more serious over time. Most of his full-length plays, including *Uncle Vanya*, *The Three Sisters*, and *The Cherry Orchard*, combine elements of tragedy and farce. Chekhov died from tuberculosis at age 44, when he was at the height of his career.

MORE ABOUT THE AUTHOR
For more on Anton Chekhov, visit the **Literature Center** at **ClassZone.com**.

Background

The Russian Gentry *A Marriage Proposal* takes place on a country estate in late-19th-century Russia. The characters are members of the privileged class known as the gentry. These wealthy landowners employed peasants to work their fields, which allowed them to enjoy a life of leisure. Writers of farces often poked fun at the habits of the gentry, including their tendency to marry for economic gain rather than affection.

A Marriage Proposal

ANTON CHEKHOV

CHARACTERS

Stepan Stepanovitch Tschubukov (styĭ-pän′ styĭ-pän′əv-yĭch chü-bü′kəf), a country farmer

Natalia Stepanovna (nə-täl′yə styĭ-pä-nôv′nə), his daughter (aged 25)

Ivan Vassiliyitch Lomov (ĭ-vän′ vəs-yēl′yĭch lô′məf), Tschubukov's neighbor

SCENE

The reception room in Tschubukov's country home in Russia. Tschubukov discovered as the curtain rises. Enter Lomov, wearing a dress suit. **A**

TIME

The present [1890s]

A READING A PLAY
What information in the **stage directions** helps you visualize the **setting** of the play?

Tschubukov (*going toward him and greeting him*). Who is this I see? My dear fellow! Ivan Vassiliyitch! I'm so glad to see you! (*shakes hands*) But this is a surprise! How are you?

Lomov. Thank you! And how are you?

Tschubukov. Oh, so-so, my friend. Please sit down. It isn't right to forget one's neighbor. But tell me, why all this ceremony? Dress clothes, white gloves, and all? Are you on your way to some engagement, my good fellow?

Lomov. No, I have no engagement except with you, Stepan Stepanovitch.

Tschubukov. But why in evening clothes, my friend? This isn't New Year's!

ANALYZE VISUALS
What **mood** is suggested by this painting?

The Promenade (1917), Marc Chagall. Oil on canvas. Russian State Museum, St. Petersburg, Russia. Photo © Scala/Art Resource, New York/Artists Rights Society (ARS), New York.

10 **Lomov.** You see, it's simply this, that— (*composing himself*) I have come to you, Stepan Stepanovitch, to trouble you with a request. It is not the first time I have had the honor of turning to you for assistance, and you have always, that is—I beg your pardon, I am a bit excited! I'll take a drink of water first, dear Stepan Stepanovitch. (*He drinks.*)

Tschubukov (*aside*). He's come to borrow money! I won't give him any! (*to* Lomov) What is it, then, dear Lomov? **B**

Lomov. You see—dear—Stepanovitch, pardon me, Stepan—Stepan—dear-vitch—I mean—I am terribly nervous, as you will be so good as to see—! What I mean to say—you are the only one who can help me, though I don't

20 deserve it, and—and I have no right whatever to make this request of you.

Tschubukov. Oh, don't beat about the bush, my dear fellow. Tell me!

Lomov. Immediately—in a moment. Here it is, then: I have come to ask for the hand of your daughter, Natalia Stepanovna.

B READING A PLAY
What does Tschubukov's **aside** reveal about him?

The Window at the Country House (1915), Marc Chagall. Tretyakov Gallery, Moscow, Russia.
© 2008 Artists Rights Society (ARS), New York/ADAGP, Paris.

Tschubukov (*joyfully*). Angel! Ivan Vassiliyitch! Say that once again! I didn't quite hear it!

Lomov. I have the honor to beg—

Tschubukov (*interrupting*). My dear, dear man. I am so happy that everything is so—everything! (*embraces and kisses him*) I have wanted this to happen for so long. It has been my dearest wish! (*He represses a tear.*) And I have always loved
30 you, my dear fellow, as my own son! May God give you his blessings and his grace and—I always wanted it to happen. But why am I standing here like a blockhead? I am completely dumbfounded with pleasure, completely dumbfounded. My whole being—! I'll call Natalia—

Lomov. Dear Stepan Stepanovitch, what do you think? May I hope for Natalia Stepanovna's acceptance?

Tschubukov. Really! A fine boy like you— and you think she won't accept on the minute? Lovesick as a cat and all that—! (*He goes out, right.*)

Lomov. I'm cold. My whole body is trembling as though I was going to take my examination! But the chief thing is to settle matters! If a person **meditates**
40 too much, or hesitates, or talks about it, waits for an ideal or for true love, he never gets it. Brrr! It's cold! Natalia is an excellent housekeeper, not at all bad looking, well educated—what more could I ask? I'm so excited my ears are roaring! (*He drinks water.*) And not to marry, that won't do! In the first place, I'm thirty-five—a critical age, you might say. In the second place, I must live a well-regulated life. I have a weak heart, continual palpitation, and I am very sensitive and always getting excited. My lips begin to tremble and the pulse in my right temple throbs terribly. But the worst of all is sleep! I hardly lie down and begin to doze before something in my left side begins to pull and tug, and something begins to hammer in my left shoulder—and in my head, too! I
50 jump up like a madman, walk about a little, lie down again, but the moment I fall asleep I have a terrible cramp in the side. And so it is all night long! (*Enter Natalia Stepanovna.*) **C**

Natalia. Ah! It's you. Papa said to go in: there was a dealer in there who'd come to buy something. Good afternoon, Ivan Vassiliyitch.

Lomov. Good day, my dear Natalia Stepanovna.

Natalia. You must pardon me for wearing my apron and this old dress: we are working today. Why haven't you come to see us oftener? You've not been here for so long! Sit down (*They sit down.*) Won't you have something to eat?

Lomov. Thank you, I have just had lunch.

60 **Natalia.** Smoke, do, there are the matches. Today it is beautiful, and only yesterday it rained so hard that the workmen couldn't do a stroke of work. How many bricks have you cut? Think of it! I was so anxious that I had the whole field mowed, and now I'm sorry I did it, because I'm afraid the hay will rot. It would have been better if I had waited. But what on earth is this? You are in evening clothes! The latest cut! Are you on your way to a ball? And you seem to be looking better, too—really. Why are you dressed up so gorgeously? **D**

meditate (mĕd′ĭ-tāt′) *v.* to consider for a long time

C CHARACTERS IN A FARCE
What main trait does Lomov exhibit in his **monologue**?

D GRAMMAR AND STYLE
Reread lines 60–66. Chekhov uses **declarative, interrogative, imperative,** and **exclamatory** sentences to reflect Natalia's scattered thoughts.

Lomov (*excited*). You see, my dear Natalia Stepanovna—it's simply this: I have decided to ask you to listen to me—of course it will be a surprise, and indeed you'll be angry, but!— (*aside*) How fearfully cold it is!

70 **Natalia.** What is it? (*a pause*) Well?

Lomov. I'll try to be brief. My dear Natalia Stepanovna, as you know, for many years, since my childhood, I have had the honor to know your family. My poor aunt and her husband, from whom, as you know, I inherited the estate, always had the greatest respect for your father and your poor mother. The Lomovs and the Tschubukovs have been for decades on the friendliest, indeed the closest, terms with each other, and furthermore my property, as you know, adjoins your own. If you will be so good as to remember, my meadows touch your birch woods.

Natalia. Pardon the interruption. You said "my meadows"—but are they yours?

80 **Lomov.** Yes, they belong to me.

Natalia. What nonsense! The meadows belong to us—not to you!

Lomov. No, to me! Now, my dear Natalia Stepanovna!

Natalia. Well, that is certainly news to me. How do they belong to you?

Lomov. How? I am speaking of the meadows lying between your birch woods and my brick earth.[1]

Natalia. Yes, exactly. They belong to us.

Lomov. No, you are mistaken, my dear Natalia Stepanovna, they belong to me.

Natalia. Try to remember exactly, Ivan Vassiliyitch. Is it so long ago that you inherited them?

90 **Lomov.** Long ago! As far back as I can remember they have always belonged to us.

Natalia. But that isn't true! You'll pardon my saying so.

Lomov. It is all a matter of record, my dear Natalia Stepanovna. It is true that at one time the title to the meadows was disputed, but now everyone knows they belong to me. There is no room for discussion. Be so good as to listen: my aunt's grandmother put these meadows, free from all costs, into the hands of your father's grandfather's peasants for a certain time while they were making bricks for my grandmother. These people used the meadows free of cost for about forty years, living there as they would on their own property. Later, however, when—

100 **Natalia.** There's not a word of truth in that! My grandfather, and my great grandfather, too, knew that their estate reached back to the swamp, so that the meadows belong to us. What further discussion can there be? I can't understand it. It is really most annoying.

Lomov. I'll show you the papers, Natalia Stepanovna.

Natalia. No, either you are joking or trying to lead me into a discussion. That's not at all nice! We have owned this property for nearly three hundred years, and

---

1. **brick earth:** clay suitable for making bricks.

now all at once we hear that it doesn't belong to us. Ivan Vassiliyitch, you will pardon me, but I really can't believe my ears. So far as I'm concerned, the meadows are worth very little. In all they don't contain more than five acres, and they are worth only a few hundred rubles,[2] say three hundred, but the injustice of the thing is what affects me. Say what you will, I can't bear injustice.

Lomov. Only listen until I have finished, please! The peasants of your respected father's grandfather, as I have already had the honor to tell you, baked bricks for my grandmother. My aunt's grandmother wished to do them a favor—

Natalia. Grandfather! Grandmother! Aunt! I know nothing of them. All I know is that the meadows belong to us, and that ends the matter.

Lomov. No, they belong to me!

Natalia. And if you keep on explaining it for two days and put on five suits of evening clothes, the meadows are still ours, ours, ours! I don't want to take your property, but I refuse to give up what belongs to us! **E**

Lomov. Natalia Stepanovna, I don't need the meadows, I am only concerned with the principle. If you are agreeable, I beg of you, accept them as a gift from me!

Natalia. But I can give them to you, because they belong to me! That is very peculiar, Ivan Vassiliyitch! Until now we have considered you as a good neighbor and a good friend; only last year we lent you our threshing machine so that we couldn't thresh until November, and you treat us like thieves! You offer to give me my own land. Excuse me, but neighbors don't treat each other that way. In my opinion, it's a very low trick—to speak frankly—

Lomov. According to you I'm a **usurper**, then, am I? My dear lady, I have never appropriated other people's property, and I shall permit no one to accuse me of such a thing! (*He goes quickly to the bottle and drinks water.*) The meadows are mine!

Natalia. That's not the truth! They are mine!

Lomov. Mine!

Natalia. Eh? I'll prove it to you! This afternoon I'll send my reapers into the meadows.

Lomov. W—h—a—t?

Natalia. My reapers will be there today!

Lomov. And I'll chase them off!

Natalia. If you dare!

Lomov. The meadows are mine, you understand? Mine!

Natalia. Really, you don't need to scream so! If you want to scream and snort and rage you may do it at home, but here please keep yourself within the limits of common decency.

E CHARACTERS IN A FARCE
Reread lines 104–120. What pattern of behavior appears evident in Natalia's responses to Lomov's claims?

usurper (yōō-sûrp′ər) *n.* someone who wrongfully takes possession of something

Woman Reaping (before 1930), Marc Chagall. National Gallery, Prague, Czech Republic. © 2008 Artists Rights Society (ARS), New York/ADAGP, Paris. Photo © Nimatallah/Art Resource, New York.

---

2. **rubles** (rōō′bəlz): units of Russian money.

The Harvest, Natalia Goncharova. Russian State Museum, St. Petersburg, Russia. © 2008 Artists Rights Society (ARS), New York/ADAGP, Paris. Photo © Scala/Art Resource, New York.

ANALYZE VISUALS
Which details in this painting suggest activities or locations that are discussed in the play?

Lomov. My dear lady, if it weren't that I were suffering from palpitation of the heart and hammering of the arteries in my temples, I would deal with you very
150 differently! (*in a loud voice*) The meadows belong to me!

Natalia. Us!

Lomov. Me! (*Enter* Tschubukov, *right.*)

Tschubukov. What's going on here? What is he yelling about?

Natalia. Papa, please tell this gentleman to whom the meadows belong, to us or to him?

Tschubukov (*to* Lomov). My dear fellow, the meadows are ours.

Lomov. But, merciful heavens, Stepan Stepanovitch, how do you make that out? You at least must be reasonable. My aunt's grandmother gave the use of the meadows free of cost to your grandfather's peasants; the peasants lived on
160 the land for forty years and used it as their own, but later when—

Tschubukov. Permit me, my dear friend. You forget that your grandfather's peasants never paid, because there had been a lawsuit over the meadows, and everyone knows that the meadows belong to us. You haven't looked at the map.

Lomov. I'll prove to you that they belong to me!

Tschubukov. Don't try to prove it, my dear fellow.

Lomov. I will!

Tschubukov. My good fellow, what are you shrieking about? You can't prove anything by yelling, you know. I don't ask for anything that belongs to you, nor do I intend to give up anything of my own. Why should I? If it has gone so far, my dear man, that you really intend to claim the meadows, I'd rather give them to the peasants than you, and I certainly shall!

Lomov. I can't believe it! By what right can you give away property that doesn't belong to you?

Tschubukov. Really, you must allow me to decide what I am to do with my own land! I'm not accustomed, young man, to have people address me in that tone of voice. I, young man, am twice your age, and I beg you to address me respectfully.

Lomov. No! No! You think I'm a fool! You're making fun of me! You call my property yours and then you expect me to stand quietly by and talk to you like a human being. That isn't the way a good neighbor behaves, Stepan Stepanovitch! You are no neighbor, you're no better than a land grabber. That's what you are!

Tschubukov. Wh—at? What did he say?

Natalia. Papa, send the reapers into the meadows this minute!

Tschubukov (*to* Lomov). What was that you said, sir?

Natalia. The meadows belong to us, and I won't give them up! I won't give them up! I won't give them up!

Lomov. We'll see about that! I'll prove in court that they belong to me.

Tschubukov. In court! You may sue in court, sir, if you like! Oh, I know you, you are only waiting to find an excuse to go to law! You're an intriguer,[3] that's what you are! Your whole family were always looking for quarrels. The whole lot!

Lomov. Kindly refrain from insulting my family. The entire race of Lomov has always been honorable! And never has one been brought to trial for embezzlement, as your dear uncle was!

Tschubukov. And the whole Lomov family were insane!

Natalia. Every one of them!

Tschubukov. Your grandmother was a dipsomaniac,[4] and the younger aunt, Nastasia Michailovna, ran off with an architect. **F**

Lomov. And your mother limped. (*He puts his hand over his heart.*) Oh, my side pains! My temples are bursting! Lord in heaven! Water!!

Tschubukov. And your dear father was a gambler—and a **glutton**!

Natalia. And your aunt was a gossip like few others.

Lomov. And you are an intriguer. Oh, my heart! And it's an open secret that you cheated at the elections—my eyes are blurred! Where is my hat?

Natalia. Oh, how low! Liar! Disgusting thing!

F **CHARACTERS IN A FARCE**
Reread lines 189–198. How does Chekhov use exaggeration to create humor in this exchange of dialogue?

glutton (glŭt′n) *n.* a person who eats too much

---

3. **intriguer** (ĭn-trē′gər): a schemer.

4. **dipsomaniac** (dĭp′sə-mā′nē-ăk′): an alcoholic.

Lomov. Where's my hat? My heart! Where shall I go? Where is the door? Oh—it seems—as though I were dying! I can't—my legs won't hold me— (*goes to the door*)

Tschubukov (*following him*). May you never darken my door again!

210 **Natalia.** Bring your suit to court! We'll see! (Lomov *staggers out, center.*)

Tschubukov (*angrily*). The devil!

Natalia. Such a good-for-nothing! And then they talk about being good neighbors!

Tschubukov. Loafer! Scarecrow! Monster!

Natalia. A swindler like that takes over a piece of property that doesn't belong to him and then dares to argue about it!

Tschubukov. And to think that this fool dares to make a proposal of marriage!

Natalia. What? A proposal of marriage?

Tschubukov. Why, yes! He came here to make you a proposal of marriage.

220 **Natalia.** Why didn't you tell me that before?

Tschubukov. That's why he had on his evening clothes! The poor fool!

Natalia. Proposal for me? (*falls into an armchair and groans*) Bring him back! Bring him back!

Tschubukov. Bring whom back!

Natalia. Faster, faster, I'm sinking! Bring him back! (*She becomes hysterical.*)

Tschubukov. What is it? What's wrong with you? (*his hands to his head*) I'm cursed with bad luck! I'll shoot myself! I'll hang myself!

Natalia. I'm dying! Bring him back!

Tschubukov. Bah! In a minute! Don't bawl! (*He rushes out, center.*)

230 **Natalia** (*groaning*). What have they done to me? Bring him back! Bring him back!

Tschubukov (*comes running in*). He's coming at once! The devil take him! Ugh! Talk to him yourself, I can't!

Natalia (*groaning*). Bring him back!

Tschubukov. He's coming, I tell you! "Oh, Lord! What a task it is to be the father of a grown daughter!" I'll cut my throat! I really will cut my throat! We've argued with the fellow, insulted him, and now you've thrown him out!—and you did it all, you!

Natalia. No, you! You haven't any manners, you are brutal! If it weren't for you, he wouldn't have gone!

240 **Tschubukov.** Oh, yes, I'm to blame! If I shoot or hang myself, remember *you'll* be to blame. You forced me to do it! (Lomov *appears in the doorway.*) There, talk to him yourself! (*He goes out.*)

Lomov. Terrible palpitation! My leg is lamed! My side hurts me—

Natalia. Pardon us, we were angry, Ivan Vassiliyitch. I remember now—the meadows really belong to you.

Lomov. My heart is beating terribly! My meadows—my eyelids tremble— (*They sit down.*) We were wrong. It was only the principle of the thing—the property isn't worth much to me, but the principle is worth a great deal.

Natalia. Exactly, the principle! Let us talk about something else. **G**

250 **Lomov.** Because I have proofs that my aunt's grandmother had, with the peasants of your good father—

Natalia. Enough, enough. (*aside*) I don't know how to begin. (*to* Lomov) Are you going hunting soon?

Lomov. Yes, heath cock shooting, respected Natalia Stepanovna. I expect to begin after the harvest. Oh, did you hear? My dog, Ugadi, you know him—limps!

Natalia. What a shame! How did that happen?

Lomov. I don't know. Perhaps it's a dislocation, or maybe he was bitten by some other dog. (*He sighs.*) The best dog I ever had—to say nothing of the price! I paid Mironov a hundred and twenty-five rubles for him.

260 **Natalia.** That was too much to pay, Ivan Vassiliyitch.

Lomov. In my opinion it was very cheap. A wonderful dog!

Natalia. Papa paid eighty-five rubles for his Otkatai, and Otkatai is much better than your Ugadi!

Lomov. Really? Otkatai is better than Ugadi? What an idea! (*He laughs.*) Otkatai better than Ugadi!

Natalia. Of course he is better. It is true Otkatai is still young; he isn't full grown yet, but in the pack or on the leash with two or three, there is no better than he, even—

Lomov. I really beg your pardon, Natalia Stepanovna, but you quite overlooked 270 the fact that he has a short lower jaw, and a dog with a short lower jaw can't snap.

Natalia. Short lower jaw? That's the first I ever heard that!

Lomov. I assure you, his lower jaw is shorter than the upper.

Natalia. Have you measured it?

Lomov. I have measured it. He is good at running though.

Natalia. In the first place, our Otkatai is pure-bred, a full-blooded son of Sapragavas and Stameskis, and as for your mongrel, nobody could ever figure out his pedigree; he's old and ugly and skinny as an old hag.

Lomov. Old, certainly! I wouldn't take five of your Otkatais for him! Ugadi is a 280 dog, and Otkatai is—it is laughable to argue about it! Dogs like your Otkatai can be found by the dozens at any dog dealer's, a whole pound full!

Natalia. Ivan Vassiliyitch, you are very **contrary** today. First our meadows belong to you, and then Ugadi is better than Otkatai. I don't like it when a person doesn't say what he really thinks. You know perfectly well that Otkatai is a hundred times better than your silly Ugadi. What makes you keep on saying he isn't?

G CHARACTERS IN A FARCE
How serious is Natalia's commitment to principle?

contrary (kŏn'trĕr'ē) *adj.* stubbornly uncooperative or contradictory

Dog Lying in the Snow (1910–1911), Franz Marc. Oil on canvas, 62.5 cm × 105 cm. Stadelsches Kunstinstitut und Stadtische Galerie, Frankfurt am Main, Germany.

Lomov. I can see, Natalia Stepanovna, that you consider me either a blind man or a fool. But at least you may as well admit that Otkatai has a short lower jaw!

Natalia. It isn't so!

290 **Lomov.** Yes, a short lower jaw!

Natalia (*loudly*). It's not so!

Lomov. What makes you scream, my dear lady?

Natalia. What makes you talk such nonsense? It's disgusting! It is high time that Ugadi was shot, and you compare him with Otkatai!

Lomov. Pardon me, but I can't carry on this argument any longer. I have palpitation of the heart!

Natalia. I have always noticed that the hunters who do the most talking know the least about hunting.

Lomov. My dear lady, I beg of you to be still. My heart is bursting! (*He shouts.*)
300 Be still!

Natalia. I won't be still until you admit that Otkatai is better! (*Enter Tschubukov.*)

Tschubukov. Well, has it begun again?

Natalia. Papa, say frankly, on your honor, which dog is better: Otkatai or Ugadi?

Lomov. Stepan Stepanovitch, I beg of you, just answer this: has your dog a short lower jaw or not? Yes or no?

Tschubukov. And what if he has? Is it of such importance? There is no better dog in the whole country.

310 **Lomov.** My Ugadi is better. Tell the truth now!

Tschubukov. Don't get so excited, my dear fellow! Permit me. Your Ugadi certainly has his good points. He is from a good breed, has a good stride, strong haunches, and so forth. But the dog, if you really want to know, has two faults; he is old and he has a short lower jaw.

Lomov. Pardon me, I have a palpitation of the heart!—Let us keep to facts— just remember in Maruskins's meadows, my Ugadi kept ear to ear with Count Rasvachai and your dog was left behind.

Tschubukov. He was behind, because the count struck him with his whip.

Lomov. Quite right. All the other dogs were on the fox's scent, but Otkatai
320 found it necessary to bite a sheep.

Tschubukov. That isn't so!—I am sensitive about that and beg you to stop this argument. He struck him because everybody looks on a strange dog of good blood with envy. Even you, sir, aren't free from sin. No sooner do you find a dog better than Ugadi than you begin to—this, that—his, mine—and so forth! I remember distinctly.

Lomov. I remember something, too!

Tschubukov (*mimicking him*). I remember something, too! What do you remember? 🅗

Lomov. Palpitation! My leg is lame—I can't—

330 **Natalia.** Palpitation! What kind of hunter are you? You ought to stay in the kitchen by the stove and wrestle with the potato peelings and not go fox hunting! Palpitation!

Tschubukov. And what kind of hunter are you? A man with your disease ought to stay at home and not jolt around in the saddle. If you were a hunter! But you only ride round in order to find out about other people's dogs and make trouble for everyone. I am sensitive! Let's drop the subject. Besides, you're no hunter.

Lomov. You only ride around to flatter the count! My heart! You intriguer! Swindler!

Tschubukov. And what of it? (*shouting*) Be still!

340 **Lomov.** Intriguer!

Tschubukov. Baby! Puppy! Walking drugstore!

Lomov. Old rat! Jesuit![5] Oh, I know you!

Tschubukov. Be still! Or I'll shoot you—with my worst gun, like a partridge! Fool! Loafer!

Lomov. Everyone knows that—oh, my heart!—that your poor late wife beat you. My leg—my temples—heavens—I'm dying—I—

Tschubukov. And your housekeeper wears the pants in your house!

🅗 **READING A PLAY**
How does the **stage direction** clarify this speech?

---

5. **Jesuit** (jĕzh′ōō-ĭt): a member of a Roman Catholic religious order that was suppressed in Russia because of its resistance to the authority of the czar, the ruler of Russia. At the time, the term had the negative meaning of "one who schemes or plots."

Lomov. Here—here—there—there—my heart has burst! My shoulder is torn apart. Where is my shoulder? I'm dying! (*He falls into a chair.*) The doctor!
350 (*faints*)

Tschubukov. Baby! Half-baked clam! Fool!

Natalia. Nice sort of hunter you are! You can't even sit on a horse. (*to* Tschubukov) Papa, what's the matter with him? (*She screams.*) Ivan Vassiliyitch! He is dead!

Lomov. I'm ill! I can't breathe! Air!

Natalia. He is dead! (*She shakes* Lomov *in the chair.*) Ivan Vassiliyitch! What have we done! He is dead! (*She sinks into a chair.*) The doctor—doctor! (*She goes into hysterics.*) ❶

Tschubukov. Ahh! What is it? What's the matter with you?

360 **Natalia** (*groaning*). He's dead! Dead!

Tschubukov. Who is dead? Who? (*looking at* Lomov) Yes, he is dead! Good God! Water! The doctor! (*holding the glass to* Lomov's *lips*) Drink! No, he won't drink! He's dead! What a terrible situation! Why didn't I shoot myself? Why have I never cut my throat? What am I waiting for now? Only give me a knife! Give me a pistol! (Lomov *moves.*) He's coming to! Drink some water—there!

Lomov. Sparks! Mists! Where am I?

Tschubukov. Get married! Quick, and then go to the devil! She's willing! (*He joins the hands of* Lomov *and* Natalia.) She's agreed! Only leave me in peace!

Lomov. Wh—what? (*getting up*) Whom?

370 **Tschubukov.** She's willing! Well? Kiss each other and—the devil take you both!

Natalia (*groans*). He lives! Yes, yes, I'm willing!

Tschubukov. Kiss each other!

Lomov. Eh? Whom? (Natalia *and* Lomov *kiss.*) Very nice! Pardon me, but what is this for? Oh, yes, I understand! My heart—sparks—I am happy. Natalia Stepanovna. (*He kisses her hand.*) My leg is lame!

Natalia. I'm happy too!

Tschubukov. Ahhh! A load off my shoulders! Ahh!

Natalia. And now at least you'll admit that Ugadi is worse that Otkatai!

Lomov. Better!

380 **Natalia.** Worse!

Tschubukov. Now the domestic joys have begun. Champagne!

Lomov. Better!

Natalia. Worse, worse, worse!

Tschubukov (*trying to drown them out*). Champagne, champagne!

Translated from the Russian by
Hilmer Baukhage and Barrett H. Clark

❶ **CHARACTERS IN A FARCE**
What is ridiculous about Natalia's reaction?

Comprehension

1. **Recall** Why does Lomov go to Tschubukov's home dressed in formal clothing?

2. **Recall** What two topics lead to **petty** arguments between Lomov and Natalia?

3. **Summarize** How does Tschubukov bring Lomov and Natalia together at the end of the play?

Literary Analysis

4. **Reading a Play** Reread lines 38–52. Why might Chekhov have chosen to have Lomov express his thoughts alone onstage in a **monologue** instead of in dialogue with other characters?

5. **Examine Characters in a Farce** Review the chart you created as you read. How does Natalia cause Lomov's main trait or pattern of behavior to become even more exaggerated in the course of the play?

6. **Interpret Character Motivation** What seems to motivate Lomov's and Natalia's desire to marry each other? Cite evidence from the play to support your answer.

7. **Analyze Irony** One important literary element that Chekhov uses in the play is irony, or the contrast between expectations and reality. Analyze the irony of the actions listed in the chart shown here.

Action	Expectation	Reality
Tschubukov sends Natalia to talk with Lomov. (line 53)		
Lomov and Natalia agree to get married. (lines 367–375)		

8. **Identify Author's Perspective** The characters in *A Marriage Proposal* are members of the gentry. What does the play suggest about Chekhov's attitude toward this class of landowners? Cite evidence to support your answer.

9. **Evaluate Characters** Are Lomov and Natalia equally responsible for their arguments, or is one character more to blame? Explain your answer.

Literary Criticism

10. **Critical Interpretations** The Russian writer Maxim Gorky said that there was always an element of sadness to Chekhov's humor: "One has only to read his 'humorous' stories with attention to see what a lot of cruel and disgusting things, behind the humorous words and situations, had been observed by the author with sorrow and were concealed by him." What sad realities underlie the humor in *A Marriage Proposal*?

OHIO STANDARDS

READING STANDARD
4.1 Compare and contrast an author's use of direct and indirect characterization

Vocabulary in Context

VOCABULARY PRACTICE

Decide if each statement is true or false.

1. If you **meditate** on something, you give it a lot of thought.
2. A **usurper** respects other people's property.
3. You might be called a **glutton** if you eat a whole pie quickly.
4. A **contrary** friend seldom agrees with you.

WORD LIST

contrary

glutton

meditate

usurper

VOCABULARY IN WRITING

Using at least three vocabulary words, describe a silly argument you had recently. You might begin as follows:

> **EXAMPLE SENTENCE**
>
> My mother always insists on being **contrary**. For example, the other day . . .

VOCABULARY STRATEGY: THE LATIN ROOT contra

The word *contrary* contains the Latin root *contra,* which means "against." When *contra* is used as a prefix with English base words, as in *contrafactual,* you can easily figure out meanings. To understand other words containing *contra,* you may need to use context clues as well as your knowledge of the root.

PRACTICE Write the word from the word web that best completes each sentence. Use context clues to help you or, if necessary, consult a dictionary.

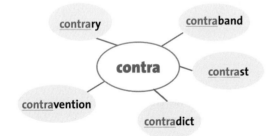

1. When you _____ yourself, you make inconsistent statements.
2. To _____ two things is to emphasize the difference between them.
3. _____ goods cannot be imported or exported abroad.
4. A _____ of international law is a serious violation.
5. He enjoys being _____ just to stir up debate.

OHIO STANDARDS

VOCABULARY STANDARD
1.5 Use knowledge of Latin roots, prefixes and suffixes to understand words

VOCABULARY PRACTICE
For more practice, go to the **Vocabulary Center** at **ClassZone.com.**

Reading-Writing Connection

Enhance your understanding of A *Marriage Proposal* by responding to these prompts. Then use **Revision: Grammar and Style** to improve your writing.

WRITING PROMPTS	SELF-CHECK
A. Short Response: Write a Dialogue Suppose that Lomov and Natalia have just gotten married. Write a **half-page dialogue** in which they discuss the behavior of their relatives at the wedding.	*A successful dialogue will ...* • resemble the style of speech used in the play • reflect the characters' personalities
B. Extended Response: Analyze an Argument Write a **three-to-five-paragraph analysis** of how each of the characters in *A Marriage Proposal* could have prevented **petty** argument or at least stopped it from escalating. Include examples of inflammatory comments and then rewrite them in a less argumentative way.	*A strong analysis will ...* • clearly state an opinion about each character's role • provide three examples and revisions of inflammatory statements

REVISION: GRAMMAR AND STYLE

VARY SENTENCE TYPES Review the **Grammar and Style** note on page 247. When writing dialogue, use a mixture of sentence types to reflect characters' thoughts and emotions. A **declarative sentence** makes a statement. An **interrogative sentence** asks a question. An **exclamatory sentence** expresses strong emotion. An **imperative sentence** gives a command, request, or direction. Here is an example of how Chekhov uses a mixture of interrogative, declarative, and imperative sentences to convey his characters' emotions.

 OHIO STANDARDS

WRITING STANDARD
5.7 Use a variety of sentence structures and lengths

> **Lomov.** *Stepan Stepanovitch, I beg of you, just answer this: has your dog a short lower jaw or not? Yes or no?*
>
> **Tschubukov.** *And what if he has? Is it of such importance? There is no better dog in the whole country.*
>
> **Lomov.** *My Ugadi is better. Tell the truth now!* (lines 306–310)

Notice how the revisions in red use a mixture of sentence types to better reflect the characters' emotions in this first draft. Revise your response to Prompt A by using similar techniques.

STUDENT MODEL

Natalia. Your uncle gobbled up the whole wedding cake! Who can eat so much?

Lomov. ~~You're~~ *Stop* lying. He only took one piece.

 **WRITING TOOLS**
For prewriting, revision, and editing tools, visit the **Writing Center** at ClassZone.com.

from **Finding Forrester**

Film Clip on (o) *MediaSmart* DVD

What makes a character BELIEVABLE?

KEY IDEA Think of a TV or movie character who captivated you. What was it about the actor's performance that convinced you of the character's **believability?** In this lesson, you'll view a movie scene that focuses on three characters. As you get a sense of each one, you'll see how film and performance techniques can influence your perceptions.

Background

Finding Friendship In the movie *Finding Forrester,* the main character is Jamal Wallace, who transfers from a high school in his tough urban neighborhood to a preparatory school with tough academic standards. Placed there on a basketball scholarship, Jamal is regarded as a star in the making. Few are aware that he is also an exceptional writer. The movie focuses on Jamal's unlikely friendship with a reclusive neighbor, William Forrester, a Pulitzer Prize-winning novelist who has begun helping Jamal tap his writing potential.

Media Literacy: Characterization in Movies

You're aware of the four basic methods in which characters are developed in fiction. In movies, characters are developed in similar ways but through camera techniques that show not only characters' physical appearance and actions but convey their emotions. In addition, actors use an array of performance techniques to add more dimension to characters.

WHAT DIRECTORS DO

Film Techniques

Directors position characters within the "frame" of a screen or image, controlling the range of distance from the characters to viewers. This draws viewers' attention to characters' behavior and emotions.

Strategies for Viewing

- Put yourself at the scene through your awareness of **camera placement.** The camera often gets closer as the tension in a scene increases. Ask yourself: What character is drawing my attention? With whom do I sympathize?

- Watch for **close-ups,** which reveal actors' facial expressions. Usually, the higher the emotional level of a scene, the more a director is likely to use close-ups.

- Observe **camera movements.** Panning is when the camera scans a location from one side to the other.

WHAT ACTORS DO

Performance Techniques

Actors rely on performance techniques to reveal characters' basic traits and to signal feelings or thoughts.

Strategies for Viewing

- Note an actor's use of **body language.** Viewers can make judgments based on a character's appearance and actions and make inferences about a character's thoughts and feelings.

- Watch **facial expressions.** Look into characters' eyes, as **close-ups** permit, to read emotional signals. How do the eyes change to reveal suspicion? fear? wonder?

- Listen to how an actor speaks the **dialogue,** which can reveal a character's personality or mood.

MediaSmart DVD

- **Film Clip:** *Finding Forrester*
- **Director:** Gus Van Sant
- **Rating:** PG-13
- **Genre:** Drama
- **Running Time:** 4.5 minutes

Viewing Guide for
Finding Forrester

In an earlier scene, Professor Crawford has told Jamal that he doubts the student's ability to succeed academically. The clip you'll view occurs later in the movie, as the professor's English composition class is in session. View the clip once in its entirety and then several more times. Use these questions as you focus on the characters and their interactions.

NOW VIEW

FIRST VIEWING: Comprehension

1. **Recall** Why does Professor Crawford deliberately single out a certain student to identify the quotation on the chalkboard?

2. **Clarify** When Jamal identifies the quotation, how does Professor Crawford react?

CLOSE VIEWING: Media Literacy

3. **Draw Conclusions** Why do you think the director chose to shoot Coleridge almost entirely in close-ups?

4. **Analyze Techniques** As the confrontation between Jamal and Professor Crawford intensifies, what film techniques does the director use to convey the building tension?

5. **Analyze Characters** Choose Jamal, Coleridge, or Professor Crawford from the clip and write a brief profile based on what you've viewed. Describe what you think are that character's thoughts and feelings throughout the scene. Cite evidence from the film clip.

6. **Evaluate Acting** In your opinion, which one of the three main actors in the scene delivers the most convincing performance? Describe what appealed to you about the actor's basic appearance, dialogue delivery, and actions.

Write or Discuss

Examine Stereotypes This pointed statement by Professor Crawford triggers the confrontation with Jamal: "Perhaps your skills *do* extend a bit beyond basketball." One of the most common shortcuts to characterization is the **stereotype,** an oversimplified representation of a person or group. This device has the virtue of saving time, but it can lead to dull predictability. To what degree do you think stereotyping is evident in this scene? What creative touches, if any, help the portrayals to rise above the usual predictability of stereotypes? Indicate specific shots, character actions, or dialogue to support your view. Keep these criteria in mind:

- your awareness of stereotypes
- the film techniques used by the director
- the nature of each actor's role and the performance techniques used

Produce Your Own Media

Create a Cast List Choose one of character-driven selections in this unit and imagine you're casting the roles for a movie version of the work. Create a cast list.

HERE'S HOW As you compose the cast list, consider these suggestions:

- For each character on the list, indicate the necessary traits to portray.
- Include the names of real-life actors whose appearance or well-known performances match the traits of the characters. Or present photos of classmates as the characters. As an "actor" poses for a shot, give directions about how to portray the character. List each character's basic traits.

> **MEDIA TOOLS**
>
> For help with creating a cast list, visit the **Media Center** at **ClassZone.com.**

Tech Tip

Have classmates pose to resemble the characters, then photograph them.

STUDENT MODEL

Cast List for "Shoofly Pie"

Ashley Chin as Mattie
sensitive
observant
good-natured
spunky

Eric Russell as Johnny
gruff exterior
uncomfortable with change
sensitive

Writing Workshop

Autobiographical Narrative

In this unit you have read descriptions of turning points, both large and small, in characters' lives. Now you have a chance to describe a significant event in your life and explain how it changed you. The **Writer's Road Map** explains how to plan and write an autobiographical narrative.

WRITER'S ROAD MAP

Autobiographical Narrative

WRITING PROMPT 1

Writing from Your Life Write an autobiographical narrative about an important experience you had. Include details that help your reader understand the people and events in your narrative. Be sure to explain why the experience matters to you.

Topics to Consider

- a funny, frightening, or sad event from your childhood
- a turning point in your life
- a success or failure that has had a lasting effect on you

WRITING PROMPT 2

Writing from Literature Choose a short story that you have read this year. Find an interesting event in that story and write an autobiographical narrative of the event from the point of view of one of the characters involved. Your narrative should show why the event was significant to the character.

Events to Consider

- the argument over the quilts in "Everyday Use"
- Johnny asking Mattie out in "Shoofly Pie"

 WRITING TOOLS
For prewriting, revision, and editing tools, visit the **Writing Center** at ClassZone.com.

KEY TRAITS

1. IDEAS
- Focuses on a single, well-defined **event**
- Includes **precise details and dialogue** that re-create the experience

2. ORGANIZATION
- Draws the reader in with an interesting **introduction**
- Has a clear **sequence** that is easy for the reader to follow
- Concludes with a summary of the **significance** of the experience

3. VOICE
- Has an individual **style** that shows the writer's beliefs and personality
- Maintains a **tone** that is appropriate for the audience and purpose

4. WORD CHOICE
- Uses **sensory details** to bring the event alive for the reader

5. SENTENCE FLUENCY
- Uses the **active voice**

6. CONVENTIONS
- Employs **correct grammar and usage**

Part 1: Analyze a Student Model

WRITING STANDARD
6.1 Write narratives

Frederick Cole
Portland High School

The Visit

It was a steamy August day, and I could feel little rivers of sweat running down my back. The sun's heat blasted up off the pavement. The grass, burnt brown, smelled like the hay bales on my cousin Luke's farm. I was ten years old, and my parents and I were walking down
5 the National Mall in Washington, D.C. We could have spent the day visiting the air-conditioned museums that line the Mall, but this day was special. We were going to see my grandfather.

Actually, my grandfather died long before I was born. He was a pilot in the armed forces, a lieutenant, and he had been sent to Vietnam to
10 fly medical evacuation helicopters during the war there. My father was ten years old, too, when Grandpa's helicopter crashed. None of the crew survived.

We were heading to the Vietnam Veterans Memorial to see my grandfather's name there and to honor his memory. I'd seen pictures of
15 Grandpa, and we had some home movies of him—clowning around with the family on Thanksgiving, teaching my dad how to ride a bike. He looked and acted like the kind of person I would like to spend time with.

When we first saw the memorial, my heart skipped a beat. I saw two long slabs of polished black granite, one pointing toward the
20 Washington Monument and the other toward the Lincoln Memorial. As we came closer, I could see the names that had been etched onto the stone—so many names, more than 58,000. They seemed to stretch

KEY TRAITS IN ACTION

Introduction reveals just enough about the event to spark the reader's curiosity. **Sensory details** help re-create the experience.

Essay focuses on a single **event.** Use of the **active voice** makes the narrative clear and direct.

Transitions help the reader follow the **sequence** of events.

on forever. What I remember most is how quiet the area was, despite the large numbers of visitors. Some people had left tokens of their

25 visits, including small bouquets of flowers and brief notes. I remember thinking, This place makes me sad, but it's beautiful.

We soon found my grandfather's name. The three of us held hands, and my father said, "Your grandpa would have been 65 this year."

Just then I noticed a woman place a piece of paper over a name

30 on the wall and begin rubbing over the paper with what looked like a charcoal pencil. *Is she trying to erase some of the names?* I asked myself.

"What's she doing, Dad?"

"She's making a tracing of the name, Fred. Would you like to make one of your grandpa's name?"

35 I said that I would, and Dad went off to find one of the vendors who provided supplies for the rubbings. After we were finished, we walked slowly along the wall, looking at the names and not saying much. Finally, we said goodbye to Grandpa.

Today, I still have that rubbing of my grandfather's name, and I

40 still think about that visit to the wall. I can remember how proud I felt seeing his name surrounded by the names of the other men and women who had died in the war. That was the first time I understood that he had played a role in our nation's history. Although I never got to meet my grandfather, I felt that I had gotten to know him on that stifling

45 morning in our nation's capital.

> Writer's **style** is honest, personal, and thoughtful. Solemn **tone** is appropriate for the subject matter.

> **Dialogue** gives the reader a "you are there" feeling.

> Conclusion explains why the experience was **significant** to the writer.

2

WRITING STANDARD
5.1 Generate writing ideas

Part 2: Apply the Writing Process

PREWRITING

What Should I Do?	What Does It Look Like?

1. Analyze the prompt.
Read the prompt carefully. (Circle) words that tell you what type of writing the prompt asks for. Then <u>underline</u> the parts that tell you what you have to include.

▶ **WRITING PROMPT** Write an (autobiographical) (narrative) about an (important experience) you had. Include <u>details that help your reader understand</u> the people and events in your narrative. Be sure to explain <u>why the experience matters</u> to you.

2. Take a trip to your past.
To get ideas for your narrative, look through photographs, journals, scrapbooks, ticket stubs, or other mementos. You might also make a list like this one to trigger memories.

▶ **summertime:** *hiking the Appalachian Trail*
accident: *breaking my ankle during a soccer game*
proudest moment: *visiting the Vietnam Veterans Memorial*
new experience: *hosting an exchange student*

3. Consider your audience and purpose.
Who's going to read your narrative? Why did you choose to tell this particular story? A chart like this one will help focus your writing.

TIP If the story you chose seems too personal to share with others, look back at your notes and choose a different topic.

▶

Topic	Purpose
visit to the Vietnam Veterans Memorial	to describe a meaningful experience from my life
Audience	**Significance**
classmates, teacher, friends, parents	made me realize that my grandpa was part of American history

4. Re-create the experience in your mind.
What sensory details do you recall from the experience? Make a list like this one. You may not need all five senses to describe your experience.

▶

Sight		Sound	
polished granite		quiet	
Touch	**Taste**		**Smell**
sweat on my back	??		dry grass

What Should I Do?	What Does It Look Like?

1. Map your narrative.
An autobiographical narrative is like a short story—it has a setting, characters, and a plot. Creating a story map can help you make sure that you've included all the important details.

TIP You can use chronological order—the order in which events happened. Or your narrative can begin in the present and include a flashback—an incident from the past.

▶
Title: The Visit
Setting: the National Mall in Washington, D.C.
Characters: Me, Mom, Dad

Plot Summary: We walk to the Vietnam Veterans Memorial to see my grandpa's name on the wall.

Sequence of Events:

1. As we walk, I recall details about Grandpa.

2. We get to the wall and find Grandpa's name.

3. I make a tracing of Grandpa's name.

4. We say goodbye to Grandpa and leave.

Significance: I learn something I'd never realized about Grandpa.

2. Make your introduction engaging.
Your introduction sets the stage for your narrative and makes your audience want to keep reading. You might begin by setting the scene or presenting a compelling detail from the narrative.

▶
Setting the scene
It was a steamy August day, and I could feel little rivers of sweat running down my back. The sun's heat blasted up off the pavement.

A compelling detail
Two slabs of black granite etched with more than 58,000 names can tell a powerful story.

3. Share your thoughts and feelings.
Don't just list a series of events. Include your thoughts and feelings by using dialogue or interior monologue—what you said to yourself as events unfolded.

See page 270: Check Your Grammar

TIP Before revising, consult the **key traits on page 264** and the **rubric and peer-reader questions on page 270.**

▶
Dialogue
   "What's she doing, Dad?" I asked.
   "She's making a tracing of the name, Fred."
Interior monologue
Is she trying to erase some of the names? I asked myself.

REVISING AND EDITING

| What Should I Do? | What Does It Look Like? |

1. Use all your senses.
- Underline words that refer to sight, sound, taste, touch, and smell.
- If your narrative has few or no underlines, add sensory words and phrases.

▶ I ~~was perspiring~~, could feel little rivers of sweat running down my back.

~~The sun was hot.~~
The sun's heat blasted up off the pavement.

~~The grass was brown.~~
The grass, burnt brown, smelled like the hay bales on my cousin Luke's farm.

2. Be active, not passive.
- (Circle) examples of passive voice in your narrative ("The wall was visited by us").
- Change these to active voice to make your narrative clearer and more interesting ("We visited the wall").

See page R57: Active and Passive Voice

▶ (~~Tokens had been left by some people.~~)
Some people had left tokens of their visits.

3. Clarify the sequence of events.
- Ask a peer reader to put a box around passages where the order of events is not clear.
- Add transitional words and phrases that tell your reader what happened when.

See page 270: Ask a Peer Reader

▶ When we first saw the memorial,

My heart skipped a beat. I saw two long slabs of polished black granite. . . .

After we were finished,

We walked slowly along the wall, looking at the names and not saying much.

4. Explain why it matters.
- [Bracket] the part of your narrative that explains why the event was special or significant.
- If you can't find a passage to put brackets around, add information so that your reader will know why the event was important to you.

▶ I can remember how proud I felt seeing his name, surrounded by the names of the other men and women who had died in the war. That was the first time I understood that he had played a role in our nation's history.

Preparing to Publish

Autobiographical Narrative

Apply the Rubric

A strong autobiographical narrative . . .

☑ has an introduction that makes the reader want to keep reading

☑ relates a significant experience in the writer's life and explains why it was important

☑ includes sensory details and dialogue to help the reader experience the incident as the writer did

☑ makes the order of events clear

☑ uses the active voice

☑ is written in a style that reflects the writer's beliefs and personality

☑ has an appropriate and consistent tone

Ask a Peer Reader

• Which passages helped you to picture and feel what I was writing about?

• Where in my narrative is the order of events unclear?

Check Your Grammar

• When including dialogue, enclose the speaker's actual words in quotation marks. Begin a new paragraph every time the speaker changes.

> " What's she doing, Dad? " I asked.
> " She's making a tracing of the name, Fred. "

• Unless the speaker's words are a question or an exclamation, use a comma to separate the speaker's words from the phrase identifying the speaker.

> " Your grandpa would have been 65 this year ," my father said.

• If the speaker's words are a question or an exclamation, use a question mark or an exclamation point instead of a comma. Place the question mark or exclamation point inside the quotation marks.

> " There's his name ! " Mom exclaimed.

See page R50: Quick Reference: Punctuation

Writing Online

PUBLISHING OPTIONS
For publishing options, visit the **Writing Center** at ClassZone.com.

ASSESSMENT PREPARATION
For writing and grammar assessment practice, go to the **Assessment Center** at ClassZone.com.

Presenting an Oral History

In Unit 2 you read about some fascinating people. Your friends and members of your family have interesting stories to tell, too. You can record those stories by producing an oral history—the story of a person's experiences, told by that person in his or her own words.

Planning the Oral History

1. **Choose someone to interview.** Perhaps someone in your autobiographical narrative would make a good subject. You might also choose someone who has lived through an important historical event or who has simply led an interesting life.

2. **Get permission to interview and videotape your subject.** Schedule a time and place for the interview. Tell your subject what you want him or her to talk about so he or she can be prepared.

3. **Prepare open-ended questions.** These questions can't be answered with a simple yes or no. They give you more material to work with as you assemble your oral history.

4. **Conduct the interview.** Videotape your subject as you conduct the interview. Try to get both long shots and medium shots. Ask if you can also film any relevant photographs or other items of interest associated with the topic of your interview. See pages R81–R82 for more interviewing tips.

5. **Consider enhancing the oral history with information from other sources.** For example, if you interviewed a family member to find out more about the Vietnam War era, you might use film clips, audio, or photographs from that time period. Be sure to credit your sources. Check each source's copyright notice or use policy; some sources allow use of their materials in student projects.

Producing the Oral History

1. **Review your footage.** Use editing software to organize the footage you shot. Alternate shots of your subject talking with shots of photographs or other items you filmed. Try to create a "you are there" feeling by choosing images that help the reader understand where and when the event took place and what it was like to experience it.

2. **Add other elements to your oral history.** Consider adding voice-over narration, a title screen, text screens that include the questions you asked, and music as appropriate.

Reading Comprehension

DIRECTIONS *Read the following selections and then answer the questions.*

from Tío Nano

Lionel G. García

Hernando Carrejo, *Tío* Nano we called him, was a master at timing his visits at mealtime. We could see him coming from the highway by the courthouse two blocks away, stooped from the weight of two suitcases full of clothes to be sold to the people living in the south Texas ranches. From his home in Laredo, he would take the bus or hitch a ride that would get him past Freer and around the ranching community of La Rosita. From there he would work his way through the ranches showing off his wares. In a few days, hungry and tired, he would find his way back to the main road and hitch a ride to San Diego to see his favorite cousin, my grandmother.

10 Then came the depression, and my grandmother grew tired of feeding and housing so many people, especially *Tío* Nano, who ate enough for two men, and we were told to be on the lookout for him. Anyone seeing *Tío* Nano coming down the road was to alert my grandmother, giving her time to hide not only the food she was cooking, but herself. We were supposed to tell him she was not home, that she had left town.

We were playing out in the street close to the courthouse one late morning when an old black car coming from the direction of Freer stopped at the corner. We heard *Tío* Nano's distinctive slurred voice thanking the driver for the ride and we saw him climb out of the car, shiny rear-end first, having

20 a difficult time getting his suitcases out from the back seat. We dropped everything and ran home before he could turn around to see us.

My grandmother was in the kitchen when we arrived.

"What in Heaven's name happened to you?" she asked.

"*Tío* Nano," Cota managed to spit out before going to the faucet to get a drink of water.

"He's here?" my grandmother inquired, her face ashen, looking at all of us one at a time.

"Yes," we said.

"God in Heaven," she cried out. "I have to hide the food."

30 She grabbed for two dirty hand towels to grasp the pot of boiling beans and rushed with it into the bathroom. She came running out of the bathroom and snatched the plate of tortillas and raced it to the bathroom where she had just hidden the beans. As she was running back out, she said, "Tell him I'm gone. Tell him I left. Went to Alice to buy groceries, and I won't return until . . . Well, not today. That won't work. Tell him I got sick and had to go see Dr. Dunlap."

from Uncles

Margaret Atwood

Once in a while Susanna's mother would make an appearance on the porch. "Susanna, don't show off," she would say, or, "Susanna, don't pester your uncles." Then an uncle would say, "She's no trouble, Mae." Mostly Susanna's mother stayed in the kitchen, doing the dishes along with the aunts, which in Susanna's opinion was where they belonged.

It was the aunts who brought most of the food for the Sunday dinners. They would arrive with roasts, lemon meringue pies, cookies, jars of their own pickles. Her mother might cook some potatoes, or make a jellied salad. Not a great deal was expected of her, because she was a war widow; she was
10 still getting over the loss, and she had a child to bring up single-handed. On the outside it didn't seem to bother her. She was cheerful and rounded, and slow-moving by nature. The uncles had clubbed together to buy her the house, because she was their little sister, they had all grown up on a farm together, they were close.

The aunts had a hard time forgiving this. It would come up at the dinner table, in oblique references to how you had to scrimp to meet two sets of mortgage payments. The uncles would look at their wives with baffled reproach, and pass their plates down to Susanna's mother for another helping of mashed potatoes. You could not turn your own flesh and blood out on the
20 streets to starve. Susanna knew this because she heard an uncle saying it as he lumbered down the front walk to his car.

"You didn't have to get such a big house," the aunt said. "It's almost as big as ours." Her high heels clipped on the cement as she hurried to keep up. All of the aunts were small, brisk women, with short legs.

Susanna was rocking in the giant white wicker rocker on the porch. She stopped rocking and scrunched down so her head was out of sight, to listen in.

"Come on, Adele," said the uncle. "You wouldn't want them living in a hut."

"She could get a job." This was an insult and the aunt knew it. It would mean that the uncle could not provide.

30 "Who would look after Susanna?" said the uncle, coming to a stop while he hunted for his keys. "Not you, that's for sure."

There was a note of bitterness in the uncle's voice that was new to Susanna. She felt sorry for him. For the aunt she felt no pity.

GO ON ➤

Comprehension

DIRECTIONS *Answer these questions about the excerpt from "Tío Nano."*

1. Which of the following characters tells the story of *Tío* Nano?
   A. the grandmother   C. a doctor
   B. a grandchild   D. an uncle

2. In lines 1–9, which of the following quotations illustrates *Tío* Nano's motives?
   A. "ate enough for two men"
   B. "We could see him coming from the highway"
   C. "stooped from the weight of two suitcases"
   D. "was a master at timing his visits at mealtime"

3. From lines 1–9, you can infer that *Tío* Nano's occupation is most likely that of a
   A. salesman   C. rancher
   B. bus driver D. lawyer

4. What motivates the grandmother in the story to change her feelings about feeding *Tío* Nano?
   A. *Tío* Nano's appetite seems to increase every time he visits.
   B. The depression has made it harder for her to feed and house her relatives.
   C. There is no room for Tío Nano and his two heavy suitcases.
   D. She is tired of cooking all day long for the children.

5. How are *Tío* Nano and the grandmother in the story alike?
   A. They both enjoy riding around in the south Texas countryside.
   B. They both become tired from working so hard.
   C. They both use the children to give other people false information.
   D. They both are ill often and cannot get their work done.

6. How does the grandmother react to news of *Tío* Nano's arrival?
   A. She prepares a big meal to welcome him to the house.
   B. She gets sick and runs out to the doctor's office.
   C. She sends the children out to play for the afternoon.
   D. She hides the food and asks the children to say she is gone.

DIRECTIONS *Answer these questions about the excerpt from "Uncles."*

7. From lines 1–5, what can you infer about the relationship between Susanna and her uncles?
   A. She annoys them.
   B. They get along well.
   C. The uncles ignore her.
   D. They don't talk much.

8. In lines 28–29, Adele knowingly insults her husband's
   A. honesty   C. self-respect
   B. loyalty   D. determination

9. What is the uncles' main motivation for buying their sister a house?

   A. They want to keep their sister and Susanna from living with them.

   B. They want to cause their wives extra work.

   C. They think their sister needs a house big enough for the Sunday dinners.

   D. They care about their sister and Susanna as family members.

10. What is the most likely reason that Susanna hides on the porch and listens to her aunt and uncle's conversation?

    A. alarm

    B. curiosity

    C. boredom

    D. indifference

11. Which generalization could you make about the aunts?

    A. They enjoy cooking and doing the dishes after dinner.

    B. They behave graciously toward Susanna and her mother.

    C. They resent their husbands' support of Susanna's mother.

    D. They are nice to Susanna because they wish they had daughters.

12. Which generalization could you make about the uncles?

    A. They expect family members to help one another.

    B. They have no disappointments in their lives.

    C. The Sunday dinners are their favorite weekly events.

    D. They sympathize with their wives' disapproval.

DIRECTIONS *Answer this question about both selections.*

13. Which of the following generalizations could you make about the main characters in both selections?

    A. They want to acquire better cars and better houses.

    B. Family relationships are important to them.

    C. They believe that children should be seen but not heard.

    D. The uncles are unpopular with everyone else in the family.

Written Response

SHORT ANSWER
Write three or four sentences to answer each question.

14. Name two ways the author reveals the grandmother's character in the excerpt from "Tío Nano." Give one example of each of these two methods of characterization.

15. Name three of Susanna's character traits in the excerpt from "Uncles." Support your answer with examples from the selection.

EXTENDED RESPONSE
Write two or three paragraphs to answer this question.

16. Compare and contrast *Tío* Nano and Susanna's uncles in terms of their behavior, their positions in life, or any other characteristics they exhibit. Support your answer with details from the selections.

GO ON

Vocabulary

DIRECTIONS *Use context clues and the Latin definitions to answer the following questions.*

1. The Latin word *ob* means "toward," and the root *liqu* means "slanting." What does the word *oblique* mean in line 16 of "Uncles"?

   A. exact

   B. indirect

   C. dishonest

   D. misunderstood

2. The prefix *dis-* means "apart," and the Latin root *stinct* means "to separate." What does *distinctive* mean in line 18 of "Tío Nano"?

   A. different

   B. common

   C. likely

   D. clear

3. The word *difficult* in line 20 of "Tío Nano" contains the root of the Latin word *facilis* and the prefix *dis-*. If *dis-* means "not" in the word *difficult*, what does *facilis* mean?

   A. fake

   B. easy

   C. dizzy

   D. challenging

DIRECTIONS *Use your knowledge of connotation and denotation to answer the following questions. The line numbers will help you find the words in the excerpt from "Uncles."*

4. What connotation does the word *clubbed* have in line 12?

   A. friendliness

   B. snobbery

   C. violence

   D. unity

5. Choose the word that has most nearly the same connotation as the word *lumbered* in line 21.

   A. walked

   B. marched

   C. trudged

   D. staggered

DIRECTIONS *Use your knowledge of connotation and denotation to answer the following questions. The line numbers will help you find the words in the excerpt from "Tío Nano."*

6. The connotation of the word *stooped* in line 3 suggests that *Tío* Nano

   A. looked down on other people

   B. had a submissive personality

   C. was weary from his work

   D. was a weak person

7. What connotation does the word *spit* have in line 24?

   A. urgency

   B. anger

   C. sloppiness

   D. disrespect

Writing & Grammar

DIRECTIONS *Read the passage and answer the following questions.*

(1) Many people aren't aware of the challenges faced by designers who customize rooms. (2) Sometimes, designers put on jumpsuits, gloves, and glasses to test a room. (3) There's a reason why they do this. (4) They want people with physical limitations to have functional homes. (5) One designer tests a kitchen by making a cup of tea. (6) She tries to open a drawer and finally has to take off her glove. (7) She puts a cup of water in the microwave. (8) Unable to see the settings, she decides to switch on a light. (9) The switch is across the room and is a struggle to reach for someone in a bulky jumpsuit—or for an elderly person. (10) Instead, she guesses which buttons to push. (11) Suddenly she hears a crackle and realizes the tea bag has caught fire.

1. Identify the abstract noun in sentence 1.

A. people   C. rooms

B. challenges   D. designers

2. Choose the best way to rewrite sentence 2 by using descriptive adjectives.

A. Sometimes, designers put on yellow jumpsuits, gloves, and glasses to test a room.

B. Sometimes, designers put on bulky jumpsuits, thick gloves, and tinted glasses to test a room.

C. Sometimes, designers put on big jumpsuits, big gloves, and glasses to test a room.

D. Sometimes, good designers have to wear jumpsuits, gloves, and glasses to test a room.

3. Choose the correct way to rewrite sentence 3 as an interrogative sentence.

A. Why do they do this?

B. There's a reason why they do this!

C. They do this for a reason.

D. Do this for a reason.

4. Choose the best way to rewrite sentence 6 by adding sensory adjectives and verbs.

A. She tries to open a blue drawer and finally has to take off her black glove.

B. She desperately tries to open a large drawer and finally has to take off her glove.

C. She tries to pull on a drawer and finally has to take off her large glove.

D. She struggles to open a drawer and finally has to yank off her cumbersome glove.

5. Identify the abstract noun in sentence 9.

A. switch   C. struggle

B. room   D. jumpsuit

6. Choose the correct way to rewrite sentence 11 as an exclamatory sentence.

A. Suddenly she hears a crackle and wonders, Has the tea bag caught fire?

B. Suddenly she hears a crackle and realizes the tea bag has caught fire!

C. Suddenly she hears a crackle; next, she realizes the tea bag has caught fire.

D. Has the tea bag caught fire?

STOP

Ideas for Independent Reading

What helps someone overcome grief? How does one person improve another's life? Find out by reading these additional works.

Is there a cure for grief?

Let Their Spirits Dance
by Stella Pope Duarte

Teresa Ramirez's brother Jesse died in Vietnam 30 years ago. When her mother, 80, decides to travel to Washington to find his name on the Vietnam Memorial wall, Teresa hopes this journey will help free her mother from her long grief.

A Death in the Family
by James Agee

This novel by one of America's most respected writers chronicles a family's grief after the father's death in an auto accident. Readers see how quickly happiness can turn to devastation.

In the Midst of Winter
edited by Mary Jane Moffat

The writers in this anthology express their grief over the loss of a family member or an animal companion. Can writing about grief help one get past it?

How good are you at judging people?

A Separate Peace
by John Knowles

The narrator of this novel remembers his high school friend Phineas, a talented athlete whom he accidentally crippled in a moment of misperception and envy.

Twelve Angry Men
by Reginald Rose

A jury must decide whether a teenager is guilty of murder. When the jurors take their first poll, all but one vote to convict the boy. Will the majority convince the holdout to change his mind?

The Heart Is a Lonely Hunter
by Carson McCullers

This classic novel portrays five outcasts in a Depression-era Southern town. McCullers reveals the complexities of humans in search of love.

Who has made you a better person?

The Color of Water: A Black Man's Tribute to His White Mother
by James McBride

McBride honors his mother, who experienced rejection, isolation, and poverty but ensured that each one of her 12 children went to college.

Death Be Not Proud
by John Gunther

The writer's son Johnny was stricken with a brain tumor when he was 17. As Johnny struggled with his illness, he never lost hope and inspired everyone around him. His father honored his memory with this book.

A Lesson Before Dying
by Ernest J. Gaines

Grant Wiggins is asked to help a young death-row inmate prepare to die. The prisoner is a victim of racism, as is Grant, who chafes at the limits it places on his life. The two men help each other resist the crippling effects of hatred.

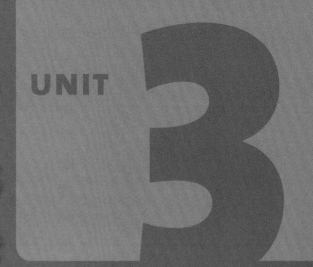

UNIT 3

A Writer's Choice

NARRATIVE DEVICES

- In Fiction
- In Nonfiction

279

Share What You Know

How do you TELL *a tale?*

Writers of stories do not follow a formula. Instead, they make deliberate **choices** about how to tell stories that will engage readers. Some writers choose narrators who observe events from an unusual vantage point. Other writers choose to tell their stories backwards. Writers might even decide to mislead readers on purpose simply for the element of surprise.

ACTIVITY With a partner, think of a book, movie, or television program that told a story in an unusual way. Discuss the techniques or devices the writer used to capture your interest and make the story memorable. Consider the following:

• Is there anything unusual about the narrator?

• Are the events arranged in any special order?

• Are there any unexpected plot twists?

OHIO STANDARDS

Preview Unit Goals

LITERARY ANALYSIS
- Identify and analyze point of view: first person, second person, third-person limited, and third-person omniscient
- Identify and analyze flashback and foreshadowing
- Read and analyze a reflective essay

READING
- Use strategies for reading, including connecting and monitoring
- Identify and analyze chronological order
- Synthesize ideas and information; support an opinion
- Make inferences and draw conclusions
- Analyze sensory details

WRITING AND GRAMMAR
- Write a short story
- Use a consistent point of view
- Add descriptive details; use similes to compare ideas
- Use appositives and appositive phrases to write concisely
- Use vocabulary and sentence structures appropriate to formal language
- Create a children's book

VOCABULARY
- Use word roots to help unlock meaning

ACADEMIC VOCABULARY
- first-person point of view
- second-person point of view
- third-person limited point of view
- flashback and foreshadowing
- third-person omniscient point of view
- reflective essay

Narrative Devices

What conflicts will drive the plot? Who will the characters be? Against what backdrop will the story develop? These are some of the questions a writer considers when crafting a story. Beyond these considerations, a writer must make two other critical choices: *who* tells the story and *how* the events will unfold in time. As a reader, you should be aware of how these choices affect your perceptions of the characters and your understanding of events.

OHIO STANDARDS

READING STANDARDS
4.6 Explain literary techniques, including foreshadowing and flashback
4.8 Analyze the author's use of point of view

Part 1: Choices About the Narrator

Point of view refers to the vantage point from which a story is told. Point of view is created by a writer's choice of **narrator,** the voice that tells the story. This choice affects whether the narrator is a character in the story or an outside observer. It also influences your opinion of the characters and how much you learn about them.

POINT OF VIEW	STRATEGIES FOR ANALYSIS
FIRST PERSON *The narrator* • is a main or minor character in the story • refers to himself or herself as *I* or *me* • presents his or her own thoughts, feelings, and interpretations • lacks direct access to the thoughts of other characters	**Consider the source.** You may feel connected to a first-person narrator because he or she seems to be talking directly to you. However, don't trust everything the narrator tells you. Ask: • Is the narrator trustworthy or unreliable? • How might the narrator's opinions of other characters affect what he or she says about them?
THIRD-PERSON LIMITED *The narrator* • is not a character in the story but an outside observer • zooms in on the thoughts and feelings of one character—usually the protagonist	**Understand the limitations.** Because you learn only one character's thoughts, you don't get the big picture. Ask: • How might the character's thoughts affect readers' impressions of characters and events? • What more would an omniscient narrator be able to convey?
THIRD-PERSON OMNISCIENT *The narrator* • is not a character in the story but an outside observer • is "all knowing"—he or she has access to the thoughts and feelings of all characters	**Take advantage of the insights.** When an omniscient narrator tells the story, you become "all knowing" too. Ask: • How do different characters react to the same event? • How do the characters perceive each other?

MODEL 1: FIRST-PERSON POINT OF VIEW

In this excerpt, the narrator learns that her sister, Lalla, has broken off her wedding engagement. How does the narrator react to this news?

from ***Lalla*** Short story by **Rosamunde Pilcher**

. . . it was a call from London and it was Allan Sutton.

"I have to speak to Lalla."

His voice sounded frantic. I said cautiously, "Is anything wrong?"

"She's broken off our engagement. I got back from the office and found a
5 letter from her and my ring. She said she was coming home. She doesn't want
to get married." . . .

I found myself caught up in a tangle of conflicting emotions. Enormous
sympathy for Allan; a reluctant admiration for Lalla, who had the courage to
take this shattering decision; but, as well, a sort of rising excitement.

Close Read

1. Review the boxed text. What do you learn about the narrator's feelings?

2. How would this scene be different if Allan were the narrator?

MODEL 2: THIRD-PERSON POINT OF VIEW

Here, a visitor prompts Luis and his father, Mr. Cintrón, to reflect on the past. Notice how the omniscient narrator lets you in on the characters' thoughts.

from ## Catch the Moon
Short story by **Judith Ortiz Cofer**

"Please call me Naomi, Señor Cintrón. You know my mother. She is the
director of the funeral home. . . ." Mr. Cintrón seemed surprised at first; he
prided himself on having a great memory. Then his friendly expression changed
to one of sadness as he recalled the day of his wife's burial. Naomi did not finish
5 her sentence. She reached over and placed her hand on Mr. Cintrón's arm for a
moment. Then she said "Adiós" softly, and got in her shiny white car. She waved
to them as she left, and her gold bracelets flashing in the sun nearly blinded Luis.

Mr. Cintrón shook his head. "How about that," he said as if to himself.
"They are the Dominican owners of Ramirez Funeral Home." And, with a sigh,
10 "She seems like such a nice young woman. Reminds me of your mother when
she was her age."

Hearing the funeral parlor's name, Luis remembered too. The day his mother
died, he had been in her room at the hospital while his father had gone for
coffee. The alarm had gone off on her monitor and nurses had come running in,
15 pushing him outside. After that, all he recalled was the anger that had made him
punch a hole in his bedroom wall.

Close Read

1. Find one example in which the narrator reveals Mr. Cintrón's thoughts. Then find one example in which Luis's thoughts are described.

2. Describe Luis's and Mr. Cintrón's feelings about their loss. What emotions is each character dealing with?

Part 2: Choices About Time

In addition to making choices about point of view, writers make choices about how time is going to unfold in a story. Most writers choose to tell a story in chronological order. Sometimes, though, a writer will use techniques such as flashback or foreshadowing to create specific effects.

If you've ever watched a horror movie, you know about **foreshadowing,** or the use of hints to build suspense about what will happen next. Those hints might be shots of foreboding settings or statements like "I'll be right back"— sure signs of lurking danger. Writers also use foreshadowing to create edge-of-your-seat effects. As you read any story, look for similar hints—repeated details or characters who make important statements or behave in unusual ways.

What clues in this familiar movie scenario hint at a disastrous plane crash?

| Flashes of lightning signal an approaching storm. | A passenger reassures others: "There's nothing to worry about." | The pilot loses control of the aircraft. | The aircraft crashes on a remote island. |

A flashback is another device frequently used in movies. In literature, a **flashback** is an account of an event or a conversation that happened before the beginning of the story. It interrupts the chronological order of events to reveal information that can help readers understand the characters or the current situation. To spot a flashback, look for phrases that signal a shift in time, such as "he remembered that day" or "as a young child."

How does this flashback help you to understand the character's emotions?

| Remnants of the crash remain on the beach. | One survivor's thoughts turn toward home. | He remembers time spent with his family years earlier. | Jolted to the present, he realizes he may never see his family again. |

MODEL: FLASHBACK

"Sophistication" is a story about a young man and woman who want to look sophisticated in each other's eyes. Here, the characters reflect on an awkward encounter from their past. As you read, consider how the flashback helps you understand the characters and their current situation.

from SOPHISTICATION

Short story by **Sherwood Anderson**

When the moment of sophistication came to George Willard his mind turned to Helen White, the Winesburg banker's daughter. . . . Once on a summer night when he was eighteen, he had walked with her on a country road and in her presence had given way to an impulse to boast, to make
5 himself appear big and significant in her eyes. Now he wanted to see her for another purpose. He wanted to . . . try to make her feel the change he believed had taken place in his nature. . . .

Helen White was thinking of George Willard even as he wandered gloomily through the crowds thinking of her. She remembered the summer evening when
10 they had walked together and wanted to walk with him again. She thought that the months she had spent in the city, the going to theaters and the seeing of great crowds wandering in lighted thoroughfares, had changed her profoundly. She wanted him to feel and be conscious of the change in her nature.

The summer evening together that had left its mark on the memory of both
15 the young man and woman had, when looked at quite sensibly, been rather stupidly spent. They had walked out of town along a country road. Then they had stopped by a fence near a field of young corn and George had taken off his coat and let it hang on his arm. "Well, I've stayed here in Winesburg—yes— I've not yet gone away but I'm growing up," he had said. "I've been reading
20 books and I've been thinking. I'm going to try to amount to something in life.

"Well," he explained, "that isn't the point. Perhaps I'd better quit talking."

The confused boy put his hand on the girl's arm. His voice trembled. The two started to walk back along the road toward town. In his desperation George boasted, "I'm going to be a big man, the biggest that ever lived here in
25 Winesburg," he declared. . . .

The boy's voice failed and in silence the two came back into town and went along the street to Helen White's house. At the gate he tried to say something impressive. Speeches he had thought out came into his head, but they seemed utterly pointless. . . .
30 On the warm fall evening as he stood in the stairway and looked at the crowd drifting through Main Street, George thought of the talk beside the field of young corn and was ashamed of the figure he had made of himself.

Close Read

1. What do you learn about George's thoughts in lines 1–7?

2. What do you learn about Helen's thoughts in lines 8–13?

3. Later, a flashback takes you to the summer evening that has loomed in George's and Helen's memories. Where does this flashback begin? Explain.

4. Review the boxed details. What do they reveal about George's behavior? Explain whether you think he impressed Helen.

5. How does the flashback help you understand George? Consider how he thinks he has changed since that evening.

Part 3: Analyze the Literature

Use what you've learned about point of view and sequence to analyze the two excerpts that follow.

The first excerpt is from a novel about a family from Bengal, India, that is making a new life in the United States. In keeping with Bengali tradition, the husband and wife are waiting for word from a family elder about what the name of their baby will be. How does the third-person omniscient point of view influence your understanding of the characters?

from # THE NAMESAKE
Novel by **Jhumpa Lahiri**

. . . they are told by Mr. Wilcox, compiler of hospital birth certificates, that they must choose a name for their son. For they learn that in America, a baby cannot be released from the hospital without a birth certificate. And that a birth certificate needs a name.

5 "But, sir," Ashima protests, "we can't possibly name him ourselves."
Mr. Wilcox, slight, bald, unamused, glances at the couple, both visibly distressed, then glances at the nameless child. "I see," he says. "The reason being?"
"We are waiting for a letter," Ashoke says, explaining the situation in detail.
"I see," Mr. Wilcox says again. "That is unfortunate. I'm afraid your only
10 alternative is to have the certificate read 'Baby Boy Ganguli.' You will, of course, be required to amend the permanent record when a name is decided upon."
Ashima looks at Ashoke expectantly. "Is that what we should do?"
"I don't recommend it," Mr. Wilcox says. "You will have to appear before a judge, pay a fee. The red tape is endless."
15 "Oh dear," Ashoke says.
Mr. Wilcox nods, and silence ensues. "Don't you have any backups?" he asks.
Ashima frowns. "What does it mean, 'backup'?"
"Well, something in reserve, in case you didn't like what your grandmother has chosen."
20 Ashima and Ashoke shake their heads. It has never occurred to either of them to question Ashima's grandmother's selection, to disregard an elder's wishes in such a way.
"You can always name him after yourself, or one of your ancestors," Mr. Wilcox suggests, admitting that he is actually Howard Wilcox III. "It's a fine
25 tradition. The kings of France and England did it," he adds.
But this isn't possible, Ashima and Ashoke think to themselves. This tradition doesn't exist for Bengalis, naming a son after father or grandfather, a daughter after mother or grandmother. This sign of respect in America and Europe, this symbol of heritage and lineage, would be ridiculed in India.
30 Within Bengali families, individual names are sacred, inviolable. They are not meant to be inherited or shared.

Close Read

1. For each character— Ashoke, Ashima, and Mr. Wilcox—find one example where you can "see" inside that character's mind.

2. This excerpt is about a clash between Bengali and American traditions. Through the omniscient narrator, what do you learn about how Ashoke's and Ashima's thoughts differ from those of Mr. Wilcox?

3. How would your impression of the characters be different if you did not know Ashoke's and Ashima's thoughts?

Now read this excerpt from a novel about friendship and growing up. In this scene, the main character visits the private school he attended as a teenager. His destination is a tree on the property, where, years earlier, something terrible happened. As you read, notice how the flashback and the point of view affect your impression of the main character.

from A *Separate* Peace

Novel by **John Knowles**

There were several trees bleakly reaching into the fog. Any one of them might have been the one I was looking for. Unbelievable that there were other trees which looked like it here. It had loomed in my memory as a huge lone spike dominating the riverbank, forbidding as an artillery piece, high
5 as the beanstalk. Yet here was a scattered grove of trees, none of them of any particular grandeur.

Moving through the soaked, coarse grass I began to examine each one closely, and finally identified the tree I was looking for by means of certain small scars rising along its trunk, and by a limb extending over the river, and
10 another thinner limb growing near it. This was the tree, and it seemed to me standing there to resemble those men, the giants of your childhood, whom you encounter years later and find that they are not merely smaller in relation to your growth, but that they are absolutely smaller, shrunken by age. In this double demotion the old giants have become pigmies[1] while you were looking
15 the other way.

The tree was not only stripped by the cold season, it seemed weary from age, enfeebled, dry. I was thankful, very thankful that I had seen it. So the more things remain the same, the more they change after all—*plus c'est la même chose, plu ça change.* Nothing endures, not a tree, not love, not even a death by violence.
20 Changed, I headed back through the mud. I was drenched; anybody could see it was time to come in out of the rain.

The tree was tremendous, an irate, steely black steeple beside the river. I was [not going to] climb it. . . . No one but Phineas could think up such a crazy idea.

He of course saw nothing the slightest bit intimidating about it. He
25 wouldn't, or wouldn't admit it if he did. Not Phineas.

"What I like best about this tree," he said in that voice of his, the equivalent in sound of a hypnotist's eyes, "what I like is that it's such a cinch!" He opened his green eyes wider and gave us his maniac look, and only the smirk on his wide mouth with its droll, slightly protruding upper lip reassured us that he
30 wasn't completely goofy.

"Is that what you like best?" I said sarcastically. I said a lot of things sarcastically that summer; that was my sarcastic summer, 1942.

---

1. **pigmies:** people of unusually small size.

Close Read

1. From what point of view is this story told? Explain how you can tell.

2. At what point does the story switch from the present to the past? Cite the clues that signaled this flashback.

3. Reread lines 3–21. What do you learn about the narrator from his own thoughts about the tree and his past?

4. Review the boxed text. What do the descriptions of the tree—in the present and in the flashback— help to emphasize?

By the Waters of Babylon
Short Story by Stephen Vincent Benét

Does KNOWLEDGE
come at a price?

OHIO STANDARDS

READING STANDARDS
2.1 Make inferences
4.11 Explain point of view

KEY IDEA How much **knowledge** should a person or society have? When, if ever, should our pursuit of knowledge be limited? In "By the Waters of Babylon," you will meet John, a character who learns through a difficult journey that knowledge can come at a price.

DISCUSS Think about a time when your desire for knowledge got you into a tough situation. Then create a cause-effect chart like the one shown to represent this experience. Share your chart with your classmates, and then discuss if pursuing knowledge is ever worth risking trouble.

What I Wanted to Know (Cause)		What I Did		What Happened (Effect)
Who my older sister liked	→	Read her electronic journal	→	I found out we both liked the same guy.

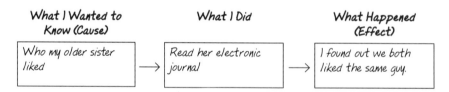

CONFIDENTIAL

288

LITERARY ANALYSIS: FIRST–PERSON POINT OF VIEW

"By the Waters of Babylon" is a short story told from the **first-person point of view.** The narrator is John, a character who speaks directly to the reader, using the pronoun *I*. He introduces himself in the following way:

My father is a priest; I am the son of a priest. I have been in the Dead Places near us, with my father—at first, I was afraid.

Everything in the story is presented through John's eyes. At times, he does not fully understand what he sees or experiences. Such a narrator is called a **naive narrator.** As you read "By the Waters of Babylon," notice how the author's choice of point of view and narrator affects what you learn about the story's characters, events, and setting.

Review: **Foreshadowing**

READING SKILL: MAKE INFERENCES

When a character narrates a story, you know only as much as the character knows. By making **inferences,** or educated guesses, you can figure out information that the narrator does not tell you. Use the following strategies to make inferences about the setting of "By the Waters of Babylon":

- Notice the names of places.
- Notice how places may resemble those you know.

As you read the story, jot down important details that help you understand the different sites John visits on his journey. Use a chart like the one shown.

Places	Important Details	My Inferences
1. Dead Places	Only priests and sons of priests can visit.	
2. the great river		
3. the Place of the Gods		

Review: **Draw Conclusions**

Author Online

Stephen Vincent Benét
1898–1943

A Literary Family
Stephen Vincent Benét (bǐ-nā') grew up in a home where literature was valued and enjoyed. When he was young, Benét and his two siblings, William and Laura, spent many evenings listening to their father, a colonel in the U.S. Army, read poetry and historical stories. Their mother was also an avid reader and occasionally wrote verse to entertain family and friends. With their upbringing, the Benét children seemed likely to lead artistic lives. In fact, each became a successful writer, making *Benét* a well-known name in American literature.

A Proud American Much of Stephen Vincent Benét's writing is based on American history and folklore. Among his most famous works is the epic Civil War poem *John Brown's Body,* for which he won a Pulitzer Prize in 1929. A second Pulitzer came in 1944, following Benét's death, for *Western Star,* a long narrative poem about the history of America. Benét also received acclaim for his fiction. His best-known story, "The Devil and Daniel Webster," won the 1937 O. Henry Award and became the basis of a play, an opera, and a film.

 MORE ABOUT THE AUTHOR
For more on Stephen Vincent Benét, visit the **Literature Center** at **ClassZone.com.**

Background

About the Title The title of this selection is an **allusion,** or reference, to Psalm 137 in the Bible. The psalm expresses the sorrow of the Jews over their enslavement in Babylon and the destruction of Zion, their homeland. The psalm begins: "By the waters of Babylon, there we sat down and wept, when we remembered thee, O Zion."

By the Waters of Babylon

Stephen Vincent Benét

The north and the west and the south are good hunting ground, but it is forbidden to go east. It is forbidden to go to any of the Dead Places except to search for metal, and then he who touches the metal must be a priest or the son of a priest. Afterwards, both the man and the metal must be purified. These are the rules and the laws; they are well made. It is forbidden to cross the great river and look upon the place that was the Place of the Gods—this is most strictly forbidden. We do not even say its name, though we know its name. It is there that spirits live, and demons—it is there that there are the ashes of the Great Burning. These things are forbidden—they have been forbidden since the beginning of time.

My father is a priest; I am the son of a priest. I have been in the Dead Places near us, with my father—at first, I was afraid. When my father went into the house to search for the metal, I stood by the door, and my heart felt small and weak. It was a dead man's house, a spirit house. It did not have the smell of man, though there were old bones in a corner. But it is not fitting that a priest's son should show fear. I looked at the bones in the shadow and kept my voice still. **A**

Then my father came out with the metal—a good, strong piece. He looked at me with both eyes, but I had not run away. He gave me the metal to hold—I took it and did not die. So he knew that I was truly his son and would be a priest in my time. That was when I was very young—nevertheless, my brothers would not have done it, though they are good hunters. After that, they gave me the good piece of meat and the warm corner by the fire. My father watched over me—he was glad that I should be a priest. But when I boasted or wept without a reason, he punished me more strictly than my brothers. That was right.

After a time, I myself was allowed to go into the dead houses and search for metal. So I learned the ways of those houses—and if I saw bones, I was no longer afraid. The bones are light and old—sometimes they will fall into dust if you touch them. But that is a great sin.

Birsay Ceremony (1996), Gloria Wallington. Monotype. Private Collection. Photo © Bridgeman Art Library.

30   I was taught the chants and the spells—I was taught how to stop the
running of blood from a wound and many secrets. A priest must know many
secrets—that was what my father said. If the hunters think we do all things by
chants and spells, they may believe so—it does not hurt them. I was taught
how to read in the old books and how to make the old writings—that was
hard and took a long time. My knowledge made me happy—it was like a fire
in my heart. Most of all, I liked to hear of the Old Days and the stories of the
gods. I asked myself many questions that I could not answer, but it was good
to ask them. At night, I would lie awake and listen to the wind—it seemed to
me that it was the voice of the gods as they flew through the air. **Ⓑ**

40   We are not ignorant like the Forest People—our women spin wool on the
wheel; our priests wear a white robe. We do not eat grubs from the tree; we
have not forgotten the old writings, although they are hard to understand.
Nevertheless, my knowledge and my lack of knowledge burned in me—I
wished to know more. When I was a man at last, I came to my father and said,
"It is time for me to go on my journey. Give me your leave."

He looked at me for a long time, stroking his beard; then he said at last,
"Yes. It is time." That night, in the house of the priesthood, I asked for and
received purification. My body hurt, but my spirit was a cool stone. It was my
father himself who questioned me about my dreams.

50   He bade me look into the smoke of the fire and see—I saw and told what
I saw. It was what I have always seen—a river, and, beyond it, a great Dead
Place and in it the gods walking. I have always thought about that. His eyes
were stern when I told him—he was no longer my father but a priest. He said,
"This is a strong dream."

"It is mine," I said, while the smoke waved and my head felt light. They
were singing the star song in the outer chamber, and it was like the buzzing of
bees in my head.

He asked me how the gods were dressed, and I told him how they were
dressed. We know how they were dressed from the book, but I saw them as if
60 they were before me. When I had finished, he threw the sticks three times and
studied them as they fell.

"This is a very strong dream," he said. "It may eat you up."

"I am not afraid," I said and looked at him with both eyes. My voice
sounded thin in my ears, but that was because of the smoke.

He touched me on the breast and the forehead. He gave me the bow and the
three arrows.

"Take them," he said. "It is forbidden to travel east. It is forbidden to cross
the river. It is forbidden to go to the Place of the Gods. All these things are
forbidden."

70   "All these things are forbidden," I said, but it was my voice that spoke and
not my spirit. He looked at me again.

Ⓑ POINT OF VIEW
Reread lines 30–39.
Think about how the
first-person point of view
affects your impression
of the narrator. What
important inner qualities
does he reveal?

"My son," he said. "Once I had young dreams. If your dreams do not eat you up, you may be a great priest. If they eat you, you are still my son. Now go on your journey." **C**

I went fasting, as is the law. My body hurt but not my heart. When the dawn came, I was out of sight of the village. I prayed and purified myself, waiting for a sign. The sign was an eagle. It flew east.

Sometimes signs are sent by bad spirits. I waited again on the flat rock, fasting, taking no food. I was very still—I could feel the sky above me and 80 the earth beneath. I waited till the sun was beginning to sink. Then three deer passed in the valley, going east—they did not wind me or see me. There was a white fawn with them—a very great sign.

I followed them, at a distance, waiting for what would happen. My heart was troubled about going east, yet I knew that I must go. My head hummed with my fasting—I did not even see the panther spring upon the white fawn. But, before I knew it, the bow was in my hand. I shouted, and the panther lifted his head from the fawn. It is not easy to kill a panther with one arrow, but the arrow went through his eye and into his brain. He died as he tried to spring—he rolled over, tearing at the ground. Then I knew I was meant to go 90 east—I knew that was my journey. When the night came, I made my fire and roasted meat.

It is eight suns' journey to the east, and a man passes by many Dead Places. The Forest People are afraid of them, but I am not. Once I made my fire on the edge of a Dead Place at night, and next morning, in the dead house, I found a good knife, little rusted. That was small to what came afterward, but it made my heart feel big. Always when I looked for game, it was in front of my arrow, and twice I passed hunting parties of the Forest People without their knowing. So I knew my magic was strong and my journey clean, in spite of the law.

100 Toward the setting of the eighth sun, I came to the banks of the great river. It was half a day's journey after I had left the god road—we do not use the god roads now, for they are falling apart into great blocks of stone, and the forest is safer going. A long way off, I had seen the water through trees, but the trees were thick. At last, I came out upon an open place at the top of a cliff. There was the great river below, like a giant in the sun. It is very long, very wide. It could eat all the streams we know and still be thirsty. Its name is Ou-dis-sun, the Sacred, the Long. No man of my tribe had seen it, not even my father, the priest. It was magic, and I prayed.

Then I raised my eyes and looked south. It was there, the Place of the Gods.
110 How can I tell what it was like—you do not know. It was there, in the red light, and they were too big to be houses. It was there with the red light upon it, mighty and ruined. I knew that in another moment the gods would see me. I covered my eyes with my hands and crept back into the forest. **D**

C MAKE INFERENCES
Why do you think the narrator's father allows the narrator to travel to the Place of the Gods, even though it is forbidden?

D MAKE INFERENCES
Reread lines 100–113. In what ways do the great river and the Place of the Gods resemble places you know?

Midsummer Night, 1994 (1994), Gloria Wallington. Monotype, 24 × 31 cm.
Private Collection. Photo © Bridgeman Art Library.

Surely, that was enough to do, and live. Surely it was enough to spend the night upon the cliff. The Forest People themselves do not come near. Yet, all through the night, I knew that I should have to cross the river and walk in the places of the gods, although the gods ate me up. My magic did not help me at all, and yet there was a fire in my bowels, a fire in my mind. When the sun rose, I thought, "My journey has been clean. Now I will go home from my journey." But, even as I thought so, I knew I could not. If I went to the Place of the Gods, I would surely die, but, if I did not go, I could never be at peace with my spirit again. It is better to lose one's life than one's spirit, if one is a priest and the son of a priest.

Nevertheless, as I made the raft, the tears ran out of my eyes. The Forest People could have killed me without fight, if they had come upon me then, but they did not come. When the raft was made, I said the sayings for the dead and painted myself for death. My heart was cold as a frog and my knees like water, but the burning in my mind would not let me have peace. As I pushed the raft from the shore, I began my death song—I had the right. It was a fine song.

130   *"I am John, son of John," I sang. "My people are the Hill People.*
They are the men.

    *I go into the Dead Places, but I am not slain. I take the metal from the Dead
Places, but I am not blasted.*

    *I travel upon the god roads and am not afraid. E-yah! I have killed the
panther; I have killed the fawn!*

    E-yah! I have come to the great river. No man has come there before.

    *It is forbidden to go east, but I have gone, forbidden to go on the great river,
but I am there.*

    Open your hearts, you spirits, and hear my song.

140   *Now I go to the Place of the Gods; I shall not return.*

    *My body is painted for death and my limbs weak, but my heart is big as I go
to the Place of the Gods!"* **E**

All the same, when I came to the Place of the Gods, I was afraid, afraid.
The current of the great river is very strong—it gripped my raft with its hands.
That was magic, for the river itself is wide and calm. I could feel evil spirits
about me, in the bright morning; I could feel their breath on my neck as I
was swept down the stream. Never have I been so much alone—I tried to
think of my knowledge, but it was a squirrel's heap of winter nuts. There was
no strength in my knowledge anymore, and I felt small and naked as a new-
150 hatched bird—alone upon the great river, the servant of the gods.

    Yet, after a while, my eyes were opened, and I saw. I saw both banks of the
river—I saw that once there had been god roads across it, though now they
were broken and fallen like broken vines. Very great they were, and wonderful
and broken—broken in the time of the Great Burning when the fire fell out of
the sky. And always the current took me nearer to the Place of the Gods, and
the huge ruins rose before my eyes.

    I do not know the customs of rivers—we are the People of the Hills. I tried
to guide my raft with the pole, but it spun around. I thought the river meant
to take me past the Place of the Gods and out into the Bitter Water of the
160 legends. I grew angry then—my heart felt strong. I said aloud, "I am a priest
and the son of a priest!" The gods heard me—they showed me how to paddle
with the pole on one side of the raft. The current changed itself—I drew near
to the Place of the Gods. **F**

    When I was very near, my raft struck and turned over. I can swim in our
lakes—I swam to the shore. There was a great spike of rusted metal sticking
out into the river—I hauled myself up upon it and sat there, panting. I had
saved my bow and two arrows and the knife I found in the Dead Place, but
that was all. My raft went whirling downstream toward the Bitter Water. I
looked after it, and thought if it had trod me under, at least I would be safely

E **POINT OF VIEW**
Think about how the
first-person point of view
helps create suspense.
How might your interest
be affected if a different
narrator told of John's
journey?

F **POINT OF VIEW**
Reread lines 157–163.
What details suggest that
John is a **naive narrator?**

170 dead. Nevertheless, when I had dried my bowstring and restrung it, I walked forward to the Place of the Gods.

It felt like ground underfoot; it did not burn me. It is not true what some of the tales say, that the ground there burns forever, for I have been there. Here and there were the marks and stains of the Great Burning, on the ruins, that is true. But they were old marks and old stains. It is not true either, what some of our priests say, that it is an island covered with fogs and enchantments. It is not. It is a great Dead Place—greater than any Dead Place we know. Everywhere in it there are god roads, though most are cracked and broken. Everywhere there are the ruins of the high towers of the gods. **G**

180 How shall I tell what I saw? I went carefully, my strung bow in my hand, my skin ready for danger. There should have been the wailings of spirits and the shrieks of demons, but there were not. It was very silent and sunny where I had landed—the wind and the rain and the birds that drop seeds had done their work—the grass grew in the cracks of the broken stone. It is a fair island— no wonder the gods built there. If I had come there, a god, I also would have built.

How shall I tell what I saw? The towers are not all broken—here and there one still stands, like a great tree in a forest, and the birds nest high. But the towers themselves look blind, for the gods are gone. I saw a fish hawk, catching

190 fish in the river. I saw a little dance of white butterflies over a great heap of broken stones and columns. I went there and looked about me—there was a carved stone with cut letters, broken in half. I can read letters, but I could not understand these. They said UBTREAS. There was also the shattered image of a man or a god. It had been made of white stone, and he wore his hair tied back like a woman's. His name was ASHING, as I read on the cracked half of a stone. I thought it wise to pray to ASHING, though I do not know that god. **H**

How shall I tell what I saw? There was no smell of man left, on stone or metal. Nor were there many trees in that wilderness of stone. There are many pigeons, nesting and dropping in the towers—the gods must have loved them,

200 or, perhaps, they used them for sacrifices. There are wild cats that roam the god roads, green-eyed, unafraid of man. At night they wail like demons, but they are not demons. The wild dogs are more dangerous, for they hunt in a pack, but them I did not meet till later. Everywhere there are the carved stones, carved with magical numbers or words.

I went north—I did not try to hide myself. When a god or a demon saw me, then I would die, but meanwhile I was no longer afraid. My hunger for knowledge burned in me—there was so much that I could not understand. After a while, I knew that my belly was hungry. I could have hunted for my meat, but I did not hunt. It is known that the gods did not hunt as we

210 do—they got their food from enchanted boxes and jars. Sometimes these are still found in the Dead Places—once, when I was a child and foolish, I opened

G MAKE INFERENCES
Reread lines 172–179. What can you infer about the events that occurred at the Place of the Gods?

H MAKE INFERENCES
Reread lines 187–196. What famous person do you think the "shattered image" depicts?

such a jar and tasted it and found the food sweet. But my father found out and punished me for it strictly, for, often, that food is death. Now, though, I had long gone past what was forbidden, and I entered the likeliest towers, looking for the food of the gods.

I found it at last in the ruins of a great temple in the mid-city. A mighty temple it must have been, for the roof was painted like the sky at night with its stars—that much I could see, though the colors were faint and dim. It went down into great caves and tunnels—perhaps they kept their slaves there.
220 But when I started to climb down, I heard the squeaking of rats, so I did not go—rats are unclean, and there must have been many tribes of them, from the squeaking. But near there, I found food, in the heart of a ruin, behind a door that still opened. I ate only the fruits from the jars—they had a very sweet taste. There was drink, too, in bottles of glass—the drink of the gods was strong and made my head swim. After I had eaten and drunk, I slept on the top of a stone, my bow at my side.

When I woke, the sun was low. Looking down from where I lay, I saw a dog sitting on his haunches. His tongue was hanging out of his mouth; he looked as if he were laughing. He was a big dog, with a gray-brown coat, as
230 big as a wolf. I sprang up and shouted at him, but he did not move—he just sat there as if he were laughing. I did not like that. When I reached for a stone to throw, he moved swiftly out of the way of the stone. He was not afraid of me; he looked at me as if I were meat. No doubt I could have killed him with an arrow, but I did not know if there were others. Moreover, night was falling.

I looked about me—not far away there was a great, broken god road, leading north. The towers were high enough, but not so high, and while many of the dead houses were wrecked, there were some that stood. I went toward this god road, keeping to the heights of the ruins, while the dog followed. When I had reached the god road, I saw that there were others behind him. If I
240 had slept later, they would have come upon me asleep and torn out my throat. As it was, they were sure enough of me; they did not hurry. When I went into the dead house, they kept watch at the entrance—doubtless they thought they would have a fine hunt. But a dog cannot open a door, and I knew, from the books, that the gods did not like to live on the ground but on high. ❶

I had just found a door I could open when the dogs decided to rush. Ha! They were surprised when I shut the door in their faces—it was a good door, of strong metal. I could hear their foolish baying beyond it, but I did not stop to answer them. I was in darkness—I found stairs and climbed. There were many stairs, turning around till my head was dizzy. At the top was another
250 door—I found the knob and opened it. I was in a long small chamber—on one side of it was a bronze door that could not be opened, for it had no handle. Perhaps there was a magic word to open it, but I did not have the word. I turned to the door in the opposite side of the wall. The lock of it was broken, and I opened it and went in.

❶ GRAMMAR AND STYLE
Reread lines 235–244. Notice how Benét uses **formal language** that lacks contractions and contains complex sentence structure.

Within, there was a place of great riches. The god who lived there must have been a powerful god. The first room was a small anteroom—I waited there for some time, telling the spirits of the place that I came in peace and not as a robber. When it seemed to me that they had had time to hear me, I went on. Ah, what riches! Few, even, of the windows had been broken—it was all as it
260 had been. The great windows that looked over the city had not been broken at all, though they were dusty and streaked with many years. There were coverings on the floors, the colors not greatly faded, and the chairs were soft and deep. There were pictures upon the walls, very strange, very wonderful—I remember one of a bunch of flowers in a jar—if you came close to it, you could see nothing but bits of color, but if you stood away from it, the flowers might have been picked yesterday. It made my heart feel strange to look at this picture— and to look at the figure of a bird, in some hard clay, on a table and see it so like our birds. Everywhere there were books and writings, many in tongues that I could not read. The god who lived there must have been a wise god and full of
270 knowledge. I felt I had a right there, as I sought knowledge also. **J**

Nevertheless, it was strange. There was a washing place but no water— perhaps the gods washed in air. There was a cooking place but no wood, and though there was a machine to cook food, there was no place to put fire in it. Nor were there candles or lamps—there were things that looked like lamps, but they had neither oil nor wick. All these things were magic, but I touched them and lived—the magic had gone out of them. Let me tell one thing to show. In the washing place, a thing said "Hot," but it was not hot to the touch—another thing said "Cold," but it was not cold. This must have been a strong magic, but the magic was gone. I do not understand—they had ways—I
280 wish that I knew.

It was close and dry and dusty in the house of the gods. I have said the magic was gone, but that is not true—it had gone from the magic things, but it had not gone from the place. I felt the spirits about me, weighing upon me. Nor had I ever slept in a Dead Place before—and yet, tonight, I must sleep there. When I thought of it, my tongue felt dry in my throat, in spite of my wish for knowledge. Almost I would have gone down again and faced the dogs, but I did not.

I had not gone through all the rooms when the darkness fell. When it fell, I went back to the big room looking over the city and made fire. There was
290 a place to make fire and a box with wood in it, though I do not think they cooked there. I wrapped myself in a floor covering and slept in front of the fire—I was very tired.

Now I tell what is very strong magic. I woke in the midst of the night. When I woke, the fire had gone out, and I was cold. It seemed to me that all around me there were whisperings and voices. I closed my eyes to shut them

J MAKE INFERENCES
Reread lines 255–270.
What does this "place of great riches" remind you of?

Selassie Monoliths, 1998 (1998), Charlie Millar. Oil on canvas, 111.7 × 96.5 cm.
Private Collection. Photo © Bridgeman Art Library.

out. Some will say that I slept again, but I do not think that I slept. I could feel
the spirits drawing my spirit out of my body as a fish is drawn on a line.

Why should I lie about it? I am a priest and the son of a priest. If there are
spirits, as they say, in the small Dead Places near us, what spirits must there
not be in that great Place of the Gods? And would not they wish to speak?
After such long years? I know that I felt myself drawn as a fish is drawn on a
line. I had stepped out of my body—I could see my body asleep in front of the
cold fire, but it was not I. I was drawn to look out upon the city of the gods.

It should have been dark, for it was night, but it was not dark. Everywhere
there were lights—lines of light—circles and blurs of light—ten thousand

300

torches would not have been the same. The sky itself was alight—you could barely see the stars for the glow in the sky. I thought to myself "This is strong magic" and trembled. There was a roaring in my ears like the rushing of rivers. Then my eyes grew used to the light and my ears to the sound. I knew that I 310 was seeing the city as it had been when the gods were alive.

That was a sight indeed—yes, that was a sight: I could not have seen it in the body—my body would have died. Everywhere went the gods, on foot and in chariots—there were gods beyond number and counting, and their chariots blocked the streets. They had turned night to day for their pleasure—they did not sleep with the sun. The noise of their coming and going was the noise of many waters. It was magic what they could do—it was magic what they did.

I looked out of another window—the great vines of their bridges were mended, and the god roads went east and west. Restless, restless, were the gods and always in motion! They burrowed tunnels under rivers—they flew in the 320 air. With unbelievable tools they did giant works—no part of the earth was safe from them, for, if they wished for a thing, they summoned it from the other side of the world. And always, as they labored and rested, as they feasted and made love, there was a drum in their ears—the pulse of the giant city, beating and beating like a man's heart.

Were they happy? What is happiness to the gods? They were great; they were mighty; they were wonderful and terrible. As I looked upon them and their magic, I felt like a child—but a little more, it seemed to me, and they would pull down the moon from the sky. I saw them with wisdom beyond wisdom and knowledge beyond knowledge. And yet not all they did was well done—even I 330 could see that—and yet their wisdom could not but grow until all was peace.

Then I saw their fate come upon them, and that was terrible past speech. It came upon them as they walked the streets of their city. I have been in the fights with the Forest People—I have seen men die. But this was not like that. When gods war with gods, they use weapons we do not know. It was fire falling out of the sky and a mist that poisoned. It was the time of the Great Burning and the Destruction. They ran about like ants in the streets of their city—poor gods, poor gods! Then the towers began to fall. A few escaped— yes, a few. The legends tell it. But, even after the city had become a Dead Place, for many years the poison was still in the ground. I saw it happen; I saw 340 the last of them die. It was darkness over the broken city, and I wept. **Ⓚ**

All this, I saw. I saw it as I have told it, though not in the body. When I woke in the morning, I was hungry, but I did not think first of my hunger, for my heart was perplexed and confused. I knew the reason for the Dead Places, but I did not see why it had happened. It seemed to me it should not have happened, with all the magic they had. I went through the house looking for an answer. There was so much in the house I could not understand—and yet I am a priest and the son of a priest. It was like being on one side of the great river, at night, with no light to show the way.

Ⓚ FORESHADOWING
John's "dream" is foreshadowed earlier in the story. Where in the story does Benét prepare the reader for this dream?

Then I saw the dead god. He was sitting in his chair, by the window, in a
350 room I had not entered before, and for the first moment, I thought that he was
alive. Then I saw the skin on the back of his hand—it was like dry leather. The
room was shut, hot and dry—no doubt that had kept him as he was. At first I
was afraid to approach him—then the fear left me. He was sitting looking out
over the city—he was dressed in the clothes of the gods. His age was neither
young nor old—I could not tell his age. But there was wisdom in his face and
great sadness. You could see that he would have not run away. He had sat at
his window, watching his city die—then he himself had died. But it is better to
lose one's life than one's spirit—and you could see from the face that his spirit
had not been lost. I knew that, if I touched him, he would fall into dust—and
360 yet, there was something unconquered in the face.

That is all of my story, for then I knew he was a man—I knew then that
they had been men, neither gods nor demons. It is a great knowledge, hard to
tell and believe. They were men—they went a dark road, but they were men.
I had no fear after that—I had no fear going home, though twice I fought off
the dogs and once I was hunted for two days by the Forest People. When I saw
my father again, I prayed and was purified. He touched my lips and my breast;
he said, "You went away a boy. You come back a man and a priest." I said,
"Father, they were men! I have been in the Place of the Gods and seen it! Now
slay me, if it is the law—but still I know they were men."

370 He looked at me out of both eyes. He said, "The law is not always the same
shape—you have done what you have done. I could not have done it my time,
but you come after me. Tell!"

I told, and he listened. After that, I wished to tell all the people, but he
showed me otherwise. He said, "Truth is a hard deer to hunt. If you eat too
much truth at once, you may die of the truth. It was not idly that our fathers
forbade the Dead Places." He was right—it is better the truth should come
little by little. I have learned that, being a priest. Perhaps, in the old days, they
ate knowledge too fast. **L**

Nevertheless, we make a beginning. It is not for the metal alone we go to
380 the Dead Places now—there are the books and the writings. They are hard
to learn. And the magic tools are broken—but we can look at them and
wonder. At least, we make a beginning. And, when I am chief priest, we
shall go beyond the great river. We shall go to the Place of the Gods—the
place newyork—not one man but a company. We shall look for the images
of the gods and find the god ASHING and the others—the gods Lincoln
and Biltmore[1] and Moses.[2] But they were men who built the city, not gods or
demons. They were men. I remember the dead man's face. They were men who
were here before us. We must build again. ◌

L DRAW CONCLUSIONS
Reread lines 376–378.
What idea about
knowledge do you
think Benét is trying
to communicate?

---

1. **Biltmore:** the name of a once-famous hotel in New York City.

2. **Moses:** Robert Moses (1888–1981), a New York City public official whose name appears
   on many bridges and other structures built during his administration.

Comprehension

1. **Recall** What profession does John plan to have?

2. **Recall** Why does John set out on his journey?

3. **Recall** What does John discover to be untrue about the Place of the Gods?

4. **Clarify** When and where does this story take place?

Literary Analysis

5. **Analyze** Why is it forbidden for anyone but a priest to visit the Dead Places? Explain your answer.

6. **Make Inferences About Setting** Review the chart you completed as you read. What can you infer about the Place of the Gods and the events that took place there long ago?

7. **Draw Conclusions** What is the **theme,** or message, of this story? Cite evidence to support your conclusion.

8. **Understand Allusion** The **Background** on page 289 explains the biblical allusion, or reference, in the story's title. How do the words of the psalm relate to the discoveries John makes about the Great Burning and the gods?

9. **Compare Points of View** With a **first-person narrator,** you see the story unfold through the eyes of one character. Think about how John reacts to other characters and the way he describes the story's events. Would a **third-person omniscient narrator**—a narrator who sees into the minds of all characters in a story—have presented a more compelling picture of the events in "By the Waters of Babylon"? Cite evidence from the story to support your opinion.

10. **Evaluate Narrative Devices** John is an example of a **naive narrator**—a narrator with limited **knowledge,** who does not fully understand what he experiences. Why did Benét choose this kind of narrator for "By the Waters of Babylon"?

Literary Criticism

11. **Historical Context** This story was published in 1937, when the threat of a second world war loomed large over the face of Europe. In what ways is this historical context reflected in the story? Explain your answer.

Reading-Writing Connection

Enrich your understanding of "By the Waters of Babylon" by responding to these prompts. Then use **Revision: Grammar and Style** to improve your writing.

WRITING PROMPTS

A. Short Response: Evaluate a Statement
Do you agree with John that too much **knowledge** can harm people and that "truth should come little by little"? Write a **one-to-two-paragraph response**, drawing on the story and real-life events.

SELF-CHECK

A successful response will . . .
- clearly state an opinion in the introduction
- provide supporting examples from the story and real life

B. Extended Response: Analyze a Character
Imagine that John's father is standing before the other priests, relating John's story and trying to convince them that John should now lead the people. Tell what he says to them in a **three-to-five-paragraph narrative**.

A good narrative will . . .
- include important events from John's journey
- use formal language like that of the original story

REVISION: GRAMMAR AND STYLE

USE APPROPRIATE LANGUAGE Review the **Grammar and Style** note on page 297. Benét uses **formal language** to convey the dark mood of the story. You, too, can use formal language when the audience and purpose require a quality of seriousness in your writing. Here are some guidelines to follow:

OHIO STANDARDS

WRITING STANDARD
5.4 Determine audience and purpose

1. **Avoid using contractions.** Contractions tend to make writing sound more like everyday speech than formal writing.

2. **Use more complex sentence structure and vocabulary.** Short, simple sentences and informal language, such as slang, are more appropriate for casual communication.

Here is an example of Benét's use of formal language:

> *How shall I tell what I saw? The towers are not all broken—here and there one still stands, like a great tree in a forest, and the birds nest high. But the towers themselves look blind, for the gods are gone.* (lines 187–189)

Notice how the revisions in red in the student model make the language of this first draft more appropriate for the audience and purpose. Use similar techniques to revise your response to Prompt B.

STUDENT MODEL

My son John is ~~a brave kid.~~ Although ~~it was a big no-no~~ to go to the
as brave as a panther. the law forbade him

Dead Places, he ~~didn't let~~ that ~~stop him. He wanted to know what was what.~~
did not fear prevent him from seeking knowledge.

WRITING TOOLS
For prewriting, revision, and editing tools, visit the **Writing Center** at ClassZone.com.

There Will Come Soft Rains
Short Story by Ray Bradbury

Is TECHNOLOGY *taking over?*

OHIO STANDARDS

READING STANDARDS
2.1 Draw conclusions
3.1 Identify and understand organizational patterns

KEY IDEA Which technological innovations have improved the quality of everyday life? Which ones have had a negative impact? In "There Will Come Soft Rains," you will read about the far-reaching consequences of **technology** on one particular home.

QUICKWRITE With a group, list the advantages and disadvantages of different technological innovations in a chart like the one shown. Then write a paragraph, telling whether you think technology overall has had a negative or a positive effect on everyday life.

Innovation	Advantages	Disadvantages
Internet	Easy access to information	Lack of human contact

● LITERARY ANALYSIS: CHRONOLOGICAL ORDER

Writers make choices about how to organize events in a story. The most straightforward way of structuring a story is to describe events in **chronological order**—the sequence in which events occur. To determine chronological order in a story, look for the following:

- words that identify time, such as *six o'clock* and *today*
- words that signal order, such as *before, next,* and *last*
- breaks in the chronological flow of events

As you read "There Will Come Soft Rains," think about the reasons Ray Bradbury might have chosen to present this science fiction story in chronological order.

● READING SKILL: DRAW CONCLUSIONS

A **conclusion** is a judgment based on evidence in the story and your own prior knowledge. Use the following strategies to analyze information about the house in the story:

- Analyze details about the family and their routine.
- Analyze details about the areas near the house.
- Identify changes in the performance of the house.

As you read the story, record and analyze important details. Later you will draw conclusions about what happened to the family and the town.

Important Details	My Thoughts
It's morning and the house is empty.	The people are gone. The house still acts as though they're there.

Review: **Compare and Contrast**

▲ VOCABULARY IN CONTEXT

Substitute a different word or phrase for each boldfaced vocabulary word.

1. The **silhouette** of the great oak is visible for miles.
2. Your increasing **paranoia** is making you a nervous wreck.
3. To **manipulate** a puppet properly requires practice.
4. The sight of the rattlesnake made Don **tremulous.**
5. She is **oblivious** to the mess all around her.
6. This is a **sublime** piece of cheesecake!

Author On|ine

**Ray Bradbury
born 1920**

Prophet of the Future
Ray Bradbury is one of America's best-known science fiction and fantasy writers. His most chilling stories comment on the human consequences of progress. "Science ran too far ahead of us too quickly," Bradbury once remarked, "and the people got lost in a mechanical wilderness." Sadly, Bradbury has lived to see some of his frightening concerns become fact.

A Magical Childhood Bradbury's interest in science fiction and fantasy emerged when he was growing up in Waukegan, Illinois. He devoured the popular culture of his day, including movies, radio shows, comics, and science fiction magazines. He was also a fan of the local library, where he enjoyed books by such early science fiction writers as H. G. Wells and Jules Verne. While various writers have influenced his style, his themes are drawn primarily from his own childhood.

 MORE ABOUT THE AUTHOR
For more on Ray Bradbury, visit the **Literature Center** at **ClassZone.com.**

Background

Technology: No Guarantee Before 1900, electric machines were used primarily in workplaces. With the spread of electricity, however, families enjoyed modern appliances in their homes. In the early 20th century, many household machines, such as the vacuum cleaner and the toaster, became available for the first time.

Science fiction writers of this period often created works featuring utopias—or ideal worlds—in which machines freed people of difficult tasks. In "There Will Come Soft Rains," Bradbury challenges this idea by presenting a society harmed by modern technology.

THERE
WILL
COME
Soft Rains

Ray Bradbury

In the living room the voice-clock sang, *Tick-tock, seven o'clock, time to get up, time to get up, seven o'clock!* as if it were afraid that nobody would. The morning house lay empty. The clock ticked on, repeating and repeating its sounds into the emptiness. *Seven-nine, breakfast time, seven-nine!*

In the kitchen the breakfast stove gave a hissing sigh and ejected from its warm interior eight pieces of perfectly browned toast, eight eggs sunnyside up, sixteen slices of bacon, two coffees, and two cool glasses of milk.

"Today is August 4, 2026," said a second voice from the kitchen ceiling, "in the city of Allendale, California." It repeated the date three times for memory's
10 sake. "Today is Mr. Featherstone's birthday. Today is the anniversary of Tilita's marriage. Insurance is payable, as are the water, gas, and light bills." **A**

Somewhere in the walls, relays[1] clicked, memory tapes glided under electric eyes.

Eight-one, tick-tock, eight-one o'clock, off to school, off to work, run, run, eight-one! But no doors slammed, no carpets took the soft tread of rubber heels. It was raining outside. The weather box on the front door sang quietly: "Rain, rain, go away; rubbers, raincoats for today . . ." And the rain tapped on the empty house, echoing.

Outside, the garage chimed and lifted its door to reveal the waiting car.
20 After a long wait the door swung down again. **B**

At eight-thirty the eggs were shriveled and the toast was like stone. An aluminum wedge scraped them into the sink, where hot water whirled them down a metal throat which digested and flushed them away to the distant sea. The dirty dishes were dropped into a hot washer and emerged twinkling dry.

---

1. **relays**: devices that automatically turn switches in electric circuits on and off.

ANALYZE VISUALS
Examine this image. What details convey the orderliness of the family that lives in the house?

A CHRONOLOGICAL ORDER
Reread lines 1–11. Which words and phrases tell you that the story is organized in chronological order?

B DRAW CONCLUSIONS
Reread lines 14–20. Which story details suggest that this is an unusual day for the family?

Nine-fifteen, sang the clock, *time to clean.*

Out of warrens in the wall, tiny robot mice darted. The rooms were acrawl with the small cleaning animals, all rubber and metal. They thudded against chairs, whirling their mustached runners, kneading the rug nap, sucking gently at hidden dust. Then, like mysterious invaders, they popped into their
30 burrows. Their pink electric eyes faded. The house was clean. **C**

Ten o'clock. The sun came out from behind the rain. The house stood alone in a city of rubble and ashes. This was the one house left standing. At night the ruined city gave off a radioactive glow which could be seen for miles.

Ten-fifteen. The garden sprinklers whirled up in golden founts, filling the soft morning air with scatterings of brightness. The water pelted windowpanes, running down the charred west side where the house had been burned evenly free of its white paint. The entire west face of the house was black, save for five places. Here the **silhouette** in paint of a man mowing a lawn. Here, as in a photograph, a woman bent to pick flowers. Still farther over, their images
40 burned on wood in one titanic instant, a small boy, hands flung into the air; higher up, the image of a thrown ball, and opposite him a girl, hands raised to catch a ball which never came down.

The five spots of paint—the man, the woman, the children, the ball— remained. The rest was a thin charcoaled layer. **D**

The gentle sprinkler rain filled the garden with falling light.

Until this day, how well the house had kept its peace. How carefully it had inquired, "Who goes there? What's the password?" and, getting no answer from lonely foxes and whining cats, it had shut up its windows and drawn shades in an old-maidenly preoccupation with self-protection which bordered
50 on a mechanical **paranoia.**

It quivered at each sound, the house did. If a sparrow brushed a window, the shade snapped up. The bird, startled, flew off! No, not even a bird must touch the house!

The house was an altar with ten thousand attendants, big, small, servicing, attending, in choirs. But the gods had gone away, and the ritual of the religion continued senselessly, uselessly.

Twelve noon.

A dog whined, shivering, on the front porch.

The front door recognized the dog voice and opened. The dog, once huge
60 and fleshy, but now gone to bone and covered with sores, moved in and through the house, tracking mud. Behind it whirred angry mice, angry at having to pick up mud, angry at inconvenience.

For not a leaf fragment blew under the door but what the wall panels flipped open and the copper scrap rats flashed swiftly out. The offending dust, hair, or paper, seized in miniature steel jaws, was raced back to the burrows. There, down tubes which fed into the cellar, it was dropped into the sighing vent of an incinerator which sat like evil Baal[2] in a dark corner.

C DRAW CONCLUSIONS
Think about the **setting** of this story. What do you learn about the society from the house's many automated features?

silhouette (sĭl′ōō-ĕt′) *n.* an outline that appears dark against a light background

D DRAW CONCLUSIONS
Reread lines 31–44. Based on the story details about the city, what do you think has happened?

paranoia (păr′ə-noi′ə) *n.* an irrational fear of danger or misfortune

---

2. **Baal** (bā′əl): an idol worshiped by certain ancient peoples of the Middle East.

The dog ran upstairs, hysterically yelping to each door, at last realizing, as the house realized, that only silence was here.

70 It sniffed the air and scratched the kitchen door. Behind the door, the stove was making pancakes which filled the house with a rich baked odor and the scent of maple syrup.

The dog frothed at the mouth, lying at the door, sniffing, its eyes turned to fire. It ran wildly in circles, biting at its tail, spun in a frenzy, and died. It lay in the parlor for an hour.

Two o'clock, sang a voice.

Delicately sensing decay at last, the regiments of mice hummed out as softly as blown gray leaves in an electrical wind.

Two-fifteen.

80 The dog was gone.

In the cellar, the incinerator glowed suddenly and a whirl of sparks leaped up the chimney. **E**

Two thirty-five.

Bridge tables sprouted from patio walls. Playing cards fluttered onto pads in a shower of pips. Martinis manifested on an oaken bench with egg-salad sandwiches. Music played.

E COMPARE AND CONTRAST
Compare the actions of the dog with those of the house. What does the dog's death suggest about the house?

But the tables were silent and the cards untouched.

At four o'clock the tables folded like great butterflies back through the paneled walls.

90 *Four-thirty.*

The nursery walls glowed.

Animals took shape: yellow giraffes, blue lions, pink antelopes, lilac panthers cavorting in crystal substance. The walls were glass. They looked out upon color and fantasy. Hidden films clocked through well-oiled sprockets, and the walls lived. The nursery floor was woven to resemble a crisp, cereal meadow. Over this ran aluminum roaches and iron crickets, and in the hot still air butterflies of delicate red tissue wavered among the sharp aroma of animal spoors! There was the sound like a great matted yellow hive of bees within a dark bellows, the lazy bumble of a purring lion. And there was the patter of 100 okapi[3] feet and the murmur of a fresh jungle rain, like other hoofs, falling upon the summer-starched grass. Now the walls dissolved into distances of parched weed, mile on mile, and warm endless sky. The animals drew away into thorn brakes and water holes.

It was the children's hour. **F**

Five o'clock. The bath filled with clear hot water.

Six, seven, eight o'clock. The dinner dishes **manipulated** like magic tricks, and in the study a *click.* In the metal stand opposite the hearth where a fire now blazed up warmly, a cigar popped out, half an inch of soft gray ash on it, smoking, waiting.

110 *Nine o'clock.* The beds warmed their hidden circuits, for nights were cool here.

Nine-five. A voice spoke from the study ceiling:

"Mrs. McClellan, which poem would you like this evening?"

The house was silent.

The voice said at last, "Since you express no preference, I shall select a poem at random." Quiet music rose to back the voice. "Sara Teasdale. As I recall, your favorite. . . .

"There will come soft rains and the
    smell of the ground,
And swallows circling with their
120   *shimmering sound;*

And frogs in the pools singing at night,
And wild plum trees in **tremulous** *white;*

Robins will wear their feathery fire,
Whistling their whims on a low fence-wire;

F DRAW CONCLUSIONS
What do the nursery's furnishings tell you about the family and their relationship to the natural world?

manipulate
(mə-nĭp′yə-lāt′) *v.* to move, operate, or handle

tremulous (trĕm′yə-ləs)
adj. trembling, unsteady

---

3. **okapi** (ō-kä′pē): an antelope-like hoofed mammal of the African jungle.

And not one will know of the war, not one
Will care at last when it is done.

Not one would mind, neither bird nor tree,
If mankind perished utterly;

And Spring herself, when she woke at dawn
130 *Would scarcely know that we were gone."* **G**

The fire burned on the stone hearth and the cigar fell away into a mound of quiet ash on its tray. The empty chairs faced each other between the silent walls, and the music played.

At ten o'clock the house began to die. **H**
The wind blew. A falling tree bough crashed through the kitchen window. Cleaning solvent, bottled, shattered over the stove. The room was ablaze in an instant!
"Fire!" screamed a voice. The house lights flashed, water pumps shot water from the ceilings. But the solvent spread on the linoleum, licking, eating,
140 under the kitchen door, while the voices took it up in chorus: "Fire, fire, fire!"
The house tried to save itself. Doors sprang tightly shut, but the windows were broken by the heat and the wind blew and sucked upon the fire.
The house gave ground as the fire in ten billion angry sparks moved with flaming ease from room to room and then up the stairs. While scurrying water rats squeaked from the walls, pistoled their water, and ran for more. And the wall sprays let down showers of mechanical rain.

G DRAW CONCLUSIONS
What do you think is the **theme,** or main message, of the poem?

H CHRONOLOGICAL ORDER
How has the marking of time changed in the story? Explain.

But too late. Somewhere, sighing, a pump shrugged to a stop. The quenching rain ceased. The reserve water supply which had filled baths and washed dishes for many quiet days was gone.

150   The fire crackled up the stairs. It fed upon Picassos and Matisses[4] in the upper halls, like delicacies, baking off the oily flesh, tenderly crisping the canvases into black shavings.

    Now the fire lay in beds, stood in windows, changed the colors of drapes! And then, reinforcements.

    From attic trapdoors, blind robot faces peered down with faucet mouths gushing green chemical.

    The fire backed off, as even an elephant must at the sight of a dead snake. Now there were twenty snakes whipping over the floor, killing the fire with a clear cold venom of green froth.

160   But the fire was clever. It had sent flame outside the house, up through the attic to the pumps there. An explosion! The attic brain which directed the pumps was shattered into bronze shrapnel on the beams.

    The fire rushed back into every closet and felt of the clothes hung there.

    The house shuddered, oak bone on bone, its bared skeleton cringing from the heat, its wire, its nerves revealed as if a surgeon had torn the skin off to let the red veins and capillaries quiver in the scalded air. Help, help! Fire! Run, run! Heat snapped mirrors like the first brittle winter ice. And the voices wailed Fire,

---

4. **Picassos and Matisses:** paintings by the famous 20th-century artists Pablo Picasso (pĭ-kä′sō) and Henri Matisse (mə-tēs′).

ANALYZE VISUALS
Review all of the illustrations in the story. Together, how effective are they at conveying the story's **chronological order** of events? Explain.

fire, run, run, like a tragic nursery rhyme, a dozen voices, high, low, like children dying in a forest, alone, alone. And the voices fading as the wires popped their sheathings like hot chestnuts. One, two, three, four, five voices died.

In the nursery the jungle burned. Blue lions roared, purple giraffes bounded off. The panthers ran in circles, changing color, and ten million animals, running before the fire, vanished off toward a distant steaming river. . . .

Ten more voices died. In the last instant under the fire avalanche, other choruses, **oblivious,** could be heard announcing the time, playing music, cutting the lawn by remote-control mower, or setting an umbrella frantically out and in the slamming and opening front door, a thousand things happening, like a clock shop when each clock strikes the hour insanely before or after the other, a scene of maniac confusion, yet unity; singing, screaming, a few last cleaning mice darting bravely out to carry the horrid ashes away! And one voice, with **sublime** disregard for the situation, read poetry aloud in the fiery study, until all the film spools burned, until all the wires withered and the circuits cracked.

The fire burst the house and let it slam flat down, puffing out skirts of spark and smoke.

In the kitchen, an instant before the rain of fire and timber, the stove could be seen making breakfasts at a psychopathic rate, ten dozen eggs, six loaves of toast, twenty dozen bacon strips, which, eaten by fire, started the stove working again, hysterically hissing!

The crash. The attic smashing into kitchen and parlor. The parlor into cellar, cellar into sub-cellar. Deep freeze, armchair, film tapes, circuits, beds, and all like skeletons thrown in a cluttered mound deep under.

Smoke and silence. A great quantity of smoke. ❶

Dawn showed faintly in the east. Among the ruins, one wall stood alone. Within the wall, a last voice said, over and over again and again, even as the sun rose to shine upon the heaped rubble and steam:

"Today is August 5, 2026, today is August 5, 2026, today is . . ." ❧

oblivious (ə-blĭv'ē-əs) *adj.* paying no attention, completely unaware

sublime (sə-blīm') *adj.* supreme, splendid

❶ **DRAW CONCLUSIONS** What idea about technology does Bradbury convey in the burning of the house?

Comprehension

1. **Recall** When and where does the story take place?

2. **Recall** List three functions the house performs.

3. **Summarize** Describe the changes the house undergoes during the story.

OHIO
STANDARDS

READING STANDARD
3.1 Identify and understand
organizational patterns

Literary Analysis

4. **Draw Conclusions** Review the chart you filled in as you read. What has happened to the McClellan family and the town? Use details to support your conclusion.

5. **Interpret Theme** What do you think is the theme, or main message, of the story? Cite evidence from the story to support your answer.

6. **Examine Point of View** In the third-person point of view, a narrator outside the action describes events and characters. How does the third-person narrator of "There Will Come Soft Rains" maintain the reader's interest in a story where there are no human characters? Explain.

7. **Analyze Chronological Order** Consider how the story would have been different if it had included numerous **flashbacks,** or scenes that recall earlier experiences. Why might Bradbury have chosen to follow chronological order? Cite evidence from the story to support your opinion.

8. **Evaluate Personification** The giving of human qualities to an object, animal, or idea is called personification. Find three examples of personification in the story. Why do you think Bradbury chose to use this technique?

9. **Compare Literary Works**
   Review Stephen Vincent Benét's "By the Waters of Babylon," pages 290–301. Use a chart to compare the characters, events, and setting of the Benét story with those in Bradbury's "There Will Come Soft Rains." Which author presents the most disturbing view of society and its **technology?**

	"By the Waters of Babylon"	"There Will Come Soft Rains"
Characters		
Events		
Setting		

Literary Criticism

10. **Author's Style** Many critics admire Bradbury for his use of **imagery,** or words and phrases that appeal to the five senses. Find three examples of imagery in "There Will Come Soft Rains," and discuss how they contribute to your experience of the story.

Vocabulary in Context

VOCABULARY PRACTICE

Choose the word that best completes the sentence.

1. Leon has overcome his_____and now enjoys friendships and social activities.
2. The cellist knows how to skillfully_____his instrument to make beautiful music.
3. In her old age, my great aunt walks in a_____manner.
4. Jenna enjoys all kinds of winter activities and is_____to the cold.
5. Critics agree that the artist's recent painting is her most_____work yet.
6. The young girl left a chalky_____of her hand on the sidewalk.

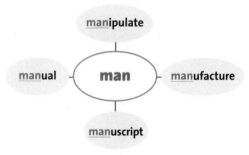

WORD LIST

manipulate
oblivious
paranoia
silhouette
sublime
tremulous

VOCABULARY IN WRITING

Imagine a time in the future when technology fails and causes widespread problems. Using at least three vocabulary words, write a paragraph describing the situation. Here is an example of how you might begin.

> **EXAMPLE SENTENCE**
>
> On October 1, 2074, a fast-acting computer virus causes global **paranoia**. . . .

OHIO STANDARDS

VOCABULARY STANDARD
1.5 Use knowledge of Latin roots, prefixes and suffixes to understand words

VOCABULARY STRATEGY: THE LATIN ROOT *man*

The vocabulary word *manipulate* stems from the Latin root *man*, which means "hand." To understand the meaning of words with *man*, use context clues as well as your knowledge of the root.

PRACTICE Write the word from the word web that best completes each sentence. Use context clues to help you, or, if necessary, consult a dictionary.

1. They_____these clothes in another country.
2. Before typewriters and printers, a book_____was written only by hand.
3. I am not sure how to_____this complicated-looking tool.
4. Many factories still depend on_____labor, rather than machines.

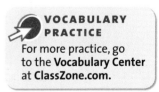

VOCABULARY PRACTICE
For more practice, go to the **Vocabulary Center** at **ClassZone.com**.

Inside the Home of the Future

Newspaper Article

Use with "There Will Come Soft Rains," page 306.

OHIO STANDARDS

READING & WRITING STANDARDS
2.2 Answer synthesizing questions to demonstrate comprehension
6.5.a Support arguments with detailed evidence

What's the Connection?

In "There Will Come Soft Rains," you read about a fictional house of the future that featured a variety of "smart" mechanical devices. The article you are about to read will tell you about actual "intelligent" houses that may be in your future.

Skill Focus: Synthesize

When you read different materials on a related topic, you **synthesize**—or put together—facts, ideas, and details from each source. As a result, you gain a fuller understanding of the topic than you would if you had simply relied on one text. Here's how you can synthesize information from two or more selections.

- Summarize the main ideas and details of each selection.
- Record questions that come to you as you learn new information.
- Note any conflicts in the information presented.
- Reread each selection to answer your questions and fill in gaps in your understanding.

To help yourself synthesize information from the Bradbury story and the following article, complete a chart like the one started here.

Source	Main Ideas and Details	Questions and New or Conflicting Information
"There Will Come Soft Rains"	Technology can improve living conditions, but it can also worsen them.	
"Inside the Home of the Future"		

Inside the Home of the Future

BY KELLY GREENE

As you pour the detergent into your last load of laundry, you realize the bottle is almost empty. But instead of making a mental note to add it to your grocery list, or running to the kitchen to scribble it down, you simply say out loud, "Remember: Buy laundry detergent." The word "remember" is picked up by a microphone in the wall and triggers a 10 computer to transcribe your words to your to-do list.

It might sound like a sci-fi vision of the future. But it's actually a project called Audio Notes, currently in the works at the Georgia Institute of Technology's 5,000-square-foot Aware Home, a combination house and laboratory in Atlanta where scientists are dreaming up futuristic housing technology.

20 "I love that shopping list," says Eileen Lange, a 68-year-old retiree from Lithonia, Ga., who toured the house and tried out some of its projects last year.

Researchers and commercial labs around the country are building experimental homes to test technology that could make domestic life easier and extend the independence of older homeowners. Such efforts go beyond so-30 called universal design, a trend toward building houses with wider doorways, grab bars and adjustable kitchen cabinets that took off in the early 1990s.

"These are lifestyle services empowered by a new generation of technology," says Joseph Coughlin, director of the Massachusetts Institute of Technology's AgeLab in Cambridge.

In many cases, the mechanics for the 40 gizmos already exist—mainly wireless sensors, cellphones, broadband access and home computers. What's been missing, and what researchers now are trying to develop, are ways to harness the hardware to run your entire house with little effort or technological savvy— letting you turn up the heat remotely, anticipating when you want the lights on, or deciding automatically how long 50 your food should cook. . . .

Here's a look at what's in store for your home of the future. **A**

The Intelligent House

Would you like your home to "know" you better? Computer scientists at the University of Texas-Arlington are building a home with this scenario as the goal:

At 6:15 A.M., the house turns up the heat, without programming, because it 60 has learned on its own that it needs 15

A **SYNTHESIZE**
Identify one or two new pieces of information that this section provides about automated homes.

minutes to warm up before your alarm goes off. At 7 A.M., when your alarm sounds, it signals the bedroom light and kitchen coffee maker to turn on. When you step into the bathroom, the morning news pops up on a video screen, and the shower turns on automatically. While you shave, the house senses (through the floor) that you are two pounds over your ideal weight; it adjusts your suggested menu and displays it in the kitchen.

When you leave home after breakfast, the house locks itself. Later that morning, it notes that the refrigerator is low on milk and cheese, and it places a grocery order to be delivered just before you get home. When you arrive, the food is there and the house has cranked up the hot tub for you.

What's powering all the automation is something called machine learning, which would enable the computer monitoring the house to observe a resident's habits for a while, and then anticipate individual needs and make decisions about what to turn on and off, says Diane Cook, the project's manager.

At the University of Florida in Gainesville, researchers are using a cell-phone to run a home. (So far, the "home" is a simulated apartment inside a lab, but there's a real house under construction that should be finished in June.) When someone rings the doorbell, you either hear it or feel your cellphone vibrating. Then you can open your phone and see a picture of the person at the door. (A video camera relays the picture.) If you recognize the visitor, you can push a button on your cellphone to unlatch the door. If it's dark and you can't see the visitor, you can push another button to turn on an outside light. **B**

The project, started three years ago, has "evolved from focusing just on smart phones to the smart house," says William Mann, who heads Florida's Rehabilitation Engineering Research Center on Technology for Successful Aging. . . .

Kicked-Up Kitchen

Scientists are devoting considerable attention to this room, where busy families can be distracted by caring for children, parents or both.

One tool on the drawing board, Georgia Tech's Cook's College, would use four cameras mounted under the kitchen cabinets to film your hands as you mix ingredients on the countertop below. The pictures, formatted like a filmstrip, would show what you've done most recently. That way, if you're interrupted by a phone call, or children needing help with homework, you can review what you've done to see whether you already had added the salt, for example, or to recall how many cups of flour you had sifted.

Since the cameras are focused on the counter, not on your face, study participants who have seen the tool haven't felt self-conscious about being filmed. "It avoids the bad-hair-day issue," says Dr. Mynatt.

At the University of Florida, researchers are working on microwave ovens that can read a new kind of label, known as radio-frequency identification tag. Such labels can store more information than bar codes and are expected to replace them eventually, says Dr. Mann, who heads the project. . . .

A range at the LifeWise Home in Bowie, Md., built by the National Center for Senior Housing Research, first acts as a refrigerator, so you can pop in a casserole in the morning, then set it to bake later in the afternoon. If two hours pass after the cooking time has finished and you haven't removed the dish from the oven, it turns back into a refrigerator.

"It's great for someone who's working, or [busy] during the day with volunteer work," says Charlotte Wade, the program director for the center. . . . It could also prevent people with memory loss from eating spoiled food. **C**

B SYNTHESIZE
Summarize the various tasks that technology can assist in completing.

C SYNTHESIZE
How positive is the view of technology presented in the article? Does "There Will Come Soft Rains" present a similar or different view?

Comprehension

1. **Recall** Describe three capabilities of the houses mentioned in the article.

2. **Recall** Who is intended to benefit from living in such homes? How?

Critical Analysis

3. **Synthesize** Review the ideas and information you noted on your chart. How is Bradbury's fictional home of the future similar to actual homes being developed by researchers? Support your answer with details from both texts.

4. **Evaluate** What is the most useful innovation described in the article? Explain your answer.

Read for Information: Support an Opinion

READING & WRITING STANDARDS
2.2 Answer synthesizing questions to demonstrate comprehension
6.5.A Support arguments with detailed evidence

WRITING PROMPT

Is technology more harmful or helpful to us? Consider both the advantages and disadvantages of living in a heavily mechanized society. Use information from both the short story and the newspaper article in your response.

To answer this prompt, you will have to support an opinion. An **opinion** is a statement that expresses an individual's beliefs, feelings, or thoughts. To support your opinion, you will need to follow these steps:

1. State your opinion on whether technology is more harmful or helpful to us.

2. Find evidence—details, facts, or direct statements—from each selection that supports your opinion.

3. Recall personal knowledge or experiences that support your opinion.

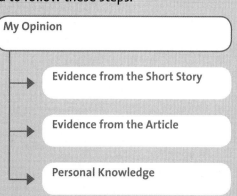

Review the evidence to make sure that your opinion is adequately supported; revise your opinion if necessary.

The Doll's House

Short Story by Katherine Mansfield

What makes someone POPULAR?

OHIO STANDARDS

READING STANDARDS
2.1 Apply reading comprehension strategies
4.11 Explain point of view

KEY IDEA How do people act when they are trying to join the "in" crowd? Sometimes they behave badly by bragging about new possessions or by making fun of others. In "The Doll's House," you will read about a group of girls whose pursuit of **popularity** brings out the worst in their nature.

SURVEY What makes someone popular at your school? With a partner, brainstorm the qualities that well-liked students seem to possess. You may choose to add to or delete from the list shown. Afterward, ask a small group of students to rank the qualities in order of importance. Tally their responses and discuss the results.

What Makes Someone Popular?
1. Sense of humor
2. Kindness
3.
4.

● LITERARY ANALYSIS: OMNISCIENT POINT OF VIEW

A story written from the **third-person point of view** has a narrator who is not a character but an outside observer. Sometimes this type of narrator is **omniscient,** or all knowing, and has the power to reveal the thoughts and feelings of more than one character. In "The Doll's House," for example, the omniscient narrator describes the private wishes of several characters, including those of the Burnell children.

The Burnell children could hardly walk to school fast enough the next morning. They burned to tell everybody, to describe, to— well—to boast about their doll's house before the school bell rang.

Unlike stories written from the first-person point of view, those with an omniscient point of view offer a wider, and perhaps more reliable, perspective. Writers often use such a point of view when they wish to examine broad social issues. As you read the story, think about how its point of view affects what you learn about the characters and the society in which they live.

Review: **Theme**

● READING STRATEGY: CONNECT

When you **connect** to a story, you relate its content to your own knowledge and experiences. This strategy can deepen your understanding of the characters, their actions, and the story's overall message. As you read "The Doll's House," make connections between the characters' world and your own. Record your observations in a chart like the one shown.

Characters' Experiences	My Experiences
The Burnell girls are thrilled by the doll's house.	I felt excited when my parents gave me my first bike.

Review: **Make Inferences**

Author Online

A Bold Spirit
Born Kathleen Beauchamp in Wellington, New Zealand, Katherine Mansfield was the third child of a wealthy merchant father and a class-conscious mother. When she was five, her family moved to the rural settlement of Karori, where she excelled in the artistic pursuits of writing and playing the cello. Although Mansfield enjoyed country life, she felt constrained by her family's traditional values. A fiercely independent teen, Mansfield, at 19, settled in London, England. There she enjoyed great creative freedom.

Katherine Mansfield
1888–1923

Breaking New Ground Although she lived only to the age of 34, Mansfield was a master of the short story and developed a distinctive prose style. Her best works reflect her use of experimental narrative techniques to offer vivid insights into characters' thoughts. Mansfield never returned to New Zealand, though she remained close to her homeland in spirit. Many of her stories, including "The Doll's House," recall her childhood experiences.

MORE ABOUT THE AUTHOR
For more on Katherine Mansfield, visit the **Literature Center** at **ClassZone.com.**

Background

The Better Sort This story is set in the late 1800s in New Zealand, which was then a colony of Great Britain. When the British emigrated there, they took with them not only their possessions but the social prejudices of their native land. At the time, British society was divided along rigid class lines. Birth usually determined a person's class, and climbing the social scale was difficult. In her fiction, Mansfield criticized this elitist system.

THE Doll's House

Katherine Mansfield

When dear old Mrs. Hay went back to town after staying with the Burnells she sent the children a doll's house. It was so big that the carter[1] and Pat carried it into the courtyard, and there it stayed, propped up on two wooden boxes beside the feed-room door. No harm could come to it; it was summer. And perhaps the smell of paint would have gone off by the time it had to be taken in. For, really, the smell of paint coming from that doll's house ("Sweet of old Mrs. Hay, of course; most sweet and generous!")—but the smell of paint was quite enough to make any one seriously ill, in Aunt Beryl's opinion. Even before the sacking was taken off. And when it was. . . . **Ⓐ**

10　　There stood the doll's house, a dark, oily, spinach green, picked out with bright yellow. Its two solid little chimneys, glued on to the roof, were painted red and white, and the door, gleaming with yellow varnish, was like a little slab of toffee. Four windows, real windows, were divided into panes by a broad streak of green. There was actually a tiny porch, too, painted yellow, with big lumps of congealed paint hanging along the edge.

　　But perfect, perfect little house! Who could possibly mind the smell? It was part of the joy, part of the newness.

　　"Open it quickly, some one!"

　　The hook at the side was stuck fast. Pat pried it open with his penknife, and 20　the whole house front swung back, and—there you were, gazing at one and the same moment into the drawing room and dining room, the kitchen and two bedrooms. That is the way for a house to open! Why don't all houses open like that? How much more exciting than peering through the slit of a door into a mean little hall with a hat stand and two umbrellas! That is—isn't it?—what you long to know about a house when you put your hand on the knocker. Perhaps it is the way God opens houses at dead of night when He is taking a quiet turn with an angel. . . .

　　"O-oh!" The Burnell children sounded as though they were in despair. It was too marvelous; it was too much for them. They had never seen anything

---

1. **carter:** delivery person.

ANALYZE VISUALS
Think about the purpose of a doll's house like the one shown. Would it be regularly played with or displayed for company? Explain.

Ⓐ POINT OF VIEW
Reread lines 1–9. What do you learn about the doll's house from the direct comments of the narrator?

30 like it in their lives. All the rooms were papered. There were pictures on the walls, painted on the paper, with gold frames complete. Red carpet covered all the floors except the kitchen; red plush chairs in the drawing room, green in the dining room; tables, beds with real bedclothes, a cradle, a stove, a dresser with tiny plates and one big jug. But what Kezia liked more than anything, what she liked frightfully, was the lamp. It stood in the middle of the dining room table, an exquisite little amber lamp with a white globe. It was even filled all ready for lighting, though, of course, you couldn't light it. But there was something inside that looked like oil, and that moved when you shook it. **B**

The father and mother dolls, who sprawled very stiff as though they had
40 fainted in the drawing room, and their two little children asleep upstairs, were really too big for the doll's house. They didn't look as though they belonged. But the lamp was perfect. It seemed to smile at Kezia, to say, "I live here." The lamp was real.

*T*he Burnell children could hardly walk to school fast enough the next morning. They burned to tell everybody, to describe, to—well—to boast about their doll's house before the school bell rang.

"I'm to tell," said Isabel, "because I'm the eldest. And you two can join in after. But I'm to tell first."

There was nothing to answer. Isabel was bossy, but she was always right, and
50 Lottie and Kezia knew too well the powers that went with being eldest. They brushed through the thick buttercups at the road edge and said nothing.

"And I'm to choose who's to come and see it first. Mother said I might."

For it had been arranged that while the doll's house stood in the courtyard they might ask the girls at school, two at a time, to come and look. Not to stay to tea, of course, or to come traipsing through the house. But just to stand quietly in the courtyard while Isabel pointed out the beauties, and Lottie and Kezia looked pleased. . . . **C**

But hurry as they might, by the time they had reached the tarred palings[2] of the boys' playground the bell had begun to jangle. They only just had time
60 to whip off their hats and fall into line before the roll was called. Never mind. Isabel tried to make up for it by looking very important and mysterious and by whispering behind her hand to the girls near her, "Got something to tell you at playtime."

Playtime came and Isabel was surrounded. The girls of her class nearly fought to put their arms around her, to walk away with her, to beam flatteringly, to be her special friend. She held quite a court under the huge pine trees at the side of the playground. Nudging, giggling together, the little girls pressed up close. And the only two who stayed outside the ring were the two who were always outside, the little Kelveys. They knew better than to come
70 anywhere near the Burnells.

2. **palings:** fence stakes.

B CONNECT
Think back to the excitement you felt when you received a favorite gift. On the basis of your experience, do you find the Burnells' reactions to the doll's house believable? Why, or why not?

C POINT OF VIEW
Reread lines 44–57. Notice what the **omniscient narrator** reveals about the Burnells. How does this information shape your opinion of the girls?

The Daughters of Edward Darley Boit (1882), John Singer Sargent. Oil on canvas, 221.93 × 222.57 cm. Gift of Mary Louisa Boit, Julia Overing Boit, Jane Hubbard Boit and Florence D. Boit in memory of Edward Darley Boit. Museum of Fine Arts, Boston. Photo © Museum of Fine Arts, Boston.

For the fact was, the school the Burnell children went to was not at all the kind of place their parents would have chosen if there had been any choice. But there was none. It was the only school for miles. And the consequence was all the children in the neighborhood, the Judge's little girls, the doctor's daughters, the storekeeper's children, the milkman's, were forced to mix together. Not to speak of there being an equal number of rude, rough little boys as well. But the line had to be drawn somewhere. It was drawn at the Kelveys. Many of the children, including the Burnells, were not allowed even to speak to them. They walked past the Kelveys with their heads in the air, and

ANALYZE VISUALS
Examine the figures and the setting in the painting. How well do they match your impression of the people and furnishings of the Burnell household? Explain.

80 as they set the fashion in all matters of behavior, the Kelveys were shunned by
   everybody. Even the teacher had a special voice for them, and a special smile
   for the other children when Lil Kelvey came up to her desk with a bunch of
   dreadfully common-looking flowers. **D**

   They were the daughters of a spry, hardworking little washerwoman, who
   went about from house to house by the day. This was awful enough. But
   where was Mr. Kelvey? Nobody knew for certain. But everybody said he was
   in prison. So they were the daughters of a washerwoman and a jailbird. Very
   nice company for other people's children! And they looked it. Why Mrs.
   Kelvey made them so conspicuous was hard to understand. The truth was they
90 were dressed in "bits" given to her by the people for whom she worked. Lil,
   for instance, who was a stout, plain child, with big freckles, came to school
   in a dress made from a green art-serge³ tablecloth of the Burnells', with red
   plush sleeves from the Logans' curtains. Her hat, perched on top of her high
   forehead, was a grown-up woman's hat, once the property of Miss Lecky, the
   postmistress. It was turned up at the back and trimmed with a large scarlet
   quill. What a little guy⁴ she looked! It was impossible not to laugh. And her
   little sister, our Else, wore a long white dress, rather like a nightgown, and a
   pair of little boy's boots. But whatever our Else wore she would have looked
   strange. She was a tiny wishbone of a child, with cropped hair and enormous
100 solemn eyes—a little white owl. Nobody had ever seen her smile; she scarcely
   ever spoke. She went through life holding on to Lil, with a piece of Lil's skirt
   screwed up in her hand. Where Lil went our Else followed. In the playground,
   on the road going to and from school, there was Lil marching in front and our
   Else holding on behind. Only when she wanted anything, or when she was out
   of breath, our Else gave Lil a tug, a twitch, and Lil stopped and turned around.
   The Kelveys never failed to understand each other. **E**

   Now they hovered at the edge; you couldn't stop them listening. When the
   little girls turned round and sneered, Lil, as usual, gave her silly, shamefaced
   smile, but our Else only looked.
110 And Isabel's voice, so very proud, went on telling. The carpet made a great
   sensation, but so did the beds with real bedclothes, and the stove with an
   oven door.

   When she finished Kezia broke in. "You've forgotten the lamp, Isabel."

   "Oh, yes," said Isabel, "and there's a teeny little lamp, all made of yellow
   glass, with a white globe that stands on the dining room table. You couldn't tell
   it from a real one."

   "The lamp's best of all," cried Kezia. She thought Isabel wasn't making half
   enough of the little lamp. But nobody paid attention. Isabel was choosing the
   two who were to come back with them that afternoon and see it. She chose
120 Emmie Cole and Lena Logan. But when the others knew they were all to have

D **POINT OF VIEW**
What do you learn about
the townspeople? Explain
how the omniscient point
of view allows you to see
problems that may affect
an entire community.

E **CONNECT**
Reread lines 84–106. Find
details that explain why
the Kelveys are disliked.
How might Lil and Else be
treated at your school?

---

3. **art-serge** (ärt-sûrj): a type of woven wool.

4. **guy:** British term for an odd-looking person.

a chance, they couldn't be nice enough to Isabel. One by one they put their arms round Isabel's waist and walked her off. They had something to whisper to her, a secret. "Isabel's my friend."

Only the little Kelveys moved away forgotten; there was nothing more for them to hear.

Days passed, and as more children saw the doll's house, the fame of it spread. It became the one subject, the rage. The one question was, "Have you seen Burnells' doll's house? Oh, ain't it lovely!" "Haven't you seen it? Oh, I say!"

Even the dinner hour was given up to talking about it. The little girls sat 130 under the pines eating their thick mutton sandwiches and big slabs of johnny cake spread with butter. While always, as near as they could get, sat the Kelveys, our Else holding on to Lil, listening too, while they chewed their jam sandwiches out of a newspaper soaked with large red blobs. . . .

"Mother," said Kezia, "can't I ask the Kelveys just once?"

"Certainly not, Kezia."

"But why not?"

"Run away, Kezia; you know quite well why not." **F**

*A*t last everybody had seen it except them. On that day the subject rather flagged. It was the dinner hour. The children stood together under the pine trees, and suddenly, as they looked at the Kelveys eating out of their paper, always by themselves, always listening, they wanted to be horrid to them. Emmie Cole started the whisper.

"Lil Kelvey's going to be a servant when she grows up."

"O-oh, how awful!" said Isabel Burnell, and she made eyes at Emmie.

Emmie swallowed in a very meaning way and nodded to Isabel as she'd seen her mother do on those occasions.

"It's true—it's true—it's true," she said.

Then Lena Logan's little eyes snapped. "Shall I ask her?" she whispered.

"Bet you don't," said Jessie May.

150 "I'm not frightened," said Lena. Suddenly she gave a little squeal and danced in front of the other girls. "Watch! Watch me! Watch me now!" said Lena. And sliding, gliding, dragging one foot, giggling behind her hand, Lena went over to the Kelveys.

Lil looked up from her dinner. She wrapped the rest quickly away. Our Else stopped chewing. What was coming now?

"Is it true you're going to be a servant when you grow up, Lil Kelvey?" shrilled Lena.

F MAKE INFERENCES
Think about how Kezia's family acts toward her. Why might she want to share the doll's house with the Kelveys?

Dead silence. But instead of answering, Lil only gave her silly, shamefaced
smile. She didn't seem to mind the question at all. What a sell for Lena! The
160 girls began to titter.

Lena couldn't stand that. She put her hands on her hips; she shot forward.
"Yah, yer father's in prison!" she hissed, spitefully.

This was such a marvelous thing to have said that the little girls rushed away
in a body, deeply, deeply excited, wild with joy. Someone found a long rope,
and they began skipping. And never did they skip so high, run in and out so
fast, or do such daring things as on that morning.

In the afternoon Pat called for the Burnell children with the buggy and
they drove home. There were visitors. Isabel and Lottie, who liked visitors,
went upstairs to change their pinafores. But Kezia thieved out at the back.
170 Nobody was about; she began to swing on the big white gates of the courtyard.

Apple Picking (1878), Winslow Homer. Watercolor and gouache on paper, laid down on board. 7″ × 8³/₈″. Terra Foundation
for the Arts, Daniel J. Terra Collection 1992.7. Photograph courtesy of Terra Foundation for the Arts, Chicago.

Presently, looking along the road, she saw two little dots. They grew bigger, they were coming towards her. Now she could see that one was in front and one close behind. Now she could see that they were the Kelveys. Kezia stopped swinging. She slipped off the gate as if she was going to run away. Then she hesitated. The Kelveys came nearer, and beside them walked their shadows, very long, stretching right across the road with their heads in the buttercups. Kezia clambered back on the gate; she had made up her mind; she swung out.

"Hullo," she said to the passing Kelveys.

They were so astounded that they stopped. Lil gave her silly smile. Our
180 Else stared.

"You can come and see our doll's house if you want to," said Kezia, and she dragged one toe on the ground. But at that Lil turned red and shook her head quickly.

"Why not?" asked Kezia.

Lil gasped, then she said, "Your ma told our ma you wasn't to speak to us."

"Oh well," said Kezia. She didn't know what to reply. "It doesn't matter. You can come and see our doll's house all the same. Come on. Nobody's looking."

But Lil shook her head still harder.

"Don't you want to?" asked Kezia.

190 Suddenly there was a twitch, a tug at Lil's skirt. She turned round. Our Else was looking at her with big, imploring eyes; she was frowning; she wanted to go. For a moment Lil looked at our Else very doubtfully. But then our Else twitched her skirt again. She started forward. Kezia led the way. Like two little stray cats they followed across the courtyard to where the doll's house stood. **G**

"There it is," said Kezia.

There was a pause. Lil breathed loudly, almost snorted; our Else was still as a stone.

"I'll open it for you," said Kezia kindly. She undid the hook and they looked inside.

200 "There's the drawing room and the dining room, and that's the—"

"Kezia!"

Oh, what a start they gave!

"Kezia!"

It was Aunt Beryl's voice. They turned round. At the back door stood Aunt Beryl, staring as if she couldn't believe what she saw.

"How dare you ask the little Kelveys into the courtyard?" said her cold, furious voice. "You know as well as I do, you're not allowed to talk to them. Run away, children, run away at once. And don't come back again," said Aunt Beryl. And she stepped into the yard and shooed them out as if they were chickens.

210 "Off you go immediately!" she called, cold and proud. **H**

G MAKE INFERENCES
Reread lines 190–194. Notice how Lil responds to Else. What does this tell you about their relationship?

H CONNECT
Aunt Beryl forbids Kezia to play with the Kelveys. How would you respond if you were in Kezia's position?

They did not need telling twice. Burning with shame, shrinking together, Lil huddling along like her mother, our Else dazed, somehow they crossed the big courtyard and squeezed through the white gate.

"*Wicked, disobedient little girl!*" said Aunt Beryl bitterly to Kezia, and she slammed the doll's house to.

The afternoon had been awful. A letter had come from Willie Brent, a terrifying, threatening letter, saying if she did not meet him that evening in Pulman's Bush, he'd come to the front door and ask the reason why! But now that she had frightened those little rats of Kelvey's and given Kezia a good 220 scolding, her heart felt lighter. That ghastly pressure was gone. She went back to the house humming. **I**

When the Kelveys were well out of sight of the Burnells', they sat down to rest on a big red drainpipe by the side of the road. Lil's cheeks were still burning; she took off the hat with the quill and held it on her knee. Dreamily they looked over the hay paddocks,[5] past the creek, to the group of wattles[6] where Logan's cows stood waiting to be milked. What were their thoughts?

Presently our Else nudged up close to her sister. But now she had forgotten the cross lady. She put out a finger and stroked her sister's quill; she smiled her rare smile.

230 "I seen the little lamp," she said, softly. **J**

Then both were silent once more. ❧

I POINT OF VIEW
Reread lines 204–221. What does the omniscient narrator reveal about Aunt Beryl and her motives for treating the Kelveys so poorly?

J THEME
Think about Kezia and Else's mutual interest in the lamp. What point do you think Mansfield makes about social status?

---

5. **paddocks** (păd′əks): areas of fenced-in land.

6. **wattles** (wŏt′lz): acacia trees.

Comprehension

OHIO STANDARDS

READING STANDARD
4.11 Explain point of view

1. **Recall** Describe the doll's house that the Burnells receive.

2. **Recall** Under what conditions are the girls' friends allowed to see the doll's house?

3. **Recall** Why are the Burnells not allowed to speak to the Kelveys?

4. **Clarify** Why does Else smile at the end of the story?

Literary Analysis

5. **Compare and Contrast Characters**
   What are the similarities and differences between Isabel Burnell and Lil Kelvey? Use a Venn diagram like the one shown to explore your answer.

   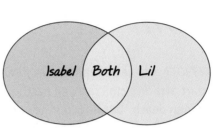

6. **Identify Symbol** A person, a place, or an object that represents something beyond itself is a symbol. For example, the doll's house might be considered a symbol for the orderly Burnell household. Think about the little lamp and the excitement it creates in both Kezia and Else. What values might the little lamp symbolize?

7. **Draw Conclusions About Theme** Think about the story's theme, or main message. What does the story reveal about **popularity?** Use evidence to support your conclusion.

8. **Connect** Writing "The Doll's House," Mansfield painted a picture of traditional New Zealand society. Despite the different location and time period, how are the characters, events, and ideas presented in the story relevant to your own experiences? Review the chart you completed as you read. Support your answer with information from the chart and the story.

9. **Analyze Point of View** In the story, the **omniscient narrator** sees into the minds of several of the story's characters. How might your sense of the town and its residents be different if the story were told through the eyes of just one character—Aunt Beryl, for example?

Literary Criticism

10. **Critical Interpretations** "The notion that human beings adopt masks and present themselves to their fellows under assumed personalities," wrote one biographer, "was one of [Mansfield's] literary obsessions." How does this comment apply to the story? Cite specific examples to support your answer.

The Seventh Man

Short Story by Haruki Murakami

Can you RECOVER *from tragedy?*

KEY IDEA We've all read stories in which a violent turn of events—a heart attack, a car crash, an earthquake—results in an individual's sudden death. But how do the survivors who are left behind **recover?** In "The Seventh Man," the main character describes the troubles and triumphs he experienced following a devastating childhood tragedy.

QUICKWRITE With a group, list several tragic events that you know about from the news. Think about the lasting effects of the events on the survivors. Select one event and write a paragraph about specific resources or methods that you think might help the survivors recover from their difficult experiences.

● LITERARY ANALYSIS: FORESHADOWING AND FLASHBACK

When crafting stories, writers often rely on two narrative techniques to help engage readers: foreshadowing and flashback.

- **Foreshadowing** is a writer's use of hints or clues to indicate situations that will occur later in a story. Writers often build suspense through foreshadowing.

- A **flashback** is an episode that interrupts the action of the story's plot to show an experience that happened at an earlier time. Writers usually provide important background information in flashbacks.

As you read "The Seventh Man," notice how the author uses both foreshadowing and flashback to build your interest in the story.

● READING STRATEGY: MONITOR

When you read, you should pause occasionally to check, or **monitor,** your understanding of a story. As you read "The Seventh Man," use the following techniques to help you monitor your own comprehension:

- **Predicting:** Predict what might happen next based on details in the story.

- **Questioning:** Ask yourself questions about ideas, events, and characters in the story.

Use a chart like the one shown to jot down places in the story where you paused to make a prediction or ask a question.

Passages Where I Paused to Check My Understanding	
Predictions	Questions

Review: **Visualize**

▲ VOCABULARY IN CONTEXT

To see how many words you know, restate each phrase, substituting a different word or words for the boldfaced term.

1. a vengeful act of **savagery**
2. **ominous** dark shadows
3. a **delirium** caused by fever
4. a **premonition** of the future
5. a farewell full of **sentiment**
6. a **reconciliation** between enemies

Author Online

Affinity with the West
Born to parents who were teachers of literature, Haruki Murakami (hä-rōō′kē mŏŏr′ä-kä′mē) grew up in Kyoto (kē-ō′tō) and Kobe (kō′bē), Japanese cities known for rich educational and cultural resources. An only child, Murakami often escaped

Haruki Murakami born 1949

loneliness and his parents' strictness by reading. As a teen, Murakami developed a taste for Western literature, favoring fiction by Leo Tolstoy, F. Scott Fitzgerald, and Truman Capote over traditional Japanese works. Today, he is a best-selling author whose novels and stories are valued for the way they elegantly combine Eastern and Western influences.

Consumer Culture Murakami often writes about the spiritual emptiness experienced by the Japanese of his generation. In his youth, the Japanese were poor but idealistic. That idealism disappeared in the late 1960s, when Japan became a prosperous nation. In its place arose a society that looked for fulfillment in consumption and found boredom and disappointment instead.

 MORE ABOUT THE AUTHOR
For more on Haruki Murakami, visit the **Literature Center** at ClassZone.com.

Background

Tsunamis and Typhoons Japan consists of four main islands and numerous smaller ones. Because the rock underlying these islands are constantly shifting, Japan is subject to frequent earthquakes. When the earthquakes occur out at sea, they whip up tsunamis, or tidal waves, which wreak havoc along the coast. The country also experiences typhoons, tropical storms that produce high winds and ocean surges.

The Seventh Man

HARUKI MURAKAMI

"A huge wave nearly swept me away," said the seventh man, almost whispering. "It happened one September afternoon when I was ten years old."

The man was the last one to tell his story that night. The hands of the clock had moved past ten. The small group that huddled in a circle could hear the wind tearing through the darkness outside, heading west. It shook the trees, set the windows to rattling, and moved past the house with one final whistle. **A**

"It was the biggest wave I had ever seen in my life," he said. "A strange wave. An absolute giant."

He paused.

10 "It just barely missed me, but in my place it swallowed everything that mattered most to me and swept it off to another world. I took years to find it again to recover from the experience—precious years that can never be replaced."

The seventh man appeared to be in his mid-fifties. He was a thin man, tall, with a moustache, and next to his right eye he had a short but deep-looking scar that could have been made by the stab of a small blade. Stiff, bristly patches of white marked his short hair. His face had the look you see on people when they can't quite find the words they need. In his case, though, the expression seemed to have been there from long before, as though it were part 20 of him. The man wore a simple blue shirt under a grey tweed coat, and every now and then he would bring his hand to his collar. None of those assembled there knew his name or what he did for a living.

He cleared his throat, and for a moment or two his words were lost in silence. The others waited for him to go on.

"In my case, it was a wave," he said. "There's no way for me to tell, of course, what it will be for each of you. But in my case it just happened to take the form of a gigantic wave. It presented itself to me all of a sudden one day, without warning. And it was devastating." **B**

A MONITOR
Why do you think the man is called "the seventh man"?

B FORESHADOWING
Reread lines 1–28. Which details suggest that you will learn more about the man's past?

Katsura Moonlight (1982), Clifton Karhu. 30/100. Woodblock, 40 × 30 cm. The Tolman Collection, Tokyo.

I grew up in a seaside town in the Province of S. It was such a small town, I doubt that any of you would recognize the name if I were to mention it. My father was the local doctor, and so I led a rather comfortable childhood. Ever since I could remember, my best friend was a boy I'll call K. His house was close to ours, and he was a grade behind me in school. We were like brothers, walking to and from school together, and always playing together when we got home. We never once fought during our long friendship. I did have a brother, six years older, but what with the age difference and differences in our personalities, we were never very close. My real brotherly affection went to my friend K. **C**

K. was a frail, skinny little thing, with a pale complexion and a face almost pretty enough to be a girl's. He had some kind of speech impediment,[1] though, which might have made him seem retarded to anyone who didn't know him. And because he was so frail, I always played his protector, whether at school or at home. I was kind of big and athletic, and the other kids all looked up to me. But the main reason I enjoyed spending time with K. was that he was such a sweet, pure-hearted boy. He was not the least bit retarded, but because of his impediment, he didn't do too well at school. In most subjects, he could barely keep up. In art class, though, he was great. Just give him a pencil or paints and he would make pictures that were so full of life that even the teacher was amazed. He won prizes in one contest after another, and I'm sure he would have become a famous painter if he had continued with his art into adulthood. He liked to do seascapes. He'd go out to the shore for hours, painting. I would often sit beside him, watching the swift, precise movements of his brush, wondering how, in a few seconds, he could possibly create such lively shapes and colors where, until then, there had been only blank white paper. I realize now that it was a matter of pure talent. **D**

One year, in September, a huge typhoon hit our area. The radio said it was going to be the worst in ten years. The schools were closed, and all the shops in town lowered their shutters in preparation for the storm. Starting early in the morning, my father and brother went around the house nailing shut all the storm doors, while my mother spent the day in the kitchen cooking emergency provisions. We filled bottles and canteens with water, and packed our most important possessions in rucksacks[2] for possible evacuation. To the adults, typhoons were an annoyance and a threat they had to face almost annually, but to the kids, removed as we were from such practical concerns, it was just a great big circus, a wonderful source of excitement.

Just after noon the color of the sky began to change all of a sudden. There was something strange and unreal about it. I stayed outside on the porch, watching the sky, until the wind began to howl and the rain began to beat against the house with a weird dry sound, like handfuls of sand. Then we closed the last storm door and gathered together in one room of the darkened house, listening to the radio. This particular storm did not have a great deal

C FLASHBACK
In lines 29–38, what information interrupts the present action of the story? Explain.

D MONITOR
Why do you think the narrator chooses to befriend K.?

---

1. **speech impediment:** an obstacle to speaking clearly, such as a lisp or stammer.

2. **rucksacks:** knapsacks.

Sudden Shower over Shin-Ohashi Bridge and Atake (1800s), Ando Hiroshige. Plate 58 from *One Hundred Famous Views of Edo*. Woodblock color print. © Brooklyn Museum of Art, Brooklyn, New York. Photo © The Bridgeman Art Library.

of rain, it said, but the winds were doing a lot of damage, blowing roofs off houses and capsizing ships. Many people had been killed or injured by flying debris. Over and over again, they warned people against leaving their homes. Every once in a while, the house would creak and shudder as if a huge hand were shaking it, and sometimes there would be a great crash of some heavy-sounding object against a storm door. My father guessed that these were tiles blowing off the neighbors' houses. For lunch we ate the rice and omelettes my mother had cooked, waiting for the typhoon to blow past.

80   But the typhoon gave no sign of blowing past. The radio said it had lost momentum almost as soon as it came ashore at S. Province, and now it was moving north-east at the pace of a slow runner. The wind kept up its savage howling as it tried to uproot everything that stood on land.

     Perhaps an hour had gone by with the wind at its worst like this when a hush fell over everything. All of a sudden it was so quiet, we could hear a bird crying in the distance. My father opened the storm door a crack and looked outside. The wind had stopped, and the rain had ceased to fall. Thick, grey clouds edged across the sky, and patches of blue showed here and there. The trees in the yard were still dripping their heavy burden of rainwater.

90   "We're in the eye of the storm," my father told me. "It'll stay quiet like this for a while, maybe fifteen, twenty minutes, kind of like an intermission. Then the wind'll come back the way it was before."

     I asked him if I could go outside. He said I could walk around a little if I didn't go far. "But I want you to come right back here at the first sign of wind." **E**

     I went out and started to explore. It was hard to believe that a wild storm had been blowing there until a few minutes before. I looked up at the sky. The storm's great "eye" seemed to be up there, fixing its cold stare on all of us below. No such "eye" existed, of course: we were just in that momentary quiet spot at the center of the pool of whirling air.

100   While the grown-ups checked for damage to the house, I went down to the beach. The road was littered with broken tree branches, some of them thick pine boughs that would have been too heavy for an adult to lift alone. There were shattered roof tiles everywhere, cars with cracked windshields, and even a doghouse that had tumbled into the middle of the street. A big hand might have swung down from the sky and flattened everything in its path.

     K. saw me walking down the road and came outside.

     "Where are you going?" he asked.

     "Just down to look at the beach," I said.

     Without a word, he came along with me. He had a little white dog that
110 followed after us.

     "The minute we get any wind, though, we're going straight back home," I said, and K. gave me a silent nod. **F**

     The shore was a 200-yard walk from my house. It was lined with a concrete breakwater—a big dyke[3] that stood as high as I was tall in those days. We had to climb a short flight of steps to reach the water's edge. This was where we came to play almost every day, so there was no part of it we didn't know well. In the eye of the typhoon, though, it all looked different: the color of the sky and of the sea, the sound of the waves, the smell of the tide, the whole expanse of the shore. We sat atop the breakwater for a time, taking in the view without
120 a word to each other. We were supposedly in the middle of a great typhoon, and yet the waves were strangely hushed. And the point where they washed against the beach was much farther away than usual, even at low tide. The

E FORESHADOWING
Reread lines 93–94.
How does the father's warning build **suspense**, or excitement?

F MONITOR
Predict what might happen next to the narrator and K.

---

3. **dyke:** a barrier built along the edge of a body of water to prevent flooding.

white sand stretched out before us as far as we could see. The whole, huge space felt like a room without furniture, except for the band of flotsam[4] that lined the beach.

We stepped down to the other side of the breakwater and walked along the broad beach, examining the things that had come to rest there. Plastic toys, sandals, chunks of wood that had probably once been parts of furniture, pieces of clothing, unusual bottles, broken crates with foreign writing on them, and
130 other, less recognizable items: it was like a big candy store. The storm must have carried these things from very far away. Whenever something unusual caught our attention, we would pick it up and look at it every which way, and when we were done, K.'s dog would come over and give it a good sniff. ⓖ

We couldn't have been doing this more than five minutes when I realized that the waves had come up right next to me. Without any sound or other warning, the sea had suddenly stretched its long, smooth tongue out to where I stood on the beach. I had never seen anything like it before. Child though I was, I had grown up on the shore and knew how frightening the ocean could be—the **savagery** with which it could strike unannounced.

140   **A**nd so I had taken care to keep well back from the waterline. In spite of that, the waves had slid up to within inches of where I stood. And then, just as soundlessly, the water drew back—and stayed back. The waves that had approached me were as unthreatening as waves can be—a gentle washing of the sandy beach. But something **ominous** about them—something like the touch of a reptile's skin—had sent a chill down my spine. My fear was totally groundless—and totally real. I knew instinctively that they were alive. They knew I was here and they were planning to grab me. I felt as if some huge, man-eating beast were lying somewhere on a grassy plain, dreaming of the moment it would pounce and tear me to pieces with its sharp
150 teeth. I had to run away.

"I'm getting out of here!" I yelled to K. He was maybe ten yards down the beach, squatting with his back to me, and looking at something. I was sure I had yelled loud enough, but my voice did not seem to have reached him. He might have been so absorbed in whatever it was he had found that my call made no impression on him. K. was like that. He would get involved with things to the point of forgetting everything else. Or possibly I had not yelled as loudly as I had thought. I do recall that my voice sounded strange to me, as though it belonged to someone else.

Then I heard a deep rumbling sound. It seemed to shake the earth. Actually,
160 before I heard the rumble I heard another sound, a weird gurgling as though a lot of water was surging up through a hole in the ground. It continued for a while, then stopped, after which I heard the strange rumbling. Even that was not enough to make K. look up. He was still squatting, looking down at

ⓖ **GRAMMAR AND STYLE**
Reread lines 126–133. To highlight the boys' intense curiosity, Murakami uses a **simile** to compare the littered beach to a candy store.

savagery (săv′ĭj-rē) *n.* extreme violence or cruelty

ominous (ŏm′ə-nəs) *adj.* menacing; threatening

---

4. **flotsam:** refuse or debris from a ship.

something at his feet, in deep concentration. He probably did not hear the rumbling. How he could have missed such an earth-shaking sound, I don't know. This may seem odd, but it might have been a sound that only I could hear—some special kind of sound. Not even K.'s dog seemed to notice it, and you know how sensitive dogs are to sound.

170 I told myself to run over to K., grab hold of him, and get out of there. It was the only thing to do. I *knew* that the wave was coming, and K. didn't know. As clearly as I knew what I ought to be doing, I found myself running the other way—running full speed toward the dyke, alone. What made me do this, I'm sure, was fear, a fear so overpowering it took my voice away and set my legs to running on their own. I ran stumbling along the soft sand beach to the breakwater, where I turned and shouted to K.

"Hurry, K.! Get out of there! The wave is coming!" This time my voice worked fine. The rumbling had stopped, I realized, and now, finally, K. heard my shouting and looked up. But it was too late. A wave like a huge snake with its head held high, poised to strike, was racing towards the shore. I had 180 never seen anything like it in my life. It had to be as tall as a three-story building. Soundlessly (in my memory, at least, the image is soundless), it rose up behind K. to block out the sky. K. looked at me for a few seconds, uncomprehending. Then, as if sensing something, he turned towards the wave. He tried to run, but now there was no time to run. In the next instant, the wave had swallowed him. **H**

The wave crashed on to the beach, shattering into a million leaping waves that flew through the air and plunged over the dyke where I stood. I was able to dodge its impact by ducking behind the breakwater. The spray wet my clothes, nothing more. I scrambled back up on to the wall and scanned the shore. By then the wave had turned and, with a wild cry, it was rushing 190 back out to sea. It looked like part of a gigantic rug that had been yanked by someone at the other end of the earth. Nowhere on the shore could I find any trace of K., or of his dog. There was only the empty beach. The receding wave had now pulled so much water out from the shore that it seemed to expose the entire ocean bottom. I stood along on the breakwater, frozen in place.

The silence came over everything again—a desperate silence, as though sound itself had been ripped from the earth. The wave had swallowed K. and disappeared into the far distance. I stood there, wondering what to do. Should I go down to the beach? K. might be down there somewhere, buried in the sand . . . But I decided not to leave the dyke. I knew from experience that big 200 waves often came in twos and threes. **I**

I'm not sure how much time went by—maybe ten or twenty seconds of eerie emptiness—when, just as I had guessed, the next wave came. Another gigantic roar shook the beach, and again, after the sound had faded, another huge wave raised its head to strike. It towered before me, blocking out the sky, like a deadly cliff. This time, though, I didn't run. I stood rooted to the sea wall, entranced, waiting for it to attack. What good would it do to run, I

ANALYZE VISUALS
Examine the illustration. How does this image of a great wave compare with your mental picture of the wave in the story?

H MONITOR
What has happened to K.? Explain.

I FORESHADOWING
Reread lines 185–200. Which details foreshadow the appearance of another wave?

Detail of *Under the Wave off Kanagawa*, Hokusai.
© Historical Picture Archive/Corbis.

thought, now that K. had been taken? Or perhaps I simply froze, overcome with fear. I can't be sure what it was that kept me standing there.

The second wave was just as big as the first—maybe even bigger. From
210 far above my head it began to fall, losing its shape, like a brick wall slowly crumbling. It was so huge that it no longer looked like a real wave. It was like something from another, far-off world, that just happened to assume the shape of a wave. I readied myself for the moment the darkness would take me. I didn't even close my eyes. I remember hearing my heart pound with incredible clarity.

The moment the wave came before me, however, it stopped. All at once it seemed to run out of energy, to lose its forward motion and simply hover there, in space, crumbling in stillness. And in its crest,[5] inside its cruel, transparent tongue, what I saw was K.

Some of you may find this impossible to believe, and if so, I don't blame
220 you. I myself have trouble accepting it even now. I can't explain what I saw any better than you can, but I know it was no illusion, no hallucination. I am telling you as honestly as I can what happened at that moment—what really happened. In the tip of the wave, as if enclosed in some kind of transparent capsule, floated K.'s body, reclining on its side. But that is not all. K. was looking straight at me, smiling. There, right in front of me, so close that I could have reached out and touched him, was my friend, my friend K. who, only moments before, had been swallowed by the wave. And he was smiling at me. Not with an ordinary smile—it was a big, wide-open grin that literally stretched from ear to ear. His cold, frozen eyes were locked on mine. He was
230 no longer the K. I knew. And his right arm was stretched out in my direction, as if he were trying to grab my hand and pull me into that other world where he was now. A little closer, and his hand would have caught mine. But, having missed, K. then smiled at me one more time, his grin wider than ever. **J**

J MONITOR
What might explain the strange image that the narrator sees in the wave?

I seem to have lost consciousness at that point. The next thing I knew, I was in bed in my father's clinic. As soon as I awoke the nurse went to call my father, who came running. He took my pulse, studied my pupils, and put his hand on my forehead. I tried to move my arm, but couldn't lift it. I was burning with fever, and my mind was clouded. I had been wrestling with a high fever for some time, apparently. "You've been asleep
240 for three days," my father said to me. A neighbor who had seen the whole thing had picked me up and carried me home. They had not been able to find K. I wanted to say something to my father. I *had* to say something to him. But my numb and swollen tongue could not form words. I felt as if some kind of creature had taken up residence in my mouth. My father asked me to tell him my name, but before I could remember what it was, I lost consciousness again, sinking into darkness.

---

5. **crest:** the top of a wave.

Altogether, I stayed in bed for a week on a liquid diet. I vomited several times, and had bouts of **delirium.** My father told me afterwards that I was so bad that he had been afraid that I might suffer permanent neurological[6] damage
250 from the shock and high fever. One way or another, though, I managed to recover—physically, at least. But my life would never be the same again.

They never found K.'s body. They never found his dog, either. Usually when someone drowned in that area, the body would wash up a few days later on the shore of a small inlet to the east. K.'s body never did. The big waves probably carried it far out to sea—too far for it to reach the shore. It must have sunk to the ocean bottom to be eaten by the fish. The search went on for a very long time, thanks to the cooperation of the local fishermen, but eventually it petered out.[7] Without a body, there was never any funeral. Half crazed, K.'s parents would wander up and down the beach every day, or they would shut
260 themselves up at home, chanting sutras.[8]

As great a blow as this had been for them, though, K.'s parents never chided me for having taken their son down to the shore in the midst of a typhoon. They knew how I had always loved and protected K. as if he had been my own little brother. My parents, too, made a point of never mentioning the incident in my presence. But I knew the truth. I knew that I could have saved K. if I had tried. I probably could have run over and dragged him out of the reach of the wave. It would have been close, but as I went over the timing of the events in my memory, it always seemed to me that I could have made it. As I said before, though, overcome with fear, I abandoned him there and saved
270 only myself. It pained me all the more that K.'s parents failed to blame me and that everyone else was so careful never to say anything to me about what had happened. It took me a long time to recover from the emotional shock. I stayed away from school for weeks. I hardly ate a thing, and spent each day in bed, staring at the ceiling. 🄚

K. was always there, lying in the wave tip, grinning at me, his hand outstretched, beckoning. I couldn't get that picture out of my mind. And when I managed to sleep, it was there in my dreams—except that, in my dreams, K. would hop out of his capsule in the wave and grab my wrist to drag me back inside with him.
280 And then there was another dream I had. I'm swimming in the ocean. It's a beautiful summer afternoon, and I'm doing an easy breaststroke far from shore. The sun is beating down on my back, and the water feels good. Then, all of a sudden, someone grabs my right leg. I feel an ice-cold grip on my ankle. It's strong, too strong to shake off. I'm being dragged down under the surface. I see K.'s face there. He has the same huge grin, split from ear to ear, his eyes locked on mine. I try to scream, but my voice will not come. I swallow water, and my lungs start to fill.

I wake up in the darkness, screaming, breathless, drenched in sweat.

---

6. **neurological:** relating to the nervous system.

7. **petered out:** came to an end.

8. **sutras:** short religious texts meant to be chanted.

delirium (dĭ-lîr′ē-əm) *n.* a temporary state of mental confusion usually resulting from high fever or shock

🄚 **MONITOR**
As you reread lines 234–274, question the narrator's reaction to the tragedy. Do you think it is believable? Explain.

At the end of the year I pleaded with my parents to let me move to another
290 town. I couldn't go on living in sight of the beach where K. had been swept
away, and my nightmares wouldn't stop. If I didn't get out of there, I'd go
crazy. My parents understood and made arrangements for me to live elsewhere.
I moved to Nagano Province in January to live with my father's family in a
mountain village near Komoro.[9] I finished elementary school in Nagano and
stayed on through junior and senior high school there. I never went home,
even for holidays. My parents came to visit me now and then.

I live in Nagano to this day. I graduated from a college of engineering in the
City of Nagano and went to work for a precision toolmaker in the area. I still
work for them. I live like anybody else. As you can see, there's nothing unusual
300 about me. I'm not very sociable, but I have a few friends I go mountain
climbing with. Once I got away from my hometown, I stopped having
nightmares all the time. They remained a part of my life, though. They would
come to me now and then, like debt collectors at the door. It happened when I
was on the verge of forgetting. And it was always the same dream, down to the
smallest detail. I would wake up screaming, my sheets soaked with sweat.

That is probably why I never married. I didn't want to wake someone
sleeping next to me with my screams in the middle of the night. I've been in
love with several women over the years, but I never spent a night with any of
them. The terror was in my bones. It was something I could never share with
310 another person.

I stayed away from my hometown for over forty years. I never went near
that seashore—or any other. I was afraid that if I did, my dream might happen
in reality. I had always enjoyed swimming, but after that day I never even
went to swim in a pool. I wouldn't go near deep rivers or lakes. I avoided
boats and wouldn't take a plane to go abroad. Despite all these precautions, I
couldn't get rid of the image of myself drowning. Like K.'s cold hand, this dark
premonition caught hold of my mind and refused to let go.

premonition
(prē′mə-nĭsh′ən) *n.*
a hunch or feeling about
the future; a foreboding

T hen, last spring, I finally revisited the beach where K. had been
taken by the wave.
320 My father had died of cancer the year before, and my brother had
sold the old house. In going through the storage shed, he had found
a cardboard carton crammed with childhood things of mine, which he sent to
me in Nagano. Most of it was useless junk, but there was one bundle of pictures
that K. had painted and given to me. My parents had probably put them away
for me as a keepsake of K., but the pictures did nothing but reawaken the
old terror. They made me feel as if K.'s spirit would spring back to life from
them, and so I quickly returned them to their paper wrapping, intending to
throw them away. I couldn't make myself do it, though. After several days of
indecision, I opened the bundle again and forced myself to take a long, hard
330 look at K.'s watercolors.

---

9. **Nagano Province . . . village near Komoro:** a northwestern area of Japan and a town in that area.

Most of them were landscapes, pictures of the familiar stretch of ocean and sand beach and pine woods and the town, and all done with that special clarity and coloration I knew so well from K.'s hand. They were still amazingly vivid despite the years, and had been executed with even greater skill than I recalled. As I leafed through the bundle, I found myself steeped in warm memories. The deep feelings of the boy K. were there in his pictures—the way his eyes were opened on the world. The things we did together, the places we went together began to come back to me with great intensity. And I realized that his eyes were my eyes, that I myself had looked upon the world back then with the same lively, unclouded vision as the boy who had walked by my side.

340

I made a habit after that of studying one of K.'s pictures at my desk each day when I got home from work. I could sit there for hours with one painting. In each I found another of those soft landscapes of childhood that I had shut out of my memory for so long. I had a sense, whenever I looked at one of K.'s works, that something was permeating my very flesh.

Perhaps a week had gone by like this when the thought suddenly struck me one evening: I might have been making a terrible mistake all those years. As he lay there in the tip of the wave, surely K. had not been looking at me with hatred or resentment; he had not been trying to take me away with him. And that terrible grin he had fixed me with: that, too, could have been an accident of angle or light and shadow, not a conscious act on K.'s part. He had probably already lost consciousness, or perhaps he had been giving me a gentle smile of eternal parting. The intense look of hatred I thought I saw on his face had been nothing but a reflection of the profound terror that had taken control of me for the moment.

350

The more I studied K.'s watercolor that evening, the greater the conviction with which I began to believe these new thoughts of mine. For no matter how long I continued to look at the picture, I could find nothing in it but a boy's gentle, innocent spirit. **L**

360

I went on sitting at my desk for a very long time. There was nothing else I could do. The sun went down, and the pale darkness of evening began to envelop the room. Then came the deep silence of night, which seemed to go on forever. At last, the scales tipped, and dark gave way to dawn. The new day's sun tinged the sky with pink.

It was then I knew I must go back.

I threw a few things in a bag, called the company to say I would not be in, and boarded a train for my old hometown.

I did not find the same quiet, little seaside town that I remembered. An industrial city had sprung up nearby during the rapid development of the Sixties, bringing great changes to the landscape. The one little gift shop by the station had grown into a mall, and the town's only movie theater had been turned into a supermarket. My house was no longer there. It had been demolished some months before, leaving only a scrape on the earth. The trees in the yard had all been cut down, and patches of weeds dotted the black

370

L MONITOR
How do you know the narrator is recovering from the tragedy?

The Wave (1800s), Ando Hiroshige. From the series *One Hundred Views of the Provinces*. Woodblock print, 37.3 × 25.5 cm. Galerie Janette Oster, Paris. Photo © The Bridgeman Art Library.

stretch of ground. K.'s old house had disappeared as well, having been replaced by a concrete parking lot full of commuters' cars and vans. Not that I was overcome by **sentiment.** The town had ceased to be mine long before.

I walked down to the shore and climbed the steps of the breakwater. On the other side, as always, the ocean stretched off into the distance, unobstructed, huge, the horizon a single straight line. The shoreline, too, looked the same as it had before: the long beach, the lapping waves, people strolling at the water's edge. The time was after four o'clock, and the soft sun of late afternoon embraced everything below as it began its long, almost meditative descent

sentiment (sĕn′tə-mənt) *n.* feeling or emotion

Ⓜ VISUALIZE
As you read lines 378–408, visualize the sea and the seventh man. What is the impact of this scene?

to the west. I lowered my bag to the sand and sat down next to it in silent
appreciation of the gentle seascape. Looking at this scene, it was impossible
to imagine that a great typhoon had once raged here, that a massive wave had
swallowed my best friend in all the world. There was almost no one left now,
surely, who remembered those terrible events. It began to seem as if the whole
thing were an illusion that I had dreamed up in vivid detail.

390   And then I realized that the deep darkness inside me had vanished.
Suddenly. As suddenly as it had come. I raised myself from the sand, and,
without bothering to take off my shoes or roll up my cuffs, walked into the
surf and let the waves lap at my ankles.

    Almost in **reconciliation,** it seemed, the same waves that had washed up on
the beach when I was a boy were now fondly washing my feet, soaking black
my shoes and pant cuffs. There would be one slow-moving wave, then a long
pause, and then another wave would come and go. The people passing by gave
me odd looks, but I didn't care.

    I looked up at the sky. A few grey cotton chunks of cloud hung there,
400 motionless. They seemed to be there for me, though I'm not sure why I felt that
way. I remembered having looked up at the sky like this in search of the "eye"
of the typhoon. And then, inside me, the axis of time gave one great heave.
Forty long years collapsed like a dilapidated house, mixing old time and new
time together in a single swirling mass. All sounds faded, and the light around
me shuddered. I lost my balance and fell into the waves. My heart throbbed at
the back of my throat, and my arms and legs lost all sensation. I lay that way for
a long time, face in the water, unable to stand. But I was not afraid. No, not at
all. There was no longer anything for me to fear. Those days were gone.

    I stopped having my terrible nightmares. I no longer wake up screaming
410 in the middle of the night. And I am trying now to start life over again. No,
I know it's probably too late to start again. I may not have much time left to
live. But even if it comes too late, I am grateful that, in the end, I was able to
attain a kind of salvation, to effect some sort of recovery. Yes, grateful: I could
have come to the end of my life unsaved, still screaming in the dark, afraid.

    The seventh man fell silent and turned his gaze upon each of the others. No
one spoke or moved or even seemed to breathe. All were waiting for the rest of
his story. Outside, the wind had fallen, and nothing stirred. The seventh man
brought his hand to his collar once again, as if in search for words. **N**

    "They tell us that the only thing we have to fear is fear itself; but I don't
420 believe that," he said. Then, a moment later, he added: "Oh, the fear is there,
all right. It comes to us in many different forms, at different times, and
overwhelms us. But the most frightening thing we can do at such times is to
turn our backs on it, to close our eyes. For then we take the most precious
thing inside us and surrender it to something else. In my case, that something
was the wave." ❧

Translated by Jay Rubin

reconciliation
(rĕkʹən-sĭlʹē-āʹshən)
n. the act of settling
or resolving

N FLASHBACK
Reread lines 415–418.
Which details tell you
that you have just
completed reading a
flashback?

INTERVIEW In this interview, the acclaimed Japanese author Haruki Murakami offers fascinating insights into his own writing process. He also demonstrates a rich understanding of contemporary world literature.

An Interview with HARUKI MURAKAMI

Larry McCaffrey and Sinda Gregory

Larry McCaffrey: I think just about all of your [stories] are in first person. Have you ever thought about not writing in first person?

Haruki Murakami: Yes, for a short time I tried to write in the third person, but it didn't work out.

LM: What's the problem? Is it not as interesting? Is it the voice?

HM: When I tried to use third person, I just felt like I became a god. But I don't want to be a god. I don't know everything. I can't write everything. I'm just myself. I would write something just as myself. I don't mean that I really am the protagonist but that I can envision what my protagonist sees and experiences. . . . I'm forty-six and married, but when I'm writing I can become twenty-five and unmarried. I can walk around in somebody else's shoes—and feel those shoes. Writing becomes your second life. That's good.

LM: Some critics, both in the U.S. and Japan, have said that your work is not really Japanese. Do you yourself think of yourself as having a distinctly Japanese sensibility?

HM: The opinion that my books are not really Japanese seems to me to be very shallow. I certainly think of myself as being a Japanese writer. . . . At first I wanted to be an international writer, but eventually saw that I was nothing but a Japanese writer. But even in the beginning I wasn't only borrowing Western styles and rules. I wanted to change Japanese literature from the inside, not the outside. So I basically made up my own rules.

Sinda Gregory: Could you give us some examples of what you mean?

HM: Most literary purists in Japan love beautiful language and appreciate sensitivity rather than energy or power. This beauty is admired for its own sake, and so their styles use a lot of very stiff, formal metaphors that don't sound natural or spontaneous at all. These writing styles get more and more refined, to the point where they resemble a kind of bonsai. I don't like such traditional forms of writing; it may sound beautiful, but it may not communicate. Besides, who knows what beauty is? So in my writing, I've tried to change that. I like to write more freely, so I use a lot of long and peculiar metaphors that seem fresh to me. . . .

SG: What's been the reaction of American readers to your work? I'm wondering especially about your younger readers.

HM: I found it very interesting when I visited universities in the U.S. that many students are interested in Japanese literature and culture. What I noticed was that they seemed to be reading contemporary Japanese books simply as novels rather than as "Japanese novels." They're reading my books or ones by Amy Yamada or Banana Yoshimoto the same way they had begun to read García Márquez and Vargas Llosa and other Latin American novelists a few years ago. It takes a while for this kind of change to take place. Writers from different countries are changing each other and finding global audiences more easily nowadays; it's a small world and a world which is getting smaller. I think that's a great thing.

Comprehension

1. **Recall** At what location does the story begin and end?

2. **Clarify** Why have the people in the group come together?

3. **Summarize** Describe the tragedy that changed the seventh man's life.

Literary Analysis

4. **Draw Conclusions** Why do you think Murakami chooses to identify the narrator simply as "the seventh man," rather than name him?

5. **Understand Cause and Effect** In what ways has the tragedy affected the seventh man? Review the story for specific examples. Use a chart like the one shown to help you organize your thoughts. An example has been filled in for you.

Cause	Effects on the Seventh Man
K.'s death $\longrightarrow$	1. He loses consciousness.

6. **Interpret Foreshadowing** Think about the point in the story that held the most **suspense,** or excitement, for you. In what way was this event foreshadowed, or hinted at, earlier in the story? Give specific examples from the story to support your answer.

7. **Analyze Flashback** "The Seventh Man" is told almost exclusively in flashback. The narrator recounts events that took place before the beginning of the story. How does this technique help you understand the seventh man and his struggle to **recover** from tragedy?

8. **Evaluate an Opinion** The seventh man concludes that the worst thing we can do when we are frightened is "to turn our backs on [fear], to close our eyes." Do you agree or disagree with this opinion? Explain your answer.

9. **Monitor** Review the notes you took as you read. What aspect of the story was the most challenging for you? How did **predicting** or **questioning** help you understand this difficult part?

10. **Compare Literary Works** In what ways does Murakami's writing seem fresh and imaginative? Use information from both "The Seventh Man" and "An Interview with Haruki Murakami" to support your answer.

Literary Criticism

11. **Critical Interpretations** In Murakami's later fiction, notes one literary critic, "we see the theme of isolation and Murakami's assertion of the need for communication and greater understanding between people." Would you say that "The Seventh Man" deals with these issues? Explain.

OHIO STANDARDS

READING STANDARD
4.6 Explain foreshadowing and flashback

Vocabulary in Context

VOCABULARY PRACTICE

Decide if each statement is true or false.

1. Individuals who commit acts of **savagery** are cruel or violent.
2. An **ominous** cloud is one that pleases or delights.
3. If you are experiencing **delirium,** your thoughts are clear.
4. A **premonition** is a recollection of the past.
5. Personal letters are often filled with **sentiment.**
6. People settle their differences in a **reconciliation.**

WORD LIST
delirium
ominous
premonition
reconciliation
savagery
sentiment

VOCABULARY IN WRITING

Using at least three vocabulary words, write a paragraph describing another type of natural disaster. Here is an example of how you might begin.

> **EXAMPLE SENTENCE**
>
> *Few experiences match the **savagery** of an avalanche.*

VOCABULARY STRATEGY: THE LATIN ROOT *sen*

The vocabulary word *sentiment* stems from the Latin root *sen,* which means "to feel." To understand the meaning of words with *sen,* use context clues as well as your knowledge of the root.

PRACTICE Write the word from the word web that best completes each sentence. Use context clues to help you, or, if necessary, consult a dictionary.

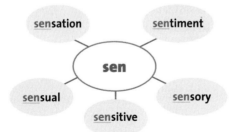

1. I choose reason over _____ when making an important decision.
2. He is very _____ to what others say about him.
3. A feather on your skin is a ticklish _____.
4. She enjoys the _____ delight of a gourmet meal.
5. A three-dimensional movie is a unique _____ experience.

OHIO STANDARDS

VOCABULARY STANDARD
1.5 Use knowledge of Latin roots, prefixes and suffixes to understand words

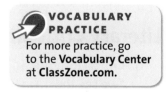

VOCABULARY PRACTICE
For more practice, go to the **Vocabulary Center** at **ClassZone.com.**

Reading-Writing Connection

Increase your understanding of "The Seventh Man" by responding to these prompts. Then use **Revision: Grammar and Style** to improve your writing.

WRITING PROMPTS	SELF-CHECK

A. Short Response: Write a Speech
Imagine that you are a friend of K.'s and have been asked to present a eulogy, or brief speech, in remembrance of him. Using details from the story, write a **one- or two-paragraph response** that captures K.'s character and life experiences. Consider including similes to clarify ideas and add interest.

A good speech will . . .
• show an understanding of K. and the story's events
• provide details that support statements

B. Extended Response: Analyze Symbols
A **symbol** is a person, a place, or an object that represents something beyond itself. In what ways does water symbolize both the painful and peaceful experiences of the seventh man? Write **three or four paragraphs** in response, using information from the story to support your answer.

A thoughtful response will . . .
• explain how water symbolizes the seventh man's experiences
• provide specific examples from the story

REVISION: GRAMMAR AND STYLE

WRITING STANDARD
6.1.b Use figurative language

ADD DESCRIPTIVE DETAILS Review the **Grammar and Style** note on page 339. Throughout the story, Murakami uses similes to clarify events and give energy to his writing. A **simile** is a direct comparison of two different things, actions, or feelings, using the words *like* or *as*. In your own writing, use similes to help readers understand unusual experiences by comparing them to more familiar things, as Murakami does. Here is an example from the story.

> *Forty long years collapsed like a dilapidated house, mixing old time and new time together in a single swirling mass.* (lines 403–404)

Notice how the revisions in red add clarity and interest to this first draft. Revise your response to Prompt A by using a similar technique.

STUDENT MODEL

K. and I were very close and ~~, like brothers,~~ spent nearly every afternoon together.

We often looked for buried treasure along the beach ~~, like two desperate pirates.~~

WRITING TOOLS
For prewriting, revision, and editing tools, visit the **Writing Center** at ClassZone.com.

The Man in the Water

Essay by Roger Rosenblatt

Can ordinary people
be HEROES?

OHIO STANDARDS

READING STANDARDS
2.1 Summarize and draw conclusions
4.5 Analyze how choice of genre affects theme or topic

KEY IDEA When disaster strikes, people react in different ways. Some struggle to save themselves, others crumble in fear, and a few rare individuals risk their own lives to save the lives of strangers. In "The Man in the Water," you will read about an ordinary man whose selfless acts made him a **hero**.

QUICKWRITE With a group, use a description wheel like the one shown to list qualities that define a hero. Then write a short paragraph about a particular person who possesses these traits. Make sure to indicate whether the hero is a public figure or an ordinary person.

Hero   caring

LITERARY ANALYSIS: REFLECTIVE ESSAY

A **reflective essay** is an essay in which the writer makes a connection between a personal observation and a universal idea—such as love, courage, or freedom. Roger Rosenblatt's essay contains narration as well as reflection. As he tells the story of a disaster, he makes choices, as a fiction writer would, about the order in which to present events and the perspective from which to present them. Notice how the choices he makes involve you in the story.

READING SKILL: IDENTIFY MAIN IDEA AND SUPPORTING DETAILS

A reflective essay, like most essays, has a thesis, or **main idea.** If you are unsure of the main idea, you can usually figure it out from the **supporting details**—that is, the facts and other evidence included in the essay to reinforce the main idea.

In "The Man in the Water," Rosenblatt explores why a 1982 airplane crash is memorable. He develops his main idea over the course of several paragraphs. Jot down each part of his main idea as you find it. Then, beneath each statement, write a few details that support it.

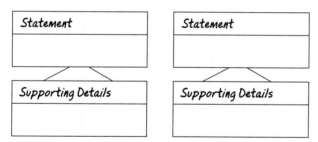

Statement	Statement
Supporting Details	Supporting Details

▲ VOCABULARY IN CONTEXT

The following words are key to understanding Rosenblatt's essay about a real-life hero. Restate each phrase, using a different word or words for the boldfaced term.

1. to straighten a **chaotic** bedroom
2. freedom **emblemized** by the American flag
3. the **flailing** goose drying its wings
4. an **implacable** child who cannot be quieted

Author Online

Star Journalist
Roger Rosenblatt is a native of New York City and holds a Ph.D. in literature and writing from Harvard University. In 1975, after teaching at his alma mater, he became a professional journalist. During his lengthy writing career, he has regularly contributed to news

Roger Rosenblatt born 1940

publications, such as the *Washington Post* and *Time,* and has won several prestigious awards. Today, he is viewed as one of the finest American essayists, approaching his work with, as one critic noted, "uncommon clarity, conciseness, eloquence and humor."

Man of the World Known for his sensitivity and literary flair, Rosenblatt has won praise for several nonfiction books on controversial topics, including *Witness: The World Since Hiroshima,* which examines the impact of the atomic bomb on different aspects of modern life. His best-known book is perhaps *Children of War,* an investigation into the lives of children in various war-torn nations.

 MORE ABOUT THE AUTHOR
For more on Roger Rosenblatt, visit the **Literature Center** at ClassZone.com.

Background

The Crash of Flight 90 One of the most publicized air disasters occurred on January 13, 1982, when Air Florida Flight 90 departed from Washington National Airport. Failing to gain enough altitude on takeoff, the passenger jet crashed into the nearby 14th Street Bridge and slid into the icy Potomac River. Seventy-eight people died in the disaster—some of them in the plane, some in their cars on the bridge, and some in the frigid waters of the Potomac. Ice on the jet's wings was the probable cause of the accident.

The Man in the Water

Roger Rosenblatt

As disasters go, this one was terrible, but not unique, certainly not among the worst on the roster of U.S. air crashes. There was the unusual element of the bridge, of course, and the fact that the plane clipped it at a moment of high traffic, one routine thus intersecting another and disrupting both. Then, too, there was the location of the event. Washington, the city of form and regulations, turned **chaotic,** deregulated, by a blast of real winter and a single slap of metal on metal. The jets from Washington National Airport that normally swoop around the presidential monuments like famished gulls are, for the moment, **emblemized** by the one that fell; so there is that detail.
10 And there was the aesthetic clash as well—blue-and-green Air Florida, the name a flying garden, sunk down among gray chunks in a black river. All that was worth noticing, to be sure. Still, there was nothing very special in any of it, except death, which, while always special, does not necessarily bring millions to tears or to attention. Why, then, the shock here?

Perhaps because the nation saw in this disaster something more than a mechanical failure. Perhaps because people saw in it no failure at all, but rather something successful about their makeup. Here, after all, were two forms of nature in collision: the elements and human character. Last Wednesday, the elements, indifferent as ever, brought down Flight 90. And
20 on that same afternoon, human nature—groping and **flailing** in mysteries of its own—rose to the occasion. **A**

Of the four acknowledged heroes of the event, three are able to account for their behavior. Donald Usher and Eugene Windsor, a park police helicopter team, risked their lives every time they dipped the skids into the water to pick up survivors. On television, side by side in bright blue jumpsuits, they described their courage as all in the line of duty. Lenny Skutnik, a twenty-eight-year-old employee of the Congressional Budget Office, said: "It's something I never thought I would do"—referring to his jumping into the water to drag an injured woman to shore. Skutnik added
30 that "somebody had to go in the water," delivering every hero's line that

A park police helicopter pulls two survivors from the Potomac River following the crash of Air Florida Flight 90.

is no less admirable for its repetitions. In fact, nobody had to go into the water. That somebody actually did so is part of the reason this particular tragedy sticks in the mind. **B**

But the person most responsible for the emotional impact of the disaster is the one known at first simply as "the man in the water." (Balding, probably in his fifties, an extravagant mustache.) He was seen clinging with five other survivors to the tail section of the airplane. This man was described by Usher and Windsor as appearing alert and in control. Every time they lowered a lifeline and flotation ring to him, he passed it on to 40 another of the passengers. "In a mass casualty, you'll find people like him," said Windsor. "But I've never seen one with that commitment." When the helicopter came back for him, the man had gone under. His selflessness was one reason the story held national attention; his anonymity another. The fact that he went unidentified invested him with a universal character. For a while he was Everyman, and thus proof (as if one needed it) that no man is ordinary. **C**

Still, he could never have imagined such a capacity in himself. Only minutes before his character was tested, he was sitting in the ordinary plane among the ordinary passengers, dutifully listening to the stewardess telling 50 him to fasten his seat belt and saying something about the "no smoking sign." So our man relaxed with the others, some of whom would owe their lives to him. Perhaps he started to read, or to doze, or to regret some harsh remark made in the office that morning. Then suddenly he knew that the trip would not be ordinary. Like every other person on that flight, he was desperate to live, which makes his final act so stunning. **D**

B **GRAMMAR AND STYLE**
Reread lines 23–25. Notice how Rosenblatt includes the **appositive phrase** "a park police helicopter team" to describe concisely who the two men are.

C **REFLECTIVE ESSAY**
In Rosenblatt's view, why did "the man in the water" give the story greater significance?

D **REFLECTIVE ESSAY**
Notice how Rosenblatt shifts back in time and assumes the perspective of the man, even though he cannot really know what the man was thinking. What does this perspective add to your impression of the man?

For at some moment in the water he must have realized that he would not live if he continued to hand over the rope and ring to others. He *had* to know it, no matter how gradual the effect of the cold. In his judgment he had no choice. When the helicopter took off with what was to be the last survivor, he
60 watched everything in the world move away from him, and he deliberately let it happen.

Yet there was something else about the man that kept our thoughts on him, and which keeps our thoughts on him still. He was *there*, in the essential, classic circumstance. Man in nature. The man in the water. For its part, nature cared nothing about the five passengers. Our man, on the other hand, cared totally. So the timeless battle commenced in the Potomac. For as long as that man could last, they went at each other, nature and man: the one making no distinctions of good and evil, acting on no principles, offering no lifelines; the other acting wholly on distinctions, principles, and,
70 one supposes, on faith. **E**

Since it was he who lost the fight, we ought to come again to the conclusion that people are powerless in the world. In reality, we believe the reverse, and it takes the act of the man in the water to remind us of our true feelings in this matter. It is not to say that everyone would have acted as he did, or as Usher, Windsor, and Skutnik. Yet whatever moved these men to challenge death on behalf of their fellows is not peculiar to them. Everyone feels the possibility in himself. That is the abiding wonder of the story. That is why we would not let go of it. If the man in the water gave a lifeline to the people gasping for survival, he was likewise giving a lifeline to those
80 who observed him.

The odd thing is that we do not even really believe that the man in the water lost his fight. "Everything in Nature contains all the powers of Nature," said Emerson. Exactly. So the man in the water had his own natural powers. He could not make ice storms, or freeze the water until it froze the blood. But he could hand life over to a stranger, and that is a power of nature too. The man in the water pitted himself against an **implacable,** impersonal enemy; he fought it with charity; and he held it to a standoff. He was the best we can do.

January 25, 1982

E MAIN IDEA
Reread lines 62–70. What distinctions does Rosenblatt make between the man in the water and nature?

implacable (ĭm-plăk′ə-bəl) *adj.* impossible to calm or satisfy; relentless

Comprehension

1. **Recall** What disaster is described in this essay?

2. **Recall** How did the anonymous man respond to the disaster?

3. **Summarize** What eventually happened to the man in the water?

Literary Analysis

4. **Clarify** Rosenblatt defines the struggle between the man and the water in broad terms. What does the struggle represent?

5. **Make Inferences** Why do you think Rosenblatt chose to focus on the anonymous man in the water rather than on one of the other three acknowledged **heroes** of the disaster?

6. **Examine Reflective Essay** Reflective essays relate a writer's personal observations to universal ideas. Such essays are loosely structured and may use some of the same narrative techniques that fictional stories do. What would this essay lose without paragraphs 5 and 6 (lines 47–61)? What would it lose without the final paragraph?

7. **Draw Conclusions About the Main Idea** Review the chart you completed as you read. What is the main idea of the essay? Cite evidence to support your answer.

8. **Analyze Tone** A writer's tone is the attitude that he or she takes toward a subject. It can be described in many different ways, including serious, bitter, playful, or sympathetic. In your own words, describe Rosenblatt's tone toward the man in the water. Cite specific words and phrases to explain your thinking.

9. **Evaluate Opinion** Rosenblatt concludes that "we do not even really believe that the man in the water lost his fight [with nature]." Do you agree or disagree with this opinion? Cite evidence to support your answer.

10. **Make Generalizations** Do you think that most people are capable of acting as heroically as the man in the water? Give examples from the essay and real life to support your opinion.

Literary Criticism

11. **Critical Interpretations** "For me," Rosenblatt once stated, "the essay is a continuous search for an answer to a question." In your opinion, what question did Rosenblatt set out to answer in "The Man in the Water"? Cite evidence to support your interpretation.

OHIO STANDARDS

READING STANDARD
2.1 Summarize and draw conclusions

Vocabulary in Context

VOCABULARY PRACTICE

Decide whether the words in each pair are synonyms or antonyms.

1. chaotic/ordered
2. emblemized/symbolized
3. flailing/waving
4. implacable/consolable

VOCABULARY IN WRITING

Using at least two vocabulary words, describe the struggle between nature and humans as presented in the essay. Here is an example of how you might begin.

> **EXAMPLE SENTENCE**
>
> Nature is **chaotic** and indifferent to how it affects the world around it.

VOCABULARY STRATEGY: THE LATIN ROOT *plac*

The word *implacable* stems from the Latin root *plac*, which means "to please or soothe." To understand the meaning of words with *plac*, use context clues as well as your knowledge of the root.

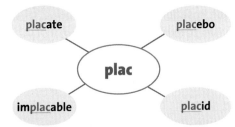

PRACTICE Choose the word from the word web that best completes each sentence. Use context clues to help you, or, if necessary, consult a dictionary.

1. The doctor prescribed a medicine-free _____ pill to satisfy the patient.
2. She gave the crying baby a pacifier to _____ her.
3. His _____ boss was so difficult to please.
4. They lived a _____, unhurried existence in the mountains.

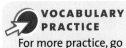

Reading-Writing Connection

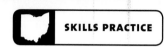

Increase your understanding of "The Man in the Water" by responding to these prompts. Then use **Revision: Grammar and Style** to improve your writing.

WRITING PROMPTS	**SELF-CHECK**

A. Short Response: Analyze a Reflective Essay
What do you learn in "The Man in the Water" that you would probably not learn in a news report of the same tragedy? Use what you know about reflective essays and narrative techniques to write a **one- or two-paragraph response.**

A successful analysis will . . .
- explain how "The Man in the Water" is an example of a reflective essay
- tell how a reflective essay differs from a news report

B. Extended Response: Imagine a Hero's Thoughts
What thoughts might the man in the water have had when he handed the rope and the ring to others? In **two or three paragraphs,** write the thoughts that might have passed through the man's mind. Draw on your own knowledge and experiences of **heroism.**

A strong response will . . .
- be consistent with the information presented in the essay
- reveal information about the man's personality and inner beliefs

REVISION: GRAMMAR AND STYLE

WRITE CONCISELY Review the **Grammar and Style** note on page 355. One way Rosenblatt is able to keep his writing concise is by using appositive phrases. An **appositive** is a noun or pronoun that identifies or renames another noun or pronoun. An **appositive phrase** is made up of an appositive plus its modifiers. By incorporating appositive phrases into your writing, you can convey information about a person or thing in one sentence. Here are two examples from the essay:

Washington, the city of form and regulations, turned chaotic . . . (lines 5–6)

Lenny Skutnik, a twenty-eight-year-old employee of the Congressional Budget Office, said . . . (lines 26–28)

Notice how the revisions in red in the student model use appositive phrases to make the writing of this first draft more concise. Revise your responses to the prompts by using a similar technique.

 OHIO STANDARDS

WRITING STANDARD
7.3 Use clauses and phrases

> **STUDENT MODEL**
>
> The scene is horrific. A woman ‸ *, the mother of two children,* is struggling to stay afloat in the water. ~~She is the mother of two children.~~ The man next to me ‸ *, a co-worker of mine,* won't last much longer. ~~He is a co-worker of mine.~~

 **WRITING TOOLS**
For prewriting, revision, and editing tools, visit the **Writing Center** at ClassZone.com.

Dyaspora
Essay by Joanne Hyppolite

Can you be from two CULTURES *at once?*

OHIO STANDARDS

READING STANDARDS
3.6 Identify appeals to emotion
4.11 Explain point of view

KEY IDEA When asked about **cultural identity,** many of us simply respond, "I'm an American." For others, however, the matter is not as clear. People who have left their native countries to settle in the United States often feel torn between two cultures. In "Dyaspora," you will read about one woman's struggles to be both Haitian and American.

DISCUSS List the aspects of home that you would miss most if you had to move abroad. Then, share your list with a partner, and discuss how you might adjust to living in a new country.

> *What I Would Miss Most About Home*
> *1. Family and friends*
> *2. Favorite TV shows*
> *3.*
> *4.*
> *5.*

LITERARY ANALYSIS: SECOND-PERSON POINT OF VIEW

Although writers of nonfiction usually choose to use the first-person or third-person points of view, they sometimes create works that use another, more unusual point of view: **second person.** In this point of view, the writer directly addresses an audience by using the pronouns *you* and *yours.* For example, in "Dyaspora," Joanne Hyppolite remarks:

In your neighborhood when you tell people you are from Haiti, they ask politely, "Where's that?" You explain and because you seem okay to them, Haiti is okay to them.

For readers, the second-person point of view often generates a sense of instant recognition. They may feel as though they know the author and share in the author's experiences. As you read "Dyaspora," think about its point of view and how that view affects you as a reader.

READING SKILL: ANALYZE SENSORY DETAILS

Sensory details are words and phrases that appeal to one or more of the five senses—sight, hearing, smell, taste, and touch. In the selection, Hyppolite offers an abundance of sensory details to help readers connect to her particular way of life. For example, she allows readers to "hear" the sounds of her home by describing her parents' accents and their favorite Haitian music. To analyze sensory details in the selection, think about

- the sense or senses to which each detail appeals
- the idea or emotion each detail is meant to evoke

As you read "Dyaspora," record sensory details that help you understand Hyppolite's experiences. Use a chart like the one shown here.

Sensory Detail	Sense(s) Appealed to	Idea or Emotion
On Sundays in your house, "Dominika-anik-anik" floats from the speakers of the record player....	Sound	

Review: **Make Inferences, Compare and Contrast**

Author Online

An Avid Reader
Joanne Hyppolite
(ē-pō′lēt′) was born
in Haiti but grew up
primarily in Boston,
Massachusetts.
When she was young,
she began visiting
her local library.
Reading ignited her
imagination. "I loved
disappearing into the
world that the writer
created," she once
stated.

Joanne Hyppolite
born 1969

A Bridge Builder At age 12, Hyppolite was inspired to write a story of her own. Soon hundreds of stories filled her notebooks. She continued to hone her craft while pursuing a bachelor's degree at the University of Pennsylvania. In 1995, Hyppolite published her first book, *Seth and Samona,* a children's story about friendship between a Haitian-American boy and an African-American girl. Today, she continues to write fiction for both children and adults. Through her books, she hopes to "debunk stereotypes" about Haitians and to build bridges between Haitian and American cultures.

 MORE ABOUT THE AUTHOR
For more on Joanne Hyppolite, visit the
Literature Center at **ClassZone.com.**

Background

The Haitian Diaspora In 1915, American troops invaded Haiti to restore order to a country ravaged by revolutions. When they left in 1934, conditions deteriorated and grew even worse during the dictatorship of François Duvalier (1957–1971). As a result, thousands of Haitians, like Hyppolite's parents, emigrated to other countries, particularly Cuba, the Dominican Republic, and the United States. In recent years, Haitians have fled in even greater numbers because of economic hardship and civil unrest.

DYASPORA

Joanne Hyppolite

When you are in Haiti they call you *Dyaspora*.[1] This word, which connotes both connection and disconnection, accurately describes your condition as a Haitian American. Disconnected from the physical landscape of the homeland, you don't grow up with a mango tree in your yard, you don't suck *kenèps* in the summer, or sit in the dark listening to stories of *Konpè* Bouki and Malis.[2] The bleat of *vaksins* or the beating of a *Yanvalou* on *Rada* drums are neither in the background or the foreground of your life.[3] Your French is nonexistent. Haiti is not where you live. **Ⓐ**

Your house in Boston is your island. As the only Haitian family on the
10 hillside street you grow up on, it represents Haiti to you. It was where your *granmè* refused to learn English, where goods like ripe mangoes, plantains, *djondjon,* and hard white blobs of mints come to you in boxes through the mail.[4] At your communion and birthday parties, all of Boston Haiti seems to gather in your house to eat *griyo* and sip *kremas*.[5] It takes forever for you to kiss every cheek, some of them heavy with face powder, some of them damp with perspiration, some of them with scratchy face hair, and some of them giving

ANALYZE VISUALS
Does the girl in this portrait look similar to how you imagine the girl described in the essay? Note **details** that influenced your answer.

Ⓐ POINT OF VIEW
Reread lines 1–8. Who do you think is the intended audience, or the "you," of this essay?

---

1. *Dyaspora,* or **diaspora** (dī-ăs′pər-ə): scattered people originally located in one place.
2. **Disconnected . . . and Malis:** Away from Haiti, you don't have a mango tree in your yard, eat Haitian fruits in the summer, or listen to Haitian stories at night.
3. **The bleat . . . your life:** The musical sounds of Haitian horns or drums playing island dances are not part of your life's experiences.
4. **It was . . . the mail:** It was where your grandmother refused to learn English and where you received packages of tropical fruits, vegetables, and mint candies sent from Haiti.
5. *griyo* (grē′yō) . . . *kremas* (krã′mäs): fried spiced pork and alcoholic drinks made with coconut.

Little Girl (1974), Luce Turnier.
Photo © Dominique Simon/Musée D'Art Haitien, Port-au-Prince, Haiti.

you a perfume head-rush as you swoop in. You are grateful for every smooth, dry cheek you encounter. In your house, the dreaded *matinèt*[6] which your parents imported from Haiti just to keep you, your brother, and your sister

20 in line sits threateningly on top of the wardrobe. It is where your mother's *andeyò Kreyòl*[7] accent and your father's *lavil*[8] French accent make sometimes beautiful, sometimes terrible music together. On Sundays in your house, "Dominika-anik-anik" floats from the speakers of the record player early in the morning and you are made to put on one of your frilly dresses, your matching lace-edged socks, and black shoes. Your mother ties long ribbons into a bow at the root of each braid. She warns you, your brother and your sister to "respect your heads" as you drive to St. Angela's, never missing a Sunday service in fourteen years. In your island house, everyone has two names. The name they were given and the nickname they have been granted so that your mother is

30 Gisou, your father is Popo, your brother is Claudy, your sister is Tinou, you are Jojo, and your grandmother is Manchoun. Every day your mother serves rice and beans and you methodically pick out all the beans because you don't like *pwa*.[9] You think they are ugly and why does all the rice have to have beans anyway? Even with the white rice or the *mayi moulen*,[10] your mother makes *sòs pwa*—bean sauce. You develop the idea that Haitians are obsessed with beans. In your house there is a mortar and a pestle as well as five pictures of Jesus, your parents drink Café Bustelo[11] every morning, your father wears *gwayabèl* shirts . . . , and you are punished when you don't get good grades at school. You learn about the behavior of husbands from conversations your aunts have.

40 You are dragged to Haitian plays, Haitian *bals,* and Haitian concerts where in spite of yourself *konpa* rhythms make you sway. You know the names of Haitian presidents and military leaders because political discussions inevitably erupt whenever there are more than three Haitian men together in the same place. Every time you are sick, your mother rubs you down with a foul-smelling liquid that she keeps in an old Barbancourt rum bottle under her bed. You splash yourself with Bien-être[12] after every bath. Your parents speak to you in *Kreyòl,* you respond in English, and somehow this works and feels natural. But when your mother speaks English, things seem to go wrong. She makes no distinction between he and she, and you become the pronoun police. Every

50 day you get a visit from some *matant* or *monnonk* or *kouzen* who is also a *marenn* or *parenn* of someone in the house.[13] In your house, your grandmother

B SENSORY DETAILS
Reread lines 13–18.
Which sensory details convey Hyppolite's discomfort as she greets guests?

C SENSORY DETAILS
Read aloud lines 40–47.
Hyppolite includes numerous Haitian words in this essay. How do these terms appeal to your sense of sound and help you to share her experiences?

---

6. **matinèt** (mä′tē-nĕt′): a small whip.

7. **andeyò Kreyòl** (än′dä-yō′ krã-yōl′): country Creole, a language spoken by Haitians, based on French and various African languages.

8. **lavil** (lä-vēl′): city.

9. **pwa** (pwä): beans.

10. **mayi moulen** (mä′yē mōō′lĕn): milled or ground corn.

11. **Café Bustelo** (kä-fā′ bōō-stä′lō): a brand of Cuban coffee.

12. **Bien-être** (byŏn-ĕt′rə): a French brand of perfumed bath products.

13. **Every day . . . the house:** Every day, you have aunts, uncles, or cousins visit.

has a porcelain *kivèt* she keeps under her bed to relieve herself at night.
You pore over photograph albums where there are pictures of you going to
school in Haiti, in the yard in Haiti, under the white Christmas tree in
Haiti, and you marvel because you do not remember anything that you
see. You do not remember Haiti because you left there too young but it
does not matter because it is as if Haiti has lassoed your house with an
invisible rope. **D**

    Outside of your house, you are forced to sink or swim in American
60 waters. For you this means an Irish-Catholic school and a Black-American
neighborhood. The school is a choice made by your parents who strongly
believe in a private Catholic education anyway, not paying any mind to
the busing crisis that is raging in the city. The choice of neighborhood is a
condition of the reality of living here in this city with its racially segregated
neighborhoods. Before you lived here, white people owned this hillside street.
After you and others who looked like you came, they gradually disappeared
to other places, leaving you this place and calling it bad because you and
others like you live there now. As any *dyaspora* child knows, Haitian parents
are not familiar with these waters. They say things to you like, "In Haiti we
70 never treated white people badly." They don't know about racism. They don't
know about the latest styles and fashions and give your brother grief every time
he sneaks out to a friend's house and gets his hair cut into a shag, a high-top,
a fade. They don't know that the ribbons in your hair, the gold loops in your
ears, and the lace that edges your socks alert other children to your difference.
So you wait until you get to school before taking them all off and out and
you put them back on at the end of your street where the bus drops you off.
Outside your house, things are black and white. You are black and white.
Especially in your school where neither you nor any of the few other Haitian
girls in your class are invited to the birthday parties of the white kids in your
80 class. You cleave to these other Haitian girls out of something that begins as
solidarity but becomes a lifetime of friendship. You make green hats in art
class every St. Patrick's day and watch Irish step-dancing shows year after year
after year. You discover books and reading and this is what you do when you
take the bus home, just you and your white schoolmates. You lose your accent.
You study about the Indians in social studies but you do not study about
Black Americans except in music class where you are forced to sing Negro
spirituals as a concession to your presence. They don't know anything about
Toussaint Louverture[14] or Jean-Jacques Dessalines.[15] **E**

    In your neighborhood when you tell people you are from Haiti, they ask
90 politely, "Where's that?" You explain and because you seem okay to them,
Haiti is okay to them. They shout "Hi, Grunny!" whenever they see your

D MAKE INFERENCES
What can you infer so far
about Hyppolite and how
she feels about being a
Haitian American?

E COMPARE AND
CONTRAST
Reread lines 59–88.
Compare Hyppolite's
Haitian values and her
American experiences.
How do you know that
she is struggling to
belong to both cultures?

---

14. **Toussaint Louverture (1743—1803)** (tōō-sā′ lōō-věr-tōōr′): a black general who struggled for Haitian
independence.

15. **Jean-Jacques Dessalines (1758—1806)** (zhô-zhôk dě′sä-lēń): African-born emperor of Haiti who defeated
the French in 1803 to win independence for the island.

grandmother on the stoop and sometimes you translate a sentence or two between them. In their houses, you eat sweet potato pie and nod because you have that too, it's made a little different and you call it *pen patat* but it's the same taste after all. From the girls on the street you learn to jump double-dutch,[16] you learn to dance the puppet and the white boy. You see a woman preacher for the first time in your life at their church. You wonder where down South is because that is where most of the boys and girls on your block go for vacations. You learn about boys . . . through these girls because this subject is not allowed in your island/house. You keep your street friends separate from your school friends and this is how it works and you are used to it. You get so you can jump between worlds with the same ease that you slide on your nightgown every evening. **F**

Then when you get to high school, things change. People in your high school and your neighborhood look at you and say, "You are Haitian?" and from the surprise in their voice you realize that they know where Haiti is now. They think they know what Haiti is now. Haiti is the boat people on the news every night. Haiti is where people have tuberculosis. Haiti is where people eat cats. You do not represent Haiti at all to them anymore. You are an aberration because you look like them and you talk like them. They do not see you. They do not see the worlds that have made you. You want to say to them that you are Haiti, too. Your house is Haiti, too, and what does that do to their perceptions? You have the choice of passing but you don't. You claim your *dyaspora* status hoping it will force them to expand their image of what Haiti is but it doesn't. Your sister who is younger and very sensitive begins to deny that she is Haitian. She is American, she says. American. **G**

You turn to books to lose yourself. You read stories about people from other places. You read stories about people from here. You read stories about people from other places who now live here. You decide you will become a writer. Through your writing they will see you, *dyaspora* child, the connections and disconnections that have made you the mosaic that you are. They will see where you are from and the worlds that have made you. They will see you. ❧

---

16. **double-dutch:** a jump-rope game involving two ropes.

Comprehension

1. **Recall** What does *dyaspora* mean?

2. **Summarize** Describe the ways in which Hyppolite's home reflects the values and customs of her native country.

3. **Clarify** What decision does Hyppolite make at the end of the essay?

Literary Analysis

4. **Examine Point of View** Consider how the second-person point of view of this essay affects you as a reader. Does Hyppolite's use of *you* and *yours* help you to relate to her unusual experiences? Cite evidence from the essay to support your answer.

5. **Analyze Sensory Details** Review the chart you created as you read. Of the sensory details you recorded, which ones were most effective in conveying Hyppolite's Haitian heritage? Explain your response.

6. **Compare and Contrast** In Hyppolite's experience, what are the similarities and differences between Haitian and American cultures? Use a graphic organizer like the one shown to record details from the essay.

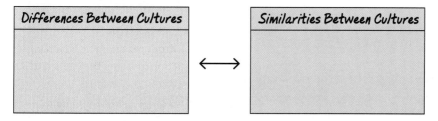

Differences Between Cultures   ⟷   Similarities Between Cultures

7. **Make Inferences** How does Hyppolite's attitude toward her own **cultural identity** change during the course of the essay? Support your answer with specific details.

8. **Evaluate** Hyppolite concludes, "Through your writing they will see you, *dyaspora* child, the connections and disconnections that have made you the mosaic that you are." Evaluate Hyppolite's essay. Does it succeed in conveying the "mosaic" quality of immigrant life in America? Cite evidence from the essay to support your response.

Literary Criticism

9. **Social Context** What does Hyppolite say about the way Americans perceive Haiti and Haitian Americans? Cite evidence to support your claim.

OHIO
STANDARDS

READING STANDARD
4.11 Explain point of view

Writing Workshop

Short Story

When you write fiction, you create a world just as you want it to be. The setting, characters, action, and dialogue are all of your own choosing. In this workshop you will write a short story, and the choices you make as a writer will determine how successful your story will be.

WRITER'S ROAD MAP

Short Story

WRITING PROMPT 1

Writing from Your Imagination To hold a reader's attention, a short story needs a central conflict. Write a story that is centered on a particular conflict that interests you.

Conflicts to Consider
- an external conflict involving nature, such as a storm or natural disaster
- an external conflict involving other people or another person
- an internal conflict—a struggle within a character

WRITING PROMPT 2

Writing from Literature A provocative question can make you see the world in a new way. Select an intriguing question from this unit or an earlier unit. Write a short story inspired by that question.

Questions to Consider
- Is technology taking over? ("There Will Come Soft Rains")
- How important is telling the truth? ("Like the Sun")
- How can you recover from tragedy? ("The Seventh Man")

 WRITING TOOLS
For prewriting, revision, and editing tools, visit the **Writing Center** at **ClassZone.com.**

KEY TRAITS

1. IDEAS
- Creates an interesting **plot** with one or more **characters**
- Develops and resolves a **central conflict**
- Includes **descriptive details** that reveal the setting and characters
- Uses **dialogue** to show characters' motivations and personalities

2. ORGANIZATION
- **Introduces** characters, setting, or action in a way that gets a reader's attention
- Presents a clear and engaging **sequence of events**
- Resolves the conflict in a convincing **conclusion**

3. VOICE
- Has a consistent **point of view** throughout

4. WORD CHOICE
- Uses **sensory language** to help a reader imagine the fictional world

5. SENTENCE FLUENCY
- Varies **sentence types and structures**

6. CONVENTIONS
- Employs **correct grammar and usage**

Part 1: Analyze a Student Model

Rose Kenwood
Central High School

Sleepless

The stairs groaned tiredly under Duane's bulk. Duane himself groaned tiredly as he plopped down at the kitchen table.

"Do we have coffee?" he muttered.

"Have you ever smelled coffee in this house?" his mother said. "You
5 know, my yoga instructor says that new class isn't full yet."

"Enough with the yoga, Ma." Duane looked blearily for the chocolate puffs cereal.

"All right, but it can really help with insomnia," she said.

Duane grunted. He could just see himself in a leotard, stretching and
10 taking deep breaths—and then his friends would walk by just as he was doing the Loser Lotus position.

Jeff, one of the linebackers, came up behind him at school.

"Hey man, you look wiped. Tackling people in your sleep now? You should get some z's. You gonna be able to practice today?"

15 "I'll be fine," Duane said, not sure if it was true. It had been nearly a week—more than six days!—since he'd managed to sleep more than a few hours. Maybe football was making him so keyed up. Plus there was this girl . . .

"You asked Tina out yet?" Jeff said.

20 "Shut up, man! You're so loud," he said, trying to look cool. "I'm just waiting for the right moment."

"Well, don't wait too long—she's cool. Somebody else'll ask her."

Duane felt his heart rate increase and his shoulders tighten even more. "Lay off, Jeff," he said as the bell rang.

KEY TRAITS IN ACTION

Introduces a central **character** in a way that captures the reader's interest.

Uses **dialogue** to make the characters come to life and to advance the **plot**.

Maintains a consistent third-person **point of view.**

Develops a **central conflict** (Duane's nervousness over asking Tina out).

25   Duane's eyelids drooped during the daily announcements. "Yoga class meets during the lunch period in the east gym. . . ." Before he knew it, the bell was ringing again.

"Duane, this is the second time this week you've fallen asleep during class. What's going on?" Mr. Trumpeter asked.

30   "Sorry, Mr. Trumpeter," Duane said, and stumbled out.

He floated in a half-wakeful state through his next four classes. At lunch, he found his stomach was too knotted to let him eat. He tried to joke with his buddies about the homecoming game but didn't have the energy.

35   He got up and started down the hall with no destination in mind, just wanting to escape the noise. A deep, loud voice startled him.

"Do you have a pass?" the security guard asked.

"Uh, no, I, uh—"

"Are you on your way to yoga class?"

40   "Yeah, yeah, it's in the east gym," he said with relief. The guard watched Duane closely as he walked down the hallway.

As soon as he opened the door to the east gym, a friendly voice said, "Hello! Grab a mat for yourself. We're just about to start."

The instructor was a big, muscular guy. He was wearing loose shorts

45   and a tank top. Duane kept his face down as he grabbed a mat and made his way to an empty spot on the floor.

"Let's start with a deep breath into your belly," the instructor said.

Breathing in, Duane dared to look around. Tina was right next to him. He choked a little and coughed. She glanced over and smiled

50   warmly. Duane smiled back and took his first deep breath in days.

> **Sequence of events** is clear. **Sensory language** draws the reader into the action.

> Varied **sentence types and structures** help keep the story lively. **Descriptive details** help the reader picture the character.

> Resolves the conflict with a satisfying **conclusion**.

2

Part 2: Apply the Writing Process

WRITING STANDARD
5.9 Use language, sensory details and colorful modifiers

PREWRITING

What Should I Do?	**What Does It Look Like?**

1. Freewrite to find ideas.

Think about interesting **characters, settings, plots,** and **conflicts.** Write down whatever comes into your mind. Circle the ideas that interest you the most.

TIP Another way to find ideas is to ask "what if" questions. What if someone you know had a serious accident? What if scientists discovered a previously unknown life form?

> Maybe something about (school) or sports or working. (Girl/boy problems.) What happens when a friend grows distant? The mall could be an interesting setting. Jocks, geeks, etc. Being (open to new experiences.)

2. Develop the details.

Once you've got an idea for your story, you need to begin fleshing out the details. Who's the central character or characters? What's the conflict, and is it internal or external? Which important details will bring the story to life?

See page 26: Plot Stages and Conflict

Character	Conflict	Details
Football player (Duane? Zach?)	Likes a girl but is too shy to ask her out—internal conflict	Conflict causes insomnia—always tired, droopy eyes, falls asleep in class, no energy. Anxiety—stomach in knots, tight muscles

3. Plan your story.

Every good story has an engaging beginning, a well-developed middle, and a satisfying ending. Use a story map, a list, a flow chart, or some other graphic organizer to plot the course your story will take. If you have trouble developing a plan, consider choosing a different idea from your freewriting.

TIP Your story might proceed chronologically, from event to event. Or you could include a flashback—an event that took place before the start of the story.

> **Beginning**
> • Meet the main character.
> • Mention insomnia and the yoga class.
>
> **Middle**
> • Main character sleepwalks through school day.
> • A friend kids him about asking Tina out.
> • He "accidentally" winds up in yoga class.
>
> **End**
> • The main character sees Tina in yoga class.
> • She smiles at him, and he knows he'll ask her out.

What Should I Do?	What Does It Look Like?

1. Grab your reader's attention.
A strong beginning will make your audience want to keep reading. You might open with dialogue, a description of the setting, or some sensory language to draw the reader into your story.
	Sensory details
	    Duane groaned tiredly as he plopped down at the kitchen table.
	
	Dialogue
	    "I am sooooo tired. Do we have coffee?" Duane muttered.

2. Use dialogue to show characters' personalities and motivations.
You can communicate a lot of information about a character through dialogue. Be sure the dialogue you write is realistic and that it helps the reader get to know and understand the character more fully.
	"You asked Tina out yet?" Jeff said.
	    "Shut up, man! You're so loud," he said, trying to look cool. "I'm just waiting for the right moment."
	    "Well, don't wait too long—she's cool. Somebody else'll ask her."

3. Consider your point of view.
Rose Kenwood chose to tell her story in the third person. You could do the same, or you might tell it in the first person.
 	
TIP Make sure that the point of view stays consistent throughout your story. Switching from *he* or *she* to *I* will confuse your reader.
	Third person
	    "Do we have coffee?" he muttered.
	    Have you ever smelled coffee in this house?" his mother said.
	
	First person
	    "Do we have coffee?" I muttered.
	    "Have you ever smelled coffee in this house?" my mother said.

4. Craft a satisfying conclusion. A strong conclusion to a short story should show how the conflict is resolved and do so in a way that readers find satisfying. **TIP** Before revising, consult the **key traits** on page 368 and the **rubric** and **peer-reader questions** on page 374.	Breathing in, Duane dared to look around. Tina was right next to him. He choked a little and coughed. She glanced over and smiled warmly. Duane smiled back and took his first deep breath in days.

REVISING AND EDITING

What Should I Do?	*What Does It Look Like?*

1. Check that your sequence is clear.
- Ask a peer reader to <u>underline</u> passages where the order of events is confusing.
- Add transitional words and phrases to make the sequence clear.

See page 374: Ask a Peer Reader

▶ through his next four classes. At lunch,
<u>He floated in a half-wakeful state, He found his
stomach was too knotted to let him eat.</u>

2. Fine-tune your dialogue.
- Read the dialogue aloud, (circling) parts that seem out of character.
- Revise your dialogue to include contractions, slang, interjections, or jargon—anything that will make the dialogue more realistic.

▶ ~~"You look tired. Are you going to be able to practice today?"~~
"Hey man, you look wiped. Tackling people in your sleep now? You should get some z's. You gonna be able to practice today?"

3. Enrich your story's descriptive details.
- Read your story and highlight sensory language and other descriptive details.
- If your story lacks highlights, add details that will enable your readers to picture the setting, follow the action, and understand the characters.

▶   Duane's eyelids drooped
~~Duane was tired~~ during the daily announcements . . .
He got up and started down the hall with
          , just wanting to escape the noise.
no destination in mind. ~~A security guard~~
          deep, loud voice startled
~~stopped~~ him.

4. Choose an appropriate title.
- Brainstorm a list of possible titles.
- Your title might refer to the introduction or conclusion, or it might be a short quotation from dialogue in the story. This writer chose a title that hints at her story's central conflict.

▶ ~~Thinking About Tina~~
~~Yoga Tales~~
Sleepless **
~~One Deep Breath~~

Apply the Rubric

A strong short story . . .

☑ begins in an interesting, attention-getting way

☑ has a well-developed plot and believable characters

☑ presents an interesting internal or external conflict

☑ includes descriptive details, sensory language, and dialogue

☑ makes the sequence of events clear and logical

☑ maintains a consistent point of view

☑ varies sentence types and structures

☑ resolves the conflict in a convincing conclusion

Ask a Peer Reader

• Can you explain in your own words the central conflict in this story?

• How can I make the sequence of events clearer?

• Where does my dialogue sound forced or unnatural?

Check Your Grammar

• Use consistent verb tenses so that your reader can keep track of what happens when. In most short stories past-tense verbs are used.

> The stairs groaned tiredly under Duane's bulk. Duane himself groaned tiredly as he plopped down at the kitchen table.

• If you want to convey drama or suspense, consider using present-tense verbs.

> The stairs groan tiredly under Duane's bulk. Duane himself groans tiredly as he plops himself down at the kitchen table.

• If you're using the present tense but your character remembers something from the past, switch to the past tense when describing that event.

> Suddenly, Duane remembers the events of yesterday, when Tina smiled warmly at him.

• Because people don't always speak in complete sentences, it's OK to use fragments to make dialogue more realistic.

> "Tackling people in your sleep now?"

See page R55: Verbs

Writing On**line**

🖱 **PUBLISHING OPTIONS**
For publishing options, visit the **Writing Center** at ClassZone.com.

ASSESSMENT PREPARATION
For writing and grammar assessment practice, go to the **Assessment Center** at ClassZone.com.

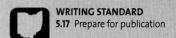

Creating a Children's Book

Children love to read and to be read to. Follow these guidelines to create an entertaining illustrated children's book.

Planning the Book

1. **Think about your audience and your purpose.** For which ages is your story appropriate? Do you want primarily to inform or to entertain your readers?

    TIP If the story you wrote for this workshop isn't suitable for children, perhaps you'd like to retell a fairy tale in your own words or share a special memory from your own childhood.

2. **Create a storyboard.** A storyboard is a series of images and text that shows the development of your book. Pictures are as important as words in children's books. Decide which parts of your story you want to illustrate, and choose images that your audience will find informative and appealing.

Producing the Book

1. **Prepare the text.** Type the text into a computer. Choose a font and type size that will be easy for your audience to read.

2. **Find or create the illustrations.** You might use paint, colored pencils, or computer software. Another method is to clip out interesting images from newspapers and magazines and use them to create collages that illustrate your story.

3. **Lay out your book.** Combine the images and text creatively on each page. You can do this by scanning images into a computer, or you can combine words and pictures by hand.

4. **Print your book.** Use a color printer or photocopier to create the finished pages. Assemble the pages within a colorful cover.

5. **Share your book with children.** As you read the story, show them the illustrations. Ask the children to tell you how they liked your book.

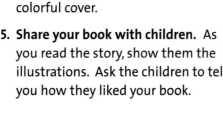

Reading Comprehension

ASSESS
The practice test items on the next few pages match skills listed on the Unit Goals page (page 281) and addressed throughout this unit. Taking this practice test will help you assess your knowledge of these skills and determine your readiness for the Unit Test.

REVIEW
After you take the practice test, your teacher can help you identify any skills you need to review.

- Flashback
- First-Person Point of View
- Third-Person Omniscient Point of View
- Chronological Order
- Make Inferences
- Latin Word Roots
- Similes
- Appositive Phrases

DIRECTIONS *Read the following selections and then answer the questions.*

from Night Calls

Lisa Fugard

As we drove up to our house now, I noticed the shabby state of the compound. The road was rutted and washed-out in many places by the spring rains. The visitors' kiosk[1] was boarded up, and the map of the sanctuary had been knocked off its post and lay on the ground. Even the pond had been neglected. When my parents had first come to Modder River, five years before I was born, my father had had the pond dug out for my mother. An avid botanist,[2] she'd planted it with indigenous water lilies that she collected, along with bulrushes, seven-weeks ferns, and floating hearts. During the two years when the Modder River was reduced to a trickle by the drought, the local

10 farmers had been astonished to hear that my father was actually pumping precious water from our borehole into the pond to prevent it from drying up. An opulent jewel in the dusty, cracked landscape, it became a haven for birds, being visited by pied kingfishers, mountain chats, spoonbills, bokmakieries, a pair of black-shouldered kites—all told, my mother counted 107 different species. Now a thick layer of brown scum covered the shallow, stagnant water. I remembered a letter that I'd received from my father several months before. The scrawled handwriting hadn't even looked like his. I'd read it once and then hidden it away, scared by the loneliness that the words hinted at.

None of this seemed to matter, however, when I stood among our dogs,
20 being pelted with paws and tails and long pink tongues: King, with his tail plumed like an ostrich feather, and Blitz, a lean, black shadow. They clattered behind me as I went into my bedroom. The room was still and dark and smelled musty. Quickly I opened the wooden shutters. I moved to the chest of drawers and found the large framed photograph of my mother, frozen at age thirty-two. She was laughing, and her head was turned slightly as a lock of hair blew across her face. I traced her jaw line with my finger and moved to the mirror with the photograph, but the dogs were demanding, barking and pawing at my legs.

---

1. **kiosk:** a small booth open on one or more sides.
2. **botanist:** one who studies plant life.

ASSESSMENT ONLINE
For more assessment practice and test-taking tips, go to the **Assessment Center** at ClassZone.com.

from The Snow Goose

Paul Gallico

She was desperately frightened of the ugly man she had come to see, for legend had already begun to gather about Rhayader, and the native wild-fowlers hated him for interfering with their sport.

But greater than her fear was the need of that which she bore. For locked in her child's heart was the knowledge, picked up somewhere in the swampland, that this ogre who lived in the lighthouse had magic that could heal injured things.

She had never seen Rhayader before and was close to fleeing in panic at the dark apparition that appeared at the studio door, drawn by her footsteps—the
10 black head and beard, the sinister hump, and the crooked claw.

She stood there staring, poised like a disturbed marsh bird for instant flight.

But his voice was deep and kind when he spoke to her.

"What is it, child?"

She stood her ground and then edged timidly forward. The thing she carried in her arms was a large white bird, and it was quite still. There were stains of blood on its whiteness and on her kirtle where she had held it to her.

The girl placed it in his arms. "I found it, sir. It's hurted. Is it still alive?"

"Yes. Yes, I think so. Come in, child, come in."

Rhayader went inside, bearing the bird, which he placed upon a table, where
20 it moved feebly. Curiosity overcame fear. The girl followed and found herself in a room warmed by a coal fire, shining with many colored pictures that covered the walls, and full of a strange but pleasant smell.

The bird fluttered. With his good hand Rhayader spread one of its immense white pinions. The end was beautifully tipped with black.

Rhayader looked and marveled, and said: "Child, where did you find it?"

"In t' marsh, sir, where fowlers had been. What—what is it, sir?"

"It's a snow goose from Canada. But how in all heaven came it here?"

The name seemed to mean nothing to the little girl. Her deep violet eyes, shining out of the dirt on her thin face, were fixed with concern on the injured
30 bird.

She said: "Can 'ee heal it, sir?"

"Yes, yes," said Rhayader. "We will try. Come, you shall help me."

There were scissors and bandages and splints on a shelf, and he was marvelously deft, even with the crooked claw that managed to hold things.

He said: "Ah, she has been shot, poor thing. Her leg is broken, and the wing tip, but not badly. See, we will clip her primaries, so that we can bandage it, but in the spring the feathers will grow and she will be able to fly again. We'll bandage it close to her body, so that she cannot move it until it has set, and then make a splint for the poor leg."

Her fears forgotten, the child watched, fascinated, as he worked, and all the more so because
40 while he fixed a fine splint to the shattered leg he told her the most wonderful story.

The bird was a young one, no more than a year old. She was born in a northern land far, far across the seas, a land belonging to England. Flying to the south to escape the snow and ice and bitter cold, a great storm had seized her and whirled and buffeted her about. It was a truly terrible storm, stronger than her great wings, stronger than anything. For days and nights it held her in its grip and there was nothing she could do but fly before it. When finally it had blown itself out and her sure instincts took her south again, she was over a different land and surrounded by strange birds that she had never seen before. At last, exhausted by her ordeal, she had sunk to rest in a friendly green marsh, only to be met by the blast from the hunter's gun.

"A bitter reception for a visiting princess," concluded Rhayader. "We will call her 'La
50 Princesse Perdue,' the Lost Princess. And in a few days she will be feeling better. See?"

Comprehension

DIRECTIONS *Answer these questions about the excerpt from "Night Calls."*

1. From what point of view is "Night Calls" told?
   A. first person
   B. second person
   C. third-person omniscient
   D. third-person limited

2. What is the correct chronological order of events during the narrator's visit to the house?
   A. they drive up to the house, the parents build a pond, the father writes a letter
   B. they drive up to the house, the dogs greet the narrator, the narrator finds the photograph
   C. the kiosk is boarded up, the mother counts bird species, the parents move
   D. the kiosk is boarded up, the parents build a pond, the mother is photographed

3. The chronological narration of the story is interrupted two times by
   A. plans
   B. tasks
   C. letters
   D. memories

4. Reread lines 23–28. What can you infer about the narrator from the information in these lines?
   A. She does not enjoy living in this house.
   B. She is very tired when she arrives.
   C. She wonders why the house is shabby.
   D. She misses her mother.

DIRECTIONS *Answer these questions about the excerpt from "The Snow Goose."*

5. The narrator of "The Snow Goose" can be described as

   A. a minor character in the story, who addresses the reader

   B. a main character in the story, who refers to himself or herself as "I"

   C. an all-knowing narrator who is outside the story

   D. a narrator who deliberately misleads the reader

6. Which of the following statements best indicates an omniscient narrator?

   A. The narrator reveals the child's fears and Rhyader's sense of marvel.

   B. The narrator describes the child carrying the injured bird.

   C. The story contains dialogue between the child and Rhyader.

   D. The narrator tells the story that Rhyader told the child.

7. Which of the following lines in the story contains the beginning of a flashback?

   A. line 4   C. line 19

   B. line 11   D. line 41

8. The flashback in the story provides background information about

   A. how Rhayader bandaged the disabled bird in the lighthouse

   B. how the snow goose most likely ended up in England, far from her home in Canada

   C. why people think Rhayader has magic that can heal injured things

   D. why the legends about Rhayader made the girl fearful of him

9. Which of the following events in the story signals that the flashback is over?

   A. The hunter shoots the snow goose.

   B. Rhayader fixes the bird's leg.

   C. Rhayader names the snow goose.

   D. The snow goose is caught in a storm.

DIRECTIONS *Answer this question about both selections.*

10. What can you infer about how the characters relate to birds and animals?

   A. They are compassionate and caring.

   B. They conduct scientific studies on them.

   C. They are uninterested in them.

   D. They know very little about their habits.

Written Response

SHORT ANSWER
Write three or four sentences to answer each question.

11. Reread lines 16–18 in "Night Calls." Rewrite those three sentences from the point of view of an omniscient narrator.

12. List in chronological order the events that occur in lines 35–48 in "The Snow Goose."

EXTENDED RESPONSE
Write three or four paragraphs to answer the following question.

13. If the author of "The Snow Goose" had told the story from the first-person point of view of the character Rhayader, some things would be missing. What are they? Explain why they would be missing.

Vocabulary

DIRECTIONS *Use context clues and the Latin root definitions to answer the following questions based on the excerpt from "Night Calls."*

1. The Latin root *sanct* means "sacred" or "holy." What is the most likely meaning of *sanctuary* as it is used in line 3?

   A. a place where criminals cannot be arrested

   B. a group of houses enclosed by a barrier

   C. an area set aside to provide safety

   D. the churchyard in a rural village

2. The Latin root *opul* means "rich" or "splendid." What is the most likely meaning of the word *opulent* in line 12?

   A. worth a lot of money

   B. extremely large

   C. greatly valued

   D. very productive

3. The Latin root *gen* means "born" or "growing." Which word in lines 3–15 means "growing naturally in a region"?

   A. neglected

   B. indigenous

   C. bulrushes

   D. stagnant

DIRECTIONS *Use context clues and the Latin word definitions to answer the following questions based on the excerpt from "The Snow Goose."*

4. The Latin word *legere* means "to read." What is the meaning of the word *legend* in line 2?

   A. a popularized myth inspired by a real person

   B. the caption for an illustration in a newspaper

   C. the title on an object, such as a coin

   D. a written story about a figure from the past

5. The Latin word *apparere* means "to appear." What is the most likely meaning of the word *apparition* in line 9?

   A. a menacing spirit

   B. a general feeling

   C. an unusual and sudden sight

   D. an easily anticipated picture

6. The Latin word *pinna* means "feather." What parts of a bird does *pinions* refer to in line 24?

   A. feet   C. wings

   B. legs   D. eyes

7. The Latin word *receptus* means "received." What is the most likely meaning of the word *reception* as it is used in line 49?

   A. a social function

   B. the catching of a forward pass

   C. mental approval

   D. a greeting or welcome

Writing & Grammar

DIRECTIONS *Read the passage and answer the following questions.*

> (1) Video games have changed a lot in the last 20 years. (2) The arcade was once the only place kids could play games with advanced graphics. (3) An arcade is a building containing video-game machines. (4) Later, Atari made it possible for kids to play some arcade games at home. (5) Atari was one of the original home gaming systems. (6) Now the Internet allows kids to play against opponents all over the world.

1. Choose the correct way to rewrite sentence 1, using a simile.

   A. Video games, along with other electronic devices, have changed a lot in the last 20 years.

   B. As any kid will tell you, video games have changed a lot in the last 20 years.

   C. The difference between video games today and those from 20 years ago is like night and day.

   D. As the times have changed, so have video games and the people who play them.

2. Choose the correct way to rewrite sentences 2 and 3 as one sentence containing an appositive phrase.

   A. The arcade, which is a building containing video-game machines, was once the only place where kids could play games with advanced graphics.

   B. Kids, interested in games with advanced graphics, had to go to the arcade, which housed video-game machines.

   C. An arcade is a building containing video-game machines and is where kids went to play games with advanced graphics.

   D. The arcade, a building containing video-game machines, was once the only place kids could play games with advanced graphics.

3. Choose the correct way to rewrite sentences 4 and 5 as one sentence containing an appositive phrase.

   A. Later, Atari made it possible for kids to play some arcade games at home, and it was one of the original home gaming systems.

   B. Later, Atari, one of the original home gaming systems, made it possible for kids to play some arcade games at home.

   C. Later, at home on their Atari, kids could play some arcade games on one of the original home gaming systems.

   D. Later, Atari became one of the original home gaming systems on which kids could play some arcade games at home.

4. Choose the correct way to rewrite sentence 6, using a simile.

   A. Now the Internet is like a global game room, allowing kids to play against opponents all over the world.

   B. Now, if kids want to play against opponents all over the world, it's as easy as turning on a computer.

   C. Now, the Internet allows kids to play against opponents from countries like China and Russia.

   D. As the Internet has developed, it has allowed kids to play against opponents all over the world.

STOP

Ideas for Independent Reading

Can learning ever harm you? Is there anything wrong with being liked?
Consider these questions when you read these works.

Does knowledge come at a price?

Fahrenheit 451
by Ray Bradbury

Montag is a fireman. His job is to burn books, which are forbidden in a future society. One day he smuggles home a book and begins to read. What will happen if he is found out?

Nervous Conditions
by Tsitsi Dangarembga

Tambudzai is delighted at the chance to leave her tiny Rhodesian village and be educated at the home of her wealthy uncle. The more she learns, however, the more critical she becomes of both her parents' and her uncle's worlds.

The Curious Incident of the Dog in the Night-Time
by Mark Haddon

When a 15-year-old autistic boy discovers his neighbor's poodle stabbed to death, he vows to solve the crime. Ultimately, he learns who killed the dog but also uncovers other secrets that turn his life upside down.

What makes someone popular?

Shattering Glass
by Gail Giles

Simon Glass is an overweight, clumsy geek until a popular clique decides to turn him into the high school Class Favorite. As they transform Simon, they begin to hate him, and the final result is chilling.

Death of a Salesman
by Arthur Miller

This classic American play tells us that salesmen don't only sell their wares; they must also sell themselves. And unpopular salesmen don't do well. The salesman Willy Loman is liked, but he's not well liked, and that is his tragedy.

Pygmalion
by George Bernard Shaw

By giving the Cockney flower-seller Eliza Doolittle lessons in speech and manners, Professor Henry Higgins transforms her into the toast of London society. But Eliza has much to teach Professor Higgins in return.

Can ordinary people be heroes?

The White Rose: Munich 1942–1943
by Inge Scholl

The German brother and sister Hans and Sophie Scholl, who hated everything Adolf Hitler stood for, worked with friends to resist the Third Reich. They were arrested, tried, and executed for distributing anti-Hitler leaflets. Their story is told by their sister.

In the Time of the Butterflies
by Julia Alvarez

Alvarez combines history and fiction in this account of the three heroic Mirabal sisters, who worked against the Trujillo dictatorship in the Dominican Republic and were assassinated. They used the code name *mariposas,* or "butterflies."

Stone Soup for the World
by Marianne Larned

This book collects 100 inspiring accounts of "everyday heroes" who improved their communities and nations. The volume also lists many volunteer organizations that interested readers can join.

Message and Meaning

THEME

- In Fiction
- In Poetry
- In Nonfiction
- Across Genres

What are life's big
LESSONS?

You can't find them in a textbook. You can't discover them in a class. The way you will learn life's most important **lessons** will be through your own experiences and through encounters with the words, accomplishments, and ideas of others. Sometimes these lessons, or themes, will show up in the fiction you read and the movies you watch.

ACTIVITY Think of a book or a movie that taught you something about life or human nature. Then answer the following:

- What lesson or theme was the author or director trying to express?

- Does the lesson reflect what your experience has shown you to be true?

- Does the lesson apply to other times and other places?

OHIO STANDARDS

Preview Unit Goals

LITERARY ANALYSIS
- Identify and analyze theme, including the roles of setting and character
- Identify and interpret symbol
- Interpret symbol and theme
- Identify and interpret verbal irony
- Analyze and compare authors' messages across genres
- Identify characteristics of a persuasive essay

READING
- Make inferences and draw conclusions
- Monitor comprehension
- Analyze reasons and evidence

WRITING AND GRAMMAR
- Write a comparison-contrast essay
- Use transitions to clarify the relationships between ideas
- Use adverbs to add descriptive detail
- Use subordinate clauses to improve sentence flow

SPEAKING, LISTENING, AND VIEWING
- Participate in a group discussion

VOCABULARY
- Understand and use connotation and denotation of words
- Use prefixes to help unlock word meanings

ACADEMIC VOCABULARY
- theme
- verbal irony
- persuasive essay
- symbol
- connotation

**OHIO
STANDARDS**

READING STANDARDS
4.4 Interpret universal themes

4.9 Explain how authors use
symbols to create broader meanings

Theme and Symbol

When a friend inquires about a movie you saw recently, you might describe it by saying something like "It's about a Guatemalan girl who moves to New York and adjusts to life in an unfamiliar world." While it is true you've described the *topic* of the movie, you're not communicating its *big idea*. If you continue by saying "It's really about finding a way to fit in without losing your uniqueness," you are talking about theme. A **theme** is an underlying message about life that a writer wants to convey. Whether that message is about fitting in, love, or another timeless topic, it can often prompt you to think about human nature in a new way.

Part 1: Universal Themes in Literature

Despite the diversity in the world, many themes show up again and again in literature, no matter what the culture, time period, or country. These **universal themes** deal with emotions and experiences that are common to all people. For example, the theme "With great power comes great responsibility" has been explored in stories as varied as ancient epics and today's comics.

"WITH GREAT POWER COMES GREAT RESPONSIBILITY"

Valmiki's *Ramayana*
India
C. 250 B.C.

Virgil's *Aeneid*
Rome
C. 20 B.C.

Spider-Man
United States
1962–present

Theme and Symbol A writer has many tools he or she can use to develop a theme. Symbols, for example, can powerfully reinforce a theme. A **symbol** is something concrete—a person, place, object, or activity—that represents an abstract idea. For example, a bird flying in the sky might represent a character's individuality and freedom. Here are some other examples of symbols and the ideas they might communicate:

- a bleak winter setting (isolation or death)

- a small child (innocence)

- a physical challenge, such as climbing a mountain (a character's emotional growth)

MODEL: THEME AND SYMBOL

In this story, a poor farm girl named Sylvia meets a hunter in search of a rare bird. Wanting to impress the hunter, Sylvia decides to help look for the heron. In the end, however, she makes a difficult choice—to protect the bird. As part of her initial effort to help, Sylvia climbs a tree to look for the heron. As you read, consider what the tree and Sylvia's climb might symbolize.

from A White Heron

Short story by **Sarah Orne Jewett**

Half a mile from home, at the farther edge of the woods, where the land was highest, a great pine tree stood, the last of its generation. Whether it was left for a boundary mark, or for what reason, no one could say; the woodchoppers who had felled its mates were dead and gone long ago, and a whole forest
5 of sturdy trees, pines and oaks and maples, had grown again. But the stately head of this old pine towered above them all and made a landmark for sea and shore miles and miles away. Sylvia knew it well. She had always believed that whoever climbed to the top of it could see the ocean; and the little girl had often laid her hand on the great rough trunk and looked up wistfully at those
10 dark boughs that the wind always stirred, no matter how hot and still the air might be below. Now she thought of the tree with a new excitement, for why, if one climbed it at break of day, could not one see all the world, and easily discover whence the white heron flew? . . .

There was the huge tree asleep yet in the paling moonlight, and small and
15 silly Sylvia began with utmost bravery to mount to the top of it. . . .

The way was harder than she thought; she must reach far and hold fast, the sharp dry twigs caught and held her and scratched her like angry talons, the pitch made her thin little fingers clumsy and stiff as she went round and round the tree's great stem. . . .
20 The tree seemed to lengthen itself out as she went up, and to reach farther and farther upward. It was like a great mainmast to the voyaging earth; it must truly have been amazed that morning through all its ponderous frame as it felt this determined spark of human spirit wending its way from higher branch to branch. Who knows how steadily the least twigs held themselves to advantage
25 this light, weak creature on her way! The old pine must have loved his new dependent. More than all the hawks, and bats, and moths, and even the sweet-voiced thrushes, was the brave, beating heart of the solitary gray-eyed child. And the tree stood still and frowned away the winds that June morning while the dawn grew bright in the east.
30 Sylvia's face was like a pale star, if one had seen it from the ground, when the last thorny bough was past, and she stood trembling and tired but wholly triumphant, high in the tree-top. Yes, there was the sea with the dawning sun making a golden dazzle over it, and toward that glorious east flew two hawks. . . . Truly it was a vast and awesome world!

Close Read

1. What is special about the pine tree? Cite details in the first paragraph to support your answer. One detail has been boxed.

2. Find three details in lines 14–32 that suggest just how challenging Sylvia's climb is. What might her climb symbolize?

3. Consider Sylvia's decision to protect the bird, as well as the symbolic meanings of the tree and the climb. What might the writer be saying about how people should treat their natural surroundings?

Part 2: Identify Theme

Sometimes the theme of a story is stated directly by a character or the narrator. Most of the time, however, the theme is implied, and readers must analyze elements in the text—for example, the setting, the characters, and the symbols—to uncover the story's deeper meaning. Use the questions shown to identify and analyze the theme of any story you read.

CLUES TO THEME

TITLE

The title may refer to a significant idea explored in the story. Ask

- To what in the story does the title refer?
- What ideas or symbols does the title highlight?
- Does the title have more than one meaning?

CHARACTERS

Characters' actions and motivations may reflect the message of the story. Ask

- What are the main character's key traits and motivations? Consider how the writer might want readers to feel about the character.
- How does the main character change?
- What lessons does the character learn?

PLOT AND CONFLICT

A story revolves around conflicts that are central to the theme. Ask

- What is the main conflict in the story?
- How is the conflict resolved?
- Is the resolution portrayed as a positive or a negative outcome?

SETTING

The setting's significance to the characters and the conflict can suggest the theme. Ask

- How does the setting influence the characters?
- How does the setting affect the plot?
- What larger idea or issue might the setting represent?

IMPORTANT STATEMENTS

The narrator or the characters may make statements that hint at the theme. Ask

- What key comments do the characters or the narrator make? Take note of statements about values and ideas.
- What message or attitude about life do these statements reveal?

SYMBOLS

Symbols can powerfully reinforce the theme. Ask

- What characters, objects, places, or events have symbolic significance in the story?
- What ideas do these symbols communicate?

Remember, some works of literature have more than one theme, but typically only one is dominant. When you describe a theme of a work, be sure to use one or two complete sentences, not single words or phrases. For example, "love" expresses a topic, not a theme. "People often find love where they least expect it," however, is a valid way to state a theme.

Part 3: Analyze the Literature

As you read the following story, use the questions provided to help you identify the theme and understand the symbolism of the cranes.

CRANES

Short story by **Hwang Sunwŏn**

BACKGROUND This story takes place at the end of the Korean War (1950–1953), a civil war that pitted the Communist government of North Korea against the more democratic government of South Korea. At the end of World War II, the Korean peninsula had been divided along the line of 38° north latitude, commonly called the 38th parallel. During the Korean War, intense fighting along this border shifted control of nearby villages back and forth between the North Koreans and South Koreans. One of these villages is the setting of "Cranes."

The northern village lay snug beneath the high, bright autumn sky, near the border at the Thirty-eighth Parallel.

White gourds lay one against the other on the dirt floor of an empty farmhouse. Any village elders who passed by extinguished their bamboo pipes 5 first, and the children, too, turned back some distance off. Their faces were marked with fear.

As a whole, the village showed little damage from the war, but it still did not seem like the same village Sŏngsam[1] had known as a boy.

At the foot of a chestnut grove on the hill behind the village he stopped and 10 climbed a chestnut tree. Somewhere far back in his mind he heard the old man with a wen[2] shout, "You bad boy, climbing up my chestnut tree again!"

The old man must have passed away, for he was not among the few village elders Sŏngsam had met. Holding on to the trunk of the tree, Sŏngsam gazed

---

1. **Sŏngsam** (sŏng′säm′).
2. **wen:** a harmless skin tumor.

Close Read

1. The title of this story is one clue to the theme. As you read, look for details that explain the significance of birds known as cranes.

2. The boxed details describe a peaceful setting—not one you might expect in a story about war. Which details in lines 1–8 suggest that the residents are unsettled by their seemingly calm surroundings?

up at the blue sky for a time. Some chestnuts fell to the ground as the dry
15 clusters opened of their own accord.

A young man stood, his hands bound, before a farmhouse that had been
converted into a Public Peace Police office. He seemed to be a stranger, so
Sŏngsam went up for a closer look. He was stunned: this young man was
none other than his boyhood playmate, Tŏkchae.[3]

20 Sŏngsam asked the police officer who had come with him from
Ch'ŏnt'ae[4] for an explanation. The prisoner was the vice-chairman of
the Farmers' Communist League and had just been flushed[5] out of
hiding in his own house, Sŏngsam learned.

Sŏngsam sat down on the dirt floor and lit a cigaret.
25 Tŏkchae was to be escorted to Ch'ŏngdan[6] by one of the peace police.
After a time, Sŏngsam lit a new cigaret from the first and stood up.
"I'll take him with me."

Tŏkchae averted his face and refused to look at Sŏngsam. The two left
the village.
30 Sŏngsam went on smoking, but the tobacco had no flavor. He just kept
drawing the smoke in and blowing it out. Then suddenly he thought that
Tŏkchae, too, must want a puff. He thought of the days when they had shared
dried gourd leaves behind sheltering walls, hidden from the adults' view. But
today, how could he offer a cigaret to a fellow like this?

35 *O*nce, when they were small, he went with Tŏkchae to steal some chestnuts
from the old man with the wen. It was Sŏngsam's turn to climb the tree.
Suddenly the old man began shouting. Sŏngsam slipped and fell to the ground.
He got chestnut burrs all over his bottom, but he kept on running. Only when
the two had reached a safe place where the old man could not overtake them
40 did Sŏngsam turn his bottom to Tŏkchae. The burrs hurt so much as they
were plucked out that Sŏngsam could not keep tears from welling up in his
eyes. Tŏkchae produced a fistful of chestnuts from his pocket and thrust them
into Sŏngsam's . . . Sŏngsam threw away the cigaret he had just lit, and then
made up his mind not to light another while he was escorting Tŏkchae.

---

3. **Tŏkchae** (tək'jă').
4. **Ch'ŏnt'ae** (chən'tă').
5. **flushed:** driven from hiding.
6. **Ch'ŏngdan** (chəng'dän').

Close Read

3. What do you think motivates Sŏngsam to take Tŏkchae with him? Explain your answer.

4. What does Sŏngsam's flashback to his childhood in lines 35–43 tell you about Tŏkchae's character and their friendship?

45   They reached the pass at the hill where he and Tŏkchae had cut fodder[7] for
cows until Sŏngsam had to move to a spot near Ch'ŏnt'ae, south of the Thirty-
eighth Parallel, two years before the liberation.
       Sŏngsam felt a sudden surge of anger in spite of himself and shouted, "So
how many have you killed?"
50   For the first time, Tŏkchae cast a quick glance at him and then looked away.
       "You! How many have you killed?" he asked again.
       Tŏkchae looked at him again and glared. The glare grew intense, and his
mouth twitched.
       "So you managed to kill quite a few, eh?" Sŏngsam felt his mind becoming
55 clear of itself, as if some obstruction had been removed. "If you were vice-
chairman of the Communist League, why didn't you run? You must have been
lying low with a secret mission."
       Tŏkchae did not reply.
       "Speak up. What was your mission?"
60   Tŏkchae kept walking. Tŏkchae was hiding something, Sŏngsam thought.
He wanted to take a good look at him, but Tŏkchae kept his face averted.
       Fingering the revolver at his side, Sŏngsam went on: "There's no need to
make excuses. You're going to be shot anyway. Why don't you tell the truth
here and now?"
65   "I'm not going to make any excuses. They made me vice-chairman of the
League because I was a hardworking farmer and one of the poorest. If that's a
capital offense,[8] so be it. I'm still what I used to be—the only thing I'm good at
is tilling the soil." After a short pause, he added, "My old man is bedridden at
home. He's been ill almost half a year." Tŏkchae's father was a widower, a poor,
70 hardworking farmer who lived only for his son. Seven years before his back had
given out, and he had contracted a skin disease.
       "Are you married?"
       "Yes," Tŏkchae replied after a time.
       "To whom?"
75   "Shorty."
       "To Shorty?" How interesting! A woman so small and plump that she knew
the earth's vastness, but not the sky's height. Such a cold fish! He and Tŏkchae
had teased her and made her cry. And Tŏkchae had married her!
       "How many kids?"
80   "The first is arriving this fall, she says."
       Sŏngsam had difficulty swallowing a laugh that he was about to let burst
forth in spite of himself. Although he had asked how many children Tŏkchae

---

7. **fodder:** coarsely chopped hay or straw used as food for farm animals.

8. **capital offense:** a crime calling for the death penalty.

Close Read

5. Reread lines 45–64. How has the war affected Sŏngsam's opinion of his former friend? Cite details that helped you to understand Sŏngsam's view of Tŏkchae.

6. What details in lines 65–80 remind Sŏngsam that Tŏkchae has a human side? One detail has been boxed.

had, he could not help wanting to break out laughing at the thought of the wife sitting there with her huge stomach, one span around. But he realized that this was no time for joking.

"Anyway, it's strange you didn't run away."

"I tried to escape. They said that once the South invaded, not a man would be spared. So all of us between seventeen and forty were taken to the North. I thought of evacuating, even if I had to carry my father on my back. But Father said no. How could we farmers leave the land behind when the crops were ready for harvesting? He grew old on that farm depending on me as the prop and the mainstay of the family. I wanted to be with him in his last moments so I could close his eyes with my own hand. Besides, where can farmers like us go, when all we know how to do is live on the land?"

Sŏngsam had had to flee the previous June. At night he had broken the news privately to his father. But his father had said the same thing: Where could a farmer go, leaving all the chores behind? So Sŏngsam had left alone. Roaming about the strange streets and villages in the South, Sŏngsam had been haunted by thoughts of his old parents and the young children, who had been left with all the chores. Fortunately, his family had been safe then, as it was now.

They had crossed over a hill. This time Sŏngsam walked with his face averted. The autumn sun was hot on his forehead. This was an ideal day for the harvest, he thought.

When they reached the foot of the hill, Sŏngsam gradually came to a halt. In the middle of a field he espied a group of cranes that resembled men in white, all bent over. This had been the demilitarized zone[9] along the Thirty-eighth Parallel. The cranes were still living here, as before, though the people were all gone.

Once, when Sŏngsam and Tŏkchae were about twelve, they had set a trap here, unbeknown to the adults, and caught a crane, a Tanjŏng crane.[10] They had tied the crane up, even binding its wings, and paid it daily visits, patting its neck and riding on its back. Then one day they overheard the neighbors whispering: someone had come from Seoul[11] with a permit from the governor-general's office to catch cranes as some kind of specimens. Then and there

Close Read

7. Line 101 marks a change in Sŏngsam's behavior. What does this change reveal about what's going on inside him? Reread lines 95–100 and explain what motivates the change.

---

9. **demilitarized zone:** an area—generally one separating two hostile nations or armies—from which military forces are prohibited.

10. **Tanjŏng** (tän′jəng′) **crane:** a type of crane found in Asia.

11. **Seoul** (sōl): the capital and largest city of South Korea.

115 the two boys had dashed off to the field. That they would be found out and punished had no longer mattered; all they cared about was the fate of their crane. Without a moment's delay, still out of breath from running, they untied the crane's feet and wings, but the bird could hardly walk. It must have been weak from having been bound.

120 The two helped the crane up. Then, suddenly, they heard a gunshot. The crane fluttered its wings once or twice and then sank back to the ground.

  The boys thought their crane had been shot. But the next moment, as another crane from a nearby bush fluttered its wings, the boys' crane stretched its long neck, gave out a whoop, and disappeared into the sky. For a long while

125 the two boys could not tear their eyes away from the blue sky up into which their crane had soared.

  "Hey, why don't we stop here for a crane hunt?" Sŏngsam said suddenly. Tŏkchae was dumbfounded.

  "I'll make a trap with this rope; you flush a crane over here."

130 Sŏngsam had untied Tŏkchae's hands and was already crawling through the weeds.

  Tŏkchae's face whitened. "You're sure to be shot anyway"—these words flashed through his mind. Any instant a bullet would come flying from Sŏngsam's direction, Tŏkchae thought.

135 Some paces away, Sŏngsam quickly turned toward him.

  "Hey, how come you're standing there like a dummy? Go flush a crane!"

  Only then did Tŏkchae understand. He began crawling through the weeds.

  A pair of Tanjŏng cranes soared high into the clear blue autumn sky, flapping their huge wings.

Translated by Peter H. Lee

Close Read

8. In what ways is Tŏkchae like the crane? Cite specific descriptions of the crane that could also apply to Tŏkchae.

9. Why does Sŏngsam push Tŏkchae to flush a crane?

10. What might the two cranes symbolize? Use details from the text to support your answer.

11. Considering the clues in the story, what do you think the writer is saying about friendship? State the story's theme and cite details that helped you arrive at your conclusion.

The Interlopers
Short Story by Saki

What's wrong with holding a GRUDGE?

OHIO STANDARDS

READING STANDARDS
2.3 Monitor comprehension
4.4 Interpret universal themes

KEY IDEA Both history and literature are full of individuals who bear **grudges,** or feelings of great resentment, against others. Recall, for example, the Montagues and Capulets—Romeo and Juliet's warring relatives. In "The Interlopers," you will read about two neighboring families whose ongoing feud has dire consequences.

ROLE-PLAY With a partner, imagine a scenario in which a long-standing grudge exists between the two of you. Think about what your relationship once involved. For example, maybe you were teammates or best friends. Also consider what event led to your disagreement. Then role-play a chance meeting. How do you behave toward each other? Do you remain angry or make up? Afterward, discuss what the hazards of holding the grudge have been.

LITERARY ANALYSIS: THEME AND SETTING

In a short story, a **theme** is a message about life or human nature that the writer wants to communicate to readers. Often, the **setting** of a story, or where and when it takes place, helps convey this message. To understand how setting might contribute to theme, ask yourself the following questions:

- What aspects of the setting are emphasized?
- How does the setting affect the characters?
- How does the setting relate to the story's main conflict?

"The Interlopers" takes place in a forest whose ownership has been disputed by two families for generations. As you read, think about what Saki is saying about human nature and how the story's setting helps make this message clear.

READING STRATEGY: MONITOR

Good readers automatically check, or **monitor,** their comprehension of what they read. One way they accomplish this is by **clarifying** difficult passages. Strategies such as rereading, reading aloud, and summarizing can make tough parts easier to understand.

As you read "The Interlopers," make sure to stop and clarify those points in the story that are confusing to you. Use a chart like the one shown to help you.

| Confusing Passage | → | How I Clarified My Understanding | → | My New Understanding |

VOCABULARY IN CONTEXT

Saki uses the following words to tell his tale of resentments and greed. Categorize each word as "Know Well," "Think I Know," or "Don't Know." Then write a brief definition of each word you are familiar with.

WORD LIST		
acquiesce	languor	pinioned
condolence	marauder	precipitous
draft	pestilential	succor
interloper		

Know Well	Think I Know	Don't Know

Author Online

Saki
1870–1916

Full of Surprises
"Saki" (sä'kē) was the pen name of Hector Hugh Munro, a British fiction writer of the early 20th century. He was considered one of the finest wits and storytellers of his generation. Written in the years leading up to World War I, his works convey the mixed sentiments of the time. Many of his short stories are **satires,** darkly humorous pieces that reveal flaws in social customs and institutions. Like the fiction of American icon O. Henry, Saki's narratives often feature surprise endings.

A World Traveler At the age of 32, Saki began a long career as a newspaper correspondent. While on assignment, he lived in various places, including the Balkans, Russia, and France. In 1908, after his father died, Saki settled in London. There, at the age of 38, he began to write fiction, incorporating many of the exotic places he had visited into his works. For example, "The Interlopers" is set in the Carpathians, a mountain range in eastern Europe that Saki knew through his many journeys.

A Tragic End Unfortunately, Saki's career as a fiction writer was short-lived. Following the outbreak of World War I, he enlisted in the British army. "I have always looked forward to the romance of a European war," he once remarked. In November 1916, he was killed by a German sniper during an attack at Beaumont-Hamel, France. He was 46 years old.

MORE ABOUT THE AUTHOR
For more on Saki, visit the **Literature Center** at **ClassZone.com.**

THE
Interlopers

SAKI

In a forest of mixed growth somewhere on the eastern spurs of the Carpathians,[1] a man stood one winter night watching and listening, as though he waited for some beast of the woods to come within the range of his vision, and, later, of his rifle. But the game[2] for whose presence he kept so keen an outlook was none that figured in the sportman's calendar as lawful and proper for the chase; Ulrich von Gradwitz[3] patrolled the dark forest in quest of a human enemy. **Ⓐ**

The forest lands of Gradwitz were of wide extent and well stocked with game; the narrow strip of **precipitous** woodland that lay on its outskirt was not remarkable for the game it harbored or the shooting it afforded, but it was the most jealously guarded of all its owner's territorial possessions. A famous lawsuit, in the days of his grandfather, had wrested it from the illegal possession of a neighboring family of petty landowners; the dispossessed party had never **acquiesced** in the judgment of the Courts, and a long series of poaching affrays[4] and similar scandals had embittered the relationships between the families for three generations. The neighbor feud had grown into a personal one since Ulrich had come to be head of his family; if there was a

interloper (ĭn'tər-lō'pər) *n.* one that intrudes in a place, situation, or activity

Ⓐ **THEME AND SETTING**
What aspects of the story's natural setting are emphasized in this introductory paragraph?

precipitous (prĭ-sĭp'ĭ-təs) *adj.* extremely steep

acquiesce (ăk'wē-ĕs') *v.* to agree or give in to

---

1. **eastern spurs of the Carpathians** (kär-pā'thē-ənz): the edges of a mountain range in central Europe.
2. **game:** animals hunted for food or sport.
3. **Ulrich von Gradwitz** (ōōl'rĭкн fôn gräd'vĭts).
4. **poaching affrays** (ə-frāz'): noisy quarrels about hunting on someone else's property.

396   UNIT 4: THEME

man in the world whom he detested and wished ill to it was Georg Znaeym,[5] the inheritor of the quarrel and the tireless game-snatcher and raider of the disputed border-forest. The feud might, perhaps, have died down or been

20 compromised if the personal ill-will of the two men had not stood in the way; as boys they had thirsted for one another's blood, as men each prayed that misfortune might fall on the other, and this wind-scourged winter night Ulrich had banded together his foresters to watch the dark forest, not in quest of four-footed quarry, but to keep a lookout for the prowling thieves whom he suspected of being afoot from across the land boundary. The roebuck,[6] which usually kept in the sheltered hollows during a storm wind, were running like driven things tonight, and there was movement and unrest among the creatures that were wont to sleep through the dark hours. Assuredly there was a disturbing element in the forest, and Ulrich could guess the quarter from

30 whence it came. **B**

He strayed away by himself from the watchers whom he had placed in ambush on the crest of the hill, and wandered far down the steep slopes amid the wild tangle of undergrowth, peering through the tree trunks and listening through the whistling and skirling[7] of the wind and the restless beating of the branches for sight or sound of the **marauders.** If only on this wild night, in this dark, lone spot, he might come across Georg Znaeym, man to man, with none to witness—that was the wish that was uppermost in his thoughts. And as he stepped around the trunk of a huge beech, he came face to face with the man he sought.

40 The two enemies stood glaring at one another for a long silent moment.

Each had a rifle in his hand, each had hate in his heart and murder uppermost in his mind. The chance had come to give full play to the passions of a lifetime. But a man who has been brought up under the code of a restraining civilization cannot easily nerve himself to shoot down his neighbor in cold blood and without a word spoken, except for an offense against his hearth and honor. And before the moment of hesitation had given way to action a deed of Nature's own violence overwhelmed them both. A fierce shriek of the storm had been answered by a splitting crash over their heads, and ere they could leap aside a mass of falling beech tree had thundered down on

50 them. Ulrich von Gradwitz found himself stretched on the ground, one arm numb beneath him and the other held almost as helplessly in a tight tangle of forked branches, while both legs were pinned beneath the fallen mass. His heavy shooting boots had saved his feet from being crushed to pieces, but if his fractures were not as serious as they might have been, at least it was evident that he could not move from his present position till someone came to release him. The descending twigs had slashed the skin of his face, and he had to wink away some drops of blood from his eyelashes before he could take in a general

B MONITOR
Clarify your understanding of why Ulrich and Georg are enemies by rereading or reading aloud lines 7–30.

marauder (mə-rôd′ər) *n.* one who raids and loots

---

5. **Georg Znaeym** (gā-ôrg′ tsnā′ēm).

6. **roebuck:** a male roe deer.

7. **skirling:** a shrill cry or sound.

view of the disaster. At his side, so near that under ordinary circumstances he could almost have touched him, lay Georg Znaeym, alive and struggling, but
60 obviously as helplessly **pinioned** down as himself. All around them lay a thick-strewn wreckage of splintered branches and broken twigs. **⊙**

Relief at being alive and exasperation at his captive plight brought a strange medley of pious thank offerings and sharp curses to Ulrich's lips. Georg, who was nearly blinded with the blood which trickled across his eyes, stopped his struggling for a moment to listen, and then gave a short, snarling laugh.

"So you're not killed, as you ought to be, but you're caught, anyway," he cried; "caught fast. Ho, what a jest, Ulrich von Gradwitz snared in his stolen forest. There's real justice for you!"

And he laughed again, mockingly and savagely.

pinioned (pĭn'yənd) *adj.* restrained or immobilized
pinion *v.*

⊙ THEME AND SETTING
How does the natural setting, particularly the fallen tree, affect Ulrich and Georg?

70   "I'm caught in my own forest land," retorted Ulrich. "When my men come to release us, you will wish, perhaps, that you were in a better plight than caught poaching on a neighbor's land, shame on you." **D**

    Georg was silent for a moment; then he answered quietly.

    "Are you sure that your men will find much to release? I have men, too, in the forest tonight, close behind me, and they will be here first and do the releasing. When they drag me out from under these branches, it won't need much clumsiness on their part to roll this mass of trunk right over on the top of you. Your men will find you dead under a fallen beech tree. For form's sake I shall send my **condolences** to your family."

80   "It is a useful hint," said Ulrich fiercely. "My men had orders to follow in ten minutes' time, seven of which must have gone by already, and when they get me out—I will remember the hint. Only as you will have met your death poaching on my lands, I don't think I can decently send any message of condolence to your family."

    "Good," snarled Georg, "good. We fight this quarrel out to the death, you and I and our foresters, with no cursed interlopers to come between us. Death . . . to you, Ulrich von Gradwitz."

    "The same to you, Georg Znaeym, forest thief, game-snatcher." **E**

    Both men spoke with the bitterness of possible defeat before them, for each
90 knew that it might be long before his men would seek him out or find him; it was a bare matter of chance which party would arrive first on the scene.

    Both had now given up the useless struggle to free themselves from the mass of wood that held them down; Ulrich limited his endeavors to an effort to bring his one partially free arm near enough to his outer coat pocket to draw out his wine flask. Even when he had accomplished that operation, it was long before he could manage the unscrewing of the stopper or get any of the liquid down his throat. But what a heaven-sent **draft** it seemed! It was an open winter,[8] and little snow had fallen as yet, hence the captives suffered less from the cold than might have been the case at that season of the year; nevertheless,
100 the wine was warming and reviving to the wounded man, and he looked across with something like a throb of pity to where his enemy lay, just keeping the groans of pain and weariness from crossing his lips.

    "Could you reach this flask if I threw it over to you?" asked Ulrich suddenly; "there is good wine in it, and one may as well be as comfortable as one can. Let us drink, even if tonight one of us dies."

    "No, I can scarcely see anything; there is so much blood caked around my eyes," said Georg, "and in any case I don't drink wine with an enemy."

    Ulrich was silent for a few minutes and lay listening to the weary screeching of the wind. An idea was slowly forming and growing in his brain, an idea that
110 gained strength every time that he looked across at the man who was fighting

D **GRAMMAR AND STYLE**
Reread lines 70–72. Saki uses the **subordinate clause** "When my men come to release us" to tell how Ulrich thinks he will be rescued.

condolence (kən-dō'ləns) *n.* an expression of sympathy

E **MONITOR**
Summarize in one or two sentences what each man threatens to do if rescued.

draft (drăft) *n.* a gulp or swallow

---

8. **open winter:** a mild winter.

so grimly against pain and exhaustion. In the pain and **languor** that Ulrich himself was feeling the old fierce hatred seemed to be dying down. **F**

"Neighbor," he said presently, "do as you please if your men come first. It was a fair compact. But as for me, I've changed my mind. If my men are the first to come, you shall be the first to be helped, as though you were my guest. We have quarreled like devils all our lives over this stupid strip of forest, where the trees can't even stand upright in a breath of wind. Lying here tonight, thinking, I've come to think we've been rather fools; there are better things in life than getting the better of a boundary dispute. Neighbor, if you will help
120 me to bury the old quarrel I—I will ask you to be my friend."

Georg Znaeym was silent for so long that Ulrich thought, perhaps, he had fainted with the pain of his injuries. Then he spoke slowly and in jerks.

"How the whole region would stare and gabble if we rode into the market square together. No one living can remember seeing a Znaeym and a von Gradwitz talking to one another in friendship. And what peace there would be among the forester folk if we ended our feud tonight. And if we choose to make peace among our people, there is none other to interfere, no interlopers from outside. . . . You would come and keep the Sylvester night[9] beneath my roof, and I would come and feast on some high day at your castle. . . . I would
130 never fire a shot on your land, save when you invited me as a guest; and you should come and shoot with me down in the marshes where the wildfowl are. In all the countryside there are none that could hinder if we willed to make peace. I never thought to have wanted to do other than hate you all my life, but I think I have changed my mind about things too, this last half-hour. And you offered me your wine flask. . . . Ulrich von Gradwitz, I will be your friend."

For a space both men were silent, turning over in their minds the wonderful changes that this dramatic reconciliation would bring about. In the cold, gloomy forest, with the wind tearing in fitful gusts through the naked branches and whistling around the tree trunks, they lay and waited for the help that
140 would now bring release and **succor** to both parties. And each prayed a private prayer that his men might be the first to arrive, so that he might be the first to show honorable attention to the enemy that had become a friend. **G**

Presently, as the wind dropped for a moment, Ulrich broke silence.

"Let's shout for help," he said; "in this lull our voices may carry a little way."

"They won't carry far through the trees and undergrowth," said Georg, "but we can try. Together, then."

The two raised their voices in a prolonged hunting call.

"Together again," said Ulrich a few minutes later, after listening in vain for an answer halloo.
150 "I heard something that time, I think," said Ulrich.

"I heard nothing but the **pestilential** wind," said Georg hoarsely.

---

9. **Sylvester night:** New Year's Eve, the feast day of Saint Sylvester (Pope Sylvester I).

languor (lăng'gər) *n.* a lack of feeling or energy

F THEME AND SETTING
In what ways are Ulrich's actions influenced by the natural setting and its conditions? Cite specifics from lines 92–112.

succor (sŭk'ər) *n.* help in a difficult situation

G THEME AND SETTING
Reread lines 113–142. How has the setting brought about changes in the **conflict** between Ulrich and Georg?

pestilential (pĕs'tə-lĕn'shəl) *adj.* likely to spread and cause disease

There was silence again for some minutes, and then Ulrich gave a joyful cry.

"I can see figures coming through the wood. They are following in the way I came down the hillside."

Both men raised their voices in as loud a shout as they could muster.

"They hear us! They've stopped. Now they see us. They're running down the hill towards us," cried Ulrich.

"How many of them are there?" asked Georg.

"I can't see distinctly," said Ulrich; "nine or ten."

160   "Then they are yours," said Georg; "I had only seven out with me."

"They are making all the speed they can, brave lads," said Ulrich gladly.

"Are they your men?" asked Georg. "Are they your men?"

"No," said Ulrich with a laugh, the idiotic chattering laugh of a man unstrung with hideous fear.

"Who are they?" asked Georg quickly, straining his eyes to see what the other would gladly not have seen.

"*Wolves.*" ✺ Ⓗ

Ⓗ **THEME AND SETTING**
How does nature seem to get the better of Ulrich and Georg at the story's conclusion?

ANALYZE VISUALS
Review the photographs in this lesson. What **mood** do they help create?

Comprehension

OHIO
STANDARDS

READING STANDARD
2.3 Monitor comprehension

1. **Recall** Why is Ulrich in the forest?

2. **Recall** Why are the von Gradwitz and Znaeym families fighting?

3. **Summarize** What happens to Ulrich and Georg when they are in the forest?

Literary Analysis

4. **Identify Conflict** Use a chart like the one shown to record an example of each kind of conflict found in the story. Then explain the nature of the conflict.

Kind of Conflict	Example from the Story	Explanation
Character vs. character		
Character vs. nature		
Character vs. self		

5. **Analyze Climax** Identify the climax of the story. How do Ulrich and Georg begin to change at this **turning point?** Cite evidence to support your claim.

6. **Understand Irony** A contrast between what is expected and what really occurs is called irony. Think about what you thought would happen at the conclusion of "The Interlopers" and what actually does happen. How is the ending of the story ironic?

7. **Interpret Title** Who or what are the interlopers? Give two interpretations of the story's title.

8. **Examine Theme and Setting** Think about the story's setting and the way it affects Ulrich and Georg. What theme related to setting do you think Saki communicates in the story? Cite evidence to support your claim.

9. **Monitor** Review the chart you created as you read. How has clarifying your reading helped you to better understand the story? Offer two personal examples to support your answer.

10. **Evaluate** Consider why the **grudge** that Ulrich and Georg hold is long-standing. Considering your own experiences, do you find the two men's feelings believable? Explain.

Literary Criticism

11. **Critical Interpretations** "Saki came to the short story as a satirist," argues one literary critic, "and never averted his eye from the darker side of human nature, a place where not only social ineptness, pomposity, and foolishness are rooted but criminality as well." What human vices or follies does Saki ridicule in the story?

Vocabulary in Context

VOCABULARY PRACTICE

Decide whether each pair of terms are similar or different.

1. precipitous/steep
2. acquiesce/dispute
3. marauder/raider
4. condolence/indifference
5. languor/energy

6. draft/sip
7. succor/assistance
8. pestilential/healthful
9. interloper/guest
10. pinioned/pinned down

VOCABULARY IN WRITING

Write three questions you might ask Ulrich and Georg about why they chose friendship over hatred. Use at least three vocabulary words. Here is an example.

> **EXAMPLE SENTENCE**
>
> In the end, why did both of you **acquiesce** in becoming friends instead of remaining enemies?

VOCABULARY STRATEGY: CONNOTATION

The term *connotation* refers to an attitude or feeling connected to a word. For example, *languor* and *sluggishness* could both be defined as "a lack of physical or mental energy," but Saki's use of *languor* to describe Ulrich's condition connotes a dreaminess not associated with *sluggishness*. Writers are aware of the connotations of words and often use them to evoke specific feelings or moods.

PRACTICE Place the words in each group on a continuum to show the positive, negative, or neutral connotations associated with each word. Then compare your answers with those of a classmate.

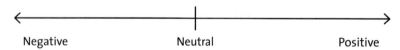

Negative   Neutral   Positive

1. pale, pasty, fair
2. exotic, strange, unusual
3. flimsy, light, feathery
4. brilliance, brightness, glare
5. discriminating, picky, selective

OHIO STANDARDS

VOCABULARY STANDARD
1.2 Analyze the relationships of pairs of words

VOCABULARY PRACTICE
For more practice, go to the **Vocabulary Center** at **ClassZone.com.**

Reading-Writing Connection

Explore the topics of context and theme in "The Interlopers" by responding to these prompts. Then use **Revision: Grammar and Style** to improve your writing.

WRITING PROMPTS	SELF-CHECK
A. Short Response: Analyze Context Saki wrote "The Interlopers" while he was fighting in World War I. How might this historical context be reflected in the story? Drawing on story details and your own prior knowledge, write a **one- or two-paragraph response.**	***A skillful response will . . .*** • mention three details that might reflect the war • organize your ideas in a coherent, logical way
B. Extended Response: Analyze Theme In the story, Saki cleverly explores the theme of hunting. In **three to five paragraphs,** analyze the message Saki conveys about hunters and their prey.	***An effective analysis will . . .*** • cite specific details that support your claims • name more than one hunter and type of prey

REVISION: GRAMMAR AND STYLE

IMPROVE SENTENCE FLOW Review the **Grammar and Style** note on page 400. Saki uses subordinate clauses to vary his sentence structures and add important details. A **subordinate** (or **dependent**) **clause** contains a subject and a verb but does not express a complete thought as a sentence does. Subordinate clauses answer the questions *how, how many, how much, to what degree, what kind, which one, why, when,* and *where.* They may be introduced by words like *because, if, since, when, where, who,* and *whom.* Here are three examples of subordinate clauses from the story:

> *The neighbor feud had grown into a personal one since Ulrich had come to be head of his family; if there was a man in the world whom he detested and wished ill to it was Georg Znaeym. . . .* (lines 15–17)

Notice how the revisions in red use subordinate clauses to join sentences. This improves the flow of the sentences and adds details to this first draft. Use similar methods to revise your responses to the prompts.

OHIO STANDARDS

WRITING STANDARD
7.3 Use clauses and phrases

> **STUDENT MODEL**
>
> Ulrich and Georg are enemies. ~~They~~ ^{who} have held a grudge against each other
>
> for a long time. ^{When}They meet in the forest. The old war picks up where it left
>
> off. ^{If} A tree ~~falls~~ ^{hadn't first fallen} on top of them, ~~Otherwise,~~ they might have killed each
>
> other immediately.

WRITING TOOLS
For prewriting, revision, and editing tools, visit the **Writing Center** at ClassZone.com.

Two Friends

Short Story by Guy de Maupassant

What would you do *for a* FRIEND?

OHIO STANDARDS

READING STANDARDS
4.1 Compare and contrast an author's use of direct and indirect characterization

4.9 Explain how authors use symbols to create broader meanings

KEY IDEA Faced with a life-or-death situation, do people who have a close **friendship** come to each other's aid? Or do they only worry about saving their own skins? In this short story, you will meet two men who remain true to each other in the face of great peril.

QUICKWRITE With a group, list meaningful acts of friendship you've witnessed or experienced. Add to or delete from the list that is shown. Then write a paragraph describing how far you would go for your closest friends.

Acts of Friendship
1. Rescued friend from a dangerous situation
2. Consoled friend when his grandparent died
3. Enjoyed many summers together at camp
4.
5.

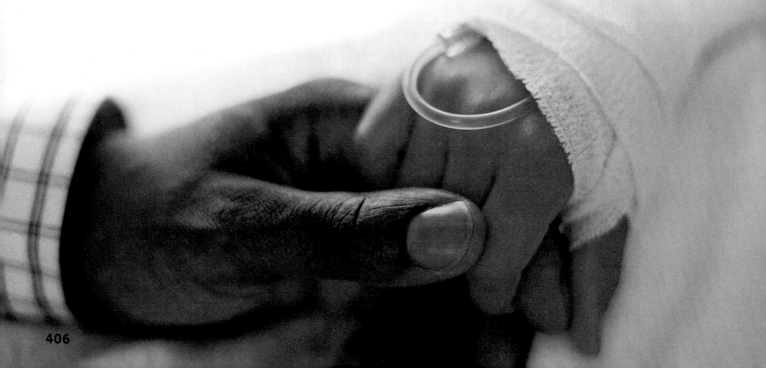

● LITERARY ANALYSIS: SYMBOL

A **symbol** is a person, place, object, or activity that represents something beyond itself. Flags, for example, often serve as symbols of national heritage and patriotism. In literature, a symbol takes its meaning from its context. In "Two Friends," for example, the bleak landscape might be said to symbolize the loss of vitality in France. To identify other symbols in the selection, use these strategies as you read:

- Note what is described at length or repeated.
- Note words that suggest broad ideas about humanity.

Review: **Setting**

● READING SKILL: MAKE INFERENCES ABOUT CHARACTER

Skilled readers **make inferences,** or logical guesses, about characters on the basis of story details and their own knowledge. Sometimes called "reading between the lines," making inferences allows readers to build a more complete understanding of the characters and the entire story.

As you read the selection, pay attention to the details that Maupassant uses to describe the two friends and the Prussian soldiers. Record your inferences about these characters in an organizer like the one shown.

Character Details	+	My Experiences	=	My Inferences
Morrisot fishes every Sunday from early morning until dark.	+	Fishing requires calm, patience, and an enjoyment of the outdoors.	=	Morrisot probably demonstrates all these qualities.

▲ VOCABULARY IN CONTEXT

To see how many vocabulary words you already know, substitute a different word or phrase for each boldfaced term.

1. She sat in her room **dejectedly** after she lost the race.
2. **Fanatical** followers of the band waited hours for tickets.
3. This relaxing vacation has **rejuvenated** my spirits!
4. Why the **pensive** look on your face?
5. The clown's **eccentric** costume made the children laugh.
6. This **atrocity** should not go unpunished.
7. This large tree will **afford** some nice shade for our picnic.
8. The child remained **unperturbed** during the storm.

Author Online

Guy de Maupassant
1850–1893

Learning from a Master In 1867, at the age of 17, Guy de Maupassant (gē′ də mō-pă-sän′) met Gustave Flaubert, a family friend and one of France's most respected novelists. Flaubert served as Maupassant's mentor, offering him advice, including the following message: "Whatever you want to say, there is only one word to express it, only one verb to give it movement, only one adjective to qualify it." Maupassant went on to become a celebrated author in his own right.

On Fire! Although Maupassant wrote several novels, his specialty was the short story, a form he helped popularize. From 1880 to 1890, Maupassant enjoyed his most prolific years as an author, remarkably producing 300 stories. His best works are often characterized by precise language and realistic portrayals of everyday life.

 MORE ABOUT THE AUTHOR
For more on Guy de Maupassant, visit the **Literature Center** at **ClassZone.com.**

Background

The Franco-Prussian War For most of the 1800s, Germany was a collection of separate German-speaking states. Among these, the northern state of Prussia emerged as the most powerful. Under the leadership of the Prussian chancellor Otto von Bismarck, the German states began to unite. In July 1870, fearing a unified Germany, Emperor Napoleon III of France began what was later called the Franco-Prussian War. "Two Friends" takes place in 1871, while Paris is under siege, or attack, by the Prussian army. The story reflects Maupassant's firsthand experiences of the war, in which he fought briefly as a young French soldier.

Two Friends

Guy de Maupassant

Paris was under siege, in the grip of famine, at its last gasp. There were few sparrows on the rooftops now, and even the sewers were losing some of their inhabitants. The fact is that people were eating anything they could get their hands on.

One bright January morning Monsieur Morissot[1] was strolling **dejectedly** along one of the outer boulevards, with an empty stomach and his hands in the pockets of his old army trousers. He was a watchmaker by trade and a man who liked to make the most of his leisure. Suddenly, he came upon one of his close friends, and he stopped short. It was Monsieur Sauvage,[2] whom he had
10 got to know on fishing expeditions.

Every Sunday before the war it was Morissot's custom to set off at the crack of dawn with his bamboo rod in his hand and a tin box slung over his back. He would catch the Argenteuil train and get off at Colombes, from where he would walk to the island of Marante. The minute he reached this land of his dreams he would start to fish—and he would go on fishing till it got dark.

And it was here, every Sunday, that he met a tubby, jolly little man by the name of Sauvage. He was a haberdasher[3] from the Rue Notre-Dame-de-Lorette, and as **fanatical** an angler[4] as Morissot himself. They often spent half the day sitting side by side, rod in hand, with their feet dangling over
20 the water. And they had become firm friends.

There were some days when they hardly spoke to each other. On other occasions they would chat all the time. But they understood each other perfectly without needing to exchange any words, because their tastes were so alike and their feelings identical. **A**

---

1. **Monsieur Morissot** (mə-syœ' mô-rē-sō').
2. **Sauvage** (sō-väzh').
3. **haberdasher:** one who sells men's clothing, such as shirts, hats, and gloves.
4. **angler:** a fisherman.

Detail of *At the Inn of Mother Anthony* (1866), Pierre Auguste Renoir. Oil on canvas. National Museum, Stockholm, Sweden. Photo © The Bridgeman Art Library.

On spring mornings at about ten o'clock, when the **rejuvenated** sun sent floating over the river that light mist which moves along with the current, warming the backs of the two enthusiastic fishermen with the welcome glow of a new season, Morissot would say to his neighbor:

"Ah! It's grand here, isn't it?"

30   And Monsieur Sauvage would reply:

"There's nothing I like better."

This simple exchange of words was all that was needed for them to understand each other and confirm their mutual appreciation.

In the autumn towards the close of day, when the sky was blood-red and the water reflected strange shapes of scarlet clouds which reddened the whole river, and the glowing sun set the distant horizon ablaze, making the two friends look as though they were on fire, and touching with gold the russet leaves which were already trembling with a wintry shudder, Monsieur Sauvage would turn to Morissot with a smile and say:

40   "What a marvelous sight!"

And Morissot, equally taken up with the wonder of it all, but not taking his eyes off his float, would answer:

"It's better than walking down the boulevards, eh?" **B**

As soon as the two friends had recognized each other, they shook hands warmly, feeling quite emotional over the fact that they had come across each other in such different circumstances. Monsieur Sauvage gave a sigh and remarked:

"What a lot has happened since we last met!"

Morissot, in mournful tones, lamented:

50   "And what awful weather we've been having! This is the first fine day of the year."

And, indeed, the sky was a cloudless blue, brilliant with light.

They started to walk on together side by side, **pensive** and melancholy. Then Morissot said:

"And what about those fishing trips, eh? *There's* something worth remembering!"

"When shall we be able to get back to it?" mused Monsieur Sauvage.

They went into a little café and drank a glass of absinthe.[5] Then they resumed their stroll along the boulevards.

60   Morissot suddenly stopped and said:

"What about another glass of the green stuff, eh?"

"Just as you wish," consented Monsieur Sauvage, and they went into a second bar.

When they came out they both felt very fuzzy, as people do when they drink alcohol on an empty stomach. The weather was very mild. A gentle breeze caressed their faces. **C**

rejuvenated
(rĭ-jōō'və-nā'tĭd) *adj.*
made new or young
again **rejuvenate** *v.*

B SYMBOL
Reread lines 25–43.
Notice that the men's
fishing trips are described
at length and in vivid
detail. What might these
experiences symbolize?

pensive (pĕn'sĭv)
adj. thoughtful in
a wistful, sad way

C MAKE INFERENCES
What inferences can you
make so far about how
the war has affected the
two men?

---

5. **absinthe:** a syrupy green alcoholic beverage that has a licorice flavor.

Monsieur Sauvage, who felt even more fuddled[6] in this warm air, stopped and said:

"What about it, then? Shall we go?"

"Go where?"

"Fishing!"

"But where can we go?"

"To our island, of course. The French frontline is near Colombes. I know the colonel in command—fellow called Dumoulin. I'm sure we'd have no trouble in getting through."

Morissot began to quiver with excitement.

"Right!" he said. "I'm your man!"

And the two friends separated and went off to get their fishing tackle.

An hour later they were striding down the main road together. They reached the villa in which the colonel had set up his headquarters. When he heard their request, he smiled at their **eccentric** enthusiasm but gave them permission. They set off once again, armed with an official pass.

They soon crossed the frontline, then went through Colombes, which had been evacuated, and now found themselves on the fringe of the area of vineyards which rise in terraces above the Seine. It was about eleven o'clock.

On the opposite bank they could see the village of Argenteuil, which looked deserted and dead. The hills of Orgemont and Sannois dominated the horizon, and the great plain which stretches as far as Nanterre was empty, completely empty, with nothing to be seen but its leafless cherry trees and gray earth.

Pointing towards the high ground Monsieur Sauvage muttered:

"The Prussians are up there."

And as the two friends gazed at the deserted countryside, they felt almost paralyzed by the sense of uneasiness which was creeping through them.

The Prussians! They had never so much as set eyes on them, but for four months now they had been aware of their presence on the outskirts of Paris, occupying part of France, looting, committing **atrocities,** reducing people to starvation . . . the invisible yet all-powerful Prussians. As they thought of them, a kind of superstitious dread was added to their natural hatred for this unknown, victorious race.

"What if we should happen to run into some of them?" said Morissot nervously.

Monsieur Sauvage gave the sort of reply which showed that cheerful Parisian banter survived in spite of everything.

"Oh, we'll just offer them some nice fish to fry!"

Even so, they were so worried by the silence of the surrounding countryside that they hesitated about going any further.

It was Monsieur Sauvage who finally made up his mind.

"Come on!" he said. "We'll go on—but we must keep a sharp lookout!" **D**

eccentric (ĭk-sĕn′trĭk) *adj.* strange; peculiar

atrocity (ə-trŏs′ĭ-tē) *n.* a very cruel or brutal act

D MAKE INFERENCES
What does the men's decision to continue their fishing trip reveal about their personalities and view of the world?

---

6. **fuddled:** drunk and confused.

And they scrambled down the slope of one of the vineyards, bent double,
110 crawling on their hands and knees, taking advantage of the cover **afforded** by
the vines, keeping their eyes wide open and their ears on the alert.

All that now separated them from the riverbank was a strip of open ground.
They ran across it, and as soon as they reached the river, they crouched
amongst the dry rushes.

Morissot pressed his ear to the ground to see if he could detect the sound of
marching feet. He could hear nothing. They were alone, completely alone.

They told each other there was nothing to worry about, and started to fish.

Opposite them the deserted island of Marante concealed them from the
other bank. The little building which once housed the restaurant was closed
120 and shuttered, and looked as though it had been abandoned for years.

It was Monsieur Sauvage who caught the first fish—a gudgeon. Morissot
caught the second, and then, almost without a pause, they jerked up their rods
time after time to find a little silvery creature wriggling away on the hook. This
really was a miraculous draft of fishes. **E**

They carefully placed each fish into a fine-meshed net which was suspended
in the water at their feet. And as they did so they were overcome by a
delightful sense of joy, the kind of joy you only experience when you resume
something you really love after being deprived of it for a long time.

afford (ə-fôrd´) *v.*
to provide or offer

E SYMBOL
A gudgeon is both a small
fish used as bait and
a person who is easily
tricked. On the basis of
this information, whom or
what might the gudgeon
symbolize?

Line fishermen, study for *La Grand Jatte* (1883), Georges Seurat. Oil on canvas, 16 cm × 25 cm. Musée d'Art Moderne, Troyes, France.
Photo © Réunion des Musées Nationaux/Art Resource, New York.

A kindly sun was shedding its warmth across their backs. They were so
130 absorbed that they no longer heard, or thought, or paid the least attention to
the outside world. What did anything matter now? They were fishing!

But suddenly, the bank beneath them shook with a dull rumble which
seemed to come from underground.

The distant cannon were starting to fire again.

Morissot turned his head, and above the bank, over to the left, he saw the
great bulk of Mont Valérien. On the mountainside was a white plume of
smoke, showing where the gunpowder had just bellowed out.

Almost immediately another jet of smoke spurted from the fort on the
summit, and a few seconds later the rumble of another detonation reached
140 their ears.

Other cannon shots followed, and every now and then the mountain spat
out its deadly breath, exhaled its clouds of milky vapor, which rose slowly into
the calm sky above. **F**

"There they go again!" said Monsieur Sauvage with a shrug of his shoulders.

Morissot, who was anxiously watching the feather on his float as it bobbed
up and down, was suddenly filled with the anger of a peace-loving man for
these maniacs who indulge in fighting.

"They've got to be really stupid," he growled, "to go on killing each other
like that!"

150 "They're worse than animals," said Monsieur Sauvage.

Morissot, who had just caught another fish, called out:

"And it'll never be any different so long as we have governments!"

"Oh, no," disagreed Monsieur Sauvage. "The Republic⁷ would never have
declared war . . ."

"Look!" interrupted Morissot. "Under kings you have war against other
countries. Under republican governments you have civil war."

And they began to argue, in a calm and friendly way, sorting out all the world's
great political problems with the commonsense approach of mild and reasonable
men. On one point they were in absolute agreement: mankind would never be
160 free. And as they talked, Mont Valérien went thundering on without respite,
demolishing French homes with its cannonades,⁸ pounding lives to dust, crushing
human beings to pulp, putting an end to so many dreams, to so many long-awaited
joys, so much long-expected happiness, tearing into the hearts of all those wives
and daughters and mothers with pain and suffering that would never be eased.

"Such is life," said Monsieur Sauvage.

"Better to call it death," laughed Morissot. **G**

But at that moment they both gave a start, scared by the feeling that
somebody had been walking just behind them. They looked round and saw
standing above them four men, four tall, bearded men, armed to the teeth,

F SETTING
Compare and contrast
this fishing trip with
earlier ones described in
the story. How has the
setting changed?

G MAKE INFERENCES
Reread lines 157–166.
Why is the argument
between Morissot and
Sauvage **ironic?**

---

7. **the Republic:** the Second Republic of France (1848–1852), which was France's first truly
   representative government.

8. **cannonades:** numerous firings of cannons.

170   dressed like liveried[9] footmen, with flat military caps on their heads—and rifles which they were pointing straight at the two friends.

    The fishing rods dropped from their hands and went floating down the river.

    In a matter of seconds they were seized, tied up, hustled along, thrown into a boat and carried across to the island. ◆

    Behind the building which they had thought deserted they saw a group of about twenty German soldiers.

    A sort of hairy giant who was sitting astride a chair and smoking a large clay pipe asked them in excellent French:

180   "Well, messieurs, did the fishing go well?"

    One of the soldiers placed at the officer's feet the net full of fish which he had been careful to bring along. The Prussian smiled and said:

    "Well, well! I can see you didn't do badly at all! . . . But I have to deal with a very different matter. Now, listen to me carefully, and don't get alarmed . . . As far as I am concerned you are a couple of spies sent out here to keep an eye on me. I've caught you and I've every right to shoot you. You were obviously pretending to fish as a cover for your real purposes. It's too bad for you that you've fallen into my hands. But war is war . . . Now, since you've come out here past your own lines, you're bound to have a password so you can get back.

190 Just give me that password and I'll spare your lives." ◼

    The two friends, ghastly pale, stood there side by side with their hands trembling. They said nothing.

    "Nobody will ever get to know about it," continued the officer. "You will go back without any trouble, and the secret will go with you . . . If you refuse to cooperate, you'll die—straight away. So take your choice!"

    They stood there motionless, keeping their mouths firmly shut.

    The Prussian, who was still quite calm, pointed in the direction of the river and said:

    "Just think! In five minutes you'll be at the bottom of that river. In five
200 minutes! You must have families. Think of them!"

    The rumbling of the cannon was still coming from Mont Valérien.

    The two fishermen simply stood there, refusing to speak. The German now gave some orders in his own language. Then he moved his chair some distance away from the prisoners. Twelve men marched up and formed a line twenty yards from them with their rifles at their sides.

    "I'll give you one minute to make up your minds," called the officer. "And not two seconds more."

    Then he jumped to his feet, went up to the two Frenchmen, took Morissot by the arm, and led him to one side. Then he said to him in a very low voice:

210   "Quick! Just let me have that password! Your friend won't know you've told me. I'll make it look as though I've taken pity on you both."

---

9. **liveried:** uniformed.

GRAMMAR AND STYLE
Reread lines 174–175. By using a **compound predicate,** Maupassant is able to describe a series of actions in one concise sentence.

MAKE INFERENCES
What can you infer about the Prussian soldiers from their actions toward the fishermen?

Morissot said nothing.

The Prussian then dragged Monsieur Sauvage to one side and made the same proposition to him.

Monsieur Sauvage said nothing. **J**

So they were pushed together again, side by side.

It was then that Morissot happened to glance down at the net full of gudgeon which was lying in the grass a few yards away.

220 A ray of sunlight fell on the heap of glittering fish, which were still quivering with life. As he looked at them he felt a momentary weakness. In spite of his efforts to hold them back, tears filled his eyes. **K**

"Farewell, Monsieur Sauvage," he mumbled.

And Monsieur Sauvage replied:

"Farewell, Monsieur Morissot."

They shook hands, trembling uncontrollably from head to foot.

"Fire!" shouted the officer.

Twelve shots rang out simultaneously.

Detail of *Execution of the Emperor Maximilian* (1867), Édouard Manet. Oil on canvas, 77¹⁄₈″ × 102¹⁄₄″.
Museum of Fine Arts, Boston. Gift of Mr. and Mrs. Frank Gair Macomber (30.444).

J MAKE INFERENCES
Why do Morissot and Sauvage refuse to offer the Prussian officer a password?

K SYMBOL
Reread lines 216–221. How does this description contribute to your understanding of the fish as a symbol in the story?

Monsieur Sauvage fell like a log onto his face. Morissot, who was taller, swayed, spun round, then collapsed on top of his friend, with his face staring
230 up at the sky and the blood welling from where his coat had been burst open across his chest.

The German shouted out more orders. His men went off and came back with some lengths of rope and a few heavy stones which they fastened to the feet of the two bodies. Then they carried them to the riverbank.

All the time Mont Valérien continued to rumble, and now it was capped by a great mountain of smoke.

Two soldiers got hold of Morissot by the head and feet. Two others lifted up Monsieur Sauvage in the same way. The two bodies were swung violently backwards and forwards, then thrown with great force. They curved through
240 the air, then plunged upright into the river, with the stones dragging them down, feet first.

The water spurted up, bubbled, swirled round, then grew calm again, with little waves rippling across to break against the bank. There was just a small amount of blood discoloring the surface.

The officer, still quite **unperturbed,** said, half aloud:

"Well, now it's the fishes' turn."

As he was going back towards the building, he noticed the net full of gudgeon lying in the grass. He picked it up, looked at the fish, then smiled, and called out:
250 "Wilhelm!"

A soldier came running up. He was wearing a white apron. The Prussian officer threw across to him the catch made by the two executed fishermen, and gave another order:

"Fry me these little creatures—straight away, while they're still alive. They'll be delicious!"

Then he lit his pipe again. ❧

Translated by Arnold Kellett

unperturbed
(ŭn′pər-tûrbd′) *adj.* calm and serene; untroubled

Comprehension

1. **Recall** Who are Morissot and Sauvage?

2. **Recall** How do the wartime conditions affect their habits?

3. **Recall** What prompts the two Frenchmen to cross the frontline of the war?

4. **Summarize** What happens to Morissot and Sauvage as a result of their venturing into enemy territory?

Literary Analysis

5. **Make Inferences** Review the chart you made as you read. Do Morissot and Sauvage seem to understand the dangers of war? Cite evidence to support your answer.

6. **Interpret Symbol** References to fish and fishing are repeated throughout the story. What do they symbolize? To help you interpret their meaning, create a chart like the one shown. Record descriptions of fish and fishing as well as the ideas you associate with them.

Descriptions of Fish/Fishing	Associations

7. **Examine Setting and Theme** Reread lines 25–40 and 118–143. Compare the conditions on the island of Marante before and during the Prussian occupation. What theme about war do these changes communicate?

8. **Analyze Irony** Explain the contrast between what you expected and what actually happens at the end of the story. Support your answer with details.

9. **Draw Conclusions** Describe how Morissot and Sauvage behave while in the enemy camp. What conclusions can you draw about their **friendship** from their final actions?

10. **Evaluate** Recall incidents you have heard about in recent years concerning the treatment of prisoners, the wounded, and civilians during times of war. Are the Prussian soldiers justified in their actions against the two Frenchmen? Explain your response.

Literary Criticism

11. **Biographical Context** "War! When I think of this word," declared Maupassant, "I feel bewildered, as though they were speaking to me of sorcery, of the Inquisition, of a distant, finished, abominable, monstrous, unnatural thing." How are Maupassant's feelings about war reflected in the story? Support your response with details.

OHIO STANDARDS

READING STANDARD
4.9 Explain how authors use symbols to create broader meanings

Vocabulary in Context

VOCABULARY PRACTICE

Decide if each statement is true or false.

1. To **afford** privacy to someone is to offer it to him or her.
2. To be **unperturbed** is to be disturbed and agitated.
3. To be **rejuvenated** is to be worn down and tired.
4. If you are **fanatical** about something, you are obsessed with it.
5. An **eccentric** person has a normal, traditional way of doing things.
6. An **atrocity** is offensive and outrageous.
7. To speak **dejectedly** is to speak with excitement and energy.
8. If you are **pensive,** you are thoughtful.

WORD LIST
afford
atrocity
dejectedly
eccentric
fanatical
pensive
rejuvenated
unperturbed

VOCABULARY IN WRITING

Using three or more vocabulary words, describe an activity you enjoy sharing with a friend. Here is an example of how you might begin.

> **EXAMPLE SENTENCE**
>
> My best friend and I feel **rejuvenated** when we go hiking.

VOCABULARY STRATEGY: ANALOGIES

Analogies express relationships between pairs of words. Some common relationships are described in the chart below.

Type	Relationship
Synonym	means the same as
Antonym	means the opposite of
Cause and effect	results in or leads to
Degree of intensity	is less (or more) than

Complete each analogy by choosing the appropriate vocabulary word. Identify the kind of relationship on which the analogy is based.

1. intelligent : clever :: strange : _____
2. annoyed : furious :: interested : _____
3. gift : delighted :: problem : _____
4. bored : excited :: fatigued : _____
5. goodwill : charity :: cruelty : _____

OHIO STANDARDS

VOCABULARY STANDARD
1.2 Analyze the relationships of pairs of words

VOCABULARY PRACTICE
For more practice, go to the **Vocabulary Center** at ClassZone.com.

Reading-Writing Connection

Deepen your understanding of "Two Friends" by responding to these prompts.
Then use **Revision: Grammar and Style** to improve your writing.

WRITING PROMPTS	SELF-CHECK

A. Short Response: Write a News Report
Imagine that you are a correspondent reporting on the latest events in the war. Using information from the selection, write a **one- or two-paragraph news report** in which you describe what has happened to the two **friends.**

▶

A well-written news report will . . .
- provide background information on the two friends
- explain the events that led to their deaths

B. Extended Response: Analyze Character
Critics have noted that many of Maupassant's characters lack higher feelings and have animal-like tendencies. Does this observation apply to the Prussians in "Two Friends"? Write a **three-to-five-paragraph response.**

▶

An effective response will . . .
- clearly state an opinion
- use details from the story to support your analysis

REVISION: GRAMMAR AND STYLE

WRITE CONCISELY Review the **Grammar and Style** note on page 414. A **predicate** indicates what a subject is or does or what happens to a subject. By combining predicates, you can avoid writing a series of short, choppy sentences that begin with the same noun or pronoun. Here are two additional examples of how Maupassant uses **compound predicates** to make his writing more concise:

Then he jumped to his feet, went up to the two Frenchmen, took Morissot by the arm, and led him to one side. (lines 208–209)

The water spurted up, bubbled, swirled round, then grew calm again . . . (line 242)

Notice how the revisions in red use compound predicates to concisely describe a series of events. Use similar methods to revise your responses to the prompts.

OHIO STANDARDS

WRITING STANDARD
5.7 Use a variety of sentence structures and lengths

STUDENT MODEL

On their last day, Morrisot and Sauvage received a pass. ~~They also~~ crossed *and*
enemy lines. ~~Morrisot and Sauvage~~ then scrambled down a hill ~~and~~ crawled *They*
on their hands and knees. Finally ~~they~~ reached their beloved fishing ground. *and*

WRITING TOOLS
For prewriting, revision, and editing tools, visit the **Writing Center** at ClassZone.com.

When Mr. Pirzada Came to Dine
Short Story by Jhumpa Lahiri

When do world CONFLICTS *affect us?*

OHIO STANDARDS

READING STANDARDS
2.3 Draw conclusions
4.4 Interpret universal themes

KEY IDEA How do you respond when you learn about a **conflict** in a distant part of the world? For some, the matter is quickly forgotten in the rush to take care of everyday concerns. For others, however, a faraway conflict can become intensely personal. In the following selection, you will read about how a young girl tries to ease the worries of a man whose loved ones live in a war-torn country.

QUICKWRITE What causes a person to identify with people engaged in a faraway conflict? With a partner, add to the graphic organizer that is shown. Then write a short paragraph about how you've reacted to conflicts you've read about or seen on television.

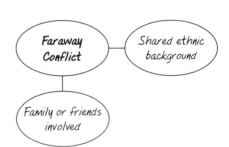

Faraway Conflict

Shared ethnic background

Family or friends involved

SECTION
2

LOCAL NE

Conflict in Middle East drives up oil prices

WASHINGTON–Sources confirmed today that the cost of a barrel of oil will increase again due to the

● LITERARY ANALYSIS: THEME AND CHARACTER

Sometimes, a story's **theme,** or central idea, is stated directly or is obvious after a first reading. More often, a theme must be pieced together after careful study. One way to discover a theme is to analyze the thoughts, words, and actions of a story's **main character.** As you read the selection, ask yourself the following questions about Lilia, the main character:

- How does she react to other characters?
- What conflicts does she experience?
- How does she change over time?

● READING SKILL: DRAW CONCLUSIONS

Remember that when you **draw conclusions,** you gather pieces of information—from your reading and from what you already know—to make judgments. Use the following strategies to help you draw conclusions about how the political events in Pakistan affect the story's characters:

- Note how the characters behave before and after the outbreak of violence in Pakistan.
- Identify any changes in the characters' habits.

As you read, use a chart like the one shown to take notes about the characters.

Details About Characters	My Thoughts
At first, Lilia and her family share relaxed meals with Mr. Pirzada.	Lilia and her family are thoughtful to include Mr. Pirzada in their meals.

▲ VOCABULARY IN CONTEXT

Jhumpa Lahiri uses the boldfaced words in her story of internal and external conflicts. Try to figure out the meaning of each boldfaced word from the context.

1. measure to **ascertain** clothing size
2. restrict an individual's **autonomy**
3. meet a **compatriot** overseas
4. celebrate a nation's **sovereignty**
5. dress **impeccably** for the occasion
6. the **imperceptible** actions of a magician
7. **assail** an enemy in battle
8. **concede** victory to an opponent

Author On|ine

Jhumpa Lahiri born 1967

Fighting to Fit In Born in London, Jhumpa Lahiri (jōōm′pə lə-hē′rē) grew up in Rhode Island, the daughter of Indian educators. As a student she often felt displaced. She recalls, "I didn't belong. I looked different and felt like an outsider." Lahiri's self-confidence improved when she began to write fiction. "I started writing ten page 'novels' during recess," she explains. "[It] allowed me to observe and make sense of things without having to participate."

Pulitzer Prize Sensation As an adult, Lahiri continued to write stories based on her own struggles as an immigrant child. In 2000, she received the prestigious Pulitzer Prize for *The Interpreter of Maladies,* her debut work of fiction. The short story collection, which includes "When Mr. Pirzada Came to Dine," depicts individuals trying hard to succeed in their adopted homeland—the United States.

 MORE ABOUT THE AUTHOR
For more on Jhumpa Lahiri, visit the **Literature Center** at **ClassZone.com.**

Background

A Nation Divided The story takes place in 1971, the year in which civil war erupted in Pakistan. At the time, Pakistan had two distinct parts, West Pakistan and East Pakistan, which were divided by more than a thousand miles of Indian soil. Major linguistic, cultural, and economic differences also separated the two sections. West Pakistan was home to many different ethnic groups. East Pakistan, on the other hand, had a more homogeneous population. East Pakistanis were resentful of the political power wielded by West Pakistanis. From this civil war came a new nation, Bangladesh.

WHEN *Mr. Pirzada Came to Dine*

Jhumpa Lahiri

In the autumn of 1971 a man used to come to our house, bearing confections in his pocket and hopes of **ascertaining** the life or death of his family. His name was Mr. Pirzada,[1] and he came from Dacca,[2] now the capital of Bangladesh, but then a part of Pakistan. That year Pakistan was engaged in civil war. The eastern frontier, where Dacca was located, was fighting for **autonomy** from the ruling regime in the west. In March, Dacca had been invaded, torched, and shelled by the Pakistani army. . . . By the end of the summer, three hundred thousand people were said to have died. In Dacca Mr. Pirzada had a three-story home, a lectureship in botany[3] at the university, a wife
10 of twenty years, and seven daughters between the ages of six and sixteen whose names all began with the letter A. "Their mother's idea," he explained one day, producing from his wallet a black-and-white picture of seven girls at a picnic, their braids tied with ribbons, sitting cross-legged in a row, eating chicken curry off of banana leaves. "How am I to distinguish? Ayesha, Amira, Amina, Aziza, you see the difficulty."

Each week Mr. Pirzada wrote letters to his wife, and sent comic books to each of his seven daughters, but the postal system, along with most everything else in Dacca, had collapsed, and he had not heard a word of them in over six months. Mr. Pirzada, meanwhile, was in America for the year, for he had
20 been awarded a grant from the government of Pakistan to study the foliage of New England. In spring and summer he had gathered data in Vermont and Maine, and in autumn he moved to a university north of Boston, where we lived, to write a short book about his discoveries. The grant was a great honor, but when converted into dollars it was not generous. As a result, Mr. Pirzada lived in a room in a graduate dormitory, and did not own a proper stove or a television set. And so he came to our house to eat dinner and watch the evening news. **A**

---

1. **Pirzada:** (pēr-zä′də).

2. **Dacca:** (dăk′ə).

3. **botany** (bŏt′n-ē): the science or study of plants.

ascertain (ăs′ər-tān′) *v.* to discover with certainty

autonomy (ô-tŏn′ə-mē) *n.* freedom; independence

ANALYZE VISUALS
In what way does the photograph help establish the **setting?**

A DRAW CONCLUSIONS
What details in lines 8–27 tell how Mr. Pirzada's life in New England is different from his life in Dacca?

At first I knew nothing of the reason for his visits. I was ten years old, and
was not surprised that my parents, who were from India, and had a number
30 of Indian acquaintances at the university, should ask Mr. Pirzada to share our
meals. It was a small campus, with narrow brick walkways and white pillared
buildings, located on the fringes of what seemed to be an even smaller town.
The supermarket did not carry mustard oil, doctors did not make house calls,
neighbors never dropped by without an invitation, and of these things, every
so often, my parents complained. In search of **compatriots,** they used to trail
their fingers, at the start of each new semester, through the columns of the
university directory, circling surnames familiar to their part of the world. It was
in this manner that they discovered Mr. Pirzada, and phoned him, and invited
him to our home.

40   I have no memory of his first visit, or of his second or his third, but by the
end of September I had grown so accustomed to Mr. Pirzada's presence in
our living room that one evening as I was dropping ice cubes into the water
pitcher, I asked my mother to hand me a fourth glass from a cupboard still out
of my reach. She was busy at the stove, presiding over a skillet of fried spinach
with radishes, and could not hear me because of the drone of the exhaust fan
and the fierce scrapes of her spatula. I turned to my father, who was leaning
against the refrigerator, eating spiced cashews from a cupped fist. **B**

      "What is it, Lilia?"

      "A glass for the Indian man."

50   "Mr. Pirzada won't be coming today. More importantly, Mr. Pirzada is
no longer considered Indian," my father announced, brushing salt from the
cashews out of his trim black beard. "Not since Partition.[4] Our country was
divided. 1947."

      When I said I thought that was the date of India's independence from
Britain, my father said, "That too. One moment we were free and then we were
sliced up," he explained, drawing an X with his finger on the countertop, "like
a pie. Hindus here, Muslims there. Dacca no longer belongs to us." He told me
that during Partition Hindus and Muslims had set fire to each other's homes.
For many, the idea of eating in the other's company was still unthinkable.

60   It made no sense to me. Mr. Pirzada and my parents spoke the same
language, laughed at the same jokes, looked more or less the same. They ate
pickled mangoes with their meals, ate rice every night for supper with their
hands. Like my parents, Mr. Pirzada took off his shoes before entering a room,
chewed fennel seeds after meals as a digestive, drank no alcohol, for dessert
dipped austere biscuits[5] into successive cups of tea. Nevertheless my father
insisted that I understand the difference, and he led me to a map of the world
taped to the wall over his desk. He seemed concerned that Mr. Pirzada might
take offense if I accidentally referred to him as an Indian, though I could not
really imagine Mr. Pirzada being offended by much of anything. "Mr. Pirzada

compatriot
(kəm-pā′trē-ət) *n.*
a person from one's
own country

B DRAW CONCLUSIONS
Which details in lines
40–47 suggest that Mr.
Pirzada is a welcome
guest in Lilia's home?

---

4. **Partition:** the division in 1947 of the Indian subcontinent into two independent countries, India and
   Pakistan, after British withdrawal.

5. **biscuits:** a British term for cookies or crackers.

70 is Bengali, but he is a Muslim," my father informed me. "Therefore he lives in East Pakistan, not India." His finger trailed across the Atlantic, through Europe, the Mediterranean, the Middle East, and finally to the sprawling orange diamond that my mother once told me resembled a woman wearing a sari[6] with her left arm extended. Various cities had been circled with lines drawn between them to indicate my parents' travels, and the place of their birth, Calcutta, was signified by a small silver star. I had been there only once and had no memory of the trip. "As you see, Lilia, it is a different country, a different color," my father said. Pakistan was yellow, not orange. I noticed that there were two distinct parts to it, one much larger than the other, separated

80 by an expanse of Indian territory; it was as if California and Connecticut constituted a nation apart from the U.S.

My father rapped his knuckles on top of my head. "You are, of course, aware of the current situation? Aware of East Pakistan's fight for **sovereignty?**"

I nodded, unaware of the situation. **C**

We returned to the kitchen, where my mother was draining a pot of boiled rice into a colander. My father opened up the can on the counter and eyed me sharply over the frames of his glasses as he ate some more cashews. "What exactly do they teach you at school? Do you study history? Geography?"

"Lilia has plenty to learn at school," my mother said. "We live here now,

90 she was born here." She seemed genuinely proud of the fact, as if it were a reflection of my character. In her estimation, I knew, I was assured a safe life, an easy life, a fine education, every opportunity. I would never have to eat rationed food, or obey curfews, or watch riots from my rooftop, or hide neighbors in water tanks to prevent them from being shot, as she and my father had. "Imagine having to place her in a decent school. Imagine her having to read during power failures by the light of kerosene lamps. Imagine the pressures, the tutors, the constant exams." She ran a hand through her hair, bobbed to a suitable length for her part-time job as a bank teller. "How can you possibly expect her to know about Partition? Put those nuts away."

100 "But what does she learn about the world?" My father rattled the cashew can in his hand. "What is she learning?"

We learned American history, of course, and American geography. That year, and every year, it seemed, we began by studying the Revolutionary War. We were taken in school buses on field trips to visit Plymouth Rock,[7] and to walk the Freedom Trail, and to climb to the top of the Bunker Hill Monument.[8] We made dioramas out of colored construction paper depicting George Washington crossing the choppy waters of the Delaware River, and

sovereignty
(sŏv′ər-ĭn-tē) *n.*
complete independence
and self-governance

C THEME AND
CHARACTER
Reread lines 50–84. In
this passage, Lilia's father
shares information about
India and Pakistan. Does
she understand the
conflict between these
two nations? Explain.

---

6. **sari** (sä′rē): a garment worn mostly by women of Pakistan and India, consisting of a length of fabric with one end wrapped around the waist to form a skirt and the other draped over the shoulder or covering the head.

7. **Plymouth Rock:** a boulder in Plymouth, Massachusetts, said to be the site where the Pilgrims disembarked from the *Mayflower*.

8. **Freedom Trail . . . Bunker Hill Monument:** historic sites in Boston, which commemorate critical events in the American struggle for independence from Great Britain.

we made puppets of King George wearing white tights and a black bow in his hair. During tests we were given blank maps of the thirteen colonies, and asked to fill in names, dates, capitals. I could do it with my eyes closed. **D**

The next evening Mr. Pirzada arrived, as usual, at six o'clock. Though they were no longer strangers, upon first greeting each other, he and my father maintained the habit of shaking hands.

"Come in, sir. Lilia, Mr. Pirzada's coat, please."

He stepped into the foyer, <u>**impeccably**</u> suited and scarved, with a silk tie knotted at his collar. Each evening he appeared in ensembles of plums, olives, and chocolate browns. He was a compact man, and though his feet were perpetually splayed, and his belly slightly wide, he nevertheless maintained an efficient posture, as if balancing in either hand two suitcases of equal weight. His ears were insulated by tufts of graying hair that seemed to block out the unpleasant traffic of life. He had thickly lashed eyes shaded with a trace of camphor,[9] a generous mustache that turned up playfully at the ends, and a mole shaped like a flattened raisin in the very center of his left cheek. **E** On his head he wore a black fez[10] made from the wool of Persian lambs, secured by bobby pins, without which I was never to see him. Though my father always offered to fetch him in our car, Mr. Pirzada preferred to walk from his dormitory to our neighborhood, a distance of about twenty minutes on foot, studying trees and shrubs on his way, and when he entered our house his knuckles were pink with the effects of the crisp autumn air.

"Another refugee, I am afraid, on Indian territory."

"They are estimating nine million at the last count," my father said.

Mr. Pirzada handed me his coat, for it was my job to hang it on the rack at the bottom of the stairs. It was made of finely checkered gray-and-blue wool, with a striped lining and horn buttons, and carried in its weave the faint smell of limes. There were no recognizable tags inside, only a hand-stitched label with the phrase "Z. Sayeed, Suitors" embroidered on it in cursive with glossy black thread. On certain days a birch or maple leaf was tucked into a pocket. He unlaced his shoes and lined them against the baseboard; a golden paste clung to the toes and heels, the result of walking through our damp, unraked lawn. Relieved of his trappings, he grazed my throat with his short, restless fingers, the way a person feels for solidity behind a wall before driving in a nail. Then he followed my father to the living room, where the television was tuned to the local news. As soon as they were seated my mother appeared from the kitchen with a plate of mincemeat kebabs with coriander chutney.[11] Mr. Pirzada popped one into his mouth.

---

9. **camphor** (kăm′fər): a fragrant compound from an Asian evergreen tree, used in skin-care products.

10. **fez** (fĕz): a man's felt hat in the shape of a flat-topped cone, worn mainly in the eastern Mediterranean region.

11. **mincemeat kebabs** (kə-bŏbz′) . . . **chutney** (chŭt′nē): an Indian or Pakistani dish consisting of pieces of spiced meat that have been placed on skewers and roasted, with an accompanying relish made of fruits, spices, and herbs.

D THEME AND CHARACTER
Which details in lines 102–110 suggest that Lilia is dissatisfied with her history class?

impeccably (ĭm-pĕk′ə-blē) *adv.* perfectly, flawlessly

E GRAMMAR AND STYLE
Reread lines 117–123. Lahiri's use of the adverbs *perpetually, slightly, thickly,* and *playfully* helps to create a vivid image of Mr. Pirzada.

"One can only hope," he said, reaching for another, "that Dacca's refugees are as heartily fed. Which reminds me." He reached into his suit pocket and gave me a small plastic egg filled with cinnamon hearts. "For the lady of the house," he said with an almost **imperceptible** splay-footed bow.

150   "Really, Mr. Pirzada," my mother protested. "Night after night. You spoil her."

"I only spoil children who are incapable of spoiling." **F**

It was an awkward moment for me, one which I awaited in part with dread, in part with delight. I was charmed by the presence of Mr. Pirzada's rotund elegance, and flattered by the faint theatricality of his attentions, yet unsettled by the superb ease of his gestures, which made me feel, for an instant, like a stranger in my own home. It had become our ritual, and for several weeks, before we grew more comfortable with one another, it was the only time he spoke to me directly. I had no response, offered no comment, betrayed no

160 visible reaction to the steady stream of honey-filled lozenges, the raspberry truffles, the slender rolls of sour pastilles. I could not even thank him, for once, when I did, for an especially spectacular peppermint lollipop wrapped in a spray of purple cellophane, he had demanded, "What is this thank-you? The lady at the bank thanks me, the cashier at the shop thanks me, the librarian thanks me when I return an overdue book, the overseas operator thanks me as she tries to connect me to Dacca and fails. If I am buried in this country I will be thanked, no doubt, at my funeral."

It was inappropriate, in my opinion, to consume the candy Mr. Pirzada gave me in a casual manner. I coveted each evening's treasure as I would a jewel, or

170 a coin from a buried kingdom, and I would place it in a small keepsake box

imperceptible
(ĭm′pər-sĕp′tə-bel) *adj.*
impossible or difficult
to notice

F **DRAW CONCLUSIONS**
What do Mr. Pirzada's
words and actions reveal
about his feelings for the
people of Dacca?

made of carved sandalwood beside my bed, in which, long ago in India, my father's mother used to store the ground areca nuts[12] she ate after her morning bath. It was my only memento of a grandmother I had never known, and until Mr. Pirzada came to our lives I could find nothing to put inside it. Every so often before brushing my teeth and laying out my clothes for school the next day, I opened the lid of the box and ate one of his treats. **G**

That night, like every night, we did not eat at the dining table, because it did not provide an unobstructed view of the television set. Instead we huddled around the coffee table, without conversing, our plates perched on the edges of our knees. From the kitchen my mother brought forth the succession of dishes: lentils[13] with fried onions, green beans with coconut, fish cooked with raisins in a yogurt sauce. I followed with the water glasses, and the plate of lemon wedges, and the chili peppers, purchased on monthly trips to Chinatown and stored by the pound in the freezer, which they liked to snap open and crush into their food.

Before eating Mr. Pirzada always did a curious thing. He took out a plain silver watch without a band, which he kept in his breast pocket, held it briefly to one of his tufted ears, and wound it with three swift flicks of his thumb and

G THEME AND CHARACTER
Consider the way Lilia cares for the gifts she receives from Mr. Pirzada. Why are they special to her?

180

12. **areca** (ə-rē′kə) **nuts:** seeds of the betel palm, chewed as a stimulant.

13. **lentils:** cooked seeds of a beanlike plant native to southwest Asia, a staple in Indian and Pakistani cuisine.

forefinger. Unlike the watch on his wrist, the pocket watch, he had explained
190 to me, was set to the local time in Dacca, eleven hours ahead. For the duration
of the meal the watch rested on his folded napkin on the coffee table. He never
seemed to consult it.

Now that I had learned Mr. Pirzada was not an Indian, I began to study him
with extra care, to try to figure out what made him different. I decided that the
pocket watch was one of those things. When I saw it that night, as he wound it
and arranged it on the coffee table, an uneasiness possessed me; life, I realized,
was being lived in Dacca first. I imagined Mr. Pirzada's daughters rising from
sleep, tying ribbons in their hair, anticipating breakfast, preparing for school.
Our meals, our actions, were only a shadow of what had already happened
200 there, a lagging ghost of where Mr. Pirzada really belonged. **H**

At six-thirty, which was when the national news began, my father raised the
volume and adjusted the antennas. Usually I occupied myself with a book, but
that night my father insisted that I pay attention. On the screen I saw tanks
rolling through dusty streets, and fallen buildings, and forests of unfamiliar
trees into which East Pakistani refugees had fled, seeking safety over the Indian
border. I saw boats with fan-shaped sails floating on wide coffee-colored rivers,
a barricaded university, newspaper offices burnt to the ground. I turned to
look at Mr. Pirzada; the images flashed in miniature across his eyes. As he
watched he had an immovable expression on his face, composed but alert, as
210 if someone were giving him directions to an unknown destination.

During the commercial my mother went to the kitchen to get more rice,
and my father and Mr. Pirzada deplored the policies of a general named
Yahyah Khan. They discussed intrigues I did not know, a catastrophe I could
not comprehend. "See, children your age, what they do to survive," my father
said as he served me another piece of fish. But I could no longer eat. I could
only steal glances at Mr. Pirzada, sitting beside me in his olive green jacket,
calmly creating a well in his rice to make room for a second helping of lentils.
He was not my notion of a man burdened by such grave concerns. I wondered
if the reason he was always so smartly dressed was in preparation to endure
220 with dignity whatever news **assailed** him, perhaps even to attend a funeral at
a moment's notice. I wondered, too, what would happen if suddenly his seven
daughters were to appear on television, smiling and waving and blowing kisses
to Mr. Pirzada from a balcony. I imagined how relieved he would be. But this
never happened.

That night when I placed the plastic egg filled with cinnamon hearts in the
box beside my bed, I did not feel the ceremonious satisfaction I normally did.
I tried not to think about Mr. Pirzada, in his lime-scented overcoat, connected
to the unruly, sweltering world we had viewed a few hours ago in our bright,
carpeted living room. And yet for several moments that was all I could
230 think about. My stomach tightened as I worried whether his wife and seven
daughters were now members of the drifting, clamoring crowd that had flashed
at intervals on the screen. In an effort to banish the image I looked around my

H THEME AND
CHARACTER
Reread lines 186–200.
What insight about Mr.
Pirzada does Lilia gain
from seeing him tend to
his pocket watch?

assail (ə-sāl′) *v.* to attack
or deliver a blow

room, at the yellow canopied bed with matching flounced curtains, at framed class pictures mounted on white and violet papered walls, at the penciled inscriptions by the closet door where my father had recorded my height on each of my birthdays. But the more I tried to distract myself, the more I began to convince myself that Mr. Pirzada's family was in all likelihood dead. Eventually I took a square of white chocolate out of the box, and unwrapped it, and then I did something I had never done before. I put the chocolate
240 in my mouth, letting it soften until the last possible moment, and then as I chewed it slowly, I prayed that Mr. Pirzada's family was safe and sound. I had never prayed for anything before, had never been taught or told to, but I decided, given the circumstances, that it was something I should do. That night when I went to the bathroom I only pretended to brush my teeth, for I feared that I would somehow rinse the prayer out as well. I wet the brush and rearranged the tube of paste to prevent my parents from asking any questions, and fell asleep with sugar on my tongue. ❶

N   o one at school talked about the war followed so faithfully in my living room. We continued to study the American Revolution, and learned
250 about the injustices of taxation without representation, and memorized passages from the Declaration of Independence. During recess the boys would divide in two groups, chasing each other wildly around the swings and seesaws, Redcoats against the colonies. In the classroom our teacher, Mrs. Kenyon, pointed frequently to a map that emerged like a movie screen from the top

❶ **THEME AND CHARACTER**
Reread lines 201–247. Think about the **internal conflict** Lilia experiences. How has her interest in Pakistan changed since the beginning of the story? Explain who or what has prompted this change.

of the chalkboard, charting the route of the *Mayflower*, or showing us the location of the Liberty Bell. Each week two members of the class gave a report on a particular aspect of the Revolution, and so one day I was sent to the school library with my friend Dora to learn about the surrender at Yorktown. Mrs. Kenyon handed us a slip of paper with the names of three books to look up in the card catalogue. We found them right away, and sat down at a low round table to read and take notes. But I could not concentrate. I returned to the blond-wood shelves, to a section I had noticed labeled "Asia." I saw books about China, India, Indonesia, Korea. Eventually I found a book titled *Pakistan: A Land and Its People*. I sat on a footstool and opened the book. The laminated jacket crackled in my grip. I began turning the pages, filled with photos of rivers and rice fields and men in military uniforms. There was a chapter about Dacca, and I began to read about its rainfall, and its jute[14] production. I was studying a population chart when Dora appeared in the aisle.

"What are you doing back here? Mrs. Kenyon's in the library. She came to check up on us."

I slammed the book shut, too loudly. Mrs. Kenyon emerged, the aroma of her perfume filling up the tiny aisle, and lifted the book by the tip of its spine as if it were a hair clinging to my sweater. She glanced at the cover, then at me.

"Is this book a part of your report, Lilia?"

"No, Mrs. Kenyon."

"Then I see no reason to consult it," she said, replacing it in the slim gap on the shelf. "Do you?" **J**

J DRAW CONCLUSIONS
How has the conflict in Pakistan affected the lives of Lilia's classmates and her history teacher, Mrs. Kenyon? Explain.

As weeks passed it grew more and more rare to see any footage from Dacca on the news. The report came after the first set of commercials, sometimes the second. The press had been censored, removed, restricted, rerouted. Some days, many days, only a death toll was announced, prefaced by a reiteration of the general situation. . . . More villages set ablaze. In spite of it all, night after night, my parents and Mr. Pirzada enjoyed long, leisurely meals. After the television was shut off, and the dishes washed and dried, they joked, and told stories, and dipped biscuits in their tea. When they tired of discussing political matters they discussed, instead, the progress of Mr. Pirzada's book about the deciduous trees[15] of New England, and my father's nomination for tenure, and the peculiar eating habits of my mother's American coworkers at the bank. Eventually I was sent upstairs to do my homework, but through the carpet I heard them as they drank more tea, and listened to cassettes of Kishore Kumar, and played Scrabble on the coffee table, laughing and arguing long into the night about the spellings of English words. I wanted to join them, wanted, above all, to console Mr. Pirzada somehow. But apart from eating a piece of candy for the sake of his family and praying for their safety, there was nothing I could do. They played Scrabble until the eleven

---

14. **jute:** the fiber from an Asian plant, used for sacking and cording.

15. **deciduous** (də-sĭj′ōō-əs) **trees:** trees that shed or lose leaves at the end of the growing season.

o'clock news, and then, sometime around midnight, Mr. Pirzada walked back to his dormitory. For this reason I never saw him leave, but each night as I drifted off to sleep I would hear them, anticipating the birth of a nation on the other side of the world. **K**

K DRAW CONCLUSIONS
How does the scarcity of news from Dacca affect Lilia's parents and Mr. Pirzada?

300   One day in October Mr. Pirzada asked upon arrival, "What are these large orange vegetables on people's doorsteps? A type of squash?"

"Pumpkins," my mother replied. "Lilia, remind me to pick one up at the supermarket."

"And the purpose? It indicates what?"

"You make a jack-o'-lantern," I said, grinning ferociously. "Like this. To scare people away."

"I see," Mr. Pirzada said, grinning back. "Very useful."

The next day my mother bought a ten-pound pumpkin, fat and round, and placed it on the dining table. Before supper, while my father and Mr. Pirzada
310 were watching the local news, she told me to decorate it with markers, but I wanted to carve it properly like others I had noticed in the neighborhood.

"Yes, let's carve it," Mr. Pirzada agreed, and rose from the sofa. "Hang the news tonight." Asking no questions, he walked into the kitchen, opened a drawer, and returned, bearing a long serrated knife. He glanced at me for approval. "Shall I?"

I nodded. For the first time we all gathered around the dining table, my mother, my father, Mr. Pirzada, and I. While the television aired unattended we covered the tabletop with newspapers. Mr. Pirzada draped his jacket over the chair behind him, removed a pair of opal cuff links, and rolled up the
320 starched sleeves of his shirt.

"First go around the top, like this," I instructed, demonstrating with my index finger.

He made an initial incision and drew the knife around. When he had come full circle he lifted the cap by the stem; it loosened effortlessly, and Mr. Pirzada leaned over the pumpkin for a moment to inspect and inhale its contents. My mother gave him a long metal spoon with which he gutted the interior until the last bits of string and seeds were gone. My father, meanwhile, separated the seeds from the pulp and set them out to dry on a cookie sheet, so that we could roast them later on. I drew two triangles against the ridged surface for
330 the eyes, which Mr. Pirzada dutifully carved, and crescents for eyebrows, and another triangle for the nose. The mouth was all that remained, and the teeth posed a challenge. I hesitated.

"Smile or frown?" I asked.

"You choose," Mr Pirzada said.

As a compromise I drew a kind of grimace, straight across, neither mournful nor friendly. Mr. Pirzada began carving, without the least bit of intimidation, as if he had been carving jack-o'-lanterns his whole life. He had nearly finished when the national news began. The reporter mentioned Dacca, and we all turned to listen: An Indian official announced that unless the world helped to relieve the burden of East Pakistani refugees, India would have to go to war against Pakistan. The reporter's face dripped with sweat as he relayed the information. He did not wear a tie or jacket, dressed instead as if he himself were about to take part in the battle. He shielded his scorched face as he hollered things to the cameraman. The knife slipped from Mr. Pirzada's hand and made a gash dipping toward the base of the pumpkin. **L**

"Please forgive me." He raised a hand to one side of his face, as if someone had slapped him there. "I am—it is terrible. I will buy another. We will try again."

"Not at all, not at all," my father said. He took the knife from Mr. Pirzada, and carved around the gash, evening it out, dispensing altogether with the teeth I had drawn. What resulted was a disproportionately large hole the size of a lemon, so that our jack-o'-lantern wore an expression of placid astonishment, the eyebrows no longer fierce, floating in frozen surprise above a vacant, geometric gaze.

For Halloween I was a witch. Dora, my trick-or-treating partner, was a witch too. We wore black capes fashioned from dyed pillowcases and conical hats with wide cardboard brims. We shaded our faces green with a broken eye shadow that belonged to Dora's mother, and my mother gave us two burlap sacks that had once contained basmati rice, for collecting candy. That year our parents decided that we were old enough to roam the neighborhood unattended. Our plan was to walk from my house to Dora's, from where I

L **DRAW CONCLUSIONS**
How does Mr. Pirzada react to the latest news report from Dacca?

was to call to say I had arrived safely, and then Dora's mother would drive me home. My father equipped us with flashlights, and I had to wear my watch and synchronize it with his. We were to return no later than nine o'clock.

When Mr. Pirzada arrived that evening he presented me with a box of chocolate-covered mints.

"In here," I told him, and opened up the burlap sack. "Trick or treat!"

"I understand that you don't really need my contribution this evening," he said, depositing the box. He gazed at my green face, and the hat secured by a string under my chin. Gingerly he lifted the hem of the cape, under which I
370 was wearing a sweater and zipped fleece jacket. "Will you be warm enough?"

I nodded, causing the hat to tip to one side.

He set it right. "Perhaps it is best to stand still."

The bottom of our staircase was lined with baskets of miniature candy, and when Mr. Pirzada removed his shoes he did not place them there as he normally did, but inside the closet instead. He began to unbutton his coat, and I waited to take it from him, but Dora called me from the bathroom to say that she needed my help drawing a mole on her chin. When we were finally ready my mother took a picture of us in front of the fireplace, and then I opened the front door to leave. Mr. Pirzada and my father, who had not gone
380 into the living room yet, hovered in the foyer. Outside it was already dark. The air smelled of wet leaves, and our carved jack-o'-lantern flickered impressively against the shrubbery by the door. In the distance came the sounds of scampering feet, and the howls of the older boys who wore no costume at all other than a rubber mask, and the rustling apparel of the youngest children, some so young that they were carried from door to door in the arms of their parents.

"Don't go into any of the houses you don't know," my father warned.

Mr. Pirzada knit his brows together. "Is there any danger?"

"No, no," my mother assured him. "All the children will be out. It's a
390 tradition."

"Perhaps I should accompany them?" Mr. Pirzada suggested. He looked suddenly tired and small, standing there in his splayed, stockinged feet, and his eyes contained a panic I had never seen before. In spite of the cold I began to sweat inside my pillowcase.

"Really, Mr. Pirzada," my mother said, "Lilia will be perfectly safe with her friend."

"But if it rains? If they lose their way?"

"Don't worry," I said. It was the first time I had uttered those words to Mr. Pirzada, two simple words I had tried but failed to tell him for weeks, had said
400 only in my prayers. It shamed me now that I had said them for my own sake.

He placed one of his stocky fingers on my cheek, then pressed it to the back of his own hand, leaving a faint green smear. "If the lady insists," he **conceded,** and offered a small bow.

concede (kən-sēd') *v.* to admit or acknowledge, often reluctantly

We left, stumbling slightly in our black pointy thrift-store shoes, and when we turned at the end of the driveway to wave good-bye, Mr. Pirzada was standing in the frame of the doorway, a short figure between my parents, waving back.

"Why did that man want to come with us?" Dora asked.

"His daughters are missing." As soon as I said it, I wished I had not. I felt
410 that my saying it made it true, that Mr. Pirzada's daughters really were missing, and that he would never see them again.

"You mean they were kidnapped?" Dora continued. "From a park or something?"

"I didn't mean they were missing. I meant, he misses them. They live in a different country, and he hasn't seen them in a while, that's all." **Ⓜ**

We went from house to house, walking along pathways and pressing doorbells. Some people had switched off all their lights for effect, or strung rubber bats in their windows. At the McIntyres' a coffin was placed in front of the door, and Mr. McIntyre rose from it in silence, his face covered with
420 chalk, and deposited a fistful of candy corns into our sacks. Several people told me that they had never seen an Indian witch before. Others performed the transaction without comment. As we paved our way with the parallel beams of our flashlights we saw eggs cracked in the middle of the road, and cars covered with shaving cream, and toilet paper garlanding the branches of trees. By the time we reached Dora's house our hands were chapped from carrying our bulging burlap bags, and our feet were sore and swollen. Her mother gave us bandages for our blisters and served us warm cider and caramel popcorn. She reminded me to call my parents to tell them I had arrived safely and when I did I could hear the television in the background. My mother did not seem
430 particularly relieved to hear from me. When I replaced the phone on the receiver it occurred to me that the television wasn't on at Dora's house at all. Her father was lying on the couch, reading a magazine, with a glass of wine on the coffee table, and there was saxophone music playing on the stereo.

After Dora and I had sorted through our plunder, and counted and sampled and traded until we were satisfied, her mother drove me back to my house. I thanked her for the ride, and she waited in the driveway until I made it to the door. In the glare of her headlights I saw that our pumpkin had been shattered, its thick shell strewn in chunks across the grass. I felt the sting of tears in my eyes, and a sudden pain in my throat, as if it had been stuffed with the sharp
440 tiny pebbles that crunched with each step under my aching feet. I opened the door, expecting the three of them to be standing in the foyer, waiting to receive me, and to grieve for our ruined pumpkin, but there was no one. In the living room Mr. Pirzada, my father, and mother were sitting side by side on the sofa. The television was turned off, and Mr. Pirzada had his head in his hands.

What they heard that evening, and for many evenings after that, was that India and Pakistan were drawing closer and closer to war. Troops from

Ⓜ THEME AND CHARACTER
Reread lines 388–415. According to Lilia, why is Mr. Pirzada protective of her? Explain how she, in turn, is protective of Mr. Pirzada.

both sides lined the border, and Dacca was insisting on nothing short of
independence. The war was soon to be waged on East Pakistani soil. The
United States was siding with West Pakistan, the Soviet Union with India and
450 what was soon to be Bangladesh. War was declared officially on December 4,
and twelve days later, the Pakistani army, weakened by having to fight three
thousand miles from their source of supplies, surrendered in Dacca. All of
these facts I know only now, for they are available to me in any history book,
in any library. But then it remained, for the most part, a remote mystery with
haphazard clues. What I remember during those twelve days of the war was
that my father no longer asked me to watch the news with them, and that
Mr. Pirzada stopped bringing me candy, and that my mother refused to serve
anything other than boiled eggs with rice for dinner. I remember some nights
helping my mother spread a sheet and blankets on the couch so that Mr.
460 Pirzada could sleep there, and high-pitched voices hollering in the middle of
the night when my parents called our relatives in Calcutta to learn more details
about the situation. Most of all I remember the three of them operating during
that time as if they were a single person, sharing a single meal, a single body, a
single silence, and a single fear.

N DRAW CONCLUSIONS
Note the way Lilia's
family and Mr. Pirzada
behave during the 12
days of war compared
with their earlier shared
experiences. How has
Pakistan's civil war
affected them?

    *I*n January, Mr. Pirzada flew back to his three-story home in Dacca, to
discover what was left of it. We did not see much of him in those final
weeks of the year; he was busy finishing his manuscript, and we went to
Philadelphia to spend Christmas with friends of my parents. Just as I have

no memory of his first visit, I have no memory of his last. My father drove him to the airport one afternoon while I was at school. For a long time we did not hear from him. Our evenings went on as usual, with dinners in front of the news. The only difference was that Mr. Pirzada and his extra watch were not there to accompany us. According to reports Dacca was repairing itself slowly, with a newly formed parliamentary government. The new leader, Sheikh Mujib Rahman, recently released from prison, asked countries for building materials to replace more than one million houses that had been destroyed in the war. Countless refugees returned from India, greeted, we learned, by unemployment and the threat of famine. Every now and then I studied the map above my father's desk and pictured Mr. Pirzada on that small patch of yellow, perspiring heavily, I imagined, in one of his suits, searching for his family. Of course, the map was outdated by then.

Finally, several months later, we received a card from Mr. Pirzada commemorating the Muslim New Year,[16] along with a short letter. He was reunited, he wrote, with his wife and children. All were well, having survived the events of the past year at an estate belonging to his wife's grandparents in the mountains of Shillong. His seven daughters were a bit taller, he wrote, but otherwise they were the same, and he still could not keep their names in order. At the end of the letter he thanked us for our hospitality, adding that although he now understood the meaning of the words "thank you" they still were not adequate to express his gratitude. To celebrate the good news my mother prepared a special dinner that evening, and when we sat down to eat at the coffee table we toasted our water glasses, but I did not feel like celebrating. Though I had not seen him for months, it was only then that I felt Mr. Pirzada's absence. It was only then, raising my water glass in his name, that I knew what it meant to miss someone who was so many miles and hours away, just as he had missed his wife and daughters for so many months. He had no reason to return to us, and my parents predicted, correctly, that we would never see him again. Since January, each night before bed, I had continued to eat, for the sake of Mr. Pirzada's family, a piece of candy I had saved from Halloween. That night there was no need to. Eventually, I threw them away. ◐ ◉

◉ **THEME AND CHARACTER**
Why does Lilia throw away her remaining candies?

---

16. **Muslim New Year:** an important Islamic holiday and observance that marks the Prophet Muhammad's emigration from Mecca to Medina, a turning point in Islamic history.

INTERVIEW In this interview, Jhumpa Lahiri describes the poignant experiences that inspired her to write the award-winning story collection *The Interpreter of Maladies*.

NewsHour

A NEWSHOUR WITH JIM LEHRER TRANSCRIPT

JHUMPA LAHIRI, PULITZER PRIZE WINNER

Elizabeth Farnsworth: Tell us about the title of [your] book. It's an unusual title, "Interpreter of Maladies." Where does it come from?

Jhumpa Lahiri: The title is . . . Well, it's the title of one of the stories in the book. And the phrase itself was something I thought of before I even wrote that story. I thought of it one day after I ran into someone I knew. I asked him what he was doing with himself, and he told me he was working as an interpreter in a doctor's office in Brookline, Massachusetts, where I was living at the time, and he was translating for a doctor who had a number of Russian patients. And he was fluent in English and Russian. And on my way home, after running into him, I thought of this . . . I just heard this phrase in my head. And I liked the way it sounded, but I wasn't quite sure what it meant, but I wrote it down. I just wrote down the phrase itself. And for years, I sort of would try to write a story that somehow fit the title. And I don't think it happened for maybe another four years that I actually thought of a story, the plot of a story that corresponded to that phrase.

EF: It occurred to me that you're kind of an interpreter of maladies yourself in these stories.

JL: I guess that's what has . . . That's the way it's turned out, yeah. But I didn't know . . . At the time, I wasn't aware of it.

EF: There's longing and loss in these stories, the longing and loss that often comes with the life of an immigrant. Is this your longing and loss, do you think, as the child of immigrants, or is this more the longing and loss of your parents' generation coming through?

JL: Both. I think that, in part, it's a reflection of what I observed my parents experiencing and their friends, their circle of fellow Indian immigrant friends. It's also, in part, drawn from my own experiences and a sense of . . . I always say that I feel that I've inherited a sense of that loss from my parents because it was so palpable all the time while I was growing up, the sense of what my parents had sacrificed in moving to the United States, and in so many ways, and yet at the same time, remaining here and building a life here and all that that entailed.

EF: One of the stories that raises these issues is called "When Mr. Pirzada Came to Dine." It begins like this: "In the autumn of 1971 a man used to come to our house bearing confections in his pocket and hopes of ascertaining the life or death of his family." I love that beginning. Tell us a little bit about the story. . . .

JL: Sure. This story is based on a gentleman who . . . used to come to my parents' house in 1971 from Bangladesh. He was at the University of Rhode Island. And I was four, four years old, at the time, and so I actually don't have any memories of this gentleman. But I've heard . . . I heard through my parents what his predicament was. And when I learned about his situation, which was that he was in the United States during the Pakistani civil war and his family was back in Dacca, I just sort of . . . I was so overwhelmed by this information that I wrote this story based on that . . . Based on that experience in my parents' life.

Comprehension

OHIO STANDARDS

READING STANDARD
4.4 Interpret universal themes

1. **Recall** Why does Mr. Pirzada begin coming to Lilia's house?

2. **Recall** How does Lilia react to the gifts Mr. Pirzada brings?

3. **Clarify** Why does Lilia's father want her to learn about Indian and Pakistani history?

Literary Analysis

4. **Analyze Character** Lilia becomes more concerned about Pakistan and its civil unrest as she becomes better acquainted with Mr. Pirzada. Show Lilia's growing cultural awareness by completing a timeline like the one shown. Fill in each blank with an appropriate story detail.

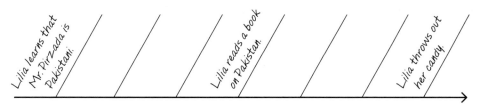

Lilia learns that Mr. Pirzada is Pakistani. / Lilia reads a book on Pakistan. / Lilia throws out her candy.

5. **Examine Character Relationship** Lilia states that Mr. Pirzada is protective of her because he misses his own daughters. How is the relationship of Lilia and Mr. Pirzada like that of a father and a daughter? Support your opinion with story details.

6. **Interpret Theme and Character** What theme do you think Lahiri is trying to communicate through the experiences of Lilia, the main character? Cite evidence to support your answer.

7. **Draw Conclusions** Review the chart you created as you read. Explain which characters are most affected by the **conflict** in Pakistan. Why do you think the conflict becomes a personal matter for some, but not for all, of the characters?

8. **Evaluate** Reread lines 482–500. Does the outcome of the story seem believable? Why or why not? In your response, explain how well the story resolves Lilia's **inner conflict.**

9. **Compare Literary Works** Reread the interview with Lahiri on page 438. What details in the interview enhance your understanding of the characters and events depicted in "When Mr. Pirzada Came to Dine"? Explain your response.

Literary Criticism

10. **Author's Style** Lahiri is admired for her penetrating insights into human behavior. Find examples of such insights in the story and discuss how they add to the story's impact.

Vocabulary in Context

VOCABULARY PRACTICE

Identify the word that is not related in meaning to the other words in the set. If necessary, use a dictionary to check the definitions of words.

1. doubt, ascertain, discover, realize
2. freedom, autonomy, independence, restriction
3. stranger, foreigner, compatriot, outsider
4. sovereignty, dependence, neediness, reliance
5. messily, sloppily, carelessly, impeccably
6. obvious, imperceptible, tangible, distinct
7. greet, assail, welcome, embrace
8. admit, allow, concede, correct

WORD LIST

ascertain

assail

autonomy

compatriot

concede

impeccably

imperceptible

sovereignty

VOCABULARY IN WRITING

Using at least three vocabulary words, write about why you think Mr. Pirzada regularly visited Lilia's home. Here is an example of how you might begin.

> **EXAMPLE SENTENCE**
>
> Unable to **ascertain** the whereabouts of his own family, perhaps Mr. Pirzada found comfort in this home away from home.

OHIO STANDARDS

VOCABULARY STANDARD
1.5 Use knowledge of Latin roots, prefixes and suffixes to understand words

VOCABULARY STRATEGY: THE PREFIX *im-*

The vocabulary word *imperceptible* contains the Latin prefix *im-*. This prefix often means "not" and is used in many English words. To understand the meanings of words that begin with *im-*, use context clues and your knowledge of the prefix.

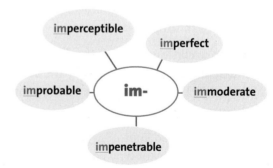

PRACTICE Write the word from the word web that best completes each sentence. Use context clues to help you or, if necessary, consult a dictionary.

1. You seem to spend an _____ amount of time with your friend Janey.
2. An _____ shirt may have one sleeve that is longer than the other.
3. The _____ fortress resisted attackers for decades.
4. Your explanation seems highly _____. What really happened?
5. The wings of a hummingbird flutter so fast as to be almost _____.

VOCABULARY PRACTICE
For more practice, go to the **Vocabulary Center** at **ClassZone.com**.

Reading-Writing Connection

Broaden your understanding of "When Mr. Pirzada Came to Dine" by responding to these prompts. Then use **Revision: Grammar and Style** to improve your writing.

WRITING PROMPTS	SELF-CHECK

A. Short Response: Describe a Dinner
Imagine that, like Mr. Pirzada, you are a dinner guest of Lilia's family. In **one or two paragraphs,** describe your experience with them, including information about their home and the meal they share with you.

▶

A strong description will . . .
• present a setting and characters consistent with those in the story
• use vivid, colorful language to describe the experience

B. Extended Response: Compare and Contrast Stories
Compare and contrast the stories you have read so far in the unit. How does each reveal the following theme about **conflict:** "After a time, hatred becomes pointless"? Using examples from the stories, write a **three-to-five-paragraph response.**

▶

An effective response will . . .
• show how the stories reveal a similar theme about conflict
• include evidence that supports your interpretation

REVISION: GRAMMAR AND STYLE

ADD DESCRIPTIVE DETAILS Review the **Grammar and Style** note on page 426. There, Lahiri uses **adverbs** to effectively convey details about her character's physical appearance. Here are two other examples of how Lahiri uses adverbs to reveal personal qualities of Lilia and Mr. Pirzada:

> *"You make a jack-o'-lantern," I said, grinning ferociously. "Like this. To scare people away."* (lines 305–306)

> *I could only steal glances at Mr. Pirzada, sitting beside me in his olive green jacket, calmly creating a well in his rice to make room for a second helping of lentils.* (lines 215–217)

Notice how the revisions in red improve the descriptive power of this first draft through the addition of adverbs. Use similar methods to revise your responses to the prompts.

OHIO STANDARDS

WRITING STANDARD
5.12 Add details

WRITING TOOLS

For prewriting, revision, and editing tools, visit the **Writing Center** at ClassZone.com.

STUDENT MODEL

As I entered Lilia's home, I was $\overset{instantly}{\wedge}$ greeted by her mother. She $\overset{kindly}{\wedge}$ asked that I remove my shoes. Not wanting to seem rude, I did so. However, I was $\overset{deeply}{\wedge}$ embarrassed because of a dime-sized hole in my right sock.

Do not weep, maiden, for war is kind
Poem by Stephen Crane

the sonnet-ballad
Poem by Gwendolyn Brooks

Who are the VICTIMS *of war?*

OHIO STANDARDS

READING STANDARDS
4.4 Interpret universal themes
4.7 Recognize how irony is used in a literary text

KEY IDEA What effect does war have on the soldiers who engage in battle and on loved ones who are left behind? These poems show how ordinary citizens can become **victims** when countries wage war.

DISCUSS Do you know anyone who has been involved in war, either as a participant or as a bystander? With a partner, discuss the effects of war as you have heard them described or as you imagine them. Then with a larger group, discuss why people have fought wars throughout history.

● LITERARY ANALYSIS: UNIVERSAL THEME

Although literary works may belong to different time periods and cultures, they often express the same message about human nature or life. In these cases, the message is called a **universal theme.** Universal themes reflect experiences that are common to most people, such as growing older or falling in love. The poems you are about to read were written 50 years apart and are the works of two distinguished authors, Stephen Crane and Gwendolyn Brooks. As you read each poem, use these strategies to discover the poems' shared message:

- Identify the **speaker,** or the voice that "talks" to the reader.
- Notice key **images** and think about their meaning.
- Identify examples of **repetition,** or words and phrases that are repeated in the poem. Think about their meaning.
- Consider the **mood,** or the overall feeling, created by the poem.

■ READING SKILL: UNDERSTAND VERBAL IRONY

Unlike fiction writers, poets typically communicate their messages in little space and few words. They often rely on different techniques to help them craft compact works of great power. One important literary technique is **verbal irony**—saying one thing but meaning the opposite. The first line of Crane's poem provides an example of such irony:

Do not weep, maiden, for war is kind.

War, by definition, cannot be considered kind. Clearly, Crane intends the reader to think something entirely different about war. Many poems, particularly those involving social criticism or protest, feature this technique. As you read the two poems, record examples of verbal irony and explain what you think they mean. Use a graphic organizer like the one shown to help you.

Poem	Examples of Verbal Irony	Explanations
Crane's poem	Do not weep, maiden, for war is kind. (line 1)	War is cruel.

Author Online

Stephen Crane: Chronicler of War

**Stephen Crane
1871–1900**

When his Civil War novella *The Red Badge of Courage,* published in 1895, achieved enormous success, Stephen Crane felt embarrassed, since he had no firsthand experience of war. However, he soon took a job as a foreign correspondent, covering wars in Cuba and Greece. His experience of spending 30 hours in a lifeboat, after being shipwrecked near Cuba, inspired his famous story "The Open Boat." Although he died at 29, Crane left behind a prodigious number of literary works, many of which are considered classics.

Gwendolyn Brooks: Poet and Activist

**Gwendolyn Brooks
1917–2000**

Raised on Chicago's South Side, Gwendolyn Brooks remained devoted to this neighborhood and its black community throughout her life. In her early poetry, Brooks was strongly influenced by traditional literary forms. Empowered by black activism, she turned to free verse in the 1960s, striving to write poems that the people she wrote about would read. In 1950, Brooks won the Pulitzer Prize for poetry, the first African American so honored.

 MORE ABOUT THE AUTHOR
For more on Stephen Crane and Gwendolyn Brooks, visit the **Literature Center** at ClassZone.com.

443

Do not weep, maiden, for war is kind

Stephen Crane

Do not weep, maiden, for war is kind.
Because your lover threw wild hands toward the sky
And the affrighted steed ran on alone,
Do not weep.
5 War is kind.

Hoarse, booming drums of the regiment,
Little souls who thirst for fight,
These men were born to drill and die.
The unexplained glory flies above them,
10 Great is the Battle-God, great, and his Kingdom—
A field where a thousand corpses lie. **A**

Do not weep, babe, for war is kind.
Because your father tumbled in the yellow trenches,
Raged at his breast, gulped and died,
15 Do not weep.
War is kind.

Swift blazing flag of the regiment,
Eagle with crest of red and gold,
These men were born to drill and die.
20 Point for them the virtue of slaughter,
Make plain to them the excellence of killing
And a field where a thousand corpses lie.

Mother whose heart hung humble as a button
On the bright splendid shroud of your son,
25 Do not weep.
War is kind. **B**

A VERBAL IRONY
Reread lines 1–11. In what way do these lines demonstrate verbal irony? Explain.

B UNIVERSAL THEME
Reread stanzas 1, 3, and 5. Identify the **images** of war presented in each stanza. What do these images have in common?

Gloria Triptych (detail of despairing woman), Giuseppe Mentessi. Right panel. Galleria d'Arte Moderna, Rome. Photo © Dagli Orti/The Art Archive.

the sonnet-ballad

Gwendolyn Brooks

Oh mother, mother, where is happiness?
They took my lover's tallness off to war,
Left me lamenting. Now I cannot guess
What I can use an empty heart-cup for.
5 He won't be coming back here any more.
Some day the war will end, but, oh, I knew
When he went walking grandly out that door
That my sweet love would have to be untrue.
Would have to be untrue. Would have to court
10 Coquettish death, whose impudent and strange
Possessive arms and beauty (of a sort)
Can make a hard man hesitate—and change.
And he will be the one to stammer, "Yes."
Oh mother, mother, where is happiness?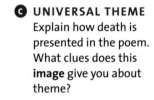

C **UNIVERSAL THEME**
Explain how death is
presented in the poem.
What clues does this
image give you about
theme?

ANALYZE VISUALS
How would you compare
the **mood** of this sculpture with that of the
painting on page 445?

Lamentation: Memorial for Ernst Barlach (1940),
Käthe Kollwitz. Bronze. © 2008 Artists Rights
Society (ARS), New York/VG Bild-Kunst, Bonn.

Comprehension

1. **Recall** Whom does the speaker address in Crane's poem?

2. **Clarify** What has happened to the father of the babe addressed in the third stanza of Crane's poem?

3. **Recall** In "the sonnet-ballad," where has the speaker's lover gone?

Literary Analysis

4. **Analyze Imagery** Think about the various images in each poem. Select one lasting image from each poem and explain its impact.

5. **Make Inferences** According to the speaker of each poem, why do people fight wars? Cite evidence to support your answer.

6. **Interpret Verbal Irony** Look back over the chart you created as you read. What does the use of verbal irony in the poems tell you about the writers' attitudes toward war? Support your answer with examples from the poems.

7. **Draw Conclusions About Universal Theme** Create a chart like the one shown, identifying the speaker, key images, examples of repetition, and mood in each poem. Then use this information to state the universal theme expressed by both poems.

	Crane's Poem	*Brooks's Poem*
Speaker		
Key images		
Repetition		
Mood		

Universal Theme

8. **Evaluate** Which poem makes the strongest statement about war and its **victims?** Give evidence from the poems to support your opinion.

Literary Criticism

9. **Historical Context** Both poems reflect the wartime experiences of earlier generations. Crane's poem was published in 1899, following Cuba's war for independence. Brooks wrote and published "the sonnet-ballad" following World War II. What aspects of these poems might be different if the authors were alive today and writing about current world events?

OHIO STANDARDS

READING STANDARD
4.7 Recognize how irony is used in a literary text

from **Tolerance**
Essay by E. M. Forster

How ACCEPTING
are you?

KEY IDEA Our global community consists of billions of people belonging to various religions, races, and ethnic groups. What is the best way to build strong alliances between different individuals, groups, and nations? According to the following selection, the answer can be found in practicing **tolerance**—or respect for the beliefs and customs of others.

SURVEY With a partner, create a brief survey about the importance of tolerance. Add to or subtract from the example shown. Ask a small group of classmates to complete the survey. Share the results with your whole class.

> **Survey About Tolerance**
> 1. How is tolerance practiced in your school? Give an example.
> 2. How is tolerance practiced in the world? Give an example.
> 3. In what ways do you practice tolerance? Give an example.

● ELEMENT OF NONFICTION: PERSUASIVE ESSAY

A **persuasive essay** is a short work of nonfiction written primarily to persuade readers to adopt the writer's message, or **thesis.** The thesis of a persuasive essay is typically a position on an issue or a topic. For example, Forster states his thesis as follows:

In public affairs, in the rebuilding of civilisation, something much less dramatic and emotional [than love] is needed, namely, tolerance.

A strong persuasive essay also uses **powerful language, persuasive techniques,** and a clear and logical **argument** to be convincing. As you read Forster's persuasive essay, be on the lookout for these elements.

● READING SKILL: ANALYZE REASONS AND EVIDENCE

To check whether Forster's essay contains a clear and logical argument, analyze the **reasons** and **evidence** he provides to support his thesis. Specifically, make sure that he backs up each reason with at least one piece of evidence. Also check to see whether each reason logically supports his thesis. Recording the reasons and evidence in a graphic organizer such as the one shown here can help you do this. Add or subtract boxes as needed.

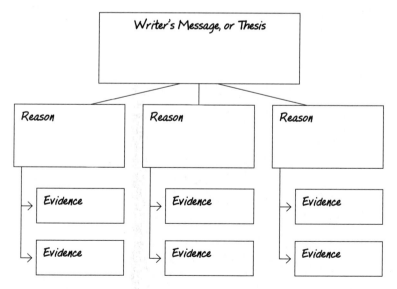

Author Online

E. M. Forster
1879–1970

The Worst Years
Edward Morgan Forster spent the early part of his life frustrated with the private boys' school that he attended in England, where he suffered the taunts of classmates and the severity of teachers. His subsequent years at Cambridge University were much happier. There, he expanded his intellectual horizons, made close friends, and dedicated himself to literature.

Literary Triumph Forster began publishing stories soon after graduation and published his first novel in 1905. A number of acclaimed novels followed. The best known of these—*A Room with a View* (1908), *Howards End* (1910), and *A Passage to India* (1924)—have enjoyed a resurgence of popularity sparked by successful film adaptations. During the 1930s and 1940s, Forster turned increasingly to social criticism and virtually gave up writing fiction.

 MORE ABOUT THE AUTHOR
For more on E. M. Forster, visit the **Literature Center** at ClassZone.com.

Background

On the Air This essay is one of several that Forster broadcast over the radio during and just after World War II (1939–1945) and later collected in his volume *Two Cheers for Democracy* (1951). In these essays, Forster often explores the means by which citizens of democracies can counter the spread of the kind of thinking that leads to brutal dictatorships—like that of Nazi Germany, Britain's foe during the war. With their claims of racial superiority and their mass murder of ethnic groups that they branded undesirable, the Nazis were the supreme example of intolerance.

TOLERANCE

E. M. Forster

Surely the only sound foundation for a civilisation is a sound state of mind. Architects, contractors, international commissioners, marketing boards, broadcasting corporations will never, by themselves, build a new world. They must be inspired by the proper spirit, and there must be the proper spirit in the people for whom they are working. . . .

What though is the proper spirit? . . . There must be a sound state of mind before diplomacy or economics or trade conferences can function. But what state of mind is sound? Here we may differ. Most people, when asked what spiritual quality is needed to rebuild civilisation, will reply "Love." Men must love one another, they say; nations must do likewise, and then the series of cataclysms which is threatening to destroy us will be checked. **A**

Respectfully but firmly, I disagree. Love is a great force in private life; it is indeed the greatest of all things: but love in public affairs does not work. It has been tried again and again: by the Christian civilisations of the Middle Ages, and also by the French Revolution, a secular movement which reasserted the brotherhood of man.[1] And it has always failed. The idea that nations should love one another, or that business concerns or marketing boards should love one another, or that a man in Portugal should love a man in Peru of whom he has never heard—it is absurd, unreal, dangerous. It leads us into perilous and vague sentimentalism.[2] "Love is what is needed," we chant and then sit back, and the world goes on as before. The fact is we can only love what we know personally. And we cannot know much. In public affairs, in the rebuilding of civilisation, something much less dramatic and emotional is needed, namely, tolerance. Tolerance is a very dull virtue. It is boring. Unlike love, it has always had a bad press. It is negative. It merely means putting up with people, being able to stand things. No one has ever written an ode[3] to tolerance or raised a

ANALYZE VISUALS
In what way does the painting illustrate **tolerance** among different people?

A PERSUASIVE ESSAY
Reread lines 1–11. According to Forster, what is needed to create a sound foundation for civilization?

"Civilization is a method of living, an attitude of equal respect for all men." From the series *Great Ideas of Western Men* (1955), George Giusti. India ink and gouache on paper, 24 7/8″ × 18 5/16″. Gift of the Container Corporation of America. Smithsonian American Art Museum, Washington, D.C. Photo © Smithsonian American Art Museum, Washington, D.C./Art Resource, New York.

1. **French Revolution . . . brotherhood of man:** The French Revolution, which lasted from 1789 to 1799, had the motto "Liberty! Equality! Brotherhood!"
2. **sentimentalism** (sĕn′tə-mĕn′tl-ĭz′əm): a tendency toward too much tender, often shallow emotion.
3. **ode** (ōd): a usually formal poem on a serious subject.

statue to her. Yet this is the quality which will be most needed after the war. This is the sound state of mind which we are looking for. This is the only force which will enable different races and classes and interests to settle down 30 together to the work of reconstruction. **B**

The world is very full of people—appallingly full; it has never been so full before, and they are all tumbling over each other. Most of these people one doesn't know, and some of them one doesn't like; doesn't like the colour of their skins, say, or the shapes of their noses, or the way they blow them or don't blow them, or the way they talk, or their smell, or their clothes, or their fondness for jazz or their dislike of jazz, and so on. Well, what is one to do? There are two solutions. One of them is the Nazi solution. If you don't like people, kill them, banish them, segregate them, and then strut up and down proclaiming that you are the salt of the earth.[4] The other way is much less 40 thrilling, but it is on the whole the way of the democracies, and I prefer it. If you don't like people, put up with them as well as you can. Don't try to love them: you can't; you'll only strain yourself. But try to tolerate them. On the basis of that tolerance a civilised future may be built. Certainly I can see no other foundation for the postwar world. **C**

For what it will most need is the negative virtues: not being huffy, touchy, irritable, revengeful. I have lost all faith in positive militant ideals; they can so seldom be carried out without thousands of human beings getting maimed or imprisoned. Phrases like "I will purge this nation," "I will clean up this city," terrify and disgust me. They might not have mattered when the world was 50 emptier: they are horrifying now, when one nation is mixed up with another, when one city cannot be organically separated from its neighbours. . . .

I don't then regard tolerance as a great eternally established divine principle, though I might perhaps quote "In my Father's house are many mansions"[5] in support of such a view. It is just a makeshift,[6] suitable for an overcrowded and overheated planet. It carries on when love gives out, and love generally gives out as soon as we move away from our home and our friends and stand among strangers in a queue[7] for potatoes. Tolerance is wanted in the queue; otherwise we think, "Why will people be so slow?"; it is wanted in the tube,[8] or "Why will people be so fat?"; it is wanted at the telephone, or "Why are they so deaf?" 60 or conversely, "Why do they mumble?" It is wanted in the street, in the office, at the factory, and it is wanted above all between classes, races, and nations. It's dull. And yet it entails imagination. For you have all the time to be putting yourself in someone else's place. Which is a desirable spiritual exercise. ✍ **D**

B **PERSUASIVE ESSAY**
Why might Forster's repetition of "this is" be considered a persuasive technique? Explain.

C **ANALYZE REASONS AND EVIDENCE**
What reasons and evidence has Forster given so far to support his message about tolerance?

D **PERSUASIVE ESSAY**
Reread lines 52–63. Think about why Forster might have chosen to include commonplace complaints. How effective are they at persuading you to agree with his position?

---

4. **salt of the earth:** the finest or noblest people. The expression derives from a statement in the New Testament of the Bible (Matthew 5:13).

5. **"In my Father's house are many mansions":** Heaven is a place of diversity. The quotation is from the New Testament of the Bible (John 14:2).

6. **makeshift:** a temporary substitute for something else.

7. **queue** (kyōō): a chiefly British expression for a line of people.

8. **tube:** a British term for the Underground, or London subway.

Comprehension

OHIO STANDARDS

READING STANDARD
3.8 Describe the features of rhetorical devices

1. **Recall** According to Forster, what quality do most people believe will improve the world?

2. **Clarify** Why does Forster disagree with this popular opinion?

3. **Recall** Why is tolerance, in Forster's eyes, a "very dull virtue"?

4. **Summarize** In your own words, restate the message, or **thesis,** of the essay.

Critical Analysis

5. **Analyze Reasons and Evidence** Review the essay and the notes you made as you read. Which reasons and evidence best support Forster's thesis? Explain your response.

6. **Understand Rhetorical Questions** When crafting persuasive essays, writers often include rhetorical questions, or questions that do not require responses. Find three different rhetorical questions in the essay. Then describe the effect the questions have on you as a reader. Use a graphic organizer like the one shown to help you.

Rhetorical Question	Effect
$\longrightarrow$	
$\longrightarrow$	
$\longrightarrow$	

7. **Draw Conclusions** Reread lines 52–61. Why do you suppose Forster uses examples drawn from everyday life to illustrate the need for **tolerance?**

8. **Interpret Text** Reread lines 62–63. What does Forster mean by his final point that tolerance requires imagination? Explain your response.

9. **Evaluate Persuasive Essay** Think about the effectiveness of the essay. After reading it, do you share Forster's position about tolerance? Why or why not?

10. **Make Judgments** Forster's essay was broadcast on British radio around the time of World War II. Who might benefit most from hearing or reading the essay today? Explain your opinion.

Letter to a Young Refugee from Another
Essay by Andrew Lam

Song of P'eng-ya
Poem by Tu Fu

What if you had to FLEE *your country?*

OHIO STANDARDS

READING STANDARDS
2.3 Apply reading strategies
4.5 Analyze how choice of genre affects theme

KEY IDEA How would you feel if political events forced you to leave your home, your belongings, and your entire community? In these two selections, you will learn about the powerful emotions and numerous hardships displaced people, or **refugees,** experience.

QUICKWRITE With a small group, create a word web that details some of the challenges a refugee might face. Then write a short paragraph in which you imagine what it would be like to live in an entirely new culture.

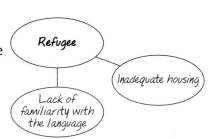

Refugee

Inadequate housing

Lack of familiarity with the language

● LITERARY ANALYSIS: AUTHOR'S MESSAGE ACROSS GENRES

When you read, it is important to keep in mind the **genre** of a work—whether it belongs to nonfiction, fiction, drama, poetry, or myth. A writer's choice of genre can greatly affect how the central message of a piece is communicated.

For example, writers of nonfiction usually rely on direct statements and evidence to convey their **messages.** Poets, on the other hand, rely more heavily on imagery, figurative language, and mood to express their **themes.** You can see this for yourself in the essay and poem that follow. Both focus on a similar topic—the experiences of a refugee—but in each the writer conveys his unique message with the elements and techniques of his particular genre. As you read, try to determine each writer's message by paying attention to the following.

In the Essay	In the Poem
• direct statements • facts, examples, and other details drawn from the writer's experiences • the list of directions for how to feel and behave • tone • the writer's final piece of advice	• words and phrases describing the speaker's thoughts and feelings • vivid imagery • figurative language • mood • the lesson or message you take away

● READING STRATEGY: SET A PURPOSE FOR READING

Sometimes people enjoy reading as a leisure activity, without a particular goal in mind. More often, and especially for school, you **set a purpose** for your reading—that is, you establish a particular reason to read a text. In this lesson, your purpose for reading is to identify the central messages of the selections. As you read, think about your impressions of the refugees and their experiences. After you read, you will use the **Points of Comparison** chart on page 462 to help you compare and contrast the messages of the two selections.

Author Online

Andrew Lam: Word Painter At the age of 11, Andrew Lam found himself thrown into an unfamiliar culture. After fleeing Saigon, South Vietnam, one day before the city fell to the North Vietnamese, Lam's family settled in northern California. In time, Lam fell in

Andrew Lam born 1964

love with his new language and way of life. Today, his passion for words is conveyed not only in his fiction but also in articles for the Pacific News Service and in commentaries for National Public Radio.

Tu Fu: Unlucky in Life Though considered one of China's greatest poets, Tu Fu (dōō' fōō') was unlucky in both his personal and his professional lives. His poetic genius went unrecognized during his lifetime, and he didn't advance far in his chosen political career. In addition,

Tu Fu 712–770

Tu Fu endured poverty and uncertainty, owing in part to the revolts and unrest that afflicted the region of China where he lived.

 MORE ABOUT THE AUTHOR For more on Tu Fu, visit the **Literature Center** at **ClassZone.com.**

Letter to a Young Refugee from Another

Andrew Lam

On the news last night I saw you amidst a sea of desperate Albanian refugees, and afterward I couldn't get the image out of my mind. You with your wide eyes and shy smile, your hand gripping your mother's as if it were a life saver, you are repeating my story of 24 years ago.

   Listen, even if I know so little about your country's tumultuous history, even if I don't know your name, I think I know what you are going through. When I was eleven, about your age, I too fled from my homeland with my mother and sister and grandmother when the communist tanks came rolling into Saigon, Vietnam. We ended up in a refugee camp[1] in Guam[2] while our father
10 was left behind. **A**

   Back then I couldn't make any sense out of what had happened to me or my family. History, after all, is always baffling to the young. One day I was reading my favorite book in my mother's rose garden, my dogs sleeping lazily at my feet, and the next day I was running for my life with a small backpack in which I only managed to save my stamp collection. Everything else was burnt: photographs, mementos, books, toys, letters, and clothes. **B**

   For the first few days in the refugee camp, I walked about as if in a kind of somnambulist[3] trance. Something had slipped loose within me, a familiar tapestry quickly unraveling. Only years later, only after many revisitations
20 to the scene in my mind, did it slowly dawn on me what I had experienced: terror—a natural reaction to the fact that I was dispossessed, an exile.

ANALYZE VISUALS
Which **details** in the photograph suggest that the woman and child are experiencing hardships?

A **AUTHOR'S MESSAGE**
Whom is the author addressing in the essay? Why?

B **AUTHOR'S MESSAGE**
Notice the **facts** and **personal anecdotes** that the author presents in lines 1–16. What does this information reveal about the author's past?

---

1. **refugee camp:** a shelter for people displaced by war, political oppression, religious persecution, or famine.

2. **Guam** (gwäm): a Pacific island that is an unincorporated territory of the United States.

3. **somnambulist** (sŏm-năm′byə-lĭst): a person who sleepwalks.

My young friend, there are so many things I want to tell you, so many experiences I want to share with you, but, most of all, I want to warn you that the road ahead is a very difficult and treacherous one, and you must be brave and strong and cunning. There are crucial things you should learn and learn quickly, and then there are things you must mull over for the rest of your life. **C**

The immediate thing is to learn to rise as early as possible. The food line is always long and no matter how early you are there, there will always be a line. You must have a hat or a scarf to protect your head from the cold and then
30 from the rising sun, since it can take half a day for food.

When you get to the end of the line, try to act as helpless and as sad as possible. Tell the server that your frail grandmother is bedridden and cannot wait in line, that you are, in fact, feeding her. Cry if you can. Try not to feel ashamed. That you never begged before in your life means nothing. Swallow your pride. Another plate will save you or your mother or sister many hours of waiting for the next meal and will give them time to stand in line for medicine or clothes, depending on your immediate needs.

Listen carefully, a new reality is upon you, and you must rise to it as best you can. It entails a drastic change in your nature and in your thinking. It
40 requires new flexibility and cunning. Be aggressive even when you are naturally shy. Be brave even when only days earlier you still hugged your teddy bear going to sleep.

Be fierce. Do not let others take advantage of you. Do not show that you are weak. In the worst circumstances, the weak get left out or beaten and robbed. Arm yourself, if you can, with a knife or a stone, and guard your family and possessions like a mad dog its bone. People can sense that you are willing to fight for what you have left, and most will back away.

Be alert. Listen to gossips and news. Find out what is coming down the line: food, donated clothes, blankets, tents, and medicines. Always get more than
50 you need, if you can manage it, because extra can be traded with others for something you don't have or can be given away to the elderly and feeble who are not as quick as you. An extra blanket is so helpful on a cold spring night, as you, I'm sure, have already found out.

Be hopeful. No, more than that. Don't give up hope. Maybe your father has made it somewhere else, to another camp possibly. The same can be said of your aunts and cousins, friends, and neighbors. Never give up hope. Soon enough the camp will organize, and there'll be a newsletter with information regarding lost relatives looking for each other, or a bulletin board with names and agencies that will track displaced loved ones. Go every day to check and
60 see whether your father has sent word. Console your inconsolable mother and sister. Hug them as often as you can. **D**

I close my eyes now and cast my mind back to that time spent in the refugee camp, and all I hear are the sounds of weeping. I imagine it is not

C **AUTHOR'S MESSAGE**
Reread lines 22–26. On the basis of this passage, what appears to be the message of the essay?

D **AUTHOR'S MESSAGE**
In lines 27–61 the author offers a **list**, or catalog, of do's and don'ts for the young Albanian refugee. **Summarize** the main points of the list.

that different than what you are hearing now each morning, each afternoon, and each night. Throughout the green tent city that flapped incessantly in the wind was the music of sorrow and grief. A woman who saw her husband shot in front of her wailed until she was hoarse and breathless. A man who left his feeble father behind cried quietly into his blanket. A woman whose teenage son was kept behind stared out into the dark as if she had lost her mind. For
70 a while, the sound of weeping was my refugee camp lullaby.

Indeed, life in limbo[4] is difficult and humiliating, but you must remember that being robbed of what you loved does not speak to your weakness or frailty. It only speaks of the inhumanity and fear and hatred of those who caused you to flee and endure in this new dispossessed reality.

By the same token, I implore you, do not give in to their hatred. I know it is very hard, if not impossible, for someone who has just been forced out of his homeland, but you must try. Those who killed and robbed and caused so much pain and suffering to you, your family, and your people are, in fact, trying to make you into their own image, even if they don't realize it yet. They
80 want you to hate just like them, and they want you to be consumed with the fire of their hatred. Don't hate. Hatred consumes oppressed and oppressors alike and its terrible expressions—revenge is chief among them—always result in blood and tears and injustice and unspeakable suffering, especially for the innocent.

Don't hate. Love instead. Love what you lost, love what you still have, and love those who suffered along with you, for their suffering and yours are part of your inheritance.

And don't forget. Commit everything—each blade of grass, each teary-eyed child, each unmarked grave—to memory. Then when you are older, tell your
90 story. Tell it on your bruised knees, if you must. Tell it at the risk of madness. Scream it from the top of your lungs, the way a wounded bird would sing its last song. For though the story of how you suffered, how you lost your home, your loved ones, and how you triumphed is not new, it must always be told. And it must be heard. It is the only light we ever have against the overwhelming darkness. ◐ **E**

E AUTHOR'S MESSAGE
What important piece of advice does the author end with?

---

4. **limbo:** a state of being disregarded or forgotten.

Song of P'eng-ya

Tu Fu

I remember when we first fled the rebels,[1]
hurrying north over dangerous trails;
night deepened on P'eng-ya Road,[2]
the moon shone over White-water Hills.
5 A whole family endlessly trudging,
begging without shame from the people we met:
valley birds sang, a jangle of soft voices;
we didn't see a single traveler returning. **F**
The baby girl in her hunger bit me;
10 fearful that tigers or wolves would hear her cries,
I hugged her to my chest, muffling her mouth,
but she squirmed and wailed louder than before.
The little boy pretended he knew what was happening;
importantly he searched for sour plums to eat.
15 Ten days, half in rain and thunder,
through mud and slime we pulled each other on.
There was no escaping from the rain,
trails slick, clothes wet and clammy;
getting past the hardest places,
20 a whole day advanced us no more than three or four li.[3]
Mountain fruits served for rations,
low-hung branches were our rafter and roof. **G**
Mornings we traveled by rock-bedded streams,
evenings camped in mists that closed in the sky.
25 We stopped a little while at the marsh of T'ung-chia,[4]
thinking to go out by Lu-tzu[5] Pass;

F **AUTHOR'S MESSAGE**
Reread lines 1–8. What has happened to the **speaker** and his family?

G **AUTHOR'S MESSAGE**
Reread lines 9–22. Which **images** strongly convey the physical hardships of refugee life?

---

1. **rebels:** troops led by the traitorous general An Lu-shan, who attacked and captured the Chinese capital of Ch'ang-an in A.D. 756.

2. **P'eng-ya** (pŭng'yä') **Road:** a road to the town of P'eng-ya, about 130 miles north of Ch'ang-an. Tu Fu and his family passed through P'eng-ya as they sought safety from the rebel forces.

3. **three or four li** (lē): less than a mile and a half.

4. **T'ung-chia** (tŏŏng'jyä').

5. **Lu-tzu** (lōō'dzŭ').

an old friend there, Sun Tsai,[6]
ideals higher than the piled-up clouds;
he came out to meet us as dusk turned to darkness,
30 called for torches, opening gate after gate,
heated water to wash our feet,
cut strips of paper to call back our souls.[7]
Then his wife and children came;
seeing us, their tears fell in streams. **H**
35 My little chicks had gone sound to sleep;
he called them to wake up and eat from his plate,
said he would make a vow with me,
the two of us to be brothers forever.
At last he cleared the room where we sat,
40 wished us goodnight, all he had at our command.
Who is willing, in the hard, bleak times,
to break open, lay bare his innermost heart?
Parting from you, a year of months has rounded,
Tartar tribes[8] still plotting evil,
45 and I think how it would be to have strong wings
that would carry me away, set me down before you. **I**

Translated by Burton Watson

H **AUTHOR'S MESSAGE**
Reread lines 27–34.
The phrase "ideals
higher than the piled-up
clouds" and "tears fell in
streams" are examples
of **figurative language.**
What ideas or emotions
do they suggest?

I **AUTHOR'S MESSAGE**
Describe the **mood,** or
feeling, conveyed by
the poem. In the end,
does the poet send a
message of hope or one
of hopelessness?

---

6. **Sun Tsai** (so͞on′ dzī′).

7. **cut strips of paper to call back our souls:** It was believed that the soul could leave the body when a person
was frightened. The ritual referred to here was intended to restore the souls of the frightened travelers.

8. **Tartar tribes:** the forces of An Lu-shan.

Comprehension

READING STANDARD
4.5 Analyze how choice of genre affects theme

1. **Recall** What do the author of the essay and the Albanian refugee have in common?

2. **Clarify** According to the essay, why should refugees love, instead of hate, those who have caused them pain?

3. **Recall** What hardships does the speaker of Tu Fu's poem face on P'eng-ya Road?

4. **Summarize** In the poem, how does Sun Tsai help the speaker's family?

Literary Analysis

5. **Analyze Point of View** Both the essay and the poem are written from first-person points of view. Think about the effect each point of view has on you as the reader. How might your understanding of **refugees** and their hardships be different if third-person observers narrated the accounts?

6. **Identify Author's Purpose** An author usually writes for one or more of the following purposes: to inform, to express an opinion or feeling, to entertain, or to persuade. For which purposes do these selections appear to have been written? Explain your answer.

7. **Examine Imagery and Mood** The feeling or atmosphere a writer creates for readers is called a mood. The mood of a piece might be described, for example, as somber, mysterious, cheerful, or joyful. Mood is often established by imagery—vivid words and phrases that appeal to the senses. Cite three examples of imagery in "Song of P'eng-ya" and tell how they help establish the mood of the poem.

Comparing Across Genres

Now that you have read both selections about refugee life, you are ready to identify each author's message. The following **Points of Comparison** chart will help you get started.

Points of Comparison	In the Essay	In the Poem
What situation does the person face?		
What living conditions are experienced?		
What qualities help the person survive?		
Write a sentence stating the **author's message** as you interpret it.		
What techniques does the author rely on most?		

Writing for Assessment

1. READ THE PROMPT

In writing assessments, you will often be asked to **compare and contrast** works of literature that explore a similar theme. You are now going to practice writing an essay that requires this type of focus.

PROMPT

Although living more than a thousand years apart, both Andrew Lam and Tu Fu experienced displacement from their homelands. In their works, both authors attempt to give readers an impression of their lives as political exiles. In a four- or five-paragraph essay, compare and contrast how the two authors explore this theme. Do the selections offer a similar message about refugee life? In what ways do the messages differ? Cite evidence to support your response.

◀ **STRATEGIES IN ACTION**

1. *I need to write an essay that will show **similarities and differences** in two selections.*

2. *I have to consider each **author's message** about refugee life.*

3. *I need to include **examples or quotations** from the two works.*

2. PLAN YOUR WRITING

- Review the answers you provided for the **Points of Comparison** chart on page 462.

- Using your chart, find examples to use as evidence for the points you will develop in your essay. If necessary, review the selections again to identify more examples.

- Create an outline to organize your main points.

I. Lam's essay
  A. Theme
  B. Author's attitude
II. Tu Fu's poem
III. Similarities
IV. Differences

3. DRAFT YOUR RESPONSE

Introduction Introduce the topic—refugee life—and then explain that you will be comparing and contrasting the messages of the selections.

Body State and explain Andrew Lam's main idea in one paragraph and Tu Fu's theme in another. In a third paragraph, compare the two messages. In a fourth paragraph, contrast the messages. Make sure to support your statements with examples and quotations from the selections.

Conclusion Wrap up your essay with a final thought about refugee life and a brief summary of your main points.

Revision Check your use of transitional words and phrases to connect your ideas within and between paragraphs. Words and phrases such as *likewise*, *both*, and *in the same way* signal similarities. *Nevertheless* and *however* signal differences.

Writing Workshop

Comparison-Contrast Essay

"This novel is much better than that one." "Which of these cameras takes better pictures?" Comparing and contrasting are important ways of understanding the world. Using this skill in writing strengthens that understanding. See for yourself by following the **Writer's Road Map**.

WRITER'S ROAD MAP

Comparison-Contrast Essay

WRITING PROMPT 1

Writing from Literature Write an essay comparing and/or contrasting two literary works. Concentrate on key aspects of the literature, such as theme, setting, and characters, and explain how those key aspects affect the works' overall meanings. Your reader should gain a new understanding of the works.

Literature to Compare
- "Two Friends" and "When Mr. Pirzada Came to Dine"
- "Do not weep, maiden, for war is kind" and "the sonnet-ballad"
- "Cranes" and "Two Friends"

WRITING PROMPT 2

Writing from the Real World Write an essay comparing two creative works that are especially interesting to you. Choose key aspects of the works as the basis of your comparison. You might consider setting, characters, time period, or theme as the focus of your comparison.

Sources to Consider
- two situation comedies on television
- two action-adventure movies
- two songs

 WRITING TOOLS
For prewriting, revision, and editing tools, visit the **Writing Center** at ClassZone.com.

KEY TRAITS

1. IDEAS
- Clearly **identifies the works** being compared and/or contrasted
- Includes a **thesis statement** that identifies the similarities and/or differences
- Uses specific **examples** to support key ideas

2. ORGANIZATION
- Includes a strong **introduction** and a satisfying **conclusion**
- Follows a consistent **organizational pattern**
- Uses **transitional words and phrases**

3. VOICE
- Uses **appropriate language** for the audience and purpose

4. WORD CHOICE
- Uses **precise words** to explain similarities and differences

5. SENTENCE FLUENCY
- Uses many different **sentence beginnings** for pacing and variety

6. CONVENTIONS
- Employs **correct grammar and usage**

Part 1: Analyze a Student Model

WRITING STANDARD
6.4 Write informational essays or reports

Jason Wilkes
Leyden High School

Defying Death: "The Interlopers" and "Two Friends"

How can people find meaning in life when death could come at any time? Philosophers and writers have pondered this question for centuries. "The Interlopers" by Saki and "Two Friends" by Guy de Maupassant are two short stories with similar messages about death and fate. However,
5 the nature of the characters' relationships, the experiences they undergo, and the circumstances of their deaths are completely different.

At the beginning of the stories, the relationships between the characters are totally dissimilar. Ulrich von Gradwitz and Georg Znaeym in "The Interlopers" are inheritors of a family land dispute and
10 share a deep, lifelong hatred: "as boys they had thirsted for one another's blood, as men each prayed that misfortune might fall on the other." Von Gradwitz jealously guards the land, hoping to find his enemy illegally hunting there and to kill him.

In "Two Friends," on the other hand, Morissot and Sauvage share
15 a deep friendship. They met while fishing and "understood each other perfectly . . . because their tastes were so alike and their feelings identical." Their relationship endures, even though they know little of each other's lives and have no contact beyond their shared hobby.

In both stories, the bond between the characters continues to draw
20 them together as the plot develops. The pairs of characters undergo very different experiences, however. In "The Interlopers," the two enemies tramp through von Gradwitz's forest, Znaeym hunting for game and von Gradwitz hunting for Znaeym. In contrast, the characters in "Two Friends" meet accidentally in the street. Overjoyed to see each other
25 after a long separation, they decide to go fishing, ignoring the fact that their country is at war.

KEY TRAITS IN ACTION

Introduction hooks readers with a question and **identifies the literary works.** The **thesis statement** spells out the differences in the two works.

Quotation and specific **examples** support the idea of the characters' hatred.

Transitional phrase clarifies the contrast between the relationships in the two stories.

Uses a point-by-point **organizational pattern. Precise words** (*bond, draw, tramp, overjoyed*) and **appropriately formal langauge** strengthen the essay.

These dissimilar experiences nevertheless lead to all four characters' deaths—deaths that are surprising and unexpected. In "The Interlopers," von Gradwitz and Znaeym meet just as a violent storm erupts. Before they can kill each other, a tree falls on them both. Realizing that they are both doomed unless someone comes to find them, von Gradwitz offers Znaeym an end to their feud and a pledge of friendship. Znaeym accepts. Together, they shout for help. With the bonds of their hatred turned to friendship, they await their death from approaching wolves.

In sharp contrast, the relationship between Morissot and Sauvage in "Two Friends" is consistent throughout the story. While the two are fishing, Prussian soldiers capture them. In the end, neither speaks because neither wants to betray the other. The soldiers shoot them both. The two men die together, victims of the same fate as von Gradwitz and Znaeym in "The Interlopers."

In these short stories, Saki and Maupassant present different characters living out different plots to come to the same unexpected end—one that comes to us all eventually. Both authors seem to be saying that, in a world full of natural or political enemies, all people have is each other. Through friendship, we can defy death and find meaning in life.

Variety of **sentence beginnings** create interest and rhythmic flow.

Conclusion summarizes and interprets the points made, explains the title of the essay, and refers back to the introduction.

2

WRITING STANDARD
5.4 Determine a purpose and audience

Part 2: Apply the Writing Process

PREWRITING

What Should I Do?	**What Does It Look Like?**

1. Analyze the prompt.
Review the writing prompt you selected. Circle words that tell you the format that your writing will take. Underline words that indicate the **topics** you should compare and contrast and the **audience** and **purpose** of your writing.

> **TIP** If the prompt does not specify your audience, write for your teacher and classmates.

WRITING PROMPT Write (an essay) comparing and/or contrasting two literary works. Concentrate on key aspects of the literature, such as theme, setting, and characters, and explain how those key aspects affect the works' overall meanings. Your reader should gain a new understanding of the works.

The format is an essay. The purpose is to compare and contrast two works of literature.

2. Focus on similarities and differences.
Reread (or re-view) the works you're comparing, looking for elements that are alike and different. Use a graphic organizer, such as a Venn diagram, to record your findings.

"The Interlopers"
* characters are enemies
* death an act of nature

Both
* die together
* death is unexpected

"Two Friends"
* characters are friends
* death an act of war

3. Write a working thesis statement.
Summarize the similarities and differences between the works in a working thesis statement. You might need to refine this statement as you draft your essay.

"The Interlopers" and "Two Friends" have similar messages about life and death. However, the characters' relationships, experiences, and deaths are very different.

4. Collect evidence.
Use a chart to record details and quotations that support the key ideas of your thesis.

> **TIP** When you use quotations from the works, copy the words precisely. Use ellipses (. . .) to show omitted material and brackets ([ ]) to add words or phrases for clarification.

Story Element	"The Interlopers"	"Two Friends"
characters' relationship	"each prayed that misfortune might fall on the other"	"they understood each other perfectly"

What Should I Do?

What Does It Look Like?

1. Choose an organizational pattern.
You can organize your comparison-contrast essay in two ways:

Point by point—Compare and contrast the works by discussing one element at a time.

Subject by subject—Discuss all the elements of one work first, then all the elements of the other.

TIP Try each pattern to see which works better.

POINT-BY-POINT ORGANIZATION

1. Characters' relationship
"The Interlopers": enemies
"Two Friends": friends

2. How they meet
"The Interlopers": want to fight each other
"Two Friends": meet by chance

3. How they die
"The Interlopers": accident, wolves
"Two Friends": soldiers

SUBJECT-BY-SUBJECT ORGANIZATION

1. "The Interlopers"
• Characters are enemies.
• They want to fight each other.
• They die by accident—tree, wolves.

2. "Two Friends"
• Characters are friends.
• They meet by chance.
• Soldiers shoot them.

2. Include specific details to show your key ideas.
Refer to the details you collected in step 4 on page 467. Incorporate these into your draft to make your writing stronger and more convincing.

In sharp contrast, the relationship between Morissot and Sauvage in "Two Friends" is consistent throughout the story. ⎤ — Key idea

While the two are fishing, Prussian soldiers capture them. In the end, neither speaks because neither wants to betray the other. ⎤ — Supporting details

3. Use transitions to clarify relationships between ideas.
Use words such as *both* and *like* to indicate similarity. Words and phrases such as *however, in contrast,* and *on the other hand* show difference.

See page 470: Add Transitions

In both stories, the bond between the characters continues to draw them together as the plot develops. The pairs of characters undergo very different experiences, however. In "The Interlopers," the two enemies tramp through von Gradwitz's forest, Znaeym hunting for game and von Gradwitz hunting for Znaeym. In contrast, the characters in "Two Friends" meet accidentally in the street.

REVISING AND EDITING

What Should I Do?	*What Does It Look Like?*

1. Make sure your introduction engages the reader.

- Read your introduction aloud. (Circle) sentences that seem obvious or boring.

- Add an interesting observation, a question, or some dialogue to catch the reader's attention.

▶

How can people find meaning in life when death could come at any time?

"The Interlopers" by Saki and "Two Friends" by Guy de Maupassant are ~~both about death.~~
two short stories with similar messages about death and fate.

2. Replace imprecise vocabulary with strong, specific words.

- <u>Underline</u> vague words and phrases, such as *really, kind of, sort of, lots,* and *things.*

- Use precise terms to make your essay more accurate and sophisticated.

▶

Their relationship ~~stays really great,~~ endures, even though

they ~~are kind of ignorant about~~ know little of each other's lives and

have no contact beyond ~~what they do.~~ their shared hobby.

3. Clearly connect your ideas.

- Draw a box around each transition that you used.

- If your essay lacks boxes, add transitions that clarify how ideas compare or contrast.

▶

Von Gradwitz jealously guards the land, hoping to find his enemy illegally hunting there and to kill him.

In "Two Friends," on the other hand, Morissot and Sauvage share a deep friendship.

4. Fine-tune your conclusion to leave a powerful impression.

- Ask a peer reader to highlight parts of your conclusion that are confusing or that need more elaboration.

- Include details or explanations to clarify your ideas and show your reader a new way of thinking about the works.

See page 470: Ask a Peer Reader

▶

~~The message of the stories is that all people have is each other.~~

Both authors seem to be saying that, in a world full of natural or political enemies, all people have is each other. Through friendship, we can defy death and find meaning in life.

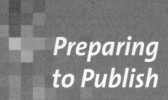

Comparison-Contrast Essay

Apply the Rubric

A strong comparison-contrast essay . . .

☑ identifies the two works in a strong introduction

☑ explains the similarities and/or differences between the works in a focused thesis statement

☑ includes well-chosen details, examples, and quotations from the works to support ideas

☑ precisely explains comparisons and contrasts

☑ develops ideas within a consistent organizational pattern

☑ uses transitions effectively

☑ varies sentence beginnings

☑ ends powerfully by drawing an overall conclusion about the works

Ask a Peer Reader

• Which statement that I made had the biggest impact on you? Why?

• Did any parts of my conclusion seem weak or confusing?

Add Transitions

For Comparing	For Contrasting
also	but
another	however
both	in contrast
in addition to	instead
similarly	on the other hand

Check Your Grammar

• Include a comma after an introductory word or phrase.

> At the beginning of the stories , the relationships between the characters are totally dissimilar.

See page R49: Quick Reference: Punctuation

• Make similar sentence elements parallel.

> Realizing that they are both doomed unless someone comes to find them, von Gradwitz offers Znaeym an end to their feud and ~~to be friends.~~ a pledge of friendship.

See page R64: Parallel Structure

Writing Online

PUBLISHING OPTIONS
For publishing options, visit the **Writing Center** at ClassZone.com.

ASSESSMENT PREPARATION
For writing and grammar assessment practice, go to the **Assessment Center** at ClassZone.com.

Participating in a Group Discussion

Taking part in a group discussion can enhance your understanding and appreciation of the works you compared and contrasted.

Planning the Discussion

1. **Form a discussion group.** Form a group with three or more classmates. Ask for volunteers or appoint group members to act as moderator and recorder. The other members will be participants.

2. **Agree on rules for the discussion.** All group members should agree to
   - speak clearly and concisely
   - listen respectfully without interrupting
   - ask thoughtful questions

3. **Review the works and your thoughts about them.** Share your main ideas with the group and try to resolve any differences.

   TIP Use your thesis statement and key points as a basis for ideas that you will contribute to the discussion.

4. **Get ready to present the results of your group's discussion.** Consider summarizing your ideas graphically in the form of a Venn diagram or a Y chart, acting out key comparisons and contrasts, or staging a debate.

> "The Interlopers"
> ~~two characters~~
> ~~with strong~~
> ~~relationship~~
> enemies because of family feud
> become friends
> ~~die unexpectedly~~
> ~~together~~
> storm and wolves kill them
> ~~friendship defies~~
> ~~death~~
>
> "Two Friends"
> ~~friendship defies~~
> ~~death~~
> friends who share a love of fishing
> ~~two characters~~
> ~~with strong~~
> ~~relationship~~
> relationship doesn't change
> ~~die unexpectedly~~
> ~~together~~
> enemy soldiers kill them
>
> **Both**
> two characters with strong relationship
> die unexpectedly together
> friendship defies death

Presenting Discussion Results

1. **Organize and run through your presentation.** Decide what each group member will contribute. Then have a brief rehearsal.

2. **Maintain eye contact.** Glance frequently at several people scattered throughout the audience. Don't forget to watch the other group members too.

3. **Speak slowly and clearly.** Adjust your pacing to stress particularly interesting or important information.

Reading Comprehension

DIRECTIONS *Read the following selection and then answer the questions.*

Witches' Loaves

O. Henry

Miss Martha Meacham kept the little bakery on the corner (the one where you go up three steps, and the bell tinkles when you open the door).

Miss Martha was forty, her bankbook showed a credit of two thousand dollars, and she possessed two false teeth and a sympathetic heart. Many people have married whose chances to do so were much inferior to Miss Martha's.

Two or three times a week a customer came in in whom she began to take an interest. He was a middle-aged man, wearing spectacles and a brown beard trimmed to a careful point.

10 He spoke English with a strong German accent. His clothes were worn and darned in places, and wrinkled and baggy in others. But he looked neat, and had very good manners.

He always bought two loaves of stale bread. Fresh bread was five cents a loaf. Stale ones were two for five. Never did he call for anything but stale bread.

Once Miss Martha saw a red and brown stain on his fingers. She was sure then that he was an artist and very poor. No doubt he lived in a garret, where he painted pictures and ate stale bread and thought of the good things to eat in Miss Martha's bakery.

Often when Miss Martha sat down to her chops and light rolls and jam
20 and tea she would sigh, and wish that the gentle-mannered artist might share her tasty meal instead of eating his dry crust in that drafty attic. Miss Martha's heart, as you have been told, was a sympathetic one.

In order to test her theory as to his occupation, she brought from her room one day a painting that she had bought at a sale, and set it against the shelves behind the bread counter.

It was a Venetian scene. A splendid marble palazzo (so it said on the picture) stood in the foreground—or rather forewater. For the rest there were gondolas (with the lady trailing her hand in the water), clouds, sky, and chiaroscuro in plenty. No artist could fail to notice it.

30 Two days afterward the customer came in.

"Two loafs of stale bread, if you blease."

"You haf here a fine bicture, madame," he said while she was wrapping up the bread.

"Yes?" says Miss Martha, reveling in her own cunning. "I do so admire art and" (no, it would not do to say "artists" thus early) "and paintings," she substituted. "You think it is a good picture?"

"Der balace," said the customer, "is not in good drawing. Der bairspective of it is not true. Goot morning, madame."

He took his bread, bowed, and hurried out.

40 Yes, he must be an artist. Miss Martha took the picture back to her room.

How gentle and kindly his eyes shone behind his spectacles! What a broad brow he had! To be able to judge perspective at a glance—and to live on stale bread! But genius often has to struggle before it is recognized.

What a thing it would be for art and perspective if genius were backed by two thousand dollars in bank, a bakery, and a sympathetic heart to— But these were daydreams, Miss Martha.

Often now when he came he would chat for a while across the showcase. He seemed to crave Miss Martha's cheerful words.

He kept on buying stale bread. Never a cake, never a pie, never one of her 50 delicious Sally Lunns.

She thought he began to look thinner and discouraged. Her heart ached to add something good to eat to his meager purchase, but her courage failed at the act. She did not dare affront him. She knew the pride of artists.

Miss Martha took to wearing her blue-dotted silk waist[1] behind the counter. In the back room she cooked a mysterious compound of quince seeds and borax. Ever so many people use it for the complexion.

One day the customer came in as usual, laid his nickel on the showcase, and called for his stale loaves. While Miss Martha was reaching for them there was a great tooting and clanging, and a fire-engine came lumbering past.

60 The customer hurried to the door to look, as anyone will. Suddenly inspired, Miss Martha seized the opportunity.

On the bottom shelf behind the counter was a pound of fresh butter that the dairyman had left ten minutes before. With bread knife Miss Martha made a deep slash in each of the stale loaves, inserted a generous quantity of butter, and pressed the loaves tight again.

When the customer turned once more she was tying the paper around them.

When he had gone, after an unusually pleasant little chat, Miss Martha smiled to herself, but not without a slight fluttering of the heart.

Had she been too bold? Would he take offense? But surely not. There was 70 no language of edibles. Butter was no emblem of unmaidenly forwardness.

For a long time that day her mind dwelt on the subject. She imagined the

---

1. **waist:** blouse.

scene when he should discover her little deception.

He would lay down his brushes and palette. There would stand his easel with the picture he was painting in which the perspective was beyond criticism.

He would prepare for his luncheon of dry bread and water. He would slice into a loaf—ah!

Miss Martha blushed. Would he think of the hand that placed it there as he ate? Would he—

80   The front door bell jangled viciously. Somebody was coming in, making a great deal of noise.

Miss Martha hurried to the front. Two men were there. One was a young man smoking a pipe—a man she had never seen before. The other was her artist.

His face was very red, his hat was on the back of his head, his hair was wildly rumpled. He clinched his two fists and shook them ferociously at Miss Martha. *At Miss Martha.*

"*Dummkopf!*" he shouted with extreme loudness; and then "*Tausendonfer!*" or something like it in German.

90   The young man tried to draw him away.

"I vill not go," he said angrily, "else I shall told her."

He made a bass drum of Miss Martha's counter.

"You haf shpoilt me," he cried, his blue eyes blazing behind his spectacles. "I vill tell you. You vas von *meddlingsome old cat!*"

Miss Martha leaned weakly against the shelves and laid one hand on her blue-dotted silk waist. The young man took the other by the collar.

"Come on," he said, "you've said enough." He dragged the angry one out at the door to the sidewalk, and then came back.

"Guess you ought to be told, ma'am," he said, "what the row is about.

100 That's Blumberger. He's an architectural draftsman. I work in the same office with him.

"He's been working hard for three months drawing a plan for a new city hall. It was a prize competition. He finished inking the lines yesterday. You know, a draftsman always makes his drawing in pencil first. When it's done he rubs out the pencil lines with handfuls of stale bread crumbs. That's better than India rubber.

"Blumberger's been buying the bread here. Well, today—well, you know, ma'am, that butter isn't—well, Blumberger's plan isn't good for anything now except to cut up into railroad sandwiches."

110   Miss Martha went into the back room. She took off the blue-dotted silk waist and put on the old brown serge she used to wear. Then she poured the quince seed and borax mixture out of the window into the ash can.

Comprehension

DIRECTIONS *Answer these questions about the story "Witches' Loaves."*

1. What can you infer about Miss Martha from lines 15–18?
   A. She has a tendency to jump to conclusions.
   B. She feels superior to artists.
   C. She wishes all artists didn't live poorly.
   D. She is proud of giving out bakery goods.

2. Miss Martha's "compound of quince seeds and borax" in lines 55–56 is a symbol of
   A. her fear of growing old and ill
   B. her pride at being successful in business
   C. her dissatisfaction with her appearance
   D. her desire for a romantic relationship

3. Which sentence best describes the main theme of the story?
   A. It takes only one mistake to ruin the work of a genius.
   B. People are sometimes too proud to accept gifts from strangers.
   C. People sometimes let their desires affect the way they see the world.
   D. It is best not to have sympathy for people.

4. What can you infer from Miss Martha's decision to wear her blue-dotted silk waist?
   A. She hopes Blumberger will mention it so that she can start a conversation.
   B. She wears it to keep her dress clean as she bakes and waits on customers.
   C. She wants to show Blumberger that she can afford expensive clothes.
   D. She wants to look attractive to Blumberger.

5. According to Miss Martha, why does Blumberger always buy only stale bread?
   A. He is too poor to afford anything better.
   B. He likes to eat stale bread.
   C. He needs it for his work.
   D. He needs an excuse to go see her.

6. What conclusion can you draw about Blumberger at the end of the story?
   A. He is insulted that Miss Martha pitied him.
   B. He is angry that his drawing was ruined.
   C. He is happy to be a draftsman.
   D. He is upset that he has to redo his drawing.

7. Why does Miss Martha throw out the quince seed and borax mixture at the end of the story?
   A. Her romantic dreams are over.
   B. She doesn't like Blumberger anymore.
   C. She wants to change her looks back.
   D. She thinks that she has been "unmaidenly."

Written Response

SHORT ANSWER
Write three or four sentences to answer this question.

8. Lines 15–18 show Miss Martha's response to Blumberger's stained fingers. How does her response illustrate the theme of the story?

EXTENDED RESPONSE
Write two or three paragraphs to answer this question.

9. Name three assumptions that Miss Martha makes about Blumberger, and give the story details on which they are based. Then tell how each assumption is shown to be wrong at the end of the story.

GO ON

Vocabulary

DIRECTIONS *Use context clues and your knowledge of prefixes to answer the following questions.*

1. The Greek prefix *sym-* means "with," and the Greek word *pathos* means "emotion." Which of the following words best conveys the meaning of *sympathetic* in lines 4, 22, and 45?

    A. dramatic

    B. understanding

    C. passionate

    D. fiery

2. The Latin prefix *af-* means "toward," and the Latin word *frons* means "face." What is the most likely meaning of *affront* in line 53?

    A. meet face to face

    B. avoid a hostile meeting

    C. go behind one's back

    D. offend openly

3. The word *inspire* comes from the Latin prefix *in-,* meaning "into," and the Latin word *spirare,* meaning "to breathe." What does the word *inspired* mean in line 61?

    A. guided by divine influence

    B. imparted courage

    C. gave life to an idea

    D. inhaled air

4. The prefix *un-* means "not" or "opposite of." The word *maiden* refers to a girl or woman who has not been married. What is the most likely meaning of *unmaidenly* in line 70?

    A. not proper or ladylike

    B. not suitable to a wife

    C. gentlemanly

    D. insulting

DIRECTIONS *Use context clues and your knowledge of connotation to answer the following questions.*

5. What connotation does the word *tinkles* have in line 2?

    A. harshness

    B. gentleness

    C. weakness

    D. alarm

6. What connotation does the word *garret* have in line 16?

    A. spaciousness

    B. loftiness

    C. creativity

    D. poverty

7. What connotation does the word *trailing* have in line 28?

    A. tranquillity

    B. closeness

    C. difficulty

    D. speed

8. What connotation does the word *meager* have in line 52?

    A. prosperity

    B. boredom

    C. humbleness

    D. toughness

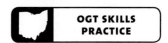

Writing & Grammar

DIRECTIONS *Read the following passage and then answer the questions.*

(1) Geologists study the origin, history, and structure of the earth. (2) Often the rocks they examine are hundreds of millions of years old. (3) Some hills and valleys have been around for a shorter period of time. (4) Just 10,000 years ago, mile-thick glaciers scraped away everything in their path, creating large basins. (5) The glaciers melted and filled the basins with water. (6) The most recent glaciers formed the Great Lakes.

1. Choose the correct way to rewrite sentence 1 by using an adverb.

   A. Geologists like to study the origin, history, and structure of the earth.

   B. Geologists study the historical origin and structure of the earth.

   C. Geologists carefully study the origin, history, and structure of the earth.

   D. Geologists study the exact origin, history, and structure of the earth.

2. Choose the correct way to combine sentences 2 and 3 by using a subordinate clause.

   A. Often the rocks they examine are hundreds of millions of years old, though some hills and valleys have been around for a shorter period of time.

   B. Often the rocks they examine are hundreds of millions of years old, and some hills and valleys have been around for a shorter period of time.

   C. Often the rocks they examine are hundreds of millions of years old, but some hills and valleys have been around for a shorter period of time.

   D. Often the rocks they examine are hundreds of millions of years old; some hills and valleys have been around for a shorter period of time.

3. Choose the correct way to rewrite sentence 4 by adding an adverb.

   A. Just 10,000 years ago, wide, mile-thick glaciers scraped away everything in their path, creating large basins.

   B. Just 10,000 years ago, mile-thick glaciers scraped away everything in their broad path, creating large basins.

   C. Just 10,000 years ago, mile-thick glaciers relentlessly scraped away everything in their path, creating large basins.

   D. Just 10,000 years ago, mile-thick glaciers scraped away almost everything in their path, creating large basins.

4. Choose the correct way to combine sentences 5 and 6 by using a subordinate clause.

   A. The most recent glaciers melted, filled the basins with water, and formed the Great Lakes.

   B. The most recent glaciers melted and filled the basins with water, forming the Great Lakes.

   C. The most recent glaciers melted and filled the basins with water; these glaciers formed the Great Lakes.

   D. As the most recent glaciers melted, they filled the basins with water and formed the Great Lakes.

STOP

UNIT 4
Great Reads

Ideas for Independent Reading

Which questions in Unit 4 did you wish you could examine further? These books can help you extend your explorations.

What would you do for a friend?

Of Mice and Men
by John Steinbeck

Farm workers George and Lennie are best friends in Depression-era California. George protects Lennie, who is bigger and stronger but mentally slow. They drift from job to job, dreaming of buying their own farm, but circumstances shatter their dreams.

Gilgamesh
trans. by Stephen Mitchell

This is a new English translation of the world's oldest book. Gilgamesh, the powerful, arrogant king of Uruk, is humanized through his close friendship with Enkidu. When Enkidu is killed, Gilgamesh sets out on a quest to find immortality.

Four Spirits
by Sena Jeter Naslund

This novel looks at a 1963 Birmingham, Alabama, church bombing through the eyes of several characters, including a black woman and a white woman who become good friends as they work in the civil rights movement.

Who are the victims of war?

The Underdogs
by Mariano Azuela

This novel of the Mexican Revolution follows a band of guerrillas over years spent fighting government forces. At first, the guerrillas are high-minded and ideal-istic; later, they become just as oppressive as their opponents.

Fallen Angels
by Walter Dean Myers

The Vietnam War is shown from the perspective of Richie Perry, a young black soldier from Harlem. His experiences confuse and terrify him and bring him to an unexpected maturity.

Catch-22
by Joseph Heller

The soldier Yossarian wants no part of war because—no surprise—people are trying to kill him. He spends his time thinking of ways to get out but is thwarted by a powerful and absurd military system.

How accepting are you?

Dreams from My Father
by Barack Obama

U.S. senator Obama was born to a white mother from Kansas and a black father from Kenya. His memoir tells how he worked to accept his racial heritage and gained success as an attorney and community organizer.

Twilight: Los Angeles, 1992
by Anna Deavere Smith

Presented are the actual words of about 45 people interviewed by Smith after the 1992 Los Angeles riots. The voices—black, white, Asian, and Latino—reveal how differently people view the world and offer insight into the causes of the riots.

Us and Them: A History of Intolerance in America
by Jim Carnes

This book explores 14 examples of intolerance in America, from the case of Mary Dyer, who was executed for her Quaker faith in 1660, to the Crown Heights riot in 1991, in which African Americans and Hasidic Jews clashed.

UNIT 5

Why Write?

AUTHOR'S PURPOSE

- In Nonfiction
- In Media
- In Fiction
- In Poetry

Why WRITE?

What if you had the ability to inspire others, or make them laugh, or change the way they think? What if you could teach people something new or share the solution to an important problem?

You can. Through writing, anyone—including you—can achieve goals like these. That's why the world is so dependent on words. People need them to accomplish a wide variety of **purposes,** from communicating weekend plans to protesting an unfair law.

ACTIVITY Think of individuals who have affected you with their words. These individuals might be songwriters, politicians, advertisers, or novelists. Write down what each person wrote, what you think his or her reason for writing was, and how you were affected.

OHIO STANDARDS

Preview Unit Goals

LITERARY ANALYSIS
- Identify and analyze author's perspective
- Identify and analyze tone and diction
- Analyze imagery and author's purpose
- Identify, analyze, and evaluate narrative elements in nonfiction

READING
- Recognize and analyze patterns of organization
- Identify and analyze author's purpose
- Use text features to locate information
- Interpret graphic aids; use graphic aids to record information

WRITING AND GRAMMAR
- Write a cause-and-effect essay
- Use transitions to show clear connections; include supporting details
- Use participles and participial phrases; use adverb clauses

SPEAKING, LISTENING, AND VIEWING
- Compare how different media cover the same event
- Evaluate the ways information is presented in nonprint sources
- Deliver an informative speech

VOCABULARY
- Use metaphor or simile to help determine word meaning

ACADEMIC VOCABULARY
- author's perspective
- tone and diction
- author's purpose
- patterns of organization
- graphic aids
- metaphor and simile

Critical Reading Workshop

Author's Purpose and Perspective

An article crammed with statistics, an essay filled with emotional appeals, a business letter, an e-mail from a friend—no matter what you are reading, usually you can scan just the first few lines to find out whether the writing is informative or persuasive, impersonal or revealing. Without realizing it, you are picking up on clues to an author's purpose and perspective, both of which affect what you read and how you read it.

OHIO STANDARDS

READING STANDARDS
3.1 Identify and understand organizational patterns
3.5 Analyze an author's perspective or viewpoint in text

Part 1: Purpose and Perspective

You already know that an **author's purpose**—a writer's reason for crafting a particular work—can be one or more of the following:

- to inform
- to persuade
- to entertain
- to express thoughts or feelings

The purpose of a text is usually obvious. Perspective, though, can be more difficult to detect. An **author's perspective** is the unique combination of ideas, values, and beliefs that influences the way a writer looks at a topic. Most writers do not intentionally broadcast their values, especially journalists, who strive to report "just the facts." In some essays and speeches, however, writers' beliefs are revealed in subtle ways.

As you read any text, look for direct statements in which the writer explicitly expresses his or her beliefs. Also pay attention to the writer's choice of words and details and his or her **tone,** or attitude toward a subject. All these elements can serve as clues to an author's perspective, as you'll notice in this example.

Can you imagine being on a waiting list that is 87,000 people long?

Last year, nearly 87,000 people were on the list for an organ transplant. My sister was one of them. A heart transplant saved her life, but not everyone on the list is as fortunate. Every day, an average of 17 people die while waiting for a compatible organ.

The thought of organ donation used to make me squeamish. But watching my sister get a second chance at life made me realize how vital this act of giving is. Learn about organ donation, and find out if you can save a life.
by Ginny García

Become an Organ Donor

PURPOSE To persuade
- **Phrases** such as *how vital this act of giving is* and the author's direct **call to action** provide clues to the purpose.
- The author makes her case by including alarming statistics.

PERSPECTIVE That of someone whose opinion of organ donation has been shaped by a personal experience
- **Words and phrases** like *second chance at life* convey an impassioned, hopeful **tone.**
- **Direct statements** reveal what the author used to think about organ donation and how she feels about it now.

MODEL 1: PURPOSE

To figure out the purpose of a particular work, you often have to examine the writer's choice of details. You should also consider the intended audience. Use these clues to determine the author's purpose in this excerpt.

from # Go Fast, Turn Easier

Feature article by **Chris Anthony**

Skiing slowly in powder[1] is like jogging through oatmeal: Not only does it feel weird and look silly, but it's downright difficult. Effortless powder skiing is fast powder skiing. You need speed to power through and rise above the snowpack. If you drive your boards under the snow without enough momentum, they'll
5 nosedive until you slow to a stop.

Most people think powder skiing means hard work. They drop in and get low in an effort to manhandle their skis around. Forget muscling the turn: The key is to be on top of the snow *before* you start turning. . . .

---

1. **powder:** deep, dry, light snow that has not yet been packed down by skiers or machines.

Close Read

1. Is this article intended for expert skiers, people with some experience in skiing, or novices? Support your answer.

2. Consider the boxed details and the intended audience. What is the author's primary purpose?

MODEL 2: PURPOSE AND PERSPECTIVE

The author of "Go Fast, Turn Easier" is a knowledgeable skier. Beyond that information, readers don't learn much about his beliefs and values. In the excerpt from "Snow Immobile," the author's perspective on a different winter sport— snowboarding—comes across clearly. As you read, look for clues that reveal both the author's purpose and his perspective.

from # SNOW IMMOBILE

Essay by **Dave Barry**

For those of you who, for whatever reason, such as a will to live, do not participate in downhill winter sports, I should explain that snowboarding is an activity that is very popular with people who do not feel that regular skiing is lethal enough. These are of course young people, fearless people, people with
5 100 percent synthetic bodies who can hurtle down a mountainside at 50 mph and knock down mature trees with their faces and then spring to their feet and go, "Cool."

Close Read

1. The author includes exaggerated details like the one in the box. Find two more examples. What do they suggest about his purpose?

2. Does this author appear to be a fan of snowboarding? Cite details that help you to detect his perspective on snowboarding.

Part 2: Organization and Format

To achieve their purpose and present ideas logically, writers use thoughtfully chosen **patterns of organization,** such as **chronological order** and **classification organization.** By noticing the organizational pattern that is used in a work, you can more easily see relationships among ideas. Here are two other patterns:

- **Cause-and-effect organization** establishes relationships between events, ideas, or trends. A writer might use this pattern to help readers understand a scientific phenomenon or to explain how one historical event brought about another. **Signal Words:** *because, as a result, consequently, since*

- **Compare-and-contrast organization** highlights similarities and differences between two or more subjects. This pattern is used to show the benefits of one subject over another or to compare an unfamiliar subject with a familiar one. **Signal Words:** *similarly, also, like, in contrast, while, but, unlike*

Sometimes readers need more than a few signal words to help them follow information. For example, think about the last time you read an in-depth feature article like the one shown here. In such complex texts, writers use **text features,** such as **titles, subheadings,** and **graphic aids,** to help readers locate information quickly.

The **title** reveals the subject of the article—the flu season.

The Flu Strikes Again

Feature article by **Faye Danahan**

Downtown resident Samantha Shaw says she always knows when winter is approaching. "The coughing and sneezing on the train, in restaurants, at the gym—I'm surrounded by germs. Let the flu season begin!"

Subheadings reflect the main ideas of the sections.

This Year More Severe Than Last
Shaw isn't the only one who's apprehensive. Experts state that flu cases are already up 5 percent from last year at this time. If this month is any indication, Chicago could see a severe 30 percent overall increase in cases this year as compared to last.

Words and phrases signal differences between this year's flu season and last year's.

How to Stay Healthy
Even if you can't get a flu vaccination, there are some precautions you can take.

Continued on page 26A

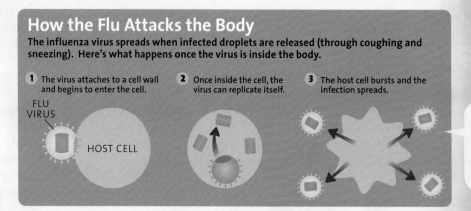

How the Flu Attacks the Body
The influenza virus spreads when infected droplets are released (through coughing and sneezing). Here's what happens once the virus is inside the body.

1. The virus attaches to a cell wall and begins to enter the cell.
2. Once inside the cell, the virus can replicate itself.
3. The host cell bursts and the infection spreads.

FLU VIRUS

HOST CELL

A **graphic aid** helps readers understand how the flu virus spreads.

MODEL: ORGANIZATION AND FORMAT

This author explains how fear and anxiety can affect athletes at pivotal moments. Notice how the author uses specific patterns of organization and text features to help you understand difficult scientific concepts.

10   20   30   40   50   60   70

from # At Home in the Discomfort Zone

Feature article by **Kevin Foley**

Fear and Anxiety   Fear is sudden and arresting, a blind-side Holyfield punch. It can start with a sloppy foothold, a hooked ski edge, or an ill-timed paddle stroke. As your body veers toward trouble—cliff, tree, Class V hole the size of a Winnebago—neurons relay electrical impulses from your eyes to your brain's gumball-size amygdala, which sounds the alarm to the hypothalamus. 5 The two structures begin gushing hormones, urging the adrenal glands to start pumping epinephrine, norepinephrine, and cortisol, three stress hormones that ramp up glucose production, increase heart rate, speed up your breathing, and often leave you sweating like a goose at a down-jacket factory. On the upside, 10 though, fear is turbocharging muscles and the brain for confrontation or evasive action—the classic fight-or-flight response—and that can help performance.

Anxiety is a more plodding matter, says 15 Mary Meagher, a psychologist in the behavioral neuroscience group at Texas A&M University, and it's a reaction that's more troublesome to athletes. "Fear and anxiety have different underlying brain circuitry," she says. "Anxiety 20 is future-oriented; it's about potential threats. You're uncertain, aroused at a low level, with clenched muscles and increased pain sensitivity." . . . | Anxiety stimulates the amygdala, triggering the production of 25 cortisol but generating less heart-whumping adrenaline than fear does. | Fear inspires alarm and action, often suddenly and acutely, outstripping thought; anxiety unfolds more slowly, disrupting thought and evaluation. 30 Thus anxiety is more insidious, magnifying injuries, hindering movements, and knocking athletes out of the blessed neural harmony of competitive flow. But it's more easily controlled than fear.

TIPS

• **Think positive.** You've heard it before, but studies by Meagher and others have shown just how well positive thinking can reduce anxiety's physical effects. . . .

• **Mentally practice overcoming adversity.** Focus on controlling your breathing (slow and deep, not rapid and shallow), on staying in the present moment (you're on the rock, not plummeting from it), and on visualizing success (you're pulling fluidly through the move).

Close Read

1. Reread lines 3–9. What pattern of organization does the author use to explain what happens when "your body veers toward trouble"?

2. In lines 14–33, the author uses compare-and-contrast organization to explain the differences between fear and anxiety. One difference is boxed. Find two other differences.

3. Identify two text features in the article, and explain how they help you as a reader.

Part 3: Compare Texts

In 1954, in *Brown v. Board of Education of Topeka,* the Supreme Court ruled that racial segregation in public schools was unconstitutional. This landmark decision overturned an earlier ruling that endorsed "separate but equal" facilities for blacks and whites. Use what you've learned in this workshop to compare two texts on this historic case.

Brown v. Board of Education of Topeka

Textbook feature

ORIGINS OF THE CASE In the early 1950s, the school system of Topeka, Kansas, operated separate schools for "the two races"—blacks and whites. Reverend Oliver Brown protested that this was unfair to his eight-year-old daughter Linda. Although the Browns lived near a "white" school, 5 Linda was forced to take a long bus ride to her "black" school across town.

THE RULING **The Court ruled that segregated public schools were "inherently" unequal and therefore unconstitutional.**

LEGAL REASONING While the correctness of the *Brown* ruling—which actually involved five segregation cases from across the nation—seems 10 obvious today, some justices had difficulty agreeing to it. One reason was the force of legal precedent. The *Plessy* v. *Ferguson* decision endorsing segregation had stood for over 50 years. It clearly stated that "separate but equal" facilities did not violate the Fourteenth Amendment.

Thurgood Marshall, the NAACP lawyer who argued *Brown,* spent 15 years laying the groundwork to chip away at Jim Crow—the local laws that required segregated facilities. Marshall had recently won two Supreme Court decisions in 1950 that challenged segregation at graduate schools. Then in 1952, the Supreme Court agreed to hear the Browns' case.
20 The Court deliberated for two years before deciding how to interpret the Fourteenth Amendment.

In the end, Chief Justice Earl Warren carefully sidestepped *Plessy,* claiming that segregated schools were not and never could be equal. On Monday, 25 May 17, 1954, Warren read the unanimous decision:

"Does segregation of children in public schools . . . deprive children of . . . equal educational opportunities? We believe that it does."

30 —*Brown* v. *Board of Education of Topeka*

LEGAL SOURCES

U.S. Constitution
Fourteenth Amendment, Equal Protection Clause (1868):

"No state shall . . . deny to any person within its jurisdiction the equal protection of the laws."

Related Case
Plessy v. *Ferguson* (1896): Established doctrine of "separate but equal"

Close Read

1. Under which subheading would you expect to find information on how the Supreme Court arrived at its decision?

2. Examine the subheadings and the boxed details. What is the author's primary purpose?

3. Identify two text features that add to your understanding of the text. Explain your choices.

4. How much can you tell about the author's perspective on *Brown v. Board of Education?* Explain your answer.

In 2004, U.S. Secretary of Education Rod Paige gave the following speech at the dedication ceremony for the *Brown* v. *Board of Education* National Historic Site. As you read Paige's remarks, try to determine his purpose and his perspective. How do they influence what you learn about the momentous case?

from Grand Opening Dedication Speech by **Rod Paige**

... *Brown* v. *Board of Education* was a triumph of the human spirit, a reaffirmation of constitutional and human rights. The decision struck down an American apartheid[1] founded on ignorance, hatred, and violence. It was, and remains today, a statement of hope and expectation, a belief that the American
5 people will rise above prejudice, ignorance, and classification to find our common humanity.

Today it is right that we remember Oliver Brown, Linda Brown, and all of the plaintiffs involved in the case. They were parents, students, and neighbors who saw the viciousness of segregation and could no longer tolerate it. These
10 parents rose above the terrible turbulence of history and conflict to fight for freedom—freedom for their children, for themselves, and for all Americans. . . .

For me, the decision was more than a legal ruling; it was a ruling on a way of life. I grew up in rural, segregated Mississippi. We lived with segregation and the racism that inspired it every single day. African Americans understood
15 the moral imperative guiding Oliver Brown and everyone involved in the case. We felt the tenacious hold of segregation on our country and our culture. And we knew its terrible consequences—centuries of prejudice, waste, division, and even death.

For us, it came as no surprise that the battleground was the educational
20 system. Our schools reflected segregationist thinking; they institutionalized separation. By example, many of our schools taught inequality, incivility, callousness, disregard, exclusion, and disrespect. It was a vicious circle. Racism was the cause, and the result, of such teaching, generation after generation, for over 250 years. It still has a hold on our schools today as we confront re-
25 segregation and the exclusion of millions of children from a quality education.

There are some who say the decision remains unfulfilled. They are right! *Brown* opened the doors of our schools. Now we must build on that decision to make education fully inclusive and fair. . . .

On May 17, 1954, thanks to a handful of Americans, a unanimous
30 Supreme Court ignited a torch for tomorrow, a torch of freedom and hope. That torch still burns brightly today. . . .

---

1. **apartheid:** "apartness"—a separation of people according to their race.

Close Read

1. How do the boxed details in the speech differ from those in the textbook feature? Explain what the details suggest about Paige's purpose.

2. Consider Paige's choice of words and phrases in lines 1–11. Would you describe his tone as inspirational or angry? Support your answer.

3. Think about Paige's tone and his description of his early years in lines 12–24. What can you infer about his perspective on the *Brown* v. *Board of Education* decision?

4. In lines 21–24, Paige uses cause-and-effect organization to talk about racism. Summarize what he says about the "vicious circle."

The Plot Against People
Humorous Essay by Russell Baker

When are little things a
BIG DEAL?

OHIO STANDARDS

READING STANDARDS
3.1 Identify and understand organizational patterns
4.8 Analyze author's point of view, mood and tone

KEY IDEA Keys get lost. Computers crash. Every day, people encounter problems, inconveniences, and other **annoyances** that make life stressful. In the following essay, Russell Baker proposes an interesting theory about why such things happen.

QUICKWRITE What are some of the things that annoy you when they break down, don't work, or get lost? Make a short list of about five items. Then choose the one that annoys you the most and explain why to a classmate.

Annoyances
1. Bus to school breaks down
2. Locker won't open
3.
4.
5.

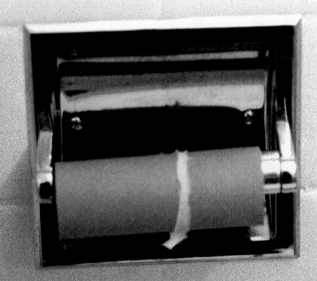

● ELEMENTS OF NONFICTION: TONE AND DICTION

While reading an essay, you might notice that the writer seems serious, mocking, or sentimental. That quality of the writing is known as the **tone,** or the expression of the writer's attitude toward a subject. One way the writer creates tone is through diction. **Diction** refers to the word choice and the arrangement of those words, or **syntax.** For example, notice how Russell Baker uses formal, scientific language in this sentence.

The goal of all inanimate objects is to resist man and ultimately to defeat him, and the three major classifications are based on the method each object uses to achieve its purpose.

Instead of using the word "things," Baker writes "inanimate objects." Also, Baker's sentence structure is complicated, or suitable for a scientific paper. The contrast between his elevated style and the everyday topic creates a humorous tone. As you read his essay, notice the diction and details Baker uses to create tone.

● READING SKILL: RECOGNIZE CLASSIFICATION

Pattern of organization refers to how a writer arranges ideas and information. Common patterns of organization include

- **cause and effect**
- **chronological order**
- **comparison and contrast**

A fourth pattern of organization is **classification.** To classify is to sort ideas or objects into groups that share common characteristics. This type of organization is revealed in Baker's thesis statement: "Inanimate objects are classified scientifically into three major categories—those that don't work, those that break down, and those that get lost."

As you read, use a chart like the one shown to identify examples of each category identified in the thesis statement. In the third column, note important characteristics of each group.

Category	Examples	Characteristics
Things that don't work		
Things that break down	car, washing machine	create maximum frustration for people
Things that get lost		

Author Online

Russell Baker
born 1925

Early Hardships
Russell Baker suffered grief and hardship early in life. He lost his father at the age of five and witnessed his suddenly widowed mother make the painful decision to leave his sister with relatives who were in a better financial position to provide for her. This sad beginning, however, did not dampen Baker's attitude or his desire to succeed in life. He credits his mother with encouraging him to set high goals: "She would make me make something of myself."

"Casual" Columnist Baker's sharp eye for detail and ability to provide insightful commentary on little things made journalism the ideal career for him. He had always loved news and the appealing stories newspapers contained. Baker knew that he eventually wanted to write for one. "I marveled at the places newspapers could take me," he once noted.

His *Observer* column, which ran from 1962 to 1998 in the *New York Times,* showcased Baker's talent for capturing details. He described it as "a casual column without anything urgent to tell humanity." Baker wrote about everyday occurrences, such as shopping for groceries and watching television, with wit and humor. His talent for relating personal stories to a universal audience has made him popular with critics and readers alike.

 MORE ABOUT THE AUTHOR
For more on Russell Baker, visit the **Literature Center** at **ClassZone.com.**

THE Plot AGAINST PEOPLE

Russell Baker

WASHINGTON, June 17 — Inanimate objects are classified scientifically into three major categories—those that don't work, those that break down, and those that get lost.

The goal of all inanimate objects is to resist man and ultimately to defeat him, and the three major classifications are based on the method each object uses to achieve its purpose. As a general rule, any object capable of breaking down at the moment when it is most needed will do so. The automobile is typical of the category.

With the cunning typical of its breed, the automobile never breaks down
10 while entering a filling station with a large staff of idle mechanics. It waits until it reaches a downtown intersection in the middle of the rush hour, or until it is fully loaded with family and luggage on the Ohio Turnpike. **A**

Thus it creates maximum misery, inconvenience, frustration, and irritability among its human cargo, thereby reducing its owner's life span.

Washing machines, garbage disposals, lawn mowers, light bulbs, automatic laundry dryers, water pipes, furnaces, electrical fuses, television tubes, hose nozzles, tape recorders, slide projectors—all are in league with the automobile to take their turn at breaking down whenever life threatens to flow smoothly for their human enemies.

20 Many inanimate objects, of course, find it extremely difficult to break down. Pliers, for example, and gloves and keys are almost totally incapable of breaking down. Therefore, they have had to evolve a different technique for resisting man.

A Plausible Theory

They get lost. Science has still not solved the mystery of how they do it, and no man has ever caught one of them in the act of getting lost. The most plausible theory is that they have developed a secret method of locomotion which they are able to conceal the instant a human eye falls upon them. **B**

ANALYZE VISUALS
How would you describe the **tone** of this painting? What qualities has the artist given to the toasters?

A TONE AND DICTION
Notice Baker's choice of the words "cunning" and "breed" in line 9. What image does this choice of words create for the reader?

B CLASSIFICATION
In lines 20–27, Baker moves from discussing the first category to describing the second. What details show how objects in this category operate?

Toasters on Hills (1998), Charles Kaufman. Acrylic on canvas, 60 cm × 80 cm. © 2002 Charles Kaufman.

It is not uncommon for a pair of pliers to climb all the way from the cellar to the attic in its single-minded determination to raise its owner's blood pressure. Keys have been known to burrow three feet under mattresses. Women's purses, despite their great weight, frequently travel through six or seven rooms to find hiding space under a couch.

Scientists have been struck by the fact that things that break down virtually never get lost, while things that get lost hardly ever break down.

A furnace, for example, will invariably break down at the depth of the first winter cold wave, but it will never get lost. A woman's purse, which after all does have some inherent capacity for breaking down, hardly ever does; it almost invariably chooses to get lost. **C**

Some persons believe this constitutes evidence that inanimate objects are not entirely hostile to man, and that a negotiated peace is possible. After all, they point out, a furnace could infuriate a man even more thoroughly by getting lost than by breaking down, just as a glove could upset him far more by breaking down than by getting lost.

Not everyone agrees, however, that this indicates a conciliatory attitude among inanimate objects. Many say it merely proves that furnaces, gloves, and pliers are incredibly stupid.

The third class of objects—those that don't work—is the most curious of all. These include such objects as barometers, car clocks, cigarette lighters, flashlights, and toy-train locomotives. It is inaccurate, of course, to say that they never work. They work once, usually for the first few hours after being brought home, and then quit. Thereafter, they never work again.

In fact, it is widely assumed that they are built for the purpose of not working. Some people have reached advanced ages without ever seeing some of these objects—barometers, for example—in working order.

Science is utterly baffled by the entire category. There are many theories about it. The most interesting holds that the things that don't work have attained the highest state possible for an inanimate object, the state to which things that break down and things that get lost can still only aspire. **D**

They Give Peace

They have truly defeated man by conditioning him never to expect anything of them, and in return they have given man the only peace he receives from inanimate society. He does not expect his barometer to work, his electric locomotive to run, his cigarette lighter to light, or his flashlight to illuminate, and when they don't, it does not raise his blood pressure.

He cannot attain that peace with furnaces and keys and cars and women's purses as long as he demands that they work for their keep. ∿ **E**

C TONE AND DICTION
Reread lines 35–38. In what ways does Baker imitate formal writing in this passage? How serious is his attitude?

D CLASSIFICATION
Why is the third class of objects "the most curious of all"?

E TONE AND DICTION
Reread lines 59–65. How do Baker's **diction** and **syntax** contribute to the humor in this passage?

Comprehension

1. **Recall** According to Baker, how does the breakdown of inanimate objects affect humans?

2. **Recall** What reason does Baker give for calling furnaces, gloves, and pliers "incredibly stupid"?

3. **Clarify** How have things that don't work "attained the highest possible state"?

OHIO STANDARDS

READING STANDARD
3.1 Identify and understand organizational patterns

Critical Analysis

4. **Recognize Classification** Review the classification chart you created. Explain what distinguishes the three classes of objects from each other and what links them. Why do you think Baker chose to discuss them in the order he did?

5. **Connect** What objects in your own life fit into the classes Baker describes?

6. **Interpret Title** What is "the plot against people"? Would "Life's Little Nuisances" be as effective a title for an essay about **annoyances?** Explain why or why not.

7. **Analyze Tone and Diction** How would you describe the overall tone of Baker's essay? What aspects of the essay created the tone—elevated diction and syntax, unexpected images, or other factors? Use a chart like the one shown to provide examples that support your answer.

Key Element	Evidence from Text	Description of Tone
Diction		
Syntax		
Images		
Other		

8. **Identify Author's Purpose** Considering Baker's tone and diction in this selection, what do you think his purpose is for writing about this subject? Use evidence from the text to support your answer.

9. **Evaluate** *New York Times* critic Christopher Buckley said this about humorous writing: "We should always treat light things humorously and serious things lightly." Evaluate Baker's essay with respect to Buckley's comment.

Why Leaves Turn Color in the Fall
Essay by Diane Ackerman

Can BEAUTY be captured in words?

OHIO STANDARDS

READING STANDARDS
3.1 Identify and understand organizational patterns

4.8 Analyze author's point of view, mood and tone

KEY IDEA How would you describe a beautiful sunset to someone who had not seen it? How would you explain this same sunset to a child who wondered why it occurred? Would explaining the sunset make it seem more beautiful, or less? In the following essay, Diane Ackerman captures the **beauty** of autumn leaves while explaining the scientific concepts behind their occurrence.

DISCUSS Describe to a partner, in as much detail as you can, a beautiful scene from nature. This might be a sunset (as mentioned before), a flock of birds taking wing, or any other natural phenomenon. Afterward, discuss how easy—or hard—it was for you to convert the scene to words and for your partner to visualize the scene.

● ELEMENTS OF NONFICTION: AUTHOR'S PURPOSE

Author's purpose is the reason why a writer writes. An author may write to explain a process, to describe a scene, to reflect on an idea, or, in the case of Diane Ackerman, to do all three. Her overall purpose in this essay is to explain why leaves turn color and fall from trees. To that end, she uses scientific terms.

A corky layer of cells forms at the leaves' slender petioles, then scars over. Undernourished, the leaves stop producing the pigment chlorophyll, and photosynthesis ceases.

Ackerman also wants to describe the beauty of autumn leaves, and to that end she uses poetic diction and **imagery,** words and phrases that re-create sensory experiences.

They glide and swoop, rocking in invisible cradles. They are all wing and may flutter from yard to yard on small whirlwinds or updrafts, swiveling as they go.

As you read, determine the main purpose of each paragraph—to explain, to describe, or to reflect.

■ READING SKILL: ANALYZE CAUSE AND EFFECT

Ackerman uses at least three **patterns of organization:**

- **cause and effect,** to explain a process
- **comparison and contrast,** to show likeness and difference
- **main idea and supporting details,** to present insights

As you read, look for cause-and-effect organization. Fill out two cause-and-effect chains—one to show why leaves turn color and another to show why they fall.

| Tree pulls nutrients back into trunk and roots. | → | | → |

▲ VOCABULARY IN CONTEXT

Diane Ackerman conveys the richness of her subject by using the following boldfaced words. Define each word.

1. **stealth** in her smooth, silent movement
2. a judge issuing an **edict** in the courtroom
3. an athlete, tall and **robustly** built
4. a painter's son, **predisposed** to the arts
5. **adaptation** of an animal to its environment
6. the monkey's **capricious,** unpredictable nature

Why Leaves Turn Color in the Fall

DIANE ACKERMAN

The **stealth** of autumn catches one unaware. Was that a goldfinch perching in the early September woods, or just the first turning leaf? A red-winged blackbird or a sugar maple closing up shop for the winter? Keen-eyed as leopards, we stand still and squint hard, looking for signs of movement. Early-morning frost sits heavily on the grass, and turns barbed wire into a string of stars. On a distant hill, a small square of yellow appears to be a lighted stage. At last the truth dawns on us: Fall is staggering in, right on schedule, with its baggage of chilly nights, macabre holidays, and spectacular, heart-stoppingly beautiful leaves. Soon the leaves will start cringing on the trees, and roll up
10 in clenched fists before they actually fall off. Dry seedpods will rattle like tiny gourds. But first there will be weeks of gushing color so bright, so pastel, so confettilike, that people will travel up and down the East Coast just to stare at it—a whole season of leaves. **A**

Where do the colors come from? Sunlight rules most living things with its golden **edicts.** When the days begin to shorten, soon after the summer solstice on June 21, a tree reconsiders its leaves. All summer it feeds them so they can process sunlight, but in the dog days of summer the tree begins pulling nutrients back into its trunk and roots, pares down, and gradually chokes off its leaves. A corky layer of cells forms at the leaves' slender petioles,[1] then scars
20 over. Undernourished, the leaves stop producing the pigment chlorophyll, and photosynthesis[2] ceases. Animals can migrate, hibernate, or store food to prepare for winter. But where can a tree go? It survives by dropping its leaves,

---

1. **petioles:** the stalks of leaves.
2. **chlorophyll . . . photosynthesis:** Chlorophyll is the green pigment in plants that is necessary for photosynthesis, the process by which plants use sunlight, water, and carbon dioxide to produce food.

stealth (stĕlth) *n.* a concealed manner of acting

A AUTHOR'S PURPOSE What seems to be Ackerman's purpose in the first paragraph? Support your answer with specific details.

edict (ē'dĭkt') *n.* a command issued by an authority

and by the end of autumn only a few fragile threads of fluid-carrying xylem[3] hold leaves to their stems. **B**

A turning leaf stays partly green at first, then reveals splotches of yellow and red as the chlorophyll gradually breaks down. Dark green seems to stay longest in the veins, outlining and defining them. During the summer, chlorophyll dissolves in the heat and light, but it is also being steadily replaced. In the fall, on the other hand, no new pigment is produced, and so we notice the other 30 colors that were always there, right in the leaf, although chlorophyll's shocking green hid them from view. With their camouflage gone, we see these colors for the first time all year, and marvel, but they were always there, hidden like a vivid secret beneath the hot glowing greens of summer. **C**

The most spectacular range of fall foliage occurs in the northeastern United States and in eastern China, where the leaves are **robustly** colored, thanks in part to a rich climate. European maples don't achieve the same flaming reds as their American relatives, which thrive on cold nights and sunny days. In Europe, the warm, humid weather turns the leaves brown or mildly yellow. Anthocyanin, the pigment that gives apples their red and turns leaves red or 40 red-violet, is produced by sugars that remain in the leaf after the supply of nutrients dwindles. Unlike the carotenoids, which color carrots, squash, and corn, and turn leaves orange and yellow, anthocyanin varies from year to year, depending on the temperature and amount of sunlight. The fiercest colors occur in years when the fall sunlight is strongest and the nights are cool and dry (a state of grace scientists find vexing to forecast). This is also why leaves

---

3. **xylem:** plant tissue through which water and nutrients are conducted.

B CAUSE AND EFFECT
In lines 14–24, the pattern of organization switches from main idea and supporting details to cause and effect. Fill out a cause-and-effect chain to show why leaves fall.

C CAUSE AND EFFECT
Why do leaves turn color? Use information in lines 25–33 to fill out a cause-and-effect chain to show this process.

robustly (rō-bŭst′lē)
adv. in a strong, powerful way

appear dizzyingly bright and clear on a sunny fall day: The anthocyanin flashes like a marquee.[4] **D**

Not all leaves turn the same colors. Elms, weeping willows, and the ancient gingko all grow radiant yellow, along with hickories, aspens, bottlebrush
50 buckeyes, cottonweeds, and tall, keening poplars. Basswood turns bronze, birches bright gold. Water-loving maples put on a symphonic display of scarlets. Sumacs turn red, too, as do flowering dogwoods, black gums, and sweet gums. Though some oaks yellow, most turn a pinkish brown. The farmlands also change color, as tepees of cornstalks and bales of shredded-wheat-textured hay stand drying in the fields. In some spots, one slope of a hill may be green and the other already in bright color, because the hillside facing south gets more sun and heat than the northern one.

An odd feature of the colors is that they don't seem to have any special purpose. We are **predisposed** to respond to their beauty, of course. They
60 shimmer with the colors of sunset, spring flowers, the tawny buff of a colt's pretty rump, the shuddering pink of a blush. Animals and flowers color for a reason—**adaptation** to their environment—but there is no adaptive reason for leaves to color so beautifully in the fall any more than there is for the sky or ocean to be blue. It's just one of the haphazard marvels the planet bestows every year. We find the sizzling colors thrilling, and in a sense they dupe us. Colored like living things, they signal death and disintegration. In time, they will become fragile and, like the body, return to dust. They are as we hope our own fate will be when we die: Not to vanish, just to sublime[5] from one beautiful state into another. Though leaves lose their green life, they bloom
70 with urgent colors, as the woods grow mummified day by day, and Nature becomes more carnal, mute, and radiant. **E**

We call the season "fall," from the Old English *feallan,* to fall, which leads back through time to the Indo-European *phol,* which also means to fall. So the word and the idea are both extremely ancient, and haven't really changed since the first of our kind needed a name for fall's leafy abundance. As we say the word, we're reminded of that other Fall, in the garden of Eden, when fig leaves never withered and scales fell from our eyes. Fall is the time when leaves fall from the trees, just as spring is when flowers spring up, summer is when we simmer, and winter is when we whine from the cold.
80 Children love to play in piles of leaves, hurling them into the air like confetti, leaping into soft unruly mattresses of them. For children, leaf fall is just one of the odder figments of Nature, like hailstones or snowflakes. Walk down a lane overhung with trees in the never-never land of autumn, and you will forget about time and death, lost in the sheer delicious spill of color. Adam and Eve concealed their nakedness with leaves, remember? Leaves have always hidden our awkward secrets. **F**

But how do the colored leaves fall? As a leaf ages, the growth hormone, auxin, fades, and cells at the base of the petiole divide. Two or three rows of

---

4. **marquee:** a lighted billboard, such as those used at movie theaters.

5. **sublime:** to transform directly into another state.

D AUTHOR'S PURPOSE
Using scientific **diction**—the terms *anthocyanin* and *carotenoids*—helps Ackerman explain the difference between the pigments found in leaves. How do they differ?

predisposed
(prē′dǐ-spōzd′) *v.*
inclined to something in advance

adaptation
(ăd′ăp-tā′shən) *n.*
the process of adjusting to suit one's surroundings

E AUTHOR'S PURPOSE
Reread lines 65–71. Here Ackerman reflects on the deaths of living things, including human beings. What does she say we hope for ourselves?

F AUTHOR'S PURPOSE
Reread lines 72–86. What seems to be Ackerman's purpose in each paragraph? Cite specific words and phrases to support your answers.

ANALYZE VISUALS
Study the photographs on this page and on pages 497 and 498. What qualities of autumn leaves are brought out in each photo?

small cells, lying at right angles to the axis of the petiole, react with water, then
90 come apart, leaving the petioles hanging on by only a few threads of xylem.
A light breeze, and the leaves are airborne. They glide and swoop, rocking in
invisible cradles. They are all wing and may flutter from yard to yard on small
whirlwinds or updrafts, swiveling as they go. Firmly tethered[6] to earth, we **G**
love to see things rise up and fly—soap bubbles, balloons, birds, fall leaves.
They remind us that the end of a season is **capricious,** as is the end of life. We
especially like the way leaves rock, careen, and swoop as they fall. Everyone
knows the motion. Pilots sometimes do a maneuver called a "falling leaf," in
which the plane loses altitude quickly and on purpose, by slipping first to the
right, then to the left. The machine weighs a ton or more, but in one pilot's
100 mind it is a weightless thing, a falling leaf. She has seen the motion before, in
the Vermont woods where she played as a child. Below her the trees radiate
gold, copper, and red. Leaves are falling, although she can't see them fall, as she
falls, swooping down for a closer view.

At last the leaves leave. But first they turn color and thrill us for weeks
on end. Then they crunch and crackle under foot. They *shush,* as children
drag their small feet through the leaves heaped along the curb. Dark, slimy
mats of leaves cling to one's heels after a rain. A damp, stuccolike mortar[7] of
semidecayed leaves protects the tender shoots with a roof until spring, and
makes a rich humus.[8] An occasional bulge or ripple in the leafy mounds signals
110 a shrew or a field mouse tunneling out of sight. Sometimes one finds in fossil
stones the imprint of a leaf, long since disintegrated, whose outlines remind us
how detailed, vibrant, and alive are the things of this earth that perish. ◗ **H**

G GRAMMAR AND STYLE
Reread lines 91–93. Ackerman effectively uses the **participial phrases** "rocking in invisible cradles" and "swiveling as they go" to vividly describe the falling leaves.

capricious
(kə-prĭsh′əs)
adj. impulsive, unpredictable

H AUTHOR'S PURPOSE
Think about Ackerman's purpose in the last paragraph. How is her purpose supported by her **diction** and use of **imagery?**

---

6. **tethered:** fastened, as if with a rope.

7. **stuccolike mortar:** a bonding material that is like a soft, sticky plaster.

8. **humus:** decomposed organic matter that provides nutrients for plants.

Comprehension

OHIO STANDARDS

READING STANDARD
3.1 Identify and understand organizational patterns

1. **Recall** How does dropping its leaves in autumn help a tree to survive?

2. **Paraphrase** What does Ackerman mean by autumn's "stealth"?

3. **Paraphrase** In what sense do the bright colors of autumn "dupe" us?

Critical Analysis

4. **Identify Author's Purpose** In which parts of her essay is Ackerman's purpose to explain? to describe? to reflect? Are these purposes compatible? Explain your answer.

5. **Analyze Cause and Effect** Use the cause-and-effect chains you created to explain why leaves turn color and why they fall. Be specific.

6. **Recognize Contrasts** What contrasts are pointed out in the essay? Cite examples.

7. **Analyze Language** Ackerman's language can be very poetic, filled with sensory **imagery**. Skim the essay and record notable examples. Which examples best describe the **beauty** of fall? Explain your answer.

Sensory Imagery
• "Early-morning frost sits heavily …" (lines 4–5)
•
•

8. **Interpret Author's Message** Explain the connection Ackerman sees between fall leaves and human beings. How close does the connection seem to you?

9. **Evaluate Interpretations** One critic has said that Ackerman's nonfiction is "a creative blend of journalism, science, and poetry; it is her poetic vision that makes her nonfiction so successful." Would you say that this is true of her essay? Cite evidence to support your answer.

Vocabulary in Context

VOCABULARY PRACTICE

Choose the word that best completes each sentence.

1. With great _____, the lioness tracked her prey.
2. Try not to be _____; think before you act!
3. Our teacher's _____ was that tardy students would be locked out.
4. _____ to a new environment ensures the survival of a species.
5. He shook my hand _____, showing great enthusiasm.
6. As an animal lover, I am _____ to veterinary school.

WORD LIST

adaptation

capricious

edict

predisposed

robustly

stealth

VOCABULARY IN WRITING

Using three or more vocabulary words, describe a season of the year.

> **EXAMPLE SENTENCE**
>
> *Animals' fur thickens in **adaptation** to winter's cold temperatures.*

VOCABULARY STRATEGY: METAPHORS AND SIMILES

A **metaphor** is a brief comparison that talks about one thing as if it were another. The comparison is implied, without the use of *like* or *as*. "She was a radiant songbird" is an example of a metaphor. A **simile** is a more easily recognizable comparison that uses *like* or *as*. "She sang like a nightingale" is an example of a simile. When an unfamiliar word appears in a sentence containing a simile or metaphor, you can sometimes figure out the meaning of the word by thinking about the comparison that is being made.

PRACTICE Note the two things compared in each simile or metaphor. What does the comparison suggest about the meaning of the boldfaced word?

1. He was as **capricious** as a child in a candy store.
2. Like burglars, the friends moved in silent **stealth.**
3. They were as **predisposed** to laugh as geese are to honk.
4. My brother was a wild mustang, running **robustly** around the yard.
5. The dictator's **edict** was a mad doctor's prescription.

OHIO STANDARDS

VOCABULARY STANDARD
1.3 Infer the literal and figurative meanings of words

VOCABULARY PRACTICE
For more practice, go to the **Vocabulary Center** at ClassZone.com.

Reading-Writing Connection

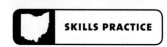

Expand your understanding of "Why Leaves Turn Color in the Fall" by responding to these prompts. Then use **Revision: Grammar and Style** to improve your writing.

WRITING PROMPTS	SELF-CHECK
A. Short Response: Describe a Scene Think back to the scene from nature that you chose to describe on page 494. Now write **one or two paragraphs** that describe this same scene. Be sure to include sensory images, as Ackerman did, to help re-create the scene.	*A successful description will . . .* • focus on details that capture the beauty of the scene • include at least two images that appeal to the senses
B. Extended Response: Reflect on Author's Message What do autumn leaves tell humans about themselves? What does their **beauty** mean? Respond in **three to five paragraphs,** drawing on Ackerman's ideas or your own original ideas.	*A strong response will . . .* • make a statement about the meaning of autumn leaves • support the statement with convincing details

REVISION: GRAMMAR AND STYLE

OHIO STANDARDS

WRITING STANDARD
7.3 Use clauses and phrases

ADD DESCRIPTIVE DETAILS Review the **Grammar and Style** note on page 500. Note how Ackerman uses participial phrases to create images of falling leaves.

A **participle** is a verb form (verbal) that acts as an adjective. It modifies a noun or a pronoun. A **participial phrase** consists of a participle plus its modifiers and complements. Here are some examples of how Ackerman uses participles and participial phrases to enrich her writing with imaginative details.

> *. . . they were always there, hidden like a vivid secret beneath the hot glowing greens of summer.* (lines 32–33)

> *Children love to play in piles of leaves, hurling them into the air like confetti, leaping into soft unruly mattresses of them.* (lines 80–81)

Notice how the revisions in red enliven this first draft by incorporating participles and participial phrases. Revise your responses to the prompts by making similar changes.

STUDENT MODEL

Deprived of the nutrients necessary to produce chlorophyll,
Leaves begin to gradually change in the fall. The pigments anthocyanin
          shocking
and carotenoids produce a display of color as they turn the leaves deep red,
blazing
~~bright~~ orange, and golden yellow.

WRITING TOOLS

For prewriting, revision, and editing tools, visit the **Writing Center** at ClassZone.com.

How a Leaf Works

Textbook Diagrams

Use with "Why Leaves Turn Color in the Fall," page 496.

OHIO STANDARDS

READING/RESEARCH STANDARDS
3.3 Evaluate the effectiveness of information found in graphic aides
8.2 Gather information from multiple sources

What's the Connection?

You just read a rather poetic yet scientific description of why leaves turn color in the fall. Now you will learn from a few well-designed graphic aids why leaves are green in the first place.

Skill Focus: Interpret Graphic Aids

A **graphic aid** is a visual illustration of a verbal statement. Graphic aids include photographs, diagrams, maps, and equations; they make complex information easier to understand. You can use these guidelines to interpret most graphic aids:

- Read the title, headings, and captions first to get the main idea.
- On maps and complex graphic aids, look for a key or legend to see how colors and symbols are used.
- Use the obvious meanings of symbols such as arrows to help you read the visual information.
- Pay attention to labels that identify specific details.
- Study the information in the graphic, looking for patterns or basic concepts.

As you read the pages that follow, complete a chart like the one shown. State in your own words what each graphic aid shows.

Type of Graphic Aid	What It Shows
Magnified photograph of a leaf cell	
Cutaway diagram of a chloroplast	
Schematic diagram of photosynthesis	
Chemical equation for photosynthesis	
Cutaway diagram of a leaf	

Photosynthesis

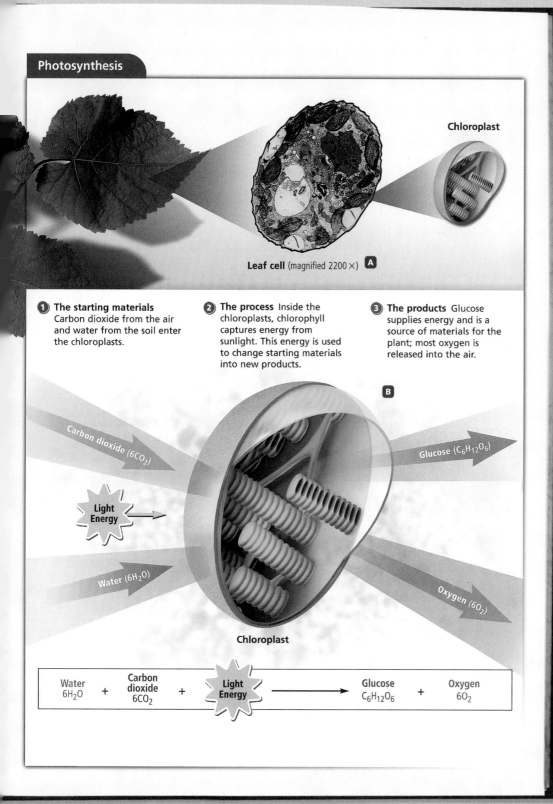

Chloroplast

Leaf cell (magnified 2200×) **A**

1 The starting materials Carbon dioxide from the air and water from the soil enter the chloroplasts.

2 The process Inside the chloroplasts, chlorophyll captures energy from sunlight. This energy is used to change starting materials into new products.

3 The products Glucose supplies energy and is a source of materials for the plant; most oxygen is released into the air.

B

Carbon dioxide (6CO$_2$)

Glucose (C$_6$H$_{12}$O$_6$)

Light Energy

Water (6H$_2$O)

Oxygen (6O$_2$)

Chloroplast

| Water 6H$_2$O | + | Carbon dioxide 6CO$_2$ | + | Light Energy | → | Glucose C$_6$H$_{12}$O$_6$ | + | Oxygen 6O$_2$ |

A INTERPRET GRAPHIC AIDS Science textbooks often include **photographs** of structures magnified to many times their actual size. What does this photo of a leaf cell show you about chloroplasts?

B INTERPRET GRAPHIC AIDS A **schematic diagram** uses lines, symbols, and words to help readers picture processes or objects not normally seen. What do the arrows in this schematic diagram communicate?

Inside a Leaf

The leaf is an organ that produces sugars. It is made up of different types of cells and tissues.

Cells at the surface produce a waxy cuticle that keeps the leaf from losing water.

Most chloroplasts are located in cells of the upper layer of the leaf.

Xylem transports water and nutrients up from the roots.

Phloem transports energy-rich compounds made in the leaf down to other parts of the plant.

Carbon dioxide, oxygen, and water vapor move into and out of the leaf through stomata.

c INTERPRET GRAPHIC AIDS
A **cutaway diagram** shows an object with the outer part removed to reveal the interior. Notice the different layers of cells in this cutaway diagram of a leaf. Where are the chloroplasts located? What do they look like?

Comprehension

1. **Recall** Where does photosynthesis take place?

2. **Recall** What does a plant do with the products of photosynthesis?

3. **Paraphrase** Review the equation at the bottom of page 505. Paraphrase this equation.

Critical Analysis

4. **Interpret Graphic Aids** What parts of a leaf are shown in the cutaway diagram on page 506, titled "Inside a Leaf"? What are their different functions?

5. **Compare Texts** How would you compare the experience of reading the graphic aids with the experience of reading "Why Leaves Turn Color in the Fall"? Which source did you find more informative? Explain your answer.

Read for Information: Use Information from Multiple Sources

OHIO STANDARDS

READING/RESEARCH STANDARDS
3.3 Evaluate the effectiveness of information found in graphic aides

8.2 Gather information from multiple sources

WRITING PROMPT

On the basis of the information in the textbook diagrams and Diane Ackerman's essay, explain (1) the process of photosynthesis, (2) the reason leaves are green in summer, and (3) the reason leaves turn color in the fall. Define scientific terms in your explanation.

To respond to this prompt, you will need to synthesize information having to do with photosynthesis and the color of leaves. Then you will need to paraphrase this information. Following these steps can help:

1. Review the chart you created as you read, noting what the schematic diagram of photosynthesis showed you.

2. Review the diagram labeled "Inside a Leaf," looking for more details you could add to your explanation. Jot them down.

3. Review Diane Ackerman's essay, identifying and taking notes on passages that discuss photosynthesis, the green color of leaves, and the process of color change.

4. Using your notes from all three sources, describe the three topics in the order listed in the prompt.

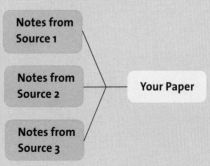

Blowup: What Went Wrong at Storm King Mountain

Narrative Nonfiction by Sebastian Junger

What can we learn from DISASTER?

OHIO STANDARDS

READING STANDARDS
2.3 Take notes
4.5 Analyze how choice of genre affects theme or topic

KEY IDEA When you hear about a **disaster,** what's your reaction? Do you pay attention to the details so you can prevent the same thing from happening to you? You wouldn't be alone in trying to learn a lesson from tragedy. People do it all the time—especially those who are paid to risk their lives when disaster strikes. The selection you are about to read is both a description and an analysis of what caused a small wildfire to flare into a deadly blaze, seemingly without warning.

DISCUSS In a small group, discuss a disaster that took lives or caused great damage to property. Note what went wrong and whether the catastrophe might have been avoided. Then write down your group's top two or three recommendations for averting a similar disaster or reducing its damage.

Earthquake

Cars forced off the road

● ELEMENTS OF NONFICTION: NARRATIVE NONFICTION

Narrative nonfiction is writing that tells a true story about real people, places, and events. Just as in a fictional story, the details in narrative nonfiction help bring the characters, settings, and events to life. For example, notice how the details in this passage from "Blowup: What Went Wrong at Storm King Mountain" convey the experiences of one firefighter who was caught in that blaze.

I was roughly one hundred and fifty feet from the top of the hill, and the fire got there in ten or twelve seconds. I made it over the top and just tumbled and rolled down the other side. . . .

As you read, notice other elements of good storytelling.

● READING STRATEGY: TAKE NOTES

When reading a text that has an obvious method of organization, it's a good idea to record the key ideas and information in that text on a graphic organizer. Here are some ideal pairings:

- a **timeline** for chronological order
- a **diagram** for spatial order, or position in space
- a **cause-and-effect chain** for cause-and-effect order

Sebastian Junger uses several patterns of organization, with chronological order being particularly important. As you read, record the main events of the disaster on a timeline.

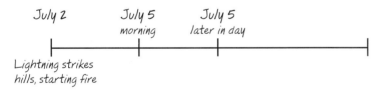

July 2   July 5   July 5
            morning   *later in day*

Lightning strikes hills, starting fire

Review: **Patterns of Organization, Graphic Aids**

▲ VOCABULARY IN CONTEXT

The following boldfaced words help the author deliver his dramatic account of a fire. To see how many you already know, substitute a different word or phrase for each one.

1. **deflect** blame from himself by accusing another
2. a rowdy **contingent** of football players at the hotel
3. forces **conspire** to create tragedy
4. a **conceivably** simple plan that went wrong
5. a **rigorous** course load at school

Author On|ine

Describing Danger
Sebastian Junger is most famous for his first book, *The Perfect Storm*—a nonfiction account of the *Andrea Gail,* a commercial fishing boat wrecked in an Atlantic storm. Originally, he had intended to write a book about people with dangerous jobs—an idea he got while recovering from a leg injury suffered while climbing trees for a tree-removal company. But a chapter on the *Andrea Gail* turned into a whole volume—and a bestseller.

Sebastian Junger
born 1962

World-Traveling Journalist Despite his success as a book author, Junger considers himself a magazine journalist. He has traveled to Kosovo, Sierra Leone, and Afghanistan on assignments for such publications as *National Geographic. Fire,* published in 2001, is a collection of his magazine articles. It includes "Blowup: What Went Wrong at Storm King Mountain." Junger says he felt compelled to write about "situations where people are in one form or another being confronted with forces that are way beyond their control."

 MORE ABOUT THE AUTHOR
For more on Sebastian Junger, visit the **Literature Center** at ClassZone.com.

Background

One of the biggest firefighting disasters in the United States occurred July 6, 1994, on Storm King Mountain in Colorado. Fourteen firefighters died in a blowup, or sudden explosion of flames, on the windy, dried-out slopes. Today the dead are memorialized with crosses at the spots where they fell and plaques along the route of the fire.

BL**O**WUP:

WHAT WENT WRONG AT STORM KING MOUNTAIN

Sebastian Junger

The main thing Brad Haugh remembers about his escape was the thunderous sound of his own heart. It was beating two hundred times a minute, and by the time he and the two smoke jumpers[1] running with him had crested a steep ridge in Colorado, everyone behind them was dead.

Their coworkers on the slope at their backs had been overrun by flames that Haugh guessed were three hundred feet high. The fire raced a quarter mile up the mountain in about two minutes, hitting speeds of eighteen miles an hour. Tools dropped in its path were completely incinerated. Temperatures reached two thousand degrees—hot enough to melt gold or fire clay.

10 "The fire blew up behind a little ridge below me," Haugh said later. "People were yelling into their radios, 'Run! Run! Run!' I was roughly one hundred and fifty feet from the top of the hill, and the fire got there in ten or twelve seconds. I made it over the top and just tumbled and rolled down the other side, and when I turned around, there was just this incredible wall of flame."

Haugh was one of forty-nine fire fighters caught in a wildfire that stunned the nation with its swiftness and its fury. Fourteen elite fire fighters perished on a spine of Storm King Mountain, seven miles west of Glenwood Springs, Colorado. They died on a steep, rocky slope in a fire initially so small that the crews had not taken it seriously. They died while cars passed within sight on 20 the interstate below and people in the valley aimed their camcorders at the fire from garage roofs.

There were many other fire fighters on Storm King when Brad Haugh crested the ridge, yet he feared that he and the two men with him were the only ones on the mountain left alive. That thought—not the flames—caused him to panic. He ran blindly and nearly knocked himself unconscious against a tree. Fires were spotting all around him as the front of the flames chased him. The roar was deafening; "a tornado on fire" was how he later described it. The light, he remembered, was a weird blood-red that fascinated him even as he ran.

ANALYZE VISUALS
How would you feel if you were photographing this scene?

---

1. **smoke jumpers:** people who fight forest fires by parachuting to remote locations. Once on the ground, they carry heavy supplies on their backs and hike over rough terrain.

The 1994 South Canyon fire on Storm King Mountain

The two smoke jumpers with him were Eric Hipke and Kevin Erickson.
30 Hipke had been so badly burned the flesh was hanging off his hands in strips. Haugh paused briefly to collect himself, then led the two men about a hundred yards down the mountain, stopping only long enough to wrap Hipke's hands in wet T-shirts. As they started down again, the fire was spreading behind them at a thousand acres an hour, oak, pinyon, and juniper spontaneously combusting[2] in the heat.

"I didn't have any nightmares about it later," said Haugh. "But I did keep waking up in the night very disoriented. . . ." **A**

The South Canyon fire, as it was called, ignited on Saturday, July 2, as a lightning strike in the steep hills outside Glenwood Springs. At first 40 people paid it little mind because dry lightning had already triggered thirty or forty fires across the drought-plagued state that day; another wisp of smoke was no big deal. But this blaze continued to grow, prompting the Bureau of Land Management[3] (BLM) district office in Grand Junction to dispatch a seven-member crew on the morning of July 5 to prepare a helicopter landing site, designated H-1, and start cutting a fire line along a ridge of Storm King. At this point the blaze was cooking slowly through the sparse pinyon and juniper covering the steep drainage below. Glenwood Springs was visible to the east, and a pricey development called Canyon Creek Estates was a mile to the west. Interstate 70 followed the Colorado River one thousand feet 50 below, and occasionally the fire fighters could see rafters in brightly colored life jackets bumping through the rapids. **B**

The BLM crew worked all day, until chain-saw problems forced them to hike down to make repairs. Replacing them were eight smoke jumpers from Idaho and Montana (eight more would be added the next morning) who parachuted onto the ridgetop to continue cutting fire line. They worked until midnight and then claimed a few hours' sleep on the rocky ground.

Just before dawn, on the morning of July 6, Incident Commander Butch Blanco led the BLM crew back up the steep slope. Arriving at the top, Blanco discussed strategy with the smoke jumper in charge, Don Mackey. At about the 60 same time, the BLM office in Grand Junction dispatched one additional crew to the fire, the twenty-member Prineville Hotshots, a crack interagency unit from Oregon whose helmet emblem is a coyote dancing over orange flame.

The smoke jumpers had cleared another landing spot, H-2, on the main ridge, and around twelve-thirty in the afternoon, a transport helicopter settled onto it. The first **contingent** of the Prineville crew ran through the rotor wash and crouched behind rocks as the chopper lifted off to pick up the rest of the unit from below. They'd been chosen alphabetically for the first flight in: Beck, Bickett, Blecha, Brinkley, Dunbar, Hagen, Holtby, Johnson, and Kelso. Rather

A NARRATIVE NONFICTION
What does Junger focus on in this seven-paragraph introduction? Why might he have chosen to begin his nonfiction narrative this way?

B TAKE NOTES
Reread lines 38–51. What is Junger able to convey through a shift back in time? Note events on your timeline.

contingent (kən-tĭn'jənt) *n.* a gathering of people representative of a larger group

---

2. **spontaneously combusting:** self-igniting through an internal chemical action.

3. **Bureau of Land Management:** an agency within the U.S. Department of the Interior, in charge of sustaining the health, diversity, and productivity of public lands.

than wait for their crew mates, these nine hotshots started downslope into the
70 burning valley. **C**

The layout of Storm King Mountain is roughly north-south, with a central spine running from the 8,793-foot summit to H-2. Another half mile south along this ridge was the larger site, H-1. The fire had started on a steep slope below these cleared safe areas and was spreading slowly.

The strategy was to cut a wide firebreak[4] along the ridgetop and a smaller line down the slope to contain the blaze on the southwestern flank of the ridge. Flare-ups would be attacked with retardant drops[5] from choppers. If there were problems, crews could easily reach H-1 in five or ten minutes and crawl under their fire shelters—light foil sheets that resemble space blankets
80 and **deflect** heat of up to six hundred degrees.

---

4. **firebreak:** a natural or constructed barrier used to stop fires that may occur.
5. **retardant drops:** the air-dropping of chemicals to help retard or delay the spread of fire.

C NARRATIVE NONFICTION
What do you learn from Junger's **characterization** of the smoke jumpers?

deflect (dĭ-flĕkt′) *v.* to fend off or avert the direction of something

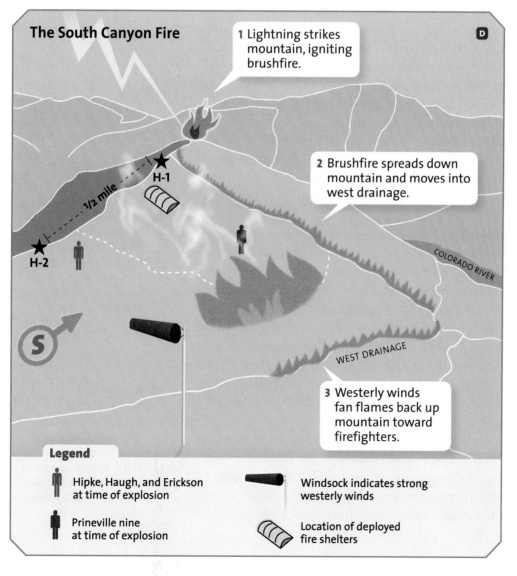

The South Canyon Fire

1 Lightning strikes mountain, igniting brushfire.

2 Brushfire spreads down mountain and moves into west drainage.

H-1

1/2 mile

H-2

COLORADO RIVER

WEST DRAINAGE

S

3 Westerly winds fan flames back up mountain toward firefighters.

Legend

Hipke, Haugh, and Erickson at time of explosion

Prineville nine at time of explosion

Windsock indicates strong westerly winds

Location of deployed fire shelters

D GRAPHIC AIDS
Study the graphic shown. What does it tell you about the progress of the fire? What other spatial relationships does it show?

"It was just an ugly little creeper," the BLM's Brad Haugh said of the early stages of the fire. Every summer, fire fighters like Haugh put out thousands of blazes like this one all over Colorado; at this point there was no reason to think South Canyon would be any different.

The second half of the Prineville crew dropped onto H-2 around 3:00 P.M. and began widening the primary fire line. Two hundred feet below, Haugh was clearing brush with his chain saw on a 33 percent slope. That meant the ground rose one foot for every yard climbed, roughly the steepness of a sand dune. The grade near the top was closer to 50 percent. He wore bulky Kevlar sawyer's chaps and a rucksack loaded with two gallons of water weighing fifteen pounds, a folding knife, freeze-dried rations, and some toilet articles. He also carried a folding fire shelter and a Stihl 056 chain saw that weighed ten or twelve pounds. Even loaded down as he was, Haugh could probably have reached the ridgetop in less than one minute if he had pushed it, and H-1 in five or ten minutes. Wildfires rarely spread faster than one or two miles an hour, and the vast majority of fire fighters are never compelled to outrun them—much less fight to survive them. By conventional fire evaluation standards, Haugh was considered safe.

About three-thirty Haugh took his second break of the day. It was so hot he had already consumed a gallon of the water he carried. The fire was burning slowly in the drainage floor, and the crews fighting it—nine from the Prineville unit and twelve smoke jumpers—were several hundred feet below him in thick Gambel oak, some of the most flammable wood in the West.

Around 3:50 Haugh and his swamper—a sawyer's helper who flings the cut brush off the fire line—were finishing their break when their crew boss announced they were pulling out. Winds were picking up from a cold front that had moved in a half hour earlier, and the fire was snapping to life. They were ordered to climb to the ridgetop and wait it out. **E**

It's rare for an entire mountainside to ignite suddenly, but it's not unheard of. If you stand near H-2 and look several miles to the west, you can see a mountain called Battlement Mesa. In 1976, three men died there in a wildfire later re-created in a training video called *Situation #8*. Every crew member on Storm King would certainly have seen it. In *Situation #8*, a crew is working upslope of a small fire in extremely dry conditions. Flames ignite Gambel oak and race up the hill, encouraged by winds. The steep terrain funnels the flames upward, and fire intensity careens off the chart, a classic blowup. Four men are overrun, three die. The survivor, who suffered horrible burns, says they were never alerted to the critical wind shift—an accusation the BLM denied at the time. . . . **F**

At about 4:00 P.M. high winds hit the mountain and pushed a wall of flames north, up the west side of the drainage. Along the ridge, the BLM crew and the upper Prineville unit began moving to the safety of H-1. Below them, Don Mackey ordered his eight jumpers to retreat up to a burned-over area beneath H-1. He then started cross-slope to join three other smoke jumpers

E TAKE NOTES
Reread lines 104–108. What happened around 3:50 P.M.? What had happened at about 3:20? Put these events on your timeline.

F NARRATIVE NONFICTION
Reread lines 109–119. Why does Junger break away from the action on Storm King Mountain to give information about the wildfire at Battlement Mesa?

deployed with the Prineville nine. Apparently, no one had advised them that the situation was becoming desperate. In the few minutes it took Mackey to join the twelve fire fighters, the fire jumped east across the drainage. "I radioed that in," said Haugh. "And then another order came to evacuate." That order came from Butch Blanco on the ridgeline, who was hurriedly conducting the evacuation. "This was a much stronger warning than the previous one," recalled Haugh. "I sent my swamper to the ridgetop with a saw and radioed that as soon as the lower Prineville contingent came into sight below me, I would bump up to the safety zone."

Suddenly, fierce westerly winds drove the fire dangerously close—though still hidden behind the thick brush—to the unsuspecting fire fighters. "The crew was unaware of what was behind them," said Haugh. "They were walking at a slow pace, tools still in hand and packs in place." As Haugh watched them, a smoke jumper appeared at his side. "He said that his brother-in-law was down in the drainage, and he wanted to take his picture."

That fellow was Kevin Erickson, and Don Mackey was his brother-in-law, now in serious trouble below. As Erickson aimed his camera, everything below him seemed to explode. "Through the viewfinder, I saw them beginning to run, with fire everywhere behind them," Erickson said. "As I took the picture, Brad grabbed me and turned me around. I took one more look back and saw a wall of fire coming uphill." Closing in on Haugh and Erickson were smoke jumper James Thrash and the twelve other fire fighters in a ragged line behind him. Though Blanco and others were now screaming, "Run! Run! Run!" on the radio, Thrash chose to stop and deploy the fire shelter he would die in. Eric Hipke ran around him and followed Haugh and Erickson up the hill. The three-hundred-foot-high flames chasing them sounded like a river thundering over a waterfall. **G**

In his book *Young Men and Fire,* Norman Maclean writes that dying in a forest fire is actually like experiencing three deaths: first the failure of your legs as you run, then the scorching of your lungs, finally the burning of your body. That, roughly, is what happens to wood when it burns. Water is driven out by the heat; then gases are superheated inside the wood and ignited; finally, the cellulose is consumed. In the end nothing is left but carbon.

This process is usually a slow one, and fires that burn more than a few acres per hour are rare. The South Canyon fire, for example, only burned fifty acres in the first three days. So why did it suddenly rip through two thousand acres in a couple of hours? Why did one hillside explode in a chain reaction that was fast enough to catch birds in midair?

Fire typically spreads by slowly heating the fuel in front of it—first drying it, then igniting it. Usually, a walking pace will easily keep fire fighters ahead of this process. But sometimes a combination of wind, fuel, and terrain **conspires** to produce a blowup in which the fire explodes out of control. One explanation for why South Canyon blew up—and the one most popular in

G TAKE NOTES
Summarize what happened at about 4:00 P.M. Then add your summary to your timeline—in proper order.

conspire (kən-spīr') *v.* to plan or plot secretly

A fire fighter observing the South Canyon fire

Glenwood Springs—was that it was just so . . . steep and dry up there and the wind blew so hard that the mountain was swept with flame. That's plausible; 170 similar conditions in other fires have certainly produced extreme fire behavior. The other explanation turns on a rare phenomenon called superheating.

Normally, radiant heat[6] drives volatile[7] gases—called turpines—out of the pinyon and juniper just minutes before they are consumed. But sometimes hot air rises up a steep slope from a blaze and drives turpines out of a whole hillside full of timber. The gases lie heavily along the contours of the slopes, and when the right combination of wind and flame reaches them, they explode. It's like leaving your gas stove burners on for a few hours and then setting a match to your kitchen.

A mountainside on the verge of combustion is a subtle but not necessarily 180 undetectable thing; there are stories of crews pulling out of a creepy-feeling canyon and then watching it blow up behind them. Turpines have an odor, and that's possibly why some of the Prineville survivors said that something had "seemed wrong." The westward-facing hillside had been drying all afternoon in the summer sun. Hot air was sucked up the drainage as if it were

---

6. **radiant heat:** heat that passes through the air, heating solid objects that in turn heat the surrounding area.

7. **volatile:** explosive.

an open flue. The powerful winds that hit around 4:00 P.M. blew the fire up the drainage at the hottest time of day. And turpines, having baked for hours, could **conceivably** have lit the whole hillside practically at once. **H**

When Storm King blew, Haugh had to run 150 feet straight up a fire line with poor footing. Despite **rigorous** conditioning—he is a runner and a bodybuilder—his heart rate shot through the roof and his adrenal glands dumped enough epinephrine[8] into his system to kill a house cat. Behind him, sheets of flame were laid flat against the hillside by 50 mph winds. The inferno roared through inherently combustible vegetation that had been desiccated,[9] first by drought, then by hot-air convection, finally by a small grass fire that flashed through a few days earlier. The moisture content of the fine dead fuels was later estimated to be as low as 2 or 3 percent—absolutely explosive. As Haugh ran, panicked shouts came over the tiny radio clipped to his vest for people to drop their equipment and flee. One brief thought flashed through his mind—"So this is what it's like to run for your life"—and he didn't think again until he reached the ridgetop.

Above him, the BLM and upper Prineville crews had abandoned hope of reaching H-1 and scrambled toward H-2. When that route too was blocked, they turned and plunged over the ridge. Due south, one hundred feet below **I** H-1, the eight smoke jumpers who had been ordered out by Don Mackey fifteen minutes earlier were crawling under their foil shelters to wait out the approaching fire storm. At Canyon Creek far below, a crew of fresh smoke jumpers who were preparing to hike in watched in horror as eight little silver squares appeared on the mountainside. Meanwhile, hidden from view by smoke, Mackey, the Prineville nine, and the three smoke jumpers were running a race only one of them, Hipke, would win.

In the end twelve of the dead were found along the lower fire line. Prineville hotshot Scott Blecha had also run past Thrash but lost his race a hundred feet from the ridgeline. The rest were in two main groups below a tree—*the* tree, as it came to be known, where Haugh had started his run—a few clumped so close together that their bodies were actually touching. Only smoke jumpers Thrash and Roger Roth had deployed their shelters, but the blistering heat disintegrated the foil. Kathi Beck died alongside Thrash, partly under his shelter. It seemed that in his last agony, Thrash may have tried to pull her in. In addition, Richard Tyler and Robert Browning, two fire fighters deployed earlier to direct helicopter operations, perished just north of H-2, only a few hundred feet from a rocky area that might have saved them. **J**

The Prineville nine's dash for safety ended after three hundred feet. They were caught just three or four seconds before Haugh himself cleared the ridgetop, and he could hear their screams over his radio. Reconstructing the details of the victims' agonized last seconds would occupy many hours of professional counseling for the survivors.

---

8. **epinephrine:** another name for adrenaline, a natural chemical released by the body that speeds up heartbeats, improves breathing, and increases blood flow to muscles during exercise.

9. **desiccated:** thoroughly dried out.

H TAKE NOTES
Based on Junger's explanation of super-heating, what might have been happening for several hours before 4:00 P.M.? Indicate this possible occurrence on your timeline.

conceivably
(kən-sēv′ə-blē) *adv.*
possibly

rigorous (rĭg′ər-əs) *adj.*
strict, uncompromising

I GRAMMAR AND STYLE
Reread lines 201–203. Notice how Junger uses the **adverb clause** "When that route too was blocked" to describe at what point the Prineville crew plunged over the ridge. Adverb clauses help to add important details to writing, telling when or where something happened, for example.

J PATTERNS OF ORGANIZATION
Why do you think Junger chose to present these details in spatial order?

Dying in a fire is often less a process of burning than of asphyxiation.[10] Their suffering was probably intense but short-lived. Pathologists looked for carbon in their lungs and upper airways and found none, which meant the victims weren't breathing when the fire passed over them. Their lungs were filled with fluid, their throats were closed in laryngeal spasms—responses to superheated air—and their blood contained toxic levels of carbon monoxide. This gas, given off during incomplete combustion, displaces oxygen in the blood and kills very quickly.

"They died after a few breaths at most," said Rob Kurtzman, a pathologist at the Grand Junction Community Hospital, "probably in less than thirty seconds. All the body changes—the charring, the muscle contractions, the bone fractures—happened after they were dead." **K**

About four-thirty Haugh, Erickson, and Hipke staggered onto Interstate 70. Just an hour before, they had enjoyed a well-earned break on the mountain; now fourteen people were dead. But all they knew at that point was that Blanco, the incident commander, was calling out names on the radio and a lot of people weren't answering.

Haugh and Erickson laid Hipke in the shade of a police cruiser and doused him with water to lower his body temperature and prevent him from going into shock. Blanco climbed back up toward the fire to look for more survivors but found none. The eight smoke jumpers who'd deployed their shelters below H-1 emerged, shaken but unhurt. They were saved not by their shelters but by having deployed them on previously burned ground. The fire was still pumping at this point, and Glenwood Springs was now in danger. Flames were racing eastward along the upper ridges, and the BLM command post at nearby Canyon Creek had begun ordering residents to evacuate.

Haugh's BLM crew had survived. The other Prineville Hotshots—the upper placements—made it out as well. They had snaked their way down the east side of the ridge through a hellish maze of spot fires and exploding trees. Two of them had tried to deploy their shelters but were dragged onward by friends. **L**

Word quickly filtered back to BLM officials in Grand Junction that something terrible had happened on Storm King. Mike Mottice, the agency's area manager, had driven past the blowup and arrived at his Glenwood Springs office around 5:00 P.M. Minutes later crews began arriving from the mountain, and Mottice realized for the first time that there were people unaccounted for. "I hoped that the fire shelters would save them," he said. "But that evening some smoke jumpers confirmed that there were deaths." . . .

The next morning investigators began to measure things, ponder the dynamics of the mountain, and coax secrets from the dead.

The first question was how fast the fire had moved, and Haugh's estimate— that the last three hundred feet were covered in about twelve seconds—turned out to be close. In the end, the investigators confirmed that the fire had

K **NARRATIVE NONFICTION**
Reread lines 227–238. Why might Junger have included this medical information in his narrative?

L **NARRATIVE NONFICTION**
What details indicate that the other Prineville Hotshots also went through a harrowing journey to survive?

---

10. **asphyxiation:** the medical term for suffocation.

A plane releasing fire retardant on the blaze

covered the quarter-mile slope in about two minutes, hitting its top speed of
270 18 mph in the dried-out Gambel oak.

The next question was why it had done that. Fire behavior is determined by
an incredibly complicated interaction of fuel, terrain, and wind, and there are
mathematical models describing the interaction. (The models are programmed
into hand-held calculators carried by most incident commanders these days.)
The deadly hillside faced west at a 33 to 50 percent slope, and the vegetation
on it possessed burning characteristics described in a formula called Fuel
Model Number Four. The moisture content of the small dead fuels on Storm
King Mountain was around 3 percent. And the live Gambel oak (which had
only been partly burned earlier) was several times drier than normal. In a light
280 wind, according to this model, those conditions would produce twenty-three-
foot flames spreading at a maximum of seven hundred feet an hour.

That's a manageable fire, or at least one that can be outrun, but an increase
in wind speed can change the situation dramatically. At 7:20 P.M. on Tuesday
(less than twenty-four hours before the blowup), the National Weather Service
issued a "Red Flag" fire warning for the area around Glenwood Springs. Dry
thunderstorms were expected the following morning, followed by southwest
winds gusting up to 30 mph. A cold front would come through sometime that
afternoon, swinging the winds to the northwest.

Fire fighter Eric Hipke revisits Storm King Mountain in 2004.

Gusts of 35 mph, plugged into Fuel Model Number Four, produce sixty-
290 four-foot flames racing up the mountain at up to fifteen feet per second. In the
superdry Gambel oak, the rate of spread would have been almost twice that—
much faster than any human can run. The lessons of the Battlement Mesa fire
(detailed in the *Situation #8* video) had not been learned: A small fire on steep
ground covered with extremely dry vegetation had once more exploded in a
mathematically predictable way—again, with tragic results. . . . **M**

"I know in my heart," said Haugh, "that the twelve persons who died
in that part of the fire were unaware of what was happening." By the time
the Prineville nine and the three smoke jumpers with them saw the horror
coming—by the time great sheets of flame hit the dry Gambel oak and frantic
300 voices over the radio screamed at them to run—they had only twenty seconds
to live. They must have died in a state of bewilderment almost as great as
their fear. ◆

M PATTERNS OF
ORGANIZATION
Reread lines 271–295.
What pattern of
organization does
Junger use to explain fire
behavior? What type of
graphic organizer would
you use to record details
from this passage?

Comprehension

1. **Recall** How were Brad Haugh and the other two men with him able to escape the fire?

2. **Recall** How did the fire originally begin on July 2?

3. **Recall** What effect did the cold front have on the fire?

4. **Clarify** Why did so many fire fighters die?

READING STANDARD
4.5 Analyze how choice of genre affects theme or topic

Critical Analysis

5. **Examine Notes** Using the timeline you created, explain what happened on Storm King Mountain. How long had the fire burned before the first crew arrived? When did the situation on the mountain become a disaster?

6. **Interpret Information** Junger has been praised for delivering a lot of technical information while telling a good story. What did you learn from the selection about wildfires and how to fight them?

7. **Analyze Cause and Effect** Junger proposes that a phenomenon called superheating could have caused the blowup. Reread the passage about superheating (lines 171–187). Then use a cause-and-effect chart to show how it occurs.

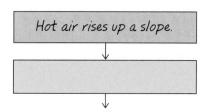

8. **Evaluate Narrative Nonfiction** Where is Junger strongest as a storyteller? Cite passages employing **suspense, foreshadowing,** vivid **characterization,** or other elements you found particularly effective.

9. **Apply Ideas** Junger believes that people with dangerous jobs are more heroic than people who participate in extreme sports. Do you think the fire fighters portrayed in "Blowup" are heroic? Explain why or why not.

Vocabulary in Context

VOCABULARY PRACTICE

Decide if each statement is true or false.

1. To **deflect** criticism means to attract it all the time.
2. A **contingent** is often a smaller group of people.
3. To **conspire** with people is to act together with them.
4. If it can **conceivably** rain today, this means there is no chance of it happening.
5. A **rigorous** course of study is easy and will teach very little.

VOCABULARY IN WRITING

Write three questions you might ask a smoke jumper about his experience on Storm King Mountain. Use at least three vocabulary words. Here is a sample question.

> **EXAMPLE SENTENCE**
>
> Did your _rigorous_ training beforehand prepare you well enough to deal with what happened that day?

VOCABULARY STRATEGY: ANALOGIES

Analogies express relationships between pairs of words. Some common relationships are described in the chart.

Type	Relationship
Part to a whole	is a part of
Antonym	means the opposite of
Cause and effect	results in or leads to
Grammar	is grammatically related to

VOCABULARY STANDARD
1.2 Analyze the relationships of pairs of words

**PRACTICE** Complete each analogy by choosing the appropriate word from the Word List. Identify the kind of relationship on which the analogy is based.

1. interruption : distract :: obstacle : _____
2. indignation : indignant :: rigor : _____
3. slightly : greatly :: impossibly : _____
4. school : class :: military : _____

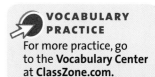

VOCABULARY PRACTICE
For more practice, go to the **Vocabulary Center** at **ClassZone.com**.

Reading-Writing Connection

Deepen your understanding of "Blowup: What Went Wrong at Storm King Mountain" by responding to these prompts. Then use **Revision: Grammar and Style** to improve your writing.

WRITING PROMPTS

SELF-CHECK

A. Short Response: Analyze Characteristics

What kind of person would volunteer to fight wildfires? On the basis of information provided in the narrative, write **one or two paragraphs** analyzing the skills and qualities a person needs to fight wildfires.

A strong analysis will . . .
- cite examples of the tasks required and the skills needed
- cite two examples of personal qualities and their importance

B. Extended Response: Identify Lesson

What is the most important lesson to be learned from the **disaster** on Storm King Mountain? Write **three to five paragraphs** discussing mistakes made and offering one or more proposals for the future.

A successful response will . . .
- identify a lesson to be learned from the disaster
- offer a proposal that would reduce loss of life in the future

REVISION: GRAMMAR AND STYLE

ADD DESCRIPTIVE DETAILS Review the **Grammar and Style** note on page 517. An **adverb clause** tells *where, why, how, when,* or *to what degree* something was done. It is typically introduced by a subordinating conjunction such as *after, as, because, since, until, when,* and *where.* In the following excerpts, notice how Junger uses adverb clauses to explain when certain events occurred.

> *As they started down again, the fire was spreading behind them at a thousand acres an hour, oak, pinyon, and juniper spontaneously combusting in the heat.* (lines 33–35)

> *All the body changes—the charring, the muscle contractions, the bone fractures—happened after they were dead.* (lines 237–238)

Notice how the revisions in red enhance the description in this first draft. Revise your responses to the prompts by including adverb clauses, making sure to set them off with a comma when they come before independent clauses.

 OHIO STANDARDS

WRITING STANDARD
7.3 Use clauses and phrases

STUDENT MODEL

As they walk up and down steep slopes,
People who fight wildfires need to be very strong. They must haul their
Since chain saws can weigh 10 to 12 pounds and two gallons of water can weigh 17 pounds,
food, water, and equipment, such as chain saws and fire shelters. This is a

difficult task.

 **WRITING TOOLS**
For prewriting, revision, and editing tools, visit the **Writing Center** at ClassZone.com.

Is the news always RELIABLE?

OHIO STANDARDS

RESEARCH STANDARD
8.3 Determine the accuracy and credibility of sources

KEY IDEA Where might you find a headline like this one: "Martians Text Message the Pentagon"? If you guessed the news source to be a supermarket tabloid, you'd probably be right. There's an endless variety of news sources out there. By critically examining two sources in this lesson, you'll explore how to make judgments about their **reliability** and usefulness.

Background

Twister Tendencies Every spring brings news of tornadoes, the most violent of all storms. Although these spiral-shaped windstorms can occur in most parts of the world, they happen most often in the United States, especially in a region known as Tornado Alley. This region includes part of Texas, Oklahoma, Kansas, Nebraska, and Iowa. The newscast and Web page you'll explore cover a series of tornadoes in Alabama that arose at the start of the 1998 tornado season.

Media Literacy: Credibility in News Reports

The ideal news report is objective, accurate, and thorough. When writing a news story, a journalist relies upon **sources**—people or published materials that provide information on the report's topic. These sources may not always be as reliable or credible as they seem. **Credibility** refers to the believability and trustworthiness of both the sources and the report itself. Since it is the journalist who chooses the sources, the reader or viewer needs to be prepared to question the credibility of both the journalist and the publisher.

QUESTIONS TO ASK ABOUT A TV NEWSCAST

- From what **news outlet**, or station, is the story broadcast? What sense do you have of the outlet's reputation and that of the **news anchor** or **field reporters?**

- Is the person delivering the report an experienced anchor with a reputation for excellence, and is he or she affiliated with a reputable news agency? If not, what background qualifies this person to deliver the news?

- Is the primary **purpose** of the report to inform, persuade, or entertain? Are there clues in the title? What other purpose is evident?

- Are the **facts** and **statistics** that appear in the report relevant and reliable? Are documented sources provided?

- What interviews are included? Are the interview **sources** witnesses to an event? Are the sources **experts** on the topic of the story?

QUESTIONS TO ASK ABOUT A WEB REPORT

- Where is the Web site published? What is the **URL** and what is the type of **domain?**

- Who is the creator or **webmaster** of the page? What is that person's educational or professional background?

- What is the report's **purpose?** Is it to inform, entertain, persuade, or give an opinion?

- Does the page offer complete details about a report?

- What **sources** are cited? Can **facts** be confirmed in other sources? Are **links** provided to related news sources or other viewpoints? Are they credible sources?

- Does the Web news report show the **date** and **time** the report was originally published?

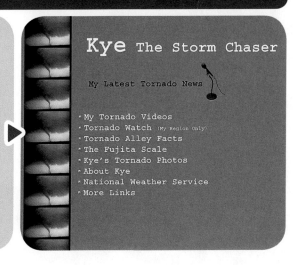

Kye The Storm Chaser

My Latest Tornado News

- My Tornado Videos
- Tornado Watch (My Region Only)
- Tornado Alley Facts
- The Fujita Scale
- Kye's Tornado Photos
- About Kye
- National Weather Service
- More Links

HOME

About Kye

When I can steal a moment from chasing storms across Tornado Alley, I'm posting news on this site to convey the excitement of being in the path of a tornado.

Viewing Guide for
News Reports

View the TV newscast clip a few times. Examine the Web page closely. As you do so, think critically about the basic purpose or purposes and judge the credibility of each news form.

NOW VIEW

FIRST VIEWING: Comprehension

1. **Summarize** In general, what does the TV newscast report that scientists are trying to learn about tornadoes?

2. **Clarify** In using Kye's Web page, which one of the links would you choose if you wanted to find out the latest information about tornadoes nationwide?

CLOSE VIEWING: Media Literacy

3. **Analyze Credibility** Explain what specific features you think give the TV newscast credibility.

4. **Make Judgments** In general, the purpose of the TV news report and the Web site is to inform. Read more details about Kye in the second small image on this page. What other purpose might there be for Kye's delivery of news?

5. **Compare Types of Sources** How do two of the sources in the newscast clip differ from Kye, the source of the Web site?

6. **Compare Credibility** Draw a credibility scale like the one shown. Number it from 1—"not at all credible"—to 5—"extremely credible." Then rate each of the two news forms according to the scale. Give at least one reason for each rating.

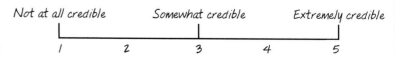

Write or Discuss

Evaluate a News Source Review the questioning strategies on page 525 for newscasts and Web news. Based on the knowledge you gained from using these strategies, evaluate the type of information you can get from each of these sources. Cite evidence in your response.

Produce Your Own Media

Highlight Credible Characteristics Find an example of a credible news story in print or electronic form. Examine the story and the news format closely, pinpointing whatever specific features make the report credible. Then redraft the report to make it seem unreliable.

HERE'S HOW Use the following suggestions when writing your new version:
- Refer to the questions on page 525 to form your criteria for credibility.
- As a class, compare news stories. Single out choices that meet all of your criteria.

> **MEDIA TOOLS**
>
> For help with drafting an alternative news report, visit the **Media Center** at **ClassZone.com.**

PROFESSIONAL MODEL

Note the characteristics that make this news story credible.

THE FAIRVIEW BULLETIN • NOVEMBER 14, 2007 **METRO** 3

Birds a Growing Hazard to Air Travel

Crashes can occur where birds and planes share airspace.

By Jen Omachi
Staff Reporter

Airplane collisions with flying birds are on the rise, according to the U.S. Department of Agriculture in a review of wildlife management.

Known as bird strikes, the in-flight encounters between birds and airplanes can result in the loss of air speed and altitude.

A Federal Aviation Administration (FAA) report claims that more than 15,000 collisions have been reported over a seven-year period in the airspace over the United States, Puerto Rico, and the U.S. Virgin Islands. Although no major crash has been connected to a bird strike, a few of the busiest airports recognize the potential for danger.

Note how the headings avoid dramatic or sensational wording.

Notice the reporter's official title.

Highlight the source of a statement or fact.

Tech Tip

If equipment is available, record a TV newscast. Pause at points to present its credible features.

And of Clay Are We Created

Short Story by Isabel Allende

Can reporters always stay OBJECTIVE?

OHIO STANDARDS

READING STANDARDS
2.3 Monitor understanding
3.5 Analyze author's perspective or viewpoint in text

KEY IDEA Should journalists remain detached and **objective** when reporting a tragedy? Or should they express their personal feelings and become involved with helping victims? What is the proper role of the news media?

QUICKWRITE Imagine that a reporter is interviewing a victim of a tragedy, such as a deadly accident or hurricane. What is usually said in such interviews? Write a brief dialogue between the reporter and the person involved. Discuss the true feelings reporters and victims might have about each other.

LITERARY ANALYSIS: AUTHOR'S PERSPECTIVE

An **author's perspective** is a unique blend of feelings, values, and beliefs that a writer brings to a subject. "And of Clay Are We Created" contains echoes of Isabel Allende's own life experiences as a former journalist and an exile from her native country. Her journalistic experience, for example, is reflected in her descriptions of a disaster scene and her exploration of a reporter's thoughts and feelings.

Carefully read the information about Allende on this page. Then, as you read her short story, draw on what you know of her life to help you understand her perspective on such subjects as news reporting, exile, suffering, and death.

Review: **Characterization**

READING STRATEGY: MONITOR

Monitoring is checking your understanding as you read and adjusting your reading strategies to improve comprehension. The following strategies may be useful:

- **adjust your reading rate**—that is, read more slowly
- **reread**—go back over the text for clarification
- **visualize**—picture characters, events, or settings
- **question**—ask about events or characters

As you read, note the passages that you are having trouble understanding, and then decide which of the strategies will best improve your comprehension. Organize your notes as in the example shown.

> **What I Don't Understand:** *where the mud came from*
> **I Should Probably:**
> • *adjust reading rate* (• *reread/clarify*) • *visualize* • *question*
> **I Now Understand:**

▲ VOCABULARY IN CONTEXT

Allende uses the following words to tell her compelling story. Put them into the categories "Words I Know Well," "Words I Think I Know," and "Words I Don't Know at All." Write a brief definition for each word in the first two categories.

WORD LIST		
embody	resignation	tenacity
fortitude	stratagem	tribulation
pandemonium	stupor	

Background

Volcanic Disaster Allende's story is based on a real event. On November 13, 1985, the Nevado del Ruiz volcano in Colombia erupted. The intense heat from the eruption melted the mountain's icecap and sent a torrent of water, ash, mud, and rocks into the valley below and onto the town of Armero. More than 20,000 people died. (See **Reading for Information** on page 542.)

AND OF *Clay* ARE WE *Created*

Isabel Allende

They discovered the girl's head protruding from the mud pit, eyes wide open, calling soundlessly. She had a First Communion name,[1] Azucena.[2] Lily. In that vast cemetery where the odor of death was already attracting vultures from far away, and where the weeping of orphans and wails of the injured filled the air, the little girl obstinately clinging to life became the symbol of the tragedy. The television cameras transmitted so often the unbearable image of the head budding like a black squash from the clay that there was no one who did not recognize her and know her name. And every time we saw her on the screen, right behind her was Rolf Carlé,[3] who had gone there on assignment, never
10 suspecting that he would find a fragment of his past, lost thirty years before.

First a subterranean[4] sob rocked the cotton fields, curling them like waves **A** of foam. Geologists had set up their seismographs[5] weeks before and knew that the mountain had awakened again. For some time they had predicted that the heat of the eruption could detach the eternal ice from the slopes of the volcano, but no one heeded their warnings; they sounded like the tales of frightened old women. The towns in the valley went about their daily life, deaf to the moaning of the earth, until that fateful Wednesday night in November when a prolonged roar announced the end of the world, and walls of snow broke loose, rolling in an avalanche of clay, stones, and water that descended
20 on the villages and buried them beneath unfathomable meters of telluric[6] vomit. As soon as the survivors emerged from the paralysis of that first awful terror, they could see that houses, plazas, churches, white cotton plantations, dark coffee forests, cattle pastures—all had disappeared. Much later, after soldiers and volunteers had arrived to rescue the living and try to assess the

---

1. **First Communion name:** a name traditionally given to a Roman Catholic child at the time of the child's first participation in the rite of Holy Communion.

2. **Azucena** (ä-sōō-sĕ′nə).

3. **Rolf Carlé** (rälf kär′lā).

4. **subterranean** (sŭb′tə-rā′nē-ən): underground.

5. **seismographs** (sīz′mə-grăfs′): instruments that record the intensity and duration of earthquakes.

6. **telluric** (tĕ-lŏŏr′ĭk): relating to the earth.

ANALYZE VISUALS
Study the painting. How do you **interpret** the girl's expression?

A **AUTHOR'S PERSPECTIVE**
Think about Allende's former job as a journalist. How is her background reflected in the following paragraph? Cite specific details to support your answers.

Niña (1943), Julia Diaz. Oil on canvas, 30 cm × 35 cm. Courtesy of the Julia Diaz Foundation.

magnitude of the cataclysm,[7] it was calculated that beneath the mud lay more than twenty thousand human beings and an indefinite number of animals putrefying in a viscous soup.[8] Forests and rivers had also been swept away, and there was nothing to be seen but an immense desert of mire.

When the station called before dawn, Rolf Carlé and I were together. I crawled out of bed, dazed with sleep, and went to prepare coffee while he hurriedly dressed. He stuffed his gear in the green canvas backpack he always carried, and we said goodbye, as we had so many times before. I had no presentiments. I sat in the kitchen, sipping my coffee and planning the long hours without him, sure that he would be back the next day. **B**

He was one of the first to reach the scene, because while other reporters were fighting their way to the edges of that morass in jeeps, bicycles, or on foot, each getting there however he could, Rolf Carlé had the advantage of the television helicopter, which flew him over the avalanche. We watched on our screens the footage captured by his assistant's camera, in which he was up to his knees in muck, a microphone in his hand, in the midst of a bedlam of lost children, wounded survivors, corpses, and devastation. The story came to us in his calm voice. For years he had been a familiar figure in newscasts, reporting live at the scene of battles and catastrophes with awesome **tenacity**. Nothing could stop him, and I was always amazed at his equanimity in the face of danger and suffering; it seemed as if nothing could shake his **fortitude** or deter his curiosity. Fear seemed never to touch him, although he had confessed to me that he was not a courageous man, far from it. I believe that the lens of a camera had a strange effect on him; it was as if it transported him to a different time from which he could watch events without actually participating in them. When I knew him better, I came to realize that this fictive distance seemed to protect him from his own emotions. **C**

Rolf Carlé was in on the story of Azucena from the beginning. He filmed the volunteers who discovered her, and the first persons who tried to reach her; his camera zoomed in on the girl, her dark face, her large desolate eyes, the plastered-down tangle of her hair. The mud was like quicksand around her, and anyone attempting to reach her was in danger of sinking. They threw a rope to her that she made no effort to grasp until they shouted to her to catch it; then she pulled a hand from the mire and tried to move but immediately sank a little deeper. Rolf threw down his knapsack and the rest of his equipment and waded into the quagmire, commenting for his assistant's microphone that it was cold and that one could begin to smell the stench of corpses.

"What's your name?" he asked the girl, and she told him her flower name. "Don't move, Azucena," Rolf Carlé directed, and kept talking to her, without a thought for what he was saying, just to distract her, while slowly he worked his way forward in mud up to his waist. The air around him seemed as murky as the mud.

7. **cataclysm** (kăt′ə-klĭz′əm): a violent and sudden change in the earth's crust.

8. **putrefying** (pyo͞o′trə-fī′ĭng) **in a viscous soup:** rotting in a thick soup.

B MONITOR
Reread lines 29–34. Who is the **narrator** of the story?

tenacity (tə-năs′ĭ-tē) *n.* the quality of holding persistently to something; firm determination

fortitude (fôr′tĭ-to͞od′) *n.* strength of mind; courage

C AUTHOR'S PERSPECTIVE
Based on the narrator's comments about the effect of a lens on Rolf Carlé, what would you say is Allende's perspective on news reporting?

It was impossible to reach her from the approach he was attempting, so he retreated and circled around where there seemed to be firmer footing. When finally he was close enough, he took the rope and tied it beneath her arms, so they could pull her out. He smiled at her with that smile that crinkles his eyes and makes him look like a little boy; he told her that everything was fine, that he was here with her now, that soon they would have her out. He signaled the others to pull, but as soon as the cord tensed, the girl screamed. They tried again, and her shoulders and arms appeared, but they could move her no farther; she was trapped. Someone suggested that her legs might be caught in the collapsed walls of her house, but she said it was not just rubble, that she was also held by the bodies of her brothers and sisters clinging to her legs. **D**

"Don't worry, we'll get you out of here," Rolf promised. Despite the quality of the transmission, I could hear his voice break, and I loved him more than ever. Azucena looked at him but said nothing.

During those first hours Rolf Carlé exhausted all the resources of his ingenuity to rescue her. He struggled with poles and ropes, but every tug was an intolerable torture for the imprisoned girl. It occurred to him to use one of the poles as a lever but got no result and had to abandon the idea. He talked a couple of soldiers into working with him for a while, but they had to leave because so many other victims were calling for help. The girl could not move, she barely could breathe, but she did not seem desperate, as if an ancestral **resignation** allowed her to accept her fate. The reporter, on the other hand, was determined to snatch her from death. Someone brought him a tire, which he placed beneath her arms like a life buoy, and then laid a plank near the hole to hold his weight and allow him to stay closer to her. As it was impossible to remove the rubble blindly, he tried once or twice to dive toward her feet but emerged frustrated, covered with mud, and spitting gravel. He concluded that he would have to have a pump to drain the water, and radioed a request for one but received in return a message that there was no available transport and it could not be sent until the next morning.

"We can't wait that long!" Rolf Carlé shouted, but in the **pandemonium** no one stopped to commiserate. Many more hours would go by before he accepted that time had stagnated and reality had been irreparably distorted. **E**

A military doctor came to examine the girl and observed that her heart was functioning well and that if she did not get too cold she could survive the night.

"Hang on, Azucena, we'll have the pump tomorrow," Rolf Carlé tried to console her.

"Don't leave me alone," she begged.

"No, of course I won't leave you."

D MONITOR
Visualize Azucena, Rolf, and the others. Why can't the rescuers pull Azucena out?

resignation
(rĕz′ĭg-nā′shən) *n.* passive acceptance of something; submission

pandemonium
(păn′də-mō′nē-əm) *n.* a wild uproar or noise

E CHARACTERIZATION
Consider Rolf's efforts to save Azucena. What do they suggest about him?

Someone brought him coffee, and he helped the girl drink it, sip by sip. The warm liquid revived her, and she began telling him about her small life, about her family and her school, about how things were in that little bit of world before the volcano erupted. She was thirteen, and she had never been outside her village. Rolf Carlé, buoyed by a premature optimism, was convinced that everything would end well: the pump would arrive, they would drain the water, move the rubble, and Azucena would be transported by helicopter to a hospital where she would recover rapidly and where he could visit her and bring her gifts. He thought, She's already too old for dolls, and I don't know what would please her; maybe a dress. I don't know much about women, he concluded, amused, reflecting that although he had known many women in his lifetime, none had taught him these details. To pass the hours he began to tell Azucena about his travels and adventures as a news hound, and when he exhausted his memory, he called upon imagination, inventing things he thought might entertain her. From time to time she dozed, but he kept talking in the darkness, to assure her that he was still there and to overcome the menace of uncertainty. **⑥**

That was a long night.

Many miles away, I watched Rolf Carlé and the girl on a television screen. I could not bear the wait at home, so I went to National Television, where I

⑥ CHARACTERIZATION
What do you learn about Rolf and Azucena in lines 108–124? What do the last two sentences suggest about Rolf's character?

Sosteniendo el Tiempo (1998), Satenik Tekyan. Mixed media, 95 cm × 80 cm. www.artesur.com/satenik.

often spent entire nights with Rolf editing programs. There, I was near his world, and I could at least get a feeling of what he lived through during those three decisive days. I called all the important people in the city, senators, commanders of the armed forces, the North American ambassador, and the president of National Petroleum, begging them for a pump to remove the silt, but obtained only vague promises. I began to ask for urgent help on radio and television, to see if there wasn't *someone* who could help us. Between calls I would run to the newsroom to monitor the satellite transmissions that periodically brought new details of the catastrophe. While reporters selected scenes with most impact for the news report, I searched for footage that featured Azucena's mud pit. The screen reduced the disaster to a single plane and accentuated the tremendous distance that separated me from Rolf Carlé; nonetheless, I was there with him. The child's every suffering hurt me as it did him; I felt his frustration, his impotence. Faced with the impossibility of communicating with him, the fantastic idea came to me that if I tried, I could reach him by force of mind and in that way give him encouragement. I concentrated until I was dizzy—a frenzied and futile activity. At times I would be overcome with compassion and burst out crying; at other times, I was so drained I felt as if I were staring through a telescope at the light of a star dead for a million years. **G**

I watched that hell on the first morning broadcast, cadavers[9] of people and animals awash in the current of new rivers formed overnight from the melted snow. Above the mud rose the tops of trees and the bell towers of a church where several people had taken refuge and were patiently awaiting rescue teams. Hundreds of soldiers and volunteers from the civil defense were clawing through rubble searching for survivors, while long rows of ragged specters awaited their turn for a cup of hot broth. Radio networks announced that their phones were jammed with calls from families offering shelter to orphaned children. Drinking water was in scarce supply, along with gasoline and food. Doctors, resigned to amputating arms and legs without anesthesia, pled that at least they be sent serum and painkillers and antibiotics; most of the roads, however, were impassable, and worse were the bureaucratic obstacles that stood in the way. To top it all, the clay contaminated by decomposing bodies threatened the living with an outbreak of epidemics. **H**

Azucena was shivering inside the tire that held her above the surface. Immobility and tension had greatly weakened her, but she was conscious and could still be heard when a microphone was held out to her. Her tone was humble, as if apologizing for all the fuss. Rolf Carlé had a growth of beard, and dark circles beneath his eyes; he looked near exhaustion. Even from that enormous distance I could sense the quality of his weariness, so different from the fatigue of other adventures. He had completely forgotten the camera; he could not look at the girl through a lens any longer. The pictures we were receiving were not his assistant's but those of other reporters

G MONITOR
Reread lines 141–147 and **clarify** what the narrator attempts to do. How does the effort make her feel?

H AUTHOR'S PERSPECTIVE
Reread lines 130–161. What would you say is Allende's perspective on politicians and other officials?

9. **cadavers** (kə-dăv′ərz): dead bodies.

who had appropriated Azucena, bestowing on her the pathetic responsibility of **embodying** the horror of what had happened in that place. With the first light Rolf tried again to dislodge the obstacles that held the girl in her tomb, but he had only his hands to work with; he did not dare use a tool for fear of injuring her. He fed Azucena a cup of the cornmeal mush and bananas the army was distributing, but she immediately vomited it up. A doctor stated that she had a fever but added that there was little he could do: antibiotics were being reserved for cases of gangrene.[10] A priest also passed by and blessed her, hanging a medal of the Virgin around her neck. By evening a gentle, persistent
180 drizzle began to fall. **❶**

"The sky is weeping," Azucena murmured, and she, too, began to cry.

"Don't be afraid," Rolf begged. "You have to keep your strength up and be calm. Everything will be fine. I'm with you, and I'll get you out somehow."

Reporters returned to photograph Azucena and ask her the same questions, which she no longer tried to answer. In the meanwhile, more television and movie teams arrived with spools of cable, tapes, film, videos, precision lenses, recorders, sound consoles, lights, reflecting screens, auxiliary motors, cartons of supplies, electricians, sound technicians, and cameramen: Azucena's face was beamed to millions of screens around the world. And all the while Rolf
190 Carlé kept pleading for a pump. The improved technical facilities bore results, and National Television began receiving sharper pictures and clearer sound, the distance seemed suddenly compressed, and I had the horrible sensation that Azucena and Rolf were by my side, separated from me by impenetrable glass. I was able to follow events hour by hour; I knew everything my love did to wrest the girl from her prison and help her endure her suffering; I overheard fragments of what they said to one another and could guess the rest; I was present when she taught Rolf to pray and when he distracted her with the stories I had told him in a thousand and one nights beneath the white mosquito netting of our bed. **❷**

200 When darkness came on the second day, Rolf tried to sing Azucena to sleep with old Austrian folk songs he had learned from his mother, but she was far beyond sleep. They spent most of the night talking, each in a **stupor** of exhaustion and hunger and shaking with cold. That night, imperceptibly, the unyielding floodgates that had contained Rolf Carlé's past for so many years began to open, and the torrent of all that had lain hidden in the deepest and most secret layers of memory poured out, leveling before it the obstacles that had blocked his consciousness for so long. He could not tell it all to Azucena; she perhaps did not know there was a world beyond the sea or time previous to her own; she was not capable of imagining Europe in the years of the war. So
210 he could not tell her of defeat, nor of the afternoon the Russians had led them to the concentration camp to bury prisoners dead from starvation. Why should he describe to her how the naked bodies piled like a mountain of firewood resembled fragile china? How could he tell this dying child about ovens and gallows? Nor did he mention the night that he had seen his mother naked,

---

10. **gangrene:** death and decay of body tissue, usually resulting from injury or disease.

embody (ĕm-bŏd′ē) *v.* to give shape to or visibly represent

❶ CHARACTERIZATION
Reread lines 165–180. What do these observations suggest has happened to Rolf? Explain your answer.

❷ AUTHOR'S PERSPECTIVE
Allende gives a behind-the-scenes view of broadcasting a news story. What criticisms of the media does she seem to be suggesting?

stupor (stoo′pər) *n.* a state of mental numbness, as from shock

Resurrection (2000), Stevie Taylor. Pastel on paper. Private Collection. Photo © Bridgeman Art Library.

shod in stiletto-heeled red boots, sobbing with humiliation. There was much
he did not tell, but in those hours he relived for the first time all the things his
mind had tried to erase. Azucena had surrendered her fear to him and so, without
wishing it, had obliged Rolf to confront his own. There, beside that hellhole
of mud, it was impossible for Rolf to flee from himself any longer, and the
220 visceral terror he had lived as a boy suddenly invaded him. He reverted to
the years when he was the age of Azucena and younger, and, like her, found
himself trapped in a pit without escape, buried in life, his head barely above
ground; he saw before his eyes the boots and legs of his father, who had
removed his belt and was whipping it in the air with the never-forgotten hiss of
a viper coiled to strike. Sorrow flooded through him, intact and precise, as if it
had lain always in his mind, waiting. He was once again in the armoire[11] where
his father locked him to punish him for imagined misbehavior, there where
for eternal hours he had crouched with his eyes closed, not to see the darkness,
with his hands over his ears to shut out the beating of his heart, trembling,
230 huddled like a cornered animal. Wandering in the mist of his memories he

---

11. **armoire** (ärm-wär'): a large wardrobe or cabinet.

found his sister, Katharina, a sweet, retarded child who spent her life hiding, with the hope that her father would forget the disgrace of her having been born. With Katharina, Rolf crawled beneath the dining room table, and with her hid there under the long white tablecloth, two children forever embraced, alert to footsteps and voices. Katharina's scent melded with his own sweat, with aromas of cooking, garlic, soup, freshly baked bread, and the unexpected odor of putrescent[12] clay. His sister's hand in his, her frightened breathing, her silk hair against his cheek, the candid gaze of her eyes. Katharina . . . Katharina materialized before him, floating on the air like a flag, clothed in the white
240   tablecloth, now a winding sheet, and at last he could weep for her death and for the guilt of having abandoned her. He understood then that all his exploits as a reporter, the feats that had won him such recognition and fame, were merely an attempt to keep his most ancient fears at bay, a **stratagem** for taking refuge behind a lens to test whether reality was more tolerable from that perspective. He took excessive risks as an exercise of courage, training by day to conquer the monsters that tormented him by night. But he had to come face to face with the moment of truth; he could not continue to escape his past. He was Azucena; he was buried in the clayey mud; his terror was not the distant emotion of an almost forgotten childhood, it was a claw sunk in his throat.
250   In the flush of his tears he saw his mother, dressed in black and clutching her imitation-crocodile pocketbook to her bosom, just as he had last seen her on the dock when she had come to put him on the boat to South America. She had not come to dry his tears, but to tell him to pick up a shovel: the war was over and now they must bury the dead. **K**

"Don't cry. I don't hurt anymore. I'm fine," Azucena said when dawn came.

"I'm not crying for you," Rolf Carlé smiled. "I'm crying for myself. I hurt all over." **L**

The third day in the valley of the cataclysm began with a pale light filtering through storm clouds. The president of the republic visited the area in his
260   tailored safari jacket to confirm that this was the worst catastrophe of the century; the country was in mourning; sister nations had offered aid; he had ordered a state of siege; the armed forces would be merciless; anyone caught stealing or committing other offenses would be shot on sight. He added that it was impossible to remove all the corpses or count the thousands who had disappeared; the entire valley would be declared holy ground, and bishops would come to celebrate a solemn mass for the souls of the victims. He went to the army field tents to offer relief in the form of vague promises to crowds of the rescued, then to the improvised hospital to offer a word of encouragement to doctors and nurses worn down from so many hours of **tribulations.** Then
270   he asked to be taken to see Azucena, the little girl the whole world had seen. He waved to her with a limp statesman's hand, and microphones recorded his emotional voice and paternal tone as he told her that her courage had served as an example to the nation. Rolf Carlé interrupted to ask for a pump, and the

---

12. **putrescent** (pyōō-trĕs´ənt): rotting and foul-smelling.

stratagem (străt´ə-jəm) *n.* a clever trick or device for obtaining an advantage

K MONITOR
In line 220 a **flashback** begins in which Rolf recalls his childhood in a defeated Austria after World War II. **Reread** this description, through line 254. What terrible memories does he have?

L AUTHOR'S PERSPECTIVE
Rolf was exiled from his homeland, as Allende was exiled from her native Chile. Given Rolf's experiences, what might Allende be saying about the consequences of burying one's past and leaving one's family?

tribulation (trĭb´yə-lā´shən) *n.* great distress or suffering

president assured him that he personally would attend to the matter. I caught a glimpse of Rolf for a few seconds kneeling beside the mud pit. On the evening news broadcast, he was still in the same position; and I, glued to the screen like a fortune teller to her crystal ball, could tell that something fundamental had changed in him. I knew somehow that during the night his defenses had crumbled and he had given in to grief; finally he was vulnerable. The girl had
280 touched a part of him that he himself had no access to, a part he had never shared with me. Rolf had wanted to console her, but it was Azucena who had given him consolation.

I recognized the precise moment at which Rolf gave up the fight and surrendered to the torture of watching the girl die. I was with them, three days and two nights, spying on them from the other side of life. I was there when she told him that in all her thirteen years no boy had ever loved her and that it was a pity to leave this world without knowing love. Rolf assured her that he loved her more than he could ever love anyone, more than he loved his mother, more than his sister, more than all the women who had slept in his arms,
290 more than he loved me, his life companion, who would have given anything to be trapped in that well in her place, who would have exchanged her life for Azucena's, and I watched as he leaned down to kiss her poor forehead, consumed by a sweet, sad emotion he could not name. I felt how in that instant both were saved from despair, how they were freed from the clay, how they rose above the vultures and helicopters, how together they flew above the vast swamp of corruption and laments. How, finally, they were able to accept death. Rolf Carlé prayed in silence that she would die quickly, because such pain cannot be borne. **M**

By then I had obtained a pump and was in touch with a general who had
300 agreed to ship it the next morning on a military cargo plane. But on the night of that third day, beneath the unblinking focus of quartz lamps and the lens of a hundred cameras, Azucena gave up, her eyes locked with those of the friend who had sustained her to the end. Rolf Carlé removed the life buoy, closed her eyelids, held her to his chest for a few moments, and then let her go. She sank slowly, a flower in the mud.

You are back with me, but you are not the same man. I often accompany you to the station, and we watch the videos of Azucena again; you study them intently, looking for something you could have done to save her, something you did not think of in time. Or maybe you study them to see yourself as if in a mirror, naked. Your cameras lie forgotten in a closet; you do not write or
310 sing; you sit long hours before the window, staring at the mountains. Beside you, I wait for you to complete the voyage into yourself, for the old wounds to heal. I know that when you return from your nightmares, we shall again walk hand in hand, as before. ❧

Translated by Margaret Sayers Peden

M MONITOR
Reread lines 284–299. In what sense are Rolf and Azucena "saved" and "freed"?

Comprehension

OHIO STANDARDS

READING STANDARD
3.5 Analyze author's perspective or viewpoint in text

1. **Recall** What disaster has happened in the town?

2. **Recall** Who is Rolf Carlé?

3. **Recall** What prevents Azucena from being rescued?

4. **Clarify** What memories disturb Rolf as he waits in the night with Azucena?

Literary Analysis

5. **Monitor Understanding** Look back at the notes you made as you read. What strategies did you use to increase your understanding?

6. **Analyze Relationships** What do Rolf and Azucena do for each other? How would you describe the relationship that develops between them? Use a chart to plan your answer.

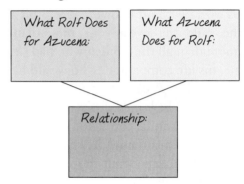

7. **Contrast Attitudes** Contrast Azucena's attitude toward her fate with Rolf's attitude. What might account for the difference?

8. **Identify Author's Perspective** Do you think Allende values **objectivity** in reporting? Support your opinion.

9. **Analyze Point of View** How does Allende's choice of narrator contribute to the story? Consider what this narrator was able to present that Rolf Carlé as narrator would not have been able to provide.

10. **Interpret Theme** State what the story suggests to you about the role of the media in a tragedy. What other messages do you draw from the story?

Literary Criticism

11. **Biographical Context** Allende, in reflecting on a photograph of Omaira Sanchez, the trapped girl who inspired her story, commented: "We've never met her and are living at the other end of the world, yet we've been brought together because of her. She never dies, this girl. . . . She's born every instant." What does this statement reveal about Allende's values?

Vocabulary in Context

VOCABULARY PRACTICE

Decide whether the words in each pair are synonyms or antonyms.

1. tenacity/laziness
2. fortitude/weakness
3. resignation/acceptance
4. pandemonium/chaos
5. stupor/enthusiasm
6. embody/represent
7. stratagem/scheme
8. tribulation/hardship

VOCABULARY IN WRITING

Briefly retell the story from the trapped girl's point of view. Use at least four vocabulary words in your new version. Here is an example of how you could begin.

> **EXAMPLE SENTENCE**
>
> Throughout the **pandemonium** of my experience, it was comforting to have my journalist friend by my side.

OHIO STANDARDS

VOCABULARY STANDARD
1.5 Use knowledge of Latin roots, prefixes and suffixes to understand words

VOCABULARY STRATEGY: THE LATIN WORD ROOT *fort*

The vocabulary word *fortitude* stems from the Latin root *fort*, which means "strong." To understand the meaning of words with *fort*, use context clues as well as your knowledge of the root.

fortissimo   fortitude

fort

forte   fortify

fortress

PRACTICE Choose the word from the word web that best completes each sentence. Use context clues to help you or, if necessary, consult a dictionary.

1. In music, to play a piece _____ is to play in a very loud manner.
2. She showed great _____ during her mother's funeral.
3. This exercise will _____ the muscles in your upper body.
4. Painting is her _____ ; she is a very talented artist.
5. Building a solid _____ will keep enemies at bay.

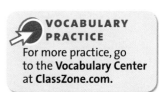

VOCABULARY PRACTICE
For more practice, go to the **Vocabulary Center** at **ClassZone.com**.

Girl, Trapped in Water for 55 Hours, Dies Despite Rescue Attempts

News Article

Use with "And of Clay Are We Created," page 530.

OHIO STANDARDS

READING STANDARDS
2.1 Compare and contrast

3.4 Assess the adequacy and appropriateness of an author's details

What's the Connection?

Often, fiction writers discover ideas for stories in real events. Isabel Allende based her short story "And of Clay Are We Created" on actual news accounts about a girl trapped in floodwater after a volcano eruption in Colombia. The news article you are about to read reports what happened to the girl, Omaira Sanchez, who was the inspiration for Allende's fictional Azucena.

Skill Focus: Analyze a News Article

A **news article** is a factual account of a real-life event. The author's purpose for writing a news article is to inform or explain. News articles typically provide the following elements:

- a **headline** summarizing the article
- photographs with **captions**, or lines of explanation
- a **lead**—the first few sentences of an article, which are meant to grab the reader's attention
- answers to the questions *who, what, when, where, why,* and *how*
- additional details arranged in order of decreasing importance

As you read the following news article, note the information it provides, and record the information on a chart like the one shown.

Elements of News Article	Information Provided
Headline	
Photos and Captions	
Lead	
Answers to who, what, when, where, why, and how questions	
Additional details	

Girl, Trapped in Water for 55 Hours, Dies Despite Rescue Attempts

Rescue efforts to save Omaira Sanchez Ⓐ

by Julia Preston

Armero, Colombia—Omaira Sanchez, a 13-year-old girl trapped up to her neck for more than 55 hours in floodwaters, died yesterday morning despite rescuers' frantic efforts to free her. Ⓑ

Omaira's legs were pinned in the ruins of what was once her home by a cement slab and by the body of an
10 aunt who drowned in the avalanche of mud that rolled over Armero Wednesday night.

Trapped in the chilly water the little girl shivered violently and her hands turned a deathly white. Finally her blood pressure dropped so low she suffered a heart attack, according to Alejandro Jimenez, 23, a medical student volunteer at the
20 disaster site who attended the child.

C ANALYZE A
NEWS ARTICLE
What information
does this photograph
convey to you?

C

Mudflow covering the fields after the Nevado del Ruiz eruption

"You can imagine how I feel," said Jimenez, looking drawn and exhausted yesterday morning. "We stayed up all night trying to save her." **D**

About a dozen 30 rescuers from the Colombian Air Force, the Red Cross, and fire departments of towns near Armero radioed increasingly desperate pleas since Thursday for an electric pump to keep the fetid waters from rising above the girl's chin. They called for 40 picks, shovels, and winches to clear away rubble trapping her.

D ANALYZE A
NEWS ARTICLE
How is Alejandro
Jimenez involved in
the events?

At 2 P.M. yesterday, four hours after Omaira died, a Colombian radio station announced that 18 water pumps 50 had just arrived in a town 45 miles from Armero. To the end, rescue workers dug with their bare hands at the cement slab leaning on Omaira's numb legs, and bailed the water with tin cans.

60 Someone stretched a dirty blue-and-white checkered tablecloth over the scene of tragedy, a scene that, displayed in newspapers around the world yesterday, came to represent the horror of the disaster.

Comprehension

1. **Recall** What caused Omaira Sanchez to be trapped?

2. **Summarize** What efforts did rescue workers make to try to save Omaira?

Critical Analysis

3. **Read a News Article** What details are provided by Alejandro Jimenez? What would have been the effect if he had not been mentioned or quoted?

4. **Analyze Details** What do the details about the pumps' arrival and the checkered tablecloth contribute to the article?

5. **Evaluate Graphic Aids** Explain what each photograph adds to your understanding of the events. Which of the two photographs has greater emotional impact? Give reasons for your answer.

Read for Information: Compare Forms

OHIO STANDARDS

READING STANDARDS
2.1 Compare and contrast
3.4 Assess the adequacy and appropriateness of an author's details

WRITING PROMPT

A news article and a short story are very different forms of writing, with different purposes and different strengths. Compare and contrast the article about Omaira Sanchez with Allende's story about Azucena. What elements do the pieces have in common? What elements are specific to each form, and what is their effect on you as a reader? Ultimately, which piece affected you more strongly? Why?

To respond to this prompt, you will need to compare and contrast, following these steps:

1. Create a large Venn diagram like the one shown.

2. On one side, note elements found only in the short story, such as the inner thoughts of the characters.

3. On the other side, note elements found only in the news article, such as photographs of the scene.

Short Story   Both   News Article

4. In the middle, note elements the two pieces have in common.

5. Weigh the elements on each side, and decide which piece affected you more strongly.

Peruvian Child
Poem by Pat Mora

Lady Freedom Among Us
Poem by Rita Dove

What do we OWE others?

**OHIO
STANDARDS**

READING STANDARDS
2.1 Make inferences

3.1 Identify and understand
techniques authors use to
accomplish purpose

KEY IDEA How do you react when you encounter a homeless person
or see a child in great need? Do you ignore the person, or do you
help? In the poems that follow, two poets express their views on the
extent of our **responsibility** toward the less fortunate.

DISCUSS Think about the following aphorisms, or
sayings: "You are your brother's keeper," "Mind your own
business," "Charity begins at home." Plot them on a
continuum ranging from no responsibility for others to
great responsibility. Then rate yourself on the continuum.
As a class, discuss how much responsibility you take for
the welfare of others.

No
Reponsibility

Great
Responsibility

• LITERARY ANALYSIS: AUTHOR'S PURPOSE AND IMAGERY

Poets do not always write poems to simply express a personal feeling. Sometimes poets write to inform or persuade readers. Even a poem that simply describes a person or a scene, such as the two poems that follow, can have a strong **purpose.**

An important clue to a poet's purpose is the way he or she uses **imagery,** or words and phrases that re-create sensory experiences. Consider this imagery from "Peruvian Child."

Still in the middle of my path is the child
with no smile who stared at us.

What picture of the child is created in your mind? How do you think the poet wants you to feel about the child?

As you read the poems, think about the images they convey and what purpose they support.

■ READING SKILL: MAKE INFERENCES

Poetry is a very compressed form of writing. Because not everything is stated explicitly, you must **make inferences,** or read between the lines, in order to enrich your understanding. For example, in "Peruvian Child," you must infer that the speaker is a person on a guided tour, though this is never stated.

Record your inferences as you read the poems, using a chart like the one shown. Include clues from the text to support your inferences.

Inferences	Clues from Text
Speaker is someone on a guided tour.	"our guide said"
	"We wanted … to hold a picture"

Author On**l**ine

Pat Mora: Upholding Heritage Pat Mora considers herself lucky to be bilingual. She grew up speaking both English and Spanish in El Paso, Texas, a city on the U.S.-Mexican border. She remembers as a child wishing that she had learned about her Mexican heritage in school. Today she

Pat Mora
born 1942

uses her writing and other activities to help kindle an interest in Latino culture. In 1997, she founded Día de los Niños/Día de los Libros (Children's Day/Book Day), which celebrates children's literacy on April 30 of each year.

Rita Dove: Poet Laureate At 41, Rita Dove was the youngest person ever to be appointed Poet Laureate of the United States. During her tenure (1993–1995), she aimed to increase literacy and bring poetry into the lives of children. In response to a request to speak

Rita Dove
born 1952

at a ceremony in Washington, D.C., commemorating the 200th anniversary of the Capitol, she wrote "Lady Freedom Among Us." "Lady Freedom" refers to the 19-foot *Statue of Freedom* that rests on top of the white dome of the Capitol. The statue depicts a woman in eagle-feathered headdress who carries a sword and shield.

MORE ABOUT THE AUTHOR
For more on Pat Mora and Rita Dove, visit the **Literature Center** at ClassZone.com.

547

Peruvian Child

Pat Mora

Still in the middle of my path is the child
with no smile who stared at us. Her eyes
even then the eyes of women who sell chickens
and onions in outdoor markets. The women
5 who stare at us as if we are guards. **Ⓐ**

She whispered to the doll with no face,
smoothed the red and blue scraps
of cloth on the path, ironed them with her hand,
wrapped and re-wrapped the doll, hair
10 mud-tangled as the child's, and the dog's,
and the llama's that followed the child's
small bare feet after she bundled the doll
in the striped *manta* on her back.

The matted group stood by the edge of the spring
15 watching us drink clear, holy water of the Inca,
a fountain of youth, our guide said.
We wanted, as usual, to hold a picture
of the child in a white border, not to hold her
mud-crusted hands or feet or face,
20 not to hold her, the child in our arms. **Ⓑ**

Ⓐ AUTHOR'S PURPOSE AND IMAGERY
Reread lines 1–5. How do the child's eyes look, and what do they suggest about her life? Speculate about the poet's purpose in describing such eyes.

Ⓑ MAKE INFERENCES
Reread lines 17–20. What do the tourists want? What does this say about their values?

Lady Freedom
Among Us

Rita Dove

don't lower your eyes
or stare straight ahead to where
you think you ought to be going

don't mutter *oh no*
5 *not another one*
get a job   fly a kite
go bury a bone **C**

with her oldfashioned sandals
with her leaden skirts
10 with her stained cheeks and whiskers and heaped up trinkets
she has risen among us in blunt reproach

she has fitted her hair under a hand-me-down cap
and spruced it up with feathers and stars
slung over one shoulder she bears
15 the rainbowed layers of charity and murmurs
all of you   even the least of you **D**

don't cross to the other side of the square
don't think *another item to fit on a tourist's agenda*

consider her drenched gaze   her shining brow
20 she who has brought mercy back into the streets
and will not retire politely to the potter's field

C MAKE INFERENCES
Think about the title of the poem. Though "Lady Freedom" refers to a famous statue, what situation is described in the poem?

D AUTHOR'S PURPOSE AND IMAGERY
Notice the similarities between the description of the homeless woman's appearance in lines 8–16 and the images of the statue on page 551. What purpose might this comparison serve?

having assumed the thick skin of this town
its gritted exhaust its sunscorch and blear
she rests in her weathered plumage
25 bigboned   resolute

don't think you can ever forget her
don't even try
she's not going to budge

no choice but to grant her space
30 crown her with sky
for she is one of the many
and she is each of us **E**

E MAKE INFERENCES
Reread lines 31–32. Who does "she" and "many" and "us" represent?

INTERVIEW Journalist Bill Moyers interviewed Rita Dove for his PBS television series *The Language of Life: A Festival of Poets.*

PBS | Bill Moyers Interviews Rita Dove

MOYERS: How is life as our poet laureate?

DOVE: Very hectic but extremely gratifying. Even more people than I had hoped are interested in poetry—I've got letters backed up to the ceiling from all kinds of people and from students of all ages. People often simply want to know where they can find poetry.

MOYERS: I can imagine Thomas Jefferson doing a double take upon finding you the poet laureate sitting here in the Jefferson Building at the Library of Congress, which houses his original library. You must know that he felt blacks were innately incapable of writing poetry. . . .

DOVE: Yes. It's troublesome to read those words and then to read other words of Jefferson's which really make a wonderful case for the equality of all men. It's a paradox I've been wrestling with. . . .

MOYERS: If Jefferson were here today, which poem would you read to him?

DOVE: I would read him "Lady Freedom Among Us," which is about his city, Washington, D.C., and which also has something to do with the body politic and with the political person. That poem would be closer than most to what he was comfortable with and knew in his life.

MOYERS: You wrote that one day after the statue of Lady Freedom was removed for cleaning and then brought back by helicopter to her place atop the Capitol Building right across from where we're sitting. That was in—

DOVE: In September 1993—about a month before the statue was brought back. Lady Freedom had been haunting me—sitting in the parking lot looking forlorn—so when the historian of Congress asked me if I would like to say a few words at the ceremony for her reinstallation I thought, "I have more than a few words to say."

MOYERS: What do you hope we'll take away from that poem?

DOVE: I would like us to think more deeply about freedom and how it affects the way human being relates to human being. That's why I wanted us to experience Lady Freedom as a human being—if we saw someone like her on the street, would we shy away from her obvious idealism and sense of herself? Hence the poem's comparisons to homeless people, who remind us that we are in this together. We really can't just imagine these people and think, "I've got my life and I'm going to keep going." They remind us that we're all connected.

Comprehension

OHIO STANDARDS

READING STANDARD
2.1 Make inferences

1. **Recall** According to the speaker in Pat Mora's poem, what does the Peruvian child look like?

2. **Recall** How does the tour group respond to the child?

3. **Clarify** What typical responses to the homeless are presented in "Lady Freedom Among Us"? What clues in the poem tell you this?

Literary Analysis

4. **Make Inferences** Review the inference chart you created. Which poem required you to infer more in order to understand its meaning? Explain.

5. **Analyze Author's Purpose and Imagery** What is Mora's purpose in "Peruvian Child"? Explain how her purpose is supported by the imagery she uses to describe the child and the tour group.

6. **Interpret Imagery and Author's Purpose** In Rita Dove's poem, what ideas are brought to mind by the imagery used to describe Lady Freedom? What might be the purpose of the poem?

7. **Synthesize** What did the interview with Rita Dove on page 552 contribute to your understanding of "Lady Freedom Among Us"?

8. **Compare and Contrast Texts** Compare and contrast the poets' views about the level of **responsibility** we have to the less fortunate. Use a Venn diagram to note the similarities and differences between Mora's and Dove's messages. Cite examples from the poems.

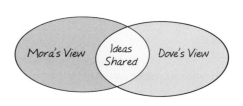

Mora's View | Ideas Shared | Dove's View

9. **Apply Ideas** Apply the ideas in these poems to your own experience. Do you accept the poets' views about how people should act toward the less fortunate? Explain.

Literary Criticism

10. **Social Context** In her interview with Bill Moyers, Dove said that she wanted people to consider freedom and how it affects the way people relate to each other. Does the freedom we value as a society make people more inclined or less inclined to take responsibility for poverty and homelessness?

Writing Workshop

Cause-and-Effect Essay

As you've seen in this unit, the world is full of tantalizing occurrences that prompt writers to explore and uncover their mysteries. You, too, can learn more about how events are connected by writing about their causes and effects. The **Writer's Road Map** will send you in the right direction.

WRITER'S ROAD MAP

Cause-and-Effect Essay

WRITING PROMPT 1

Writing from the Real World Write an essay in which you explain a cause-and-effect relationship that you consider important or interesting. You can explore how multiple causes lead to a single effect or how a single cause leads to multiple effects.

Topics to Consider
- an accomplishment of yours, such as winning a game or dramatically improving your grade in a class
- a scientific phenomenon, such as an eclipse or a comet
- a historical event, such as the French Revolution or the stock market crash of 1929

WRITING PROMPT 2

Writing from Literature Write an essay that traces a cause-and-effect relationship in a work of fiction or nonfiction.

Topics to Consider
- the causes and effects of a tragedy ("Blowup: What Went Wrong at Storm King Mountain")
- the causes and effects that drive a particular character's actions ("The Possibility of Evil")

 WRITING TOOLS
For prewriting, revision, and editing tools, visit the **Writing Center at ClassZone.com.**

KEY TRAITS

1. IDEAS
- Clearly identifies a true **cause-and-effect relationship**
- Presents a **thesis statement** that explains the connection between cause(s) and effect(s)
- Includes facts, examples, and other **details** to illustrate each cause and effect

2. ORGANIZATION
- Has an interesting **introduction** and a satisfying **conclusion**
- Presents cause(s) and effect(s) in a sensible **order**
- Uses **transitions** to signal clear connections between cause(s) and effect(s)

3. VOICE
- Has a **tone** appropriate for the audience and purpose

4. WORD CHOICE
- Uses **precise language** to explain each cause and effect

5. SENTENCE FLUENCY
- Varies **sentence lengths** to add interest and energy

6. CONVENTIONS
- Employs **correct grammar and usage**

Part 1: Analyze a Student Model

 **Jason Nemo**
Evanston Township High School

Moments

I've just run in the state championship 3,200-meter relay race with three teammates. We won! In the past I usually chalked up our wins to raw talent, but winning this event in a state meet made me realize how far from raw my talent is. I had actually started working out in seventh

5 or eighth grade. The training that began back then made this victory possible. After the race, I jogged around the track to cool off, and I reflected on the stages of training that led me to this moment.

The summer before I entered high school I joined a track club, where I was able to compete against other clubs for the first time. We were

10 often pitted against imposing relay teams of 12- and 13-year-olds who looked like cousins of the Incredible Hulk. Even though we were just in training for the upcoming school year, I felt more inadequate than I have felt at any other time in my running career. The effect of those competitions was that I learned to overcome whatever doubts I had

15 about myself and just run as well as I knew I could.

That fall I ran cross-country for my school. If running two to three miles in a cross-country meet across rugged terrain in pouring rain doesn't build your stamina, I don't know what will. Daily practices throughout the fall and spring paid off when I was named best

20 freshman in the conference in the 400-meter event. It was the first time I had distinguished myself in my sport. Consequently, my pride and confidence increased, and I was ready to push myself to the next level.

KEY TRAITS IN ACTION

Upbeat **introduction** captures the reader's interest.

Thesis statement identifies a true **cause-and-effect relationship** (training caused Jason to win).

Writer describes events in a logical **order**. Competing in the track club is the cause, and overcoming doubts is the effect.

Essay includes precise **details** of the training regimen. The **tone** is friendly and conversational.

Transitional word clarifies the connection between praise and its effect—increased confidence.

The following summer, I practiced every morning for the fall cross-
country season. By steamy August we were pushing six to eight miles a
25 day. The highlight of my career came months later, in the last meet of
the track season, on our archrival's track. I won all three races, including
the 400-meter, which I won with my fastest time ever. As a result, I
knew that expectations would be high for next year. That was fine with
me. My expectations for myself had been increasing with each new
30 success.

Because of all our success, everyone was expecting us to go all the
way. Our hard work and training paid off, and we made it to the big
show—the state finals. I was a wreck before the race. I had been nervous
about races before, though, so I knew that I could overcome it. I
35 stepped onto that big blue track, looking into the huge crowd with my
whole season on the line. If I could excel at all the meets before now, I
told myself, I could do the same here at the state championship.

My legs felt like lead. When the gun went off, the jitters wouldn't go
away, and I hardly noticed the race. I finished my leg of the race in less
40 than two minutes, which was a record for me. Even in my nervous state,
I had exceeded my expectations for myself. A couple of minutes later my
teammate crossed the finish line. I looked up and saw that we had won.
Still exhausted, I hobbled over to my teammates to share the victory.

Thanks to four years of training, facing intimidating opponents, and
45 demonstrating my abilities to myself and others, my team and I had
proved ourselves winners. With sweat still pouring off my face, I was
already thinking about next year's team.

Varied **sentence lengths** help the reader experience the excitement and energy of the race.

Writer uses **precise language** and sensory details.

Dynamic **conclusion** summarizes the causes and effect and leaves the reader thinking about the writer's future.

2

WRITING STANDARD
5.1 Generate writing ideas

Part 2: Apply the Writing Process

PREWRITING

What Should I Do?	*What Does It Look Like?*

1. Brainstorm to find a topic.
Create a cluster diagram, and fill in the circles with any ideas that come to mind. Think about events in your own life, what's happening in the world, natural phenomena, and anything else that intrigues you. Then circle the topic that interests you most.

2. Chart causes and effects.
Outline the cause-and-effect relationships of your topic. Remember that a cause can have several effects and that several causes can combine to produce one effect.

> **TIP** Make sure you have picked a true cause-and-effect relationship. The fact that one event follows another doesn't necessarily mean that the first event causes the second.

Overall cause: training	→ **Overall effect:** winning at state finals
Cause: joined summer track club	→ **Effect:** learned to overcome doubts
Cause: ran cross-country	→ **Effect:** increased confidence and stamina
Cause: practiced all summer	→ **Effect:** won three races in last meet of season

3. Consider your audience and purpose.
Write a sentence or two stating whom you'll be addressing and what you want to accomplish in your essay.

> **Audience:** This essay is mainly for my classmates. Of course, my teacher will read it too.
> **Purpose:** I want to inform my classmates about the requirements and rewards of running track. (It would be great if my essay entertained them too.)

4. List details that support your main points.
Gather facts, statistics, quotations, and anecdotes that help you explain the causes and effects. Be concrete and specific.

> **Track club**
> • Faced stiff competition
> • Overcame self-doubt
> **Freshman cross-country team**
> • Practiced daily
> • Ran in all kinds of weather

DRAFTING

What Should I Do?	What Does It Look Like?

1. Choose an organizational pattern.
You might organize your essay by describing an effect and then analyzing its causes. Another way to organize your essay is to begin with a cause or causes and trace the effect or effects. The writer of the student model analyzed a series of related causes and effects.

▶

Summer before high school
   Cause: joined track club (competitors looked like Incredible Hulk!)
   Effect: overcame self-doubt
Fall and spring of freshman year
   Cause: ran cross-country, with daily practices
   Effects: was named best freshman, self-confidence increased
Summer before sophomore year
   Cause: practiced every morning
   Effect: won three races in the last meet of the season
Junior year: state finals
   Cause: hard work and preparation
   Effect: won the 3,200-meter relay despite nervousness

2. Include specific details about each cause and effect.
Refer back to the details you collected in step 4 on page 557. Incorporate these into your draft to help the reader experience the events you're describing rather than just read that "this happened, then that happened."

▶

The summer before I entered high school I joined a track club, where I was able to compete against other clubs for the first time. } — Key point

We were often pitted against imposing relay teams of 12- and 13-year-olds who looked like cousins of the Incredible Hulk. The effect of those competitions was that I learned to overcome whatever doubts I had about myself and just run as well as I knew I could. } — Support

3. Make it memorable.
Create a strong **conclusion** that does more than just summarize the points you've made. Try showing why the information is important or how it might affect your life or your reader's life.

TIP Before revising, review the key traits on page 554 and the rubric and peer-reader questions on page 560.

▶

Thanks to four years of training, facing intimidating opponents, and demonstrating my abilities to myself and others, my team and I had proved ourselves winners. With sweat still pouring off my face, I was already thinking about next year's team.

Shows readers that the writer will continue running because it is such a satisfying experience

REVISING AND EDITING

What Should I Do?	**What Does It Look Like?**

1. Grab the reader's attention in your introduction.

- Read the first paragraph aloud. <u>Underline</u> phrases or sentences that might bore or confuse a reader.
- Add examples, facts, or other details to create excitement and interest.

▶

~~My essay is about being on the track team because it has changed me in many ways.~~
I've just run in the state championship 3,200-meter relay race with three teammates. We won! Winning this event in a state meet made me realize how far from raw my talent is. I had actually started working out in seventh or eighth grade. The training that began back then made this victory possible.

2. Clearly connect your ideas.

- Draw a (circle) around sentences that make you ask: How is this related to what I just said?
- Insert transitions that clarify how the ideas are connected.

See page 560: Clarify with Transitions

▶

I won all three races, including the 400-meter, which
As a result,
I won with my fastest time ever. I knew that expectations would be high for next year.

3. Consider your audience.

- Ask a peer reader to [bracket] words or statements in your essay that he or she has questions about.
- Add background information to explain these ideas.

See page 560: Ask a Peer Reader

▶

That fall I ran cross-country for my school. [~~It was really difficult.~~] I was named best freshman in the conference in the 400-meter event.
If running two to three miles in a cross-country meet across rugged terrain in pouring rain doesn't build your stamina, I don't know what will. Daily practices throughout the fall and spring paid off when

4. Vary the lengths of your sentences.

- Draw a |box| around sentences that seem choppy because they are all the same length.
- Combine or split up some of these sentences to make your writing more lively and rhythmic.

▶

When
My legs felt like lead. The gun went off. The jitters
, and
wouldn't go away. I hardly noticed the race.

Cause-and-Effect Essay

Apply the Rubric

A strong cause-and-effect essay . . .

☑ discusses a true cause-and-effect relationship

☑ begins strongly, explaining the connection between cause(s) and effect(s) in a thesis statement

☑ includes supporting examples, facts, and other details

☑ organizes cause(s) and effect(s) logically

☑ uses appropriate transitions

☑ varies sentence lengths to create rhythm and interest

☑ uses precise language and an appropriate tone

☑ goes beyond a summary to create a satisfying conclusion

Ask a Peer Reader

- Which connection between cause and effect that I presented seems weakest to you? Why?

- What background information do you need to help you understand my essay?

- What did you like best about my essay? Why?

Clarify with Transitions

Cause	Effect
because	as a result
provided that	consequently
if	then
since	therefore

Check Your Grammar

Punctuate compound and compound-complex sentences correctly. Independent clauses can be joined with (1) a comma and a coordinating conjunction, (2) a semicolon, or (3) a semicolon followed by a conjunctive adverb and a comma.

1. After the race, I jogged around the track to cool off, and I reflected on my training.

2. That was fine with me; my expectations for myself had been increasing.

3. It was the first time I had distinguished myself in my sport; consequently, my pride and confidence increased.

See pages R63–R64: The Structure of Sentences

Writing Online

PUBLISHING OPTIONS
For publishing options, visit the **Writing Center** at ClassZone.com.

ASSESSMENT PREPARATION
For writing and grammar assessment practice, go to the **Assessment Center** at ClassZone.com.

COMMUNICATION STANDARD
9.8 Deliver informational presentations

Delivering an Informative Speech

A good way to reach a broad audience is to present your essay orally.

Planning Your Informative Speech

1. **Reread your essay.** Review your main points, including each cause and effect. Think about ways to state these ideas simply and forcefully.

2. **Create a script.** Highlight sentences that you want to emphasize, and note how to use your voice and body language to stress this material. If you are using primary or secondary sources, check that you have quoted the material accurately. Also, be sure to explain any terms that audience members might not understand. For example, the writer of the student model explained how long a distance 3,200 meters is. He also included a photograph to show the difficult handoff of the baton.

3. **Rehearse your speech as many times as you can.** Practice by yourself and with friends and family.

Delivering Your Informative Speech

1. **Address your audience directly.** You might want to ask a question, such as: How many of you have been nervous before a big test or performance? If you are using visuals, display them where they can be seen easily or pass them around the room.

2. **Invite listeners to ask questions.** If you don't know an answer, say so, and offer to find out and get back to the questioner. You might want to conclude by asking your audience to rate your presentation and suggest ways to improve your next informative speech.

See page R78: Evaluate an Informative Speech

Reading Comprehension

DIRECTIONS *Read the following selection and then answer the questions.*

from Spiders Up Close

Of the more than 34,000 species of spiders named so far (with another estimated 136,000 yet to be named), all are predators, their bodies designed to catch and consume their prey: insects.

Top-notch Predators

Hanging head-down from the hub of her web, the silver argiope (*Argiope argentata*) feels her trap begin to quiver, indicating the presence of prey. Determining direction by the vibration of the radial web spokes, she scrambles toward a grasshopper that is frantically struggling in a sticky thread. Working quickly, she wraps her victim in silk. Then she gives it a paralyzing bite with
10 her jaws, or chelicerae, and regurgitates digestive enzymes that begin to liquefy the insect. Leaving her mummified meal suspended from the web, the spider returns to her control post to wait for more victims.

Ingenious Hunters   Few creatures have developed more varied techniques to capture their prey than the spider. Although 60 percent of spiders, including the orb-weaving *A. argentata,* fashion some sort of aerial trap with silk, the rest do not spin webs at all but pursue their prey in other deadly ways.

A jumping spider (family Salticidae) can leap on its prey from a distance, impaling it with venom-delivering fangs. Its leaping prowess is astonishing, especially considering that it has no enlarged muscular hindlegs to propel it.
20 Researchers suggest that hydrostatic pressure builds up in the legs, suddenly releasing and popping the spider forward—as much as forty times its own body length.

Jumping spiders are stalkers like cats, but some spiders simply run down their prey. Wolf spiders (family Lycosidae) have earned their name for their speedy pursuit of prey. The much larger tarantulas are also generally runners, often lurking in underground burrows until they detect vibrations of prey on the soil outside their lair.

Bolas spiders (family Araneidae) do their hunting with a short silk thread tipped with a drop of glue; they hold one end of the thread and fling the sticky
30 end at passing prey. To improve their chances, these spiders emit a pheromone that mimics that of female moths; approaching male moths looking for a mate are likely to become lunch instead. . . .

Dolomedes, the fishing spiders (family Pisauridae), venture right onto the water surface to hunt, sometimes diving to capture insects and small fish. The

surface of the water acts as their web. By touching the water with their legs, these spiders detect vibrations of passing insects. Supported by surface tension, they dash out to subdue prey. The king of the fishers is the water spider *(Argyroneta aquatica)*; it weaves an air-filled diving bell out of silk and can remain submerged in the water inside it for weeks.

Comprehension

DIRECTIONS *Answer these questions about the excerpt from "Spiders Up Close."*

1. Which text features help you recognize the article's pattern of organization?

   A. captions

   B. diagrams

   C. title and subheadings

   D. boldfaced words in text

2. Which overall pattern of organization does the author use?

   A. cause and effect

   B. comparison and contrast

   C. chronological order

   D. classification

3. Which pattern of organization does the author use in lines 23–27 to describe how different spiders catch their prey?

   A. comparison and contrast

   B. classification

   C. main idea and supporting details

   D. cause and effect

4. Which word best describes the author's tone?

   A. gloomy   C. alarmed

   B. admiring   D. ironic

5. The author's two purposes for writing the article are to

   A. inform and express feelings

   B. inform and persuade

   C. express feelings and entertain

   D. inform and entertain

Written Response

SHORT ANSWER
Write three or four sentences to answer this question.

6. Find two words in lines 13–22 that express the author's attitude toward spiders. Explain how those words reflect that attitude.

EXTENDED RESPONSE
Write two to three paragraphs to answer this question.

7. The author achieves two purposes in lines 28–32. Identify each of those purposes and cite words and images that the author uses to convey each purpose.

GO ON

from How to Write a Letter

Garrison Keillor

A blank white eight-by-eleven sheet can look as big as Montana if the pen's not so hot—try a smaller page and write boldly. Or use a note card with a piece of fine art on the front; if your letter ain't good, a least they get the Matisse. Get a pen that makes a sensuous line, get a comfortable typewriter, a friendly word processor—whichever feels easy to the hand.

Sit for a few minutes with the blank sheet in front of you, and meditate on the person you will write to, let your friend come to mind until you can almost see her or him in the room with you. Remember the last time you saw each other and how your friend looked and what you said and what perhaps was 10 unsaid between you, and when your friend becomes real to you, start to write.

Write a salutation—*Dear* You—and take a deep breath and plunge in. A simple declarative sentence will do, followed by another and another and another. Tell us what you're doing and tell it like you were talking to us. Don't think about grammar, don't think about lit'ry style, don't try to write dramatically, just give us your news. Where did you go, who did you see, what did they say, what do you think?

If you don't know where to begin, start with the present moment: *I'm sitting at the kitchen table on a rainy Saturday morning. Everyone is gone and the house is quiet.* Let your simple description of the present moment lead to something 20 else, let the letter drift gently along.

The toughest letter to crank out is one that is meant to impress, as we all know from writing job applications; if it's hard work to slip off a letter to a friend, maybe you're trying too hard to be terrific. A letter is only a report to someone who already likes you for reasons other than your brilliance. Take it easy.

Don't worry about form. It's not a term paper. When you come to the end of one episode, just start a new paragraph. You can go from a few lines about the sad state of pro football to the fight with your mother to your fond memories of Mexico to your cat's urinary-tract infection to a few thoughts on personal indebtedness and on to the kitchen sink and what's in it. The more 30 you write, the easier it gets, and when you have a True True Friend to write to, a *compadre,* a soul sibling, then it's like driving a car down a country road, you just get behind the keyboard and press on the gas.

Comprehension

DIRECTIONS *Answer these questions about the excerpt from "How to Write a Letter."*

8. Which statement best describes the author's perspective?

 A. He is tired of receiving poorly written letters.

 B. He thinks writing a good letter is hard work.

 C. He believes letter writing is a way to impress your friends.

 D. He thinks letter writing should be like having a conversation.

9. The author's perspective is most clearly revealed in his

 A. references to job applications and term papers

 B. list of letter-writing do's and don'ts

 C. suggestion for an appropriate salutation

 D. use of slang and sincere expressions

10. Which word best describes the tone of "How to Write a Letter"?

 A. sarcastic

 B. monotonous

 C. superior

 D. reassuring

11. Which tone does the author adopt in lines 26–29 to help convey his purpose?

 A. showy

 B. humorous

 C. agitated

 D. conciliatory

12. The author's purpose for writing this essay is to

 A. clarify

 B. complain

 C. give advice

 D. persuade

Written Response

SHORT ANSWER
Write two or three sentences to answer this question.

13. How do these sentences from lines 23–24 illustrate the tone of the essay?

 "A letter is only a report to someone who already likes you for reasons other than your brilliance. Take it easy."

EXTENDED RESPONSE
Write two to three paragraphs to answer this question.

14. What is the author's perspective on writing in general? Give at least three examples of images or word choices in this essay that reveal his perspective, and explain how they do so.

Vocabulary

DIRECTIONS *Use context clues and your knowledge of similes and metaphors to answer the following questions.*

1. In the article "Spiders Up Close," which spider name is a metaphor?
   A. jumping spider
   B. wolf spider
   C. tarantula
   D. silver argiope spider

2. Which expression from "Spiders Up Close" contains a metaphor?
   A. "Hanging head-down from the hub of her web"
   B. "Jumping spiders are stalkers like cats"
   C. "The much larger tarantulas are also generally runners"
   D. "The king of the fishers is the water spider"

3. Which expression from "Spiders Up Close" contains a metaphor?
   A. "she scrambles toward a grasshopper that is frantically struggling in a sticky thread"
   B. "To improve their chances, these spiders emit a pheromone that mimics that of female moths"
   C. "venture right onto the water surface to hunt, sometimes diving to capture insects and small fish"
   D. "it weaves an air-filled diving bell out of silk and can remain submerged in the water inside it for weeks"

4. Which expression from "How to Write a Letter" contains a simile?
   A. "A blank white eight-by-eleven sheet can look as big as Montana"
   B. "let your friend come to mind until you can almost see her or him"
   C. "The toughest letter to crank out is one that is meant to impress"
   D. "A letter is only a report to someone who already likes you"

5. Which expression from "How to Write a Letter" contains a simile?
   A. "take a deep breath and plunge in"
   B. "When you come to the end of one episode"
   C. "it's like driving a car down a country road"
   D. "you can almost see her or him in the room"

6. Which expression from "How to Write a Letter" contains a metaphor?
   A. "get a comfortable typewriter"
   B. "Sit for a few minutes"
   C. "don't try to write dramatically"
   D. "let the letter drift gently along"

Writing & Grammar

DIRECTIONS *Read this passage and then answer the questions that follow.*

> (1) American history has many famous heroes, but Sybil Ludington is one who is less well known. (2) In 1777, Sybil was just 16 years old. (3) Her father was an officer in the New York militia. (4) One night, the British attacked a nearby town. (5) Someone had to alert the militiamen in the area. (6) Sybil volunteered to call the soldiers to arms. (7) She rode 40 miles that night.

1. Choose the correct way to add an adverb clause to sentence 2.

   A. In 1777, Sybil was just 16 years old, and the Revolutionary War was raging.

   B. In 1777, during the Revolutionary War, Sybil was just 16 years old.

   C. Sybil was just 16 years old in 1777, when the Revolutionary War was raging.

   D. Sybil was a 16-year-old girl in 1777.

2. Choose the correct way to add a participial phrase to sentence 3.

   A. Her father was an officer in the New York militia, leading a force of local soldiers.

   B. Her father led a force of local soldiers as an officer in the New York militia.

   C. An officer in the New York militia, her father led a force of local soldiers.

   D. Her father was an officer in the New York militia who led a force of local soldiers.

3. Choose the correct way to add a participial phrase to sentence 4.

   A. One night, the British attacked a nearby town; the colonists had stored supplies there.

   B. One night, the British attacked a nearby town and stole supplies.

   C. One night, the British attacked a nearby town, stealing colonists' supplies.

   D. One night, the British attacked a nearby town where the colonists had stored supplies.

4. Choose the correct way to add an adverb clause to sentence 6.

   A. Because the messenger and his horse were too weary to travel, Sybil volunteered to call the soldiers to arms.

   B. The messenger and his horse were too weary to travel, so Sybil volunteered to call the soldiers to arms.

   C. The messenger and his horse were too weary to call the soldiers to arms, but Sybil felt fine.

   D. The messenger and his horse were too weary to travel; Sybil volunteered to call the soldiers to arms.

5. Choose the correct way to add a participial phrase to sentence 7.

   A. She rode 40 miles that night and roused the militia to action.

   B. She rode 40 miles that night, rousing the militia to action.

   C. She rode 40 miles that night to rouse the militia to action.

   D. She rode 40 miles that night; she roused the militia to action.

Ideas for Independent Reading

If you enjoyed discussing the questions and selections in Unit 5, you may enjoy the following books as well.

Can beauty be captured in words?

Cultivating Delight: A Natural History of My Garden
by Diane Ackerman

A naturalist and writer, Ackerman celebrates the color, the animals, and the changing seasons in her garden. She also digresses into such topics as the origins of the word *tulip*.

Pilgrim at Tinker Creek
by Annie Dillard

This is a highly spiritual and poetic meditation on nature, modeled on Thoreau's *Walden*. Dillard records and reflects on the beauty and cruelty she sees around her home near Tinker Creek in Virginia.

West with the Night
by Beryl Markham

Much of this memoir describes the stunning beauty of East Africa, where Markham grew up. She recalls the varied landscapes, wildlife, and people of the region.

What can we learn from disaster?

Triangle: The Fire That Changed America
by David Von Drehle

In 1911, a fire at the Triangle Shirtwaist Company factory killed 146 people—most of them Jewish and Italian immigrant women. The tragedy led to massive labor organizing and widespread factory reforms.

Fitzgerald's Storm: The Wreck of the Edmund Fitzgerald
by Dr. Joseph MacInnis

Part natural history, part investigative history, this book describes the sinking of the *Edmund Fitzgerald,* an ore carrier that went down in a storm on Lake Superior in 1975. Twenty-nine men died.

The Greatest Disaster Stories Ever Told
edited by Lamar Underwood

This book offers accounts of 17 disasters, including the deadly chemical spill in Bhopal, India; the space shuttle *Challenger* explosion; and the September 11 terrorist attack on the World Trade Center.

What do we owe others?

There Are No Children Here
by Alex Kotlowitz

Kotlowitz, a *Wall Street Journal* reporter, follows the lives of two young boys growing up in a Chicago housing project. They live in constant terror of gang violence and worry that they will not reach adulthood.

Alabanza
by Martín Espada

Alabanza means "praise" in Spanish, and the title poem of this collection remembers the immigrant restaurant workers killed in the World Trade Center attack. The remaining poems also praise the poor and forgotten.

Family Matters
by Rohinton Mistry

A grandfather in Bombay is increasingly unable to care for himself. His daughter and her family, living in straitened circumstances, take him in, and each family member learns something about responsibility for others.

6

Making a Case

ARGUMENT AND PERSUASION

- In Nonfiction
- In Fiction
- Across Genres
- In Media

Can you be PERSUADED?

We all like to think that we're strong-minded, that we know what we believe and want. We also like to imagine that we're not easily swayed by what others might say or do. But is this really the case?

Every day we are bombarded with persuasive messages. How many of these messages are you aware of? How actively do you analyze the ideas being presented?

DISCUSS With a group of classmates, record the different kinds of persuasive messages you encounter in a day. Rank them according to how effective you think they are, and discuss why the good ones work so well. Here are some ideas to get you started.

- **Media:** commercials, nightly news shows, radio talk shows, Internet pop-ups, essays and editorials

- **Oral communication:** speeches, meetings, phone solicitors

- **Images:** on TV shows, in magazines, on billboards

OHIO STANDARDS

Preview Unit Goals

LITERARY ANALYSIS
- Analyze theme
- Interpret didactic literature

READING
- Use reading strategies, including monitoring and setting a purpose for reading
- Draw conclusions; summarize
- Distinguish fact from opinion
- Analyze and evaluate an argument, including claim, support, reasons, evidence, and counterargument
- Analyze inductive and deductive reasoning
- Identify and analyze persuasive and rhetorical devices

WRITING AND GRAMMAR
- Write an editorial
- Use repetition and rhetorical questions to add impact
- Use compound-complex sentences to vary sentence structure

SPEAKING, LISTENING, AND VIEWING
- Recognize and analyze persuasive techniques in advertising
- Recognize persuasive media forms

VOCABULARY
- Understand the meaning of specialized vocabulary
- Use a thesaurus and a dictionary etymology

ACADEMIC VOCABULARY
- fact and opinion
- argument
- claim; support
- persuasive devices
- rhetorical devices
- inductive and deductive reasoning

Critical Reading Workshop

Argument and Persuasion

In today's world, you are faced with choices every day, from which brand of gym shoes you should buy to which presidential candidate deserves your support. Along with every choice comes a barrage of persuasive messages. TV ads, speeches, editorials, petitions—all are aimed at influencing your beliefs and actions. How do you separate the logical arguments from powerful appeals that aren't based on sound reasoning? By learning how to analyze arguments, you will be better able to make informed choices about decisions that matter.

OHIO STANDARDS

READING STANDARDS
3.4 Identify persuasive techniques
3.5 Analyze an author's implicit and explicit argument
3.8 Describe the features of rhetorical devices

Part 1: The Analysis of an Argument

Like a pair of gym shoes, an argument may be constructed of high-quality parts, or it might be poorly made—attractive at first glance but flimsy upon closer inspection. To analyze an argument, you first need to understand its parts. A strong argument typically includes

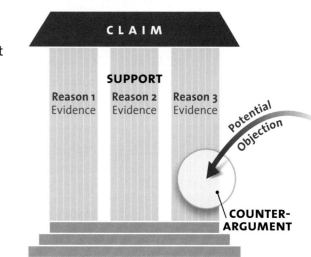

- a **claim**, or the writer's position on a problem or an issue

- **support**, which includes reasons and evidence that help to justify the claim

- a **counterargument**, or a brief argument that negates objections to the claim that "the other side" is likely to raise

STRATEGIES FOR EVALUATING AN ARGUMENT

- **Check the claim.** What is the writer trying to convince you to do or believe? Consider whether the reasons given actually support the claim.

- **Examine the evidence.** Does the information come from a trustworthy source? Is there enough of it to make the case?

- **Look for logic.** Watch for errors in logic, such as **hasty generalizations**, or conclusions drawn from too little evidence. (Example: "Our student president is a football player, and he's doing a terrible job. Athletes shouldn't be elected to the student council.")

- **Consider the counterargument.** Has the writer adequately dealt with likely objections?

MODEL 1: CLAIM AND SUPPORT

As you read this excerpt from a feature article, look for the claim that the author is making. Is it effectively supported?

from **Youth ✓oter Participation**

Feature article from **Ad Council**

The right to vote for the leaders of our state and nation is a freedom that separates our country from so many others in the world. In order for democracy to work in America, people must exercise this privilege.

Voting is a way to have a voice in our government—whether you want to
5 ensure that your children receive the best education; or that you will collect your social security benefits upon retirement; or that your taxes will support research for life-threatening diseases. Our leaders, whether it be your local mayor or the President, make decisions that affect your life.

Close Read

1. Identify the author's claim, or position.

2. What reason is given to support the claim? In your opinion, is the reason strong? Support your answer.

MODEL 2: COUNTERARGUMENT

The same article continues with a counterargument. As you read, notice the potential objection that the author anticipates. How does the author counter the opposing viewpoint?

Why don't people vote? Many people say that it's because they don't think it will matter. Imagine if everyone felt that way—we could never elect a president or a congressman. There have been many, many elections, locally and nationally, that have been decided by less than 100 votes.

5 **1776**—One vote gave America the English language instead of German.

1845—One vote brought Texas into the Union.

1868—One vote allowed Andrew Johnson to escape impeachment.

1920—The 19th Amendment to the U.S. Constitution gave women the right to vote.

Close Read

1. Reread the boxed text. In your own words, explain the opposing argument that the author anticipates. What is the author's response?

2. Reread the evidence that the author gives to counter the opposing viewpoint. Is this evidence effective? Support your viewpoint.

Part 2: The Craft of Persuasion

Even when you know how to evaluate an argument, it's easy to be swayed by appeals that bypass your brain and go straight to your heart. Allowing feelings to influence your decisions is not always a mistake. However, you should be aware of how powerful language and emotion can be used to enhance airtight arguments or distract you from holes in inadequate ones.

PERSUASIVE TECHNIQUES

Many of the following techniques are probably familiar to you. What additional examples have you encountered in speeches, ads, and other types of persuasive writing?

TECHNIQUE	EXAMPLE
Appeals by Association	
Bandwagon Appeal Taps into people's desire to belong or be a part of a group	Audiences everywhere are raving about *Deception*. Don't be the only one to miss out on the most suspenseful film in years!
"Plain Folks" Appeal Implies that ordinary people are on "our side" or that a candidate is like a regular person	At last, an investment plan created with real families and real budgets in mind.
Testimonial Relies on endorsements from celebrities or satisfied customers	I lost twenty pounds in six weeks—thanks to the new TurboCycle exercise program. You can too!
Transfer Connects a product, a candidate, or a cause with a positive image or idea	Take pride in being an American. Re-elect Governor Frank.
Emotional Appeals	
Appeal to Pity, Fear, or Vanity Uses strong feelings, rather than facts and evidence, to persuade	**Appeal to Vanity** Choose the Enigma XRB—because you deserve a car that's as stylish as you are.
Appeal to Values	
Ethical Appeal Taps into people's values or moral standards	If you believe in education, vote against cutting after-school programs. With your help, we can keep these programs going strong.
Word Choice	
Loaded Language Uses words with positive or negative connotations to stir people's emotions	Smooth. Silky. Luxuriously creamy. You'll never go back to ordinary low-fat margarine.

MODEL 1: PERSUASION IN SPEECHES

Here, a senator tries to persuade his audience—the U.S. Congress—to work harder to combat the country's hunger crisis. What techniques does he use to enhance his argument?

from HUNGER AWARENESS

Speech by **Senator Edward Kennedy**

Today is National Hunger Awareness Day, and it is an opportunity for all of us in Congress to pledge a greater effort to deal effectively with this festering problem that shames our nation and has grown even more serious in recent years.

5   The number of Americans living in hunger, or on the brink of hunger, . . . now includes 13 million children. . . .

These Americans deserve higher priority by all of us in Congress. Day in and day out, the needs of millions of Americans living in poverty have been overlooked, and too often their voices have been silenced.

10   These are real people, struggling every day to get by. They are single mothers serving coffee at the local diner at 5 A.M. and cleaning houses in the afternoon, yet are still unable to afford both shelter and food. They are low-wage workers holding down two jobs, yet still forced to make impossible choices between feeding their family, paying the rent, and obtaining decent

15 medical care. They are children who go to bed hungry every night whose parents can't afford to give them more than a single slim meal a day.

Close Read

1. One example of loaded language is boxed. Find two more examples.

2. Identify another persuasive technique, used in lines 10–16. Is it effective? Explain your opinion.

MODEL 2: PERSUASION IN THE MEDIA

On this billboard, language and visuals work together to send a persuasive message.

Close Read

1. Reread the text on this billboard. What techniques are being used to persuade you? Cite specific words or phrases to support your answer.

2. Consider the photographs and the layout. Do these visual elements contribute to the power of the message? Explain your opinion.

RHETORICAL DEVICES

Without powerful language—or **rhetoric**—even skillfully crafted arguments can seem uninspired. To make their messages more memorable, writers use rhetorical devices, such as repetition, parallelism, analogies, and rhetorical questions. Notice how the use of language strengthens the arguments shown.

RHETORICAL DEVICE	EXAMPLE
REPETITION Uses the same word or words more than once for emphasis	Freedom leads to prosperity. Freedom replaces the ancient hatreds among the nations with comity and peace. Freedom is the victor. —Ronald Reagan, speech at Brandenburg Gate
PARALLELISM Uses similar grammatical constructions to express ideas that are related or equal in importance. Often creates a rhythm.	Let us rise up tonight with a greater readiness. Let us stand with a greater determination. And let us move on in these powerful days, these days of challenge to make America what it ought to be. —Martin Luther King Jr., "I've been to the mountaintop" speech

Here, the journalist Anna Quindlen gives advice to graduating students. How does she enhance her message with rhetorical devices?

from COMMENCEMENT ADDRESS

Speech by **Anna Quindlen**

Set aside the old traditional notion of female as nurturer and male as leader; set aside, too, the new traditional notions of female as superwoman and male as oppressor. Begin with that most terrifying of all things, a clean slate. Then look, every day, at the choices you are making, and when you ask yourself why
5 you are making them, find this answer: for me, for me. Because they are who and what I am, and mean to be.

This is the hard work of your life in the world, to make it all up as you go along, to acknowledge the introvert, the clown, the artist, the reserved, the distraught, the goofball, the thinker. You will have to bend all your will not
10 to march to the music that all of those great "theys" out there pipe on their flutes. They want you to go to professional school, to wear khakis, to pierce your navel, to bare your soul. These are the fashionable ways. The music is tinny, if you listen close enough. Look inside. That way lies dancing to the melodies spun out by your own heart. This is a symphony. All the rest are jingles.

Close Read

1. Find one example each of repetition and parallelism. For each example, explain what the wording helps to emphasize.

2. Another device that Quindlen uses is an **analogy,** or a comparison between two things. Explain the analogy in the boxed text. Why might it appeal to students?

Part 3: Analyze the Text

Through the AmeriCorps network, young volunteers do service work while earning money toward their college education. As you read this article from the AmeriCorps Web site, use what you have learned to evaluate the argument being presented. What techniques are used to persuade you to join the organization?

BACK   FORWARD   STOP   REFRESH   HOME   PRINT

Are You Up to the CHALLENGE?

AmeriCorps: Are you up to the challenge?
Put your idealism to work through AmeriCorps. Make a community safer. Help a kid get a real education. Protect the environment. Whatever your interest, there's an AmeriCorps program that needs your courage, your skills, and your dedication.

Do something special, something unique, something exciting. Are you up to the challenge?

You decide where and how to serve.
Each year, more than 40,000 members serve with programs in every state in the nation. You can tutor kids in your own community, or build new homes for families far away from your home. Restore coastlines or help families traumatized by domestic violence. You might do the work yourself, or help others serve by organizing projects and recruiting volunteers. Whatever you do, there's an AmeriCorps challenge just waiting for you.

Get an education, experience, and skills.
You'll learn teamwork, communication, responsibility, and other essential skills that will help you for the rest of your life. And you'll gain the personal satisfaction of taking on a challenge and seeing results.

You will be able to pay your bills.
After successfully completing a term of service, AmeriCorps members who are enrolled in the National Service Trust are eligible to receive an education award. The education award can be used to pay education costs at qualified institutions of higher education or training, or to repay qualified student loans. The award currently is $4,725 for a year of full-time service, with correspondingly lesser awards for part-time and reduced part-time service. A member has up to seven years after his or her term of service has ended to claim the award. . . .

Ready to take the next step and apply to AmeriCorps?

Close Read

1. One reason that the author uses to persuade readers to join AmeriCorps is boxed. Identify two other reasons. In your opinion, are they convincing?

2. What persuasive techniques are being used in this article? Give specific examples to support your answer.

3. Find one example of parallelism and explain its effect.

4. Reread the boxed reason. Does the evidence that follows support the reason? (Consider: How much does four years of college cost?)

5. How do the images and the use of color add to the article's message?

Doing Nothing Is Something
Persuasive Essay by Anna Quindlen

How should you spend your
FREE TIME?

READING STANDARDS
3.4 Identify persuasive techniques
3.5 Analyze an author's implicit and explicit argument

KEY IDEA What is your typical day like? School and homework must take up a lot of time. If you have other commitments, such as a job, sports practice, or family chores, then there's probably not much room in your life for **leisure.** In this essay, Anna Quindlen explores whether young people have enough leisure time or are too busy for their own good.

DISCUSS If you had more free time, how would you spend it? Make a list of things you would do—or not do. Then discuss with a partner how you would benefit from the extra free time.

Free Time
1. Draw cartoons.
2. Take long walks.
3.
4.
5.

● ELEMENTS OF NONFICTION: ARGUMENT

At the heart of every argument is a **claim,** the writer's position on an issue. For example, in "Doing Nothing Is Something," Anna Quindlen expresses a claim about the role of downtime in children's lives. To convince readers that a claim is valid, a writer must offer **support,** which may consist of

- reasons that explain or justify an action, a belief, or a decision
- evidence in the form of facts, statistics, examples, or the views of experts

As you read, use a chart like the one shown to help you identify Anna Quindlen's claim and the support she provides.

Claim: We need to allow children to have downtime in the summer.	
Reason	*Evidence*
Children are overscheduled.	*A suburb set aside one night free of homework, athletic practices, and after-school events.*

● READING SKILL: DISTINGUISH FACT FROM OPINION

A **fact** is a statement that can be proved, such as, "A majority of U.S. households now have Internet access." An **opinion** is a statement of belief or feeling, such as, "I think most people rely too much on the Internet."

People often use words and phrases such as *I think, I believe, perhaps,* and *maybe* to state their opinions—but not always. To identify opinions that lack such telltale words and phrases, remember that an opinion cannot be proved; at best, an opinion can only be supported. Keep these points in mind as you read Quindlen's essay.

▲ VOCABULARY IN CONTEXT

The following vocabulary words help Quindlen make her point about free time. To see how many words you know, match each word from the list with its synonym.

WORD LIST	contemptuous	hiatus	prestigious
	deficit	laudable	

1. prominent
2. shortfall
3. break
4. disdainful
5. praiseworthy

Author On line

Anna Quindlen born 1952

A Fresh Voice Anna Quindlen was hired as a reporter by the *New York Times* in 1977, just three years after graduating from college. She gave up her full-time job in 1985 to stay home with her children and work on a novel. However, an editor convinced her to write a column about marriage and parenthood. Quindlen's voice stood out among the *Times* columnists, most of whom were men who focused on politics. She has earned widespread acclaim for her ability to address important social issues through her personal experiences. In 1992, she won a Pulitzer Prize for the columns she had initially viewed as "a way to make a little bit of money while writing my novel."

Family Portraits While Quindlen achieved success as a columnist, she continued to pursue her dream of writing fiction. Her first novel, *Object Lessons,* became a bestseller when it was published in 1991, and other successful novels have followed. Although she tackles controversial subjects, such as domestic violence, Quindlen's fiction, like her columns, is rooted in observations of family life. She said that anyone who reads her books would realize that "family is central to my existence."

 MORE ABOUT THE AUTHOR
For more on Anna Quindlen, visit the **Literature Center** at ClassZone.com.

Doing Nothing Is Something

by Anna Quindlen

Summer is coming soon.
I can feel it in the softening of the air,
but I can see it, too, in the textbooks
on my children's desks. The number
of uncut pages at the back grows
smaller and smaller. The looseleaf
is ragged at the edges, the binder
plastic ripped at the corners. An
old remembered glee rises inside me.
10 Summer is coming. Uniform skirts in
mothballs. Pencils with their points
left broken. Open windows. Day
trips to the beach. Pickup games.
Hanging out.

ANALYZE VISUALS
What **mood** does this
photograph suggest
to you?

How boring it was.

Of course, it was the making of me, as a human being and a writer. Downtime is where we become ourselves, looking into the middle distance, kicking at the curb, lying on the grass or sitting on the stoop and staring at the tedious blue of the summer sky. I don't believe you can write poetry, or compose music, or become an actor without downtime, and plenty of it, a **hiatus** that passes for boredom but is really the quiet moving of the wheels inside that fuel creativity.

And that, to me, is one of the saddest things about the lives of American children today. Soccer leagues, acting classes, tutors—the calendar of the average middle-class kid is so over the top that soon Palm handhelds will be sold in Toys "R" Us. Our children are as overscheduled as we are, and that is saying something. **A**

This has become so bad that parents have arranged to schedule times for unscheduled time. Earlier this year the privileged suburb of Ridgewood, N.J., announced a Family Night, when there would be no homework, no athletic practices and no after-school events. This was terribly exciting until I realized that this was not one night a week, but one single night. There is even a free-time movement, and Web site: familylife1st.org. Among the frequently asked questions provided online: "What would families do with family time if they took it back?"

Let me make a suggestion for the kids involved: how about nothing? It is not simply that it is pathetic to consider the lives of children who don't have a moment between piano and dance and homework to talk about their day or just search for split ends, an enormously satisfying leisure-time activity of my youth. There is also ample psychological research suggesting that what we might call "doing nothing" is when human beings actually do their best thinking, and when creativity comes to call. Perhaps we are creating an entire generation of people whose ability to think outside the box, as the current parlance[1] of business has it, is being systematically stunted by scheduling.

A study by the University of Michigan quantified[2] the downtime **deficit;** in the last 20 years American kids have lost about four unstructured hours a week. There has even arisen a global Right to Play movement: in the Third World it is often about child labor, but in the United States it is about the sheer labor of being a perpetually busy child. In Omaha, Neb., a group of parents recently lobbied for additional recess. Hooray, and yikes. **B**

How did this happen? Adults did it. There is a culture of adult distrust that suggests that a kid who is not playing softball or attending science-enrichment programs—or both—is huffing or boosting cars: if kids are left alone, they will not stare into the middle distance and consider

---

1. **parlance** (pär'ləns): a particular manner of speaking.

2. **quantified:** expressed as a number or quantity.

hiatus (hī-ā'təs) *n.* a gap or break in continuity

deficit (dĕf'ĭ-sĭt) *n.* a shortfall or deficiency

A DISTINGUISH FACT FROM OPINION
Is the last statement in this paragraph a fact or an opinion? Explain your answer.

B ARGUMENT
What evidence does Quindlen supply in lines 76–88 to support her claim? Add this evidence to your chart.

the meaning of life and how come your nose in pictures never looks the way you think it should, but 100 instead will get into trouble. There is also the culture of cutthroat and unquestioning competition that leads even the parents of preschoolers to gab about **prestigious** colleges without a trace of irony: this suggests that any class in which you do not enroll your first grader will put him at a disadvantage in, say, law school.

Finally, there is a culture of 110 workplace presence (as opposed to productivity). Try as we might to suggest that all these enrichment activities are for the good of the kid, there is ample evidence that they are really for the convenience of parents with way too little leisure time of their own. Stories about the resignation of presidential aide Karen Hughes unfailingly reported her 120 dedication to family time by noting that she arranged to get home at 5:30 one night a week to have dinner with her son. If one weekday dinner out of five is considered **laudable,** what does that say about what's become commonplace? **C**

Summer is coming. It used to be a time apart for kids, a respite from the clock and the copybook, the 130 organized day. Every once in a while, either guilty or overwhelmed or tired of listening to me keen³ about my monumental boredom, my mother would send me to some rinky-dink park program that consisted almost entirely of three-legged races and making things out of Popsicle sticks.

Now, instead, there are music camps, sports camps, fat camps, probably 140 thin camps. I mourn hanging out in the backyard. I mourn playing Wiffle ball in the street without a sponsor and matching shirts. I mourn drawing in the dirt with a stick.

Maybe that kind of summer is gone for good. Maybe this is the leading edge of a new way of living that not only has no room for contemplation but is **contemptuous** 150 of it. But if downtime cannot be squeezed during the school year into the life of frantic and often joyless activity with which our children are saddled while their parents pursue frantic and often joyless activity of their own, what about summer? Do most adults really want to stand in line for Space Mountain or sit in traffic to get to a shore house that 160 doesn't have enough saucepans? Might it be even more enriching for their children to stay at home and do nothing? For those who **D** say they will only watch TV or play on the computer, a piece of technical advice: the cable box can be unhooked, the modem removed. Perhaps it is not too late for American kids to be given the 170 gift of enforced boredom for at least a week or two, staring into space, bored out of their gourds, exploring the inside of their own heads. "To contemplate is to toil, to think is to do," said Victor Hugo. "Go outside and play," said Prudence Quindlen. Both of them were right.

prestigious
(prĕ-stē′jəs) *adj.* having a great reputation; highly respected

contemptuous
(kən-tĕmp′chōō-əs) *adj.* scornful or disrespectful

laudable (lô′də-bəl) *adj.* worthy of high praise

C DISTINGUISH FACT FROM OPINION
Reread lines 109–126. What fact does Quindlen include to support her opinion that parents have too little leisure time?

D GRAMMAR AND STYLE
Reread lines 150–163. Quindlen uses **rhetorical questions** to make the idea of doing nothing sound more appealing than the usual summertime activities.

Comprehension

1. **Recall** What were Quindlen's summers like when she was a child?

2. **Recall** What does she believe many children lack today?

3. **Recall** What change does Quindlen propose in her essay?

4. **Clarify** What does the word *nothing* mean in the essay's title?

Critical Analysis

5. **Analyze an Argument** Review the chart you created as you read. What are two reasons Quindlen provides to support her claim?

6. **Distinguish Fact from Opinion** Identify whether each statement listed in the chart is a fact or an opinion. Use a chart like the one shown to record your answers.

Statement	Fact or Opinion?
"I don't believe you can write poetry, or compose music, or become an actor without downtime...." (lines 23–26)	
"...in the last 20 years American kids have lost about four unstructured hours a week." (lines 78–80)	
"I mourn hanging out in the backyard." (lines 140–141)	

7. **Examine Support** How does the Victor Hugo quotation in lines 173–175 support Quindlen's **claim?**

8. **Make Judgments** Quindlen notes that children today are enrolled in soccer leagues, acting classes, music camps, and sports camps—pursuits that may be quite enjoyable. Explain whether you agree with her that such activities do not qualify as **leisure.**

9. **Synthesize Concepts** What does the essay suggest about our society's values? Cite evidence in your response.

10. **Evaluate an Argument** How effective is Quindlen's argument in this essay? Support your opinion with evidence from the text.

OHIO STANDARDS

READING STANDARD
3.5 Analyze an author's implicit and explicit argument

Vocabulary in Context

VOCABULARY PRACTICE

Choose the letter of the word that is most different in meaning from the others. If necessary, use a dictionary to check the precise meanings of words you are unsure of.

1. (a) prestigious, (b) reputable, (c) infamous, (d) eminent
2. (a) hiatus, (b) gap, (c) respite, (d) renewal
3. (a) surplus, (b) excess, (c) sufficiency, (d) deficit
4. (a) despicable, (b) admirable, (c) laudable, (d) commendable
5. (a) disdainful, (b) deferential, (c) scornful, (d) contemptuous

WORD LIST

contemptuous

deficit

hiatus

laudable

prestigious

VOCABULARY IN WRITING

Using three or more vocabulary words, write about why you think young people often lack free time. Here is an example of how you could begin.

> **EXAMPLE SENTENCE**
>
> *Students who want to get into a **prestigious** college not only study hard but also involve themselves in many extracurricular activities.*

VOCABULARY STRATEGY: ETYMOLOGY

The **etymology** of a word, or its origin and history, can provide insight into the word's meaning. You can learn about a word's etymology by looking up the word or its root in a dictionary. Information about the etymology will appear near the beginning or end of the dictionary entry.

OHIO STANDARDS

VOCABULARY STANDARD
1.6 Determine meanings of unknown words by using dictionaries

> **hi•a•tus** (hī-ā′təs) *n., pl.* **–tus•es** or **hiatus 1.** A gap or interruption in space, time, or continuity; a break: *"We are likely to be disconcerted by . . . hiatuses of thought"* (Edmund Wilson). **2.** *Linguistics* A slight pause that occurs when two immediately adjacent vowels in consecutive syllables are pronounced, as in *reality* and *naive*. **3.** *Anatomy* A separation, aperture, fissure, or short passage in an organ or body part. [Latin *hiātus,* from past participle of *hiāre,* to gape.] —**hi•a′tal** (-āt′l) *adj.*

PRACTICE Look up the following italicized words in a dictionary, noting each word's derivation and meaning. Also look for clues to explain its spelling. Then answer the questions.

1. What language is the original source of the word *deficit*?
2. Through which languages can the history of *laudable* be traced?
3. From which Latin word does *contemptuous* derive, and what does the Latin word mean?

VOCABULARY PRACTICE
For more practice, go to the **Vocabulary Center** at **ClassZone.com.**

Reading-Writing Connection

Explore the ideas presented in "Doing Nothing Is Something" by responding to these prompts. Then use **Revision: Grammar and Style** to improve your writing.

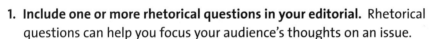

WRITING PROMPTS	SELF-CHECK

A. Short Response: Describe Free Time
What is it like to "do nothing"? Write a **one- or two-paragraph description** of how you have spent a period of **leisure**.

▶

A strong description will . . .
- explain how you were affected by the experience
- use words and phrases that appeal to readers' senses

B. Extended Response: Write an Editorial
Write a **three-to-five-paragraph editorial** in which you argue that children reap greater benefits from participating in structured activities.

▶

An effective editorial will . . .
- clearly state a claim
- provide reasons and evidence to support the claim

REVISION: GRAMMAR AND STYLE

OHIO STANDARDS

WRITING STANDARD
5.9 Use language appropriate to audience and purpose

ADD RHETORICAL QUESTIONS Review the **Grammar and Style** note on page 582. Quindlen uses **interrogative sentences** to pose a series of **rhetorical questions,** or questions that do not require answers, encouraging readers to think about issues. Revise your response to Prompt B by employing these techniques:

1. **Include one or more rhetorical questions in your editorial.** Rhetorical questions can help you focus your audience's thoughts on an issue.

2. **Use rhetorical questions sparingly so that they retain their impact.** Add rhetorical questions only when you really need to underscore a point. Here is one student's example.

> **STUDENT MODEL**
>
> Are we supposed to feel sorry for kids who are lucky enough to participate in a variety of activities? Do we really think kids are too overscheduled just because they spend their days at soccer practice and music lessons instead of looking up at the sky?

Notice how the revision in red helps to highlight the message in this first draft.

> **STUDENT MODEL**
>
> I know plenty of kids who do volunteer work in the summer or take courses in subjects not taught at school. ∧ *Would they really be better off hanging out at the pool?*

WRITING TOOLS
For prewriting, revision, and editing tools, visit the **Writing Center** at ClassZone.com.

Abolishing the Penny Makes Good Sense

Editorial by Alan S. Blinder

Why keep what is no longer USEFUL?

OHIO STANDARDS

READING STANDARDS
3.4 Assess accuracy of author's details
3.5 Analyze an author's implicit and explicit argument

KEY IDEA Are there old tools or appliances in your home that nobody ever uses? What keeps your family from throwing them away? In "Abolishing the Penny Makes Good Sense," economist Alan Blinder denies the **usefulness** of one of the most common objects in our society.

QUICKWRITE Write a paragraph about a device or an object that has outlived its usefulness. Explain what caused it to lose value, and discuss why some people might be reluctant to get rid of it.

● ELEMENTS OF NONFICTION: EVIDENCE

Writers use **evidence** to try to convince readers that their claims are valid. Alan Blinder presents a variety of evidence in "Abolishing the Penny Makes Good Sense," including family anecdotes and observations such as the following:

Few people nowadays even bend down to pick a penny off the sidewalk.

Evidence may also consist of examples, statistics, and the views of experts. Sound evidence is

- relevant to the writer's argument
- sufficient to support a claim or reason

As you read, evaluate the evidence Blinder presents.

● READING SKILL: ANALYZE DEDUCTIVE REASONING

When you arrive at a conclusion by applying a general principle to a specific situation, you are using **deductive reasoning.** Here is an example:

General Principle: Any student caught cheating will be suspended.
Specific Situation: Jeremiah was caught cheating.
Conclusion: Jeremiah will be suspended.

Writers often use deductive reasoning in arguments without stating the general principle. They just assume that readers will recognize and agree with the principle.

Careful readers don't always assume the general principle is sound, however. They identify it, as well as the other parts of the argument, and then ask whether each part is really true.

To analyze Alan Blinder's deductive reasoning, one reader began the chart shown here. As you read Blinder's editorial, complete the chart.

> *General Principle (Implied)*
> *Any coin that has outlived its usefulness should be abolished.*
>
> ↓
>
> *Specific Situation*
>
> ↓
>
> *Reasons and Evidence*
>
> ↓
>
> *Conclusion*

Author Onine

Money Matters
Alan S. Blinder is a professor of economics at Princeton University. The author of numerous articles and essays, Blinder has also influenced economic policy from within government. He served on the Council of Economic Advisors, which advises the president on economic issues, and from 1994 to 1996 he helped oversee the nation's banking system as vice chairman of the Federal Reserve Board. An economist who collaborated on a textbook with Blinder noted that "when Alan offered a criticism of something I had done, it was almost invariably right. I never could think of a good counterargument."

Alan S. Blinder
born 1945

🔎 **MORE ABOUT THE AUTHOR**
For more on Alan S. Blinder, visit the **Literature Center** at ClassZone.com.

Background

The Ever-Changing Penny The first U.S. penny was minted in 1793. Made of solid copper, it was about the size of a quarter. Since that time, the penny has been redesigned 11 times, with the Lincoln penny making its debut in 1909 to mark the 100th anniversary of Lincoln's birth. The composition of the penny has changed over the years as well. In 1982 the government switched from a mostly copper penny to one that is 97% zinc with a copper coating. Had the mint continued to make pennies out of copper, the cost to produce each one would have been greater than one cent.

Diminishing Value A penny doesn't go as far as it once did. In the 1930s a penny could buy a lollipop, a pencil, or a handful of peanuts. Today, you would be hard-pressed to find anything that costs only one cent.

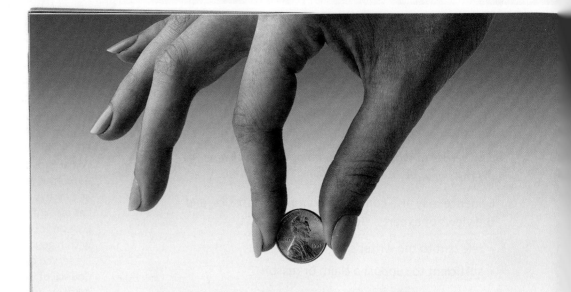

Abolishing the Penny Makes Good Sense

by Alan S. Blinder

An economist rarely has the opportunity to recommend a policy change that benefits 200 million people, imposes costs on virtually no one, and saves the government money to boot. But I have such a suggestion to offer the nation as a holiday gift: Let's abolish the penny.

Yes, the old copperhead has outlived its usefulness and is by now a public nuisance—something akin to the gnat. Pennies get in the way when
10 we make change. They add unwanted weight to our pockets and purses. Few people nowadays even bend down to pick a penny off the sidewalk. Doesn't that prove that mining and minting[1] copper into pennies is wasteful? Today, if it rained pennies from heaven, only a fool would turn his umbrella upside down: The money caught would be worth less than the ruined umbrella. **A**

---

1. **minting:** stamping coins from metal.

A DEDUCTIVE REASONING
Reread lines 7–17. What is the specific situation Blinder intends to prove exists? Restate this situation in your own words on your chart.

I have been antipenny for years, but final proof came about two years ago. I used to dump my pennies into a shoe box. Eventually, I accumulated several hundred. Dismayed by the ever-growing collection of useless copper, I offered the box to my son William, then 8, warning him that the bank would take the pennies only if he neatly wrapped them in rolls of 50. William, obviously a keen, intuitive economist, thought the matter over carefully for about two seconds before responding: "Thanks, Dad, but it's not worth it." If it's not worth the time of an 8-year-old to wrap pennies, why does the U.S. government keep producing the things? **Ⓑ**

91 Billion in Circulation

More than the time of 8-year-olds is involved. Think how often you have waited in line while the customers ahead of you fumbled through their pockets or purses for a few—expletive deleted—pennies. A trivial problem? Yes, until you multiply your wasted seconds by the billions of cash transactions that take place in our economy each year. I estimate that all this penny-pinching wastes several hundred million hours annually. Valuating[2] that at, say, $10 an hour adds up to several billion dollars per year, which is more than enough to justify this column.

We also must consider the cost of minting and maintaining the penny supply. There are roughly 91 billion pennies circulating, and every year the U.S. Treasury produces 12 billion to 14 billion more, at a cost of about $90 million. Since this expenditure just produces a nuisance for society, it should be at the top of everyone's list of budget cuts.

There are no coherent objections to abolishing the penny. It has been claimed, apparently with a straight face, that eliminating pennies would be inflationary,[3] because all those $39.99 prices would rise to $40. Apart from the fact that such increases would be penny-ante,[4] the claim itself is ludicrous. A price such as $39.99 is designed to keep a four from appearing as the first digit—something the retailer deems psychologically important. In a penny-less society merchants probably would change the number to $39.95, not raise it to $40. Even if only one-fifth of all merchants reacted this way, abolishing the penny would be disinflationary.

Sales tax poses a problem. How would a penny-free economy cope with, for instance, a 7% sales tax on a $31 purchase, which comes to $2.17? The answer leads to the second part of my suggestion. Let all states and localities amend their sales taxes to round all tax bills to the next-highest nickel. In the example, the state would collect $2.20 instead of $2.17. The customer would lose 3¢ but—if my previous arguments are correct—would actually be better off without the pennies. What other tax leaves the taxpayer happier for having paid it?

Ⓑ EVIDENCE
In your opinion, is the anecdote Blinder offers in lines 18–35 truly "final proof" that the penny has no value? Why or why not?

---

2. **valuating:** placing a value on.

3. **inflationary:** causing an increase in the price of goods.

4. **penny-ante** (ăn'tē): a business deal on a trivial scale.

After pennies are struck at the U.S. Mint, they must be inspected for imperfections before they can be released.

Sentimental Value

Only tradition explains our stubborn attachment to the penny. But sometimes traditions get ridiculous. Surely the smallest currency unit a country uses should be related to its average income. Yet countries with lower standards of living than the United States have minimum currency units worth more than 1¢—while we have been minting the penny for two centuries.

Even England, as tradition-bound a nation as they come, is more progressive in this matter than the United States. Years ago the smallest unit of British currency was the farthing, equal to one-quarter of what was then called a penny. As England grew richer, the farthing gave way to the half-penny, then to the old penny, and finally to the new penny, which is the equivalent of 9.6 farthings. During this same time, all the stodgy United States did was abolish the half-penny. **C**

Sure, the penny has sentimental value. That motivates the last part of my suggestion. Rather than call in all the pennies and melt them, which would be too expensive and perhaps heartrending, the government should simply announce that it is demonetizing[5] the penny as of next January—and let collectors take many of the pesky coppers out of circulation. After hobbyists and investors accumulated whatever stockpiles they desired, the rest could be redeemed by the government—wrapped neatly in rolls of 50, of course.

Let's get penny-wise and abolish the 1¢ piece. The idea is so logical, so obviously correct, that I am sure the new Congress will enact it during its first days in office.

5. **demonetizing** (dē-mŏn′ĭ-tī′zĭng): depriving of value.

C EVIDENCE
Reread lines 107–120. How relevant to the author's **argument** is the evidence about currency in other countries?

Comprehension

OHIO STANDARDS

READING STANDARD
3.5 Analyze an author's implicit and explicit argument

1. **Recall** What is the author's opinion of the penny?

2. **Recall** In what ways does the penny inconvenience people?

3. **Summarize** According to the author, how will customers be affected at checkout lines if the penny is abolished?

Critical Analysis

4. **Examine an Argument** For each objection to abolishing the penny listed in the chart shown, summarize the **counterargument** that the author makes to refute the objection.

5. **Analyze Deductive Reasoning** Review the chart you created as you read. What is the strongest reason that the author presents to support his conclusion that the penny has lost its **usefulness?** Explain your answer.

Objection	Counterargument
Inflation would result.	
People would pay more in sales taxes.	
The penny is part of our tradition.	

6. **Analyze Tone** What tone does the author use when discussing arguments in favor of keeping the penny? Cite examples from the text.

7. **Interpret a Statement** What does the author intend to suggest in the last paragraph when he says that his "idea is so logical, so obviously correct, that I am sure the new Congress will enact it during its first days in office"?

8. **Predict an Outcome** The author speculates about how merchants and consumers would respond if the penny is abolished. What do you predict will happen if the penny is removed from circulation? Give reasons for your prediction.

9. **Make Judgments** The author states in the opening paragraph that abolishing the penny would impose "costs on virtually no one." Do you agree with his characterization of how the change would affect people? Cite evidence to support your opinion.

10. **Evaluate Evidence** Does the author provide sufficient evidence to support his conclusion that the penny should be abolished? Explain why or why not.

11. **Evaluate an Unstated Assumption** Look at the chart on page 587 and note Blinder's unstated general principle. Do you agree with this basis for Blinder's argument? Explain why or why not.

On Nuclear Disarmament

Speech by Carl Sagan

What would make the world SAFER?

OHIO STANDARDS

READING STANDARDS
3.5 Analyze an author's implicit and explicit argument
3.8 Describe the features of rhetorical devices

KEY IDEA The newspapers are full of reports about war, epidemics, terrorism, and environmental crises. Some problems are so serious that they may threaten civilization. In his speech on nuclear disarmament, delivered in 1988, scientist Carl Sagan argues for rethinking ideas about how to maintain **security.**

SURVEY Ask six people to identify something that can be done to make the world a safer place. Present the results of your survey to the class.

● ELEMENTS OF NONFICTION: RHETORICAL DEVICES

In persuasive writing, rhetorical devices can make the writer's ideas more compelling and memorable. Carl Sagan uses the following devices in his speech "On Nuclear Disarmament":

- **Repetition**—the use of the same word, phrase, or sentence more than once for emphasis

- **Parallelism**—the use of similar grammatical constructions to express related ideas. Sagan opens his speech with a sentence that includes the parallel phrases "ancestors of some of us, brothers of us all."

As you read, notice how Sagan uses these rhetorical devices to drive home his persuasive argument.

● READING SKILL: ANALYZE INDUCTIVE REASONING

When you are led by specific evidence to form a general principle, or generalization, you are following **inductive reasoning.** Carl Sagan uses inductive reasoning when he presents examples and facts from past wars and then, from these, makes a generalization about warfare in general.

When you encounter inductive reasoning, examine the evidence and the concluding generalization to see whether

- the evidence is valid and provides sufficient support for the conclusion

- the writer overgeneralizes, or draws a conclusion that is too broad

As you read, use a graphic organizer like the one shown to help you analyze Sagan's inductive reasoning.

Evidence		Evidence		General Conclusion
Cannons and rifles killed 51,000 in three days at Gettysburg.	→		→	

▲ VOCABULARY IN CONTEXT

In the speech you are about to read, Sagan makes use of the following words. Which words do you already know? Write a sentence for each of those words. After you have read the selection, check to see if you used those words correctly.

WORD LIST	annihilate	contending	precursor
	carnage	malice	reconcile

Author Online

Popular Scientist
Carl Sagan's gift for explaining science to the general public helped make him one of the most famous scientists of his time. The astronomer is best known for writing and narrating a television series about astronomy and related topics. The series, *Cosmos,*

Carl Sagan
1934–1996

was watched by 400 million viewers, or, as Sagan put it, 3 percent of the world's population.

No Nukes! A staunch opponent of nuclear weapons, Sagan promoted the idea that even a limited nuclear war would devastate life on Earth by causing global temperatures to plunge. Although some scientists disputed this "nuclear winter" theory, it probably helped spur efforts in the 1980s to reduce the number of nuclear weapons held by the United States and the Soviet Union.

 MORE ABOUT THE AUTHOR
For more on Carl Sagan, visit the **Literature Center** at **ClassZone.com.**

Background

The Cold War In 1988, Carl Sagan delivered "On Nuclear Disarmament" in Gettysburg, Pennsylvania, to mark the 125th anniversary of a famous Civil War battle. At the time of the speech, the United States and the Soviet Union were still locked in a decades-long rivalry known as the cold war. Both nations had tens of thousands of nuclear warheads in their arsenals. According to some military strategists, these weapons prevented direct conflict because each side knew that it could be destroyed in a counterattack. This state of affairs was known as a balance of terror. However, many people feared that a crisis could spark a nuclear war between the superpowers.

On Nuclear Disarmament

Carl Sagan

Fifty-one thousand human beings were killed or wounded here, ancestors of some of us, brothers of us all. This was the first full-fledged example of an industrialized war, with machine-made arms and railroad transport of men and materiel. This was the first hint of an age yet to come, our age; an intimation of what technology bent to the purposes of war might be capable. The new Spencer repeating rifle was used here. In May 1863, a reconnaissance balloon of the Army of the Potomac[1] detected movement of Confederate troops across the Rappahannock River, the beginning of the campaign that led to the Battle of Gettysburg. That balloon was a **precursor** of air forces and strategic
10 bombing and reconnaissance satellites.

A few hundred artillery pieces were deployed in the three-day battle of Gettysburg. What could they do? What was the war like then? . . . Ballistic projectiles, launched from the cannons that you can see all over this Gettysburg Memorial, had a range, at best, of a few miles. The amount of explosive in the most formidable of them was some twenty pounds, roughly one-hundredth of a ton of TNT.[2] It was enough to kill a few people. **Ⓐ**

But the most powerful chemical explosives used eighty years later, in World War II, were the blockbusters, so-called because they could destroy a city block. Dropped from aircraft, after a journey of hundreds of miles, each

---

1. **Army of the Potomac:** the Union army that defeated Confederate forces near the town of Gettysburg, Pennsylvania. The battle was a turning point in the Civil War.

2. **TNT:** a chemical compound used as an explosive.

precursor (prĭ-kûr′sər) *n.* something that comes before and signals or prepares the way for what will follow

Ⓐ INDUCTIVE REASONING
What statistics does Sagan provide as **evidence** in lines 1–16?

The Soldiers' National Cemetery in Gettysburg National Military Park

20 carried about ten tons of TNT, a thousand times more than the most powerful weapon at the Battle of Gettysburg. A blockbuster could kill a few dozen people.

At the very end of World War II, the United States used the first atomic bombs to **annihilate** two Japanese cities. Each of those weapons had the equivalent power of about ten thousand tons of TNT, enough to kill a few hundred thousand people. One bomb.

A few years later the United States and the Soviet Union developed the first thermonuclear[3] weapons, the first hydrogen bombs. Some of them had an explosive yield equivalent to ten million tons of TNT; enough to kill a few million people. One bomb. Strategic nuclear weapons can now be launched to 30 any place on the planet. Everywhere on earth is a potential battlefield now. **B**

Each of these technological triumphs advanced the art of mass murder by a factor of a thousand. From Gettysburg to the blockbuster, a thousand times more explosive energy; from the blockbuster to the atomic bomb, a thousand times more; and from the atomic bomb to the hydrogen bomb, a thousand times still more. A thousand times a thousand, times a thousand is a billion; in less than one century, our most fearful weapon has become a billion times more deadly. But we have not become a billion times wiser in the generations that stretch from Gettysburg to us. **C**

annihilate (ə-nī′ə-lāt′) v. to destroy completely

B INDUCTIVE REASONING
How is the **evidence** in this paragraph related to evidence provided earlier in the speech?

C RHETORICAL DEVICES
Reread lines 32–38. What idea does Sagan stress through the use of **parallelism?**

---

3. **thermonuclear** (thûr′mō-nōō′klē-ər): based on the process of nuclear fusion, in which atomic nuclei combine at high temperatures, releasing energy.

The souls that perished here would find the **carnage** of which we are now
40 capable unspeakable. Today, the United States and the Soviet Union have
booby-trapped our planet with almost sixty thousand nuclear weapons. Sixty
thousand nuclear weapons! Even a small fraction of the strategic arsenals
could without question annihilate the two **contending** superpowers, probably
destroy the global civilization, and possibly render the human species extinct.
No nation, no man should have such power. We distribute these instruments
of apocalypse[4] all over our fragile world, and justify it on the grounds that it
has made us safe. We have made a fool's bargain.

The 51,000 casualties here at Gettysburg represented one-third of the
Confederate army and one-quarter of the Union army. All those who died,
50 with one or two exceptions, were soldiers. The best-known exception was a
civilian in her own house who thought to bake a loaf of bread and, through
two closed doors, was shot to death; her name was Jennie Wade. But in the
global thermonuclear war, almost all the casualties will be civilians, men,
women, and children, including vast numbers of citizens of nations that
had no part in the quarrel that led to the war, nations far removed from the
northern mid-latitude "target zone." There will be billions of Jennie Wades.
Everyone on earth is now at risk. . . . **D**

Two months before Gettysburg, on May 3, 1863, there was a Confederate
triumph, the Battle of Chancellorsville. On the moonlit evening following the
60 victory, General Stonewall Jackson and his staff, returning to the Confederate
lines, were mistaken for Union cavalry. Jackson was shot twice in error by his
own men. He died of his wounds.

We make mistakes. We kill our own.

There are some who claim that since we have not yet had an accidental
nuclear war, the precautions being taken to prevent one must be adequate.
But not three years ago we witnessed the disasters of the *Challenger*[5] space
shuttle and the Chernobyl[6] nuclear power plant, high-technology systems, one
American, one Soviet, into which enormous quantities of national prestige had
been invested. There were compelling reasons to prevent these disasters. In
70 the preceding year, confident assertions were made by officials of both nations
that no accidents of that sort could happen. We were not to worry. The experts
would not permit an accident to happen. We have since learned that such
assurances do not amount to much.

We make mistakes. We kill our own. **E**

This is the century of Hitler and Stalin, evidence—if any were needed—that
madmen can seize the reins of power of modern industrial states. If we are
content in a world with nearly sixty thousand nuclear weapons, we are betting
our lives on the proposition that no present or future leaders, military or
civilian—of the United States, the Soviet Union, Britain, France, China, Israel,

---

4. **apocalypse** (ə-pŏk′ə-lĭps′): total devastation.

5. *Challenger:* an American space shuttle that exploded in 1986, killing all seven crew members.

6. **Chernobyl** (chər-nō′bəl): a town in the Ukraine (then part of the Soviet Union) that was the
site of a major nuclear power plant accident in 1986.

carnage (kär′nĭj) *n.*
massive slaughter

contending
(kən-tĕn′dĭng) *adj.*
struggling in rivalry
contend *v.*

D INDUCTIVE REASONING
What new point does
Sagan make with the
historical **evidence** he
discusses in lines 48–57?

E GRAMMAR AND STYLE
The two simple sentences
in line 74 also appear
earlier and later in the
speech. Consider how
this **repetition** serves
to link and emphasize
essential points.

80 India, Pakistan, South Africa, and whatever other nuclear powers there will be—will ever stray from the strictest standards of prudence. We are gambling on their sanity and sobriety even in times of great personal and national crisis, all of them, for all times to come. I say this is asking too much of us. Because we make mistakes. We kill our own. . . .

We have made a fool's bargain. We have been locked in a deadly embrace with the Soviet Union, each side always propelled by the abundant malefactions of the other; almost always looking to the short term—to the next congressional or presidential election, to the next party congress—and almost never seeing the big picture.

90 Dwight Eisenhower, who was closely associated with this Gettysburg community, said, "The problem in defense spending is to figure out how far you should go without destroying from within what you are trying to defend from without." I say we have gone too far. . . .

The Civil War was mainly about union; union in the face of differences. A million years ago, there were no nations on the planet. There were no tribes. The humans who were here were divided into small family groups of a few dozen people each. They wandered. That was the horizon of our identification, an itinerant family group. Since them, the horizons have expanded. From a handful of hunter-gatherers, to a tribe, to a horde, to a small city-state, to 100 a nation, and today to immense nation-states. The average person on the earth today owes his or her primary allegiance to a group of something like a hundred million people. It seems very clear that if we do not destroy ourselves first, the unit of primary identification of most human beings will before long be the planet Earth and the human species. To my mind, this raises the key question: whether the fundamental unit of identification will expand to embrace the planet and the species, or whether we will destroy ourselves first. I'm afraid it's going to be very close.

The identification horizons were broadened in this place 125 years ago, and at great cost to North and South, to blacks and whites. But we recognize that 110 expansion of identification horizons as just. Today there is an urgent, practical necessity to work together on arms control, on the world economy, on the global environment. It is clear that the nations of the world now can only rise and fall together. It is not a question of one nation winning at the expense of another. We must all help one another or all perish together. **F**

On occasions like this it is customary to quote homilies; phrases by great men and women that we've all heard before. We hear, but we tend not to focus. Let me mention one, a phrase that was uttered not far from this spot by Abraham Lincoln: "With **malice** toward none, with charity for all. . . ." *Think* of what that means. This is what is expected of us, not merely because 120 our ethics command it, or because our religions preach it, but because it is necessary for human survival.

F INDUCTIVE REASONING
What **conclusion** does Sagan draw in lines 108–114?

malice (măl'ĭs) *n.* a desire to harm others

Here's another: "A house divided against itself cannot stand." Let me vary it a little: A species divided against itself cannot stand. A planet divided against itself cannot stand. And [to be] inscribed on this Eternal Light Peace Memorial, which is about to be rekindled and rededicated, is a stirring phrase: "A World United in the Search for Peace."

The real triumph of Gettysburg was not, I think, in 1863 but in 1913, when the surviving veterans, the remnants of the adversary forces, the Blue and the Gray, met in celebration and solemn memorial. It had been the war that set
130 brother against brother, and when the time came to remember, on the fiftieth anniversary of the battle, the survivors fell, sobbing, into one another's arms. They could not help themselves.

It is time now for us to emulate them, NATO and the Warsaw Pact,[7] Israelis and Palestinians, whites and blacks, Americans and Iranians, the developed and the underdeveloped worlds.

We need more than anniversary sentimentalism and holiday piety and patriotism. Where necessary, we must confront and challenge the conventional wisdom. It is time to learn from those who fell here. Our challenge is to **reconcile,** not *after* the carnage and the mass murder, but *instead* of the
140 carnage and the mass murder.

It is time to act. ✷

reconcile (rĕk′ən-sīl′) *v.* to restore friendly relations

---

7. **Warsaw Pact:** an alliance of the Soviet Union and other Communist nations.

Comprehension

1. **Recall** What weapons were used in the Battle of Gettysburg?

2. **Recall** What developments in warfare occurred during and shortly after World War II?

3. **Summarize** According to Sagan, why should we reject assurances that a nuclear war will not occur?

Critical Analysis

4. **Examine a Rhetorical Device** What idea does Sagan emphasize with his **repetition** of the statement, "We have made a fool's bargain"?

5. **Examine an Argument** Sagan states that as society has evolved, humans have gone from identifying with small groups to identifying with enormous nation-states. How does this idea relate to the main **claim** of his argument?

6. **Interpret a Statement** What does Sagan mean when he says that "the real triumph of Gettysburg" was the behavior of surviving veterans who attended the 50th anniversary of the battle, in 1913?

7. **Analyze Inductive Reasoning** Review the graphic organizer you created as you read. Does Sagan provide sufficient **support** for his conclusion about nuclear weapons and **security?** Explain why or why not.

8. **Analyze a Conclusion** At the end of his speech, Sagan says it is "time to act" to prevent nuclear war. In a chart like the one shown, identify specific actions that individuals and groups can take in response to Sagan's call for action.

Preventing Nuclear War	
Individual Actions	Group Activities
•	•
•	•
•	•

9. **Compare Texts** Compare and contrast the techniques of argument used in Sagan's speech and Alan Blinder's editorial "Abolishing the Penny Makes Good Sense."

10. **Evaluate Explanations** Sagan became famous for helping the general public understand scientific concepts. How well does he explain the complex issues involved with nuclear weapons? Cite evidence to support your opinion.

OHIO STANDARDS

READING STANDARD
3.8 Describe the features of rhetorical devices

Vocabulary in Context

WORD LIST
annihilate
carnage
contending
malice
precursor
reconcile

VOCABULARY PRACTICE

Decide whether the words in each pair are synonyms or antonyms.

1. annihilate/preserve
2. carnage/bloodshed
3. contending/cooperating
4. malice/hatred
5. precursor/aftermath
6. reconcile/antagonize

VOCABULARY IN WRITING

Create four questions that you would like to ask a politician or military leader about war, using at least one vocabulary word in each question. Here is a sample.

EXAMPLE SENTENCE

Is this harsh criticism of the country's ruler a **_precursor_** to war?

VOCABULARY STRATEGY: SPECIALIZED VOCABULARY

Specialized vocabulary is vocabulary specifically suited to a particular occupation or field of study. Politicians and military personnel often use specialized vocabulary when talking about war. This vocabulary includes terms such as *ballistic,* which refers to the movements of missiles and other weapons propelled through the air. It is often possible to figure out the meaning of a specialized vocabulary term from context. Otherwise, look up the term in a dictionary.

PRACTICE Write the term that matches each definition. If you need to, check a dictionary.

> arsenal casualties deploy disarmament reconnaissance

1. military people lost through death, injury, sickness, or capture
2. a stock of weapons
3. the reduction of a nation's military forces and equipment
4. an inspection of an area to gather military information
5. to position troops or equipment in readiness for combat

OHIO STANDARDS

VOCABULARY STANDARD
1.6 Determine meanings of unknown words by using dictionaries

VOCABULARY PRACTICE
For more practice, go to the **Vocabulary Center** at **ClassZone.com.**

Reading-Writing Connection

Explore the message in "On Nuclear Disarmament" by responding to these prompts. Then use **Revision: Grammar and Style** to improve your writing.

WRITING PROMPTS	SELF-CHECK
A. Short Response: Write Across Texts Is the world a safer place today than it was when Sagan gave his speech? Use Sagan's speech and the nuclear weapons chart on page 603 to write a **one- or two-paragraph response.**	*A thoughtful response will . . .* • compare current security risks with the situation Sagan describes in his speech • synthesize ideas and information from the speech and chart
B. Extended Response: Explain Views There are often disagreements about the best ways to maintain national and international **security.** In **three to five paragraphs,** explain your own views on this topic.	*A strong explanation will . . .* • express clear opinions on maintaining security • discuss how your own views compare with those of Sagan

REVISION: GRAMMAR AND STYLE

USE RHETORICAL DEVICES Review the **Grammar and Style** note on page 597. Using **repetition,** as Sagan does in his speech, can reinforce important messages and ideas. Use these techniques to revise your responses to the prompts:

OHIO STANDARDS

WRITING STANDARD
5.13 Rearrange words and sentences to maintain consistent style, tone and voice.

1. **Repeat powerful words or phrases that will draw attention to a key point.** In this example, Sagan repeats the participial phrase "divided against itself" to stress the necessity of nations working together:

   . . . *"A house divided against itself cannot stand." Let me vary it a little: A species divided against itself cannot stand. A planet divided against itself cannot stand.* (lines 122–124)

2. **Use repetition to link related ideas.** Repeating important words or phrases in a persuasive essay or speech can indicate to readers that ideas appearing at different points in the piece are related.

Notice how the revisions in red strengthen the message in this first draft.

WRITING TOOLS
For prewriting, revision, and editing tools, visit the **Writing Center** at ClassZone.com.

> **STUDENT MODEL**
>
> Sagan believes it is ~~a mistake~~ *foolish* to seek safety in terrible weapons, *foolish to* trust
>
> politicians to make the right decisions, and *foolish to* set nation against nation.

Reading for Information

STATISTICAL ILLUSTRATION When Carl Sagan delivered his speech "On Nuclear Disarmament" in 1988, the United States and the Soviet Union had about 60,000 nuclear weapons pointed at each other. This chart shows estimated amounts of nuclear weapons 14 years later. Note that the end of the cold war led to reductions in some nuclear stockpiles.

Stockpiles of Nuclear Weapons,

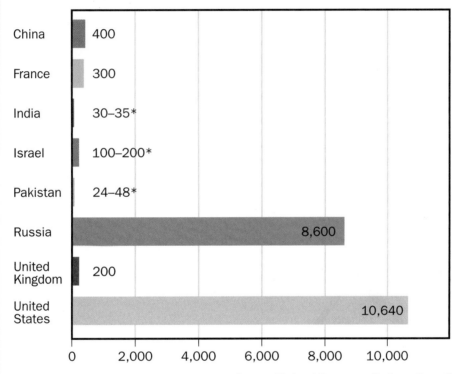

China	400
France	300
India	30–35*
Israel	100–200*
Pakistan	24–48*
Russia	8,600
United Kingdom	200
United States	10,640

Source: National Resources Defense Council

*Estimates of the nuclear stockpiles of these countries are much harder to make because the countries have never joined with other nations in signing the Treaty on the Non-Proliferation of Nuclear Weapons, which was established to limit the spread of nuclear weapons.

I Acknowledge Mine

Essay by Jane Goodall

Do animals have RIGHTS?

OHIO STANDARDS

READING STANDARD
2.1 Summarize
3.4 Identify persuasive techniques

KEY IDEA People express their love for animals in a variety of ways, such as pampering pets or contributing money to protect natural habitats. But we often buy products that were tested on animals, and such tests can cause suffering or even death. In this selection, Jane Goodall raises questions about our moral responsibility toward chimpanzees used in medical labs and the importance of **animal rights.**

DEBATE Should our society recognize animal rights? With a group of classmates, list the reasons for your position on the issue. Then debate the topic with another group.

● ELEMENTS OF NONFICTION: PERSUASIVE TECHNIQUES

Writers use **persuasive techniques** to help convince readers about an issue. Such techniques include **emotional appeals**—statements intended to stir up strong feelings. In the following example, Jane Goodall includes disturbing details and emotionally charged words to arouse pity in readers:

. . . young chimpanzees, in similar tiny prisons, rocked back and forth or from side to side, far gone in misery and despair.

Emotional appeals can be an important element of an effective argument. However, writers sometimes exaggerate problems or use appeals to cover up flawed reasoning. As you read "I Acknowledge Mine," notice Goodall's use of emotional appeals.

■ READING STRATEGY: SUMMARIZE

When you **summarize** an argument, you briefly restate the text's main ideas and important information. Summarizing can help you understand and remember what you read. When you summarize, you should

- present ideas and information in the same order in which they appear in the text
- leave out examples and details that are not essential for understanding the writer's key points

As you read, use a chart like the one shown to help you summarize important ideas and information.

Main Idea	Details
Chimpanzees in the lab suffered from overcrowding and isolation.	The youngest were kept in pairs in small, dark cages.
	Older ones lived alone, without any companionship or stimulation.

▲ VOCABULARY IN CONTEXT

To see how many vocabulary words you know, substitute a different word or phrase for each boldfaced word.

1. Criminals feared the **stark** prison.
2. The crowd was loud and **boisterous.**
3. This pill can **alleviate** pain.
4. Must you disagree so **stridently?**
5. I admit my **complicity** in the error.

Author Online

Call of the Wild
Beginning in 1960, British naturalist and author Jane Goodall devoted herself to observing the behavior of wild chimpanzees in the Gombe Stream Chimpanzee Reserve in Tanzania. There, Goodall made some startling discoveries. For example, she saw chimpanzees make and use tools, disproving the theory that only humans use them. She also observed a chimpanzee "adopt" a younger, orphaned chimpanzee.

**Jane Goodall
born 1934**

Championing Chimps Goodall's observations over several decades support her belief that chimpanzees are highly intelligent creatures capable of feeling emotions and forming long-term relationships. As a leading authority on chimpanzee behavior, Goodall has written dozens of books, ranging from scholarly works to illustrated children's books. Today, she dedicates her time to lecturing about wildlife conservation and animal welfare.

 MORE ABOUT THE AUTHOR
For more on Jane Goodall, visit the **Literature Center** at ClassZone.com.

Background

Chimpanzees and Research Because about 98 percent of chimpanzees' genetic material is identical to ours, they have long been used by researchers for studying the progression and treatment of human diseases. In recent years, they have been used in the study of hepatitis C and HIV. The use of chimpanzees in research has grown increasingly controversial, however, and has been banned in some nations, including Great Britain, Sweden, and New Zealand.

I Acknowledge Mine   Jane Goodall

It was on December 27, 1986, that I watched the videotape that would
change the pattern of my life. I had spent a traditional Christmas with my
family in Bournemouth, England. We all sat watching the tape, and we were
all shattered. Afterward, we couldn't speak for a while. The tape showed scenes
from inside a biomedical research laboratory, in which monkeys paced round
and round, back and forth, within incredibly small cages stacked one on top
of the other, and young chimpanzees, in similar tiny prisons, rocked back and
forth or from side to side, far gone in misery and despair. I had, of course, known
about the chimpanzees who were locked away in medical research laboratories.
10 But I had deliberately kept away, knowing that to see them would be utterly
depressing, thinking that there would be nothing I could do to help them.
After seeing the video I knew I had to try. . . . **A**

   The videotape had revealed conditions inside Sema, a federally funded
laboratory in Maryland. Goodall took action, criticizing Sema for violating
government standards and causing psychological harm to chimpanzees. The
president of Sema denied these charges. Several months after Goodall first
viewed the videotape, she received permission to visit the laboratory.

   Even repeated viewing of the videotape had not prepared me for the **stark**
reality of that laboratory. I was ushered, by white-coated men who smiled
20 nervously or glowered, into a nightmare world. The door closed behind us.
Outside, everyday life went on as usual, with the sun and the trees and the
birds. Inside, where no daylight had ever penetrated, it was dim and colorless.
I was led along one corridor after another, and I looked into room after room

ANALYZE VISUALS
What aspects of this
photograph give it an
emotional appeal?

A SUMMARIZE
How would you
summarize the
information in
lines 1–12?

stark (stärk) *adj.*
harsh or grim

lined with small, bare cages, stacked one above the other. I watched as monkeys paced around their tiny prisons, making bizarre, abnormal movements.

Then came a room where very young chimpanzees, one or two years old, were crammed, two together, into tiny cages that measured (as I found out later) some twenty-two inches by twenty-two inches at the base. They were two feet high. These chimp babies peered out from the semidarkness of their
30 tiny cells as the doors were opened. Not yet part of any experiment, they had been waiting in their cramped quarters for four months. They were simply objects, stored in the most economical way, in the smallest space that would permit the continuation of life. At least they had each other, but not for long. Once their quarantine was over they would be separated, I was told, and placed singly in other cages, to be infected with hepatitis or AIDS or some other viral disease. And all the cages would then be placed in isolettes.

What could they see, these infants, when they peered out through the tiny panel of glass in the door of their isolette? The blank wall opposite their prison. What was in the cage to provide occupation, stimulation, comfort? For those
40 who had been separated from their companions—nothing. I watched one isolated prisoner, a juvenile female, as she rocked from side to side, sealed off from the outside world in her metal box. A flashlight was necessary if one wanted to see properly inside the cage. All she could hear was the constant loud sound of the machinery that regulated the flow of air through vents in her isolette. **B**

A "technician" (for so the animal-care staff are named, after training) was told to lift her out. She sat in his arms like a rag doll, listless, apathetic. He did not speak to her. She did not look at him or try to interact with him in any way. Then he returned her to her cage, latched the inner door, and closed her isolette, shutting her away again from the rest of the world.
50 I am still haunted by the memory of her eyes, and the eyes of the other chimpanzees I saw that day. They were dull and blank, like the eyes of people who have lost all hope, like the eyes of children you see in Africa, refugees, who have lost their parents and their homes. Chimpanzee children are so like **C** human children, in so many ways. They use similar movements to express their feelings. And their emotional needs are the same—both need friendly contact and reassurance and fun and opportunity to engage in wild bouts of play. And they need love.

Dr. James Mahoney, veterinarian at the Laboratory for Experimental Medicine and Surgery in Primates (LEMSIP), recognized this need when he began
60 working for Jan Moor-Jankowski.[1] Several years ago he started a "nursery" in that lab for the infant chimpanzees when they are first taken from their mothers. It was not long after my visit to Sema that I went for the first of a number of visits to LEMSIP.

Once I was suitably gowned and masked and capped, with paper booties over my shoes, Jim took me to see his nursery. Five young chimps were there at the time, ranging in age from about nine months to two years. Each one was

---

1. **Jan Moor-Jankowski:** director of LEMSIP.

B PERSUASIVE TECHNIQUES
Reread lines 37–44. Why might Goodall have chosen to include **rhetorical questions**—questions that do not require answers—in her appeal to the reader's sympathy?

C GRAMMAR AND STYLE
Reread lines 50–53. Notice how Goodall uses **imagery** and **figurative language**—comparing the chimpanzees to orphaned refugee children—to convey a sad **tone**.

dressed in children's clothes—"to keep their diapers on, really," said the staff member who was with them. (Someone is always with them throughout the day.) The infants played vigorously around me as I sat on the soft red carpet,

70 surrounded by toys. I was for the moment more interesting than any toy, and almost immediately they had whisked off my cap and mask. Through a window these infants could look into a kitchen and work area where, most of the time, some human activity was going on. They had been taken from their mothers when they were between nine and eighteen months old, Jim said. He brings them into the nursery in groups, so that they can all go through the initial trauma together, which is why some were older than others. And, he explained, he tries to do this during summer vacation so that there will be no shortage of volunteer students to help them over their nightmares. Certainly these **boisterous** youngsters were not depressed.

80   I stayed for about forty minutes, then Jim came to fetch me. He took me to a room just across the corridor where there were eight young chimpanzees who had recently graduated from the nursery. This new room was known as "Junior Africa," I learned. Confined in small, bare cages, some alone, some paired, the youngsters could see into the nursery through the window. They could look back into their lost childhood. For the second time in their short lives, security and joy had been abruptly brought to an end through no fault of their own. Junior Africa: the name seems utterly appropriate until one remembers all the infants in Africa who are seized from their mothers by hunters, rescued and cared for in human families, and then, as they get older, banished into

90 small cages or tied to the ends of chains. Only the reasons, of course, are different. Even these very young chimpanzees at LEMSIP may have to go through grueling experimental procedures, such as repeated liver biopsies[2] and the drawing of blood. Jim is always pleading for a four-year childhood before research procedures commence, but the bodies of these youngsters, like those of other experimental chimps, are rented out to researchers and pharmaceutical companies. The chimpanzees, it seems, must earn their keep from as early an age as possible.

    During a subsequent visit to LEMSIP, I asked after one of the youngsters I had met at the nursery, little Josh. A real character he had been there, a born group leader. I was led to one of the cages in Junior Africa, where that

100 once-assertive infant, who had been so full of energy and zest for life, now sat huddled in the corner of his barred prison. There was no longer any fun in his eyes. "How can you bear it?" I asked the young woman who was caring for him. Her eyes, above the mask, filled with tears. "I can't," she said. "But if I leave, he'll have even less."

    This same fear of depriving the chimpanzees of what little they have is what keeps Jim at LEMSIP. After I had passed through Junior Africa that first day, Jim took me to the windowless rooms to meet ten adult chimps. No carpets or toys for them, no entertainment. This was the hard, cold world of the adult research

boisterous (boiʹstər-əs) *adj.* noisy and lacking in restraint or discipline

---

2. **biopsies:** removals of tissue samples from a living body for examination.

110 chimps at LEMSIP. Five on each side of the central corridor, each in his own
small prison, surrounded by bars—bars on all sides, bars above, bars below. Each
cage measured five feet by five feet and was seven feet high, which was the legal
minimum cage size at that time for storing adult chimpanzees. Each cage was
suspended above the ground, so that feces and food remains would fall to the
floor below. Each cage contained an old car tire and a chimpanzee. That was all.

JoJo's cage was the first on the right as we went in. I knelt down, new cap
and mask in place, along with overalls and plastic shoe covers and rubber
gloves. I looked into his eyes and talked to him. He had been in his cage at least
ten years. He had been born in the African forest. . . . Could he remember, I
120 wondered? Did he sometimes dream of the great trees with the breeze rustling
through the canopy, the birds singing, the comfort of his mother's arms? Very
gently JoJo reached one great finger through the steel bars and touched one of
the tears that slipped out above my mask, then went on grooming the back of
my wrist. So gently. Ignoring the rattling of cages, the clank of steel on steel,
the violent sway of imprisoned bodies beating against the bars, as the other
male chimps greeted the veterinarian.

His round over, Jim returned to where I still crouched before JoJo. The
tears were falling faster now. "Jane, please don't," Jim said, squatting beside

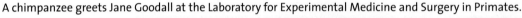

A chimpanzee greets Jane Goodall at the Laboratory for Experimental Medicine and Surgery in Primates.

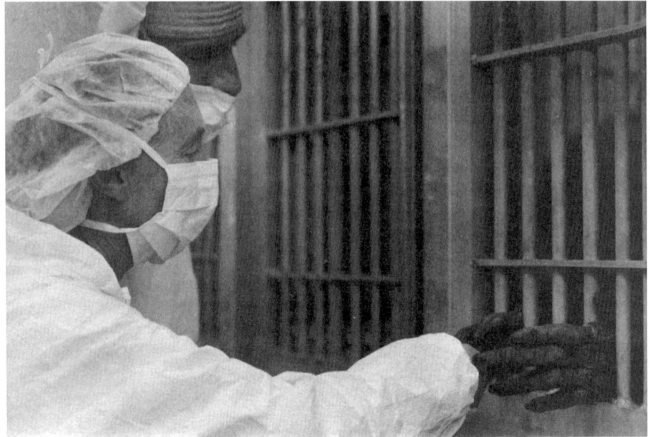

me and putting his arm around me. "Please don't. I have to face this every morning of my life." **D**

I also visited [the pharmaceutical company] Immuno's two labs in Austria. The first of these, where hepatitis research is conducted and where chimpanzees are used to test batches of vaccine, was built some time ago. There I got no farther than the administration building. I was not allowed into the chimpanzee rooms because I had not had a hepatitis shot. And—how unfortunate!—the closed-circuit TV monitors could not, for some reason, be made to work that day. In the lobby, though, there were two demonstration cages, set there so the public could see for itself the magnificent and spacious housing that Immuno was planning for its chimpanzee colony. (This they felt was necessary because of all the criticisms that were being made about the small size of the existing cages, dangerous criticisms leading to expensive lawsuits.) The present cages, I knew, were not very large. The new ones looked identical to those at LEMSIP. . . .

To my mind, it should be required that all scientists working with laboratory animals, whatever the species, not only know something about the animals and their natural behavior, but see for themselves how their protocols[3] affect individual animals. Researchers should observe firsthand any suffering they cause, so that they can better balance the benefit (or hoped-for benefit) to humanity against the cost in suffering to the animal. Laboratory chimpanzees are prisoners, but they are guilty of no crimes. Rather, they are helping—perhaps—to **alleviate** human suffering. Yet in some of the labs I have described, and in others around the world, they are subjected to far harsher treatment than we give to hardened criminals. Surely we owe them more than that. **E**

Even if all research labs could be redesigned to provide the best possible environment for the chimpanzee subjects, there would still be one nagging question—should chimpanzees be used at all? . . . Of course I wish I could wave a wand and see the lab cages standing empty. Of course I hate the suffering that goes on behind the closed doors of animal labs. I hate even more the callous attitude that lab personnel so often show toward the animals in their power—deliberately cultivated, no doubt, to try to protect themselves from any twinge of guilt. . . . Our children are gradually desensitized to animal suffering. ("It's all right, darling; it's only an animal.") The process goes on throughout school, culminating in the frightful things that zoology, psychology, veterinary, and medical students are forced to do to animals in the process of acquiring knowledge. They have to quell empathy if they are to survive in their chosen fields, for scientists do things to animals that, from the animals' point of view, are torture and would be regarded as such by almost everyone if done by nonscientists.

Animals in labs are used in different ways. In the quest for knowledge, things are done to them to see what happens. To test the safety of various products, animals are injected with or forced to swallow different amounts

D PERSUASIVE TECHNIQUES
Reread lines 116–130. What details help make this passage a powerful **emotional appeal**?

alleviate (ə-lē′vē-āt′) v. to make easier or provide relief

E SUMMARIZE
Briefly restate the key point that Goodall makes in lines 144–153.

---

3. **protocols** (prō′tə-kôlz′): plans for scientific experiments.

to see how sick they get, or if they survive. The effectiveness of medical procedures and drugs are tried out on animals. Surgical skills are practiced on animals. Theories of all sorts, ranging from the effects of various substances to psychological trauma, are tested on animals. What is so shocking is the lack of respect for the victims, the almost total disregard for their living, feeling, sometimes agonizing bodies. And often the tortures are inflicted for nothing. There is an angry debate, ongoing and abrasive, about the role of animals in medicine. Even though I am not qualified to judge a dispute of this

180 magnitude, which has become so polarized, it seems obvious that extremists on both sides are wrong. The scientists who claim that medical research could never have progressed at all without the use of animals are as incorrect as the animal-rights activists who declare **stridently** that no advances in medicine have been made due to animal research.

Let me return to chimpanzees and to the question of whether we are justified in using them in our search for medical knowledge. Approximately three thousand of them languish in medical research laboratories around the world, somewhat more than half this number (about one thousand eight hundred) in the United States. Today, as we have seen, they are primarily

190 used in infectious-disease research and vaccine testing; even though they have seldom shown even minor symptoms of either AIDS or hepatitis, the experimental procedures are often stressful, the conditions in which they are maintained typically bleak. . . .

Humans are a species capable of compassion, and we should develop a heightened moral responsibility for beings who are so like ourselves. Chimpanzees form close, affectionate bonds that may persist throughout life. Like us, they feel joy and sorrow and despair. They show many of the intellectual skills that until recently we believed were unique to ourselves. They may look into mirrors and see themselves as individuals—beings who have consciousness

200 of "self." Do they not, then, deserve to be treated with the same kind of consideration that we accord to other highly sensitive, conscious beings— ourselves? Granted, we do not always show much consideration to one another. That is why there is so much anguish over human rights. That is why it makes little sense to talk about the "rights" of chimpanzees. But at least where we desist from doing certain things to human beings for ethical reasons, we should desist also from doing them to chimpanzee beings. We no longer perform certain experiments on humans, for ethical reasons. I suggest that it would be logical to refrain also from doing these experiments on chimpanzees. **F**

F **SUMMARIZE**
Summarize Goodall's proposal for determining whether experiments on chimpanzees are justified.

Why do I care so much? Why, in order to try to change attitudes and

210 actions in the labs, do I subject myself repeatedly to the personal nightmare of visiting these places, knowing that I shall be haunted endlessly by memories of my encounters with the prisoners there? Especially in their eyes, those bewildered or sad or angry eyes. The answer is simple. I have spent so many years in the forests of Gombe, being with and learning from the chimpanzees. I consider myself one of the luckiest people on earth. It is time to repay something of the debt I owe the chimpanzees, for what they have taught me

about themselves, about myself, about the place of humans and chimpanzees in the natural world.

When I visit JoJo in his tiny steel prison I often think of David Greybeard, 220 that very special chimpanzee who, by his calm acceptance of my presence, first helped me to open the door into the magic world of the chimpanzees of Gombe. I learned so much from him. It was he who introduced me to his companions, Goliath and Mike and the Flo family and all the other unique, fascinating personalities who made up his community at that time. David even allowed me to groom him. A fully adult male chimpanzee who had lived all his life in the wild actually tolerated the touch of a human hand.

There was one especially memorable event. I had been following David one day, struggling through dense undergrowth near a stream. I was thankful when he stopped to rest, and I sat near him. Close by I noticed the fallen red fruit of 230 an oil nut palm, a favorite food of chimpanzees. I picked it up and held it out to David on the palm of my hand. For a moment I thought he would ignore my gesture. But then he took the nut, let it fall to the ground and, with the same movement, very gently closed his fingers around my hand. He glanced at my face, let go of my hand, and turned away. I understood his message: "I don't want the nut, but it was nice of you to offer it." We had communicated most truly, relying on shared primate signals that are deeper and more ancient than words. It was a moment of revelation. I did not follow David when he wandered off into the forest. I wanted to be alone, to ponder the significance of what had happened, to enshrine those moments permanently in my mind.

240   And so, when I am with JoJo, I remember David Greybeard and the lessons he taught me. I feel deep shame—shame that we, with our more sophisticated intellect, with our greater capacity for understanding and compassion, have deprived JoJo of almost everything. Not for him the soft colors of the forest, the dim greens and browns entwined, or the peace of the afternoon when the sun flecks the canopy and small creatures rustle and flit and creep among the leaves. Not for him the freedom to choose, each day, how he will spend his time and where and with whom. Nature's sounds are gone, the sounds of running water, of wind in the branches, of chimpanzee calls that ring out so clear and rise up through the treetops to drift away in the hills. The comforts
250 are gone, the soft leafy floor of the forest, the springy branches from which sleeping nests can be made. All are gone. Here, in the lab, the world is concrete and steel; it is loud, horrible sounds, clanging bars, banging doors, and the deafening volume of chimpanzee calls confined in underground rooms. It is a world where there are no windows, nothing to look at, nothing to play with. A world where family and friends are torn apart and where sociable beings are locked away, innocent of crime, into solitary confinement. **G**

    It is we who are guilty. I look again into JoJo's clear eyes. I acknowledge my own **complicity** in this world we have made, and I feel the need for forgiveness. He reaches out a large, gentle finger and once again touches the
260 tear trickling down into my mask. ᘉ

Some of the laboratories discussed in this selection have changed their practices, partly in response to Jane Goodall's criticism and recommendations. For example, Sema, which is now called Diagnon, no longer keeps chimpanzees in isolettes. The chimpanzees now live in more spacious, well-lit cubicles, and they are sometimes allowed to have contact with other chimpanzees.

G PERSUASIVE TECHNIQUES
Reread lines 240–256. What words and images in this passage appeal to your emotions?

complicity
(kəm-plĭs′ĭ-tē) *n.* association or partnership in a crime or offense

Comprehension

1. **Recall** What made Goodall decide to investigate research laboratories?

2. **Recall** What conditions did she find in the laboratories that she visited?

3. **Recall** How did the chimpanzee named David Greybeard behave when he came in contact with Goodall in the forests of Gombe?

4. **Clarify** Why does Goodall believe it is important for scientists who work with laboratory animals to know about their natural behavior?

Critical Analysis

5. **Examine an Argument** Review the chart you created as you read. How would you **summarize** Goodall's proposals to improve the treatment of chimpanzees in laboratories?

6. **Interpret a Statement** Reread lines 194–208. How do you interpret Goodall's remarks about human rights and the **rights** of chimpanzees?

7. **Analyze Support** How does the example of Goodall's experiences with David Greybeard support her argument?

8. **Make Inferences** How does Goodall seem to feel about James Mahoney, the veterinarian who guided her visit to LEMSIP?

9. **Identify an Author's Perspective** What beliefs, values, and feelings influence the way Goodall views experimentation on chimpanzees? Support your answer with evidence.

10. **Draw Conclusions** Does Goodall think that chimpanzees should be treated differently from other animals used in laboratory experiments? Cite evidence to support your conclusion.

11. **Evaluate Persuasive Techniques** Does Goodall use **emotional appeals** appropriately in her argument, or are these appeals exaggerated or excessive? Provide examples to support your opinion.

OHIO STANDARDS

READING STANDARD
3.4 Identify persuasive techniques

Vocabulary In Context

VOCABULARY PRACTICE

Decide whether each statement is true or false.

1. To **alleviate** a problem is to make it worse.
2. A **boisterous** child may disrupt a quiet restaurant.
3. If you have **complicity** in a crime, you had involvement in it.
4. An elegantly decorated room can be described as **stark.**
5. To speak **stridently** is to ask in a sweet, quiet manner.

WORD LIST
alleviate
boisterous
complicity
stark
stridently

VOCABULARY IN WRITING

Using at least two vocabulary words, write about an issue that has inspired public debate. Here is an example of how you might begin.

> **EXAMPLE SENTENCE**
>
> *For years politicians have **stridently** debated how to limit our country's dependence on imported fuel.*

VOCABULARY STRATEGY: ANALOGIES

Analogies express relationships between pairs of words. Some common relationships are described in the chart.

OHIO STANDARDS

VOCABULARY STANDARD
1.2 Analyze the relationships of pairs of words

Type	Relationship
Object to purpose	is used for
Synonyms	means the same as
Antonyms	means the opposite of
Cause to effect	results in or leads to
Grammar	is grammatically related to

PRACTICE Complete each analogy by choosing the appropriate vocabulary word. Identify the kind of relationship on which the analogy is based.

1. generosity : gratitude :: _____ : guilt
2. grateful : gratefully :: strident : _____
3. selfish : generous :: calm : _____
4. alarm : protect :: aspirin : _____
5. practical : useful :: bleak : _____

VOCABULARY PRACTICE
For more practice, go to the **Vocabulary Center** at ClassZone.com.

Reading-Writing Connection

Deepen your understanding of "I Acknowledge Mine" by responding to these prompts. Then use **Revision: Grammar and Style** to improve your writing.

WRITING PROMPTS	SELF-CHECK
A. Short Response: Write a Speech Suppose that Jane Goodall received an award for her efforts to help chimpanzees. Write a **one- or two-paragraph acceptance speech** for her, referring to experiences she describes in the selection.	*A strong speech will . . .* • summarize Goodall's observations of chimpanzees in laboratories • reflect the values she reveals in her essay
B. Extended Response: Analyze an Argument Write a **three-to-five-paragraph personal response** in which you analyze Goodall's argument and explain how it affected your view on **animal rights.**	*A thoughtful analysis will . . .* • clearly state a personal opinion on animal rights • evaluate Goodall's use of emotional appeals

REVISION: GRAMMAR AND STYLE

WRITING STANDARD
5.9 Use precise language: sensory details

SET THE TONE Review the **Grammar and Style** note on page 608. **Tone** is a writer's attitude toward a subject—humorous, angry, or sarcastic, for example—as expressed through **word choice, imagery,** and **formal** or **informal language.** In her writing, Goodall uses imagery and figurative language to express sadness and outrage over the treatment of chimpanzees. Note how she effectively uses nouns, adjectives, and participles to create disturbing images in the following example:

> *Here, in the lab, the world is concrete and steel; it is loud, horrible sounds, clanging bars, banging doors, and the deafening volume of chimpanzee calls confined in underground rooms.* (lines 251–253)

Notice how the revisions in red help to establish tone in this first draft. Revise your responses to the prompts by making sure your choice of language and use of imagery match the tone you want to convey.

STUDENT MODEL

These chimpanzees spend all day and night in confinement,ₐ *, like prisoners.*

When they look out from theirₐcages, ~~there is nothing to provide~~
small, dark   *they can only*
see a blank wall.
~~them with stimulation.~~

WRITING TOOLS
For prewriting, revision, and editing tools, visit the **Writing Center** at ClassZone.com.

Use of Animals in Biomedical Research

Position Paper by the American Medical Association

Do the E N D S
justify the means?

OHIO STANDARDS

READING STANDARDS
2.3 Monitor comprehension
3.5 Analyze an author's implicit and explicit argument

KEY IDEA You have read about Jane Goodall's objections to some aspects of **animal research.** In "Use of Animals in Biomedical Research," the American Medical Association addresses the issue of whether improving human health outweighs the suffering of animals in medical laboratories.

DISCUSS Think of a situation in which an unpleasant or disturbing action may lead to a worthy outcome. Create a balance scale like the one shown. Jot down the possible benefits of the action in one box and the harm caused by it in the other. Share your balance scale with your classmates, and discuss whether the possible benefits outweigh the harm.

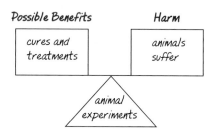

● ELEMENTS OF NONFICTION: COUNTERARGUMENTS

Although the American Medical Association is firmly in favor of using animals in research, it does not ignore the views of opponents. Instead, it states the opponents' views and then disputes them with **counterarguments.** As you read "Use of Animals in Biomedical Research," use a chart like the one shown to keep track of counterarguments in the selection.

Opposing Viewpoint	Counterargument	Support for Counterargument
Animal experimentation isn't needed.	Most modern medical advances have required such experiments.	Many Nobel Prizes have been awarded for medical research involving animals.

● READING STRATEGY: MONITOR

When you **monitor** as you read, you check your comprehension and use strategies to improve it. For example, if you find an argument difficult to follow, you might slow your reading pace. The following strategies may be helpful for reading "Use of Animals in Biomedical Research":

- Ask questions about ideas in the text, and read to find the answers.
- Reread difficult passages. Paraphrase if necessary.

As you read, note passages or words that are unclear to you, and use these strategies to increase your understanding.

▲ VOCABULARY IN CONTEXT

Figure out the meaning of each word from the context provided, and write a sentence that shows your understanding.

1. support from a **proponent** of this plan
2. a **speculative** and unreliable conclusion
3. a speech full of insincere **rhetoric**
4. obstacles that **impede** our progress

Background

American Medical Association
Founded in Philadelphia in 1847, the American Medical Association (AMA) is the largest professional organization for physicians in the United States. The AMA identifies its core purpose as the promotion of "the science and art of medicine and the betterment of public health." The AMA formulates policies on a wide range of health care and ethical issues, such as tobacco use and discrimination against AIDS patients. Many important studies have been published in the prestigious *Journal of the American Medical Association.*

Animal Rights Versus Animal Welfare
Discussions of animal protection often distinguish between the animal rights and animal welfare movements. Animal rights advocates believe that all experimentation on animals is wrong, even if it relieves human suffering. According to People for the Ethical Treatment of Animals (PETA), the world's largest animal rights organization, "animals, like humans, have interests that cannot be sacrificed or traded away just because it might benefit others.... Animals are not ours to use for food, clothing, entertainment, or experimentation." Animal welfare advocates, on the other hand, do not entirely rule out the use of animals in research, but they believe that the animals should be treated as humanely as possible. The animal welfare movement also calls for a reduction in the numbers of animals used in research and for the development of experimental procedures that do not require animals.

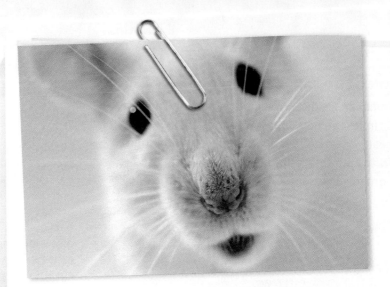

Use of Animals in Biomedical Research

American Medical Association

Animals have been used in experiments for at least 2,000 years, with the first reference made in the third century B.C. in Alexandria, Egypt, when the philosopher and scientist Erisistratus used animals to study body functions.

Five centuries later, the Roman physician Galen used apes and pigs to prove his theory that veins carry blood rather than air. In succeeding centuries, animals were employed to discover how the body functions or to confirm or disprove theories developed through observation. Advances in knowledge made through these experiments included Harvey's demonstration of the circulation of blood in 1622, the effect of anesthesia on the body in 1846, and the relationship between bacteria and disease in 1878.

Today, animals are used in experiments for three general purposes: (1) biomedical and behavioral research, (2) education, (3) drug and product testing. . . . Biomedical research increases understanding of how biological systems function and advances medical knowledge. . . . Educational experiments are conducted to educate and train students in medicine, veterinary medicine, physiology,[1] and general science. In many instances, these experiments are conducted with dead animals. . . . Animals also are employed to determine the safety and efficacy[2] of new drugs or the toxicity[3] of chemicals to which humans or animals may be exposed. Most of these experiments are conducted by commercial firms to fulfill government requirements. . . . **A**

Use of Animals Rather than Humans

A basic assumption of all types of research is that man should relieve human and animal suffering. One objection to the use of animals in

A MONITOR
What additional information might help you understand lines 20–39?

---

1. **physiology** (fĭz'ē-ŏl'ə-jē): a branch of biology that deals with the functioning of organisms.

2. **efficacy** (ĕf'ĭ-kə-sē): the capacity to produce a desired effect.

3. **toxicity** (tŏk-sĭs'ĭ-tē): the quality of being poisonous or harmful.

biomedical research is that the animals are used as surrogates for human beings. This objection presumes the equality of all forms of life; animal rights advocates argue that if the tests are for the benefit of man, then man should serve as the subject of the experiments. There are limitations, however, to the use of human subjects both ethically, such as in the testing of a potentially toxic drug or chemical, and in terms of what can be learned. The process of aging, for instance, can best be observed through experiments with rats, which live an average of two to three years, or with some types of monkeys, which live 15 to 20 years. Some experiments require numerous subjects of the same weight or genetic makeup or require special diets or physical environments; these conditions make the use of human subjects difficult or impossible. By using animals in such tests, researchers can observe subjects of uniform age and background in sufficient numbers to determine if findings are consistent and applicable to a large population. **B**

Animals are important in research precisely because they have complex body systems that react and interact with stimuli much as humans do. The more true this is with a particular animal, the more valuable that animal is for a particular type of research. One important property to a researcher is discrimination—the extent to which an animal exhibits the particular quality to be investigated. The greater the degree of discrimination, the greater the reliability and predictability of the information gathered from the experiment.

For example, dogs have been invaluable in biomedical research because of the relative size of their organs compared to humans. The first successful kidney transplant was performed in a dog, and the techniques used to save the lives of "blue babies," babies with structural defects in their hearts, were developed with dogs. Open-heart surgical techniques, coronary bypass surgery,[4] and heart transplantation all were developed using dogs.

Another important factor is the amount of information available about a particular animal. Mice and rats play an extensive role in research and testing, in part because repeated experiments and controlled breeding have created a pool of data to which the findings from a new experiment can be related and given meaning. Their rapid rate of reproduction also has made them important in studies of genetics and other experiments that require observation over a number of generations. Moreover, humans cannot be bred to produce "inbred strains"[5] as can be done with animals; therefore, humans cannot be substituted for animals in studies where an inbred strain is essential. **C**

Scientists argue repeatedly that research is necessary to reduce human and animal suffering and disease. Biomedical advances depend on research with animals, and not using them would be unethical because it would deprive humans and animals of the benefits of research. . . .

Benefits of Animal Experimentation

The arguments advanced by animal rights activists in opposing the use of animals in biomedical research . . . are scientific, emotional, and philosophic. . . . The scientific challenge raised by animal rights activists goes to the heart

B COUNTERARGUMENTS
What counterargument is given to dispute the view that humans should be the subjects of experiments that benefit humans?

C MONITOR
How would you paraphrase the main idea in lines 110–114?

---

4. **coronary bypass surgery:** open-heart surgery to improve the blood supply to the heart.

5. **inbred strains:** groups of animals produced by the mating of siblings over at least 20 generations, resulting in individuals as genetically similar as possible.

of the issue by asking whether animal experiments are necessary for scientific and medical progress and whether all the experiments being performed and all the animals being used are justified and required. Scientists insist that they are; animal rights activists insist that they are not.

Scientists justify use of animals in biomedical research on two grounds: the contribution that the information makes to human and animal health and welfare, and the lack of any alternative way to gain the information and knowledge. Animal rights activists contest experiments that utilize animals on both these grounds and assert that this practice no longer is necessary because alternative methods of experimentation exist for obtaining the same information. **D**

In an appearance on the *Today* show in 1985, Ingrid Newkirk, representing People for the Ethical Treatment of Animals (PETA), stated: "If it were such a valuable way to gain knowledge, we should have eternal life by now." This statement is similar in spirit to one made in 1900 by an antivivisectionist[6] who stated that, given the number of experiments on the brain done up to then, the insane asylums of Washington, D.C. should be empty.

Scientists believe that such assertions miss the point. The issue is not what *has not* been accomplished by animal use in biomedical research, but what *has* been accomplished. A longer life span has been achieved, decreased infant mortality[7] has occurred, effective treatments have been developed for many diseases, and the quality of life has been enhanced for mankind in general.

One demonstration of the critical role that animals play in medical and scientific advances is that 54 of 76 Nobel Prizes awarded in physiology or medicine since 1901 have been for discoveries and advances made through the use of experimental animals. Among these have been the Prize awarded in 1985 for the studies (using dogs) that documented the relationship between cholesterol and heart disease; the 1966 Prize for the studies (using chickens) that linked viruses and cancer; and the 1960 Prize for studies (using cattle, mice, and chicken embryos) that established that a body can be taught to accept tissue from different donors if it is inoculated[8] with different types of tissue prior to birth or during the first year of life, a finding expected to help simplify and advance organ transplants in the future. Studies using animals also resulted in successful culture of the poliomyelitis[9] virus; a Nobel Prize was awarded for this work in 1954. The discovery of insulin and treatment of diabetes, achieved through experiments using dogs, also earned the Prize in 1923.

In fact, virtually every advance in medical science in the 20th century, from antibiotics and vaccines to antidepressant drugs and organ transplants, has been achieved either directly or indirectly through the use of animals in laboratory experiments. The result of these experiments has been the elimination or control of many infectious diseases—smallpox, poliomyelitis, measles—and the development of numerous life-saving techniques—blood transfusions, burn therapy, open-heart and brain surgery.

D MONITOR
Reread lines 137–148. What questions do you have about the ideas in this passage?

---

6. **antivivisectionist** (ăn′tē-vĭv′ĭ-sĕk′shən-ĭst): someone opposed to the act of operating on live animals for science experiments.

7. **infant mortality:** the death rate during the first year of life.

8. **inoculated** (ĭ-nŏk′yə-lā′tĭd): injected.

9. **poliomyelitis** (pō′lē-ō-mī′ə-lī′tĭs): a highly infectious viral disease that generally affects children and may lead to paralysis and deformity. Also called *polio*.

A boy is vaccinated for polio in 1955 under the gaze of his sister, who became paralyzed from a polio infection. The first polio vaccine was developed through experiments on animals.

This has meant a longer, healthier, better life with much less pain and suffering. For many, it has meant life itself. Often forgotten in the **rhetoric** is the fact that humans *do* participate in biomedical research in the form of clinical trials. They experience pain and are injured, 220 and in fact, some of them die from this participation. Hence, scientists are not asking animals to be "guinea pigs" alone for the glory of science. . . . **E**

Scientists feel that it is essential for the public to understand that had scientific research been restrained in the first decade of the 20th century as antivivisectionists and activists were then and are today urging, many millions of 230 Americans alive and healthy today would never have been born or would have suffered a premature death. Their parents or grandparents would have died from diphtheria, scarlet fever, tuberculosis, diabetes, appendicitis, and countless other diseases and disorders. . . .

The Danger of Restricting Research

The activities and arguments of animal rights and animal welfare activists and organizations present the American 240 people with some fundamental decisions that must be made regarding the use of animals in biomedical research.

The fundamental issue raised by the philosophy of the animal rights movement is whether man has the right to use animals in a way that causes them to suffer and die. To accept the philosophical and moral viewpoint of the animal rights movement would require a total ban 250 on the use of animals in any scientific research and testing. The consequences of such a step were set forth by the Office of Technology Assessment (OTA) in its report to Congress: "Implementation of this option would effectively arrest most basic biomedical and behavioral research and toxicological testing in the United States." The economic and public health consequences of that, the OTA warned 260 Congress, "are so unpredictable and **speculative** that this course of action should be considered dangerous." **F**

No nation and no jurisdiction within the United States has yet adopted such a ban. Although . . . laws to ban the use of animals in biomedical research have been introduced into a number of state legislatures, neither a majority of the American people nor their elected representatives 270 have ever supported these bills.

Another aspect of the use of animals in biomedical research that has received little consideration is the economic consequences of regulatory change. Clearly, other nations are not curtailing the use of animals to any significant degree. Some of these, like Japan, are major competi-

rhetoric (rĕt'ər-ĭk) *n.* grand but empty talk

E COUNTERARGUMENTS
What opposing viewpoints are disputed in lines 200–223?

speculative (spĕk'yə-lə-tĭv) *adj.* based on guesses and theories rather than fact

F MONITOR
What strategy would you use to gain a deeper understanding of lines 251–262?

◆ **GRAMMAR AND STYLE**
Reread lines 313–325.
Because this is a paper
written for a professional
audience, it contains
elements of **formal
language,** including
complex vocabulary
and sentence structure,
standard punctuation,
and a lack of contractions.

proponent (prə-pō′nənt)
n. a person who pleads for
or supports a cause

impede (ĭm-pēd′) *v.* to
obstruct or hinder

⬤ **COUNTERARGUMENTS**
What counterargument
is made in response
to the animal welfare
movement in lines
326–336?

tors of the United States in biomedical research. Given the economic climate
280 in the United States, our massive trade imbalance, and our loss of leadership in many areas, can the United States afford not to keep a leading industry, i.e., biomedical science, developing as rapidly as possible? Many nations are in positions to assume leadership roles, and the long-term economic impact on our citizens could be profound. This economic impact would be expressed in
290 many ways, not the least of which would certainly be a reduction in the quality and number of health services available for people who need them.

Through polls and by other means, the American people have indicated that they support the use of animals in research and testing. At the same time they have expressed a strong wish that the animals be protected against
300 any unnecessary pain and suffering. The true question, therefore, is how to achieve this without interfering with the performance of necessary research. Scientists already comply with a host of federal, state, municipal, and institutional guidelines and laws. However, in this era of cost containment, they fear that overregulation will become so costly that research progress will suffer.
310 Scientists emphasize that a reasonable balance must be achieved between increased restrictions and increased cost.

What must be recognized, say scientists, is that it is not possible to protect all animals against pain and still conduct meaningful research. No legislation and no standard of humane care can eliminate this necessity. The only alternative is either to eliminate
320 the research, as animal rights adherents urge, and forego the knowledge and the benefits of health-related research that would result, or to inflict the pain

and suffering on human beings by using them as research subjects. ◆

The desire by animal welfare **proponents** to ensure maximum comfort and minimal pain to research animals is understandable and appeals
330 to scientists, the public, and to legislators. But what also must be recognized and weighed in the balance is the price paid in terms of human pain and suffering if overly protective measures are adopted that **impede** or prevent the use of animals in biomedical research. ⬤

In short, the American people should not be misled by emotional appeals and philosophic rhetoric on this issue.
340 Biomedical research using animals is essential to continued progress in clinical medicine. Animal research holds the key for solutions to AIDS, cancer, heart disease, aging, and congenital defects.[10] In discussing legislation concerning animal experimentation, the prominent physician and physiologist Dr. Walter B. Cannon stated in 1896 that ". . . the antivivisectionists are the second of the
350 two types Theodore Roosevelt described when he said, 'Common sense without conscience may lead to crime, but conscience without common sense may lead to folly, which is the handmaiden of crime.'"

The American Medical Association has been an outspoken proponent of biomedical research for over 100 years, and that tradition continues today.
360 The Association believes that research involving animals is absolutely essential to maintaining and improving the health of the American people. The Association is opposed to any legislation or regulation that would inappropriately limit such research, and actively supports all legislative efforts to ensure the continued use of animals in research, while providing for their humane treatment.

---

10. **congenital defects:** defects present at birth.

Comprehension

1. **Recall** What is the AMA's position on the use of animals in medical research?

2. **Recall** How important has **animal research** been to medical science?

3. **Clarify** How do the animal rights and animal welfare movements differ from each other?

4. **Summarize** According to the AMA, what consequences will result from banning or restricting the use of animals in medical experiments?

OHIO STANDARDS

READING STANDARD
2.3 Monitor comprehension

Critical Analysis

5. **Recognize Monitoring Techniques** Identify the passage in the selection that you found most difficult to understand. Discuss how one or more strategies helped you monitor your comprehension of the passage.

6. **Interpret Statements** Reread lines 301–336. Does the AMA favor any changes in current practice to minimize the pain and suffering of research animals? Give reasons for your interpretation.

7. **Draw Conclusions** What values have influenced the AMA's position on animal research? Cite evidence to support your conclusion.

8. **Make Judgments** Does the AMA fairly represent the opposing viewpoints of the animal rights movement in this paper? Explain why or why not.

9. **Evaluate Support** Consider the **reasons** and **evidence** that the AMA gives to support the view that animal research is necessary for medical science. Does the AMA provide sufficient support for its claim? Explain your opinion.

10. **Evaluate Counterargument** Supporters of animal rights argue that it is morally wrong for humans to use animals in a way that causes them to suffer or die. Review the chart you created as you read. Does the AMA offer a satisfactory counterargument to this viewpoint? Cite evidence to support your opinion.

11. **Compare Texts** The AMA's position on animal research differs greatly from the views expressed by Jane Goodall in "I Acknowledge Mine." Compare and contrast the techniques that the AMA and Goodall use to persuade readers.

Vocabulary in Context

VOCABULARY PRACTICE

Choose the word from the list that best completes each sentence.

1. Until we get the facts from the proper sources, everything is _____.
2. Concrete actions speak louder than empty _____.
3. As a _____ of conservation, she signed a petition for the preservation of wetlands.
4. I do not want to _____ your work, so please let me know if I'm a distraction.

WORD LIST
impede
proponent
rhetoric
speculative

VOCABULARY IN WRITING

Using two or more vocabulary words, write about the importance of science in your life. Here is an example of how you might begin.

> **EXAMPLE SENTENCE**
>
> I am a **proponent** of increased funding for science education because I believe that people need to make informed decisions about scientific issues, such as the use of animals in research.

VOCABULARY STRATEGY: CONNOTATION

A word's **connotation** is the overtone of meaning that it has beyond its basic meaning. Some connotations may be positive or negative. For example, although the nouns *rhetoric* and *discourse* can both be used to refer to written or oral expression in language, *rhetoric* can have a negative connotation because it can suggest language that is empty or insincere. When you choose words in writing, be sure to consider whether their connotations fit the context.

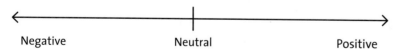

OHIO STANDARDS

VOCABULARY STANDARD
1.2 Analyze the relationships of pairs of words

PRACTICE Place the words in each group on a continuum like the one shown, to identify whether they have positive, negative, or neutral connotations. Then compare your answers with those of a classmate.

Negative   Neutral   Positive

1. sentimental, overemotional, romantic
2. childlike, youthful, immature
3. thrifty, economical, stingy
4. strange, quaint, peculiar

VOCABULARY PRACTICE
For more practice, go to the **Vocabulary Center** at **ClassZone.com**.

Reading-Writing Connection

Explore the ideas presented in "Use of Animals in Biomedical Research" by responding to these prompts. Then use **Revision: Grammar and Style** to improve your writing.

WRITING PROMPTS	SELF-CHECK
A. Short Response: Write a Speech Suppose that you were invited to speak at the opening of a new medical research laboratory. Write a **one- or two-paragraph speech** in which you discuss the benefits of **animal research.**	*An effective speech will . . .* • explain why animals are used in medical research • include information from the selection on achievements made possible by animal research
B. Extended Response: Write a Letter How do you feel about animal rights, animal welfare, and the use of animals in experiments? Write a **three-to-five-paragraph letter** to the AMA in which you express your views on these issues.	*A strong letter will . . .* • clearly state your personal views • provide reasons and evidence to support those views

REVISION: GRAMMAR AND STYLE

CONSIDER AUDIENCE Review the **Grammar and Style** note on page 624. When deciding how to craft a particular piece of writing, it is important to consider your audience. For example, your writing style in an e-mail to a friend will probably differ from the style you use in a research paper. For most school and business communication, you should use **formal language.** Typically, this style of language does not contain contractions and consists of standard punctuation and more complex vocabulary and sentence structure. Here is an example of how the American Medical Association uses formal language in its position paper.

> *Animal rights activists contest experiments that utilize animals on both these grounds and assert that this practice no longer is necessary because alternative methods of experimentation exist for obtaining the same information.* (lines 143–148)

Notice how the revisions in red create a more formal writing style. Use similar methods to revise your responses to the prompts.

OHIO STANDARDS

WRITING STANDARD
5.4 Plan strategies to address purpose and audience

STUDENT MODEL

This wonderful new research facility is part of a tradition that goes back *hundreds of years. Many* ~~a long ways. Lots of~~ people contributed to its completion. ~~This~~ *which* shows

that support for science remains strong.

WRITING TOOLS
For prewriting, revision, and editing tools, visit the **Writing Center** at ClassZone.com.

A Chip of Glass Ruby
Short Story by Nadine Gordimer

What would you SACRIFICE *for justice?*

OHIO STANDARDS

READING STANDARDS
2.1 Draw conclusions

4.6 Explain how literary techniques are used to shape the plot

KEY IDEA During times of injustice, change often comes from ordinary people who are willing to **sacrifice** their comfort or security to stand up for an ideal. "A Chip of Glass Ruby" portrays one such person, a housewife who struggles against South Africa's system of racial segregation.

QUICKWRITE Make a list of important problems in society. Choose the problem that you care about the most, and write a paragraph explaining what you would be willing to sacrifice to help overcome it.

Problems
1. Homelessness
2. Racism
3.
4.
5.

● LITERARY ANALYSIS: THEME AND PERSUASION

Just as essayists and speech writers can **persuade** readers to take action or adopt a certain position, fiction writers can persuade readers to feel differently about important issues. By creating stories in which characters must grapple with injustice, for example, a fiction writer can develop important **themes** about society and its values.

As you read "A Chip of Glass Ruby," notice how Nadine Gordimer makes use of narrative techniques to tell a story that is both interesting and persuasive.

● READING SKILL: DRAW CONCLUSIONS

When you **draw conclusions** about a character in a story, you use information from the story and your own prior knowledge to make judgments. For example, if a character often exaggerates his own problems and does not show sympathy for other characters, you would probably conclude that the character is self-centered.

As you read "A Chip of Glass Ruby," note the behavior of the main characters and their attitudes toward events. Use a chart like the one shown to organize your observations.

Event	Behavior/Attitude	
	Bamjee	Mrs. Bamjee
Arrival of duplicating machine		

▲ VOCABULARY IN CONTEXT

Gordimer uses the following boldfaced words to help illuminate the faults of racial segregation in South Africa. Use context clues to determine the meaning of these words.

1. I was **disarmed** by his friendly smile.
2. She looked **morose** after hearing the bad news.
3. Don't **patronize** people just because they lack experience.
4. The stranger's **presumption** caused great offense.
5. His fine **repute** was ruined by scandal.

Author Online

A Voice Against Racism One of South Africa's leading authors, Nadine Gordimer often explores the destructive influence of racism on people's daily lives. Gordimer's highly acclaimed novels and short stories deliver a powerful political message; several of her books were banned in her homeland for many years. Although Gordimer has stated that she does not consider herself to be a political writer, she recognizes that her work has been strongly affected by the extreme politics she experienced in South Africa when it was racially segregated. Gordimer won the Nobel Prize in literature in 1991.

Nadine Gordimer born 1923

 MORE ABOUT THE AUTHOR For more on Nadine Gordimer, visit the **Literature Center** at ClassZone.com.

Background

Life Under Apartheid "A Chip of Glass Ruby" is set in South Africa during the period of apartheid, a system of racial segregation and discrimination that was formally established in the 1950s. Every citizen was classified as either white, colored (mixed race), Asian (of East Indian ancestry), or Bantu (native black). Strictly enforced laws set limits on the lives of the nonwhite majority. The Group Areas Act forced nonwhites to live in certain areas, and "pass laws" required black South Africans to carry passes identifying where they could and could not go. Although Asians did not have to carry passes, their movements were restricted. For decades, activists struggled to overturn apartheid. Many blacks died during strikes and protests; others were imprisoned. Apartheid was officially abolished in 1991.

A Chip of Glass Ruby

Nadine Gordimer

When the duplicating machine was brought into the house, Bamjee said, "Isn't it enough that you've got the Indians' troubles on your back?" Mrs. Bamjee said, with a smile that showed the gap of a missing tooth but was confident all the same, "What's the difference, Yusuf? We've all got the same troubles."

"Don't tell me that. We don't have to carry passes; let the natives protest against passes on their own; there are millions of them. Let them go ahead with it." **A**

The nine Bamjee and Pahad children were present at this exchange as they were always; in the small house that held them all there was no room for
10 privacy for the discussion of matters they were too young to hear, and so they had never been too young to hear anything. Only their sister and half-sister, Girlie, was missing; she was the eldest, and married. The children looked expectantly, unalarmed and interested, at Bamjee, who had neither left the room nor settled down again to the task of rolling his own cigarettes, which had been interrupted by the arrival of the duplicator. He had looked at the thing that had come hidden in a washbasket and conveyed in a black man's taxi, and the children turned on it too, their black eyes surrounded by thick lashes like those still, open flowers with hairy tentacles that close on whatever touches them.

A DRAW CONCLUSIONS
How do Bamjee and Mrs. Bamjee differ in their attitudes toward native black people?

Untitled, Chandragupta
Thenuwara. Oil on canvas/bayvon.com.

20   "A fine thing to have on the table where we eat," was all he said at last. They smelled the machine among them; a smell of cold black grease. He went out, heavily on tiptoe, in his troubled way.

    "It's going to go nicely on the sideboard!" Mrs. Bamjee was busy making a place by removing the two pink glass vases filled with plastic carnations and the hand-painted velvet runner with the picture of the Taj Mahal.[1]

    After supper she began to run off leaflets on the machine. The family lived in that room—the three other rooms in the house were full of beds—and they were all there. The older children shared a bottle of ink while they did their homework, and the two little ones pushed a couple of empty milk bottles in

30 and out the chair legs. The three-year-old fell asleep and was carted away by one of the girls. They all drifted off to bed eventually; Bamjee himself went before the older children—he was a fruit-and-vegetable hawker[2] and was up at half past four every morning to get to the market by five. "Not long now," said Mrs. Bamjee. The older children looked up and smiled at him. He turned his back on her. She still wore the traditional clothing of a Moslem woman, and her body, which was scraggy and unimportant as a dress on a peg when it was not host to a child, was wrapped in the trailing rags of a cheap sari,[3] and her thin black plait was greased. When she was a girl, in the Transvaal[4] town where they lived still, her mother fixed a chip of glass ruby in her nostril; but she had

40 abandoned that adornment as too old-style, even for her, long ago.

    She was up until long after midnight, turning out leaflets. She did it as if she might have been pounding chilies.

Bamjee did not have to ask what the leaflets were. He had read the papers. All the past week Africans had been destroying their passes and then presenting themselves for arrest. Their leaders were jailed on charges of incitement,[5] campaign offices were raided—someone must be helping the few minor leaders who were left to keep the campaign going without offices or equipment. What was it the leaflets would say—"Don't go to work tomorrow," "Day of Protest," "Burn Your Pass for Freedom"? He didn't want to see. **B**

50   He was used to coming home and finding his wife sitting at the table deep in discussion with strangers or people whose names were familiar by **repute**. Some were prominent Indians, like the lawyer, Dr. Abdul Mohammed Khan, or the big businessman, Mr. Moonsamy Patel, and he was flattered, in a suspicious way, to meet them in his house. As he came home from work next day, he met Dr. Khan coming out of the house, and Dr. Khan—a highly educated man—said to him, "A wonderful woman." But Bamjee had never

B DRAW CONCLUSIONS
What does Bamjee's reaction to the leaflets suggest about him?

repute (rĭ-pyōot′) *n.* reputation; fame

---

1. **Taj Majal** (täzh mä-häl′): a beautiful white marble building in India.

2. **hawker:** a peddler who sells goods by calling out.

3. **sari** (sä′rē): a garment worn by East Indian women and girls, consisting of a long cloth wrapped around the body, with one end draped over the shoulder.

4. **Transvaal** (trăns-väl′): a province in northeast South Africa.

5. **charges of incitement:** accusations that the defendants have tried to persuade others to commit illegal actions.

caught his wife out in any **presumption;** she behaved properly, as any Moslem woman should, and once her business with such gentlemen was over would never, for instance, have sat down to eat with them. He found her now back in the kitchen, setting about the preparation of dinner and carrying on a conversation on several different wavelengths with the children. "It's really a shame if you're tired of lentils, Jimmy, because that's what you're getting—Amina, hurry up, get a pot of water going—don't worry, I'll mend that in a minute; just bring the yellow cotton, and there's a needle in the cigarette box on the sideboard."

"Was that Dr. Khan leaving?" said Bamjee.

"Yes, there's going to be a stay-at-home on Monday. Desai's ill, and he's got to get the word around by himself. Bob Jali was up all last night printing leaflets, but he's gone to have a tooth out." She had always treated Bamjee as if it were only a mannerism that made him appear uninterested in politics, the way some woman will persist in interpreting her husband's bad temper as an endearing gruffness hiding boundless goodwill, and she talked to him of these things just as she passed on to him neighbors' or family gossip.

"What for do you want to get mixed up with these killings and stonings and I don't know what? Congress[6] should keep out of it. Isn't it enough with the Group Areas?"

She laughed. "Now, Yusuf, you know you don't believe that. Look how you said the same thing when the Group Areas started in Natal. You said we should begin to worry when we get moved out of our own houses here in the Transvaal. And then your own mother lost her house in Noorddorp,[7] and there you are; you saw that nobody's safe. Oh, Girlie was here this afternoon; she says Ismail's brother's engaged—that's nice, isn't it? His mother will be pleased; she was worried." **C**

"Why was she worried?" asked Jimmy, who was fifteen, and old enough to **patronize** his mother.

"Well, she wanted to see him settled. There's a party on Sunday week at Ismail's place—you'd better give me your suit to give to the cleaners tomorrow, Yusuf."

One of the girls presented herself at once. "I'll have nothing to wear, Ma."

Mrs. Bamjee scratched her sallow face. "Perhaps Girlie will lend you her pink, eh? Run over to Girlie's place now and say I say will she lend it to you."

The sound of commonplaces often does service as security, and Bamjee, going to sit in the armchair with the shiny armrests that was wedged between the table and the sideboard, lapsed into an unthinking doze that, like all times of dreamlike ordinariness during those weeks, was filled with uneasy jerks and starts back into reality. The next morning, as soon as he got to market, he heard that Dr. Khan had been arrested. But that night Mrs. Bamjee sat up making a new dress for her daughter; the sight **disarmed** Bamjee, reassured him again, against his will, so that the resentment he had been making ready

Line numbers: 60, 70, 80, 90

presumption
(prĭ-zŭmp′shən) *n.*
behavior or language that is boldly arrogant or offensive

C THEME AND PERSUASION
Reread lines 66–83. What does this dialogue suggest about the responsibilities of individuals?

patronize (pā′trə-nīz′) *v.*
to behave in a manner that shows feelings of superiority

disarm (dĭs-ärm′) *v.* to win over; to make less hostile

---

6. **Congress:** the African National Congress (ANC), one of the main groups that opposed apartheid.

7. **Natal** (nə-tăl′) . . . **Noorddorp** (nōrt′dôrp): provinces in South Africa.

all day faded into a **morose** and accusing silence. Heaven knew, of course, who
100 came and went in the house during the day. Twice in that week of riots, raids,
and arrests, he found black women in the house when he came home; plain
ordinary native women in doeks,[8] drinking tea. This was not a thing other
Indian women would have in their homes, he thought bitterly; but then his
wife was not like other people, in a way he could not put his finger on, except
to say what it was not: not scandalous, not punishable, not rebellious. It was,
like the attraction that had led him to marry her, Pahad's widow with five
children, something he could not see clearly.

morose (mə-rōs') *adj.*
gloomy; sullen

When the Special Branch[9] knocked steadily on the door in the small
hours of Thursday morning, he did not wake up, for his return to
110 consciousness was always set in his mind to half past four, and that was more
than an hour away. Mrs. Bamjee got up herself, struggled into Jimmy's raincoat
which was hanging over a chair, and went to the front door. The clock on
the wall—a wedding present when she married Pahad—showed three o'clock
when she snapped on the light, and she knew at once who it was on the other
side of the door. Although she was not surprised, her hands shook like a very
old person's as she undid the locks and the complicated catch on the wire
burglar-proofing. And then she opened the door and they were there—two
colored policemen in plain clothes. "Zanip Bamjee?"
"Yes."
120 As they talked, Bamjee woke up in the sudden terror of having overslept.
Then he became conscious of men's voices. He heaved himself out of bed in
the dark and went to the window, which, like the front door, was covered
with a heavy mesh of thick wire against intruders from the dingy lane it
looked upon. Bewildered, he appeared in the room, where the policemen were
searching through a soapbox of papers beside the duplicating machine. "Yusuf,
it's for me," Mrs. Bamjee said.
At once, the snap of a trap, realization came. He stood there in an old shirt
before the two policemen, and the woman was going off to prison because of
the natives. "There you are!" he shouted, standing away from her. "That's what
130 you've got for it. Didn't I tell you? Didn't I? That's the end of it now. That's the
finish. That's what it's come to." She listened with her head at the slightest tilt
to one side, as if to ward off a blow, or in compassion.
Jimmy, Pahad's son, appeared at the door with a suitcase; two or three of the
girls were behind him. "Here, Ma, you take my green jersey." "I've found your
clean blouse." Bamjee had to keep moving out of their way as they helped their
mother to make ready. It was like the preparation for one of the family festivals
his wife made such a fuss over; wherever he put himself, they bumped into
him. Even the two policemen mumbled, "Excuse me," and pushed past into
the rest of the house to continue their search. They took with them a tome

ANALYZE VISUALS
How does the painting
reflect what is happening
in the story?

---

8. **doeks** (düks): cloth head coverings.

9. **Special Branch:** the South African secret police.

Untitled, Jagath Weerasinghe/bayvon.com.

A CHIP OF GLASS RUBY

140 that Nehru[10] had written in prison; it had been bought from a persevering traveling salesman and kept, for years, on the mantelpiece. "Oh, don't take that, please," Mrs. Bamjee said suddenly, clinging to the arm of the man who had picked it up.

The man held it away from her.

"What does it matter, Ma?"

It was true that no one in the house had ever read it; but she said, "It's for my children."

"Ma, leave it." Jimmy, who was squat and plump, looked like a merchant advising a client against a roll of silk she had set her heart on. She went into
150 the bedroom and got dressed. When she came out in her old yellow sari with a brown coat over it, the faces of the children were behind her like faces on the platform at a railway station. They kissed her goodbye. The policemen did not hurry her, but she seemed to be in a hurry just the same.

"What am I going to do?" Bamjee accused them all.

The policemen looked away patiently.

"It'll be all right. Girlie will help. The big children can manage. And Yusuf—" The children crowded in around her; two of the younger ones had awakened and appeared, asking shrill questions.

"Come on," said the policemen.

160 "I want to speak to my husband." She broke away and came back to him, and the movement of her sari hid them from the rest of the room for a moment. His face hardened in suspicious anticipation against the request to give some message to the next fool who would take up her pamphleteering until he, too, was arrested. "On Sunday," she said. "Take them on Sunday." He did not know what she was talking about. "The engagement party," she whispered, low and urgent. "They shouldn't miss it. Ismail will be offended." **D**

They listened to the car drive away. Jimmy bolted and barred the front door and then at once opened it again; he put on the raincoat that his mother had taken off. "Going to tell Girlie," he said. The children went back to bed. Their
170 father did not say a word to any of them; their talk, the crying of the younger ones and the argumentative voices of the older, went on in the bedrooms. He found himself alone; he felt the night all around him. And then he happened to meet the clock face and saw with a terrible sense of unfamiliarity that this was not the secret night but an hour he should have recognized: the time he always got up. He pulled on his trousers and his dirty white hawker's coat and wound his grey muffler up to the stubble on his chin and went to work.

The duplicating machine was gone from the sideboard. The policemen had taken it with them, along with the pamphlets and the conference reports and the stack of old newspapers that had collected on top of the
180 wardrobe in the bedroom—not the thick dailies of the white men but the

D DRAW CONCLUSIONS
What conclusions can you draw about Mrs. Bamjee based on her behavior in lines 160–166?

---

10. **Nehru** (nä′roo): Jawaharlal (jə-wä′hər-läl′) Nehru, nationalist leader in India's movement for self-governance and the first prime minister of independent India.

thin, impermanent-looking papers that spoke up, sometimes interrupted by suppression or lack of money, for the rest. It was all gone. When he had married her and moved in with her and her five children, into what had been the Pahad and became the Bamjee house, he had not recognized the humble, harmless, and apparently useless routine tasks—the minutes of meetings being written up on the dining-room table at night, the government blue books that were read while the latest baby was suckled, the employment of the fingers of the older children in the fashioning of crinkle-paper Congress rosettes—as activity intended to move mountains. For years and years he had not noticed it, and now it was gone.

The house was quiet. The children kept to their lairs, crowded on the beds with the doors shut. He sat and looked at the sideboard, where the plastic carnations and the mat with the picture of the Taj Mahal were in place. For the first few weeks he never spoke of her. There was the feeling, in the house, that he had wept and raged at her, that boulders of reproach had thundered down upon her absence, and yet he had said not one word. He had not been to inquire where she was; Jimmy and Girlie had gone to Mohammed Ebrahim, the lawyer, and when he found out that their mother had been taken—when she was arrested, at least—to a prison in the next town, they had stood about outside the big prison door for hours while they waited to be told where she had been moved from there. At last they had discovered that she was fifty miles away, in Pretoria.[11] Jimmy asked Bamjee for five shillings to help Girlie pay the train fare to Pretoria, once she had been interviewed by the police and had been given a permit to visit her mother; he put three two-shilling pieces on the table for Jimmy to pick up, and the boy, looking at him keenly, did not know whether the extra shilling meant anything, or whether it was merely that Bamjee had no change.

It was only when relations and neighbors came to the house that Bamjee would suddenly begin to talk. He had never been so expansive in his life as he was in the company of these visitors, many of them come on a polite call rather in the nature of a visit of condolence. "Ah, yes, yes, you can see how I am— you see what has been done to me. Nine children, and I am on the cart all day. I get home at seven or eight. What are you to do? What can people like us do?"

"Poor Mrs. Bamjee. Such a kind lady."

"Well, you see for yourself. They walk in here in the middle of the night and leave a houseful of children. I'm out on the cart all day; I've got a living to earn." Standing about in his shirtsleeves, he became quite animated; he would call for the girls to bring fruit drinks for the visitors. When they were gone, it was as if he, who was orthodox if not devout and never drank liquor, had been drunk and abruptly sobered up; he looked dazed and could not have gone over in his mind what he had been saying. And as he cooled, the lump of resentment and wrongedness stopped his throat again. **F**

E GRAMMAR AND STYLE
Reread lines 196–201. Notice how Gordimer forms a **compound-complex sentence** by connecting a series of independent and subordinate clauses.

F DRAW CONCLUSIONS
Reread lines 208–222. Why does Bamjee feel so resentful about his wife's imprisonment?

---

11. **Pretoria** (prĭ-tôr′ē-ə): the administrative capital of South Africa.

Bamjee found one of the little boys the center of a self-important group of championing brothers and sisters in the room one evening. "They've been cruel to Ahmed."

"What has he done?" said the father.

"Nothing! Nothing!" The little girl stood twisting her handkerchief excitedly.

An older one, thin as her mother, took over, silencing the others with a gesture of her skinny hand. "They did it at school today. They made an example of him."

230 "What is an example?" said Bamjee impatiently.

"The teacher made him come up and stand in front of the whole class, and he told them, 'You see this boy? His mother's in jail because she likes the natives so much. She wants the Indians to be the same as natives.' "

"It's terrible," he said. His hands fell to his sides. "Did she ever think of this?"

"That's why Ma's *there*," said Jimmy, putting aside his comic and emptying out his schoolbooks upon the table. "That's all the kids need to know. Ma's there because things like this happen. Petersen's a colored teacher, and it's his black blood that's brought him trouble all his life, I suppose. He hates anyone who says everybody's the same because that takes away from him his bit of whiteness that's

240 all he's got. What d'you expect? It's nothing to make too much fuss about." **G**

"Of course, you are fifteen and you know everything," Bamjee mumbled at him.

"I don't say that. But I know Ma, anyway." The boy laughed.

There was a hunger strike among the political prisoners, and Bamjee could not bring himself to ask Girlie if her mother was starving herself too. He would not ask; and yet he saw in the young woman's face the gradual weakening of her mother. When the strike had gone on for nearly a week, one of the elder children burst into tears at the table and could not eat. Bamjee pushed his own plate away in rage.

250 Sometimes he spoke out loud to himself while he was driving the vegetable lorry.[12] "What for?" Again and again: "What for?" She was not a modern woman who cut her hair and wore short skirts. He had married a good plain Moslem woman who bore children and stamped her own chilies. He had a sudden vision of her at the duplicating machine, that night just before she was taken away, and he felt himself maddened, baffled, and hopeless. He had become the ghost of a victim, hanging about the scene of a crime whose motive he could not understand and had not had time to learn.

The hunger strike at the prison went into the second week. Alone in the rattling cab of his lorry, he said things that he heard as if spoken by

260 someone else, and his heart burned in fierce agreement with them. "For a crowd of natives who'll smash our shops and kill us in our houses when their time comes." "She will starve herself to death there." "She will die there." "Devils who will burn and kill us." He fell into bed each night like a stone and dragged himself up in the mornings as a beast of burden is beaten to its feet.

---

12. **lorry:** truck.

G THEME AND PERSUASION
How does Jimmy view his mother's political activity?

One of these mornings, Girlie appeared very early, while he was wolfing bread and strong tea—alternate sensations of dry solidity and stinging heat—at the kitchen table. Her real name was Fatima, of course, but she had adopted the silly modern name along with the clothes of the young factory girls among whom she worked. She was expecting her first baby in a week or two, and her small face, her cut and curled hair, and the sooty arches drawn over her eyebrows did not seem to belong to her thrust-out body under a clean smock. She wore mauve lipstick and was smiling her cocky little white girl's smile, foolish and bold, not like an Indian girl's at all.

270

A Sketch of Two Figures at a Window, Nicholai Uvarov. 29.2 cm × 23.4 cm. Bonhams, London/Photo © Bridgeman Art Library.

"What's the matter?" he said.

She smiled again. "Don't you know? I told Bobby he must get me up in time this morning. I wanted to be sure I wouldn't miss you today."

"I don't know what you're talking about."

She came over and put her arm up around his unwilling neck and kissed the grey bristles at the side of his mouth. "Many happy returns! Don't you
280 know it's your birthday?"

"No," he said. "I didn't know, didn't think—" He broke the pause by swiftly picking up the bread and giving his attention desperately to eating and drinking. His mouth was busy, but his eyes looked at her, intensely black. She said nothing but stood there with him. She would not speak, and at last he said, swallowing a piece of bread that tore at his throat as it went down, "I don't remember these things."

The girl nodded, the Woolworth baubles in her ears swinging. "That's the first thing she told me when I saw her yesterday—don't forget it's Bajie's birthday tomorrow."

290 He shrugged over it. "It means a lot to children. But that's how she is. Whether it's one of the old cousins or the neighbor's grandmother, she always knows when the birthday is. What importance is my birthday, while she's sitting there in a prison? I don't understand how she can do the things she does when her mind is always full of woman's nonsense at the same time—that's what I don't understand with her." **H**

"Oh, but don't you see?" the girl said. "It's because she doesn't want anybody to be left out. It's because she always remembers; remembers everything— people without somewhere to live, hungry kids, boys who can't get educated— remembers all the time. That's how Ma is."

300 "Nobody else is like that." It was half a complaint.

"No, nobody else," said his stepdaughter.

She sat herself down at the table, resting her belly. He put his head in his hands. "I'm getting old"—but he was overcome by something much more curious, by an answer. He knew why he had desired her, the ugly widow with five children; he knew what way it was in which she was not like the others; it was there, like the fact of the belly that lay between him and her daughter. ❧

H DRAW CONCLUSIONS
How has Mrs. Bamjee been affected by her imprisonment?

Comprehension

1. **Recall** What political struggle is Mrs. Bamjee engaged in?

2. **Recall** How does Bamjee feel about his wife's political activities?

3. **Recall** What happens when the government finds out about Mrs. Bamjee's activities?

4. **Summarize** How do the members of Mrs. Bamjee's family react to what happens to her?

OHIO STANDARDS

READING STANDARD
2.1 Draw conclusions

Literary Analysis

5. **Examine Character Traits** What traits does Gordimer give Mrs. Bamjee to make her a sympathetic character? Identify the traits in a graphic organizer like the one shown.

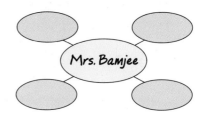

Mrs. Bamjee

6. **Analyze Theme** What main theme does Gordimer develop in the story to **persuade** readers? Is she successful? Support your responses.

7. **Interpret a Statement** Reread lines 296–299. What do you make of Girlie's explanation of Mrs. Bamjee's commitment to both her family and the anti-apartheid movement?

8. **Make Inferences** Reread lines 302–306. What does Bamjee come to realize about his feelings for his wife at the end of the story?

9. **Draw Conclusions** Review the chart you created as you read. What conclusion would you draw about the relationship between Bamjee and Mrs. Bamjee? Provide examples to support your conclusion.

10. **Make Judgments** Mrs. Bamjee's family makes **sacrifices** as a result of the government's actions against her. Should she have avoided political activity out of concern for their welfare? Give reasons for your opinion.

Literary Criticism

11. **Critical Interpretations** The critic Brigitte Weeks once wrote that "Gordimer insists that her readers face South African life as she does: with affection and horror." How might this statement apply to "A Chip of Glass Ruby"?

Vocabulary in Context

VOCABULRY PRACTICE

Choose the vocabulary word that is a synonym for each of the following words.

1. disrespect
2. fame
3. condescend
4. soothe
5. sullen

WORD LIST

disarm

morose

patronize

presumption

repute

VOCABULARY IN WRITING

Using three or more vocabulary words, write a description of a disagreement between two people. Here is how you might begin.

EXAMPLE SENTENCE

*The coach thought that Mike showed **presumption** in challenging his authority.*

VOCABULARY STRATEGY: USING A THESAURUS

A **thesaurus** is a book of synonyms and antonyms. You can use it to find a replacement for an overused word or to find a word with the precise shade of meaning that you need. The synonyms in a thesaurus entry are not always interchangeable. For example, *assumption* and *impudence* are both synonyms for the word *presumption,* but only *assumption* would be an appropriate replacement in the following sentence:

It is my presumption that the plane is late due to the bad weather.

OHIO STANDARDS

WRITING STANDARD
5.14 Use dictionaries and thesauruses to select effective and precise vocabulary

PRACTICE Use a thesaurus to find appropriate synonyms for the boldfaced words.

1. The judge was **partial** to the defendant in the case.
2. We received a generous **legacy** from our benefactor.
3. She spoke with impressive **gravity** on the topic.
4. I was completely **immersed** in my studies.
5. His comment **provoked** laughter in the audience.

VOCABULARY PRACTICE
For more practice, go to the **Vocabulary Center** at **ClassZone.com.**

Reading-Writing Connection

Explore the themes of "A Chip of Glass Ruby" by responding to these prompts. Then use **Revision: Grammar and Style** to improve your writing.

WRITING PROMPTS	SELF-CHECK
A. Short Response: Analyze Theme A character in one of Gordimer's novels says, "The real definition of loneliness is to live without responsibility." Write **one or two paragraphs** in which you discuss how this quotation relates to the main theme of "A Chip of Glass Ruby."	*A strong analysis will . . .* • include a statement of the story's theme • provide examples from the story that are relevant to the quotation
B. Extended Response: Write an Editorial Suppose that you were working for a South African newspaper at the time of Mrs. Bamjee's arrest. Write a **three-to-five-paragraph editorial** about Mrs. Bamjee's **sacrifice** in the fight against apartheid.	*A successful editorial will . . .* • summarize Mrs. Bamjee's political activities and the circumstances of her arrest • express an opinion about the government's actions

REVISION: GRAMMAR AND STYLE

VARY SENTENCE STRUCTURE Review the **Grammar and Style** note on page 637. A **compound-complex sentence** consists of two or more independent clauses and at least one subordinate clause. By using this particular sentence structure, Gordimer, in just one sentence, connects ideas and answers such questions as *where, why, when, what kind,* and *which one.* In the following example, notice how Gordimer combines a subordinate clause (in green) with a series of independent clauses (in yellow) to form a compound-complex sentence:

> When the Special Branch knocked steadily on the door in the small hours of Thursday morning, he did not wake up, for his return to consciousness was always set in his mind to half past four, and that was more than an hour away.
> (lines 108–111)

In the following student model, the revisions in red demonstrate how a series of simple sentences can be combined to form one compound-complex sentence. Note the use of independent and subordinate clauses, and make similar revisions in your responses to the prompts.

OHIO STANDARDS

WRITING STANDARD
5.7 Use a variety of sentence structures and lengths

STUDENT MODEL

Since
^Mrs. Bamjee has never done harm to anyone. ~~T~~here is no excuse for her
incarceration~~,~~ *, and* ^~~W~~e must recognize this extreme sacrifice on her part.

WRITING TOOLS
For prewriting, revision, and editing tools, visit the **Writing Center** at ClassZone.com.

How Much Land Does a Man Need?
Short Story by Leo Tolstoy

from The New Testament
Scriptural Writing

How important is WEALTH?

OHIO STANDARDS

READING STANDARDS
2.1 Apply reading comprehension strategies
4.5 Analyze how choice of genre affects theme or topic

KEY IDEA We all need a certain amount of money just to survive. But many people strive to achieve more than a basic level of comfort, and some can't be satisfied unless they are rich. The two selections you will read address the dangers of pursuing **wealth.**

DISCUSS Think of three activities that make you happy. Then discuss with a partner what role money plays in these activities. Consider whether you would find it easier or harder to pursue the activities if you were wealthy.

● LITERARY ANALYSIS: DIDACTIC LITERATURE

The short story and the Bible excerpt you are about to read are examples of **didactic literature**—literature intended mainly to instruct or to convey a moral message. Although both selections address how people are affected by the desire for wealth, they convey their messages on this topic through different methods. As you read, try to determine the moral message of each selection by paying attention to the following literary techniques:

In the Short Story	In the Bible Excerpt
plot and foreshadowing	direct statements
character traits and motivation	figurative language
irony	word choice and tone

Review: **Suspense**

● READING STRATEGY: SET A PURPOSE FOR READING

When you **set a purpose** for reading, you identify specific goals to accomplish as you read. In this case, you'll be asked, after reading these selections, to write an essay in which you compare each selection's message. As you read, keep the following goals in mind:

- to determine the moral message of each selection
- to identify similarities and differences in the two messages

Review: **Predict**

▲ VOCABULARY IN CONTEXT

To see how many words you already know, substitute a different word or phrase for each boldfaced term.

1. You should not praise people and then **disparage** them behind their backs.

2. The club meeting was friendly and free of **discord.**

3. I was so hungry that I could not **forbear** eating my lunch early.

4. He lay **prostrate** on the table during the doctor's exam.

Author Online

**Leo Tolstoy
1828–1910**

Rise to Fame Leo Tolstoy was born into an aristocratic Russian family. He became internationally famous for his novels *War and Peace* and *Anna Karenina,* which are among the finest ever written. However, shortly after *Anna Karenina* was published in 1877, Tolstoy suffered a profound spiritual crisis that led him to question whether his life and literary works had any meaning.

Tolstoy's New Faith As a result of his crisis, Tolstoy began preaching a personal faith that emphasized love of humanity and rejection of traditional authority. Tolstoy worked among the poor and simplified his own life in the belief that material possessions—money or land—were not the answer to society's problems. He also became a pacifist and a vegetarian. Tolstoy's new outlook on life is reflected in his later fiction, including "How Much Land Does a Man Need?"

 MORE ABOUT THE AUTHOR
For more on Leo Tolstoy, visit the **Literature Center** at ClassZone.com.

Background

The New Testament: Paul and His Letters Paul the Apostle dedicated his life to promoting Christianity in parts of Asia and Europe during the first century A.D. His letters to followers, which make up a good portion of the New Testament, helped shape Christian beliefs. The passage you will read is from a letter traditionally thought to have been written by Paul to his disciple Timothy.

How Much Land Does a Man *Need?*

Leo Tolstoy

❧ I ❧

An elder sister came to visit her younger sister in the country. The elder was married to a tradesman in town, the younger to a peasant in the village. As the sisters sat over their tea talking, the elder began to boast of the advantages of town life: saying how comfortably they lived there, how well they dressed, what fine clothes her children wore, what good things they ate and drank, and how she went to the theater, promenades, and entertainments.

The younger sister was piqued, and in turn **disparaged** the life of a tradesman, and stood up for that of a peasant.

"I would not change my way of life for yours," said she. "We may live
10 roughly, but at least we are free from anxiety. You live in better style than we do, but though you often earn more than you need, you are very likely to lose all you have. You know the proverb, 'Loss and gain are brothers twain.'[1] It often happens that people who are wealthy one day are begging their bread the next. Our way is safer. Though a peasant's life is not a fat one, it is a long one. We shall never grow rich, but we shall always have enough to eat." **Ⓐ**

The elder sister said sneeringly:

"Enough? Yes, if you like to share with the pigs and the calves! What do you know of elegance or manners! However much your goodman may slave, you will die as you are living—on a dung heap—and your children the same."

---

1. **twain:** two.

disparage (dĭ-spăr′ĭj) v. to speak of in a negative or insulting way

Ⓐ DIDACTIC LITERATURE
What values does the younger sister express in her speech? Cite specific words and phrases.

Late Night Guest (2002), A. Kurzov. Tradestone Gallery.

20   "Well, what of that?" replied the younger. "Of course our work is rough and coarse. But, on the other hand, it is sure, and we need not bow to any one. But you, in your towns, are surrounded by temptations; today all may be right, but tomorrow the Evil One may tempt your husband with cards, wine, or women, and all will go to ruin. Don't such things happen often enough?"

Pakhom, the master of the house, was lying on the top of the stove[2] and he listened to the women's chatter.

"It is perfectly true," thought he. "Busy as we are from childhood tilling[3] mother earth, we peasants have no time to let any nonsense settle in our heads. Our only trouble is that we haven't land enough. If I had plenty of land, I
30 shouldn't fear the Devil himself!"

The women finished their tea, chatted a while about dress, and then cleared away the tea-things and lay down to sleep.

But the Devil had been sitting behind the stove, and had heard all that was said. He was pleased that the peasant's wife had led her husband into boasting, and that he had said that if he had plenty of land he would not fear the Devil himself.

"All right," thought the Devil. "We will have a tussle. I'll give you land enough; and by means of that land I will get you into my power."

~ II ~

C lose to the village there lived a lady, a small landowner who had an
40 estate of about three hundred acres. She had always lived on good terms with the peasants until she engaged as her steward[4] an old soldier, who took to burdening the people with fines. However careful Pakhom tried to be, it happened again and again that now a horse of his got among the lady's oats, now a cow strayed into her garden, now his calves found their way into her meadows—and he always had to pay a fine.

Pakhom paid up, but grumbled, and going home in a temper, was rough with his family. All through that summer, Pakhom had much trouble because of this steward, and he was even glad when winter came and the cattle had to be stabled. Though he grudged the fodder[5] when they could no longer graze
50 on the pasture-land, at least he was free from anxiety about them.

In the winter the news got about that the lady was going to sell her land and that the keeper of the inn on the high road was bargaining for it. When the peasants heard this they were very much alarmed.

---

2. **Pakhom** (pâ-kōm′) . . . **lying on the top of the stove:** The stoves and ovens in Russian peasant homes had large tops that were often used for sleeping because they provided extra warmth.

3. **tilling:** plowing land to prepare it for planting.

4. **steward:** a person in charge of the household affairs of a large estate.

5. **fodder:** food for livestock, such as hay or straw.

"Well," thought they, "if the innkeeper gets the land, he will worry us with fines worse than the lady's steward. We all depend on that estate."

So the peasants went on behalf of their commune,[6] and asked the lady not to sell the land to the innkeeper, offering her a better price for it themselves. The lady agreed to let them have it. Then the peasants tried to arrange for the commune to buy the whole estate, so that it might be held by them all in

60 common. They met twice to discuss it, but could not settle the matter; the Evil One sowed **discord** among them and they could not agree. So they decided to buy the land individually, each according to his means; and the lady agreed to this plan as she had to the other.

Presently Pakhom heard that a neighbor of his was buying fifty acres, and that the lady had consented to accept one half in cash and to wait a year for the other half. Pakhom felt envious.

"Look at that," thought he, "the land is all being sold, and I shall get none of it." So he spoke to his wife.

"Other people are buying," said he, "and we must also buy twenty acres

70 or so. Life is becoming impossible. That steward is simply crushing us with his fines."

So they put their heads together and considered how they could manage to buy it. They had one hundred rubles[7] laid by. They sold a colt and one half of their bees, hired out one of their sons as a laborer and took his wages in advance; borrowed the rest from a brother-in-law, and so scraped together half the purchase money.

Having done this, Pakhom chose out a farm of forty acres, some of it wooded, and went to the lady to bargain for it. They came to an agreement, and he shook hands with her upon it and paid her a deposit in advance. Then

80 they went to town and signed the deeds; he paying half the price down, and undertaking to pay the remainder within two years.

So now Pakhom had land of his own. He borrowed seed, and sowed it on the land he had bought. The harvest was a good one, and within a year he had managed to pay off his debts both to the lady and to his brother-in-law. So he became a landowner, plowing and sowing his own land, making hay on his own land, cutting his own trees, and feeding his cattle on his own pasture. When he went out to plow his fields, or to look at his growing corn, or at his grass-meadows, his heart would fill with joy. The grass that grew and the flowers that bloomed there seemed to him unlike any that grew elsewhere.

90 Formerly, when he had passed by that land, it had appeared the same as any other land, but now it seemed quite different. **B**

discord (dĭs'kôrd') *n.* disagreement; lack of harmony

B PREDICT
Will Pakhom remain content with the land that he has purchased? Why or why not?

---

6. **commune:** in late 19th-century Russia, a local organization of peasants that held land in common for its members. A peasant could also own land individually while still belonging to the commune.

7. **rubles** (rōō'bəlz): The ruble is the basic monetary unit of Russia.

∼ III ∼

So Pakhom was well-contented, and everything would have been right if the neighboring peasants would only not have trespassed on his corn-fields and meadows. He appealed to them most civilly, but they still went on: now the communal herdsmen would let the village cows stray into his meadows, then horses from the night pasture would get among his corn. Pakhom turned them out again and again, and forgave their owners, and for a long time he **forbore** to prosecute any one. But at last he lost patience and complained to the district court. He knew it was the peasants' want of land, and no evil intent on their part, that caused the trouble, but he thought:

"I cannot go on overlooking it or they will destroy all I have. They must be taught a lesson."

So he had them up, gave them one lesson, and then another, and two or three of the peasants were fined. After a time Pakhom's neighbors began to bear him a grudge for this, and would now and then let their cattle on to his land on purpose. One peasant even got into Pakhom's wood at night and cut down five young lime trees for their bark. Pakhom passing through the wood one day noticed something white. He came nearer and saw the stripped trunks lying on the ground, and close by stood the stumps where the trees had been. Pakhom was furious.

forbear (fôr-bâr') *v.* to refrain from; resist

Woodland Scenery with Cows, Ivanchuk.
Vika's Russia Direct.

"If he had only cut one here and there it would have been bad enough," thought Pakhom, "but the rascal has actually cut down a whole clump. If I could only find out who did this, I would pay him out."[8]

He racked his brains as to who it could be. Finally he decided: "It must be Simon—no one else could have done it." So he went to Simon's homestead to have a look round, but he found nothing, and only had an angry scene. However, he now felt more certain than ever that Simon had done it, and he lodged a complaint. Simon was summoned. The case was tried, and retried, and at the end of it all Simon was acquitted, there being no evidence against
120 him. Pakhom felt still more aggrieved, and let his anger loose upon the elder and the judges.

"You let thieves grease your palms,"[9] said he. "If you were honest folk yourselves you would not let a thief go free."

So Pakhom quarreled with the judges and with his neighbors. Threats to burn his building began to be uttered. So though Pakhom had more land, his place in the commune was much worse than before. **C**

About this time a rumor got about that many people were moving to new parts.

"There's no need for me to leave my land," thought Pakhom. "But some of
130 the others might leave our village and then there would be more room for us. I would take over their land myself and make my estate a bit bigger. I could then live more at ease. As it is, I am still too cramped to be comfortable."

One day Pakhom was sitting at home when a peasant, passing through the village, happened to call in. He was allowed to stay the night, and supper was given him. Pakhom had a talk with this peasant and asked him where he came from. The stranger answered that he came from beyond the Volga[10] where he had been working. One word led to another, and the man went on to say that many people were settling in those parts. He told how some people from his village had settled there. They had joined the commune, and had had twenty-
140 five acres per man granted them. The land was so good, he said, that the rye sown on it grew as high as a horse, and so thick that five cuts of a sickle made a sheaf. One peasant, he said, had brought nothing with him but his bare hands, and now he had six horses and two cows of his own.

Pakhom's heart kindled with desire. He thought:

"Why should I suffer in this narrow hole, if one can live so well elsewhere? I will sell my land and my homestead here, and with the money I will start afresh over there and get everything new. In this crowded place one is always having trouble. But I must first go and find out all about it myself."

C DIDACTIC LITERATURE
Reread lines 101–126. What **message** about private ownership does Tolstoy convey through this description of Pakhom's encounters with his neighbors?

---

8. **pay him out:** get even with him.

9. **grease your palms:** bribe you.

10. **Volga** (vôl′gə): the longest river in Russia, flowing from north of Moscow to the Caspian Sea.

Storm Is Coming V. V. Sindyukov.
Vika's Russia Direct.

Towards summer he got ready and started. He went down the Volga on a
150 steamer to Samara,[11] then walked another three hundred miles on foot, and
at last reached the place. It was just as the stranger had said. The peasants had
plenty of land: every man had twenty-five acres of communal land given him
for his use and any one who had money could buy, besides, at two shillings an
acre as much good freehold[12] land as he wanted.

Having found out all he wished to know, Pakhom returned home as autumn
came on, and began selling off his belongings. He sold his land at a profit,
sold his homestead and all his cattle, and withdrew from membership of the
commune. He only waited till the spring, and then started with his family for
the new settlement.

ANALYZE VISUALS
How does the **mood**
of this image relate to
Pakhom's experiences on
his new farm?

---

11. **Samara** (sə-mâr′ə): a city in western Russia on the Volga River.

12. **freehold:** land held for life with the right to pass it along to one's heirs.

∾ IV ∾

160   As soon as Pakhom and his family reached their new abode, he applied for admission into the commune of a large village. He stood treat[13] to the elders and obtained the necessary documents. Five shares of communal land were given him for his own and his sons' use: that is to say—125 acres (not all together, but in different fields) besides the use of the communal pasture. Pakhom put up the buildings he needed, and bought cattle. Of the communal land alone he had three times as much as at his former home, and the land was good corn-land. He was ten times better off than he had been. He had plenty of arable[14] land and pasturage, and could keep as many head of cattle as he liked.

   At first, in the bustle of building and settling down, Pakhom was pleased
170 with it all, but when he got used to it he began to think that even here he had not enough land. The first year, he sowed wheat on his share of the communal land and had a good crop. He wanted to go on sowing wheat, but had not enough communal land for the purpose, and what he had already used was not available; for in those parts wheat is only sown on virgin soil or on fallow[15] land. It is sown for one or two years, and then the land lies fallow till it is again overgrown with prairie grass. There were many who wanted such land and there was not enough for all; so that people quarreled about it. Those who were better off wanted it for growing wheat, and those who were poor wanted it to let to dealers, so that they might raise money to pay their taxes.
180 Pakhom wanted to sow more wheat, so he rented land from a dealer for a year. He sowed much wheat and had a fine crop, but the land was too far from the village—the wheat had to be carted more than ten miles. After a time Pakhom noticed that some peasant-dealers were living on separate farms and were growing wealthy; and he thought:

   "If I were to buy some freehold land and have a homestead on it, it would be a different thing altogether. Then it would all be nice and compact."

   The question of buying freehold land recurred to him again and again.

   He went on in the same way for three years, renting land and sowing wheat. The seasons turned out well and the crops were good, so that he began to lay
190 money by. He might have gone on living contentedly, but he grew tired of having to rent other people's land every year, and having to scramble for it. Wherever there was good land to be had, the peasants would rush for it and it was taken up at once, so that unless you were sharp about it you got none. It happened in the third year that he and a dealer together rented a piece of pasture land from some peasants; and they had already plowed it up, when there was some dispute and the peasants went to law about it, and things fell out so that the labor was all lost.

---

13. **stood treat:** paid for the cost of drinks or entertainment.

14. **arable:** land suitable for farming.

15. **fallow:** land left unplowed and unseeded during a growing season, usually to restore its fertility.

"If it were my own land," thought Pakhom, "I should be independent, and there would not be all this unpleasantness."

So Pakhom began looking out for land which he could buy; and he came across a peasant who had bought thirteen hundred acres, but having got into difficulties was willing to sell again cheap. Pakhom bargained and haggled with him, and at last they settled the price at 1,500 rubles, part in cash and part to be paid later. They had all but clinched the matter when a passing dealer happened to stop at Pakhom's one day to get a feed for his horses. He drank tea with Pakhom and they had a talk. The dealer said that he was just returning from the land of the Bashkirs,[16] far away, where he had bought thirteen thousand acres of land, all for 1,000 rubles. Pakhom questioned him further, and the tradesman said:

"All one need do is to make friends with the chiefs. I gave away about one hundred rubles worth of silk robes and carpets, besides a case of tea, and I gave wine to those who would drink it; and I got the land for less than a penny an acre." And he showed Pakhom the title-deeds, saying:

"The land lies near a river, and the whole prairie is virgin soil."

Pakhom plied him with questions, and the tradesman said:

"There is more land there than you could cover if you walked a year, and it all belongs to the Bashkirs. They are as simple as sheep, and land can be got almost for nothing."

"There now," thought Pakhom, "with my one thousand rubles, why should I get only thirteen hundred acres, and saddle myself with a debt besides? If I take it out there, I can get more than ten times as much for the money."

∽ V ∾

Pakhom inquired how to get to the place, and as soon as the tradesman had left him, he prepared to go there himself. He left his wife to look after the homestead, and started on his journey taking his man with him. They stopped at a town on their way and bought a case of tea, some wine, and other presents, as the tradesman had advised. On and on they went until they had gone more than three hundred miles, and on the seventh day they came to a place where the Bashkirs had pitched their tents. It was all just as the tradesman had said. The people lived on the steppes,[17] by a river, in felt-covered tents. They neither tilled the ground, nor ate bread. Their cattle and horses grazed in herds on the steppe. The colts were tethered behind the tents, and the mares were driven to them twice a day. The mares were milked, and from the milk kumiss[18] was made. It was the women who prepared kumiss, and they also made cheese. As far as the men were concerned, drinking kumiss

---

16. **Bashkirs:** a group of people of Asiatic origin who lived in southwestern Russia.

17. **steppes:** vast semi-arid, grass-covered plains.

18. **kumiss:** a liquor made from fermented mare's or camel's milk.

and tea, eating mutton, and playing on their pipes, was all they cared about. They were all stout and merry, and all the summer long they never thought of doing any work. They were quite ignorant, and knew no Russian, but were good-natured enough. **D**

240 As soon as they saw Pakhom, they came out of their tents and gathered round their visitor. An interpreter was found, and Pakhom told them he had come about some land. The Bashkirs seemed very glad; they took Pakhom and led him into one of the best tents, where they made him sit on some down cushions placed on a carpet, while they sat round him. They gave him some tea and kumiss, and had a sheep killed, and gave him mutton to eat. Pakhom took presents out of his cart and distributed them among the Bashkirs, and divided the tea amongst them. The Bashkirs were delighted. They talked a great deal among themselves, and then told the interpreter to translate.

"They wish to tell you," said the interpreter, "that they like you, and that it is our custom to do all we can to please a guest and to repay him for his gifts. 250 You have given us presents, now tell us which of the things we possess please you best, that we may present them to you."

"What pleases me best here," answered Pakhom, "is your land. Our land is crowded and the soil is exhausted; but you have plenty of land and it is good land. I never saw the like of it."

The interpreter translated. The Bashkirs talked among themselves for a while. Pakhom could not understand what they were saying, but saw that they were much amused and that they shouted and laughed. Then they were silent and looked at Pakhom while the interpreter said:

"They wish me to tell you that in return for your presents they will gladly 260 give you as much land as you want. You have only to point it out with your hand and it is yours."

The Bashkirs talked again for a while and began to dispute. Pakhom asked what they were disputing about, and the interpreter told him that some of them thought they ought to ask their chief about the land and not act in his absence, while others thought there was no need to wait for his return.

∼ VI ∼

While the Bashkirs were disputing, a man in a large fox-fur cap appeared on the scene. They all became silent and rose to their feet. The interpreter said, "This is our chief himself."

Pakhom immediately fetched the best dressing-gown and five pounds of tea, 270 and offered these to the chief. The chief accepted them, and seated himself in the place of honor. The Bashkirs at once began telling him something. The chief listened for a while, then made a sign with his head for them to be silent, and addressing himself to Pakhom, said in Russian:

D DIDACTIC LITERATURE
Note how the Bashkirs' way of life compares with that of Pakhom and the other Russian peasants. What lesson does this comparison help teach?

Dervishes Wearing Their Festive Clothes (1869), Vasilii Vasilievich Vereshchagin. Oil on canvas. © The State Tretyakov Gallery, Moscow.

"Well, let it be so. Choose whatever piece of land you like; we have plenty of it."

"How can I take as much as I like?" thought Pakhom. "I must get a deed to make it secure, or else they may say, 'It is yours,' and afterwards may take it away again."

"Thank you for your kind words," he said aloud. "You have much land, and I only want a little. But I should like to be sure which bit is mine. Could it not be measured and made over to me? Life and death are in God's hands. You good people give it to me, but your children might wish to take it away again."

"You are quite right," said the chief. "We will make it over to you."

"I heard that a dealer had been here," continued Pakhom, "and that you gave him a little land, too, and signed title-deeds to that effect. I should like to have it done in the same way."

The chief understood.

"Yes," replied he, "that can be done quite easily. We have a scribe, and we will go to town with you and have the deed properly sealed."

290   "And what will be the price?" asked Pakhom.

"Our price is always the same: one thousand rubles a day."

Pakhom did not understand.

"A day? What measure is that? How many acres would that be?"

"We do not know how to reckon it out," said the chief. "We sell it by the day. As much as you can go round on your feet in a day is yours, and the price is one thousand rubles a day."

Pakhom was surprised.

"But in a day you can get round a large tract of land," he said.

The chief laughed.

300   "It will all be yours!" said he. "But there is one condition: If you don't return on the same day to the spot whence you started, your money is lost."

"But how am I to mark the way that I have gone?"

"Why, we shall go to any spot you like, and stay there. You must start from that spot and make your round, taking a spade with you. Wherever you think necessary, make a mark. At every turning, dig a hole and pile up the turf; then afterwards we will go round with a plow from hole to hole. You may make as large a circuit as you please, but before the sun sets you must return to the place you started from. All the land you cover will be yours." **E**

Pakhom was delighted. It was decided to start early next morning. They

310 talked a while, and after drinking some more kumiss and eating some more mutton, they had tea again, and then the night came on. They gave Pakhom a feather-bed to sleep on, and the Bashkirs dispersed for the night, promising to assemble the next morning at day-break and ride out before sunrise to the appointed spot.

E PREDICT
What do you think will happen to Pakhom on the day he claims his new land?

∼ VII ∽

Pakhom lay on the feather-bed, but could not sleep. He kept thinking about the land.

"What a large tract I will mark off!" thought he. "I can easily do thirty-five miles in a day. The days are long now, and within a circuit of thirty-five miles what a lot of land there will be! I will sell the poorer land, or let it to peasants,

320 but I'll pick out the best and farm it. I will buy two ox-teams, and hire two more laborers. About a hundred and fifty acres shall be plow-land, and I will pasture cattle on the rest."

Pakhom lay awake all night, and dozed off only just before dawn. Hardly were his eyes closed when he had a dream. He thought he was lying in that same tent and heard somebody chuckling outside. He wondered who it could be, and rose and went out, and he saw the Bashkir chief sitting in front of the tent holding his sides and rolling about with laughter. Going nearer to the chief, Pakhom asked: "What are you laughing at?" But he saw that it was no longer the chief, but the dealer who had recently stopped at his house and had

330 told him about the land. Just as Pakhom was going to ask, "Have you been

here long?" he saw that it was not the dealer, but the peasant who had come up from the Volga, long ago, to Pakhom's old home. Then he saw that it was not the peasant either, but the Devil himself with hoofs and horns, sitting there and chuckling, and before him lay a man barefoot, **prostrate** on the ground, with only trousers and a shirt on. And Pakhom dreamt that he looked more attentively to see what sort of man it was that was lying there, and he saw that the man was dead, and that it was himself! He awoke horror-struck.

"What things one does dream," thought he.

Looking round he saw through the open door that the dawn was breaking.

"It's time to wake them up," thought he. "We ought to be starting."

He got up, roused his man (who was sleeping in his cart), bade him harness; and went to call the Bashkirs.

"It's time to go to the steppe to measure the land," he said.

The Bashkirs rose and assembled, and the chief came too. Then they began drinking kumiss again, and offered Pakhom some tea, but he would not wait.

"If we are to go, let us go. It is high time," said he.

～ VIII ～

The Bashkirs got ready and they all started: some mounted on horses, and some in carts. Pakhom drove in his own small cart with his servant and took a spade with him. When they reached the steppe, the morning red was beginning to kindle. They ascended a hillock (called by the Bashkirs a *shikhan*[19]) and dismounting from their carts and their horses, gathered in one spot. The chief came up to Pakhom and stretching out his arm toward the plain:

"See," said he, "all this, as far as your eye can reach, is ours. You may have any part of it you like."

Pakhom's eyes glistened: it was all virgin soil, as flat as the palm of your hand, as black as the seed of a poppy, and in the hollows different kinds of grasses grew breast high.

The chief took off his fox-fur cap, placed it on the ground and said:

"This will be the mark. Start from here, and return here again. All the land you go round shall be yours."

Pakhom took out his money and put it on the cap. Then he took off his outer coat, remaining in his sleeveless under-coat. He unfastened his girdle[20] and tied it tight below his stomach, put a little bag of bread into the breast of his coat, and tying a flask of water to his girdle, he drew up the tops of his boots, took the spade from his man, and stood ready to start. He considered for some moments which way he had better go—it was tempting everywhere.

"No matter," he concluded, "I will go towards the rising sun."

He turned his face to the east, stretched himself, and waited for the sun to appear above the rim.

prostrate (prŏs′trāt′) *adj.*
lying in a flat, horizontal position

---

19. *shikhan* (shĭ-kân′).

20. **girdle:** a belt or sash that fastens around the waist.

370   "I must lose no time," he thought, "and it is easier walking while it is still cool."

The sun's rays had hardly flashed above the horizon, before Pakhom, carrying the spade over his shoulder, went down into the steppe.

Pakhom started walking neither slowly nor quickly. After having gone a thousand yards he stopped, dug a hole, and placed pieces of turf one on another to make it more visible. Then he went on; and now that he had walked off his stiffness he quickened his pace. After a while he dug another hole.

Pakhom looked back. The hillock could be distinctly seen in the sunlight, with the people on it, and the glittering tires of the cart-wheels. At a rough
380 guess Pakhom concluded that he had walked three miles. It was growing warmer; he took off his under-coat, flung it across his shoulder, and went on again. It had grown quite warm now; he looked at the sun, it was time to think of breakfast.

"The first shift is done, but there are four in a day, and it is too soon yet to turn. But I will just take off my boots," said he to himself.

He sat down, took off his boots, stuck them into his girdle, and went on. It was easy walking now.

"I will go on for another three miles," thought he, "and then turn to the left. This spot is so fine, that it would be a pity to lose it. The further one goes,
390 the better the land seems."

Forest Road. A. Karapaev.
Vika's Russia Direct.

He went straight on for a while, and when he looked round, the hillock was scarcely visible and the people on it looked like black ants, and he could just see something glistening there in the sun.

"Ah," thought Pakhom, "I have gone far enough in this direction, it is time to turn. Besides I am in a regular sweat, and very thirsty."

He stopped, dug a large hole, and heaped up pieces of turf. Next he untied his flask, had a drink, and then turned sharply to the left. He went on and on; the grass was high, and it was very hot.

Pakhom began to grow tired: he looked at the sun and saw that it was noon.

400 "Well," he thought, "I must have a rest."

He sat down, and ate some bread and drank some water; but he did not lie down, thinking that if he did he might fall asleep. After sitting a little while, he went on again. At first he walked easily: the food had strengthened him; but it had become terribly hot and he felt sleepy, still he went on, thinking: "An hour to suffer, a life-time to live."

He went a long way in this direction also, and was about to turn to the left again, when he perceived a damp hollow: "It would be a pity to leave that out," he thought. "Flax[21] would do well there." So he went on past the hollow, and dug a hole on the other side of it before he turned the corner. Pakhom

410 looked towards the hillock. The heat made the air hazy: it seemed to be quivering, and through the haze the people on the hillock could scarcely be seen.

"Ah!" thought Pakhom, "I have made the sides too long; I must make this one shorter." And he went along the third side, stepping faster. He looked at the sun: it was nearly half-way to the horizon, and he had not yet done two miles of the third side of the square. He was still ten miles from the goal.

"No," he thought, "though it will make my land lop-sided, I must hurry back in a straight line now. I might go too far, and as it is I have a great deal of land."

So Pakhom hurriedly dug a hole, and turned straight towards the hillock.

∼ IX ∼

420 Pakhom went straight towards the hillock, but he now walked with difficulty. He was done up with the heat, his bare feet were cut and bruised, and his legs began to fail. He longed to rest, but it was impossible if he meant to get back before sunset. The sun waits for no man, and it was sinking lower and lower.

"Oh dear," he thought, "if only I have not blundered trying for too much! What if I am too late?"

He looked towards the hillock and at the sun. He was still far from his goal, and the sun was already near the rim.

---

21. **flax:** a plant grown for its seed and for its fine fibers.

Pakhom walked on and on; it was very hard walking but he went quicker
430 and quicker. He pressed on, but was still far from the place. He began running,
threw away his coat, his boots, his flask, and his cap, and kept only the spade
which he used as a support.

"What shall I do?" he thought again, "I have grasped too much and ruined
the whole affair. I can't get there before the sun sets."

And this fear made him still more breathless. Pakhom went on running, his
soaking shirt and trousers stuck to him and his mouth was parched. His breast
was working like a blacksmith's bellows,[22] his heart was beating like a hammer,
and his legs were giving way as if they did not belong to him. Pakhom was
seized with terror lest he should die of the strain.

440 Though afraid of death, he could not stop. "After having run all that way
they will call me a fool if I stop now," thought he. And he ran on and on, and
drew near and heard the Bashkirs yelling and shouting to him, and their cries
inflamed his heart still more. He gathered his last strength and ran on.

The sun was close to the rim, and cloaked in mist looked large, and red as
blood. Now, yes now, it was about to set! The sun was quite low, but he was
also quite near his aim. Pakhom could already see the people on the hillock
waving their arms to hurry him up. He could see the fox-fur cap on the
ground and the money on it, and the chief sitting on the ground holding his
sides. And Pakhom remembered his dream.

450 "There is plenty of land," thought he, "but will God let me live on it? I have
lost my life, I have lost my life! I shall never reach that spot!" **F**

Pakhom looked at the sun, which had reached the earth: one side of it had
already disappeared. With all his remaining strength he rushed on, bending
his body forward so that his legs could hardly follow fast enough to keep him
from falling. Just as he reached the hillock it suddenly grew dark. He looked
up—the sun had already set! He gave a cry: "All my labor has been in vain,"
thought he, and was about to stop, but he heard the Bashkirs still shouting,
and remembered that though to him, from below, the sun seemed to have
set, they on the hillock could still see it. He took a long breath and ran up the
460 hillock. It was still light there. He reached the top and saw the cap. Before it
sat the chief laughing and holding his sides. Again Pakhom remembered his
dream, and he uttered a cry: his legs gave way beneath him, he fell forward
and reached the cap with his hands.

"Ah, that's a fine fellow!" exclaimed the chief. "He has gained much land!"

Pakhom's servant came running up and tried to raise him, but he saw that
blood was flowing from his mouth. Pakhom was dead!

The Bashkirs clicked their tongues to show their pity.

His servant picked up the spade and dug a grave long enough for Pakhom to lie
in, and buried him in it. Six feet from his head to his heels was all he needed. ◕

F SUSPENSE
How does Tolstoy create
suspense in lines 429–451?

---

22. **bellows:** a device with a flexible chamber that can be expanded to draw air in and
contracted to force air out.

The Money Lender and his Wife (1514), Quentin Metsys. Louvre, Paris. Photo © Erich Lessing/ Art Resource, New York.

ANALYZE VISUALS
What details indicate that the people depicted in the painting are wealthy?

The New Testament

There is great gain in godliness with contentment; for we brought nothing into the world, and we cannot take anything out of the world; but if we have food and clothing, with these we shall be content. But those who desire to be rich fall into temptation, into a snare, into many senseless and hurtful desires that plunge men into ruin and destruction. For the love of money is the root of all evils; it is through this craving that some have wandered away from the faith and pierced their hearts with many pangs. . . .

As for the rich of this world, charge them not to be haughty, nor to set their hopes on uncertain riches but on God who richly furnishes us with everything
10 to enjoy. They are to do good, to be rich in good deeds, liberal and generous, thus laying up for themselves a good foundation for the future, so that they may take hold of the life which is life indeed. ❧ **G**

G **DIDACTIC LITERATURE**
Reread lines 8–12. How do you interpret the phrase "the life which is life indeed"?

Comprehension

1. **Recall** In "How Much Land Does a Man Need?" what conflicts does Pakhom have after buying his first farm?

2. **Recall** Why does Pakhom want to buy land from the Bashkirs?

3. **Summarize** What happens to Pakhom at the end of the story?

OHIO STANDARDS

READING STANDARD
4.5 Analyze how choice of genre affects theme or topic

Literary Analysis

4. **Interpret Didactic Literature** Explain the meaning of the statement from the New Testament that "money is the root of all evils."

5. **Examine Irony** A contrast between what is expected and what actually happens is called irony. Reread lines 468–469 of "How Much Land Does a Man Need?" What irony does Tolstoy develop in this description?

6. **Make Judgments** Is Pakhom's fate inevitable? If so, why? If not, at what point could he have avoided his downfall?

Comparing Across Genres

Now that you have read both selections, you are ready to identify the moral message in each one. The questions in the **Points of Comparison** chart will help you get started. If a point of comparison is not applicable to one of the selections, leave the box blank.

Points of Comparison	In the Short Story	In the Bible Excerpt
What problem is identified with the desire for **wealth?**		
What idea, if any, does the title emphasize?		
What images strike you as important?		
Write a sentence stating the message as you interpret it.		
Which literary techniques are most important in conveying the message?		

Vocabulary in Context

VOCABULARY PRACTICE

Identify the word that is not related in meaning to the other words in the set. If necessary, use a dictionary to look up the precise meanings of words you are unsure of.

1. disparage, compliment, belittle, insult
2. harmony, peace, discord, agreement
3. forbear, refrain, commence, withhold
4. vertical, prostrate, horizontal, flat

VOCABULARY IN WRITING

Use two or more vocabulary words to write about Pakhom's experiences in the story. Here is an example of how you might begin.

> **EXAMPLE SENTENCE**
>
> *Pakhom could not **forbear** acquiring more land, although his gains never brought him happiness.*

VOCABULARY STRATEGY: SIMILES AND METAPHORS

A **simile** is a figure of speech that compares two things that are basically unlike each other but have something in common. In a simile, a word such as *like* or *as* signals the comparison. A **metaphor** is also a figure of speech that compares two things. However, unlike a simile, a metaphor does not use the words *like* or *as*. When an unfamiliar word appears in a sentence containing a simile or metaphor, you can often figure out its meaning by examining the comparison being made.

PRACTICE Explain what is being compared in each of the following sentences, and identify whether the figure of speech is a simile or a metaphor. Then decide what each comparison adds to your understanding of the boldfaced word.

1. The **discord** in the room was a dark, ominous cloud.
2. When I **forbear** sleeping, I'm as cranky as an alligator.
3. My heart was shattered glass after they **disparaged** me.
4. The man lay as **prostrate** as a rug on the floor.

OHIO STANDARDS

VOCABULARY STANDARD
1.3 Infer the literal and figurative meanings of words

VOCABULARY PRACTICE
For more practice, go to the **Vocabulary Center** at **ClassZone.com.**

Writing for Assessment

1. READ THE PROMPT

In writing assessments, you will often be asked to compare and contrast works that have a similar subject or purpose, such as the two selections you have just read. You are now going to practice writing an essay that involves this type of comparison.

PROMPT

The desire for wealth raises moral issues in many cultures. Consider how this subject is addressed in "How Much Land Does a Man Need?" and in the passage from the New Testament. In a well-developed essay, compare and contrast the selections, identifying the moral message in each selection and the techniques used to convey it. Note examples and details in the Tolstoy story that illustrate the points made in the Bible passage.

◀ **STRATEGIES IN ACTION**

1. I need to write an essay that points out similarities and differences between the Bible passage and the Tolstoy story.

2. I need to discuss the techniques used to convey a **moral message** in each selection.

3. I need to identify **examples** of how the Tolstoy story supports ideas in the Bible passage.

2. PLAN YOUR WRITING

- Review the **Points of Comparison** chart you created on page 663.
- Using your chart, find examples to use as evidence for the points you plan to develop in your essay. If necessary, review the selections again to identify more examples.
- Create an outline to organize your main points. You might want to base your outline on the **Points of Comparison** chart, as shown.

I. Problems with wealth
   A. Story
   B. Scripture
II. Title
   A. Story
   B. Scripture

3. DRAFT YOUR RESPONSE

Introduction Explain that you will be comparing a short story and scriptural writing that both deal with the desire for wealth. Be sure to identify the title of each work.

Body Cover each key point of comparison in its own paragraph. In one paragraph, for example, you might compare and contrast problems associated with the desire for wealth in each selection. Within each paragraph you write, give specific details to back up your points.

Conclusion Wrap up your essay by summarizing your main points.

Revision Be sure you have included details from both selections to support each key comparison. Also, check your use of transitional words and phrases to connect your ideas within and between paragraphs.

Daisy
America's Back

Political Ads on *MediaSmart* DVD

How do candidates
get your VOTE?

OHIO STANDARDS

READING STANDARD
3.4 Identify persuasive techniques and examples of propaganda, bias and stereotyping

KEY IDEA Experience, leadership, honesty, compassion—in politics, a candidate's image is just as important as the issues he or she represents. In this lesson, you'll learn how political campaign advertisers use **persuasive techniques** to influence the way voters perceive candidates.

Background

Selling Candidates In a TV ad, most candidates have 30 seconds or less to "sell" their message and appeal to voters. Just how important is a 30-second commercial? In 1964, President Lyndon B. Johnson ran one of the most memorable ad campaigns in advertising and political history. The ad "Daisy" aired at a time when the threat of a nuclear war between the Soviet Union and the United States was a key issue for voters. It ran only one day, but it had a profound impact. Johnson's opponent, Barry Goldwater, lost the election.

While "Daisy" addressed viewers' deepest fears, President Ronald Reagan's 1984 ad "America's Back," captured the public's attention in a different way. The ad shows a series of images that highlighted the theme of the campaign: America is "Prouder, Stronger, Better." By sending an optimistic message, the ad helped viewers associate positive feelings with the Reagan campaign.

Media Literacy: Persuasion in Political Ads

A well-designed ad can define a candidate's beliefs, values, and issues, but it can also present a deliberately distorted or misleading view of a candidate or his or her opponent. By using carefully chosen visuals, sounds, and persuasive techniques, political ads have the potential to sway voters' attitudes about candidates. The following types of political ads are commonly used by candidates, political organizations, and interest groups:

- **Biography ads** emphasize the candidate's personal and professional accomplishments.

- **Vision ads** provide a "vision" of the candidate's policies. These ads are intended to make viewers feel good about the country and the politician.

- **Negative ads** portray a candidate's opponent in an unfavorable light, often distorting the facts by citing false or misleading statements.

- **Scare ads** play on voters' fears and are usually combined with negative ads.

STRATEGIES FOR ANALYZING PERSUASION IN POLITICAL ADS

Visual Elements

- Notice a candidate's **physical appearance** and **body language.** A candidate's physical appearance and behavior are carefully planned to create an impression on a **target audience.** Members of a target audience often share such characteristics as age, gender, ethnicity, economic level, or values. For example, a target audience of voters who prefer a likeable, approachable candidate will respond well to images of one who is dressed casually and shakes hands.

- **Symbols** are images that represent certain ideas or values. An image of the Statue of Liberty, for example, might be used to symbolize freedom.

Persuasive Techniques

- **Emotional appeals** create strong feelings such as fear, security, anger, patriotism, optimism, distrust, and loyalty. Ask yourself: What emotions is the ad trying to create?

- **Glittering generalities** are general statements that sound important but are often vague or abstract. Their intended effect is to create a positive feeling about a candidate (for example, "A vote for Evan Smith is a vote for freedom and democracy").

- **"Plain folks" appeals** are attempts to persuade viewers that the candidate understands the average person, because he or she is one.

Sound Elements

- **Music** is used to trigger emotions such as optimism or nostalgia. Upbeat music inspires voters, while jarring or disturbing music gives a sense of mistrust.

- Some **voice-over** narrations can inspire trust or confidence. Other voice-overs can give a sense of unease or mistrust. Ask yourself: How is voice-over used to create a positive or negative image of a candidate?

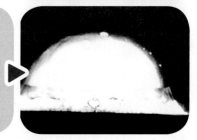

Viewing Guide for
Political Ads

As you view the political ads, consider the times in which they were created. Both ads are regarded as classic by today's standards. "Daisy" capitalizes on voters' fears of a nuclear war with the Soviet Union. The ad was meant to scare viewers into voting for Johnson. "America's Back" uses images of peace and prosperity to persuade Americans to re-elect President Reagan.

Quickly review the persuasive techniques that appear on page 667 of this lesson as well as those listed on page 574. To analyze how persuasive techniques are used in political ads, view each ad more than once and answer the following questions.

NOW VIEW

FIRST VIEWING: Comprehension

1. **Summarize** Summarize the message in each ad.

2. **Recall** What symbol appears repeatedly in "America's Back"?

CLOSE VIEWING: Media Literacy

3. **Identify Type of Ad** How would you categorize each ad—biography ad, vision ad, negative ad, or scare ad? Give reasons.

4. **Identify Target Audience** Who do you think is the target audience of each ad—for example, new voters, retired voters, wealthy voters? Explain.

5. **Analyze Emotional Appeals** In "Daisy," what emotions do you think the visuals and voice-over are attempting to trigger?

6. **Analyze Persuasive Techniques** Identify the persuasive techniques used in "America's Back." How do these techniques help convey the ad's message?

Write or Discuss

Evaluate the Message By contrasting the image of a little girl counting daisy petals with an image of a nuclear explosion, "Daisy" made a powerful and persuasive suggestion about Goldwater's position on war. Based on your viewing of "Daisy," do you think the ad's creators went too far to win votes for Johnson? Why or why not? Use evidence to support your opinion and also consider the following:

- persuasive techniques used in the ad to attract voters' attention and to influence their actions
- the use of visual and sound elements
- any information that you think is missing from the ad
- your reaction to the ad and how you think viewers responded

Produce Your Own Media

MEDIA TOOLS

For help with creating a campaign poster, visit the **Media Center** at **ClassZone.com.**

Design a Campaign Poster Imagine that you are a political consultant whose job it is to create a campaign poster for a candidate. Choose an existing candidate, a historical figure, or someone running for student government, and create a poster that projects a positive image of the candidate.

Tech Tip

Use a software program to add design elements, such as color and special fonts, to your campaign poster.

HERE'S HOW To help you create your poster, consider the following suggestions:

- Determine whether you will focus on the candidate's image or the issues.
- Create a **slogan** that captures a major theme of a campaign or that highlights the candidate's personality and image. Remember that slogans are catchy phrases that voters remember and associate with a candidate.
- Plan the layout of the poster. What images or words will stand out? What symbols or colors will get voters' attention?

Writing Workshop

Editorial

Persuasion is much more than a skill; it's an art. You've seen many persuasive techniques at work in Unit 6. Now you'll get to build a persuasive argument as you write an editorial about an issue that matters to you.

WRITER'S ROAD MAP

Editorial

WRITING PROMPT 1

Writing for the Real World An eloquent and well-supported argument can get readers thinking and talking. Choose an issue you feel strongly about. Write an editorial for your school newspaper in support of your position.

Issues to Consider
- censorship of school newspapers
- helmet laws for motorcyclists, bicyclists, or in-line skaters
- whether it is morally wrong to wear fur
- whether school districts should pay students for getting good grades

WRITING PROMPT 2

Writing from Literature Choose an issue that you care about from one of the selections in this unit. Write an editorial for your local newspaper, using the piece you read as a starting point.

Selections to Explore
- "A Chip of Glass Ruby" (civil disobedience)
- "I Acknowledge Mine" (animal research)
- "On Nuclear Disarmament" (eradicating nuclear weapons)

 WRITING TOOLS
For prewriting, revision, and editing tools, visit the **Writing Center** at ClassZone.com.

KEY TRAITS

1. **IDEAS**
   - **Identifies the issue** clearly
   - Presents a clear, logical **claim** in a **thesis statement**
   - **Supports** the thesis with relevant and convincing reasons and evidence
   - Anticipates and answers **opposing viewpoints** with **counterarguments**

2. **ORGANIZATION**
   - Has an **introduction** that describes the issue in a memorable and thought-provoking way
   - Uses a **pattern of organization** that clarifies ideas and relationships between them
   - Uses **transitions** to connect ideas
   - Concludes with a **summary** of main points and a **call to action**

3. **VOICE**
   - Uses a **tone** that is suited to the audience and purpose

4. **WORD CHOICE**
   - Uses **persuasive language** effectively

5. **SENTENCE FLUENCY**
   - Varies **sentence structures** for interest and flow

6. **CONVENTIONS**
   - Employs **correct grammar and usage**

Part 1: Analyze a Student Model

WRITING STANDARD
6.5 Write persuasive compositions

Alec Kincaid
Clearwater High School

Let the Punishment Fit the Offender

Last month, 15-year-old Jonathan Herr walked boldly into a convenience store, pulled a weapon out of his backpack, and demanded that the cashier hand over the contents of the cash register. As he ran out of the store with $95, an off-duty police officer caught him. Herr told
5 police he had robbed the store after friends dared him to. Police charged the high school freshman with aggravated armed robbery, and state prosecutors announced that the boy would be tried as an adult. He faces a maximum sentence of 25 years in prison.

Increasingly, youths who commit crimes in the United States—
10 especially violent crimes—are being transferred out of the juvenile justice system to be tried in adult court. In 2005, our state had 466 offenders under the age of 18 in its adult prison system, the most of any state in the nation. This is a dangerous trend that must be reversed. Society should treat young offenders differently from adults.

15 Proponents of trying youths as adults argue that offenders like Jonathan Herr are old enough to know right from wrong and must be held accountable for their actions. Certainly, this is true. At the same time, however, society must recognize that a high school freshman is not a mature, responsible adult. Being a teenager can be difficult.
20 Pressure at school, at home, and from peers simply overwhelms many teens. Furthermore, teens are impulsive; often they do not take the time to think through the consequences of their actions. These are the very reasons we have a juvenile justice system.

KEY TRAITS IN ACTION

Introduces the issue with a compelling real-life incident.

Writer clarifies the issue with a statistic.

This statement of opinion is the writer's **thesis,** or **claim.**

Writer anticipates and addresses **opposing viewpoints** with **counterarguments.**

Precise words are **persuasive** without being overly emotional. The writer varies **sentence structures** throughout the essay.

Proponents also argue that the punishment must fit the crime, so
that anyone convicted of a violent offense should be punished harshly
whether that person is 15 or 35. Again, this is true, but what is harsh
for a 35-year-old may well be cruel and unusual for someone just out of
middle school. In adult court, youths face the same penalties as adults,
including life with no possibility of parole. What's more, studies show
that youths sent to adult court are much more likely to commit new
crimes than those sent to juvenile court. Also, youths in adult prisons
receive little education, mental health treatment, or rehabilitation.

Recently, science weighed in on this issue. Using magnetic resonance
imaging, researchers have learned that the teenage brain is still very
much a work in progress, especially when it comes to reasoning,
judgment, and impulse control. A teenager's brain is just not as
sophisticated as an adult's. As Dr. Jay Giedd, a neuroscientist at the
National Institute of Mental Health, has said, "It's sort of unfair to
expect [teens] to have adult levels of organizational skills or decision-
making before their brains are finished being built."

Trying youths as adults makes prosecutors look tough and may even
make society feel safer, but it's unfair to young offenders. Yes, Jonathan
Herr must be punished for his actions, but his life shouldn't be thrown
away. Young people are still learning about life, and they have great
potential for change. Society should use the juvenile justice system to
give them that chance.

> **Transitions** give order and focus to the writer's arguments. The formal **tone** is appropriate for the serious subject matter.

> Writer **supports** his argument by including interesting, relevant evidence, such as this quotation from an expert.

> Carefully chosen words make the argument more **persuasive.** The conclusion **summarizes** the argument and ends with a **call to action.**

2

Part 2: Apply the Writing Process

WRITING STANDARD
5.4 Plan strategies to address purpose and audience

PREWRITING

What Should I Do?

1. **Analyze the prompt.**
   Read the prompt carefully. Circle the part of the prompt that tells you what form your writing will take. Underline the part that tells you what your subject matter should be.

2. **Think about issues that interest you and your readers.**
   List some "hot-button" issues of today. Choose one that you believe you could make an audience care about. Then create a chart like this one to help you evaluate whether that issue would make an effective editorial.

3. **Make your claim.**
   You want your audience to know exactly how you feel about the issue your editorial addresses. A straightforward **thesis statement** will do just that.

4. **Collect evidence.**
   How will you support the statement you just made? Your best bet is to bolster each reason you give with evidence, such as relevant statistics and convincing quotations.

What Does It Look Like?

▶ **WRITING PROMPT** An eloquent and well-supported argument can get readers thinking and talking. Choose <u>an issue you feel strongly about.</u> Write (an) (editorial for your school) (newspaper) in support of your position.

▶ *Interesting issue:* trying youthful offenders as adults

Places to look:	Questions to think about:
magazines	Does my audience feel strongly
TV news	about this issue? Yes
Internet	Does this issue have two clear sides
newspapers	to it? Yes
	Is this issue narrow enough to
	be discussed persuasively in an
	editorial? Yes

▶ *More and more young people are being tried in adult courts. This is wrong. Society should treat young offenders differently from adults.*

Reason	Supporting Evidence
A high school freshman is not an adult.	• Teens are impulsive. • There is a separate justice system for juveniles.
A teenager's brain is less sophisticated than an adult's.	• Magnetic resonance imaging shows differences in impulse control. • Quotation from Dr. Giedd: "It's sort of unfair ..."

What Should I Do?	What Does It Look Like?
1. Grab your reader's attention. The first few sentences of your editorial are critical to holding your audience's attention. You might begin by describing a hypothetical situation ("What if . . .") or by sharing a real-life incident.	▶ **A dramatic question** *How would you react if someone told you, at age 15, that you were going to spend the rest of your life locked up?* **A real-life incident** *Last month, 15-year-old Jonathan Herr walked boldly into a convenience store, pulled a weapon out . . .*
2. Develop your argument. Think about what reasons and evidence someone opposed to your position might use to attack it. Develop counterarguments to show why your position is the right one.	▶ ***Opposing argument:*** *All offenders, even young ones, must be punished harshly.* ***Counterarguments:*** • *Studies show that youths sent to adult court commit more new crimes than youths sent to juvenile court.* • *Youths in adult prisons don't get much education or mental health treatment.*
3. Watch your language. Use language that is strongly persuasive. However, don't let your words become so emotionally charged that your audience will conclude that you're overstating your case.	▶ **Overemotional** *What is harsh for a 35-year-old will be absolutely inhuman and exceedingly barbaric for some poor child.* **Strongly persuasive** *What is harsh for a 35-year-old may well be cruel and unusual for someone just out of middle school.*
4. Issue a call to action. Your conclusion is an opportunity to restate your argument and issue a **call to action**—an invitation to your reader or to society as a whole to do something that brings about change.	▶ *Yes, Jonathan Herr must be punished for his actions, but his life shouldn't be thrown away. Young people are still learning about life, and they have great potential for change.* ⎤ Restated argument *Society should use the juvenile justice system to give them that chance.* ⎤ Call to action

REVISING AND EDITING

What Should I Do?	**What Does It Look Like?**

1. Choose persuasive language.

- Read your editorial and <u>underline</u> words that seem weak, such as *good, nice, should, is, really,* and *very.*

- Replace these words with vivid verbs and forceful modifiers that add persuasive punch to your writing.

▶

Last month, 15-year-old Jonathan Herr walked_∧ into ⟨boldly⟩
a convenience store, t̶o̶o̶k̶_∧ a weapon out of his ⟨pulled⟩
backpack, and a̶s̶k̶e̶d̶_∧ that the cashier hand over the ⟨demanded⟩
contents of the cash register.

Pressure at school, at home, and from peers i̶s̶ ̶v̶e̶r̶y̶_∧ ⟨simply overwhelms⟩
d̶i̶f̶f̶i̶c̶u̶l̶t̶ ̶f̶o̶r̶ many teens.

2. Counter opposing viewpoints.

- Ask a peer reader to highlight any parts of your editorial that do not address opposing viewpoints completely and honestly.

- Add further explanation to sharpen your argument.

See page 676: Ask a Peer Reader

▶

~~Some people want to try youths as adults, but that's cruel and unusual.~~

Proponents of trying youths as adults argue that offenders are old enough to know right from wrong and therefore must be held accountable. Certainly, this is true. However, society must recognize that a high school freshman is not a mature, responsible adult.

3. Smooth out your sentences.

- (Circle) the three longest or most complex sentences in your editorial. Read each one aloud.

- Shorten confusing sentences by breaking each up into two or more sentences or by deleting unnecessary information.

▶

Youths in adult prisons receive little education_∧, ~~which is important for their futures, and they don't get much~~ mental health treatment, ⟨or⟩
_∧ ~~plus there isn't much~~ rehabilitation.

4. Don't use faulty reasoning.

- Read your editorial aloud. Draw a ⬚box⬚ around examples of name-calling, oversimplification, or other errors in logic.

- Replace these examples with reasoned, persuasive language.

See page 676: Errors in Logic

▶

Proponents also argue that the punishment must fit the crime, so that anyone convicted of a violent offense should be punished harshly whether that person is 15 or 35. ⟦That attitude is so ignorant.⟧ Again, this is true, but what is harsh for a 35-year-old may well be cruel and unusual for someone just out of middle school.

Preparing to Publish   Editorial

Apply the Rubric

A strong editorial . . .

☑ has a compelling opening

☑ identifies the issue and includes a clear and focused thesis statement

☑ offers supporting reasons and evidence, such as facts, statistics, examples, or quotations

☑ is logically organized

☑ connects ideas with transitions

☑ anticipates and addresses opposing arguments

☑ maintains an appropriate tone

☑ uses persuasive language effectively

☑ concludes by restating the writer's position and calling the reader to action

Ask a Peer Reader

• What issue am I addressing?

• How could I address opposing viewpoints more effectively?

• Can you explain why the editorial either did or did not change your mind about the issue?

Errors in Logic

Name-calling: an attempt to discredit an idea by attacking the person or group holding it ("These rigid, vindictive people are living in the 18th century.")

Oversimplification: an explanation of a complex situation or problem as if it were much simpler than it is ("It's clear to anyone that young adults do not belong in prisons.")

See page 1070 for more types of errors in logic.

Check Your Grammar

• *Who* is always a subject or a predicate pronoun.

> *Subject:* Who robbed the convenience store?
> *Predicate pronoun:* It was who?

• *Whom* is always an object.

> *Direct object:* Whom would you try as an adult?
> *Indirect object:* They gave whom a life sentence?
> *Object of preposition:* Against whom were charges brought?

See page R54: Interrogative Pronouns

Writing Online

PUBLISHING OPTIONS
For publishing options, visit the **Writing Center** at ClassZone.com.

ASSESSMENT PREPARATION
For writing and grammar assessment practice, go to the **Assessment Center** at ClassZone.com.

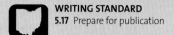

Creating a Brochure

One way to reach a wide audience with your editorial message is to create a brochure. A brochure is an illustrated booklet, often just a few pages long, that presents information in a very focused way. In addition to text, a brochure may contain photographs, charts, graphs, or illustrations. The goal of a brochure is to make an important message clear, concise, and compelling.

Planning the Brochure

1. **Consider your audience and your purpose.** Who is going to read your brochure? Is your goal to inform, to entertain, to persuade, or some combination of these?

2. **Plan the "look" of your brochure—its layout and composition.** How many pages will the brochure have? Will it be tall and thin, or will it look more like a book? What background colors will you use? Will you draw illustrations, include photographs, or create charts or graphs? Will the brochure be folded or stapled?

3. **Create thumbnail sketches of the pages.** A thumbnail sketch is a simple illustration that shows where headings, text, and illustrations will be placed.

4. **Write the text.** Adapt the language of your editorial for your brochure. Be concise. You may be able to delete some text if you are using compelling visuals. Prepare headings and captions for the visuals as necessary.

> The Problem
>
> photo of J. Herr
>
> Youthful Offenders Are Different
>
> chart

Producing the Brochure

1. **Use software to create the brochure.** Word-processing programs include templates for different types of documents, including brochures. A template can guide you as you assemble the pieces.

2. **Scan visuals.** Scan into a computer the visuals you want to use. Then paste them into your word-processed document.

3. **Copy and distribute your brochure.** Give your finished brochure to friends, family members, and classmates.

Reading Comprehension

DIRECTIONS *Read these selections and answer the questions that follow.*

from Why Go Back to the Moon?

Michael D. Lemonick

Using the moon as a launching pad for Mars, as President Bush suggested last week, may not be the most sensible route to the Red Planet. But that doesn't mean a return to the moon shouldn't be part of a reinvigorated human spaceflight program. There are plenty of reasons to go back to the world we abandoned 30 years ago—some fanciful and futuristic, others quite practical.

At the more practical end, the moon offers unique opportunities for scientific research. Going there is the only way to figure out where the moon came from, for example. Current theory says it was blasted from Earth in a collision with a planet-size object billions of years ago, but the moon rocks we
10 have in hand from the Apollo missions don't offer enough mineralogical clues to prove or refute the idea.

The moon would also be a terrific place to build astronomical observatories. With no atmosphere to interfere with precision optics, it offers both the clarity of outer space and a surface solid enough to support enormous structures. . . .

Another good reason to go is the one disdained by straight-to-Mars boosters: learning how to live off the land—manufacturing some of what we need from soil that contains oxygen, silicon, aluminum, iron, calcium, magnesium and titanium, plus a dusting of helium, hydrogen, nitrogen and carbon deposited by solar winds.

20 To some dreamers, the presence of silicon, especially, suggests a way to make a return to the moon pay—and maybe even save the environment back home. If you could set up automated lunar factories to extract the silicon and turn it into solar cells, says David Criswell, director of the Institute for Space Systems Operations at the University of Houston, the moon could become a solar power station, beaming clean energy via microwaves back to Earth. . . .

The fact that solar power isn't yet cost effective on Earth makes this high-tech scenario seem a bit farfetched. The same goes for another energy-producing idea: extracting helium-3, an isotope rare on Earth but relatively abundant on the lunar surface, and shipping it back to fuel nuclear-fusion
30 power plants. First, though, somebody would have to demonstrate that fusion reactors actually work.

from In Defense of Space Exploration

Matt Silver

While many in the Massachusetts Institute of Technology community are likely thrilled by President Bush's newly announced initiative to return men to the moon, others remain more skeptical. Let's take a moment to review both the plan and benefits of space exploration in general.

Regarding cost, let's put some things in perspective. NASA's FY03 budget[1] was roughly $15.5 billion. The Bush initiative calls for $1 billion in new funds spread over the next five years, and $11 billion re-allocated from existing NASA programs, resulting in an increase of $200 million a year. For comparison, the U.S. will spend roughly $400 billion on defense in 2004—more
10 than the next fifteen countries combined.

Those opposed to space programs will here point out that federal over-spending in one area does not justify it in another. There are many reasons, however, why that increase and the plan that goes with it constitute wise resource allocation. First, the initiative opens the possibility for much needed change at NASA. The Columbia tragedy threw light on major internal and organizational problems at the agency. The Columbia Accident Investigation Board report describes the tragedy not as an isolated incident, but as symptomatic of a broken safety and management culture in which innovation and safety often take a back seat to bureaucracy and political infighting. The
20 bold mandate for an $11 billion internal re-organization coming from the highest levels of government will finally give NASA headquarters the authority to cancel unnecessary programs, streamline operations not consistent with the stated goal, and override political pressure that otherwise stifled change.

Some, of course, maintain that the U.S. should simply not be involved in human space flight to begin with. This brings us to the classic argument of whether human space exploration in general is a good thing, worth reviewing in light of the current plans.

First, money spent on space research and development does not disappear into thin air. It goes toward creating knowledge, jobs, new businesses, and
30 technologies, many of which have direct application to other activities.

---

1. National Aeronautics and Space Administration's budget for fiscal year 2003.

There will also be important scientific returns. The NASA Hubble Space Telescope has literally changed our understanding of the universe. A telescope on the moon, shielded from both solar and earth radiation, has the potential to see further into the universe than anything previously built. During the Apollo moon landings, we arguably learned more about lunar geology and the solar system in general than we could have in many decades of robotic probes. This kind of science merits government funding.

An often-ignored benefit of space activities involves its capacity to increase international cooperation and generate goodwill. A return to the moon will bring the international community together in an activity that pits man against the cosmos. An international effort will
40 not only lower costs through the pooling of resources, it will create concrete links between the U.S., Russia, Japan, Europe, even China; and this will have tremendous symbolic overtones.

Reach for the stars ... and one day you may get there.

Public service announcement, 2007

Comprehension

DIRECTIONS *Answer these questions about the excerpt from "Why Go Back to the Moon?"*

1. In lines 1–11, what claim does the author make about the value of moon exploration?

   A. The president supports moon exploration.

   B. Travel to the moon is the best route to Mars.

   C. Good reasons exist for exploring the moon.

   D. A return to the moon is an outdated idea.

2. Which statement is a fact that supports setting up a solar power station on the moon?

   A. It is the best way to provide clean energy through microwaves.

   B. Silicon, which is available on the moon, is useful in producing power.

   C. The moon has a surface that is solid enough to support enormous structures.

   D. Someone needs to show that nuclear fusion reactors can produce power.

3. Which argument is used to counter the "straight-to-Mars boosters" (lines 15–16)?

A. People could use the moon's element-rich soil to manufacture necessities.

B. People who want to use solar power and make money from the moon are dreamers.

C. Nuclear fusion power plants would be a better source of energy than solar power.

D. Solar power isn't cost-effective on Earth.

DIRECTIONS *Answer these questions about the excerpt from "In Defense of Space Exploration."*

4. Which one of the following statements is an opinion?

A. NASA's budget for 2003 was roughly $15.5 billion. (lines 5–6)

B. We arguably learned more about space from the moon landings than we could have from robotic probes. (lines 34–35)

C. Money spent on space research and development provides jobs. (lines 28–30)

D. The Hubble telescope has provided scientific information. (lines 31–32)

5. Which argument does the author counter in lines 25–36?

A. More money should be given to NASA.

B. Many countries do not agree with the United States about space programs.

C. Human space exploration is not a good enterprise.

D. NASA needs the authority to cancel unnecessary programs.

6. Which words and images in lines 31–41 make the strongest appeal to your emotions?

A. solar system, moon landings, lunar geology

B. earth radiation, potential, robotic probes

C. goodwill, man against the cosmos, tremendous

D. capacity, return to the moon, effort

DIRECTIONS *Answer this question about both selections.*

7. Which idea is presented by both authors in support of space exploration?

A. reorganizing NASA

B. pooling resources among nations

C. setting up a space observatory on the moon

D. turning silicon into solar cells

DIRECTIONS *Answer this question about the advertisement.*

8. Which feeling does the ad try to convey by showing a smiling child looking up at the stars?

A. optimism   C. patriotism

B. reverence   D. playfulness

Written Response

SHORT ANSWER *Write three or four sentences to answer this question.*

9. Is the following sentence from "Why Go Back to the Moon?" a statement of fact or opinion? Briefly explain your reasoning.

"The moon would also be a terrific place to build astronomical observatories." (line 12)

EXTENDED RESPONSE *Write two or three paragraphs to answer this question.*

10. Which selection in favor of space exploration do you think is more persuasive? Identify the reasons, evidence, and persuasive techniques that you think make it more effective.

Vocabulary

DIRECTIONS *Use context clues to answer the following questions about specialized vocabulary words.*

1. Which expression in lines 8–10 of "Why Go Back to the Moon?" gives the best clue to the meaning of *mineralogical?*

   A. blasted from Earth

   B. planet-size object

   C. moon rocks

   D. Apollo missions

2. In line 12 of "Why Go Back to the Moon?" the word *astronomical* refers to

   A. outer space

   B. enormous size

   C. microwaves

   D. optics

3. Which word in lines 34–35 of "In Defense of Space Exploration" gives the best clue to the meaning of *lunar?*

   A. moon

   B. geology

   C. solar

   D. robotic

DIRECTIONS *Read the thesaurus entries and answer the questions.*

> **farfetched** *adjective*
> bizarre, grotesque, fantastic, remote, distant, imaginary, antic, strained

4. Which word could be substituted for the word *farfetched* as it is used in line 27 of "Why Go Back to the Moon?"

   A. strained

   B. grotesque

   C. fantastic

   D. antic

> **bold** *adjective*
> rude, pushy, noticeable, adventurous, conspicuous, obvious, shameless

5. Which word could be substituted for the word *bold* as it is used in line 20 of "In Defense of Space Exploration"?

   A. rude

   B. pushy

   C. obvious

   D. adventurous

> **consistent** *adjective*
> compatible, unchanging, constant, unfailing, even, loyal, valid

6. Which word could be substituted for the word *consistent* as it is used in line 22 of "In Defense of Space Exploration"?

   A. compatible

   B. unchanging

   C. constant

   D. unfailing

Writing & Grammar

DIRECTIONS *Read the passage and answer the questions that follow.*

(1) Space tourism is a lucrative business. (2) One company found two willing candidates. (3) The candidates wanted to fly to the International Space Station. (4) Each was ready to pay $20 million. (5) In the future, the company will offer more-affordable trips. (6) People will be able to take suborbital flights for just $100,000. (7) Civilian spaceships need to be built first. (8) Some people might want the experience without going to space. (9) To meet this need, the company will offer a training-only session. (10) Others might be interested in a short flight. (11) They'll have the option to fly just 15 miles high.

1. Choose the correct way to rewrite sentences 2, 3, and 4 as one compound-complex sentence.

   A. One company found two willing candidates wanting to fly to the International Space Station, and each was ready to pay $20 million.

   B. One company found two willing candidates who wanted to fly to the International Space Station, and each was ready to pay $20 million.

   C. When one company found two willing candidates wanting to fly to the International Space Station, they discovered that each was ready to pay $20 million.

   D. One company found two willing candidates wanting to fly to the International Space Station, with each ready to pay $20 million.

2. Choose the correct way to rewrite sentences 5, 6, and 7 as one compound-complex sentence.

   A. In the future, the company will offer more-affordable trips to people who will be able to take suborbital flights for just $100,000 when civilian spaceships are built.

   B. In the future, when civilian spaceships are built, the company will offer more-affordable trips to people who will be able to take suborbital flights for just $100,000.

   C. In the future, when civilian spaceships are built, the company will offer more-affordable trips, and people will be able to take suborbital flights for just $100,000.

   D. In the future, civilian spaceships will be built, and the company will offer more-affordable flights to people for just $100,000.

3. Choose the correct way to rewrite sentences 9, 10, and 11 as one compound-complex sentence.

   A. To meet this need, the company will offer a training-only session, or if people are interested in a short flight, they'll have the option to fly just 15 miles high.

   B. To meet this need, the company will offer a training-only session, or people will have the option to fly just 15 miles high for a short flight.

   C. To meet this need, the company will offer a training-only session to interested people who also will have the option to fly just 15 miles high.

   D. To meet this need, the company will offer a training-only session; people also will have the option to fly just 15 miles high.

STOP

Ideas for Independent Reading

What should people do to protect the rights of animals? to protect the rights of other people? The following books explore such questions.

Do animals have rights?

The Pig Who Sang to the Moon
by Jeffrey Moussaieff Masson

Masson's observations of farm animals suggest that they, too, are capable of fear, happiness, and grief. Masson argues that if animals feel, their lives matter to them, and it is not right to confine and slaughter them for human food.

The Ten Trusts
by Jane Goodall and Marc Bekoff

The authors set out ways in which people can protect animals and the environment. True stories of animals are matched with the ten trusts, which include "Respect all life" and "Refrain from harming life in order to learn about it."

Speaking Out for Animals
edited by Kim W. Stallwood

A collection of interviews, this book sheds light on the reasons people have adopted the animal rights cause. Some names are well-known, such as that of the ex-Beatle Paul McCartney, but most of the subjects are ordinary people.

What would you sacrifice for justice?

To Kill a Mockingbird: The Screenplay
by Horton Foote

In the South before the civil rights era, the lawyer Atticus Finch courageously (and unpopularly) defends a black man against unjust charges. His story is told from the viewpoint of his young daughter, Scout.

Silver Rights
by Constance Curry

This book tells the true story of the Carters, a black Mississippi family who worked for justice by having 7 of their 13 children desegregate an all-white school system in 1965. There were threats and bullets in the middle of the night, but the family endured.

Eyewitness: A Filmmaker's Memoir of the Chicano Movement
by Jesús Salvador Treviño

Treviño's memoir reflects on the Mexican-American civil rights movement, which he helped document through his work as a filmmaker. This experience shaped the political principles that guide his work as a television producer and director.

How important is wealth?

A Christmas Carol
by Charles Dickens

This classic introduces readers to Ebenezer Scrooge, a wealthy and disagreeable 19th-century businessman. One Christmas Eve he receives a series of ghostly visits that change the way he lives his life.

The Pearl
by John Steinbeck

When Kino, a poor Mexican fisherman, finds a huge pearl, he thinks it will bring his family wealth and happiness. Instead, it places him in danger and causes him to lose what he values most.

Mean Spirit
by Linda Hogan

Based on historical events, this novel is set in 1920s Oklahoma, where oil was discovered on Osage Indian lands. The murder of Grace Blanket, the richest woman in the territory, is followed by other mysterious deaths. Who is responsible?

Sound and Sense

**THE LANGUAGE
OF POETRY**

Where do you find POETRY?

We drove to the cafe in silence.
When we arrived,
She whispered to the piano player,
Then took my hand. We danced.
And suddenly, something we had lost was back.

Where do you think these lines are from? Could they appear somewhere else in this anthology? in a volume of love poems? Perhaps they're from a song.

It might surprise you to learn that lines like these appeared in a magazine ad for a car. So are they poetry or not? Your answer probably depends on what you think poetry is and on the role it plays in your life.

MAKE A LIST On a sheet of paper, write your own definition of what poetry is. Then, on the basis of that definition, make a list of all the places you think poetry lives. When you're done, compare your definition and list with those of others in your class. Do any of the responses surprise you?

OHIO STANDARDS

Preview Unit Goals

LITERARY ANALYSIS
- Recognize characteristics of a variety of forms of poetry, including lyric poetry, ode, ballad, sonnet, and free verse
- Analyze form, including line and stanza
- Analyze imagery
- Analyze figurative language, including metaphor, simile, and personification
- Analyze sound devices, including repetition, alliteration, assonance, consonance, onomatopoeia, rhyme, rhythm, rhyme scheme, and meter

READING
- Compare and contrast
- Develop strategies for reading poetry
- Understand and analyze dialect
- Take notes and evaluate poems

WRITING AND GRAMMAR
- Write a literary analysis
- Use precise language to express rhythm, sound, and imagery
- Use parallelism to create rhythm

SPEAKING, LISTENING, AND VIEWING
- Deliver an oral interpretation

ACADEMIC VOCABULARY
- form
- line
- stanza
- figurative language
- sound devices
- imagery
- literary analysis
- oral interpretation

The Language of Poetry

Emily Dickinson once wrote, "If I feel physically as if the top of my head were taken off, I know that is poetry." A good poem can make readers look at the world in a new way. A simple fork becomes the foot of a strange and unearthly bird; death itself appears as the driver of a carriage. After reading a poem, you might find yourself repeating lines in your mind or remembering images that "spoke" to you from the page. What gives poetry such power? Read a poem closely, and you'll see how it has been carefully crafted to affect you.

OHIO STANDARDS

READING STANDARDS
4.5 Analyze how choice of genre affects theme or topic
4.10 Describe the effect of using sound devices in literary texts
4.11 Explain ways author develops point of view and style

Part 1: Form

What you'll most likely notice first about a poem is its **form,** or the distinctive way the words are arranged on the page. Form refers to the length and placement of **lines** and the way they are grouped into **stanzas.** Similar to a paragraph in narrative writing, each stanza conveys a unified idea and contributes to a poem's overall meaning.

Poems can be traditional or organic in form. Regardless of its structure, though, a poem's form is often deliberately chosen to echo its meaning.

TRADITIONAL	**ORGANIC**
Characteristics • follows fixed rules, such as a specified number of lines • has a regular pattern of rhythm and rhyme • includes the following forms: sonnet, ode, haiku, limerick, ballad, epic	*Characteristics* • does not have a regular pattern of rhythm and may not rhyme • may use unconventional spelling, punctuation, and grammar • includes the following forms: free verse, concrete poetry
▼	▼

Example
Does the road wind up-hill all the way?
    Yes, to the very end.
Will the day's journey take the whole long day?
    From morn to night, my friend.
 	
    —from "Up-hill" by Christina Rossetti
	Example
	wear your colors
	like a present person
	        today is
	        here & now
	
	    —from "Look Not to Memories"
	        by Angela de Hoyos

Analyze the Example • Identify the rhyming words at the ends of the lines to see the rhyme pattern of the stanza. • Read the lines aloud to hear their regular rhythm. • Notice how the singsong musical quality emphasizes the comforting message.	**Analyze the Example** • Notice that this poem has no capitalization or end punctuation. • Note the lack of rhyme and the use of an ampersand (&). • Think about why this structure suits the "seize the day" message.

MODEL 1: TRADITIONAL FORM

The following two stanzas are from an **ode,** a complex lyric poem that addresses a serious theme, such as justice, truth, or the passage of time. While odes can follow just about any structure, "The Fire of Driftwood" is traditional in form because of its regular stanzas, rhythm, and rhyme. Here, the **speaker**—the voice that talks to the reader—sadly reflects on how he and his friends have grown apart.

from THE FIRE *of* DRIFTWOOD
Poem by **Henry Wadsworth Longfellow**

We spake of many a vanished scene,
    Of what we once had thought and said,
Of what had been, and might have been,
    And who was changed, and who was dead;

5 And all that fills the hearts of friends,
    When first they feel, with secret pain,
Their lives thenceforth have separate ends,
    And never can be one again.

Close Read

1. How is the form of the first stanza similar to that of the second? Consider the number and length of the lines, the pattern of the rhyme, and the rhythm.

2. Summarize the different ideas expressed in each stanza.

MODEL 2: ORGANIC FORM

This poem is written in **free verse,** with no regular pattern of rhythm and rhyme. Notice how its form differs from that of Longfellow's poem.

i am not done   yet
Poem by **Lucille Clifton**

as possible as yeast
as imminent as bread
a collection of safe habits
a collection of cares
5 less certain than i seem
more certain than i was
a changed changer
i continue to continue
where i have been
10 most of my lives is
where i'm going

Close Read

1. Using the chart on the preceding page, identify two characteristics that make this poem organic in form.

2. Read the poem aloud. The short lines and the rhythm help to emphasize the ideas expressed in each line. Choose two lines and explain what the speaker is saying.

Part 2: Poetic Elements

What gives one poem a brisk rhythm and another the sound of an everyday conversation? How can two poems on the same subject—for example, the simplicity of nature—create dramatically different images in your mind? Sound devices and imagery are the techniques that give dimension to words on a page.

SOUND DEVICES

Much of the power of poetry depends on **rhythm**—the pattern of stressed and unstressed syllables in each line. Poets use rhythm to emphasize important words or ideas and to create a mood that suits their subject. Some poems have a regular pattern of rhythm, which is called **meter.** Analyzing the effects of a poem's rhythm begins with **scanning,** or marking, the meter. Unstressed syllables are marked with a (˘) and stressed syllables with a (´), as in these lines from "A Dirge" by Percy Bysshe Shelley:

Rough wind, / that moan / est loud   a

Grief / too sad / for song;   b

Wild wind / when sul / len cloud   a

Knells / all the night / long.   b

A regular pattern of rhyme is called a **rhyme scheme.** Rhyme scheme is charted by assigning a letter of the alphabet to matching end rhymes, as shown in "A Dirge."

Poets also use many other sound devices to create specific effects. In each of the following examples, notice how the device helps to establish a mood, create a rhythm, and suggest different sounds and sights of the sea.

REPETITION
a sound, word, phrase, or line that is repeated for emphasis and unity

Break, break, break,
   On thy cold gray stones, O Sea!
—from "Break, Break, Break" by Alfred, Lord Tennyson

ALLITERATION
the repetition of consonant sounds at the beginnings of words

The scraggy rock spit shielding the town's blue bay
         —from "Departure" by Sylvia Plath

ASSONANCE
the repetition of vowel sounds in words that do not end with the same consonant

The waves break fold on jewelled fold.
        —from "Moonlight" by Sara Teasdale

CONSONANCE
the repetition of consonant sounds within and at the ends of words

And black are the waters that sparkled so green.
      —from "Seal Lullaby" by Rudyard Kipling

MODEL 1: RHYTHM AND RHYME

The speakers in this next poem could be understood to be the collective voice of the pool players mentioned underneath the title. Read the poem aloud to hear its unique rhyme scheme and rhythm. In what ways do these elements reflect the fast-lane lifestyle that the speakers describe?

We Real Cool

The Pool Players.
Seven at The Golden Shovel.

Poem by **Gwendolyn Brooks**

We real cool. We
Left school. We

Lurk late. We
Strike straight. We

5   Sing sin. We
Thin gin. We

Jazz June. We
Die soon.

Close Read

1. Even though the rhyming words in this poem fall in the middle of the lines, they sound like end rhymes. If you treat these words as end rhymes, what is the rhyme scheme?

2. One way to read this poem is to stress every syllable. How would you describe the rhythm? Explain how it echoes the speakers' attitude toward life.

MODEL 2: OTHER SOUND DEVICES

This poem immerses you in the edge-of-your-seat excitement of a close baseball game. What sound devices has the poet used to create this effect?

THE BASE STEALER

Poem by **Robert Francis**

Poised between going on and back, pulled
Both ways taut like a tightrope-walker,
Fingertips pointing the opposites,
Now bouncing tiptoe like a dropped ball

5   Or a kid skipping rope, come on, come on,
Running a scattering of steps sidewise,
How he teeters, skitters, tingles, teases,
Taunts them, hovers like an ecstatic bird,
He's only flirting, crowd him, crowd him,

10   Delicate, delicate, delicate, delicate—now!

Close Read

1. Read the boxed text aloud. The use of alliteration emphasizes the tension that the base stealer feels. Find another example of alliteration and explain its effect.

2. Identify two other sound devices that the poet uses and describe their effects.

IMAGERY AND FIGURATIVE LANGUAGE

I can remember wind-swept streets of cities
on cold and blustery nights, on rainy days;
heads under shabby felts and parasols
and shoulders hunched against a sharp concern.

—from "Memory" by Margaret Walker

Do these lines make you want to stay indoors, nestled under layers of blankets? If so, the reason is **imagery**, or words and phrases that re-create sensory experiences for readers. Through the highlighted images, the poet helps readers visualize the bleak scene—the way it looks, sounds, and even *feels*—in striking detail.

One way poets create strong imagery is through the use of **figurative language**, which conveys meanings beyond the literal meanings of words. Figurative language pops up all the time in everyday speech. For example, if you say "My heart sank when I heard the disappointing news," your friends will understand that your heart did not literally sink. Through this figurative expression, you are conveying the emotional depth of your disappointment.

In the following examples, notice what each technique helps to emphasize about the subject described.

FIGURATIVE LANGUAGE	EXAMPLE
SIMILE a comparison between two unlike things using the words *like, as,* or *as if*	I remember how you sang in your stone shoes light-voiced as dusk or feathers. —from "Elegy for My Father" by Robert Winner
METAPHOR a comparison between two unlike things but without the words *like* or *as*	The door of winter is frozen shut. —from "Wind Chill" by Linda Pastan
PERSONIFICATION a description of an object, an animal, a place, or an idea in human terms	Death, be not proud, though some have callèd thee Mighty and dreadful, for thou art not so. —from "Sonnet 10" by John Donne
HYPERBOLE an exaggeration for emphasis or humorous effect	Here once the embattled farmers stood And fired the shot heard round the world. —from "The Concord Hymn" by Ralph Waldo Emerson

MODEL 3: IMAGERY

Notice the imagery this poet uses to transport you to the hot sands of an island in the West Indies.

Midsummer, *Tobago*

Poem by **Derek Walcott**

Broad sun-stoned beaches.

White heat.
A green river.

A bridge,
5   scorched yellow palms

from the summer-sleeping house
drowsing through August.

Days I have held,
days I have lost,

10   days that outgrow, like daughters,
my harbouring arms.

Close Read

1. The boxed image appeals to the senses of sight and touch. Identify three other images and describe the scene they conjure up in your mind.

2. How does the speaker feel about the summer days he or she describes? Explain how the image in lines 10–11 helps you to understand the speaker's emotions.

MODEL 4: FIGURATIVE LANGUAGE

The use of figurative language in this poem strengthens the contrast between a lifeless winter day and the vibrancy of the horses.

from Horses

Poem by **Pablo Neruda**, translated by Alastair Reid

I was in Berlin, in winter. The light
was without light, the sky skyless.

The air white like a moistened loaf.

From my window, I could see a deserted arena,
5   a circle bitten out by the teeth of winter.

All at once, led out by a man,
ten horses were stepping into the snow.

Emerging, they had scarcely rippled into existence
like flame, than they filled the whole world of my eyes,
10   empty till now. Faultless, flaming,
they stepped like ten gods on broad, clean hooves.

Close Read

1. One example of a simile is boxed. What does this comparison tell you about the air? Find another simile and explain the comparison.

2. In line 5, the poet uses personification to describe winter. What characteristics of winter does this comparison emphasize?

Part 3: Analyze the Literature

Apply what you have just learned about the forms, techniques, and effects of poetry by comparing the next two poems. The first describes the dead-end life of Flick Webb, a former high school basketball star. Read the poem a first time, looking for details that help you to understand the character of Flick. Then read the poem aloud to get the full impact.

EX-*Basketball Player*

Poem by **John Updike**

Pearl Avenue runs past the high-school lot,
Bends with the trolley tracks, and stops, cut off
Before it has a chance to go two blocks,
At Colonel McComsky Plaza. Berth's Garage
5 Is on the corner facing west, and there,
Most days, you'll find Flick Webb, who helps Berth out.

Flick stands tall among the idiot pumps—
Five on a side, the old bubble-head style,
Their rubber elbows hanging loose and low.
10 One's nostrils are two S's, and his eyes
An E and O. And one is squat, without
A head at all—more of a football type.

Once Flick played for the high-school team, the Wizards.
He was good: in fact, the best. In '46
15 He bucketed three hundred ninety points,
A county record still. The ball loved Flick.
I saw him rack up thirty-eight or forty
In one home game. His hands were like wild birds.

He never learned a trade, he just sells gas,
20 Checks oil, and changes flats. Once in a while,
As a gag, he dribbles an inner tube,
But most of us remember anyway.
His hands are fine and nervous on the lug wrench.
It makes no difference to the lug wrench, though.

25 Off work, he hangs around Mae's Luncheonette.
Grease-gray and kind of coiled, he plays pinball,
Smokes those thin cigars, nurses lemon phosphates.
Flick seldom says a word to Mae, just nods
Beyond her face toward bright applauding tiers
30 Of Necco Wafers, Nibs, and Juju Beads.

Close Read

1. In the second stanza, Flick stands next to gas pumps, which are personified as athletes. Citing details in the stanza, describe this image as you see it in your mind's eye.

2. Identify the simile in the third stanza. What does it tell you about Flick's athletic ability in high school?

3. Now that you know more about the character of Flick, reread lines 1–3. How does the image of Pearl Avenue remind you of him?

4. The poet uses alliteration in the last stanza. One example is boxed. Find two more examples.

The description of basketball players in this poem provides a sharp contrast to the sad portrait of Flick Webb in "Ex-Basketball Player."

SLAM,

DUNK, &

HOOK

Poem by **Yusef Komunyakaa**

Fast breaks. Lay ups. With Mercury's
Insignia on our sneakers,
We outmaneuvered to footwork
Of bad angels. Nothing but a hot
5   Swish of strings like silk
Ten feet out. In the roundhouse
Labyrinth our bodies
Created, we could almost
Last forever, poised in midair
10   Like storybook sea monsters.
A high note hung there
A long second. Off
The rim. We'd corkscrew
Up & dunk balls that exploded
15   The skullcap of hope & good
Intention. Lanky, all hands
& feet . . . sprung rhythm.
We were metaphysical when girls
Cheered on the sidelines.
20   Tangled up in a falling,
Muscles were a bright motor
Double-flashing to the metal hoop
Nailed to our oak.
When Sonny Boy's mama died
25   He played nonstop all day, so hard
Our backboard splintered.
Glistening with sweat,
We rolled the ball off
Our fingertips. Trouble
30   Was there slapping a blackjack
Against an open palm.
Dribble, drive to the inside,
& glide like a sparrow hawk.
Lay ups. Fast breaks.
35   We had moves we didn't know
We had. Our bodies spun
On swivels of bone & faith,
Through a lyric slipknot
Of joy, & we knew we were
40   Beautiful & dangerous.

Close Read

1. Is the form of this poem traditional or organic? Support your answer with specific examples.

2. Read the boxed lines aloud and identify two sound devices that are used. What does the rhythm in these lines remind you of?

3. The speaker describes the players as "Beautiful & dangerous" in line 40. Find two examples of figurative language that suggest either of these qualities. Explain your choices.

4. Contrast the two poems, citing three differences. Think about each poet's treatment of the subject, as well as his use of poetic techniques.

There Will Come Soft Rains
Poem by Sara Teasdale

Meeting at Night
Poem by Robert Browning

The Sound of Night
Poem by Maxine Kumin

What is our place in NATURE?

OHIO STANDARDS

READING & COMM STANDARDS
4.10 Describe the effect of using sound devices in literary texts
9.6 Adjust volume, phrasing, enunciation, voice modulation and inflection

KEY IDEA Are humans more powerful than **nature?** Think of how we change landscapes, drive other species to extinction, and otherwise use nature for our own ends. Or are humans insignificant in the face of nature's power?

DISCUSS Think about a recent encounter you had with nature. What attitude did you express—admiration? indifference? In a small group, discuss your overall attitudes toward nature.

● LITERARY ANALYSIS: SOUND DEVICES

One common sound device used in poetry is **rhyme,** the repetition of sounds at the ends of words. **End rhyme** is rhyme at the ends of lines, as in this excerpt:

Whose woods these are I think I <u>know</u>.
His house is in the village <u>though</u>.

Another sound device is **alliteration,** the repetition of consonant sounds at the beginnings of words, as in *<u>D</u>roning a <u>d</u>rowsy syncopated tune.*

   Still another sound device is **onomatopoeia,** the use of words that imitate sounds, as in *The <u>buzz</u> saw <u>snarled</u> and <u>rattled</u> in the yard.* As you read the following poems about nature, notice their sound devices. Record examples on a chart.

Title	End Rhyme	Alliteration	Onomatopoeia
"There Will Come Soft Rains"	ground / sound (lines 1 and 2)		

● READING STRATEGY: READING POETRY

Reading poetry requires paying attention not only to the meaning of the words but to the way they look and sound. The following strategies will help you.

- Notice how the lines are arranged on the page. Are they long lines, or short? Are they grouped into regular **stanzas** or irregular stanzas, or are they not divided into stanzas at all? Stanza breaks usually signal the start of a new idea.

- Pause in your reading where punctuation marks appear, just as you would when reading prose. Note that in poetry, punctuation does not always occur at the end of a line; a thought may continue for several lines.

- Read a poem aloud several times. As you read, notice whether the rhythm is regular or varied. Is there a **rhyme scheme,** or regular pattern of end rhyme? For example, you'll notice that "There Will Come Soft Rains" is written in **couplets,** two-line units with an *aa* rhyme scheme. Regular patterns of rhythm and rhyme give a musical quality to poems.

Review: **Make Inferences**

Author Online

Sara Teasdale: Love and War Sara Teasdale explored the topic of love in all of its aspects. Drawing on her own experiences, she wrote about the beauty, pleasure, fragility, and heartache of love in exquisitely crafted lyric poems. In reaction to World War I, she also wrote antiwar poems, such as "There Will Come Soft Rains."

Sara Teasdale
1884–1933

Robert Browning: Painter of Portraits Robert Browning was a master at capturing psychological complexity. Using the **dramatic monologue,** a poem addressed to a silent listener, he conveyed the personalities of both fictional and historical figures. "Meeting at Night" is one of his shorter lyric poems.

Robert Browning
1812–1889

Maxine Kumin: Poet of Place The poetry of Maxine Kumin is rooted in New England rural life. Using traditional verse forms, Kumin explores changes in nature, people's relationship to the land and its creatures, and human mortality, loss, and survival.

Maxine Kumin
born 1925

 MORE ABOUT THE AUTHOR
For more on these poets, visit the **Literature Center** at **ClassZone.com.**

There Will Come Soft Rains

Sara Teasdale

There will come soft rains and the smell of the ground,
And swallows circling with their shimmering sound; **A**

And frogs in the pools singing at night,
And wild plum-trees in tremulous white;

5 Robins will wear their feathery fire
Whistling their whims on a low fence-wire; **B**

And not one will know of the war, not one
Will care at last when it is done.

Not one would mind, neither bird nor tree
10 If mankind perished utterly;

And Spring herself, when she woke at dawn,
Would scarcely know that we were gone.

A READING POETRY
Read the first stanza aloud. Notice that it is a rhymed **couplet.** What expectations are set up by this **end rhyme?**

B SOUND DEVICES
What examples of **alliteration** can you identify in lines 1–6?

ANALYZE VISUALS
What overall feeling do you get from this landscape?

Spring Landscape (1909), Constant Permeke. Constant Permeke Museum, Jabbeke, Belgium. © 2008 Artists Rights Society (ARS), New York/SABAM, Brussels.

Moonrise (1906), Guillermo Gomez y Gil. Oil on canvas. Musée des Beaux-Arts, Pau, France. Photo © Giraudon/Bridgeman Art Library.

Meeting *at* Night
Robert Browning

1

The gray sea and the long black land;
And the yellow half-moon large and low;
And the startled little waves that leap
In fiery ringlets from their sleep,
5 As I gain the cove[1] with pushing prow,[2]
And quench its speed i' the slushy sand. **C**

2

Then a mile of warm sea-scented beach;
Three fields to cross till a farm appears;
A tap at the pane, the quick sharp scratch
10 And blue spurt of a lighted match,
And a voice less loud, through its joys and fears,
Than the two hearts beating each to each! **D**

---

1. **cove:** a small, partly enclosed body of water.

2. **prow** (prou): the front part of a boat.

C READING POETRY
Read the first stanza aloud. What **rhyme scheme** do you notice?

D MAKE INFERENCES
Where does the speaker arrive, and what happens once he is there?

The *Sound of Night*

Maxine Kumin

Trees at Night (c. 1900), Thomas Meteyard. Berry Hill Gallery, New York. Photo © Edward Owen/Art Resource, New York.

And now the dark comes on, all full of chitter noise.
Birds huggermugger[1] crowd the trees,
the air thick with their vesper[2] cries,
and bats, snub seven-pointed kites,
5 skitter across the lake, swing out,
squeak, chirp, dip, and skim on skates
of air, and the fat frogs wake and prink
wide-lipped, noisy as ducks, drunk
on the boozy black, gloating chink-chunk. **E**

10 And now on the narrow beach we defend ourselves from dark.
The cooking done, we build our firework
bright and hot and less for outlook
than for magic, and lie in our blankets
while night nickers around us. Crickets
15 chorus hallelujahs; paws, quiet
and quick as raindrops, play on the stones
expertly soft, run past and are gone;
fish pulse in the lake; the frogs hoarsen.

Now every voice of the hour—the known, the supposed, the strange,
20 the mindless, the witted, the never seen—
sing, thrum, impinge,[3] and rearrange
endlessly; and debarred[4] from sleep we wait
for the birds, importantly silent,
for the crease of first eye-licking light,
25 for the sun, lost long ago and sweet.
By the lake, locked black away and tight,
we lie, day creatures, overhearing night.

E **SOUND DEVICES**
What examples of **onomatopoeia** can you identify in the first stanza? What do they add to the poem?

---

1. **huggermugger:** disorderly.
2. **vesper:** pertaining to the evening; a type of swallow that sings in the evening.
3. **impinge** (ĭm-pĭnj′): to strike or push upon.
4. **debarred:** prevented or hindered.

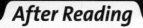

Comprehension

 **OHIO STANDARDS**

READING STANDARD
4.10 Describe the effect of using sound devices in literary texts

1. **Clarify** According to the speaker in Teasdale's poem, how would the natural world react if "mankind perished utterly"?

2. **Clarify** Whom does the speaker in Browning's poem meet when he arrives at his destination?

3. **Clarify** What time and place are described in Kumin's poem?

Literary Analysis

4. **Reading Poetry** Which poem did you appreciate most when read aloud? Explain the qualities that were brought out in an oral reading.

5. **Analyze Rhyme** Describe how **end rhyme** is used in each poem. Which poems employ a regular **rhyme scheme?** What ideas are emphasized through end rhyme? Use a chart like the one shown to plan your answer.

	Rhyme Scheme	Important Rhyming Words
"There Will Come Soft Rains"		
"Meeting at Night"		
"The Sound of Night"		

6. **Recognize Alliteration** Which poem makes the most obvious use of alliteration? What feelings or ideas are suggested by these repeated consonant sounds?

7. **Relate Theme and Sound Devices** Describe the qualities of **nature** conveyed in each poem. How are sound devices used to suggest these qualities? Refer to your sound devices chart to plan your answer.

8. **Draw Conclusions** What does each poem suggest about humans and nature?

Literary Criticism

9. **Critical Interpretations** According to one critic, Teasdale's poetry "expresses the fragility of human life where the only real certainty comes from nature." How does this comment apply to "There Will Come Soft Rains"?

Reading-Writing Connection

Broaden your understanding of the poems by responding to these prompts. Then use **Revision: Grammar and Style** to improve your writing.

WRITING PROMPTS	SELF-CHECK
A. Short Response: Support an Opinion Which of the three poems expresses the greatest appreciation of **nature?** Defend your choice in **one or two paragraphs,** using examples from the poems.	*A strong opinion statement will . . .* • identify one poem as expressing the most appreciation of nature • show how the imagery and tone of the poem express this appreciation
B. Extended Response: Interpret Theme What is the theme or message of each poem that you read? Drawing on details from the poems, write a **three-to-five-paragraph response.**	*An effective response will . . .* • give a clearly stated interpretation of each poem • present details that support the interpretation

REVISION: GRAMMAR AND STYLE

WRITING STANDARD
5.9 Use precise language: action verbs

USE PRECISE LANGUAGE It is important for writers to choose words that effectively express the rhythm, sound, and imagery they wish to convey to their audience. Notice how Maxine Kumin's use of **precise verbs** in "The Sound of Night" makes the description livelier and more specific than if she had used verbs such as "fly" or "communicate."

> *and bats, snub seven-pointed kites,*
> *skitter across the lake, swing out,*
> *squeak, chirp, dip, and skim on skates*
> *of air . . .* (lines 4–7)

Careful consideration of word choice can be given to all types of writing, not just poetry. Notice that the revisions in red are precise verbs that enhance the description in this first draft. Revise your responses to the prompts by changing any dull, general verbs to more precise ones.

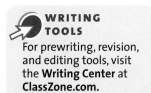

WRITING TOOLS
For prewriting, revision, and editing tools, visit the **Writing Center** at ClassZone.com.

STUDENT MODEL

In "There Will Come Soft Rains," Sara Teasdale ~~asks~~ *urges* us to consider that nature will go on long after humans have ~~done away with~~ *annihilated* themselves.

I dwell in Possibility—

Poem by Emily Dickinson

Variation on a Theme by Rilke

Poem by Denise Levertov

blessing the boats

Poem by Lucille Clifton

What if you couldn't FAIL?

OHIO STANDARDS

READING STANDARDS
4.5 Analyze how choice of genre affects theme or topic
4.11 Explain ways author develops point of view and style

KEY IDEA Think about living in a world of endless **possibility.** You have no limitations, and you have every advantage available to you. If you want to sing, you have an extraordinary voice. If you want to feed the hungry, world leaders adopt your plans. What would you do in life if you knew that you could only succeed?

QUICKWRITE Make a short to-do list of things you'd like to accomplish if success were assured. Then, with a partner, discuss your list. What are some of the entries? How do you feel inside as you imagine completing these tasks?

To-Do List
1. Compete in the Olympics
2.
3.

● POETIC FORM: LYRIC POETRY

A **lyric poem** is a short poem in which a single speaker expresses personal thoughts and feelings on a subject. In ancient Greece, lyric poets expressed their feelings in song, accompanied by a lyre. While modern lyric poems are no longer sung, they still retain common characteristics such as:

- a sense of rhythm and melody
- imaginative language
- exploration of a single feeling or thought

Reading the lyric poems on the following pages aloud will help you appreciate these characteristics.

● LITERARY ANALYSIS: FIGURATIVE LANGUAGE

Figurative language is an expression of ideas beyond what the words literally mean. Three basic types of figurative language, or **figures of speech**, follow:

- A **simile** compares two unlike things that have something in common, using *like* or *as*. (*bats, sailing like kites*)
- A **metaphor** compares two unlike things by saying that one thing actually is the other. (*bats, snub seven-pointed kites*)
- **Personification** lends human qualities to an object, animal, or idea. (*bats, performing a graceful ballet*)

Poets use figurative language both to convey abstract thoughts and to offer a fresh outlook on everyday things. As you read the following poems, use a chart like this one to record and analyze examples of simile, metaphor, and personification.

Example	Type	Two Things Compared	Ideas Suggested
"I dwell in Possibility—/ A fairer House than Prose—"	metaphor	poetry/possibility and a house	

● READING SKILL: COMPARE AND CONTRAST

Comparing and contrasting the poems—identifying the similarities and the differences between them—will help you understand each poem's central theme. As you read, compare the feelings expressed and the figurative language used.

Author Online

Emily Dickinson: Passionate Poet
As an adult, Emily Dickinson rarely left her father's home or welcomed visitors. Yet she managed to write poems that are remarkable for their originality and awareness of human passion. Using unusual imagery and syntax, she explored such powerful emotions as love, despair, and ecstasy.

**Emily Dickinson
1830–1886**

Denise Levertov: A Poetic Vocation
Denise Levertov's view that writing poetry should be like a religious calling was influenced by the early 20th-century poet Rainer Maria Rilke, whom she claimed as a role model. Levertov often used her art in service of political ideals, tackling such issues as the Vietnam War and the nuclear arms race.

**Denise Levertov
1923–1997**

Lucille Clifton: Honoring Heritage
Lucille Clifton's poetry honors African heritage and expresses optimism about life. Clifton is a professor of humanities at St. Mary's College, which boasts a premier varsity sailing program. Sailboat races there may have inspired "blessing the boats."

**Lucille Clifton
born 1936**

MORE ABOUT THE AUTHOR
For more on these poets, visit the **Literature Center** at ClassZone.com.

I dwell in Possibility—

EMILY DICKINSON

I dwell in Possibility—
A fairer House than Prose—
More numerous of Windows—
Superior—for Doors—Ⓐ

5 Of Chambers as the Cedars—
Impregnable[1] of Eye—
And for an Everlasting Roof
The Gambrels[2] of the Sky—Ⓑ

Of Visitors—the fairest—
10 For Occupation—This—
The spreading wide my narrow Hands
To gather Paradise—

Ⓐ **FIGURATIVE LANGUAGE**
The speaker is not literally living in a House of Possibility. What idea is really being conveyed in this **metaphor**?

Ⓑ **FIGURATIVE LANGUAGE**
An **extended metaphor** compares two unlike things in more than one way. The house metaphor continues from the first stanza to the next. In lines 5–8, what is Dickinson saying about the size and scope of this house?

---

1. **Impregnable:** unconquerable.
2. **Gambrels:** a type of roof with two slopes on each side.

Detail of *Cape Cod Morning* (1950), Edward Hopper. Oil on canvas, 34¹/₈″ × 40¹/₄″. Smithsonian American Art Museum, Washington, D.C. © Heirs of Josephine N. Hopper, licensed by the Whitney Museum of American Art.

ANALYZE VISUALS
In what way does this image illustrate the feelings expressed in Dickinson's poem? Give specific **details.**

Variation on a Theme by Rilke
(The Book of Hours, *Book I, Poem I, Stanza I*)

DENISE LEVERTOV

A certain day became a presence to me;
there it was, confronting me—a sky, air, light:
a being. And before it started to descend
from the height of noon, it leaned over
5 and struck my shoulder as if with
the flat of a sword, granting me
honor and a task. The day's blow **C**
rang out, metallic—or it was I, a bell awakened,
and what I heard was my whole self
10 saying and singing what it knew: *I can.* **D**

C FIGURATIVE LANGUAGE
In this poem, a day is given human qualities. What idea does Levertov highlight through this use of **personification**?

D COMPARE AND CONTRAST
How similar are the feelings expressed in this poem and Dickinson's poem?

blessing the boats
(at St. Mary's)

LUCILLE CLIFTON

may the tide
that is entering even now
the lip of our understanding
carry you out
5 beyond the face of fear
may you kiss
the wind then turn from it
certain that it will
love your back   may you
10 open your eyes to water
water waving forever
and may you in your innocence
sail through this to that **E**

E LYRIC POETRY
What feeling is the
speaker expressing?

Comprehension

1. **Recall** In Dickinson's poem, what is the speaker's house "fairer than"?

2. **Recall** What did the speaker of Levertov's poem hear when "the day's blow rang out"?

3. **Paraphrase** What does the speaker of Clifton's poem wish?

Literary Analysis

4. **Interpret Metaphor** In Dickinson's poem, the house is the basis for a metaphor that is carried throughout the poem. What does this **extended metaphor** suggest about being a poet and living a life of the imagination?

5. **Interpret Figurative Language** Reread lines 4–7 in Levertov's poem and identify two examples of figurative language. What idea is conveyed? How does the figurative language illustrate the relationship between the speaker and the day?

6. **Analyze Personification** Find two or three examples of personification in Clifton's poem. What is given human qualities, and to what effect?

7. **Evaluate Figurative Language** Refer to the chart you created as you read. Which poem made the best use of figurative language? Explain your choice.

8. **Compare and Contrast Themes** Complete a chart like the one shown. Based on this information, do the poems suggest similar or different ideas about **possibility?**

	Feelings Expressed	Figurative Language Used
"I dwell in Possibility"		
"Variation on a Theme by Rilke"		
"blessing the boats"		

9. **Evaluate Lyric Poems** Review the characteristics of lyric poetry listed on page 705. Which poem would work best as the lyrics of a song, and why?

Literary Criticism

10. **Critical Interpretations** French poet Jean de La Fontaine said, "Man is so made that when anything fires his soul, impossibilities vanish." Evaluate the three poems against his statement. Do they support his claim? Why or why not?

Reading-Writing Connection

Broaden your understanding of the poems by responding to these prompts. Then use **Revision: Grammar and Style** to improve your writing.

WRITING PROMPTS	SELF-CHECK

A. Short Response: Write a Lyric Poem

In four or more lines, write a **poem** about a feeling you've had. Incorporate at least two examples of figurative language.

A successful poem will . . .
- describe a single impression
- include similes, metaphors, or personification

B. Extended Response: Analyze Theme

Who or what inspires the speakers of the three poems to be open to **possibility?** Write **three to five paragraphs** in which you explore the people, places, ideas, or things that embolden the three speakers.

An effective analysis will . . .
- include statements about the speakers' inspiration
- present details from the poems to support conclusions
- devote at least one paragraph to each poem

REVISION: GRAMMAR AND STYLE

CREATE RHYTHM **Parallelism** is the use of similar grammatical constructions to express ideas that are related or equal in importance. In the following excerpt from her poem "blessing the boats," Lucille Clifton uses parallelism to add rhythmic cadence to her writing. Notice how, in two different instances, she uses an inverted sentence structure that begins with the words "may you," followed by predicates.

OHIO STANDARDS

WRITING STANDARD
5.7 Use parallel sentence structure

> *may you kiss*
> *the wind then turn from it*
> *certain that it will*
> *love your back   may you*
> *open your eyes to water*
> *water waving forever* (lines 6–11)

Note how the revisions in red use parallelism to improve this first draft. Revise your responses to the prompts by making similar changes.

WRITING TOOLS
For prewriting, revision, and editing tools, visit the **Writing Center** at ClassZone.com.

STUDENT MODEL

Through poetry, the speaker sees the unseen. *And through* ~~Poetry~~ ~~also helps~~ the speaker experience *s* heaven on earth.

The Fish
Poem by Elizabeth Bishop

Christmas Sparrow
Poem by Billy Collins

The Sloth
Poem by Theodore Roethke

What ANIMAL *reminds you of yourself?*

OHIO STANDARDS

READING STANDARDS
4.5 Analyze how choice of genre affects theme or topic

4.9 Explain how authors use symbols to create broader meanings

KEY IDEA Think about your pets or other animals you've seen at the zoo or on TV nature shows. Do they ever behave in a way that seems almost human? Have you ever thought you knew what they were feeling? In the poems that follow, you will meet three **animals** with distinctive "human" qualities.

DISCUSS Choose one animal you identify with the most. Explain to a partner why you relate to it and what characteristics you share with it.

POETIC FORM: FREE VERSE

Most modern poems are written in **free verse,** a poetic form with no regular pattern of rhyme or rhythm. A free verse poem can be structured as one long, unbroken stanza, as in "The Fish," or with many stanzas of varying length, as in "Christmas Sparrow." The lines in free verse poems may also vary in length. Without a strict meter, the rhythm of free verse poetry often seems more like everyday speech. As you read, notice how the line length, sounds of words, and punctuation create a rhythm in each poem.

LITERARY ANALYSIS: IMAGERY

Sometimes a poem can seem like a portrait of a moment, a person, an animal, or an object. **Imagery,** or words and phrases that appeal to the reader's senses, can help create these types of portraits and often reinforce certain ideas about the subject described. For example, in "The Fish," Bishop appeals to the senses of sight and touch when she describes the fish's skin. Lines like these help depict a beautifully fragile old fish.

hung in strips / like ancient wallpaper

shapes like full-blown roses / stained and lost through age

As you read the poems, record strong, evocative imagery on a chart like the one shown. Identify

• the sense the word or phrase appeals to
• the associations the imagery conjures up
• the idea that is being reinforced

Poem Title:			
Imagery	Sense(s)	Associations	Idea Reinforced

READING STRATEGY: VISUALIZE

As you read the following poems, notice how the imagery, descriptions, and specific words help you **visualize** the animals, settings, and events in the poems. Use your imagination to "see" what they might look like. For example, what image of a fish comes to mind when you read the following description?

He hung a grunting weight, / battered and venerable / and homely. . . .

The Fish

Elizabeth Bishop

I caught a tremendous fish
and held him beside the boat
half out of water, with my hook
fast in a corner of his mouth.
5 He didn't fight.
He hadn't fought at all.
He hung a grunting weight,
battered and venerable
and homely. Here and there Ⓐ
10 his brown skin hung in strips
like ancient wallpaper,
and its pattern of darker brown
was like wallpaper:
shapes like full-blown roses
15 stained and lost through age.
He was speckled with barnacles,
fine rosettes of lime,
and infested
with tiny white sea-lice,
20 and underneath two or three
rags of green weed hung down.
While his gills were breathing in
the terrible oxygen
—the frightening gills,
25 fresh and crisp with blood,
that can cut so badly—
I thought of the coarse white flesh
packed in like feathers,
the big bones and the little bones,
30 the dramatic reds and blacks
of his shiny entrails,

Ⓐ **FREE VERSE**
Notice how the lines of
this poem are unequal in
length. How do the short
lines affect the rhythm in
the poem?

and the pink swim-bladder
like a big peony.
I looked into his eyes
35 which were far larger than mine
but shallower, and yellowed,
the irises backed and packed
with tarnished tinfoil
seen through the lenses
40 of old scratched isinglass.
They shifted a little, but not
to return my stare.
—It was more like the tipping
of an object toward the light. **B**
45 I admired his sullen face,
the mechanism of his jaw,
and then I saw
that from his lower lip
—if you could call it a lip—
50 grim, wet, and weaponlike,
hung five old pieces of fish-line,
or four and a wire leader
with the swivel still attached,
with all their five big hooks
55 grown firmly in his mouth.
A green line, frayed at the end
where he broke it, two heavier lines,
and a fine black thread
still crimped from the strain and snap
60 when it broke and he got away.
Like medals with their ribbons
frayed and wavering,
a five-haired beard of wisdom
trailing from his aching jaw. **C**
65 I stared and stared
and victory filled up
the little rented boat,
from the pool of bilge
where oil had spread a rainbow
70 around the rusted engine
to the bailer rusted orange,
the sun-cracked thwarts,
the oarlocks on their strings,
the gunnels—until everything
75 was rainbow, rainbow, rainbow!
And I let the fish go.

B VISUALIZE
Reread lines 34–44. What aspects of the fish's character can you "see" in this description of its eyes?

C IMAGERY
What senses does this description of the fish's face appeal to? What associations form in your mind about the fish?

CHRISTMAS SPARROW

BILLY COLLINS

The first thing I heard this morning
was a rapid flapping sound, soft, insistent—

wings against glass as it turned out
downstairs when I saw the small bird
5 rioting in the frame of a high window,
trying to hurl itself through
the enigma of glass into the spacious light. **D**

Then a noise in the throat of the cat
who was hunkered on the rug
10 told me how the bird had gotten inside,
carried in the cold night
through the flap of a basement door,
and later released from the soft grip of teeth.

On a chair, I trapped its pulsations
15 in a shirt and got it to the door,
so weightless it seemed
to have vanished into the nest of cloth.

But outside, when I uncupped my hands,
it burst into its element,
20 dipping over the dormant garden
in a spasm of wingbeats
then disappeared over a row of tall hemlocks.

D IMAGERY
What images describe the
bird in lines 1–7? What
senses do these images
appeal to?

For the rest of the day,
I could feel its wild thrumming
25 against my palms as I wondered about
the hours it must have spent
pent in the shadows of that room,
hidden in the spiky branches
of our decorated tree, breathing there
30 among the metallic angels, ceramic apples, stars of yarn,
its eyes open, like mine as I lie in bed tonight **E**
picturing this rare, lucky sparrow
tucked into a holly bush now,
a light snow tumbling through the windless dark.

E VISUALIZE
What details help you
imagine how the bird
looks and feels as it hides
in the Christmas tree?

The Sloth

Theodore Roethke

In moving-slow he has no Peer.[1]
You ask him something in his Ear,
He thinks about it for a Year;

And, then, before he says a Word
5 There, upside down (unlike a Bird),
He will assume that you have Heard—

A most Ex-as-per-at-ing Lug.
But should you call his manner Smug,
He'll sigh and give his Branch a Hug;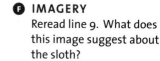

10 Then off again to Sleep he goes,
Still swaying gently by his Toes,
And you just *know* he knows he knows.

F IMAGERY
Reread line 9. What does
this image suggest about
the sloth?

---

1. **peer:** equal.

Comprehension

1. **Recall** How does the fish in Bishop's poem react when it is caught?

2. **Recall** How did the bird in Collins's poem get trapped inside the house?

3. **Summarize** What is the sloth's response when asked a question?

OHIO STANDARDS

READING STANDARD
4.9 Explain how authors use symbols to create broader meanings.

Literary Analysis

4. **Visualize** Describe in detail the mental picture you form of each animal in the poems.

5. **Analyze Imagery** Review the examples of imagery you recorded in your chart. Identify some images that appeal to your sense of sight and others that appeal to your sense of touch. What is the most striking image in each poem? Why?

6. **Analyze Free Verse** How is the experience of reading Bishop's and Collins's free verse poems different from reading Roethke's more traditional poem?

7. **Interpret Themes** How are the three **animals** in these poems like people? What does each poem suggest about the relationship between human beings and animals?

8. **Compare and Contrast Texts** Compare and contrast the Bishop and Collins poems. In a chart like the one shown, consider subject, mood, and theme in your answer.

	"The Fish"	"Christmas Sparrow"	Similarities	Differences
Subject				
Mood				
Theme				

Literary Criticism

9. **Critical Interpretations** According to Billy Collins, the best poems begin in clarity and end in mystery. Would you say that this is true for each of the three poems in this lesson? Why or why not?

Piano
Poem by D. H. Lawrence

Fifteen
Poem by William Stafford

Tonight I Can Write . . . / Puedo Escribir Los Versos . . .
Poem by Pablo Neruda

Which MEMORIES *last?*

KEY IDEA Think back to a moment from your past that evokes powerful feelings in you. Why has this **memory** made such a lasting impression? Was it the person you shared the experience with, or the activity itself? In the poems that follow, three speakers recall moments that have had a lasting impact.

QUICKWRITE In a short paragraph, describe a particular memory. Why is this recollection special? What feelings do you remember? Include sensory details that help present a clear picture.

LITERARY ANALYSIS: SOUND DEVICES

In the poems that follow, the poets use rhyme and other **sound devices** to convey rhythm and meaning:

- **Assonance**—the repetition of vowel sounds in words that don't rhyme

  We could find the end of a road, meet
  the sky on out Seventeenth. . . .

- **Consonance**—the repetition of consonant sounds within and at the ends of words

  Softly, in the dusk, a woman is singing to me;
  Taking me back down the vista of years, till I see

- **Repetition**—a sound, word, phrase, or line that is repeated

  I loved her, and sometimes she loved me too.
  She loved me, sometimes I loved her too.

Listen for the various sound devices that establish each poem's rhythmic flow, and notice how they help to evoke specific memories. Record examples in a chart.

	Assonance	Consonance	Repetition
"Piano"			
"Fifteen"			
"Tonight I Can Write…"			

READING SKILL: UNDERSTAND LINE BREAKS

End-stopped lines of poetry end at a normal speech pause, as in these lines from "Tonight I Can Write . . .":

The same night whitening the same trees.
We, of that time, are no longer the same.

This emphasizes the line endings and makes a reader view each line as a complete unit of meaning.

Enjambed lines run on without a natural pause, as in "Fifteen":

South of the bridge on Seventeenth
I found back of the willows one summer
day a motorcycle with engine running

Enjambment can create a tension and momentum until the thought is complete. As you read each poem, think about how line breaks affect rhythm and meaning.

Review: **Make Inferences**

The Spinet (1902), Thomas Wilmer Dewing. Oil on wood, 15¹/₂″ × 20″. Smithsonian American Art Museum, Washington, D.C. Photo © Smithsonian American Art Museum, Washington, D.C./Art Resource, New York.

Piano

D. H. Lawrence

Softly, in the dusk, a woman is singing to me;
Taking me back down the vista of years, till I see
A child sitting under the piano, in the boom of the
    tingling strings
And pressing the small, poised feet of a mother who
    smiles as she sings.

5 In spite of myself, the insidious mastery of song
Betrays me back, till the heart of me weeps to belong
To the old Sunday evenings at home, with winter outside
And hymns in the cozy parlour, the tinkling piano
    our guide. **Ⓐ**

So now it is vain for the singer to burst into clamour
10 With the great black piano appassionato. The glamour
Of childish days is upon me, my manhood is cast
Down in the flood of remembrance, I weep like a child
    for the past.

Ⓐ SOUND DEVICES
Reread lines 5–9 aloud. Where can you find **assonance** and **consonance** in this stanza?

Fifteen

William Stafford

South of the bridge on Seventeenth
I found back of the willows one summer
day a motorcycle with engine running
as it lay on its side, ticking over
5 slowly in the high grass. I was fifteen.

I admired all that pulsing gleam, the
shiny flanks, the demure headlights
fringed where it lay; I led it gently
to the road and stood with that
10 companion, ready and friendly. I was fifteen. **B**

We could find the end of a road, meet
the sky on out Seventeenth. I thought about
hills, and patting the handle got back a
confident opinion. On the bridge we indulged
15 a forward feeling, a tremble. I was fifteen.

Thinking, back farther in the grass I found
the owner, just coming to, where he had flipped
over the rail. He had blood on his hand, was pale—
I helped him walk to his machine. He ran his hand
20 over it, called me good man, roared away.

I stood there, fifteen.

B **LINE BREAKS**
Notice how Stafford
continues a thought
or sentence from one
line to the next. How
does this **enjambment**
affect the way you
read the lines?

Tonight I Can Write . . .

Pablo Neruda

Tonight I can write the saddest lines.

Write, for example, 'The night is shattered
and the blue stars shiver in the distance.'

The night wind revolves in the sky and sings.

5 Tonight I can write the saddest lines.
I loved her, and sometimes she loved me too.

Through nights like this one I held her in my arms.
I kissed her again and again under the endless sky.

She loved me, sometimes I loved her too.
10 How could one not have loved her great still eyes.

Tonight I can write the saddest lines. **C**
To think that I do not have her. To feel that I have lost her.

To hear the immense night, still more immense without her.
And the verse falls to the soul like dew to the pasture.

15 What does it matter that my love could not keep her.
The night is shattered and she is not with me.

This is all. In the distance someone is singing. In the distance.
My soul is not satisfied that it has lost her.

My sight searches for her as though to go to her.
20 My heart looks for her, and she is not with me.

The same night whitening the same trees.
We, of that time, are no longer the same.

I no longer love her, that's certain, but how I loved her.
My voice tried to find the wind to touch her hearing.

25 Another's. She will be another's. Like my kisses before.
Her voice. Her bright body. Her infinite eyes.

I no longer love her, that's certain, but maybe I love her.
Love is so short, forgetting is so long.

Because through nights like this one I held her in my arms
30 my soul is not satisfied that it has lost her.

Though this be the last pain that she makes me suffer
and these the last verses that I write for her. **D**

Translated by W. S. Merwin

C SOUND DEVICES
What impact is created
by the **repetition** of
"Tonight I can write the
saddest lines"?

D MAKE INFERENCES
Reread lines 27–32. Do
you think the speaker still
loves the woman? Why or
why not?

Puedo Escribir Los Versos . . .
Pablo Neruda

Puedo escribir los versos más tristes esta noche.

Escribir, por ejemplo: 'La noche está estrellada,
y tiritan, azules, los astros, a lo lejos.'

El viento de la noche gira en el cielo y canta.

5 Puedo escribir los versos más tristes esta noche.
Yo la quise, y a veces ella también me quiso.

En las noches como ésta la tuve entre mis brazos.
La besé tantas veces bajo el cielo infinito.

Ella me quiso, a veces yo también la quería.
10 Cómo no haber amado sus grandes ojos fijos.

Puedo escribir los versos más tristes esta noche.
Pensar que no la tengo. Sentir que la he perdido.

Oir la noche inmensa, más inmensa sin ella.
Y el verso cae al alma como al pasto el rocío.

15 Qué importa que mi amor no pudiera guardarla.
La noche está estrellada y ella no está conmigo.

Eso es todo. A lo lejos alguien canta. A lo lejos.
Mi alma no se contenta con haberla perdido.

Como para acercarla mi mirada la busca.
20 Mi corazón la busca, y ella no está conmigo.

La misma noche que hace blanquear los mismos árboles.
Nosotros, los de entonces, ya no somos los mismos.

Ya no la quiero, es cierto, pero cuánto la quise.
Mi voz buscaba el viento para tocar su oído.

25 De otro. Será de otro. Como antes de mis besos.
Su voz, su cuerpo claro. Sus ojos infinitos.

Ya no la quiero, es cierto, pero tal vez la quiero.
Es tan corto el amor, y es tan largo el olvido.

Porque en noches como ésta la tuve entre mis brazos,
30 mi alma no se contenta con haberla perdido.

Aunque éste sea el último dolor que ella me causa,
y éstos sean los últimos versos que yo le escribo.

Waiting (2001), Ben McLaughlin. Oil on board, 30.5 cm × 30.5 cm. Private collection. Photo © Bridgeman Art Library.

JOURNAL ARTICLE In 1971, nearly 50 years after writing "Tonight I Can Write . . ." Pablo Neruda was awarded the Nobel Prize in literature. For Neruda, this meant a prize of $450,000 and worldwide fame, although he was already quite famous in and around Chile, his native country. The following selection gives background on this prestigious award.

The Nobel Prize in Literature

In 1888, the well-known scientist and inventor Alfred Nobel experienced the shock of reading his own obituary. A French journalist had mistakenly reported his passing and described him as a "merchant of Death." The name was a reference to Nobel's most famous invention: dynamite.

This description troubled Nobel. He had often spoken out against violence and considered himself a pacifist. Many believe that he was moved to create a more positive legacy; for when he did die, his will specified that his fortune be used to honor people whose achievements enrich human life.

Since 1900, the Nobel Prize has rewarded some of the world's most dazzling achievements in the fields of physics, chemistry, medicine, economics, peace, and literature. Given out each year by the Swedish Academy, the prize consists of a gold medal, a diploma, and money (in 2000, it reached one million dollars), but its actual worth is much higher. Nobel winners, or laureates, are considered among the most important and influential people in the world. The Nobel Prize has both launched new careers and brought closure to long and successful ones.

Nobel's will required that a prize winner's work provide "the greatest benefit to mankind." For achievements in literature, however, Nobel had a second requirement: this work must also be "in an ideal direction." Over the past century, there has been debate over what "ideal direction" means, and why any particular writer should be chosen. As a result, the prize has been used at different times to honor different things: talented but unknown writers, for example, or writers who pioneer new styles. Pablo Neruda falls into the "pioneers" category, while recent winning poets Seamus Heaney (1995) and Wislawa Szymborska (1996), were honored as "unknown masters."

When Neruda won his Nobel Prize in 1971, the Academy's presentation speech stated that "his work benefits mankind precisely because of its direction." Neruda's early poems describing "isolation and dissonance" gave way to later ones declaring "harmony with Man and the Earth." The Academy saw this as an "ideal direction" for all of mankind to take. Neruda's work was also praised for its political content, particularly as it criticized the oppression of writers and artists.

In recent years, the Academy has moved away from determining "ideal direction" in favor of simply honoring writers for work which "furthers knowledge of man and his condition." This tendency might have pleased Neruda, who once stated, "The books that help you most are those which make you think the most . . . a great book that comes from a great thinker is a ship of thought, deep freighted with truth and beauty."

Comprehension

1. **Recall** How does the speaker in Stafford's poem react to finding the motorcycle?

2. **Recall** What are some nature images in Neruda's poem?

3. **Summarize** In Lawrence's poem, what is the speaker remembering?

Literary Analysis

4. **Visualize** Cite specific lines from both Lawrence's and Stafford's poems that helped you to visualize what the speakers remember. For example, what mental pictures did you form when reading lines 3 and 4 of Lawrence's poem?

5. **Analyze Sound Devices** What examples of sound devices did you list as you read? Explain what ideas are emphasized through **repetition** of words and phrases.

6. **Analyze Figurative Language** For each poem, record one or two effective examples of figurative language on a chart like the one shown. Note whether each example is a **simile**, **metaphor**, or **personification**. Also indicate what ideas each comparison suggests.

Poem	Example	Type of Figurative Language	Ideas Suggested

READING STANDARD
4.10 Describe the effect of using sound devices in literary texts

7. **Examine Line Breaks** Compare and contrast the poets' use of **end-stopped** and **enjambed** lines. How do their choices affect the rhythm of the poems?

8. **Compare and Contrast Themes** Compare and contrast the speakers' **memories.** In your opinion, why have these memories endured?

9. **Evaluate** Read "The Nobel Prize in Literature" on page 726, and consider "Tonight I Can Write . . ." in light of the Swedish Academy's comments on Neruda's work. Does the poem have more to do with isolation and dissonance, or harmony?

Reading-Writing Connection

WRITING PROMPT	**SELF-CHECK**
Extended Response: Analyze Imagery What do the images from nature in Neruda's poem reveal about the speaker's relationship with the woman? What do they tell the reader about the speaker's emotions? Use details from the poem to write a response in **three to five paragraphs.**	*An effective analysis will . . .* • cite examples of nature imagery • describe what feelings are evoked in these examples

Sonnet 18
Poem by William Shakespeare

Sonnet XXX of *Fatal Interview*
Poem by Edna St. Vincent Millay

What makes a good
LOVE POEM?

OHIO STANDARDS

READING STANDARDS
2.3 Monitor comprehension
4.5 Analyze how choice of genre affects theme or topic

KEY IDEA How do you describe something you cannot see or taste or touch? Like a love song, a **love poem** uses familiar objects and experiences to make sense of the mysterious feelings of love. As you'll see in "Sonnet 18" and "Sonnet XXX," the results can be as different as day and night.

BRAINSTORM In a group, brainstorm a list of comparisons you might use to describe how it feels to be in love. Think of song lyrics you know or poems you have read. As you create your list, discuss what aspect or quality of love each comparison communicates.

Love is like . . .
1. Fever
2. A red, red rose
3. A faucet

● POETIC FORM: SONNET

The sonnet has been a popular poetic form for centuries, and, traditionally, love has been its subject. While different types of sonnets have been developed by various poets, there are some characteristics that are common to all sonnets.

- Typically, the **sonnet** is a 14-line lyric poem written with a strict pattern of rhyme and rhythm.

- The **English,** or **Shakespearean, sonnet** has a rhyme scheme of *abab cdcd efef gg.* Notice how this divides the poem into four distinct line groups: three **quatrains,** or four-line units, followed by a **couplet**—a pair of rhymed lines, or two-line unit.

- The **meter,** or the repeated pattern of rhythm, in each line of a sonnet is typically **iambic pentameter.** Each rhythmic unit of meter is known as a **foot.** The most commonly used metrical foot is an **iamb,** which is an unstressed syllable followed by a stressed syllable. Note the iambs in the following example from Shakespeare's "Sonnet 18":

> Sŏ lóng ăs mén căn bréathe, ŏr éyes căn sée,
>
> Sŏ lóng lĭves thís, ănd thís gĭves lífe tŏ thée.

In each line, notice that there are five units of iambs. When a line has five feet in it, it is referred to as **pentameter.** Therefore, this meter is called iambic pentameter.

As you read the poems in this lesson, compare their rhyme schemes and meter.

● READING STRATEGY: READING SONNETS

Through their structure, sonnets often express complex ideas. These strategies will help you better understand sonnets:

1. Identify the situation, problem, or question introduced at the beginning of the poem.
2. Identify the turning point, if there is one.
3. Determine how the situation is clarified, the problem resolved, or the question answered.

As you read, apply these strategies and record the results on a chart like the one shown.

Strategy	Sonnet 18	Sonnet XXX
Situation/Problem/Question		
Turning Point		
Solution/Resolution/Answer		

Author Online

William Shakespeare: Renaissance Man

Although Shakespeare is best known for his plays, he was also a brilliant poet. When Shakespeare began his career in the 1590s, the sonnet was a literary fashion in England, usually written as a longing tribute to a faraway beloved.

**William Shakespeare
1564–1616**

In fact, many of Shakespeare's sonnets are addressed to a "dark lady" whose identity has never been discovered. First published in 1609, the complete series of 154 sonnets includes some of the finest love poems written in English. For more about Shakespeare, see the extended biography on page 1084.

Edna St. Vincent Millay: A True Original

Edna St. Vincent Millay was only 19 when her poem "Renascence" made her an instant celebrity. Although Millay's youth and free-spirited lifestyle fit the image of the rebellious artist, her highly crafted poems often took on traditional

**Edna St. Vincent Millay
1892–1950**

poetic forms, such as the sonnet. In 1923 she became the first woman to win the Pulitzer Prize in poetry, a tribute to her technical skill.

MORE ABOUT THE AUTHOR
For more on William Shakespeare and Edna St. Vincent Millay, visit the **Literature Center** at **ClassZone.com.**

ANALYZE VISUALS
Describe the relationship
of the figures shown.
What specific details
support your **inferences?**

Sonnet 18

William Shakespeare

Shall I compare thee to a summer's day?
Thou art more lovely and more temperate:[1]
Rough winds do shake the darling buds of May,
And summer's lease hath all too short a date:
5 Sometime too hot the eye of heaven shines,
And often is his gold complexion dimmed;
And every fair from fair sometime declines,
By chance or nature's changing course untrimmed;[2] **A**
But thy eternal summer shall not fade,
10 Nor lose possession of that fair thou owest;[3]
Nor shall Death brag thou wander'st in his shade,
When in eternal lines to time thou growest:
    So long as men can breathe, or eyes can see,
    So long lives this, and this gives life to thee.

A READING SONNETS
Reread the second
quatrain, or grouping of
four lines. What situation
does it describe?

---

1. **temperate** (tĕm′pər-ĭt): moderate, mild.
2. **untrimmed:** stripped of beauty.
3. **thou owest** (*thou* ō′ĭst): you own; you possess.

Offering of the Heart (1400-1410).
French tapestry from Arras. Wool
and silk, 247 cm × 209 cm. Louvre,
Paris. Photo © Réunion des Musées
Nationaux/Art Resource, New York.

The Cathedral (1908), Auguste
Rodin. Bronze, 24^1/$_2$″ × 10^3/$_4$″ ×
11^3/$_4$″. Photo © Timothy
McCarthy/Art Resource, New York.

Sonnet XXX
OF FATAL INTERVIEW

Edna St. Vincent Millay

Love is not all: it is not meat nor drink
Nor slumber nor a roof against the rain;
Nor yet a floating spar[1] to men that sink
And rise and sink and rise and sink again;
5 Love can not fill the thickened lung with breath,
Nor clean the blood, nor set the fractured bone;
Yet many a man is making friends with death
Even as I speak, for lack of love alone. **B**
It well may be that in a difficult hour,
10 Pinned down by pain and moaning for release,
Or nagged by want[2] past resolution's power,
I might be driven to sell your love for peace,
Or trade the memory of this night for food.
It well may be. I do not think I would.

B SONNET
How does the **rhyme
scheme** of lines 1–8
compare with that of
Shakespeare's sonnet?

---

1. **spar:** a pole used to support a ship's sails.

2. **want:** need.

Comprehension

1. **Recall** What is the main comparison developed in "Sonnet 18"?

2. **Clarify** In "Sonnet 18," the speaker promises the subject of the poem that "thy eternal summer shall not fade." What is the basis for this promise?

3. **Recall** What contrast opens "Sonnet XXX"?

4. **Paraphrase** Reread the second quatrain of "Sonnet XXX." What is the speaker's claim about love in these lines?

Literary Analysis

5. **Identify Metaphor** In poetry, an **extended metaphor** is a comparison between two distinctive things that is continued across a number of lines. Consider the extended metaphor used in "Sonnet 18." What qualities does this metaphor help communicate?

6. **Interpret Imagery** Consider the images that Millay presents in describing what love is not, or what it cannot do. These images are examples of what kinds of human needs? What is the point of contrasting love with these needs? Use a chart like the one shown to record the images from the poem.

Love Is Not	Love Cannot
meat	fill the lung with breath

7. **Analyze Sonnet Structure** Review the chart you developed as you read. How do the ideas expressed in the sonnet relate to its quatrains and couplets? Cite evidence from the poems to explain your answer.

READING STANDARD
4.5 Analyze how choice of genre affects theme or topic

8. **Compare Form** Although separated by more than 300 years, Millay and Shakespeare both wrote poetry using the sonnet form. Determine the rhyme scheme and meter for both sonnets. Then reread the top of page 729. Is Millay's poem a Shakespearean sonnet? Explain your answer.

Reading-Writing Connection

WRITING PROMPT

Extended Response: Interpret Theme
How would the speaker of each poem respond to the statement "Love lasts forever"? Use details from "Sonnet 18" and "Sonnet XXX" to **write a three- to five-paragraph response.**

SELF-CHECK

A successful response will . . .
- describe each speaker's concept of love
- provide examples to support your opinion

Lord Randall
Anonymous Ballad

Ballad / Balada
Poem by Gabriela Mistral

Midwinter Blues
Poem by Langston Hughes

When does poetry SING?

OHIO STANDARDS

READING STANDARDS
4.1 Compare and contrast an author's use of dialect
4.5 Analyze how choice of genre affects theme or topic

KEY IDEA Have you ever found yourself singing lines from a song you'd forgotten you knew? As you'll see in this lesson, poems based on **musical** forms can be as catchy as song lyrics.

QUICKWRITE With a small group, write out the lyrics of a well-known song. Discuss the patterns you notice in the song, such as repetition and rhyme. Then, write a brief response to this question: What qualities make a poem "songlike"?

Song Patterns
1. Repetition
2. Rhyme

● POETIC FORM: BALLAD

The earliest **ballads** were stories told in song, using the voice and language of everyday people. They were composed orally, and singers often added or changed details to make the songs meaningful for their audience. These early ballads, typical of the medieval period, are known as **folk ballads.**

Like a work of fiction, a ballad has characters, setting, and dialogue. Like a song, it uses repetition and has regular rhyme and meter. A **traditional ballad**—such as "Lord Randall," the written version of an older folk ballad—has these characteristics:

- consists of four-line stanzas with a simple rhyme scheme
- narrates a single tragic incident through dialogue

A ballad's rhyme scheme may be very loose or seem inconsistent. A loose rhyme scheme gave the singer more freedom to improvise lyrics. And, because pronunciations change over time, words that once rhymed may no longer sound alike.

As you read "Ballad" and "Midwinter Blues," consider how these poems expand the traditional ballad form.

● READING SKILL: UNDERSTAND DIALECT

People who inhabit a particular region or who belong to a particular social or ethnic group may speak in a **dialect,** a variation of a language. Their speech may differ in pronunciation, vocabulary, and grammar from the standard form of the language.

Dialect often provides clues about a poem's setting, as in "Lord Randall," which uses an 18th-century Scottish dialect. It can also reveal information about the speaker's identity, such as ethnicity and social class, as in "Midwinter Blues."

As you read "Lord Randall," record on a graphic organizer words and phrases written in dialect, and then rewrite them in standard English. Make a similar graphic organizer for "Midwinter Blues."

Title: "Lord Randall"	
Speaker's English	Standard English
What gat ye to your dinner?	What did you eat?

Author On|ine

Gabriela Mistral:
Voice of the Poor
Chilean poet Gabriela Mistral (mē-sträl′) wrote about the lives of everyday people. She believed the poet had a duty to speak for his or her own people and age. "What the soul is to the body," she once remarked, "so is the artist to his people."

Gabriela Mistral
1899–1957

Mistral's themes include love and loss, faith, childbearing, and motherhood. Many of her finest poems grappled with the suicide of her fiancé Romelio Ureta, who had left Mistral prior to his death. In 1945, Mistral became the first Latin American writer to receive the Nobel Prize for literature.

Langston Hughes:
Man of the People
Langston Hughes was a central figure of the Harlem Renaissance, a cultural movement of the 1920s and 1930s celebrating African-American artistic expression. He was one of the first to champion the artistry of blues

Langston Hughes
1902–1967

songs, which he called music from "black, beaten, but unbeatable throats." Blues songs, and the "low-down folks" who sang them, were a lifelong inspiration to Hughes, who drew on their rhythms, motifs, and themes in his poems, short stories, essays, and novels.

MORE ABOUT THE AUTHOR
For more on these poets, visit the **Literature Center** at ClassZone.com.

Lord Randall
Anonymous

"Oh where ha'e ye[1] been, Lord Randall my son?
O where ha'e ye been, my handsome young man?"
"I ha'e been to the wild wood: mother, make my bed soon,
For I'm weary wi'[2] hunting, and fain[3] wald[4] lie down." **A**

5 "Where gat ye[5] your dinner, Lord Randall my son?
Where gat ye your dinner, my handsome young man?"
"I dined wi' my true love: mother, make my bed soon,
For I'm weary wi' hunting, and fain wald lie down."

"What gat ye to your dinner, Lord Randall my son?
10 What gat ye to your dinner, my handsome young man?"
"I gat eels boiled in broo:[6] mother, make my bed soon,
For I'm weary wi' hunting and fain wald lie down."

"What became of your bloodhounds, Lord Randall my son?
What became of your bloodhounds, my handsome young man?"
15 "O they swelled and they died: mother, make my bed soon,
For I'm weary wi' hunting and fain wald lie down."

"O I fear ye are poisoned, Lord Randall my son!
O I fear ye are poisoned, my handsome young man!"
"Oh yes, I am poisoned: mother, make my bed soon,
20 For I'm sick at the heart, and I fain wald lie down." **B**

A DIALECT
Reread the first stanza. What words capture the qualities of spoken language?

B BALLAD
How does the ballad's pattern of repetition change in this stanza?

---

1. **ha'e ye** (hā' yē'): have you.
2. **wi'** (wĭ): with.
3. **fain** (fān): gladly, eagerly.
4. **wald** (wăld): would.
5. **gat ye** (găt yē): did you get.
6. **broo** (brōō): brew, broth.

The Vitriol Thrower (1894), Eugene Grasset. Color lithograph. Cecil Higgins Art Gallery, Bedford, Bedfordshire, United Kingdom. Photo © Bridgeman Art Library.

Ballad

Gabriela Mistral

He passed by with another;
I saw him pass by.
The wind ever sweet
and the path full of peace.
5 And these eyes of mine, wretched,
saw him pass by!

He goes loving another
over the earth in bloom.
The hawthorn[1] is flowering
10 and a song wafts by.
He goes loving another
over the earth in bloom! **C**

He kissed the other
by the shores of the sea.
15 The orange-blossom moon
skimmed over the waves.
And my heart's blood did not taint[2]
the expanse of the sea!

He will go with another
20 through eternity.
Sweet skies will shine.
(God wills to keep silent.)
And he will go with another
through eternity!

Translated by Doris Dana

C BALLAD
Reread stanzas 1
and 2. What patterns
of repetition can
you identify?

---

1. **hawthorn:** a spring-flowering shrub.
2. **taint** (tānt): contaminate.

Balada

Gabriela Mistral

El pasó con otra;
yo le vi pasar.
Siempre dulce el viento
y el camino en paz.
5 ¡Y estos ojos míseros
le vieron pasar!

El va amando a otra
por la tierra en flor.
Ha abierto el espino;
10 pasa una canción.
¡Y él va amando a otra
por la tierra en flor!

El besó a la otra
a orillas del mar;
15 resbaló en las olas
la luna de azahar.
¡Y no untó mi sangre
la extensión del mar!

El irá con otra
20 por la eternidad
Habrá cielos dulces.
(Dios quiere callar.)
¡Y él irá con otra
por la eternidad!

Melancholy, Edvard Munch. National Gallery, Oslo, Norway. © 2008 The Munch Museum/The Munch-Ellingsen Group/ Artists Rights Society (ARS), New York. Photo © Scala/Art Resource, New York.

Midwinter Blues

Langston Hughes

Graffiti Divas (2003), Jen Thario. Spray paint on paper,
22″ × 22″. © Jen Thario.

In the middle of the winter,
Snow all over the ground.
In the middle of the winter,
Snow all over the ground—
5 'Twas the night befo' Christmas
My good man turned me down. **D**

Don't know's I'd mind his goin'
But he left me when the coal was low.
Don't know's I'd mind his goin'
10 But he left when the coal was low.
Now, if a man loves a woman
That ain't no time to go. **E**

He told me that he loved me
But he must a been tellin' a lie.
15 He told me that he loved me.
He must a been tellin' a lie.
But he's the only man I'll
Love till the day I die.

I'm gonna buy me a rose bud
20 An' plant it at my back door,
Buy me a rose bud,
Plant it at my back door,
So when I'm dead they won't need
No flowers from the store.

D BALLAD
Compare this opening
stanza with that of "Lord
Randall." What qualities
do the poems share?

E DIALECT
Based on the dialect used
in this poem, what do you
learn about the speaker's
identity?

Comprehension

1. **Recall** Where has Lord Randall been, and what has happened to him?

2. **Clarify** Why is the speaker of "Ballad" so distressed?

3. **Summarize** In "Midwinter Blues," what is the speaker's situation?

Literary Analysis

4. **Identify Ballad** Reread "Lord Randall" and "Ballad." Using a chart like the one shown, compare how the elements of the traditional ballad are used in both poems. How does Mistral's poem depart from a traditional ballad?

Ballad Characteristics	Examples from "Lord Randall"	Examples from "Ballad"
Single tragic incident		
Repetition		
Dialogue		
Four-line stanzas		
Regular rhyme and meter		

OHIO STANDARDS

READING STANDARD
4.1 Compare and contrast an author's use of dialect

5. **Analyze Dialect** Review your dialect chart. How does dialect help establish the voices of the speakers in "Lord Randall" and "Midwinter Blues"?

6. **Contrast Speakers** Contrast the attitudes of the speakers in "Ballad" and "Midwinter Blues." How does the language used in each poem communicate the speaker's emotional state?

7. **Compare Styles** Consider qualities that make a poem **musical.** How do poems based on song forms differ from others you have read?

Reading-Writing Connection

WRITING PROMPT	SELF-CHECK
Extended Response: Support an Opinion Compare and contrast the experiences of each speaker. What do their experiences suggest about the nature of romantic love? Support your argument with details from the poems in a **three-to five-paragraph response.**	*A successful response will . . .* • point out similarities and differences between the speakers' experiences • formulate a conclusion that is supported by details

from **Blues Poems**

Essay by Kevin Young

Use with "Lord Randall," "Ballad," and "Midwinter Blues," pages 736–740.

OHIO STANDARDS

READING & WRITING STANDARDS
2.3 Take notes

5.5 Use organizational strategies (e.g., notes, outlines) to plan writing

What's the Connection?

The speakers of the poems you just read all share the experience of lost love, a theme that runs through blues music. But sorrow isn't the only way to face hard times. In the following selection, you'll learn how people transform sorrow into solace by singing the blues.

Skill Focus: Take Notes

Note taking is a strategy for organizing information by showing how ideas relate to one another. To take notes effectively, you need to identify which ideas are important (**main ideas**) and which facts or examples support those ideas (**supporting details**). Using a chart will enable you to see at a glance how main ideas connect with supporting details. To complete such a chart, follow these steps:

• Identify the topic of the selection—in this case, the blues. Write it at the top of the chart.

• On a first reading, examine the supporting details used to elaborate the topic, and organize them into categories. In this essay, you can organize the details the author provides into four main categories: the origin of the blues, the feeling of the blues, the form of blues music and poetry, and the subjects of the blues.

As you read the selection a second time, fill in the chart started here by relating the supporting details to the appropriate categories. This will prepare you to identify the main ideas the author presents about the blues.

The Blues	
Origin • Originated in African-American culture	**Feeling**
Form	**Subjects**

BLUES POEMS

FOREWORD BY KEVIN YOUNG

There are feelings and states of mind that are hard to describe—some might say that don't properly exist—until we have a word for them. *Catharsis, angst, schadenfreude, duende, ennui:* all feelings we now know in English, but that still retain the tenor of their country and culture of origin. One could easily add *the blues* to this list. Indeed, you might say that the blues contain all these other words in one.

The blues, after all, describe a state of being, a feeling, a form and sound not yet named until their 12 bars and repeated refrains came into being—and now that black folks have invented and named the blues, 10 people all over the world speak them. Being part of our common language in no way denies the blues' origins in African American culture and mouths and hands. Too many people, however, mistake the feeling of the blues with the form of the blues themselves.

For in spite of navigating the depths of despair, the blues ultimately are **A** about triumphing over that despair—or at least surviving it long enough to sing about it. With the blues, the form fights the feeling. Survival and loss, sin and regret, boasts and heartbreak, leaving and loving, a pigfoot and a bottle of beer—the blues are a series of reversals, of finding love and losing it, of wanting to see yourself dead in the depths of despair, and then soon 20 as the train comes down the track, yanking your fool head back. . . . As one saying goes, the blues ain't nothin' but a good man (or woman) feelin' bad.

A TAKE NOTES
Paraphrase the first sentence of this paragraph. What point is the author making?

B TAKE NOTES
How are contradictory
emotions important to
the form of the blues?

But another saying knows the opposite is true: the blues ain't nothin' but a bad woman (or man) feelin' good. **B**

. . . As Langston Hughes often said, the blues are "laughing to keep from crying"; the fact that this line also appears in the song "Trouble in Mind" tells us that even when there's trouble, we still can laugh about it. We must, the blues insist. Ralph Ellison puts it this way:

> The blues is an impulse to keep the painful details and episodes of a brutal experience alive in one's aching consciousness, to finger its
30   jagged grain, and then transcend it, not by the consolation of philosophy but by squeezing from it a near-tragic, near-comic lyricism. As a form, the blues is an autobiographical chronicle of personal catastrophe expressed lyrically.

Indeed, for me the blues provide a fresh way to express the lyric poem's mix of emotion and intensity, all the while evoking not so much strict autobiography as a personal metaphor for life's daily struggles. "You've been a good old wagon, but you done broke down."

The blues can be about work, or the lack of it; about losing hope or your home, your lover or your mind or your faith; or all of these at once! The
40 blues are unafraid of talking about violence, whether of the physical kind (as reflected in Hughes' "Beale Street Love" and Ma Rainey's "See See Rider Blues") or the often more troubling psychological sort. Still, the heartbreak the blues rails against and trains us to overcome is never far from ironic and even comic, and for every "Nobody Knows You When You're Down and Out," Bessie Smith declares "Tain't Nobody's Business if I Do." That Nobody sure is fickle. **C**

The blues ain't polite—they don't say please, though sometimes they say "Good Morning." They are, in the end, often more loyal than the sweet mistreater whom the singer loves but wants "to lay low". . . after feeling
50 low for days. Or nights—the blues after all, began as Saturday night entertainment, making us laugh and move and maybe even forget our troubles, not by pretending everything's all right, but by admitting it's a hard road full of forks and crossroad devils. By finding out that the powerful voice onstage, or on the jukebox, or coming from the radio, has been there too. The blues are loyal to a fault.

C TAKE NOTES
Review the author's
list of blues subjects.
What attitude do blues
songs express about
these subjects?

Comprehension

1. **Recall** According to Young, what do the blues describe?

2. **Recall** What are some typical subjects found in blues music?

3. **Clarify** According to Ralph Ellison, how do the blues help us transcend personal tragedy?

Critical Analysis

4. **Analyze Notes** Review the details you recorded in your chart. Based on these details, what are the main characteristics of blues music?

5. **Identify Tone** What tone, or attitude, toward blues music does Young convey in his essay? Cite specific words and phrases that help convey this tone.

Read for Information: Evaluate Poems

OHIO STANDARDS

READING & WRITING STANDARDS
2.3 Take notes

5.5 Use organizational strategies (e.g., notes, outlines) to plan writing

WRITING PROMPT

Of the three poems on pages 736–740, which best matches Young's description of the blues? Use excerpts from the poems and descriptive details from the essay to support your response.

To answer this prompt, follow these steps:

1. Review your chart to make sure you understand Young's main points about the blues. Restate his main points in your own words.

2. Analyze the poems to see how many characteristics of blues songs you can find in each. Decide which poem best matches Young's description of the blues.

3. State your conclusion(s) in a topic sentence. Then, support those conclusions with ideas and details from the poems.

Characteristics of the Blues	Characteristics of Poem 1	Characteristics of Poem 2	Characteristics of Poem 3
	✓		
		✓	✓
			✓

Conclusion:

Writing Workshop

Literary Analysis

As you've seen in this unit, carefully chosen words can express very private feelings or open up new worlds of experience. Analyzing how poets use elements of style can help you understand what they are saying and why it affects you the way it does. To get started writing a literary analysis, read the **Writer's Road Map.**

WRITER'S ROAD MAP

Literary Analysis

WRITING PROMPT 1

Writing from Literature Choose one or more poems and write an essay examining their meaning. In your essay, you should focus on one or more specific literary elements in the poem(s) and explain how those elements contribute to the meaning.

Literary Elements to Consider
- imagery in "Sonnet 18"
- theme in "Tonight I Can Write . . ." and in "Ballad"
- symbolism and imagery in "The Fish"

WRITING PROMPT 2

Writing for the Real World Write an essay for a music Web site, in which you analyze the lyrics of a particular song. Give specific examples to help readers understand why these lyrics are important to you.

Types of Music to Consider
- country
- rock or pop
- rap or hip-hop
- blues

WRITING TOOLS
For prewriting, revision, and editing tools, visit the **Writing Center** at ClassZone.com.

KEY TRAITS

1. IDEAS
- Presents a **thesis statement** that clearly identifies the key points of the discussion
- Uses **examples** from the text, such as quotations and paraphrases, to illustrate each key point

2. ORGANIZATION
- Identifies the poem or lyrics and their author in a thoughtful **introduction**
- Has a logical **organizational pattern**
- Summarizes ideas and makes broader judgments about the poem or lyrics in a satisfying **conclusion**

3. VOICE
- Maintains a **tone** that is suitable for the audience and purpose

4. WORD CHOICE
- Uses **literary terms** accurately

5. SENTENCE FLUENCY
- Varies **sentence structures** to add interest and sophistication

6. CONVENTIONS
- Employs **correct grammar and usage**

Part 1: Analyze a Student Model

Allison Chen
Markham High School

Being Fifteen

Have you ever wanted to escape into another world? In his poem "Fifteen," William Stafford creates a powerful snapshot of the dreams and realities of one particular teenager. Stafford's plain, direct language and rhythms make this poem easy to read, but it is his use of personification

5 and repetition that helps readers enter the world of that fifteen-year-old and experience his feelings.

Stafford draws readers into that world from the first stanza. The speaker is vague about where and when the action takes place—"back of the willows one summer / day." He does not reveal his name or describe

10 himself except for the statement "I was fifteen." He seems to assume that we already know him. However, there is nothing vague about the motorcycle the boy finds: "it lay on its side, ticking over / slowly in the high grass." This description makes the machine sound almost like a living thing with a heartbeat.

15 In the second stanza of the poem, Stafford shows us how much the motorcycle has captured the speaker's imagination by using personification. The speaker relates to the motorcycle as he would to a person, calling it a "companion, ready and friendly." We begin to wonder what adventures he is dreaming up for himself and his two-

20 wheeled friend. In the next stanza he tells us, sharing his vision that he will "meet / the sky" and escape to faraway, mysterious places.

KEY TRAITS IN ACTION

Interesting **introduction** identifies the literary work and its author. **Thesis statement** presents the key points of the analysis.

Includes quotations from "Fifteen" as **examples** to support the analysis.

Uses accurate **literary terms.** *Personification* means "giving human qualities to an object, animal, or idea."

By this time, we have identified so strongly with the speaker that
we want to climb onto that motorcycle with him and roar off into the
unknown, completely free and fearless. So why does he keep repeating
"I was fifteen"? I believe Stafford uses this repetition to show how
25   complicated teenagers—and their feelings—can be. Each time the
speaker makes that statement, it tells us something else about him. At
the end of the first stanza, it reveals how excited he feels after finding
the motorcycle, as if anything is possible. At the end of the second
stanza, it shows how lonely he is and how much he needs a friend.
30   When he says it again after describing his wild fantasies in the third
stanza, though, it seems that he's beginning to realize that his fantasy
and the real world don't match up. The motorcycle is not his, and
he probably doesn't even have a driver's license. He isn't ready for
35   independence and the adult world.

Sure enough, in the next stanza the speaker starts thinking
realistically about the situation. He goes looking for the owner of
the motorcycle and finds him lying injured in the grass. When the
motorcyclist thanks the speaker for his help, calling him "good man,"
40   we clearly see the contrast between the two characters. Though the
speaker dreams of being an adult who can climb on a roaring machine
and take off for exciting adventures, he is still just a boy who is left
behind as the motorcyclist speeds away.

Stafford uses personification and repetition to show us what it feels
45   like to be trapped between childhood and adulthood. "I stood there,
fifteen," the boy says in the last line of the poem. Soon, but not yet, he
will be adult enough to "meet / the sky on out Seventeenth."

Varied **sentence structures** throughout the essay create rhythm, sophistication, and interest.

Organizational pattern is logical, discussing the stanzas of the poem in order.

Tone is formal enough for a literary analysis, yet appropriate for the writer's teacher and classmates.

Conclusion summarizes the main points and explains why the poem's message is important.

2

Part 2: Apply the Writing Process

WRITING STANDARD
5.3 Establish and develop a clear thesis statement

PREWRITING

What Should I Do?	*What Does It Look Like?*

1. Reread the work you have chosen.
Keep a reading log in which you record the questions and comments that specific words and ideas bring to mind. Look for elements of style as well as for the message of the work.

▶

Quotations	Reactions
"South of the bridge on Seventeenth"	Should I know where that is?
"We could ... meet / the sky"	Yeah, escape sounds great!
"companion, ready and friendly"	Acting like the bike is alive = personification
"I was fifteen."	Why is this line repeated so much?

2. Focus on the main point you want to make.
Figure out the most important point you want to make about the work. Then jot down a working thesis statement that identifies that idea and the literary elements that help the author get it across.

TIP Think about the literary elements you have studied this year, such as rhyme, repetition, word choice, and figurative language.

See page 752: Review Literary Terms

▶

Working thesis statement:

In "Fifteen," William Stafford draws readers into the confusing world of a teenager. He uses personification and repetition to help readers experience the boy's feelings, dreams, and realities.

3. Find examples in the work that support your key points.
Read through the work again. List quotations, details, and other examples that back up the main ideas in your working thesis statement.

▶

Evidence	What It Means
Boy describes motorcycle as a "companion."	He must be really lonely.
"called me good man"	The boy isn't really a man, but he wants to think he is.
Boy is left behind as motorcyclist roars off.	He's stuck between childhood and adulthood.

DRAFTING

What Should I Do?	**What Does It Look Like?**

1. Organize your ideas.
Try different ways of presenting your material. You might want to discuss your points in the order they appear in the work you're analyzing, as this writer did (Pattern 1). You could also discuss each stylistic element separately (Pattern 2) or begin—or end—with your most important or interesting idea.

▶

TIP Make sure that each of your key points directly relates to your thesis statement.

PATTERN 1

Introduction and thesis

A. *Stanza 1—boy finds motorcycle, which seems alive to him (personification)*

B. *Stanza 2—treats it like a friend*

C. *Stanza 3—dreams of adventures (repetition shows his complex feelings)*

D. *Stanza 4—finds cyclist and is left behind, stuck between childhood and adulthood*

Conclusion

PATTERN 2

Introduction and thesis

A. *Personification of motorcycle*
   1. *Heartbeat*
   2. *Friendly, confident*
   3. *Shows speaker's loneliness*

B. *Repetition of "I was fifteen"*
   1. *Shows complex feelings of teen*
   2. *Stuck between childhood and adulthood*

Conclusion

2. Create a strong introduction.
Capture your reader's attention immediately by beginning with a question, a quotation, or a statement that relates to his or her own life. Then identify the work you are analyzing, along with its author, and state your thesis.

▶

Statement that relates to reader's life
Sooner or later, everyone feels the urge to run away from everything that is familiar and start a new life. The poet William Stafford describes...

Question
Have you ever wanted to escape into another world?

3. Give details from the text to support each key point.
Back up with evidence every statement that you make. Explain exactly how each detail supports your ideas.

TIP Before revising, consult the key traits on page 746 and the rubric and peer-reader questions on page 752.

▶

He's beginning to realize that his fantasy and the real world don't match up.... ⎫ Key point

Sure enough, in the next stanza the speaker starts thinking realistically about the situation. He goes looking for the owner of the motorcycle and finds him lying injured in the grass. ⎫ Support

REVISING AND EDITING

What Should I Do?	What Does It Look Like?

1. Use literary terms accurately.
- Have a peer reader <u>underline</u> words and phrases that should be replaced with literary terms.
- Turn to "Review Literary Terms" on page 752 to make sure you substitute the correct terms.

  See page 752: Ask a Peer Reader

▶

In the second stanza of the poem, Stafford shows us how much the motorcycle has captured the speaker's imagination by using ~~statements that make us think it's alive~~ personification.

2. Match your tone to your audience.
- Read your analysis aloud. (Circle) passages that contain slang terms or other types of informal writing.
- Rewrite these sections, using formal language like that in books and newspapers.

▶

we have identified so strongly with the speaker
By this time, ~~you're so totally into the stuff the guy~~
                                                    we
~~is thinking about~~ that ~~you kind of~~ want to climb onto that motorcycle with him and roar off into the unknown.

3. Vary the structures of your sentences.
- Review your sentences. Draw a ☐box☐ around ones that repeat the same subject-verb-object structure.
- Rewrite, separate, or combine some of these sentences to give your writing some variety.

▶

The speaker is vague about where and when the action takes place. ~~He says it is~~ "back of the willows one summer / day." He does not reveal his name or
        except for the statement
describe himself. ~~He just tells readers~~ "I was fifteen."

4. Strengthen your conclusion.
- Highlight the last paragraph of your analysis.
- Make sure you have summarized your key points and commented on the overall meaning of the work.

▶

Stafford uses personification and repetition ~~in the poem in a really effective way~~ to show us what it feels like to be trapped between childhood and adulthood. "I stood there, fifteen," the boy says in the last line of the poem. Soon, but not yet, he will be old enough to "meet / the sky on out Seventeenth."

Apply the Rubric

A strong literary analysis . . .

☑ catches the reader's attention with a strong introduction that identifies the author and work

☑ states the key points in a clear thesis statement

☑ organizes ideas logically

☑ supports statements with details and examples from the text

☑ includes appropriate literary terms

☑ uses a tone suited to the audience and purpose

☑ varies sentence structures

☑ concludes with a summary and an overall comment about the work

Ask a Peer Reader

• What did you like most about my analysis? Why?

• Which of my key points need more explanation or support?

• What literary terms did I either use inaccurately or fail to use when I should have?

Review Literary Terms

Figurative language: words and phrases that communicate more than their literal meanings (The speaker in "Fifteen" is a *blank book.*)

Imagery: words and phrases that re-create sensory experiences for the reader (The motorcycle had a *"pulsing gleam."*)

Personification: description of inanimate objects, animals, or ideas as if they were human (The motorcycle *trembled with anticipation.*)

Symbolism: the use of one idea or object to represent another (The motorcycle symbolizes freedom.)

Check Your Grammar

• When quoting from a poem, use slashes (/) to show line breaks.

> The action takes place "back of the willows one summer / day."

• When using a quotation of three or more lines, begin the quotation on a new line, indent the quotation ten spaces, and use the same line breaks that the poet did.

Writing Online

PUBLISHING OPTIONS
For publishing options, visit the **Writing Center** at **ClassZone.com.**

ASSESSMENT PREPARATION
For writing and grammar assessment practice, go to the **Assessment Center** at **ClassZone.com.**

Delivering an Oral Interpretation

Literature—especially poetry—is meant for your ears as well as your eyes. A good way to share both the sound and the sense of the poem you've analyzed is to deliver an oral interpretation.

Planning the Oral Interpretation

1. **Mark up a copy of the poem to create a script.** Highlight words to stress and places to change your pacing. Show where to include gestures and other body language.

> We could find the end of a road, meet the sky on out Seventeenth. I thought about hills, and patting the handle got back a confident opinion. On the bridge we indulged a forward feeling, a tremble. I was fifteen.
>
> Smile and nod. →
> Lean forward → while picking up pace.
>
> **Notes**
> Blue = Use stress here. Green = Speak more quickly.

2. **Tape-record your delivery.** Listen to the tape and adjust the volume, tone, and pace of your voice to make the poem clearer to listeners.
3. **Practice in front of a mirror or a test audience.** Rehearse your gestures and facial expressions until they come naturally and work well with your voice.

Delivering the Oral Interpretation

1. **Be confident.** Use a proud but relaxed posture.
2. **Look at your listeners.** Face your audience at all times. Hold your script so that you can glance at it without lowering your head.
3. **Make sure your body and voice help clarify, not confuse, the poem's meaning.** Remember that you are not the focus of the oral interpretation—the poem is. So don't go overboard with your voice and gestures. Just keep it natural.

See page R80: Evaluate an Oral Interpretation

Reading Comprehension

DIRECTIONS *Read these poems and answer the questions that follow.*

The Taxi

Amy Lowell

When I go away from you
The world beats dead
Like a slackened drum.
I call out for you against the jutted stars
5 And shout into the ridges of the wind.
Streets coming fast,
One after the other,
Wedge you away from me,
And the lamps of the city prick my eyes
10 So that I can no longer see your face.
Why should I leave you,
To wound myself upon the sharp edges of the night?

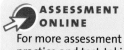

Reprise

Ogden Nash

Geniuses of countless nations
Have told their love for generations
Till all their memorable phrases
Are common as goldenrod or daisies.
5 Their girls have glimmered like the moon,
Or shimmered like a summer noon,
Stood like lily, fled like fawn,
Now the sunset, now the dawn,
Here the princess in the tower
10 There the sweet forbidden flower.
Darling, when I look at you
Every aged phrase is new,
And there are moments when it seems
I've married one of Shakespeare's dreams.

Comprehension

DIRECTIONS *Answer these questions about "The Taxi."*

1. "The Taxi" is an example of

A. concrete poetry

B. a ballad

C. free verse

D. a sonnet

2. The repetition of the *w* sound throughout the poem is an example of

A. rhyme

B. consonance

C. assonance

D. alliteration

3. What sound devices used in lines 2–3 suggest the thump of a drum?

A. alliteration and consonance

B. rhyme and onomatopoeia

C. assonance and end rhyme

D. repetition and dialect

4. The images in lines 4–5 reinforce the idea that

A. the taxi is traveling too fast

B. the speaker is distressed

C. nature is full of violence

D. the city is a dangerous place

5. Which image best conveys the speaker's feeling of vulnerability?

A. "Streets coming fast, / One after the other"

B. "And shout into the ridges of the wind"

C. "So that I can no longer see your face"

D. "To wound myself upon the sharp edges of the night"

6. The poet presents one image after another in rapid succession to

A. paint a detailed picture of the city

B. create a sensation of movement

C. express the excitement of traveling

D. stress the transient beauty of nature

DIRECTIONS *Answer these questions about "Reprise."*

7. Which of the following terms best describes the rhymed lines of this poem?

A. quatrain

B. stanza

C. couplet

D. iambic pentameter

8. Which pair of words is an example of alliteration in the poem?

A. girls, glimmered (line 5)

B. fawn, dawn (lines 7, 8)

C. every, aged (line 12)

D. seems, dreams (lines 13, 14)

9. Lines 2–3 contain examples of alliteration, consonance, and

A. metaphor

B. onomatopoeia

C. end rhyme

D. assonance

10. Which of the following lines contains a metaphor?

A. "Geniuses of countless nations" (line 1)

B. "Are common as goldenrod or daisies" (line 4)

C. "Or shimmered like a summer noon" (line 6)

D. "There the sweet forbidden flower" (line 10)

11. Line 7, "Stood like lily, fled like fawn," contains examples of

  A. metaphor

  B. personification

  C. simile

  D. onomatopoeia

12. The speaker lists similes and metaphors used by other writers and calls them "memorable phrases" to emphasize that

  A. only geniuses can describe love

  B. love is as common as goldenrod

  C. love has been around for generations

  D. love is hard to describe in new ways

DIRECTIONS *Answer the following questions about both poems.*

13. Which statement accurately compares the emotional state of the speakers in the two poems?

  A. Both speakers are lonely.

  B. Both speakers are angry.

  C. One speaker is content and one is unhappy.

  D. One speaker is frightened and one is optimistic.

14. In these poems, both poets reflect on

  A. the sorrows that accompany being in love

  B. the strong feelings of someone in love

  C. the beauty and uniqueness of the loved one

  D. nature as a great comfort to those in love

Written Response

SHORT ANSWER *Write three or four sentences to answer this question.*

15. Why is the taxi a suitable image for Lowell's poem? Support your answer with details from the poem.

EXTENDED RESPONSE *Write two or three paragraphs to answer this question.*

16. Compare and contrast the nature imagery in "The Taxi" and "Reprise." What do these images reveal about the two speakers' attitudes toward love?

Writing & Grammar

DIRECTIONS *Read the passage and answer the questions that follow.*

(1) Although they are separated by nearly 3,000 years, Homer and hip-hop performers share certain traits. (2) Both have created works that <u>use</u> poetry and singing, for example. (3) In Homer's epics and in hip-hop, poetry is linked to song by rhyme and rhythmically. (4) Like hip-hop artists on tour, poets of the seventh-century B.C. were storytellers who <u>went</u> from town to town. (5) They sang epic works like Homer's *Odyssey*, educating the crowd and to entertain. (6) With the advent of the printing press, poetry became more of a written art form. (7) Then, in the 1950s, poetry readings <u>caused</u> a strong resurgence in the oral tradition. (8) Further energizing spoken poetry were poetry slams and hip-hop music in the 1980s and 1990s.

(9) Today, hip-hop <u>has</u> worldwide attention. (10) The United States, France, and Japan are the three largest markets for hip-hop music, but also producing and appreciating it are countries in Africa and South America. (11) Hip-hop music and culture are even studied in universities. (12) Students and scholars <u>are given</u> grants to travel the world, visiting countries such as Senegal, Tanzania, Cuba, Mongolia, and Brazil to research this emerging musical form.

1. Choose the most precise verb to replace the underlined word in sentence 2.

A. contain

B. meld

C. utilize

D. have

2. Choose how to rewrite sentence 3 so that its elements are parallel.

A. In Homer's epics and poetry and in hip-hop, there is a link to song by rhyme and rhythmically.

B. In Homer's epics and in hip-hop, poetry is linked to song by rhyming and rhythm.

C. In Homer's epics and in hip-hop, poetry is linked to song by rhyme and rhythm.

D. Through rhyme and rhythmically, Homer's epics and hip-hop link poetry to song.

3. Choose the most precise verb to replace the underlined word in sentence 4.

A. advanced

B. moved

C. journeyed

D. passed

4. Choose how to rewrite sentence 5 so that its elements are parallel.

A. They sang epic works like Homer's *Odyssey* to educate and entertain the crowd.

B. They sang epic works like Homer's *Odyssey*, educating and to entertain the crowd.

C. Singing epic works like Homer's *Odyssey*, they educated and were entertaining the crowd.

D. They sang epic works like Homer's *Odyssey* and educate and entertain the crowd.

5. Choose the most precise verb to replace the underlined word in sentence 7.

A. started

B. promoted

C. sparked

D. generated

6. Choose how to rewrite sentence 8 so that it is parallel in structure to sentence 7.

A. Further energizing spoken poetry, poetry slams and hip-hop music became popular in the 1980s and 1990s.

B. The 1980s' and 1990s' energy from poetry slams and hip-hop music was part of spoken poetry.

C. The spoken poetry of the 1980s and 1990s was further energized by poetry slams and hip-hop music.

D. In the 1980s and 1990s, poetry slams and hip-hop music further energized spoken poetry.

7. Choose the most precise verb to replace the underlined word in sentence 9.

A. receives

B. produces

C. elicits

D. gets

8. Choose how to rewrite sentence 10 so that its elements are parallel.

A. The three largest markets for hip-hop music are the United States, France, and Japan, but countries in Africa and South America are also producing and appreciating it.

B. Becoming the three largest markets for hip-hop music are the United States, France, and Japan, but in countries in Africa and South America, hip-hop music is also produced and appreciated.

C. The United States, France, and Japan are the three largest markets for hip-hop music, but countries in Africa and South America also produce and appreciate it.

D. The United States, France, and Japan are the three largest markets for hip-hop music, but it is also produced and appreciated in countries in Africa and South America.

9. Choose the most precise verb phrase to replace the underlined words in sentence 12.

A. are awarded

B. are allowed

C. are left

D. are permitted

Ideas for Independent Reading

Which topics in Unit 7 inspired you most? Nature? Memories? Love?
Explore them further with these additional works.

What is our place in nature?

Any Small Thing Can Save You
by Christina Adam

A bestiary is a collection of writing about animals. This prose bestiary considers animals throughout the alphabet—from asp to goose, from porcupine to vulture—and the effect each has on humans.

Why I Wake Early
by Mary Oliver

Oliver is regarded as one of America's best nature poets. In this collection she describes elements of the natural world—toads, water, flowers—that cause her to wake early each morning, so as not to miss something extraordinary.

Danger on Peaks
by Gary Snyder

Several poems in this collection are about Washington State's Mount St. Helens, which Snyder first climbed in 1945. Pristine and quiet when he first scaled it, the mountain signaled its 1980 volcanic eruption with "growl stamp-dance, quiver swell, glow."

Which memories last?

An American Childhood
by Annie Dillard

In Dillard's memoir of her childhood years, she tells of diving into experiences fearlessly and without hesitation, whether pitching, throwing snowballs, or observing the natural world. Her full engagement in life provided many rich memories.

The Woman I Kept to Myself
by Julia Alvarez

Born in the Dominican Republic, Alvarez writes poems about her past and the forces and people that helped make her what she is today. Family, friends, animals, and jobs all formed her, and she looks to her past as a way of understanding who she is now.

I Can Hear the Cowbells Ring
by Lionel G. García

These hilarious autobiographical stories describe growing up in an extended Mexican-American family in south Texas after World War II. García creates indelible portraits of his stern grandmother and eccentric aunts and uncles.

What makes a good love poem?

Sonnets from the Portuguese
by Elizabeth Barrett Browning

These 44 sonnets that Browning wrote to her husband, Robert, are considered to be classics of love poetry. They celebrate the pair's marriage and the lasting nature of true love. Included is the famous "How do I love thee? ..."

The Radiation Sonnets
by Jane Yolen

While her husband underwent 43 days of radiation and chemotherapy for an inoperable tumor, Jane Yolen wrote a sonnet a day to express her love and her fear, as well as her anger over the threat to his life. The sonnets have been inspirational to other cancer patients and their families.

Mother Love
by Rita Dove

Dove, the former poet laureate of the United States, examines the strong tie of love between mother and daughter in these sonnets. Several explore the classical myth of Demeter and Persephone, and one of Dove's major themes is a mother's obligation to let go.

8

Signatures

AUTHOR'S STYLE AND VOICE

- In 19th-Century Writing
- In 20th-Century Writing

Share What You Know

Who's got STYLE?

People in the public eye often cultivate an image that sets them apart from others. Some do it with the way they dress, others through the way they speak or act, and some with what they design or create. You recognize these people or their work by their **style**—that special blend of appearance, expression, and attitude that makes each person unique.

ACTIVITY Choose an individual whose personal or professional style you admire. This person could be someone you know, or a public figure such as a performer, a politician, or a businessperson. Draw a sketch or create a collage or illustration like the one shown to represent the elements of that person's style.

OHIO STANDARDS

Preview Unit Goals

LITERARY ANALYSIS
- Identify elements of style, including diction, tone, and imagery
- Recognize author's style
- Recognize style of specific authors, including Poe, Whitman, Frost, and Cisneros

READING
- Make inferences about speaker
- Identify author's purpose
- Paraphrase
- Use evidence from multiple sources

WRITING AND GRAMMAR
- Write a critical review
- Use evidence from a work to support an opinion
- Use personification to create vivid images and details
- Understand and use infinitives

SPEAKING, LISTENING, AND VIEWING
- Create a Web site

VOCABULARY
- Use figurative language to help determine the meaning of words
- Use a dictionary etymology

ACADEMIC VOCABULARY
- elements of style
- tone
- diction
- imagery
- author's style
- critical review
- evidence
- etymology

OHIO STANDARDS

READING STANDARDS
4.5 Analyze how choice of genre affects theme or topic
4.10 Describe the effect of using sound devices in literary texts
4.11 Explain ways author develops point of view and style

Author's Style and Voice

Jane Austen, Edgar Allan Poe, and Maya Angelou—why do works by authors such as these continue to captivate generations of readers? Not only have these authors crafted compelling stories, but they have expressed themselves in such individual, memorable ways. Austen's witty observations of society, Poe's dark tales of terror, and Angelou's deeply personal anecdotes all leave lasting impressions largely because of each author's distinctive style.

Part 1: Style in Literature

Style refers to the way a work of literature is written—not what is said, but *how* it is said. The "how" depends on many elements, including a writer's tone, sentence structures, and language. In the first example shown, notice how Ernest Hemingway's direct, journalistic style results from his use of simple words and sentences, among other elements.

Distinctive styles extend beyond individual writers, however. Sometimes writing produced during a particular time period, such as 19th-century England, has a recognizable style, as you'll notice in the second example.

STYLE OF AN INDIVIDUAL

Ernest Hemingway
Hemingway, who wrote during the 20th century, is known for his simple style. He avoided flowery language in favor of no-frills storytelling and short sentences.

Example

"Don't talk about the war," I said. The war was a long way away. Maybe there wasn't any war. There was no war here. Then I realized it was over for me. But I did not have the feeling that it was really over.

—from *A Farewell to Arms*

Characteristics of Hemingway's Style
- everyday words and sparse details
- simple sentence structures
- informal tone
- matter-of-fact descriptions of characters' feelings

STYLE OF A TIME PERIOD

Victorian England
Much of the writing produced in 19th-century England has an elaborate, formal style. Sentences are complex, and the vocabulary is sophisticated.

Example

Anyone who had looked at him as the red light shone upon his pale face, strange straining eyes, and meager form, would perhaps have understood the mixture of contemptuous pity, dread, and suspicion with which he was regarded by his neighbors. . . .

—from *Silas Marner* by George Eliot

Characteristics of Victorian Style
- elevated language and vivid imagery
- complex sentence structures
- formal tone
- involved focus on the narrator's and characters' observations and thoughts

MODEL 1: STYLE OF AN INDIVIDUAL

Now that you have learned the characteristics of Hemingway's style and have read a passage from *A Farewell to Arms,* examine this excerpt from one of his short stories.

> ### from BIG TWO-HEARTED RIVER
> #### Short story by **Ernest Hemingway**
>
> Nick was hungry. He did not believe he had ever been hungrier. He opened and emptied a can of pork and beans and a can of spaghetti into the frying pan.
> "I've got a right to eat this kind of stuff, if I'm willing to carry it," Nick said. His voice sounded strange in the darkening woods. He did not speak again.
> 5   He started a fire with some chunks of pine he got with the ax from a stump. Over the fire he stuck a wire grill, pushing the four legs down into the ground with his boot. Nick put the frying pan on the grill over the flames. He was hungrier. The beans and spaghetti warmed. Nick stirred them and mixed them together.

Close Read

1. Identify two characteristics of Hemingway's style that are evident in the boxed text.

2. Compare the excerpt from *A Farewell to Arms* with this one. What is the most striking stylistic similarity between them? Explain.

MODEL 2: STYLE OF A TIME PERIOD

Like George Eliot, Emily Brontë wrote in the sophisticated, ornate style that characterizes 19th-century English literature. In this excerpt from one of Brontë's novels, the narrator visits the estate of his landlord, Heathcliff.

> ### from *Wuthering Heights*
> #### Novel by **Emily Brontë**
>
> Yesterday afternoon set in misty and cold. I had half a mind to spend it by my study fire, instead of wading through heath and mud to Wuthering Heights. On coming up from dinner, however, (N.B.[1]—I dine between twelve and one o'clock; the housekeeper, a matronly lady, taken as a fixture along with the house, could not, or would not, comprehend my request that I might be
> 5 served at five)—on mounting the stairs with this lazy intention, and stepping into the room, I saw a servant-girl on her knees surrounded by brushes and coal-scuttles, and raising an infernal dust as she extinguished the flames with heaps of cinders. This spectacle drove me back immediately; I took my hat, and, after a four-miles' walk, arrived at Heathcliff's garden-gate just in time to
> 10 escape the first feathery flakes of a snow-shower.
>
> ---
> 1. **N.B.:** an abbreviation of the Latin *nota bene,* "take notice."

Close Read

1. In what ways do Brontë's sentences— especially the one in the box—differ from Hemingway's?

2. Identify two stylistic similarities between Brontë's writing here and Eliot's writing in the excerpt from *Silas Marner* on the preceding page.

Part 2: Style and Voice

You've started to consider how elements such as sentence structure and word choice help to create style. A closer look at the unique blend of three other key elements—**diction, tone,** and **imagery**—will help you to compare writing styles. You will also grasp how these elements contribute to a writer's or narrator's **voice**—the personality that comes across on the page.

Here, notice how diction, tone, and imagery help to distinguish Nathaniel Hawthorne's formal, ornate style from Gloria Naylor's playfully informal one.

COMPARING STYLES

She had dark and abundant hair, so glossy that it threw off the sunshine with a gleam, and a face which, besides being beautiful from regularity of feature and richness of complexion, had the impressiveness belonging to a marked brow and deep black eyes.

—from *The Scarlet Letter* by Nathaniel Hawthorne

She loaded that baby down with every name in the book: Charles Somebody Harrison Somebody-Else Duvall. We called him Chick. That's what he looked like, toddling around: little pecan head sitting on a scrawny neck, two bright buttons for eyes, and a feathery mess of hair she couldn't keep slicked down for nothing.

—from *Mama Day* by Gloria Naylor

DICTION

Diction includes both a writer's choice of words and his or her **syntax,** or arrangement of words into sentences. Hawthorne's formal style comes from his use of elevated vocabulary ("abundant hair"), complex phrases ("richness of complexion" rather than "great skin"), and long sentences. In contrast, Naylor's use of informal language, such as "slicked down for nothing," creates a conversational style.

TONE

Tone is a writer's attitude toward a subject, as expressed through choice of words and details. Naylor establishes a playful tone in her description of Chick's real name: "Charles Somebody Harrison Somebody-Else Duvall." Naylor's tone also helps readers to "hear" the no-nonsense voice of the narrator. Hawthorne's elegant diction, however, conveys a formal tone and style.

IMAGERY

You already know that **imagery** consists of words and phrases that re-create sensory experiences for readers. "Abundant hair, so glossy that it threw off the sunshine with a gleam" and "little pecan head"—image-laden descriptions like these are signatures of both Hawthorne's and Naylor's styles. The *kinds* of images the writers include, though, dramatically set their styles apart.

MODEL 1: ELEMENTS OF STYLE

Jamaica Kincaid's writing is rich with images that evoke the settings she describes. In this excerpt from one of Kincaid's novels, the narrator is leaving her home on the island of Antigua. As she rides a launch to her ship, she is overcome with emotion.

from

A WALK TO THE JETTY

from Annie John
Novel by **Jamaica Kincaid**

... My heart shriveled up and the words "I shall never see this again" stabbed at me. I don't know what stopped me from falling in a heap at my parents' feet.

When we were all on board, the launch headed out to sea. Away from the
5   jetty, the water became the customary blue, and the launch left a wide path in it that looked like a road. I passed by sounds and smells that were so familiar that I had long ago stopped paying any attention to them. But now here they were, and the ever-present "I shall never see this again" bobbed up and down inside me. There was the sound of the seagull diving down into the water and
10   coming up with something silverish in its mouth. There was the smell of the sea and the sight of small pieces of rubbish floating around in it.

Close Read

1. Identify two images that allow you to visualize the setting.

2. Reread the boxed details, noting such words as *stabbed* and *bobbed*. What does Kincaid's unique diction tell you about the narrator?

3. Would you describe Kincaid's tone as sympathetic or harsh? Explain your answer.

MODEL 2: ELEMENTS OF STYLE

Here, David Copperfield, the narrator of Charles Dickens's classic novel, reflects on an exciting time in his childhood—when he was preparing to leave *his* home. As you read, pay attention to the stylistic elements that help distinguish Dickens's writing from Kincaid's.

from

David Copperfield

Novel by **Charles Dickens**

The day soon came for our going. It was such an early day that it came soon, even to me, who was in a fever of expectation, and half afraid that an earthquake or a fiery mountain, or some other great convulsion of nature, might interpose to stop the expedition. We were to go in a carrier's cart, which
5   departed in the morning after breakfast. I would have given any money to have been allowed to wrap myself up overnight, and sleep in my hat and boots.

It touches me nearly now, although I tell it lightly, to recollect how eager I was to leave my happy home; to think how little I suspected what I did leave for ever.

Close Read

1. Consider Dickens's formal, dramatic diction, particularly evident in the boxed phrases. Through this stylistic element, what do you learn about young David?

2. What is the greatest difference between Kincaid's and Dickens's styles? Explain.

Part 3: Analyze the Literature

Apply what you now know about style as you analyze these two excerpts. Each describes a connection between three people, one of whom will end up disappointed and unlucky in love.

This excerpt is taken from Jane Austen's novel *Emma.* Austen, who wrote during the early 19th century, is known for her ironic, amused observations of middle-class society in England. Here, Emma bemoans her foiled attempt to pair the sought-after Mr. Elton with her friend Harriet. Mr. Elton has fallen for Emma instead.

from
Emma
Novel by **Jane Austen**

The hair was curled, and the maid sent away, and Emma sat down to think and be miserable.—It was a wretched business, indeed!—Such an overthrow of every thing she had been wishing for!—Such a development of every thing most unwelcome!—Such a blow for Harriet!—That was the worst of all. Every
5 part of it brought pain and humiliation, of some sort or other; but, compared with the evil to Harriet, all was light; and she would gladly have submitted to feel yet more mistaken—more in error—more disgraced by mis-judgment, than she actually was, could the effects of her blunders have been confined to herself.

"If I had not persuaded Harriet into liking the man, I could have born any
10 thing. He might have doubled his presumption to me—But poor Harriet!"

How she could have been so deceived!—He protested that he had never thought seriously of Harriet—never! She looked back as well as she could; but it was all confusion. She had taken up the idea, she supposed, and made every thing bend to it. His manners, however, must have been unmarked, wavering,
15 dubious, or she could not have been so misled.

Close Read

1. Consider the tone Austen uses to describe Emma's predicament. Is it mocking or serious? Support your answer.

2. Describe Austen's diction, citing details in the boxed text. What does her diction help to emphasize about Emma's current state of mind?

3. Austen's use of dashes and exclamation points helps to suggest Emma's personality and manner. What does this stylistic element tell you about the kind of person Emma is?

F. Scott Fitzgerald lived and wrote more than a century after Austen. Like Austen, he was a keen observer and recorder of society's manners and constraints. Though the authors explored similar subjects, their writing styles differed dramatically. As you read this excerpt from a short story by Fitzgerald, notice the stylistic elements that help to create this difference.

from

BERNICE BOBS HER HAIR

Short story by **F. Scott Fitzgerald**

Warren, who had grown up across the street from Marjorie, had long been "crazy about her." Sometimes she seemed to reciprocate his feeling with a faint gratitude, but she had tried him by her infallible test and informed him gravely that she did not love him. Her test was that when she was away from him she
5 forgot him and had affairs with other boys. Warren found this discouraging, especially as Marjorie had been making little trips all summer, and for the first two or three days after each arrival home he saw great heaps of mail on the Harveys' hall table addressed to her in various masculine handwritings. To make matters worse, all during the month of August she had been visited by her
10 cousin Bernice from Eau Claire, and it seemed impossible to see her alone. It was always necessary to hunt round and find some one to take care of Bernice. As August waned this was becoming more and more difficult.

Much as Warren worshiped Marjorie, he had to admit that Cousin Bernice was sorta dopeless. She was pretty, with dark hair and high color, but she was no
15 fun on a party. Every Saturday night he danced a long arduous duty dance with her to please Marjorie, but he had never been anything but bored in her company.

"Warren"—a soft voice at his elbow broke in upon his thoughts, and he turned to see Marjorie, flushed and radiant as usual. She laid a hand on his shoulder and a glow settled almost imperceptibly over him.
20 "Warren," she whispered, "do something for me—dance with Bernice. She's been stuck with little Otis Ormonde for almost an hour."

Warren's glow faded.

"Why—sure," he answered half-heartedly.

Close Read

1. Reread lines 1–8. In your opinion, is the writer's tone mocking or sympathetic toward the emotions and attitudes of young people in (and out of) love?

2. Through the boxed image, Fitzgerald helps readers to understand Warren's feeling of disappointment. Identify two more images.

3. Describe Fitzgerald's style, explaining whether you see any similarities between his writing and Austen's.

The Pit and the Pendulum
Short Story by Edgar Allan Poe

The Lake
Poem by Edgar Allan Poe

What breeds TERROR?

OHIO STANDARDS

READING STANDARDS
2.3 Monitor comprehension

4.11 Explain ways author develops point of view and style

KEY IDEA What causes your heart to race and your palms to sweat? Perhaps it's a deserted alley, a snarling dog, or a shadowy stranger. In the following selections by Edgar Allan Poe, you will read about both the physical and the psychological effects of **fear.**

DISCUSS With a large group, categorize the things that terrify people. What distinguishes the fear of snakes from the fear of being buried alive, for example? What categories do you come up with?

● LITERARY ANALYSIS: POE'S STYLE

A writer's **style** is the particular way he or she uses language to communicate ideas. Some writers are famous for their distinctive, innovative styles. This is true of Edgar Allan Poe, whose dark, suspenseful works helped create the genre of modern horror literature. The following characteristics frequently mark his style:

- a **first-person point of view** in which the narrator expresses emotional intensity
- repeated or italicized words
- unusual choice of words, phrases, and expressions
- long sentences or sentences with interruptions
- strange or grotesque **sensory images**

As you read, think about how Poe's stylistic choices help make the selections remarkably compelling.

● READING STRATEGY: PARAPHRASE

Poe's works can be challenging because they often feature unfamiliar words and complex sentences. One way that you can make sense of his writing as you read is to **paraphrase**, or restate information in your own words. A paraphrase is usually the same length as the original text but contains simpler language.

Poe's Words	Paraphrase
"Very suddenly there came back to my soul motion and sound...." (line 66)	I very quickly regained consciousness and was able to see and hear.

Review: **Make Inferences**

▲ VOCABULARY IN CONTEXT

Many of Poe's words may seem unusual or old-fashioned. Review the list, noting any familiar roots, prefixes, or suffixes that might help you unlock the meanings of these words.

WORD LIST		
confound	lethargy	pervade
eloquent	lucid	supposition
indeterminate	pertinacity	voracity
insuperable		

Author Online

Edgar Allan Poe
1809–1849

Living a Nightmare
Edgar Allan Poe was born in Boston, the son of traveling actors. Following Poe's birth, his father deserted the family, and his mother moved to Virginia. She died in 1811, shortly after the move. An orphan, Poe was raised by his mother's friend Frances Allan and her husband, John, a merchant. In 1831, after brief studies at the University of Virginia and West Point, Poe, 21, sought work as a writer. Allan did not approve of Poe's literary ambitions and, in time, severed all ties with his foster son.

A Valuable Legacy The 1845 publication of his eerie poem "The Raven" made Poe famous. His success, however, was soon marred by personal tragedy. In 1847, his wife, Virginia, fell victim to tuberculosis. Two years later, at, the age of 40, Poe himself grew ill and died. Although Poe's life was brief, his contribution to literature was great. He is widely credited with the invention of modern horror and detective literature.

 MORE ABOUT THE AUTHOR
For more on Edgar Allan Poe, visit the **Literature Center** at **ClassZone.com.**

Background

Tortured Times "The Pit and the Pendulum" is set in the Spanish city of Toledo during the grim age of the Spanish Inquisition. Since the Middle Ages, the Roman Catholic Church had authorized priests to try heretics—people who opposed the teachings of the church. The priests, or inquisitors, frequently misused their power. Some suspects were tortured, and those found guilty were often executed at elaborate public ceremonies called autos-da-fé.

THE PIT AND THE
Pendulum

Edgar Allan Poe

Impia tortorum longos hic turba furores
Sanguinis innocui, non satiata, aluit.
Sospite nunc patriâ, fracto nunc funeris antro,
Mors ubi dira fuit vita salusque patent.[1]

[Quatrain composed for the gates of a market to be erected
upon the site of the Jacobin[2] Club House at Paris.]

I was sick—sick unto death with that long agony; and when they at length
unbound me, and I was permitted to sit, I felt that my senses were leaving
me. The sentence—the dread sentence of death—was the last of distinct
accentuation which reached my ears. After that, the sound of the inquisitorial
voices seemed merged in one dreamy **indeterminate** hum. It conveyed to
my soul the idea of *revolution*—perhaps from its association in fancy with
the burr of a millwheel. This only for a brief period; for presently I heard no
more. Yet, for a while, I saw; but with how terrible an exaggeration! I saw the
lips of the black-robed judges. They appeared to me white—whiter than the
10 sheet upon which I trace these words—and thin even to grotesqueness; thin
with the intensity of their expression of firmness—of immoveable resolution—of
stern contempt of human torture. I saw that the decrees of what to me was Fate,
were still issuing from those lips. I saw them writhe with a deadly locution.[3] **Ⓐ**
I saw them fashion the syllables of my name; and I shuddered because no
sound succeeded. I saw, too, for a few moments of delirious horror, the soft
and nearly imperceptible waving of the sable draperies which enwrapped the
walls of the apartment.[4] And then my vision fell upon the seven tall candles
upon the table. At first they wore the aspect of charity, and seemed white

indeterminate
(ĭn′dĭ-tûr′mə-nĭt) *adj.*
not precisely known or
determined

Ⓐ POE'S STYLE
Reread lines 1–13, noting
Poe's use of **repeated
words** and **dashes.** What
do these reveal about the
narrator's state of mind?

---

1. **Impia . . . patent** *Latin:* Here the wicked crowd of tormentors, unsated, fed their long-time lusts
   for innocent blood. Now that our homeland is safe, now that the tomb is broken, life and health
   appear where once was dread death.
2. **Jacobin** (jăk′ə-bĭn): belonging to a radical French political group famous for its terrorist policies
   during the French Revolution.
3. **locution** (lō-kyōō′shən): speech.
4. **apartment:** room.

ANALYZE VISUALS
What details create the
frightening **mood** of this
illustration?

Illustrations © Cliff Nielson.

slender angels who would save me; but then, all at once, there came a most
20 deadly nausea over my spirit, and I felt every fiber in my frame thrill as if
I had touched the wire of a galvanic[5] battery, while the angel forms became
meaningless specters, with heads of flame, and I saw that from them there
would be no help. And then there stole into my fancy, like a rich musical note,
the thought of what sweet rest there must be in the grave. The thought came
gently and stealthily, and it seemed long before it attained full appreciation;[6]
but just as my spirit came at length properly to feel and entertain it, the figures
of the judges vanished, as if magically, from before me; the tall candles sank
into nothingness; their flames went out utterly; the blackness of darkness
supervened; all sensations appeared swallowed up in a mad rushing descent as of
30 the soul into Hades.[7] Then silence, and stillness, and night were the universe. **B**

I had swooned;[8] but still will not say that all of consciousness was lost. What
of it there remained I will not attempt to define, or even to describe; yet all
was not lost. In the deepest slumber—no! In delirium—no! In a swoon—no!
In death—no! even in the grave all *is not* lost. Else there is no immortality for
man. Arousing from the most profound of slumbers, we break the gossamer
web of *some* dream. Yet in a second afterward, (so frail may that web have
been) we remember not that we have dreamed. In the return to life from
the swoon there are two stages; first, that of the sense of mental or spiritual;
secondly, that of the sense of physical, existence. It seems probable that if,
40 upon reaching the second stage, we could recall the impressions of the first, we
should find these impressions **eloquent** in memories of the gulf beyond. And
that gulf is—what? How at least shall we distinguish its shadows from those
of the tomb? But if the impressions of what I have termed the first stage, are
not, at will, recalled, yet, after long interval, do they not come unbidden, while
we marvel whence[9] they come? He who has never swooned, is not he who
finds strange palaces and wildly familiar faces in coals that glow; is not he who
beholds floating in midair the sad visions that the many may not view; is not
he who ponders over the perfume of some novel flower—is not he whose brain
grows bewildered with the meaning of some musical cadence which has never
50 before arrested his attention.
　　Amid frequent and thoughtful endeavors to remember; amid earnest
struggles to regather some token of the state of seeming nothingness into
which my soul had lapsed, there have been moments when I have dreamed
of success; there have been brief, very brief periods when I have conjured
up remembrances which the **lucid** reason of a later epoch assures me could
have had reference only to that condition of seeming unconsciousness. These

B PARAPHRASE
Paraphrase lines 23–30.
What are the narrator's
thoughts immediately
following his trial? How
do these thoughts affect
him?

eloquent (ĕl′ə-kwənt) *adj.*
vividly expressive

lucid (lōō′sĭd) *adj.* clear;
mentally sound

---

5. **galvanic** (găl-văn′ĭk): electric.

6. **attained full appreciation:** was fully understood.

7. **Hades** (hā′dēz): the underworld in Greek mythology.

8. **swooned:** passed out from weakness or distress.

9. **whence:** from where.

shadows of memory tell, indistinctly, of tall figures that lifted and bore me in silence down—down—still down—till a hideous dizziness oppressed me at the mere idea of the interminableness of the descent. They tell also of a vague

60 horror at my heart, on account of that heart's unnatural stillness. Then comes a sense of sudden motionlessness throughout all things; as if those who bore me (a ghastly train!) had outrun, in their descent, the limits of the limitless, and paused from the wearisomeness of their toil. After this I call to mind flatness and dampness; and that all is *madness*—the madness of a memory which busies itself among forbidden things.

VERY suddenly there came back to my soul motion and sound—the tumultuous motion of the heart, and, in my ears, the sound of its beating. Then a pause in which all is blank. Then again sound, and motion, and touch—a tingling sensation **pervading** my frame. Then the mere

70 consciousness of existence, without thought—a condition which lasted long. Then, very suddenly, *thought,* and shuddering terror, and earnest endeavor to comprehend my true state. Then a strong desire to lapse into insensibility. Then a rushing revival of soul and a successful effort to move. And now a full memory of the trial, of the judges, of the sable draperies, of the sentence, of the sickness, of the swoon. Then entire forgetfulness of all that followed; of all that a later day and much earnestness of endeavor have enabled me vaguely to recall. **C**

So far, I had not opened my eyes. I felt that I lay upon my back, unbound. I reached out my hand, and it fell heavily upon something damp and hard.

80 There I suffered[10] it to remain for many minutes, while I strove to imagine where and *what* I could be. I longed, yet dared not to employ my vision. I dreaded the first glance at objects around me. It was not that I feared to look upon things horrible, but that I grew aghast lest there should be *nothing* to see. At length, with a wild desperation at heart, I quickly unclosed my eyes. My worst thoughts, then, were confirmed. The blackness of eternal night encompassed me. I struggled for breath. The intensity of the darkness seemed to oppress and stifle me. The atmosphere was intolerably close. I still lay quietly, and made effort to exercise my reason. I brought to mind the inquisitorial proceedings, and attempted from that point to deduce my real

90 condition. The sentence had passed; and it appeared to me that a very long interval of time had since elapsed. Yet not for a moment did I suppose myself actually dead. Such a **supposition,** notwithstanding what we read in fiction, is altogether inconsistent with real existence;—but where and in what state was I? The condemned to death, I knew, perished usually at the *autos-da-fé,*[11] and

pervade (pər-vād') *v.* to spread throughout

C MAKE INFERENCES
In lines 66–77, the narrator regains consciousness after having fainted. How does this account help create tension, or **suspense?**

supposition (sŭp'ə-zĭsh'ən) *n.* something supposed; an assumption

---

10. **suffered:** allowed.

11. *autos-da-fé* (ou'tōz-də-fā') *Portuguese:* acts of faith—public executions of people tried by the Inquisition, carried out by the civil authorities.

one of these had been held on the very night of the day of my trial. Had I been remanded to my dungeon, to await the next sacrifice, which would not take place for many months? This I at once saw could not be. Victims had been in immediate demand. Moreover, my dungeon, as well as all the condemned cells at Toledo, had stone floors, and light was not altogether excluded.

100　　A fearful idea now suddenly drove the blood in torrents upon my heart, and for a brief period, I once more relapsed into insensibility. Upon recovering, I at once started to my feet, trembling convulsively in every fiber. I thrust my arms wildly above and around me in all directions. I felt nothing; yet dreaded to move a step, lest I should be impeded by the walls of the *tomb*. Perspiration burst from every pore and stood in cold big beads on my forehead. The agony of suspense grew at length intolerable, and I cautiously moved forward, with my arms extended, and my eyes straining from their sockets, in the hope of catching some faint ray of light. I proceeded for many paces; but still all was blackness and vacancy. I breathed more freely. It seemed evident that mine
110　was not, at least, the most hideous of fates. **ⓓ**

　　And now, as I still continued to step cautiously onward, there came thronging upon my recollection a thousand vague rumors of the horrors of Toledo. Of the dungeons there had been strange things narrated—fables I

ⓓ POE'S STYLE
Reread lines 100–110. What **unusual words and phrases** express the narrator's dread of the dungeon?

had always deemed them—but yet strange, and too ghastly to repeat, save in a whisper. Was I left to perish of starvation in the subterranean world of darkness; or what fate, perhaps even more fearful, awaited me? That the result would be death, and a death of more than customary bitterness, I knew too well the character of my judges to doubt. The mode and the hour were all that occupied or distracted me. **E**

120   My outstretched hands at length encountered some solid obstruction. It was a wall, seemingly of stone masonry—very smooth, slimy, and cold. I followed it up! stepping with all the careful distrust with which certain antique narratives had inspired me. This process, however, afforded me no means of ascertaining the dimensions of my dungeon; as I might make its circuit, and return to the point whence I set out, without being aware of the fact; so perfectly uniform seemed the wall. I therefore sought the knife which had been in my pocket, when led into the inquisitorial chamber; but it was gone; my clothes had been exchanged for a wrapper of coarse serge.[12] I had thought of forcing the blade in some minute crevice of the masonry, so as to
130 identify my point of departure. The difficulty, nevertheless, was but trivial; although, in the disorder of my fancy, it seemed at first **insuperable.** I tore a part of the hem from the robe and placed the fragment at full length, and at right angles to the wall. In groping my way around the prison I could not fail to encounter this rag upon completing the circuit. So, at least I thought: but I had not counted upon the extent of the dungeon, or upon my own weakness. The ground was moist and slippery. I staggered onward for some time, when I stumbled and fell. My excessive fatigue induced me to remain prostrate; and sleep soon overtook me as I lay.

140   UPON awakening, and stretching forth an arm, I found beside me a loaf and a pitcher with water. I was too much exhausted to reflect upon this circumstance, but ate and drank with avidity. Shortly afterward, I resumed my tour around the prison, and with much toil, came at last upon the fragment of the serge. Up to the period when I fell I had counted fifty-two paces, and upon resuming my walk, I counted forty-eight more;—when I arrived at the rag. There were in all, then, a hundred paces; and, admitting two paces to the yard, I presumed the dungeon to be fifty yards in circuit. I had met, however, with many angles in the wall, and thus I could form no guess at the shape of the vault; for vault I could not help supposing it to be. **F**

      I had little object—certainly no hope—in these researches; but a vague
150 curiosity prompted me to continue them. Quitting the wall, I resolved to cross the area of the enclosure. At first I proceeded with extreme caution, for the floor, although seemingly of solid material, was treacherous with slime. At length, however, I took courage, and did not hesitate to step firmly; endeavoring

E PARAPHRASE
Paraphrase lines 111–119. What important realization about his situation does the narrator come to?

insuperable
(ĭn-sōō'pər-ə-bəl) *adj.* impossible to overcome

F POE'S STYLE
In lines 139–148, the narrator seems more clear minded than in earlier passages. What aspects of Poe's style help you understand this change in the narrator?

12. **serge** (sûrj): a woolen cloth.

to cross in as direct a line as possible. I had advanced some ten or twelve paces in this manner, when the remnant of the torn hem of my robe became entangled between my legs. I stepped on it, and fell violently on my face.

In the confusion attending my fall, I did not immediately apprehend a somewhat startling circumstance, which yet, in a few seconds afterward, and while I still lay prostrate, arrested my attention. It was this—my chin rested upon the floor of the prison, but my lips and the upper portion of my head, although seemingly at a less elevation than the chin, touched nothing. At the same time my forehead seemed bathed in a clammy vapor, and the peculiar smell of decayed fungus arose to my nostrils. I put forward my arm, and shuddered to find that I had fallen at the very brink of a circular pit, whose extent, of course, I had no means of ascertaining at the moment. Groping about the masonry just below the margin, I succeeded in dislodging a small fragment, and let it fall into the abyss. For many seconds I hearkened to its reverberations as it dashed against the sides of the chasm in its descent; at length there was a sullen plunge into water, succeeded by loud echoes. At the same moment there came a sound resembling the quick opening, and as rapid closing of a door overhead, while a faint gleam of light flashed suddenly through the gloom, and as suddenly faded away. **G**

I saw clearly the doom which had been prepared for me, and congratulated myself upon the timely accident by which I had escaped. Another step before my fall, and the world had seen me no more. And the death just avoided, was of that very character which I had regarded as fabulous and frivolous in the tales respecting the Inquisition. To the victims of its tyranny, there was the choice of death with its direst physical agonies, or death with its most hideous moral horrors. I had been reserved for the latter. By long suffering my nerves had been unstrung, until I trembled at the sound of my own voice, and had become in every respect a fitting subject for the species of torture which awaited me.

Shaking in every limb, I groped my way back to the wall; resolving there to perish rather than risk the terrors of the wells, of which my imagination now pictured many in various positions about the dungeon. In other conditions of mind I might have had courage to end my misery at once by a plunge into one of these abysses; but now I was the veriest of cowards. Neither could I forget what I had read of these pits—that the *sudden* extinction of life formed no part of their most horrible plan. **H**

Agitation of spirit kept me awake for many long hours; but at length I again slumbered. Upon arousing, I found by my side as before, a loaf and a pitcher of water. A burning thirst consumed me, and I emptied the vessel at a draft. It must have been drugged; for scarcely had I drunk, before I became irresistibly drowsy. A deep sleep fell upon me—a sleep like that of death. How long it lasted of course, I know not; but when, once again, I unclosed my eyes, the

160

170

180

190

G POE'S STYLE
Reread lines 157–172, noting Poe's **sensory images**—words and phrases that appeal to the senses. Which details communicate the foulness of the pit?

H PARAPHRASE
Paraphrase this brief paragraph. Think about the narrator's opinion of himself. Do you agree or disagree with his view?

objects around me were visible. By a wild sulphurous luster,[13] the origin of which I could not at first determine, I was enabled to see the extent and aspect of the prison.

IN its size I had been greatly mistaken. The whole circuit of its walls did not exceed twenty-five yards. For some minutes this fact occasioned me a world of vain trouble;[14] vain indeed! for what could be of less importance, under the terrible circumstances which environed me, than the mere dimensions of my dungeon? But my soul took a wild interest in trifles, and I busied myself in endeavors to account for the error I had committed in my measurement. The truth at length flashed upon me. In my first attempt at exploration I had counted fifty-two paces, up to the period when I fell; I must then have been within a pace or two of the fragments of serge; in fact, I had nearly performed the circuit of the vault. I then slept, and upon awaking, I must have returned upon my steps—thus supposing the circuit nearly double what it actually was. My confusion of mind prevented me from observing that I began my tour with the wall to the left, and ended it with the wall to the right.

---

13. **sulphurous** (sŭl'fə-rəs) **luster:** fiery glow.

14. **occasioned . . . trouble:** caused me a great deal of useless worry.

I had been deceived, too, in respect to the shape of the enclosure. In feeling my way around I had found many angles, and thus deduced an idea of great irregularity; so potent is the effect of total darkness upon one arousing from **lethargy** or sleep! The angles were simply those of a few slight depressions, or niches, at odd intervals. The general shape of the prison was square. What I had taken for masonry seemed now to be iron, or some other metal, in huge plates, whose sutures or joints occasioned the depression. The entire surface of this metallic enclosure was rudely daubed in all the hideous and repulsive

220 devices to which the charnel superstitions[15] of the monks has given rise. The figures of fiends in aspects of menace, with skeleton forms, and other more really fearful images, overspread and disfigured the walls. I observed that the outlines of these monstrosities were sufficiently distinct, but that the colors seemed faded and blurred, as if from the effects of a damp atmosphere. I now noticed the floor, too, which was of stone. In the center yawned the circular pit from whose jaws I had escaped; but it was the only one in the dungeon. **I**

ALL this I saw distinctly and by much effort: for my personal condition had been greatly changed during slumber. I now lay upon my back, and at full length, on a species of low framework of wood. To this I was securely

230 bound by a long strap resembling a surcingle.[16] It passed in many convolutions about my limbs and body, leaving at liberty only my head, and my left arm to such extent that I could, by dint[17] of much exertion, supply myself with food from an earthen dish which lay by my side on the floor. I saw, to my horror, that the pitcher had been removed. I say to my horror; for I was consumed with intolerable thirst. This thirst it appeared to be the design of my persecutors to stimulate: for the food in the dish was meat pungently seasoned.

Looking upward I surveyed the ceiling of my prison. It was some thirty or forty feet overhead, and constructed much as the side walls. In one of its panels a very singular figure riveted my whole attention. It was the painted figure of

240 Time as he is commonly represented, save that, in lieu of a scythe, he held what, at a casual glance, I supposed to be the pictured image of a huge pendulum such as we see on antique clocks. There was something, however, in the appearance of this machine which caused me to regard it more attentively. While I gazed directly upward at it (for its position was immediately over my own) I fancied that I saw it in motion. In an instant afterward the fancy was confirmed. Its sweep was brief, and of course slow. I watched it for some minutes, somewhat in fear, but more in wonder. Wearied at length with observing its dull movement, I turned my eyes upon the other objects in the cell. **J**

lethargy (lĕth′ər-jē) *n.* prolonged sluggishness; unconsciousness

◆ **GRAMMAR AND STYLE**
In lines 225–226, Poe uses **personification**—describing the pit as an open mouth—to make the image seem particularly disturbing.

J PARAPHRASE
Paraphrase lines 227–248. What situation does the narrator find himself in?

---

15. **charnel** (chär′nəl) **superstitions:** ghastly irrational beliefs.

16. **surcingle** (sûr′sĭng′gəl): a band used to tie a pack or saddle to a horse.

17. **dint:** force.

A slight noise attracted my notice, and, looking to the floor, I saw several
250 enormous rats traversing it. They had issued from the well, which lay just
within view to my right. Even then, while I gazed, they came up in troops,
hurriedly, with ravenous eyes, allured by the scent of the meat. From this it
required much effort and attention to scare them away.

It might have been half an hour, perhaps even an hour, (for I could take but
imperfect note of time) before I again cast my eyes upward. What I then saw
confounded and amazed me. The sweep of the pendulum had increased in
extent by nearly a yard. As a natural consequence, its velocity was also much
greater. But what mainly disturbed me was the idea that it had perceptibly
descended. I now observed—with what horror it is needless to say—that its
260 nether extremity was formed of a crescent of glittering steel, about a foot in
length from horn to horn; the horns upward, and the under edge evidently as
keen as that of a razor. Like a razor also, it seemed massy and heavy, tapering
from the edge into a solid and broad structure above. It was appended to a
weighty rod of brass, and the whole *hissed* as it swung through the air.

I could no longer doubt the doom prepared for me by monkish ingenuity
in torture. My cognizance of the pit had become known to the inquisitorial
agents—*the pit* whose horrors had been destined for so bold a recusant[18] as
myself—*the pit,* typical of hell, and regarded by rumor as the Ultima Thule[19]
of all their punishments. The plunge into this pit I had avoided by the merest
270 of accidents, and I knew that surprise, or entrapment into torment, formed
an important portion of all the grotesquerie of these dungeon deaths. Having
failed to fall, it was no part of the demon plan to hurl me into the abyss; and
thus (there being no alternative) a different and a milder destruction awaited
me. Milder! I half smiled in my agony as I thought of such application of such
a term. **K**

What boots it[20] to tell of the long, long hours of horror more than mortal,
during which I counted the rushing vibrations of the steel! Inch by inch—
line by line—with a descent only appreciable at intervals that seemed ages—
down and still down it came! Days passed—it might have been that many
280 days passed—ere it swept so closely over me as to fan me with its acrid breath.
The odor of the sharp steel forced itself into my nostrils. I prayed—I wearied
heaven with my prayer for its more speedy descent. I grew frantically mad,
and struggled to force myself upward against the sweep of the fearful
scimitar.[21] And then I fell suddenly calm, and lay smiling at the glittering
death, as a child at some rare bauble.

confound (kən-found´) *v.*
to confuse or astonish

K POE'S STYLE
In lines 254–275, Poe
includes various **italicized
words.** What effect do
they have on you as a
reader?

---

18. **recusant** (rĕk´yə-zənt): a religious dissenter; heretic.

19. **Ultima Thule** (ŭl´tə-mə thōō´lē): according to ancient geographers, the most remote region of
    the habitable world—here used figuratively to mean "most extreme achievement; summit."

20. **what boots it:** what good is it.

21. **scimitar** (sĭm´ĭ-tər): a curved, single-edged Asian sword.

THERE was another interval of utter insensibility; it was brief; for, upon again lapsing into life there had been no perceptible descent in the pendulum. But it might have been long; for I knew there were demons who took note of my swoon, and who could have arrested the vibration at pleasure. Upon my recovery, too, I felt very—oh, inexpressibly sick and weak, as if through long inanition.[22] Even amid the agonies of that period, the human nature craved food. With painful effort I outstretched my left arm as far as my bonds permitted, and took possession of the small remnant which had been spared me by the rats. As I put a portion of it within my lips, there rushed to my mind a half formed thought of joy—of hope. Yet what business had I with hope? It was, as I say, a half formed thought—man has many such which are never completed. I felt that it was of joy—of hope; but I felt also that it had perished in its formation. In vain I struggled to perfect—to regain it. Long suffering had nearly annihilated all my ordinary powers of mind. I was an imbecile—an idiot.

The vibration of the pendulum was at right angles to my length. I saw that the crescent was designed to cross the region of the heart. It would fray the serge of my robe—it would return and repeat its operations—again—and again. Notwithstanding its terrifically wide sweep (some thirty feet or more) and the hissing vigor of its descent, sufficient to sunder these very walls of iron, still the fraying of my robe would be all that, for several minutes, it would accomplish. And at this thought I paused. I dared not go farther than this reflection. I dwelt upon it with a **pertinacity** of attention—as if, in so dwelling, I could arrest *here* the descent of the steel. I forced myself to ponder upon the sound of the crescent as it should pass across the garment—upon the peculiar thrilling sensation which the friction of cloth produces on the nerves. I pondered upon all this frivolity until my teeth were on edge.

Down—steadily down it crept. I took a frenzied pleasure in contrasting its downward with its lateral velocity. To the right—to the left—far and wide—with the shriek of a . . . spirit; to my heart with the stealthy pace of the tiger! I alternately laughed and howled as the one or the other idea grew predominant.

Down—certainly, relentlessly down! It vibrated within three inches of my bosom! I struggled violently, furiously, to free my left arm. This was free only from the elbow to the hand. I could reach the latter, from the platter beside me, to my mouth, with great effort, but no farther. Could I have broken the fastenings above the elbow, I would have seized and attempted to arrest the pendulum. I might as well have attempted to arrest an avalanche!

Down—still unceasingly—still inevitably down! I gasped and struggled at each vibration. I shrunk convulsively at its every sweep. My eyes followed its outward or upward whirls with the eagerness of the most unmeaning despair; they closed themselves spasmodically at the descent, although death would have been a relief, oh! how unspeakable! Still I quivered in every nerve to think how slight a sinking of the machinery would precipitate that keen, glistening

pertinacity
(pûr′tn-ăs′ĭ-tē) *n.*
unyielding persistence or adherence

ANALYZE VISUALS
How effectively does this image convey the terror of the narrator's situation?

---

22. **inanition** (ĭn′ə-nĭsh′ən): wasting away from lack of food.

axe upon my bosom. It was *hope* that prompted the nerve to quiver—the frame
330 to shrink. It was *hope*—the hope that triumphs on the rack[23]—that whispers
to the death-condemned even in the dungeons of the Inquisition. **L**

I saw that some ten or twelve vibrations would bring the steel in actual
contact with my robe, and with this observation there suddenly came over
my spirit all the keen, collected calmness of despair. For the first time during
many hours—or perhaps days—I *thought*. It now occurred to me that the
bandage, or surcingle, which enveloped me, was *unique*. I was tied by no
separate cord. The first stroke of the razor-like crescent athwart[24] any portion
of the band, would so detach it that it might be unwound from my person
by means of my left hand. But how fearful, in that case, the proximity of the
340 steel! The result of the slightest struggle how deadly! Was it likely, moreover,
that the minions[25] of the torturer had not foreseen and provided for this
possibility! Was it probable that the bandage crossed my bosom in the track
of the pendulum? Dreading to find my faint, and, as it seemed, my last hope
frustrated, I so far elevated my head as to obtain a distinct view of my breast.
The surcingle enveloped my limbs and body close in all directions—*save in
the path of the destroying crescent.*

Scarcely had I dropped my head back into its original position, when there
flashed upon my mind what I cannot better describe than as the unformed half
of that idea of deliverance to which I have previously alluded, and of which a
350 moiety[26] only floated indeterminately through my brain when I raised food to
my burning lips. The whole thought was now present—feeble, scarcely sane,
scarcely definite,—but still entire. I proceeded at once, with the nervous
energy of despair, to attempt its execution.

For many hours the immediate vicinity of the low framework upon which
I lay, had been literally swarming with rats. They were wild, bold, ravenous;
their red eyes glaring upon me as if they waited but for motionlessness on
my part to make me their prey. "To what food," I thought, "have they been
accustomed in the well?"

They had devoured, in spite of all my efforts to prevent them, all but a
360 small remnant of the contents of the dish. I had fallen into an habitual see-
saw, or wave of the hand about the platter, and, at length, the unconscious
uniformity of the movement deprived it of effect. In their **voracity** the vermin
frequently fastened their sharp fangs into my fingers. With the particles of
the oily and spicy viand[27] which now remained, I thoroughly rubbed the
bandage wherever I could reach it; then, raising my hand from the floor, I lay
breathlessly still. **M**

At first the ravenous animals were startled and terrified at the change—at
the cessation of movement. They shrank alarmedly back; many sought the

---

23. **rack:** a device for torturing people by gradually stretching their bodies.

24. **athwart:** across.

25. **minions** (mĭn'yənz): followers; servants.

26. **moiety** (moi'ĭ-tē): half.

27. **viand** (vī'ənd): food.

L POE'S STYLE
Reread lines 313–331.
Which stylistic devices
help convey the narrator's
growing fear?

voracity (vô-răs'ĭ-tē) *n.*
greed for food

M PARAPHRASE
Paraphrase lines 359–366.
What does the narrator
hope to accomplish by
wiping his greasy hands
on his bindings?

well. But this was only for a moment. I had not counted in vain upon their voracity. Observing that I remained without motion, one or two of the boldest leaped upon the framework, and smelt at the surcingle. This seemed the signal for a general rush. Forth from the well they hurried in fresh troops. They clung to the wood—they overran it, and leaped in hundreds upon my person. The measured movement of the pendulum disturbed them not at all. Avoiding its strokes they busied themselves with the anointed bandage. They pressed—they swarmed upon me in ever accumulating heaps. They writhed upon my throat; their cold lips sought my own; I was half stifled by their thronging pressure; disgust, for which the world has no name, swelled my bosom, and chilled, with a heavy clamminess, my heart. Yet one minute, and I felt that the struggle would be over. Plainly I perceived the loosening of the bandage. I knew that in more than one place it must be already severed. With a more than human resolution I lay *still*.

Nor had I erred in my calculations—nor had I endured in vain. I at length felt that I was *free*. The surcingle hung in ribands[28] from my body. But the stroke of the pendulum already pressed upon my bosom. It had divided the serge of the robe. It had cut through the linen beneath. Twice again it swung, and a sharp sense of pain shot through every nerve. But the moment of escape

---

28. **ribands** (rĭb′əndz): ribbons.

had arrived. At a wave of my hand my deliverers hurried tumultuously away. With a steady movement—cautious, sidelong, shrinking, and slow—I slid from the embrace of the bandage and beyond the reach of the scimitar. For the moment, at least, *I was free.*

Free!—and in the grasp of the Inquisition! I had scarcely stepped from my wooden bed of horror upon the stone floor of the prison, when the motion of the hellish machine ceased and I beheld it drawn up, by some invisible force, through the ceiling. This was a lesson which I took desperately to heart. My every motion was undoubtedly watched. Free!—I had but escaped death in one form of agony, to be delivered unto worse than death in some other. With that thought I rolled my eyes nervously around the barriers of iron that hemmed me in. Something unusual—some change which at first I could not appreciate distinctly—it was obvious, had taken place in the apartment. For many minutes in a dreamy and trembling abstraction, I busied myself in vain, unconnected conjecture. During this period, I became aware, for the first time, of the origin of the sulphurous light which illuminated the cell. It proceeded from a fissure, about half an inch in width, extending entirely around the prison at the base of the walls, which thus appeared, and were, completely separated from the floor. I endeavored, but of course in vain, to look through the aperture.[29]

As I arose from the attempt, the mystery of the alteration in the chamber broke at once upon my understanding. I have observed that, although the outlines of the figures upon the walls were sufficiently distinct, yet the colors seemed blurred and indefinite. These colors had now assumed, and were momentarily assuming, a startling and most intense brilliancy, that gave to the spectral and fiendish portraitures an aspect that might have thrilled even firmer nerves than my own. Demon eyes, of a wild and ghastly vivacity, glared upon me in a thousand directions, where none had been visible before, and gleamed with the lurid luster of a fire that I could not force my imagination to regard as unreal.

Unreal!—Even while I breathed there came to my nostrils the breath of the vapor of heated iron! A suffocating odor pervaded the prison! A deeper glow settled each moment in the eyes that glared at my agonies! A richer tint of crimson diffused itself over the pictured horrors of blood. I panted! I gasped for breath! There could be no doubt of the design of my tormentors—oh! most unrelenting! oh! most demoniac of men! I shrank from the glowing metal to the center of the cell. Amid the thought of the fiery destruction that impended, the idea of the coolness of the well came over my soul like balm. I rushed to its deadly brink. I threw my straining vision below. The glare from the enkindled roof illumined its inmost recesses. Yet, for a wild moment, did my spirit refuse to comprehend the meaning of what I saw. At length it forced—it wrestled its way into my soul—it burned itself in upon

---

29. **aperture** (ăp′ər-chər): opening.

430 my shuddering reason.—Oh! for a voice to speak!—oh! horror!—oh! any horror but this! With a shriek, I rushed from the margin, and buried my face in my hands—weeping bitterly. ⊙

The heat rapidly increased, and once again I looked up, shuddering as with a fit of the ague.[30] There had been a second change in the cell—and now the change was obviously in the form. As before, it was in vain that I, at first, endeavored to appreciate or understand what was taking place. But not long was I left in doubt. The Inquisitorial vengeance had been hurried by my two-fold escape, and there was to be no more dallying with the King of Terrors. The room had been square. I saw that two of its iron angles were now acute—
440 two, consequently, obtuse. The fearful difference quickly increased with a low rumbling or moaning sound. In an instant the apartment had shifted its form into that of a lozenge. But the alteration stopped not here—I neither hoped nor desired it to stop. I could have clasped the red walls to my bosom as a garment of eternal peace. "Death," I said, "any death but that of the pit!" Fool! might I have not known that *into the pit* it was the object of the burning iron to urge me? Could I resist its glow? or, if even that, could I withstand its pressure? And now, flatter and flatter grew the lozenge, with a rapidity that left me no time for contemplation. Its center, and of course, its greatest width, came just over the yawning gulf. I shrank back—but the closing walls pressed
450 me resistlessly onward. At length for my seared and writhing body there was no longer an inch of foothold on the firm floor of the prison. I struggled no more, but the agony of my soul found vent in one loud, long, and final scream of despair. I felt that I tottered upon the brink—I averted my eyes—

There was a discordant hum of human voices! There was a loud blast of many trumpets! There was a harsh grating as of a thousand thunders! The fiery walls rushed back! An outstretched arm caught my own as I fell, fainting, into the abyss. It was that of General Lasalle. The French army had entered Toledo. The Inquisition was in the hands of its enemies. ⌒

⊙ **POE'S STYLE**
Reread lines 418–432. What does the **punctuation** used by Poe suggest about the narrator's emotional state?

---

30. **the ague** (āʹgyōō): a feverish illness.

Timeless, 2002, Lee Campbell. Private collection. Photo © The Bridgeman Art Library.

THE
Lake

Edgar Allan Poe

In youth's spring, it was my lot
To haunt of the wide earth a spot
The which I could not love the less;
So lovely was the loneliness
5 Of a wild lake, with black rock bound,
And the tall pines that tower'd around.
But when the night had thrown her pall
Upon that spot—as upon all,
And the wind would pass me by
10 In its still melody,
My infant spirit would awake
To the terror of that lone lake.
Yet that terror was not fright—
But a tremulous delight,
15 And a feeling undefin'd,
Springing from a darken'd mind. **P**
Death was in that poison'd wave
And in its gulf a fitting grave
For him who thence could solace bring
20 To his dark imagining;
Whose wild'ring thought could even make
An Eden of that dim lake. **Q**

P POE'S STYLE
Reread lines 1–16.
Which words and phrases
help communicate the
emotional intensity of
the speaker?

Q PARAPHRASE
Paraphrase lines 17–22.
What comfort does the
speaker find in visiting
the eerie lake?

Comprehension

1. **Recall** What are the first two dangers the narrator faces in the story?

2. **Recall** How does the narrator break free from his bonds?

3. **Clarify** Who or what seems to save the narrator at the end?

4. **Summarize** In the poem, what effect does the lake have on the speaker?

READING STANDARD
4.11 Explain ways author develops point of view and style

Literary Analysis

5. **Make Inferences About Character** Consider the narrator's words, thoughts, and actions in "The Pit and the Pendulum." What can you infer are his greatest strengths in his battle against the inquisitors? Support your answer with details from the story.

6. **Interpret Ending** Paraphrase the story's conclusion, lines 454–458. Do you think the narrator is truly saved, or is he simply imagining a rescue as he falls? Cite evidence to support your opinion.

7. **Examine Sound Devices** Reread "The Lake," looking for examples of **alliteration** (repetition of consonant sounds at the beginnings of words) and **assonance** (repetition of vowel sounds). Which sound device does Poe use more extensively? What effect does this have on the reader?

8. **Analyze Imagery and Mood** Find several examples of sensory imagery— words and phrases that appeal to the senses—in the story and in the poem. In what way do these images help convey a mood of **fear** and anxiety?

9. **Analyze Poe's Style** Poe has fascinated generations of readers with his tales of horror and haunting poetry. Identify the stylistic characteristics that are common to both selections you have just read. Use the following list to help you:

   • a first-person point of view that expresses emotional intensity

   • repeated or italicized words

   • unusual choice of words, phrases, and expressions

   • long sentences or sentences with interruptions

   • strange or grotesque sensory images

Literary Criticism

10. **Critical Interpretations** One literary critic has noted that Poe's "imagination is visual and three-dimensional. . . . If he had been alive today he probably would be a filmmaker." How do you think "The Pit and the Pendulum" would succeed as a movie? Consider what would have to be changed in order to adapt the story for the screen.

Vocabulary in Context

VOCABULARY PRACTICE

Indicate whether the words in each pair are synonyms or antonyms.

1. precise/indeterminate
2. eloquent/inarticulate
3. lucid/clear
4. spread/pervade
5. supposition/evidence
6. insuperable/unconquerable
7. lethargy/excitement
8. bewilder/confound
9. reluctance/pertinacity
10. hunger/voracity

VOCABULARY IN WRITING

Imagine that you are able to view the narrator in the dungeon. Write a paragraph to describe your feelings about him and his circumstances. Use at least three vocabulary words. You might begin as shown.

> **EXAMPLE SENTENCE**
>
> *The darkness and slipperiness **confound** the poor man.*

VOCABULARY STRATEGY: METAPHORS AND SIMILES

Figurative language is language that communicates ideas beyond the literal meanings of the words. Two common forms of figurative language—metaphors and similes—make comparisons between unlike things. A **metaphor** makes a direct comparison, without signal words: "Her voice is pure honey." A **simile** signals a comparison with *like* or *as:* "Her voice is like pure honey." Metaphors and similes can provide clues to the meanings of unfamiliar words.

PRACTICE Identify whether each sentence contains a simile or a metaphor. What does the figurative language suggest about the meaning of the underlined term?

1. His <u>lethargy</u> was a fog that would not lift.
2. She could feel peace <u>pervade</u> her body like a soothing wave.
3. The single flower was as <u>eloquent</u> as a poem.
4. Her <u>voracity</u> became a beast eager to be satisfied.

OHIO STANDARDS

VOCABULARY STANDARD
1.3 Infer the literal and figurative meanings of words

VOCABULARY PRACTICE
For more practice, go to the **Vocabulary Center** at **ClassZone.com.**

Reading-Writing Connection

Broaden your understanding of Poe's works by responding to these prompts.
Then use **Revision: Grammar and Style** to improve your writing.

WRITING PROMPTS	SELF-CHECK

A. Short Response: Describe a Setting
In each work, Poe depicts a terrifying place or situation.
What setting—real or imaginary—strikes **fear** in
you? Write a **one- or two-paragraph description** that
communicates the sights, sounds, and smells of this
dreaded place.

A powerful description will...
- focus on one particular place
  or situation
- include strong sensory images
  that create a frightening mood

B. Extended Response: Write Across Texts
According to one critic, Poe's work is concerned with
"death-in-life" and "life-in-death." How do "The Pit
and the Pendulum" and "The Lake" deal with these
themes? Using examples from the texts, write a **three-
to-five-paragraph response.**

An effective response will...
- include a thesis statement
  in the introduction
- cite specific details that
  support your conclusions

REVISION: GRAMMAR AND STYLE

USE PERSONIFICATION Review the **Grammar and Style** note on page 780.
Poe uses a type of figurative language known as **personification,** in which a
writer gives human characteristics to an animal, a thing, or an idea. To create
personification within a description, choose **nouns, verbs,** and **adjectives** that
are usually used to refer to people. In the following example, Poe refers to the
pendulum that moves to "fan" the narrator with its "breath":

> *Days passed—it might have been that many days passed—ere it swept
> so closely over me as to fan me with its acrid breath.* (lines 279–280)

Notice how the revisions in red make the images in this first draft more
memorable. Revise your response to Prompt A by incorporating examples
of personification.

OHIO
STANDARDS

WRITING STANDARD
6.1.b Use literary devices including
figurative language

**WRITING
TOOLS**
For prewriting, revision,
and editing tools, visit
the **Writing Center** at
ClassZone.com.

> **STUDENT MODEL**
>
> As I walk through the ~~empty~~ *lonely* town, night ~~falls~~ *creeps in* around me. I listen for
>
> footsteps or voices, but all I hear is the ~~sound~~ *moan* of the wind.

When I Heard the Learn'd Astronomer
Poem by Walt Whitman

The Artilleryman's Vision
Poem by Walt Whitman

What do we learn from EXPERIENCE?

OHIO STANDARDS

READING STANDARDS
4.8 Analyze author's use of mood and tone

4.11 Explain ways author develops point of view and style

KEY IDEA We often gain valuable information through reading, watching television, and listening to people share their knowledge. But sometimes **experience** can be the most powerful teacher. In the following poems by Walt Whitman, you will meet two men who learn very different lessons through their life experiences.

QUICKWRITE Think about a time in which experiencing something firsthand helped you to learn about it. For example, maybe you gained appreciation for a distant city by actually visiting it. Or perhaps breaking a leg made you aware of some barriers to the disabled. Explain to a classmate how experience fostered your new understanding.

LITERARY ANALYSIS: WHITMAN'S STYLE

Like other poets of his day, Walt Whitman was deeply committed to celebrating the beauty and richness of America. Yet, while many of his contemporaries relied on conventional poetic forms such as sonnets and ballads, Whitman did not. Instead, he invented a new form to capture the spirit of the nation. Called **free verse,** this poetic form lacks any regular patterns of rhyme and meter. As a result, the lines in free verse flow easily, resembling natural speech. Other aspects of style that distinguish Whitman's work are as follows:

- **repetition**—or repeated words and phrases
- **parallelism**—or ideas phrased in similar ways
- **onomatopoeia**—or words that imitate sounds
- **catalogs**—or lists of things, people, or attributes

As you read each poem, notice how Whitman's choice of form and stylistic devices help convey the speaker's experience.

READING SKILL: ANALYZE SENSORY DETAILS

In his poetry, Whitman praised life in all of its diversity. He often relied on sensory details to communicate a wealth of experiences to readers. You probably remember that **sensory details** are words and phrases that appeal to the five senses: sight, hearing, taste, smell, and touch. As you read Whitman's poetry, record various examples of sensory details and analyze their effectiveness. For each poem, use a chart like the one shown.

"When I Heard the Learn'd Astronomer"		
Details	Sense(s)	Why Effective
"When I heard ... When the proofs, the figures, were ranged in columns before me" (lines 1–2)	hearing and sight	They clearly place the speaker in a lecture hall.

Author Online

**Walt Whitman
1819–1892**

Jack-of-All-Trades
Born in 1819, Walt Whitman grew up in a hurry. He left school at age 11, and within a few years he was living on his own in New York City. He drifted from job to job, working as a printer, journalist, and carpenter. He loved to stroll around the city, taking in sights and sounds that he would later use in his poetry.

Pioneer of Poetry In 1855, Whitman published *Leaves of Grass,* a volume of poems that captured the variety and tumult of 19th-century American life. Upon receiving a copy, the poet Ralph Waldo Emerson declared, "It is the most extraordinary piece of wit and wisdom that America has yet contributed." However, other writers denounced the book for its unorthodox form and content. Over the years, Whitman added to, revised, and rearranged the poems in *Leaves of Grass,* producing nine editions in total. Today, it is often regarded as the most influential collection of poetry in American literature.

Whitman and the Civil War When Whitman learned that his younger brother had been wounded in Fredericksburg, Virginia, he immediately traveled to the front. There he saw the aftermath of one of the war's bloodiest battles. This experience convinced him to work in Washington, D.C., as a volunteer nurse. In caring for the wounded, Whitman witnessed the effects of war on men's bodies and minds. During this time, he wrote numerous poems, including the poignant "The Artilleryman's Vision." His years of nursing, he once wrote, were "the greatest privilege and satisfaction . . . and, of course, the most profound lesson of my life."

 MORE ABOUT THE AUTHOR
For more on Walt Whitman, visit the **Literature Center** at ClassZone.com.

WHEN I HEARD
THE LEARN'D
ASTRONOMER

Walt Whitman

When I heard the learn'd astronomer,
When the proofs,[1] the figures, were ranged in columns before me,
When I was shown the charts and diagrams, to add, divide, and
    measure them,
When I sitting heard the astronomer where he lectured with much
    applause in the lecture-room, **Ⓐ**
5 How soon unaccountable I became tired and sick,
Till rising and gliding out I wander'd off by myself,
In the mystical moist night air, and from time to time,
Look'd up in perfect silence at the stars. **Ⓑ**

Ⓐ WHITMAN'S STYLE
Notice Whitman's use of
parallelism in lines 1–4.
What other distinctive
features of his style can
you see in this poem?

Ⓑ SENSORY DETAILS
Of the various sensory
details, which most
effectively conveys the
speaker's enjoyment of
the night sky?

---

1. **proofs:** formal scientific statements of evidence.

THE Artilleryman's VISION

Walt Whitman

While my wife at my side lies slumbering, and the wars are over
    long,
And my head on the pillow rests at home, and the vacant midnight
    passes,
And through the stillness, through the dark, I hear, just hear, the
    breath of my infant,
There in the room as I wake from sleep this vision presses upon me;
5 The engagement[1] opens there and then in fantasy unreal,
The skirmishers[2] begin, they crawl cautiously ahead, I hear the
    irregular snap! snap! **C**
I hear the sounds of the different missiles, the short *t-h-t! t-h-t!* of
    the rifle balls,
I see the shells exploding leaving small white clouds, I hear the great
    shells shrieking as they pass,
The grape[3] like the hum and whirr of wind through the trees,
    (tumultuous now the contest rages,)
10 All the scenes at the batteries[4] rise in detail before me again,
The crashing and smoking, the pride of the men in their pieces,
The chief-gunner ranges and sights his piece and selects a fuse of the
    right time,
After firing I see him lean aside and look eagerly off to note the
    effect;
Elsewhere I hear the cry of a regiment charging, (the young colonel
    leads himself this time with brandish'd[5] sword,)

C **SENSORY DETAILS**
Reread lines 1–6. Which
sensory details help
you to understand the
situation described at the
beginning of the poem?

---

1. **engagement:** battle.
2. **skirmishers:** soldiers sent out in advance of a main attack.
3. **grape:** grapeshot—small iron balls shot in a bunch from a cannon.
4. **batteries:** groups of cannons.
5. **brandish'd:** raised and waving.

15 I see the gaps cut by the enemy's volleys,[6] (quickly fill'd up, no
   delay,)
I breathe the suffocating smoke, then the flat clouds hover low
   concealing all;
Now a strange lull for a few seconds, not a shot fired on either side, **D**
Then resumed the chaos louder than ever, with eager calls and
   orders of officers,
While from some distant part of the field the wind wafts to my ears
   a shout of applause, (some special success,)
20 And ever the sound of the cannon far or near, (rousing even in
   dreams a devilish exultation and all the old mad joy in the depths
   of my soul,)
And ever the hastening of infantry shifting positions, batteries,
   cavalry, moving hither and thither,
(The falling, dying, I heed not, the wounded dripping and red I heed
   not, some to the rear are hobbling,)
Grime, heat, rush, aide-de-camps[7] galloping by or on a full run,
With the patter of small arms, the warning *s-s-t* of the rifles, (these
   in my vision I hear or see,)
25 And bombs bursting in air, and at night the vari-color'd rockets. **E**

D WHITMAN'S STYLE
Reread lines 7–17, noting
the long **catalog** of
combat activities. In
what way is this stylistic
element in keeping with
the poem's speaker—a
dreaming soldier?

E WHITMAN'S STYLE
What overall effect does
Whitman create by using
free verse in this poem?

---

6. **volleys:** groups of cannonballs fired at the same time.

7. **aide-de-camps** (ād′dĭ-kămps′): assistants to military commanders.

LETTER In this letter to his mother, Walt Whitman describes a meaningful encounter with a wounded Union soldier following the Battle of Fredericksburg.

January 29, 1865

Dear Mother—

Here is a case of a soldier I found among the crowded cots in the Patent hospital — (they have removed most of the men of late and broken up that hospital). He likes to have some one to talk to, and we will listen to him. He got badly wounded in the leg and side at Fredericksburg that eventful Saturday, 13th December. He lay the succeeding two days and nights helpless on the field, between the city and those grim batteries, for his company and his regiment had been compelled to leave him to his fate. To make matters worse, he lay with his head slightly down hill, and could not help himself. At the end of some fifty hours he was brought off, with other wounded, under a flag of truce.

We ask him how the Rebels treated him during those two days and nights within reach of them — whether they came to him — whether they abused him? He answers that several of the Rebels, soldiers and others, came to him, at one time and another. A couple of them, who were together, spoke roughly and sarcastically, but did no act. One middle-aged man, however, who seemed to be moving around the field among the dead and wounded for benevolent purposes, came to him in a way he will never forget. This man treated our soldier kindly, bound up his wounds, cheered him, gave him a couple of biscuits, gave him a drink and water, asked him if he could eat some beef. This good Secesh,[1] however, did not change our soldier's position, for it might have caused the blood to burst from the wounds where they were clotted and stagnated. Our soldier is from Pennsylvania; has had a pretty severe time; the wounds proved to be bad ones. But he retains a good heart, and is at present on the gain. . . .

Walt

---

1. **Secesh** (sĭ-sĕsh'): a secessionist from the Union; a Confederate.

Comprehension

1. **Recall** In "When I Heard the Learn'd Astronomer," what methods does the astronomer use to teach about the stars?

2. **Recall** In "The Artilleryman's Vision," where is the artilleryman when he experiences his vision?

3. **Summarize** Describe the sequence of events in "The Artilleryman's Vision."

Literary Analysis

4. **Interpret Mood** Reread "When I Heard the Learn'd Astronomer." At what point does the mood, or atmosphere, of the poem change? Explain which words and phrases signal this shift.

5. **Understand Whitman's Style** In his poetry, Whitman often celebrates nature and its beauty. Which aspects of Whitman's style in "When I Heard the Learn'd Astronomer" help communicate the beauty of nature? If necessary, review the list of aspects of Whitman's style on page 793.

6. **Examine Diction and Tone** Reread lines 18–22 of "The Artilleryman's Vision," reviewing Whitman's diction, or choice of words. Considering phrases such as "devilish exultation" and "old mad joy," describe Whitman's tone, or attitude, toward war.

7. **Analyze Sensory Details** Review the charts that you created and your conclusions about Whitman's use of sensory details. Select one poem and explain how sensory details help make the speaker's firsthand **experience** vivid and engaging. Use examples from the poem to support your answer.

8. **Generalize About Poetic Form** Whitman uses **free verse** in both selections. How might your sense of the speakers and their experiences be different if the poems had been written in a form with a conventional metrical pattern and rhyme scheme?

9. **Compare Literary Works** Compare Whitman's depictions of Civil War soldiers in "The Artilleryman's Vision" and in his letter to his mother on page 798. Which offers a more disturbing view of the after-effects of war—the poem or the personal letter? Use information from both pieces to support your response.

Literary Criticism

10. **Historical Context** When Whitman wrote "The Artilleryman's Vision" in the mid-1860s, psychology had yet to become a modern science. What does this fact reveal about Whitman and his handling of the poem's subject?

OHIO STANDARDS

READING STANDARD
4.11 Explain ways author develops point of view and style

Birches
Poem by Robert Frost

Mending Wall
Poem by Robert Frost

How can NATURE *inspire you?*

OHIO STANDARDS

READING STANDARDS
2.1 Make inferences
4.11 Explain ways author develops point of view and style

KEY IDEA Spending time in **nature** often inspires us to think of things beyond our ordinary routines. Whether it's hiking through woods or canoeing down a river, for example, being in "the great outdoors" can help us appreciate our place in the world at large. In the following poems by Robert Frost, the speakers gain new insights into their own lives through their experiences with nature.

QUICKWRITE Think of an outdoor activity that says something about you and what you're like—such as birdwatching, fishing, climbing, or swimming. Write a paragraph describing the activity and what it has helped you realize about yourself.

LITERARY ANALYSIS: FROST'S STYLE

In many ways, Robert Frost is a transitional figure between the 19th and 20th centuries. Like his predecessors, Frost loved and wrote about the natural world, particularly rural New England. His poems, however, contain more than his impressions of simple country life. In them, Frost often uses humor to point to more serious matters, such as themes of solitude and isolation. In this way, his writing anticipates later works of modern poetry and fiction. The following are key aspects of Frost's style:

- conversational or **colloquial language**
- rich sensory **imagery**
- imaginative **similes** and **metaphors**
- realistic **dialogue**
- a playful, mocking **tone**

As you read, notice how these stylistic elements help make "Birches" and "Mending Wall" works of rare beauty and complexity.

READING SKILL: MAKE INFERENCES

In modern poetry, speakers do not often make direct statements about how they view the world. Instead, readers must use clues in the texts to **make inferences,** or logical guesses, about the speakers' ideas and feelings. For example, speculate about what the following lines from "Birches" reveal about the speaker's desires:

So was I once myself a swinger of birches.
And so I dream of going back to be.

As you read each poem, try to "read between the lines," and then record your inferences in a chart like the one shown.

"Birches"		
Poem Details	My Associations	Inferences
"When I see birches bend to left and right/ Across the lines of straighter darker trees/ I like to think some boy's been swinging them."	Birches are white, flexible trees.	Seeing bent birches makes the speaker invent a playful explanation for them.

Author Online

Robert Frost
1874–1963

Unruly Youth
Although Robert Frost is linked with rural New England in the public imagination, he spent his early years in cities. At age 11, Frost moved with his mother and sister from his birthplace, San Francisco, to the industrial city of Lawrence, Massachusetts. Undisciplined in grade school, Frost became co-valedictorian of his high school graduating class. However, he dropped out of the two universities he attended—Harvard and Dartmouth—because he disliked the discipline of academic life.

Farmer-Poet In his 20s and 30s, Frost worked a 30-acre farm in Derry, New Hampshire. Captivated by Derry's inhabitants and rugged landscape, Frost wrote many of his most beloved poems while living there. He used traditional poetic devices—such as rhyme and meter—to capture the speech patterns of rural New Englanders. Frost's immense achievement was recognized with four Pulitzer Prizes in poetry and 44 honorary college degrees.

 MORE ABOUT THE AUTHOR
For more on Robert Frost, visit the **Literature Center** at ClassZone.com.

Background

Nature's Splendor In the selections, Frost captures the stark beauty of rural New England. In "Birches," he paints a vivid picture of the white-barked trees that adorn much of the countryside. The birch is a tall, delicate tree with a slender white trunk that can bend easily in a moderate wind. The title "Mending Wall" refers to the act of repairing the stone walls that divide farms and fields in New England. Farmers typically build these walls with stones removed from their own land.

Birches
Robert Frost

When I see birches bend to left and right
Across the lines of straighter darker trees,
I like to think some boy's been swinging them.
But swinging doesn't bend them down to stay
5 As ice-storms do. Often you must have seen them
Loaded with ice a sunny winter morning
After a rain. They click upon themselves
As the breeze rises, and turn many-colored
As the stir cracks and crazes their enamel.
10 Soon the sun's warmth makes them shed crystal shells
Shattering and avalanching on the snow-crust—
Such heaps of broken glass to sweep away
You'd think the inner dome of heaven had fallen. **A**
They are dragged to the withered bracken¹ by the load,
15 And they seem not to break; though once they are bowed
So low for long, they never right themselves:
You may see their trunks arching in the woods
Years afterwards, trailing their leaves on the ground
Like girls on hands and knees that throw their hair
20 Before them over their heads to dry in the sun. **B**
But I was going to say when Truth broke in
With all her matter-of-fact about the ice-storm
I should prefer to have some boy bend them
As he went out and in to fetch the cows—
25 Some boy too far from town to learn baseball,
Whose only play was what he found himself,
Summer or winter, and could play alone. **C**

---

1. **bracken:** weedy ferns having large triangular fronds and often forming dense thickets.

A FROST'S STYLE
Frost uses plain and **colloquial words**— such as contractions— throughout this poem. Find one or two examples in lines 1–13. What effect do these everyday words create?

B FROST'S STYLE
Which sensory details presented so far help the **image** of the birches come alive for you?

C MAKE INFERENCES
Reread lines 21–27. What can you infer about the speaker?

One by one he subdued[2] his father's trees
By riding them down over and over again
30 Until he took the stiffness out of them,
And not one but hung limp, not one was left
For him to conquer. He learned all there was
To learn about not launching out too soon
And so not carrying the tree away
35 Clear to the ground. He always kept his poise[3]
To the top branches, climbing carefully
With the same pains you use to fill a cup
Up to the brim, and even above the brim.
Then he flung outward, feet first, with a swish,
40 Kicking his way down through the air to the ground. **D**
So was I once myself a swinger of birches.
And so I dream of going back to be.
It's when I'm weary of considerations,
And life is too much like a pathless wood
45 Where your face burns and tickles with the cobwebs
Broken across it, and one eye is weeping
From a twig's having lashed across it open. **E**
I'd like to get away from earth awhile
And then come back to it and begin over.
50 May no fate willfully misunderstand me
And half grant what I wish and snatch me away
Not to return. Earth's the right place for love:
I don't know where it's likely to go better.
I'd like to go by climbing a birch tree,
55 And climb black branches up a snow-white trunk
Toward heaven, till the tree could bear no more,
But dipped its top and set me down again.
That would be good both going and coming back.
One could do worse than be a swinger of birches. **F**

D FROST'S STYLE
In lines 28–40, Frost describes a boy swinging in the birches. Which words or phrases convey Frost's playful and energetic **tone?**

E FROST'S STYLE
Identify the **simile** used in lines 41–47. What ideas beyond the literal meaning of the words does this simile communicate?

F MAKE INFERENCES
Reread lines 48–59. Think of what this final passage suggests about the speaker. Does he accept or deny reality? Explain.

---

2. **subdued:** brought under control.

3. **poise:** balance.

Mending Wall
Robert Frost

Cotswold Landscape (1981), Derold Page. Private collection. Photo © The Bridgeman Art Library.

ANALYZE VISUALS
In what ways might the **setting** shown in the painting represent that of "Mending Wall"? In what ways might it be different?

Something there is that doesn't love a wall,
That sends the frozen-ground-swell under it
And spills the upper boulders in the sun,
And makes gaps even two can pass abreast. **G**
5 The work of hunters is another thing:
I have come after them and made repair
Where they have left not one stone on a stone,
But they would have the rabbit out of hiding,
To please the yelping dogs.[1] The gaps I mean,
10 No one has seen them made or heard them made,
But at spring mending-time we find them there.

G **FROST'S STYLE**
Think about Frost's decision to use the informal, plain word *something* in line 1. In your opinion, would a more descriptive word have provided a better effect? Explain your opinion.

---

1. **The work . . . yelping dogs:** The speaker has replaced the stones hunters have removed from the wall when they have been pursuing rabbits.

I let my neighbor know beyond the hill;
And on a day we meet to walk the line
And set the wall between us once again. **H**
15 We keep the wall between us as we go.
To each the boulders that have fallen to each.
And some are loaves and some so nearly balls
We have to use a spell to make them balance:
"Stay where you are until our backs are turned!"
20 We wear our fingers rough with handling them.
Oh, just another kind of outdoor game,
One on a side. It comes to little more:
There where it is we do not need the wall:
He is all pine and I am apple orchard.
25 My apple trees will never get across
And eat the cones under his pines, I tell him.
He only says, "Good fences make good neighbors."
Spring is the mischief in me, and I wonder
If I could put a notion in his head:
30 "*Why* do they make good neighbors? Isn't it
Where there are cows? But here there are no cows. **I**
Before I built a wall I'd ask to know
What I was walling in or walling out,
And to whom I was like to give offense.
35 Something there is that doesn't love a wall,
That wants it down." I could say "Elves" to him,
But it's not elves exactly, and I'd rather
He said it for himself. I see him there,
Bringing a stone grasped firmly by the top
40 In each hand, like an old-stone savage armed.
He moves in darkness as it seems to me,
Not of woods only and the shade of trees.
He will not go behind his father's saying,
And he likes having thought of it so well
45 He says again, "Good fences make good neighbors." **J**

H **MAKE INFERENCES**
Describe the speaker's feelings so far about mending the stone wall. Which words and phrases helped you make your inference?

I **MAKE INFERENCES**
Reread lines 23–31, looking for details that convey the speaker's opinion of his neighbor. Does the speaker admire him? Why or why not?

J **FROST'S STYLE**
Consider Frost's overall **tone,** or attitude, in this poem. Do you think the poet himself approves or disapproves of walls between neighbors? Explain.

Comprehension

1. **Recall** In "Birches," what two explanations does the speaker give for the bent trees?

2. **Clarify** Which explanation does the speaker seem to prefer? Explain.

3. **Recall** According to the speaker of "Mending Wall," what two forces cause the stone wall to fall apart?

4. **Clarify** Why is there no practical need for the wall?

Literary Analysis

5. **Make Inferences** Review the charts you made as you read. Think about the key inferences that helped you understand each speaker. What personality traits and values does each speaker appear to have?

6. **Draw Conclusions** In "Birches," the speaker concludes, "One could do worse than be a swinger of birches." Why does **nature** hold such strong appeal for the speaker? Support your answer with details from the poem.

7. **Interpret** In "Mending Wall," the neighbor reminds the speaker that "good fences make good neighbors." Paraphrase this statement. Do you agree or disagree? Explain your response.

8. **Analyze Tone Through Imagery** In his works, Frost often reveals a mischievous attitude toward his subjects through his choice of images. Review lines 23–42 in "Birches" and lines 15–26 in "Mending Wall." Which **sensory details** in each poem strongly convey Frost's playful tone?

9. **Analyze Frost's Style** One hallmark of Frost's style is his use of imaginative **similes** and **metaphors.** Identify two similes and two metaphors in the poems. Explain how they convey ideas beyond the literal meaning of the words.

10. **Generalize About Poetic Form** Frost often relied on conventional verse forms in his work. Both "Birches" and "Mending Wall" are written in **blank verse**— a form of unrhymed iambic pentameter favored by many English poets, including William Shakespeare. What does Frost's regular use of this poetic form suggest about him and his writing style?

Literary Criticism

11. **Biographical Context** Sharing his understanding of good poetry, Frost once said: "A poem is never a put-up job, so to speak. It begins as a lump in the throat, a sense of wrong, a homesickness, a lovesickness.... It is at its best when it is a tantalizing vagueness." Select either poem and explain how it might fit Frost's standards. Use examples from the poem to support your response.

OHIO STANDARDS

READING STANDARD
2.1 Make inferences

Reading-Writing Connection

Broaden your understanding of Frost's poems by responding to these prompts. Then use **Revision: Grammar and Style** to improve your writing.

WRITING PROMPTS	SELF-CHECK
A. Short Response: Analyze Dialogue How does the dialogue in "Mending Wall" help illuminate the differences between the speaker and his neighbor? Write a **one- or two-paragraph response.**	*A successful analysis will . . .* • clearly contrast the speaker with his neighbor • cite specific dialogue
B. Extended Response: Examine Theme According to the critic Peter Davison, Frost is "one of the great poets of loneliness." In what ways do both poems explore the theme of solitude? Using examples from the poems, write a **three-to-five-paragraph response.**	*An effective response will . . .* • include a thesis statement in the introduction • offer specific details that support your conclusions

REVISION: GRAMMAR AND STYLE

USE LANGUAGE EFFECTIVELY Poetry consists of words and phrases that are carefully chosen to create particular rhythms and effects. One kind of phrase that often appears in poetry is the **infinitive phrase,** which consists of an infinitive—a verb form that begins with *to*—plus its modifiers and complements. Infinitive phrases function as nouns, adjectives, or adverbs, but often they are able to provide more information than would one-word examples of these parts of speech. Here are some instances of Frost's use of infinitive phrases. Note how they function as adverbs and a noun in the poem.

> *I should prefer to have some boy bend them*
> *As he went out and in to fetch the cows—*
> *Some boy too far from town to learn baseball* ("Birches," lines 23–25)

In the following revision, notice how the writer uses an infinitive phrase to better describe the neighbor's wish. Use similar techniques to revise your responses to the prompts.

OHIO STANDARDS

WRITING STANDARD
7.3 Use clauses and phrases

WRITING TOOLS
For prewriting, revision, and editing tools, visit the **Writing Center** at ClassZone.com.

STUDENT MODEL

The speaker in "Mending Wall" doesn't understand his neighbor's wish. *to erect a wall between their properties*

The Pond
Poem by Amy Lowell

Fourth of July Night
Poem by Carl Sandburg

The Red Wheelbarrow
Poem by William Carlos Williams

Can you paint a PICTURE *with words?*

OHIO STANDARDS

READING STANDARDS
2.1 Apply reading comprehension strategies

4.11 Explain ways author develops point of view and style

KEY IDEA Think of a favorite photo and picture in your mind the scene it shows. What details help you visualize the scene? As you'll see, through carefully chosen details, a poem can capture the **image** of a moment in time.

QUICKWRITE William Carlos Williams famously remarked that a poem can be made out of anything. With a group, think of an animal or object that could be the subject of a poem. Without naming the animal or object, list details that illustrate its physical qualities and the feeling it creates in people who view it. Then, see if other groups can guess your subject from the details you chose.

LITERARY ANALYSIS: IMAGISM

A style can be unique to an author, or it can reflect the shared artistic vision of a literary movement. **Imagism** was a style embraced by several influential English and American poets in the 1910s and 1920s. Rebelling against structured verse forms like the sonnet, imagists wanted poetry to be "swift, uncluttered, functional." Different poets interpreted the style in different ways, but most imagist poems include these characteristics:

- simple, unpretentious **language**
- flexible, natural **rhythms** instead of strict meter and rhyme
- concise, precise **descriptions**
- clear, vivid **images,** usually drawn from everyday life

While many poets use imagery, imagists wrote poems about single striking images or series of images. Every element of a poem—words, rhythm, structure—was carefully chosen to re-create the experience of seeing an image, whose meaning was never stated but only implied.

Imagism borrowed from several poetic traditions, including classical Greek lyric, Japanese haiku, and French symbolist poetry. **Free verse,** or unrhymed lines with irregular rhythms, was a hallmark of imagist style. As you read, note the elements of imagist style you find in each poem.

READING STRATEGY: VISUALIZE

When you **visualize,** you form mental pictures based on the details a writer supplies. Visualizing can help you understand the experience an imagist poem presents. Use the following strategies to visualize the scenes in these poems:

- Note **sensory details** in each poem, such as the "cold, wet leaves" in Amy Lowell's "The Pond."
- Think about the **mood** or idea each detail conveys. Are "cold, wet leaves" happy or sad?
- Sketch the mental images you "see" as you read each poem. What new details do you notice?

For each poem, use a chart to record descriptive phrases and words and the mental images that they evoke for you.

Title: "The Pond"	
Descriptive Words	Mental Pictures
"cold, wet leaves"	shivering; fallen leaves

Author Online

Amy Lowell: Imagist Leader Born into a well-known New England family, Amy Lowell was 28 when she decided to become a poet. She learned about imagism early in her career and became a tireless advocate for the new style. Her literary lectures and essays, as much as her creative work, helped transform American poetry.

**Amy Lowell
1874–1925**

Carl Sandburg: American Bard A poet, reporter, folk musician, and traveler, Carl Sandburg chronicled the lives and landscapes of everyday America. His simple verse forms captured the bracing reality of a world he observed firsthand. Sandburg's colorful career and his best-selling biographies of Abraham Lincoln made him an American icon.

**Carl Sandburg
1878–1967**

William Carlos Williams: Local Visionary William Carlos Williams wrote nearly 50 books of fiction, drama, poetry, and essays while working full-time as a doctor in Rutherford, New Jersey. Using informal language and experimental forms, Williams wrote poems about objects, scenes, and people from his own life.

**William Carlos Williams
1883–1963**

MORE ABOUT THE AUTHOR
For more on these poets, visit the **Literature Center** at ClassZone.com.

The Pond

Amy Lowell

Cold, wet leaves
Floating on moss-coloured water,
And the croaking of frogs—
Cracked bell-notes in the twilight. **Ⓐ**

Ⓐ IMAGISM
What elements of imagist style can you identify in this poem?

ANALYZE VISUALS
Compare this image with the one on page 811. Which elements, such as color, subject, and composition, help establish the **mood** of each image?

Fourth of July Night

Carl Sandburg

The little boat at anchor
in black water sat murmuring
to the tall black sky.

     A white sky bomb fizzed on a black line.
5   A rocket hissed its red signature into the west.
     Now a shower of Chinese fire alphabets,
     a cry of flower pots broken in flames,
     a long curve to a purple spray,
     three violet balloons—
10   Drips of seaweed tangled in gold,
         shimmering symbols of mixed numbers,
         tremulous arrangements of cream gold folds
         of a bride's wedding gown— **B**

A few sky bombs spoke their pieces,
15 then velvet dark.

The little boat at anchor
in black water sat murmuring
to the tall black sky.

B VISUALIZE
Reread the second stanza.
Which image is most
vivid, and why?

The Red Wheelbarrow

William Carlos Williams

so much depends
upon

a red wheel
barrow

5 glazed with rain
water

beside the white
chickens. **C**

C **VISUALIZE**
What visual contrast does
this poem present?

Comprehension

1. **Recall** What phrase does the speaker of "The Pond" use to describe the croaking of frogs?

2. **Clarify** What contrast does "Fourth of July Night" include?

3. **Recall** What sensory details does "The Red Wheelbarrow" provide about its subject?

OHIO STANDARDS

READING STANDARD
4.11 Explain ways author develops point of view and style

Literary Analysis

4. **Describe Mood** Amy Lowell's "The Pond" uses one simple image to communicate its message. Describe the mood of this poem. How does the image chosen help establish this mood?

5. **Interpret Form** In what way does the structure of "Fourth of July Night" mimic the action it describes?

6. **Make Inferences** Reread "The Red Wheelbarrow" without its opening stanza. How does the first stanza change your understanding of the poem?

7. **Visualize** Imagist poems present compact descriptions that leave many details implied or unstated. Choose an **image** from one of the charts you created earlier. Using the visualization strategy, write a more detailed description of the image.

8. **Evaluate Imagist Style** Use a chart to identify features of imagist style in each poem. Which of the poems is the best example of imagist style? Cite details to support your conclusion.

Title:

Imagist Element	Example
Simple language	
Free verse	
Concise descriptions	
Striking images	

Literary Criticism

9. **Historical Context** In the early decades of the 20th century, Europe and the United States experienced rapid technological and social change, as well as the outbreak of a devastating world war. How might these challenges to established traditions have fueled an experimental artistic movement like imagism?

Only Daughter
Personal Essay by Sandra Cisneros

from Caramelo
Fiction by Sandra Cisneros

What is your ROLE *in your household?*

KEY IDEA Think about the different **roles** that you play in your family and how you feel about them. Has your gender helped to determine these roles? In the following selections by Sandra Cisneros, you will learn what it means to be a daughter in a traditional Mexican-American family.

DISCUSS During the 1960s, many people began reexamining the role of women both at home and in society. Since then, ideas about the proper roles of males and females have changed dramatically. In a large group, share your thoughts about the roles of males and females today. Discuss gender roles at home, at school, in the workplace, and in the community.

● LITERARY ANALYSIS: CISNEROS'S STYLE AND VOICE

Sandra Cisneros is a contemporary writer who is known for her vibrant writing style. Her work is easily recognizable because of her distinctive voice. In literature, a **voice** is a writer's use of language in a way that allows readers to "hear" a personality in his or her writing. In "Only Daughter," Cisneros states:

At Christmas, I flew home to Chicago. The house was throbbing, same as always; hot tamales *and sweet* tamales *hissing in my mother's pressure cooker, and everybody—my mother, six brothers, wives, babies, aunts, cousins—talking too loud and at the same time. . . .*

Cisneros's use of conversational language, vivid images, and lyrical sentences gives readers a sense of her own lively spirit. As you read the two selections, think about the other stylistic elements that contribute to her voice.

● READING SKILL: IDENTIFY AUTHOR'S PURPOSE

You may recall that an **author's purpose** is the reason why he or she creates a particular work. Often, an author's purpose directly relates to the form, or genre, of a text. Cisneros is a versatile writer whose body of work comprises different forms, including poetry, nonfiction, and fiction. As you read each selection, jot down answers to the following questions:

- What is the form, or genre, of this work?
- Why do writers usually write this type of work?
- What is the subject?
- Which words or phrases suggest a specific purpose?

Later, you will use your answers to help you draw conclusions about Cisneros's purpose in each selection.

▲ VOCABULARY IN CONTEXT

The words in boldface help reveal what it's like to grow up in a traditional household. Restate each phrase, substituting a different word or words for each boldfaced word.

1. an **anthology** of short stories
2. fulfilling one's **destiny**
3. viewing events in **retrospect**
4. a **trauma** to the head
5. **nostalgia** for earlier days

Author On|ine

A Writer Under Wraps Born in Chicago in 1954, Sandra Cisneros (sĭs-nĕ′rôs) grew up with her Mexican father, Mexican-American mother, and six brothers. As a young girl, she had few friends because her family moved frequently between Chicago and Mexico City. To ward off loneliness, she often read stories and wrote poetry. As a teenager, she continued to write but was careful to keep her work away from family members, who disapproved of her writing.

Sandra Cisneros born 1954

A Proud Latina While in graduate school, Cisneros began to embrace her own cultural heritage and experiences. She learned that the people and events that had shaped her life were different from those that had influenced the lives of her classmates. This discovery helped her find her own literary voice—one that reflected her unique Mexican-American background. In 1984, Cisneros published *The House on Mango Street*—a series of prose vignettes told by a girl living in a Chicago neighborhood. Since then, she has continued to tell stories drawn from her personal history.

 MORE ABOUT THE AUTHOR
For more on Sandra Cisneros, visit the **Literature Center** at ClassZone.com.

Background

Traditional Roles In "Only Daughter," Cisneros describes her father's ideas about the proper role of females. Coming from the culture of old Mexico, Cisneros's father held the patriarchal beliefs of many traditional cultures—that is, he considered men the heads of families and the leaders of society. According to his values, a woman needed only to "become someone's wife" and devote herself to her home and family.

ONLY DAUGHTER

Sandra Cisneros

Once, several years ago, when I was just starting out my writing career, I was asked to write my own contributor's note for an **anthology** I was part of. I wrote: "I am the only daughter in a family of six sons. *That* explains everything."

Well, I've thought about that ever since, and yes, it explains a lot to me, but for the reader's sake I should have written: "I am the only daughter in a *Mexican* family of six sons." Or even: "I am the only daughter of a Mexican father and a Mexican-American mother." Or: "I am the only daughter of a working-class family of nine." All of these had everything to do with who I am today.

I was/am the only daughter and *only* a daughter. Being an only daughter in a family of six sons forced me by circumstance to spend a lot of time by myself because my brothers felt it beneath them to play with a *girl* in public. But that aloneness, that loneliness, was good for a would-be writer—it allowed me time to think and think, to imagine, to read and prepare myself. **Ⓐ**

Being only a daughter for my father meant my **destiny** would lead me to become someone's wife. That's what he believed. But when I was in the fifth grade and shared my plans for college with him, I was sure he understood. I remember my father saying, "*Que bueno, mi'ja,*[1] that's good." That meant a lot to me, especially since my brothers thought the idea hilarious. What I didn't realize was that my father thought college was good for girls—good for finding a husband. After four years in college and two more in graduate school and still no husband, my father shakes his head even now and says I wasted all that education.

In **retrospect,** I'm lucky my father believed daughters were meant for husbands. It meant it didn't matter if I majored in something silly like English. After all, I'd find a nice professional eventually, right? This allowed me the liberty to putter about embroidering my little poems and stories without my father interrupting with so much as a "What's that you're writing?"

anthology (ăn-thŏl′ə-jē) *n.* a collection of written works—such as poems, short stories, or plays— in a single book or set

Ⓐ AUTHOR'S PURPOSE Reread lines 11–15. What specific experience is the **subject** of this personal essay? Identify the details that helped you draw your conclusion.

destiny (dĕs′tə-nē) *n.* the determined fate of a particular person or thing; lot in life

retrospect (rĕt′rə-spĕkt′) *n.* a view or contemplation of something past

---

1. **Que bueno, mi'ja** (kĕ bwĕ′nô mē′hä) *Spanish:* That's good, my daughter. (*Mi'ja* is a shortened form of *mi hija.*)

Sandra Cisneros (2000), Raquel Valle Sentíes. Oil, 20″ × 20″.

30   But the truth is, I wanted him to interrupt. I wanted my father to understand what it was I was scribbling, to introduce me as "My only daughter, the writer." Not as "This is only my daughter. She teaches." *Es maestra*[2]—teacher. Not even *profesora*.[3]

In a sense, everything I have ever written has been for him, to win his approval even though I know my father can't read English words, even though my father's only reading includes the brown-ink *Esto* sports magazines from Mexico City and the bloody *¡Alarma!* magazines that feature yet another sighting of *La Virgen de Guadalupe*[4] on a tortilla or a wife's revenge on her philandering[5] husband by bashing his skull in with a *molcajete*[6] (a kitchen
40 mortar[7] made of volcanic rock). Or the *fotonovelas*,[8] the little picture paperbacks with tragedy and **trauma** erupting from the characters' mouths in bubbles. **B**

My father represents, then, the public majority. A public who is disinterested in reading, and yet one whom I am writing about and for and privately trying to woo.

When we were growing up in Chicago, we moved a lot because of my father. He suffered bouts of **nostalgia.** Then we'd have to let go our flat, store the furniture with mother's relatives, load the station wagon with baggage and bologna sandwiches, and head south. To Mexico City.

50   We came back, of course. To yet another Chicago flat, another Chicago neighborhood, another Catholic school. Each time, my father would seek out the parish priest in order to get a tuition break and complain or boast: "I have seven sons."

He meant *siete hijos*,[9] seven children, but he translated it as "sons." "I have seven sons." To anyone who would listen. The Sears Roebuck employee who sold us the washing machine. The short-order cook where my father ate his ham-and-eggs breakfasts. "I have seven sons." As if he deserved a medal from the state.

My papa. He didn't mean anything by that mistranslation, I'm sure. But
60 somehow I could feel myself being erased. I'd tug my father's sleeve and whisper: "Not seven sons. Six! and *one daughter*." **C**

When my oldest brother graduated from medical school, he fulfilled my father's dream that we study hard and use this—our heads, instead of this—our hands. Even now my father's hands are thick and yellow, stubbed by a history of hammer and nails and twine and coils and springs. "Use this,"

trauma (trô′mə) *n.* severe physical or emotional distress

B **STYLE AND VOICE**
Reread lines 34–42. Describe Cisneros's **tone**, or attitude, toward her father and his reading habits. Which details strongly convey her feelings?

nostalgia (nŏ-stăl′jə) *n.* a wistful longing for the past or the familiar

C **AUTHOR'S PURPOSE**
In personal essays, writers often express opinions on subjects. Which details in lines 46–61 suggest Cisneros's opinions?

---

2. *Es maestra* (ĕs mä-ĕs′trä) *Spanish:* She is a teacher.

3. *profesora* (prô-fĕ-sô′rä) *Spanish:* professor.

4. *La Virgen de Guadalupe* (lä vēr′hĕn dĕ gwä-dä-lōō′pĕ) *Spanish:* the Virgin of Guadalupe—a vision of Mary, the virgin mother of Jesus, said to have appeared on a hill outside Mexico City in 1531.

5. *philandering:* engaging in many casual love affairs.

6. *molcajete* (môl-kä-hĕ′tĕ) *Spanish.*

7. *mortar:* bowl for grinding grain.

8. *fotonovelas* (fô-tô-nô-vĕ′läs) *Spanish.*

9. *siete hijos* (syĕ′tĕ ē′hôs) *Spanish. (Hijos* can mean either "children" or "sons.")

my father said, tapping his head, "and not this," showing us those hands. He always looked tired when he said it.

Wasn't college an investment? And hadn't I spent all those years in college? And if I didn't marry, what was it all for? Why would anyone go to college
70 and then choose to be poor? Especially someone who had always been poor.

Last year, after ten years of writing professionally, the financial rewards started to trickle in. My second National Endowment for the Arts Fellowship.[10] A guest professorship at the University of California, Berkeley. My book, which sold to a major New York publishing house.

At Christmas, I flew home to Chicago. The house was throbbing, same as always; hot *tamales*[11] and sweet *tamales* hissing in my mother's pressure cooker, and everybody—my mother, six brothers, wives, babies, aunts, cousins— talking too loud and at the same time, like in a Fellini[12] film, because that's just how we are.

80 I went upstairs to my father's room. One of my stories had just been translated into Spanish and published in an anthology of Chicano[13] writing, and I wanted to show it to him. Ever since he recovered from a stroke two years ago, my father likes to spend his leisure hours horizontally. And that's how I found him, watching a Pedro Infante[14] movie on Galavisión[15] and eating rice pudding.

There was a glass filmed with milk on the bedside table. There were several vials of pills and balled Kleenex. And on the floor, one black sock and a plastic urinal that I didn't want to look at but looked at anyway. Pedro Infante was about to burst into song, and my father was laughing. **D**

90 I'm not sure if it was because my story was translated into Spanish or because it was published in Mexico or perhaps because the story dealt with Tepeyac,[16] the *colonia* my father was raised in and the house he grew up in, but at any rate, my father punched the mute button on his remote control and read my story.

I sat on the bed next to my father and waited. He read it very slowly. As if he were reading each line over and over. He laughed at all the right places and read lines he liked out loud. He pointed and asked questions: "Is this So-and-so?"

"Yes," I said. He kept reading.

When he was finally finished, after what seemed like hours, my father
100 looked up and asked: "Where can we get more copies of this for the relatives?"

Of all the wonderful things that happened to me last year, that was the most wonderful. ♋

D STYLE AND VOICE
Reread lines 86–89, noting Cisneros's use of vivid **sensory images**. What do you learn about Cisneros's **voice**, or personality, through these details?

---

10. **National Endowment for the Arts Fellowship:** The National Endowment for the Arts (NEA)—a U.S. government agency—awards money in the form of fellowships to artists and writers.

11. *tamales* (tä-mä'lĕs) *Spanish:* rolls of cornmeal dough filled with meat and peppers and steamed in cornhusk wrappings.

12. **Fellini:** the Italian movie director Federico Fellini (1920–1993), famous for his noisy, energetic films.

13. **Chicano:** Mexican-American.

14. **Pedro Infante** (pā'drō ĭn-fän'tā): a popular Mexican film star.

15. **Galavisión:** cable TV network that features movies and programs in Spanish.

16. **Tepeyac** (tĕ-pĕ-yäk'): a district of Mexico City.

CARAMELO

Sandra Cisneros

Acuérdate de Acapulco,
de aquellas noches,
María bonita, María del alma;
acuérdate que en la playa,
con tus manitas las estrellitas
las enjuagabas.[1]
—*"María bonita," by Augustín Lara, version sung by the composer while
playing the piano, accompanied by a sweet, but very, very sweet violin*

We're all little in the photograph above Father's bed. We were little in
Acapulco. We will always be little. For him we are just as we were then.

Here are the Acapulco waters lapping just behind us, and here we are sitting
on the lip of land and water. The little kids, Lolo and Memo, making devil
horns behind each other's head; the Awful Grandmother holding them even
though she never held them in real life. Mother seated as far from her as
politely possible; Toto slouched beside her. The big boys, Rafa, Ito, and Tikis,
stand under the roof of Father's skinny arms. Aunty Light-Skin hugging
Antonieta Araceli to her belly. Aunty shutting her eyes when the shutter
10 clicks, as if she chooses not to remember the future, the house on Destiny
Street sold, the move north to Monterrey. **E**

Here is Father squinting that same squint I always make when I'm photographed. He isn't *acabado*[2] yet. He isn't *finished*, worn from working, from
worrying, from smoking too many packs of cigarettes. There isn't anything on
his face but his face, and a tidy, thin mustache, like Pedro Infante, like Clark
Gable.[3] Father's skin pulpy and soft, pale as the belly side of a shark.

The Awful Grandmother has the same light skin as Father, but in elephant
folds, stuffed into a bathing suit the color of an old umbrella with an amber
handle.

20 I'm not here. They've forgotten about me when the photographer walking
along the beach proposes a portrait, *un recuerdo,* a remembrance literally. No
one notices I'm off playing by myself building sand houses. They won't realize
I'm missing until the photographer delivers the portrait to Catita's house, and
I look at it for the first time and ask,—When was this taken? Where?

Then everyone realizes the portrait is incomplete. It's as if I didn't exist. It's
as if I'm the photographer walking along the beach with the tripod camera on
my shoulder asking.—*¿Un recuerdo?* A souvenir? A memory? **F**

E AUTHOR'S PURPOSE
Reread lines 3–11.
Consider your own
reaction to phrases
such as "making devil
horns" and "the Awful
Grandmother." What
purpose do they suggest?

F STYLE AND VOICE
Cisneros's style is often
characterized by loosely
structured sentences, such
as those in lines 20–27.
What aspect of Cisneros's
voice comes through in
this type of writing?

---

1. **Acuérdate de Acapulco . . . las enjuagabas** *Spanish:* Remember Acapulco, those nights, beautiful Maria,
   Maria of my soul; remember that in the sand, you washed the stars with your hands.
2. *acabado* (ä-kä-bä′dô) *Spanish:* finished.
3. **Clark Gable:** an American film star of the 1940s.

Comprehension

1. **Recall** According to "Only Daughter," what expectations did Cisneros's father have for her?

2. **Recall** In what way did Cisneros go against her father's expectations?

3. **Summarize** Describe the different family members included in the souvenir photograph in the excerpt from *Caramelo*. Who is missing from the picture?

4. **Clarify** Reread lines 25–27 of the excerpt. Why does the narrator compare herself to the photographer?

OHIO STANDARDS

READING STANDARD
4.11 Explain ways author develops point of view and style

Literary Analysis

5. **Identify Theme** In "Only Daughter," what theme about female **roles** does Cisneros communicate through her relationship with her father? Support your answer with evidence from the essay.

6. **Examine Cisneros's Style and Voice** Cisneros's writing style is often marked by a use of conversational language and fragmented sentences. How might your sense of Cisneros and her experiences be different if "Only Daughter" had been written with more formal words and sentence structures?

7. **Interpret Symbol** A person, a place, an activity, or an object that represents something beyond itself is called a symbol. In the excerpt from *Caramelo*, what does the souvenir photograph seem to symbolize to the narrator?

8. **Relate Imagery and Tone** Reread lines 12–19 of the excerpt, reviewing Cisneros's use of vivid sensory images. Considering words such as "squinting," "elephant folds," and "the color of an old umbrella," describe the narrator's tone, or attitude, toward her father and her grandmother.

9. **Compare Author's Purposes** Review your answers to the questions on page 815. Identify Cisneros's purpose for writing each selection. What similarities or differences in purpose do you see between "Only Daughter" and the excerpt from *Caramelo?* Explain your response.

Literary Criticism

10. **Social Context** "Only Daughter" was first published in *Glamour,* a monthly magazine that is read almost exclusively by women, many of whom are young and single. Does this information affect your understanding of Cisneros's purpose for writing the personal essay? Explain your response.

Vocabulary in Context

VOCABULARY PRACTICE

Select the vocabulary word that best completes each sentence.

1. Josh believed that his _____ would lead him to become a famous actor.
2. Someone with _____ often relives happy memories of earlier times.
3. Shirley is often seen carrying a(n) _____ of the works of Langston Hughes, her favorite author.
4. In _____, I wish I had done things differently.
5. The _____ of the accident would never completely leave Kyra.

VOCABULARY IN WRITING

Using two or more vocabulary words, write about something positive or negative you remember from your own childhood. Here is how you might begin.

> **EXAMPLE SENTENCE**
>
> It is easy to feel **nostalgia** for a childhood that was happy and carefree.

VOCABULARY STRATEGY: ETYMOLOGY

Etymology is the history of words, and knowing this history can often help you remember a word's meaning. For example, the word *nostalgia* derives from two Greek words: *nostos,* which means "homecoming," and *algos,* meaning "pain, grief, or distress." In modern English, this translates to "a sad or wistful yearning for the past."

> **nos•tal•gi•a** (nŏ-stăl'jə) *n.* **1.** a bittersweet longing. **2.** a sad or wistful yearning for the past. [Greek *nostos,* homecoming + Greek *algos,* pain, grief, or distress.]

PRACTICE Use the dictionary or an online reference to research the etymology of each word below. Study each word's derivation, meaning, and spelling.

1. anthology
2. retrospect
3. trauma

OHIO STANDARDS

VOCABULARY STANDARD
1.6 Determine the meaning of words using dictionaries

VOCABULARY PRACTICE
For more practice, go to the **Vocabulary Center** at **ClassZone.com.**

Author Brings Back Memories of Not So Long Ago

Newspaper Column

Use with "Only Daughter" and excerpt from *Caramelo*, pages 816 and 820.

OHIO STANDARDS

READING/RESEARCH STANDARDS
3.2 Critique the treatment, scope and organization of ideas

8.4 Select appropriate sources to support central ideas, concepts and themes

What's the Connection?

In the previous selections by Sandra Cisneros, you discovered how the author and one of her fictional characters feel about living in a Mexican-American family. In the newspaper column you are about to read, you will learn what one Latino writer thinks about Cisneros's 1984 novel *The House on Mango Street*.

Skill Focus: Identify the Characteristics of a Column

A **column** is a feature article that appears regularly in a newspaper or magazine. It is written by the same writer, or columnist, every time. While columns vary in subject matter and purpose, each is characterized by its particular area of focus, author's perspective, and voice. In fact, it is the columnist's specific focus, views, and voice that make his or her column popular—or not.

As you read Yvette Cabrera's article, think about how you would describe various aspects of her column. Record your descriptions in a chart like the one shown.

Elements of Any Column	In Cabrera's Column
Area of focus	
Author's perspective, or unique views, beliefs, and experiences	
Primary purpose	
Intended audience	
Tone	
Voice	

Author Brings Back Memories of Not So Long Ago

by Yvette Cabrera

Forget the boxes and the cobwebs; I was determined to find the book. I looked at my watch and out the window at the gray, misty morning outside my garage. It was already late.

I dived in frantically. It has to be here somewhere, but where in this mass of boxes and old furniture?

Five minutes later, still no luck. From
10 behind an old bookcase my boyfriend heard me half scream/half wail in frustration, as I pulled out box after box searching through my old college books.

Finally, the last box of books. My last hope. Please, I prayed, let this be my lucky day. In the last box, there it was: *The House on Mango Street* by Sandra Cisneros.

Slightly yellowed, with that com-
20 forting, worn appeal of your favorite pajamas, the book was just as I had left it.

A $9 soft-cover (the best a "working-three-jobs-a-week" college student could afford), its pages were dog-eared, my favorite paragraphs highlighted in fluorescent purples and pinks, and my notes scribbled on the borders.

With little time to spare, I sped off to work. Today, I was going to meet the
30 author of one of my favorite books.

Growing up, I studied books my high school English teachers said were written by the literary "greats"—must reads for a well-rounded education. Books like J.D. Salinger's *Catcher in the Rye,* Fyodor

Author Sandra Cisneros

Dostoyevsky's *Crime and Punishment* and Thomas Hardy's *Tess of the d'Urbervilles.*

It was literature with profound meaning that imparted important lessons. But
40 still, I felt a disconnection. *Beowulf* was an epic poem, but as my high school teacher went into great detail explaining what a mail[1] shirt was, I wondered what that had to do with my life.

It was that way all through high school, until the day in college when I was assigned to read *The House on Mango Street.* **A**

Mango. The word alone evoked
50 memories of my childhood—weekends when my family and I would pile into our sky-blue Chevrolet Malibu and head to Olvera Street's plaza in downtown Los Angeles.

At the time, the plaza was home to the Mexican consulate where my parents, Mexican immigrants, would deal with passport and residency paperwork.

The treat, for my sisters and I, for
60 behaving ourselves during the long

---

1. **mail:** flexible armor made of metal rings.

A CHARACTERISTICS
OF A COLUMN
On the basis of lines 16–48, what seems to be the **subject** of the column?

waits at the consulate, was a juicy mango on a stick sold at a fruit stand near the plaza's kiosk. Peeled and impaled on a stick for easy grip, we would squeeze lemon and sprinkle chile and salt over the bright yellow slices. **B**

Later, as an adult, whenever I had a reporting assignment near Olvera Street, I'd always take a minute to stop. There, amid the smell of sizzling carne asada[2] in a nearby restaurant, the sounds of vendors negotiating prices in Spanish, and children licking a rainbow of raspados (shaved ice treats), I would bite into my mango and feel at home.

That's what *The House on Mango Street* did for me. A coming-of-age, Chicana-feminist novel, the protagonist Esperanza, like Cisneros, grows up in a mainly Latino neighborhood in Chicago.

From the first page, when Esperanza explains how at school they say her name funny "as if the syllables were made out of tin and hurt the roof of your mouth," I was hooked. . . .

That was a dozen years ago. Today, Latinos are the majority in cities like Santa Ana, California, where Cisneros spoke last week at Valley High School to more than 1,000 students, as part of the Pathway Project, a collaborative effort among the University of California, Irvine, Santa Ana College and the city's school district.

Today, these students can pick from bookstore shelves filled with authors such as Julia Alvarez, Victor Villaseñor and Judith Ortiz Cofer—authors who go beyond census numbers to explain what U.S. Latino life is about. **C**

It's about, as Cisneros explained to the students as she read from her novel *Caramelo,* a journey between two worlds.

It's about relishing truck-stop doughnut shops and bologna sandwiches on this side of the border, just as much as the strawberries in cream, the gelatins, and fruity *tejocote* bathed in caramel sauce on the other side of the border.

It was an hour of humorous storytelling that had the students busting with laughter and then crowding in line afterward, giddily waiting to get her autograph. . . .

Later, as I talk to Cisneros, she explains how much the literary world has changed since she finished writing *The House on Mango Street* 20 years ago. Back then, forget trying to get *The New York Times* to review your book if you were Latino or getting a major bookseller to carry it, she says.

"I never questioned the Jim Crow[3] aspect of how our books were never reviewed—I was young," says Cisneros, 47, of San Antonio.

One thing has remained constant, something that Cisneros can see by the question that's most asked by students.

"They want to know, 'Is this real? Did this happen to you,'" Cisneros says. "They're so concerned and want to make sure this is my story, because it's their story, too."

As Cisneros autographed my book, I felt that same excitement I felt 12 years ago when I first discovered *The House on Mango Street.*

"Para la Yvette,[4] Sandra Cisneros," it read. I chuckled. Mexicans just love to give nicknames, but sans[5] a nickname you attach a simple "la" in front of the name and suddenly you're extra special. Not just "Sandra," but "la Sandra" (that Sandra).

Even her autographs are authentic! **D**

B CHARACTERISTICS OF A COLUMN
Describe the kinds of words Cabrera uses in lines 49–66. What do they reveal about her **voice,** or personality?

C CHARACTERISTICS OF A COLUMN
Reread lines 86–100. What **audience** does Cabrera seem particularly interested in reaching?

D CHARACTERISTICS OF A COLUMN
Reread lines 135–145. Which details reveal Cabrera's **tone,** or attitude, toward Sandra Cisneros and her writing?

---

2. **carne asada** (kär′nĕ ä-sä′dä): grilled marinated steak.
3. **Jim Crow:** upholding or practicing discrimination against a minority population.
4. **para la Yvette** *Spanish:* for that Yvette.
5. **sans** (sănz): without.

Comprehension

1. **Recall** What childhood memory does the word *mango* evoke for Cabrera?

2. **Clarify** What question do students typically ask Cisneros, and why?

Literary Analysis

3. **Identify Author's Purpose** Scan the first page of Cabrera's column, including its title. What, in your opinion, is the main purpose of the column? Explain your response.

4. **Analyze Column** Review the chart you developed as you read the article. What do you think makes Cabrera's column distinctive? Support your answer with evidence from the text.

5. **Compare Authors** What does Yvette Cabrera have in common with Sandra Cisneros? How were their childhoods different?

Read for Information: Cite Evidence from Multiple Sources

OHIO STANDARDS

READING/RESEARCH STANDARDS
3.2 Critique the treatment, scope and organization of ideas

8.4 Select appropriate sources to support central ideas, concepts and themes

WRITING PROMPT

Many writing instructors believe that students should "write what they know." Find evidence in the nonfiction works of Sandra Cisneros and Yvette Cabrera that shows they have followed this advice.

The following steps will help you respond to the prompt:

1. Reread Cisneros's "Only Daughter" and Cabrera's column, looking for direct statements, facts, and anecdotes about living as a Mexican American.

2. Record direct quotations and summarize longer passages that seem relevant to your response. For each, note the author, source, and page number.

3. Review your notes and evaluate each item's usefulness in writing your response.

4. As you compose your response, support your statements with direct quotations and citations of facts or anecdotes in the two sources. Make sure to use quotation marks around any direct quotations.

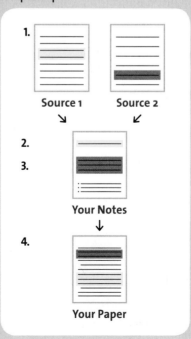

Writing Workshop

Critical Review

Every reader is a critic. In this workshop, you'll write a critical review of a work of fiction, nonfiction, or poetry. In your review, you'll express your opinion about whether the author succeeded in fulfilling your expectations.

WRITER'S ROAD MAP

Critical Review

WRITING PROMPT 1

Writing from Literature Write a critical review of a literary work. Consider how the author's use of style elements (such as word choice, figurative language, imagery, mood, or theme) affected your appreciation of the work. Your review should state your opinion of the work, explain the criteria you used to judge it, and tell whether you would recommend it to others.

Literary Works and Style Elements to Consider
• theme and word choice in "A Chip of Glass Ruby"
• imagery and tone in "Birches"

WRITING PROMPT 2

Writing for the Real World Write a critical review of a story you have viewed or read. Your review should state your opinion of the work, explain the criteria you used to judge it, and tell whether you would recommend it to others.

Types of Stories to Consider
• a movie or documentary that gave you a better understanding of a particular issue
• a play or television program that changed the way you see the world

 WRITING TOOLS
For prewriting, revision, and editing tools, visit the **Writing Center** at ClassZone.com.

KEY TRAITS

1. IDEAS

• Presents an **opinion statement** that includes an explanation of the criteria the writer used in judging the work

• Uses quotations, paraphrases, or other **evidence** from the work to support the opinion statement

• Provides **background information** to help the reader understand the review

2. ORGANIZATION

• Identifies the work being analyzed in a thoughtful **introduction**

• Is clearly **organized**

• Uses **transitions** to connect ideas

• Summarizes the writer's opinion in a persuasive **conclusion**

3. VOICE

• Considers the potential **audience** for the review

• Maintains a **tone** that matches the writer's purpose

4. WORD CHOICE

• Uses accurate **literary, film, or drama terms** to discuss the work

5. SENTENCE FLUENCY

• Varies **sentence lengths** to keep the review from becoming choppy or long-winded

6. CONVENTIONS

• Employs **correct grammar and usage**

Part 1: Analyze a Student Model

WRITING STANDARD
6.2 Write responses to literature

Julie Nagib
Pomona High School

Increasing Terror

With so many horror-themed movies, novels, and video games available these days, it's reasonable to ask whether a short story from the mid-1800s is scary enough for a modern audience. To be successful, a work of horror must include enough suspense to ratchet up the reader's
5 anxiety level. In "The Pit and the Pendulum," Edgar Allan Poe succeeds at creating an extremely high level of suspense by using vivid sensory details, dramatic repetition, and a sympathetic point of view.

The story takes place in Spain during the Spanish Inquisition. The Inquisition was a series of trials in which people whose beliefs differed
10 from those of the Roman Catholic Church were imprisoned, tortured, and even burned at the stake. As the story opens, the Inquisition's judges are sentencing the narrator to death. He faints and then wakes up in a dungeon. As the plot unfolds, the reader feels the narrator's dread and horror as he slowly discovers the diabolical terrors his captors have
15 planned for him.

Poe uses sensory details to help the reader share the narrator's fears. When the narrator first opens his eyes, panic grips him: "The blackness of eternal night encompassed me. I struggled for breath. The intensity of the darkness seemed to oppress and stifle me." When he almost falls into
20 the pit, the narrator uses his sense of smell to perceive what he cannot see: ". . . the peculiar smell of decayed fungus arose to my nostrils." Later, as he lies strapped to the table, the blade of the pendulum "swept so closely over me as to fan me with its acrid breath." Because Poe describes so precisely what the narrator was able to see, smell, and feel, the reader can't
25 help but imagine what it would be like to suffer such dread and panic.

KEY TRAITS IN ACTION

Introduction identifies the work being reviewed, states the writer's **opinion** of it, and explains the criteria the writer used to judge it.

Background information about the work helps the reader understand the review. **Tone** is consistent and appropriate for the intended **audience** (teacher and classmates).

The reviewer supports her opinion with **evidence**—quotations from the story.

Poe also uses repetition to show the narrator's terror. Three consecutive paragraphs begin with the word *down* followed by adverbs to mark the progress of the descending blade. "Down—steadily down it crept. . . . Down—certainly, relentlessly down! . . . Down—still unceasingly—still inevitably down!" And as the hot steel walls of the dungeon move ever closer to him, forcing the narrator to choose between being burned and crushed or being pushed into the pit, he curses his tormentors: ". . . oh! most unrelenting! oh! most demoniac of men! . . . Oh! for a voice to speak!—oh! horror!—oh! any horror but this!" Although some readers might find this passage melodramatic, it perfectly illustrates the anxiety and horror that the narrator feels.

The most effective suspense-building technique that Poe uses is his choice of a first-person narrator. This helps the reader experience what the narrator is experiencing. As the narrator discovers each new horror of the dungeon, so does the reader. When the narrator is confused or panicky or nearly driven insane by his ordeal, the reader shares his emotions. At the end of the story, when the suspense has grown nearly unbearable, the reader experiences sudden relief along with the narrator.

Few writers share Poe's talent for creating and sustaining suspense. "The Pit and the Pendulum" sweeps the reader along, paragraph by paragraph, horror by horror, on a wave of tension and terror. It's a ride that modern readers shouldn't miss.

Varies **sentence lengths** to avoid the monotony of sentences that are all either very long or very short.

Uses accurate **literary terms** throughout the review.

Transitions help the reader understand how the review is **organized.**

Conclusion summarizes the reviewer's opinion and offers a recommendation to the reader.

2

WRITING STANDARD
5.2 Apply prewriting strategies

Part 2: Apply the Writing Process

PREWRITING

What Should I Do?	**What Does It Look Like?**

1. Revisit the work you are reviewing.
Reread or rewatch the work. Freewrite about your overall impression of the work and about details that caught your attention. Circle any words or phrases that could become the focus for your critical review.

TIP Choose a work that stirs your emotions—either positively or negatively.

▶ Suspense is almost unbearable. I feel like I'm being tortured along with the narrator! Lots of stuff about what the guy can see, smell, feel. The Inquisition was a terrible time in history.

2. Focus on a few key elements.
Take another look at your freewriting. Which elements of the work most influenced your overall impression? Questions like the ones shown here can help you.

▶ **People**
• Do the people seem real?
• Which ones do I care about?

Places
• How does the setting affect the work?

Dialogue
• Does it sound as if real people said it?
• What does the dialogue tell me about the people and places in the work?

3. Develop an opinion statement.
An opinion statement summarizes your judgment of the work you are reviewing. It also lists the **criteria,** or standards, you used to reach that judgment.

▶ "The Pit and the Pendulum" is exciting to read even though it's really old. The writer, Edgar Allan Poe, made the story suspenseful by describing sights and smells, repeating certain words, and making the narrator a very sympathetic character.

4. Find evidence that supports your opinion.
In your prewriting notes, list the criteria you used in forming your opinion. Then find examples and details in the work that support your point.

▶ **Sensory details:** "The blackness of eternal night encompassed me."

Narrator: First-person narrator; I feel what the narrator experiences.

What Should I Do?	What Does It Look Like?

1. Outline your review.
Creating an informal outline will help you focus your thoughts and organize the information you want to present.

TIP Consider putting your most convincing point last to give your review a strong ending.

▶

1. **Introduction**
   • opinion: great suspense
   • criteria: sensory details, repetition, point of view
2. **Background information**
   • explanation of Inquisition
   • brief recap of story beginning
3. **Sensory details**
   • three quotations: see, smell, feel
4. **Repetition**
   • two quotations: "down" and "oh!"
5. **Most effective technique: first-person narration**
   • reader shares the narrator's experiences
6. **Conclusion**
   • summary and recommendation

---

2. Make your introduction appealing.
This writer began her review with her audience in mind. She wanted to convince her classmates that a story from the 1800s is still worth reading.

▶

With so many horror-themed movies, novels, and video games available these days, it's reasonable to ask whether a short story from the mid-1800s is scary enough for a modern audience.

---

3. Use accurate terminology.
If you're reviewing a work of fiction, use literary terms. If you're reviewing a production of a play, discuss sets, costumes, lighting, and so on.

See page 834: Literary Terms

▶

Edgar Allan Poe succeeds at creating an extremely high level of suspense by using vivid sensory details, dramatic repetition, and a sympathetic point of view. . . . The most effective suspense-building technique that Poe uses is his choice of a first-person narrator.

---

4. Conclude your review with a recommendation.
Summarize your review and offer the reader your opinion on whether the work is worth seeking out.

▶

"The Pit and the Pendulum" sweeps the reader along, paragraph by paragraph, horror by horror, on a wave of tension and terror. ⎤ Summary

It's a ride that modern readers shouldn't miss. ⎤ Opinion

REVISING AND EDITING

What Should I Do?	**What Does It Look Like?**

1. Make sure your tone is appropriate.

- <u>Underline</u> places where your tone is too casual or jargon-filled for your audience.

- Rewrite the passages you've underlined so that the tone is appropriate and consistent.

▶ When the narrator first opens his eyes, he ~~freaks out completely~~; panic grips him.

        Few writers share Poe's talent for
~~Poe is way better~~ than ~~most other writers at~~ creating and sustaining suspense.

2. Vary the length of your sentences.

- Too many long sentences can confuse a reader, while too many short sentences can make your review sound choppy and immature. **[Bracket]** your longest sentence and two or three short sentences in a row, if you have them.

- Try to break up long sentences and combine short sentences.

▶ [Poe also uses repetition to show the narrator's terror, as when three consecutive paragraphs begin with the word "down" followed by adverbs to mark the progress of the descending blade.]

3. Think about how much background information you are providing.

- Background information helps readers understand your review. However, if you include too much, you risk crowding out your own thoughts about the work.

- On the basis of a peer reader's comments, shorten your summary or add details to it.

See page 834: Ask a Peer Reader

▶ As the story opens, the Inquisition's judges are sentencing the narrator to death. ~~He is so sick and scared that he has trouble seeing the judges, who are wearing black robes, and the seven white candles on the table. Anyway,~~ he faints and then wakes up in a dungeon.

4. State your opinions clearly.

- (Circle) vague, overused opinion words, such as *great, nice, interesting, boring, stupid,* or *terrible.*

- Replace them with specific words, such as *fast-paced, imaginative, surprising, outdated, melodramatic,* or *predictable.*

▶ ~~Some readers might think this part is too much, but I think it's great.~~
Although some readers might find this passage melodramatic, it perfectly illustrates the anxiety and horror that the narrator feels.

Preparing to Publish

Critical Review

Apply the Rubric

A strong critical review . . .

☑ has an engaging introduction that identifies the work being reviewed

☑ states the reviewer's overall opinion of the work and makes clear the criteria used to judge it

☑ supports opinions with accurate details and well-chosen examples

☑ uses literary, film, or drama terms appropriately

☑ is logically and effectively organized

☑ varies sentence lengths

☑ maintains a tone that matches the intended audience and purpose

☑ concludes with a brief summary of the reviewer's opinion and a recommendation to the reader

Ask a Peer Reader

• How would you summarize my overall impression of this work?

• What places need more background information?

• Which supporting detail is the strongest or most convincing?

Literary Terms

Narrator: the character or voice that tells a story

Mood: the feeling, or atmosphere, that a writer creates for the reader

Setting: the time and place of the actions of a story

Suspense: excitement or tension readers feel as they wait to find out how a story ends or how a conflict is resolved

Check Your Grammar

• **Titles:** Capitalize the first and last words and all other words except articles and prepositions of less than five letters.

> "The Pit and the Pendulum"

See page R51: Quick Reference: Capitalization

• **Quotations:** Use ellipses (. . .) to show where you have left out words. If you are leaving out the end of a sentence, put a period, an exclamation point, or a question mark before the ellipses.

> "Down—steadily down it crept. . . . Down—certainly, relentlessly down! . . . Down—still unceasingly—still inevitably down!"

See page R50: Quick Reference: Punctuation

Writing Online

PUBLISHING OPTIONS
For publishing options, visit the **Writing Center** at **ClassZone.com.**

ASSESSMENT PREPARATION
For writing and grammar assessment practice, go to the **Assessment Center** at **ClassZone.com.**

RESEARCH STANDARD
8.7 Use a variety of communication techniques

Creating an Online Database

You and your classmates can build a Web site to house not only the critical reviews you wrote for this workshop but also reviews of books, movies, television shows, video games, or restaurants that interest you.

Planning the Database

1. **Make a flow chart that illustrates the organization of the site.** Will you organize the content by the types of reviews, by the names of the reviewers, or alphabetically by the titles of the materials being reviewed? (Remember that if you want to post reviews that you did not write yourself, you will need the writers' permission.)

2. **Sketch a design for the site's home page.** Your sketch should show the placement of the site's title, any visuals you want to include, and the placement and design of navigation buttons.

3. **Select appropriate visuals to accompany reviews.** Drawings, maps, photographs, and charts can add both interest and information to the reviews.

   TIP Some visuals may be copyrighted. Always include a source line that tells where the visual came from. In some cases, you may need to get permission from the work's creator to use a visual.

Producing the Database

1. **Build your site.** Ask your school's computer specialist which authoring program to use. An authoring program lets you import word-processed text and other media elements into a Web site document.

2. **Test and revise.** Test the completed site thoroughly to make sure it's easy to read and simple to navigate. Proofread the content and fix any faulty links.

3. **Upload your site.** Ask your school's computer administrator for assistance in making your site available on the World Wide Web.

Mr. Swenson's Class

REVIEWS
@
RATINGS

ENTER ▶

Reading Comprehension

DIRECTIONS *Read these selections and answer the questions that follow.*

from The House of the Seven Gables
Nathaniel Hawthorne

On entering the shop, she found an old man there, a humble resident of Pyncheon-street, and whom, for a great many years past, she had suffered to be a kind of familiar of the house. He was an immemorial personage, who seemed always to have had a white head and wrinkles, and never to have possessed but a single tooth, and that a half-decayed one, in the front of the upper jaw. Well advanced as Hepzibah was, she could not remember when Uncle Venner, as the neighborhood called him, had not gone up and down the street, stooping a little and drawing his feet heavily over the gravel or pavement. But still there was something tough and vigorous about him, that
10 not only kept him in daily breath, but enabled him to fill a place which would else have been vacant, in the apparently crowded world. To go of errands, with his slow and shuffling gait, which made you doubt how he ever was to arrive anywhere; to saw a small household's foot or two of firewood, or knock to pieces an old barrel, or split up a pine board, for kindling-stuff; in summer, to dig the few yards of garden-ground, appertaining to a low-rented tenement, and share the produce of his labor at the halves; in winter, to shovel away the snow from the sidewalk, or open paths to the wood-shed, or along the clothesline; —such were some of the essential offices which Uncle Venner performed among at least a score of families.

Old Man at the Bridge
Ernest Hemingway

An old man with steel rimmed spectacles and very dusty clothes sat by the side of the road. There was a pontoon bridge across the river and carts, trucks, and men, women and children were crossing it. The mule-drawn carts staggered up the steep bank from the bridge with soldiers helping push against the spokes of the wheels. The trucks ground up and away heading out of it all and the peasants plodded along in the ankle deep dust. But the old man sat there without moving. He was too tired to go any farther.

It was my business to cross the bridge, explore the bridgehead beyond and find out to what point the enemy had advanced. I did this and returned over

10   the bridge. There were not so many carts now and very few people on foot, but
the old man was still there.

"Where do you come from?" I asked him.

"From San Carlos," he said, and smiled.

That was his native town and so it gave him pleasure to mention it and he
smiled.

"I was taking care of animals," he explained.

"Oh," I said, not quite understanding.

"Yes," he said. "I stayed, you see, taking care of animals. I was the last one to
leave the town of San Carlos."

20   He did not look like a shepherd nor a herdsman and I looked at his black
dusty clothes and his gray dusty face and his steel rimmed spectacles and said,
"What animals were they?"

"Various animals," he said, and shook his head. "I had to leave them."

I was watching the bridge and the African looking country of the Ebro
Delta and wondering how long now it would be before we would see the
enemy, and listening all the while for the first noises that would signal that ever
mysterious event called contact, and the old man still sat there.

"What animals were they?" I asked.

"There were three animals altogether," he explained." "There were two goats
30   and a cat and then there were four pairs of pigeons."

"And you had to leave them?" I asked.

"Yes. Because of the artillery. The captain told me to go because of the
artillery."

"And you have no family?" I asked, watching the far end of the bridge where
a few last carts were hurrying down the slope of the bank.

"No," he said, "only the animals I stated. The cat, of course, will be all right.
A cat can look out for itself, but I cannot think what will become of the others."

"What politics have you?" I asked.

"I am without politics," he said. "I am seventy-six years old. I have come
40   twelve kilometers now and I think now I can go no further."

"This is not a good place to stop," I said. "If you can make it, there are
trucks up the road where it forks for Tortosa."

"I will wait a while," he said. "and then I will go. Where do the trucks go?"

"Towards Barcelona," I told him.

"I know no one in that direction," he said. "but thank you very much.
Thank you again very much."

He looked at me very blankly and tiredly, then said, having to share his
worry with some one, "The cat will be alright, I am sure. There is no need

GO ON ➤

to be unquiet about the cat. But the others. Now what do you think about the
50 others?"

"Why they'll probably come through it all right."

"You think so?"

"Why not," I said, watching the far bank where now there were no carts.

"But what will they do under the artillery when I was told to leave because
of the artillery?"

"Did you leave the dove cage unlocked?" I asked.

"Yes."

"Then they'll fly."

"Yes, certainly they'll fly. But the others. It's better not to think about the
60 others," he said.

"If you are rested I would go," I urged. "Get up and try to walk now."

"Thank you," he said and got to his feet, swayed from side to side and then
sat down backwards in the dust.

"I was taking care of animals," he said dully, but no longer to me. "I was
only taking care of animals."

There was nothing to do about him. It was Easter Sunday and the Fascists
were advancing toward the Ebro. It was a gray overcast day with a low ceiling
so their planes were not up. That and the fact that cats know how to look after
themselves was all the good luck that old man would ever have.

Comprehension

DIRECTIONS *Answer these questions about the excerpt from* The House of the Seven Gables.

1. The author's style includes his use of sentences that are

    A. all short sentences

    B. all long sentences

    C. mostly short sentences

    D. a mix of long and short sentences

2. What can you infer about Uncle Venner from the imagery in lines 9–11?

    A. He succeeds through his charm.

    B. He survives by being useful.

    C. He is somewhat overweight.

    D. He has breathing problems.

3. The author's style can best be characterized by his use of

    A. long descriptions and a harsh tone

    B. lyrical language and an informal tone

    C. flowery language and a monotonous tone

    D. detailed descriptions and a good-natured tone

4. The author's purpose in this excerpt is most likely to

    A. paint an affectionate portrait of a local character

    B. ridicule an eccentric old man

    C. illustrate the hardships of poverty

    D. highlight the indifference of the community

DIRECTIONS *Answer these questions about "Old Man at the Bridge."*

5. One element of the author's style is his use of

A. mostly long sentences

B. all very short short sentences

C. long sentences and some incomplete sentences

D. mostly short, simple sentences and some long sentences

6. The author's choice of words can best be characterized as

A. flowery

B. conversational

C. exaggerated

D. technical

7. Which word describes the tone conveyed in lines 1–7?

A. somber   C. sarcastic

B. playful   D. bitter

8. The author repeats variations of the phrase "the old man still sat there" in lines 6–7, 11, and 27 to create an image of

A. stubbornness   C. impatience

B. weariness   D. foolishness

9. The author's primary purpose in writing this story is to

A. describe an elderly man's fondness for his animals

B. persuade people that politics is unimportant

C. portray the effects of war on the citizens of a country

D. evaluate the duties of a soldier in times of war

DIRECTIONS *Answer the following question about both selections.*

10. What can you infer about the old men in the two selections?

A. They are tired from all of the work that they do.

B. One of them is sad and one is angry because they must work for other people.

C. Because they are elderly, both must rely on others to care for them.

D. Both take their work and responsibilities seriously.

Written Response

SHORT ANSWER *Write three or four sentences to answer these questions.*

11. Why do you think the author has a soldier narrate "Old Man at the Bridge"? In what way does this help the author achieve his purpose?

12. List five words or images from *The House of the Seven Gables* that describe Uncle Venner. What can you infer about Venner from these words and images?

EXTENDED RESPONSE *Write two or three paragraphs to answer this question.*

13. Describe the differences in the two authors' writing styles. Give examples of word choices, sentence structure, and tone in your answer.

GO ON

Vocabulary

DIRECTIONS *Use the underlined etymology clues to help you choose the correct word that is missing from each of the following sentences.*

1. You can travel over (<u>Middle English, from Old French, diminutive of</u> *grave,* <u>"pebbly shore,"</u> <u>of Celtic origin</u>) to reach the houses near the sea.
   A. kindling-stuff
   B. pavement
   C. gait
   D. gravel

2. In his role as a (<u>Middle English, from Old French, Latin</u> *famulus,* <u>"servant"</u>) among the Winterthorns, he ran errands and cleaned the outbuildings.
   A. resident
   B. family
   C. familiar
   D. clergyman

3. He was described as a (<u>Middle English, from Old French, from Latin</u> *humilis,* <u>"low," from</u> *humus,* <u>"ground"</u>) person, as much for his lack of pride as for his station in life.
   A. household
   B. vigorous
   C. humble
   D. garden-ground

4. By (<u>Middle English, from Old English,</u> *stupian,* <u>"to bow, bend"</u>), their parents could exit from the front door of the playhouse.
   A. shuffling
   B. entering
   C. appertaining
   D. stooping

5. The exhausted climbers (<u>alteration of Middle English</u> *stakerem,* <u>from Old Norse</u> *stakra, staka,* <u>"to push"</u>) to the top of the mountain, driven forward by sheer willpower.
   A. plodded
   B. staggered
   C. advanced
   D. swayed

6. The soldiers' first (<u>Latin, from past participle of</u> *con-* <u>"together"</u>+ *tangere* <u>"to touch"</u>) with the enemy was one that they would not forget.
   A. bridgehead
   B. signal
   C. contact
   D. bank

7. Her interest in local (<u>Middle English, from Old French, from Latin, from Greek</u> *polites,* <u>"citizen," from</u> *polis,* <u>"city"</u>) led to a career as a congresswoman.
   A. politics
   B. business
   C. towns
   D. planes

Writing & Grammar

DIRECTIONS *Read this passage and answer the questions that follow.*

(1) Pablo Picasso's painting *Guernica* portrays the destruction of a town during the Spanish Civil War. (2) It is an abstract composition of colors and forms. (3) Tormented animals and tortured human images fill the canvas. (4) In the painting, a snorting bull and a writhing horse seem uncomfortable. (5) The painting also depicts human suffering. (6) Picasso painted a woman clutching her dead child. (7) His purpose was to expose the horrors of war.

1. How might you rewrite sentence 2 so that it incorporates personification?

   A. It is an abstract composition that requires close inspection of its colors and forms.

   B. It is a provocative abstract composition of colors and forms.

   C. It is an abstract composition that grabs the viewer with its colors and forms.

   D. It is a powerful composition of somber colors and contorted forms.

2. How might you incorporate an infinitive phrase into sentence 4?

   A. In the painting, a snorting bull and a writhing horse seem to be in great pain.

   B. In the painting, a snorting bull seems uncomfortable and so does a writhing horse.

   C. A snorting bull and a writhing horse, which seem to be uncomfortable, appear in the painting.

   D. In the painting, a snorting bull seems unhappy, and a writhing horse seems uncomfortable.

3. How might you rewrite sentence 5 so that it incorporates personification?

   A. The painting also shows human suffering in great detail.

   B. The painting also cries out against human suffering.

   C. The painting also demonstrates examples of human suffering.

   D. The painting also displays images of human suffering.

4. How might you incorporate an infinitive phrase into sentence 6?

   A. To illustrate this suffering, Picasso painted a woman clutching her dead child.

   B. Picasso painted a woman, who is screaming, clutching her dead child.

   C. Picasso painted a woman, with her mouth open, clutching her dead child.

   D. A woman clutching a dead child illustrates this human suffering.

STOP

Ideas for Independent Reading

Extend your exploration of authors' styles and of provocative questions raised in this unit by reading the following works.

What breeds terror?

Dracula
by Bram Stoker

Though books, films, and television series about vampires are now common, nothing terrifies readers like the original tale of Dracula, the undead count who hunts for young women he can turn into vampires.

It
by Stephen King

Readers could argue forever about which of King's horror novels is the most terrifying. This one pits seven teenagers against a clown-faced evil. They unite to banish it, only to see it reappear after they've grown to adulthood.

The Collector of Hearts: New Tales of the Grotesque
by Joyce Carol Oates

Oates, who claims Edgar Allan Poe as an influence, offers 27 macabre tales written in her own distinctive style. Several stories center on children, such as "Handpuppet," in which a ragged toy alters its young owner.

What do we learn from experience?

On the Blue Shores of Silence: Poems of the Sea
by Pablo Neruda

Chile's national poet, who admired Walt Whitman, loved to watch the sea outside his island home. In these poems Neruda captures the sea's continual movements—at times wild, at times calm— and its changes of color.

. . . And the Earth Did Not Devour Him
by Tomás Rivera

This kaleidoscopic collection of stories centers on a Mexican-American migrant community. The stories detail the people's hardships and hopes as they complete the yearly cycle of travel, labor, and return to Texas.

A Raisin in the Sun
by Lorraine Hansberry

In this famous play, an African-American family in Chicago dreams of what they will do with a $10,000 life insurance check. The son's rash decision teaches the family a painful yet ultimately ennobling lesson.

What is your role in your household?

The Joy Luck Club
by Amy Tan

This novel-in-stories explores the relationships of Chinese-immigrant mothers and their American-born daughters. The mothers struggle with painful memories as they adjust to a new culture. The daughters struggle with their mothers' high expectations of them.

Invent Radium, or I'll Pull Your Hair
by Doris Drucker

Doris Drucker grew up in an assimilated German-Jewish family who hoped they could outlast the Nazis. Her mother wanted her to be a scientist and forbade Doris to have opinions that differed from hers. This witty memoir gives insight into German culture under Hitler.

The Prize Winner of Defiance, Ohio
by Terry Ryan

Ryan's mother began entering contests as a young wife. She wrote jingles for products and earned enough to support ten children through years when her husband was unable to work. The family lived on her monetary winnings and the products that came with them.

9

Product of the Times

HISTORY, CULTURE, AND THE AUTHOR

- In Nonfiction
- In Fiction
- In Poetry
- In Media

What SHAPES *your world?*

Popular reality shows are fond of placing individuals in unfamiliar settings and situations. These shows can be fascinating because viewers see how a different environment, culture, or situation can transform the people involved.

Our own daily reality **shapes** each of us, usually without our even being aware of it. It affects how we live, how we behave, even how we think. It influences artists, musicians, and writers, as well; the times and places in which they work can affect their choice of subject matter, their perspective, and their popularity.

ACTIVITY In a small group, think of at least two events that have occurred in your lifetime and changed the way people think or act. Examples might include an election, a natural disaster, or a war. Discuss the impact each event had on you personally or on society as a whole.

OHIO
STANDARDS

Preview Unit Goals

LITERARY ANALYSIS
- Identify cultural characteristics
- Analyze influence of historical and cultural context
- Analyze influence of author's background
- Analyze influence of a literary period
- Identify and analyze sensory details

READING
- Use reading strategies, including connecting, monitoring, and predicting
- Cite evidence to support an opinion
- Analyze rhetorical devices

WRITING AND GRAMMAR
- Write an informative essay
- Use simple, compound, complex, and compound-complex sentences; use gerund phrases

SPEAKING, LISTENING, AND VIEWING
- Conduct an interview
- Determine cultural influences in the creation of media messages

VOCABULARY
- Understand and use prefixes and suffixes to determine word meaning
- Use a dictionary to help determine word meaning

ACADEMIC VOCABULARY
- cultural context
- historical context
- cultural characteristics
- author's background

History, Culture, and the Author

Behind every work of literature is a writer—the individual responsible for crafting the words on the page. A writer's words may entertain, inform, or inspire, but they may also reveal glimpses into his or her background, beliefs, or times. Perhaps the writer endured the horrors of a war you've only read about, or grew up in a family very different from your own. Learning more about writers and the forces that shaped their lives can help you discover unexpected layers of meaning in the literature you read.

OHIO STANDARDS

READING STANDARDS
4.2 Analyze the features of setting and their importance in a literary text
4.11 Explain ways in which an author develops a point of view and style

Part 1: The Writer's Background

"Write what you know" is often the first piece of advice that writers receive. Whether they intentionally follow it or not, many writers produce works that are influenced by personal factors in their lives, such as heritage, national identity, customs, and values. For example, consider the following excerpt from Paule Marshall's short story "To Da-duh, in Memoriam." On one level, the work is a poignant story about family. But by reading the background and asking yourself a few questions, you can discover just how personal the story is.

---

from To Da-duh, in Memoriam

Short story by **Paule Marshall**

BACKGROUND Paule Marshall was born in Brooklyn, New York, but her family came from the island of Barbados. Her story draws on her memories of a childhood visit to her grandmother (nicknamed Da-duh). "Ours was a complex relationship," she has written, "close, affectionate yet rivalrous." Marshall has said that the rivalry between the grandmother and the granddaughter in the story is supposed to represent a struggle between cultures, old and new.

... She stopped before an incredibly tall royal palm which rose cleanly out of the ground, and drawing the eye up with it, soared high above the trees around it into the sky. It appeared to be touching the blue dome of sky, to be flaunting its dark crown of fronds right in the blinding white face of the late morning sun.

5 Da-duh watched me a long time before she spoke, and then she said, very quietly, "All right, now, tell me if you've got anything this tall in that place you're from."

I almost wished, seeing her face, that I could have said no. "Yes," I said. "We've got buildings hundreds of times this tall in New York."

QUESTIONS TO ASK

What beliefs and values are reflected in the writing?
Through the interaction between the characters, Marshall conveys a respect for the old (the palm tree) and an acknowledgment of the new (skyscrapers).

What aspects of the author's background are evident?
Though Marshall was born in New York, she too visited her grandmother in Barbados as a child.

What does the background reveal about the author's motivation for writing this story?
Marshall is communicating her understanding of cultural conflicts.

MODEL 1: ANALYZING A POEM

Read this poem "cold" first, noticing what images it calls to mind.

Women

Poem by **Alice Walker**

They were women then
My mama's generation
Husky of voice—Stout of
Step
5 With fists as well as
Hands
How they battered down
Doors
And ironed
10 Starched white
Shirts
How they led
Armies
Headragged Generals
15 Across mined
Fields
Booby-trapped
Kitchens
To discover books
20 Desks
A place for us
How they knew what we
Must know
Without knowing a page
25 Of it
Themselves.

Close Read

1. "Women" is full of images that suggest physical force. One is boxed. Find two more images.

2. What one word would you use to describe the women in the poem? Explain your choice.

3. Reread lines 19–26. What do you think the women did for their children?

MODEL 2: THE WRITER'S BACKGROUND

Now read this background information about Alice Walker. How does learning about the poet change or enhance your understanding of her poem?

BACKGROUND Alice Walker was born in Eatonton, Georgia, in 1944, a time of legal segregation and organized violence against African Americans. The eighth child in a family of sharecroppers, she grew up in a black community that nurtured and protected its children. Her mother and aunts were strong
5 women who maintained their independence despite racism and poverty and fought for a better future for the young. Inspired by these role models, Walker became a civil rights activist and writer.

Close Read

1. In line 14 of the poem, the speaker describes the women as generals. What might she see as the enemy they were fighting?

2. Using information from the background and the poem, explain why Walker may admire women of her mother's generation.

Part 2: Historical and Cultural Influences

What effect would Anne Frank's diary have on you if you knew nothing of the horrors of the Holocaust or her ultimate fate? To fully understand some works of literature, you need a sense of their **historical** and **cultural context**—the social and cultural conditions that influenced their creation. What was happening at the time a work was written, both in the writer's hometown and in the world at large? What issues or social problems were people grappling with? By uncovering answers to questions like these, you can often gain deeper insights into literature.

When John Steinbeck's novel *The Grapes of Wrath* was published in 1939, the Great Depression had been going on for ten long years. The novel presents a sympathetic portrayal of farmers who are forced to leave their land. Notice how reading the background and asking some questions can help you understand Steinbeck's work as social commentary on the harsh injustices of the time.

from The Grapes of Wrath

Novel by **John Steinbeck**

BACKGROUND During the Great Depression, life was especially difficult for farmers on the Great Plains, where a severe drought turned the land to desert. High winds brought terrible dust storms that killed crops and livestock and blotted out the sun for days. Some farmers gave up, abandoning their land. Others struggled to hold on, relying on government aid— "relief"—in the form of food, money, and jobs. Many were evicted when they couldn't pay their mortgages or when wealthy landowners replaced sharecroppers with mechanical tractors. Many farmers fled to California in search of promising jobs, only to find backbreaking, low-paying work.

This is an exchange between landowners and sharecroppers they are about to evict:

But if we go, where'll we go? How'll we go? We got no money.

We're sorry, said the owner men. The bank, the fifty-thousand-acre owner can't be responsible. You're on land that isn't yours. Once over the line maybe you can pick cotton in the fall. Maybe you go on relief. Why don't you

5 go on west to California? There's work there, and it never gets cold. Why, you can reach out anywhere and pick an orange. Why, there's always some kind of crop to work in. Why don't you go there? And the owner men started their cars and rolled away.

QUESTIONS TO ASK

How does the conflict reflect the struggles of the times?
The sharecroppers' conflict— being evicted from their land—was one that many poor farmers experienced during the Great Depression.

How are the characters portrayed?
The pleas of the sharecroppers make them seem desperate. Expressions like "rolled away" make the landowners seem indifferent.

How does your knowledge of history help you understand what you are reading?
Steinbeck knew that the reality of life in California did not measure up to the promise of "reach[ing] out anywhere and pick[ing] an orange." Therefore, the portrayal of California as a paradise becomes ironic.

MODEL 1: ANALYZING FICTION

This excerpt is from a short story that is set several years after the California gold rush of the mid-1800s. As you read it, consider what you already know about that time.

from The Californian's Tale
Short story by **Mark Twain**

Now and then, half an hour apart, one came across solitary log cabins of the earliest mining days, built by the first gold miners. . . . In some few cases these cabins were still occupied; and when this was so, you could depend upon it that the occupant was the very pioneer who had built the cabin; and . . .
5 that he was there because he had once had his opportunity to go home to the States rich, and had not done it; had rather lost his wealth, and had then in his humiliation resolved to sever all communication with his home relatives and friends, and be to them thenceforth as one dead. Round about California in that day were scattered a host of these living dead men— pride-smitten
10 poor fellows, grizzled and old at forty, whose secret thoughts were made all of regrets and longings —regrets for their wasted lives, and longings to be out of the struggle and done with it all.
It was a lonesome land! Not a sound in all those peaceful expanses of grass and woods but the drowsy hum of insects; no glimpse of man or beast;
15 nothing to keep up your spirits and make you glad to be alive.

Close Read

1. What do you learn about the men who live in the cabins? Cite details that help you understand their situation.

2. Identify four phrases or details that suggest a sense of desolation and hopelessness.

MODEL 2: HISTORICAL AND CULTURAL CONTEXT

The following background explains how the promise of gold lured thousands to California in 1848. As you read, consider how this information enhances your understanding of the "wasted lives" of the men in Twain's story.

BACKGROUND On a winter morning in 1848, workers discovered gold east of Sacramento, setting off an epidemic of "gold fever." Thousands of young men left their homes and traveled west in the hope that they would strike it rich. The first to arrive found that there was plenty of gold to go around—but
5 not much else. Prices for food and other supplies shot sky-high in the rough frontier towns. Newly rich miners let their fortunes slip away, confident they could get more. By mid-1849, however, gold became much harder to find. Soon, many gave up and left, turning the "boom" towns into ghost towns.
By the time Samuel Clemens went west in the early 1860s, the wild hopes
10 of the gold rush years had turned to bitter disillusionment. After a few unsuccessful months of working as a miner, Clemens gave up and began a new career as the writer Mark Twain."

Close Read

1. Reread the boxed details in Twain's story. What information in the background helps you understand the narrator's description of the land and its inhabitants?

2. In your opinion, is Twain's tone toward the miners sympathetic? Explain.

Part 3: Analyze the Literature

Zhang Jie is one of the most acclaimed writers from the People's Republic of China. Her story "Love Must Not Be Forgotten" takes place during the 1970s, when Communist ideals affected how people viewed the institution of marriage. Read this background about China during that time and about the life of Zhang Jie. Then use the information in the background to help you analyze an excerpt from her story.

BACKGROUND

A Writer in the People's Republic

Zhang Jie

For the Greater Good In 1949, Mao Zedong and his Communist forces took control of China. In 1966, Mao felt that new blood was needed to keep the ideals of
5 communism alive, so he implemented the Cultural Revolution. For the next several years, groups of young radicals removed and replaced older Communist Party leaders, who were executed or imprisoned.

10 Despite sweeping political changes, many Chinese customs were slow to change. For example, centuries-old traditions dictated that marriages be arranged by couples' families when the
15 couples were still young children. New laws enacted by the Communists allowed individuals to choose their own marriage partners. However, marrying for love was still frowned upon, because Communist
20 teachings encouraged individuals to suppress personal desires for the greater social good.

The Fight Against Injustice Both personal hardships and the harsh political
25 climate in Communist China helped shape the life of the writer Zhang Jie. She has written, "These circumstances made me sensitive to all injustice and inequality. . . . I determined to fight
30 injustice all my life." Born in 1937, Zhang Jie grew up in poverty during the war-torn years before communism. She dreamed of studying literature at the great university in Beijing and of

35 becoming a writer. Zhang Jie's dreams were put on hold when the government assigned her to a subject considered more useful to the nation: economics.

After graduation, Zhang Jie worked
40 as a statistician. She married a colleague and gave birth to their daughter in 1963. Then came the Cultural Revolution, when millions of educated white-collar workers were sent to harsh work camps to be "re-
45 educated" in Communist thought. Despite her loyalty to communism, Zhang Jie was sent thousands of miles away to a labor camp, where she spent four years tending pigs and slogging through rice paddies.

50 **A Writer at Last** Zhang Jie was 40 when she finally was able to publish her first story, which won a major award. Soon she was one of the most popular writers in China—and one of the most controversial.
55 "Love Must Not Be Forgotten" raised a storm of protest from party officials, who thought the story undermined traditional attitudes toward marriage.

from

LOVE MUST NOT BE FORGOTTEN

Short story by **Zhang Jie**

I am thirty, the same age as our People's Republic. For a republic thirty is still young. But a girl of thirty is virtually on the shelf.

Actually, I have a bona fide suitor. Have you seen the Greek sculptor Myron's Discobolus? Qiao Lin is the image of that discus thrower. Even the padded
5   clothes he wears in winter fail to hide his fine physique. Bronzed, with clear-cut features, a broad forehead and large eyes, his appearance alone attracts most girls to him.

But I can't make up my mind to marry him. I'm not clear what attracts me to him, or him to me.
10   I know people are gossiping behind my back, "Who does she think she is, to be so choosy?"

To them, I'm a nobody playing hard to get. They take offense at such preposterous behavior.

Of course, I shouldn't be captious.[1] In a society where commercial production
15   still exists, marriage like most other transactions is still a form of barter.

I have known Qiao Lin for nearly two years, yet still cannot fathom whether he keeps so quiet from aversion to talking or from having nothing to say. When, by way of a small intelligence test, I demand his opinion of this or that, he says "good" or "bad" like a child in kindergarten.
20   Once I asked, "Qiao Lin, why do you love me?" He thought the question over seriously for what seemed an age. I could see from his normally smooth but now wrinkled forehead that the little grey cells in his handsome head were hard at work cogitating. I felt ashamed to have put him on the spot.

Finally he raised his clear childlike eyes to tell me, "Because you're good!"
25   Loneliness flooded my heart. "Thank you, Qiao Lin!" I couldn't help wondering, if we were to marry, whether we could discharge our duties to each other as husband and wife. Maybe, because law and morality would have bound us together. But how tragic simply to comply with law and morality! Was there no stronger bond to link us?
30   When such thoughts cross my mind, I have the strange sensation that instead of being a girl contemplating marriage I am an elderly social scientist.

Perhaps I worry too much. We can live like most married couples, bringing up children together, strictly true to each other according to the law. . . . Although living in the seventies of the twentieth century, people still consider marriage the
35   way they did millennia ago, as a means of continuing the race, a form of barter or a business transaction in which love and marriage can be separated.

---

1.   **captious:** overly critical.

Close Read

1. Which details in the background help you understand why Zhang Jie chose to write about a woman who questions social values?

2. What values do you think Zhang Jie and her narrator share? Support your answer.

3. Reread the boxed text. How was marriage viewed in China during the 1970s? Does the narrator support this view? Explain.

4. What aspects of this story might Communist Party officials have considered controversial? Support your answer, using details from both texts.

from **Night**
Memoir by Elie Wiesel

Can HUMANITY
triumph over evil?

OHIO STANDARDS

READING STANDARDS
2.1 Apply reading comprehension strategies
4.5 Analyze how choice of genre affects theme or topic

KEY IDEA Elie Wiesel was imprisoned in a Nazi concentration camp when he was only 15. He later wrote his memoir *Night* so that the world would never forget the horrors he and his fellow prisoners experienced. Yet his book also shows how people in the most desperate circumstances can retain their **humanity** through acts of kindness and self-sacrifice.

DISCUSS As a class, recall two or three examples of world events in which cruelty was inflicted on groups of people. Discuss how individuals and governments responded to these events, and then list actions that should be taken to prevent similar tragedies from occurring.

Triumphing Over Evil
1. Expose violations of human rights.
2. Prosecute leaders responsible for crimes.
3.
4.

LITERARY ANALYSIS: MEMOIR

A **memoir** is a personal account of the significant events and people in the author's life. In Elie Wiesel's memoir *Night*, for example, readers view through his eyes the terrifying experience of being imprisoned in a Nazi concentration camp. Unlike strictly historical accounts, most memoirs

- are first-person narratives in the writer's voice
- express the writer's feelings and opinions about events, giving insight into the impact of history on people's lives

As you read, record the insights you gain from Wiesel's personal history. Use a chart like the one shown.

Wiesel's Experience	Historical Insight
"I had been transferred to another unit . . . where, twelve hours a day, I had to drag heavy blocks of stone about."	In the concentration camps, inmates were brutally overworked.

READING STRATEGY: CONNECT

Because a memoir offers a personal view of events, you will often have the opportunity to **connect** the content to your own experiences and knowledge. Although Wiesel describes cruel treatment that few readers will have experienced, at some point in your life you probably have felt emotions that he expresses, such as his sense of relief in this example:

"Well? So you passed?"
"Yes. And you?"
"Me too."
How we breathed again, now!

As you read, look for opportunities to connect with Wiesel's reactions to incidents in the concentration camp.

▲ VOCABULARY IN CONTEXT

The following words help to convey Wiesel's harrowing experience. To see how many words you know, substitute a different word or phrase for each boldfaced word.

1. She heard the **din** of a dozen car horns.
2. I appeared **emaciated** after my long fast.
3. The basketball player had an imposing **stature**.
4. That long concert seemed **interminable**.

Author Online

Holocaust Survivor
Elie Wiesel was born in Transylvania, a region of Romania controlled by Hungary during World War II. In April 1944, the Nazis ordered the deportation of all Jews in the area. Wiesel and his family were forced to board a cattle train bound for the

Elie Wiesel
born 1928

Auschwitz concentration camp in Poland, where his mother and one of his sisters were murdered. Wiesel and his father were later sent to another camp, Buchenwald, in Germany; his father died just three months before the camp was liberated. Wiesel's Holocaust experiences have led him to speak out against human rights violations in countries around the world. A U.S. citizen since 1963, Wiesel was awarded the Nobel Peace Prize in 1986.

 MORE ABOUT THE AUTHOR
For more on Elie Wiesel, visit the **Literature Center** at **ClassZone.com**.

Background

The Holocaust Soon after Adolf Hitler became chancellor of Germany in 1933, he began to persecute German Jews, gradually stripping them of their rights. Germany's invasion of Poland in 1939 marked the beginning of World War II. Two of Hitler's goals were to expand his empire across Europe and to eliminate the Jewish population. Jews from all areas under Nazi control were transported to concentration camps, along with gypsies, homosexuals, political opponents, and others. Prisoners at Auschwitz, the largest camp, had numbers tattooed on their arms for identification. Most of the 6 million Jews killed in the Holocaust died in concentration camps—in gas chambers, before firing squads, or from starvation, torture, or disease.

Night

Elie Wiesel

The SS[1] gave us a fine New Year's gift.

We had just come back from work. As soon as we had passed through the door of the camp, we sensed something different in the air. Roll call did not take so long as usual. The evening soup was given out with great speed and swallowed down at once in anguish.

I was no longer in the same block as my father. I had been transferred to another unit, the building one, where, twelve hours a day, I had to drag heavy blocks of stone about. The head of my new block was a German Jew, small of **stature,** with piercing eyes. He told us that evening that no one would
10 be allowed to go out after the evening soup. And soon a terrible word was circulating—selection.

We knew what that meant. An SS man would examine us. Whenever he found a weak one, a *musulman* as we called them, he would write his number down: good for the crematory.

After soup, we gathered together between the beds. The veterans said:

"You're lucky to have been brought here so late. This camp is paradise today, compared with what it was like two years ago. Buna[2] was a real hell then. There was no water, no blankets, less soup and bread. At night we slept almost naked, and it was below thirty degrees. The corpses were collected in
20 hundreds every day. The work was hard. Today, this is a little paradise. The Kapos[3] had orders to kill a certain number of prisoners every day. And every week—selection. A merciless selection. . . . Yes, you're lucky."

"Stop it! Be quiet!" I begged. "You can tell your stories tomorrow or on some other day."

They burst out laughing. They were not veterans for nothing.

"Are you scared? So were we scared. And there was plenty to be scared of in those days." **A**

---

1. **SS:** an elite military unit of the Nazi party that served as Hitler's personal guard and as a special security force.

2. **Buna** (bōō′nə): a forced-labor camp in Poland, near the Auschwitz concentration camp.

3. **Kapos** (kä′pōz): the prisoners who served as foremen, or heads, of each building or cell block.

ANALYZE VISUALS
The painting shows a portion of a uniform worn by a concentration camp prisoner. What do the details on the uniform **symbolize?**

stature (stăch′ər) *n.* the height of a person, animal, or object in an upright position

A MEMOIR
Reread lines 15–27. What insights did you gain from this conversation between Wiesel and the camp veterans?

Auschwitz Prisoner's Uniform, from the series *Reclaiming My Family History* (1998), Lina Eve. Mixed media on canvas.

The old men stayed in their corner, dumb, motionless, haunted. Some were praying. ⓑ

30   An hour's delay. In an hour, we should know the verdict—death or a reprieve.

And my father? Suddenly I remembered him. How would he pass the selection? He had aged so much. . . .

The head of our block had never been outside concentration camps since 1933. He had already been through all the slaughterhouses, all the factories of death. At about nine o'clock, he took up his position in our midst:

"Achtung!"[4]

There was instant silence.

"Listen carefully to what I am going to say." (For the first time, I heard his voice quiver.) "In a few moments the selection will begin. You must get
40 completely undressed. Then one by one you go before the SS doctors. I hope you will all succeed in getting through. But you must help your own chances. Before you go into the next room, move about in some way so that you give yourselves a little color. Don't walk slowly, run! Run as if the devil were after you! Don't look at the SS. Run, straight in front of you!"

He broke off for a moment, then added:

"And, the essential thing, don't be afraid!"

Here was a piece of advice we should have liked very much to be able to follow.

I got undressed, leaving my clothes on the bed. There was no danger of anyone stealing them this evening.

50   Tibi and Yossi, who had changed their unit at the same time as I had, came up to me and said:

"Let's keep together. We shall be stronger."

Yossi was murmuring something between his teeth. He must have been praying. I had never realized that Yossi was a believer. I had even always thought the reverse. Tibi was silent, very pale. All the prisoners in the block stood naked between the beds. This must be how one stands at the last judgment.

"They're coming!"

There were three SS officers standing around the notorious Dr. Mengele,[5] who had received us at Birkenau.[6] The head of the block, with an attempt at a
60 smile, asked us:

"Ready?"

Yes, we were ready. So were the SS doctors. Dr. Mengele was holding a list in his hand: our numbers. He made a sign to the head of the block: "We can begin!" As if this were a game!

The first to go by were the "officials" of the block: *Stubenaelteste,*[7] Kapos, foremen, all in perfect physical condition of course! Then came the ordinary

---

4. **Achtung!** (ŏk-tōong´) *German:* Attention!

5. **Dr. Mengele** (mŭng´gĕ·lə): Josef Mengele, a German doctor who personally selected nearly half a million prisoners to die in gas chambers at Auschwitz. He also became infamous for his medical experiments on inmates.

6. **Birkenau** (bûr´kĭn-ou´): a large section of the Auschwitz concentration camp.

7. *Stubenaelteste* (shtyōō´bə-nĭl-tŭs´-tə): a rank of Kapos; literally "elders of the rooms."

prisoners' turn. Dr. Mengele took stock of them from head to foot. Every now and then, he wrote a number down. One single thought filled my mind: not to let my number be taken; not to show my left arm.

70   There were only Tibi and Yossi in front of me. They passed. I had time to notice that Mengele had not written their numbers down. Someone pushed me. It was my turn. I ran without looking back. My head was spinning: you're too thin, you're too weak, you're too thin, you're good for the furnace. . . . The race seemed **interminable.** I thought I had been running for years. . . . You're too thin, you're too weak. . . . At last I had arrived exhausted. When I regained my breath, I questioned Yossi and Tibi:

"Was I written down?"

"No," said Yossi. He added, smiling: "In any case, he couldn't have written you down, you were running too fast. . . ."

80   I began to laugh. I was glad. I would have liked to kiss him. At that moment, what did the others matter! I hadn't been written down. **C**

Those whose numbers had been noted stood apart, abandoned by the whole world. Some were weeping in silence.

The SS officers went away. The head of the block appeared, his face reflecting the general weariness.

"Everything went off all right. Don't worry. Nothing is going to happen to anyone. To anyone."

Again he tried to smile. A poor, **emaciated,** dried-up Jew questioned him avidly in a trembling voice:

90   "But . . . but, *Blockaelteste*,[8] they did write me down!"

The head of the block let his anger break out. What! Did someone refuse to believe him!

"What's the matter now? Am I telling lies then? I tell you once and for all, nothing's going to happen to you! To anyone! You're wallowing in your own despair, you fool!"

The bell rang, a signal that the selection had been completed throughout the camp.

With all my might I began to run to Block 36. I met my father on the way. He came up to me:

100   "Well? So you passed?"

"Yes. And you?"

"Me too."

How we breathed again, now! My father had brought me a present—half a ration of bread obtained in exchange for a piece of rubber, found at the warehouse, which would do to sole a shoe. **D**

The bell. Already we must separate, go to bed. Everything was regulated by the bell. It gave me orders, and I automatically obeyed them. I hated it. Whenever I dreamed of a better world, I could only imagine a universe with no bells.

interminable
(ĭn-tûr′mə-nə-bəl) *adj.*
having no limit or end

C CONNECT
What experiences in your own life help you understand Wiesel's reaction after he gets through the selection process?

emaciated
(ĭ-mā′shē-ā′tĭd) *adj.*
excessively thin as a result of starvation
emaciate *v.*

D MEMOIR
What do you learn in lines 103–105 about actions that prisoners could take to improve their situation?

---

8. *Blockaelteste* (blä′kĭl-tŭs′tə): a rank of Kapos; literally, "elders of the building."

The Food of the Dead for the Living, David Olère. 102 cm × 76 cm. Gift of the Olère family. Museum of Jewish Heritage, a Living Memorial to the Holocaust, New York.

ANALYZE VISUALS
In what ways does this painting reflect Wiesel's experiences in the camp?

110   Several days had elapsed. We no longer thought about the selection. We went to work as usual, loading heavy stones into railway wagons. Rations had become more meager: this was the only change.

  We had risen before dawn, as on every day. We had received the black coffee, the ration of bread. We were about to set out for the yard as usual. The head of the block arrived, running.

  "Silence for a moment. I have a list of numbers here. I'm going to read them to you. Those whose numbers I call won't be going to work this morning; they'll stay behind in the camp."

  And, in a soft voice, he read out about ten numbers. We had understood.
120 These were numbers chosen at the selection. Dr. Mengele had not forgotten.

  The head of the block went toward his room. Ten prisoners surrounded him, hanging onto his clothes:

  "Save us! You promised . . . ! We want to go to the yard. We're strong enough to work. We're good workers. We can . . . we will . . . ."

  He tried to calm them to reassure them about their fate, to explain to them that the fact that they were staying behind in the camp did not mean much, had no tragic significance.

  "After all, I stay here myself every day," he added.

  It was a somewhat feeble argument. He realized it, and without another
130 word went and shut himself up in his room.

  The bell had just rung.

  "Form up!"

  It scarcely mattered now that the work was hard. The essential thing was to be as far away as possible from the block, from the crucible of death, from the center of hell.

  I saw my father running toward me. I became frightened all of a sudden.

  "What's the matter?"

Out of breath, he could hardly open his mouth.

"Me, too . . . me, too . . . ! They told me to stay behind in the camp."

140 They had written down his number without his being aware of it.

"What will happen?" I asked in anguish.

But it was he who tried to reassure me.

"It isn't certain yet. There's still a chance of escape. They're going to do another selection today . . . a decisive selection."

I was silent.

He felt that his time was short. He spoke quickly. He would have liked to say so many things. His speech grew confused; his voice choked. He knew that I would have to go in a few moments. He would have to stay behind alone, so very alone.

150 "Look, take this knife," he said to me. "I don't need it any longer. It might be useful to you. And take this spoon as well. Don't sell them. Quickly! Go on. Take what I'm giving you!"

The inheritance.

"Don't talk like that, Father." (I felt that I would break into sobs.) "I don't want you to say that. Keep the spoon and knife. You need them as much as I do. We shall see each other again this evening, after work." **E**

He looked at me with his tired eyes, veiled with despair. He went on:

"I'm asking this of you. . . . Take them. Do as I ask, my son. We have no time. . . . Do as your father asks."

160 Our Kapo yelled that we should start.

The unit set out toward the camp gate. Left, right! I bit my lips. My father had stayed by the block, leaning against the wall. Then he began to run, to catch up with us. Perhaps he had forgotten something he wanted to say to me. . . . But we were marching too quickly . . . Left, right!

We were already at the gate. They counted us, to the **din** of military music. We were outside.

The whole day, I wandered about as if sleepwalking. Now and then Tibi and Yossi would throw me a brotherly word. The Kapo, too, tried to reassure me. He had given me easier work today. I felt sick at heart. How well they were treating me! Like an orphan! I thought: even now, my father is still helping me.

170 I did not know myself what I wanted—for the day to pass quickly or not. I was afraid of finding myself alone that night. How good it would be to die here!

At last we began the return journey. How I longed for orders to run!

The military march. The gate. The camp.

I ran to Block 36.

Were there still miracles on this earth? He was alive. He had escaped the second selection. He had been able to prove that he was still useful. . . . I gave him back his knife and spoon. ❧

E CONNECT
Think about a time when you received some painful news. Why might Wiesel have been reluctant to accept the spoon and knife?

din (dĭn) *n.* a deafening noise

SPEECH The following is an excerpt from the speech that Elie Wiesel gave in 1986 at the ceremony in Oslo, Norway, where he was awarded the Nobel Peace Prize.

Nobel Prize Acceptance Speech

ELIE WIESEL

It is with a profound sense of humility that I accept the honor you have chosen to bestow upon me. I know: your choice transcends me. This both frightens and pleases me.

It frightens me because I wonder: do I have the right to represent the multitudes who have perished? Do I have the right to accept this great honor on their behalf? I do not. That would be presumptuous. No one may speak for the dead, no one may interpret their mutilated dreams and visions.

It pleases me because I may say that this honor belongs to all the survivors and their children, and through us, to the Jewish people with whose destiny I have always identified.

I remember: it happened yesterday or eternities ago. A young Jewish boy discovered the kingdom of night. I remember his bewilderment, I remember his anguish. It all happened so fast. The ghetto. The deportation. The sealed cattle car. The fiery altar upon which the history of our people and the future of mankind were meant to be sacrificed.

I remember: he asked his father: "Can this be true? This is the 20th century, not the Middle Ages. Who would allow such crimes to be committed? How could the world remain silent?"

And now the boy is turning to me: "Tell me," he asks. "What have you done with my future? What have you done with your life?"

And I tell him that I have tried. That I have tried to keep memory alive, that I have tried to fight those who would forget. Because if we forget, we are guilty, we are accomplices.

And then I explained to him how naive we were, that the world did know and remained silent. And that is why I swore never to be silent whenever and wherever human beings endure suffering and humiliation. We must always take sides. Neutrality helps the oppressor, never the victim. Silence encourages the tormentor, never the tormented.

Comprehension

1. **Recall** What is the purpose of the camp's selection process?

2. **Recall** How do the prisoners try to avoid being chosen?

3. **Recall** Why does Wiesel's father give him his knife and spoon?

4. **Summarize** What happens after Wiesel's father stays behind at the camp?

Literary Analysis

5. **Connect** How did the connections you made as you read deepen your understanding of Wiesel's experiences? Discuss specific examples in the selection.

6. **Analyze Memoir** Review the chart you created as you read. What insights did you gain about the hardships faced by the concentration camp prisoners? Support your response with examples from the text.

7. **Make Inferences** Reread lines 84–95. Why does the head of Wiesel's block insist so firmly that none of the prisoners is in danger? Cite evidence to support your answer.

8. **Draw Conclusions** Wiesel describes an encounter with veteran prisoners in lines 15–27. Based on this description, what would you conclude about the effects of living in a concentration camp over a long period of time?

9. **Interpret Title** Why do you think Wiesel chose to call his memoir *Night?*

10. **Examine Author's Purpose** What does the excerpt from Wiesel's Nobel Prize acceptance speech on page 860 suggest about his purpose for writing *Night?* Cite specific statements in your response.

Literary Criticism

11. **Different Perspectives** Elie Wiesel once said, "Just as despair can come to one only from other human beings, hope, too, can be given to one only by other human beings." Which details or incidents in the selection from *Night* give you reason to be hopeful about **humanity?**

OHIO STANDARDS

READING STANDARD
4.5 Analyze how choice of genre affects theme or topic

Vocabulary in Context

VOCABULARY PRACTICE

Decide whether the words in each pair are synonyms or antonyms.

1. stature/height
2. interminable/finite
3. emaciated/portly
4. din/commotion

WORD LIST

din

emaciated

interminable

stature

VOCABULARY IN WRITING

Using two or more vocabulary words, describe a scene in which people are forced to live in harsh conditions.

> **EXAMPLE SENTENCE**
>
> *Although relief agencies had started to bring food to the refugee camp, many of the children looked **emaciated**.*

VOCABULARY STRATEGY: CONNOTATION AND DENOTATION

A word's **denotation** is its basic dictionary meaning. Its **connotation** is the overtones of meaning that it may take on. For example, *emaciated* and *skinny* both mean "very thin," but the connotation of *emaciated* makes it a better choice to describe someone who is suffering from starvation or illness. When you choose words in writing, be sure to consider whether their connotations fit the context.

OHIO STANDARDS

VOCABULARY STANDARD
1.2 Analyze the relationships of pairs of words

PRACTICE From the choice of words supplied in each sentence, choose the one that fits best.

1. I feel (anxious/fearful) about my upcoming math quiz.
2. She admired his easy and (confident/presumptuous) attitude.
3. You are young and (naive/foolish), but you have a good head on your shoulders.
4. The new employee will not last long if he continues to be (lazy/leisurely).
5. I appreciate your (meticulous/picky) review of my term paper.

VOCABULARY PRACTICE
For more practice, go to the **Vocabulary Center** at **ClassZone.com**.

Reading-Writing Connection

Broaden your understanding of the selection from *Night* by responding to these prompts. Then use **Revision: Grammar and Style** to improve your writing.

WRITING PROMPTS	**SELF-CHECK**
A. Short Response: Write an Analysis Wiesel and his father were under the control of fellow prisoners as well as the Nazis. Write a **one- or two-paragraph analysis** of the status of each group of people in the camp.	*A strong analysis will . . .* • explain how the head of the block and the other Kapos help keep the prisoners under control • discuss the actions of Dr. Mengele
B. Extended Response: Write a Journal Entry Suppose that you were one of the soldiers who liberated Auschwitz from the Nazis. In **three to five paragraphs,** write a journal entry describing what you found in the camp.	*An effective journal entry will . . .* • discuss harsh conditions in the camp • use details from *Night* and the illustrations to describe the appearance of prisoners

REVISION: GRAMMAR AND STYLE

ESTABLISH TONE Review the **Grammar and Style** note on page 856. Tone, or the writer's attitude toward a subject, is established through the use of **imagery, word choice,** and **formal** or **informal language.** Wiesel's short, simple sentences and stark imagery help to convey the serious tone of his piece, allowing the tragic events to speak for themselves. In your own writing, make sure the language you choose matches the tone you wish to convey to your reader. Here is another example from the text:

> *Those whose numbers had been noted stood apart, abandoned by the whole world. Some were weeping in silence.*
>
> *The SS officers went away. The head of the block appeared, his face reflecting the general weariness.* (lines 82–85)

Notice how the revisions in red give this first draft a more serious tone. Revise your responses to the prompts by making sure your word choice, sentence structure, and use of imagery match the desired tone.

 **OHIO STANDARDS**

WRITING STANDARD
5.9 Use language and style as appropriate to audience and purpose

---

STUDENT MODEL

Although the Kapos ~~could push around~~ ⟨had some authority over⟩ other prisoners, they were completely under the control of Dr. Mengele. He had the power ~~to kill off~~ ⟨of life and death⟩ ~~any guy.~~

 **WRITING TOOLS**
For prewriting, revision, and editing tools, visit the **Writing Center** at ClassZone.com.

from **Farewell to Manzanar**

Memoir by Jeanne Wakatsuki Houston and James D. Houston

What if your government declared you the ENEMY?

OHIO STANDARDS

READING STANDARDS
2.3 Monitor comprehension
4.11 Explain ways author develops point of view and style

KEY IDEA What sort of government would harm innocent people just because of their ancestry? Unfortunately, such persecution has occurred in many nations, including our own. During World War II, the United States declared Japanese Americans to be **enemy** aliens and forced them into internment camps, a tragic event described in *Farewell to Manzanar.*

QUICKWRITE Governments often take unusual measures during times of crisis. Write one or two paragraphs discussing whether it is ever justifiable to limit the rights of citizens or legal residents who have committed no crimes.

● LITERARY ANALYSIS: CULTURAL CHARACTERISTICS

In memoirs, writers often provide information about their culture or about a particular time period in which they lived. When reading such accounts, readers can learn about the beliefs, values, traditions, and customs that are characteristic of a culture. For example, in *Farewell to Manzanar,* Wakatsuki makes the following statement about the customs of the Japanese diet:

Among the Japanese . . . rice is never eaten with sweet foods, only with salty or savory foods.

As you read about the Wakatsuki family, identify cultural beliefs, customs, traditions, or values and how these influence the family's actions and perceptions of events.

● READING STRATEGY: MONITOR

Memoirs often mix personal details with references to historical events. When you find it difficult to keep track of such information, you can use techniques such as the following to **monitor** your reading:

- Ask questions about events or ideas that are unclear, and then read to find the answers.
- Clarify your understanding by rereading passages, summarizing, or slowing down your reading pace.

As you read the excerpt from *Farewell to Manzanar,* use a chart to improve your comprehension of difficult passages.

Passage	Monitoring Technique
lines 1–13	I reread the paragraph to clear up my confusion about the different locations that are mentioned.

Review: **Make Inferences**

▲ VOCABULARY IN CONTEXT

The following words are used in *Farewell to Manzanar* to describe a family's ordeal. Which words do you already know? Use each of those words in a sentence. After you have read the selection, check your sentences to make sure you used the words correctly.

WORD LIST	inevitable	permeate	subordinate
	irrational	sinister	

Author On|ine

Coming to Terms
Jeanne Wakatsuki (wä-käts-ōō′kē) Houston was only seven when her family was forced to leave their home in California. The Wakatsukis were among the first Japanese Americans sent to the Manzanar internment camp and among the last to be released. Houston waited 25 years before describing her experience in *Farewell to Manzanar,* which she co-authored with her husband, James D. Houston. She says that writing was "a way of coming to terms with the impact these years have had on my entire life." The book won critical praise upon its publication in 1973 and helped publicize the unjust treatment of Japanese Americans during World War II.

Jeanne Wakatsuki Houston (born 1934) and James D. Houston (born 1933)

 MORE ABOUT THE AUTHOR
For more on Jeanne Wakatsuki Houston and James D. Houston, visit the **Literature Center** at **ClassZone.com.**

Background

Internment of Japanese Americans After Japan attacked Pearl Harbor and drew the United States into World War II, some officials feared that Japanese Americans would secretly aid Japan's war effort, although there was no evidence of their disloyalty. In February 1942, President Franklin Roosevelt signed an order that led to the removal of almost 120,000 Japanese Americans from their homes on the West Coast. With little notice, they were bused to ten "relocation" centers in Western states and Arkansas, where they were confined for the duration of the war.

Farewell *to* Manzanar

Jeanne Wakatsuki Houston and
James D. Houston

The American Friends Service[1] helped us find a small house in Boyle Heights, another minority ghetto, in downtown Los Angeles, now inhabited briefly by a few hundred Terminal Island refugees.[2] Executive Order 9066 had been signed by President Roosevelt, giving the War Department authority to define military areas in the western states and to exclude from them anyone who might threaten the war effort. There was a lot of talk about internment, or moving inland, or something like that in store for all Japanese Americans. I remember my brothers sitting around the table talking very intently about what we were going to do, how we would keep the family together. They had
10 seen how quickly Papa was removed, and they knew now that he would not be back for quite a while. Just before leaving Terminal Island, Mama had received her first letter, from Bismarck, North Dakota. He had been imprisoned at Fort Lincoln, in an all-male camp for enemy aliens.

Papa had been the patriarch. He had always decided everything in the family. With him gone, my brothers, like councilors in the absence of a chief, worried about what should be done. The ironic thing is, there wasn't much left to decide. These were mainly days of quiet, desperate waiting for what seemed at the time to be **inevitable.** There is a phrase the Japanese use in such situations, when something difficult must be endured.
20 You would hear the older heads, the Issei,[3] telling others very quietly, *"Shikata ga nai"* (It cannot be helped). *"Shikata ga nai"* (It must be done). Ⓐ

---

1. **American Friends Service:** a Quaker charity that often aids political and religious refugees and other displaced persons.

2. **Terminal Island refugees:** Shortly after Pearl Harbor was attacked, Japanese fishermen and cannery workers were forced to leave Terminal Island, which is located near Los Angeles.

3. **Issei** (ē′sā): people born in Japan who immigrate to the United States.

ANALYZE VISUALS
Surrounded by her family's belongings, a young girl awaits transportation to an internment camp. Why might this photograph be used to support criticism of the internment policy?

inevitable (ĭn-ĕv′ĭ-tə-bəl) *adj.* unavoidable

Ⓐ **CULTURAL CHARACTERISTICS**
Reread lines 14–21. What does this passage reveal about traditional Japanese attitudes toward adversity?

Mama and Woody went to work packing celery for a Japanese produce dealer. Kiyo and my sister May and I enrolled in the local school, and what sticks in my memory from those few weeks is the teacher—not her looks, her remoteness. In Ocean Park my teacher had been a kind, grandmotherly woman who used to sail with us in Papa's boat from time to time and who wept the day we had to leave. In Boyle Heights the teacher felt cold and distant. I was confused by all the moving and was having trouble with the classwork, but she would never help me out. She would have nothing to do with me. **B**

30   This was the first time I had felt outright hostility from a Caucasian. Looking back, it is easy enough to explain. Public attitudes toward the Japanese in California were shifting rapidly. In the first few months of the Pacific war, America was on the run. Tolerance had turned to distrust and **irrational** fear. The hundred-year-old tradition of anti-Orientalism on the west coast soon resurfaced, more vicious than ever. Its result became clear about a month later, when we were told to make our third and final move.

The name Manzanar meant nothing to us when we left Boyle Heights. We didn't know where it was or what it was. We went because the government ordered us to. And, in the case of my older brothers and sisters, we went with
40   a certain amount of relief. They had all heard stories of Japanese homes being attacked, of beatings in the streets of California towns. They were as frightened of the Caucasians as Caucasians were of us. Moving, under what appeared to be government protection, to an area less directly threatened by the war seemed not such a bad idea at all. For some it actually sounded like a fine adventure.

Our pickup point was a Buddhist church in Los Angeles. It was very early, and misty, when we got there with our luggage. Mama had bought heavy coats for all of us. She grew up in eastern Washington and knew that anywhere inland in early April would be cold. I was proud of my new coat, and I remember sitting on a duffel bag trying to be friendly with the Greyhound driver. I smiled at him.
50 He didn't smile back. He was befriending no one. Someone tied a numbered tag to my collar and to the duffel bag (each family was given a number, and that became our official designation until the camps were closed), someone else passed out box lunches for the trip, and we climbed aboard.

I had never been outside Los Angeles County, never traveled more than ten miles from the coast, had never even ridden on a bus. I was full of excitement, the way any kid would be, and wanted to look out the window. But for the first few hours the shades were drawn. Around me other people played cards, read magazines, dozed, waiting. I settled back, waiting too, and finally fell sleep. The bus felt very secure to me. Almost half its passengers were immediate relatives.
60 Mama and my older brothers had succeeded in keeping most of us together, on the same bus, headed for the same camp. I didn't realize until much later what a job that was. The strategy had been, first, to have everyone living in the same district when the evacuation began, and then to get all of us included under the same family number, even though names had been changed by marriage. Many families weren't as lucky as ours and suffered months of anguish while trying to arrange transfers from one camp to another.

B MONITOR
What might explain the unfriendly behavior of the teacher in Boyle Heights? To clarify, read on and check your answer.

irrational (ĭ-răsh′ə-nəl) *adj.* not possessed with reason or understanding

These Japanese Americans are riding to an assembly center, where they will be held until their transfer to an internment camp.

We rode all day. By the time we reached our destination, the shades were up. It was late afternoon. The first thing I saw was a yellow swirl across a blurred, reddish setting sun. The bus was being pelted by what sounded like splattering
70 rain. It wasn't rain. This was my first look at something I would soon know very well, a billowing flurry of dust and sand churned up by the wind through Owens Valley.[4]

We drove past a barbed-wire fence, through a gate, and into an open space where trunks and sacks and packages had been dumped from the baggage trucks that drove out ahead of us. I could see a few tents set up, the first rows of black barracks, and beyond them, blurred by sand, rows of barracks that seemed to spread for miles across this plain. People were sitting on cartons or milling around, with their backs to the wind, waiting to see which friends or relatives might be on this bus. As we approached, they turned or stood up,
80 and some moved toward us expectantly. But inside the bus no one stirred. No one waved or spoke. They just stared out the windows, ominously silent. I didn't understand this. Hadn't we finally arrived, our whole family intact? I opened a window, leaned out, and yelled happily. "Hey! This whole bus is full of Wakatsukis!" **C**

Outside, the greeters smiled. Inside there was an explosion of laughter, hysterical, tension-breaking laughter that left my brothers choking and whacking each other across the shoulders.

C MAKE INFERENCES
Why were people in the bus "ominously silent" upon their arrival at the camp?

---

4. **Owens Valley:** the valley of the Owens River in south-central California west of Death Valley, where Manzanar was built. The once lush and green valley had become dry and deserted in the 1930s after water was diverted to an aqueduct supplying Los Angeles.

We had pulled up just in time for dinner. The mess halls weren't completed yet. An outdoor chow line snaked around a half-finished building that broke
90 a good part of the wind. They issued us army mess kits, the round metal kind that fold over, and plopped in scoops of canned Vienna sausage, canned string beans, steamed rice that had been cooked too long, and on top of the rice a serving of canned apricots. The Caucasian servers were thinking that the fruit poured over rice would make a good dessert. Among the Japanese, of course, rice is never eaten with sweet foods, only with salty or savory foods. Few of us could eat such a mixture. But at this point no one dared protest. It would have been impolite. I was horrified when I saw the apricot syrup seeping through my little mound of rice. I opened my mouth to complain. My mother jabbed me in the back to keep quiet. We moved on through the line and joined the
100 others squatting in the lee[5] of half-raised walls, dabbing courteously at what was, for almost everyone there, an inedible concoction. **D**

After dinner we were taken to Block 16, a cluster of fifteen barracks that had just been finished a day or so earlier—although finished was hardly the word for it. The shacks were built of one thickness of pine planking covered with tarpaper. They sat on concrete footings, with about two feet of open space between the floorboards and the ground. Gaps showed between the planks,

D CULTURAL CHARACTERISTICS
How does the cultural information in lines 90–101 help you understand the experience of the Japanese Americans?

---

5. **lee:** the side sheltered from the wind.

In the mess halls of internment camps, Japanese Americans were served unfamiliar foods such as sausages.

and as the weeks passed and the green wood dried out, the gaps widened. Knotholes gaped in the uncovered floor.

Each barracks was divided into six units, sixteen by twenty feet, about
110 the size of a living room, with one bare bulb hanging from the ceiling and an oil stove for heat. We were assigned two of these for the twelve people in our family group; and our official family "number" was enlarged by three digits—16 plus the number of this barracks. We were issued steel army cots, two brown army blankets each, and some mattress covers, which my brothers stuffed with straw. **E**

The first task was to divide up what space we had for sleeping. Bill and Woody contributed a blanket each and partitioned off the first room: one side for Bill and Tomi, one side for Woody and Chizu and their baby girl. Woody also got the stove, for heating formulas.

120 The people who had it hardest during the first few months were young couples like these, many of whom had married just before the evacuation began, in order not to be separated and sent to different camps. Our two rooms were crowded, but at least it was all in the family. My oldest sister and her husband were shoved into one of those sixteen-by-twenty-foot compartments with six people they had never seen before—two other couples, one recently married like themselves, the other with two teenage boys. Partitioning off a room like that wasn't easy. It was bitter cold when we arrived, and the wind did not abate. All they had to use for room dividers were those army blankets, two of which were barely enough to keep one person warm. They argued over whose blanket should
130 be sacrificed and later argued about noise at night—the parents wanted their boys asleep by 9:00 P.M.—and they continued arguing over matters like that for six months, until my sister and her husband left to harvest sugar beets in Idaho. It was grueling work up there, and wages were pitiful, but when the call came through camp for workers to alleviate the wartime labor shortage, it sounded better than their life at Manzanar. They knew they'd have, if nothing else, a room, perhaps a cabin of their own.

That first night in Block 16, the rest of us squeezed into the second room— Granny; Lillian, age fourteen; Ray, thirteen; May, eleven; Kiyo, ten; Mama; and me. I didn't mind this at all at the time. Being youngest meant I got to
140 sleep with Mama. And before we went to bed I had a great time jumping up and down on the mattress. The boys had stuffed so much straw into hers, we had to flatten it some so we wouldn't slide off. I slept with her every night after that until Papa came back.

We woke early, shivering and coated with dust that had blown up through the knotholes and in through the slits around the doorway. During the night Mama had unpacked all our clothes and heaped them on our beds for warmth. Now our cubicle looked as if a great laundry bag had exploded and then been sprayed with fine dust. A skin of sand covered the floor. I looked over Mama's shoulder at Kiyo, on top of his fat mattress, buried under jeans and overcoats
150 and sweaters. His eyebrows were gray, and he was starting to giggle. He was looking at me, at my gray eyebrows and coated hair, and pretty soon we were

E MONITOR
What strategy would you use to clarify the information in lines 109–115?

both giggling. I looked at Mama's face to see if she thought Kiyo was funny. She lay very still next to me on our mattress, her eyes scanning everything— bare rafters, walls, dusty kids—scanning slowly, and I think the mask of her face would have cracked had not Woody's voice just then come at us through the wall. He was rapping on the planks as if testing to see if they were hollow.

"Hey!" he yelled. "You guys fall into the same flour barrel as us?"

"No," Kiyo yelled back. "Ours is full of Japs."

All of us laughed at this.

160   "Well, tell 'em it's time to get up," Woody said. "If we're gonna live in this place, we better get to work."

He gave us ten minutes to dress, then he came in carrying a broom, a hammer, and a sack full of tin can lids he had scrounged somewhere. Woody would be our leader for a while now, short, stocky, grinning behind his mustache. He had just turned twenty-four. In later years he would tour the country with Mr. Moto, the Japanese tag-team wrestler, as his **sinister** assistant Suki— karate chops through the ropes from outside the ring, a chunky leg reaching from under his kimono to trip up Mr. Moto's foe. In the ring Woody's smile looked sly and crafty; he hammed it up. Offstage it was whimsical, as if

170 some joke were bursting to be told.

"Hey, brother Ray, Kiyo," he said. "You see these tin can lids?"

"Yeah, yeah," the boys said drowsily, as if going back to sleep. They were both young versions of Woody.

"You see all them knotholes in the floor and in the walls?"

They looked around. You could see about a dozen.

Woody said, "You get those covered up before breakfast time. Any more sand comes in here through one of them knotholes, you have to eat it off the floor with ketchup."

"What about sand that comes in through the cracks?" Kiyo said.

180 Woody stood up very straight, which in itself was funny, since he was only about five-foot-six.

"Don't worry about the cracks," he said. "Different kind of sand comes in through the cracks."

He put his hands on his hips and gave Kiyo a sternly comic look, squinting at him through one eye the way Papa would when he was asserting his authority. Woody mimicked Papa's voice: "And I can tell the difference. So be careful."

The boys laughed and went to work nailing down lids. May started sweeping out the sand. I was helping Mama fold the clothes we'd used for cover, when Woody came over and put his arms around her shoulder. He was

190 short; she was even shorter, under five feet.

He said softly, "You okay, Mama?"

She didn't look at him, she just kept folding clothes and said, "Can we get the cracks covered too, Woody?"

Outside the sky was clear, but icy gusts of wind were buffeting our barracks every few minutes, sending fresh dust puffs up through the floorboards. May's broom could barely keep up with it, and our oil heater could scarcely hold its own against the drafts. **F**

sinister (sĭn′ĭ-stər) *adj.* threatening or foreshadowing evil

F MONITOR
Why is sand still entering the room even though the knotholes have been covered? If necessary, do some rereading or skimming to find the answer.

Dust storms frequently blew through the 550-acre Manzanar internment camp, which was located 200 miles northeast of Los Angeles at the foot of the Sierra Nevada mountains.

"We'll get this whole place as tight as a barrel, Mama. I already met a guy who told me where they pile all the scrap lumber."

200 "Scrap?"

"That's all they got. I mean, they're still building the camp, you know. Sixteen blocks left to go. After that, they say maybe we'll get some stuff to fix the insides a little bit."

Her eyes blazed then, her voice quietly furious. "Woody, we can't live like this. Animals live like this."

It was hard to get Woody down. He'd keep smiling when everybody else was ready to explode. Grief flickered in his eyes. He blinked it away and hugged her tighter. "We'll make it better, Mama. You watch."

We could hear voices in other cubicles now. Beyond the wall Woody's baby
210 girl started to cry.

"I have to go over to the kitchen," he said, "see if those guys got a pot for heating bottles. That oil stove takes too long—something wrong with the fuel line. I'll find out what they're giving us for breakfast."

"Probably hotcakes with soy sauce," Kiyo said, on his hands and knees between the bunks.

"No." Woody grinned, heading out the door. "Rice. With Log Cabin syrup and melted butter."

I don't remember what we ate that first morning. I know we stood for half an hour in cutting wind waiting to get our food. Then we took it back to the

Internees at Manzanar used boxes and scrap material to make their housing more comfortable.

ANALYZE VISUALS
How does this photograph reflect the attitudes of people depicted in the selection?

220　cubicle and ate huddled around the stove. Inside, it was warmer than when we
left, because Woody was already making good his promise to Mama, tacking
up some ends of lath[6] he'd found, stuffing rolled paper around the door frame.

　　Trouble was, he had almost nothing to work with. Beyond this temporary
weather stripping, there was little else he could do. Months went by, in fact,
before our "home" changed much at all from what it was the day we moved in—
bare floors, blanket partitions, one bulb in each compartment dangling from a
roof beam, and open ceilings overhead so that mischievous boys like Ray and
Kiyo could climb up into the rafters and peek into anyone's life.

　　The simple truth is the camp was no more ready for us when we got there
230　than we were ready for it. We had only the dimmest ideas of what to expect.
Most of the families, like us, had moved out from southern California with
as much luggage as each person could carry. Some old men left Los Angeles
wearing Hawaiian shirts and Panama hats and stepped off the bus at an altitude
of 4000 feet, with nothing available but sagebrush and tarpaper to stop the
April winds pouring down off the back side of the Sierras.[7]

　　The War Department was in charge of all the camps at this point. They
began to issue military surplus from the First World War—olive-drab knit caps,
earmuffs, peacoats, canvas leggings. Later on, sewing machines were shipped
in, and one barracks was turned into a clothing factory. An old seamstress
240　took a peacoat of mine, tore the lining out, opened and flattened the sleeves,
added a collar, put arm holes in and handed me back a beautiful cape. By fall,
dozens of seamstresses were working full-time transforming thousands of these

---

　6.　**lath** (lăth): a thin strip of wood.

　7.　**Sierras** (sē-ĕr′əz): the Sierra Nevada mountain range in eastern California.

old army clothes into capes, slacks, and stylish coats. But until that factory got going and packages from friends outside began to fill out our wardrobes, warmth was more important than style. I couldn't help laughing at Mama walking around in army earmuffs and a pair of wide-cuffed, khaki-colored wool trousers several sizes too big for her. Japanese are generally smaller than Caucasians, and almost all these clothes were oversize. They flopped, they dangled, they hung.

250   It seems comical, looking back; we were a band of Charlie Chaplins[8] marooned in the California desert. But at the time, it was pure chaos. That's the only way to describe it. The evacuation had been so hurriedly planned, the camps so hastily thrown together, nothing was completed when we got there, and almost nothing worked.

I was sick continually, with stomach cramps and diarrhea. At first it was from the shots they gave us for typhoid, in very heavy doses and in assembly-line fashion: swab, jab, swab, *Move along now,* swab, jab, swab, *Keep it moving.* That knocked all of us younger kids down at once, with fevers and vomiting. Later, it was the food that made us sick, young and old alike. The kitchens
260 were too small and badly ventilated. Food would spoil from being left out too long. That summer, when the heat got fierce, it would spoil faster. The refrigeration kept breaking down. The cooks, in many cases, had never cooked before. Each block had to provide its own volunteers. Some were lucky and had a professional or two in their midst. But the first chef in our block had been a gardener all his life and suddenly found himself preparing three meals a day for 250 people. **G**

"The Manzanar runs" became a condition of life, and you only hoped that when you rushed to the latrine,[9] one would be in working order.

That first morning, on our way to the chow line, Mama and I tried to use the
270 women's latrine in our block. The smell of it spoiled what little appetite we had. Outside, men were working in an open trench, up to their knees in muck—a common sight in the months to come. Inside, the floor was covered with excrement, and all twelve bowls were erupting like a row of tiny volcanoes.

Mama stopped a kimono-wrapped woman stepping past us with her sleeve pushed up against her nose and asked, "What do you do?"

"Try Block Twelve," the woman said, grimacing. "They have just finished repairing the pipes."

It was about two city blocks away. We followed her over there and found a line of women waiting in the wind outside the latrine. We had no choice but
280 to join the line and wait with them.

Inside it was like all the other latrines. Each block was built to the same design just as each of the ten camps, from California to Arkansas, was built to a common master plan. It was an open room, over a concrete slab. The sink was a long metal trough against one wall, with a row of spigots for hot and cold

G MONITOR
How would you summarize the information in lines 255–266?

8. **Charlie Chaplins:** Charlie Chaplin, an actor and director, portrayed a tramp in baggy clothing in comedy films of the 1920s and 1930s.

9. **latrine:** a communal toilet in a camp or barracks.

water. Down the center of the room twelve toilet bowls were arranged in six pairs, back to back, with no partitions. My mother was a very modest person, and this was going to be agony for her, sitting down in public, among strangers.

One old woman had already solved the problem for herself by dragging in a large cardboard carton. She set it up around one of the bowls, like a three-sided screen. OXYDOL was printed in large black letters down the front. I remember this well, because that was the soap we were issued for laundry; later on, the smell of it would **permeate** these rooms. The upended carton was about four feet high. The old woman behind it wasn't much taller. When she stood, only her head showed over the top.

She was about Granny's age. With great effort she was trying to fold the sides of the screen together. Mama happened to be at the head of the line now. As she approached the vacant bowl, she and the old woman bowed to each other from the waist. Mama then moved to help her with the carton, and the old woman said very graciously, in Japanese, "Would you like to use it?"

Happily, gratefully, Mama bowed again and said, *"Arigato"* (Thank you). *"Arigato gozaimas"* (Thank you very much). "I will return it to your barracks."

"Oh, no. It is not necessary. I will be glad to wait."

The old woman unfolded one side of the cardboard, while Mama opened the other; then she bowed again and scurried out the door.

Those big cartons were a common sight in the spring of 1942. Eventually sturdier partitions appeared, one or two at a time. The first were built of scrap lumber. Word would get around that Block such and such had partitions now, and Mama and my older sisters would walk halfway across the camp to use them. Even after every latrine in camp was screened, this quest for privacy continued. Many would wait in line at night. Ironically, because of this, midnight was often the most crowded time of all. **H**

Like so many of the women there, Mama never did get used to the latrines. It was a humiliation she just learned to endure: *shikata ga nai,* this cannot be helped. She would quickly **subordinate** her own desires to those of the family or the community, because she knew cooperation was the only way to survive. At the same time, she placed a high premium on personal privacy, respected it in others and insisted upon it for herself. Almost everyone at Manzanar had inherited this pair of traits from the generations before them who had learned to live in a small, crowded country like Japan. Because of the first, they were able to take a desolate stretch of wasteland and gradually make it livable. But the entire situation there, especially in the beginning—the packed sleeping quarters, the communal mess halls, the open toilets—all this was an open insult to that other, private self, a slap in the face you were powerless to challenge. ❧

290

300

310

320

permeate (pûr′mē-āt′) *v.* to spread or flow throughout

H **GRAMMAR AND STYLE**
Reread lines 305–311. Notice how the authors use a variety of **simple, complex,** and **compound-complex sentences** to add rhythm and interest to their writing.

subordinate (sə-bôr′dn-āt′) *v.* to lower in rank or importance

Comprehension

1. **Recall** Why were the Wakatsukis sent to Manzanar?

2. **Recall** What kind of housing were they given?

3. **Recall** Why did Mama have to borrow the cardboard box?

4. **Summarize** How did the Wakatsukis and other Japanese Americans improve conditions at the camp?

OHIO STANDARDS

READING STANDARD
2.3 Monitor comprehension

Literary Analysis

5. **Examine Monitoring Strategies** Review the chart you created as you read. Identify the strategy that you used most often to monitor your comprehension, and discuss why it was helpful.

6. **Identify Cultural Characteristics** What did you learn about Japanese beliefs, values, and customs as you read the excerpt from *Farewell to Manzanar*? Cite examples.

7. **Analyze Character Traits** What character traits helped Jeanne and her siblings adjust to life at Manzanar? Cite evidence from the text to support your answer.

8. **Analyze Cause and Effect** The people in charge of Manzanar knew little about Japanese culture. How did their lack of knowledge affect conditions in the camp? Provide examples to support your answer.

9. **Compare Texts** Both Elie Wiesel and Jeanne Wakatsuki Houston were treated unjustly by their governments. Use a graphic organizer like the one shown to compare and contrast their experiences.

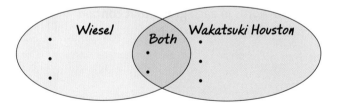

Wiesel — Both — Wakatsuki Houston

10. **Draw Conclusions** In the foreword to *Farewell to Manzanar*, Jeanne Wakatsuki Houston says, "It has taken me 25 years to reach the point where I could talk openly about Manzanar." Why might it have taken her so long to be able to discuss her experience?

Literary Criticism

11. **Historical Context** In your opinion, could a forced internment, like the one experienced by the Wakatsuki family, happen in the United States today? Explain why or why not.

Vocabulary in Context

VOCABULARY PRACTICE

Decide whether each statement is true or false.

1. Something **inevitable** can be easily avoided.
2. A person who displays sound reasoning and judgment is **irrational.**
3. The stench of garbage can **permeate** the room.
4. A letter that talks of evil to come can be described as **sinister.**
5. To **subordinate** your feelings is to share them openly with others.

VOCABULARY IN WRITING

Use three or more vocabulary words to write about the decision to intern Japanese Americans during World War II. Here is an example of how you might begin.

> **EXAMPLE SENTENCE**
>
> We should not assume that this tragic decision was ***inevitable.***

VOCABULARY STRATEGY: THE PREFIX *in-*

In- at the beginning of a word may be a prefix meaning "not," as in the vocabulary word *inevitable,* which means "not evitable (avoidable)." When the prefix *in-* precedes certain letters, it is spelled *il-, im-,* or *ir-.* For example, the vocabulary word *irrational,* meaning "not rational," begins with *ir-.* If you can identify a root or a base word in words like these, you can often figure out their meanings.

PRACTICE Use a dictionary to help you find two words in each group that contain a prefix meaning "not." Then write a short definition of each word.

1. inconsiderate, incentive, incompetent
2. insensitive, inattentive, indulge
3. illiterate, illogical, illuminate
4. imaginary, impartial, immortal
5. irresponsible, irritable, irreversible

OHIO STANDARDS

VOCABULARY STANDARD
1.5 Use knowledge of prefixes to understand words

VOCABULARY PRACTICE
For more practice, go to the **Vocabulary Center** at **ClassZone.com.**

Reading-Writing Connection

Enhance your understanding of the selection from *Farewell to Manzanar* by responding to these prompts. Then use **Revision: Grammar and Style** to improve your writing.

WRITING PROMPTS	SELF-CHECK

A. Short Response: Write an Analysis

In *Farewell to Manzanar*, Jeanne and her siblings are especially concerned about Mama. In **one or two paragraphs,** analyze why Mama found it more difficult than her children to adjust to life at Manzanar.

An insightful analysis will . . .

- discuss the absence of Jeanne's father and his role in the family
- consider how younger generations of Japanese Americans differed from older generations

B. Extended Response: Write an Editorial

Suppose that you worked for a newspaper during World War II. Write a **three-to-five-paragraph editorial** about the government's policy of interning **"enemy"** Japanese Americans.

An effective editorial will . . .

- clearly state a position on the internment policy
- include details about life in an internment camp

REVISION: GRAMMAR AND STYLE

VARY SENTENCE STRUCTURE Review the **Grammar and Style** note on page 876. To improve the cadence of your writing, be sure to employ a variety of sentence structures. A **simple** sentence consists of one independent clause and no subordinate clauses. A **compound** sentence consists of two or more independent clauses joined together. A **complex** sentence consists of one independent clause and one or more subordinate clauses. A **compound-complex** sentence consists of two or more independent clauses and one or more subordinate clauses. In the following example, notice how the writers use a variety of simple, complex, and compound-complex sentences to create an effective description.

OHIO STANDARDS

WRITING STANDARD
5.7 Use simple, compound and complex sentences

> *I remember this well, because that was the soap we were issued for laundry; later on, the smell of it would permeate these rooms. The upended carton was about four feet high. The old woman behind it wasn't much taller. When she stood, only her head showed over the top.* (lines 290–294)

Notice how the revisions in red relieve the monotony of this first draft by changing simple sentences to complex and compound-complex sentences.

STUDENT MODEL

Although
~~T~~he Japanese Americans in the camps have done nothing wrong, ~~Yet~~ they receive worse treatment than most criminals. They live in drafty barracks, *and* They must use filthy latrines. *that* Often ~~the latrines~~ do not work.

WRITING TOOLS
For prewriting, revision, and editing tools, visit the **Writing Center** at ClassZone.com.

Montgomery Boycott

Memoir by Coretta Scott King

How can we
CHANGE *society?*

OHIO STANDARDS

READING STANDARDS
3.5 Analyze an author's argument
4.2 Analyze the features of setting and their importance in a literary text

KEY IDEA You don't have to be rich or powerful to **change** society. In "Montgomery Boycott," Coretta Scott King describes how a major triumph in the civil rights movement started when a seamstress refused to give up her seat on a bus.

DISCUSS Think of something you would like to change in your community. For example, you might see a need for more parks or afterschool programs. With a classmate, discuss specific actions you could take to help make this change.

● LITERARY ANALYSIS: HISTORICAL EVENTS IN MEMOIRS

Memoirs often contain information about historical events in which the writer was involved. For example, in "Montgomery Boycott," Coretta Scott King shares her memory of the events that sparked the 1955 bus boycott in Montgomery, Alabama. While reading a memoir such as King's, you can gain a new perspective on a historical event as well as learn in-depth information about it.

As you read, look for statements that convey information about the Montgomery bus boycott, the events leading up to it, and Martin Luther King Jr.'s involvement.

● READING SKILL: DISTINGUISH FACT FROM OPINION

Memoirs can offer an intimate view of the past through a mixture of facts and opinions. A **fact** is a statement that can be verified using a reliable source, such as an encyclopedia. An **opinion** is a personal belief that cannot be proved. King often expresses opinions when she uses adjectives to describe people or historical circumstances.

As you read, use a chart like this one to identify important facts and the opinions of King or her husband. Underline parts of opinion statements that cannot be proved.

Facts	Opinions
"…in March 1955, … fifteen-year-old Claudette Colvin refused to give up her seat to a white passenger."	"Of all the facets of segregation in Montgomery, <u>the most degrading</u> were the rules of the Montgomery City Bus Lines."

▲ VOCABULARY IN CONTEXT

King uses the following boldfaced words to describe a crucial event in the civil rights movement. Figure out the meaning of each word from the context of the phrase.

1. employees humiliated by **degrading** work conditions
2. a **boycott** of the company until our demands are met
3. a clever **tactic** to get what they want
4. angry members urging a more **militant** protest
5. ending the **perpetuation** of injustice
6. authorities using **coercion** to control people

Author Online

Civil Rights Champion
As a child in Alabama, Coretta Scott had to walk five miles a day to a one-room schoolhouse while white children rode past her on a school bus. That experience and others made her determined to struggle for racial equality. She worked fearlessly with her

Coretta Scott King
1927–2006

husband, Martin Luther King Jr., during his leadership of the civil rights movement, refusing to be intimidated after the 1956 bombing of their home. After her husband's assassination in 1968, she remained a tireless champion in the struggle for racial justice, most notably as founder of the Martin Luther King Jr. Center for Nonviolent Social Change in Atlanta, Georgia. "Montgomery Boycott" is taken from her book *My Life with Martin Luther King, Jr.*, which she wrote shortly after his death.

 MORE ABOUT THE AUTHOR
For more on Coretta Scott King, visit the **Literature Center** at **ClassZone.com**.

Background

The Civil Rights Movement Prior to 1954, many states, especially in the South, had laws to ensure segregation, the complete separation of the races in public places. After World War II, however, opponents of these laws began to challenge their legality. In 1954, the Supreme Court ruled that it was unconstitutional to force whites and blacks to attend separate schools. Soon afterward, African Americans in Montgomery, Alabama, began the bus boycott that is the subject of this selection. The Montgomery boycott, which lasted for 381 days, brought about an end to segregation on public buses.

MONTGOMERY *BOYCOTT*

CORETTA SCOTT KING

Of all the facets of segregation in Montgomery, the most **degrading** were the rules of the Montgomery City Bus Lines. This northern-owned corporation outdid the South itself. Although seventy percent of its passengers were black, it treated them like cattle—worse than that, for nobody insults a cow. The first seats on all buses were reserved for whites. Even if they were unoccupied and the rear seats crowded, blacks would have to stand at the back in case some whites might get aboard; and if the front seats happened to be occupied and more white people boarded the bus, black people seated in the rear were forced to get up and give them their seats. Furthermore—and I don't think
10 northerners ever realized this—blacks had to pay their fares at the front of the bus, get off, and walk to the rear door to board again. Sometimes the bus would drive off without them after they had paid their fare. This would happen to elderly people or pregnant women, in bad weather or good, and was considered a joke by the drivers. Frequently the white bus drivers abused their passengers, calling them . . . black cows, or black apes. Imagine what it was like, for example, for a black man to get on a bus with his son and be subjected to such treatment. **A**

There had been one incident in March 1955, when fifteen-year-old Claudette Colvin refused to give up her seat to a white passenger. The high
20 school girl was handcuffed and carted off to the police station. At that time Martin served on a committee to protest to the city and bus-company officials. The committee was received politely—and nothing was done.

The fuel that finally made that slow-burning fire blaze up was an almost routine incident. On December 1, 1955, Mrs. Rosa Parks, a forty-two-year-old seamstress whom my husband aptly described as "a charming person with a

degrading (dĭ-grā′dĭng) *adj.* tending or intended to cause dishonor or disgrace

A HISTORICAL EVENTS
What information in lines 1–17 helps you understand the motivation for the boycott?

ANALYZE VISUALS
What impression of Martin Luther King Jr. do you get from this photograph?

Rosa Parks being fingerprinted by a Montgomery sheriff after she refused to give up her seat on a bus

radiant personality," boarded a bus to go home after a long day working and shopping. The bus was crowded, and Mrs. Parks found a seat at the beginning of the black section. At the next stop more whites got on. The driver ordered Mrs. Parks to give her seat to a white man who boarded; this meant that she 30 would have to stand all the way home. Rosa Parks was not in a revolutionary frame of mind. She had not planned to do what she did. Her cup had run over. As she said later, "I was just plain tired, and my feet hurt." So she sat there, refusing to get up. The driver called a policeman, who arrested her and took her to the courthouse. From there Mrs. Parks called E. D. Nixon, who came down and signed a bail bond for her.

Mr. Nixon was a fiery Alabamian. He was a Pullman porter who had been active in A. Philip Randolph's Brotherhood of Sleeping Car Porters,[1] and in civil rights activities. Suddenly he also had had enough; suddenly, it seemed, almost every African American in Montgomery had had enough. It was 40 spontaneous combustion.[2] Phones began ringing all over the black section of the city. The Women's Political Council suggested a one-day **boycott** of the buses as a protest. E. D. Nixon courageously agreed to organize it. **B**

boycott (boi′kŏt′) *n.* a form of protest in which a group stops using a specific service or product in order to force a change

B DISTINGUISH FACT FROM OPINION
Which details in lines 36–42 are factual, and which ones are opinion?

---

1. **Pullman . . . Sleeping Car Porters:** Pullman porters were railroad employees who served passengers on Pullman sleeping cars, which had seats that could be converted into beds. The Brotherhood of Sleeping Car Porters was the first successful black labor union.

2. **spontaneous combustion** (spŏn-tā′nē-əs kəm-bŭs′chən): literally, the situation that occurs when something bursts into flames on its own, without the addition of heat from an outside source.

The first we knew about it was when Mr. Nixon called my husband early in the morning of Friday, December 2. He had already talked to Ralph Abernathy.[3] After describing the incident, Mr. Nixon said, "We have taken this type of thing too long. I feel the time has come to boycott the buses. It's the only way to make the white folks see that we will not take this sort of thing any longer."

Martin agreed with him and offered the Dexter Avenue Church as a meeting place. After much telephoning, a meeting of black ministers and civic leaders
50 was arranged for that evening. Martin said later that as he approached his church Friday evening, he was nervously wondering how many leaders would really turn up. To his delight, Martin found over forty people, representing every segment of African-American life, crowded into the large meeting room at Dexter. There were doctors, lawyers, businessmen, federal-government employees, union leaders, and a great many ministers. The latter were particularly welcome, not only because of their influence, but because it meant that they were beginning to accept Martin's view that "religion deals with both heaven and earth. . . . Any religion that professes to be concerned with the souls of men and is not concerned with the slums that doom them, the economic
60 conditions that strangle them, and the social conditions that cripple them, is dry-as-dust religion." From that very first step, the Christian ministry provided the leadership of our struggle, as Christian ideals were its source. **C**

Martin told me after he got home that the meeting was almost wrecked because questions or suggestions from the floor were cut off. However, after a stormy session, one thing was clear: however much they differed on details, everyone was unanimously for a boycott. It was set for Monday, December 5. Committees were organized; all the ministers present promised to urge their congregations to take part. Several thousand leaflets were printed on the church mimeograph machine, describing the reasons for the boycott and urging all
70 blacks not to ride buses "to work, to town, to school, or anyplace on Monday, December 5." Everyone was asked to come to a mass meeting at the Holt Street Baptist Church on Monday evening for further instructions. The Reverend A. W. Wilson had offered his church because it was larger than Dexter and more convenient, being in the center of the black district.

Saturday was a busy day for Martin and the other members of the committee. They hustled around town talking with other leaders, arranging with the black-owned taxi companies for special bulk fares and with the owners of private automobiles to get the people to and from work. I could do little to help because Yoki[4] was only two weeks old, and my physician, Dr. W.
80 D. Pettus, who was very careful, advised me to stay in for a month. However, I was kept busy answering the telephone, which rang continuously, and coordinating from that central point the many messages and arrangements.

Our greatest concern was how we were going to reach the fifty thousand black people of Montgomery, no matter how hard we worked. The white press,

C HISTORICAL EVENTS
What disagreement within the African-American community did King need to overcome in order to build an effective movement?

---

3. **Ralph Abernathy** (1926–1990): a minister who became a close colleague of Martin Luther King Jr.'s, and an important civil rights leader.

4. **Yoki:** nickname of the Kings' daughter Yolanda.

in an outraged exposé, spread the word for us in a way that would have been impossible with only our own resources.

As it happened, a white woman found one of our leaflets, which her black maid had left in the kitchen. The irate woman immediately telephoned the newspapers to let the white community know what the blacks were up to. We laughed a lot about this, and Martin later said that we owed them a great debt.

On Sunday morning, from their pulpits, almost every African-American minister in town urged people to honor the boycott.

Martin came home late Sunday night and began to read the morning paper. The long articles about the proposed boycott accused the NAACP[5] of planting Mrs. Parks on the bus—she had been a volunteer secretary for the Montgomery chapter—and likened the boycott to the **tactics** of the White Citizens Councils.[6] This upset Martin. That awesome conscience of his began to gnaw at him, and he wondered if he was doing the right thing. Alone in his study, he struggled with the question of whether the boycott method was basically unchristian. Certainly it could be used for unethical ends. But, as he said, "We were using it to give birth to freedom . . . and to urge men to comply with the law of the land. Our concern was not to put the bus company out of business, but to put justice in business." He recalled Thoreau's[7] words, "We can no longer lend our cooperation to an evil system," and he thought, "He who accepts evil without protesting against it is really cooperating with it." Later Martin wrote, "From this moment on I conceived of our movement as an act of massive noncooperation. From then on I rarely used the word 'boycott.'"

Serene after his inner struggle, Martin joined me in our sitting room. We wanted to get to bed early, but Yoki began crying and the telephone kept ringing. Between interruptions we sat together talking about the prospects for the success of the protest. We were both filled with doubt. Attempted boycotts had failed in Montgomery and other cities. Because of changing times and tempers, this one seemed to have a better chance, but it was still a slender hope. We finally decided that if the boycott was sixty percent effective we would be doing all right, and we would be satisfied to have made a good start.

A little after midnight we finally went to bed, but at five-thirty the next morning we were up and dressed again. The first bus was due at six o'clock at the bus stop just outside our house. We had coffee and toast in the kitchen; then I went into the living room to watch. Right on time, the bus came, headlights blazing through the December darkness, all lit up inside. I shouted, "Martin! Martin, come quickly!" He ran in and stood beside me, his face lit with excitement. There was not one person on that usually crowded bus!

We stood together waiting for the next bus. It was empty too, and this was

tactic (tăk′tĭk) *n.* a planned action or maneuver to reach a certain goal

---

5. **NAACP:** the National Association for the Advancement of Colored People, a prominent civil rights organization.

6. **White Citizens Councils:** groups that formed, first in Mississippi and then throughout the South, to resist the 1954 Supreme Court decision to desegregate the schools.

7. **Thoreau** (thə-rō′): Henry David Thoreau (1817–1862), American writer whose famous essay "Civil Disobedience" helped inspire the ideas of nonviolent resistance used in the civil rights movement.

African Americans walking to work during the third month of the bus boycott

the most heavily traveled line in the whole city. Bus after empty bus paused at the stop and moved on. We were so excited we could hardly speak coherently. Finally Martin said, "I'm going to take the car and see what's happening other places in the city."

He picked up Ralph Abernathy and they cruised together around the city. Martin told me about it when he got home. Everywhere it was the same—a few
130 white people and maybe one or two blacks in otherwise empty buses. Martin and Ralph saw extraordinary sights—the sidewalks crowded with men and women trudging to work; the students of Alabama State College walking or thumbing rides; taxicabs with people clustered in them. Some of our people rode mules; others went in horse-drawn buggies. But most of them were walking, some making a round-trip of as much as twelve miles. Martin later wrote, "As I watched them I knew that there is nothing more majestic than the determined courage of individuals willing to suffer and sacrifice for their freedom and dignity."

Martin rushed off again at nine o'clock that morning to attend the trial of Mrs. Parks. She was convicted of disobeying the city's segregation ordinance
140 and fined ten dollars and costs. Her young attorney, Fred D. Gray, filed an appeal. It was one of the first clear-cut cases of an African American being convicted of disobeying the segregation laws—usually the charge was disorderly conduct or some such thing.

The leaders of the Movement called a meeting for three o'clock in the afternoon to organize the mass meeting to be held that night. Martin was a bit late, and as he entered the hall, people said to him, "Martin, we have elected you to be our president. Will you accept?"

Fear was an invisible presence at the meeting, along with courage and hope. Proposals were voiced to make the organization, which the leaders decided to
150 call the Montgomery Improvement Association, or MIA, a sort of secret society, because if no names were mentioned it would be safer for the leaders. E. D. Nixon opposed that idea. "We're acting like little boys," he said. "Somebody's name will be known, and if we're afraid, we might just as well fold up right now.

The white folks are eventually going to find out anyway. We'd better decide now if we are going to be fearless men or scared little boys." **D**

That settled that question. It was also decided that the protest would continue until certain demands were met. Ralph Abernathy was made chairman of the committee to draw up the demands.

Martin came home at six o'clock. He said later that he was nervous about
160 telling me he had accepted the presidency of the protest movement, but he need not have worried, because I sincerely meant what I said when I told him that night: "You know that whatever you do, you have my backing."

Reassured, Martin went to his study. He was to make the main speech at the mass meeting that night. It was now six-thirty and—this was the way it was usually to be—he had only twenty minutes to prepare what he thought might be the most decisive speech of his life. He said afterward that thinking about the responsibility and the reporters and television cameras, he almost panicked. Five minutes wasted and only fifteen minutes left. At that moment he turned to prayer. He asked God "to restore my balance and be with me in a time
170 when I need Your guidance more than ever."

How could he make his speech **militant** enough to rouse people to action and yet devoid of hate and resentment? He was determined to do both.

Martin and Ralph went together to the meeting. When they got within four blocks of the Holt Street Baptist Church, there was an enormous traffic jam. Five thousand people stood outside the church listening to loudspeakers and singing hymns. Inside it was so crowded, Martin told me, the people had to lift Ralph and him above the crowd and pass them from hand to hand over their heads to the platform. The crowd and the singing inspired Martin, and God answered his prayer. Later Martin said, "That night I understood what the older preachers
180 meant when they said, 'Open your mouth and God will speak for you.'"

First the people sang "Onward, Christian Soldiers" in a tremendous wave of five thousand voices. This was followed by a prayer and a reading of the Scriptures. Martin was introduced. People applauded; television lights beat upon him. Without any notes at all he began to speak. Once again he told the story of Mrs. Parks, and rehearsed some of the wrongs black people were suffering. Then he said,

> *But there comes a time when people get tired. We are here this evening to say to those who have mistreated us so long, that we are tired. Tired of being segregated and humiliated; tired of being kicked about by the brutal feet of oppression.*

The audience cheered wildly, and Martin said,

190 > *We have no alternative but to protest. We have been amazingly patient . . . but we come here tonight to be saved from that patience that makes us patient with anything less than freedom and justice.*

Taking up the challenging newspaper comparison with the White Citizens Councils and the Klan,[8] Martin said,

D DISTINGUISH FACT FROM OPINION
What factual evidence supports the statement of opinion in line 148?

militant (mĭl′ĭ-tənt) *adj.* aggressive or combative

---

8. **Klan:** the Ku Klux Klan, a secret society trying to establish white power and authority by unlawful and violent methods directed against African Americans and other minority groups.

Martin Luther King Jr., speaking at a church in Montgomery

ANALYZE VISUALS
How does the photograph reflect the author's description of King's speaking ability?

*They are protesting for the **perpetuation** of injustice in the community; we're protesting for the birth of justice . . . their methods lead to violence and lawlessness. But in our protest there will be no cross-burnings, no white person will be taken from his home by a hooded Negro mob and brutally murdered . . . We will be guided by the highest principles of law and order.*

perpetuation
(pər-pĕch′o͞o-ā′shən) *n.*
the act of continuing or prolonging something

200 Having roused the audience for militant action, Martin now set limits upon it. His study of nonviolence and his love of Christ informed his words. He said,

*No one must be intimidated to keep them from riding the buses. Our method must be persuasion, not **coercion**. We will only say to the people, "Let your conscience be your guide." . . . Our actions must be guided by the deepest principles of the Christian faith. . . . Once again we must hear the words of Jesus, "Love your enemies. Bless them that curse you. Pray for them that despitefully use you." If we fail to do this, our protest will end up as a meaningless drama on the stage of history and its memory will be shrouded in the ugly garments of shame. . . . We must not become bitter and end up by*
210 *hating our white brothers. As Booker T. Washington*[9] *said, "Let no man pull you so low as to make you hate him."*

coercion (kō-ûr′zhən) *n.*
the act of compelling by force or authority

Finally, Martin said,

If you will protest courageously, and yet with dignity and Christian love, future historians will say, "There lived a great people—a black people—who injected new meaning and dignity into the veins of civilization." This is our challenge and our overwhelming responsibility.

As Martin finished speaking, the audience rose cheering in exaltation. And in that speech my husband set the keynote and the tempo of the Movement he was to lead, from Montgomery onward. ↶

---

9. **Booker T. Washington** (1856–1915): an African-American educator and writer.

Comprehension

OHIO STANDARDS

READING STANDARD
3.5 Analyze an author's argument

1. **Recall** What rules did African Americans have to follow on buses in Montgomery?

2. **Recall** What incident set off the bus boycott?

3. **Recall** How successful was the first day of the boycott?

4. **Summarize** What did Martin Luther King Jr. urge his followers to avoid in his speech at the Holt Street Baptist Church?

Literary Analysis

5. **Analyze Opinions** Review the chart you created as you read. Both the author and Martin Luther King Jr. express opinions about the protesters who participated in the boycott. What character traits of the protesters are emphasized in these opinions?

6. **Interpret Passage** Reread lines 98–108. How did King justify the use of boycotts to **change society?**

7. **Examine Historical Events in Memoir** According to the author, how did the Montgomery boycott influence the civil rights movement? Use a chart like the one shown to record your answer.

Aspects of Civil Rights Movement	Influence of Boycott
Leadership	
Strategies	

8. **Analyze Memoir** In what ways might this selection have been different if the author had intended to write a standard historical account instead of a memoir? Be specific.

9. **Draw Conclusions About Leadership** What values influenced King's leadership during the boycott? Cite evidence from the text.

10. **Compare Texts** Compare and contrast the experiences of the African Americans in Montgomery with the experiences of Japanese Americans described in the excerpt from *Farewell to Manzanar*, which begins on page 866. What circumstances might explain the different ways in which these two groups responded to injustice?

Literary Criticism

11. **Critical Interpretations** Some reviewers of Coretta Scott King's memoir *My Life with Martin Luther King, Jr.* complained that her portrayal of the civil rights leader is too idealized. Do you think that she should have shown more of her husband's flaws or weaknesses in "Montgomery Boycott"? Explain why or why not.

Vocabulary in Context

VOCABULARY PRACTICE

Choose the word that is not related in meaning to the other words in the set.

1. boycott, cooperation, acceptance, participation
2. tactic, strategy, maneuver, hindrance
3. perpetuation, conclusion, cessation, interruption
4. compliant, militant, submissive, passive
5. coercion, compulsion, intimidation, influence
6. humiliating, demeaning, uplifting, degrading

WORD LIST

boycott

coercion

degrading

militant

perpetuation

tactic

VOCABULARY IN WRITING

Using three or more vocabulary words, write questions that you would ask Martin Luther King Jr. if he were alive today. Here is an example.

> **EXAMPLE SENTENCE**
>
> Why do you think the Montgomery **boycott** was so successful?

VOCABULARY STRATEGY: THE SUFFIX -*ion*

The suffix –*ion* means "the act, state, or result of." When this suffix is added to a verb, it changes the word to a noun. For example, in the vocabulary word *coercion*, the suffix –*ion* has changed the verb *coerce* into a noun meaning "the act of coercing." Notice that the final *e* in a word is dropped when a suffix that begins with a vowel is added. Sometimes a final consonant in a word is doubled or letters are changed when a suffix is added. If you can identify the root or the base word in a word with the suffix –*ion*, you can often figure out the word's meaning.

PRACTICE Add the suffix –*ion* to each word below, changing the last letter or letters of the base word if necessary. Then write a short definition of each word, referring to a dictionary if necessary.

1. perpetuate
2. conciliate
3. evacuate
4. imitate
5. expand
6. suspect

OHIO STANDARDS

VOCABULARY STANDARD
1.5 Use knowledge of roots, prefixes and suffixes to understand words

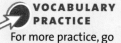

VOCABULARY PRACTICE
For more practice, go to the **Vocabulary Center** at **ClassZone.com**.

A Eulogy for Dr. Martin Luther King Jr.

Speech

Use with "Montgomery Boycott," page 882.

OHIO STANDARDS

READING/RESEARCH STANDARDS
3.1 Identify techniques authors use to accomplish their purpose
8.4 Select appropriate sources to support central ideas

What's the Connection?

In "Montgomery Boycott," Coretta Scott King recalls an important event in the civil rights movement that was also a turning point in Martin Luther King Jr.'s career. Now, in "A Eulogy for Dr. Martin Luther King Jr.," you will read a moving speech that Robert F. Kennedy delivered on the day of King's assassination.

Skill Focus: Analyze Rhetorical Devices

Rhetorical devices are techniques that allow writers to communicate ideas more effectively. Speeches often contain rhetorical devices, because they help keep an audience's attention. By analyzing rhetorical devices, you can gain insight into what makes a speech powerful or memorable.

One common rhetorical device is the **repetition** of the same word, phrase, or sentence for emphasis. Another device is **parallelism,** the use of similar grammatical constructions to express related ideas. The chart shows examples of these rhetorical devices from a speech delivered by Martin Luther King Jr. during the Montgomery bus boycott. Use a similar chart to identify examples of rhetorical devices in the following selection.

Device	Example
Repetition	"Tired of being segregated and humiliated; tired of being kicked about by the brutal feet of oppression."
Parallelism	"They are protesting for the perpetuation of injustice in the community; we're protesting for the birth of justice. . . ."

A Eulogy for Dr. Martin Luther King Jr.

by Robert F. Kennedy

On April 4, 1968, hundreds of African Americans gathered for what they thought would be an exciting political event. Presidential candidate Robert F. Kennedy was coming to speak to them. Before he was to deliver his speech, however, Kennedy was informed that Martin Luther King Jr. had been assassinated earlier that day. He nevertheless went to the rally, where he found the people upbeat in anticipation of his appearance. Realizing that they were unaware of the tragic event, he began his speech with the following words.

I have bad news for you, for all of our fellow citizens, and people who love peace all over the world, and that is that Martin Luther King was shot and killed tonight.

Martin Luther King dedicated his life to love and to justice for his fellow human beings, and he died because of that effort.

In this difficult day, in this difficult time for the United States, it is perhaps well to ask what kind of a nation we are and what direction we want to move in. For those of you who are black—considering the evidence there evidently is that there were white people who were
10 responsible—you can be filled with bitterness, with hatred, and a desire for revenge. We can move in that direction as a country, in great polarization—black people amongst black, white people amongst white, filled with hatred toward one another. **Ⓐ**

Or we can make an effort, as Martin Luther King did, to understand and to comprehend, and to replace that violence, that stain of bloodshed that has spread across our land, with an effort to understand with compassion and love.

For those of you who are black and are tempted to be filled with hatred and distrust at the injustice of such an act, against all white people, I can
20 only say that I feel in my own heart the same kind of feeling. I had a member of my family killed, but he was killed by a white man. But we have to make an effort in the United States, we have to make an effort to understand, to go beyond these rather difficult times.

My favorite poet was Aeschylus. He wrote, "In our sleep, pain which cannot forget falls drop by drop upon the heart until, in our own despair, against our will, comes wisdom through the awful grace of God."

Ⓐ RHETORICAL DEVICES
How does Kennedy use **parallelism** to emphasize the potential for American society to become more divided?

What we need in the United States is not division; what we need in the United States is not hatred; what we need in the United States is not violence or lawlessness but love and wisdom, and compassion toward one
30 another, and a feeling of justice towards those who still suffer within our country, whether they be white or they be black.

So I shall ask you tonight to return home, to say a prayer for the family of Martin Luther King, that's true, but more importantly to say a prayer for our own country, which all of us love—a prayer for understanding and that compassion of which I spoke.

We can do well in this country. We will have difficult times. We've had difficult times in the past. We will have difficult times in the future. It is not the end of violence; it is not the end of lawlessness; it is not the end of disorder. **B**

40 But the vast majority of white people and the vast majority of black people in this country want to live together, want to improve the quality of our life, and want justice for all human beings who abide in our land.

Let us dedicate ourselves to what the Greeks wrote so many years ago: to tame the savageness of man and to make gentle the life of this world.

Let us dedicate ourselves to that, and say a prayer for our country and for our people. **C**

B RHETORICAL DEVICES
What idea does Kennedy call attention to through **parallelism** in lines 36–39?

C RHETORICAL DEVICES
What does Kennedy suggest through the **repetition** of the phrase "let us dedicate ourselves" in lines 43–46?

Shown (left to right) are King, Kennedy, Roy Wilkins, and Lyndon Johnson.

Comprehension

1. **Recall** What personal experience has helped Kennedy understand the feelings of African Americans following King's assassination?

2. **Summarize** What kinds of reactions does Kennedy hope his speech will prevent?

Critical Analysis

3. **Analyze Rhetorical Devices** Review the examples of rhetorical devices in the chart you created as you read. Choose an example of each device, and explain how it helps make the speech effective.

4. **Interpret Statement** What do you make of the statement by Aeschylus that Kennedy quotes in lines 24–26?

Read for Information: Cite Evidence

OHIO STANDARDS

READING/RESEARCH STANDARDS
3.1 Identify techniques authors use to accomplish their purpose

8.4 Select appropriate sources to support central ideas

WRITING PROMPT

In "A Eulogy for Dr. Martin Luther King Jr.," Kennedy urges the audience to follow King's approach to fighting injustice. How do Martin Luther King Jr.'s words and actions in "Montgomery Boycott" support the message of Kennedy's speech?

To answer this prompt, you will need to identify Kennedy's message and cite evidence from "Montgomery Boycott" that supports this message. Use the following steps:

1. Reread Kennedy's speech, looking for statements about injustice to help you identify his message.

2. Reread "Montgomery Boycott" and keep track of statements, facts, and anecdotes that are relevant to Kennedy's message. Indicate line numbers for each item in your notes.

3. Review your notes and evaluate each item to see whether it supports Kennedy's message.

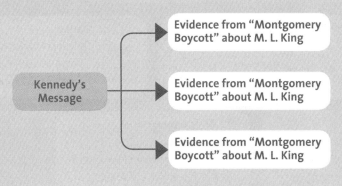

Marriage Is a Private Affair

Short Story by Chinua Achebe

Whose LIFE is it, anyway?

OHIO STANDARDS

READING STANDARDS
2.1 Make predictions
4.3 Distinguish how conflicts affect text

KEY IDEA Growing up means learning to make your own decisions. But parents are often reluctant to let go of their authority. In the traditional culture that Chinua Achebe portrays in the following selection, even adults are expected to get **parental approval** for some big decisions.

SURVEY Take this survey about parental involvement. Then form a small group with two to four classmates, and find out which topics you generally agree on and which ones lead to strong differences of opinion.

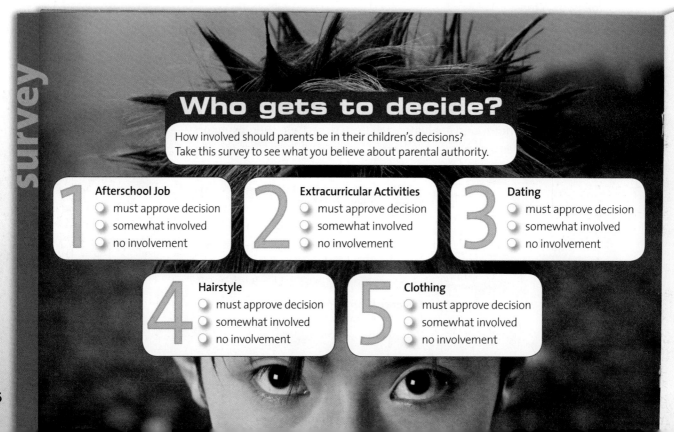

survey

Who gets to decide?

How involved should parents be in their children's decisions? Take this survey to see what you believe about parental authority.

1 Afterschool Job
- must approve decision
- somewhat involved
- no involvement

2 Extracurricular Activities
- must approve decision
- somewhat involved
- no involvement

3 Dating
- must approve decision
- somewhat involved
- no involvement

4 Hairstyle
- must approve decision
- somewhat involved
- no involvement

5 Clothing
- must approve decision
- somewhat involved
- no involvement

● LITERARY ANALYSIS: CULTURAL CONFLICT

When you read a story that is set in a foreign country, knowledge of the culture can help you understand why characters behave a certain way or why **cultural conflicts** sometimes develop.

Fiction writers often use indirect methods of providing cultural information. For example, in "Marriage Is a Private Affair," Chinua Achebe reveals a tension between Nigerian city ways and village ways of life through a character's thoughts:

In the cosmopolitan atmosphere of the city it had always seemed to her something of a joke that a person's tribe could determine whom he married.

As you read, look for examples of conflicts that arise from cultural friction.

● READING STRATEGY: PREDICT

You can use text clues in a story to make **predictions,** reasonable guesses about what will happen next. When making predictions,

- analyze the words, thoughts, and actions of characters to gain a sense of how they might react in a situation
- tap into your own experiences and knowledge of human behavior

As you read, use a chart like the one shown to record your predictions and to see how they compare with actual outcomes in the story.

Prediction	Reason for Prediction	Actual Outcome
Nnaemeka's father will be upset about the engagement.	Nnaemeka says villagers are unhappy when they do not get to arrange an engagement.	

▲ VOCABULARY IN CONTEXT

Achebe uses the following boldfaced words to portray family conflict. Determine the meaning of each word from the context.

1. Her travels had given her a **cosmopolitan** attitude.

2. He **vehemently** denied any wrongdoing on his part.

3. She would not accept attempts at **dissuasion;** her mind was set.

4. It is important to show **deference** to your elders.

5. We can still **persevere,** despite all the obstacles ahead.

Marriage Is a **PRIVATE** Affair

Chinua Achebe

"Have you written to your dad yet?" asked Nene[1] one afternoon as she sat with Nnaemeka[2] in her room at 16 Kasanga Street, Lagos.

"No. I've been thinking about it. I think it's better to tell him when I get home on leave!"

"But why? Your leave is such a long way off yet—six whole weeks. He should be let into our happiness now."

Nnaemeka was silent for a while and then began very slowly as if he groped for his words: "I wish I were sure it would be happiness to him."

"Of course it must," replied Nene, a little surprised. "Why shouldn't it?"

10 "You have lived in Lagos all your life, and you know very little about people in remote parts of the country."

"That's what you always say. But I don't believe anybody will be so unlike other people that they will be unhappy when their sons are engaged to marry."

"Yes. They are most unhappy if the engagement is not arranged by them. In our case it's worse—you are not even an Ibo."

This was said so seriously and so bluntly that Nene could not find speech immediately. In the **cosmopolitan** atmosphere of the city it had always seemed to her something of a joke that a person's tribe could determine whom he married.

At last she said, "You don't really mean that he will object to your marrying 20 me simply on that account? I had always thought you Ibos were kindly disposed to other people."

"So we are. But when it comes to marriage, well, it's not quite so simple. And this," he added, "is not peculiar to the Ibos. If your father were alive and lived in the heart of Ibibio-land, he would be exactly like my father." **A**

"I don't know. But anyway, as your father is so fond of you, I'm sure he will forgive you soon enough. Come on then, be a good boy and send him a nice lovely letter . . ."

---

1. **Nene** (nĕ′-nĕ).
2. **Nnaemeka** (ĕn-nä′ĕ-mĕ′kä).

ANALYZE VISUALS
What does the painting suggest about the story's characters and setting?

cosmopolitan
(kŏz′mə-pŏl′ĭ-tn) *adj.* containing elements from all over the world; sophisticated

A CULTURAL CONFLICT
Reread lines 1–24. What do you learn about the cultural backgrounds of Nene and Nnaemeka?

Woman and Husband in Floating Agbada 1 (1997), D. Gbenga Orimoloye. Gouache, 25 cm × 20 cm. © www.Orimoloye.com.

"It would not be wise to break the news to him by writing. A letter will **B**
bring it upon him with a shock. I'm quite sure about that."

30   "All right, honey, suit yourself. You know your father."

As Nnaemeka walked home that evening, he turned over in his mind different ways of overcoming his father's opposition, especially now that he had gone and found a girl for him. He had thought of showing his letter to Nene but decided on second thoughts not to, at least for the moment. He read it again when he got home and couldn't help smiling to himself. He remembered Ugoye[3] quite well, an Amazon[4] of a girl who used to beat up all the boys, himself included, on the way to the stream, a complete dunce at school.

I have found a girl who will suit you admirably—Ugoye Nweke, the eldest daughter of our neighbor, Jacob Nweke. She has a proper Christian
40   *upbringing. When she stopped schooling some years ago, her father (a man of sound judgment) sent her to live in the house of a pastor where she has received all the training a wife could need. Her Sunday school teacher has told me that she reads her Bible very fluently. I hope we shall begin negotiations when you come home in December.*

On the second evening of his return from Lagos Nnaemeka sat with his father under a cassia tree. This was the old man's retreat where he went to read his Bible when the parching December sun had set and a fresh, reviving wind blew on the leaves.

"Father," began Nnaemeka suddenly, "I have come to ask for forgiveness."

50   "Forgiveness? For what, my son?" he asked in amazement.

"It's about this marriage question."

"Which marriage question?"

"I can't—we must—I mean it is impossible for me to marry Nweke's daughter."

"Impossible? Why?" asked his father.

"I don't love her."

"Nobody said you did. Why should you?" he asked.

"Marriage today is different . . ."

"Look here, my son," interrupted his father, "nothing is different. What one
60 looks for in a wife are a good character and a Christian background." **C**

Nnaemeka saw there was no hope along the present line of argument.

"Moreover," he said, "I am engaged to marry another girl who has all of Ugoye's good qualities, and who . . ."

His father did not believe his ears. "What did you say?" he asked slowly and disconcertingly.

"She is a good Christian," his son went on, "and a teacher in a girls' school in Lagos."

"Teacher, did you say? If you consider that a qualification for a good wife,

3. **Ugoye** (ū-gō′yĕ).
4. **Amazon:** a woman who is tall, strong-willed, and aggressive.

B GRAMMAR AND STYLE
Reread line 28. Rather than writing, "It would not be wise to write to him to break the news to him," Achebe uses the **gerund** *writing,* a verb form that functions as a noun.

C CULTURAL CONFLICT
What does the exchange of dialogue in lines 49–60 reveal about Nnaemeka's and his father's beliefs about marriage?

I should like to point out to you, Emeka, that no Christian woman should
70   teach. St. Paul in his letter to the Corinthians says that women should keep
silence." He rose slowly from his seat and paced forwards and backwards. This
was his pet subject, and he condemned **vehemently** those church leaders who
encouraged women to teach in their schools. After he had spent his emotion
on a long homily, he at last came back to his son's engagement, in a seemingly
milder tone.

"Whose daughter is she, anyway?"

"She is Nene Atang."

"What!" All the mildness was gone again. "Did you say Neneataga; what
does that mean?"

80   "Nene Atang from Calabar.⁵ She is the only girl I can marry." This was a
very rash reply, and Nnaemeka expected the storm to burst. But it did not.
His father merely walked away into his room. This was most unexpected and
perplexed Nnaemeka. His father's silence was infinitely more menacing than a
flood of threatening speech. That night the old man did not eat. **D**

When he sent for Nnaemeka a day later, he applied all possible ways of
dissuasion. But the young man's heart was hardened, and his father eventually
gave him up as lost.

"I owe it to you, my son, as a duty to show you what is right and what is
wrong. Whoever put this idea into your head might as well have cut your
90   throat. It is Satan's work." He waved his son away.

"You will change your mind, Father, when you know Nene."

"I shall never see her" was the reply. From that night the father scarcely
spoke to his son. He did not, however, cease hoping that he would realize
how serious was the danger he was heading for. Day and night he put him
in his prayers.

Nnaemeka, for his own part, was very deeply affected by his father's grief.
But he kept hoping that it would pass away. If it had occurred to him that
never in the history of his people had a man married a woman who spoke a
different tongue, he might have been less optimistic. "It has never been heard,"
100 was the verdict of an old man speaking a few weeks later. In that short sentence
he spoke for all of his people. This man had come with others to commiserate
with Okeke⁶ when news went round about his son's behavior. By that time the
son had gone back to Lagos.

"It has never been heard," said the old man again with a sad shake of his head.

"What did Our Lord say?" asked another gentleman. "Sons shall rise against
their fathers; it is there in the Holy Book."

"It is the beginning of the end," said another.

The discussion thus tending to become theological, Madubogwu, a highly
practical man, brought it down once more to the ordinary level.

110   "Have you thought of consulting a native doctor about your son?" he asked
Nnaemeka's father.

---

5. **Calabar:** a seaport in southeastern Nigeria.

6. **Okeke** (ō-kě'-kě).

vehemently
(vē'ə-mənt-lē) *adv.* in a
fierce, intense manner

D   PREDICT
Will Nnaemeka's father
change his mind after
thinking about his son's
marriage plans?

dissuasion (dǐ-swā'zhən)
n. an attempt to deter a
person from a course of
action

"He isn't sick" was the reply.

"What is he then? The boy's mind is diseased, and only a good herbalist[7] can bring him back to his right senses. The medicine he requires is *Amalile,* the same that women apply with success to recapture their husbands' straying affection."

"Madubogwu is right," said another gentleman. "This thing calls for medicine."

"I shall not call in a native doctor." Nnaemeka's father was known to be obstinately ahead of his more superstitious neighbors in these matters. "I will not be another Mrs. Ochuba. If my son wants to kill himself, let him do it with his own hands. It is not for me to help him."

"But it was her fault," said Madubogwu. "She ought to have gone to an honest herbalist. She was a clever woman, nevertheless."

"She was a wicked murderess," said Jonathan, who rarely argued with his neighbors because, he often said, they were incapable of reasoning. "The medicine was prepared for her husband, it was his name they called in its preparation, and I am sure it would have been perfectly beneficial to him. It was wicked to put it into the herbalist's food and say you were only trying it out." **E**

Six months later, Nnaemeka was showing his young wife a short letter from his father:

It amazes me that you could be so unfeeling as to send me your wedding picture. I would have sent it back. But on further thought I decided just to cut off your wife and send it back to you because I have nothing to do with her. How I wish that I had nothing to do with you either.

When Nene read through this letter and looked at the mutilated picture, her eyes filled with tears, and she began to sob.

"Don't cry, my darling," said her husband. "He is essentially good-natured and will one day look more kindly on our marriage." But years passed, and that one day did not come.

For eight years, Okeke would have nothing to do with his son, Nnaemeka. Only three times (when Nnaemeka asked to come home and spend his leave) did he write to him.

"I can't have you in my house," he replied on one occasion. "It can be of no interest to me where or how you spend your leave—or your life, for that matter."

The prejudice against Nnaemeka's marriage was not confined to his little village. In Lagos, especially among his people who worked there, it showed itself in a different way. Their women, when they met at their village meeting, were not hostile to Nene. Rather, they paid her such excessive **deference** as to make her feel she was not one of them. But as time went on, Nene gradually broke through some of this prejudice and even began to make friends among them. Slowly and grudgingly they began to admit that she kept her home much better than most of them.

The story eventually got to the little village in the heart of the Ibo country that Nnaemeka and his young wife were a most happy couple. But his father

E CULTURAL CONFLICT
What beliefs and practices do you learn about in lines 113–127?

deference (dĕf′ər-əns) *n.* polite respect; submission to someone else's wishes

---

7. **herbalist** (ûr′bə-lĭst): a person who is expert in the use of medicinal herbs.

Portrait 1 (1999), D. Gbenga Orimoloye. Watercolor, 30 cm × 20 cm. © www.Orimoloye.com.

was one of the few people in the village who knew nothing about this. He always displayed so much temper whenever his son's name was mentioned that everyone avoided it in his presence. By a tremendous effort of will he had succeeded in pushing his son to the back of his mind. The strain had nearly killed him, but he had **persevered** and won.

Then one day he received a letter from Nene, and in spite of himself he
160 began to glance through it perfunctorily until all of a sudden the expression on his face changed and he began to read more carefully.

> *. . . Our two sons, from the day they learnt that they have a grandfather, have insisted on being taken to him. I find it impossible to tell them that you will not see them. I implore you to allow Nnaemeka to bring them home for a short time during his leave next month. I shall remain here in Lagos . . .* **F**

The old man at once felt the resolution he had built up over so many years falling in. He was telling himself that he must not give in. He tried to steel his heart against all emotional appeals. It was a reenactment of that other struggle. He leaned against a window and looked out. The sky was overcast with heavy
170 black clouds, and a high wind began to blow, filling the air with dust and dry leaves. It was one of those rare occasions when even Nature takes a hand in a human fight. Very soon it began to rain, the first rain in the year. It came down in large sharp drops and was accompanied by the lightning and thunder which mark a change of season. Okeke was trying hard not to think of his two grandsons. But he knew he was now fighting a losing battle. He tried to hum a favorite hymn, but the pattering of large raindrops on the roof broke up the tune. His mind immediately returned to the children. How could he shut his door against them? By a curious mental process he imagined them standing, sad and forsaken, under the harsh angry weather—shut out from his house.
180 That night he hardly slept, from remorse—and a vague fear that he might die without making it up to them. ❧

persevere (pûr′sə-vîr′) *v.* to persist in an action or belief despite difficulty

F PREDICT
How will Nnaemeka's father react to this letter? Cite evidence.

Comprehension

1. **Recall** Why does Okeke oppose Nnaemeka's choice of a wife?

2. **Recall** What does Okeke do when his son sends him a wedding photo?

3. **Summarize** What happens at the end of the story?

Literary Analysis

4. **Examine Predictions** Review the chart you created as you read. How accurate were your predictions about Okeke? Cite specific examples in your response.

5. **Analyze Cultural Conflict** What beliefs cause conflict to develop between Nnaemeka and Okeke? Record your answer in a diagram like the one shown.

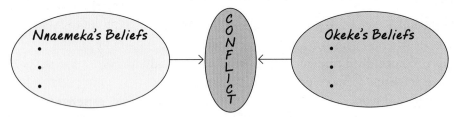

6. **Interpret Cultural Context** Why might living in a city influence Nnaemeka's attitude toward Ibo traditions?

7. **Make Inferences** Why does Nene's letter have such a powerful effect on Okeke?

8. **Draw Conclusions** Reread lines 166–181. Does the ending of the story suggest that Okeke will finally offer **parental approval** of Nnaemeka's marriage? Cite evidence for your conclusion.

9. **Make Judgments** How much sympathy do you have for Okeke as a character? Give reasons for your answer.

Literary Criticism

10. **Critical Interpretations** The critic G. D. Killam has said about Achebe's work, "Through it all the spirit of man and the belief in the possibility of triumph endures." How might this comment apply to "Marriage Is a Private Affair"?

OHIO STANDARDS

READING STANDARD
4.3 Distinguish how conflicts affect text

Vocabulary in Context

VOCABULARY PRACTICE

Decide whether the words in each pair are synonyms or antonyms.

1. cosmopolitan/provincial
2. vehemently/fiercely
3. persuasion/dissuasion
4. deference/respect
5. abandon/persevere

VOCABULARY IN WRITING

Using three or more vocabulary words, write about the conflict between Nnaemeka and Okeke. Here is how you might begin.

> **EXAMPLE SENTENCE**
>
> *Okeke expected Nnaemeka to respond with __deference__ when he found a wife for him.*

OHIO STANDARDS

VOCABULARY STANDARD
1.6 Use dictionaries

VOCABULARY STRATEGY: THE *kosmos* WORD FAMILY

The root of the vocabulary word *cosmopolitan* can be traced to the Greek word *kosmos*, which means "world." This root has given rise to a family of words. If you are familiar with the other word parts in a word with the root *cosmo* or *cosm*, you can often figure out the word's meaning.

PRACTICE Using a dictionary, find four words containing the root *cosmo* or *cosm*. Define each word.

VOCABULARY PRACTICE
For more practice, go to the **Vocabulary Center** at **ClassZone.com**.

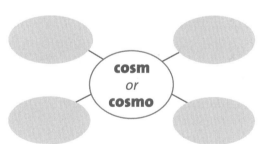

cosm
or
cosmo

Reading-Writing Connection

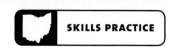

Enhance your understanding of "Marriage Is a Private Affair" by responding to these prompts. Then use **Revision: Grammar and Style** to improve your writing.

WRITING PROMPTS	SELF-CHECK
A. Short Response: Write a Letter Write a **one- or two-paragraph letter** that Okeke might send in response to Nene's letter.	*A strong letter will . . .* • respond to the points brought up in Nene's letter • reflect Okeke's personality and change of heart
B. Extended Response: Write Across Texts What do you think is gained or lost when people let go of traditions such as **parental approval** of children's spouses? Write **three to five paragraphs** in response, using examples from "Marriage Is a Private Affair" and the transcript "Adam and Rosie" (page 907).	*A successful response will . . .* • clearly state an opinion • support the opinion with appropriate examples from the story and the transcript

REVISION: GRAMMAR AND STYLE

OHIO STANDARDS

WRITING STANDARD
7.3 Use clauses and phrases

WRITE CONCISELY Review the **Grammar and Style** note on page 900. Like Achebe, you can use **gerunds** and **gerund phrases** to make your writing more fluid and concise. A gerund is a verb form that ends in *–ing* and functions as a noun. A gerund phrase is a gerund plus its modifiers and complements. Here is an example of Achebe's use of a gerund phrase. Notice how "pattering of large raindrops on the roof" functions as a noun in the sentence.

> *He tried to hum a favorite hymn, but the pattering of large raindrops on the roof broke up the tune.* (lines 175–177)

The revisions in red use a gerund phrase to make the following first draft more concise. Revise your responses to the prompts by incorporating gerunds and gerund phrases into your writing.

WRITING TOOLS
For prewriting, revision, and editing tools, visit the **Writing Center** at ClassZone.com.

> **STUDENT MODEL**
> ~~e~~When you choos~~e~~ ^ing^ a spouse, ~~you are making a decision that~~ is too personal
> ^a decision^ to put in anyone else's hands.

Reading for Information

TRANSCRIPT In "Marriage Is a Private Affair," a son comes into conflict with his father when he marries someone outside his ethnic group. The following selection, from *Mixed Matches,* describes how a Korean family dealt with a similar situation.

Case Study #51

Adam and Rosie

When we were first going out, Rosie's parents were extremely upset by her dating a non-Korean. They refused to meet me. One day Rosie decided to take me to visit her grandmother, who lived only a few blocks from Rosie's parents. It was hard to read her reaction. She didn't speak much English, and I didn't speak Korean. She offered us tea, and after a half hour we left. We started to visit her regularly, and even though Rosie's parents wouldn't accept our relationship, it was clear that her grandmother enjoyed our coming over. Finally she had a talk with Rosie's mother, and soon after that we received our first invitation to the house.

Now we have a child, and Rosie's parents have relaxed. I was really touched when her father said at the baby naming, "After a hundred generations our family tree has a different color branch grafted onto it. I was very worried about the colors harmonizing, but now that I can see the results, I am pleased."

I think if it wasn't for her grandmother, we would never have made it as a couple. When I visit my in-laws these days, I take my mother-in-law's hands and kiss them in front of her friends. She and her friends giggle like schoolgirls. In their culture they're not used to direct expressions of affection—especially between men and women. It wouldn't be considered proper nor would they tolerate that kind of behavior if Rosie had married another Korean. But my being white puts me in a different category. I think for them, as upset as they initially were by Rosie getting involved with me, they enjoy the novelty I have introduced into their lives.

On the Rainy River
Short Story by Tim O'Brien

What is
COWARDICE?

OHIO STANDARDS

READING STANDARDS
3.5 Analyze an author's perspective or viewpoint

4.2 Analyze the features of setting and their importance in a literary text

KEY IDEA Some people take great risks to avoid being accused of **cowardice.** Yet daring actions are not necessarily brave ones, especially if they are done for the wrong reasons. In "On the Rainy River," a young man must decide whether to risk his life fighting in a war he opposes.

DISCUSS With a small group of classmates, discuss the difference between physical cowardice and moral cowardice. Come up with several examples of each type of cowardice.

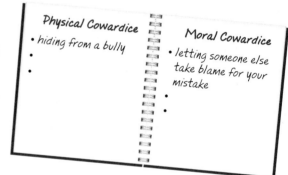

Physical Cowardice
• hiding from a bully
•
•

Moral Cowardice
• letting someone else take blame for your mistake
•
•

● LITERARY ANALYSIS: HISTORICAL CONTEXT

When you look at literature in its **historical context,** you examine the social conditions that inspired or influenced the creation of a literary work. Sometimes you can obtain historical information from the work you are reading. For example, the narrator of Tim O'Brien's story often directly comments on the Vietnam War era:

America was divided on these and a thousand other issues. . . . The only certainty that summer was moral confusion.

You may also need to read background information to learn more about a work's historical context. Before you read "On the Rainy River," study the background information on this page. Then, as you read the story, use this information to gain insight into the narrator's actions and beliefs.

● READING SKILL: IDENTIFY AUTHOR'S PERSPECTIVE

An **author's perspective** is the combination of beliefs, values, and feelings through which a writer views a subject. Tim O'Brien's perspective was influenced by his rural upbringing, his education, and his experiences in Vietnam. These influences are reflected in statements by the narrator of "On the Rainy River," whose background and experiences are very similar to those of the author.

As you read, use a chart like the one shown to identify statements that reveal the author's perspective.

Statements	O'Brien's Perspective
"It was my view then, and still is, that you don't make war without knowing why."	The United States should not have entered the Vietnam War.

Review: **Make Inferences, Predict**

▲ VOCABULARY IN CONTEXT

O'Brien uses the following words to describe characters and attitudes. Put them into the categories "Words I Know Well," "Words I Think I Know," and "Words I Don't Know at All." Write brief definitions for words in the first two categories.

WORD LIST	acquiescence	compassionate	preoccupied
	censure	naive	reticence

Author On|ine

Fact and Fiction
"On the Rainy River" appears in *The Things They Carried* (1990), Tim O'Brien's collection of interrelated stories about the Vietnam War. Although the stories are fictional, they were inspired by O'Brien's wartime experiences. He even gave his own name to

Tim O'Brien born 1946

the narrator, who, like the real Tim O'Brien, grew up in Minnesota and was drafted into the U.S. Army after graduating from college. For O'Brien, the truths a story conveys are more important than whether the story is literally true: "I want you to feel what I felt. I want you to know why story truth is truer sometimes than happening truth."

 MORE ABOUT THE AUTHOR For more on Tim O'Brien, visit the **Literature Center** at **ClassZone.com.**

Background

The Vietnam War The Vietnam War (1954–1975) was one of the most controversial military conflicts in U.S. history. The United States entered the war in the 1960s to prevent the spread of Communism throughout Southeast Asia. During the course of the war, nearly 3 million Americans were sent overseas to defend the South Vietnamese government against a takeover by Communist North Vietnam and the Viet Cong, a South Vietnamese Communist rebel force. Although many volunteered for service, about two-thirds of American soldiers were drafted into the military. Draftees who opposed the war faced a difficult decision: whether to risk their lives in a foreign war they did not believe in or risk imprisonment at home by refusing to serve. Some chose to leave the country, most often by crossing the border into Canada.

ON THE
Rainy River

Tim O'Brien

ANALYZE VISUALS
Based on details in the collage, what do you **predict** the story will be about?

This is one story I've never told before. Not to anyone. Not to my parents, not to my brother or sister, not even to my wife. To go into it, I've always thought, would only cause embarrassment for all of us, a sudden need to be elsewhere, which is the natural response to a confession. Even now, I'll admit, the story makes me squirm. For more than twenty years I've had to live with it, feeling the shame, trying to push it away, and so by this act of remembrance, by putting the facts down on paper, I'm hoping to relieve at least some of the pressure on my dreams.

Still, it's a hard story to tell. All of us, I suppose, like to believe that in a
10 moral emergency we will behave like the heroes of our youth, bravely and forthrightly, without thought of personal loss or discredit. Certainly that was my conviction back in the summer of 1968. Tim O'Brien: a secret hero. The Lone Ranger. If the stakes ever became high enough—if the evil were evil enough, if the good were good enough—I would simply tap a secret reservoir of courage that had been accumulating inside me over the years. Courage, I seemed to think, comes to us in finite quantities, like an inheritance, and by being frugal and stashing it away, and letting it earn interest, we steadily increase our moral capital in preparation for that day when the account must be drawn down. It was a comforting theory. It dispensed with all those
20 bothersome little acts of daily courage; it offered hope and grace to the repetitive coward; it justified the past while amortizing the future. **A**

A AUTHOR'S PERSPECTIVE
Reread lines 9–21. What does this passage suggest about the way the narrator's perspective has changed over time?

In June of 1968, a month after graduating from Macalester College, I was drafted to fight a war I hated. I was twenty-one years old. Young, yes, and politically **naive,** but even so the American war in Vietnam seemed to me wrong. Certain blood was being shed for uncertain reasons. I saw no unity of purpose, no consensus on matters of philosophy or history or law. The very facts were shrouded in uncertainty: Was it a civil war? A war of national liberation or simple aggression? Who started it, and when, and why? What really happened to the U.S.S. *Maddox* on that dark night in the Gulf of
30 Tonkin?[1] Was Ho Chi Minh[2] a Communist stooge, or a nationalist savior, or both, or neither? What about the Geneva Accords?[3] What about SEATO[4] and the Cold War?[5] What about dominoes?[6] America was divided on these and a thousand other issues, and the debate had spilled out across the floor of the United States Senate and into the streets, and smart men in pinstripes could not agree on even the most fundamental matters of public policy. The only certainty that summer was moral confusion. It was my view then, and still is, that you don't make war without knowing why. Knowledge, of course, is always imperfect, but it seemed to me that when a nation goes to war it must have reasonable confidence in the justice and imperative of its cause. You can't
40 fix your mistakes. Once people are dead, you can't make them undead. **B**

In any case those were my convictions, and back in college I had taken a modest stand against the war. Nothing radical, no hothead stuff, just ringing

naive (nī-ēv′) *adj.* unsophisticated, lacking worldly experience

B HISTORICAL CONTEXT
Reread lines 22–40. Cite details that explain why the narrator is opposed to the Vietnam War.

---

1. **U.S.S. *Maddox* . . . Gulf of Tonkin** (tŏn′kĭn′): a reference to the alleged attack in 1964 on the U.S. destroyer *Maddox* in the Gulf of Tonkin, off the coast of North Vietnam, which provided a basis for expanding U.S. involvement in the Vietnam conflict.

2. **Ho Chi Minh** (hō′ chē′ mĭn′): a political leader who waged a successful fight against French colonial rule and established a Communist government in North Vietnam.

3. **Geneva Accords:** a 1954 peace agreement providing for the temporary division of Vietnam into North and South Vietnam and calling for national elections.

4. **SEATO:** the Southeast Asia Treaty Organization, an alliance of eight nations, including the United States, formed to halt Communist expansion in Southeast Asia after Communist forces defeated France in Indochina.

5. **Cold War:** the post–World War II struggle for influence between Communist and democratic nations.

6. **dominoes:** a reference to the domino theory, which holds that if a nation becomes a Communist state, it it will cause neighboring nations to also become Communist, as a falling domino will cause neighboring dominoes to fall too.

a few doorbells for Gene McCarthy,[7] composing a few tedious, uninspired editorials for the campus newspaper. Oddly, though, it was almost entirely an intellectual activity. I brought some energy to it, of course, but it was the energy that accompanies almost any abstract endeavor; I felt no personal danger; I felt no sense of an impending crisis in my life. Stupidly, with a kind of smug removal that I can't begin to fathom, I assumed that the problems of killing and dying did not fall within my special province.

50   The draft notice arrived on June 17, 1968. It was a humid afternoon, I remember, cloudy and very quiet, and I'd just come in from a round of golf. My mother and father were having lunch out in the kitchen. I remember opening up the letter, scanning the first few lines, feeling the blood go thick behind my eyes. I remember a sound in my head. It wasn't thinking, it was just a silent howl. A million things all at once—I was too *good* for this war. Too smart, too **compassionate,** too everything. It couldn't happen. I was above it. I had the world—Phi Beta Kappa and summa cum laude and president of the student body and a full-ride scholarship for grad studies at Harvard. A mistake, maybe—a foul-up in the paperwork. I was no soldier. I hated Boy Scouts. I

60 hated camping out. I hated dirt and tents and mosquitoes. The sight of blood made me queasy, and I couldn't tolerate authority, and I didn't know a rifle from a slingshot. I was a *liberal*: If they needed fresh bodies, why not draft some back-to-the-stone-age hawk? Or some dumb jingo[8] in his hardhat and Bomb Hanoi button? Or one of LBJ's[9] pretty daughters? Or Westmoreland's[10] whole family—nephews and nieces and baby grandson? There should be a law, I thought. If you support a war, if you think it's worth the price, that's fine, but you have to put your own life on the line. You have to head for the front and hook up with an infantry unit and help spill the blood. And you have to bring along your wife, or your kids, or your lover. A *law*, I thought.

70   I remember the rage in my stomach. Later it burned down to a smoldering self-pity, then to numbness. At dinner that night my father asked what my plans were.

compassionate
(kəm-păsh′ə-nĭt) *adj.*
feeling or sharing the
suffering of others

---

7. **Gene McCarthy:** Eugene McCarthy, the U.S. senator from Minnesota and a critic of the Vietnam War, who unsuccessfully sought the 1968 Democratic presidential nomination.

8. **jingo** (jĭng′gō): one who aggressively supports his or her country and favors war as a means of settling political disputes.

9. **LBJ:** Lyndon B. Johnson, the U.S. president from 1963 to 1969.

10. **Westmoreland:** General William Westmoreland, the senior commander of U.S. forces in Vietnam from 1964 to 1968.

"Nothing," I said. "Wait."

I spent the summer of 1968 working in an Armour meat-packing plant in my hometown of Worthington, Minnesota. The plant specialized in pork products, and for eight hours a day I stood on a quarter-mile assembly line—more properly, a disassembly line—removing blood clots from the necks of dead pigs. My job title, I believe, was Declotter. After slaughter, the hogs were decapitated, split down the length of the belly, pried open, eviscerated,[11] and strung up by the hind hocks on a high conveyer belt. Then gravity took
80 over. By the time a carcass reached my spot on the line, the fluids had mostly drained out, everything except for thick clots of blood in the neck and upper chest cavity. To remove the stuff, I used a kind of water gun. The machine was heavy, maybe eighty pounds, and was suspended from the ceiling by a heavy rubber cord. There was some bounce to it, an elastic up-and-down give, and the trick was to maneuver the gun with your whole body, not lifting with the arms, just letting the rubber cord do the work for you. At one end was a trigger; at the muzzle end was a small nozzle and a steel roller brush. As a carcass passed by, you'd lean forward and swing the gun up against the clots and squeeze the trigger, all in one motion, and the brush would whirl and
90 water would come shooting out and you'd hear a quick splattering sound as the clots dissolved into a fine red mist. It was not pleasant work. Goggles were a necessity, and a rubber apron, but even so it was like standing for eight hours a day under a lukewarm blood-shower. At night I'd go home smelling of pig. I couldn't wash it out. Even after a hot bath, scrubbing hard, the stink was always there—like old bacon, or sausage, a dense greasy pig-stink that soaked deep into my skin and hair. Among other things, I remember, it was tough getting dates that summer. I felt isolated; I spent a lot of time alone. And there was also that draft notice tucked away in my wallet.

In the evenings I'd sometimes borrow my father's car and drive aimlessly
100 around town, feeling sorry for myself, thinking about the war and the pig factory and how my life seemed to be collapsing toward slaughter. I felt paralyzed. All around me the options seemed to be narrowing, as if I were hurtling down a huge black funnel, the whole world squeezing in tight. There was no happy way out. The government had ended most graduate school deferments; the waiting lists for the National Guard and Reserves[12] were impossibly long; my health was solid; I didn't qualify for CO status[13]—no religious grounds, no history as a pacifist. Moreover, I could not claim to be opposed to war as a matter of general principle. There were occasions, I believed, when a nation was justified in using military force to achieve its
110 ends, to stop a Hitler or some comparable evil, and I told myself that in such circumstances I would've willingly marched off to the battle. The problem, though, was that a draft board did not let you choose your war. **G**

G HISTORICAL CONTEXT
Reread lines 99–112, and then review the Background on page 909. What circumstances from that period are depicted here?

---

11. **eviscerated** (ĭ-vĭs′ə-rā′tĭd): having guts removed.

12. **National Guard and Reserves:** military reserve units run by each state in the United States. Some men joined these units to avoid service in Vietnam.

13. **CO status:** the status of a conscientious objector, a person exempted from military service because of strongly held moral or religious beliefs that do not permit participation in war.

Beyond all this, or at the very center, was the raw fact of terror. I did not want to die. Not ever. But certainly not then, not there, not in a wrong war. Driving up Main Street, past the courthouse and the Ben Franklin store, I sometimes felt the fear spreading inside me like weeds. I imagined myself dead. I imagined myself doing things I could not do—charging an enemy position, taking aim at another human being. **D**

120 At some point in mid-July I began thinking seriously about Canada. The border lay a few hundred miles north, an eight-hour drive. Both my conscience and my instincts were telling me to make a break for it, just take off and run like hell and never stop. In the beginning the idea seemed purely abstract, the word Canada printing itself out in my head; but after a time I could see particular shapes and images, the sorry details of my own future— a hotel room in Winnipeg, a battered old suitcase, my father's eyes as I tried to explain myself over the telephone. I could almost hear his voice, and my mother's. Run, I'd think. Then I'd think, Impossible. Then a second later I'd think, *Run.*

It was a kind of schizophrenia.[14] A moral split. I couldn't make up my mind.
130 I feared the war, yes, but I also feared exile. I was afraid of walking away from my own life, my friends and my family, my whole history, everything that mattered to me. I feared losing the respect of my parents. I feared the law. I feared ridicule and **censure.** My hometown was a conservative little spot on the prairie, a place where tradition counted, and it was easy to imagine people sitting around a table at the old Gobbler Café on Main Street, coffee cups poised, the conversation slowly zeroing in on the young O'Brien kid, how the damned sissy had taken off for Canada. At night, when I couldn't sleep, I'd sometimes carry on fierce arguments with those people. I'd be screaming at them, telling them how much I detested their blind, thoughtless, automatic
140 **acquiescence** to it all, their simple-minded patriotism, their prideful ignorance, their love-it-or-leave-it platitudes, how they were sending me off to fight a war they didn't understand and didn't want to understand. I held them responsible. By God, yes I *did.* All of them—I held them personally and individually responsible—the polyestered Kiwanis boys, the merchants and farmers, the pious churchgoers, the chatty housewives, the PTA and the Lions club and the Veterans of Foreign Wars and the fine upstanding gentry out at the country club. They didn't know Bao Dai[15] from the man in the moon. They didn't know history. They didn't know the first thing about Diem's[16] tyranny, or the nature of Vietnamese nationalism, or the long colonialism of
150 the French—this was all too damned complicated, it required some reading— but no matter, it was a war to stop the Communists, plain and simple, which was how they liked things, and you were treasonous if you had second thoughts about killing or dying for plain and simple reasons. **E**

> **D** **GRAMMAR AND STYLE**
> Reread lines 113–118. Notice how O'Brien uses short sentences, sentence fragments, and figurative language to establish his **voice,** or the "sound" of his writing.

censure (sĕn'shər) *n.* harsh criticism or disapproval

acquiescence (ăk'wē-ĕs'əns) *n.* passive agreement; acceptance without protest

> **E** **AUTHOR'S PERSPECTIVE**
> What can you infer about the author's values based on the narrator's statements regarding people in his hometown?

---

14. **schizophrenia** (skĭt'sə-frē'nē-ə): a mental disorder. Here, the narrator refers to a split personality.

15. **Bao Dai** (bä'ō dä'ē): the last emperor of Vietnam (1926–1945) and chief of state from 1949 to 1955.

16. **Diem:** Ngo Dinh Diem (nyō' dǐn' dē-ĕm'), the brutal and dictatorial first president of South Vietnam, who was murdered by his own generals in 1963.

I was bitter, sure. But it was so much more than that. The emotions went from outrage to terror to bewilderment to guilt to sorrow and then back again to outrage. I felt a sickness inside me. Real disease.

Most of this I've told before, or at least hinted at, but what I have never told is the full truth. How I cracked. How at work one morning, standing on the pig line, I felt something break open in my chest. I don't know what 160 it was. I'll never know. But it was real. I know that much, it was a physical rupture—a cracking-leaking-popping feeling. I remember dropping my water gun. Quickly, almost without thought, I took off my apron and walked out of the plant and drove home. It was midmorning, I remember, and the house was empty. Down in my chest there was still that leaking sensation, something very warm and precious spilling out, and I was covered with blood and hogstink, and for a long while I just concentrated on holding myself together. I remember taking a hot shower. I remember packing a suitcase and carrying it out to the kitchen, standing very still for a few minutes, looking carefully at the familiar objects all around me. The old chrome toaster, the telephone, the 170 pink and white Formica on the kitchen counters. The room was full of bright sunshine. Everything sparkled. My house, I thought. My life. I'm not sure how long I stood there, but later I scribbled out a short note to my parents.

What it said exactly, I don't recall now. Something vague. Taking off, will call, love Tim.

I drove north.

It's a blur now, as it was then, and all I remember is a sense of high velocity and the feel of the steering wheel in my hands. I was riding on adrenaline.[17] A giddy feeling, in a way, except there was the dreamy edge of impossibility to it—like running a dead-end maze—no way out—it couldn't 180 come to a happy conclusion and yet I was doing it anyway because it was all I could think to do. It was pure flight, fast and mindless. I had no plan. Just hit the border at high speed and crash through and keep on running. Near dusk I passed through Bemidji, then turned northeast toward International Falls. I spent the night in the car behind a closed-down gas station a half mile from the border. In the morning, after gassing up, I headed straight west along the Rainy River, which separates Minnesota from Canada, and which for me separated one life from another. The land was mostly wilderness. Here and there I passed a motel or bait shop, but otherwise the country unfolded in great sweeps of pine and birch and sumac. Though it was still August, the air already 190 had the smell of October, football season, piles of yellow-red leaves, everything crisp and clean. I remember a huge blue sky. Off to my right was the Rainy River, wide as a lake in places, and beyond the Rainy River was Canada.

For a while I just drove, not aiming at anything, then in the late morning I began looking for a place to lie low for a day or two. I was exhausted, and

---

17. **adrenaline** (ə-drĕn′ə-lĭn): a hormone that is released into the bloodstream in response to physical or mental stress, such as fear, and that initiates or heightens several physical responses, including an increase in heart rate.

scared sick, and around noon I pulled into an old fishing resort called the Tip Top Lodge. Actually, it was not a lodge at all, just eight or nine tiny yellow cabins clustered on a peninsula that jutted northward into the Rainy River. The place was in sorry shape. There was a dangerous wooden dock, an old minnow tank, a flimsy tar paper boathouse along the shore. The main building,

200 which stood in a cluster of pines on high ground, seemed to lean heavily to one side, like a cripple, the roof sagging toward Canada. Briefly, I thought about turning around, just giving up, but then I got out of the car and walked up to the front porch.

The man who opened the door that day is the hero of my life. How do I say this without sounding sappy? Blurt it out—the man saved me. He offered exactly what I needed, without questions, without any words at all. He took me in. He was there at the critical time—a silent, watchful presence. Six days later, when it ended, I was unable to find a proper way to thank him, and I never have, and so, if nothing else, this story represents a small gesture of

210 gratitude twenty years overdue.

Even after two decades I can close my eyes and return to that porch at the Tip Top Lodge. I can see the old guy staring at me. Elroy Berdahl: eighty-one years old, skinny and shrunken and mostly bald. He wore a flannel shirt and brown work pants. In one hand, I remember, he carried a green apple, a small paring knife in the other. His eyes had the bluish gray color of a razor blade, the same polished shine, and as he peered up at me I felt a strange sharpness, almost painful, a cutting sensation, as if his gaze were somehow

slicing me open. In part, no doubt, it was my own sense of guilt, but even so
I'm absolutely certain that the old man took one look and went right to the
220 heart of things—a kid in trouble. When I asked for a room, Elroy made a little
clicking sound with his tongue. He nodded, led me out to one of the cabins,
and dropped a key in my hand. I remember smiling at him. I also remember
wishing I hadn't. The old man shook his head as if to tell me it wasn't worth
the bother.

"Dinner at five-thirty," he said. "You eat fish?"

"Anything," I said.

Elroy grunted and said, "I'll bet."

e spent six days together at the Tip Top Lodge.
Just the two of us. Tourist season was over, and there were no
230 boats on the river, and the wilderness seemed to withdraw into a
great permanent stillness. Over those six days Elroy Berdahl and I took most of
our meals together. In the mornings we sometimes went out on long hikes into
the woods, and at night we played Scrabble or listened to records or sat reading
in front of his big stone fireplace. At times I felt the awkwardness of an intruder,
but Elroy accepted me into his quiet routine without fuss or ceremony. He took
my presence for granted, the same way he might've sheltered a stray cat—no
wasted sighs or pity—and there was never any talk about it. Just the opposite.
What I remember more than anything is the man's
willful, almost ferocious silence. In all that time
240 together, all those hours, he never asked the obvious
questions: Why was I there? Why alone? Why so
preoccupied? If Elroy was curious about any of this,
he was careful never to put it into words.

My hunch, though, is that he already knew. At
least the basics. After all, it was 1968, and guys were
burning draft cards, and Canada was just a boat ride
away. Elroy Berdahl was no hick. His bedroom, I
remember, was cluttered with books and newspapers.
He killed me at the Scrabble board, barely
250 concentrating, and on those occasions when speech
was necessary, he had a way of compressing large
thoughts into small, cryptic packets of language.
One evening, just at sunset, he pointed up at an owl
circling over the violet-lighted forest to the west.

"Hey, O'Brien," he said. "There's Jesus."

The man was sharp—he didn't miss much. Those
razor eyes. Now and then he'd catch me staring out
at the river, at the far shore, and I could almost hear
the tumblers clicking in his head. Maybe I'm wrong,
260 but I doubt it.

preoccupied
(prē-ŏk'yə-pīd') *adj.*
absorbed in one's
thoughts; distracted

One thing for certain, he knew I was in desperate trouble. And he knew I couldn't talk about it. The wrong word—or even the right word—and I would've disappeared. I was wired and jittery. My skin felt too tight. After supper one evening I vomited and went back to my cabin and lay down for a few moments and then vomited again; another time, in the middle of the afternoon, I began sweating and couldn't shut it off. I went through whole days feeling dizzy with sorrow. I couldn't sleep; I couldn't lie still. At night I'd toss around in bed, half awake, half dreaming, imagining how I'd sneak down to the beach and quietly push one of the old man's boats out into the river and start paddling my way toward Canada. There were times when I thought I'd gone off the psychic edge. I couldn't tell up from down, I was just falling, and late in the night I'd lie there watching weird pictures spin through my head. Getting chased by the Border Patrol—helicopters and searchlights and barking dogs—I'd be crashing through the woods, I'd be down on my hands and knees—people shouting out my name—the law closing in on all sides—my hometown draft board and the FBI and the Royal Canadian Mounted Police. It all seemed crazy and impossible. Twenty-one years old, an ordinary kid with all the ordinary dreams and ambitions, and all I wanted was to live the life I was born to—a mainstream life—I loved baseball and hamburgers and cherry Cokes—and now I was off on the margins of exile, leaving my country forever, and it seemed so impossible and terrible and sad. **F**

I'm not sure how I made it through those six days. Most of it I can't remember. On two or three afternoons, to pass some time, I helped Elroy get the place ready for winter, sweeping down the cabins and hauling in the boats, little chores that kept my body moving. The days were cool and bright. The nights were very dark. One morning the old man showed me how to split and stack firewood, and for several hours we just worked in silence out behind his house. At one point, I remember, Elroy put down his maul[18] and looked at me for a long time, his lips drawn as if framing a difficult question, but then he shook his head and went back to work. The man's self-control was amazing. He never pried. He never put me in a position that required lies or denials. To an extent, I supposed, his **reticence** was typical of that part of Minnesota, where privacy still held value, and even if I'd been walking around with some horrible deformity—four arms and three heads—I'm sure the old man would've talked about everything except those extra arms and heads. Simple politeness was part of it. But even more than that, I think, the man understood that words were insufficient. The problem had gone beyond discussion. During that long summer I'd been over and over the various arguments, all the pros and cons, and it was no longer a question that could be decided by an act of pure reason. Intellect had come up against emotion. My conscience told me to run, but some irrational and powerful force was resisting, like a weight pushing me toward the war. What it came down to, stupidly, was a sense of shame. Hot, stupid shame. I did not want people to think badly of me. Not my parents, not my brother and sister, not even the folks down at the Gobbler Café. I was

F HISTORICAL CONTEXT
How does the historical context of the work help you understand the narrator's feelings in lines 261–281?

reticence (rĕt′ĭ-səns) *n.* the quality of keeping silent or reserved

---

18. **maul** (môl): a heavy hammer with a wedge-shaped head.

ashamed to be there at the Tip Top Lodge. I was ashamed of my conscience, ashamed to be doing the right thing.

Some of this Elroy must've understood. Not the details, of course, but the plain fact of crisis.

Although the old man never confronted me about it, there was one occasion
310 when he came close to forcing the whole thing out into the open. It was early evening, and we'd just finished supper, and over coffee and dessert I asked him about my bill, how much I owed so far. For a long while the old man squinted down at the tablecloth.

"Well, the basic rate," he said, "is fifty bucks a night. Not counting meals. This makes four nights, right?"

I nodded. I had three hundred and twelve dollars in my wallet.

Elroy kept his eyes on the tablecloth. "Now that's an on-season price. To be fair, I suppose we should knock it down a peg or two." He leaned back in his chair. "What's a reasonable number, you figure?"
320 "I don't know," I said. "Forty?"

"Forty's good. Forty a night. Then we tack on food—say another hundred? Two hundred sixty total?"

"I guess."

He raised his eyebrows. "Too much?"

"No, that's fair. It's fine. Tomorrow, though . . . I think I'd better take off tomorrow."

Elroy shrugged and began clearing the table. For a time he fussed with the dishes, whistling to himself as if the subject had been settled. After a second he slapped his hands together.
330 "You know what we forgot?" he said. "We forgot wages. Those odd jobs you done. What we have to do, we have to figure out what your time's worth. Your last job—how much did you pull in an hour?"

"Not enough," I said.

"A bad one?"

"Yes. Pretty bad."

Slowly then, without intending any long sermon, I told him about my days at the pig plant. It began as a straight recitation of the facts, but before I could stop myself I was talking about the blood clots and the water gun and how the smell had soaked into my skin and how I couldn't wash it away. I went on for
340 a long time. I told him about wild hogs squealing in my dreams, the sounds of butchery, slaughterhouse sounds, and how I'd sometimes wake up with that greasy pig-stink in my throat.

When I was finished, Elroy nodded at me.

"Well, to be honest," he said, "when you first showed up here, I wondered about that. The aroma, I mean. Smelled like you was awful damned fond of pork chops." The old man almost smiled. He made a snuffling sound, then sat down with a pencil and a piece of paper. "So what'd this crud job pay? Ten bucks an hour? Fifteen?"

"Less."

ANALYZE VISUALS
What details in the photograph help you form an impression of the Tip Top Lodge?

350   Elroy shook his head. "Let's make it fifteen. You put in twenty-five hours here, easy. That's three hundred seventy-five bucks total wages. We subtract the two hundred sixty for food and lodging. I still owe you a hundred and fifteen."

He took four fifties out of his shirt pocket and laid them on the table.

"Call it even," he said.

"No."

"Pick it up. Get yourself a haircut."

The money lay on the table for the rest of the evening. It was still there when I went back to my cabin. In the morning though, I found an envelope tacked to my door. Inside were the four fifties and a two-word note that said

360 EMERGENCY FUND.

The man knew.

Looking back after twenty years, I sometimes wonder if the events of that summer didn't happen in some other dimension, a place where your life exists before you've lived it, and where it goes afterward. None of it ever seemed real. During my time at the Tip Top Lodge I had the feeling that I'd slipped out of my own skin, hovering a few feet away while some poor yo-yo with my name and face tried to make his way toward a future he didn't

understand and didn't want. Even now I can see myself as I was then. It's like watching an old home movie: I'm young and tan and fit. I've got hair—lots of
370 it. I don't smoke or drink. I'm wearing faded blue jeans and a white polo shirt. I can see myself sitting on Elroy Berdahl's dock near dusk one evening, the sky a bright shimmering pink, and I'm finishing up a letter to my parents that tells what I'm about to do and why I'm doing it and how sorry I am that I've never found the courage to talk to them about it. I ask them not to be angry. I try to explain some of my feelings, but there aren't enough words, and so I just say that it's a thing that has to be done. At the end of the letter I talk about the vacations we used to take up in this north country, at a place called Whitefish Lake, and how the scenery here reminds me of those good times. I tell them I'm fine. I tell them I'll write again from Winnipeg or Montreal or wherever I
380 end up.

On my last full day, the sixth day, the old man took me out fishing on the Rainy River. The afternoon was sunny and cold. A stiff breeze came in from the north, and I remember how the little fourteen-foot boat made sharp rocking motions as we pushed off from the dock. The current was fast. All around us, I remember, there was a vastness to the world, an unpeopled rawness, just the trees and the sky and the water reaching out toward nowhere. The air had the brittle scent of October.

For ten or fifteen minutes Elroy held a course upstream, the river choppy and silver-gray, then he turned straight north and put the engine on full
390 throttle. I felt the bow lift beneath me. I remember the wind in my ears, the sound of the old outboard Evinrude. For a time I didn't pay attention to anything, just feeling the cold spray against my face, but then it occurred to me that at some point we must've passed into Canadian waters, across that dotted line between two different worlds, and I remember a sudden tightness in my chest as I looked up and watched the far shore come at me. This wasn't a daydream. It was tangible and real. As we came in toward land, Elroy cut the engine, letting the boat fishtail lightly about twenty yards off shore. The old man didn't look at me or speak. Bending down, he opened up his tackle box and busied himself with a bobber and a piece of wire leader, humming to
400 himself, his eyes down.

It struck me then that he must've planned it. I'll never be certain, of course, but I think he meant to bring me up against the realities, to guide me across the river and to take me to the edge and to stand a kind of vigil as I chose a life for myself. **G**

I remember staring at the old man, then at my hands, then at Canada. The shoreline was dense with brush and timber. I could see tiny red berries on the bushes. I could see a squirrel up in one of the birch trees, a big crow looking at me from a boulder along the river. That close—twenty yards—and I could see the delicate latticework of the leaves, the texture of the soil, the browned
410 needles beneath the pines, the configurations of geology and human history.

G PREDICT
What choices will O'Brien make now that he can easily reach Canada? Cite evidence to support your prediction.

Twenty yards. I could've done it. I could've jumped and started swimming for my life. Inside me, in my chest, I felt a terrible squeezing pressure. Even now, as I write this, I can still feel that tightness. And I want you to feel it—the wind coming off the river, the waves, the silence, the wooded frontier. You're at the bow of a boat on the Rainy River. You're twenty-one years old, you're scared, and there's a hard squeezing pressure in your chest.

What would you do?

Would you jump? Would you feel pity for yourself? Would you think about the family and your childhood and your dreams and all you're leaving behind? Would it hurt? Would it feel like dying? Would you cry, as I did?

I tried to swallow it back. I tried to smile, except I was crying.

Now, perhaps, you can understand why I've never told this story before. It's not just the embarrassment of tears. That's part of it, no doubt, but what embarrasses me much more, and always will, is the paralysis that took my heart. A moral freeze: I couldn't decide, I couldn't act, I couldn't comport myself with even a pretense of modest human dignity. **H**

All I could do was cry. Quietly, not bawling, just the chest-chokes.

At the rear of the boat Elroy Berdahl pretended not to notice. He held a fishing rod in his hands, his head bowed to hide his eyes. He kept humming a soft, monotonous little tune. Everywhere, it seemed, in the trees and water and sky, a great worldwide sadness came pressing down on me, a crushing sorrow, sorrow like I had never known before. And what was so sad, I realized, was that Canada had become a pitiful fantasy. Silly and hopeless. It was no longer a possibility. Right then, with the shore so close, I understood that I would not do what I should do. I would not swim away from my hometown and my country and my life. I would not be brave. That old image of myself as a hero, as a man of conscience and courage, all that was just a threadbare pipe dream.[19] Bobbing there on the Rainy River, looking back at the Minnesota shore, I felt a sudden swell of helplessness come over me, a drowning sensation, as if I had toppled overboard and was being swept away by the silver waves. Chunks of my own history flashed by. I saw a seven-year-old boy in a white cowboy hat and a Lone Ranger mask and a pair of holstered six-shooters; I saw a twelve-year-old Little League shortstop pivoting to turn a double play; I saw a sixteen-year-old kid decked out for his first prom, looking spiffy in a white tux and a black bow tie, his hair cut short and flat, his shoes freshly polished. My whole life seemed to spill out into the river, swirling

H **AUTHOR'S PERSPECTIVE**
Reread lines 422–426. What insight into the author's values do you gain from this passage?

---

19. **pipe dream:** a daydream or fantasy that will never happen; vain hope.

away from me, everything I had ever been or ever wanted to be. I couldn't get my breath; I couldn't stay afloat; I couldn't tell which way to swim. A hallucination, I suppose, but it was as real as anything I would ever feel. I saw my parents calling to me from the far shoreline. I saw my brother and sister, all the townsfolk, the mayor and the entire Chamber of Commerce and all my old teachers and girlfriends and high school buddies. Like some weird
460 sporting event: everybody screaming from the sidelines, rooting me on—a loud stadium roar. Hotdogs and popcorn—stadium smells, stadium heat. A squad of cheerleaders did cartwheels along the banks of the Rainy River; they had megaphones and pompoms and smooth brown thighs. The crowd swayed left and right. A marching band played fight songs. All my aunts and uncles were there, and Abraham Lincoln and Saint George,[20] and a nine-year-old girl named Linda who had died of a brain tumor back in fifth grade, and several members of the United States Senate, and a blind poet scribbling notes, and LBJ, and Huck Finn, and Abbie Hoffman,[21] and all the dead soldiers back from the grave, and the many thousands who were later to die—villagers
470 with terrible burns, little kids without arms or legs—yes, and the Joint Chiefs of Staff[22] were there, and a couple of popes, and a first lieutenant named Jimmy Cross, and the last surviving veteran of the American Civil War, and Jane Fonda dressed up as Barbarella,[23] and an old man sprawled beside a pigpen, and my grandfather, and Gary Cooper,[24] and a kind-faced woman carrying an umbrella and a copy of Plato's *Republic*,[25] and a million ferocious citizens waving flags of all shapes and colors—people in hardhats, people in headbands—they were all whooping and chanting and urging me toward one shore or the other. I saw faces from my distant past and distant future. My wife was there. My unborn daughter waved at me, and my two sons hopped
480 up and down, and a drill sergeant named Blyton sneered and shot up a finger and shook his head. There was a choir in bright purple robes. There was a cabbie from the Bronx. There was a slim young man I would one day kill with a hand grenade along a red clay trail outside the village of My Khe.[26] ∎

The little aluminum boat rocked softly beneath me. There was the wind and the sky.

I tried to will myself overboard.

I gripped the edge of the boat and leaned forward and thought, *Now.*

MAKE INFERENCES
Notice the **extended simile** in lines 457–483 of a sporting event in which people are cheering for the narrator from both shores of the river. What can you infer about the narrator's state of mind from this simile?

---

20. **Saint George:** a Christian martyr and the patron saint of England. According to legend, he slew a frightening dragon.

21. **Abbie Hoffman:** a social organizer and radical anti–Vietnam War activist known for his humor and politically inspired pranks.

22. **Joint Chiefs of Staff:** the principal military advisors of the U.S. president, including the chiefs of the army, navy, and air force and the commandant of the marines.

23. **Jane Fonda dressed up as Barbarella:** the actress and anti–Vietnam War activist Jane Fonda, who played the title character in the 1968 science fiction film *Barbarella*.

24. **Gary Cooper:** an American actor famous for playing strong, quiet heroes.

25. **Plato's *Republic*:** a famous work in which the ancient Greek philosopher Plato describes the ideal state or society.

26. **My Khe** (mē' kā').

I did try. It just wasn't possible.

All those eyes on me—the town, the whole universe—and I couldn't risk
490 the embarrassment. It was as if there were an audience to my life, that swirl
of faces along the river, and in my head I could hear people screaming at
me. Traitor! they yelled. Turncoat! I felt myself blush. I couldn't tolerate it. I
couldn't endure the mockery, or the disgrace, or the patriotic ridicule. Even in
my imagination, the shore just twenty yards away, I couldn't make myself be
brave. It had nothing to do with morality. Embarrassment, that's all it was.

And right then I submitted.

I would go to the war—I would kill and maybe die—because I was
embarrassed not to.

That was the sad thing. And so I sat in the bow of the boat and cried. It was
500 loud now. Loud, hard crying. **J**

Elroy Berdahl remained quiet. He kept fishing. He worked his line with
the tips of his fingers, patiently, squinting out at his red and white bobber on
the Rainy River. His eyes were flat and impassive. He didn't speak. He was
simply there, like the river and the late-summer sun. And yet by his presence,
his mute watchfulness, he made it real. He was the true audience. He was a
witness, like God, or like the gods, who look on in absolute silence as we live
our lives, as we make our choices or fail to make them.

"Ain't biting," he said.

Then after a time the old man pulled in his line and turned the boat back
510 toward Minnesota.

I don't remember saying goodbye. That last night we had dinner together,
and I went to bed early, and in the morning Elroy fixed breakfast for me.
When I told him I'd be leaving, the old man nodded as if he already knew.
He looked down at the table and smiled.

At some point later in the morning it's possible that we shook hands—I just
don't remember—but I do know that by the time I'd finished packing the old
man had disappeared. Around noon, when I took my suitcase out to the car, I
noticed that his old black pickup truck was no longer parked in front of the
house. I went inside and waited for a while, but I felt a bone certainty that
520 he wouldn't be back. In a way, I thought, it was appropriate. I washed up the
breakfast dishes, left his two hundred dollars on the kitchen counter, got into
the car, and drove south toward home.

The day was cloudy. I passed through towns with familiar names, through
the pine forests and down to the prairie, and then to Vietnam, where I was a
soldier, and then home again. I survived, but it's not a happy ending. I was a
coward. I went to the war. ◖

J AUTHOR'S
PERSPECTIVE
How might the author
view his character's
decision to go to war?

Comprehension

1. **Recall** What kind of notice does the narrator receive in the mail after graduating from college?

2. **Recall** Why does the narrator drive toward the Canadian border?

3. **Recall** How does the narrator meet Elroy Berdahl?

4. **Summarize** What happens when Elroy's boat brings the narrator within 20 yards of the Canadian shoreline?

READING STANDARD
3.5 Analyze an author's perspective or viewpoint

Literary Analysis

5. **Analyze Historical Context** The 1960s was a period in which many young people rebelled against the beliefs and traditions of older generations. How does "On the Rainy River" reflect this historical context?

6. **Identify Author's Perspective** Review the chart you created as you read. How might the author's upbringing in a small Minnesota town have influenced his view of events and people in the story? Cite evidence from the text.

7. **Analyze Symbol** A symbol is a person, a place, an object, or an activity that represents something beyond itself. What does the narrator's job at the meat-packing plant symbolize? Explain your answer.

8. **Draw Conclusions** The narrator describes Elroy as "the hero of my life." In a graphic organizer like the one shown, identify some of Elroy's admirable traits and actions. Then explain why he was so important to the narrator.

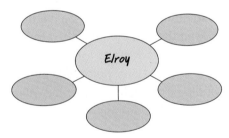

9. **Make Judgments** Do you agree with the narrator that his decision to go to Vietnam was an act of **cowardice?** Give reasons for your answer.

10. **Evaluate** Would this story be as effective if Tim O'Brien had not served in Vietnam? Explain why or why not.

Literary Criticism

11. **Social Context** How do the experiences of people entering the military today compare with the experiences of people in Tim O'Brien's generation? Cite examples from the text in your response.

Vocabulary in Context

VOCABULARY PRACTICE

Choose the vocabulary word that best completes each sentence.

1. We have to rely on _____ people to look out for the needy.
2. His _____ made him reluctant to take part in group discussions.
3. I am _____ with this issue; I can't think of anything else.
4. She was a _____ girl who knew nothing of the world outside her door.
5. The corrupt politician wanted to avoid public _____.
6. I have come to regret my _____ in this terrible decision.

WORD LIST

acquiescence

censure

compassionate

naive

preoccupied

reticence

VOCABULARY IN WRITING

Using three or more vocabulary words, write a brief letter from the narrator to his parents after he entered the military. Here is how you might begin:

> **EXAMPLE SENTENCE**
>
> I was too **preoccupied** with my basic training to write to you until now.

VOCABULARY STRATEGY: USING A DICTIONARY

In addition to the spellings and definitions of words, a **dictionary** contains other helpful features. Following the entry word is the pronunciation guide, a respelling of the word using symbols that stand for sounds. These symbols are explained in a pronunciation key. A dictionary also indicates the part of speech of each entry word and its etymology, or origin and history. When a word has more than one meaning, the different definitions are numbered. Usually the most common meaning appears first.

PRACTICE Use a dictionary to answer the following questions.

1. What syllable would you emphasize the most when pronouncing the word *acquiescence*?
2. What parts of speech can *censure* be?
3. What is the most common meaning of *preoccupy*?
4. What is a synonym for *compassionate*?
5. From which language did the word *reticent* originate?
6. Which meaning of *naive* is expressed in the following sentence? *Although the poem is full of clichés, the naive reader considered it a masterpiece.*

OHIO STANDARDS

VOCABULARY STANDARD
1.6 Use dictionaries

VOCABULARY PRACTICE
For more practice, go to the **Vocabulary Center** at **ClassZone.com.**

Reading-Writing Connection

Broaden your understanding of "On the Rainy River" by responding to these prompts. Then use **Revision: Grammar and Style** to improve your writing.

WRITING PROMPTS	SELF-CHECK

A. Short Response: Analyze Cowardice
The narrator concludes that he was a coward for going to fight in Vietnam. Write **one or two paragraphs** in which you analyze his view of **cowardice.**

An insightful analysis will . . .
- explain how the narrator uses the word *coward* at the end of the story
- provide examples from the story that illustrate the narrator's view of cowardice

B. Extended Response: Write a New Ending
Imagine that instead of remaining in the boat, the narrator swims to Canada. Write a **three-to-five-paragraph alternative ending** to the story that reflects this choice.

A powerful ending will . . .
- describe Elroy's reactions to the narrator's choice
- suggest how the narrator later felt about avoiding military service in Vietnam

REVISION: GRAMMAR AND STYLE

ESTABLISH VOICE Review the **Grammar and Style** note on page 915. Voice is the unique way a writer uses vocabulary, sentence structure, and figurative language to express himself or herself. The particular characteristics of a writer's voice help to identify a piece as belonging to that writer. In "On the Rainy River," for example, O'Brien's use of short, simple sentences, sentence fragments, and similes distinguishes his writing from that of other writers. Here is an example:

> *His eyes were flat and impassive. He didn't speak. He was simply there, like the river and the late-summer sun. And yet by his presence, his mute watchfulness, he made it real. He was the true audience. He was a witness, like God, or like the gods, who look on in absolute silence as we live our lives. . . .* (lines 503–507)

In this first draft, notice how the revisions in red better capture O'Brien's voice. Revise your response to Prompt B by tailoring your sentence structures and use of figurative language to make it seem as if O'Brien wrote the alternative ending.

OHIO STANDARDS

WRITING STANDARD
5.9 Use language and techniques to convey a personal style and voice

STUDENT MODEL

I jumped overboard, ~~and into the cool, clean water, leaving behind~~ *trailing behind me like tracks in sand* my life ~~as I knew it.~~ From now on, I was an outlaw, a draft dodger, ~~and~~ a criminal. But it felt right, *as if all my fears were being washed away.*

WRITING TOOLS
For prewriting, revision, and editing tools, visit the **Writing Center** at ClassZone.com.

The New Colossus
Poem by Emma Lazarus

Who Makes the Journey
Poem by Cathy Song

How does it feel to START OVER?

OHIO STANDARDS

READING STANDARDS
4.5 Analyze how choice of genre affects theme or topic
4.8 Analyze the author's use of mood and tone

KEY IDEA The United States has welcomed millions of people fleeing religious and political persecution, as well as those who simply wanted to make a better life for themselves and their families. In the following poems, Emma Lazarus and Cathy Song reflect upon the ideals and the reality of the **immigrant** experience.

DISCUSS If your family moved away from the United States, what challenges would you face? With a group of classmates, make a list of challenges and discuss how hard they would be to overcome.

Challenges
1. Learning a new language
2. Meeting friends
3.
4.
5.

LITERARY ANALYSIS: LITERARY PERIODS

Just as there are trends in fashion and music, there are trends in literature. For example, poems from the same **literary period** often have similarities in style. The opening lines of "The New Colossus" exemplify the formal tone and diction common in 19th-century poetry.

Not like the brazen giant of Greek fame,
With conquering limbs astride from land to land;

In contrast, the opening of "Who Makes the Journey" has a relaxed, conversational tone that is more typical of contemporary poetry.

In most cases,
it is the old woman
who makes the journey;

Contemporary poets are also less likely than poets from earlier periods to follow regular patterns of rhyme and meter.

As you read, note how the two poems differ in style and form, and consider how the poets' attitudes toward their subjects may have been influenced by their literary periods.

READING SKILL: ANALYZE SENSORY DETAILS

Each of the poems you will read has a vivid central image—a towering statue or an old woman crossing the street. To create these images, Lazarus and Song use **sensory details,** appealing to the senses of sight, hearing, taste, smell, or touch.

As you read, use a chart like the one shown to analyze sensory details in each poem.

"Who Makes the Journey"		
Detail	Sense	What It Suggests
"the stooped gnome figure" (line 30)	sight	small and worn down

Author Online

Emma Lazarus: Voice of Liberty In her brief lifetime, Emma Lazarus (lăz'ər-əs) saw the United States being transformed by a surge in immigration. Although her family had been in America since the 1600s, she strongly identified with immigrants, especially fellow Jews who had left eastern Europe to escape violence and oppression. She wrote her poem about the Statue of Liberty, "The New Colossus," in 1883 to raise funds to build a pedestal for the statue. The poem was later inscribed on the pedestal.

Emma Lazarus
1849–1887

Cathy Song: Family Ties Born in Hawaii of Korean and Chinese ancestry, Cathy Song often writes about the experiences of her immigrant grandparents and other family members. She has been widely praised for her beautiful imagery and her ability to draw meaning from seemingly minor incidents. Song came to national attention when her first book of poems won the prestigious Yale Series of Younger Poets competition in 1983.

Cathy Song
born 1955

 MORE ABOUT THE AUTHOR
For more on Emma Lazarus and Cathy Song, visit the **Literature Center** at **ClassZone.com.**

The New COLOSSUS

Emma Lazarus

Not like the brazen giant of Greek fame,[1]
With conquering limbs astride from land to land;
Here at our sea-washed, sunset gates shall stand
A mighty woman with a torch, whose flame
5 Is the imprisoned lightning, and her name
Mother of Exiles. From her beacon-hand
Glows world-wide welcome; her mild eyes command
The air-bridged harbor that twin cities[2] frame.
"Keep, ancient lands, your storied pomp!"[3] cries she
10 With silent lips. "Give me your tired, your poor,
Your huddled masses yearning to breathe free,
The wretched refuse of your teeming shore.
Send these, the homeless, tempest-tost[4] to me,
I lift my lamp beside the golden door!" **A**

A SENSORY DETAILS
What do the sensory
details in lines
10–14 suggest about
immigrants?

---

1. **giant of Greek fame:** the Colossus of Rhodes, a huge Greek statue
   of the sun god Helios.
2. **harbor . . . twin cities:** New York Harbor, where the Statue of Liberty
   is located. Brooklyn was a city separate from New York until 1898.
3. **storied pomp:** the splendor of your history.
4. **tempest-tost:** tossed by violent windstorms.

Who Makes the JOURNEY

Cathy Song

In most cases,
it is the old woman
who makes the journey;
the old man having had
5 the sense to stay
put and die at home.

You see her scurrying
behind her
newly arrived family.
10 She comes from the Azores[1]
and she comes from the Orient.
It makes no difference.
You have seen her before: **B**

the short substantial
15 legs buckle
under the weight
of the ghost child
she carried centuries

ago like a bundle of rags
20 who now turns in front
of your windshield,
transformed in Western clothes.

The grown woman stops
impatiently
25 and self-consciously
to motion *Hurry* to her mother.

---

1. **Azores:** a group of islands in the
   northern Atlantic Ocean.

B **LITERARY PERIODS**
What words and phrases
in lines 7–13 help give
the stanza a casual,
contemporary tone?

Seeping into your side view
mirror like a black mushroom
blooming in a bowl of water,
30 the stooped gnome figure
wades through the river
of cars hauling

her sack of cabbages,
the white and curved,
35 translucent leaves of which
she will wash individually
as if they were porcelain cups. **C**

Like black seed buttons
sewn onto a shapeless dress,
40 those cryptic eyes
rest on your small reflection

for an instant. Years pass.
History moves like an old woman
crossing the street.

C SENSORY DETAILS
What do the sensory
details in lines 33–37
reveal about the old
woman?

ANALYZE VISUALS
How does the photograph
reflect Song's description
of the old woman?

Comprehension

1. **Clarify** Who is being welcomed in "The New Colossus"?

2. **Recall** How does the old woman in "Who Makes the Journey" differ from her daughter?

3. **Clarify** What journey does the title of Cathy Song's poem refer to?

Literary Analysis

4. **Compare and Contrast** In what ways is the Statue of Liberty unlike the ancient Greek colossus that Lazarus describes in lines 1–2 of "The New Colossus"? Cite evidence from the text.

5. **Analyze Literary Periods** How might Lazarus's poem be different if she had written it today? Be specific.

6. **Interpret Figurative Language** A **simile** is figurative language that makes a comparison using *like* or *as*. Reread lines 43–44 of "Who Makes the Journey." Explain the meaning of the simile at the end of Song's poem.

7. **Identify Sensory Details** Review the chart you created as you read "Who Makes the Journey." What details does Song include to help you visualize the old woman as if you were watching her from a car?

8. **Analyze Tone and Author's Purpose** How would you describe the tone and purpose of "Who Makes the Journey"? Cite passages to support your response.

9. **Synthesize** On the basis of these two poems, what conclusion can you draw about the **immigrant** experience? Use a graphic organizer like the one shown to record your answer.

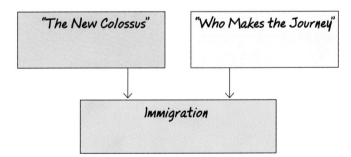

Literary Criticism

10. **Biographical Context** During the early 1880s, Emma Lazarus met many Jewish refugees who had recently fled Russia to escape a wave of anti-Semitic massacres. What details in "The New Colossus" reflect this personal experience?

**OHIO
STANDARDS**

READING STANDARD
4.8 Analyze the author's use of mood and tone

The Aftermath of September 11

Image Collection on  **MediaSmart** DVD

What are the SIGNS of the times?

OHIO STANDARDS

READING STANDARD
3.6 Identify appeals to emotion

KEY IDEA Any major event—a war, a natural disaster, or a political crisis—causes ripple effects. In this lesson, you'll examine images that are **reflections** of a life-altering event in U.S. history. To explore what might have motivated or influenced the creation of these images, it's helpful to have background about the event.

Background

Total Impact On September 11, 2001, terrorist hijackers crashed jetliners into the World Trade Center in New York City and into the Pentagon in Washington, D.C. Another hijacked plane bound for Washington crashed in rural Pennsylvania. Nearly 3,000 people died. The simple term for this catastrophic event became *9/11*.

The first image in this lesson is a cartoon from the *New Yorker*, a magazine known for its depictions of sophisticated city dwellers. The second image is the book cover of *9-11: September 11, 2001*, published by a collection of comic-book writers and artists. The third image is the top page of a Web site designed to help keep American citizens on alert.

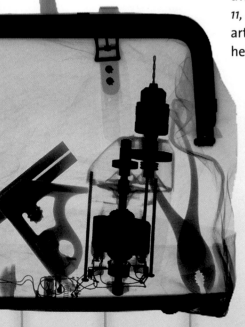

Media Literacy: History Through Media

Media images and messages are deeply influenced by the history and culture in which they are created. These images from 9/11 reflect the event's wide-ranging impact on the American way of life and the values and concerns of the time period.

CULTURAL INFLUENCES

IMAGES

Cartoon Since the 1920s, the cartoons of the *New Yorker* have made witty comments about major American events. In the aftermath of 9/11, the magazine's staff wanted to uphold its tradition of humorous commentary while acknowledging the heightened public anxiety about security.

Book Cover Following 9/11, comic book artists shifted the emphasis from imaginary superheroes to salute the heroism of the ordinary citizens—the first responders to the 9/11 attacks.

- Note the top of the cover. The shadow cast by the numbered title is in the shape of the twin towers of the World Trade Center.

- Notice the sizes of the people depicted on the billboard in relation to the size of Superman.

Web Site 9/11 marked a new era of homeland security.

- Sites like this one addressed the public's need for preparedness and tapped into a new sense of patriotism.

- Possible threats to security are menu items at the left of the page. At the center, the same links are categorized under headings worded as calls to action.

- Phrases such as "terrorism forces us" and "keep America safe" convey a sense of urgency and a need for watchfulness.

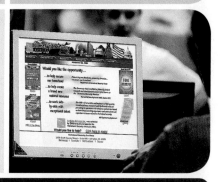

STRATEGIES FOR EXAMINING IMAGES

Use these questions to guide your examination of each image:

- What might the subject matter of the image reveal about the creator's life and times?

- What message does the image convey? Is any part of the image a potential symbol?

- What mood does the work reflect? what beliefs or values?

- What is the tone expressed through the image? What does this work pay tribute to or criticize?

- How do the design elements of **color, line, texture, shape,** and **words** work together to reinforce the work's message?

Viewing Guide for

The Aftermath of September 11

Access the full-sized images of the cartoon, book cover, and Web site on the DVD. Begin by examining each image individually and carefully, jotting down your own initial impressions. To help you examine each in terms of color, line, texture, and shape, refer to the **Elements of Design** section of the **Media Handbook** (pages R91–R92). Then quickly review the purposes, additional details, and strategies on page 937 and study the images again. Use questions like the following as well.

NOW VIEW

FIRST VIEWING: Comprehension

1. **Recall** What does Superman say as he looks at the billboard?

2. **Clarify** On the Web site of the U.S. Department of Homeland Security, what does the slogan encourage the public to do in response to terrorism?

CLOSE VIEWING: Media Literacy

3. **Analyze the Cartoon** In the aftermath of 9/11, airports, the White House, and other public buildings enforced stricter security measures. Nationwide, Americans had to adjust to the inconvenience of additional security checkpoints. In your own words, describe the message the cartoonist conveys in the *New Yorker* cartoon.

4. **Draw Conclusions** Look closely at the *9-11* book cover. What evidence can you find in the image that shows the artist is expressing America's strength and determination in the face of terrorism?

5. **Analyze the Web Site** Look at the images at the top of the homeland security Web site. The left-to-right presentation shows the official symbol of the U.S. Department of Homeland Security, the U.S. flag, and an ordinary citizen who appears calm, alert, and proud. What impressions do you think these images are intended to convey?

Write or Discuss

Compare the Images You've focused on three images that in some way reflect the aftermath of September 11, 2001. In your opinion, which image communicates the mood of these times most effectively? Give specific reasons for your views. Think about

- the original purpose for each image and any message it conveys
- how clearly the message comes across years after the event
- the use of color, line, texture, shape, and words in the images

Produce Your Own Media

Create a Signs-of-the-Times Collage What are the signs of *your* times? In recent times, you've probably witnessed—directly and indirectly—a number of happenings on the American scene, involving social and cultural issues, technological advances, music, fashion, the environment, media, and so on. Depict the times in which you live in the form of a collage. Use the design template shown as a guide in selecting images or quotations.

HERE'S HOW Here are a few suggestions for making the collage:

- Individually or in small groups, brainstorm a list of current events and trends.
- Decide on a tone for the piece. It can be humorous, serious, or a combination.
- Clip images and relevant headlines or quotations from a variety of old newspapers and magazines. Reflect what you believe to be the mood of the times.
- Think about how to incorporate such elements as color, line, texture, and shape into your collage.

MEDIA TOOLS
For help with creating a collage, visit the **Media Center** at **ClassZone.com**.

DESIGN TEMPLATE

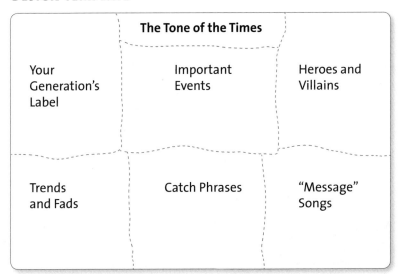

The Tone of the Times

| Your Generation's Label | Important Events | Heroes and Villains |
| Trends and Fads | Catch Phrases | "Message" Songs |

Tech Tip
You can use a word processing program to vary the typefaces of any headlines or quotes.

Writing Workshop

Informative Essay and Interview

Hearing about an event from someone who lived through it is a good way to understand what really happened. By interviewing someone and incorporating his or her experiences into an informative essay, you can make readers feel as if they were there. To get started, consult the **Writer's Road Map.**

WRITER'S ROAD MAP

Informative Essay and Interview

WRITING PROMPT 1

Writing from Literature Choose an event that you have read about. Find someone who remembers that event. Interview him or her and write an informative essay based on your interview and your reading. Your essay should briefly summarize the event, give the name of the person you interviewed, and explain that person's reaction to the event.

Events and Literary Works to Consider
- the assassination of Dr. Martin Luther King Jr. ("A Eulogy for Dr. Martin Luther King Jr.")
- one immigrant's story ("The New Colossus")

WRITING PROMPT 2

Writing from the Real World Choose a historical period or event that interests you. Interview someone who lived through that period or experienced that event. Then write an informative essay that identifies the person you chose to interview and explains what you learned about the subject from him or her.

Topics to Consider
- life during wartime
- a hurricane or another disaster
- popular culture in the 1950s, 1960s, 1970s, or 1980s

 WRITING TOOLS
For prewriting, revision, and editing tools, visit the **Writing Center** at **ClassZone.com.**

KEY TRAITS

1. IDEAS
- Presents a **thesis statement** that identifies the key points of the essay
- Clearly **identifies** the person interviewed and the topic discussed
- Includes **descriptive details** to give the reader a "you are there" feeling

2. ORGANIZATION
- **Introduces** the subject in an interesting, informative way
- Is logically **organized**
- Summarizes the significance of the event in a well-developed **conclusion**

3. VOICE
- Uses a **tone** appropriate for the topic, audience, and purpose

4. WORD CHOICE
- Includes **quotations** from the person interviewed
- Uses **precise language** to describe the situation

5. SENTENCE FLUENCY
- Uses a variety of **sentence structures** to help maintain the reader's interest

6. CONVENTIONS
- Employs **correct grammar and usage**

Part 1: Analyze a Student Model

WRITING STANDARD
6.4 Write informational essays or reports

Tyler Stone
Sun Valley High School

The Death of a President

At 43 years old, John F. Kennedy was the youngest man ever elected president. When he took office in 1961, racial tensions at home and the cold war with the Soviet Union were heating up. Kennedy's youth, energy, and eloquence captured Americans' hearts and gave them a new
5   vision for their country. People responded strongly to Kennedy's direct appeal and looked to the future with hope. Tragically, the president's own future would be cut short less than three years later, on November 22, 1963. People who lived through that day say that they will never forget where they were, what they were doing, and how they felt when
10 they heard the news of President Kennedy's assassination. My aunt, Sarah Stone, was one of those people, and she agreed to share some of her memories with me.

Aunt Sarah was a senior in high school in 1963, and she remembers that November 22 was an unusually warm day, more like spring than
15 the end of fall. "It was a Friday," she began, "which meant Driver's Ed rather than having to change for gym class. So I wore my new mohair sweater, which was very 'in' at the time. I remember sitting in study hall doing my math homework and rubbing my hand over the sleeve of the sweater, loving the way its softness tickled my palm and created static
20 electricity. That was when the loudspeaker began to crackle."

No one could recognize the principal's voice, my aunt said, because it sounded halting and confused as he announced, "The President has been shot." The students thought it was a joke at first. Things like that don't happen in America, they protested. But the loudspeaker had been

KEY TRAITS IN ACTION

Writer **introduces** the subject (President Kennedy's assassination) with specific details.

Thesis statement identifies the key points of the essay. The writer introduces his aunt as the person he interviewed.

Quotations and **descriptive details** help the reader understand what Sarah Stone experienced.

25 hooked into a radio, and as newscasters kept giving details and naming
places—Dallas, Dealey Plaza, Parkland Memorial Hospital—the reality
began to set in. "We still didn't know what Kennedy's condition was,"
Aunt Sarah recalled, "but we knew we would never be the same. And we
all cried—even the boys."

30   Then the principal broke into the radio broadcast and, although it
was still early afternoon, dismissed classes for the day. Numb and silent,
the students trooped home. "We sat in front of the television set the
whole weekend," she went on, "watching the horrible events unfold in
endless replay. We couldn't look away, as if seeing it enough times would
35 change the outcome." But nothing could change what had happened.
President Kennedy was dead.

     Police arrested the assassin, Lee Harvey Oswald. Then, with the
whole world watching, Jack Ruby shot Oswald. Although few people
had ever heard those names before, no one would ever forget them. "I
40 remember thinking," Aunt Sarah concluded, "that with almost 12 years
of education behind me, I didn't understand the first thing about the
world or the people in it. When President Kennedy died, the innocence
of a whole generation died with him."

     Aunt Sarah has never forgotten that day or President Kennedy's
45 famous words: "Ask not what your country can do for you—ask what
you can do for your country." She went on to serve in the Peace Corps
that Kennedy began, helping to keep his legacy alive by doing what she
could for her country.

Precise words describe the situation.

Essay is **organized** logically, presenting events in the order in which they happened.

Varied **sentence structures** keep the reader involved in the flow of events. The writer chooses quotations with an appropriate **tone** to discuss this serious topic.

Conclusion summarizes the lasting effects of the president's assassination on the writer's aunt.

2

Part 2: Apply the Writing Process

WRITING STANDARD
5.3 Establish and develop a clear thesis statement for informational writing

PREWRITING

| *What Should I Do?* | *What Does It Look Like?* |

1. Explore possible topics.
With a small group, brainstorm events that interest you. Use the bulleted items in the prompts on page 940 to get you started.

TIP Because you'll need to find someone to interview in addition to locating other information about your topic, try to come up with several workable ideas.

▶

Event	When It Happened
Iraq war	2000s
Early rock 'n' roll music	1950s
Assassination of President Kennedy	1963
Hurricane Katrina	2005

2. Identify people to interview.
List people who have personal information about your topics, such as relatives, neighbors, or teachers.

▶

People to interview:

Iraq war—talk to my cousin who's in the Marine Corps

Kennedy assassination—interview Aunt Sarah by phone

Rock 'n' roll—e-mail Mr. Johnson's brother

3. Choose a topic and contact a person who knows about it.
Tell the person who you are, explain what topic you're investigating, and ask if he or she is willing to be interviewed. If the answer is yes, set a time and date.

TIP Before the interview, make a list of open-ended questions—ones that require more than a yes-or-no answer.

▶

Questions for Aunt Sarah:

How old were you when Kennedy was assassinated?

What were you doing that day?

What actually happened?

How did you feel at the time?

What lasting effects did the event have on you?

4. Conduct and summarize the interview.
See pages R81–R82 for information on conducting an interview. Take detailed notes, even if you are audiotaping or videotaping the interview. Write a transcript of the questions and answers as soon as possible afterward.

▶

Q: How did you react when you heard that the president had been shot?

A: We all thought it was a joke at first, that this couldn't happen in America. But as we heard more and more details—Dallas, Dealey Plaza, Parkland Memorial Hospital—it became all too real.

What Should I Do?	**What Does It Look Like?**
1. Focus on the most important point you want to make. Consider all the information you've gathered from your reading and interviewing. Zero in on the idea that will serve as the thesis statement, or organizing principle, of your essay. **TIP** Think about what surprised, interested, or moved you.	*Main idea:* *The assassination of John F. Kennedy made a lasting impression. People who lived through that day say they will never forget where they were, what they were doing, and how they felt when they heard that awful news.*
2. Outline your material. Many informative essays follow this pattern: • introduction—captures the reader's interest and identifies the topic and the person being interviewed • body—includes quotations and details that help the reader understand what the event was like • conclusion—summarizes what the writer learned and leaves the reader with something to think about	*Introduction* • *brief facts about Kennedy* • *Aunt Sarah's role as interviewee* *Body* • *Aunt Sarah in school* • *details of shooting and students' reactions* • *closing of school and reliance on TV* • *Ruby shooting Oswald* • *Aunt Sarah's feelings* *Conclusion* • *quotation from Kennedy inauguration* • *Aunt Sarah's Peace Corps service* • *Kennedy's legacy*
3. Start with an attention grabber. Because you will be presenting a lot of information in your essay, be sure to grab your reader's attention with the first sentence. A powerful quotation, a brief anecdote, a memorable description, or an interesting fact can work well.	A memorable quotation *"Ask not what your country can do for you—ask what you can do for your country."* An intriguing fact *At 43 years old, John F. Kennedy was the youngest man ever elected president of the United States. He was also the youngest to die in office.*

REVISING AND EDITING

| *What Should I Do?* | *What Does It Look Like?* |

1. Include accurate quotations and rich descriptive details.
- (Circle) parts of your essay that have few quotations or descriptions.
- Replace some information with direct quotations and add lively sensory details.

▶ Aunt Sarah was a senior in high school in 1963, and she remembers that November 22 was an unusually warm day, more like spring than the end of fall. ⟨She was wearing a special sweater.⟩

"It was a Friday," she began, "which meant Driver's Ed rather than having to change for gym class. So I wore my new mohair sweater, which was very 'in' at the time."

2. Keep your language and tone appropriate.
- <u>Underline</u> examples of slang or jargon.
- Substitute words appropriate for your teacher and other adults.

  TIP It's fine to include slang or other informal language when quoting your interviewee.

▶ People ~~thought the guy was amazing and knew he was gonna make everything OK~~ responded strongly to Kennedy's direct appeal and looked to the future with hope.

3. Anticipate and answer readers' questions.
- Ask a peer reader to draw a ⃞box⃞ around statements that need more explanation.
- Add details or reasons to clarify your ideas.

  See page 946: Ask a Peer Reader

▶ The students thought it was a joke at first. Things like that don't happen in America, they protested. But the loudspeaker had been hooked into a radio, and as newscasters kept ⃞giving details and naming places⃞ the reality began to set in.
—Dallas, Dealey Plaza, Parkland Memorial Hospital—

4. Add punch to your conclusion.
- Read your conclusion aloud. [Bracket] statements that seem too general or obvious, such as "Things were really different back then."
- Replace these sentences with a strong explanation of the importance of your topic.

▶ Aunt Sarah has never forgotten that day, [~~It was an unusual experience that will be etched into her heart forever.~~] or President Kennedy's famous words: "Ask not what your country can do for you—ask what you can do for your country." She went on to serve in the Peace Corps that Kennedy began, helping to keep his legacy alive by doing what she could for her country.

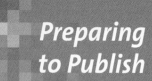

Preparing to Publish

Informative Essay and Interview

Apply the Rubric

A strong informative essay and interview . . .

☑ includes a clear thesis statement

☑ states the topic and identifies the person who was interviewed

☑ organizes information logically

☑ develops ideas by using quotations and sharp, descriptive details

☑ has a tone geared to the topic, purpose, and intended audience

☑ uses precise language to describe the situation

☑ varies sentence structures to keep the reader interested

☑ concludes by summarizing the significance of the topic

Ask a Peer Reader

• Why do you think I chose to write about this topic?

• Which of my statements need more explanation or specific details?

• What new information did you learn from reading my essay?

Check Your Grammar

• Use the active voice as much as possible. Including the doer of an action helps the reader identify with the doer and experience the event personally and powerfully.

> Police arrested
> ~~The~~ assassin, Lee Harvey Oswald, ~~was taken into custody.~~ Then, with the whole world watching, ~~Oswald was shot by~~ Jack Ruby, shot Oswald.

See page R57: Active and Passive Voice

• Insert a comma after every item in a series except the last one. Remember that in some cases these items might be phrases or clauses rather than single words.

> Kennedy's youth, energy, and eloquence captured Americans' hearts.
>
> People who lived through that day say that they will never forget where they were, what they were doing, and how they felt when they heard the news of President Kennedy's assassination.

See page R49: Quick Reference: Punctuation

Writing Online

PUBLISHING OPTIONS
For publishing options, visit the **Writing Center** at ClassZone.com.

ASSESSMENT PREPARATION
For writing and grammar assessment practice, go to the **Assessment Center** at ClassZone.com.

RESEARCH STANDARD
8.7 Use a variety of communication techniques to present information

PUBLISHING WITH TECHNOLOGY

Creating a Documentary

You can add depth and interest to your informative essay by turning it into a documentary. Your presentation can be any length and can focus on any aspect of your subject—or on a totally different subject if you wish.

Planning the Documentary

1. **Outline your plan.** Briefly list the goals, audience, main message, and approximate length of your documentary. This plan is called a treatment.

2. **Think about materials that you can use.** Do you have a video or audio recording of your interview? What people and places can you record locally? Are there Web sites with photographs, audio, and video that you can use? (Check each site's use policy. Some sites allow use of their materials in student projects.)

3. **Review your resources and budget.** Find out what audio-visual equipment is available at your school or in your community. If you have access to an editing program, you can videotape material in any order and organize it later. If not, you'll need to do in-camera editing—shooting the scenes in the order in which they will appear in the documentary.

4. **Create a shooting script.** Your script should describe the actions and sounds you want to include in your documentary—for example, narration, dialogue, sound effects, onscreen text, and music. Develop your ideas further in a storyboard, which is a series of simple sketches that illustrate, shot by shot, exactly what viewers will see. For an example of a storyboard, see page 133.

Producing the Documentary

1. **Let the camera roll.** Frame each scene and present the setting with a long- or medium-range establishing shot. Then bring the camera in closer as you give the audience more information about the subject. Consider using close-ups to stress important points.

2. **Put it all together.** Review your video footage. If you have the equipment to do postproduction editing, assemble and organize the best scenes. You might also want to create a title screen and credits and record voice-overs.

3. **Do a test screening.** Show your documentary to your family or friends and ask for feedback. Use your test audience's comments to fine-tune and improve your final product.

Reading Comprehension

DIRECTIONS *Read these prose poems and the two supplementary selections about the historical and cultural context and the author. Use this background material to help you answer the questions that follow.*

Freedom to Breathe

Alexander Solzhenitsyn

A shower fell in the night and now dark clouds drift across the sky, occasionally sprinkling a fine film of rain.

I stand under an apple tree in blossom and I breathe. Not only the apple tree but the grass round it glistens with moisture; words cannot describe the
5 sweet fragrance that pervades the air. I inhale as deeply as I can, and the aroma invades my whole being; I breathe with my eyes open, I breathe with my eyes closed—I cannot say which gives me the greater pleasure.

This, I believe, is the single most precious freedom that prison takes away from us: the freedom to breathe freely, as I now can. No food on earth, no
10 wine, not even a woman's kiss is sweeter to me than this air steeped in the fragrance of flowers, of moisture and freshness.

No matter that this is only a tiny garden, hemmed in by five-story houses like cages in a zoo. I cease to hear the motorcycles backfiring, radios whining, the burble of loudspeakers. As long as there is fresh air to breathe under an
15 apple tree after a shower, we may survive a little longer.

The Bonfire and the Ants

Alexander Solzhenitsyn

I threw a rotten log onto the fire without noticing that it was alive with ants.

The log began to crackle, the ants came tumbling out and scurried around in desperation. They ran along the top and writhed as they were scorched by the flames. I gripped the log and rolled it to one side. Many of the ants then
5 managed to escape onto the sand or the pine needles.

But, strangely enough, they did not run away from the fire.

They had no sooner overcome their terror than they turned, circled, and some kind of force drew them back to their forsaken homeland. There were many who climbed back onto the burning log, ran about on it, and perished
10 there.

Historical Background

In 1917, disgruntled Russian workers forced Czar Nicholas II to leave the throne. A year later, he and other members of the royal family were executed. Known as the Bolshevik Revolution, the uprising was led by Vladimir Lenin with the goal of creating a Communist state in which citizens would share in the common wealth. When Lenin died, his successor, Joseph Stalin, tightened state control over all aspects of life in the Soviet Union, including citizens' private lives. His economic policies were strictly enforced through successive Five-Year Plans. Many people were forced to give up their private lands to work on collective farms, while others had to relocate to cities to work in factories.

Stalin stifled political criticism through the use of propaganda, censorship, secret police, deportations, forced labor, and executions. A prominent feature of his regime was a network of forced labor camps known as the Gulag. By 1934, the Gulag's population numbered in the millions and included hardened criminals, as well as artists, political and religious dissenters, and prisoners of war. The main camps were located in remote regions where inmates worked on forestry, mining, and construction projects.

Many Communist Party members thought the Gulag went against the Bolshevik ideal of a workers' state—an ideal they believed could be restored when Stalin died. Critics viewed the Gulag as the essence of communism's evil core and a symbol of its repression.

During its nearly 40 years of operation, the Gulag had a deep economic and cultural impact on Soviet society. The prisoners gave the state a ready source of cheap labor to develop remote regions. At the same time, many people voiced their criticism of the harsh Soviet system—and their hope for a brighter future—in novels, memoirs, poems, and songs.

Author's Background

Alexander Solzhenitsyn was born in 1918. As a young man, he joined the Soviet army and fought in World War II, rising to the rank of captain. His fortunes changed in 1945, when he was sentenced to eight years of hard labor for criticizing Russian leader Joseph Stalin in a private letter. Because of his mathematical expertise, he served part of that sentence at a research institute before being transferred to a labor camp in Kazakhstan to work as a bricklayer. He was not allowed to return to Russia until 1956.

Solzhenitsyn transformed his harsh experiences in the labor camp into *One Day in the Life of Ivan Denisovich*. In 1970, he received the Nobel Prize in literature for that work and other writings, all of which had been smuggled out of the country to avoid censorship. Three years later, the first volume of *The Gulag Archipelago*, his

GO ON

literary-historical account of the vast network of Soviet prison camps, was published in Paris. Upon its publication, the government charged him with treason. He was then deported in 1974. Eventually, Solzhenitsyn traveled to the United States and settled in Vermont, where he continued to write. Although he was welcomed in the United States, he didn't feel comfortable outside his homeland. His wife said, "They can separate a Russian writer from his native land, but no one has the power and strength to sever his spiritual link with it." He returned to Russia in 1994 after the collapse of the Soviet Union.

'Caution, comrades! He's armed with the most dangerous weapon in the Soviet Union!'

Comprehension

DIRECTIONS *Use the Historical Background and Author's Background information to help you answer these questions about "Freedom to Breathe."*

1. Which experience in Solzhenitsyn's life most likely influenced him to write "Freedom to Breathe"?

   A. serving as a soldier in World War II

   B. being imprisoned in a Soviet labor camp

   C. winning a Nobel Prize in literature

   D. being deported from the Soviet Union

2. Which details convey the sensation of "freshness" referred to in the poem?

   A. "eyes open," "eyes closed"

   B. "dark clouds," "cages in a zoo"

   C. "a woman's kiss," "a burble of loudspeakers"

   D. "a fine film of rain," "the fragrance of flowers"

3. Which sensory detail creates a visual image of crowding?

   A. "dark clouds"

   B. "radios whining"

   C. "cages in a zoo"

   D. "an apple tree in blossom"

4. Which statement is most clearly supported by images in the poem?

   A. One can derive pleasure from simple things.

   B. Freedom can be experienced only through nature.

   C. Flowers are sweeter than a woman's kiss.

   D. People live like caged animals.

5. The connection made between freedom and breathing supports the idea that

   A. nature holds the key to freedom

   B. freedom is essential to life

   C. people can live freely in a city

   D. fresh air is as sweet as freedom

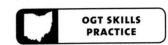

DIRECTIONS *Use the Historical Background and Author's Background information to help you answer these questions about "The Bonfire and the Ants."*

6. Which experience in Solzhenitsyn's life most likely influenced him to write the piece?

A. living under a repressive government

B. moving to the United States

C. smuggling his writings out of the Soviet Union

D. working as a bricklayer in Kazakhstan

7. Which group mentioned in the Historical Background material do the ants in the poem most likely represent?

A. the secret police

B. Soviet citizens

C. hardened criminals

D. the royal family

8. The log being tossed into the flames suggests what kind of event in Russian history?

A. violent political upheaval

B. tightening of government control

C. termination of the Gulag

D. rapid economic development

9. The "crackle" of the burning log in line 2 appeals to the reader's sense of

A. taste   C. touch

B. smell   D. hearing

10. Solzhenitsyn believes that a homeland has a powerful pull. You can find evidence of this belief in the image of the ants

A. running away from the burning log

B. scurrying around in desperation

C. climbing back onto the burning log

D. writhing in the flames

DIRECTIONS *Use the Historical Background and Author's Background information to help you answer this question about both prose poems.*

11. In the two poems, Solzhenitsyn uses contrasting images of nature to convey his feelings about

A. truth and propaganda

B. censorship and exile to a Gulag

C. war and political unrest

D. freedom and love of one's country

DIRECTIONS *Answer this question about the cartoon.*

12. Which statement best expresses the message of the political cartoon?

A. Actions speak louder than words.

B. A mind opens wider than a window.

C. Three men are stronger than one man.

D. Words are more powerful than weapons.

Written Response

SHORT ANSWER *Write three or four sentences to answer this question.*

13. Which senses does the author use to experience freedom in "Freedom to Breathe"? Cite sensory details from the poem to support your choices.

EXTENDED RESPONSE *Write two or three paragraphs to answer this question.*

14. What can you infer about Solzhenitsyn's views on communism from "Freedom to Breathe" and "The Bonfire and the Ants"? Cite evidence from the Historical Background and Author's Background material to support your viewpoint.

GO ON ➤

Vocabulary

DIRECTIONS *Read this dictionary entry and answer the following questions.*

> **film** (f lm) *noun.* **1.** A thin skin or membrane.
> **2.** A thin covering or coating. **3.** A thin
> sheet of flexible material, such as a cellulose
> derivative or a thermoplastic resin, coated with
> a photosensitive emulsion and used to make
> photographic negatives or transparencies.
> **4.** A movie.—**film** *verb.* **filmed, film·ing, films**
> —*tr.* **1.** To cover with a film. **2.** To make a movie
> of. [Middle English, from Old English *filmen.*]

1. Which parts of speech can *film* be?

   A. noun and pronoun

   B. verb and adverb

   C. noun and verb

   D. noun, verb, and interjection

2. Which definition of the noun *film* is used in line 2 of "Freedom to Breathe"?

   A. definition 1

   B. definition 2

   C. definition 3

   D. definition 4

3. From which language does the word *film* originate?

   A. Modern English

   B. Old English

   C. Middle English

   D. uncertain origin

DIRECTIONS *Use context clues and your knowledge of suffixes to answer the following questions.*

4. What is the meaning of the word *moisture* as it is used in lines 4 and 11 of "Freedom to Breathe?"

   A. wetness

   B. dampen

   C. liquefy

   D. humidifier

5. What is the meaning of the word *fragrance* as it is used in line 5 of "Freedom to Breathe"?

   A. smelly

   B. scented

   C. aroma

   D. perfumed

6. What is the meaning of the word *desperation* as it is used in line 3 of "The Bonfire and the Ants"?

   A. great need

   B. a state of distress

   C. an aimless way

   D. an irrational manner

Writing & Grammar

DIRECTIONS *Read the passage and answer the questions that follow.*

> (1) In the 1950s, the United States investigated citizens. (2) They were considered Communist sympathizers. (3) Senator Joseph McCarthy led the charge. (4) McCarthy was known for his reckless accusations. (5) As a result of these accusations, many people lost their jobs. (6) Even people who read foreign magazines were under suspicion. (7) This accusatory technique became known as McCarthyism. (8) Today, the term still describes the use of unfounded accusations.

1. Choose the correct way to combine sentences 1 and 2 to form one complex sentence.

  A. In the 1950s, the United States investigated citizens who were considered Communist sympathizers.

  B. In the 1950s, the United States investigated citizens, thinking they were Communist sympathizers.

  C. In the 1950s, the United States investigated citizens; they were considered Communist sympathizers.

  D. In the 1950s, the United States investigated citizens and considered them Communist sympathizers.

2. Choose the correct way to rewrite sentences 4 and 5 as one sentence, using a gerund phrase.

  A. McCarthy was known for his reckless accusations, and many people lost their jobs as a result.

  B. Known for making reckless accusations, McCarthy caused many people to lose their jobs.

  C. McCarthy made reckless accusations; as a result, many people lost their jobs.

  D. McCarthy was making reckless accusations and causing many people to lose their jobs.

3. Choose the correct way to rewrite sentence 6 by using a gerund phrase.

  A. To read a foreign magazine was enough cause for suspicion.

  B. McCarthy was even suspicious of people who read foreign magazines.

  C. Even reading foreign magazines made people seem suspicious.

  D. To be considered suspicious, people read foreign magazines.

4. Choose the correct way to combine sentences 7 and 8 to form one compound sentence.

  A. This accusatory technique became known as McCarthyism, a term still used today to describe unfounded accusations.

  B. This accusatory technique became known as McCarthyism, a term that still today describes the use of unfounded accusations.

  C. This accusatory technique became known as McCarthyism, which is a term that still today describes the use of unfounded accusations.

  D. This accusatory technique became known as McCarthyism; today, the term still describes the use of unfounded accusations.

STOP

Ideas for Independent Reading

Several profound questions were raised in Unit 9. Reading the following books may deepen your perspective on these questions.

Can humanity triumph over evil?

Lord of the Flies
by William Golding

In this novel by a former schoolmaster, a group of English schoolboys is marooned with no adults on a Pacific island. They organize their own society, which soon disintegrates into savagely warring factions.

Jubilee
by Margaret Walker

The character Vyry, based on the novelist's great-grandmother, survives the brutality of slavery in the Old South only to have her family terrorized by the Ku Klux Klan after slavery's end. Through all her trials, she manages to keep a loving heart.

Schindler's List
by Thomas Keneally

Oskar Schindler was a German factory owner who managed to save 1,300 Polish Jews during the Holocaust by claiming that he needed their labor. Keneally's novel, based on true events, explores how a person can do good in the midst of the worst evil.

What if your government declared you the enemy?

Farewell to Manzanar
by Jeanne Wakatsuki Houston and James D. Houston

Read more about the Wakatsuki family's experiences in an internment camp. Learn how internees made the camp more homelike, planting gardens and setting up schools. Also discover how hard it was to adjust to life outside the camps once they were closed.

Resistance
by Barry Lopez

This collection of short fiction shows Americans abroad who are targeted by U.S. authorities for challenging government power. Each story is a farewell, explaining the events that are causing the narrator to flee and go underground.

Torn Between Two Cultures
by Maryam Qudrat Aseel

Aseel is a Muslim woman born in the United States to Afghan immigrant parents. She reflects on being considered an enemy in her own country after the terrorist attacks of September 11, 2001, and she attempts to correct misperceptions about Afghan culture and Islam.

What is cowardice?

Lord Jim
by Joseph Conrad

Jim, a ship's crew member, unthinkingly leaves the ship when it catches fire and sinks. Though the captain and other officials have also fled, Jim alone is tried for abandoning the passengers. For the rest of this novel, Jim tries to make up for this act of cowardice.

Confronting the War Machine
by Michael S. Foley

They were called cowards and worse. The men profiled in this book did not hide or seek draft deferments but refused to serve in Vietnam and were willing to take the consequences. Their resistance powered the U.S. antiwar movement.

Refusenik! Israel's Soldiers of Conscience
by Peretz Kidron

Refuseniks are Israeli soldiers who refuse orders on moral grounds. They believe in defending their country but oppose its occupation of territories outside its borders. Though praised by peace groups, refuseniks have not always had an easy time within Israeli society.

Upholding Honor

GREEK TRAGEDY AND MEDIEVAL ROMANCE

- In Drama
- In Fiction
- Across Genres

What QUESTS *live on?*

Jason and the Argonauts sailed from their homes to find the Golden Fleece. The knights of King Arthur spent years seeking the Holy Grail. Ponce de León explored unknown lands, hoping to discover the Fountain of Youth. All of these quests live on in history and legend. Why do they capture our imaginations so powerfully?

ACTIVITY On a chart, list each of the great quests mentioned above, and add to them any other historical quests that come to mind. Then think of modern quests that are equally captivating: the search for life on other planets, the plan to raise the *Titanic*. With a partner, try to identify the characteristics you think raise each quest to the level of legend. What do all of these quests have in common?

OHIO STANDARDS

Preview Unit Goals

LITERARY ANALYSIS
- Identify characteristics of classical drama
- Identify and analyze characteristics of Greek tragedy, including tragic hero and tragic flaw
- Identify and analyze conventions of medieval romance, including romance hero
- Identify characteristics of a parody
- Identify and analyze theme and conflict
- Analyze and evaluate style

READING
- Make inferences
- Use strategies for reading a classical drama

WRITING AND GRAMMAR
- Write a persuasive essay
- Vary sentence structure by inverting sentences
- Vary sentence beginnings by using a variety of phrases and clauses

SPEAKING, LISTENING, AND VIEWING
- Debate an issue

VOCABULARY
- Use dictionary etymology to research word origins
- Understand and use connotations of words

ACADEMIC VOCABULARY
- classical drama
- tragic hero
- medieval romance
- parody
- connotation
- Greek tragedy
- tragic flaw
- romance hero
- etymology

Literary Analysis Workshop

Greek Tragedy and Medieval Romance

In today's popular culture, heroes are celebrated in movies and TV shows. Centuries ago, other cultures immortalized their heroes in literature. Consider ancient Greek tragedy and medieval romance. One features ill-fated heroes who face defeat with dignity, and the other follows gallant, knightly heroes on perilous quests. Each type of hero reflects the values of its time and its society, but these values still appeal to us, many centuries later.

OHIO STANDARDS

READING STANDARDS
4.1 Compare and contrast an author's use of characterization

4.5 Analyze how choice of genre affects theme or topic

Part 1: Greek Tragedy

Misfortune, anguish, death—these are some of the elements you might associate with any tragedy. In literature, however, a **tragedy** is a form of drama that shows the downfall of a dignified, superior character who participates in events of great significance. The ancient Greeks, who developed tragedy, used it to explore ideas about humans' relationship to the gods, often delving into such serious subjects as duty, suffering, and fate.

Familiarize yourself with the characteristics of Greek tragedy by examining this chart.

CHARACTERISTICS OF GREEK TRAGEDY

Tragic Hero

At the center of a tragedy is its hero, the main character, or **protagonist.** The tragic hero is a person of high rank who accepts his or her downfall with dignity.

Tragic Flaw

A **tragic flaw**—an error in judgment or a weakness in character, such as pride or arrogance—helps bring about the hero's downfall. The tragic hero recognizes this flaw and its consequences but only after it is too late to change the course of events.

Catastrophe

A tragedy ends with a **catastrophe,** a disastrous conclusion that usually involves multiple deaths. If the tragic hero does not die, then he or she suffers complete ruin.

Chorus

Throughout a tragedy, the **chorus**—a masked group of actors—observe and comment on the action through songs. Their responses and values were supposed to reflect those of the audience.

CENTRAL BELIEF

Fate

The ancient Greeks believed in the idea of **fate,** or a destiny preordained by the gods no matter what action a person takes in the present. The Fates, or *Moirai*, were three goddesses who determined the length of a person's life and how much suffering it would contain. Greeks held that it was impossible to escape one's fate. This belief is reflected in such ancient tragedies as *Oedipus the King* and *Antigone*.

MODEL: CHARACTERISTICS OF GREEK TRAGEDY

Oedipus the King is one of the most famous Greek tragedies; the philosopher Aristotle based his definition of *tragedy* on this play. Which characteristics of Greek tragedy do you notice in this excerpt?

from
OEDIPUS THE KING

Tragedy by **Sophocles,** translated by Robert Fagles

Oedipus. My father was Polybus, king of Corinth.
My mother, a Dorian, Merope. And I was held
the prince of the realm among the people there,
till something struck me out of nowhere,
5   something strange . . . worth remarking perhaps,
hardly worth the anxiety I gave it.
Some man at a banquet who had drunk too much
shouted out—he was far gone, mind you—
that I am not my father's son. Fighting words!
10 I barely restrained myself that day
but early the next I went to mother and father,
questioned them closely, and they were enraged
at the accusation and the fool who let it fly.
So as for my parents I was satisfied,
15 but still this thing kept gnawing at me,
the slander spread—I had to make my move.
                            And so,
unknown to mother and father I set out for Delphi,
and the god Apollo spurned me, sent me away
denied the facts I came for,
20 but first he flashed before my eyes a future
great with pain, terror, disaster—I can hear him cry,
"You are fated to couple with your mother, you will bring
a breed of children into the light no man can bear to see—
you will kill your father, the one who gave you life!"
25 I heard all that and ran. I abandoned Corinth. . . .

At the end of the scene, the chorus sings.

Chorus. Destiny guide me always
Destiny find me filled with reverence
  pure in word and deed.
Great laws tower above us, reared on high
30 born for the brilliant vault of heaven—
  Olympian sky their only father,
nothing mortal, no man gave them birth. . . .

Close Read

1. What do you learn about the tragic hero Oedipus in lines 1–3? Consider his background and how others regard him.

2. What incident disturbs Oedipus' happy existence?

3. According to the god Apollo, what tragic fate awaits Oedipus?

4. Reread the boxed text. Consider Oedipus' response to the disturbing news at the banquet and the vision that Apollo flashes before his eyes. What possible tragic flaw does Oedipus display?

5. Summarize what the chorus says about destiny and the laws that rule human life.

Part 2: Medieval Romance

The heroes who populate the pages of medieval romances are not suffering, flawed figures but knights in shining armor. A **romance** is an adventure tale that features extravagant characters, exotic places, heroic events, passionate love, and supernatural forces. Romances first appeared in Old French literature of the 12th century and quickly spread throughout Europe. The best-known English romances concern the legendary King Arthur and his Knights of the Round Table.

Romance literature expresses the ideals of chivalry, an elaborate code of honor that is described in the chart. As the stories entertain readers, they also convey medieval values of loyalty and Christian faith.

CONVENTIONS OF MEDIEVAL ROMANCE

Romance Hero

The **romance hero** is a knight of superhuman strength, intelligence, and virtue who follows the code of chivalry.

A Quest

The hero of a romance often proves his worth by undertaking a **quest,** a journey motivated by love, religious faith, or a desire for adventure. He must overcome many obstacles on this quest.

Exotic Setting

Romances are set in imaginary kingdoms with great castles, enchanted lakes, and forests populated with giants and monsters.

Supernatural Elements

Sorcerers and magic spells, giants and dragons, mysterious evil forces and foreknowledge of future events—such supernatural elements all play a part in romances.

Hidden Identities

In a romance, others are often unaware of a character's true identity. The truth is usually revealed at the climax of the tale.

Episodic Structure

Romances are not tightly structured; characters simply go from one adventure to the next.

CENTRAL BELIEF

Chivalry

The code of chivalry required that a knight

- swear allegiance to his lord
- fight to uphold Christianity
- seek to redress all wrongs
- honor truth by word and deed
- be faithful to one lady
- act with bravery, courtesy, and modesty

These ideals guide the behavior of the knights in the romance literature you will read.

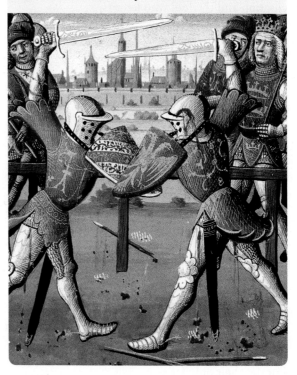

MODEL: CONVENTIONS OF MEDIEVAL ROMANCE

Sir Gawain and the Green Knight is a famous romance originally composed
in verse. Gawain is a knight of King Arthur's Round Table. On New Year's
Day, when all are gathered at the court, a giant green knight issues
an unusual challenge: any man may strike him with an axe, provided
the Green Knight can return the blow a year later. Notice how Gawain
responds to the challenge.

from Sir Gawain and the
Green Knight

Romance retold by **Constance Hieatt**

The knight leaped down from his horse and handed the great axe to the
king. While Arthur swung it to test its weight, the tall knight waited calmly.
He tossed off his cloak, with no sign of fear.

But now Sir Gawain, who had remained quietly in his place at the table,
5 spoke courteously to Arthur: "I beg you, let this contest be mine, dear lord—
allow me to take your place. It is not seemly that you, our king, should accept
such a challenge when all around you sit the bravest knights in the world. I am
the least of them, and my life is worth little. But I am the first to ask. Let me
be the one to take this knight's dare."

After Gawain accepts the challenge, the Green Knight prepares for Gawain's blow.

10 The knight in green bent and pulled his long hair forward over his head,
so that his neck was bare. Gawain gripped the weapon with both hands and
raised it high over his head. He leaned forward on his left foot, and swung the
axe down with such force that it went straight through the neck and bit into
the floor. The Green Knight's head fell to the ground and tumbled toward the
15 high table, where knights and ladies drew back in horror as it rolled.

Yet the bleeding, headless body did not fall! The green man stood up,
walked briskly over to his head, and picked it up by the long hair. Then he
turned to his horse, caught hold of the bridle, and swung into the saddle,
sitting there as easily as if nothing had happened. He held up the head,
20 turning it to face the high table. It opened its red eyes and spoke: "Gawain,
Gawain, remember the promise you made before your king and this company.
I am the knight of the Green Chapel. Next New Year's Day you will find me
there. If you will look for me, you will find me. Therefore come, or be called
coward by all men!"

Close Read

1. Reread Gawain's speech in the [boxed] text. In what ways does he show the traits of a romance hero?

2. What elements of the supernatural are evident in this tale? Cite specific details to support your answer.

3. If Gawain does not meet the Green Knight next New Year's Day, how will he violate the code of chivalry?

Part 3: Analyze the Literature

Now you will read two excerpts from works you will study in this unit. The first excerpt is from *Antigone* (ăn-tĭg′ə-nē), which tells the story of Oedipus' grown daughter and her conflict with Creon, her uncle and the king of Thebes. Here, Antigone tells her sister, Ismene, that she intends to bury their brother Polyneices, who died on the battlefield fighting against their country. Burying the dead is a sacred act, but Creon, by law, has forbidden this particular burial.

from ANTIGONE

Tragedy by **Sophocles,** translated by Dudley Fitts
and Robert Fitzgerald, Lines 47–72

Ismene. We cannot fight with men, Antigone!
The law is strong, we must give in to the law
In this thing, and in worse. I beg the dead
50 To forgive me, but I am helpless: I must yield
To those in authority. And I think it is dangerous business
To be always meddling.

Antigone.   If that is what you think,
I should not want you, even if you asked to come.
You have made your choice; you can be what you want to be.

55 But I will bury him [our brother]; and if I must die,
I say that this crime is holy: I shall lie down
With him in death, and I shall be as dear
To him as he to me.
          It is the dead,
Not the living, who make the longest demands:
60 We die forever. . . .
          You may do as you like,
Since apparently the laws of the gods mean nothing to you.

Ismene. They mean a great deal to me; but I have no strength
To break laws that were made for the public good.

Antigone. That must be your excuse, I suppose. But as for me,
65 I will bury the brother I love.

Ismene.   Antigone,
I am so afraid for you!

Antigone.   You need not be:
You have yourself to consider, after all.

Ismene. But no one must hear of this; you must tell no one!
I will keep it a secret, I promise!

Antigone.   Oh tell it! Tell everyone!
70 Think how they'll hate you when it all comes out
If they learn that you knew about it all the time!

Ismene. So fiery! You should be cold with fear.

Close Read

1. Reread the boxed text. What is Antigone's motivation for wanting to bury her brother?

2. What contrasting Greek social values are represented through the argument between Antigone and Ismene?

3. What traits of a tragic hero does Antigone exhibit? In your opinion, does she seem to have a tragic flaw? Explain.

4. A fearful Ismene hints that Antigone will have to face the terrible consequences of her future actions. What tragic outcome do you predict?

This excerpt is from *Le Morte d'Arthur,* a 15th-century English collection of Arthurian romances. Here, King Arthur discovers that King Pellinore has injured a young knight. Angered, Arthur challenges King Pellinore to a joust, a form of medieval combat in which two mounted knights armed with long spears try to unseat each other from their horses. Merlin, a prophet and magician, has accompanied Arthur to the challenge.

from Le Morte d'Arthur

Romance by **Sir Thomas Malory,** retold by Keith Baines

Merlin accompanied Arthur to the well, and when they arrived they found King Pellinore seated outside his pavilion. "Sir," said Arthur, "it would seem that no knight can pass this well without your challenging him."

"That is so," said King Pellinore.

5 "I have come to force you to change this custom of yours, so defend yourself!"

They jousted three times, each time breaking their spears, until the third time, when Arthur was flung from his horse. "Very well," said Arthur, "you have won the advantage jousting; now let us see what you can do on foot." King Pellinore was reluctant to dismount and lose the advantage he had

10 won; however, when Arthur rushed at him boldly with drawn sword, he grew ashamed and did dismount.

They fought until both collapsed from pain and exhaustion; their armor was splintered and the blood flowed from their wounds. They fought again, until Arthur's sword broke in his hand. "Now," said King Pellinore, "you shall

15 yield to me, or die."

"Not so!" Arthur shouted as he sprang at him, and grabbing him around the waist, threw him to the ground. Arthur was unlacing his helmet when, with a sudden fearful effort, King Pellinore overturned Arthur and clambered on top of him. King Pellinore had loosened Arthur's helmet and raised his

20 sword to strike off his head when Merlin spoke.

"Hold your hand!" he said; "you will endanger the whole realm. You do not realize who it is you are about to kill."

"Who is it, then?"

"King Arthur."

25 Hearing this, King Pellinore feared that he would receive little mercy from Arthur if he spared him—so he raised his sword once more. Merlin adroitly put him to sleep with a magic spell.

"You have killed him with your magic," said Arthur hotly. "I would rather that my whole realm were lost, and myself killed; he was a magnificent fighter."

30 "He is more whole than you are," Merlin replied. "He will not only live, but serve you excellently: It is to him that you will give your sister in marriage, and she will bear two sons—Sir Percivale and Sir Lamerok—who will be two of the most famous of the Knights of the Round Table."

Close Read

1. The code of chivalry required that knights act with bravery and courtesy. How are these qualities reflected in Arthur's and Pellinore's behavior and actions? Support your answer with specific details.

2. What common characteristic of medieval romance is revealed in the boxed lines?

3. How does the supernatural play a role in the story? Is it a force for good or evil?

4. Which knight—Pellinore or Arthur—displays more qualities of a romance hero? Cite details from the excerpt to support your opinion.

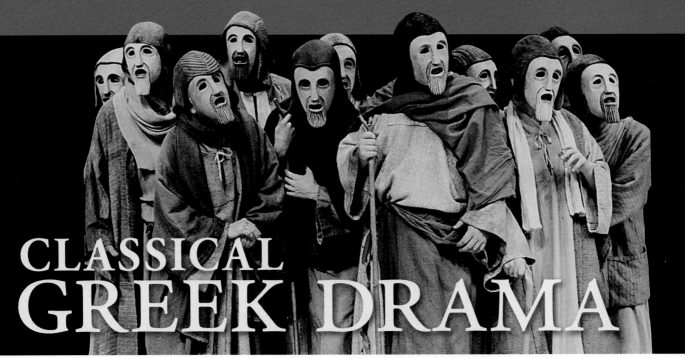

CLASSICAL GREEK DRAMA

Masked chorus in a production of a classical Greek drama

Religious Origins The drama of ancient Greece and Rome is referred to as **classical drama.** It arose in Athens from religious celebrations in honor of the Greek god Dionysus (dī'ə-nī'səs). These celebrations included ritual chants and songs performed by a group called a chorus. Drama evolved from these celebrations during the sixth century B.C., when individual actors began entering into dialogue with the chorus to tell a story.

The Theater Greek drama was filled with the spectacle and pageantry of a religious festival. Attended by thousands, plays were performed during the day in an outdoor theater with seats built into a hillside. The action of each play was presented at the foot of the hill, often on a raised platform. A long building, called the **skene,** served as a backdrop for the action and as a dressing room. A spacious floor, the **orchestra,** was located between the skene and the audience, who sat in the **theatron.**

Actors and Chorus The actors—all men—wore elegant robes, huge masks, and often elevated shoes, all of which added to the grandeur of the spectacle. Sophocles (sŏf'ə-klēz'), an innovator in classical drama, used three actors in his plays;

between scenes, they changed costumes and masks when they needed to portray different characters. The **chorus**—a group of about 15—commented on the action, and the leader of the chorus, the **choragus** (kə-rā'gəs), participated in the dialogue. Between scenes, the chorus sang and danced to musical accompaniment in the orchestra, giving insights into the message of the play. The chorus has often been considered a kind of ideal spectator, representing the response of ordinary citizens to the events unfolding in the play. Typically, the chorus communicated the values, beliefs, and ideals that were central to Athenian society.

Tragedy and the Tragic Hero During Sophocles' lifetime, three playwrights were chosen each year to enter a theatrical competition in the festival of Dionysus. Each playwright would produce three tragedies, along with a satyr (sā'tər) play, a short comic interlude.

As you recall, a **tragedy** is a drama that recounts the downfall of a dignified, superior character—a **tragic hero**—who is involved in

Greek drama was first performed at festivals honoring Dionysus, depicted in this sculpture.

This illustration shows what scholars believe a Greek theater looked like.

1 skene

2 orchestra

3 theatron

historically or socially significant events. The philosopher Aristotle was the first to define tragedy, theorizing that the form evokes both pity and fear in audiences—pity because they feel sorry for the tragic hero, fear because they realize that the hero's struggles are perhaps a necessary part of human life. At the end of a tragedy, an audience generally feels a sense of waste because a person who is in some way superior has been destroyed. Aristotle based his ideas about tragedy on Sophocles' *Oedipus the King,* which he considered the perfect tragedy. Other Greek tragedies, such as *Antigone,* may not fit his model so perfectly.

Mythological Sources The subjects of Greek tragedy are myths and legends that were very familiar to a Greek audience. **Myths,** as you may know, are traditional stories about gods and goddesses; **legends** are stories about people believed to have once lived. Gods and goddesses are often characters in tragedies, and even when they do not appear on stage, they influence the fates of human characters. Usually a tragic hero's downfall is the result of having offended the gods. The gods' wishes are frequently made known through specially gifted characters—such as the blind prophet Teiresias in *Antigone*—who

communicate with the gods. Because the myths and legends were so familiar, the audience already knew the outcome of events and could realize the significance of words and actions the characters were blind to. When the audience knows more than the characters do, the result is **dramatic irony.**

Greek Deities Some knowledge of Greek deities is needed to understand classical drama, as the dialogue is filled with allusions to gods and rituals. The ancient Greeks believed that their gods ruled the world from the top of Mount Olympus, Greece's highest mountain. The gods' ruler was Zeus, whose weapons were thunderbolts. Other deities included Ares, the god of war; Aphrodite, the goddess of love and beauty; Athena, the goddess of wisdom, for whom Athens was named; and Dionysus, the god of wine and fertility in whose honor dramas were first performed. The characters in tragedies honor and fear their gods and struggle to live in proper relationship to them. These characters' struggles continue to fascinate audiences today.

Antigone

Drama by Sophocles

What is your ultimate
LOYALTY?

OHIO STANDARDS

READING STANDARDS
2.1 Apply reading comprehension strategies
4.5 Analyze how choice of genre affects theme or topic

KEY IDEA Do you feel more loyal to your family or your friends? to yourself or your country? Which of these gets your greatest **loyalty?**

DISCUSS Rank the principles shown on the list in order of their importance to you. Imagine situations that might bring these principles into conflict and think about which you would choose. With a small group, discuss your rankings and your reasoning.

> loyalty to family
> obedience to civil law
> protection of nation
> protection of personal dignity

● LITERARY ANALYSIS: CLASSICAL DRAMA

Keep these characteristics of classical drama in mind as you read Sophocles' *Antigone*:

- A major form of classical drama is the **tragedy,** which recounts the downfall of a dignified, superior character—a **tragic hero.** An error or weakness—the hero's **tragic flaw**—may contribute to his or her ruin.

- An important element of classical drama is the **chorus,** a group of actors who comment on the action in the play. Their leader is the **choragus.**

- **Dramatic irony**—the audience's awareness of things the characters do not know—is often present in classical drama.

Review: **Character, Conflict, Theme**

● READING STRATEGY: READING CLASSICAL DRAMA

Use the following strategies to help you understand *Antigone:*

- **Visualize** the staging of the play, with its masked actors.
- **Clarify** unfamiliar references by using the marginal notes.
- **Infer** the traits, values, and motivations of the two main characters, Antigone and Creon. **Evaluate** these characters, who are in conflict.
- **Relate** the songs of the chorus to the action of the play. Use a chart to record notes about the song the chorus sings at the end of each scene.

	Summary of Song	Function of Song
Parodos	Polyneices attacked Thebes but was defeated.	gives background for Creon's order not to bury Polyneices
Ode I		

▲ VOCABULARY IN CONTEXT

Define each vocabulary word you're familiar with. After reading the play, define the words that were unfamiliar.

Background

Sophocles
496?–406 B.C.

Doomed King
Sophocles was one of the great dramatists of ancient Greece, and his play *Antigone* is regarded as one of the finest examples of classical Greek tragedy. Along with *Oedipus the King* and *Oedipus at Colonus*, it is part of Sophocles' Theban trilogy. These three plays are based on the legend of Oedipus (ĕd′ə-pəs), the doomed Theban king who unknowingly killed his father and married his mother. Antigone (ăn-tĭg′ə-nē) is the daughter of Oedipus.

Family Feud As the play begins, Antigone and her sister, Ismene (ĭs-mē′nē), recall their dead father. Upon discovering the truth about his marriage, Oedipus blinded himself and went into exile, where he was cared for by his two daughters until his death. His sons, Eteocles (ĭ-tē′ə-klēz′) and Polyneices (pŏl′ə-nī′sēz), agreed to share the kingship of Thebes, ruling in alternate years. However, after Eteocles had served his first term as king, he refused to relinquish the throne to Polyneices, claiming that Polyneices was unfit to rule. Polyneices then enlisted an army from Argos, a long-standing enemy of Thebes, to fight his brother. In the course of battle, the brothers killed each other. Their uncle, Creon, who has become king, now faces the task of restoring order in Thebes. He plans to honor one corpse and dishonor the other.

 MORE ABOUT THE AUTHOR
For more on Sophocles, visit the **Literature Center** at ClassZone.com.

ANTIGONE

SOPHOCLES

CAST OF CHARACTERS

Antigone, daughter of Oedipus, former king of Thebes

Ismene, daughter of Oedipus

Creon (krē′ŏn′), king of Thebes, uncle of Antigone and Ismene

Haemon (hē′mŏn′), Creon's son, engaged to Antigone

Eurydice (yŏŏ-rĭd′ĭ-sē), wife of Creon

Teiresias (tī-rē′sē-əs), a blind prophet

Chorus, made up of about 15 elders of Thebes

Choragus, leader of the chorus

A Sentry

A Messenger

SCENE

Before the palace of Creon, king of Thebes. A central double door, and two doors at the side. A platform extends the length of the stage, and from this platform three steps lead down into the orchestra, or chorus ground.

TIME

Dawn of the day after the repulse of the Argive army from the assault on Thebes

PROLOGUE

(Antigone *and* Ismene *enter from the central door of the palace.*)

Antigone. Ismene, dear sister,
You would think that we had already suffered enough
For the curse on Oedipus:
I cannot imagine any grief
5 That you and I have not gone through. And now—
Have they told you the new decree of our king Creon?

Ismene. I have heard nothing: I know
That two sisters lost two brothers, a double death
In a single hour; and I know that the Argive army
10 Fled in the night; but beyond this, nothing.

9 Argive (är′jīv′): of Argos.

Martha Henry as Antigone and Philip Bosco as Creon in the Lincoln Center Repertory 1971 production

Antigone. I thought so. And that is why I wanted you
To come out here with me. There is something we must do.

Ismene. Why do you speak so strangely?

Antigone. Listen, Ismene:
15 Creon buried our brother Eteocles
With military honors, gave him a soldier's funeral,
And it was right that he should; but Polyneices,
Who fought as bravely and died as miserably—
They say that Creon has sworn
20 No one shall bury him, no one mourn for him,
But his body must lie in the fields, a sweet treasure
For carrion birds to find as they search for food.
That is what they say, and our good Creon is coming here
To announce it publicly; and the penalty—
25 Stoning to death in the public square!

                                   There it is,
And now you can prove what you are:
A true sister, or a traitor to your family.

Ismene. Antigone, you are mad! What could I possibly do?

Antigone. You must decide whether you will help me or not.

30 **Ismene.** I do not understand you. Help you in what?

Antigone. Ismene, I am going to bury him. Will you come?

Ismene. Bury him! You have just said the new law forbids it.

Antigone. He is my brother. And he is your brother, too.

Ismene. But think of the danger! Think what Creon will do!

35 **Antigone.** Creon is not strong enough to stand in my way.

Ismene. Ah sister!
Oedipus died, everyone hating him
For what his own search brought to light, his eyes
Ripped out by his own hand; and Jocasta died,
40 His mother and wife at once: she twisted the cords
That strangled her life; and our two brothers died,
Each killed by the other's sword. And we are left:
But oh, Antigone,
Think how much more terrible than these
45 Our own death would be if we should go against Creon
And do what he has forbidden! We are only women;
We cannot fight with men, Antigone!
The law is strong, we must give in to the law
In this thing, and in worse. I beg the dead
50 To forgive me, but I am helpless: I must yield
To those in authority. And I think it is dangerous business
To be always meddling.

20–22 No one shall bury . . . search for food: The obligation to bury the dead with appropriate rites was considered sacred by the ancient Greeks. They believed that the soul of someone left unburied would never find peace.

39 Jocasta (jō-kăs′tə): the mother of Antigone and Ismene, who hanged herself when she realized the truth about her relationship with Oedipus.

Antigone.   If that is what you think,
I should not want you, even if you asked to come.
You have made your choice; you can be what you want to be.
55 But I will bury him; and if I must die,
I say that this crime is holy: I shall lie down
With him in death, and I shall be as dear
To him as he to me. **Ⓐ**
                    It is the dead,
Not the living, who make the longest demands:
60 We die forever. . . .
                    You may do as you like,
Since apparently the laws of the gods mean nothing to you.

Ismene. They mean a great deal to me; but I have no strength
To break laws that were made for the public good.

Antigone. That must be your excuse, I suppose. But as for me,
65 I will bury the brother I love.

Ⓐ CONFLICT
Note the seriousness of the conflict that is introduced. What is Antigone going to do, and what may happen to her as a result?

Tandy Cronyn as Ismene and Martha Henry as Antigone in the Lincoln Center Repertory 1971 production

Ismene.   Antigone,
I am so afraid for you!

Antigone.   You need not be:
You have yourself to consider, after all.

Ismene. But no one must hear of this; you must tell no one!
I will keep it a secret, I promise!

Antigone.   Oh tell it! Tell everyone!
70 Think how they'll hate you when it all comes out
If they learn that you knew about it all the time!

Ismene. So fiery! You should be cold with fear.

Antigone. Perhaps. But I am doing only what I must.

Ismene. But can you do it? I say that you cannot.

75 **Antigone.** Very well: when my strength gives out, I shall do no more.

Ismene. Impossible things should not be tried at all.

Antigone. Go away, Ismene:
I shall be hating you soon, and the dead will too,
For your words are hateful. Leave me my foolish plan:
80 I am not afraid of the danger; if it means death,
It will not be the worst of deaths—death without honor.

Ismene. Go then, if you feel that you must.
You are unwise,
But a loyal friend indeed to those who love you. **B**

(*Exit into the palace.* Antigone *goes off, left. Enters the* Chorus,
with Choragus.)

PARODOS

Chorus. Now the long blade of the sun, lying
Level east to west, touches with glory
Thebes of the Seven Gates. Open, unlidded
Eye of golden day! O marching light
5 Across the eddy and rush of Dirce's stream,
Striking the white shields of the enemy
Thrown headlong backward from the blaze of morning!

Choragus. Polyneices their commander
Roused them with windy phrases,
10 He the wild eagle screaming
Insults above our land,

B CHARACTER
So far, what have you learned about
Antigone, the **protagonist** of the
play? How would you contrast her
with her sister, Ismene?

Parodos (păr′ə-dŏs′): a song that marks
the entry of the chorus, which represents
the leading citizens of Thebes.

5 Dirce's (dûr′sēz) **stream:** a stream
flowing past Thebes. The stream is
named for a murdered queen who
was thrown into it.

His wings their shields of snow,
His crest their marshaled helms.

Chorus. Against our seven gates in a yawning ring
15 The famished spears came onward in the night;
But before his jaws were **sated** with our blood,
Or pine fire took the garland of our towers,
He was thrown back; and as he turned, great Thebes—
No tender victim for his noisy power—
20 Rose like a dragon behind him, shouting war.

Choragus. For God hates utterly
The bray of bragging tongues;
And when he beheld their smiling,
Their swagger of golden helms,
25 The frown of his thunder blasted
Their first man from our walls.

Chorus. We heard his shout of triumph high in the air
Turn to a scream; far out in a flaming arc
He fell with his windy torch, and the earth struck him.
30 And others storming in fury no less than his
Found shock of death in the dusty joy of battle.

Choragus. Seven captains at seven gates
Yielded their clanging arms to the god
That bends the battle line and breaks it.
35 These two only, brothers in blood,
Face to face in matchless rage,
Mirroring each the other's death,
Clashed in long combat.

Chorus. But now in the beautiful morning of victory
40 Let Thebes of the many chariots sing for joy!
With hearts for dancing we'll take leave of war:
Our temples shall be sweet with hymns of praise,
And the long night shall echo with our chorus. **C**

14–15 seven gates: Thebes had seven gates, which the Argives attacked all at once.

sate (sāt) *v.* to satisfy fully

21–26 Zeus, the king of the gods, threw a thunderbolt, which killed the first Argive attacker.

32–34 When the seven captains were killed, their armor was offered as a sacrifice to Ares (âr′ēz), the god of war.

C READING CLASSICAL DRAMA
Summarize the background information that the **chorus** gives in its song. How does the chorus view Polyneices?

🌿 SCENE 1

Choragus. But now at last our new king is coming:
Creon of Thebes, Menoeceus' son.
In this **auspicious** dawn of his reign
What are the new complexities
5 That shifting Fate has woven for him?
What is his counsel? Why has he summoned
The old men to hear him?

(*Enter* Creon *from the palace. He addresses the* Chorus *from the top step.*)

Creon. Gentlemen: I have the honor to inform you that our ship of
state, which recent storms have threatened to destroy, has come
10 safely to harbor at last, guided by the merciful wisdom of heaven.
I have summoned you here this morning because I know that I
can depend upon you: your devotion to King Laius was absolute;
you never hesitated in your duty to our late ruler Oedipus; and
when Oedipus died, your loyalty was transferred to his children.
15 Unfortunately, as you know, his two sons, the princes Eteocles and
Polyneices, have killed each other in battle; and I, as the next in
blood, have succeeded to the full power of the throne.

   I am aware, of course, that no ruler can expect complete loyalty
from his subjects until he has been tested in office. Nevertheless,
20 I say to you at the very outset that I have nothing but **contempt**
for the kind of governor who is afraid, for whatever reason, to
follow the course that he knows is best for the state; and as for
the man who sets private friendship above the public welfare—
I have no use for him, either. I call God to witness that if I
25 saw my country headed for ruin, I should not be afraid to
speak out plainly; and I need hardly remind you that I would
never have any dealings with an enemy of the people. No one
values friendship more highly than I; but we must remember
that friends made at the risk of wrecking our ship are not real
30 friends at all. **D**

   These are my principles, at any rate, and that is why I have
made the following decision concerning the sons of Oedipus:
Eteocles, who died as a man should die, fighting for his country,
is to be buried with full military honors, with all the ceremony
35 that is usual when the greatest heroes die; but his brother
Polyneices, who broke his exile to come back with fire and
sword against his native city and the shrines of his fathers'
gods, whose one idea was to spill the blood of his blood and
sell his own people into slavery—Polyneices, I say, is to have no
40 burial: no man is to touch him or say the least prayer for him;
he shall lie on the plain, unburied; and the birds and the
scavenging dogs can do with him whatever they like.

2 Menoeceus' (mə-nē′syōōs).

auspicious (ô-spĭsh′əs) *adj.* promising success; favorable

12 Laius (lā′əs): the father of Oedipus.

contempt (kən-tĕmpt′) *n.* an attitude of regarding someone or something as worthless or inferior

D CHARACTER
This speech introduces Creon, who acts as Antigone's **antagonist.** According to him, what deserves the highest loyalty? Read on to learn his motives for forbidding Polyneices' burial.

Philip Bosco as Creon in the Lincoln Center Repertory 1971 production

This is my command, and you can see the wisdom behind it.
As long as I am king, no traitor is going to be honored with the
45 loyal man. But whoever shows by word and deed that he is on
the side of the state—he shall have my respect while he is
living, and my **reverence** when he is dead.

reverence (rĕv′ər-əns) *n.* awe and respect

Choragus. If that is your will, Creon son of Menoeceus,
You have the right to enforce it: we are yours.

50 **Creon.** That is my will. Take care that you do your part.

Choragus. We are old men: let the younger ones carry it out.

Creon. I do not mean that: the sentries have been appointed.

Choragus. Then what is it that you would have us do?

Creon. You will give no support to whoever breaks this law.

55 **Choragus.** Only a crazy man is in love with death!

Creon. And death it is; yet money talks, and the wisest
Have sometimes been known to count a few coins too many.

(*Enter* Sentry.)

Sentry. I'll not say that I'm out of breath from running, King, because every
time I stopped to think about what I have to tell you, I felt like going back.
60 And all the time a voice kept saying, "You fool, don't you know you're walking
straight into trouble?"; and then another voice: "Yes, but if you let somebody
else get the news to Creon first, it will be even worse than that for you!" But
good sense won out, at least I hope it was good sense, and here I am with a
story that makes no sense at all; but I'll tell it anyhow, because, as they say,
65 what's going to happen's going to happen, and—

Creon. Come to the point. What have you to say?

Sentry. I did not do it. I did not see who did it. You must not punish me for
what someone else has done.

Creon. A comprehensive defense! More effective, perhaps,
70 If I knew its purpose. Come: what is it?

Sentry. A dreadful thing . . . I don't know how to put it—

Creon. Out with it!

Sentry.   Well, then;
The dead man—
                Polyneices—

(*Pause. The* Sentry *is overcome, fumbles for words.* Creon *waits **impassively**.*)
                out there—
                        someone—
New dust on the slimy flesh!

impassively (ĭm-păs′ĭv-lē) *adv.* in a way that shows no emotion or feeling

(*Pause. No sign from* Creon.)

75 Someone has given it burial that way, and
Gone. . . .

(*Long pause.* Creon *finally speaks with deadly control.*)

Creon. And the man who dared do this? **E**

Sentry.   I swear I
Do not know! You must believe me!
                          Listen:
The ground was dry, not a sign of digging, no,
80 Not a wheel track in the dust, no trace of anyone.
It was when they relieved us this morning: and one of them,
The corporal, pointed to it.
                          There it was,
The strangest—
                          Look:
The body, just mounded over with light dust: you see?
85 Not buried really, but as if they'd covered it
Just enough for the ghost's peace. And no sign
Of dogs or any wild animal that had been there.

And then what a scene there was! Every man of us
Accusing the other: we all proved the other man did it;
90 We all had proof that we could not have done it.
We were ready to take hot iron in our hands,
Walk through fire, swear by all the gods,
It was not I!
I do not know who it was, but it was not I!

(Creon's *rage has been mounting steadily, but the* Sentry *is too
intent upon his story to notice it.*)

95 And then, when this came to nothing, someone said
A thing that silenced us and made us stare
Down at the ground: you had to be told the news,
And one of us had to do it! We threw the dice,
And the bad luck fell to me. So here I am,
100 No happier to be here than you are to have me:
Nobody likes the man who brings bad news. **F**

Choragus. I have been wondering, King: can it be that the gods
  have done this? **G**

Creon (*furiously*). Stop!
Must you doddering wrecks
105 Go out of your heads entirely? "The gods!"
Intolerable!
The gods favor this corpse? Why? How had he served them?

E CLASSICAL DRAMA
Who do you think buried the body?
Note the **dramatic irony** arising from
Creon's assumption that it was a
man.

F CHARACTER
Notice how the sentry, a **minor
character,** relates to Creon.
What does his attitude tell you
about Creon?

G CLASSICAL DRAMA
The **choragus** poses a reasonable
question. Judge Creon's response,
noting what attitude he shows
toward the gods.

Tried to loot their temples, burn their images,
Yes, and the whole state, and its laws with it!
110 Is it your senile opinion that the gods love to honor bad men?
A pious thought!—
                          No, from the very beginning
There have been those who have whispered together,
Stiff-necked **anarchists,** putting their heads together,
Scheming against me in alleys. These are the men,
115 And they have bribed my own guard to do this thing.
(*sententiously*) Money!
There's nothing in the world so demoralizing as money.
Down go your cities,
Homes gone, men gone, honest hearts corrupted,
120 Crookedness of all kinds, and all for money!
                          (*to* Sentry)   But you—!
I swear by God and by the throne of God,
The man who has done this thing shall pay for it!
Find that man; bring him here to me, or your death
Will be the least of your problems: I'll string you up
125 Alive, and there will be certain ways to make you
Discover your employer before you die;
And the process may teach you a lesson you seem to have missed:
The dearest profit is sometimes all too dear.
That depends on the source. Do you understand me?
130 A fortune won is often misfortune.

Sentry. King, may I speak?

Creon.   Your very voice distresses me.

Sentry. Are you sure that it is my voice, and not your conscience?

Creon. By God, he wants to analyze me now!

Sentry. It is not what I say, but what has been done, that hurts you.

135 **Creon.** You talk too much.

Sentry.   Maybe; but I've done nothing.

Creon. Sold your soul for some silver: that's all you've done.

Sentry. How dreadful it is when the right judge judges wrong!

Creon. Your figures of speech
May entertain you now; but unless you bring me the man,
140 You will get little profit from them in the end. **H**

(*Exit* Creon *into the palace.*)

Sentry. "Bring me the man"—!
I'd like nothing better than bringing him the man!
But bring him or not, you have seen the last of me here.
At any rate, I am safe!

(*Exit* Sentry.)

anarchist (ăn'ər-kĭst) *n.* a person favoring the overthrow of government

sententiously (sĕn-tĕn'shəs-lē) *adv.* in a pompous, moralizing manner

H CHARACTER
What do you think of Creon so far? What seem to be his virtues? his flaws?

ODE 1

Ode: a song chanted by the chorus.

Chorus. Numberless are the world's wonders, but none ◆ ❶
More wonderful than man; the storm-grey sea
Yields to his prows; the huge crests bear him high;
Earth, holy and inexhaustible, is graven
5 With shining furrows where his plows have gone
Year after year, the timeless labor of stallions.

The light-boned birds and beasts that cling to cover,
The lithe fish lighting their reaches of dim water,
All are taken, tamed in the net of his mind;
10 The lion on the hill, the wild horse windy-maned,
Resign to him; and his blunt yoke has broken
The sultry shoulders of the mountain bull.

Words also, and thought as rapid as air,
He fashions to his good use; statecraft is his,
15 And his the skill that deflects the arrows of snow,
The spears of winter rain: from every wind
He has made himself secure—from all but one:
In the late wind of death he cannot stand.

O clear intelligence, force beyond all measure!
20 O fate of man, working both good and evil!
When the laws are kept, how proudly his city stands!
When the laws are broken, what of his city then?
Never may the anarchic man find rest at my hearth,
Never be it said that my thoughts are his thoughts. ❶

❶ **GRAMMAR AND STYLE**
Reread line 1 of the ode. Notice how
the subject *wonders* comes after,
rather than before, the verb *are*.
Writers sometimes use **inverted
sentences** like this to add variety or
emphasis to their writing.

❷ **READING CLASSICAL DRAMA**
In your chart, summarize the
message that this choral **ode**
conveys about human beings.
How would you relate the ode to
the preceding scene?

⚜ SCENE 2

(*Reenter* Sentry *leading* Antigone.)

Choragus. What does this mean? Surely this captive woman
Is the princess, Antigone. Why should she be taken?

Sentry. Here is the one who did it! We caught her
In the very act of burying him. Where is Creon?

5 **Choragus.** Just coming from the house.

(*Enter* Creon, *center.*)

Creon.   What has happened?
Why have you come back so soon?

Sentry (*expansively*).   O King,
A man should never be too sure of anything: Ⓐ
I would have sworn
That you'd not see me here again: your anger
10 Frightened me so, and the things you threatened me with;
But how could I tell then
That I'd be able to solve the case so soon?

No dice throwing this time: I was only too glad to come!

Here is this woman. She is the guilty one:
15 We found her trying to bury him.

Take her, then; question her; judge her as you will.
I am through with the whole thing now, and glad of it.

Creon. But this is Antigone! Why have you brought her here?

Sentry. She was burying him, I tell you!

Creon (*severely*).   Is this the truth?

20 **Sentry.** I saw her with my own eyes. Can I say more?

Creon. The details: come, tell me quickly!

Sentry.   It was like this:
After those terrible threats of yours, King,
We went back and brushed the dust away from the body.
The flesh was soft by now, and stinking,
25 So we sat on a hill to windward and kept guard.
No napping this time! We kept each other awake.
But nothing happened until the white round sun
Whirled in the center of the round sky over us:
Then, suddenly,
30 A storm of dust roared up from the earth, and the sky
Went out, the plain vanished with all its trees

Ⓐ **CLASSICAL DRAMA**
Reread line 7, and note the **dramatic irony.** How might the sentry's statement that "a man should never be too sure of anything" apply to Creon?

Martha Henry as Antigone and Philip Bosco as Creon in the Lincoln Center Repertory 1971 production

In the stinging dark. We closed our eyes and endured it.
The whirlwind lasted a long time, but it passed;
And then we looked, and there was Antigone!
35 I have seen
A mother bird come back to a stripped nest, heard
Her crying bitterly a broken note or two
For the young ones stolen. Just so, when this girl
Found the bare corpse, and all her love's work wasted,
40 She wept, and cried on heaven to damn the hands
That had done this thing.

                    And then she brought more dust
And sprinkled wine three times for her brother's ghost.

We ran and took her at once. She was not afraid,
Not even when we charged her with what she had done.
45 She denied nothing.

             And this was a comfort to me,
And some uneasiness: for it is a good thing
To escape from death, but it is no great pleasure
To bring death to a friend. **B**

                 Yet I always say
There is nothing so comfortable as your own safe skin!

50 **Creon** (*slowly, dangerously*). And you, Antigone,
You with your head hanging—do you confess this thing?

Antigone. I do. I deny nothing.

Creon (*to* Sentry).   You may go.

(*Exit* Sentry.)

(*to* Antigone) Tell me, tell me briefly:
Had you heard my proclamation touching this matter?

55 **Antigone.** It was public. Could I help hearing it?

Creon. And yet you dared defy the law.

Antigone.   I dared.
It was not God's proclamation. That final Justice
That rules the world below makes no such laws.

Your edict, King, was strong,
60 But all your strength is weakness itself against
The immortal unrecorded laws of God.
They are not merely now: they were, and shall be,
Operative forever, beyond man utterly.

I knew I must die, even without your decree:
65 I am only mortal. And if I must die
Now, before it is my time to die,

B CLASSICAL DRAMA
In classical drama, much of the action takes place offstage and is reported by **minor characters.** How does the sentry's speech create sympathy for Antigone?

Surely this is no hardship: can anyone
Living, as I live, with evil all about me,
Think Death less than a friend? This death of mine
70 Is of no importance; but if I had left my brother
Lying in death unburied, I should have suffered.
Now I do not. **C**

           You smile at me. Ah Creon,
Think me a fool, if you like; but it may well be
That a fool convicts me of folly.

75 **Choragus.** Like father, like daughter: both headstrong, deaf to reason!
She has never learned to yield.

Creon.   She has much to learn.
The inflexible heart breaks first, the toughest iron
Cracks first, and the wildest horses bend their necks
At the pull of the smallest curb.

                        Pride? In a slave?
80 This girl is guilty of a double **insolence,**
Breaking the given laws and boasting of it.
Who is the man here,
She or I, if this crime goes unpunished? **D**
Sister's child, or more than sister's child,
85 Or closer yet in blood—she and her sister
Win bitter death for this!

           (*to servants*) Go, some of you,
Arrest Ismene. I accuse her equally.
Bring her: you will find her sniffling in the house there.

Her mind's a traitor: crimes kept in the dark
90 Cry for light, and the guardian brain shudders;
But how much worse than this
Is brazen boasting of barefaced anarchy!

Antigone. Creon, what more do you want than my death?

Creon.   Nothing.
That gives me everything.

Antigone.   Then I beg you: kill me.
95 This talking is a great weariness: your words
Are distasteful to me, and I am sure that mine
Seem so to you. And yet they should not seem so:
I should have praise and honor for what I have done.
All these men here would praise me
100 Were their lips not frozen shut with fear of you.
(*bitterly*) Ah the good fortune of kings,
Licensed to say and do whatever they please! **E**

C CHARACTER
Reread lines 57–72. What does
Antigone believe is the supreme law?
What is her attitude toward death?

insolence (īn′sə-ləns) *n.* rudeness
and disrespect

D CONFLICT
How does Creon's perception of
Antigone as a threat to his manhood
heighten the **conflict** between them?

E THEME
Reread lines 99–102. What is
Antigone suggesting about the rule
of kings and its effect on citizens?

Creon. You are alone here in that opinion.

Antigone. No, they are with me. But they keep their tongues in leash.

105 **Creon.** Maybe. But you are guilty, and they are not.

Antigone. There is no guilt in reverence for the dead.

Creon. But Eteocles—was he not your brother too?

Antigone. My brother too.

Creon.   And you insult his memory?

Antigone (*softly*). The dead man would not say that I insult it.

110 **Creon.** He would: for you honor a traitor as much as him.

Antigone. His own brother, traitor or not, and equal in blood.

Creon. He made war on his country. Eteocles defended it.

Antigone. Nevertheless, there are honors due all the dead.

Creon. But not the same for the wicked as for the just.

115 **Antigone.** Ah Creon, Creon,
Which of us can say what the gods hold wicked? **F**

F **CLASSICAL DRAMA**
Greek **tragedy** explores humans' relationship to the gods. How does Antigone's thinking about the gods differ from Creon's thinking?

Creon. An enemy is an enemy, even dead.

Antigone. It is my nature to join in love, not hate.

Creon (*finally losing patience*). Go join them, then; if you must have your love,
120 Find it in hell!

Choragus. But see, Ismene comes:

(*Enter* Ismene, *guarded.*)

Those tears are sisterly; the cloud
That shadows her eyes rains down gentle sorrow.

Creon. You too, Ismene,
125 Snake in my ordered house, sucking my blood
Stealthily—and all the time I never knew
That these two sisters were aiming at my throne!

                                                Ismene,
Do you confess your share in this crime or deny it?
Answer me.

130 **Ismene.** Yes, if she will let me say so. I am guilty.

Martha Henry as Antigone and Philip Bosco as Creon in the Lincoln Center Repertory 1971 production

Antigone (*coldly*). No, Ismene. You have no right to say so.
You would not help me, and I will not have you help me.

Ismene. But now I know what you meant; and I am here
To join you, to take my share of punishment.

135 **Antigone.** The dead man and the gods who rule the dead
Know whose act this was. Words are not friends.

Ismene. Do you refuse me, Antigone? I want to die with you:
I too have a duty that I must discharge to the dead.

Antigone. You shall not lessen my death by sharing it.

140 **Ismene.** What do I care for life when you are dead?

Antigone. Ask Creon. You're always hanging on his opinions.

Ismene. You are laughing at me. Why, Antigone?

Antigone. It's a joyless laughter, Ismene.

Ismene.   But can I do nothing?

Antigone. Yes. Save yourself. I shall not envy you.
145 There are those who will praise you; I shall have honor, too.

Ismene. But we are equally guilty!

Antigone.   No, more, Ismene.
You are alive, but I belong to Death. **G**

Creon (*to the* Chorus). Gentlemen, I beg you to observe these girls:
One has just now lost her mind; the other,
150 It seems, has never had a mind at all.

Ismene. Grief teaches the steadiest minds to waver, King.

Creon. Yours certainly did, when you assumed guilt with the guilty!

Ismene. But how could I go on living without her?

Creon.   You are.
She is already dead.

Ismene.   But your own son's bride!

155 **Creon.** There are places enough for him to push his plow.
I want no wicked women for my sons!

Ismene. O dearest Haemon, how your father wrongs you! **H**

Creon. I've had enough of your childish talk of marriage!

Choragus. Do you really intend to steal this girl from your son?

160 **Creon.** No; Death will do that for me.

Choragus.   Then she must die?

Creon. You dazzle me.

                    —But enough of this talk!

G CHARACTER
What does Antigone's treatment of her sister reveal about her character?

H CONFLICT
Ismene reveals that Antigone is engaged to Creon's son Haemon. What new issues could arise from the conflict between Antigone and Creon?

(*to guards*) You, there, take them away and guard them well:
For they are but women, and even brave men run
When they see Death coming.

(*Exeunt* Ismene, Antigone, *and guards.*)

ODE 2

Chorus. Fortunate is the man who has never tasted God's vengeance!
Where once the anger of heaven has struck, that house is shaken
Forever: damnation rises behind each child
Like a wave cresting out of the black northeast,
5 When the long darkness under sea roars up
And bursts drumming death upon the wind-whipped sand.

I have seen this gathering sorrow from time long past
Loom upon Oedipus' children: generation from generation
Takes the compulsive rage of the enemy god.
10 So lately this last flower of Oedipus' line
Drank the sunlight! but now a passionate word
And a handful of dust have closed up all its beauty. **I**

What mortal arrogance
Transcends the wrath of Zeus?
15 Sleep cannot lull him, nor the effortless long months
Of the timeless gods: but he is young forever,
And his house is the shining day of high Olympus.
All that is and shall be,
And all the past, is his.
20 No pride on earth is free of the curse of heaven.

The straying dreams of men
May bring them ghosts of joy:
But as they drowse, the waking embers burn them;
Or they walk with fixed eyes, as blind men walk.
25 But the ancient wisdom speaks for our own time:
Fate works most for woe
With Folly's fairest show.
Man's little pleasure is the spring of sorrow. **J**

I **READING CLASSICAL DRAMA**
Judging from this choral **ode,** how do the gods feel toward the family of Oedipus? Make notes in your chart.

J **READING CLASSICAL DRAMA**
Explain the last three lines of the **ode.** Whom do you think these lines apply to?

❧ SCENE 3

Choragus. But here is Haemon, King, the last of all your sons.
Is it grief for Antigone that brings him here,
And bitterness at being robbed of his bride?

(*Enter* Haemon.)

Creon. We shall soon see, and no need of diviners.

                                     —Son,

5 You have heard my final judgment on that girl:
Have you come here hating me, or have you come
With deference and with love, whatever I do?

Haemon. I am your son, Father. You are my guide.
You make things clear for me, and I obey you.
10 No marriage means more to me than your continuing wisdom.

Creon. Good. That is the way to behave: subordinate
Everything else, my son, to your father's will.
This is what a man prays for, that he may get
Sons attentive and dutiful in his house,
15 Each one hating his father's enemies,
Honoring his father's friends. But if his sons
Fail him, if they turn out unprofitably,
What has he fathered but trouble for himself
And amusement for the malicious? **Ⓐ**

                              So you are right
20 Not to lose your head over this woman.
Your pleasure with her would soon grow cold, Haemon,
And then you'd have a hellcat in bed and elsewhere.
Let her find her husband in hell!
Of all the people in this city, only she
25 Has had contempt for my law and broken it.

Do you want me to show myself weak before the people?
Or to break my sworn word? No, and I will not.
The woman dies.

I suppose she'll plead "family ties." Well, let her.
30 If I permit my own family to rebel,
How shall I earn the world's obedience?
Show me the man who keeps his house in hand,
He's fit for public authority.

                           I'll have no dealings
With lawbreakers, critics of the government:
35 Whoever is chosen to govern should be obeyed—
Must be obeyed, in all things, great and small,

4 diviners (dĭ-vī′nərz): those who predict the future.

Ⓐ THEME
Reread lines 11–19. What is Creon's view of family relationships?

Philip Bosco as Creon in the Lincoln Center Repertory 1971 production

Just and unjust! O Haemon,
The man who knows how to obey, and that man only,
Knows how to give commands when the time comes.
40 You can depend on him, no matter how fast
The spears come: he's a good soldier; he'll stick it out.

Anarchy, anarchy! Show me a greater evil!
This is why cities tumble and the great houses rain down;
This is what scatters armies! **B**

45 No, no: good lives are made so by discipline.
We keep the laws then, and the lawmakers,
And no woman shall seduce us. If we must lose,
Let's lose to a man, at least! Is a woman stronger than we? **C**

Choragus. Unless time has rusted my wits,
50 What you say, King, is said with point and dignity.

Haemon (*boyishly earnest*). Father:
Reason is God's crowning gift to man, and you are right
To warn me against losing mine. I cannot say—
I hope that I shall never want to say!—that you
55 Have reasoned badly. Yet there are other men
Who can reason, too; and their opinions might be helpful.
You are not in a position to know everything
That people say or do, or what they feel:
Your temper terrifies them—everyone
60 Will tell you only what you like to hear. **D**
But I, at any rate, can listen; and I have heard them
Muttering and whispering in the dark about this girl.
They say no woman has ever, so unreasonably,
Died so shameful a death for a generous act:
65 "She covered her brother's body. Is this indecent?
She kept him from dogs and vultures. Is this a crime?
Death? She should have all the honor that we can give her!"

This is the way they talk out there in the city.

You must believe me:
70 Nothing is closer to me than your happiness.
What could be closer? Must not any son
Value his father's fortune as his father does his?
I beg you, do not be unchangeable:
Do not believe that you alone can be right.
75 The man who thinks that,

B THEME
Reread lines 35–44. What are
Creon's views about government
and his role as king?

C CONFLICT
How does Creon's perception of
women contribute to his conflict
with Antigone?

D THEME
Reread lines 55–60. How do
Haemon's views of government
differ from Creon's?

The man who maintains that only he has the power
To reason correctly, the gift to speak, the soul—
A man like that, when you know him, turns out empty.

It is not reason never to yield to reason!

80 In flood time you can see how some trees bend,
And because they bend, even their twigs are safe,
While stubborn trees are torn up, roots and all.
And the same thing happens in sailing:
Make your sheet fast, never slacken—and over you go,
85 Head over heels and under: and there's your voyage. **E**
Forget you are angry! Let yourself be moved!
I know I am young; but please let me say this:
The ideal condition
Would be, I admit, that men should be right by instinct;
90 But since we are all too likely to go astray,
The reasonable thing is to learn from those who can teach.

Choragus. You will do well to listen to him, King,
If what he says is sensible. And you, Haemon,
Must listen to your father. Both speak well. **F**

95 **Creon.** You consider it right for a man of my years and experience
To go to school to a boy?

Haemon.   It is not right
If I am wrong. But if I am young, and right,
What does my age matter?

Creon. You think it right to stand up for an anarchist?

100 **Haemon.** Not at all. I pay no respect to criminals.

Creon. Then she is not a criminal?

Haemon. The city would deny it, to a man.

Creon. And the city proposes to teach me how to rule?

Haemon. Ah. Who is it that's talking like a boy now?

105 **Creon.** My voice is the one voice giving orders in this city!

Haemon. It is no city if it takes orders from one voice.

Creon. The state is the king!

Haemon.   Yes, if the state is a desert. **G**

(*pause*)

Creon. This boy, it seems, has sold out to a woman.

Haemon. If you are a woman: my concern is only for you.

110 **Creon.** So? Your "concern"! In a public brawl with your father!

E THEME
Compare Haemon's words to Creon with Creon's words in Scene 2, beginning "The inflexible heart breaks first . . ." (line 77, page 983). What do both speeches suggest about inflexibility?

F CLASSICAL DRAMA
How does the **choragus** respond to Creon's and Haemon's arguments? How similar is your response?

G THEME
Interpret Haemon's reply.

Haemon. How about you, in a public brawl with justice?

Creon. With justice, when all that I do is within my rights?

Haemon. You have no right to trample on God's right.

Creon (*completely out of control*). Fool, adolescent fool! Taken in by a woman!

115 **Haemon.** You'll never see me taken in by anything vile.

Creon. Every word you say is for her!

Haemon (*quietly, darkly*). And for you.
And for me. And for the gods under the earth.

Creon. You'll never marry her while she lives.

Haemon. Then she must die. But her death will cause another.

120 **Creon.** Another?
Have you lost your senses? Is this an open threat? ⓗ

Haemon. There is no threat in speaking to emptiness.

Creon. I swear you'll regret this superior tone of yours!
You are the empty one!

Haemon. If you were not my father,
125 I'd say you were **perverse**.

Creon. You girl-struck fool, don't play at words with me!

Haemon. I am sorry. You prefer silence.

Creon. Now, by God—!
I swear, by all the gods in heaven above us,
You'll watch it; I swear you shall!
(*to the servants*) Bring her out!
130 Bring the woman out! Let her die before his eyes,
Here, this instant, with her bridegroom beside her!

Haemon. Not here, no; she will not die here, King.
And you will never see my face again.
Go on raving as long as you've a friend to endure you.
(*Exit* Haemon.)

135 **Choragus.** Gone, gone.
Creon, a young man in a rage is dangerous!

Creon. Let him do, or dream to do, more than a man can.
He shall not save these girls from death.

Choragus. These girls?
You have sentenced them both?

Creon. No, you are right.
140 I will not kill the one whose hands are clean.

ⓗ **CLASSICAL DRAMA**
Note the **dramatic irony.** What might Haemon mean? What does Creon think he means?

perverse (pər-vûrs') *adj.* willfully determined to go against what is expected or desired

Choragus. But Antigone?

Creon (*somberly*).   I will carry her far away,
Out there in the wilderness, and lock her
Living in a vault of stone. She shall have food,
As the custom is, to absolve the state of her death.
145 And there let her pray to the gods of hell:
They are her only gods:
Perhaps they will show her an escape from death,
Or she may learn,
                    though late,
That piety shown the dead is pity in vain. ●

(*Exit* Creon.)

ODE 3

Chorus. Love, unconquerable [J]
Waster of rich men, keeper
Of warm lights and all-night vigil
In the soft face of a girl:
5 Sea wanderer, forest visitor!
Even the pure immortals cannot escape you,
And mortal man, in his one day's dusk,
Trembles before your glory.

Surely you swerve upon ruin
10 The just man's consenting heart,
As here you have made bright anger
Strike between father and son—
And none has conquered but Love!
A girl's glance working the will of heaven:
15 Pleasure to her alone who mocks us,
Merciless Aphrodite.

● **CHARACTER**
What do you make of Creon's decision to bury a person alive when he has refused to bury a person who is dead?

[J] **READING CLASSICAL DRAMA**
In your chart, summarize the message about love expressed in this **ode**. How does the ode relate to the exchange between Creon and Haemon?

16 Aphrodite (ăf′rə-dī′tē): the goddess of love and beauty.

❀ SCENE 4

Choragus (*as* Antigone *enters, guarded*). But I can no longer stand
   in awe of this,
Nor, seeing what I see, keep back my tears.
Here is Antigone, passing to that chamber
Where all find sleep at last.

5 **Antigone.** Look upon me, friends, and pity me
Turning back at the night's edge to say
Good-bye to the sun that shines for me no longer;
Now sleepy Death
Summons me down to Acheron, that cold shore:
10 There is no bride song there, nor any music.

   Chorus. Yet not unpraised, not without a kind of honor,
You walk at last into the underworld;
Untouched by sickness, broken by no sword.
What woman has ever found your way to death?

15 **Antigone.** How often I have heard the story of Niobe,
Tantalus' wretched daughter, how the stone
Clung fast about her, ivy-close: and they say
The rain falls endlessly
And sifting soft snow; her tears are never done.
20 I feel the loneliness of her death in mine.

   Chorus. But she was born of heaven, and you
Are woman, woman-born. If her death is yours,
A mortal woman's, is this not for you
Glory in our world and in the world beyond?

25 **Antigone.** You laugh at me. Ah, friends, friends,
Can you not wait until I am dead? O Thebes,
O men many-charioted, in love with Fortune,
Dear springs of Dirce, sacred Theban grove,
Be witnesses for me, denied all pity,
30 Unjustly judged! and think a word of love
For her whose path turns
Under dark earth, where there are no more tears.

   Chorus. You have passed beyond human daring and come at last
Into a place of stone where Justice sits.
35 I cannot tell
What shape of your father's guilt appears in this.

   Antigone. You have touched it at last: that bridal bed
Unspeakable, horror of son and mother mingling:
Their crime, infection of all our family!
40 O Oedipus, father and brother!
Your marriage strikes from the grave to murder mine.

9 Acheron (ăk′ə-rŏn′): in Greek
mythology, one of the rivers bordering
the underworld, the place inhabited by
the souls of the dead.

15–20 Niobe (nī′ə-bē) was a queen of
Thebes whose children were killed by
the gods because she had boasted that
she was greater than a goddess. After
their deaths, she was turned to stone
but continued to shed tears.

Martha Henry as Antigone in the
Lincoln Center Repertory 1971
production

I have been a stranger here in my own land:
All my life
The blasphemy of my birth has followed me.

45 **Chorus.** Reverence is a virtue, but strength
Lives in established law: that must prevail.
You have made your choice;
Your death is the doing of your conscious hand. **(A)**

Antigone. Then let me go, since all your words are bitter,
50 And the very light of the sun is cold to me.
Lead me to my vigil, where I must have
Neither love nor **lamentation**; no song, but silence.

(Creon *interrupts impatiently.*)

Creon. If dirges and planned lamentations could put off death,
Men would be singing forever.
          (*to the servants*) Take her, go!
55 You know your orders: take her to the vault
And leave her alone there. And if she lives or dies,
That's her affair, not ours: our hands are clean.

Antigone. O tomb, vaulted bride-bed in eternal rock,
Soon I shall be with my own again
60 Where Persephone welcomes the thin ghosts underground:
And I shall see my father again, and you, Mother,
And dearest Polyneices—
                    dearest indeed
To me, since it was my hand
That washed him clean and poured the ritual wine:
65 And my reward is death before my time!

And yet, as men's hearts know, I have done no wrong;
I have not sinned before God. Or if I have,
I shall know the truth in death. But if the guilt
Lies upon Creon who judged me, then, I pray,
70 May his punishment equal my own. **(B)**

Choragus.   O passionate heart,
Unyielding, tormented still by the same winds!

Creon. Her guards shall have good cause to regret their delaying.

Antigone. Ah! That voice is like the voice of death!

Creon. I can give you no reason to think you are mistaken.

75 **Antigone.** Thebes, and you my fathers' gods,
And rulers of Thebes, you see me now, the last
Unhappy daughter of a line of kings,
Your kings, led away to death. You will remember
What things I suffer, and at what men's hands,

80 Because I would not **transgress** the laws of heaven.
(*to the guards, simply*) Come: let us wait no longer. **C**
(*Exit* Antigone, *left, guarded.*)

ODE 4

Chorus. All Danae's beauty was locked away
In a brazen cell where the sunlight could not come:
A small room, still as any grave, enclosed her.
Yet she was a princess too,
5 And Zeus in a rain of gold poured love upon her.
O child, child,
No power in wealth or war
Or tough sea-blackened ships
Can prevail against untiring Destiny!

10 And Dryas' son also, that furious king,
Bore the god's prisoning anger for his pride:
Sealed up by Dionysus in deaf stone,
His madness died among echoes.
So at the last he learned what dreadful power
15 His tongue had mocked:
For he had profaned the revels
And fired the wrath of the nine
Implacable sisters that love the sound of the flute.

And old men tell a half-remembered tale
20 Of horror done where a dark ledge splits the sea
And a double surf beats on the grey shores:
How a king's new woman, sick
With hatred for the queen he had imprisoned,
Ripped out his two sons' eyes with her bloody hands
25 While grinning Ares watched the shuttle plunge
Four times: four blind wounds crying for revenge,

Crying, tears and blood mingled. Piteously born,
Those sons whose mother was of heavenly birth!
Her father was the god of the north wind,
30 And she was cradled by gales;
She raced with young colts on the glittering hills
And walked untrammeled in the open light:
But in her marriage deathless Fate found means
To build a tomb like yours for all her joy. **D**

---

transgress (trăns-grĕs′) *v.* to violate
or break (a law, command, or moral
code)

C THEME
What is Antigone's highest **loyalty**?

1–5 The princess Danae (dăn′ə-ē′) was
imprisoned by her father because it had
been predicted that her son would one
day kill him. After Zeus visited Danae
in the form of a shower of gold, she
gave birth to his son Perseus, who did
eventually kill his grandfather.

10–18 King Lycurgus (lī-kûr′gəs), son of
Dryas (drī′əs), was driven mad and eaten
by horses for objecting to the worship of
Dionysus. The **nine implacable sisters** are
the Muses, the goddesses who presided
over literature, the arts, and the sciences.
Once offended, they were impossible to
appease.

19–34 These lines refer to the myth of
King Phineus (fĭn′yŏōs), who imprisoned
his first wife, the daughter of the north
wind, and allowed his new wife to blind
his sons from his first marriage.

D READING CLASSICAL DRAMA
What insights into Antigone's
situation do you get from the **myths**
that this **ode** alludes to? Summarize
your thoughts in your chart.

❀ SCENE 5

(Enter blind Teiresias, *led by a boy. The opening speeches of* Teiresias *should be in singsong contrast to the realistic lines of* Creon.)

Teiresias. This is the way the blind man comes, princes, princes,
Lock step, two heads lit by the eyes of one.

Creon. What new thing have you to tell us, old Teiresias?

Teiresias. I have much to tell you: listen to the prophet, Creon.

5 **Creon.** I am not aware that I have ever failed to listen.

Teiresias. Then you have done wisely, King, and ruled well.

Creon. I admit my debt to you. But what have you to say?

Teiresias. This, Creon: you stand once more on the edge of fate.

Creon. What do you mean? Your words are a kind of dread.

10 **Teiresias.** Listen, Creon:
I was sitting in my chair of augury, at the place
Where the birds gather about me. They were all a-chatter,
As is their habit, when suddenly I heard
A strange note in their jangling, a scream, a
15 Whirring fury; I knew that they were fighting,
Tearing each other, dying
In a whirlwind of wings clashing. And I was afraid.
I began the rites of burnt offering at the altar,
But Hephaestus failed me: instead of bright flame,
20 There was only the sputtering slime of the fat thigh-flesh
Melting: the entrails dissolved in grey smoke;
The bare bone burst from the welter. And no blaze!

This was a sign from heaven. My boy described it,
Seeing for me as I see for others.

25 I tell you, Creon, you yourself have brought
This new calamity upon us. Our hearths and altars
Are stained with the corruption of dogs and carrion birds
That glut themselves on the corpse of Oedipus' son.
The gods are deaf when we pray to them; their fire
30 Recoils from our offering; their birds of omen
Have no cry of comfort, for they are gorged
With the thick blood of the dead. **Ⓐ**
                O my son,
These are no trifles! Think: all men make mistakes,
But a good man yields when he knows his course is wrong,
35 And repairs the evil. The only crime is pride.

Give in to the dead man, then: do not fight with a corpse—
What glory is it to kill a man who is dead?

1–7 Teiresias is physically blind but spiritually sighted. As a prophet, he is an agent of the gods in their dealings with humans. His revelation of the truth to Oedipus had led Oedipus to leave Thebes, thus indirectly helping Creon to become king.

11–17 chair of augury: the place where Teiresias sits to hear the birds, whose sounds reveal the future to him. The fighting among the birds suggests that the anarchy infecting Thebes has spread even to the world of nature.

19 Hephaestus (hĭ-fĕs′təs): the god of fire.

26–32 According to Teiresias, the birds and dogs that have eaten the corpse of Polyneices have become corrupt, causing the gods to reject the Thebans' offerings and prayers.

Ⓐ CLASSICAL DRAMA
Reread lines 18–32. What do they suggest about how the gods view Creon's refusal to allow Polyneices to be buried?

Sydney Walker as Teiresias in the Lincoln Center Repertory 1971 production

Think, I beg you:
It is for your own good that I speak as I do.
40 You should be able to yield for your own good.

Creon. It seems that prophets have made me their especial province.
All my life long
I have been a kind of butt for the dull arrows
Of doddering fortunetellers!
                        No, Teiresias:
45 If your birds—if the great eagles of God himself—
Should carry him stinking bit by bit to heaven,
I would not yield. I am not afraid of pollution:
No man can **defile** the gods.
                        Do what you will;
Go into business, make money, speculate
50 In India gold or that synthetic gold from Sardis,
Get rich otherwise than by my consent to bury him.
Teiresias, it is a sorry thing when a wise man
Sells his wisdom, lets out his words for hire!

Teiresias. Ah Creon! Is there no man left in the world—

55 **Creon.** To do what? Come, let's have the aphorism!

Teiresias. No man who knows that wisdom outweighs any wealth?

Creon. As surely as bribes are baser than any baseness.

Teiresias. You are sick, Creon! You are deathly sick!

Creon. As you say: it is not my place to challenge a prophet.

60 **Teiresias.** Yet you have said my prophecy is for sale.

Creon. The generation of prophets has always loved gold.

Teiresias. The generation of kings has always loved brass.

Creon. You forget yourself! You are speaking to your king.

Teiresias. I know it. You are a king because of me.

65 **Creon.** You have a certain skill; but you have sold out.

Teiresias. King, you will drive me to words that—

Creon.   Say them, say them!
Only remember: I will not pay you for them.

Teiresias. No, you will find them too costly.

Creon.   No doubt. Speak:
Whatever you say, you will not change my will.

70 **Teiresias.** Then take this, and take it to heart!
The time is not far off when you shall pay back
Corpse for corpse, flesh of your own flesh.
You have thrust the child of this world into living night;
You have kept from the gods below the child that is theirs:

defile (dĭ-fīl´) *v.* to make dirty,
unclean, or impure

50 Sardis (sär´dĭs): the capital of ancient
Lydia, where metal coins were first
produced.

75 The one in a grave before her death, the other,
Dead, denied the grave. This is your crime:
And the Furies and the dark gods of hell
Are swift with terrible punishment for you.

Do you want to buy me now, Creon?

                              Not many days,
80 And your house will be full of men and women weeping,
And curses will be hurled at you from far
Cities grieving for sons unburied, left to rot before the walls of Thebes.

These are my arrows, Creon: they are all for you.

(*to boy*) But come, child: lead me home.
85 Let him waste his fine anger upon younger men.
Maybe he will learn at last
To control a wiser tongue in a better head. **B**

(*Exit* Teiresias.)

Choragus. The old man has gone, King, but his words
Remain to plague us. I am old, too,
90 But I cannot remember that he was ever false.

Creon. That is true. . . . It troubles me.
Oh it is hard to give in! but it is worse
To risk everything for stubborn pride.

Choragus. Creon: take my advice.

Creon.   What shall I do?

95 **Choragus.** Go quickly: free Antigone from her vault
And build a tomb for the body of Polyneices.

Creon. You would have me do this?

Choragus.   Creon, yes!
And it must be done at once: God moves
Swiftly to cancel the folly of stubborn men.

100 **Creon.** It is hard to deny the heart! But I
Will do it: I will not fight with destiny. **C**

Choragus. You must go yourself; you cannot leave it to others.

Creon. I will go.

                    —Bring axes, servants:
Come with me to the tomb. I buried her; I
105 Will set her free.

                    Oh quickly!
My mind misgives—
The laws of the gods are mighty, and a man must serve them
To the last day of his life!

(*Exit* Creon.)

> **77 Furies:** three goddesses who avenge crimes, especially those that violate family ties.

> **B** CHARACTER
> What does Creon's exchange with the **minor character** Teiresias reveal about Creon's view of himself and others? Predict how Teiresias' prophecy might be fulfilled.

> **C** CHARACTER
> Why does Creon change his mind?

PAEAN

Choragus. God of many names

Chorus.   O Iacchus

                              son

of Cadmean Semele

                    O born of the thunder!

guardian of the West

                    regent

of Eleusis' plain

                    O prince of maenad Thebes

5   and the Dragon Field by rippling Ismenus:

Choragus. God of many names

Chorus.   the flame of torches

flares on our hills

                    the nymphs of Iacchus

dance at the spring of Castalia:

from the vine-close mountain

                              come ah come in ivy:

10 *Evohé evohé!* sings through the streets of Thebes

Choragus. God of many names

Chorus.   Iacchus of Thebes

heavenly child

                    of Semele bride of the Thunderer!

The shadow of plague is upon us:

                              come

with clement feet

                    oh come from Parnassus

15 down the long slopes

                    across the lamenting water

Choragus. Io Fire! Chorister of the throbbing stars!

O purest among the voices of the night!

Thou son of God, blaze for us!

Chorus. Come with choric rapture of circling Maenads

20 Who cry *Io Iacche!*

                    God of many names! **D**

Paean (pē′ən): a hymn that is an appeal to the gods for assistance. In this paean, the chorus praises Dionysus, or Iacchus (yä′kəs), and calls on him to come to Thebes to show mercy and drive out evil.

2 Cadmus was the legendary founder of Thebes. Dionysus was the son of Cadmus' daughter **Semele** (sə-mē′lē) and Zeus, who is referred to here as thunder.

4–5 These lines name locations near Athens and Thebes. A **maenad** (mē′năd′) was a priestess of Dionysus.

8–9 Castalia: a spring on the sacred mountain Parnassus. Grapevines and ivy were symbols of Dionysus.

10 evohé (ĕ-woi′): hallelujah.

D READING CLASSICAL DRAMA
What **mood** is created by this **paean** to the god Dionysus?

EXODOS

Exodos: the last episode in the play. It is followed by a final speech made by the choragus and addressed directly to the audience.

(*Enter* Messenger.)

Messenger. Men of the line of Cadmus, you who live
Near Amphion's citadel:
                       I cannot say
Of any condition of human life, "This is fixed,
This is clearly good, or bad." Fate raises up,
5 And Fate casts down the happy and unhappy alike:
No man can foretell his fate.
                          Take the case of Creon:
Creon was happy once, as I count happiness:
Victorious in battle, sole governor of the land,
Fortunate father of children nobly born.
10 And now it has all gone from him! Who can say
That a man is still alive when his life's joy fails?
He is a walking dead man. Grant him rich;
Let him live like a king in his great house:
If his pleasure is gone, I would not give
15 So much as the shadow of smoke for all he owns.

Choragus. Your words hint at sorrow: what is your news for us?

Messenger. They are dead. The living are guilty of their death.

Choragus. Who is guilty? Who is dead? Speak!

Messenger.   Haemon.
Haemon is dead; and the hand that killed him
20 Is his own hand.

Choragus.   His father's? or his own?

Messenger. His own, driven mad by the murder his father had done.

Choragus. Teiresias, Teiresias, how clearly you saw it all!

Messenger. This is my news: you must draw what conclusions you can from it.

Choragus. But look: Eurydice, our queen:
25 Has she overheard us?

(*Enter* Eurydice *from the palace, center.*)

Eurydice. I have heard something, friends:
As I was unlocking the gate of Pallas' shrine,
For I needed her help today, I heard a voice
Telling of some new sorrow. And I fainted
30 There at the temple with all my maidens about me.
But speak again: whatever it is, I can bear it:
Grief and I are no strangers.

2 Amphion (ăm-fī′ən), Niobe's husband, built a wall around Thebes by charming the stones into place with music.

27 Pallas' (păl′əs): of Athena, the goddess of wisdom.

32 Megareus (mə-găr′yōōs), the older son of Eurydice and Creon, had died in the battle for Thebes.

Messenger.   Dearest lady,
I will tell you plainly all that I have seen.
I shall not try to comfort you: what is the use,
35 Since comfort could lie only in what is not true?
The truth is always best.
                                   I went with Creon
To the outer plain where Polyneices was lying,
No friend to pity him, his body shredded by dogs.
We made our prayers in that place to Hecate
40 And Pluto, that they would be merciful. And we bathed
The corpse with holy water, and we brought
Fresh-broken branches to burn what was left of it,
And upon the urn we heaped up a towering barrow
Of the earth of his own land.
                                   When we were done, we ran
45 To the vault where Antigone lay on her couch of stone.
One of the servants had gone ahead,
And while he was yet far off he heard a voice
Grieving within the chamber, and he came back
And told Creon. And as the king went closer,
50 The air was full of wailing, the words lost,
And he begged us to make all haste. "Am I a prophet?"
He said, weeping. "And must I walk this road,
The saddest of all that I have gone before?
My son's voice calls me on. Oh quickly, quickly!
55 Look through the crevice there, and tell me
If it is Haemon, or some deception of the gods!"

We obeyed; and in the cavern's farthest corner
We saw her lying:
She had made a noose of her fine linen veil
60 And hanged herself. Haemon lay beside her,
His arms about her waist, lamenting her,
His love lost underground, crying out
That his father had stolen her away from him.
When Creon saw him, the tears rushed to his eyes,
65 And he called to him: "What have you done, child? Speak to me.
What are you thinking that makes your eyes so strange?
O my son, my son, I come to you on my knees!"
But Haemon spat in his face. He said not a word,
Staring—
            and suddenly drew his sword
70 And lunged. Creon shrank back; the blade missed, and the boy,
Desperate against himself, drove it half its length
Into his own side and fell. And as he died,
He gathered Antigone close in his arms again,

39–40 Hecate (hĕk′ə-tē) **and Pluto:** other names for Persephone and Hades, the queen and king of the underworld.

43–44 Note the contrast between the barrow, or burial mound, erected by Creon and the handful of dirt used by Antigone to cover her brother.

60 Note that this is the same way in which Jocasta, Antigone's mother, killed herself.

Choking, his blood bright red on her white cheek.
75 And now he lies dead with the dead, and she is his
At last, his bride in the houses of the dead. **E**

(*Exit* Eurydice *into the palace.*)

Choragus. She has left us without a word. What can this mean?

Messenger. It troubles me, too; yet she knows what is best;
Her grief is too great for public lamentation,
80 And doubtless she has gone to her chamber to weep
For her dead son, leading her maidens in his dirge.

Choragus. It may be so: but I fear this deep silence.

(*pause*)

Messenger. I will see what she is doing. I will go in.

(*Exit* Messenger *into the palace. Enter* Creon *with attendants, bearing* Haemon's *body.*)

Choragus. But here is the king himself: oh look at him,
85 Bearing his own damnation in his arms.

Creon. Nothing you say can touch me any more.
My own blind heart has brought me
From darkness to final darkness. Here you see
The father murdering, the murdered son—
90 And all my civic wisdom!
Haemon my son, so young, so young to die,
I was the fool, not you; and you died for me.

Choragus. That is the truth; but you were late in learning it.

Creon. This truth is hard to bear. Surely a god
95 Has crushed me beneath the hugest weight of heaven,
And driven me headlong a barbaric way
To trample out the thing I held most dear.

The pains that men will take to come to pain! **F**

(*Enter* Messenger *from the palace.*)

Messenger. The burden you carry in your hands is heavy,
100 But it is not all: you will find more in your house.

Creon. What burden worse than this shall I find there?

Messenger. The queen is dead.

Creon. O port of death, deaf world,
Is there no pity for me? And you, angel of evil,
105 I was dead, and your words are death again.
Is it true, boy? Can it be true?
Is my wife dead? Has death bred death?

Messenger. You can see for yourself.

E CLASSICAL DRAMA
Summarize the **tragic** catastrophe that events have led to.

F CLASSICAL DRAMA
Reread lines 86–98. How does Creon view his actions?

(The doors are opened, and the body of Eurydice *is disclosed within.)*

Creon. Oh pity!
110 All true, all true, and more than I can bear!
O my wife, my son!

Messenger. She stood before the altar, and her heart
Welcomed the knife her own hand guided,
And a great cry burst from her lips for Megareus dead,
115 And for Haemon dead, her sons; and her last breath
Was a curse for their father, the murderer of her sons.
And she fell, and the dark flowed in through her closing eyes.

Creon. O God, I am sick with fear.
Are there no swords here? Has no one a blow for me?

120 **Messenger.** Her curse is upon you for the deaths of both.

Creon. It is right that it should be. I alone am guilty.
I know it, and I say it. Lead me in,
Quickly, friends.
I have neither life nor substance. Lead me in. **G**

125 **Choragus.** You are right, if there can be right in so much wrong.
The briefest way is best in a world of sorrow.

Creon. Let it come;
Let death come quickly and be kind to me.
I would not ever see the sun again.

130 **Choragus.** All that will come when it will; but we, meanwhile,
Have much to do. Leave the future to itself.

Creon. All my heart was in that prayer!

Choragus. Then do not pray any more: the sky is deaf.

Creon. Lead me away. I have been rash and foolish.
135 I have killed my son and my wife.
I look for comfort; my comfort lies here dead.
Whatever my hands have touched has come to nothing.
Fate has brought all my pride to a thought of dust.

(As Creon *is being led into the house, the* Choragus *advances and speaks directly to the audience.)*

Choragus. There is no happiness where there is no wisdom;
140 No wisdom but in submission to the gods.
Big words are always punished,
And proud men in old age learn to be wise. **H**

Translated by Dudley Fitts and Robert Fitzgerald

G CLASSICAL DRAMA
Creon assumes responsibility for the terrible events that have occurred. To what extent is he a **tragic hero?**

H THEME
What theme does the **choragus** express in the final words of the play?

Comprehension

1. **Recall** Why is Antigone determined to bury her brother?

2. **Recall** What punishment does Antigone receive for disobeying Creon?

3. **Clarify** How does Antigone die?

Literary Analysis

4. **Identify Conflict** Describe the conflict between Antigone and Creon. What arguments support each one's position? You may want to reread Scene 2, lines 105–118 (pages 984–985).

5. **Understand Classical Drama** In what way do the comments and songs of the **chorus** influence your understanding of characters and events? Refer to the chart you filled out as you read.

6. **Make Judgments** How responsible is Creon for the deaths of Antigone, Haemon, and Eurydice?

7. **Analyze Minor Characters** How do the minor characters—such as Ismene, Teiresias, Haemon, Eurydice, the sentry, and the messenger—help you judge Antigone and Creon?

8. **Analyze Tragedy** Who better fits the definition of a **tragic hero**, Antigone or Creon? Use a chart like the one shown to help you plan your answer.

	Antigone	Creon
Dignified, Superior Character		
Meets Tragic End		
Possesses Tragic Flaw		
Recognizes Flaw and Consequences		

9. **Analyze Dramatic Irony** Discuss the effects of dramatic irony in the play. At what points do you know more than the characters know?

10. **Interpret Themes** What does the play suggest about where a person's highest **loyalty** should lie? What other themes are revealed in the play? Give evidence to support your interpretations.

11. **Apply Themes** What relevance do the themes of *Antigone* have in modern times? Explain your opinion, offering examples.

Literary Criticism

12. **Biographical Context** Sophocles was not only a playwright; he served in the Athenian government. What messages does *Antigone* contain about democracy and the government of states?

Vocabulary in Context

VOCABULARY PRACTICE

Decide if each statement is true or false.

1. To **sate** a desire is to make it stronger.
2. An **auspicious** event is promising and hopeful.
3. To have **contempt** for someone is to show scorn and disdain.
4. To have **reverence** for others is to love and respect them.
5. To do something **impassively** is to do it with energy and enthusiasm.
6. An **anarchist** wants to overthrow a country's government.
7. To speak **sententiously** is to do so in a respectful, humble manner.
8. Teachers appreciate **insolence** in their students.
9. A **perverse** child is one who is obedient.
10. A **lamentation** might occur at a funeral or burial site.
11. People who **transgress** the law are those who enforce it.
12. To **defile** something is to make it more beautiful in appearance.

WORD LIST

anarchist
auspicious
contempt
defile
impassively
insolence
lamentation
perverse
reverence
sate
sententiously
transgress

VOCABULARY IN WRITING

Using three or more vocabulary words, write some questions you might ask Creon about his situation. Here is an example.

> **EXAMPLE SENTENCE**
>
> Why did you think your son Haemon was showing **insolence** to you?

VOCABULARY STRATEGY: ETYMOLOGY

An etymology is the history of a word. Knowing a word's history can often help you remember the word's meaning. For example, the word *contempt* derives from the Latin *contemptus,* which means "despised." Use the dictionary or an online reference to research the etymology of each word below. Study each word's derivation, meaning, and spelling.

1. anarchist: _____
2. trangress: _____
3. insolence: _____
4. perverse: _____

OHIO STANDARDS

VOCABULARY STANDARD
1.6 Determine the meaning of words using dictionaries

VOCABULARY PRACTICE
For more practice, go to the **Vocabulary Center** at ClassZone.com.

Reading-Writing Connection

Broaden your understanding of the play by responding to these prompts. Then use **Revision: Grammar and Style** to improve your writing.

WRITING PROMPTS	SELF-CHECK
A. Short Response: Compare Characters In **one or two paragraphs,** describe a modern person who reminds you of Antigone. Perhaps this person also defied authority or suffered for deeply held beliefs.	***A strong comparison will . . .*** • name a person who is similar to Antigone in some way • demonstrate the similarity with examples
B. Extended Response: Persuade an Audience Who has more right on his or her side—Antigone or Creon? Write a **three-to-five-paragraph response** to persuade citizens of Thebes. You might discuss the idea of **loyalty** in your argument.	***An effective response will . . .*** • state which character is more right • support your opinion with reasons

REVISION: GRAMMAR AND STYLE

VARY SENTENCE STRUCTURE Review the **Grammar and Style** note on page 979. Most sentences you write will have subjects preceding verbs; however, you may occasionally use inverted sentences when you want to add variety or emphasis. In an inverted sentence, the subject comes after the verb or part of the verb phrase. Here is an example from *Antigone*:

> **Chorus.** *Fortunate is the man who has never tasted God's vengeance!*
> (Ode 2, line 1)

Notice how the revisions in red in this response to Prompt B make the writing more interesting and effective.

 **OHIO STANDARDS**

WRITING STANDARD
5.7 Use a variety of sentence structures and lengths

STUDENT MODEL

Creon is very harsh in dealing with his niece Antigone. Although she speaks forcefully when she is brought before Creon, he refuses to change his mind. ~~A woman~~ has ~~never~~ ^*a woman* been treated so mercilessly.

 **WRITING TOOLS**
For prewriting, revision, and editing tools, visit the **Writing Center** at ClassZone.com.

from Le Morte d'Arthur
The Crowning of Arthur
Sir Launcelot du Lake

Romance by Sir Thomas Malory

Retold by Keith Baines

Could you be a KNIGHT?

OHIO STANDARDS

READING/RESEARCH STANDARDS
4.5 Analyze how choice of genre affects theme or topic

8.4 Evaluate and systematically organize important information

KEY IDEA The time of knights—roughly 1100 to 1400—is often called the age of **chivalry.** The term *chivalry* refers to the code of conduct that medieval knights were expected to follow. Chivalry promoted the idea of the knight as both a warrior and a gentleman. He was to be courageous, honest, loyal, generous to enemies, and protective of women and the weak. In the following selections, you will read about the legendary King Arthur and his Knights of the Round Table and see how they lived up to the standards of medieval knighthood.

DISCUSS Could you be a knight? With a partner, discuss the traits associated with knights. Then try to provide examples from your own life that demonstrate each trait. Afterward, review your partner's responses. Four or five examples mean that he or she is worthy to join the company of the Round Table.

Chivalric Traits	My Examples
1. Courage	
2. Honesty	
3. Loyalty	
4. Generosity	
5. Kindness	

● LITERARY ANALYSIS: MEDIEVAL ROMANCE

In the 12th century, a new literary form—the **romance**—developed in France and spread throughout Europe. The main purpose of a romance was to recount the heroic deeds of knights and to celebrate their chivalric way of life. A famous romance is Sir Thomas Malory's *Le Morte d'Arthur,* which features King Arthur and the Knights of the Round Table. As you read the selections, notice the conventions of medieval romance:

- idealized noble characters
- exaggerated or larger-than-life behavior
- a hero's quest, which is motivated by love, religious faith, or a desire for adventure
- supernatural or magical elements
- unusual or exotic settings
- incidents involving hidden or mistaken identity

● READING SKILL: EVALUATE

The chivalric code is of great importance in the world Malory describes. As you read, **evaluate,** or make judgments about, how well the main characters follow the code. Complete a chart like the one shown. For each character listed, place a check mark by the chivalric traits he demonstrates.

	Uther	Arthur	Launcelot	Tarquine
Courage				
Honesty				
Loyalty				
Generosity				
Kindness				

▲ VOCABULARY IN CONTEXT

The following words are used in the selections. Some of these words may seem unusual or antiquated. Review the list, noting any familiar roots, prefixes, and suffixes that might help you unlock the meanings of the words.

WORD LIST			
	abash	ignominiously	succession
	adversary	prowess	vindicate
	fidelity	recompense	

Author Online

A Knight Himself The man who wrote *Le Morte d'Arthur* called himself "Syr Thomas Maleore, knight." He also indicated that he completed this work in the ninth year of Edward IV's reign (1469 or 1470), and he added a prayer that he be delivered from prison. Although his precise identity remains uncertain, most historians believe him to be Sir Thomas Malory (1405?–1471), an English knight who lived at the end of the Middle Ages.

Behind Bars As a youth, Malory fought bravely for England during the Hundred Years' War with France. In the 1440s, however, he embarked on a life of crime. From 1451 on, Malory was imprisoned several times, accused of such crimes as highway robbery and attempted murder. In 1462, he joined rebel forces opposing Edward IV in the Wars of the Roses. Accused of treason, he spent the remainder of his life in London's Newgate Prison, where historians believe he wrote *Le Morte d'Arthur.*

 MORE ABOUT THE AUTHOR
For more on Sir Thomas Malory, visit the **Literature Center** at ClassZone.com.

Background

Legendary King The legend of King Arthur is one of the most popular and enduring legends in Western culture. Some scholars believe the tales of King Arthur were inspired by the heroic deeds of an actual Celtic chieftain or warlord who defended Britain against Anglo-Saxon (Germanic) invaders during the 5th or 6th century. However, the historical Arthur was undoubtedly very different from the king of legend, who ruled an idealized world of knights, damsels, and dragons.

The earliest tales of Arthur come from Welsh literature. Malory drew upon these ancient tales and several 13th-century French romances in writing *Le Morte d'Arthur.* Most English-speaking readers know of the Arthurian legend through this work or one of its modern retellings.

The Crowning of Arthur

Sir Thomas Malory

ANALYZE VISUALS
The two scenes shown are from a medieval manuscript about King Arthur. What event does each scene seem to depict?

King Uther Pendragon,[1] ruler of all Britain, had been at war for many years with the Duke of Tintagil in Cornwall when he was told of the beauty of Lady Igraine,[2] the duke's wife. Thereupon he called a truce and invited the duke and Igraine to his court, where he prepared a feast for them, and where, as soon as they arrived, he was formally reconciled to the duke through the good offices of his courtiers.[3]

In the course of the feast, King Uther grew passionately desirous of Igraine and, when it was over, begged her to become his paramour.[4] Igraine, however, being as naturally loyal as she was beautiful, refused him.

10 "I suppose," said Igraine to her husband, the duke, when this had happened, "that the king arranged this truce only because he wanted to make me his mistress. I suggest that we leave at once, without warning, and ride overnight to our castle." The duke agreed with her, and they left the court secretly.

The king was enraged by Igraine's flight and summoned his privy council.[5] They advised him to command the fugitives' return under threat of renewing the war; but when this was done, the duke and Igraine defied his summons. He then warned them that they could expect to be dragged from their castle within six weeks.

The duke manned and provisioned[6] his two strongest castles: Tintagil for
20 Igraine, and Terrabyl, which was useful for its many sally ports,[7] for himself. Soon King Uther arrived with a huge army and laid siege to Terrabyl; but despite the ferocity of the fighting, and the numerous casualties suffered by both sides, neither was able to gain a decisive victory. **A**

Still enraged, and now despairing, King Uther fell sick. His friend Sir Ulfius came to him and asked what the trouble was. "Igraine has broken my heart," the king replied, "and unless I can win her, I shall never recover."

A EVALUATE
Summarize the events that lead King Uther to renew his battle with the duke of Tintagil. Do you think King Uther behaves honorably? Why or why not?

---

1. **Uther Pendragon** (ōō'thər pĕn-drăg'ən): Uther took the name *Pendragon* after seeing a dragon-shaped comet, which foretold his ascension to power. *Pendragon* refers to a supreme chief or leader.
2. **Igraine** (ē-grān').
3. **offices of his courtiers** (kôrt'tē-ərz): services of his court attendants.
4. **paramour** (păr'ə-mŏŏr'): sweetheart or lover.
5. **privy** (prĭv'ē) **council:** a group of advisers who serve a ruler.
6. **provisioned:** supplied.
7. **sally ports:** gates or doors in the walls of fortifications, from which troops can make sudden attacks.

Arthur Extracting the Sword (1280) from *Histoire de Merlin.* MS Fr.95, f.159v 14tr. Bibliothèque Nationale de France, Paris. Photo © Bibliotheque Nationale de France, Paris.

"Sire," said Sir Ulfius, "surely Merlin the Prophet[8] could find some means to help you? I will go in search of him."

Sir Ulfius had not ridden far when he was accosted by a hideous beggar.
30 "For whom are you searching?" asked the beggar; but Sir Ulfius ignored him.

"Very well," said the beggar, "I will tell you: you are searching for Merlin, and you need look no further, for I am he. Now go to King Uther and tell him that I will make Igraine his if he will reward me as I ask; and even that will be more to his benefit than to mine."

"I am sure," said Sir Ulfius, "that the king will refuse you nothing reasonable."

"Then go, and I shall follow you," said Merlin.

Well pleased, Sir Ulfius galloped back to the king and delivered Merlin's message, which he had hardly completed when Merlin himself appeared at the entrance to the pavilion.[9] The king bade him welcome.

40 "Sire," said Merlin, "I know that you are in love with Igraine; will you swear, as an anointed[10] king, to give into my care the child that she bears you, if I make her yours?"

The king swore on the gospel that he would do so, and Merlin continued: "Tonight you shall appear before Igraine at Tintagil in the likeness of her husband, the duke. Sir Ulfius and I will appear as two of the duke's knights: Sir Brastius and Sir Jordanus. Do not question either Igraine or her men, but say that you are sick and retire to bed. I will fetch you early in the morning, and do not rise until I come; fortunately Tintagil is only ten miles from here."

The plan succeeded: Igraine was completely deceived by the king's
50 impersonation of the duke, and gave herself to him, and conceived Arthur. The king left her at dawn as soon as Merlin appeared, after giving her a farewell kiss. But the duke had seen King Uther ride out from the siege on the previous night and, in the course of making a surprise attack on the king's army, had been killed. When Igraine realized that the duke had died three hours before he had appeared to her, she was greatly disturbed in mind; however, she confided in no one. **B**

Once it was known that the duke was dead, the king's nobles urged him to be reconciled to Igraine, and this task the king gladly entrusted to Sir Ulfius, by whose eloquence it was soon accomplished. "And
60 now," said Sir Ulfius to his fellow nobles, "why should not the king marry the beautiful Igraine? Surely it would be as well for us all."

The marriage of King Uther and Igraine was celebrated joyously thirteen days later; and then, at the king's request, Igraine's sisters were also married: Margawse, who later bore Sir Gawain, to King Lot of Lowthean and Orkney; Elayne, to King Nentres of Garlot. Igraine's daughter, Morgan le Fay, was put to school in a nunnery; in after years she was to become a witch, and to be married to King Uryens of Gore, and give birth to Sir Uwayne of the Fair Hands.

B MEDIEVAL ROMANCE
Reread lines 29–56. Describe the ways in which Merlin demonstrates his **magical powers** to Sir Ulfius and King Uther.

---

8. **Merlin the Prophet:** Merlin possesses the ability to prophesy, or predict future events.

9. **pavilion:** a large tent, often with a peaked top.

10. **anointed:** installed in office with a religious ceremony.

A few months later it was seen that Igraine was with child, and one night, as she lay in bed with King Uther, he asked her who the father might be. Igraine was greatly **abashed.**

"Do not look so dismayed," said the king, "but tell me the truth, and I swear I shall love you the better for it."

"The truth is," said Igraine, "that the night the duke died, about three hours after his death, a man appeared in my castle—the exact image of the duke. With him came two others who appeared to be Sir Brastius and Sir Jordanus. Naturally I gave myself to this man as I would have to the duke, and that night, I swear, this child was conceived."

"Well spoken," said the king; "it was I who impersonated the duke, so the child is mine." He then told Igraine the story of how Merlin had arranged it, and Igraine was overjoyed to discover that the father of her child was now her husband. **C**

Sometime later, Merlin appeared before the king. "Sire," he said, "you know that you must provide for the upbringing of your child?"

"I will do as you advise," the king replied.

"That is good," said Merlin, "because it is my reward for having arranged your impersonation of the duke. Your child is destined for glory, and I want him brought to me for his baptism.[11] I shall then give him into the care of foster parents who can be trusted not to reveal his identity before the proper time. Sir Ector would be suitable: he is extremely loyal, owns good estates, and his wife has just borne him a child. She could give her child into the care of another woman, and herself look after yours."

Sir Ector was summoned and gladly agreed to the king's request, who then rewarded him handsomely. When the child was born, he was at once wrapped in a gold cloth and taken by two knights and two ladies to Merlin, who stood waiting at the rear entrance to the castle in his beggar's disguise. Merlin took the child to a priest, who baptized him with the name of Arthur, and thence to Sir Ector, whose wife fed him at her breast. **D**

Two years later King Uther fell sick, and his enemies once more overran his kingdom, inflicting heavy losses on him as they advanced. Merlin prophesied that they could be checked only by the presence of the king himself on the battlefield, and suggested that he should be conveyed there on a horse litter.[12] King Uther's army met the invader on the plain at St. Albans, and the king duly appeared on the horse litter. Inspired by his presence, and by the lively leadership of Sir Brastius and Sir Jordanus, his army quickly defeated the enemy, and the battle finished in a rout. The king returned to London to celebrate the victory.

But his sickness grew worse, and after he had lain speechless for three days and three nights, Merlin summoned the nobles to attend the king in his chamber on the following morning. "By the grace of God," he said, "I hope to make him speak."

abash (ə-băsh′) v. to make ashamed or embarrass

C MEDIEVAL ROMANCE
Think about Malory's depiction of Igraine up to this point. What details suggest that she is an **idealized character?**

D EVALUATE
Reread lines 82–97. In what way does Merlin show his loyalty to King Uther and the Britons?

---

11. **baptism:** a religious sacrament that marks the admission of a person into the Christian faith. In Arthurian legend, Arthur represents the ideal Christian knight and monarch.

12. **horse litter:** a stretcher pulled by a horse.

110   In the morning, when all the nobles were assembled, Merlin addressed the
king: "Sire, is it your will that Arthur shall succeed to the throne, together with
all its prerogatives?"[13]

The king stirred in his bed and then spoke so that all could hear: "I bestow
on Arthur God's blessing and my own, and Arthur shall succeed to the throne
on pain of forfeiting my blessing." Then King Uther gave up the ghost.[14] He
was buried and mourned the next day, as befitted his rank, by Igraine and the
nobility of Britain.

D uring the years that followed the death of King Uther, while Arthur
was still a child, the ambitious barons fought one another for the
120   throne, and the whole of Britain stood in jeopardy. Finally the
day came when the Archbishop of Canterbury,[15] on the advice of Merlin,
summoned the nobility to London for Christmas morning. In his message the
archbishop promised that the true **succession** to the British throne would be
miraculously revealed. Many of the nobles purified themselves during their
journey, in the hope that it would be to them that the succession would fall.

The archbishop held his service in the city's greatest church (St. Paul's),
and when matins[16] were done, the congregation filed out to the yard. They
were confronted by a marble block into which had been thrust a beautiful
sword. The block was four feet square, and the sword passed through a steel
130   anvil which had been struck in the stone, and which projected a foot from it.
The anvil had been inscribed with letters of gold:

WHOSO PULLETH OUTE THIS SWERD OF THIS STONE AND ANVYLD
IS RIGHTWYS KYNGE BORNE OF ALL BRYTAYGNE[17]

The congregation was awed by this miraculous sight, but the archbishop
forbade anyone to touch the sword before mass had been heard. After mass,
many of the nobles tried to pull the sword out of the stone, but none was
able to, so a watch of ten knights was set over the sword, and a tournament
proclaimed for New Year's Day, to provide men of noble blood with the
opportunity of proving their right to the succession.

140   Sir Ector, who had been living on an estate near London, rode to the
tournament with Arthur and his own son Sir Kay, who had been recently
knighted. When they arrived at the tournament, Sir Kay found to his
annoyance that his sword was missing from its sheath, so he begged Arthur
to ride back and fetch it from their lodging.

Arthur found the door of the lodging locked and bolted, the landlord and
his wife having left for the tournament. In order not to disappoint his brother,
he rode on to St. Paul's, determined to get for him the sword which was lodged

succession (sək-sĕsh′ən)
n. the sequence in which
one person after another
acquires a title, dignity, or
estate

---

13. **prerogatives:** rights and privileges.

14. **gave up the ghost:** died.

15. **Archbishop of Canterbury:** the leader of the Christian community in England.

16. **matins** (măt′nz): morning prayers.

17. **Whoso pulleth . . . all Brytaygne:** Whoever pulls this sword from this stone and anvil is rightfully king of
all Britain.

in the stone. The yard was empty, the guard also having slipped off to see the tournament, so Arthur strode up to the sword, and, without troubling

150 to read the inscription, tugged it free. He then rode straight back to Sir Kay and presented him with it.

Sir Kay recognized the sword and, taking it to Sir Ector, said, "Father, the succession falls to me, for I have here the sword that was lodged in the stone." But Sir Ector insisted that they should all ride to the churchyard, and once there bound Sir Kay by oath to tell how he had come by the sword. Sir Kay then admitted that Arthur had given it to him. Sir Ector turned to Arthur and said, "Was the sword not guarded?"

"It was not," Arthur replied.

"Would you please thrust it into the stone again?" said Sir Ector. Arthur

160 did so, and first Sir Ector and then Sir Kay tried to remove it, but both were unable to. Then Arthur, for the second time, pulled it out. Sir Ector and Sir Kay both knelt before him.

"Why," said Arthur, "do you both kneel before me?"

"My lord," Sir Ector replied, "there is only one man living who can draw the sword from the stone, and he is the true-born King of Britain." Sir Ector then told Arthur the story of his birth and upbringing.

"My dear father," said Arthur, "for so I shall always think of you—if, as you say, I am to be king, please know that any request you have to make is already granted."

170 Sir Ector asked that Sir Kay should be made Royal Seneschal,[18] and Arthur declared that while they both lived it should be so. Then the three of them visited the archbishop and told him what had taken place. **E**

All those dukes and barons with ambitions to rule were present at the tournament on New Year's Day. But when all of them had failed, and Arthur alone had succeeded in drawing the sword from the stone, they protested against one so young, and of ignoble[19] blood, succeeding to the throne.

The secret of Arthur's birth was known only to a few of the nobles surviving from the days of King Uther. The archbishop urged them to make Arthur's cause their own; but their support proved ineffective. The tournament was

180 repeated at Candlemas and at Easter, and with the same outcome as before.

Finally at Pentecost,[20] when once more Arthur alone had been able to remove the sword, the commoners arose with a tumultuous cry and demanded that Arthur should at once be made king. The nobles, knowing in their hearts that the commoners were right, all knelt before Arthur and begged forgiveness for having delayed his succession for so long. Arthur forgave them and then, offering his sword at the high altar, was dubbed[21] first knight of the realm. The coronation took place a few days later, when Arthur swore to rule justly, and the nobles swore him their allegiance. **∿ F**

E EVALUATE
Compare the behavior of Sir Kay with that of Arthur. Which character better illustrates the chivalric traits of a knight? Explain.

F MEDIEVAL ROMANCE
Reread lines 173–188. How do Arthur's actions fit the conventions of medieval romance?

---

18. **Royal Seneschal** (sĕn'ə-shəl): the representative of a king in judicial and domestic matters.

19. **ignoble:** not noble; common.

20. **Candlemas . . . Easter . . . Pentecost** (pĕn'tĭ-kôst'): Christian holidays.

21. **dubbed:** granted knighthood by being tapped on the shoulder.

from LE MORTE D'ARTHUR

Sir Launcelot du Lake

Sir Thomas Malory

When King Arthur returned from Rome, he settled his court at Camelot, and there gathered about him his knights of the Round Table, who diverted themselves with jousting[22] and tournaments. Of all his knights one was supreme, both in **prowess** at arms and in nobility of bearing, and this was Sir Launcelot, who was also the favorite of Queen Gwynevere, to whom he had sworn oaths of **fidelity.**

One day Sir Launcelot, feeling weary of his life at the court, and of only playing at arms,[23] decided to set forth in search of adventure. He asked his nephew Sir Lyonel to accompany him, and when both were suitably armed 10 and mounted, they rode off together through the forest. **G**

At noon they started across a plain, but the intensity of the sun made Sir Launcelot feel sleepy, so Sir Lyonel suggested that they should rest beneath the shade of an apple tree that grew by a hedge not far from the road. They dismounted, tethered their horses, and settled down.

"Not for seven years have I felt so sleepy," said Sir Launcelot, and with that fell fast asleep, while Sir Lyonel watched over him.

Soon three knights came galloping past, and Sir Lyonel noticed that they were being pursued by a fourth knight, who was one of the most powerful he had yet seen. The pursuing knight overtook each of the others in turn and, 20 as he did so, knocked each off his horse with a thrust of his spear. When all three lay stunned, he dismounted, bound them securely to their horses with the reins, and led them away.

Without waking Sir Launcelot, Sir Lyonel mounted his horse and rode after the knight and, as soon as he had drawn close enough, shouted his challenge. The knight turned about, and they charged at each other, with the result that Sir Lyonel was likewise flung from his horse, bound, and led away a prisoner.

prowess (prou′ĭs) *n.* superior skill, strength, or courage, especially in battle

fidelity (fĭ-dĕl′ĭ-tē) *n.* faithfulness to duties; loyalty and devotion

G **MEDIEVAL ROMANCE**
Reread lines 7–10. What motivates Sir Launcelot to begin his **quest?**

ANALYZE VISUALS
How does the use of color and active figures affect the **mood** of this illustration? Contrast the mood with that of the illustration on page 1013.

---

22. **jousting:** combat between two knights who charge each other with lances while riding horses.

23. **playing at arms:** fighting with weapons as sport.

Tournament jousting at the court of Caerleon (1468). *Les chroniques de Hainaut.* MS 9243, fol. 45. Bibliothèque Royale Albert I, Brussels, Belgium. Photo © Art Resource, New York.

The victorious knight, whose name was Sir Tarquine,[24] led his prisoners to his castle and there threw them on the ground, stripped them naked, and beat them with thorn twigs. After that he locked them in a dungeon where many
30 other prisoners, who had received like treatment, were complaining dismally.

Meanwhile, Sir Ector de Marys,[25] who liked to accompany Sir Launcelot on his adventures, and finding him gone, decided to ride after him. Before long he came upon a forester.

"My good fellow, if you know the forest hereabouts, could you tell me in which direction I am most likely to meet with adventure?"

"Sir, I can tell you: less than a mile from here stands a well-moated castle. On the left of the entrance you will find a ford where you can water your horse, and across from the ford a large tree from which hang the shields of many famous knights. Below the shields hangs a caldron, of copper and
40 brass: strike it three times with your spear, and then surely you will meet with adventure—such, indeed, that if you survive it, you will prove yourself the foremost knight in these parts for many years."

"May God reward you!" Sir Ector replied.

The castle was exactly as the forester had described it, and among the shields Sir Ector recognized several as belonging to knights of the Round Table. After watering his horse, he knocked on the caldron, and Sir Tarquine, whose castle it was, appeared. **H**

They jousted, and at the first encounter Sir Ector sent his opponent's horse spinning twice about before he could recover.
50 "That was a fine stroke; now let us try again," said Sir Tarquine.

This time Sir Tarquine caught Sir Ector just below the right arm and, having impaled him on his spear, lifted him clean out of the saddle and rode with him into the castle, where he threw him on the ground.

"Sir," said Sir Tarquine, "you have fought better than any knight I have encountered in the last twelve years; therefore, if you wish, I will demand no more of you than your parole[26] as my prisoner."

"Sir, that I will never give."

"Then I am sorry for you," said Sir Tarquine, and with that he stripped and beat him and locked him in the dungeon with the other prisoners. There Sir
60 Ector saw Sir Lyonel. **I**

"Alas, Sir Lyonel, we are in a sorry plight. But tell me, what has happened to Sir Launcelot? for he surely is the one knight who could save us."

"I left him sleeping beneath an apple tree, and what has befallen him since I do not know," Sir Lyonel replied; and then all the unhappy prisoners once more bewailed their lot.

H MEDIEVAL ROMANCE
Reread lines 31–47, and think about the **setting** in which Sir Ector de Marys finds himself. What details suggest that this is an unusual or exotic place?

I EVALUATE
Consider Sir Tarquine's behavior up to this point. Does he treat his opponents fairly both on and off the battlefield? Explain.

---

24. **Tarquine** (tär′kwĭn).

25. **Sir Ector de Marys** (măr′əs): the brother of Launcelot.

26. **parole:** the promise of a prisoner to abide by certain conditions in exchange for full or partial freedom.

hile Sir Launcelot still slept beneath the apple tree, four queens started across the plain. They were riding white mules and accompanied by four knights who held above them, at the tips of their spears, a green silk canopy, to protect them from the sun. The party was startled by the neighing of Sir Launcelot's horse and, changing direction, rode up to the apple tree, where they discovered the sleeping knight. And as each of the queens gazed at the handsome Sir Launcelot, so each wanted him for her own.

"Let us not quarrel," said Morgan le Fay. "Instead, I will cast a spell over him so that he remains asleep while we take him to my castle and make him our prisoner. We can then oblige him to choose one of us for his paramour."

Sir Launcelot was laid on his shield and borne by two of the knights to the Castle Charyot, which was Morgan le Fay's stronghold. He awoke to find himself in a cold cell, where a young noblewoman was serving him supper.

"What cheer?"[27] she asked.

"My lady, I hardly know, except that I must have been brought here by means of an enchantment."

"Sir, if you are the knight you appear to be, you will learn your fate at dawn tomorrow." And with that the young noblewoman left him. Sir Launcelot spent an uncomfortable night, but at dawn the four queens presented themselves and Morgan le Fay spoke to him:

"Sir Launcelot, I know that Queen Gwynevere loves you, and you her. But now you are my prisoner, and you will have to choose: either to take one of us for your paramour, or to die miserably in this cell—just as you please. Now I will tell you who we are: I am Morgan le Fay, Queen of Gore; my companions are the queens of North Galys, of Estelonde, and of the Outer Isles. So make your choice."

"A hard choice! Understand that I choose none of you, lewd sorceresses that you are; rather will I die in this cell. But were I free, I would take pleasure in proving it against any who would champion you that Queen Gwynevere is the finest lady of this land."

"So, you refuse us?" asked Morgan le Fay.

"On my life, I do," Sir Launcelot said finally, and so the queens departed. **J**

Sometime later, the young noblewoman who had served Sir Launcelot's supper reappeared.

"What news?" she asked.

"It is the end," Sir Launcelot replied.

"Sir Launcelot, I know that you have refused the four queens, and that they wish to kill you out of spite. But if you will be ruled by me, I can save you. I ask that you will champion my father at a tournament next Tuesday, when he has to combat the King of North Galys, and three knights of the Round Table, who last Tuesday defeated him **ignominiously**."

"My lady, pray tell me, what is your father's name?"

J EVALUATE
Reread lines 87–98. What does Launcelot's response to the ultimatum of the four queens reveal about his character?

ignominiously
(ĭg′nə-mĭn′ē-əs-lē) *adv.*
shamefully

---

27. **What cheer?:** How are you?

"King Bagdemagus."[28]

110 "Excellent, my lady; I know him for a good king and a true knight, so I shall be happy to serve him."

"May God reward you! And tomorrow at dawn I will release you and direct you to an abbey[29] which is ten miles from here, and where the good monks will care for you while I fetch my father."

"I am at your service, my lady."

As promised, the young noblewoman released Sir Launcelot at dawn. When she had led him through the twelve doors to the castle entrance, she gave him his horse and armor, and directions for finding the abbey.

"God bless you, my lady; and when the time comes, I promise I shall not
120 fail you." **K**

Sir Launcelot rode through the forest in search of the abbey but at dusk had still failed to find it and, coming upon a red silk pavilion, apparently unoccupied, decided to rest there overnight and continue his search in the morning.

He had not been asleep for more than an hour, however, when the knight who owned the pavilion returned and got straight into bed with him. Having made an assignation[30] with his paramour, the knight supposed at first that Sir Launcelot was she and, taking him into his arms, started kissing him. Sir Launcelot awoke with a start and, seizing his sword, leaped out of bed and out
130 of the pavilion, pursued closely by the other knight. Once in the open they set to with their swords, and before long Sir Launcelot had wounded his unknown **adversary** so seriously that he was obliged to yield.

The knight, whose name was Sir Belleus, now asked Sir Launcelot how he came to be sleeping in his bed and then explained how he had an assignation with his lover, adding:

"But now I am so sorely wounded that I shall consider myself fortunate to escape with my life."

"Sir, please forgive me for wounding you; but lately I escaped from an enchantment, and I was afraid that once more I had been betrayed. Let us go
140 into the pavilion, and I will staunch your wound." **L**

Sir Launcelot had just finished binding the wound when the young noblewoman who was Sir Belleus's paramour arrived and, seeing the wound, at once rounded in fury on Sir Launcelot.

"Peace, my love," said Sir Belleus. "This is a noble knight, and as soon as I yielded to him, he treated my wound with the greatest care." Sir Belleus then described the events which had led up to the duel.

"Sir, pray tell me your name, and whose knight you are," the young noblewoman asked Sir Launcelot.

"My lady, I am called Sir Launcelot du Lake."

K MEDIEVAL ROMANCE
Review the exchange between Sir Launcelot and the noblewoman in lines 99–120. Why might they be considered **idealized characters**?

adversary (ăd'vər-sĕr'ē) *n.* an opponent; enemy

L MEDIEVAL ROMANCE
Hidden identity is a common element in romances. Compare the scene in lines 121–140 with the scene in lines 40–56 on page 1014. What different effects do these scenes create?

---

28. **Bagdemagus** (băg'də-măg'əs).

29. **abbey:** a place where monks or nuns live.

30. **assignation** (ăs'ĭg-nā'shən): an appointment for a meeting between lovers.

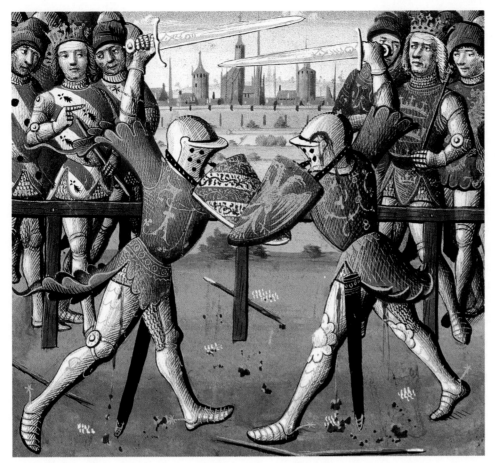

Combat between Lancelot and Gawain (1400s) from the *Cycle de Lancelot.* MS Fr. 120, f. 590v.107a. Bibliothèque Nationale de France, Paris. Photo © Bibliothèque Nationale de France, Paris.

150   "As I guessed, both from your appearance and from your speech; and indeed I know you better than you realize. But I ask you, in **recompense** for the injury you have done my lord, and out of the courtesy for which you are famous, to recommend Sir Belleus to King Arthur, and suggest that he be made one of the knights of the Round Table. I can assure you that my lord deserves it, being only less than yourself as a man-at-arms, and sovereign of many of the Outer Isles."

"My lady, let Sir Belleus come to Arthur's court at the next Pentecost.[31] Make sure that you come with him, and I promise I will do what I can for him; and if he is as good a man-at-arms as you say he is, I am sure Arthur will accept him."

160   As soon as it was daylight, Sir Launcelot armed, mounted, and rode away in search of the abbey, which he found in less than two hours. King Bagdemagus's daughter was waiting for him and, as soon as she heard his horse's footsteps in the yard, ran to the window and, seeing that it was Sir Launcelot, herself ordered the servants to stable his horse. She then led him to her chamber, disarmed him, and gave him a long gown to wear, welcoming him warmly as she did so.

recompense
(rĕk′əm-pĕns′) *n.* amends for damage or payment for service

---

31. **Pentecost:** In Arthurian legend, Pentecost is one of the times at which the knights meet at Camelot to renew their oaths and receive new missions.

King Bagdemagus's castle was twelve miles away, and his daughter sent for him as soon as she had settled Sir Launcelot. The king arrived with his retinue[32] and embraced Sir Launcelot, who then described his recent enchantment, and the great obligation he was under to his daughter for releasing him.

"Sir, you will fight for me on Tuesday next?"

"Sire, I shall not fail you; but please tell me the names of the three Round Table knights whom I shall be fighting."

"Sir Modred, Sir Madore de la Porte, and Sir Gahalantyne. I must admit that last Tuesday they defeated me and my knights completely."

"Sire, I hear that the tournament is to be fought within three miles of the abbey. Could you send me three of your most trustworthy knights, clad in plain armor, and with no device,[33] and a fourth suit of armor which I myself shall wear? We will take up our position just outside the tournament field and watch while you and the King of North Galys enter into combat with your followers; and then, as soon as you are in difficulties, we will come to your rescue and show your opponents what kind of knights you command."

This was arranged on Sunday, and on the following Tuesday Sir Launcelot and the three knights of King Bagdemagus waited in a copse,[34] not far from the pavilion which had been erected for the lords and ladies who were to judge the tournament and award the prizes.

The King of North Galys was the first on the field, with a company of ninescore knights; he was followed by King Bagdemagus with fourscore[35] knights, and then by the three knights of the Round Table, who remained apart from both companies. At the first encounter King Bagdemagus lost twelve knights, all killed, and the King of North Galys six.

With that, Sir Launcelot galloped on to the field, and with his first spear unhorsed five of the King of North Galys's knights, breaking the backs of four of them. With his next spear he charged the king and wounded him deeply in the thigh.

"That was a shrewd blow," commented Sir Madore and galloped onto the field to challenge Sir Launcelot. But he too was tumbled from his horse, and with such violence that his shoulder was broken.

Sir Modred was the next to challenge Sir Launcelot, and he was sent spinning over his horse's tail. He landed headfirst, his helmet became buried in the soil, and he nearly broke his neck, and for a long time lay stunned.

Finally Sir Gahalantyne tried; at the first encounter both he and Sir Launcelot broke their spears, so both drew their swords and hacked vehemently at each other. But Sir Launcelot, with mounting wrath, soon struck his opponent a blow on the helmet which brought the blood streaming from eyes, ears, and

---

32. **retinue** (rĕt'n-ōō'): attendants.

33. **device:** an emblem or design used as an identifying mark.

34. **copse** (kŏps): a thicket of small trees.

35. **ninescore . . . fourscore:** A score is a set of 20; thus, ninescore is 180 and fourscore is 80.

mouth. Sir Gahalantyne slumped forward in the saddle, his horse panicked, and he was thrown to the ground, useless for further combat.

Sir Launcelot took another spear and unhorsed sixteen more of the King of North Galys's knights and, with his next, unhorsed another twelve; and in each case with such violence that none of the knights ever fully recovered. The King of North Galys was forced to admit defeat, and the prize was awarded to King Bagdemagus. **Ⓜ**

That night Sir Launcelot was entertained as the guest of honor by King Bagdemagus and his daughter at their castle and before leaving was loaded with gifts.

"My lady, please, if ever again you should need my services, remember that I shall not fail you."

The next day Sir Launcelot rode once more through the forest and by chance came to the apple tree where he had previously slept. This time he met a young noblewoman riding a white palfrey.[36]

"My lady, I am riding in search of adventure; pray tell me if you know of any I might find hereabouts."

"Sir, there are adventures hereabouts if you believe that you are equal to them; but please tell me, what is your name?"

"Sir Launcelot du Lake."

"Very well, Sir Launcelot, you appear to be a sturdy enough knight, so I will tell you. Not far away stands the castle of Sir Tarquine, a knight who in fair combat has overcome more than sixty opponents whom he now holds prisoner. Many are from the court of King Arthur, and if you can rescue them, I will then ask you to deliver me and my companions from a knight who distresses us daily, either by robbery or by other kinds of outrage."

"My lady, please first lead me to Sir Tarquine; then I will most happily challenge this miscreant knight of yours."

When they arrived at the castle, Sir Launcelot watered his horse at the ford and then beat the caldron until the bottom fell out. However, none came to answer the challenge, so they waited by the castle gate for half an hour or so. Then Sir Tarquine appeared, riding toward the castle with a wounded prisoner slung over his horse, whom Sir Launcelot recognized as Sir Gaheris, Sir Gawain's brother and a knight of the Round Table.

"Good knight," said Sir Launcelot, "it is known to me that you have put to shame many of the knights of the Round Table. Pray allow your prisoner, who I see is wounded, to recover, while I **vindicate** the honor of the knights whom you have defeated."

"I defy you, and all your fellowship of the Round Table," Sir Tarquine replied.

"You boast!" said Sir Launcelot.

At the first charge the backs of the horses were broken and both knights stunned. But they soon recovered and set to with their swords, and both struck so lustily that neither shield nor armor could resist, and within two hours they

---

36. **palfrey:** a gentle riding-horse.

Ⓜ EVALUATE
Reread lines 192–212. Which aspects of the chivalric code does Sir Launcelot uphold in his performance at the jousting tournament?

vindicate (vĭn′dĭ-kāt′) *v.* to clear of suspicion, doubt, or blame

were cutting each other's flesh, from which the blood flowed liberally. Finally
250 they paused for a moment, resting on their shields.

"Worthy knight," said Sir Tarquine, "pray hold your hand for a while and, if
you will, answer my question."

"Sir, speak on."

"You are the most powerful knight I have fought yet, but I fear you may be
the one whom in the whole world I most hate. If you are not, for the love of
you I will release all my prisoners and swear eternal friendship."

"What is the name of the knight you hate above all others?"

"Sir Launcelot du Lake; for it was he who slew my brother, Sir Carados
of the Dolorous Tower, and it is because of him that I have killed a hundred
260 knights and maimed as many more, apart from the sixty-four I still hold
prisoner. And so, if you are Sir Launcelot, speak up, for we must then fight
to the death."

"Sir, I see now that I might go in peace and good fellowship or otherwise
fight to the death; but being the knight I am, I must tell you: I am Sir
Launcelot du Lake, son of King Ban of Benwick, of Arthur's court, and a
knight of the Round Table. So defend yourself!"

"Ah! this is most welcome."

Now the two knights hurled themselves at each other like two wild bulls;
swords and shields clashed together, and often their swords drove into the
270 flesh. Then sometimes one, sometimes the other, would stagger and fall, only
to recover immediately and resume the contest. At last, however, Sir Tarquine
grew faint and unwittingly lowered his shield. Sir Launcelot was swift to
follow up his advantage and, dragging the other down to his knees, unlaced his
helmet and beheaded him. **N**

Sir Launcelot then strode over to the young noblewoman: "My lady, now I
am at your service, but first I must find a horse."

Then the wounded Sir Gaheris spoke up: "Sir, please take my horse. Today
you have overcome the most formidable knight, excepting only yourself, and
by so doing have saved us all. But before leaving, please tell me your name."

280 "Sir Launcelot du Lake. Today I have fought to vindicate the honor of the
knights of the Round Table, and I know that among Sir Tarquine's prisoners
are two of my brethren, Sir Lyonel and Sir Ector, also your own brother, Sir
Gawain. According to the shields there are also Sir Brandiles, Sir Galyhuddis,[37]
Sir Kay, Sir Alydukis,[38] Sir Marhaus, and many others. Please release the
prisoners and ask them to help themselves to the castle treasure. Give them all
my greetings and say I will see them at the next Pentecost. And please request
Sir Ector and Sir Lyonel to go straight to the court and await me there." ☙

N **MEDIEVAL ROMANCE**
Reread lines 246–274.
Which details suggest
that the clash between
Sir Tarquine and Sir
Launcelot is **exaggerated**
or larger than life?

---

37. **Galyhuddis** (găl′ĭ-hōōd′əs).

38. **Alydukis** (ăl′ĭ-dōō′kəs).

HISTORICAL ACCOUNT In *A Distant Mirror*, the historian Barbara Tuchman offers a glimpse of the actual conditions medieval knights faced in battle.

from A Distant Mirror:
The Calamitous 14th Century

Barbara Tuchman

To fight on horseback or foot wearing 55 pounds of plate armor, to crash in collision with an opponent at full gallop while holding horizontal an eighteen-foot lance half the length of an average telephone pole, to give and receive blows with sword or battle-ax that could cleave a skull or slice off a limb at a stroke, to spend half of life in the saddle through all weathers and for days at a time, was not a weakling's work. Hardship and fear were part of it. "Knights who are at the wars . . . are forever swallowing their fear," wrote the companion and biographer of Don Pero Niño, the "Unconquered Knight" of the late 14th century. "They expose themselves to every peril; they give up their bodies to the adventure of life in death. Moldy bread or biscuit, meat cooked or uncooked; today enough to eat

The knight (1400s). *Livre des eschecs moralisés,* translated by Jean Ferron from the Latin of Jacques de Cessoles. MS 3066, fol. 21. Bibliothèque Municipale, Rouen, France. Photo © Giraudon/Art Resource, New York.

and tomorrow nothing, little or no wine, water from a pond or a butt,[1] bad quarters, the shelter of a tent or branches, a bad bed, poor sleep with their armor still on their backs, burdened with iron, the enemy an arrow-shot off. 'Ware! Who goes there? To arms! To arms!' With the first drowsiness, an alarm; at dawn, the trumpet. 'To horse! To horse! Muster! Muster!' As lookouts, as sentinels, keeping watch by day and by night, fighting without cover, as foragers, as scouts, guard after guard, duty after duty. 'Here they come! Here! They are so many—No, not as many as that—This way—that—Come this side— Press them there—News! News! They come back hurt, they have prisoners—no, they bring none back. Let us go! Let us go! Give no ground! On!' Such is their calling."

---

1. **butt:** water cask.

Comprehension

1. **Recall** What motivates King Uther to resume war against the duke of Tintagil?

2. **Summarize** Describe the reign of King Uther following Arthur's birth.

3. **Recall** How does Sir Launcelot repay the noblewoman who releases him from the four queens?

4. **Clarify** Why does Sir Tarquine wish to kill Sir Launcelot?

Literary Analysis

5. **Make Inferences** Reread lines 82–97 of "The Crowning of Arthur" (page 1015). Why does Merlin want Arthur to be raised in secrecy and away from the royal court?

6. **Draw Conclusions** In "The Crowning of Arthur," the nobles repeatedly reject Arthur as their true-born ruler. Why do you think Arthur chooses to forgive them rather than punish them once he is crowned king?

7. **Analyze Character** In "Sir Launcelot du Lake," identify at least three of Sir Launcelot's actions that are worthy of a chivalric knight. What, if anything, does he do that seems unworthy of his position?

8. **Compare Characters** Who seems to pose a greater threat to Launcelot's honor—Morgan le Fay or Sir Tarquine? Cite evidence to support your answer.

9. **Examine Medieval Romance** Review the conventions of medieval romance on page 1011. Choose one selection and try to find examples of each convention. To what extent does the selection reflect all of these conventions? Explain your response.

10. **Evaluate** Review the chart you created as you read. In your opinion, which of the four characters most closely follows the code of **chivalry?** Support your answer with details from your chart.

11. **Compare Literary Texts** Compare "Sir Launcelot du Lake" with the excerpt from *A Distant Mirror* on page 1027. How do these two pieces—a medieval romance and a historical account—differ in their depictions of knighthood? Use information from both texts to support your response.

Literary Criticism

12. **Historical Context** At the end of the 15th century, England was recovering from both the Hundred Years' War with France and its own civil conflicts—the Wars of the Roses. Why do you think Malory wrote *Le Morte d'Arthur* during this turbulent period?

Vocabulary in Context

VOCABULARY PRACTICE

Decide whether each pair of words are synonyms or antonyms.

1. abash/encourage
2. sequence/succession
3. prowess/skill
4. disloyalty/fidelity
5. ignominiously/disgracefully
6. supporter/adversary
7. recompense/payment
8. accuse/vindicate

VOCABULARY IN WRITING

Using three or more vocabulary words, describe a past challenge of yours and the way you faced it. Here is an example of how you might begin.

> **EXAMPLE SENTENCE**
>
> My **prowess** on the tennis court did not always come so easily.

VOCABULARY STRATEGY: ANALOGIES

Analogies express relationships between pairs of words. Some common relationships are described in the chart that follows.

Type	Relationship
synonym	means the same as
antonym	means the opposite of
characteristic	distinguishes or describes

Write the letter of the word pair that expresses a relationship similar to that of the first pair. Indicate what kind of relationship is being expressed.

1. dog : fidelity :: (a) chicken : egg, (b) fox : cleverness, (c) wolf : timidity, (d) whale : mammal
2. prowess : gladiator :: (a) tact : diplomat, (b) honesty : thief, (c) wisdom : fool, (d) shyness : actor
3. adversary : friend :: (a) cat : pet, (b) hunter : trapper, (c) servant : ruler, (d) member : club

VOCABULARY STANDARD

1.2 Analyze the relationships of pairs of words

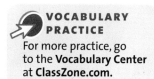

VOCABULARY PRACTICE

For more practice, go to the **Vocabulary Center** at **ClassZone.com.**

from **The Acts of King Arthur and His Noble Knights**

Romance by John Steinbeck

Do heroes get to be
HUMAN?

KEY IDEA Think about people whom you regard as heroes. How do you expect them to behave? What kinds of virtues should they possess? In this modern retelling of Arthurian legend, John Steinbeck depicts Sir Lancelot as a knight whose private ambitions clash with his public image of **perfection.**

QUICKWRITE Write a paragraph or two about what it might be like to live in the public eye and be held to a high standard of behavior. Then discuss when, if ever, we allow our heroes to show human weaknesses.

LITERARY ANALYSIS: STYLE

In his introduction to *The Acts of King Arthur and His Noble Knights,* John Steinbeck states his aim: to set down the story of King Arthur in "present-day speech," avoiding the archaic language of Malory's version. As you read the selection, notice how the following stylistic techniques help create a retelling that appeals to modern readers:

- plain, contemporary language
- detailed characterizations
- vivid sensory images
- rich figurative language, including similes and metaphors
- long, flowing sentences
- realistic dialogue
- a sympathetic tone

READING SKILL: MAKE INFERENCES

In his work, Steinbeck presents Lancelot (spelled *Launcelot* by Malory) as a complex character—one who struggles to maintain integrity in both his public and his private life. To fully appreciate Lancelot, you will need to use details in the text and your own knowledge to **make inferences,** or logical guesses, about his feelings and behavior. As you read, keep track of your inferences in a chart like the one shown.

Details About Lancelot	My Experiences	My Inferences
"Some said he nodded and perhaps dozed...." (line 26)	Traveling can be tiring. Award ceremonies can be tedious.	Lancelot is weary from his journey and bored by the speeches.

▲ VOCABULARY IN CONTEXT

To see how many vocabulary words you already know, match each boldfaced vocabulary word in the first column with a word that has a similar meaning in the second column.

1. disparagement   a. revenge
2. exalt   b. exhausted
3. haggard   c. wandering
4. intemperate   d. praise
5. reprisal   e. denigration
6. vagrant   f. excessive

Author Online

**John Steinbeck
1902–1968**

Voice of the Common People John Steinbeck, who believed that a writer's first duty is to "set down his time as nearly as he can understand it," managed perhaps better than anyone else to tell the stories of ordinary people caught up in the Great Depression of the 1930s. His masterpiece, *The Grapes of Wrath,* depicts the hardships of an Oklahoma farm family forced to migrate west for work. Like his other novels, it shows deep sympathy for working people and outrage over social injustice.

"Dazzled and Swept Up" Steinbeck was born in Salinas, California, in one of the nation's most productive farming regions. A shy young man, he enjoyed spending time alone by the seashore in Monterey, where he basked in the raw, untamed power of nature. For adventure, he turned to literature. In particular, he felt "dazzled and swept up" by the legends of King Arthur.

Steinbeck and Arthur As an adult, Steinbeck attempted to set down a retelling of Arthurian legend that his two sons could enjoy. He researched the legend in England and Italy, studying rare manuscripts, and wrote in a room he named Joyous Garde, after Lancelot's castle. Unfortunately, Steinbeck died before he completed his version of the legend. In 1976, his unfinished work was published as *The Acts of King Arthur and His Noble Knights.* The excerpt you are about to read offers a fresh perspective on some of the events in Malory's tale of Sir Launcelot.

 MORE ABOUT THE AUTHOR
For more on John Steinbeck, visit the **Literature Center** at **ClassZone.com.**

The Acts of King Arthur
and His Noble Knights

JOHN STEINBECK

King Arthur held Whitsun[1] court at Winchester, that ancient royal town favored by God and His clergy as well as the seat and tomb of many kings. The roads were clogged with eager people, knights returning to stamp in court the record of their deeds, of bishops, clergy, monks, of the defeated fettered to their paroles,[2] the prisoners of honor. And on Itchen water, pathway from Solent[3] and the sea, the little ships brought succulents, lampreys, eels and oysters, plaice and sea trout, while barges loaded with casks of whale oil and casks of wine came tide borne. Bellowing oxen walked to the spits on their own four hooves, while geese and swans, sheep and swine, waited their turn
10 in hurdle pens. Every householder with a strip of colored cloth, a ribbon, any textile gaiety, hung it from a window to flap its small festival, and those in lack tied boughs of pine and laurel over their doors. **Ⓐ**

In the great hall of the castle on the hill the king sat high, and next below the fair elite company of the Round Table, noble and decorous as kings themselves, while at the long trestle boards the people were as fitted as toes in a tight shoe.

Then while the glistening meat dripped down the tables, it was the custom for the defeated to celebrate the deeds of those who had overcome them, while the victor dipped his head in **disparagement** of his greatness and fended off
20 the compliments with small defensive gestures of his hands. And as at public penitence sins are given stature they do not deserve, little sins grow up and baby sins are born, so those knights who lately claimed mercy perchance might raise the exploits of the brave and merciful beyond reasonable gratitude for their lives and in anticipation of some small notice of value.

This no one said of Lancelot, sitting with bowed head in his golden-lettered seat at the Round Table. Some said he nodded and perhaps dozed, for the testimony to his greatness was long and the monotony of his victories

Ⓐ STYLE
Reread lines 1–12, noting Steinbeck's **long, flowing sentences.** Why do you think Steinbeck begins this part of his retelling of Arthurian legend in this way?

disparagement
(dĭ-spăr′ĭj-mənt) *n.* belittlement

ANALYZE VISUALS
What **character traits** are suggested in this portrait of King Arthur?

---

1. **Whitsun:** another name for Pentecost. In Arthurian legend, Pentecost is one of the times at which the knights meet at Camelot to renew their oaths and receive new missions.
2. **fettered to their paroles:** bound by their word of honor to lay down arms.
3. **Itchen . . . Solent:** waterways in southern England.

Detail of *King Arthur* (1903), Charles Ernest Butler. Oil on canvas, 123.2 cm × 73.7 cm. Private collection. Christopher Wood Gallery, London. © Bridgeman Art Library.

continued for many hours. Lancelot's immaculate fame had grown so great that men took pride in being unhorsed by him—even this notice was an honor. And since he had won many victories, it is possible that knights he had never seen claimed to have been overthrown by him. It was a way to claim attention for a moment. And as he dozed and wished to be otherwhere, he heard his deeds **exalted** beyond his recognition, and some mighty exploits once attributed to other men were brought bright-painted out and laid on the shining pile of his achievements. There is a seat of worth beyond the reach of envy whose occupant ceases to be a man and becomes the receptacle of the wishful longings of the world, a seat most often reserved for the dead, from whom neither **reprisal** nor reward may be expected, but at this time Sir Lancelot was its unchallenged tenant. And he vaguely heard his strength favorably compared with elephants, his ferocity with lions, his agility with deer, his cleverness with foxes, his beauty with the stars, his justice with Solon,[4] his stern probity with St. Michael, his humility with newborn lambs; his military niche would have caused the Archangel Gabriel[5] to raise his head. Sometimes the guests paused in their chewing the better to hear, and a man who slopped his metheglin[6] drew frowns. **B**

Arthur on his dais[7] sat very still and did not fiddle with his bread, and beside him sat lovely Guinevere, still as a painted statue of herself. Only her inward eyes confessed her **vagrant** thoughts. And Lancelot studied the open pages of his hands—not large hands, but delicate where they were not knobby and scarred with old wounds. His hands were fine-textured—soft of skin and very white, protected by the pliant leather lining of his gauntlets. **C**

The great hall was not still, not all upturned listening. Everywhere was movement as people came and went, some serving huge planks of meat and baskets of bread, round and flat like a plate. And there were restless ones who could not sit still, while everyone under burden of half-chewed meat and the floods and freshets of mead and beer found necessity for repeated departures and returns.

Lancelot exhausted the theme of his hands and squinted down the long hall and watched the movement with eyes so nearly closed that he could not see faces. And he thought how he knew everyone by carriage. The knights in long full floor-brushing robes walked lightly or thought their feet barely touched the ground because their bodies were released from their crushing boxes of iron. Their feet were long and slender because, being horsemen, they had never widened and flattened their feet with walking. The ladies, full-skirted, moved like water, but this was schooled and designed, taught to little girls with the help of whips on raw ankles, while their shoulders were bound back with nail-studded harnesses and their heads held high and rigid by painful collars

---

4. **Solon:** an Athenian statesman and lawgiver who lived in the sixth century B.C.

5. **St. Michael . . . Archangel Gabriel:** In several religious traditions, Michael and Gabriel are archangels, the chief messengers of God. Both are celebrated as warriors against evil.

6. **metheglin** (mə-thĕg′lĭn): a liquor made from honey.

7. **dais** (dā′ĭs): a raised platform used for a seat of honor.

of woven willow or, for the forgetful, by supports of painted wire, for to learn the high proud head on a swan's neck, to learn to flow like water, is not easy
70 for a little girl as she becomes a gentlewoman. But knights and ladies both matched their movements to their garments; the sweep and rhythm of a long gown informs the manner of its moving. It is not necessary to inspect a serf or a slave, his shoulder wide and sloping from burdens, legs short and thick and crooked, feet splayed and widespread, the whole frame slowly crushed by weights. In the great hall the serving people walked under burdens with the slow weight of oxen and scuttled like crabs, crooked and nervous when the weight was gone. **D**

A pause in the recital of his virtues drew Lancelot's attention. The knight who had tried to kill him in a tree had finished, and among the benches Sir
80 Kay was rising to his feet. Lancelot could hear his voice before he spoke, reciting deeds like leaves and bags and barrels. Before his friend could reach the center of the hall, Sir Lancelot wriggled to his feet and approached the dais. "My lord king," he said, "forgive me if I ask leave to go. An old wound has broken open."

Arthur smiled down on him. "I have the same old wound," he said. "We'll go together. Perhaps you will come to the tower room when we have attended to our wounds." And he signed the trumpets to end the gathering, and the bodyguards to clear the hall. **E**

The stone stairway to the king's room was in the thickness of the wall of
90 the round tower of the keep. At short intervals a deep embrasure[8] and a long, beveled arrow slit commanded some aspect of the town below.

No armed men guarded this stairway. They were below and had passed Sir Lancelot in. The king's room was round, a horizontal slice of the tower, windowless save for the arrow slits, entered by a narrow arched door. It was a sparsely furnished room, carpeted with rushes. A wide bed, and at its foot a carved oaken chest, a bench before the fireplace, and several stools completed the furnishing. But the raw stone of the tower was plastered over and painted with solemn figures of men and angels walking hand in hand. Two candles and the reeky fire gave the only light. **F**

100 When Lancelot entered, the queen stood up from the bench before the fire, saying, "I will retire, my lords."

"No, stay," said Arthur.

"Stay," said Lancelot.

The king was stretched comfortably in the bed. His bare feet projecting from his long saffron[9] robe caressed each other, the toes curled downward.

The queen was lovely in the firelight, all lean, down-flowing lines of green samite.[10] She wore her little mouth-corner smile of concealed amusement, and

D STYLE
In lines 60–77, Steinbeck describes various members of medieval society. What **similes** and **metaphors** help you understand these people and their differences?

E MAKE INFERENCES
Reread lines 78–88. What can you infer about Lancelot and Arthur on the basis of their sudden departure from the banquet hall?

F GRAMMAR AND STYLE
Reread lines 92–99. Notice how Steinbeck varies the beginnings of his sentences, here through the use of adjectives, conjunctions, pronouns, and articles.

---

8. **embrasure** (ĕm-brā′zhər): an opening in a wall, narrowing toward the outside.

9. **saffron**: golden yellow, like the spice of that name.

10. **samite**: a heavy silk fabric.

Queen Guinevere's Maying, John Collier. Bradford Art Galleries and Museums, West Yorkshire, UK. Photo © Bridgeman Art Library.

her bold golden eyes were the same color as her hair, and odd it was that her lashes and slender brows were dark, an oddity contrived with kohl[11] brought in a small enameled pot from an outland by a far-wandering knight.

"How are you holding up?" Arthur asked.

"Not well, my lord. It's harder than the quest."

"Did you really do all the things they said you did?"

Lancelot chuckled. "Truthfully, I don't know. It sounds different when they tell about it. And most of them feel it necessary to add a little. When I remember leaping eight feet, they tell it at fifty, and frankly I don't recall several of those giants at all." **G**

The queen made room for him on the fire bench, and he took his seat, back to the fire.

Guinevere said, "The damsel—what's her name—talked about fair queen enchantresses,[12] but she was so excited that her words tumbled over each other. I couldn't make out what happened."

Lancelot looked nervously away. "You know how excitable young girls are," he said. "A little back-country necromancy[13] in a pasture."

"But she spoke particularly of queens."

"My lady, I think everyone is a queen to her. It's like the giants—makes the story richer."

"Then they were not queens?"

"Well, for that matter, when you get into the field of enchantment, everyone is a queen, or thinks she is. Next time she tells it, the little damsel will be a queen. I do think, my lord, there's too much of that kind of thing going on. It's a bad sign, a kind of restlessness, when people go in for fortunetelling and all such things. Maybe there should be a law about it."

"There is," said Arthur. "But it's not in secular hands. The Church is supposed to take care of that."

"Yes, but some of the nunneries are going in for it."

"Well, I'll put a bug in the archbishop's ear."[14]

The queen observed, "I gather you rescued damsels by the dozen." She put her fingers on his arm and a searing shock ran through his body, and his mouth opened in amazement at a hollow ache that pressed upward against his ribs and shortened his breath. **H**

After a moment she said, "How many damsels did you rescue?"

His mouth was dry. "Of course there were a few, madame. There always are."

"And all of them made love to you?"

"That they did not, madame. There you protect me."

"I?"

"Yes. Since with my lord's permission I swore to serve you all my life

---

11. **kohl:** a cosmetic preparation used as eye makeup.

12. **fair queen enchantresses:** Morgan le Fay and three other queens, the four of whom, as related in "Sir Launcelot du Lake," imprisoned Launcelot, demanding that he take one of them as his lover.

13. **necromancy:** magic.

14. **put a bug in the archbishop's ear:** alert the archbishop in a quiet way.

G MAKE INFERENCES
How are Lancelot's remarks in lines 114–117 consistent with his earlier behavior at the banquet? Explain.

H STYLE
Review the **dialogue** in lines 120–138. Which words and phrases in this exchange sound particularly realistic? Explain.

and gave my knightly courtly love[15] to you, I am sheltered from damsels by your name."

150   "And do you want to be sheltered?"

"Yes, my lady. I am a fighting man. I have neither time nor inclination for any other kind of love. I hope this pleases you, my lady. I sent many prisoners to ask your mercy."

"I never saw such a crop of them," Arthur said. "You must have swept some counties clean."

Guinevere touched him on the arm again and with side-glancing golden eyes saw the spasm that shook him. "While we are on this subject, I want to mention one lady you did not save. When I saw her, she was a headless corpse and not in good condition, and the man who brought her in was
160 half crazed."[16]

"I am ashamed of that," said Lancelot. "She was under my protection, and I failed her. I suppose it was my shame that made me force the man to do it. I'm sorry. I hope you released him from the burden."

"Not at all," she said. "I wanted him away before the feast reeked up the heavens. I sent him with his burden to the Pope. His friend will not improve on the way. And if his loss of interest in ladies continues, he may turn out to be a very holy man, a hermit or something of that nature, if he isn't a maniac first."

The king rose on his elbow. "We will have to work out some system," he said. "The rules of errantry[17] are too loose, and the quests overlap. Besides, I
170 wonder how long we can leave justice in the hands of men who are themselves unstable. I don't mean you, my friend. But there may come a time when order and organization from the crown will be necessary."

The queen stood up. "My lords, will you grant me permission to leave you now? I know you will wish to speak of great things foreign and perhaps tiresome to a lady's ears."

The king said, "Surely, my lady. Go to your rest."

"No, sire—not rest. If I do not lay out the designs for the needlepoint, my ladies will have no work tomorrow."

"But these are feast days, my dear."

180   "I like to give them something every day, my lord. They're lazy things and some of them so woolly in the mind that they forget how to thread a needle from day to day. Forgive me, my lords."

She swept from the room with proud and powerful steps, and the little breeze she made in the still air carried a strange scent to Lancelot, a perfume which sent a shivering excitement coursing through his body. It was an odor he did not, could not, know, for it was the smell of Guinevere distilled by her

I MAKE INFERENCES
Reread lines 138–157. Describe Lancelot's feelings for Guinevere. Which details helped you make your inference?

ANALYZE VISUALS
How does this painting depict Lancelot as an ideal knight?

---

15. **courtly love:** a sentimental reflection of the feudal relationship between a knight and his lord. The knight serves his chosen lady with the same obedience and loyalty he owes his lord. The knight's love for the lady inspires him to seek adventure and achieve great deeds.

16. **When I saw her . . . half crazed:** Guinevere is referring to a woman Lancelot was unable to save—a woman who was beheaded by her jealous husband. As punishment, Lancelot commanded the husband to take the woman's body to Guinevere and to throw himself on her mercy.

17. **errantry** (ĕr′ən-trē): the knightly pursuit of adventure.

Detail of *Lancelot and Guinevere,* Herbert James Draper. Private collection. Bohams, London. Photo © Bridgeman Art Library.

own skin. And as she passed through the door and descended the steps, he saw himself leap up and follow her, although he did not move. And when she was gone, the room was bleak, and the glory was gone from it, and Sir Lancelot 190 was dog-weary, tired almost to weeping. **J**

"What a queen she is," said King Arthur softly. "And what a woman equally. Merlin was with me when I chose her. He tried to dissuade me with his usual doomful prophecies. That was one of the few times I differed with him. Well, my choice has proved him fallible. She has shown the world what a queen should be. All other women lose their sheen when she is present."

Lancelot said, "Yes, my lord," and for no reason he knew, except perhaps the **intemperate** dullness of the feast, he felt lost, and a cold knife of loneliness pressed against his heart. **K**

The king was chuckling. "It is the device of ladies that their lords have great 200 matters to discuss, when if the truth were told, we bore them. And I hope the truth is never told. Why, you look **haggard,** my friend. Are you feverish? Did you mean that about an old wound opening?"

"No. The wound was what you thought it was, my lord. But it is true that I can fight, travel, live on berries, fight again, go without sleeping, and come out fresh and fierce, but sitting still at Whitsun feast has wearied me to death."

Arthur said, "I can see it. We'll discuss the realm's health another time. Go to your bed now. Have you your old quarters?"

"No—better ones. Sir Kay has cleared five knights from the lovely lordly rooms over the north gate. He did it in memory of an adventure which we, 210 God help us, will have to listen to tomorrow. I accept your dismissal, my lord."

And Lancelot knelt down and took the king's beloved hand in both of his and kissed it. "Good night, my liege[18] lord, my liege friend," he said and then stumbled blindly from the room and felt his way down the curving stone steps past the arrow slits.

As he came to the level of the next landing, Guinevere issued silently from a darkened entrance. He could see her in the thin light from the arrow slit. She took his arm and led him to her dark chamber and closed the oaken door.

"A strange thing happened," she said softly. "When I left you, I thought you followed me. I was so sure of it I did not even look around to verify it. You 220 were there behind me. And when I came to my own door, I said good night to you, so certain I was that you were there."

He could see her outline in the dark and smell the scent which was herself. "My lady," he said, "when you left the room, I saw myself follow you as though I were another person looking on."

Their bodies locked together as though a trap had sprung. Their mouths met, and each devoured the other. Each frantic heartbeat at the walls of ribs trying to get to the other until their held breaths burst out and Lancelot, dizzied, found the door and blundered down the stairs. And he was weeping bitterly. ᴥ **L**

J STYLE
Reread lines 183–190, noting Steinbeck's **imagery**—words that appeal to the senses. Which images help you understand Guinevere and her effect on Lancelot?

intemperate
(ĭn-tĕm′pər-ĭt) *adj.* extreme

K STYLE
Consider Steinbeck's **tone,** or attitude, in lines 191–198. What details suggest that he has great sympathy for both Arthur and Lancelot?

haggard (hăg′ərd) *adj.* appearing worn and exhausted

L MAKE INFERENCES
Reread the final paragraph of the selection. Why does Lancelot weep?

Comprehension

1. **Recall** Why is Lancelot praised at the feast?

2. **Clarify** Why does Lancelot leave the feast?

3. **Summarize** Describe what happens after Lancelot leaves the king's room.

Literary Analysis

4. **Make Inferences** Review the chart you created as you read. Do you think Lancelot sees himself as others do—as a model of **perfection?** Cite evidence.

5. **Analyze Characters** Think about the way Lancelot and Arthur interact in lines 83–88. Which details suggest that they are close friends?

6. **Draw Conclusions** Reread lines 183–198. What conclusions can you draw about the **internal conflict** Lancelot experiences? Support your answer.

7. **Interpret Theme** What theme about knighthood does Steinbeck communicate in the selection? Cite evidence to support your answer.

8. **Understand Style** Steinbeck's style features many tightly constructed **characterizations.** Choose a passage of at least five lines that illustrates the author's ability to create a brief, effective portrait. Explain your choice.

9. **Examine Figurative Language** Identify three examples of figurative language—similes and metaphors—in the selection. Explain how each helps to clarify an idea or enliven a scene.

10. **Compare Literary Texts** Review Keith Baines's retelling of Malory's *Le Morte d'Arthur* on pages 1012–1026. Then compare Baines's writing style with Steinbeck's. Complete a chart like the one shown, noting key aspects of each author's **style.** In your opinion, which author presents the more exciting version of Arthurian legend? Explain your response.

	Baines	Steinbeck
Characterization		
Sensory Details		
Dialogue		
Word Choice		
Tone		

Literary Criticism

11. **Social Context** In *King Arthur and His Noble Knights,* what does Steinbeck suggest were the roles and responsibilities of noblewomen in medieval society? Cite evidence to support your response.

OHIO STANDARDS

READING STANDARD
2.1 Make inferences

Vocabulary in Context

VOCABULARY PRACTICE

Choose the letter of the word that differs most in meaning from the others in the set. If necessary, use a dictionary to check the precise meanings of words you are unsure of.

1. (a) encouragement, (b) belittlement, (c) disparagement, (d) ridicule
2. (a) motionless, (b) vagrant, (c) drifting, (d) wandering
3. (a) mercy, (b) reprisal, (c) punishment, (d) revenge
4. (a) glorify, (b) condemn, (c) exalt, (d) acclaim
5. (a) intemperate, (b) excessive, (c) mild, (d) extreme
6. (a) refreshed, (b) rundown, (c) worn, (d) haggard

WORD LIST

disparagement

exalt

haggard

intemperate

reprisal

vagrant

VOCABULARY IN WRITING

Using three or more vocabulary words, describe Lancelot's complex feelings for both Arthur and Guinevere. Here is how you might begin.

> **EXAMPLE SENTENCE**
>
> Nobles and peasants alike **exalt** Lancelot, but his love for Guinevere . . .

VOCABULARY STRATEGY: CONNOTATION

A **connotation** is an attitude or a feeling associated with a word. For example, *vagrant* and *rambling* could both be defined as "moving in a random fashion," but Steinbeck's use of *vagrant* to describe Guinevere's thoughts does not convey the negativity associated with *rambling*. Writers are aware of the connotations of words and often use them to evoke particular moods.

PRACTICE Place the words in each group on a continuum to show the positive, neutral, or negative connotation of each word. Then compare your answers with those of a classmate.

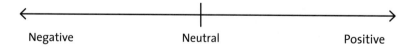

Negative   Neutral   Positive

1. intemperate, bold, extreme
2. worn, haggard, tired
3. exalt, boast, praise
4. retaliation, reprisal, revenge

OHIO STANDARDS

VOCABULARY STANDARD
1.2 Analyze the relationships of pairs of words

VOCABULARY PRACTICE
For more practice, go to the **Vocabulary Center** at **ClassZone.com.**

Reading-Writing Connection

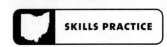

SKILLS PRACTICE

Broaden your understanding of the selections by responding to these prompts.
Then use **Revision: Grammar and Style** to improve your writing.

WRITING PROMPTS	SELF-CHECK
A. Short Response: Examine the Influence of Medieval Romance Review the conventions of medieval romance on page 1011. In **one or two paragraphs,** describe how the influence of medieval romance can be seen in contemporary novels, movies, and television shows. Cite specific examples to support your response.	***A successful response will . . .*** • show a good understanding of medieval romance ▶ • state how aspects of medieval romance can be seen in modern literature and media
B. Extended Response: Compare Literary Texts How does Malory's portrayal of Launcelot (also spelled Lancelot) differ from Steinbeck's? Compare and contrast the way the two authors depict this famous knight in a **three-to-five-paragraph response.**	***A strong response will . . .*** • explain how the character's personality traits differ from story to story ▶ • provide specific examples to support your conclusions

REVISION: GRAMMAR AND STYLE

VARY SENTENCE BEGINNINGS Review the **Grammar and Style** note on page 1035. In the selection, Steinbeck uses a variety of sentence beginnings that help to enliven his work. Your writing, too, will be more interesting if you use an assortment of **phrases, clauses,** and **words** to begin sentences. In the following examples, notice how Steinbeck starts one sentence with a series of prepositional phrases and another sentence with an adverbial clause:

> *In the great hall of the castle on the hill the king sat high . . . while at the long trestle boards the people were as fitted as toes in a tight shoe.* (lines 13–16)
> *Then while the glistening meat dripped down the tables, it was the custom for the defeated to celebrate the deeds of those who had overcome them. . . .* (lines 17–18)

Note how the revisions in red make the following draft less repetitive. Revise your responses to the prompts by varying your sentence beginnings.

OHIO STANDARDS

WRITING STANDARD
5.7 Use a variety of sentence structures and lengths

STUDENT MODEL

In Le Morte d'Arthur,
⋀ Malory portrays Launcelot as the true gallant knight. ~~Malory's~~ *His* Launcelot

clanks swords with sworn enemies before dramatically riding off across the

While
countryside. ⋀ Steinbeck's Lancelot is just as brave as Malory's, *he* ~~Steinbeck's~~

~~Lancelot~~ is much more distracted by thoughts of Guinevere₆ ~~though.~~

WRITING TOOLS
For prewriting, revision, and editing tools, visit the **Writing Center** at **ClassZone.com.**

from **Don Quixote**
Novel by Miguel de Cervantes

from **Man of La Mancha**
Musical Play by Dale Wasserman

Why do we admire DREAMERS?

OHIO STANDARDS

READING STANDARDS
2.1 Apply reading comprehension strategies
4.5 Analyze how choice of genre affects theme or topic

KEY IDEA Think of people you know or have heard of who have pursued their dreams even when the dreams seemed foolish or impossible to achieve. Which of their qualities do you admire the most? In these two selections, you will meet a character whose devotion to an impossible **dream** has inspired countless readers.

DISCUSS With a small group, generate a list of people who have been considered dreamers—Mahatma Gandhi, for example. Then discuss these questions: What traits do these individuals share? How have their actions affected the way you look at the world?

● LITERARY ANALYSIS: PARODY ACROSS GENRES

A **parody** is a comic imitation of another work or of a type of literature. The following two selections are parodies of medieval romances, rambling tales of heroic knights and their fearless search for adventure. Romance heroes were devoted to the ideals of chivalry, the knightly code of honor. Use the descriptions on pages 1010 and 1011 to review characteristics of the chivalric code and of medieval romance.

The novel and play excerpts you will read both portray the same ridiculous hero on his hopeless quest, but they use different techniques to get the joke across. The following chart shows how genre influences the comic strategies each writer uses.

In the Novel	In the Play
• character traits and motivations conveyed through description	• character traits and motivations conveyed through dialogue, song, and action
• verbal humor, such as exaggerated descriptions, puns, and irony	• visual humor, such as non-realistic staging, sight gags, and pratfalls
• language that imitates the style of a chivalric romance	• comic misunderstandings that highlight the unrealistic ideals of the chivalric code
• absurd situations that parallel the actions of a chivalric hero	

As you read, think about how these techniques are used to play with the conventions of the romance.

● READING STRATEGY: SET A PURPOSE FOR READING

When you **set a purpose for reading,** you decide what to look for as you read. In this lesson, you are reading to compare and contrast two selections that parody the medieval romance. As you read, note the specific ideas each writer is mocking and the techniques he uses to achieve his comic effects. After you read, you will use the **Points of Comparison** chart on page 1061 to analyze the two selections.

▲ VOCABULARY IN CONTEXT

Test your knowledge by substituting a different word or phrase for each boldfaced term.

1. **resurrect** the dead
2. expose the **fictitious** alibi
3. a smiling and **affable** host
4. **burnish** the silver
5. his **incongruous** garb
6. swore undying **enmity**
7. split up the **hapless** couple
8. a mile-long **cavalcade**

Don Quixote

Miguel de Cervantes

❧ *Part 1, Chapter 1* ❧

In a village of La Mancha[1] the name of which I have no desire to recall, there lived not so long ago one of those gentlemen who always have a lance in the rack, an ancient buckler,[2] a skinny nag, and a greyhound for the chase. A stew with more beef than mutton in it, chopped meat for his evening meal, scraps for a Saturday, lentils on Friday, and a young pigeon as a special delicacy for Sunday, went to account for three-quarters of his income.

The rest of it he laid out on a broadcloth greatcoat[3] and velvet stockings for feast days, with slippers to match, while the other days of the week he cut a figure in a suit of the finest homespun. Living with him were a housekeeper in
10 her forties, a niece who was not yet twenty, and a lad of the field and market place who saddled his horse for him and wielded the pruning knife.

This gentleman of ours was close on to fifty, of a robust constitution but with little flesh on his bones and a face that was lean and gaunt. He was noted for his early rising, being very fond of the hunt. They will try to tell you that his surname was Quijada or Quesada—there is some difference of opinion among those who have written on the subject—but according to the most likely conjectures we are to understand that it was really Quejana.[4] But all this means very little so far as our story is concerned, providing that in the telling of it we do not depart one iota from the truth. **A**

20 You may know, then, that the aforesaid gentleman, on those occasions when he was at leisure, which was most of the year around, was in the habit of reading books of chivalry with such pleasure and devotion as to lead him almost wholly to forget the life of a hunter and even the administration of his estate. So great was his curiosity and infatuation in this regard that he even sold many acres of tillable land in order to be able to buy and read the books that he loved, and he would carry home with him as many of them as he could obtain.

---

1. **La Mancha:** a high, flat, barren region in central Spain.
2. **buckler:** a small, round shield carried or worn on the arm.
3. **broadcloth greatcoat:** a heavy wool overcoat.
4. **Quijada** (kē-hä′dä) . . . **Quesada** (kě-sä′dä) . . . **Quejana** (kě-hä′nä).

ANALYZE VISUALS
What details in this photograph evoke the heroic image of the ideal knight?

A PARODY
Reread the opening paragraphs. Compare this passage with the idealized descriptions of Malory's heroes. What details establish a pointed contrast with the romance hero?

John Lithgow in the TNT production of *Don Quixote*

Of all those that he thus devoured none pleased him so well as the ones that had been composed by the famous Feliciano de Silva,[5] whose lucid prose style and involved conceits[6] were as precious to him as pearls; especially when he
30 came to read those tales of love and amorous challenges that are to be met with in many places, such a passage as the following, for example: "The reason of the unreason that afflicts my reason, in such a manner weakens my reason that I with reason lament me of your comeliness." And he was similarly affected when his eyes fell upon such lines as these: ". . . the high Heaven of your divinity divinely fortifies you with the stars and renders you deserving of that desert your greatness doth deserve."

The poor fellow used to lie awake nights in an effort to disentangle the meaning and make sense out of passages such as these, although Aristotle[7] himself would not have been able to understand them, even if he had been
40 **resurrected** for that sole purpose. He was not at ease in his mind over those wounds that Don Belianís[8] gave and received; for no matter how great the surgeons who treated him, the poor fellow must have been left with his face and his entire body covered with marks and scars. Nevertheless, he was grateful to the author for closing the book with the promise of an interminable adventure to come; many a time he was tempted to take up his pen and literally finish the tale as had been promised, and he undoubtedly would have done so, and would have succeeded at it very well, if his thoughts had not been constantly occupied with other things of greater moment. **B**

He often talked it over with the village curate,[9] who was a learned man, a
50 graduate of Sigüenza,[10] and they would hold long discussions as to who had been the better knight, Palmerin of England or Amadis of Gaul; but Master Nicholas, the barber of the same village, was in the habit of saying that no one could come up to the Knight of Phoebus,[11] and that if anyone could compare with him it was Don Galaor, brother of Amadis of Gaul, for Galaor was ready for anything—he was none of your finical[12] knights, who went around whimpering as his brother did, and in point of valor he did not lag behind him.

In short, our gentleman became so immersed in his reading that he spent whole nights from sundown to sunup and his days from dawn to dusk in poring over his books, until, finally, from so little sleeping and so much
60 reading, his brain dried up and he went completely out of his mind. He had

resurrect (rĕz′ə-rĕkt′) v. to bring back to life

B PARODY
Describe the **tone** of lines 27–48. How does the narrator seem to view books of chivalry and Quejana's passion for them?

---

5. **Feliciano de Silva:** a Spanish author of fictional books about knights.
6. **conceits:** lengthy, exaggerated comparisons.
7. **Aristotle:** a Greek philosopher (384–322 B.C.) widely known for his wisdom.
8. **Don Belianís** (dôn bĕ-lyä-nēs′): the hero of a chivalric romance.
9. **curate** (kyŏŏr′ĭt): a religious official in charge of a parish.
10. **Sigüenza** (sē-gwĕn′sä): a "minor" university of Spain, whose graduates were often mocked.
11. **Palmerin of England . . . Amadis** (ä′mə-dĭs) **of Gaul . . . Knight of Phoebus** (fē′bəs): romance heroes who exemplified knightly perfection.
12. **finical** (fĭn′ĭ-kəl): finicky; picky.

filled his imagination with everything that he had read, with enchantments, knightly encounters, battles, challenges, wounds, with tales of love and its torments, and all sorts of impossible things, and as a result had come to believe that all these **fictitious** happenings were true; they were more real to him than anything else in the world. He would remark that the Cid Ruy Díaz[13] had been a very good knight, but there was no comparison between him and the Knight of the Flaming Sword,[14] who with a single backward stroke had cut in half two fierce and monstrous giants. He preferred Bernardo del Carpio,[15] who at Roncesvalles had slain Roland despite the charm the latter bore, availing
70   himself of the stratagem which Hercules employed when he strangled Antaeus, the son of Earth, in his arms.

He had much good to say for Morgante[16] who, though he belonged to the haughty, overbearing race of giants, was of an **affable** disposition and well brought up. But, above all, he cherished an admiration for Rinaldo of Montalbán,[17] especially as he beheld him sallying forth from his castle to rob all those that crossed his path, or when he thought of him overseas stealing the image of Mohammed which, so the story has it, was all of gold. And he would have liked very well to have had his fill of kicking that traitor Galalón,[18] a privilege for which he would have given his housekeeper with his niece
80   thrown into the bargain.

At last, when his wits were gone beyond repair, he came to conceive the strangest idea that ever occurred to any madman in this world. It now appeared to him fitting and necessary, in order to win a greater amount of honor for himself and serve his country at the same time, to become a knight-errant[19] and roam the world on horseback, in a suit of armor; he would go in quest of adventures, by way of putting into practice all that he had read in his books; he would right every manner of wrong, placing himself in situations of the greatest peril such as would redound[20] to the eternal glory of his name. As a reward for his valor and the might of his arm, the poor fellow could already
90   see himself crowned Emperor of Trebizond[21] at the very least; and so, carried away by the strange pleasure that he found in such thoughts as these, he at once set about putting his plan into effect.

fictitious (fĭk-tĭsh′əs) *adj.* fabricated; created by the imagination

affable (ăf′ə-bəl) *adj.* warm and friendly

---

13. **Cid Ruy Díaz** (sēd′ rwē′ dē′äs): Rodrigo (or Ruy) Díaz de Vivar, known as the Cid, was an actual Spanish military leader and national hero about whom an epic poem was written.

14. **Knight of the Flaming Sword:** Amadis of Greece, a romance hero whose symbol was a red sword.

15. **Bernardo del Carpio** (kär′pyô): a legendary Spanish hero who, in some tales, killed the hero of *The Song of Roland* by strangling him in midair, as Hercules had done to the giant Antaeus.

16. **Morgante** (môr-gän′tĕ): a ferocious giant, in an Italian romantic poem, who later became sweet and loving.

17. **Rinaldo of Montalbán** (môn-täl-bän′): the hero in a series of French epic poems.

18. **Galalón** (gä-lä-lôn′): Ganelon, the stepfather and betrayer of Roland, the French epic hero.

19. **knight-errant:** a knight who wanders the countryside in search of adventure to prove his chivalry.

20. **redound:** contribute.

21. **Trebizond:** a former Greek empire, often mentioned in stories of knighthood.

The first thing he did was to **burnish** up some old pieces of armor, left him by his great-grandfather, which for ages had lain in a corner, moldering and forgotten. He polished and adjusted them as best he could, and then he noticed that one very important thing was lacking: there was no closed helmet, but only a morion, or visorless headpiece, with turned up brim of the kind foot soldiers wore. His ingenuity, however, enabled him to remedy this, and he proceeded to fashion out of cardboard a kind of half-helmet, which, when
100 attached to the morion, gave the appearance of a whole one. True, when he went to see if it was strong enough to withstand a good slashing blow, he was somewhat disappointed; for when he drew his sword and gave it a couple of thrusts, he succeeded only in undoing a whole week's labor. The ease with which he had hewed it to bits disturbed him no little, and he decided to make it over. This time he placed a few strips of iron on the inside, and then, convinced that it was strong enough, refrained from putting it to any further test; instead, he adopted it then and there as the finest helmet ever made.

After this, he went out to have a look at his nag; and although the animal had more *cuartos,* or cracks, in its hoof than there are quarters in a real,[22]
110 and more blemishes than Gonela's steed[23] which *tantum pellis et ossa fuit,*[24] it nonetheless looked to its master like a far better horse than Alexander's Bucephalus or the Babieca of the Cid.[25] He spent all of four days in trying to think up a name for his mount; for—so he told himself—seeing that it belonged to so famous and worthy a knight, there was no reason why it should not have a name of equal renown. The kind of name he wanted was one that would at once indicate what the nag had been before it came to belong to a knight-errant and what its present status was; for it stood to reason that, when the master's worldly condition changed, his horse also ought to have a famous, high-sounding appellation, one suited to the new order of things and the new
120 profession that it was to follow.

After he in his memory and imagination had made up, struck out, and discarded many names, now adding to and now subtracting from the list, he finally hit upon "Rocinante," a name that impressed him as being sonorous and at the same time indicative of what the steed had been when it was but a hack, whereas now it was nothing other than the first and foremost of all the hacks[26] in the world. **C**

Having found a name for his horse that pleased his fancy, he then desired to do as much for himself, and this required another week, and by the end of that period he had made up his mind that he was henceforth to be known as

burnish (bûr′nĭsh) *v.*
to polish

C PARODY
What does the horse's name imply about the hero's lofty goals?

---

22. **quarters in a real** (rā-äl′): A real was a coin worth about five cents.

23. **Gonela's steed:** the horse of the Italian court comedian Pietro Gonela, which was famous for having gas.

24. *tantum pellis et ossa fuit Latin:* was only skin and bones.

25. **Alexander's Bucephalus** (byōō-sĕf′ə-ləs) **or the Babieca** (bä-byĕ′kä) **of the Cid:** famous horses. Alexander is Alexander the Great, the early conqueror of Asia.

26. **Rocinante** (rô-sĕ-nän′tĕ) . . . **foremost of all the hacks:** *Rocin* means "nag" or "hack" in Spanish; *ante* means "before" or "first." So the name Rocinante indicates that the horse is the first, or chief, nag.

130 Don Quixote,[27] which, as has been stated, has
led the authors of this veracious history to assume
that his real name must undoubtedly have been
Quijada, and not Quesada as others would have
it. But remembering that the valiant Amadis
was not content to call himself that and nothing
more, but added the name of his kingdom and
fatherland that he might make it famous also, and
thus came to take the name Amadis of Gaul, so
our good knight chose to add his place of origin

140 and become "Don Quixote de la Mancha"; for by
this means, as he saw it, he was making very plain
his lineage and was conferring honor upon his
country by taking its name as his own.

And so, having polished up his armor and made
the morion over into a closed helmet, and having
given himself and his horse a name, he naturally
found but one thing lacking still: he must seek out
a lady of whom he could become enamored; for
a knight-errant without a ladylove was like a tree

150 without leaves or fruit, a body without a soul.

"If," he said to himself, "as a punishment for
my sins or by a stroke of fortune I should come
upon some giant hereabouts, a thing that very commonly happens to knights-
errant, and if I should slay him in a hand-to-hand encounter or perhaps cut
him in two, or, finally, if I should vanquish and subdue him, would it not
be well to have someone to whom I may send him as a present, in order
that he, if he is living, may come in, fall upon his knees in front of my sweet
lady, and say in a humble and submissive tone of voice, 'I, lady, am the giant
Caraculiambro,[28] lord of the island Malindrania, who has been overcome in

160 single combat by that knight who never can be praised enough, Don Quixote
de la Mancha, the same who sent me to present myself before your Grace that
your Highness may dispose of me as you see fit'?" **D**

Oh, how our good knight reveled in this speech, and more than ever when
he came to think of the name that he should give his lady! As the story goes,
there was a very good-looking farm girl who lived near by, with whom he
had once been smitten, although it is generally believed that she never knew
or suspected it. Her name was Aldonza Lorenzo, and it seemed to him that
she was the one upon whom he should bestow the title of mistress of his
thoughts. For her he wished a name that should not be **incongruous** with his

170 own and that would convey the suggestion of a princess or a great lady; and,

John Lithgow and Vanessa Williams in the TNT production
of *Don Quixote*

D **PARODY**
Reread lines 127–162, and
note Cervantes's imitation
of the style of medieval
romance. What romance
conventions does
Cervantes mock here?

incongruous
(ĭn-kŏng′grōō-əs) *adj.*
unsuitable; incompatible

---

27. **Quixote** (kē-hô′tĕ): The word literally denotes a piece of armor that protects the thigh.

28. **Caraculiambro** (kä-rä-kōō-lyäm′brô).

accordingly, he resolved to call her "Dulcinea del Toboso,"[29] she being a native of that place. A musical name to his ears, out of the ordinary and significant, like the others he had chosen for himself and his appurtenances.[30]

After completing his preparations, Don Quixote sets off on his first adventure, which lasts three days. He persuades an innkeeper to dub him a knight. Then he "rescues" a servant boy from his master's beating, but as soon as "our knight" leaves, the master beats the boy even harder. Next, Don Quixote mistakes a traveling group of merchants for hostile knights. After insulting the merchants for failing to swear to the beauty of Dulcinea del Toboso, he is badly beaten. A neighbor finds him on the road and carries him home, to the great relief of his family and friends. They blame Don Quixote's mad behavior on his reading habits, so for his own good they decide to burn his books.

ᥱᥩ *from Part 1, Chapter 7* ᥩᥱ

. . . That night the housekeeper burned all the books there were in the stable yard and in all the house; and there must have been some that went up in smoke which should have been preserved in everlasting archives, if the one who did the scrutinizing had not been so indolent. Thus we see the truth of the old saying, to the effect that the innocent must sometimes pay for the sins of the guilty.

One of the things that the curate and the barber advised as a remedy for
180 their friend's sickness was to wall up the room where the books had been, so that, when he arose, he would not find them missing—it might be that the cause being removed, the effect would cease—and they could tell him that a magician had made away with them, room and all. This they proceeded to do as quickly as possible. Two days later, when Don Quixote rose from his bed, the first thing he did was to go have a look at his library, and, not finding it where he had left it, he went from one part of the house to another searching for it. Going up to where the door had been, he ran his hands over the wall and rolled his eyes in every direction without saying a word; but after some little while he asked the housekeeper where his study was with all his books.
190 She had been well instructed in what to answer him. "Whatever study is your Grace talking about?" she said. "There is no study, and no books, in this house; the devil took them all away."

"No," said the niece, "it was not the devil but an enchanter who came upon a cloud one night, the day after your Grace left here; dismounting from a serpent that he rode, he entered your study, and I don't know what all he did there, but after a bit he went flying off through the roof, leaving the house full of smoke;

---

29. **Dulcinea del Toboso** (do͞ol-sē-nē′ä dĕl tô-bô′sô): The name comes from *dulce,* the Spanish word for sweet.

30. **appurtenances:** appendages; accessories.

and when we went to see what he had done, there was no study and not a book in sight. There is one thing, though, that the housekeeper and I remember very well: at the time that wicked old fellow left, he cried out in a loud voice that it
200 was all on account of a secret **enmity** that he bore the owner of those books and that study, and that was why he had done the mischief in this house which we would discover. He also said that he was called Muñatón the Magician."

"Frestón, he should have said," remarked Don Quixote.

"I can't say as to that," replied the housekeeper, "whether he was called Frestón or Fritón;[31] all I know is that his name ended in a *tón*."

"So it does," said Don Quixote. "He is a wise enchanter, a great enemy of mine, who has a grudge against me because he knows by his arts and learning that in the course of time I am to fight in single combat with a knight whom he favors, and that I am to be the victor and he can do nothing to prevent
210 it. For this reason he seeks to cause me all the trouble that he can, but I am warning him that it will be hard to gainsay or shun that which Heaven has ordained." . . . **E**

In the meanwhile Don Quixote was bringing his powers of persuasion to bear upon a farmer who lived near by, a good man—if this title may be applied to one who is poor—but with very few wits in his head. The short of it is, by pleas and promises, he got the **hapless** rustic to agree to ride forth with him and serve him as his squire. Among other things, Don Quixote told him that

enmity (ĕn′mĭ-tē) *n.* hostility and ill will

E PARODY
Would Don Quixote's response in lines 206–212 make sense in the context of a traditional romance? Explain.

hapless (hăp′lĭs) *adj.* pitiful; unfortunate

---

31. **Frestón** (frĕs-tôn′) **or Fritón** (frē-tôn′): Frestón, a magician, was thought to be the author of *History of Belianís of Greece.*

Bob Hoskins and John Lithgow in the TNT production of *Don Quixote*

he ought to be more than willing to go, because no telling what adventure might occur which would win them an island, and then he (the farmer) would
220 be left to be the governor of it. As a result of these and other similar assurances, Sancho Panza forsook his wife and children and consented to take upon himself the duties of squire to his neighbor.

Next, Don Quixote set out to raise some money, and by selling this thing and pawning that and getting the worst of the bargain always, he finally scraped together a reasonable amount. He also asked a friend of his for the loan of a buckler and patched up his broken helmet as well as he could. He advised his squire, Sancho, of the day and hour when they were to take the road and told him to see to laying in a supply of those things that were most necessary, and, above all, not to forget the saddlebags. Sancho replied that he
230 would see to all this and added that he was also thinking of taking along with him a very good ass that he had, as he was not much used to going on foot.

With regard to the ass, Don Quixote had to do a little thinking, trying to recall if any knight-errant had ever had a squire thus asininely[32] mounted. He could not think of any, but nevertheless he decided to take Sancho with the intention of providing him with a nobler steed as soon as occasion offered; he had but to appropriate the horse of the first discourteous knight he met. Having furnished himself with shirts and all the other things that the innkeeper had recommended, he and Panza rode forth one night unseen by anyone and without taking leave of wife and children, housekeeper or niece.
240 They went so far that by the time morning came they were safe from discovery had a hunt been started for them. . . .

ᕦ *from Part 1, Chapter 8* ᕤ

At this point they caught sight of thirty or forty windmills which were standing on the plain there, and no sooner had Don Quixote laid eyes upon them than he turned to his squire and said, "Fortune is guiding our affairs better than we could have wished; for you see there before you, friend Sancho Panza, some thirty or more lawless giants with whom I mean to do battle. I shall deprive them of their lives, and with the spoils from this encounter we shall begin to enrich ourselves; for this is righteous warfare, and it is a great service to God to remove so accursed a breed from the face of the earth."
250 "What giants?" said Sancho Panza.

"Those that you see there," replied his master, "those with the long arms some of which are as much as two leagues in length."

"But look, your Grace, those are not giants but windmills, and what appear to be arms are their wings which, when whirled in the breeze, cause the millstone to go."

---

32. **asininely:** foolishly; ridiculously (derived from Latin *asinus*, "ass"). The statement is both a literal description and a sly joke about Sancho's unheroic appearance.

"It is plain to be seen," said Don Quixote, "that you have had little experience in this matter of adventures. If you are afraid, go off to one side and say your prayers while I am engaging them in fierce, unequal combat."

Saying this, he gave spurs to his steed Rocinante, without paying any heed to Sancho's warning that these were truly windmills and not giants that he was riding forth to attack. Nor even when he was close upon them did he perceive what they really were, but shouted at the top of his lungs, "Do not seek to flee, cowards and vile creatures that you are, for it is but a single knight with whom you have to deal!"

At that moment a little wind came up and the big wings began turning.

"Though you flourish as many arms as did the giant Briareus,"[33] said Don Quixote when he perceived this, "you still shall have to answer to me."

He thereupon commended himself with all his heart to his lady Dulcinea, beseeching her to succor him in this peril; and, being well covered with his shield and with his lance at rest, he bore down upon them at a full gallop and fell upon the first mill that stood in his way, giving a thrust at the wing, which was whirling at such a speed that his lance was broken into bits and both horse and horseman went rolling over the plain, very much battered indeed. Sancho upon his donkey came hurrying to his master's assistance as fast as he could, but when he reached the spot, the knight was unable to move, so great was the shock with which he and Rocinante had hit the ground.

"God help us!" exclaimed Sancho, "did I not tell your Grace to look well, that those were nothing but windmills, a fact which no one could fail to see unless he had other mills of the same sort in his head?"

"Be quiet, friend Sancho," said Don Quixote. "Such are the fortunes of war, which more than any other are subject to constant change. What is more, when I come to think of it, I am sure that this must be the work of that magician Frestón, the one who robbed me of my study and my books, and who has thus changed the giants into windmills in order to deprive me of the glory of overcoming them, so great is the enmity that he bears me; but in the end his evil arts shall not prevail against this trusty sword of mine." **F**

"May God's will be done," was Sancho Panza's response. And with the aid of his squire the knight was once more mounted on Rocinante, who stood there with one shoulder half out of joint. And so, speaking of the adventure that had just befallen them, they continued along the Puerto Lápice[34] highway; for there, Don Quixote said, they could not fail to find many and varied adventures, this being a much traveled thoroughfare.... ✒

Translated by Samuel Putnam

F PARODY
Compare Don Quixote's quest with the heroic journeys of the knights-errant of romance. What point is Cervantes making about using chivalry as a practical guide to life?

---

33. **Briareus** (brē-ăr′yŏŏs): a mythological giant with 100 arms.

34. **Puerto Lápice** (pwĕr′tô lä′pē-sĕ).

Man of *La Mancha*

A Musical Play by Dale Wasserman
Lyrics by Joe Darion, Music by Mitch Leigh

Brian Stokes Mitchell as Don Quixote in a 2002 Broadway
production of *Man of La Mancha*

ANALYZE VISUALS
What details establish the subject
of the photo as a comic character?

Basing his work partly on Cervantes's life experiences, Wasserman set his play in a Spanish prison, where Cervantes and his fellow prisoners act out scenes from Don Quixote.

Cervantes. I shall impersonate a man . . . enter into my imagination and see him! His name is Alonso Quijana . . . a country squire, no longer young. Bony and hollow-faced . . . eyes that burn with the fire of inner vision. Being retired, he has much time for books. He studies them from morn to night, and often through the night as well. And all he reads oppresses him . . . fills him with indignation at man's murderous ways toward man. He broods . . . and broods . . . and broods—and finally from so much brooding his brains dry up! He lays down the melancholy burden of sanity and conceives the

10 strangest project ever imagined . . . to become a knight-errant and sally forth into the world to right all wrongs. No longer shall he be plain Alonso Quijana . . . but a dauntless knight known as—Don Quixote de La Mancha!!!

(*The* Prisoners *giggle appreciatively as the transformation of* Cervantes *into* Don Quixote *takes place before their eyes. The* Manservant, *who will become* Sancho Panza, *assists with costume elements, props, and so forth.*)

Don Quixote (*singing, a little tongue-in-cheek; an actor aware that he's performing*).

20 Hear me now, oh thou bleak and unbearable world!
Thou art base and debauched as can be;
And a knight with his banners all bravely unfurled
Now hurls down his gauntlet to thee!

I am I, Don Quixote,
The Lord of La Mancha,
My destiny calls and I go;
And the wild winds of fortune will carry me onward,
Oh whithersoever they blow.

Whithersoever they blow,
30 Onward to glory I go! **G**

Sancho.
I'm Sancho! Yes, I'm Sancho!
I'll follow my master till the end.
I'll tell all the world proudly
I'm his squire! I'm his friend!

G PARODY
Reread lines 1–30. What dramatic techniques does the playwright use to introduce Don Quixote and explain his transformation?

Don Quixote.
Hear me, heathens and wizards and serpents of sin!
All your dastardly doings are past;
For a holy endeavor is now to begin,
And virtue shall triumph at last!

40 (*They mount the "horses"—two dancers with wooden frames attached— and ride away. As they ride, the horses dance a spirited flamenco and* Don Quixote *points out to* Sancho *the sights along the way. They sing together.*)

Don Quixote.	**Sancho.**
I am I, Don Quixote,	I'm Sancho! Yes, I'm
The Lord of La Mancha,	Sancho!
My destiny calls and I go;	I'll follow my master till
And the wild winds of	the end.
fortune will carry	I'll tell all the world
me onward,	proudly
Oh whithersoever they	I'm his squire!
blow!	I'm his friend!

Don Quixote and Sancho.
50   Whithersoever they blow,
    Onward to glory we go!

(*At the conclusion of the song, they dismount and* Sancho *leads the "horses" to the well to drink.*)

Don Quixote. Well, Sancho—how dost thou like adventuring?

Sancho. Oh, marvelous, Your Grace. But it's peculiar—to me this great highway to glory looks exactly like the road to El Toboso where you can buy chickens cheap.

Don Quixote. Like beauty, my friend, 'tis all in the eyes of the beholder. Only wait and thou shalt see amazing sights. **H**

60 **Sancho.** What kind?

Don Quixote. There will be knights and nations, warlocks, wizards . . . a **cavalcade** of vast, unending armies!

Sancho. They sound dangerous!

Don Quixote. They *are* dangerous. But one there'll be who leads them . . . and he will be most dangerous of all!

Sancho. Well, who is he? Who?

Don Quixote. The Great Enchanter. Beware him, Sancho . . . for his thoughts are cold and his spirit shriveled. He has eyes like little machines, and where he walks the earth is blighted. But one day I
70 shall meet him face to face . . . and on that day—!

(*He shakes his lance ferociously.*)

H **PARODY**
What character contrast does the **dialogue** in lines 54–59 establish?

cavalcade (kăv'əl-kād') *n.* a procession of people on horseback

Sancho (*sensibly*). Well, I wouldn't get upset, Your Grace. As I always say, have patience and shuffle the cards.

Don Quixote. Do you never run out of proverbs?

Sancho. No, Your Grace. I was born with a bellyful of them. I always say—

Don Quixote (*looking off as the projected shadows of a great windmill's sails cross the stage*). Aah-hah!

Sancho. What is it?

80 **Don Quixote.** How long since we sallied forth?

Sancho. About two minutes?

Don Quixote. So soon shall I engage in brave, unequal combat!

Sancho. Combat? Where?

Don Quixote. Can'st not see? (*pointing*) A monstrous giant of infamous repute!

Sancho (*looking vainly; the "horses" are interested, too*). *What* giant?

Don Quixote.
It is that dark and dreaded ogre
By the name of Matagoger!
You can tell him by the four great arms awhirling on his back!

90 **Sancho.** It's a windmill.

Don Quixote (*shouting*).
Ho! Feckless giant standing there!
Avast! Avaunt! On guard! Beware!

(*He charges off.*)

Sancho. No, no, Your Grace, I swear by my wife's little black mustache, that's not a giant, it's only a— (*Offstage a crash; the horses run for cover. To musical accompaniment the combat continues as* Sancho *dances about, dodging first* Quixote's *helmet which comes flying back onstage, then the butt of his lance, splayed and splintered. The final crash;*

100 *and* Quixote *crawls back into view, his sword a corkscrew. A doleful picture, he comes rolling downstage as* Sancho *hurries to plump himself down and stop him.*) Didn't I tell you? Didn't I say, "Your Grace, that's a windmill"? ❶

Don Quixote (*hollowly*). The work of my enemy.

Sancho. The Enchanter?

Don Quixote. He changed that giant into a windmill at the last moment. He will take any advantage in order to— (*a pause; an illumination*) Sancho, it comes to me!

Sancho. What, Your Grace?

❶ **PARODY**
Identify three examples of **visual humor** in lines 96–102.

110 **Don Quixote.** How he was able to upset me. It is because I have never properly been dubbed a knight.

Sancho. That's no problem. Just tell me how it's done and I'll be glad to take care of this drubbing.

Don Quixote. Dubbing. Thank you, my friend, but it may only be done by another knight.

Sancho (*dismayed*). *That's* a problem. I've never *seen* another knight.

Don Quixote. The lord of some castle would do. Or a king or a duke.

Sancho (*helping* Quixote *to his feet*). Very well. I'll keep an eye out for any kings or dukes as we go.

120 **Don Quixote** (*looking off*). Ahaaa!

Sancho (*apprehensively*). Now what?

Don Quixote. The very place!

Sancho. Where?

Don Quixote. There!

Sancho. If Your Grace would just give me a hint . . . ?

Don Quixote. There in the distance. A castle!

Sancho (*peering vainly*). Castle.

Don Quixote. Rockbound amidst the crags!

Sancho. Crags.

130 **Don Quixote.** And the banners—ah, the brave banners flaunting in the wind!

Sancho. Anything on 'em?

Don Quixote (*shielding his eyes*). I see a cat crouching on a field tawny . . . and beneath it the inscription "Miau"!

Sancho. Oh, that's fine, Your Grace. Maybe this is where you can get yourself drubbed.

Don Quixote. Dubbed. (*excitedly*) Blow thy bugle that a dwarf may mount the battlements and announce our coming!

Sancho (*under the spell, lifts his bugle then hesitates*). But I don't *see*
140 a castle. I do see something . . . maybe it's an inn. ❶

Don Quixote (*sadly*). An inn.

Sancho. We'd better pass it by, Your Grace. Those roadside places are full of rough men and women.

Don Quixote. Come. We shall ride straight to the drawbridge of yon castle, and there thy vision may improve!

(*The lights fade to transition lighting as* Quixote *and* Sancho *drop out of character.*)

❶ **PARODY**
Reread lines 120–140. What causes the misunderstanding between Sancho Panza and Don Quixote?

Comprehension

1. **Recall** What causes Don Quixote to lose his mind?

2. **Clarify** Why does Don Quixote decide to become a knight-errant?

3. **Clarify** Why does Sancho Panza agree to become Don Quixote's squire?

OHIO STANDARDS

READING STANDARD
4.5 Analyze how choice of genre affects theme or topic

Literary Analysis

4. **Identify Hyperbole** The romances Cervantes parodied often used hyperbole, or exaggerated descriptions, to emphasize the perfection of their heroes. Reread the description of Don Quixote's horse in lines 108–126 (page 1050), and give two examples of exaggerated details in this description. What kinds of details does Cervantes choose to exaggerate?

5. **Analyze Character Traits** A **foil** is a character whose traits contrast sharply with those of a main character. List three traits that make Sancho Panza a foil for Don Quixote. How does the contrast between these characters bring out the humor of Don Quixote's behavior?

6. **Interpret Dialogue** Both Cervantes and Wasserman use **diction,** or unique word choices and speech patterns, to make Don Quixote a vivid character. Describe what is distinctive about Don Quixote's manner of speaking in the play and in the novel. In what ways does the hero's diction help the authors communicate the point of their **parodies?**

7. **Draw Conclusions** Recall the main points of your discussion on **dreamers.** Which of the qualities that you associate with dreamers does Don Quixote exhibit?

Comparing Across Genres

Now that you've read both selections about Don Quixote, you are ready to compare the ways in which the authors parody chivalric romances. To get started, complete the following Points of Comparison chart. If a point of comparison is not covered in one of the selections, leave the box blank.

Points of Comparison	In the Novel	In the Play
What motivates the main character?		
How do the main character's traits compare with those of a romance hero?		
What absurd events occur in the story?		
What romance conventions are being mocked?		
Which descriptions, dialogue, or visual images were particularly funny?		

Vocabulary in Context

VOCABULARY PRACTICE

Choose the word that best completes the sentence.

WORD LIST
affable
burnish
cavalcade
enmity
fictitious
hapless
incongruous
resurrect

1. Her quirky courtroom outfit looked _____ next to the conservative suits of those around her.
2. This _____ child seems always to have bad luck.
3. That noise was loud enough to _____ the dead!
4. He was distressed and puzzled by the _____ of his rival.
5. Although they seem real, the characters in her story are _____.
6. The _____ of mounted police led the parade.
7. She left orders to _____ the trophies until they gleamed.
8. People easily warm up to your _____ personality.

VOCABULARY IN WRITING

Using three or more vocabulary words, describe the character of Don Quixote to someone who knows nothing about him. Here is how you might begin.

> **EXAMPLE SENTENCE**
>
> The **hapless** Don Quixote has no more success at adventure than he had at managing his estate.

VOCABULARY STRATEGY: SIMILES AND METAPHORS

A **simile** is a figure of speech in which *like, as,* or *as if* signals that a comparison is being made. A **metaphor** is a comparison in which one thing is talked about as if it were another. The comparison is implied; there are no signal words to show that it is not literal. Similes and metaphors can provide clues to the meanings of unfamiliar words.

PRACTICE Indicate whether each sentence contains a simile or a metaphor. Ask yourself what two things are being compared. Then ask what the comparison suggests about the meaning of the boldfaced word.

1. He was **hapless** and confused, like a boy who had lost his mother in a store.
2. The **enmity** of his former friend was a dark cloud over his happiness.
3. The comment was as **incongruous** as a pink tutu on a hippo.
4. The story was **fictitious,** a richly embroidered veil for the truth.
5. The **cavalcade** of invaders stretched to the horizon like a deadly carpet.

OHIO STANDARDS

VOCABULARY STANDARD
1.3 Infer the literal and figurative meanings of words

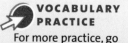

VOCABULARY PRACTICE
For more practice, go to the **Vocabulary Center** at **ClassZone.com.**

Writing for Assessment

1. READ THE PROMPT

In writing-assessment tests, you will often be asked to **compare and contrast** two works of literature that treat a similar subject. You are now going to practice writing an essay that requires this type of focus.

PROMPT

Both Cervantes and Wasserman poke fun at the form of medieval romances and at the chivalric code of behavior. Compare and contrast the writers' parodies of romances. Do they mock the same ideas, customs, and behaviors? In what ways do their parodies differ? Support your points with evidence from the texts.

◀ **STRATEGIES IN ACTION**

*1. I need to consider how each writer ridicules the style and content of **chivalric romances.***

*2. I need to write an essay that **compares and contrasts** two parodies.*

*3. I need to support my ideas with **details and quotations** from each work.*

2. PLAN YOUR WRITING

- Review the **Points of Comparison** chart you created on page 1061.
- Using your chart, find examples to use as evidence for the points you will develop in your essay. If necessary, review the selections to identify more examples.
- Create an outline to organize your main points.

3. DRAFT YOUR RESPONSE

Introduction Introduce the topic—making fun of chivalric romances—and then explain that you will discuss how the two works accomplish this goal.

Organization Use the topics in your **Points of Comparison** chart as a guide to the key points of your comparison. In one paragraph, for example, you might point out how the authors choose similar targets for their humor. In another, you might focus on the different comic techniques the authors use.

Conclusion Wrap up your essay with a restatement of your main idea and a brief summary of your main points.

Revision Check to make sure that your essay is not repetitive or bland. Add interest to your writing by replacing dull language with vivid and fresh nouns, adjectives, and verbs.

Writing Workshop

Persuasive Essay

Do you want to help protect endangered animals, work with senior citizens, or speak out for the rights of children? Just about everyone values something enough to stand up and fight for it. Like the writers in this unit, you can use your words to influence readers and stir them to action. The **Writer's Road Map** will get you started.

WRITER'S ROAD MAP

Persuasive Essay

WRITING PROMPT 1

Writing from the Real World The literature in this unit deals with the universal ideals of honor, loyalty, and service to others. Think about how these ideals are connected to today's issues. Choose an issue you feel strongly about, and write an essay to persuade your readers to agree with you.

Issues to Consider
- helping the homeless
- voting
- serving your country
- stopping others from cheating

WRITING PROMPT 2

Writing from Literature Choose one of the great ideals you encountered in this unit. Write a persuasive essay to encourage others to support the ideal. Refer to the literature in your essay, but be sure you make a connection to an issue in today's world.

Literature to Consider
- *Antigone* (Is the government always right?)
- *Le Morte d'Arthur* (What does loyalty mean?)
- *Don Quixote* (Are ideals worth fighting for?)

 WRITING TOOLS
For prewriting, revision, and editing tools, visit the **Writing Center** at **ClassZone.com.**

KEY TRAITS

1. IDEAS
- Presents a **thesis statement** taking a position on a clearly identified issue
- Uses **relevant and convincing evidence** to support the position
- Anticipates and answers **opposing arguments and counterclaims**

2. ORGANIZATION
- **Introduces** the issue in a memorable and thoughtful way
- Uses **transitional words and phrases** to connect ideas
- Concludes with a **summary,** a **call to action,** or both

3. VOICE
- Uses a **tone** that is suited to the audience and purpose
- Reflects a **commitment** to the writer's own ideas

4. WORD CHOICE
- Uses **persuasive language** effectively

5. SENTENCE FLUENCY
- Varies **sentence beginnings** for interest and flow

6. CONVENTIONS
- Employs **correct grammar and usage**

Part 1: Analyze a Student Model

Brianna S. Willoughby
Sacred Heart Academy

Help Wipe Out Illiteracy

Imagine that you are trying to hold down a job and raise a family—and that you can't read this sentence. How would you understand the directions on a medicine bottle, the warning on a road sign, or the information asked for on a job application? Shockingly, this imaginary situation is all too real: more than 44 million adult Americans cannot read or write at the first-grade level. This lack of basic skills drastically limits what they can accomplish in life and contribute to society. Illiteracy is everyone's problem, and everyone needs to take a stand to wipe it out.

According to a study by the National Assessment of Educational Progress, 73 percent of 21- to 25-year-olds couldn't understand a typical newspaper story. Think about how this lack of reading skills affects their day-to-day lives. The jobs they qualify for are almost always low-paying service positions that give them no training, skills, or chance to advance. The U.S. Department of Education reports that illiterate adults earn an average of 42 percent less than high school graduates. Some people assume that this situation affects only the illiterate adults themselves. In fact, though, the children of illiterate parents are twice as likely to be illiterate as are children whose parents can read. Illiteracy also has an enormous economic impact on our entire society. At least half of the unemployed are illiterate, and their public assistance costs taxpayers about $5 billion a year.

KEY TRAITS IN ACTION

Introduces the issue with a powerful example that appeals to the reader's emotions.

Thesis statement presents a clear position on illiteracy and uses **persuasive language** (*everyone's problem, needs, take a stand, wipe it out*).

Varies **sentence beginnings** to provide interest. Includes **relevant and convincing evidence** to support statements.

Nevertheless, as depressing as these statistics are, there is hope. You and I and other citizens are that hope. I believe that each of us

25 can, and must, help turn this situation around. Many opportunities to volunteer exist in our community. For example, the library offers individual tutoring to adults who want to improve their reading ability. Anyone over the age of 14 can volunteer to be a tutor. Volunteers receive intensive training and ongoing support. They also experience

30 the satisfaction of seeing someone gain confidence as well as essential life skills. Tutoring takes little time, but it has lasting payoffs. Statistics collected by the Literacy Volunteers of America show that only 35 to 45 hours of tutoring can improve reading scores a full grade level. I've been a tutor and have seen the results myself.

35 Some people might object to volunteer tutoring programs because tutors are inexperienced and may not even be particularly good readers themselves. However, any successful high school student is knowledgeable enough to provide accurate basic information—or to get it from the tutoring staff. In addition, tutors who have had trouble

40 learning to read themselves can offer helpful understanding and encouragement to the people they tutor.

It's easy for those of us who have no trouble reading to take this vital skill for granted. We need to confront the terrible problem of illiteracy, though, and not turn away. Volunteer to do your part today.

Transitional word clarifies connection between ideas.

Straightforward, serious **tone** shows the writer's **commitment** to ideas and awareness of the audience.

Anticipates **opposing arguments and counterclaims** and answers them.

Summary restates the issue, appeals to the reader's ethical beliefs, and makes a clear **call to action.**

2

Part 2: Apply the Writing Process

WRITING STANDARD
5.4 Determine a purpose and audience

PREWRITING

| What Should I Do? | What Does It Look Like? |

What Should I Do?

1. Analyze the prompt.
Choose a prompt on page 1064 that interests you. Underline words that state the type of issue you should focus on. Circle words that describe the audience, the purpose, and the format of your writing.

What Does It Look Like?

► **WRITING PROMPT** The literature in this unit deals with the universal ideals of <u>honor, loyalty, and service to others.</u> Think about how these ideals are connected to <u>today's issues.</u> Choose <u>an issue you feel strongly about,</u> and write an (essay) to (persuade) your readers to agree with you.

I need to come up with an issue I really care about. The audience isn't stated, so I can assume it's my classmates and my teacher.

2. List issues that really matter to you.
Jot down situations that make you want to take action. Include some comments or questions about each issue.

TIP Be sure that the issue you choose has two sides to some aspect of it. Remember, you need to convince people who disagree with you, not those who have similar views.

►

What I Care About	Comments/Questions
Illiteracy	Nobody supports illiteracy, but people should do more about it.
Lying	One-sided issue? Does anyone support lying?
World peace	Too vague

3. Draft a thesis statement to guide you.
Think carefully about the main point you want to make in your essay. Then state that idea clearly in a sentence or two.

► *A huge number of American adults cannot read or write at the first-grade level. Illiteracy is everyone's problem, and everyone needs to help wipe it out.*

4. Gather background information and evidence.
Search the Internet and talk to experts to find facts and statistics related to your position. Think about what your readers already know and what arguments and reasons will convince them.

►

Idea	Support
Illiteracy is a serious problem.	It affects more than 44 million adults and their families.
Literacy tutoring works.	Reading level improves a grade level after 35 to 45 hours of tutoring.

What Should I Do?	What Does It Look Like?

1. Organize your arguments.

Two ways to organize your arguments are shown. Do you want to present each opposing argument and answer it immediately (Pattern 1) or list all the opposing arguments and then address them as a whole (Pattern 2)?

TIP Think about what claims opponents might make and how you should answer them. For example, nobody favors illiteracy, but some people may disagree about how serious the problem is and what should be done about it.

PATTERN 1

A. Opposing argument: Illiteracy is a limited problem—it affects only the illiterate.

B. My argument: It puts children at risk and costs society billions.

C. Opposing argument: Tutoring doesn't help because volunteers may lack experience.

D. My argument: Tutors have training and support.

PATTERN 2

A. Opposing arguments

1. Illiteracy affects only the illiterate.

2. Tutoring doesn't help because volunteers may lack experience.

B. My arguments

1. It puts children at risk for illiteracy and costs society billions.

2. Tutors have training and support.

2. Make your language persuasive.

Keep in mind the connotations of the words you choose. Using words with strong positive or negative connotations shows your commitment to your ideas and stirs your reader's emotions.

See page 574: Persuasive Techniques

Strongly negative connotations

This lack of basic skills drastically limits what people can accomplish.

Strongly positive connotations

Volunteers experience the satisfaction of seeing someone gain confidence as well as essential life skills.

3. Support your statements with solid evidence.

You need to give your readers facts, statistics, and logical reasons to convince them to agree with your position. Be sure to explain exactly how each piece of evidence backs up your ideas.

Tutoring takes little time, but it has lasting payoffs. ⎤— Key point

Statistics collected by the Literacy Volunteers of America show that only 35 to 45 hours of tutoring can improve reading scores a full grade level. I've been a tutor and have seen the results myself. ⎤— Support

REVISING AND EDITING

What Should I Do?	*What Does It Look Like?*

1. Correct errors in logic.
- Read your essay aloud and (circle) statements that don't make sense.
- Revise these statements to be logical and clear.

See page 1070: Avoid Errors in Logic

▶ Illiteracy is important because ~~it is a serious problem,~~ it has an enormous economic impact on our entire society.

2. Energize your language.
- <u>Underline</u> language that is vague or general.
- Replace these words with specific words that express your strong feelings about the topic. This writer included a **testimonial:** "I've been a tutor and have seen the results myself." For more examples of testimonials and other persuasive techniques, see page 574.

▶ Volunteers <u>~~have help~~</u>∧ receive intensive training and ongoing support.

       experience
They ~~get~~∧ the satisfaction of seeing someone ~~change,~~∧ gain confidence as well as essential life skills. I've been a tutor and have seen the results myself.

3. Answer opposing arguments completely.
- Ask a peer reader to draw a box around statements that need more explanation.
- Add details and reasons that help you fully defeat opposing arguments.

See page 1070: Ask a Peer Reader

▶ Some people assume that this situation affects only the illiterate adult themselves. In fact, though, ~~it does,~~∧ the children of illiterate parents are twice as likely to be illiterate as are children whose parents can read. Illiteracy also has an enormous economic impact on our entire society. At least half of the unemployed are illiterate, and their public assistance costs taxpayers about #5 billion a year.

4. Strengthen your conclusion.
- [Bracket] your conclusion. Ask yourself: If I heard or read this message somewhere, would it be enough to convince me?
- Fine-tune your conclusion. Does it clearly summarize your points? If you make a call to action, is it a strong one?

▶   *take this vital skill for granted.*
[It's easy for those of us who have no trouble reading to ~~not care.~~ We need to confront the terrible problem of illiteracy, though, and not turn away.]∧ Volunteer to do your part today.

Apply the Rubric

A strong persuasive essay . . .

- ☑ begins by identifying the issue and the writer's position in a thesis statement
- ☑ supports the position with sound reasons and solid facts or statistics
- ☑ acknowledges opposing arguments and counterclaims and answers them thoroughly
- ☑ makes the organization clear by using transitions effectively
- ☑ uses persuasive language
- ☑ varies sentence beginnings
- ☑ has a tone that makes sense for the audience and purpose
- ☑ shows the writer's commitment to his or her ideas
- ☑ finishes with a concise summary, a rousing call to action, or both

Ask a Peer Reader

- How would you restate my position on this issue in your own words?
- Which statements could use more details or supporting evidence?
- Which of my arguments is the strongest? Which is the weakest? Why?

Avoid Errors in Logic

Circular reasoning: supporting a statement by simply repeating it in other words ("People are illiterate because they can't read.")

Overgeneralization: making a statement that is too broad or general to be proved ("Everybody wants to become a literacy tutor.")

Either/or fallacy: a statement that suggests that there are only two possible ways to view a situation or only two options to choose from ("If you don't become a volunteer tutor, illiteracy will double.")

See page 676 for more types of logical fallacies.

Check Your Grammar

The subject and verb of a sentence must agree in number.

> This lack of basic skills drastically limit͜s what they can accomplish. (singular subject, singular verb)

See page R65: Subject-Verb Agreement

Writing Online

PUBLISHING OPTIONS
For publishing options, visit the **Writing Center** at ClassZone.com.

ASSESSMENT PREPARATION
For writing and grammar assessment practice, go to the **Assessment Center** at ClassZone.com.

COMMUNICATION STANDARD
9.10 Deliver persuasive presentations

Debating an Issue

Further explore both sides of your issue by holding a debate.

Planning the Debate

1. **Find someone to debate with you.** Ask one or more classmates or adults to participate. Explain that the purpose of the debate is to get people to think about an important issue, not to bully anyone or to make a debater look foolish.

2. **State the issue you will debate as a resolution.** Here is an example: *Students should volunteer to work as literacy tutors.*

3. **Decide who will argue for, and who against, the resolution.** One debater or team will take the affirmative position; the other will take the negative position.

   TIP As a challenge, consider arguing a different position than you took in your essay.

4. **Gather support.** Plan the statements you will make in defending your position and the answers you will give to possible arguments from the opposition.

5. **Find someone to act as a moderator.** Ask for a volunteer or appoint someone to introduce the debate resolution and the participants and to keep the debate running smoothly.

Holding the Debate

1. **Make your voice and body language work for you.** Speak clearly and confidently. Maintain eye contact with the audience, and use facial expressions and gestures for emphasis.

2. **Vary the pace and volume of your delivery.** Slowing down and raising your voice slightly can help you stress important points. After making a particularly powerful statement, pause briefly to let your words sink into audience members' minds.

3. **State your position strongly and calmly.** Use the information you included in your essay, but talk to your audience rather than reading to them.

   TIP If you find yourself becoming too emotional, take a deep breath and focus on the issues.

4. **Find out how you did.** Use a questionnaire, a whole-class discussion, or individual interviews to find out which of your arguments were successful and which need refining.

   See page R79: Evaluate a Team in a Debate

Reading Comprehension

DIRECTIONS *Read these selections and answer the questions that follow.*

In this excerpt from Scene 2, Creon confronts Antigone for disobeying his proclamation.

from Antigone
Sophocles

Creon (*slowly, dangerously*). And you, Antigone,
You with your head hanging—do you confess this thing?

Antigone. I do. I deny nothing.

Creon (*to* Sentry).   You may go.

(*Exit* Sentry.)

(*to* Antigone) Tell me, tell me briefly:
Had you heard my proclamation touching this matter?

55 **Antigone.** It was public. Could I help hearing it?

Creon. And yet you dared defy the law.

Antigone.   I dared.
It was not God's proclamation. That final Justice
That rules the world below makes no such laws.

Your edict, King, was strong,
60 But all your strength is weakness itself against
The immortal unrecorded laws of God.
They are not merely now: they were, and shall be,
Operative forever, beyond man utterly.

I knew I must die, even without your decree:
65 I am only mortal. And if I must die
Now, before it is my time to die,
Surely this is no hardship: can anyone
Living, as I live, with evil all about me,
Think Death less than a friend? This death of mine
70 Is of no importance; but if I had left my brother
Lying in death unburied, I should have suffered.
Now I do not.
                    You smile at me. Ah Creon,
Think me a fool, if you like; but it may well be
That a fool convicts me of folly.

75 **Choragus.** Like father, like daughter: both headstrong, deaf to reason!
She has never learned to yield.

Creon.   She has much to learn.
The inflexible heart breaks first, the toughest iron
Cracks first, and the wildest horses bend their necks
At the pull of the smallest curb.
                              Pride? In a slave?
80 This girl is guilty of a double insolence,
Breaking the given laws and boasting of it.
Who is the man here,
She or I, if this crime goes unpunished?
Sister's child, or more than sister's child,
85 Or closer yet in blood—she and her sister
Win bitter death for this!
              (*to servants*) Go, some of you,
Arrest Ismene. I accuse her equally.
Bring her: you will find her sniffling in the house there.
Her mind's a traitor: crimes kept in the dark
90 Cry for light, and the guardian brain shudders;
But how much worse than this
Is brazen boasting of barefaced anarchy!

Antigone. Creon, what more do you want than my death?

Creon.   Nothing.
That gives me everything.

Antigone.   Then I beg you: kill me.
95 This talking is a great weariness: your words
Are distasteful to me, and I am sure that mine
Seem so to you. And yet they should not seem so:
I should have praise and honor for what I have done.
All these men here would praise me
100 Were their lips not frozen shut with fear of you.
(*bitterly*) Ah the good fortune of kings,
Licensed to say and do whatever they please!

Creon. You are alone here in that opinion.

Antigone. No, they are with me. But they keep their tongues in leash.

105 **Creon.** Maybe. But you are guilty, and they are not.

Antigone. There is no guilt in reverence for the dead.

GO ON ▶

from Le Morte d' Arthur

Sir Thomas Malory

"Good knight," said Sir Launcelot, "it is known to me that you have put to shame many of the knights of the Round Table. Pray allow your prisoner, who I see is wounded, to recover, while I vindicate the honor of the knights whom you have defeated."

"I defy you, and all your fellowship of the Round Table," Sir Tarquine replied.

"You boast!" said Sir Launcelot.

At the first charge the backs of the horses were broken and both knights stunned. But they soon recovered and set to with their swords, and both struck so lustily that neither shield nor armor could resist, and within two hours they
10 were cutting each other's flesh, from which the blood flowed liberally. Finally they paused for a moment, resting on their shields.

"Worthy knight," said Sir Tarquine, "pray hold your hand for a while and, if you will, answer my question."

"Sir, speak on."

"You are the most powerful knight I have fought yet, but I fear you may be the one whom in the whole world I most hate. If you are not, for the love of you I will release all my prisoners and swear eternal friendship."

"What is the name of the knight you hate above all others?"

"Sir Launcelot du Lake; for it was he who slew my brother, Sir Carados of the
20 Dolorous Tower, and it is because of him that I have killed a hundred knights and maimed as many more, apart from the sixty-four I still hold prisoner. And so, if you are Sir Launcelot, speak up, for we must then fight to the death."

"Sir, I see now that I might go in peace and good fellowship or otherwise fight to the death; but being the knight I am, I must tell you: I am Sir Launcelot du Lake, son of King Ban of Benwick, of Arthur's court, and a knight of the Round Table. So defend yourself!"

"Ah! this is most welcome."

Now the two knights hurled themselves at each other like two wild bulls; swords and shields clashed together, and often their swords drove into the
30 flesh. Then sometimes one, sometimes the other, would stagger and fall, only to recover immediately and resume the contest. At last, however, Sir Tarquine grew faint and unwittingly lowered his shield. Sir Launcelot was swift to follow up his advantage and, dragging the other down to his knees, unlaced his helmet and beheaded him.

Comprehension

DIRECTIONS *Answer these questions about the excerpt from* Antigone.

1. Creon is angry with Antigone because she
   A. spoke rudely to him in public
   B. buried her brother and boasted about it
   C. tried to seize his throne and kill him
   D. lied to protect herself and her sister

2. In which of the following statements does Antigone most clearly express her defiance?
   A. "I do. I deny nothing." (line 52)
   B. "Could I help hearing it?" (line 55)
   C. "Creon, what more do you want than my death?" (line 93)
   D. "I should have praise and honor for what I have done." (line 98)

3. The function of the choragus in lines 75–76 is to
   A. foreshadow the action
   B. comment on the characters
   C. provide a musical backdrop
   D. influence Creon

4. Which quality of a tragic hero does Antigone exhibit in the face of Creon's anger?
   A. descent from royal lineage
   B. respect for political authority
   C. ability to control emotions
   D. willingness to accept fate

5. According to Antigone in lines 65–72, which experience would cause her the most suffering?
   A. being condemned to death by Creon
   B. leaving her brother unburied
   C. dying while she is still young
   D. saving her sister's life

DIRECTIONS *Answer these questions about the excerpt from* Le Morte d'Arthur.

6. Which element of medieval romance is reflected in this battle scene?
   A. a supernatural occurrence
   B. a hidden identity
   C. an exotic setting
   D. a romantic quest

7. You can identify Launcelot as a hero in a medieval romance because he fights to
   A. defend the honor of his fellow knights
   B. establish his reputation as a warrior
   C. exhibit his magical powers in battle
   D. bring public shame upon Tarquine

DIRECTIONS *Answer this question about both excerpts.*

8. Which trait motivates Antigone and Launcelot in their heroic endeavors?
   A. personal loyalty
   B. desire for adventure
   C. reverence for God
   D. excessive ambition

SHORT ANSWER *Write three or four sentences to answer this question.*

9. Identify two ways in which Tarquine and Launcelot practice the code of chivalry.

EXTENDED RESPONSE *Write two or three paragraphs to answer this question.*

10. What do the actions of Antigone and Creon reveal about their individual views of loyalty? Support your answer with details from the excerpt.

 GO ON

Vocabulary

DIRECTIONS *Use the underlined etymology clues to help you choose the correct word that is missing from each of the following sentences.*

1. Carried out in broad daylight, the robbery was a (<u>Middle English, from Old English *bræsen,* "made of brass"</u>) act.

   A. public

   B. strong

   C. bitter

   D. brazen

2. The opposing attorneys were quick to (<u>Middle English, from Old French *desfier,* from Vulgar Latin *disfidare,* "absence of" + "faithful"</u>) each other's arguments.

   A. vindicate

   B. defy

   C. resist

   D. defend

3. The carpenter was (<u>Middle English *stonen,* Old French *estoner,* from Latin *tonare,* "to thunder"</u>) when the beam hit his head.

   A. stunned

   B. maimed

   C. beheaded

   D. struck

DIRECTIONS *Use context clues and your knowledge of connotation to answer the following questions.*

4. The word *sniffling* in line 88 of *Antigone* has a connotation of

   A. weakness

   B. secretiveness

   C. meanness

   D. desperation

5. The word *barefaced* in line 92 of *Antigone* has a connotation of

   A. shamelessness

   B. honesty

   C. rareness

   D. courtesy

6. The word *hurled* in line 28 of *Le Morte d'Arthur* has a connotation of

   A. hesitation

   B. forcefulness

   C. clumsiness

   D. speed

Writing & Grammar

DIRECTIONS *Read the passage and answer the questions that follow.*

> (1) Medieval nobles were much more powerful than peasants under the feudal system. (2) Still, medieval nobles and peasants endured similarly harsh living conditions. (3) Medieval castles were built for defense, not comfort. (4) So, though a lord's castle might be large, <u>it was rarely inviting</u>. (5) It was built of thick stone and had few windows. (6) It had damp, dark, and cold rooms. (7) It had bedrooms with lice-infested mattresses.

1. Choose the best way to vary the beginnings of sentences 1–3.

  A. Medieval nobles and peasants held different levels of power under the feudal system. Nobles and peasants endured similarly harsh living conditions, though. Castles were built for defense, not comfort.

  B. Under the feudal system, medieval nobles were much more powerful than peasants. Still, when it came to daily life, the two endured similarly harsh conditions. Castles were built for defense, not comfort.

  C. In medieval times, nobles held much more power than peasants did. In this time, nobles and peasants nonetheless endured similarly harsh conditions. Defense, not comfort, is what medieval castles were built for.

  D. Under the feudal system, medieval nobles were much more powerful than peasants. Still, under the feudal system, nobles and peasants endured similarly harsh conditions. Castles were built for defense, not comfort.

2. Choose the correct way to add emphasis by inverting the underlined portion of sentence 4.

  A. rarely was it inviting

  B. inviting it was, rarely

  C. it was inviting rarely

  D. it rarely was inviting

3. Choose the best way to vary the beginnings of sentences 5–7.

  A. The castle was built of thick stone with few windows. The rooms were damp, dark, and cold. The mattresses in the bedrooms were lice infested.

  B. The castle had thick stone walls and few windows. The rooms were damp, dark, and cold. Lice-infested mattresses were in the bedrooms.

  C. The castle had thick stone walls with few windows. In the rooms, it was damp, dark, and cold. In the bedrooms were lice-infested mattresses.

  D. Built of thick stone, it had few windows. Rooms were damp, dark, and cold. In the bedrooms, the mattresses were lice infested.

STOP

Ideas for Independent Reading

What ideas about honor did you gain from reading Greek drama and medieval romances? Expand on your thoughts with these related readings.

What is your ultimate loyalty?

Antigone
by Jean Anouilh

French playwright Anouilh wrote his version of *Antigone* when the Nazis occupied France during World War II. The play is often interpreted as an allegory of the French Resistance. Read to see how it differs from the original.

Jane Eyre
by Charlotte Bronte

Poor, plain, and honest Jane Eyre is a governess. Her employer, Mr. Rochester, is attracted by her directness, and the two fall in love. On the day of their wedding, Jane learns a secret that forces her to make a hard choice.

Grey Is the Color of Hope
by Irina Ratushinskaya

This memoir is by a deeply religious Russian poet who spent four years as a political prisoner in a Soviet labor camp. She and other female prisoners refused to submit to rules that would strip them of their humanity.

Could you be a knight?

The Once and Future King
by T. H. White

White's retelling of Malory's *Le Morte d'Arthur* is a classic of English literature. Written at the outbreak of World War II, it entertains while commenting on political ideas of the time. King Arthur rejects the philosophy that "might makes right" and conceives the Round Table to use might *for* right.

Perceval: The Story of the Grail
by Chrétien de Troyes

This 12th-century French romance in verse introduced the legend of the Holy Grail. Perceval is a naïve boy who lives in the forest with his mother. Awestruck after seeing a knight for the first time, he vows to become one. Eventually he joins the Round Table.

Ramón Lull's Book of Knighthood and Chivalry
by Ramón Lull

This "training manual for squires" was written by a 13th-century Spanish knight who later became a theologian. Among the advice it offers: "The knight must possess such riches as to support his office, lest he be forced to robbery."

Why do we admire dreamers?

Encounters with the Archdruid
by John McPhee

The author describes conversations between David Brower, one of America's most uncompromising conservationists, and three of his opponents—a developer, a mining engineer, and a dam builder.

Mountains Beyond Mountains
by Tracy Kidder

Kidder profiles Dr. Paul Farmer, a Harvard-trained physician and anthropologist whose mission is to fight disease among the world's poor. Much of Farmer's work was done in rural Haiti, battling drug-resistant tuberculosis.

They All Laughed . . .
by Ira Flatow

This book is subtitled "From Light Bulbs to Lasers: The Fascinating Stories Behind the Great Inventions That Have Changed Our Lives." Many of these discoveries were ridiculed when first publicized.

Shakespearean Drama

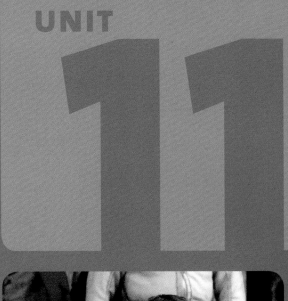

THE TRAGEDY OF JULIUS CAESAR

- In Drama
- In Media

When does ambition lead to TRAGEDY?

History, politics, and literature are filled with stories of people who sought power or fame at any cost. But success can ultimately have a dark side, as many of those individuals learned. Some were stripped of the power they found, while others found that their success came at an unexpected cost. Why do you think so many of these stories end in **tragedy?**

ACTIVITY As a class, brainstorm examples of individuals whose ambition led to tragedy. These can be characters from literature or real people from business, politics, or history. Analyze what happened in each case, and draw conclusions about what led to each person's downfall.

OHIO STANDARDS

Preview Unit Goals

LITERARY ANALYSIS
- Identify characteristics of Shakespearean drama
- Identify characteristics of Shakespearean tragedy, including tragic hero and tragic flaw
- Identify and analyze soliloquy and aside
- Identify and analyze dramatic irony and rhetorical devices
- Identify and analyze blank verse

READING
- Use strategies for reading Shakespearean language and drama
- Draw conclusions
- Analyze a theater review

WRITING AND GRAMMAR
- Compare a film and a play
- Add descriptive details by using adjective clauses

SPEAKING, LISTENING, AND VIEWING
- Identify, analyze, and evaluate mise en scène
- Compare your response to a critical review
- Create a shooting script
- Deliver a dramatic reading

ACADEMIC VOCABULARY
- Shakespearean tragedy
- soliloquy
- aside
- dramatic irony
- blank verse
- mise en scène

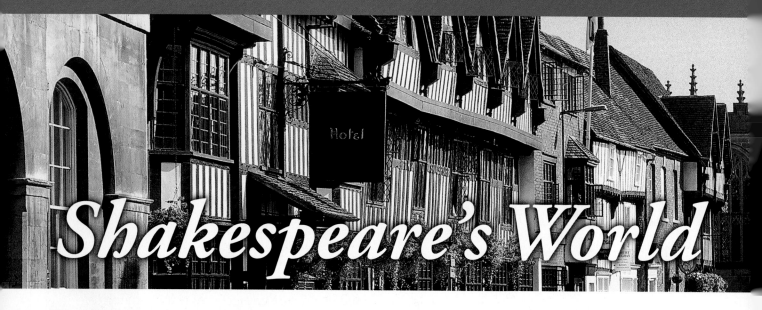

Shakespeare's World

Shakespeare's England

Cultural Blossoming
William Shakespeare is considered by many to be the world's greatest playwright. Shakespeare lived in England during the Renaissance, the blossoming of European learning that followed the Middle Ages. During the Middle Ages, the European world view had focused on God

**William Shakespeare
1564–1616**

and the afterlife, but with the Renaissance came a renewal of interest in individual human achievement. This new emphasis spurred human beings to expand their horizons in all sorts of ways—scientifically, geographically, commercially, philosophically, artistically. In 1564, when Shakespeare was born, England had already embraced the spirit of Renaissance creativity. In the decades that followed, Shakespeare himself would help carry the Renaissance to even greater heights.

Queen of the Arts Six years before Shakespeare was born, Elizabeth I became queen of England, and the period of her reign, from 1558 to 1603, is known as the Elizabethan Age. Elizabeth I supported all the arts—literature, painting,

sculpture, music, and theater. She was also a frugal and clever leader who, despite frequent political in-fighting and religious turmoil, managed to steer England down a middle road to stability and prosperity.

During Elizabeth's reign, London, the capital of the nation, flourished as a great commercial center, the hub of England's growing overseas empire. London was also the hub of the artistic efforts that Elizabeth championed, and it attracted talented and ambitious individuals from all over the land.

**Queen Elizabeth I
1533–1603**

Because a true Renaissance figure was supposed to excel in many fields, Elizabeth's courtiers often dabbled in writing. In fact, some of them, like Sir Walter Raleigh, produced memorable poetry that is still being read today. Topping the list of the era's fine literature, however, was its verse drama, plays in which the dialogue consists mostly or entirely of poetry. Several outstanding dramatists appeared, none more notable than William Shakespeare; and by the end of the 16th century, London had more theaters than any other city in Europe.

Shakespeare's Theater

The World's a Stage From the early 1590s, Shakespeare was affiliated with a theater company known as the Lord Chamberlain's Men. Its chief sponsors were a father and son who served consecutively as England's Lord Chamberlain, an influential member of Elizabeth's court. Shakespeare not only wrote the company's plays but also was a company shareholder, or part owner, and even performed occasionally as an actor. In 1599, with the other company shareholders, he became part owner of the Globe Theatre, the new London home of the Lord Chamberlain's Men. Four years later, when Queen Elizabeth died, the company at the Globe acquired a new sponsor, King James I, and became known as the King's Men.

Located on the south bank of the Thames (tĕmz) River, just outside of central London, the Globe Theatre was a three-story wooden building that held up to 3,000 theatergoers. In the center was an open-air courtyard with a platform stage on which the plays were performed. Those paying the lowest admission charges, known as groundlings, stood in the pit, the part of the courtyard right near the stage. Wealthier theatergoers sat in the building's interior galleries, which surrounded all sides of the courtyard except for the part of the building directly behind the stage.

Insight and Excitement Judging from the success of Shakespeare's company, all classes of theatergoers seem to have enjoyed his plays. That's probably because they included something for everyone—powerful speeches, fancy sword fights, humor, eerie supernatural events, and insightful observations about human nature. Such a mixture was important to Shakespeare. As a playwright, he wanted to explore human behavior, to understand how different people deal with universal problems. Yet he was also part of a commercial venture, writing for an audience that wanted, first and foremost, to be entertained. He made sure that his plays included enough action and excitement to keep just about anyone interested. The groundlings were particularly loud in their appreciation, cheering the heroes, yelling insults at the villains, and laughing loudly at humorous characters and jokes. In fact, by the standards of today's theater, Elizabethan performances were rather rowdy events.

Since the Globe had no artificial lighting or heat, performances were given in daylight in warmer weather. The stage also had no scenery; usually, lines of dialogue told the audience where a scene was taking place.

Despite the lack of scenery, productions were by no means drab. Costumes could be quite ornate, and props such as swords, shields, and swirling banners added to the colorful display. From behind the stage came sound effects—the chiming of a clock, for instance, or the sound of a cannon. The stage had no curtain. Instead, performers usually walked on and off in full view of the audience.

THE GLOBE THEATRE

The Globe was rebuilt in 1996.

1 raised platform stage **3** inner balconies

2 the pit **4** doors for actors' entrances

Shakespeare's Life

Mystery Man Though the works of William Shakespeare have probably been seen or read by more people worldwide than those of any other author, the man himself remains something of a mystery. This is particularly true of his early life, before he became a famous playwright. Literary biographies were uncommon in the Elizabethan period, and Shakespeare did not belong to a prominent family. What we know of his early life and family background comes from scanty documentary evidence—church records and property deeds, for example.

A Small-Town Boy According to those records, an infant named William Shakespeare was baptized in April 1564 in the local church in Stratford-upon-Avon, a bustling town on the River Avon, northwest of London. His father was a tanner and glove-maker and also served as a local politician. It is likely that Shakespeare attended Stratford's grammar school, where he would have studied Latin, the language of ancient Rome; classical literature written in Latin; and translations from ancient Greek. It is here that he would have been introduced to the writings of the ancient Greek biographer Plutarch, whose *Parallel Lives* provides the historical basis for the events in *Julius Caesar.*

Shakespeare's birthplace at Stratford-upon-Avon

Off to London Records further tell us that in 1582 William Shakespeare married one Anne Hathaway, probably the daughter of a well-to-do Stratford farm family, and that over the next three years the couple had three children, an older daughter named Susanna and twins named Hamnet (a male) and Judith. After the birth of the twins in 1585, nothing is known about Shakespeare for the next several years, after which he turns up again, living in London and working as an actor and a playwright. Clearly he was recognized as a promising talent, for he became a shareholder in the prestigious acting company the Lord Chamberlain's Men, which had strong ties to Elizabeth's court. Shakespeare's plays helped make the company even more successful, and he was soon allowed—probably even encouraged—to give up acting in order to focus on his writing.

The Years of Fame By 1599, the year in which *Julius Caesar* was first produced, Shakespeare is known to have written 18 of his 38 plays, including early pieces such as his history *Richard III,* his comedy *The Taming of the Shrew,* and his tragedy *Romeo and Juliet.* He was also a rich man. As a shareholder in the Lord Chamberlain's Men, he was now one of the owners of the company's new home, the Globe Theatre. He also made money by having his plays produced and by publishing some of his nondramatic poetry, although his sonnets did not appear in print until 1609.

The Final Years About a year before the sonnets appeared, Shakespeare began curtailing his theater activities. He seems to have spent less time in London and more back in Stratford. He wrote no plays after 1613, when he probably moved back to Stratford permanently. No ones knows for sure just when, where, or how he died, but his gravestone in Stratford's Holy Trinity Church lists the date of his death as April 23, 1616.

A scene from Franco Zeffirelli's 1990 film *Hamlet*

A scene from the film *O*, Tim Blake Nelson's 2001 update of *Othello*

Shakespeare's Legacy

The Test of Time Some of the most familiar lines in the English language come from the plays of Shakespeare: "Friends, Romans, countrymen, lend me your ears" *(Julius Caesar),* "O Romeo, Romeo! wherefore art thou Romeo?" *(Romeo and Juliet),* "To be or not to be" *(Hamlet).* Why do readers and theatergoers continue to enjoy Shakespeare's plays four centuries after they were written? One answer is that Shakespeare thoroughly understood the theater and knew all the tricks of stagecraft—how to move an audience, create an exciting scene, and sketch out a setting using only the spoken word. Another answer lies in Shakespeare's language— the beautiful lines and phrases that resound in the minds of all who experience his plays. No other writer, before or since, has developed the potential of the English language to such heights. Still another answer lies in Shakespeare's profound understanding of human psychology, revealed in the unforgettable characters he created. Today, as much as ever, to understand Shakespeare's plays is to understand what is most important about human beings and about life.

OTHER PLAYS BY WILLIAM SHAKESPEARE

As You Like It (1599)

King Lear (1605)

Macbeth (1606)

The Merchant of Venice (1596–1597)

A Midsummer Night's Dream (1595–1596)

Richard II (1595)

The Tempest (1611)

Twelfth Night (1601–1602)

MORE ABOUT THE AUTHOR
For more on William Shakespeare, visit the **Literature Center** at ClassZone.com.

OHIO STANDARDS

READING STANDARDS
4.1 Compare and contrast ways that characters reveal traits about themselves

4.5 Analyze how choice of genre affects theme or topic

4.7 Recognize irony

Shakespearean Drama

In Elizabethan times, Shakespeare's plays captivated diverse crowds of theatergoers, ranging from wealthy nobility to common groundlings. But even Shakespeare may have been surprised that his works have so resonated with contemporary audiences, centuries after the plays were first performed. One reason Shakespeare has endured may be that his characters—figures from history and his imagination—transcend any particular time or place. For example, the scheming characters and conspiracies at the heart of *The Tragedy of Julius Caesar* are as relevant today as they were in Shakespeare's time. From plotting the removal of a dictator to betraying each other, the characters go to great lengths to serve their own ambitions.

Part 1: Characteristics of Shakespearean Tragedy

Perhaps the most powerful of Shakespeare's plays are his tragedies. A **tragedy** is a drama in which a series of actions leads to the downfall of the main character, called the **tragic hero.** The plot builds to a **catastrophe,** or a disastrous final outcome, that usually involves the death of the hero and many others.

To create suspense before this inevitable outcome and to help the audience understand the characters, Shakespeare used certain dramatic conventions—the **soliloquy,** the **aside,** and **dramatic irony**—which are described in the chart.

MAIN CHARACTER

Tragic Hero

- is of high social rank—a king, a prince, or a general

- has a **tragic flaw**—an error in judgment or a character defect—that ultimately leads to his or her downfall

- suffers complete ruin or death

- faces his or her downfall with courage and dignity

DRAMATIC CONVENTIONS

Dramatic Irony

- results when the audience knows more than one or more of the characters—for example, Caesar does not know that people are plotting against him, but the audience does

- helps build suspense

Soliloquy

- is a speech given by a character alone on stage, used to reveal his or her private thoughts and feelings

- may help the audience understand a character's motivation

Aside

- is a character's remark, either to the audience or to another character, that no one else on stage is supposed to hear

- lets the audience in on a character's thoughts or secrets

MODEL 1: TRAGIC HERO

Many critics believe that the tragic hero in *Julius Caesar* is not Caesar himself but Brutus, a respected Roman. As you read this excerpt, consider what Brutus' words reveal about his character.

from **Act One**

Scene 2

Lines 79–89

Brutus. What means this shouting? I do fear the people
80 Choose Caesar for their king.

Cassius.   Ay, do you fear it?
Then must I think you would not have it so.

Brutus. I would not, Cassius, yet I love him well.
But wherefore do you hold me here so long?
What is it that you would impart to me?
85 If it be aught toward the general good,
Set honor in one eye and death i' the other,
And I will look on both indifferently;
For let the gods so speed me as I love
The name of honor more than I fear death.

85–87 Brutus declares that he would not care whether he faced death if the matter Cassius has in mind concerns the public welfare (**general good**).

Close Read

1. Reread the boxed lines. What noble qualities does Brutus display? Cite specific details to support your answer.

2. What possible flaw might Brutus' mindset suggest?

MODEL 2: SOLILOQUY

Early in the play, Brutus must make a critical choice. Should he continue to live under Caesar's rule, or should he assassinate Caesar before the dictator becomes too power-hungry? Notice what you learn about Brutus from this soliloquy.

from **Act Two**

Scene 1

Lines 10–17

10 **Brutus.** It must be by his death; and for my part,
I know no personal cause to spurn at him,
But for the general. He would be crowned.
How that might change his nature, there's the question.
It is the bright day that brings forth the adder,
15 And that craves wary walking. Crown him that,
And then I grant we put a sting in him
That at his will he may do danger with.

10–12 It must ... general: Caesar would need to be killed, and I have no personal reason to attack him, only concern for the general welfare.

15 craves: demands.

Close Read

1. In the boxed text, Brutus compares Caesar to a poisonous snake (adder). Explain how this analogy helps you understand Brutus' concern about Caesar.

2. What is Brutus' motive for opposing Caesar? Given what you've just learned about Brutus, does his motive surprise you? Explain.

Part 2: The Language of Shakespeare

Shakespearean language is more grand, more rhythmic, and, admittedly, less comprehensible than everyday modern speech. If you familiarize yourself with Shakespeare's language, though, you will find yourself getting caught up in the intriguing plot that drives *Julius Caesar.*

BLANK VERSE

Shakespeare's plays are **verse dramas,** in which most of the dialogue is written in the metrical patterns of poetry. Shakespeare wrote primarily in **blank verse,** or unrhymed lines of iambic pentameter. **Iambic pentameter** is a pattern of rhythm that has five unstressed syllables (ˇ), each followed by a stressed syllable (ʹ). Read these lines aloud, noticing how the rhythm mimics that of everyday speech:

> *Such men as he be never at heart's ease*
> *Whiles they behold a greater than themselves,*

Most of *Julius Caesar* is written in blank verse. In some places, however, Shakespeare broke the pattern to vary the rhythm, create dramatic tension, or distinguish certain characters from others.

RHETORICAL DEVICES

Julius Caesar is about power, ambition, and betrayal. The characters are constantly trying to persuade themselves, each other, and the audience of the rightness of their cause. As a result, the play is full of speeches that make masterful use of rhetorical devices, such as those shown in the chart.

ELIZABETHAN WORDS TO KNOW

Here are words that you will encounter often while reading *Julius Caesar:*

an: if.

aught: anything.

beseech: beg.

but: only.

durst: dared.

ere: before.

hie: hurry.

hither: here.

mark: notice.

marry: a short form of "by the Virgin Mary" and so a mild exclamation.

prithee: pray thee, or please.

save: except.

soft: wait a minute.

thither: there.

wherefore: why.

whither: when.

withal: also.

RHETORICAL DEVICE	EXAMPLE
REPETITION the use of words and phrases more than once to emphasize ideas	Therein, ye gods, you make the weak most strong; Therein, ye gods, you tyrants do defeat. —Act One, Scene 3, Lines 91–92
PARALLELISM the repetition of grammatical structures to express ideas that are related or of equal importance	Not that I loved Caesar less, but that I loved Rome more. —Act Three, Scene 2, Line 20
RHETORICAL QUESTIONS the use of questions that require no answer to make the speaker's rightness seem self-evident	Wherein hath Caesar thus deserved your loves? Alas, you know not! —Act Three, Scene 2, Lines 232–233

MODEL 1: BLANK VERSE

In the following excerpt, Casca, one conspirator plotting against Caesar, speaks excitedly to the senator Cicero about a violent thunderstorm that is occurring. As you read, notice the rhythmic variation in the lines.

from

Scene 3

Lines 3–13

> **Casca.** Are you not moved when all the sway of earth
> Shakes like a thing unfirm? O Cicero,
> 5   I have seen tempests when the scolding winds
> Have rived the knotty oaks, and I have seen
> The ambitious ocean swell and rage and foam
> To be exalted with the threat'ning clouds;
> But never till tonight, never till now,
> 10   Did I go through a tempest dropping fire.
> Either there is a civil strife in heaven,
> Or else the world, too saucy with the gods,
> Incenses them to send destruction.

3 sway of earth: the natural order of things.

5 tempests: storms.

6 rived: torn.

8 To be exalted with: to raise themselves to the level of.

11–13 Either . . . destruction: Either there is a civil war in heaven or the world has so insulted the gods that they want to destroy us.

Close Read

1. Read the [boxed] lines aloud and scan the stressed and unstressed syllables. Where are the breaks in the pattern?

2. Point out the key words that are emphasized by the rhythm in lines 3–7. Why might Shakespeare have chosen to stress them?

MODEL 2: RHETORICAL DEVICES

This speech is given by Marullus, a Roman official loyal to Caesar's rival, Pompey. As the play opens, Romans take to the streets to celebrate Caesar's victory over Pompey, an occasion that spurs the official's anger. What rhetorical devices does Marullus use in his address to the crowd?

from

Scene 1

Lines 36–42 and 48–51

> **Marullus.** . . . O you hard hearts, you cruel men of Rome!
> Knew you not Pompey? Many a time and oft
> Have you climbed up to walls and battlements,
> To tow'rs and windows, yea, to chimney tops,
> 40   Your infants in your arms, and there have sat
> The livelong day, with patient expectation,
> To see great Pompey pass the streets of Rome. . . .
>
> And do you now put on your best attire?
> And do you now cull out a holiday?
> 50   And do you now strew flowers in his way
> That comes in triumph over Pompey's blood?

37 Pompey: a former Roman ruler defeated by Caesar in 48 B.C. Pompey was murdered a year after his defeat.

49 cull out: select.

Close Read

1. Consider the use of parallelism in the [boxed] lines. What words or phrases are parallel?

2. Notice the rhetorical questions that Marullus asks in line 37 and in lines 48–51. Through this rhetorical device, what is he trying to emphasize?

Part 3: Reading Shakespearean Drama

Understanding Shakespearean drama can be challenging for modern readers. Unusual vocabulary and grammatical structures can be difficult to decipher, and certain dramatic conventions can be tricky to track. Use these strategies to help you appreciate and analyze *Julius Caesar*.

READING TRAGEDY

- Study the opening **cast of characters,** which in *Julius Caesar* will tell you who is conspiring against the title character and who is supporting him.

- Try to visualize the setting and the action by using information in the **stage directions,** the **dialogue,** and the **synopsis** at the beginning of each scene.

- Keep track of the characters, and think about what their speech and actions reveal about their traits. Caesar, Cassius, Brutus, and Mark Antony are the ones to watch in *Julius Caesar*. At the end, consider how closely each fits the model of a **tragic hero.**

- Note examples of **foreshadowing,** using a chart like the one shown. Think about how each example can help you both **predict** events and better understand the characters' personalities.

- Look for **cause-and-effect relationships** between events, especially those events that lead to the tragic outcome.

- Keep in mind the **historical background** on page 1095 as you read the play. *Julius Caesar* is based on ancient Roman figures and events that Shakespeare views from an Elizabethan perspective. Shakespeare knew his audience had divided opinions about Caesar, and he exploits that tension throughout the play.

STRATEGIES IN ACTION

Scene 2   Lines 22–24

Caesar. What say'st thou to me now? Speak once again.

Soothsayer. Beware the ides of March.

Caesar. He is a dreamer; let us leave him. Pass.

Example of Foreshadowing	My Impressions
Soothsayer (fortune-teller) gives Caesar a mysterious warning about March 15 (ides)	• shows that Caesar is not superstitious or easily rattled • suggests that something terrible may happen to Caesar on that day

READING SHAKESPEARE'S LANGUAGE

- Use the **side notes,** context clues, and the word list on page 1088 to help you understand the meanings of unfamiliar words and expressions.

- Be aware that the English spoken in Shakespeare's time contains grammatical forms and structures that are no longer used today. Using a chart like the one shown, jot down difficult lines and then reword them to read like modern speech.

- Remember that the end of a line does not necessarily mean the end of a thought. Look closely at each line's punctuation, and try to figure out the meaning of the complete sentence or phrase.

- Paraphrase passages to help you understand characters' public personas as well as their private schemes. When you **paraphrase** a passage, you restate its key points in your own words.

Lines from Play	Modern Rewording
"...you and I will yet ere day See Brutus at his house. Three parts of him Is ours already, and the man entire Upon the next encounter yields him ours." *(Act One, Scene 3, Lines 153–156)*	Before the end of the day, you and I will see Brutus at his house. We've already won over three parts of him. The next time we see him, we'll win him over entirely.

MODEL: READING SHAKESPEAREAN DRAMA

This scene takes place on the streets as Caesar returns from a public festival. Many characters are on stage at the same time, but Brutus and Cassius speak privately in asides, as do Caesar and Antony. Use the stage directions and sidenotes to help you understand the scene.

from

Scene 2

Lines 178–201

[*Voices and music are heard approaching.*]

Brutus. The games are done, and Caesar is returning.

Cassius. As they pass by, pluck Casca by the sleeve,
180 And he will (after his sour fashion) tell you
What hath proceeded worthy note today.

> **181 worthy note:** worthy of notice.

[*Reenter* Caesar *and his train of followers.*]

Brutus. I will do so. But look you, Cassius!
The angry spot doth glow on Caesar's brow,
And all the rest look like a chidden train.
185 Calpurnia's cheek is pale, and Cicero
Looks with such ferret and such fiery eyes
As we have seen him in the Capitol,
Being crossed in conference by some senators.

> **184 chidden train:** a group of followers who have been scolded.
>
> **185–188** Cicero was a highly respected senator. Brutus says he has the angry look of a **ferret** (a fierce little animal), the look he gets when other senators disagree with him.

Cassius. Casca will tell us what the matter is.

[Caesar *looks at* Cassius *and turns to* Antony.]

190 **Caesar.** Antonius.

Antony. Caesar?

Caesar. Let me have men about me that are fat,
Sleek-headed men, and such as sleep o' nights.
Yond Cassius has a lean and hungry look;
195 He thinks too much, such men are dangerous.

> **190–214** Brutus and Cassius take Casca aside. The conversation Caesar has with Antony is not heard by any of the other characters around them.

Antony. Fear him not, Caesar, he's not dangerous.
He is a noble Roman, and well given.

Caesar. Would he were fatter! But I fear him not.
Yet if my name were liable to fear,
200 I do not know the man I should avoid
So soon as that spare Cassius. . . .

> **197** Antony says that Cassius, despite his appearance, is a supporter of Caesar.

Close Read

1. Paraphrase what Cassius is saying to Brutus in lines 179–181.

2. Reread the boxed lines and visualize the action unfolding in your mind. Cite details from the stage directions and Brutus' dialogue that helped you form a mental image of the characters' movements.

3. Consider what Caesar says about Cassius in lines 192–195. What do his words reveal about the character traits of Cassius and of Caesar himself?

4. How do you think Caesar will act toward Cassius in the future? Give reasons to support your prediction.

Part 4: Analyze the Literature

Use what you've learned about Shakespearean drama to analyze this scene from the beginning of *Julius Caesar*. In the scene, Cassius finally persuades Casca to join the conspiracy against Caesar. It is night, and a thunderstorm is raging. When Cinna, another conspirator, enters, they discuss winning over Brutus. Notice how Cassius manipulates the others.

from

Scene 3

Cassius. And why should Caesar be a tyrant then?
Poor man! I know he would not be a wolf
105 But that he sees the Romans are but sheep;
He were no lion, were not Romans hinds.
Those that with haste will make a mighty fire
Begin it with weak straws. What trash is Rome,
What rubbish and what offal, when it serves
110 For the base matter to illuminate
So vile a thing as Caesar! But, O grief,
Where hast thou led me? I, perhaps, speak this
Before a willing bondman. Then I know
My answer must be made. But I am armed,
115 And dangers are to me indifferent.

Casca. You speak to Casca, and to such a man
That is no fleering telltale. Hold, my hand.
Be factious for redress of all these griefs,
And I will set this foot of mine as far
120 As who goes farthest.

Cassius.   There's a bargain made.
Now know you, Casca, I have moved already
Some certain of the noblest-minded Romans
To undergo with me an enterprise
Of honorable-dangerous consequence;
125 And I do know, by this they stay for me
In Pompey's Porch; for now, this fearful night,
There is no stir or walking in the streets,
And the complexion of the element
In favor's like the work we have in hand,
130 Most bloody, fiery, and most terrible.

[*Enter* Cinna.]

Casca. Stand close awhile, for here come one in haste.

Cassius. 'Tis Cinna. I do know him by his gait.
He is a friend. Cinna, where haste you so?

Lines 103–164

103–111 Cassius says the only reason for Caesar's strength is the weakness of the Romans, who are female deer (**hinds**) and trash (**offal**) for allowing such a person as Caesar to come to power.

111–114 Cassius says that he will have to pay the penalty for his words if Casca is a submissive slave (**willing bondsman**).

117 fleering telltale: sneering tattletale.

118–120 Be factious ... farthest: Form a group, or faction, to correct (**redress**) these wrongs, and I will go as far as any other man.

125–126 by this ... Porch: Right now, they wait (**stay**) for me at the entrance to the theater Pompey built.

128–130 the complexion ... terrible: The sky (**element**) looks like the work we have ahead of us—bloody, full of fire, and terrible.

132 gait: manner of walking.

Close Read

1. Find examples of rhetorical questions and parallelism that Cassius uses in lines 103–115. What ideas does he want Casca to accept?

2. Reword the exchange between Cassius and Casca in lines 111–120 to sound like modern speech. Use the sidenotes to help you.

3. Read lines 121–124 aloud as you think Cassius would say them. What words are emphasized by the variation in the rhythm of line 124?

LITERARY ANALYSIS: SHAKESPEAREAN TRAGEDY

A **tragedy** is a drama in which a series of actions leads to the downfall of the main character, or **tragic hero.** In Shakespeare's tragedies, the hero is usually the title character. However, many critics believe that the tragic hero of *Julius Caesar* is not Caesar but another character, a prominent Roman named Brutus.

As you read, pay attention to these characteristics of Shakespearean tragedy:

- Because the tragic hero is a person of high rank, his or her fate has an impact on all of society.

- The hero has a **tragic flaw**—a fatal error in judgment or a weakness in character—that contributes to his or her downfall.

- Characters sometimes reveal their motives in **soliloquies** or **asides,** speeches that express thoughts that are hidden from other characters.

READING STRATEGY: READING SHAKESPEAREAN DRAMA

Shakespeare's plays, with their unusual vocabulary, grammar, and word order, can be challenging for modern readers. The following strategies can help:

- Read the synopsis, or summary, at the beginning of each scene to get an idea of what will happen in the scene.

- If you have trouble understanding a passage, use the sidenotes to figure out the meaning of unfamiliar words and gain helpful information. However, you do not necessarily need to understand every word to understand and enjoy the play.

- Rearrange sentences with unusual word order to create a familiar sentence structure.

- Use the stage directions and details in dialogue to help you visualize the play's settings and action.

- As you read, use a chart like the one shown to help you identify and analyze important characters in the play. Revise the chart as you learn more about the characters.

Important Characters	Who Are They?	Personality
Julius Caesar	dictator of Rome	

Background

Past and Present

Julius Caesar is a history play as well as a tragedy. For the Elizabethans, the ancient past offered important lessons about their own political problems. Like Rome under Caesar, England was governed by a strong ruler, Elizabeth I. The queen had survived

Bust of Julius Caesar

several plots against her life, and by 1599, when Shakespeare wrote his play, she was an elderly woman. Many English people feared that her death would lead to civil unrest.

Caesar's Rise to Power The story of Julius Caesar, a Roman general, politician, and orator who lived from 100 to 44 B.C., was well-known in Shakespeare's time. One of the greatest military leaders in Roman history, Caesar is famous for conquering Gaul, a land that corresponds roughly to modern-day France and Belgium. Caesar's growing power alarmed Rome's senators, who feared that he would seize control of the government. In 49 B.C., the Senate ordered him to give up his command in one of Rome's provinces. Caesar refused the order and crossed with his troops into Italy, starting a civil war. Caesar was opposed by Pompey, a former friend and ally. By 45 B.C., Caesar had defeated his opponents and was governing as an absolute ruler. Generous in victory, Caesar gave important positions to men who had recently been his enemies. However, many members of the nobility resented his disregard for their traditional authority, and some began to plot against him.

BUILDING BACKGROUND
To learn more about Julius Caesar and ancient Rome, visit the **Literature Center** at **ClassZone.com.**

Go Behind the Curtain

This photograph shows the interior of London's Globe Theatre, a reconstruction of Shakespeare's original theater. As you read the play, you will see photographs from the Globe Theatre Company's 1999 production of *Julius Caesar*. Photographs from other productions appear in the **Behind the Curtain** feature pages, which explore the stagecraft used to create exciting theatrical productions of this famous play.

The Tragedy of
JULIUS CÆSAR
William Shakespeare

CAST OF CHARACTERS

Julius Caesar

TRIUMVIRS AFTER THE DEATH OF JULIUS CAESAR

Octavius Caesar

Marcus Antonius

M. Aemilius Lepidus

SENATORS

Cicero

Publius

Popilius Lena

CONSPIRATORS AGAINST JULIUS CAESAR

Marcus Brutus

Cassius

Casca

Trebonius

Ligarius

Decius Brutus

Metellus Cimber

Cinna

Flavius and Marullus, *tribunes of the people*

Artemidorus of Cnidos, *a teacher of Rhetoric*

A Soothsayer

Cinna, *a poet*

Another Poet

FRIENDS TO BRUTUS AND CASSIUS

Lucilius

Titinius

Messala

Young Cato

Volumnius

SERVANTS TO BRUTUS

Varro

Clitus

Claudius

Strato

Lucius

Dardanius

Pindarus, *servant to Cassius*

Calpurnia, *wife to Caesar*

Portia, *wife to Brutus*

The Ghost of Caesar

Senators, Citizens, Guards, Attendants, Servants, etc.

TIME

44 B.C.

PLACE

Rome; the camp near Sardis; the plains of Philippi

Act One

Scene 1 *A street in Rome.*

The play begins on February 15, the religious feast of Lupercal. Today the people have a particular reason for celebrating. Julius Caesar has just returned to Rome after a long civil war in which he defeated the forces of Pompey, his rival for power. Caesar now has the opportunity to take full control of Rome.

In this opening scene, a group of workmen, in their best clothes, celebrate in the streets. They are joyful over Caesar's victory. The workers meet Flavius and Marullus, two tribunes—government officials—who supported Pompey. The tribunes express their anger at the celebration, and one worker responds with puns. Finally, the two tribunes scatter the crowd.

Flavius. Hence! home, you idle creatures, get you home!
Is this a holiday? What, know you not,
Being mechanical, you ought not walk
Upon a laboring day without the sign
5 Of your profession? Speak, what trade art thou?

First Commoner. Why, sir, a carpenter.

Marullus. Where is thy leather apron and thy rule?
What dost thou with thy best apparel on?
You, sir, what trade are you?

10 **Second Commoner.** Truly sir, in respect of a fine workman I am
but, as you would say, a cobbler.

Marullus. But what trade art thou? Answer me directly.

Second Commoner. A trade, sir, that I hope I may use with a safe
conscience, which is indeed, sir, a mender of bad soles.

15 **Flavius.** What trade, thou knave? Thou naughty knave, what trade?

Second Commoner. Nay, I beseech you, sir, be not out with me.
Yet if you be out, sir, I can mend you.

Marullus. What mean'st thou by that? Mend me, thou saucy fellow?

Second Commoner. Why, sir, cobble you.

20 **Flavius.** Thou art a cobbler, art thou?

Second Commoner. Truly, sir, all that I live by is with
the awl. I meddle with no tradesman's matters nor
women's matters, but with all. I am indeed, sir, a
surgeon to old shoes. When they are in great
25 danger, I recover them. As proper men as ever trod
upon neat's leather have gone upon my handiwork.

2–5 What, know ... profession: Since you are craftsmen (**mechanical**), you should not walk around on a workday without your work clothes and tools (**sign / Of your profession**). *What is Flavius' attitude toward these workers?*

10–26 In this conversation, a shoemaker (**cobbler**) makes a series of puns about his trade, which Marullus and Flavius fail to understand. Imagine the workmen laughing as Marullus and Flavius grow increasingly angry, wondering what is so funny.

15–16 Flavius accuses the commoner of being a wicked, sly person (**naughty knave**), but the commoner begs Flavius not to be angry with him (**be not out with me**).

18 Marullus thinks the cobbler means "I can mend your behavior." He accuses the cobbler of being disrespectful (**saucy**).

21–23 The cobbler jokes about the similarity of **awl** (a shoemaker's tool) to the word *all*.

26 neat's leather: calfskin, used to make expensive shoes. The cobbler means that even rich people come to him for shoes.

Julius Caesar in the Globe Theatre's 1999 production

Flavius. But wherefore art not in thy shop today?
Why dost thou lead these men about the streets?

Second Commoner. Truly, sir, to wear out their shoes, to get
30 myself into more work. But indeed, sir, we make holiday to see
Caesar and to rejoice in his triumph.

Marullus. Wherefore rejoice? What conquest brings he home?
What tributaries follow him to Rome
To grace in captive bonds his chariot wheels?
35 You blocks, you stones, you worse than senseless things!
O you hard hearts, you cruel men of Rome!
Knew you not Pompey? Many a time and oft
Have you climbed up to walls and battlements,
To tow'rs and windows, yea, to chimney tops,
40 Your infants in your arms, and there have sat
The livelong day, with patient expectation,
To see great Pompey pass the streets of Rome.
And when you saw his chariot but appear,
Have you not made an universal shout,
45 That Tiber trembled underneath her banks
To hear the replication of your sounds
Made in her concave shores?
And do you now put on your best attire?
And do you now cull out a holiday?
50 And do you now strew flowers in his way
That comes in triumph over Pompey's blood?
Be gone!
Run to your houses, fall upon your knees,
Pray to the gods to intermit the plague
55 That needs must light on this ingratitude.

Flavius. Go, go, good countrymen, and for this fault
Assemble all the poor men of your sort;
Draw them to Tiber banks, and weep your tears
Into the channel, till the lowest stream
60 Do kiss the most exalted shores of all.

[*Exeunt all the* Commoners.]

See, whe'r their basest metal be not moved.
They vanish tongue-tied in their guiltiness.
Go you down that way towards the Capitol;
This way will I. Disrobe the images
65 If you do find them decked with ceremonies.

Marullus. May we do so?
You know it is the feast of Lupercal.

Flavius. It is no matter. Let no images
Be hung with Caesar's trophies. I'll about

27 wherefore: why.

33–34 What ... wheels: What captured prisoners march chained to the wheels of his chariot?

37 Pompey: a former Roman ruler, defeated by Caesar in 48 B.C. Pompey was murdered a year after his defeat.

45 Tiber: a river that runs through Rome.

46 replication: echo.

49 cull out: select.

51 Pompey's blood: Caesar is returning to Rome in triumph after defeating Pompey's sons in Spain.

54–55 intermit ... ingratitude: hold back the deadly illness that might be just punishment for your behavior.

58–60 weep ... of all: weep into the Tiber River until it overflows.

Exeunt (Latin): They leave.

61 Flavius and Marullus are now alone, having shamed the workers into leaving the street. Flavius says that they will now see if they have touched (**moved**) the workers' poor characters (**basest metal**).

64–65 Disrobe ... ceremonies: Strip the statues of any decorations you find on them.

70 And drive away the vulgar from the streets.
   So do you too, where you perceive them thick.
   These growing feathers plucked from Caesar's wing
   Will make him fly an ordinary pitch,
   Who else would soar above the view of men
75 And keep us all in servile fearfulness.

   [*Exeunt.*]

69–71 I'll about...thick: I'll go around and scatter the rest of the commoners. Do the same yourself wherever they are forming a crowd.

72–75 These...fearfulness: Flavius compares Caesar to a bird. He hopes that turning away some of Caesar's supporters (**growing feathers**) will prevent him from becoming too powerful.

Scene 2   *A public place in Rome.*

As Caesar attends the traditional race at the festival of Lupercal, a soothsayer warns him to beware the ides of March, or March 15. (The middle day of each month was called the ides.) When Caesar leaves, Cassius and Brutus speak. Cassius tries to turn Brutus against Caesar by using flattery, examples of Caesar's weaknesses, and sarcasm about Caesar's power. Caesar passes by again, expressing his distrust of Cassius. Cassius and Brutus learn of Caesar's reluctant rejection of a crown that his friend Antony has offered him. They agree to meet again to discuss what must be done about Caesar.

[*A flourish of trumpets announces the approach of Caesar. A large crowd of Commoners has assembled; a Soothsayer is among them. Enter* Caesar, *his wife* Calpurnia, Portia, Decius, Cicero, Brutus, Cassius, Casca, *and* Antony, *who is stripped for running in the games.*]

Caesar. Calpurnia.

Casca.   Peace, ho! Caesar speaks.

Caesar.   Calpurnia.

Calpurnia. Here, my lord.

Caesar. Stand you directly in Antonius' way
When he doth run his course. Antonius.

5 **Antony.** Caesar, my lord?

Caesar. Forget not in your speed, Antonius,
To touch Calpurnia; for our elders say
The barren, touched in this holy chase,
Shake off their sterile curse.

Antony.   I shall remember.
10 When Caesar says "Do this," it is performed.

Caesar. Set on, and leave no ceremony out.

[*Flourish of trumpets.* Caesar *starts to leave.*]

Soothsayer. Caesar!

Caesar. Ha! Who calls?

Casca. Bid every noise be still. Peace yet again!

15 **Caesar.** Who is it in the press that calls on me?
I hear a tongue shriller than all the music

3–9 Stand...curse: Antony (Antonius) is about to run in a race that is part of the Lupercal celebration. Caesar refers to the superstition that a **sterile** woman (one unable to bear children) can become fertile if touched by one of the racers.

9–10 I shall...performed: *What do these lines tell you about Antony's attitude toward Caesar?*

12–15 The fortuneteller (**soothsayer**) who calls out Caesar's name can hardly be heard above the noise of the crowd (**press**). Casca tells the crowd to quiet down.

Cry "Caesar!" Speak. Caesar is turned to hear.

Soothsayer. Beware the ides of March.

Caesar.   What man is that?

Brutus. A soothsayer bids you beware the ides of March.

20 **Caesar.** Set him before me; let me see his face.

Cassius. Fellow, come from the throng; look upon Caesar.

Caesar. What say'st thou to me now? Speak once again.

Soothsayer. Beware the ides of March.

Caesar. He is a dreamer; let us leave him. Pass.

[*Trumpets sound. Exeunt all but* Brutus *and* Cassius.]

25 **Cassius.** Will you go see the order of the course?

Brutus. Not I.

Cassius. I pray you do.

Brutus. I am not gamesome. I do lack some part
Of that quick spirit that is in Antony.

30 Let me not hinder, Cassius, your desires.
I'll leave you.

Cassius. Brutus, I do observe you now of late;
I have not from your eyes that gentleness
And show of love as I was wont to have.

35 You bear too stubborn and too strange a hand
Over your friend that loves you.

Brutus.   Cassius,
Be not deceived. If I have veiled my look,
I turn the trouble of my countenance
Merely upon myself. Vexed I am

40 Of late with passions of some difference,
Conceptions only proper to myself,
Which give some soil, perhaps, to my behaviors;
But let not therefore my good friends be grieved
(Among which number, Cassius, be you one)

45 Nor construe any further my neglect
Than that poor Brutus, with himself at war,
forgets the shows of love to other men.

Cassius. Then, Brutus, I have much mistook your passion,
By means whereof this breast of mine hath buried

50 Thoughts of great value, worthy cogitations.
Tell me, good Brutus, can you see your face?

Brutus. No, Cassius, for the eye sees not itself
But by reflection, by some other things.

18 **ides of March:** March 15.

25–28 Cassius asks if Brutus is going to watch the race (**the order of the course**), but Brutus says he is not fond of sports (**gamesome**).

32–34 **I do observe . . . to have:** Lately I haven't seen the friendliness in your face that I used to see (**was wont to have**).

37–42 Brutus explains that if he has seemed distant, it is only because he has been preoccupied with conflicting emotions (**passions of some difference**), and that these private thoughts may have stained his conduct.

48–50 **I have . . . cogitations:** I have misunderstood your feelings. As a result, I have kept certain thoughts to myself.

Cassius. 'Tis just.

55　And it is very much lamented, Brutus,
　　That you have no such mirrors as will turn
　　Your hidden worthiness into your eye,
　　That you might see your shadow. I have heard
　　Where many of the best respect in Rome
60　(Except immortal Caesar), speaking of Brutus
　　And groaning underneath this age's yoke,
　　Have wished that noble Brutus had his eyes.

Brutus. Into what dangers would you lead me, Cassius,
　　That you would have me seek into myself
65　For that which is not in me?

Cassius. Therefore, good Brutus, be prepared to hear;
　　And since you know you cannot see yourself
　　So well as by reflection, I, your glass,
　　Will modestly discover to yourself
70　That of yourself which you yet know not of.
　　And be not jealous on me, gentle Brutus.
　　Were I a common laugher, or did use
　　To stale with ordinary oaths my love
　　To every new protester; if you know
75　That I do fawn on men and hug them hard,
　　And after scandal them; or if you know
　　That I profess myself in banqueting
　　To all the rout, then hold me dangerous.

[*Flourish and shout.*]

Brutus. What means this shouting? I do fear the people
80　Choose Caesar for their king.

Cassius.　　　　　　　　　　　Ay, do you fear it?
　　Then must I think you would not have it so.

Brutus. I would not, Cassius, yet I love him well.
　　But wherefore do you hold me here so long?
　　What is it that you would impart to me?
85　If it be aught toward the general good,
　　Set honor in one eye and death i' the other,
　　And I will look on both indifferently;
　　For let the gods so speed me as I love
　　The name of honor more than I fear death.

90　**Cassius.** I know that virtue to be in you, Brutus,
　　As well as I do know your outward favor.
　　Well, honor is the subject of my story.
　　I cannot tell what you and other men
　　Think of this life, but for my single self,
95　I had as lief not be as live to be

55–62 it is ... eyes: It is too bad you don't have a mirror that would show you your inner qualities (**hidden worthiness**). In fact, many respected citizens suffering under Caesar's rule (**this age's yoke**) have wished that Brutus could see how things stand. *What is Cassius suggesting to Brutus?*

66–70 Therefore ... not of: Listen, Brutus, since you cannot see yourself, I will be your mirror (**glass**) and show you what you truly are.

71 jealous on me: suspicious of me.

72–78 Were I ... dangerous: If you think I am a fool (**common laugher**) or someone who pretends to be the friend of everyone I meet, or if you believe that I show friendship and then talk evil about my friends (**scandal them**) behind their backs, or that I try to win the affections of the common people (**all the rout**), then consider me dangerous.

85–87 Brutus declares that he would not care whether he faced death if the matter Cassius has in mind concerns the public welfare (**general good**).

91 outward favor: physical appearance.

In awe of such a thing as I myself.
I was born free as Caesar, so were you;
We both have fed as well, and we can both
Endure the winter's cold as well as he.
100 For once, upon a raw and gusty day,
The troubled Tiber chafing with her shores,
Caesar said to me, "Dar'st thou, Cassius, now
Leap in with me into this angry flood
And swim to yonder point?" Upon the word,
105 Accoutered as I was, I plunged in
And bade him follow. So indeed he did.
The torrent roared, and we did buffet it
With lusty sinews, throwing it aside
And stemming it with hearts of controversy.
110 But ere we could arrive the point proposed,
Caesar cried, "Help me, Cassius, or I sink!"
I, as Aeneas, our great ancestor,
Did from the flames of Troy upon his shoulder
The old Anchises bear, so from the waves of Tiber
115 Did I the tired Caesar. And this man
Is now become a god, and Cassius is
A wretched creature and must bend his body
If Caesar carelessly but nod on him.
He had a fever when he was in Spain,
120 And when the fit was on him, I did mark
How he did shake. 'Tis true, this god did shake.
His coward lips did from their color fly
And that same eye whose bend doth awe the world
Did lose his luster. I did hear him groan.
125 Ay, and that tongue of his that bade the Romans
Mark him and write his speeches in their books,
Alas, it cried, "Give me some drink, Titinius,"
As a sick girl! Ye gods! it doth amaze me
A man of such a feeble temper should
130 So get the start of the majestic world
And bear the palm alone.

[*Shout. Flourish.*]

Brutus. Another general shout?
I do believe that these applauses are
For some new honors that are heaped on Caesar.

135 **Cassius.** Why, man, he doth bestride the narrow world
Like a Colossus, and we petty men
Walk under his huge legs and peep about
To find ourselves dishonorable graves.

95–96 I had . . . I myself: I would rather not live, than to live in awe of someone no better than I am.

101 troubled . . . shores: The Tiber River was rising in the middle of a storm.

105 Accoutered: dressed.

107–109 we did . . . controversy: We fought the raging river with strong muscles (**lusty sinews**), conquering it with our spirit of competition (**hearts of controversy**).

110 ere: before.

112–115 I, as Aeneas . . . Caesar: Aeneas (ĭ-nē′əs), the mythological founder of Rome, carried his father, Anchises (ăn-kī′sēz′), out of the burning city of Troy. Cassius says he did the same for Caesar when he became exhausted.

117 bend his body: bow.

122 His coward . . . fly: His lips turned pale.

123 bend: glance.

125–131 that tongue . . . alone: The same tongue that has led Romans to memorize his speeches cried out in the tone of a sick girl. I'm amazed that such a weak man should get ahead of the rest of the world and appear as the victor (**bear the palm**) all by himself. (A palm leaf was a symbol of victory in war.)

135–136 he doth . . . Colossus: Cassius compares Caesar to Colossus, the huge statue of the Greek god Apollo at Rhodes. The statue supposedly spanned the entrance to the harbor and was so high that ships could sail through the space between its legs. *What is Cassius' tone in these lines?*

Men at some time are masters of their fates.
140 The fault, dear Brutus, is not in our stars,
But in ourselves, that we are underlings.
"Brutus," and "Caesar." What should be in that "Caesar"?
Why should that name be sounded more than yours?
Write them together: yours is as fair a name.
145 Sound them, it doth become the mouth as well.
Weigh them, it is as heavy. Conjure with 'em:
"Brutus" will start a spirit as soon as "Caesar."
Now in the names of all the gods at once,
Upon what meat doth this our Caesar feed
150 That he is grown so great? Age, thou are shamed!
Rome, thou hast lost the breed of noble bloods!
When went there by an age since the great Flood
But it was famed with more than with one man?
When could they say (till now) that talked of Rome
155 That her wide walls encompassed but one man?
Now is it Rome indeed, and room enough,
When there is in it but one only man!
O, you and I have heard our fathers say
There was a Brutus once that would have brooked
160 The eternal devil to keep his state in Rome
As easily as a king.

Brutus. That you do love me I am nothing jealous.
What you would work me to, I have some aim.
How I have thought of this, and of these times,
165 I shall recount hereafter. For this present,
I would not (so with love I might entreat you)
Be any further moved. What you have said
I will consider; what you have to say
I will with patience hear, and find a time
170 Both meet to hear and answer such high things.
Till then, my noble friend, chew upon this:
Brutus had rather be a villager
Than to repute himself a son of Rome
Under these hard conditions as this time
175 Is like to lay upon us.

Cassius.   I am glad
That my weak words have struck but thus much show
Of fire from Brutus.

[*Voices and music are heard approaching.*]

Brutus. The games are done, and Caesar is returning.

Cassius. As they pass by, pluck Casca by the sleeve,
180 And he will (after his sour fashion) tell you

140–141 **The fault . . . underlings:** It is not the stars that have determined our fate; we are inferiors through our own fault.

146 **Conjure:** call up spirits.

150 **Age . . . shamed:** It is a shameful time (**Age**) in which to be living.

159–161 **There was . . . a king:** Cassius is referring to an ancestor of Brutus who drove the last of the ancient kings from Rome.

162 **am nothing jealous:** am sure.

163 **have some aim:** can guess.

164–167 **How I have . . . moved:** I will tell you later (**recount hereafter**) my thoughts about this topic. For now, I ask you as a friend not to try to convince me further. *What does this request suggest about Brutus' character?*

170 **meet:** appropriate.

What hath proceeded worthy note today.

[*Reenter* Caesar *and his train of followers.*]

Brutus. I will do so. But look you, Cassius!
The angry spot doth glow on Caesar's brow,
And all the rest look like a chidden train.
185 Calpurnia's cheek is pale, and Cicero
Looks with such ferret and such fiery eyes
As we have seen him in the Capitol,
Being crossed in conference by some senators.

Cassius. Casca will tell us what the matter is.

[Caesar *looks at* Cassius *and turns to* Antony.]

190 **Caesar.** Antonius.

Antony. Caesar?

Caesar. Let me have men about me that are fat,
Sleek-headed men, and such as sleep o' nights.
Yond Cassius has a lean and hungry look;
195 He thinks too much, such men are dangerous.

Antony. Fear him not, Caesar, he's not dangerous.
He is a noble Roman, and well given.

Caesar. Would he were fatter! But I fear him not.
Yet if my name were liable to fear,
200 I do not know the man I should avoid
So soon as that spare Cassius. He reads much,
He is a great observer, and he looks
Quite through the deeds of men. He loves no plays
As thou dost, Antony; he hears no music.
205 Seldom he smiles, and smiles in such a sort
As if he mocked himself and scorned his spirit
That could be moved to smile at anything.
Such men as he be never at heart's ease
Whiles they behold a greater than themselves,
210 And therefore are they very dangerous.
I rather tell thee what is to be feared
Than what I fear, for always I am Caesar.
Come on my right hand, for this ear is deaf,
And tell me truly what thou think'st of him. **Ⓐ**

[*Trumpets sound. Exeunt* Caesar *and all his train except* Casca, *who stays behind.*]

215 **Casca.** You pulled me by the cloak. Would you speak with me?

Brutus. Ay, Casca. Tell us what hath chanced today
That Caesar looks so sad.

Casca. Why, you were with him, were you not?

181 worthy note: worthy of notice.

184 chidden train: a group of followers who have been scolded.

185–188 Cicero was a highly respected senator. Brutus says he has the angry look of a **ferret** (a fierce little animal), the look he gets when other senators disagree with him.

190–214 Brutus and Cassius take Casca aside. The conversation Caesar has with Antony is not heard by any of the other characters around them.

197 Antony says that Cassius, despite his appearance, is a supporter of Caesar.

202–203 he looks . . . deeds of men: He sees hidden motives in men's actions.

Ⓐ BLANK VERSE
Reread lines 208–214 aloud, tapping out the stressed syllables with your finger. Which line in this passage vary from strict iambic pentameter?

216 hath chanced: has happened.

Brutus. I should not then ask Casca what had chanced.

220 **Casca.** Why, there was a crown offered him; and being offered him, he put it by with the back of his hand, thus. And then the people fell a-shouting.

Brutus. What was the second noise for?

Casca. Why, for that too.

225 **Cassius.** They shouted thrice. What was the last cry for?

Casca. Why, for that too.

Brutus. Was the crown offered him thrice?

Casca. Ay, marry, was't! and he put it by thrice, every time gentler than other; and at every putting-by mine honest
230 neighbors shouted.

Cassius. Who offered him the crown?

Casca. Why, Antony.

Brutus. Tell us the manner of it, gentle Casca.

Casca. I can as well be hanged as tell the manner of it. It was
235 mere foolery; I did not mark it. I saw Mark Antony offer him a crown—yet 'twas not a crown neither, 'twas one of these coronets—and, as I told you, he put it by once. But for all that, to my thinking, he would fain have had it. Then he offered it to him again; then he put it by again; but to my thinking, he was
240 very loath to lay his fingers off it. And then he offered it the third time. He put it the third time by; and still as he refused it, the rabblement hooted, and clapped their chapped hands, and threw up their sweaty nightcaps, and uttered such a deal of stinking breath because Caesar refused the crown that it had,
245 almost, choked Caesar; for he swounded and fell down at it. And for mine own part, I durst not laugh, for fear of opening my lips and receiving the bad air.

Cassius. But soft, I pray you. What, did Caesar swound?

Casca. He fell down in the market place and foamed at mouth
250 and was speechless.

Brutus. 'Tis very like. He hath the falling sickness.

Cassius. No, Caesar hath not it; but you, and I, And honest Casca, we have the falling sickness.

Casca. I know not what you mean by that, but I am sure Caesar
255 fell down. If the tag-rag people did not clap him and hiss him, according as he pleased and displeased them, as they use to do the players in the theater, I am no true man.

Brutus. What said he when he came unto himself?

---

221 put it by: pushed it aside.

228 Ay, marry, was't: Yes, indeed, it was. *Marry* was a mild oath used in Shakespeare's time (but not in ancient Rome). The word means "by the Virgin Mary."

237 coronets: small crowns.

238 fain: gladly.

240 loath: reluctant.

242 rabblement: unruly crowd.

245 swounded: fainted.

248 soft: Wait a moment.

251 falling sickness: epilepsy.

252–253 Cassius' pun on the term **falling sickness** suggests that they have fallen low under Caesar's rule.

Casca. Marry, before he fell down, when he perceived the
260 common herd was glad he refused the crown, he plucked me ope
his doublet and offered them his throat to cut. An I had been a
man of any occupation, if I would not have taken him at a word
I would I might go to hell among the rogues. And so he fell.
When he came to himself again, he said, if he had done or said
265 anything amiss, he desired their worships to think it was his
infirmity. Three or four wenches where I stood cried, "Alas,
good soul!" and forgave him with all their hearts. But there's no
heed to be taken of them. If Caesar had stabbed their mothers,
they would have done no less. **B**

270 **Brutus.** And after that, he came thus sad away?

Casca. Ay.

Cassius. Did Cicero say anything?

Casca. Ay, he spoke Greek.

Cassius. To what effect?

275 **Casca.** Nay, an I tell you that, I'll ne'er look you i' the face again.
But those that understood him smiled at one another and shook
their heads; but for mine own part, it was Greek to me. I could
tell you more news, too. Marullus and Flavius, for pulling scarfs
off Caesar's images, are put to silence. Fare you well. There was
280 more foolery yet, if I could remember it.

Cassius. Will you sup with me tonight, Casca?

Casca. No, I am promised forth.

Cassius. Will you dine with me tomorrow?

Casca. Ay, if I be alive, and your mind hold, and your
285 dinner worth eating.

Cassius. Good. I will expect you.

Casca. Do so. Farewell both.

[*Exit.*]

Brutus. What a blunt fellow is this grown to be!
He was quick mettle when he went to school.

290 **Cassius.** So is he now in execution
Of any bold or noble enterprise,
However he puts on this tardy form.
This rudeness is a sauce to his good wit,
Which gives men stomach to digest his words
295 With better appetite.

Brutus. And so it is. For this time I will leave you.
Tomorrow, if you please to speak with me,
I will come home to you; or if you will,
Come home to me, and I will wait for you.

260–261 plucked me ... doublet: tore open his jacket.

261–263 An ... rogues: If (**An**) I had been a worker with a proper tool, may I go to hell with the sinners (**rogues**) if I would not have done as he asked (**taken him at a word**).

265 amiss: wrong.

265–266 his infirmity: due to his sickness.

266 wenches: common women.

B BLANK VERSE
Notice that Shakespeare uses prose instead of blank verse for Casca's speeches. Which of Casca's **character traits** may have inspired this choice?

279 put to silence: silenced by removal from office, exile, or death. *What does this detail suggest about Caesar's rule?*

282 I am promised forth: I have another appointment.

289 quick mettle: clever, intelligent.

290–295 So is ... appetite: Casca can still be intelligent in carrying out an important project. He only pretends to be slow (**tardy**). His rude manner makes people more willing to accept (**digest**) the things he says.

Set Design

In a theatrical production, the **set design** helps audiences imagine the time and place in which the action occurs. Some designers use scenery and props to create the illusion of specific rooms or outdoor locations. Others try to suggest the essence of a play's setting through elements such as platforms, stairs, and columns. How do the features of these sets for *Julius Caesar* differ?

Set for the Shakespeare Theatre's 1993–1994 production

Set for a 2005 production at the Warf1 Theatre

Set for a 2005 production at the Belasco Theatre

300 **Cassius.** I will do so. Till then, think of the world.

[*Exit* Brutus.]

Well, Brutus, thou art noble; yet I see
Thy honorable mettle may be wrought
From that it is disposed. Therefore it is meet
That noble minds keep ever with their likes;
305 For who so firm that cannot be seduced?
Caesar doth bear me hard, but he loves Brutus.
If I were Brutus now and he were Cassius,
He should not humor me. I will this night,
In several hands, in at his windows throw,
310 As if they came from several citizens,
Writings, all tending to the great opinion
That Rome holds of his name; wherein obscurely
Caesar's ambition shall be glanced at.
And after this let Caesar seat him sure,
315 For we will shake him, or worse days endure. **Ⓒ**

[*Exit.*]

> **302 Thy...wrought:** Your honorable nature can be manipulated.

> **306 bear me hard:** hold a grudge against me.

> **308 He should...me:** I wouldn't let him influence me.

> **308–312 I will...his name:** Cassius plans to leave messages at Brutus' home that appear to be from several people.

> **Ⓒ SOLILOQUY**
> Why would Cassius not want Brutus to hear the thoughts he expresses in lines 301–315?

Scene 3   *A street in Rome.*

It is the night of March 14. Amid violent thunder and lightning, a terrified Casca fears that the storm and other omens predict terrible events to come. Cassius interprets the storm as a sign that Caesar must be overthrown. Cassius and Casca agree that Caesar's rise to power must be stopped by any means. Cinna, another plotter, enters, and they discuss how to persuade Brutus to follow their plan.

[*Thunder and lightning. Enter, from opposite sides,* Casca, *with his sword drawn, and* Cicero.]

Cicero. Good even, Casca. Brought you Caesar home?
Why are you breathless? and why stare you so?

Casca. Are not you moved when all the sway of earth
Shakes like a thing unfirm? O Cicero,
5 I have seen tempests when the scolding winds
Have rived the knotty oaks, and I have seen
The ambitious ocean swell and rage and foam
To be exalted with the threat'ning clouds;
But never till tonight, never till now,
10 Did I go through a tempest dropping fire.
Either there is a civil strife in heaven,
Or else the world, too saucy with the gods,
Incenses them to send destruction.

Cicero. Why, saw you anything more wonderful?

15 **Casca.** A common slave—you know him well by sight—
Held up his left hand, which did flame and burn

> **3 sway of earth:** the natural order of things.

> **5 tempests:** storms.

> **6 rived:** torn.

> **8 To be exalted with:** to raise themselves to the level of.

> **11–13 Either...destruction:** Either there is a civil war in heaven, or the world has so insulted the gods that they want to destroy us.

> **14 saw...wonderful:** Did you see anything else that was strange?

Like twenty torches joined; and yet his hand,
Not sensible of fire, remained unscorched.
Besides—I ha' not since put up my sword—
20 Against the Capitol I met a lion,
Who glared upon me, and went surly by
Without annoying me. And there were drawn
Upon a heap a hundred ghastly women,
Transformed with their fear, who swore they saw
25 Men, all in fire, walk up and down the streets.
And yesterday the bird of night did sit
Even at noonday upon the market place,
Hooting and shrieking. When these prodigies
Do so conjointly meet, let not men say,
30 "These are their reasons, they are natural,"
For I believe they are portentous things
Unto the climate that they point upon. **D**

Cicero. Indeed it is a strange-disposed time.
But men may construe things after their fashion,
35 Clean from the purpose of the things themselves.
Comes Caesar to the Capitol tomorrow?

Casca. He doth, for he did bid Antonius
Send word to you he would be there tomorrow.

Cicero. Good night then, Casca. This disturbed sky
40 Is not to walk in.

Casca.   Farewell, Cicero.

[*Exit* Cicero.]

[*Enter* Cassius.]

Cassius. Who's there?

Casca.   A Roman.

Cassius.   Casca, by your voice.

Casca. Your ear is good. Cassius, what night is this!

Cassius. A very pleasing night to honest men.

Casca. Who ever knew the heavens menace so?

45 **Cassius.** Those that have known the earth so full of faults.
For my part, I have walked about the streets,
Submitting me unto the perilous night,
And, thus unbraced, Casca, as you see,
Have bared my bosom to the thunder-stone;
50 And when the cross blue lightning seemed to open
The breast of heaven, I did present myself
Even in the aim and very flash of it.

18 Not sensible of fire: not feeling the fire.

19–20 I ha' not . . . lion: I haven't put my sword back into its scabbard since I saw a lion at the Capitol building.

22–23 drawn . . . heap: huddled together.

23 ghastly: ghostly white.

26 bird of night: the owl, usually seen only at night.

28–32 When these . . . upon: When strange events (**prodigies**) like these happen at the same time (**conjointly meet**), no one should say there are natural explanations for them. I believe they are bad omens (**portentous things**) for the place where they happen.

33–35 Cicero agrees that the times are strange, but he says that people can misinterpret events.

D TRAGEDY
How does Casca's speech in lines 15–32 help build **suspense?**

41 Who's there?: Cassius probably has his sword out; with no light other than moonlight, it could be dangerous to come upon a stranger in the street.

46–52 Cassius brags that he offered himself to the dangerous night, with his coat open (**unbraced**), exposing his chest to the lightning. *Why might he do this?*

Casca. But wherefore did you so much tempt the heavens?
It is the part of men to fear and tremble
55 When the most mighty gods by tokens send
Such dreadful heralds to astonish us.

Cassius. You are dull, Casca, and those sparks of life
That should be in a Roman you do want,
Or else you use not. You look pale, and gaze,
60 And put on fear, and cast yourself in wonder,
To see the strange impatience of the heavens.
But if you would consider the true cause
Why all these fires, why all these gliding ghosts,
Why birds and beasts, from quality and kind;
65 Why old men fool and children calculate;
Why all these things change from their ordinance,
Their natures, and preformed faculties,
To monstrous quality, why, you shall find
That heaven hath infused them with these spirits
70 To make them instruments of fear and warning
Unto some monstrous state.
Now could I, Casca, name to thee a man
Most like this dreadful night
That thunders, lightens, opens graves, and roars
75 As doth the lion in the Capitol;
A man no mightier than thyself or me
In personal action, yet prodigious grown
And fearful, as these strange eruptions are.

Casca. 'Tis Caesar that you mean. Is it not, Cassius?

80 **Cassius.** Let it be who it is. For Romans now
Have thews and limbs like to their ancestors.
But woe the while! our fathers' minds are dead,
And we are governed with our mothers' spirits,
Our yoke and sufferance show us womanish.

85 **Casca.** Indeed, they say the senators tomorrow
Mean to establish Caesar as king,
And he shall wear his crown by sea and land
In every place save here in Italy.

Cassius. I know where I will wear this dagger then;
90 Cassius from bondage will deliver Cassius.
Therein, ye gods, you make the weak most strong;
Therein, ye gods, you tyrants do defeat.
Nor stony tower, nor walls of beaten brass,
Nor airless dungeon, nor strong links of iron,
95 Can be retentive to the strength of spirit;
But life, being weary of these worldly bars,

54–56 It is ... astonish us: Men are supposed to be frightened when the gods send dreadful signs (**tokens**) of what is to come.

58 want: lack.

62–71 Cassius insists that heaven has brought about such things as birds and animals that change their natures (**from quality and kind**) and children who predict the future (**calculate**)—all these beings that act unnaturally (**change from their ordinance / Their natures, and preformed faculties**). Heaven has done all this, he says, to warn the Romans of an evil condition that they should correct.

77 prodigious grown: become enormous and threatening.

80–84 Romans ... womanish: Modern Romans have muscles (**thews**) and limbs like our ancestors, but we have the minds of our mothers, not our fathers. Our acceptance of servitude (**yoke and sufferance**) shows us to be like women, not like men. (In Shakespeare's time—and in ancient Rome—women were considered weak creatures.)

88 save: except.

89–90 I know ... deliver Cassius: I will free myself from slavery (**bondage**) by killing myself (**wear this dagger**).

91 Therein: through suicide.

95 be retentive to: hold in.

Never lacks power to dismiss itself.
If I know this, know all the world besides,
That part of tyranny that I do bear
100 I can shake off at pleasure.

[*Thunder still.*]

Casca.   So can I.
So every bondman in his own hand bears
The power to cancel his captivity.

Cassius. And why should Caesar be a tyrant then?
Poor man! I know he would not be a wolf
105 But that he sees the Romans are but sheep;
He were no lion, were not Romans hinds.
Those that with haste will make a mighty fire
Begin it with weak straws. What trash is Rome,
What rubbish and what offal, when it serves
110 For the base matter to illuminate
So vile a thing as Caesar! But, O grief,
Where hast thou led me? I, perhaps, speak this
Before a willing bondman. Then I know
My answer must be made. But I am armed,
115 And dangers are to me indifferent.

Casca. You speak to Casca, and to such a man
That is no fleering telltale. Hold, my hand.
Be factious for redress of all these griefs,
And I will set this foot of mine as far
120 As who goes farthest.

Cassius.   There's a bargain made.
Now know you, Casca, I have moved already
Some certain of the noblest-minded Romans
To undergo with me an enterprise
Of honorable-dangerous consequence;
125 And I do know, by this they stay for me
In Pompey's Porch; for now, this fearful night,
There is no stir or walking in the streets,
And the complexion of the element
In favor's like the work we have in hand,
130 Most bloody, fiery, and most terrible.

[*Enter* Cinna.]

Casca. Stand close awhile, for here comes one in haste.

Cassius. 'Tis Cinna. I do know him by his gait.
He is a friend. Cinna, where haste you so?

Cinna. To find out you. Who's that? Metellus Cimber?

89–100 *What impression does Cassius convey of himself in this speech?*

103–111 Cassius says the only reason for Caesar's strength is the weakness of the Romans, who are female deer (**hinds**) and trash (**offal**) for allowing such a person as Caesar to come to power.

111–114 Cassius says that he will have to pay the penalty for his words if Casca is a submissive slave (**willing bondsman**). *Why does Cassius suggest that he may have spoken too freely to Casca?*

117 fleering telltale: sneering tattletale.

118–120 Be factious...farthest: Form a group, or faction, to correct (**redress**) these wrongs, and I will go as far as any other man.

125–126 by this...Porch: Right now, they wait (**stay**) for me at the entrance to the theater Pompey built.

128–130 the complexion...terrible: The sky (**element**) looks like the work we have ahead of us—bloody, full of fire, and terrible.

132 gait: manner of walking.

135 **Cassius.** No, it is Casca, one incorporate
To our attempts. Am I not stayed for, Cinna?

Cinna. I am glad on't. What a fearful night is this!
There's two or three of us have seen strange sights.

Cassius. Am I not stayed for? Tell me.

Cinna.   Yes, you are.
140 O Cassius, if you could
But win the noble Brutus to our party—

Cassius. Be you content. Good Cinna, take this paper
And look you lay it in the praetor's chair,
Where Brutus may but find it, and throw this
145 In at his window. Set this up with wax
Upon old Brutus' statue. All this done,
Repair to Pompey's Porch, where you shall find us.
Is Decius Brutus and Trebonius there?

Cinna. All but Metellus Cimber, and he's gone
150 To seek you at your house. Well, I will hie
And so bestow these papers as you bade me.

Cassius. That done, repair to Pompey's Theater.

[*Exit* Cinna.]

Come, Casca, you and I will yet ere day
See Brutus at his house. Three parts of him
155 Is ours already, and the man entire
Upon the next encounter yields him ours.

Casca. O, he sits high in all the people's hearts,
And that which would appear offense in us,
His countenance, like richest alchemy,
160 Will change to virtue and to worthiness.

Cassius. Him and his worth and our great need of him
You have right well conceited. Let us go,
For it is after midnight, and ere day
We will awake him and be sure of him.

[*Exeunt.*]

135–136 it is . . . stayed for: This is Casca, who is now part of our plan (**incorporate / To our attempts**). Are they waiting for me?

142–146 Cassius tells Cinna to place letters for Brutus at several locations, including the seat of the praetor, a position held by Brutus.

150–151 I will . . . bade me: I'll hurry (**hie**) to place (**bestow**) these papers as you instructed me.

154–156 Three parts . . . yields him ours: We've already won over three parts of Brutus. The next time we meet him, he will be ours completely.

157–160 he sits . . . worthiness: The people love Brutus. What would seem offensive if we did it will, like magic (**alchemy**), become good and worthy because of his involvement.

162 conceited: judged.

Comprehension

1. **Recall** Why do the tribunes Flavius and Marullus become angry with the commoners at the beginning of the play?

2. **Recall** How does Caesar respond to the Soothsayer's warning?

3. **Recall** According to Casca, what happened at the games when Mark Antony offered Caesar a crown?

4. **Clarify** Why does Cassius send letters to Brutus that appear to have been written by other people?

OHIO STANDARDS

READING STANDARD
4.5 Analyze how choice of genre affects theme or topic

Literary Analysis

5. **Examine Blank Verse** Identify which characters speak in blank verse and which ones speak in prose in Act One, Scene 1. What can you tell about the characters in this scene based on whether their dialogue is in verse or prose?

6. **Analyze Suspense** In Scene 3, Shakespeare creates excitement about what will happen next in the play. Use a graphic organizer like the one shown to identify details in the scene that help build suspense.

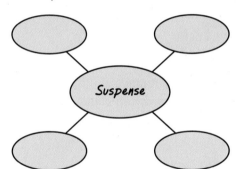

7. **Reading Shakespearean Drama** Review the chart you created as you read, and compare the personalities of Brutus and Cassius. In your opinion, which character would make a better leader? Give reasons for your answer.

8. **Draw Conclusions About Motivation** In Scenes 2 and 3, Cassius explains why he is opposed to Caesar. Does Cassius seem motivated more by personal rivalry or concern for the future of Rome? Cite details to support your conclusion.

9. **Make Judgments** Reread Casca's description of Caesar's behavior at the games in lines 215–287 of Scene 2. Do Caesar's words and actions suggest that he is becoming a tyrant? Support your answer with evidence from the play.

Literary Criticism

10. **Historical Context** When Shakespeare wrote *Julius Caesar,* Europe did not have any democratically elected leaders; most nations were governed by powerful monarchs such as England's Queen Elizabeth I. How might a modern audience's reaction to the events in Act One differ from the reaction of an Elizabethan audience? Discuss specific examples in your response.

Act Two

Scene 1 *Brutus' orchard in Rome.*

It is a few hours before dawn on March 15—the ides of March. Brutus, unable to sleep, walks in his garden. He faces a crucial decision: accept Caesar's growing power or kill Caesar and thus end his rule. While considering the problem, Brutus receives an anonymous letter (from Cassius) suggesting that Brutus take action against Caesar. Shortly after, Cassius and the conspirators visit Brutus, and they all agree to assassinate Caesar that day. After the conspirators leave, Brutus' wife, Portia, asks him to confide what has been troubling him.

Brutus. What, Lucius, ho!
I cannot by the progress of the stars
Give guess how near to day. Lucius, I say!
I would it were my fault to sleep so soundly.

5 When, Lucius, when? Awake, I say! What, Lucius!

[*Enter* Lucius *from the house.*]

Lucius. Called you, my lord?

Brutus. Get me a taper in my study, Lucius.
When it is lighted, come and call me here.

Lucius. I will, my lord.

[*Exit.*]

[Brutus *returns to his brooding.*]

10 **Brutus.** It must be by his death; and for my part,
I know no personal cause to spurn at him,
But for the general. He would be crowned.
How that might change his nature, there's the question.
It is the bright day that brings forth the adder,

15 And that craves wary walking. Crown him that,
And then I grant we put a sting in him
That at his will he may do danger with.
The abuse of greatness is when it disjoins
Remorse from power. And to speak truth of Caesar,

20 I have not known when his affections swayed
More than his reason. But 'tis a common proof
That lowliness is young ambition's ladder,
Whereto the climber-upward turns his face;
But when he once attains the upmost round,

25 He then unto the ladder turns his back,
Looks in the clouds, scorning the base degrees
By which he did ascend. So Caesar may.

4 I would … soundly: I wish I could sleep so soundly.

7 taper: candle.

10–12 It must … general: Caesar would need to be killed; and I have no personal reason to attack him, only concern for the general welfare.

15 craves: demands.

19 Remorse: compassion.

20 affections swayed: passions ruled.

21–27 Brutus says that for an ambitious person, humility (**lowliness**) is like a ladder that only remains useful until the climber reaches the top rung (**round**). *How does this metaphor relate to the argument for overthrowing Caesar?*

Brutus and Portia in the Globe Theatre's 1999 production

Then lest he may, prevent. And since the quarrel
Will bear no color for the thing he is,
30 Fashion it thus: that what he is, augmented,
Would run to these and these extremities;
And therefore think him as a serpent's egg,
Which, hatched, would as his kind grow mischievous,
And kill him in the shell.

[*Reenter Lucius with a letter.*]

35 **Lucius.** The taper burneth in your closet, sir.
Searching the window for a flint, I found
This paper, thus sealed up, and I am sure
It did not lie there when I went to bed.

[*Gives him the letter.*]

Brutus. Get you to bed again; it is not day.
40 Is not tomorrow, boy, the ides of March?

Lucius. I know not, sir.

Brutus. Look in the calendar and bring me word.

Lucius. I will, sir.

[*Exit.*]

Brutus. The exhalations, whizzing in the air,
45 Give so much light that I may read by them.

[*Opens the letter and reads.*]

"Brutus, thou sleep'st. Awake, and see thyself!
Shall Rome, etc. Speak, strike, redress!"
"Brutus, thou sleep'st. Awake!"
Such instigations have been often dropped
50 Where I have took them up.
"Shall Rome, etc." Thus must I piece it out:
Shall Rome stand under one man's awe? What, Rome?
My ancestors did from the streets of Rome
The Tarquin drive when he was called a king.
55 "Speak, strike, redress!" Am I entreated
To speak and strike? O Rome, I make thee promise,
If the redress will follow, thou receivest
Thy full petition at the hand of Brutus!

[*Reenter Lucius.*]

Lucius. Sir, March is wasted fifteen days.

[*Knocking within.*]

60 **Brutus.** 'Tis good. Go to the gate, somebody knocks.

[*Exit Lucius.*]

Since Cassius first did whet me against Caesar,
I have not slept.

28–34 lest ... shell: Rather than let Caesar do that, I should take steps to prevent it. Since our case against Caesar is weak (**Will bear no color**) at present, we must shape (**Fashion**) our argument against him in the following way: We know what kind of person Caesar is now. If his true nature were allowed to develop (**augmented**), it would reach terrible extremes. So we must treat him as a serpent's egg and kill him before he hatches.

35 closet: private room.

44 exhalations: meteors.

47 redress: right a wrong. The letter is meant to suggest certain things to Brutus, without actually spelling them out.

49 instigations: suggestions.

51 Thus ... out: I must guess the rest of the sentence.

52 Shall ... awe: Should Rome have such fear and respect for just one man?

53–54 My ancestors ... king: Brutus refers to an ancestor who drove out Rome's last king. After that, rule by the Senate was established.

56–58 I make ... Brutus: I promise you, Rome, if a remedy for our troubles can follow from my action, you will get what you need from Brutus.

61 whet me: sharpen my appetite.

Between the acting of a dreadful thing
And the first motion, all the interim is
65 Like a phantasma or a hideous dream.
The genius and the mortal instruments
Are then in council, and the state of man,
Like to a little kingdom, suffers then
The nature of an insurrection.

[*Reenter* Lucius.]

70 **Lucius.** Sir, 'tis your brother Cassius at the door,
Who doth desire to see you.

Brutus.   Is he alone?

Lucius. No, sir, there are more with him.

Brutus.   Do you know them?

Lucius. No, sir. Their hats are plucked about their ears
And half their faces buried in their cloaks,
75 That by no means I may discover them
By any mark of favor.

Brutus.   Let 'em enter.

[*Exit* Lucius.]

They are the faction. O conspiracy,
Sham'st thou to show thy dang'rous brow by night,
When evils are most free? O, then by day
80 Where wilt thou find a cavern dark enough
To mask thy monstrous visage? Seek none,
conspiracy, hide it in smiles and affability!
For if thou path, thy native semblance on,
No Erebus itself were dim enough
85 To hide thee from prevention. Ⓐ

[*Enter the conspirators,* Cassius, Casca, Decius, Cinna, Metellus
Cimber, *and* Trebonius.]

Cassius. I think we are too bold upon your rest.
Good morrow, Brutus. Do we trouble you?

Brutus. I have been up this hour, awake all night.
Know I these men that come along with you?

90 **Cassius.** Yes, every man of them; and no man here
But honors you; and every one doth wish
You had but that opinion of yourself
Which every noble Roman bears of you.
This is Trebonius.

Brutus.   He is welcome hither.

95 **Cassius.** This, Decius Brutus.

Brutus.   He is welcome too.

63–69 **Between . . . insurrection:** The
time between the earliest thought of a
terrible act and the actual performance
of it is a nightmare. The soul (**genius**) and
body (**mortal instruments**) debate the
subject, while the man himself feels like a
kingdom undergoing a civil war.

70 **brother:** Cassius, the husband of
Brutus' sister, is his brother-in-law.

75–76 **by no . . . favor:** There is no way I
can tell who they are.

77–85 **O conspiracy . . . prevention:** If these
plotters are afraid to be seen at night, how
will they keep these terrible plans from
showing on their faces during the day?
They must smile and show friendliness
(**affability**). If they go out showing their
true natures (**native semblance**), even the
dark gateway to hell (**Erebus** ĕr'ə-bəs)
could not hide them.

Ⓐ **SOLILOQUY**
Reread lines 61–69 and 77–85. What
feelings does Brutus reveal in these
two soliloquies?

86 **I think . . . rest:** I think we may have
come too early.

Cassius. This, Casca; this, Cinna; and this, Metellus Cimber.

Brutus. They are all welcome.
What watchful cares do interpose themselves
Betwixt your eyes and night?

100 **Cassius.** Shall I entreat a word?

[*They whisper.*]

Decius. Here lies the east. Doth not the day break here?

Casca. No.

Cinna. O, pardon, sir, it doth; and yon grey lines
That fret the clouds are messengers of day.

105 **Casca.** You shall confess that you are both deceived.
Here, as I point my sword, the sun arises,
Which is a great way growing on the south,
Weighing the youthful season of the year.
Some two months hence, up higher toward the north
110 He first presents his fire; and the high east
Stands as the Capitol, directly here.

[Brutus *and* Cassius *rejoin the others.*]

Brutus. Give me your hands all over, one by one.

Cassius. And let us swear our resolution.

Brutus. No, not on oath. If not the face of men,
115 The sufferance of our souls, the time's abuse—
If these be motives weak, break off betimes,
And every man hence to his idle bed.
So let high-sighted tyranny range on
Till each man drop by lottery. But if these
120 (As I am sure they do) bear fire enough
To kindle cowards and to steel with valor
The melting spirits of women, then, countrymen,
What need we any spur but our own cause
To prick us to redress? what other bond
125 Than secret Romans that have spoke the word
And will not palter? and what other oath
Than honesty to honesty engaged
That this shall be, or we will fall for it?
Swear priests and cowards and men cautelous,
130 Old feeble carrions and such suffering souls
That welcome wrongs; unto bad causes swear
Such creatures as men doubt; but do not stain
The even virtue of our enterprise,
Nor the insuppressive mettle of our spirits,
135 To think that or our cause or our performance
Did need an oath when every drop of blood

98–99 What watchful . . . night: What troubles keep you awake at night?

100 Shall I entreat a word?: Cassius asks Brutus to step aside and talk privately with him. While they talk, the others chatter about the sky (lines 101–111), pretending to be not at all interested in what Cassius and Brutus are discussing.

104 fret: stripe.

107–108 Which is . . . year: from a southerly direction, since it is still early in the year.

114–119 If not . . . lottery: We do not need to swear our loyalty to one another. The sadness of people's faces, our own suffering, and the awful time we live in—if these aren't strong enough to hold us together, then let us all go back to bed. In that case, let tyranny live, while we die off, one at a time, by chance (**by lottery**).

126 palter: go back on our word.

129–131 Swear priests . . . wrongs: Swearing oaths is for priests, crafty men, old men on the verge of death, and wretches who welcome injustice.

134 insuppressive mettle: unconquerable courage.

135 or our cause . . . performance: either our cause or our actions.

That every Roman bears, and nobly bears,
Is guilty of a several bastardy
If he do break the smallest particle
140 Of any promise that hath passed from him.

Cassius. But what of Cicero? Shall we sound him?
I think he will stand very strong with us.

Casca. Let us not leave him out.

Cinna.   No, by no means.

Metellus. O, let us have him! for his silver hairs
145 Will purchase us a good opinion
And buy men's voices to commend our deeds.
It shall be said his judgment ruled our hands;
Our youths and wildness shall no whit appear,
But all be buried in his gravity.

150 **Brutus.** O, name him not! Let us not break with him,
For he will never follow anything
That other men begin.

Cassius.   Then leave him out.

Casca. Indeed he is not fit. **B**

Decius. Shall no man else be touched but only Caesar?

155 **Cassius.** Decius, well urged. I think it is not meet
Mark Antony, so well beloved of Caesar,
Should outlive Caesar. We shall find of him
A shrewd contriver; and you know, his means,
If he improve them, may well stretch so far
160 As to annoy us all; which to prevent,
Let Antony and Caesar fall together.

Brutus. Our course will seem too bloody, Caius Cassius,
To cut the head off and then hack the limbs,
Like wrath in death and envy afterwards;
165 For Antony is but a limb of Caesar.
Let us be sacrificers, but not butchers, Caius.
We all stand up against the spirit of Caesar,
And in the spirit of men there is no blood.
O that we then could come by Caesar's spirit
170 And not dismember Caesar! But, alas,
Caesar must bleed for it! And, gentle friends,
Let's kill him boldly, but not wrathfully;
Let's carve him as a dish fit for the gods,
Not hew him as a carcass fit for hounds.
175 And let our hearts, as subtle masters do,
Stir up their servants to an act of rage
And after seem to chide 'em. This shall make

138 guilty . . . bastardy: not truly Roman.

141 sound him: see what he thinks of the matter.

144–146 his silver . . . deeds: his old age will win us popular support.

B TRAGEDY
The development of the conspiracy is an important part of the **plot** of *Julius Caesar*. Who seems to be in charge in lines 112–153, Brutus or Cassius? Cite details to support your answer.

169–170 Brutus wishes they could remove Caesar's soul without having to destroy his body.

174 Not . . . hounds: Let's not chop him up like the body of an animal to be fed to dogs.

Our purpose necessary, and not envious;
Which so appearing to the common eyes,
180 We shall be called purgers, not murderers.
And for Mark Antony, think not of him;
For he can do no more than Caesar's arm
When Caesar's head is off.

Cassius.   Yet I fear him,
For in the ingrafted love he bears to Caesar—

185 **Brutus.** Alas, good Cassius, do not think of him!
If he love Caesar, all that he can do
Is to himself—take thought, and die for Caesar.
And that were much he should; for he is given
To sports, to wildness, and much company.

190 **Trebonius.** There is no fear in him. Let him not die,
For he will live and laugh at this hereafter.

[*Clock strikes.*]

Brutus. Peace! Count the clock.

Cassius.   The clock hath stricken three.

Trebonius. 'Tis time to part.

Cassius.   But it is doubtful yet
Whether Caesar will come forth today or no;
195 For he is superstitious grown of late,
Quite from the main opinion he held once
Of fantasy, of dreams, and ceremonies.
It may be these apparent prodigies,
The unaccustomed terror of this night,
200 And the persuasion of his augurers
May hold him from the Capitol today.

Decius. Never fear that. If he be so resolved,
I can o'ersway him; for he loves to hear
That unicorns may be betrayed with trees
205 And bears with glasses, elephants with holes,
Lions with toils, and men with flatterers;
But when I tell him he hates flatterers,
He says he does, being then most flattered.
Let me work,
210 For I can give his humor the true bent,
And I will bring him to the Capitol.

Cassius. Nay, we will all of us be there to fetch him.

Brutus. By the eighth hour. Is that the uttermost?

Cinna. Be that the uttermost, and fail not then.

175–180 **let our hearts . . . murderers:** Let our hearts treat our hands (**servants**) the way sly masters do; we will let our hands do our dirty work, then later scold (**chide**) them for what they have done. This attitude will make us seem to the public (**common eyes**) to be healers (**purgers**) instead of murderers.

184 **ingrafted:** deep-rooted.

188–189 **And that . . . company:** And that is unlikely, for he loves sports, wild times, and socializing.

190 **There is no fear in him:** We have nothing to fear from Antony.

193–201 **But it is . . . Capitol today:** We don't know if Caesar will leave his house (**come forth**) today. Lately he has become superstitious, in contrast to the strong views (**main opinion**) he once had of such beliefs. The cause may be these strange events and the arguments of his fortunetellers (**augurers**). These things may keep him from coming to the Capitol today.

203 **o'ersway him:** change his mind.

204–208 Decius tells of ways to trap shrewd animals. He says that Caesar, who loves to hear such stories, can also be trapped—by flattery.

210 **I can give . . . true bent:** I can get him into the right mood.

213 **By the . . . uttermost:** By eight o'clock. Do we all agree that eight is the latest we will be there?

215 **Metellus.** Caius Ligarius doth bear Caesar hard,
Who rated him for speaking well of Pompey.
I wonder none of you have thought of him.

Brutus. Now, good Metellus, go along by him.
He loves me well, and I have given him reasons.
220 Send him but hither, and I'll fashion him.

Cassius. The morning comes upon's. We'll leave you, Brutus.
And, friends, disperse yourselves; but all remember
What you have said and show yourselves true Romans.

Brutus. Good gentlemen, look fresh and merrily.
225 Let not our looks put on our purposes,
But bear it as our Roman actors do,
With untired spirits and formal constancy.
And so good morrow to you every one.

[*Exeunt all but* Brutus.]

Boy! Lucius! Fast asleep? It is no matter.
230 Enjoy the honey-heavy dew of slumber.
Thou hast no figures nor no fantasies
Which busy care draws in the brains of men;
Therefore thou sleep'st so sound.

[*Enter* Portia, *Brutus' wife.*]

Portia.   Brutus, my lord!

Brutus. Portia! What mean you? Wherefore rise you now?
235 It is not for your health thus to commit
Your weak condition to the raw cold morning.

Portia. Nor for yours neither. Y'have ungently, Brutus,
Stole from my bed. And yesternight at supper
You suddenly arose and walked about,
240 Musing and sighing with your arms across;
And when I asked you what the matter was,
You stared upon me with ungentle looks.
I urged you further, then you scratched your head
And too impatiently stamped with your foot.
245 Yet I insisted, yet you answered not,
But with an angry wafture of your hand
Gave sign for me to leave you. So I did,
Fearing to strengthen that impatience
Which seemed too much enkindled, and withal
250 Hoping it was but an effect of humor,
Which sometime hath his hour with every man.
It will not let you eat nor talk nor sleep,
And could it work so much upon your shape
As it hath much prevailed on your condition,

215–217 Caius . . . of him: Caius Ligarius has a grudge against Caesar, who criticized him for supporting Pompey. I don't know why you haven't asked him to join our plot.

220 fashion: persuade.

225 Let not . . . purposes: Let's not let our appearances give away (**put on**) what we are planning to do.

233 *As you read the conversation between Brutus and his wife, think about the kind of relationship they have.*

245 Yet: still.

246 wafture: waving.

249 withal: also.

250 humor: mood.

255 I should not know you Brutus. Dear my lord,
Make me acquainted with your cause of grief.

Brutus. I am not well in health, and that is all.

Portia. Brutus is wise and, were he not in health,
He would embrace the means to come by it.

260 **Brutus.** Why, so I do. Good Portia, go to bed.

Portia. Is Brutus sick, and is it physical
To walk unbraced and suck up the humors
Of the dank morning? What, is Brutus sick,
And will he steal out of his wholesome bed
265 To dare the vile contagion of the night,
And tempt the rheumy and unpurgéd air,
To add unto his sickness? No, my Brutus.
You have some sick offense within your mind,
Which by the right and virtue of my place
270 I ought to know of; and upon my knees
I charm you, by my once commended beauty,
By all your vows of love, and that great vow
Which did incorporate and make us one,
That you unfold to me, yourself, your half,
275 Why you are heavy, and what men tonight
Have had resort to you; for here have been
Some six or seven, who did hide their faces
Even from darkness.

Brutus. Kneel not, gentle Portia.

Portia. I should not need if you were gentle Brutus.
280 Within the bond of marriage, tell me, Brutus,
Is it excepted I should know no secrets
That appertain to you? Am I yourself
But, as it were, in sort or limitation?
To keep with you at meals, comfort your bed,
285 And talk to you sometimes? Dwell I but in the suburbs
Of your good pleasure? If it be no more,
Portia is Brutus' harlot, not his wife.

Brutus. You are my true and honorable wife,
As dear to me as are the ruddy drops
290 That visit my sad heart.

Portia. If this were true, then should I know this secret.
I grant I am a woman, but withal
A woman that Lord Brutus took to wife.
I grant that I am a woman, but withal
295 A woman well reputed, Cato's daughter.
Think you I am no stronger than my sex,
Being so fathered and so husbanded?

253–255 And could . . . you Brutus: If a mood like that could change your appearance (**shape**) the way it has changed your personality (**condition**), I would not recognize you.

257 *Why do you think Brutus lies to Portia?*

261–267 Is Brutus . . . sickness: Do you expect me to believe that you're sick? Is it healthy to walk without a coat (**unbraced**) and breathe the air of a damp morning or the unhealthy night air that is not yet cleansed (**unpurged**) by the sun?

268–270 You have . . . know of: You have a sickness of the mind; as your wife, I have a right to know what it is.

275 heavy: sad.

281 excepted: made an exception that.

283 in sort or limitation: only in part.

289–290 the ruddy . . . heart: my blood.

Brutus and Portia in the Shakespeare Theatre's 1993–1994 production

Casting

When **casting** roles for a Shakespearean play, directors don't necessarily try to match the race or even the gender of a character. (Originally, all of the roles were played by males.) However, physical traits are still important; a plump actor would generally not be chosen to play the "lean and hungry" Cassius. These photographs show three pairs of actors who have played Brutus and Portia. What traits set them apart? Which actors would you have chosen for the roles? Explain your response.

Brutus and Portia in the New York Shakespeare Festival's 1988 production

Brutus and Portia in the Globe Theatre's 1999 production

Tell me your counsels; I will not disclose 'em.
I have made strong proof of my constancy,
300 Giving myself a voluntary wound
Here, in the thigh. Can I bear that with patience,
And not my husband's secrets?

Brutus.   O ye gods,
Render me worthy of this noble wife!

[*Knocking within.*]

Hark, hark! one knocks. Portia, go in awhile,
305 And by-and-by thy bosom shall partake
The secrets of my heart.
All my engagements I will construe to thee,
All the charactery of my sad brows.
Leave me with haste.

[*Exit* Portia.]

                              Lucius, who's that knocks?

[*Reenter* Lucius *with* Caius Ligarius.]

310 **Lucius.** Here is a sick man that would speak with you.

Brutus. Caius Ligarius, that Metellus spake of.
Boy, stand aside. Caius Ligarius, how?

Caius. Vouchsafe good morrow from a feeble tongue.

Brutus. O, what a time have you chose out, brave Caius,
315 To wear a kerchief! Would you were not sick!

Caius. I am not sick if Brutus have in hand
Any exploit worthy the name of honor.

Brutus. Such an exploit have I in hand, Ligarius,
Had you a healthful ear to hear of it.

320 **Caius.** By all the gods that Romans bow before,
I here discard my sickness! Soul of Rome!
Brave son, derived from honorable loins!
Thou like an exorcist has conjured up
My mortified spirit. Now bid me run,
325 And I will strive with things impossible;
Yea, get the better of them. What's to do?

Brutus. A piece of work that will make sick men whole.

Caius. But are not some whole that we must make sick?

Brutus. That must we also. What it is, my Caius,
330 I shall unfold to thee as we are going
To whom it must be done.

Caius.   Set on your foot,
And with a heart new-fired I follow you,
To do I know not what; but it sufficeth

296–302 Think you . . . secrets: How can you consider me merely a typical woman when I am the daughter of Cato (**a highly respected Roman**) and the wife of Brutus? So tell me your secret. I have proven my strength by wounding myself here in the thigh. If I can put up with that pain, I can certainly deal with my husband's secrets.

307–308 All may . . . brows: I will explain all my dealings and the reason for my sad looks.

313 Vouchsafe . . . tongue: Accept a good morning from a sick man.

315 kerchief: a covering to protect the head during sickness.

317 exploit: deed.

322 derived . . . loins: descended from noble Romans.

323 exorcist: someone who can call up spirits.

328 *What is Caius hinting at?*

331 Set on your foot: Lead the way.

333 it sufficeth: It is enough.

That Brutus leads me on.

[*Thunder.*]

Brutus.   Follow me then.

[*Exeunt.*]

Scene 2 *Caesar's house in Rome.*

It is now past dawn on March 15. Like everyone else in Rome, Caesar and his wife have slept badly because of the storm. There is still some lightning and thunder. Caesar prepares to go to the Capitol; but because of the many threatening omens, his wife, Calpurnia, insists that he stay home. Caesar agrees, for Calpurnia's sake. He changes his mind, however, when Decius, one of the conspirators, persuades him that he must not seem swayed by his wife's superstitions. Although Caesar doesn't know it, the other conspirators are on their way to his house to make sure he does not decide to stay at home.

[*Enter* Caesar *in his nightgown.*]

Caesar. Nor heaven nor earth have been at peace tonight.
Thrice hath Calpurnia in her sleep cried out
"Help, ho! They murder Caesar!" Who's within?

[*Enter a* Servant.]

Servant. My lord?

5 **Caesar.** Go bid the priests do present sacrifice,
And bring me their opinions of success.

Servant. I will, my lord.

[*Exit.*]

[*Enter* Caesar's *wife,* Calpurnia, *alarmed.*]

Calpurnia. What mean you, Caesar? Think you to walk forth?
You shall not stir out of your house today.

10 **Caesar.** Caesar shall forth. The things that threatened me
Ne'er looked but on my back. When they shall see
The face of Caesar, they are vanished.

Calpurnia. Caesar, I never stood on ceremonies,
Yet now they fright me. There is one within,
15 Besides the things that we have heard and seen,
Recounts most horrid sights seen by the watch.
A lioness hath whelped in the streets,
And graves have yawned and yielded up their dead.
Fierce fiery warriors fought upon the clouds
20 In ranks and squadrons and right form of war,
Which drizzled blood upon the Capitol.
The noise of battle hurtled in the air,
Horses did neigh, and dying men did groan,
And ghosts did shriek and squeal about the streets.

5–6 Go bid . . . success: Roman priests would kill an animal as a sacrifice to the gods. Then they would cut the animal open and examine its internal organs for signs of future events.

10–12 The things . . . vanished: When I turn to face the things that threaten me, they disappear.

13–26 Caesar, I never . . . fear them: Calpurnia tells Caesar that she has never before believed in omens (**stood on ceremonies**), but now she is frightened. She describes the terrible things she has heard of from the men who were on guard during the night.

25 O Caesar, these things are beyond all use,
And I do fear them!

Caesar.   What can be avoided
Whose end is purposed by the mighty gods?
Yet Caesar shall go forth, for these predictions
Are to the world in general as to Caesar.

30 **Calpurnia.** When beggars die there are no comets seen;
The heavens themselves blaze forth the death of princes.

Caesar. Cowards die many times before their deaths;
The valiant never taste of death but once.
Of all the wonders that I yet have heard,
35 It seems to me most strange that men should fear,
Seeing that death, a necessary end,
Will come when it will come. **C**

[*Reenter* Servant.]

                What say the augurers?

Servant. They would not have you to stir forth today.
Plucking the entrails of an offering forth,
40 They could not find a heart within the beast.

Caesar. The gods do this in shame of cowardice.
Caesar should be a beast without a heart
If he should stay at home today for fear.
No, Caesar shall not. Danger knows full well
45 That Caesar is more dangerous than he.
We are two lions littered in one day,
And I the elder and more terrible,
And Caesar shall go forth.

Calpurnia.   Alas, my lord!
Your wisdom is consumed in confidence.
50 Do not go forth today. Call it my fear
That keeps you in the house and not your own.
We'll send Mark Antony to the Senate House,
And he shall say you are not well today.
Let me upon my knee prevail in this.

55 **Caesar.** Mark Antony shall say I am not well,
And for thy humor I will stay at home.

[*Enter* Decius.]

Here's Decius Brutus, he shall tell them so.

Decius. Caesar, all hail! Good morrow, worthy Caesar!
I come to fetch you to the Senate House.

60 **Caesar.** And you are come in very happy time
To bear my greetings to the senators

---

25 beyond all use: unlike anything we are accustomed to.

26–29 Caesar insists that if these are omens and if the gods have destined that certain things will happen, no one can avoid them. He will go out, since the predictions, he believes, apply to the whole world, not only to himself.

C TRAGIC HERO
Reread lines 32–37. What is Caesar's attitude toward his fate?

46 littered in one day: born at the same time.

And tell them that I will not come today.
Cannot, is false; and that I dare not, falser.
I will not come today. Tell them so, Decius.

65 **Calpurnia.** Say he is sick.

Caesar.   Shall Caesar send a lie?
Have I in conquest stretched mine arm so far
To be afeard to tell greybeards the truth?
Decius, go tell them Caesar will not come.

Decius. Most mighty Caesar, let me know some cause,
70 Lest I be laughed at when I tell them so.

Caesar. The cause is in my will: I will not come.
That is enough to satisfy the Senate;
But for your private satisfaction,
Because I love you, I will let you know.
75 Calpurnia here, my wife, stays me at home.
She dreamt tonight she saw my statue,
Which, like a fountain with an hundred spouts,
Did run pure blood, and many lusty Romans
Came smiling and did bathe their hands in it.
80 And these does she apply for warnings and portents
And evils imminent, and on her knee
Hath begged that I will stay at home today.

Decius. This dream is all amiss interpreted;
It was a vision fair and fortunate.
85 Your statue spouting blood in many pipes,
In which so many smiling Romans bathed,
Signifies that from you great Rome shall suck
Reviving blood, and that great men shall press
For tinctures, stains, relics, and cognizance.
90 This by Calpurnia's dream is signified.

Caesar. And this way have you well expounded it.

Decius. I have, when you have heard what I can say:
And know it now, the Senate have concluded
To give this day a crown to mighty Caesar.
95 If you shall send them word you will not come,
Their minds may change. Besides, it were a mock
Apt to be rendered, for some one to say
"Break up the Senate till another time,
When Caesar's wife shall meet with better dreams."
100 If Caesar hide himself, shall they not whisper
"Lo, Caesar is afraid"?
Pardon me, Caesar, for my dear dear love
To your proceeding bids me tell you this,
And reason to my love is liable.

65–68 Shall . . . not come: Caesar is appalled by his wife's suggestion that he lie to a bunch of old men (**greybeards**) about his reason for not going to the Senate.

80 portents: signs of evil to come.

83 amiss: wrongly.

83–90 Decius has to think fast. He promised the others that he could flatter Caesar into believing anything. Now he must give Caesar a new interpretation of Calpurnia's dream, one that will get him out of the house.

88–89 great men . . . cognizance: Great men will come to you for honors and souvenirs to remember you by.

96–97 it were . . . rendered: It's likely that someone will make a sarcastic comment.

102–104 my dear . . . liable: My sincere interest in your career (**proceeding**) makes me tell you this. My feeling for you overtakes my intelligence (**reason**).

What arguments does Decius use to change Caesar's mind?

105 **Caesar.** How foolish do your fears seem now, Calpurnia!
I am ashamed I did yield to them.
Give me my robe, for I will go.

[*Enter* Brutus, Ligarius, Metellus, Casca, Trebonius, Cinna, *and* Publius.]

And look where Publius is come to fetch me.

Publius. Good morrow, Caesar.

Caesar.   Welcome Publius.
110 What Brutus, are you stirred so early too?
Good morrow, Casca. Caius Ligarius,
Caesar was ne'er so much your enemy
As that same ague which hath made you lean.
What is't o'clock?

Brutus.   Caesar, 'tis strucken eight.

115 **Caesar.** I thank you for your pains and courtesy.

[*Enter* Antony.]

See! Antony, that revels long o'nights,
Is notwithstanding up. Good morrow, Antony.

Antony. So to most noble Caesar.

Caesar.   Bid them prepare within.
I am to blame to be thus waited for.
120 Now, Cinna, now, Metellus. What, Trebonius!
I have an hour's talk in store for you;
Remember that you call on me today;
Be near me, that I may remember you.

Trebonius. Caesar, I will. [*Aside.*] And so near will I be
125 That your best friends shall wish I had been further.

Caesar. Good friends, go in and taste some wine with me,
And we (like friends) will straightway go together. **D**

Brutus. [*Aside.*] That every like is not the same, O Caesar,
The heart of Brutus yearns to think upon.

[*Exeunt.*]

Scene 3   *A street in Rome near the Capitol.*

In this brief scene, Caesar has still another chance to avoid the path that leads to his death. Artemidorus, a supporter of Caesar, has learned about the plot. He reads a letter he has written to warn Caesar, and then waits in the street for Caesar to pass by on his way to the Capitol.

[*Enter* Artemidorus, *reading a paper.*]

Artemidorus. "Caesar, beware of Brutus; take heed of Cassius; come not near Casca; have an eye to Cinna;

113 **ague:** sickness.

116–117 **Antony...up:** Even Antony, who parties (**revels**) late into the night, is up early today.

124 **Aside:** privately, in a way that keeps the other characters from hearing what is said. Think of it as a whisper that the audience happens to overhear.

D DRAMATIC IRONY
Why are Caesar's remarks in lines 126–127 an example of dramatic irony?

trust not Trebonius; mark well Metellus Cimber;
Decius Brutus loves thee not; thou hast wronged Caius
5 Ligarius. There is but one mind in all these men,
and it is bent against Caesar. If thou beest not
immortal, look about you. Security gives way to
conspiracy. The mighty gods defend thee!

"Thy Lover,
10 "ARTEMIDORUS."

Here will I stand till Caesar pass along
And as a suitor will I give him this.
My heart laments that virtue cannot live
Out of the teeth of emulation.
15 If thou read this, O Caesar, thou mayst live;
If not, the Fates with traitors do contrive.

[*Exit.*]

9 Lover: devoted friend.

12 suitor: a person making a petition or request.

13–14 My heart . . . emulation: My heart is sad that Caesar's greatness cannot escape jealousy (**the teeth of emulation**).

16 contrive: plot.

Scene 4   *In front of Brutus' house.*

Brutus' wife, Portia, feels anxious about the conspiracy. She nervously orders the servant Lucius to go and see what is happening at the Capitol. She next meets the Soothsayer, who makes her even more anxious as he continues to predict danger for Caesar.

[*Enter* Portia *and* Lucius.]

Portia. I prithee, boy, run to the Senate House.
Stay not to answer me, but get thee gone!
Why dost thou stay?

Lucius.   To know my errand, madam.

Portia. I would have had thee there and here again
5 Ere I can tell thee what thou shouldst do there.
O constancy, be strong upon my side,
Set a huge mountain 'tween my heart and tongue!
I have a man's mind, but a woman's might.
How hard it is for women to keep counsel!
10 Art thou here yet?

Lucius.   Madam, what should I do?
Run to the Capitol and nothing else?
And so return to you and nothing else?

Portia. Yes, bring me word, boy, if thy lord look well,
For he went sickly forth; and take good note
15 What Caesar doth, what suitors press to him.
Hark, boy! What noise is that?

Lucius. I hear none, madam.

5 ere: before.

6 constancy: determination

9 keep counsel: keep a secret. *What does Portia seem to have learned from Brutus since their last scene together?*

15 what suitors press to him: what petitioners stand near him.

Portia. Prithee, listen well.
I heard a bustling rumor like a fray,
And the wind brings it from the Capitol.

20 **Lucius.** Sooth, madam, I hear nothing.

[*Enter the* Soothsayer.]

Portia. Come hither, fellow. Which way hast thou been?

Soothsayer. At mine own house, good lady.

Portia. What is't o'clock?

Soothsayer About the ninth hour, lady.

Portia. Is Caesar yet gone to the Capitol?

25 **Soothsayer.** Madam, not yet. I go to take my stand,
To see him pass on to the Capitol.

Portia. Thou hast some suit to Caesar, hast thou not?

Soothsayer. That I have, lady. If it will please Caesar
To be so good to Caesar as to hear me,
30 I shall beseech him to befriend himself.

Portia. Why, know'st thou any harm's intended towards him?

Soothsayer. None that I know will be, much that I fear may chance.
Good morrow to you. Here the street is narrow.
The throng that follows Caesar at the heels,
35 Of senators, of praetors, common suitors,
Will crowd a feeble man almost to death.
I'll get me to a place more void and there
Speak to great Caesar as he comes along.

[*Exit.*]

Portia. I must go in. Ay me, how weak a thing
40 The heart of woman is! O Brutus,
The heavens speed thee in thine enterprise—
Sure the boy heard me.—Brutus hath a suit
That Caesar will not grant.—O, I grow faint.—
Run, Lucius, and commend me to my Lord;
45 Say I am merry. Come to me again
And bring me word what he doth say to thee. **E**

[*Exeunt severally.*]

18 **a bustling . . . fray:** a noise like a fight.

20 **Sooth:** truly.

21 The Soothsayer is the same fortune-teller who warned Caesar to beware the ides of March. He is now on his way to the street near the Capitol building where he usually sits.

27 **suit:** petition.

32 **None . . . chance:** I'm not sure of any danger, but I fear that some may occur.

37 **void:** empty.

42–43 Fearing that Lucius has overheard her mention of the plot against Caesar, Portia pretends to worry about a petition that Brutus is going to present today.

E **TRAGEDY**
Which details in this scene help build **suspense?**

severally: separately.

Comprehension

1. **Recall** Why is Portia upset with Brutus?

2. **Recall** What has made Calpurnia concerned about Caesar's safety?

3. **Recall** Why are Artemidorus and the Soothsayer trying to reach Caesar as he makes his way to the Capitol?

4. **Summarize** How does Decius convince Caesar to change his mind about staying home?

Literary Analysis

5. **Reading Shakespearean Drama** Review the chart you created. What have you learned about Caesar in Act Two?

6. **Analyze Soliloquy and Aside** Using a chart like the one shown, identify soliloquies and asides in Act Two, and explain what each one reveals about the speaker. Which technique gives you more insight into a character's way of thinking? Explain your response.

Scene and Line Nos.	Speaker	Soliloquy or Aside?	What It Reveals

7. **Identify Mood** What mood do the two brief scenes at the end of Act Two help create? Cite details in your response.

8. **Make Inferences About Characters** Contrast the relationship between Caesar and Calpurnia with the relationship between Brutus and Portia. What do the differences suggest about the character of each man?

9. **Draw Conclusions** Is Brutus' decision to join the conspiracy driven more by his **conscience** or by Cassius' manipulation? Support your conclusion with evidence from the text.

10. **Evaluate Argument** Reread Brutus' soliloquy in lines 10–34 of Scene 1. Are you persuaded by his argument on the need to kill Caesar? Why or why not?

Literary Criticism

11. **Critical Interpretations** According to some critics, one reason *Julius Caesar* is so complex is that it offers widely differing views of the title character. Do you agree that the play allows you to form different impressions of Caesar as you read, or is his character portrayed consistently? Cite evidence to support your opinion.

OHIO STANDARDS

READING STANDARD
4.1 Compare and contrast ways that characters reveal traits about themselves

Act Three

Scene 1   *The Capitol in Rome.*

Outside the Capitol, Caesar refuses to look at Artemidorus' letter of warning. Caesar next moves into the Capitol. There, the conspirators surround him, pretending to plead a case. Suddenly, they stab him to death. Mark Antony flees, but Brutus persuades the conspirators to let him live. Brutus himself promises to explain the killing and its reasons to the Roman people. Antony returns and pretends to be an ally of the conspirators. Secretly, however, he plans to strike back with help from Octavius Caesar, who is now on his way to Rome.

[*The Senate sits on a higher level, waiting for* Caesar *to appear.* Artemidorus *and the* Soothsayer *are among the crowd. A flourish of trumpets. Enter* Caesar, Brutus, Cassius, Casca, Decius, Metellus, Trebonius, Cinna, Antony, Lepidus, Popilius, *and others.* Caesar *stops in front of the* Soothsayer.]

Caesar. The ides of March are come.

Soothsayer. Ay, Caesar, but not gone.

[Artemidorus *steps up to* Caesar *with his warning.*]

Artemidorus. Hail, Caesar! Read this schedule.

[Decius *steps up quickly with another paper.*]

Decius. Trebonius doth desire you to o'erread
5 (At your best leisure) this his humble suit.

Artemidorus. O Caesar, read mine first, for mine's a suit
That touches Caesar nearer. Read it, great Caesar!

Caesar. What touches us ourself shall be last served.

[Caesar *pushes the paper aside and turns away.*]

Artemidorus. Delay not, Caesar! Read it instantly!

10 **Caesar.** What, is the fellow mad?

Publius.   Sirrah, give place.

[Publius *and the conspirators force* Artemidorus *away from* Caesar.]

Cassius. What, urge you your petitions in the street?
Come to the Capitol.

[Caesar *goes into the Senate House, the rest following.* Popilius *speaks to* Cassius *in a low voice.*]

Popilius. I wish your enterprise today may thrive.

Cassius. What enterprise, Popilius?

Popilius.   Fare you well.

[*Advances to* Caesar.]

---

3 **schedule:** document.

4–5 **o'erread:** read over. *Why does Decius interrupt Artemidorus' request by presenting Caesar with a petition from someone else?*

7 **touches Caesar nearer:** more closely concerns Caesar.

10 **Sirrah:** a form of address used toward a servant or inferior, often to express anger or disrespect; **give place:** get out of the way.

13 **I wish . . . thrive:** I hope your venture is successful.

Antony mourns Julius Caesar in the Globe Theatre's 1999 production

15 **Brutus.** What said Popilius Lena?

Cassius. He wished today our enterprise might thrive.
I fear our purpose is discovered.

Brutus. Look how he makes to Caesar. Mark him.

Cassius. Casca, be sudden, for we fear prevention.
20 Brutus, what shall be done? If this be known,
Cassius or Caesar never shall turn back,
For I will slay myself.

Brutus.   Cassius, be constant.
Popilius Lena speaks not of our purposes,
For look, he smiles, and Caesar doth not change. Ⓐ

25 **Cassius.** Trebonius knows his time, for look you, Brutus,
He draws Mark Antony out of the way.

[*Exeunt* Antony *and* Trebonius.]

Decius. Where is Metellus Cimber? Let him go
And presently prefer his suit to Caesar.

Brutus. He is addressed. Press near and second him.

30 **Cinna.** Casca, you are the first that rears your hand.

[Caesar *seats himself in his high Senate chair.*]

Caesar. Are we all ready? What is now amiss
That Caesar and his Senate must redress?

Metellus. Most high, most mighty, and most puissant Caesar,
Metellus Cimber throws before thy seat
35 An humble heart.

[*Kneeling.*]

Caesar.   I must prevent thee, Cimber.
These couchings and these lowly courtesies
Might fire the blood of ordinary men
And turn preordinance and first decree
Into the law of children. Be not fond
40 To think that Caesar bears such rebel blood
That will be thawed from the true quality
With that which melteth fools—I mean, sweet words,
Low-crookèd curtsies, and base spaniel fawning.
Thy brother by decree is banished.
45 If thou dost bend and pray and fawn for him,
I spurn thee like a cur out of my way.
Know, Caesar doth not wrong, nor without cause
Will he be satisfied.

Metellus. Is there no voice more worthy than my own,
50 To sound more sweetly in great Caesar's ear
For the repealing of my banished brother?

19 **prevention:** being prevented from carrying out our task.

22 **constant:** calm.

Ⓐ **TRAGIC HERO**
How does Brutus' behavior in this dangerous moment compare with that of Cassius?

28 **presently prefer:** immediately present.

29 **addressed:** ready.

33 **puissant:** powerful.

36–46 Caesar declares that he will not be influenced by low bows and humble appeals, which might cause ordinary men to overlook established laws (**preordinance and first decree**). No amount of pleading will cause him to end the banishment of Metellus' brother.

Brutus. I kiss thy hand, but not in flattery, Caesar,
Desiring thee that Publius Cimber may
Have an immediate freedom of repeal.

54 freedom of repeal: the right to return to Rome from exile.

55 **Caesar.** What, Brutus?

Cassius.   Pardon, Caesar! Caesar, pardon!
As low as to thy foot doth Cassius fall
To beg enfranchisement for Publius Cimber.

57 enfranchisement: restoration of citizenship.

Caesar. I could be well moved, if I were as you;
If I could pray to move, prayers would move me;

59 If I . . . move: if, like you, I could plead with others to change their minds.

60 But I am constant as the Northern Star,
Of whose true-fixed and resting quality
There is no fellow in the firmament.
The skies are painted with unnumbered sparks,
They are all fire, and every one doth shine;
65 But there's but one in all doth hold his place.
So in the world: 'tis furnished well with men.
And men are flesh and blood, and apprehensive,
Yet in the number I do not know but one
That unassailable holds on his rank,
70 Unshaked of motion; and that I am he,
Let me a little show it, even in this,
That I was constant Cimber should be banished
And constant do remain to keep him so.

60–70 Caesar compares himself to the North Star, which always appears at the same place in the sky. Like that star, which has no equal in the sky (**fellow in the firmament**), Caesar cannot be moved from his decisions. *Has Caesar been as firm in his decisions as he claims to be?*

Cinna. O Caesar!

Caesar.   Hence! Wilt thou lift up Olympus?

74 Olympus: the mountain where the Greek gods were believed to live.

75 **Decius.** Great Caesar!

Caesar.   Doth not Brutus bootless kneel?

75 Doth not . . . kneel: Can't you see that even Brutus' kneeling is useless?

Casca. Speak hands for me!

[*They stab* Caesar. Casca, *the others in turn, then* Brutus.]

Caesar. *Et tu, Brute?*—Then fall Caesar!

[*Dies.*]

77 Et tu, Brute? (ĕt tōō brōō-tā) *Latin:* Even you, Brutus?

Cinna. Liberty! Freedom! Tyranny is dead!
Run hence, proclaim, cry it about the streets!

80 **Cassius.** Some to the common pulpits and cry out
"Liberty, freedom, and enfranchisement!"

80–83 Some . . . pulpits: Some of you go to the speakers' platforms. *What do Cassius and Brutus fear might occur following the assassination?*

Brutus. People and Senators, be not affrighted.
Fly not; stand still. Ambition's debt is paid.

Casca. Go to the pulpit, Brutus.

Decius   And Cassius, too.

85 **Brutus.** Where's Publius?

Cinna. Here, quite confounded with this mutiny.

86 confounded with this mutiny: stunned by this turmoil.

Blocking

During theater rehearsals, the director works out the positions and movements of actors on stage in a process called **blocking.** Some of these decisions are simple ones, such as figuring out how an actor will enter and exit. But blocking can have an important influence on the impact of a scene. How does the blocking of Caesar's assassination differ in these photographs? Which photograph gives the greatest impression of violence, and why?

Caesar's assassination in the Royal Shakespeare Company's 2004 production

Caesar's assassination in the Stratford 1993 production

Caesar's assassination in the Royal Shakespeare Company's 2001 production

Metellus. Stand fast together, lest some friend of Caesar's
Should chance—

Brutus. Talk not of standing! Publius, good cheer.
90 There is no harm intended to your person
Nor to no Roman else. So tell them, Publius.

Cassius. And leave us, Publius, lest that the people,
Rushing on us, should do your age some mischief.

Brutus. Do so, and let no man abide this deed
95 But we the doers.

[*Reenter* Trebonius.]

Cassius.   Where is Antony?

Trebonius. Fled to his house amazed.
Men, wives, and children stare, cry out, and run,
As it were doomsday.

Brutus.   Fates, we will know your pleasures.
That we shall die, we know; 'tis but the time,
100 And drawing days out, that men stand upon.

Cassius. Why, he that cuts off twenty years of life
Cuts off so many years of fearing death.

Brutus. Grant that, and then is death a benefit.
So are we Caesar's friends, that have abridged
105 His time of fearing death. Stoop, Romans, stoop,
And let us bathe our hands in Caesar's blood
Up to the elbows and besmear our swords.
Then walk we forth, even to the market place,
And waving our red weapons o'er our heads,
110 Let's all cry, "Peace, freedom, and liberty!" **B**

Cassius. Stoop then and wash. How many ages hence
Shall this our lofty scene be acted over
In states unborn and accents yet unknown!

Brutus. How many times shall Caesar bleed in sport,
115 That now on Pompey's basis lies along
No worthier than the dust!

Cassius.   So oft as that shall be.
So often shall the knot of us be called
The men that gave their country liberty.

Decius. What, shall we forth?

Cassius.   Ay, every man away.
120 Brutus shall lead, and we will grace his heels
With the most boldest and best hearts of Rome.

[*Enter a* Servant.]

Brutus. Soft! who comes here? A friend of Antony's.

92–93 Cassius wants Publius, an old man, to leave before he gets hurt by the crowd.

94 abide: suffer for.

B TRAGEDY
What message is Brutus trying to convey by having the conspirators go out in public smeared with Caesar's blood?

111–113 Cassius predicts that far into the future, the assassination will be reenacted in plays performed around the world. *Why might Shakespeare have added this speech?*

115 Pompey's basis: the base of Pompey's statue.

Servant. Thus, Brutus, did my master bid me kneel;
Thus did Mark Antony bid me fall down;
125 And being prostrate, thus he bade me say:
Brutus is noble, wise, valiant, and honest;
Caesar was mighty, bold, royal, and loving.
Say I love Brutus and I honor him;
Say I feared Caesar, honored him, and loved him.
130 If Brutus will vouchsafe that Antony
May safely come to him and be resolved
How Caesar hath deserved to lie in death,
Mark Antony shall not love Caesar dead
So well as Brutus living, but will follow
135 The fortunes and affairs of noble Brutus
Through the hazards of this untrod state
With all true faith. So says my master Antony.

Brutus. Thy master is a wise and valiant Roman.
I never thought him worse.
140 Tell him, so please him come unto this place,
He shall be satisfied and, by my honor,
Depart untouched.

Servant.   I'll fetch him presently.
[*Exit.*]

Brutus. I know that we shall have him well to friend.

Cassius. I wish we may. But yet have I a mind
145 That fears him much; and my misgiving still
Falls shrewdly to the purpose.

[*Reenter* Antony.]

Brutus. But here comes Antony. Welcome, Mark Antony.

Antony. O mighty Caesar! Dost thou lie so low?
Are all thy conquests, glories, triumphs, spoils,
150 Shrunk to this little measure? Fare thee well.
I know not, gentlemen, what you intend,
Who else must be let blood, who else is rank.
If I myself, there is no hour so fit
As Caesar's death's hour; nor no instrument
155 Of half that worth as those your swords, made rich
With the most noble blood of all this world.
I do beseech ye, if you bear me hard,
Now, whilst your purpled hands do reek and smoke,
Fulfill your pleasure. Live a thousand years,
160 I shall not find myself so apt to die;
No place will please me so, no mean of death,
As here by Caesar, and by you cut off,
The choice and master spirits of this age.

130–137 **If Brutus . . . faith:** If Brutus will guarantee Antony's safety so that he may come and receive a satisfactory explanation for Caesar's death, then Antony will faithfully support Brutus through the dangers of this crisis.

142 **presently:** immediately.

144–146 Unlike Brutus, Cassius doesn't trust Antony. He adds that his doubts (**misgiving**) in matters like this are usually accurate.

152 **Who else . . . rank:** who else is so diseased (**rank**) that they must be "cured" by bloodshed.

153–163 Antony says that if they have hard feelings toward him, he would be honored to be killed at this time and place by the same great men who killed Caesar. *Does Antony seem sincere? Why or why not?*

Brutus. O Antony, beg not your death of us!
165 Though now we must appear bloody and cruel,
As by our hands and this our present act
You see we do, yet see you but our hands
And this the bleeding business they have done.
Our hearts you see not. They are pitiful;
170 And pity to the general wrong of Rome
(As fire drives out fire, so pity pity)
Hath done this deed on Caesar. For your part,
To you our swords have leaden points, Mark Antony.
Our arms in strength of malice, and our hearts
175 Of brothers' temper, do receive you in
With all kind of love, good thoughts, and reverence.

Cassius. Your voice shall be as strong as any man's
In the disposing of new dignities.

Brutus. Only be patient till we have appeased
180 The multitude, beside themselves with fear,
And then we will deliver you the cause
Why I, that did love Caesar when I struck him,
Have thus proceeded.

Antony. I doubt not of your wisdom.
Let each man render me his bloody hand.
185 First, Marcus Brutus, will I shake with you;
Next, Caius Cassius, do I take your hand;
Now, Decius Brutus, yours; now yours, Metellus;
Yours, Cinna; and, my valiant Casca, yours.
Though last, not least in love, yours, good Trebonius.
190 Gentlemen all—Alas, what shall I say?
My credit now stands on such slippery ground
That one of two bad ways you must conceit me,
Either a coward or a flatterer.
That I did love thee, Caesar, O, 'tis true!
195 If then thy spirit look upon us now,
Shall it not grieve thee dearer than thy death
To see thy Antony making his peace,
Shaking the bloody fingers of thy foes,
Most noble! in the presence of thy corse?
200 Had I as many eyes as thou hast wounds,
Weeping as fast as they stream forth thy blood,
It would become me better than to close
In terms of friendship with thine enemies.
Pardon me, Julius! Here wast thou bayed, brave hart;
205 Here didst thou fall; and here thy hunters stand,
Signed in thy spoil, and crimsoned in thy lethe.
O world, thou wast the forest to his hart;

169 **pitiful:** full of pity.

171 **As fire ... pity:** Just as one fire may extinguish another, our pity for Rome overcame our pity for Caesar.

172–176 Brutus assures Antony that as far as he is concerned, their swords are harmless, and their arms as well as their hearts are friendly toward him.

191 **credit:** reputation.

192 **conceit:** think of.

194–210 These lines are addressed to the corpse (**corse**) of Caesar.

204 **Here ... hart:** This is the place where you were trapped (**bayed**) like a hunted deer (**hart**).

206 **Signed ... lethe:** marked with the signs of your slaughter and reddened by your bloodshed.

And this indeed, O world, the heart of thee!
How like a deer, strucken by many princes,
210 Dost thou here lie!

Cassius. Mark Antony—

Antony.   Pardon me, Caius Cassius.
The enemies of Caesar shall say this;
Then, in a friend, it is cold modesty.

Cassius. I blame you not for praising Caesar so;
215 But what compact mean you have with us?
Will you be pricked in number of our friends,
Or shall we on, and not depend on you?

Antony. Therefore I took your hands; but was indeed
Swayed from the point by looking down on Caesar.
220 Friends am I with you all, and love you all,
Upon this hope, that you shall give me reasons
Why and wherein Caesar was dangerous.

Brutus. Or else were this a savage spectacle.
Our reasons are so full of good regard
225 That were you, Antony, the son of Caesar,
You should be satisfied.

Antony.   That's all I seek;
And am moreover suitor that I may
Produce his body to the market place
And in the pulpit, as becomes a friend,
230 Speak in the order of his funeral.

Brutus. You shall, Mark Antony.

Cassius.   Brutus, a word with you.

[*Aside to* Brutus.]

You know not what you do. Do not consent
That Antony speak in his funeral.
Know you how much the people may be moved
235 By that which he will utter?

Brutus.   By your pardon,

[*Aside to* Cassius.]

I will myself into the pulpit first
And show the reason of our Caesar's death.
What Antony shall speak, I will protest
He speaks by leave and by permission,
240 And that we are contented Caesar shall
Have all true rites and lawful ceremonies.
It shall advantage more than do us wrong.

215 **compact:** agreement.

216 **pricked:** listed; marked down.

218 **Therefore . . . hands:** That is why I shook hands with all of you (because I intend to be counted as an ally of yours).

223 **Or else . . . spectacle:** If we could not give you reasons for what we have done, it would be nothing but a display of savagery.

226–230 Antony asks permission to present Caesar's body in public and make a funeral speech.

238 **protest:** explain.

242 **It shall . . . wrong:** His speech will do us more good (**advantage more**) than harm.

Cassius.

[*Aside to* Brutus.]

I know not what may fall. I like it not. **C**

Brutus. Mark Antony, here, take you Caesar's body.

245 You shall not in your funeral speech blame us,
But speak all good you can devise of Caesar,
And say you do't by our permission.
Else shall you not have any hand at all
About his funeral. And you shall speak

250 In the same pulpit whereto I am going,
After my speech is ended.

Antony.   Be it so.
I do desire no more.

Brutus. Prepare the body then, and follow us.

[*Exeunt all but* Antony, *who looks down at* Caesar's *body.*]

Antony. O, pardon me, thou bleeding piece of earth,

255 That I am meek and gentle with these butchers!
Thou art the ruins of the noblest man
That ever lived in the tide of times.
Woe to the hand that shed this costly blood!
Over thy wounds now do I prophesy

260 (Which, like dumb mouths, do ope their ruby lips
To beg the voice and utterance of my tongue),
A curse shall light upon the limbs of men;
Domestic fury and fierce civil strife
Shall cumber all the parts of Italy;

265 Blood and destruction shall be so in use
And dreadful objects so familiar
That mothers shall but smile when they behold
Their infants quartered with the hands of war,
All pity choked with custom of fell deeds;

270 And Caesar's spirit, ranging for revenge,
With Até by his side come hot from hell,
Shall in these confines with a monarch's voice
Cry "Havoc!" and let slip the dogs of war,
That this foul deed shall smell above the earth

275 With carrion men, groaning for burial.

[*Enter* Octavius' Servant.]

You serve Octavius Caesar, do you not?

Servant. I do, Mark Antony.

Antony. Caesar did write for him to come to Rome.

C TRAGEDY
Cassius remains concerned about Brutus' decision to let Antony give a funeral speech. How might this decision lead to complications in the play's **plot?**

254–275 Now that Antony is alone with Caesar's corpse, he speaks truthfully. His speech shows what he really thinks of the men who have just left and what he intends to do about the murder.

257 in the tide of times: in all of history.

263–269 Domestic fury ... deeds: Rome (**Italy**) will be torn by civil war. People will become so accustomed to horrible sights that mothers will simply smile when they see their children cut into pieces (**quartered**). Pity will disappear among so much cruelty.

271 Até (ā′tē): the Greek goddess of revenge.

273 "Havoc!": Kill without mercy.

275 With carrion ... burial: like rotting corpses begging to be buried.

276 Antony is interrupted by a servant of Octavius, Caesar's grandnephew and adopted son.

Servant. He did receive his letters and is coming,
280 And bid me say to you by word of mouth—
O Caesar!

Antony. Thy heart is big. Get thee apart and weep.
Passion, I see, is catching, for mine eyes,
Seeing those beads of sorrow stand in thine,
285 Began to water. Is thy master coming?

Servant. He lies tonight within seven leagues of Rome.

Antony. Post back with speed and tell him what hath chanced.
Here is a mourning Rome, a dangerous Rome,
No Rome of safety for Octavius yet.
290 Hie hence and tell him so. Yet stay awhile.
Thou shalt not back till I have borne this corse
Into the market place. There shall I try
In my oration how the people take
The cruel issue of these bloody men,
295 According to the which thou shall discourse
To young Octavius of the state of things.
Lend me your hand.

[*Exeunt with* Caesar's *body.*]

Scene 2   *The forum in Rome.*

Brutus speaks before a group of "citizens," or common people of Rome. He explains why Caesar had to be slain for the good of Rome. Then Brutus leaves and Antony speaks to the citizens. A far better judge of human nature than Brutus, Antony cleverly manages to turn the crowd against the conspirators by telling them of Caesar's good works and his concern for the people, as proven by the slain ruler's will. He has left all his wealth to the people. As Antony stirs the citizens to pursue the assassins and kill them, he learns that Octavius has arrived in Rome and that Brutus and Cassius have fled.

[*Enter* Brutus *and* Cassius *and a throng of* Citizens, *disturbed by the death of* Caesar.]

Citizens. We will be satisfied! Let us be satisfied!

Brutus. Then follow me and give me audience, friends.
Cassius, go you into the other street
And part the numbers.
5 Those that will hear me speak, let 'em stay here;
Those that will follow Cassius, go with him;
And public reasons shall be rendered
Of Caesar's death.

First Citizen.   I will hear Brutus speak.

Second Citizen. I will hear Cassius, and compare their reasons
10 when severally we hear them rendered.

286 **He lies . . . Rome:** Octavius will set up camp tonight about 21 miles (**seven leagues**) outside Rome.

287–297 Antony tells the servant to hurry back and tell Octavius what has happened. Then he tells the servant to wait. He wants the servant to listen to his funeral speech and report to Octavius how the crowd responds to it.

3–8 Brutus tells Cassius to divide the crowd (**part the numbers**) so they can explain their reasons for killing Caesar to separate groups.

[*Exit* Cassius, *with some of the* Citizens. Brutus *goes into the pulpit.*]

Third Citizen. The noble Brutus is ascended. Silence!

Brutus. Be patient till the last.
Romans, countrymen, and lovers, hear me for my cause, and be silent, that you may hear. Believe me for mine honor, and have
15 respect to mine honor, that you may believe. Censure me in your wisdom, and awake your senses, that you may the better judge. If there be any in this assembly, any dear friend of Caesar's, to him I say that Brutus' love to Caesar was no less than his. If then that friend demand why Brutus rose against Caesar, this is my answer:
20 Not that I loved Caesar less, but that I loved Rome more. Had you rather Caesar were living, and die all slaves, than that Caesar were dead, to live all freemen? As Caesar loved me, I weep for him; as he was fortunate, I rejoice at it; as he was valiant, I honor him; but—as he was ambitious, I slew him. There is tears for his love; joy for his
25 fortune; honor for his valor; and death for his ambition. Who is here so base that would be a bondman? If any, speak, for him have I offended. Who is here so rude that would not be a Roman? If any, speak, for him have I offended. Who is here so vile that will not love his country? If any, speak, for him have I offended. I pause
30 for a reply.

All. None, Brutus, none!

Brutus. Then none have I offended. I have done no more to Caesar than you shall do to Brutus. The question of his death is enrolled in the Capitol; his glory not extenuated, wherein he was
35 worthy, nor his offenses enforced, for which he suffered death.

[*Enter* Antony *and others, with* Caesar's *body.*]

Here comes his body, mourned by Mark Antony, who though he had no hand in his death, shall receive the benefit of his dying, a place in the commonwealth, as which of you shall not? With this ◆ **D**
I depart, that, as I slew my best lover for the good of Rome, I
40 have the same dagger for myself when it shall please my country to need my death.

All. Live, Brutus! live, live!

First Citizen. Bring him with triumph home unto his house.

Second Citizen. Give him a statue with his ancestors.

45 **Third Citizen.** Let him be Caesar.

Fourth Citizen.   Caesar's better parts
Shall be crowned in Brutus.

First Citizen. We'll bring him to his house with shouts and clamors.

Brutus. My countrymen—

Second Citizen.   Peace! silence! Brutus speaks.

13 lovers: friends.

15 Censure me: Judge me.

16 senses: reason.

25–26 Who is ... bondman: Which of you is so low that you would prefer to be a slave?

27 rude: uncivilized.

33–35 The question ... death: The reasons for his death are on record in the Capitol. We have not belittled (**extenuated**) his accomplishments or overemphasized (**enforced**) the failings for which he was killed.

D GRAMMAR AND STYLE
Reread lines 36–38. Here, Shakespeare uses the **adjective clause** "who ... shall receive the benefit of his dying" to convey Brutus' implication that Antony will gain from Caesar's death.

42–48 *What is the mood of the crowd as Brutus finishes his speech?*

45 parts: qualities.

First Citizen. Peace ho!

50 **Brutus.** Good countrymen, let me depart alone,
And, for my sake, stay here with Antony.
Do grace to Caesar's corpse, and grace his speech
Tending to Caesar's glories which Mark Antony,
By our permission, is allowed to make.
55 I do entreat you, not a man depart,
Save I alone, till Antony have spoke.

[*Exit.*]

First Citizen. Stay, ho! and let us hear Mark Antony.

Third Citizen. Let him go up into the public chair.
We'll hear him. Noble Antony, go up.

60 **Antony.** For Brutus' sake I am beholding to you.

[*Goes into the pulpit.*]

Fourth Citizen. What does he say of Brutus?

Third Citizen.   He says for Brutus'
Sake he finds himself beholding to us all.

Fourth Citizen. 'Twere best he speak no harm of Brutus here!

65 **First Citizen.** This Caesar was a tyrant.

Third Citizen.   Nay, that's certain.
We are blest that Rome is rid of him.

Second Citizen. Peace! Let us hear what Antony can say.

Antony. You gentle Romans—

All.   Peace, ho! Let us hear him.

70 **Antony.** Friends, Romans, countrymen, lend me your ears;
I come to bury Caesar, not to praise him.
The evil that men do lives after them;
The good is oft interred with their bones.
So let it be with Caesar. The noble Brutus
75 Hath told you Caesar was ambitious.
If it were so, it was a grievous fault,
And grievously hath Caesar answered it.
Here, under leave of Brutus and the rest
(For Brutus is an honorable man;
80 So are they all, all honorable men),
Come I to speak in Caesar's funeral.
He was my friend, faithful and just to me;
But Brutus says he was ambitious,
And Brutus is an honorable man.
85 He hath brought many captives home to Rome,
Whose ransoms did the general coffers fill.
Did this in Caesar seem ambitious?

52 **grace his speech:** Listen to him respectfully.

56 **Save:** except.

58 **public chair:** speaker's platform.

60 **beholding:** indebted.

70–134 In this famous speech, notice how Antony gradually turns the citizens away from their support of the conspirators.

72–74 Antony says that Caesar's good deeds should be buried (**interred**) with him; let him be remembered by his faults.

76 **grievous:** serious.

78 **under leave of:** with the permission of.

86 **general coffers:** the Roman government's treasury.

When that the poor have cried, Caesar hath wept;
Ambition should be made of sterner stuff.
90 Yet Brutus says he was ambitious;
And Brutus is an honorable man.
You all did see that on the Lupercal
I thrice presented him a kingly crown,
Which he did thrice refuse. Was this ambition?
95 Yet Brutus says he was ambitious;
And sure he is an honorable man. **E**
I speak not to disprove what Brutus spoke,
But here I am to speak what I do know.
You all did love him once, not without cause.
100 What cause withholds you then to mourn for him?
O judgment, thou art fled to brutish beasts,
And men have lost their reason! Bear with me,
My heart is in the coffin there with Caesar,
And I must pause till it come back to me.

105 **First Citizen.** Methinks there is much reason in his sayings.

Second Citizen. If thou consider rightly of the matter,
Caesar has had great wrong.

Third Citizen.   Has he, masters?
I fear there will a worse come in his place.

Fourth Citizen. Marked ye his words? He would not take the crown;
110 Therefore 'tis certain he was not ambitious.

First Citizen. If it be found so, some will dear abide it.

Second Citizen. Poor soul! his eyes are red as fire with weeping.

Third Citizen. There's not a nobler man in Rome than Antony.

Fourth Citizen. Now mark him. He begins again to speak.

115 **Antony.** But yesterday the word of Caesar might
Have stood against the world. Now lies he there,
And none so poor to do him reverence.
O masters! If I were disposed to stir
Your hearts and minds to mutiny and rage,
120 I should do Brutus wrong, and Cassius wrong,
Who, you all know, are honorable men.
I will not do them wrong. I rather choose
To wrong the dead, to wrong myself and you,
Than I will wrong such honorable men.
125 But here's a parchment with the seal of Caesar.
I found it in his closet; 'tis his will.
Let but the commons hear this testament,
Which (pardon me) I do not mean to read,
And they would go and kiss dead Caesar's wounds
130 And dip their napkins in his sacred blood;

93 **thrice:** three times.

E **RHETORICAL DEVICES**
Reread lines 74–96 and pay
attention to Antony's **repetition** of
the words *ambitious* and *honorable*.
What does he emphasize through
the repetition of these words?

111 **some will dear abide it:** Some will pay
dearly for it.

115 **But:** only.

117 **And none . . . reverence:** And no one is
low enough to show respect for him.

127–134 Antony says that if the people
heard Caesar's will, they would dip their
handkerchiefs (**napkins**) in his blood or
beg for one of his hairs, and then upon
their own deaths their children (**issue**)
would inherit these valuable mementos.
*Why does Antony tell the crowd that he
does not plan to read the will?*

Yea, beg a hair of him for memory,
And dying, mention it within their wills,
Bequeathing it as a rich legacy
Unto their issue.

135 **Fourth Citizen.** We'll hear the will! Read it, Mark Antony.

All. The will, the will! We will hear Caesar's will!

Antony. Have patience, gentle friends, I must not read it.
It is not meet you know how Caesar loved you.
You are not wood, you are not stones, but men;
140 And being men, hearing the will of Caesar,
It will inflame you, it will make you mad.
'Tis good you know not that you are his heirs,
For if you should, O, what would come of it?

Fourth Citizen. Read the will! We'll hear it, Antony!
145 You shall read us the will, Caesar's will!

Antony. Will you be patient? Will you stay awhile?
I have o'ershot myself to tell you of it.
I fear I wrong the honorable men
Whose daggers have stabbed Caesar; I do fear it.

150 **Fourth Citizen.** They were traitors. Honorable men!

All. The will! the testament!

Second Citizen. They were villains, murderers! The will!
Read the will!

Antony. You will compel me then to read the will?
155 Then make a ring about the corpse of Caesar
And let me show you him that made the will.
Shall I descend? and will you give me leave? **F**

All. Come down.

Second Citizen. Descend.

160 **Third Citizen.** You shall have leave.

[Antony *comes down.*]

Fourth Citizen. A ring! Stand round.

First Citizen. Stand from the hearse! Stand from the body!

Second Citizen. Room for Antony, most noble Antony!

Antony. Nay, press not so upon me. Stand far off.

165 **All.** Stand back! Room! Bear back!

Antony. If you have tears, prepare to shed them now.
You all do know this mantle. I remember
The first time ever Caesar put it on.
'Twas on a summer's evening in his tent,
170 That day he overcame the Nervii.

138 **meet:** proper.

147 **I have . . . of it:** I have gone too far in even mentioning it to you.

F RHETORICAL DEVICES
Reread lines 146–157. What does Antony's use of **rhetorical questions** suggest about his relationship with the crowd?

167 **mantle:** Caesar's toga.

170 **the Nervii:** a Belgian tribe that Caesar defeated 13 years earlier.

Look, in this place ran Cassius' dagger through.
See what a rent the envious Casca made.
Through this the well-beloved Brutus stabbed;
And as he plucked his cursed steel away,
175 Mark how the blood of Caesar followed it,
As rushing out of doors to be resolved
If Brutus so unkindly knocked or no;
For Brutus, as you know, was Caesar's angel.
Judge, O you gods, how dearly Caesar loved him!
180 This was the most unkindest cut of all;
For when the noble Caesar saw him stab,
Ingratitude, more strong than traitors' arms,
Quite vanquished him. Then burst his mighty heart;
And in his mantle muffling up his face,
185 Even at the base of Pompey's statue
(Which all the while ran blood) great Caesar fell.
O, what a fall was there, my countrymen!
Then I, and you, and all of us fell down,
Whilst bloody treason flourished over us.
190 O, now you weep, and I perceive you feel
The dint of pity. These are gracious drops.
Kind souls, what, weep you when you but behold
Our Caesar's vesture wounded? Look you here!
Here is himself, marred, as you see, with traitors.

[*Pulls the cloak off* Caesar's *body.*]

195 **First Citizen.** O piteous spectacle!

Second Citizen. O noble Caesar!

Third Citizen. O woeful day!

Fourth Citizen. O traitors, villains!

First Citizen. O most bloody sight!

200 **Second Citizen.** We will be revenged.

All. Revenge! About! Seek! Burn! Fire! Kill! Slay!
Let not a traitor live!

Antony. Stay, countrymen.

First Citizen. Peace there! Hear the noble Antony.

205 **Second Citizen.** We'll hear him, we'll follow him, we'll die with him!

Antony. Good friends, sweet friends, let me not stir you up
To such a sudden flood of mutiny.
They that have done this deed are honorable.
What private griefs they have, alas, I know not,
210 That made them do it. They are wise and honorable,
And will no doubt with reasons answer you.
I come not, friends, to steal away your hearts.

172 rent: tear, hole.

175 Mark: notice.

176–177 As rushing . . . or no: as if it rushed out of that opening to find out if it really was Brutus who had made the wound.

183 vanquished: defeated.

191 dint: force.

192–194 weep you . . . traitors: Do you cry when you look only at his wounded clothing (**vesture**)? Here, look at his body!

I am no orator, as Brutus is,
But (as you know me all) a plain blunt man
215 That love my friend; and that they know full well
That gave me public leave to speak of him.
For I have neither wit, nor words, nor worth,
Action, nor utterance, nor the power of speech
To stir men's blood. I only speak right on.
220 I tell you that which you yourselves do know,
Show you sweet Caesar's wounds, poor poor dumb mouths,
And bid them speak for me. But were I Brutus,
And Brutus Antony, there were an Antony
Would ruffle up your spirits, and put a tongue
225 In every wound of Caesar that should move
The stones of Rome to rise and mutiny. **G**

All. We'll mutiny.

First Citizen.   We'll burn the house of Brutus.

Third Citizen. Away then! Come, seek the conspirators.

Antony. Yet hear me, countrymen. Yet hear me speak.

230 **All.** Peace, ho! Hear Antony, most noble Antony!

Antony. Why, friends, you go to do you know not what.
Wherein hath Caesar thus deserved your loves?
Alas, you know not! I must tell you then.
You have forgot the will I told you of.

235 **All.** Most true! The will! Let's stay and hear the will.

Antony. Here is the will, under Caesar's seal.
To every Roman citizen he gives,
To every several man, seventy-five drachmas.

Second Citizen. Most noble Caesar! We'll revenge his death!

240 **Third Citizen.** O royal Caesar!

Antony. Hear me with patience.

All. Peace, ho!

Antony. Moreover, he hath left you all his walks,
His private arbors, and new-planted orchards,
245 On this side Tiber; he hath left them you,
And to your heirs for ever—common pleasures,
To walk abroad and recreate yourselves.
Here was a Caesar! When comes such another?

First Citizen. Never, never! Come, away, away!
250 We'll burn his body in the holy place
And with the brands the traitors' houses.
Take up the body.

Second Citizen. Go fetch fire!

G **RHETORICAL DEVICES**
Identify examples of rhetorical
devices in Antony's funeral speech,
lines 70–226. What is **ironic** about
his claim in lines 213–219?

238 several: individual; **drachmas:** silver
coins, worth quite a bit to poor people
such as those in the crowd.

243–247 Antony tells the crowd that
Caesar has left all his private parks and
gardens on this side of the Tiber River to
be used by the public.

251 brands: pieces of burning wood.

Third Citizen. Pluck down benches!

255 **Fourth Citizen.** Pluck down forms, windows, anything!

[*Exeunt* Citizens *with the body.*]

Antony. Now let it work. Mischief, thou art afoot,
Take thou what course thou wilt.

[*Enter a* Servant.]

How now, fellow?

Servant. Sir, Octavius is already come to Rome.

Antony. Where is he?

260 **Servant.** He and Lepidus are at Caesar's house.

Antony. And thither will I straight to visit him.
He comes upon a wish. Fortune is merry,
And in this mood will give us anything.

Servant. I heard him say Brutus and Cassius

265 Are rid like madmen through the gates of Rome.

Antony. Belike they had some notice of the people,
How I had moved them. Bring me to Octavius.

[*Exeunt.*]

256–257 Now let . . . wilt: Alone, Antony gloats over what he has just accomplished. Let things take their course, he says. Whatever happens, happens.

261 thither . . . him: I will go right there to see him.

262–263 Antony says that Octavius has arrived just as he hoped. Antony believes that Fortune, the goddess of fate, is on his side.

265 Are rid: have ridden.

266 Belike: probably.

Scene 3   *A street in Rome.*

This scene involves a famous Roman poet named Cinna. (He is not the same Cinna who took part in the assassination.) The angry Roman citizens come upon the poet and believe he is Cinna the conspirator. Soon they realize he is the wrong man, yet they are so enraged that they slay him anyway. Then they rush through the city after the true killers of Caesar.

[*Enter Cinna, the poet, and after him the* Citizens, *armed with sticks, spears, and swords.*]

Cinna. I dreamt tonight that I did feast with Caesar,
And things unluckily charge my fantasy.
I have no will to wander forth of doors,
Yet something leads me forth.

5 **First Citizen.** What is your name?

Second Citizen. Whither are you going?

Third Citizen. Where do you dwell?

Fourth Citizen. Are you a married man or a bachelor?

Second Citizen. Answer every man directly.

10 **First Citizen.** Ay, and briefly.

Fourth Citizen. Ay, and wisely.

Third Citizen. Ay, and truly, you were best.

2 things . . . fantasy: Recent events have caused me to imagine awful things.

6 Whither: where.

Cinna. What is my name? Whither am I going? Where do I dwell? Am I a married man or a bachelor? Then, to answer every man
15 directly and briefly, wisely and truly: wisely I say, I am a bachelor.

Second Citizen. That's as much to say they are fools that marry. You'll bear me a bang for that, I fear. Proceed—directly.

Cinna. Directly I am going to Caesar's funeral.

First Citizen. As a friend or an enemy?

20 **Cinna.** As a friend.

Second Citizen. That matter is answered directly.

Fourth Citizen. For your dwelling—briefly.

Cinna. Briefly, I dwell by the Capitol.

Third Citizen. Your name, sir, truly.

25 **Cinna.** Truly, my name is Cinna.

First Citizen. Tear him to pieces! He's a conspirator.

Cinna. I am Cinna the poet! I am Cinna the poet!

Fourth Citizen. Tear him for his bad verses! Tear him for his bad verses!

30 **Cinna.** I am not Cinna the conspirator.

Fourth Citizen. It is no matter; his name's Cinna! Pluck but his name out of his heart, and turn him going.

Third Citizen. Tear him, tear him!

[*They attack* Cinna.]

Come, brands, ho! To Brutus', to Cassius'! Burn all!
35 Some to Decius' house and some to Casca's; some to Ligarius'! Away, go!

[*Exeunt all the* Citizens.]

16–17 That's . . . fear: This response shows that Cinna is in danger. The citizen threatens to beat him (**You'll bear me a bang**), even though Cinna's comment was not meant to be insulting.

31–32 Pluck . . . going: Let's just tear the name out of his heart and send him away.

Comprehension

1. **Recall** What request do the conspirators make just before killing Caesar?

2. **Recall** What disagreement do Brutus and Cassius have about the plans for Caesar's funeral?

3. **Recall** What information does Antony reveal to the crowd during his funeral speech?

4. **Clarify** Why does the crowd attack Cinna the poet?

OHIO STANDARDS

READING STANDARD
4.7 Recognize irony

Literary Analysis

5. **Reading Shakespearean Drama** Review the chart you created. How do the events in Act Three affect your impression of Brutus?

6. **Examine Dramatic Irony** What dramatic irony does Shakespeare create in lines 1–2 of Act Three, Scene 1?

7. **Identify Motivation** Reread Mark Antony's soliloquy in lines 254–275 of Scene 1. What does this speech reveal about the motivation for Antony's actions in the rest of Act Three?

8. **Analyze Rhetorical Devices** In a chart like the one shown, analyze examples of rhetorical devices in the funeral speeches delivered by Brutus and Antony in Act Three, Scene 2, lines 13–42 and 70–248. How does Antony use **repetition** to contradict assertions in Brutus' speech?

Example	Speaker	Type of Rhetorical Device	What It Suggests or Emphasizes

9. **Compare and Contrast** Why does Antony's funeral speech have a much more powerful effect on the crowd than Brutus' speech? Cite details in your response.

10. **Draw Conclusions About Plot** Act Three begins and ends with violent events. What does the murder of Cinna the poet in Scene 3 suggest about the use of violence to achieve political goals? Cite evidence to support your conclusion.

Literary Criticism

11. **Critical Interpretations** The novelist and critic E. M. Forster wrote that Brutus "cannot realize that men seek their own interests, for he has never sought his own, he has lived nobly among noble thoughts, wedded to a noble wife." How is this limitation reflected in Brutus' words and actions in Act Three? Cite examples from the text.

Act Four

Scene 1   *At a table in Antony's house in Rome.*

Antony, Octavius, and Lepidus now rule Rome as a triumvirate—a committee of three. The scene opens on the triumvirate, meeting to draw up a list of their enemies who must be killed. They also discuss changing Caesar's will. As Lepidus goes to fetch the will, Antony expresses his low opinion of Lepidus as a leader. Then, Antony and Octavius begin to discuss how to defeat the armies of Brutus and Cassius.

[*Enter* Antony, Octavius, *and* Lepidus.]

Antony. These many, then, shall die; their names are pricked.

Octavius. Your brother too must die. Consent you, Lepidus?

Lepidus. I do consent.

Octavius.   Prick him down, Antony.

Lepidus. Upon condition Publius shall not live,
5 Who is your sister's son, Mark Antony.

Antony. He shall not live. Look, with a spot I damn him.
But Lepidus, go you to Caesar's house.
Fetch the will hither, and we shall determine
How to cut off some charge in legacies.

10 **Lepidus.** What? shall I find you here?

Octavius. Or here or at the Capitol.

[*Exit* Lepidus.]

Antony. This is a slight unmeritable man,
Meet to be sent on errands. Is it fit,
The threefold world divided, he should stand
15 One of the three to share it?

Octavius.   So you thought him,
And took his voice who should be pricked to die
In our black sentence and proscription.

Antony. Octavius, I have seen more days than you;
And though we lay these honors on this man
20 To ease ourselves of divers sland'rous loads,
He shall but bear them as the ass bears gold,
To groan and sweat under the business,
Either led or driven as we point the way;
And having brought our treasure where we will,
25 Then take we down his load, and turn him off
(Like to the empty ass) to shake his ears
And graze in commons.

---

1 pricked: marked down.

6 with a spot . . . him: I condemn him by marking him on this list.

8–9 Fetch . . . legacies: Bring Caesar's will here, so we can figure out how to lower the amounts left to the people. *What impression of Antony do you get from this remark?*

13 meet: fit.

13–15 Antony questions whether it is fitting for Lepidus to share control of Rome's lands in Europe, Asia, and Africa (**the threefold world**).

17 black sentence and proscription: death sentences.

19–27 Antony says that they are giving Lepidus temporary power only so that he will bear the burden of public criticism of their actions.

27 commons: public land for grazing.

Cassius and Brutus in the Globe Theatre's 1999 production

Behind the Curtain

Brutus and Cassius in the Royal Shakespeare Company's 2001 production

Brutus and Cassius in the New York Shakespeare Festival's 1988 production

Brutus and Cassius in the Shakespeare Theatre's 1993–1994 production

Costume Design

In addition to providing information about a character's occupation and social class, a **stage costume** may offer clues to the character's personality. Costume designers often have to do careful research to create historically accurate styles of clothing. For a production that is not realistic, the designer may mix fashions from different periods. How do the costumes of Brutus and Cassius differ in these photographs? What do they suggest about the characters?

But for supporting robbers—shall we now
Contaminate our fingers with base bribes,
25 And sell the mighty space of our large honors
For so much trash as may be grasped thus?
I had rather be a dog and bay the moon
Than such a Roman.

Cassius.   Brutus, bait not me!
I'll not endure it. You forget yourself
30 To hedge me in. I am a soldier, I,
Older in practice, abler than yourself
To make conditions.

Brutus.   Go to! You are not, Cassius.

Cassius. I am.

Brutus. I say you are not.

35 **Cassius.** Urge me no more! I shall forget myself.
Have mind upon your health, tempt me no farther.

Brutus. Away, slight man!

Cassius. Is't possible?

Brutus.   Hear me, for I will speak.
Must I give way and room to your rash choler?
40 Shall I be frighted when a madman stares?

Cassius. O ye gods, ye gods! Must I endure all this?

Brutus. All this? Ay, more! Fret till your proud heart break.
Go show your slaves how choleric you are
And make your bondmen tremble. Must I budge?
45 Must I observe you? Must I stand and crouch
Under your testy humor? By the gods,
You shall digest the venom of your spleen,
Though it do split you; for from this day forth
I'll use you for my mirth, yea, for my laughter,
50 When you are waspish. **B**

Cassius.   Is it come to this?

Brutus. You say you are a better soldier;
Let it appear so. Make your vaunting true,
And it shall please me well. For mine own part,
I shall be glad to learn of noble men.

55 **Cassius.** You wrong me every way! You wrong me, Brutus!
I said an elder soldier, not a better.
Did I say "better"?

Brutus.   If you did, I care not.

Cassius. When Caesar lived he durst not thus have moved me.

Brutus. Peace, peace! You durst not so have tempted him.

---

23 But for supporting robbers: because he supported corrupt officials. (This is not one of the charges the conspirators originally made against Caesar.)

27 bay: howl at.

28 bait: provoke.

32 make conditions: arrange matters.

B TRAGIC HERO
In lines 39–50, Brutus refers to Cassius' quick temper (**rash choler**), irritable mood (**testy humor**), and his spleen, which was once believed to be the source of emotions such as anger and spite. What **character trait** does Brutus imply is necessary in a good leader?

52 vaunting: bragging. *What challenge does Brutus make?*

58 he durst ... me: Even Caesar would not have dared to provoke me this way.

60 **Cassius.** I durst not?

Brutus. No.

Cassius. What, durst not tempt him?

Brutus.   For your life you durst not.

Cassius. Do not presume too much upon my love.
I may do that I shall be sorry for.

65 **Brutus.** You have done that you should be sorry for.
There is no terror, Cassius, in your threats;
For I am armed so strong in honesty
That they pass by me as the idle wind,
Which I respect not. I did send to you
70 For certain sums of gold, which you denied me,
For I can raise no money by vile means—
By heaven, I had rather coin my heart
And drop my blood for drachmas than to wring
From the hard hands of peasants their vile trash
75 By any indirection. I did send
To you for gold to pay my legions,
Which you denied me. Was that done like Cassius?
Should I have answered Caius Cassius so?
When Marcus Brutus grows so covetous
80 To lock such rascal counters from his friends,
Be ready, gods, with all your thunderbolts,
Dash him to pieces! **C**

Cassius.   I denied you not.

Brutus. You did.

Cassius. I did not. He was but a fool that brought
85 My answer back. Brutus hath rived my heart.
A friend should bear his friend's infirmities,
But Brutus makes mine greater than they are.

Brutus. I do not, till you practice them on me.

Cassius. You love me not.

Brutus.   I do not like your faults.

90 **Cassius.** A friendly eye could never see such faults.

Brutus. A flatterer's would not, though they do appear
As huge as high Olympus.

Cassius. Come, Antony, and young Octavius, come!
Revenge yourselves alone on Cassius.
95 For Cassius is aweary of the world:
Hated by one he loves; braved by his brother;
Checked like a bondman, all his faults observed,
Set in a notebook, learned and conned by rote
To cast into my teeth. O, I could weep

71–75 **For I can . . . indirection:** I cannot raise money by dishonest (**vile**) methods. I would rather make coins out of my heart and blood than steal money from peasants by lying (**indirection**).

76 **legions:** armies.

79–82 **When . . . pieces:** When I become such a miser as to deny cheap coins (**rascal counters**) to my friends, may the gods destroy me.

C TRAGIC HERO
What conclusion would you draw about Brutus' honesty in light of his request for money from Cassius? Explain your answer.

85 **rived:** torn apart.

86 **infirmities:** shortcomings.

96 **braved:** defied.

97 **Checked like a bondman:** scolded like a slave.

98 **conned by rote:** memorized by repetition.

100 My spirit from mine eyes! There is my dagger,
And here my naked breast; within, a heart
Dearer than Pluto's mine, richer than gold:
If that thou be'st a Roman, take it forth.
I, that denied thee gold, will give my heart.
105 Strike as thou didst at Caesar; for I know,
When thou didst hate him worst, thou lov'dst him better
Than ever thou lov'dst Cassius.

Brutus.   Sheathe your dagger.
Be angry when you will; it shall have scope.
Do what you will; dishonor shall be humor.
110 O Cassius, you are yoked with a lamb
That carries anger as the flint bears fire;
Who, much enforced, shows a hasty spark,
And straight is cold again.

Cassius.   Hath Cassius lived
To be but mirth and laughter to his Brutus
115 When grief and blood ill-tempered vexeth him?

Brutus. When I spoke that, I was ill-tempered too.

Cassius. Do you confess so much? Give me your hand.

Brutus. And my heart too.

Cassius.   O Brutus!

Brutus.   What's the matter?

Cassius. Have you not love enough to bear with me
120 When that rash humor which my mother gave me
Makes me forgetful?

Brutus.   Yes, Cassius, and from henceforth,
When you are over-earnest with your Brutus,
He'll think your mother chides, and leave you so.

[*Enter a* Poet *followed by* Lucilius, Titinius, *and* Lucius.]

Poet. Let me go in to see the generals!
125 There is some grudge between 'em. 'Tis not meet
They be alone.

Lucilius. You shall not come to them.

Poet. Nothing but death shall stay me.

Cassius. How now? What's the matter?

130 **Poet.** For shame, you generals! What do you mean?
Love and be friends, as two such men should be,
For I have seen more years, I'm sure, than ye.

Cassius. Ha, ha! How vilely doth this cynic rhyme!

Brutus. Get you hence, sirrah! Saucy fellow, hence!

135 **Cassius.** Bear with him, Brutus. 'Tis his fashion.

108–113 Brutus tells Cassius not to restrain his anger; he will no longer take offense at Cassius' insults. He describes himself as a mild man (**lamb**) who may flare up when provoked but whose anger immediately cools.

113–115 Recalling Brutus' remark in lines 49–50, Cassius asks whether his moodiness has made him a joke to Brutus.

120 rash humor: quick temper.

124–138 The poet who interrupts Brutus and Cassius is called a rude fellow (**cynic**) and other insulting terms. *Why might Shakespeare have included this brief scene with the poet?*

Cassius and Poet in the Globe Theatre's 1999 production

Brutus. I'll know his humor when he knows his time.
What should the wars do with these jigging fools?
Companion, hence!

Cassius.   Away, away, be gone!

[*Exit* Poet.]

Brutus. Lucilius and Titinius, bid the commanders
140 Prepare to lodge their companies tonight.

Cassius. And come yourselves, and bring Messala with you
Immediately to us.

[*Exeunt* Lucilius *and* Titinius.]

Brutus.   Lucius, a bowl of wine.

[*Exit* Lucius.]

Cassius. I did not think you could have been so angry.

Brutus. O Cassius, I am sick of many griefs.

145 **Cassius.** Of your philosophy you make no use
If you give place to accidental evils.

Brutus. No man bears sorrow better. Portia is dead.

Cassius. Ha! Portia?

Brutus. She is dead.

150 **Cassius.** How scaped I killing when I crossed you so?

145–146 Of your . . . evils: You aren't making use of your philosophy if you let chance happenings get you down. (Brutus was a Stoic, one who believed that pain and suffering should be endured calmly.)

148 Ha: Cassius is not laughing but is so shocked by the news of Portia's death that he gasps.

150 How . . . so: How did I escape being killed when I angered you, with such a terrible thing on your mind?

O insupportable and touching loss!
Upon what sickness?

Brutus.   Impatient of my absence,
And grief that young Octavius with Mark Antony
Have made themselves so strong—for with her death
155 That tidings came—with this she fell distract,
And (her attendants absent) swallowed fire.

Cassius. And died so?

Brutus.   Even so.

Cassius.   O ye immortal gods!

[*Reenter* Lucius, *with wine and tapers.*]

Brutus. Speak no more of her. Give me a bowl of wine.
In this I bury all unkindness, Cassius.

[*Drinks.*]

160 **Cassius.** My heart is thirsty for that noble pledge.
Fill, Lucius, till the wine o'erswell the cup.
I cannot drink too much of Brutus' love.

[*Drinks. Exit* Lucius.]

[*Reenter* Titinius, *with* Messala.]

Brutus. Come in, Titinius! Welcome, good Messala.
Now sit we close about this taper here
165 And call in question our necessities.

Cassius. Portia, art thou gone?

Brutus.   No more, I pray you.
Messala, I have here received letters
That young Octavius and Mark Antony
Come down upon us with a mighty power,
170 Bending their expedition toward Philippi.

Messala. Myself have letters of the selfsame tenure.

Brutus. With what addition?

Messala. That by proscription and bills of outlawry
Octavius, Antony, and Lepidus
175 Have put to death an hundred senators.

Brutus. Therein our letters do not well agree.
Mine speak of seventy senators that died
By their proscriptions, Cicero being one.

Cassius. Cicero one?

Messala.   Cicero is dead,
180 And by that order of proscription.
Had you your letters from your wife, my lord?

152–156 Impatient . . . fire: She was worried about my absence and about the armies of Antony and Octavius. These things made her insane (**she fell distract**). When her servants were not around, she swallowed burning coals.

161 o'erswell: overflow.

164–165 Now sit . . . necessities: Let's sit around this candle and talk about what we must do.

170 Bending . . . Philippi: leading their armies to Philippi (**a city in northern Greece**).

171 Myself . . . tenure: I have received letters that say the same thing.

173 proscription . . . outlawry: death sentences and lists of condemned people.

Brutus. No, Messala.

Messala. Nor nothing in your letters writ of her?

Brutus. Nothing, Messala.

Messala.   That methinks is strange.

185 **Brutus.** Why ask you? Hear you aught of her in yours?

Messala. No, my lord.

Brutus. Now as you are a Roman, tell me true.

Messala. Then like a Roman bear the truth I tell,
For certain she is dead, and by strange manner.

190 **Brutus.** Why, farewell, Portia. We must die, Messala.
With meditating that she must die once,
I have the patience to endure it now.

Messala. Even so great men great losses should endure.

Cassius. I have as much of this in art as you,
195 But yet my nature could not bear it so.

Brutus. Well, to our work alive. What do you think
Of marching to Philippi presently?

Cassius. I do not think it good.

Brutus.   Your reason?

Cassius.   This it is:
'Tis better that the enemy seek us.
200 So shall he waste his means, weary his soldiers,
Doing himself offense, whilst we, lying still,
Are full of rest, defense, and nimbleness.

Brutus. Good reasons must of force give place to better.
The people 'twixt Philippi and this ground
205 Do stand but in a forced affection,
For they have grudged us contribution.
The enemy, marching along by them,
By them shall make a fuller number up,
Come on refreshed, new-added, and encouraged;
210 From which advantage we cut him off
If at Philippi we do face him there,
These people at our back.

Cassius.   Hear me, good brother.

Brutus. Under your pardon. You must note beside
That we have tried the utmost of our friends,
215 Our legions are brimful, our cause is ripe.
The enemy increaseth every day;
We, at the height, are ready to decline.
There is a tide in the affairs of men
Which, taken at the flood, leads on to fortune;

181–195 Brutus seems to know nothing about Portia's death in this passage, although earlier he describes her fate to Cassius in lines 149–158. Many scholars believe that the first account of Portia's death was a revision and that Shakespeare intended to delete this second account. *How does Brutus' reaction to Portia's death differ in the two accounts?*

194 **in art:** in theory, in my beliefs.

203–212 **Good . . . our back:** Good reasons have to give way to better ones. The people between (**'twixt**) here and Philippi are friendly only because they have to be (**stand but in a forced affection**). They have given us aid grudgingly. If the enemy marches through, they will find recruits. If we face them at Philippi, we'll eliminate this advantage and keep these unfriendly people behind us.

213–217 Brutus interrupts with another reason for his plan: Their army is now at peak strength, while the enemy is growing stronger.

218–221 Comparing life to a sea voyage, Brutus says that if you miss the high tide when it comes, you can be stuck at shore forever.

220 Omitted, all the voyage of their life
Is bound in shallows and in miseries.
On such a full sea are we now afloat,
And we must take the current when it serves
Or lose our ventures. **D**

    Cassius.   Then, with your will, go on.
225 We'll along ourselves and meet them at Philippi.

    Brutus. The deep of night is crept upon our talk
And nature must obey necessity,
Which we will niggard with a little rest.
There is no more to say?

    Cassius.   No more. Good night.
230 Early tomorrow will we rise and hence.

    Brutus. Lucius!

[*Reenter* Lucius.]

My gown.

[*Exit* Lucius.]

Farewell, good Messala.
Good night, Titinius. Noble, noble Cassius,
235 Good night and good repose!

    Cassius.   O my dear brother,
This was an ill beginning of the night!
Never come such division 'tween our souls!
Let it not, Brutus.

[*Reenter* Lucius, *with the gown.*]

    Brutus.   Everything is well.

    Cassius. Good night, my lord.

    Brutus.   Good night, good brother.

240 **Titinius and Messala.** Good night, Lord Brutus.

    Brutus.   Farewell every one.

[*Exeunt all but* Brutus *and* Lucius.]

Give me the gown. Where is thy instrument?

    Lucius. Here in the tent.

    Brutus.   What, thou speak'st drowsily?
Poor knave, I blame thee not, thou art o'erwatched.
Call Claudius and some other of my men;
245 I'll have them sleep on cushions in my tent.

    Lucius. Varro and Claudius!

[*Enter* Varro *and* Claudius.]

    Varro. Calls my lord?

    Brutus. I pray you, sirs, lie in my tent and sleep.

D TRAGIC HERO
Reread lines 196–224. What **tragic flaw** does Brutus reveal in his response to Cassius' concerns about marching their armies to Philippi? Cite details to support your answer.

228 Which . . . rest: We will reluctantly satisfy nature by getting a little rest.

232 gown: nightgown.

242–243 What . . . o'erwatched: I see you're sleepy. It's no wonder, since you've been watching and waiting for so long.

It may be I shall raise you by-and-by
250 On business to my brother Cassius.

Varro. So please you, we will stand and watch your pleasure.

Brutus. I will not have it so. Lie down, good sirs.
It may be I shall otherwise bethink me.

[Varro *and* Claudius *lie down.*]

Look, Lucius, here's the book I sought for so;
255 I put it in the pocket of my gown.

Lucius. I was sure your lordship did not give it me.

Brutus. Bear with me, good boy, I am much forgetful.
Canst thou hold up by thy heavy eyes awhile,
And touch thy instrument a strain or two?

260 **Lucius.** Ay, my lord, an't please you.

Brutus.   It does, my boy.
I trouble thee too much, but thou art willing.

Lucius. It is my duty, sir.

Brutus. I should not urge thy duty past thy might.
I know young bloods look for a time of rest.

265 **Lucius.** I have slept, my lord, already.

Brutus. It was well done; and thou shalt sleep again;
I will not hold thee long. If I do live,
I will be good to thee. **E**

[*Music, and a song.* Lucius *falls asleep as he sings.*]

This is a sleepy tune. O murd'rous slumber!
270 Layest thou thy leaden mace upon my boy,
That plays thee music? Gentle knave, good night.
I will not do thee so much wrong to wake thee.
If thou dost nod, thou break'st thy instrument;
I'll take it from thee; and, good boy, good night.
275 Let me see, let me see. Is not the leaf turned down
Where I left reading? Here it is, I think.

[*Sits.*]

[*Enter the* Ghost of Caesar.]

How ill this taper burns! Ha! Who comes here?
I think it is the weakness of mine eyes
That shapes this monstrous apparition.
280 It comes upon me. Art thou anything?
Art thou some god, some angel, or some devil,
That mak'st my blood cold and my hair to stare?
Speak to me what thou art.

Ghost. Thy evil spirit, Brutus.

249–253 It may . . . bethink me: Brutus
wants them to be handy in case he
needs to send a message to Cassius.
Varro offers to stand guard all night.
Brutus insists the men sleep, not stand
guard. He says he may change his mind
(**otherwise bethink me**) about sending
messages to Cassius.

E TRAGIC HERO
What **character traits** are revealed in
Brutus' dialogue with Lucius?

270 **mace:** a rod used as a symbol of
authority. Brutus is addressing slumber
as though it were an officer of the law
who has arrested Lucius.

277 **How . . . burns:** How poorly this
candle burns. Everyone in the tent is
asleep except Brutus. At first he thinks
the thing he sees is only the result of
poor eyesight. Then he realizes that
something is really there.

282 **stare:** stand on end.

Brutus. Why com'st thou?

285 **Ghost.** To tell thee thou shalt see me at Philippi.

Brutus. Well; then I shall see thee again?

Ghost. Ay, at Philippi.

Brutus. Why, I will see thee at Philippi then.

[*Exit* Ghost.]

Now I have taken heart thou vanishest.
290 Ill spirit, I would hold more talk with thee.
Boy! Lucius! Varro! Claudius! Sirs! Awake!
Claudius!

Lucius. The strings, my lord, are false.

Brutus. He thinks he still is at his instrument.
295 Lucius, awake!

Lucius. My lord?

Brutus. Didst thou dream, Lucius, that thou so criedst out?

Lucius. My lord, I do not know that I did cry.

Brutus. Yes, that thou didst. Didst thou see anything?

300 **Lucius.** Nothing, my lord.

Brutus. Sleep again, Lucius. Sirrah Claudius!

[*To* Varro.]

Fellow thou, awake!

Varro. My lord?

Claudius. My lord?

305 **Brutus.** Why did you so cry out, sirs, in your sleep?

Both. Did we, my lord?

Brutus. Ay. Saw you anything?

Varro. No, my lord, I saw nothing.

Claudius. Nor I, my lord.

Brutus. Go and commend me to my brother Cassius.
Bid him set on his pow'rs betimes before,
310 And we will follow.

Both. It shall be done, my lord.

[*Exeunt.*]

289 Now . . . vanishest: Now that I have my courage back, you disappear.

293 false: out of tune. Lucius, only half awake, thinks he is playing the instrument that Brutus took from him earlier.

308 commend me: give my respects to.

309 Bid . . . before: Tell him to get his army (**pow'rs**) moving early in the morning.

Comprehension

OHIO STANDARDS

READING STANDARD
4.5 Analyze how choice of genre affects theme or topic

1. **Recall** Which three characters have taken control of Rome after Caesar's assassination?

2. **Recall** What has strained the relationship between Brutus and Cassius?

3. **Recall** What happened to Portia after Brutus fled from Rome?

4. **Paraphrase** What arguments do Brutus and Cassius make regarding whether they should march to Philippi to fight their enemies?

Literary Analysis

5. **Analyze Tragic Hero** What flaw or flaws does Brutus show in Act Four, Scene 3? Cite details to support your answer.

6. **Reading Shakespearean Drama** Review your notes on Antony's personality in the chart you created as you read. Are Antony's words and actions in Act Four, Scene 1, consistent with your impression of him earlier in the play? Support your answer with evidence from the text.

7. **Make Inferences** Why might Brutus choose to tell Cassius the news about Portia after they have resolved their quarrel?

8. **Predict Outcome** What do you predict will be the outcome of Brutus' decision to meet his enemies at Philippi? Give reasons for your prediction.

9. **Draw Conclusions** Do the Romans seem better or worse off under their new rulers than they were under Julius Caesar? Cite evidence to support your answer.

10. **Make Judgments** Reread lines 1–123 of Scene 3. Is Brutus justified in his complaints about Cassius? Explain why or why not.

Literary Criticism

11. **Critical Interpretations** Some critics have argued that *Julius Caesar* dramatizes the difficulty of balancing private values and public leadership. Do you agree that this conflict between values and effective leadership is an important **theme** in the play? Provide specific examples in your response.

Act Five

Scene 1 *The plains of Philippi in Greece.*

Antony and Octavius enter the battlefield with their army. Brutus and Cassius enter with their forces. The four leaders meet, but they only exchange insults and taunts. Antony and Octavius leave to prepare for battle. Cassius expresses his fears to Messala. Finally, Brutus and Cassius say their final farewells, in case they should die in battle.

[*Enter* Octavius, Antony, *and their Army.*]

Octavius. Now Antony, our hopes are answered.
You said the enemy would not come down
But keep the hills and upper regions.
It proves not so, their battles are at hand.
5 They mean to warn us at Philippi here,
Answering before we do demand of them.

Antony. Tut! I am in their bosoms and I know
Wherefore they do it. They could be content
To visit other places, and come down
10 With fearful bravery, thinking by this face
To fasten in our thoughts that they have courage.
But 'tis not so.

[*Enter a* Messenger.]

Messenger.   Prepare you, generals,
The enemy comes on in gallant show;
Their bloody sign of battle is hung out,
15 And something to be done immediately.

Antony. Octavius, lead your battle softly on
Upon the left hand of the even field.

Octavius. Upon the right hand I. Keep thou the left.

Antony. Why do you cross me in this exigent?

20 **Octavius.** I do not cross you; but I will do so.

[*March.*]

[*Drum. Enter* Brutus, Cassius, *and their Army;* Lucilius, Titinius, Messala, *and others.*]

Brutus. They stand and would have parley.

Cassius. Stand fast, Titinius. We must out and talk.

Octavius. Mark Antony, shall we give sign of battle?

Antony. No, Caesar, we will answer on their charge.
25 Make forth. The generals would have some words.

3 keep ... regions: stay in the higher areas (where they could defend themselves more easily).

5 warn: challenge.

7–11 I am ... courage: I know their secrets (**am in their bosoms**) and why they have done this. They would rather be in other places, but they come down with a show of bravery, thinking they will convince us they have courage.

14 sign of battle: a red flag symbolizing readiness for battle.

19 exigent: moment of crisis.

21 They ... parley: They are standing and waiting for a conference.

24 answer on their charge: respond to their attack.

Antony speaks over the body of Brutus in the Globe Theatre's 1999 production.

Octavius. Stir not until the signal.

[Brutus, Cassius, Octavius, *and* Antony *meet in the center of the stage.*]

Brutus. Words before blows. Is it so, countrymen?

Octavius. Not that we love words better, as you do.

Brutus. Good words are better than bad strokes, Octavius.

30 **Antony.** In your bad strokes, Brutus, you give good words;
Witness the hole you made in Caesar's heart,
Crying "Long live! Hail, Caesar!"

Cassius.   Antony,
The posture of your blows are yet unknown;
But for your words, they rob the Hybla bees,
35 And leave them honeyless.

Antony.   Not stingless too.

Brutus. O yes, and soundless too!
For you have stol'n their buzzing, Antony,
And very wisely threat before you sting.

Antony. Villains! you did not so when your vile daggers
40 Hacked one another in the sides of Caesar.
You showed your teeth like apes, and fawned like hounds,
And bowed like bondmen, kissing Caesar's feet;
Whilst damned Casca, like a cur, behind
Struck Caesar on the neck. O you flatterers!

45 **Cassius.** Flatterers? Now, Brutus, thank yourself!
This tongue had not offended so today
If Cassius might have ruled.

Octavius. Come, come, the cause! If arguing make us sweat,
The proof of it will turn to redder drops.
50 Look,
I draw a sword against conspirators.
When think you that the sword goes up again?
Never, till Caesar's three-and-thirty wounds
Be well avenged, or till another Caesar
55 Have added slaughter to the sword of traitors.

Brutus. Caesar, thou canst not die by traitors' hands
Unless thou bring'st them with thee.

Octavius.   So I hope.
I was not born to die on Brutus' sword.

Brutus. Oh, if thou wert the noblest of thy strain,
60 Young man, thou couldst not die more honorable.

Cassius. A peevish schoolboy, worthless of such honor,
Joined with a masker and a reveller!

Antony. Old Cassius still.

33–35 The posture . . . honeyless: We don't know yet how effective you'll be as a soldier, but your words are sweeter than honey. (Hybla is a mountain in Sicily known for its sweet honey.)

39–44 you did not so . . . neck: You didn't give warning before you killed Caesar. Instead, you acted like loving pets and slaves while Casca, like a dog (**cur**), stabbed Caesar in the neck.

45–47 Cassius angrily tells Brutus that they wouldn't be listening to these insults if he had gotten his way (**ruled**) when arguing that Antony should be killed.

48 cause: business at hand.

49 proof of it: testing of the argument in battle.

54–55 or till . . . traitors: or until a second Caesar (that is, Octavius himself—Caesar's grandnephew and adopted son) has been killed by the traitors.

59 strain: family line.

62–63 Cassius insults Antony by calling him a partygoer and a playboy. Same old Cassius (**Old Cassius still**), Antony replies.

Octavius.   Come, Antony. Away!
Defiance, traitor, hurl we in your teeth.
65 If you dare fight today, come to the field;
If not, when you have stomachs.

[*Exeunt* Octavius, Antony, *and their Army.*]

Cassius. Why, now blow wind, swell billow, and swim bark!
The storm is up, and all is on the hazard.

Brutus. Ho, Lucilius! Hark, a word with you.

[Lucilius *and* Messala *stand forth.*]

Lucilius.   My lord?

[Brutus *and* Lucilius *converse apart.*]

70 **Cassius.** Messala.

Messala   What says my general?

Cassius.   Messala,
This is my birthday; as this very day
Was Cassius born. Give me thy hand, Messala.
Be thou my witness that against my will
(As Pompey was) am I compelled to set
75 Upon one battle all our liberties.
You know that I held Epicurus strong
And his opinion. Now I change my mind
And partly credit things that do presage.
Coming from Sardis, on our former ensign
80 Two mighty eagles fell, and there they perched,
Gorging and feeding from our soldiers' hands,
Who to Philippi here consorted us.
This morning are they fled away and gone,
And in their steads do ravens, crows, and kites
85 Fly o'er our heads and downward look on us
As we were sickly prey. Their shadows seem
A canopy most fatal, under which
Our army lies, ready to give up the ghost.

Messala. Believe not so.

Cassius.   I but believe it partly,
90 For I am fresh of spirit and resolved
To meet all perils very constantly.

Brutus. Even so, Lucilius.

Cassius.   Now, most noble Brutus,
The gods today stand friendly, that we may,
Lovers in peace, lead on our days to age!
95 But since the affairs of men rest still incertain,
Let's reason with the worst that may befall.

66 **stomachs:** enough nerve.

68 **all . . . hazard:** Everything is at stake.

74–75 **to set . . . liberties:** to gamble our freedom in one battle.

76–88 Epicurus was a philosopher who did not believe omens. Cassius says that he once was a follower of this philosophy, but now he sometimes believes in things that predict the future (**credit things that do presage**). Cassius then tells Messala of two eagles that accompanied the army from Sardis to Philippi. The eagles have been replaced by ravens, crows, and hawks (**kites**)—birds that symbolize death.

79 **former ensign:** the flag that was carried at the head of the army's march.

91 **constantly:** with determination.

96 **Let's . . . befall:** Let's think about the worst that might happen to us.

Cassius carrying laurel wreath and banner in the Globe Theatre's 1999 production

If we do lose this battle, then is this
The very last time we shall speak together.
What are you then determined to do?

100 **Brutus.** Even by the rule of that philosophy
By which I did blame Cato for the death
Which he did give himself—I know not how,
But I do find it cowardly and vile,
For fear of what might fall, so to prevent
105 The time of life—arming myself with patience
To stay the providence of some high powers
That govern us below.

     Cassius.   Then, if we lose this battle,
You are contented to be led in triumph
Through the streets of Rome.

110 **Brutus.** No, Cassius, no. Think not, thou noble Roman,
That ever Brutus will go bound to Rome.
He bears too great a mind. But this same day
Must end that work the ides of March begun,
And whether we shall meet again I know not.
115 Therefore our everlasting farewell take.

100–107 Even . . . govern us below: According to the Stoic philosophy that Brutus follows, people should endure their troubles. Brutus therefore finds suicide to be dishonorable (**cowardly and vile**). He mentions Cato, a famous Roman who killed himself after Pompey lost to Caesar.

108 in triumph: as a captive in a victory parade.

115 our . . . take: Let's make a final farewell to each other.

For ever and for ever farewell, Cassius!
If we do meet again, why, we shall smile;
If not, why then this parting was well made. **Ⓐ**

Cassius. For ever and for ever farewell, Brutus!
120 If we do meet again, we'll smile indeed;
If not, 'tis true this parting was well made.

Brutus. Why then, lead on. O that a man might know
The end of this day's business ere it come!
But it sufficeth that the day will end,
125 And then the end is known. Come, ho! Away!

[*Exeunt.*]

Ⓐ TRAGIC HERO
Reread lines 110–112. What **character trait** would lead Brutus to overlook his philosophical objection to suicide if he were captured?

Scene 2 *The battlefield.*

Brutus sends Messala with orders for the forces across the field.

[*Alarum. Enter* Brutus *and* Messala.]

Brutus. Ride, ride, Messala, ride, and give these bills
Unto the legions on the other side.

[*Loud alarum.*]

Let them set on at once; for I perceive
But cold demeanor in Octavius' wing,
5 And sudden push gives them the overthrow.
Ride, ride, Messala! Let them all come down.

[*Exeunt.*]

4 cold demeanor: lack of courage.
How does Brutus feel about the battle at this point?

Scene 3 *Another part of the battlefield.*

Cassius retreats, losing the battle to Antony's forces. He sends Titinius to see if nearby forces are friend or enemy. From a hill, Pindarus believes he sees Titinius killed. Completely discouraged, Cassius asks Pindarus to kill him. Titinius returns to find Cassius' body and kills himself. Brutus and others arrive, having defeated Octavius army. Messala has brought them to see the body of Cassius. Now they see that Titinius is also dead. Brutus mourns the two, but also looks to a second battle with his enemies.

[*Enter* Cassius *and* Titinius.]

Cassius. O, look, Titinius, look! The villains fly!
Myself have to mine own turned enemy.
This ensign here of mine was turning back;
I slew the coward and did take it from him.

5 **Titinius.** O Cassius, Brutus gave the word too early,
Who, having some advantage on Octavius,
Took it too eagerly. His soldiers fell to spoil,
Whilst we by Antony are all enclosed.

[*Enter* Pindarus.]

1–4 Dismayed that his troops are fleeing from the battle, Cassius says that when he saw his flag-bearer (**ensign**) start to retreat, he killed him and took his flag.

7 His . . . spoil: Brutus' soldiers began looting (instead of fighting the enemy).

Pindarus. Fly further off, my lord! fly further off!
10 Mark Antony is in your tents, my lord.
Fly, therefore, noble Cassius, fly far off!

Cassius. This hill is far enough. Look, look, Titinius!
Are those my tents where I perceive the fire?

Titinius. They are, my lord.

Cassius.   Titinius, if thou lovest me,
15 Mount thou my horse and hide thy spurs in him
Till he have brought thee up to yonder troops
And here again, that I may rest assured
Whether yond troops are friend or enemy.

Titinius. I will be here again even with a thought.

[*Exit.*]

20 **Cassius.** Go, Pindarus, get higher on that hill.
My sight was ever thick. Regard Titinius,
And tell me what thou not'st about the field.

[*Pindarus ascends the hill.*]

This day I breathed first. Time is come round,
And where I did begin, there shall I end.
25 My life is run his compass. Sirrah, what news?

Pindarus.

[*Above.*]

O my lord!

Cassius. What news?

Pindarus.

[*Above.*]

Titinius is enclosed round about
With horsemen that make to him on the spur.
30 Yet he spurs on. Now they are almost on him.
Now, Titinius!
Now some light. O, he lights too! He's ta'en.

[*Shout.*]

And hark!
They shout for joy.

Cassius.   Come down; behold no more.
35 O coward that I am to live so long
To see my best friend ta'en before my face!

[*Enter* Pindarus *from above.*]

Come hither, sirrah.
In Parthia did I take thee prisoner,
And then I swore thee, saving of thy life,

15–18 Mount . . . enemy: Ride my horse to those troops over there, and come back to tell me if they are friend or enemy.

19 even with a thought: as fast as you can think of it.

25 is run his compass: has come full circle.

29 make to . . . spur: ride to him at top speed.

32 light: dismount; **ta'en:** taken prisoner.

38–46 In Parthia . . . the sword: When I saved your life in Parthia (an ancient Asian land), you swore to do whatever I asked. Now keep your oath and become a free man. I'll cover my face as you stab me (**search this bosom**) with the same sword that killed Caesar. Don't argue (**Stand not to answer**). *Why does Cassius finally decide to kill himself?*

40 That whatsoever I did bid thee do,
Thou shouldst attempt it. Come now, keep thine oath.
Now be a freeman, and with this good sword,
That ran through Caesar's bowels, search this bosom.
Stand not to answer. Here, take thou the hilts,
45 And when my face is covered, as 'tis now,
Guide thou the sword.

[Pindarus *stabs him.*]

                     —Caesar, thou are revenged
Even with the sword that killed thee.

[*Dies.*]

Pindarus. So, I am free, yet would not so have been,
Durst I have done my will. O Cassius!
50 Far from this country Pindarus shall run,
Where never Roman shall take note of him.

[*Exit.*]

[*Reenter* Titinius *with* Messala.]

Messala. It is but change, Titinius; for Octavius
Is overthrown by noble Brutus' power,
As Cassius' legions are by Antony.

55 **Titinius.** These tidings will well comfort Cassius.

Messala. Where did you leave him?

Titinius.   All disconsolate,
With Pindarus his bondman, on this hill.

Messala. Is not that he that lies upon the ground?

Titinius. He lies not like the living. O my heart!

60 **Messala.** Is not that he?

Titinius.   No, this was he, Messala,
But Cassius is no more. O setting sun,
As in thy red rays thou does sink to night
So in his red blood Cassius' day is set!
The sun of Rome is set. Our day is gone;
65 Clouds, dews, and dangers come; our deeds are done!
Mistrust of my success hath done this deed. **B**

Messala. Mistrust of good success hath done this deed.
O hateful Error, Melancholy's child,
Why dost thou show to the apt thoughts of men
70 The things that are not? O Error, soon conceived,
Thou never com'st unto a happy birth,
But kill'st the mother that engend'red thee!

Titinius. What, Pindarus! Where art thou, Pindarus?

Messala. Seek him, Titinius, whilst I go to meet

48–49 So...will: I am free, but I wouldn't have been if I had done what I wanted (that is, refused to kill Cassius).

52–54 It is...Antony: It's an even exchange. Just as Antony has defeated Cassius, Brutus has defeated Octavius.

56 disconsolate: extremely sad.

B TRAGEDY
Titinius says that Cassius killed himself because he believed that Titinius had failed in his mission. How might Cassius' decision to commit suicide affect the final outcome of the **plot**?

68–72 Messala says that depression can lead people to misperceive events; such errors end up killing the minds that gave birth to them.

75 The noble Brutus, thrusting this report
Into his ears. I may say "thrusting" it;
For piercing steel and darts envenomed
Shall be as welcome to the ears of Brutus
As tidings of this sight.

Titinius.   Hie you, Messala,
80 And I will seek for Pindarus the while.

[*Exit* Messala.]

[Titinius *looks at* Cassius.]

Why didst thou send me forth, brave Cassius?
Did I not meet thy friends, and did not they
Put on my brows this wreath of victory
And bid me give it thee? Didst thou not hear their shouts?
85 Alas, thou hast misconstrued everything!
But hold thee, take this garland on thy brow.
Thy Brutus bid me give it thee, and I
Will do his bidding. Brutus, come apace
And see how I regarded Caius Cassius.
90 By your leave, gods. This is a Roman's part.
Come, Cassius' sword, and find Titinius' heart.

[*Dies.*]

[*Alarum. Enter* Brutus, Messala, Young Cato, Strato, Volumnius, *and* Lucilius.]

Brutus. Where, where, Messala, doth his body lie?

Messala. Lo, yonder, and Titinius mourning it.

Brutus. Titinius' face is upward.

Cato.   He is slain.

95 **Brutus.** O Julius Caesar, thou art mighty yet!
Thy spirit walks abroad and turns our swords
In our own proper entrails. **C**

[*Low alarums.*]

Cato.   Brave Titinius!
Look whe'r he have not crowned dead Cassius.

Brutus. Are yet two Romans living such as these?
100 The last of all the Romans, fare thee well!
It is impossible that ever Rome
Should breed thy fellow. Friends, I owe more tears
To this dead man than you shall see me pay.
I shall find time, Cassius; I shall find time.
105 Come therefore, and to Thasos send his body.
His funerals shall not be in our camp,
Lest it discomfort us. Lucilius, come;
And come, young Cato. Let us to the field.

77 darts envenomed: poisoned darts.

79 Hie you: Hurry.

88 apace: quickly.

90 This ... part: This (killing myself) is the proper thing for a brave Roman to do.

C TRAGEDY
What **theme** is expressed in Brutus' remark about Caesar's spirit?

98 whe'r: whether.

102 fellow: equal.

105 Thasos (thā'sŏs'): an island near Philippi.

107 discomfort us: discourage our troops.

Labeo and Flavius set our battles on.
110 'Tis three o'clock; and, Romans, yet ere night
We shall try fortune in a second fight.

[*Exeunt.*]

Scene 4 *Another part of the battlefield.*

During the battle, Young Cato is killed, and Lucilius is taken prisoner. Brought to Antony, Lucilius insists that Brutus will never be taken alive.

[*Alarum. Enter* Brutus, Messala, Young Cato, Lucilius, *and* Flavius.]

Brutus. Yet, countrymen, O, yet hold up your heads!

Cato. What fellow doth not? Who will go with me?
I will proclaim my name about the field.
I am the son of Marcus Cato, ho!
5 A foe to tyrants, and my country's friend.
I am the son of Marcus Cato, ho!

[*Enter Soldiers and fight.*]

Brutus. And I am Brutus, Marcus Brutus I!
Brutus, my country's friend! Know me for Brutus!

[*Exit.*]

[*Young Cato falls.*]

Lucilius. O young and noble Cato, art thou down?
10 Why, now thou diest as bravely as Titinius,
And mayst be honored, being Cato's son.

First Soldier. Yield, or thou diest.

Lucilius.   Only I yield to die.

[*Offering money.*]

There is so much that thou wilt kill me straight.
Kill Brutus, and be honored in his death.

15 **First Soldier.** We must not. A noble prisoner!

[*Enter* **Antony.**]

Second Soldier. Room ho! Tell Antony Brutus is ta'en.

First Soldier. I'll tell the news. Here comes the general.
Brutus is ta'en! Brutus is ta'en, my lord!

Antony. Where is he?

20 **Lucilius.** Safe, Antony; Brutus is safe enough.
I dare assure thee that no enemy
Shall ever take alive the noble Brutus.
The gods defend him from so great a shame!
When you do find him, or alive or dead,
25 He will be found like Brutus, like himself.

Antony. This is not Brutus, friend; but, I assure you,

4 Marcus Cato: Portia's father, a greatly respected Roman.

12 Yield: surrender.

13–14 Pretending to be Brutus, Lucilius offers the soldier money to kill him immediately. *Why would Lucilius want the enemy to think he is Brutus?*

24 or alive or dead: either alive or dead.
How do you interpret Lucilius' remark that Brutus will be found "like Brutus, like himself"?

A prize no less in worth. Keep this man safe;
Give him all kindness. I had rather have
Such men my friends than enemies. Go on,
30 And see whe'r Brutus be alive or dead;
And bring us word unto Octavius' tent
How everything is chanced.

[*Exeunt.*]

Scene 5   *Another part of the battlefield.*

Facing defeat, Brutus' forces rest. Brutus feels that all is lost. He asks three men to kill him, but each refuses. Finally, Strato agrees to hold the sword as Brutus kills himself on it. Antony, Octavius, and others arrive. Antony mourns Brutus, calling him the "noblest Roman." Octavius promises him a noble funeral as the play ends.

[*Enter* Brutus, Dardanius, Clitus, Strato, *and* Volumnius.]

Brutus. Come, poor remains of friends, rest on this rock.

Clitus. Statilius showed the torchlight but, my lord,
He came not back. He is or ta'en or slain.

Brutus. Sit thee down, Clitus. Slaying is the word.
5 It is a deed in fashion. Hark thee, Clitus.

[*Whispers.*]

Clitus. What, I, my lord? No, not for all the world!

Brutus. Peace then. No words.

Clitus.   I'll rather kill myself.

Brutus. Hark thee, Dardanius.

[*Whispers.*]

Dardanius.   Shall I do such a deed?

Clitus. O Dardanius!

10 **Dardanius.** O Clitus!

Clitus. What ill request did Brutus make to thee?

Dardanius. To kill him, Clitus. Look he meditates.

Clitus. Now is that noble vessel full of grief,
That it runs over even at his eyes.

15 **Brutus.** Come hither, good Volumnius. List a word.

Volumnius. What says my lord?

Brutus.   Why this, Volumnius.
The ghost of Caesar hath appeared to me
Two several times by night—at Sardis once,
And this last night here in Philippi fields.
20 I know my hour is come.

Volumnius.   Not so, my lord.

2–3 **Statilius . . . slain:** Statilius (our scout) signaled with his torch that all was well at our camp. But since he hasn't come back, he has been either captured or killed.

4–5 Brutus says that it has become fashionable to kill, not to capture.

15 **List:** listen to.

18 **Two several times:** twice.

Brutus. Nay, I am sure it is, Volumnius.
Thou seest the world, Volumnius, how it goes.
Our enemies have beat us to the pit.

[*Low alarums.*]

It is more worthy to leap in ourselves
25 Than tarry till they push us. Good Volumnius,
Thou know'st that we two went to school together.
Even for that our love of old, I prithee
Hold thou my sword-hilts whilst I run on it.

Volumnius. That's not an office for a friend, my lord.

[*Alarum still.*]

30 **Clitus.** Fly, fly, my lord! There is no tarrying here.

Brutus. Farewell to you; and you; and you, Volumnius.
Strato, thou hast been all this while asleep.
Farewell to thee too, Strato. Countrymen,
My heart doth joy that yet in all my life
35 I found no man but he was true to me.
I shall have glory by this losing day
More than Octavius and Mark Antony
By this vile conquest shall attain unto.
So fare you well at once, for Brutus' tongue
40 Hath almost ended his life's history.
Night hangs upon mine eyes; my bones would rest,
That have but labored to attain this hour. **D**

[*Alarum. Cry within:* Fly, fly, fly!]

Clitus. Fly, my lord, fly!

Brutus.   Hence! I will follow.

[*Exeunt* Clitus, Dardanius, *and* Volumnius.]

I prithee, Strato, stay thou by thy lord.
45 Thou art a fellow of a good respect;
Thy life hath had some smatch of honor in it.
Hold then my sword, and turn away thy face
While I do run upon it. Wilt thou, Strato?

Strato. Give me your hand first. Fare you well, my lord.

50 **Brutus.** Farewell, good Strato. Caesar, now be still.
I killed not thee with half so good a will.

[*Dies.*]

[*Alarum. Retreat. Enter* Octavius, Antony, Messala, Lucilius, *and the* Army.]

Octavius. What man is that?

Messala. My master's man. Strato, where is thy master?

Strato. Free from the bondage you are in, Messala.

---

23 pit: a hole into which hunted animals are forced.

25 tarry: wait.

27–28 I prithee ... on it: I beg you to hold my sword while I run into it.

29 That's ... friend: That's no duty for a friend to perform.

41–42 my bones ... hour: My tired bones have worked to reach this final hour.

D TRAGIC HERO
Reread lines 31–42. Which details in Brutus' farewell speech show his courage and dignity in defeat?

46 smatch: little bit.

51 I killed ... will: I didn't kill you (Caesar) half as willingly as I kill myself.

52 man: servant.

55 The conquerors can but make a fire of him;
For Brutus only overcame himself,
And no man else hath honor by his death.

Lucilius. So Brutus should be found. I thank thee, Brutus,
That thou hast proved Lucilius' saying true.

60 **Octavius.** All that served Brutus, I will entertain them.
Fellow, wilt thou bestow thy time with me?

Strato. Ay, if Messala will prefer me to you.

Octavius. Do so, good Messala.

Messala. How died my master, Strato?

65 **Strato.** I held the sword, and he did run on it.

Messala. Octavius, then take him to follow thee,
That did the latest service to my master.

Antony. This was the noblest Roman of them all.
All the conspirators save only he
70 Did that they did in envy of great Caesar;
He, only in a general honest thought
And common good to all, made one of them.
His life was gentle, and the elements
So mixed in him that Nature might stand up
75 And say to all the world, "This was a man!"

Octavius. According to his virtue let us use him,
With all respect and rites of burial.
Within my tent his bones tonight shall lie,
Most like a soldier, ordered honorably.
80 So call the field to rest, and let's away
To part the glories of this happy day.

[*Exeunt.*]

58–59 So Brutus . . . true: That is just how Brutus should be found. Thank you, Brutus, for proving me correct (in saying you would never be taken alive).

60 All . . . them: All those who served Brutus will now be welcome in my army.

62 prefer: recommend.

66–67 Octavius . . . master: Octavius, I recommend him for your army; he performed the last favor for Brutus (**my master**).

69 save: except.

72 made one of them: joined the conspirators.

76 According . . . him: Let us treat him as he deserves.

81 part: divide up.

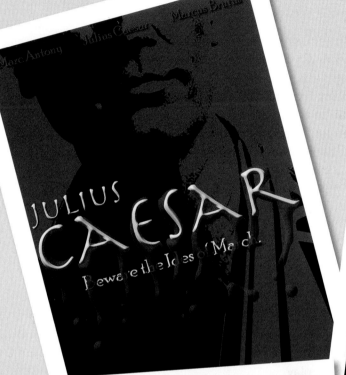

Promotion

How do producers get people to see a new Shakespeare production? They mainly rely on good reviews and **promotional** items, such as posters. What do the images in these posters suggest about how the producers have chosen to "sell" the play? Which poster do you find most interesting? Explain your responses.

Comprehension

1. **Recall** What misunderstanding leads to Cassius' death?

2. **Recall** Why does Brutus commit suicide?

3. **Clarify** What distinction does Antony make between Brutus and the other conspirators?

OHIO STANDARDS

READING STANDARD
2.1 Make inferences

Literary Analysis

4. **Examine Tragedy** Throughout *Julius Caesar,* characters make flawed decisions that contribute to the play's **catastrophe.** In a chart like the one shown, list important decisions and their consequences. Then identify decisions in Act Five that lead to the death of Brutus. Cite details from the chart in your answer.

Decisions	Consequences

5. **Analyze Tragedy** Brutus and Julius Caesar both have traits that are associated with tragic heroes. In your opinion, which character is really the **tragic hero** of the play? Explain your response.

6. **Reading Shakespearean Drama** Review the chart you created as you read. How did your impression of Cassius change over the course of *Julius Caesar*? Support your response with details from the play.

7. **Identify Cause and Effect** Which of Brutus' and Cassius' actions in Act Five may have been influenced by an omen or supernatural occurrence? Cite evidence.

8. **Make Inferences** Reread lines 1–20 of Act Five, Scene 1. What does this exchange of dialogue suggest about the relationship between Octavius and Antony?

9. **Make Judgments** Reread lines 33–38 of Scene 5. Do you agree with Brutus' statement that despite his defeat, he will gain more glory from the Battle of Philippi than Octavius and Antony? Explain why or why not.

Literary Criticism

10. **Critical Interpretations** According to the critic Maurice Charney, *Julius Caesar* is "deeply ambiguous. We grow increasingly certain after the middle of the play that the conspirators will lose, but we feel a strange balancing of values between the party of Brutus and the party of Caesar." Do you agree that Shakespeare offers a balanced view of the conflict, or does he portray one side more favorably than the other? Support your opinion with evidence from the play.

Reading-Writing Connection

Broaden your understanding of *Julius Caesar* by responding to these prompts.
Then use **Revision: Grammar and Style** to improve your writing.

WRITING PROMPTS	SELF-CHECK

A. Short Response: Analyze Character Motives

To what extent do you consider Mark Antony to be motivated by **conscience?** Using examples from the text, write a **one- or two-paragraph response** that explains how Antony's decisions reflect his internal sense of what is right and wrong.

An insightful analysis will . . .

- discuss what Antony's soliloquies and asides reveal about his thoughts
- consider the consequences of Antony's decisions

B. Extended Response: Examine Theme

In Act One, Scene 3, Cicero observes that "men may construe things after their fashion/Clean from the purpose of the things themselves." How do misunderstandings and false interpretations influence the main characters? In **three to five paragraphs,** discuss how this theme is developed in the play.

A thoughtful response will . . .

- include a restatement of the theme suggested by Cicero's comment
- show a cause-and-effect relationship between characters' misunderstandings and their actions

REVISION: GRAMMAR AND STYLE

ADD DESCRIPTIVE DETAILS Review the **Grammar and Style** note on page 1145. **Adjective clauses** are subordinate clauses that modify nouns and pronouns in the same way adjectives do. They are useful for adding details that help to explain, support, and connect ideas. Adjective clauses are introduced by the **relative pronouns** *that, which, who, whom,* and *whose,* and the **relative adverbs** *where, when,* and *why.* Note Shakespeare's use of adjective clauses in the following excerpts.

> *Against the Capitol I met a lion,/Who glared upon me.* . . . (Act One, Scene 3, lines 20–21)

> *All this done,/Repair to Pompey's Porch, where you shall find us.* (Act One, Scene 3, lines 146–147)

Notice how the revisions in red add more descriptive details to the following first draft. Revise your responses to the prompts by using adjective clauses to help support your ideas.

OHIO STANDARDS

WRITING STANDARD
7.3 Use clauses and phrases

WRITING TOOLS
For prewriting, revision, and editing tools, visit the **Writing Center** at ClassZone.com.

STUDENT MODEL

Mark Antony proves himself to be a good friend ~~to Caesar.~~ *who remains loyal to Caesar even after his death.* Through a powerful speech ^*that he delivers at Caesar's funeral,* he turns Rome's citizens against the conspirators.

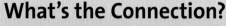

Reading for Information

Julius Caesar at the Public Theater

Theater Reviews

Use with *Julius Caesar*, page 1096.

OHIO STANDARDS

READING/RESEARCH STANDARDS
2.1 Draw conclusions
8.4 Evaluate and systematically organize important information

What's the Connection?

Now that you have read *Julius Caesar*, you are familiar with the characters and plot of William Shakespeare's tragedy. But the text is just the starting point for a play, which comes to life through the artistic choices of directors, actors, set designers, and other theater professionals. In the following selections, two critics respond very differently to the same production at the Public Theater in New York City.

Skill Focus: Analyze a Theater Review

A **theater review** is an essay in which the writer presents opinions about a theatrical production. Use the following steps to analyze a theater review:

- Identify the reviewer's **criteria,** the standards on which his or her opinions are based. For example, a reviewer might evaluate an actor's performance on how clearly the actor delivers lines of dialogue and on his or her ability to suggest a character's emotions. Sometimes a reviewer states criteria, but often you must infer the criteria from the reviewer's opinions.

- Note **details** about the production that the reviewer uses to support opinions. These details might include descriptions of the stage set and costumes or particular movements and gestures that actors make in their performances.

- Identify the **tone,** the writer's attitude toward the production. For example, does the writer seem enthusiastic, even-handed, or sarcastic? Consider what the tone suggests about the reviewer's general opinion of the production.

As you read, use a chart like the one shown to help you analyze each review.

Review by Thomas Disch	
Criteria	A production of Julius Caesar should be judged by its stateliness, pageantry, and music.
Details of the Performance	
Tone	
General Opinion	

Review of
Julius Caesar

by Thomas M. Disch

Julius Caesar is at once the dullest and the most familiar of Shakespeare's tragedies. It has become the most familiar precisely because it is the dullest, a tale so flensed[1] of dramatic meat that it can be presented to any group of teenagers, however rowdy, without danger of awakening their interest.

10 Given all these liabilities, the best one can hope for from any production of *Julius Caesar* is stateliness, pageantry and music, . . . and these aren't qualities likely to be in large supply at the Public Theater, which undertook *Julius Caesar* as the second production of its six-year assault on the whole oeuvre.[2] It was stoically[3] done. Without the ghost of an idea for making it new, director Stuart Vaughan had his cast trot through their 20 lines as best they could and the devil take the hindmost.[4] The hindmost was indisputably Martin Sheen as Brutus. He declaimed every line in the same hoarse timbre[5] and indicated every statement with alphabet-block simplicity: a thump of his hand to his heart when that organ was mentioned, or a finger pointing to his head, when "thoughts" had to be glossed. He was not left to die 30 entirely by himself, however, but fell upon his sword with careful choreography, and nothing in his role became him like the leaving of it. **A**

Al Pacino as Mark Antony seemed ill. This was an Antony whose protestations of a lack of eloquence can be taken at face value. Had he had to contend against any Brutus but Sheen's, the Romans' preference for him would have 40 been unaccountable. But he did remember all the lines of that long oration, which, you'll recall, is very long indeed. Bravo, Al. Now, my advice to you is get some rest, eat sensibly, exercise, and take Geritol every day. **B**

A THEATER REVIEW
Reread lines 17–29. What **details** does the reviewer include to support his opinion of Martin Sheen's performance as Brutus?

B THEATER REVIEW
Describe the reviewer's **tone** in lines 34–45.

---

1. **flensed** (flĕnsd): stripped of the fat or skin; said of an animal.
2. **oeuvre** (œˈvrə): the sum of the lifework of an artist, a writer, or a composer.
3. **stoically** (stōˈĭk-ə-lē): in a manner unaffected by pain or pleasure.
4. **devil take the hindmost**: let others manage as best as they can.
5. **timbre** (tămˈbər): the distinctive tone of an instrument or a voice.

Hail, Caesar!

by Edith Oliver

C THEATER REVIEW
Reread lines 4–42, and
note the qualities that the
reviewer admires in the
performances of Edward
Herrmann, Martin Sheen,
and Al Pacino. What
can you infer about her
criteria for evaluating the
casting of a play?

Herewith some impressions of "Julius Caesar," the second entry in the Shakespeare Marathon, at the Public:

This is the first "Caesar" I've ever seen that is dominated by Cassius, in Edward Herrmann's towering performance— towering physically, too, with a lean, but hardly hungry, look. Mr. Herrmann brings an intellectual clarity and force
10 to the character which make him seem the focus of the play, the instigator of the action. And the rest of the casting, as is usual at the Public, is mostly very good. Martin Sheen, a memorable Hamlet there twenty years ago (he recited the "To be, or not to be" soliloquy in a Hispanic accent), now makes the step to Brutus seem inevitable. His Brutus is self-questioning, often melancholy,
20 and virtuous and brave—a man whose honesty, even innocence, makes him an easy mark for more devious types. Which, of course, brings us to Al Pacino's Mark Antony, a devious type if ever there was one, so obviously scheming and sinister right from the start that I doubt he could fool even this Brutus into allowing him to deliver Caesar's funeral oration. (He doesn't fool
30 Cassius.) A sullen, sharp-witted Antony,

Mr. Pacino takes the curse of "set piece" off that oration. John McMartin is a surprising but, as it turns out, excellent choice for a Caesar who is aristocratic, cheerful, and friendly—just the sort of ruler to inspire the devotion of Brutus, among others, and perhaps the distrust of Cassius. His very soft "Et tu, Brute!" at the stabbing is indelible. I also admired
40 Joan MacIntosh, in her one passionate, loving scene with Brutus, and, come to think of it, almost everyone else. **C**

Under the sensible direction of Stuart Vaughan, the performance as a whole is always absorbing and always clear. If you sense some extra enthusiasm in my praise, you're probably right. It is the fervor of the convert;[1] it took me a long time to enjoy and appreciate the kind
50 of American Shakespeare presented by Joseph Papp at the Public or in the Park. (There have been some lemons, too.) The handsome setting for "Julius Caesar"—a bare stage with a flight of steps at center leading to a platform and surrounded by square, sky-high columns of brick—was designed by Bob Shaw and effectively lighted by Arden Fingerhut; the appropriate costumes
60 were designed by Lindsay W. Davis.

---

1. **fervor of the convert:** the intensity of emotion experienced by one who has changed one set of beliefs for another.

Comprehension

1. **Recall** According to Thomas Disch, which actor gave the worst performance in *Julius Caesar?*

2. **Recall** Why did Edward Herrmann's performance as Cassius surprise Edith Oliver?

3. **Summarize** What general opinion does each reviewer express about the production?

Critical Analysis

4. **Analyze a Theater Review** Look over the charts you created as you read. Which reviewer offers better support for the opinions expressed in his or her review? Cite evidence to support your response.

5. **Make Inferences** A theater review may be influenced by factors outside of the production, such as the reviewer's opinion of the play itself and past experiences with the theater company. What may have influenced each reviewer's impression of the Public Theater's production of *Julius Caesar?*

Read for Information: Draw Conclusions

OHIO STANDARDS

READING/RESEARCH STANDARDS
2.1 Draw conclusions

8.4 Evaluate and systematically organize important information

WRITING PROMPT

What choices in casting, set design, and costumes would you make if you were in charge of a production of *Julius Caesar?* How do you suppose Thomas Disch or Edith Oliver would respond to your production?

To answer this prompt, you will need to **draw conclusions,** making judgments based on information from the two reviews and your own knowledge of the play. Use the following steps:

1. Reread both reviews to remind yourself of the reviewers' opinions about casting, set design, and costumes. Use these opinions as the starting point for your planning.

2. Describe the choices you would make about the casting, the set design, and the costumes in a production of the play.

3. Draw conclusions about how Disch and Oliver would likely respond to your production. Cite evidence from the reviews to support your prediction.

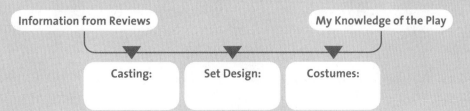

from **Julius Caesar**

Film Clip on ⊙ **MediaSmart** DVD

What gives a SCENE *its power?*

OHIO STANDARDS

COMMUNICATION STANDARD
9.4 Identify how language choice and delivery styles contribute to meaning

KEY IDEA Some of the world's greatest **speeches** have inspired and moved audiences. Others have initiated change by creating cultural and political awareness. A few, like Shakespeare's version of Mark Antony's funeral oration, have stirred a crowd to mob action. In this lesson, you'll see how certain filmmaking techniques enhance the **performance** of Mark Antony's famous speech.

Background

"**Friends, Romans, Countrymen . . .**" If you've ever seen a live performance of a Shakespearean play, then you understand why film directors have long been interested in bringing Shakespearean drama to film. Shakespeare's understanding of human nature—the flaws, strengths, and ambitions of his characters—remains universal and timeless.

One of the most memorable speeches in literary history. Mark Antony's funeral oration is brief. However, its ability to stir an audience from sadness and compassion to anger and rage shows the emotional range of Shakespearean drama.

Media Literacy: Shakespearean Drama on Film

One key ingredient directors use to bring Shakespearean drama to the big screen is **mise en scène** (mēz′ äɴ sĕn′). This French term refers to the arrangement and the use of setting, props, costumes, lighting, and acting in a scene. Once the visual elements come together, directors use a careful selection of **camera shots.** Here are some of the ways directors use these techniques.

FILMMAKING TECHNIQUES	STRATEGIES FOR VIEWING	
Mise en Scène Directors use elements of mise en scène to provide clues about the setting, to create relationships between characters, and to show the behavior and motivation of characters.	• Pay close attention to the **setting,** the **props,** and the **costumes.** They not only establish the time and place in which a story is set but may also be essential to the plot in other ways. For example, a director may use a prop as a symbol. Keep track of when and how a prop is used. • Study the **performances.** An actor's performance consists of his or her appearance, body movements, facial expressions, gestures, and voice. • Notice how characters are positioned within a frame. For example, a main character may be placed in the center of the frame to emphasize his or her importance in a scene.	 
Camera Shots In the realm of theater, directors achieve effective onstage performances through precise positioning of the actors. Film directors do this as well, but they also use camera shots to draw viewers' attention to something important, and to create an impression or feeling in the audience.	• Study the types of shots a director uses to convey the action in a scene. An **extreme long shot,** or **establishing shot,** is used to provide a view of a large area or to establish the scene. To show how characters interact within their surroundings, a director may use a **long shot.** • Notice how **close-up shots** can suggest a character's inner thoughts and feelings. Likewise, a **reaction shot** may be used to show how a character reacts to something in a previous shot.	

MediaSmart DVD

- **Film Clip:** *Julius Caesar*, 1970
- **Director:** Stuart Burge
- **Genre:** Drama
- **Running Time:** 10 minutes

Viewing Guide for
Julius Caesar

Prepare to view an interpretation of one of the most famous speeches in Shakespearean drama. How might the experience of watching this scene performed on screen differ from the experience of reading or watching the stage performance? As you view, think about these questions.

NOW VIEW

FIRST VIEWING: Comprehension

1. **Recall** What type of **camera shot** is used to open the scene?

2. **Recall** Name one prop that is used in this scene.

CLOSE VIEWING: Media Literacy

3. **Make Inferences** Throughout the scene, the director cuts to the reactions of three men. What do the **reaction shots** convey about these men?

4. **Analyze Mise en Scène** What elements of mise en scène indicate that the film takes place in the past?

5. **Analyze Camera Shots** Which camera shot is used the most? Why do you think this shot is important to the scene?

6. **Evaluate the Performance** The actor's performance is an important element of **mise en scène.** How would you rate the performance of the actor who plays Mark Antony? Think about

   - how the actor uses facial expressions and gestures to convey the character's emotions
   - the actor's tone of voice and delivery of the lines
   - your own expectations of the character of Mark Antony and how the actor would portray any traits you associate with him

Write or Discuss

Evaluate the Film Clip The 1970 adaptation of *Julius Caesar* received mixed reviews. Read an excerpt from a review by critic Roger Ebert. Explain whether you agree or disagree with his statements. Support your opinion with evidence from the clip you've viewed.

> When the crowds gather for Mark Antony's funeral oration, they group themselves like refugees from a particularly orderly Renaissance painting. When we get close-ups of the conspirators, they're arranged like mannequins in a department-store window. . . . And then Charlton Heston leaps in with his Mark Antony speech. Heston does a fine job. . . . But just when Heston gets into high gear, we cut away to a long shot of the crowd and lose all the personal emotion in Heston's face.
>
> Roger Ebert, *Chicago Sun-Times,* March 17, 1971

Produce Your Own Media

Write a Shooting Script Before filming, directors often create a **shooting script.** A shooting script is a split-page document that describes camera shots on the left, and sound (dialogue, voice-over narration, music, and sound effects) on the right. Choose a scene (or part of a scene) from *Julius Caesar* and create a shooting script that describes how the scene is shot.

HERE'S HOW Use the model and the tip to help you create a shooting script.

- Determine the setting, the place and time in which the scene takes place.
- Vary the **camera placement** to show characters' actions and emotions.
- Consider how **sound** contributes to the scene.

> **MEDIA TOOLS**
>
> For help with creating a shooting script, visit the **Media Center** at **ClassZone.com.**

STUDENT MODEL

SHOT DESCRIPTIONS	SOUND	
FADE IN EXT—DAY		
1. MS, CASCA AND BRUTUS. Begin slow zoom out to reveal Brutus pulling Casca's cloak. Casca has turned to face Brutus.	**CASCA:**	You pulled me by the cloak. Would you speak with me?
	BRUTUS:	Ay, Casca. Tell us what hath chanced today that Caesar looks so sad.
2. CU—CASCA LOOKS CONFUSED.	**CASCA:**	Why you were with him, were you not?

PRODUCTION TIP

Use the following abbreviations to indicate camera placement:

ELS = extreme long shot

LS = long shot

CU = close-up shot

MS = medium shot

POV = point-of-view shot

Writing Workshop

Comparing a Play and a Film

"The book was better than the movie." Have you ever heard someone say that, or have you said it yourself? In this workshop, you will compare a work of literature with its screen adaptation. The **Writer's Road Map** will show you how.

WRITER'S ROAD MAP

Comparing a Play and a Film

WRITING PROMPT 1

Writing from Literature Write an essay in which you compare one scene from a filmed adaptation of *Julius Caesar* with the same scene in Shakespeare's play.

Scenes to Compare

- Calpurnia's begging Caesar not to go to the Senate (Act Two, Scene 2)
- Caesar's murder (Act Three, Scene 1)
- Mark Antony's "Friends, Romans, countrymen" speech (Act Three, Scene 2)

WRITING PROMPT 2

Writing for the Real World Choose a short story, novel, or play that you have read and enjoyed and that has been made into a film. Write a review for a movie Web site that compares the literary work with the film it inspired.

Subjects to Consider

- "A Sound of Thunder"
- *I, Robot*
- *Jaws*

WRITING TOOLS
For prewriting, revision, and editing tools, visit the **Writing Center** at **ClassZone.com.**

KEY TRAITS

1. IDEAS

- Clearly states the **focus** of the comparison
- Includes a **thesis statement** that identifies similarities and/or differences
- Uses relevant **details** from the two works to support ideas

2. ORGANIZATION

- Follows a clear, logical **organizational pattern**
- Connects ideas with **transitions**
- Provides **background information** for the reader
- Ends with a **summary** and a broader **conclusion** about ideas in the two works

3. VOICE

- Uses **appropriate language** for the audience and purpose

4. WORD CHOICE

- Includes precise **literary and media terms** when discussing the written work and the film

5. SENTENCE FLUENCY

- Uses different **sentence lengths** for interest and variety

6. CONVENTIONS

- Employs **correct grammar and usage**

Part 1: Analyze a Student Model

WRITING STANDARD
6.2 Write responses to literature

Andre Davis
Austin College Prep

The Tragedy of Julius Caesar

When director Stuart Burge decided to film a Shakespeare play, he had to confront the many differences between stage and screen. What works on stage is sometimes awkward or unnecessary on film, and filmmakers create effects that theater directors can't achieve. In his
5 version of *Julius Caesar,* Burge cut dialogue and used camera shots, symbols, and sound effects to make the movie powerful and dramatic. These moviemaking techniques are on display in Act One, Scene 2, when the conspiracy against Caesar begins to take shape.

In both the play and the film, Scene 2 opens during a festival called
10 Lupercal. The film's script for this scene is faithful to Shakespeare's play, although some dialogue has been deleted to keep the story moving. For example, Cassius' description of saving Caesar from drowning is missing from the movie version. This is unfortunate because the description in the play offers revealing details about Caesar's physical weakness and
15 Cassius' resentment of him.

As Caesar strolls through a plaza in Rome, a soothsayer warns: "Beware the ides of March." The play offers no description of the soothsayer and no stage directions telling how the soothsayer should act. Burge presents Shakespeare's soothsayer as a gaunt, hooded man.
20 The film cuts, or suddenly jumps, to his face as he howls his warning. Caesar summons him to repeat the message. As the camera lingers on a close-up of Caesar's face, his worried look slowly changes to a faint smile, indicating he doesn't take the warning seriously. This dramatic effect would not be possible in a theater because theatergoers far back in the
25 auditorium would never be able to see so slight a smile.

KEY TRAITS IN ACTION

Focus of the comparison is clearly stated.

Thesis statement identifies how the film differs from the play.

Uses a **transition** to introduce the **organizational pattern,** comparing the play and the film one point at a time.

Background information about the characters helps the reader understand the point the writer is making.

Uses **appropriately formal language.** Different **sentence lengths** make the writing more dramatic.

Burge uses a visual symbol to make Shakespeare's words even more dramatic. In the play, Cassius complains to Brutus about how unfair it is that the Romans love Caesar so much. In the film, however, Cassius picks up a dagger, an example of visual foreshadowing that hints at the
30 means by which Caesar will be killed. Then, as Cassius asks, "Upon what meat does this our Caesar feed / That he is grown so great," he whirls around to face Brutus and stabs his dagger into a table—more visual foreshadowing of Caesar's fate.

At the end of Scene 2, the director uses another visual symbol and a
35 sound effect. In both the play and the film, Cassius delivers a soliloquy in which he predicts that Brutus will join the conspiracy. In the movie, Cassius walks up to a statue of Caesar that has a garland of flowers on it. As he snarls, "For we will shake him, or worse days endure," he rips down the flowers. The film cuts to the sky as thunder crashes and
40 lightning flashes, foreshadowing the chaos to come. Finally, the film cuts back to Caesar's statue, to a close-up shot of his stony face as it flickers in the lightning of the approaching storm.

Stuart Burge's adaptation of *Julius Caesar* remains faithful to the plot and themes of Shakespeare's play while skillfully using cinematic
45 techniques to showcase the ideas within it. In doing so, Burge shows how film can expand and enrich a playwright's vision.

Throughout the essay, the writer supports his ideas with **relevant details** from both works.

Precise **literary and media terms** help the reader see how the director has interpreted Shakespeare.

Ends with a **summary** and a broader **conclusion** about the playwright and the director.

2

Part 2: Apply the Writing Process

WRITING STANDARD
5.6 Create a coherent whole : introduction, body and conclusion

PREWRITING

What Should I Do?

What Does It Look Like?

1. **Choose a scene.**
   Watch the movie, making notes about which scenes are most interesting. If possible, turn on the English-language subtitles or closed captioning to aid your understanding. When you have chosen a scene, watch it several times, taking notes as you do.

   TIP Think about which scenes affect you emotionally and which seem most different from the original work.

   > *Act One, Scene 2: Conspiracy begins. Caesar's death foreshadowed. The dagger scene with Cassius. Cassius plots with Brutus.*
   >
   > *Act Three, Scene 1: Caesar assassinated, extremely violent, blood everywhere. Caesar killed in the name of peace and freedom.*
   >
   > *Act Three, Scene 2: "Friends, Romans, . . ."—very powerful speech. Lots of irony. Antony sways the crowd to rioting, burning.*

2. **Reread the same scene in the literary work.**
   Make a chart showing the similarities and differences on screen and on the page.
   Think about

   - characters or events that are different in the play and in the film
   - dialogue that has been expanded, edited, or deleted
   - ways that the director uses costumes, props, sets, music, or effects to interpret the playwright's words

   See page 1200: Techniques of the Stage and Screen

Play	Film
• *story about Cassius saving Caesar from drowning*	• *drowning story missing*
• *no description of soothsayer*	• *soothsayer is thin, wears a hood, yells Caesar's name*
• *Cassius to Brutus: unfair that the Romans love Caesar*	• *same dialogue, but Cassius has dagger— foreshadows assassination*

3. **Develop a working thesis statement.**
   An effective thesis statement not only tells the reader what you're going to write about but also helps you keep your writing focused.

   TIP If your writing leads you in unexpected directions, you may need to revise your thesis statement after drafting your essay.

   > *Working thesis statement:*
   >
   > *In his version of <u>Julius Caesar</u>, Stuart Burge made changes to the play so that the movie would be powerful and dramatic.*
   > *1. dialogue*
   > *2. camera shots*
   > *3. visual symbols*
   > *4. sound effects*

What Should I Do?

What Does It Look Like?

1. **Decide on an organizational pattern.**
Here is an informal outline Andre Davis created to organize his essay. He chose a **point-by-point** organization, comparing the play and the movie one point at a time. He could have used a **subject-by-subject** organization instead, discussing the play in the first half of his essay and the film in the second half.

   TIP Experiment with both kinds of organization to find out which works better for your comparison.

> Introduction: Act One, Scene 2
> **Point 1: Dialogue**
>   **Play:** Cassius tells how he saved Caesar from drowning.
>   **Film:** Dialogue has been cut.
> **Point 2: Character Interpretation**
>   **Play:** There is no description of the soothsayer.
>   **Film:** He is thin and hooded; Caesar smiles slightly at his warning.
> **Point 3: Visual Symbol**
>   **Play:** Cassius complains to Brutus.
>   **Film:** Cassius stabs a dagger into the table.
> **Point 4: Sound Effect**
>   **Play:** Cassius predicts that Brutus will join the conspiracy.
>   **Film:** Director adds thunder for effect.
> Conclusion

2. **Gather your evidence.**
As you compare the play and the film, you must offer the reader evidence to back up your comparisons. Your evidence may include bits of dialogue, costumes, visual symbols, camera movements, stage directions, music, sound effects, special effects, and so on.

> The director visually foreshadows Caesar's fate.
> - Cassius picks up a dagger as he complains about Caesar.
> - Cassius tears flowers off a statue of Caesar.
> - The director shows a close-up of the statue's face as lightning flashes.

3. **Consider your audience's needs.**
If audience members are not familiar with the play or the film, you may need to give information about a character or an event to enhance their understanding of your comparison.

   TIP Before revising, consult the key traits on page 1194 and the rubric and peer-reader questions on page 1200.

> For example, Cassius' description of saving Caesar from drowning is missing from the movie version. This is unfortunate because the description in the play offers revealing details about Caesar's physical weakness and Cassius' resentment of him.

REVISING AND EDITING

What Should I Do?

1. Use language that is appropriate to your audience and purpose.
- Ask a peer reader to <u>underline</u> passages that are too informal or that contain language that the reader might not understand.
- Revise your essay so that your tone and language are appropriate to your audience.

See page 1200: Ask a Peer Reader

2. Make sure transitions are clear.
- (Circle) the transitional words and phrases you have used.
- If you have few or no circles, add transitions that connect ideas and show your organizational pattern.

3. Explain technical terms.
- Draw a box around any technical terms you have used.
- Add definitions where necessary to make your writing clear.

4. Write a conclusion that does more than just summarize.
- Highlight your conclusion. Ask yourself if you're just repeating your thesis statement.
- Revise your conclusion so that it not only summarizes your comparison but also explains why it matters.

What Does It Look Like?

What works on stage sometimes ~~looks bad~~ *is awkward or unnecessary* on film, and filmmakers ~~can do stuff that theater guys can't.~~ *create effects that theater directors can't achieve.*

Scene 2 opens during *a festival called* Lupercal.

In the film, *however,* Cassius picks up a dagger, an example of visual foreshadowing that hints at the means by which Caesar will be killed. (Finally,) the film cuts back to Caesar's statue.

The film [cuts] *, or suddenly jumps,* to his face as he howls his warning.

~~The movie and the play of Julius Caesar are similar in some ways and different in others.~~ Stuart Burge's adaptation of <u>Julius Caesar</u> remains faithful to the plot and themes of Shakespeare's play while skillfully using cinematic techniques to showcase the ideas within it. In doing so, Burge shows how film can expand and enrich a playwright's vision.

Comparing a Play and a Film

Apply the Rubric

A strong essay that compares a play and a film . . .

☑ states the focus of the comparison

☑ has a thesis that identifies similarities (and differences, if applicable)

☑ includes helpful background information

☑ supports the thesis with evidence from both works

☑ uses literary and media terms accurately

☑ is sensibly organized, with effective transitions

☑ varies sentence lengths

☑ maintains an appropriate tone

☑ has a thoughtful conclusion

Ask a Peer Reader

• Which parts of my comparison are strongest? weakest?

• Where have I used language that is too informal or that is difficult to understand?

• Where does my conclusion explain why my comparison matters?

Techniques of the Stage and Screen

Lighting can help set the mood. For example, heavy shadows can seem mysterious or threatening.

Sound effects, such as thunder, can add drama. **Music** can set a tone for a production.

Sets are locations where the action takes place. **Props, costumes,** and **backdrops** can make an ordinary set look like a Roman marketplace.

Check Your Grammar

• Use the comparative form of an adjective or adverb to compare two things.

> *Cassius is angrier than Brutus.*
>
> *Caesar is more suspicious than Antony.*

• Use the superlative form to compare three or more things.

> *Of all the conspirators, Cassius is the angriest.*
>
> *Caesar is the most powerful Roman citizen.*

See pages R57–R58: Comparison of Modifiers

Writing On|ine

PUBLISHING OPTIONS
For publishing options, visit the **Writing Center** at **ClassZone.com.**

ASSESSMENT PREPARATION
For writing and grammar assessment practice, go to the **Assessment Center** at **ClassZone.com.**

SPEAKING AND LISTENING

Delivering a Dramatic Reading

A dramatic reading of a passage from the work you wrote about can increase your audience's appreciation of the author's style and ideas.

Planning the Dramatic Reading

1. **Choose an excerpt to read.** Look for a passage that is especially dramatic or gives insight into a character. If the passage includes another speaker, ask a classmate to help you.

2. **Prepare a script of the excerpt.** Highlight words and phrases you want to stress. Note places where you want to pause or shift your pacing or emphasis. Ask your teacher for help with meaning, pronunciation, and rhythm.

> [NOTE: Emphasize highlighted words.]
>
> Why, man, he doth bestride the narrow world
>
> Like a Colossus, and we petty men
>
> [frown] Walk under his huge legs and peep about
>
> To find ourselves dishonorable graves. ←————— lower voice
>
> [pause] Men at some times are masters of their fates.

3. **Rehearse.** Make recordings—audio or video—of your rehearsals. Refine your pacing, tone, emphasis, and gestures.

Presenting the Dramatic Reading

1. **Speak directly to your audience.** Vary your eye contact throughout your performance. Establish and maintain a posture that is appropriate for the excerpt you are presenting.

2. **Remember, it's a *dramatic* reading.** If you want to engage your audience, let them see and hear your commitment to the passage you chose. Your voice, facial expressions, and gestures can help your audience understand the meaning of what you are saying. Laugh, point, frown, yell, or whisper—whatever it takes to bring your reading to life.

See page R80: Evaluate an Oral Interpretation

Reading Comprehension

DIRECTIONS *Read this excerpt from* The Tragedy of Julius Caesar, *Act Two, Scene 1, and answer the questions that follow.*

from The Tragedy of Julius Caesar

William Shakespeare

Lucius. Sir, March is wasted fifteen days.

[*Knocking within.*]

60 **Brutus.** 'Tis good. Go to the gate, somebody knocks.

[*Exit* Lucius.]

Since Cassius first did whet me against Caesar,
I have not slept.
Between the acting of a dreadful thing
And the first motion, all the interim is

65 Like a phantasma or a hideous dream.
The genius and the mortal instruments
Are then in council, and the state of man,
Like to a little kingdom, suffers then
The nature of an insurrection.

[*Reenter* Lucius.]

70 **Lucius.** Sir, 'tis your brother Cassius at the door,
Who doth desire to see you.

Brutus.   Is he alone?

Lucius. No, sir, there are more with him.

Brutus.   Do you know them?

Lucius. No, sir. Their hats are plucked about their ears
And half their faces buried in their cloaks,

75 That by no means I may discover them
By any mark of favor.

Brutus.   Let 'em enter.

[*Exit* Lucius.]

They are the faction. O conspiracy,
Sham'st thou to show thy dang'rous brow by night,
When evils are most free? O, then by day

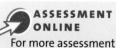

80 Where wilt thou find a cavern dark enough
To mask thy monstrous visage? Seek none,
conspiracy, Hide it in smiles and affability!
For if thou path, thy native semblance on,
No Erebus itself were dim enough
85 To hide thee from prevention.

[*Enter the conspirators,* Cassius, Casca, Decius, Cinna, Metellus
Cimber, *and* Trebonius.]

Cassius. I think we are too bold upon your rest.
Good morrow, Brutus. Do we trouble you?

Brutus. I have been up this hour, awake all night.
Know I these men that come along with you?

90 **Cassius.** Yes, every man of them; and no man here
But honors you; and every one doth wish
You had but that opinion of yourself
Which every noble Roman bears of you.
This is Trebonius.

Brutus.   He is welcome hither.

95 **Cassius.** This, Decius Brutus.

Brutus.   He is welcome too.

Cassius. This, Casca; this, Cinna; and this, Metellus Cimber.

Brutus. They are all welcome.
What watchful cares do interpose themselves
Betwixt your eyes and night?

100 **Cassius.** Shall I entreat a word?

[*They whisper.*]

Decius. Here lies the east. Doth not the day break here?

Casca. No.

Cinna. O, pardon, sir, it doth; and yon grey lines
That fret the clouds are messengers of day.

105 **Casca.** You shall confess that you are both deceived.
Here, as I point my sword, the sun arises,
Which is a great way growing on the south,
Weighing the youthful season of the year.

GO ON

Some two months hence, up higher toward the north
110 He first presents his fire; and the high east
Stands as the Capitol, directly here.

[Brutus *and* Cassius *rejoin the others.*]

Brutus. Give me your hands all over, one by one.

Cassius. And let us swear our resolution.

Brutus. No, not on oath. If not the face of men,
115 The sufferance of our souls, the time's abuse—
If these be motives weak, break off betimes,
And every man hence to his idle bed.
So let high-sighted tyranny range on
Till each man drop by lottery. But if these
120 (As I am sure they do) bear fire enough
To kindle cowards and to steel with valor
The melting spirits of women, then, countrymen,
What need we any spur but our own cause
To prick us to redress? what other bond
125 Than secret Romans that have spoke the word
And will not palter? and what other oath
Than honesty to honesty engaged
That this shall be, or we will fall for it?
Swear priests and cowards and men cautelous,
130 Old feeble carrions and such suffering souls
That welcome wrongs; unto bad causes swear
Such creatures as men doubt; but do not stain
The even virtue of our enterprise,
Nor the insuppressive mettle of our spirits,
135 To think that or our cause or our performance
Did need an oath when every drop of blood
That every Roman bears, and nobly bears,
Is guilty of a several bastardy
If he do break the smallest particle
140 Of any promise that hath passed from him.

Comprehension

DIRECTIONS *Answer these questions about the excerpt from* The Tragedy of Julius Caesar.

1. Reread lines 61–69. In this soliloquy, Brutus reflects on his sleeplessness and tells the audience that it is caused by
   A. bad dreams of phantoms
   B. thoughts of going against Caesar
   C. pains suffered in battle
   D. dreadful acts he has witnessed

2. In lines 66–69 of his soliloquy, Brutus compares an uprising in a kingdom to
   A. his internal conflict
   B. a conflict between rulers
   C. Caesar's internal conflict
   D. battlefield conflicts

3. Brutus' sleeplessness is a sign of his
   A. nervous energy
   B. strength of character
   C. feelings of guilt
   D. mental instability

4. This excerpt is written mostly in iambic pentameter, a meter that is always used in
   A. prose
   B. dialogue
   C. blank verse
   D. regular speech

5. In his soliloquy in lines 77–85, Brutus reveals his opinion that the conspirators
   A. lack the courage to murder Caesar
   B. should reveal their true feelings about the conspiracy
   C. are consumed with evil thoughts
   D. must disguise their plot with friendliness

6. In which statement does Brutus reveal his willingness to engage in trickery?
   A. "Hide it in smiles and affability!" (line 82)
   B. "Give me your hands all over, one by one." (line 112)
   C. "So let high-sighted tyranny range on / Till each man drop by lottery." (lines 118–119)
   D. "what other bond / Than secret Romans that have spoke the word" (lines 124–125)

7. Cassius and the conspirators visit Brutus before the sun has risen because
   A. it is the only time of day they can all agree to meet
   B. they are afraid of being detected as they conspire
   C. they are kept awake by their concern for Rome's citizens
   D. they must set off early so that they can return by nightfall.

8. Which motive is most likely behind Cassius' comment to Brutus that "every one doth wish / You had but that opinion of yourself / Which every noble Roman bears of you." (lines 91–93)?
   A. He wants to encourage Brutus to be more confident in his leadership abilities.
   B. He knows that Caesar respects Brutus more than any other Roman citizen.
   C. He hopes to flatter Brutus so that he will join the conspiracy.
   D. He thinks Brutus does not know that most Romans admire him.

9. Why do Decius, Casca, and Cinna argue in lines 101–111?

   A. to define their roles in the conspiracy

   B. because they want to justify swearing an oath

   C. because they do not trust Cassius or Brutus

   D. to pass the time while Cassius and Brutus speak privately

10. The rhythm of iambic pentameter in line 116 comes from the occurrence of

    A. two stressed syllables followed by an unstressed syllable

    B. an unstressed syllable followed by a stressed syllable

    C. a stressed syllable followed by an unstressed syllable

    D. two rhyming words within the line

11. In lines 112–128, Brutus and Cassius disagree about whether they should

    A. swear allegiance to one another

    B. proceed with their plans for assassination

    C. be willing to die for their cause

    D. involve women in the conspiracy

12. Which character trait does Brutus reveal in his speech in lines 114–140?

    A. cowardice

    B. valor

    C. nobility

    D. tyranny

13. Brutus believes that swearing an oath of allegiance is unnecessary because he has

    A. ulterior motives

    B. personal integrity

    C. powerful friends

    D. Roman ancestors

Written Response

SHORT ANSWER *Write three or four sentences to answer each question.*

14. In this excerpt, what action does Brutus take that will lead to his downfall?

15. Brutus is engaged in an internal and an external conflict in this excerpt. Identify each of these conflicts and give a short quote from the excerpt that illustrates each one.

EXTENDED RESPONSE *Write two or three paragraphs to answer this question.*

16. List the main actions of Cassius and Brutus in this excerpt. Explain how their actions further the plot. Support your explanation with details from the excerpt.

Writing & Grammar

DIRECTIONS *Read the passage and answer the questions that follow.*

> (1) The word *ides* was a calendar term used during the time of Caesar. (2) The term dates back to the earliest Roman calendar. (3) The ides fell on the 15th day in March, May, July, and October and on the 13th day in the other months. (4) The ides' significance grew upon the death of Caesar. (5) From then on, the ides of March was viewed as a day of foreboding and gloom.

1. How might you add descriptive details to sentence 1 by using an adjective clause?

A. In ancient Rome, people used the word *ides* as a calendar term.

B. The word *ides* was a calendar term used during the time of Caesar, a Roman general and politician.

C. The word *ides* was a calendar term used in ancient Rome; it means "to divide."

D. The word *ides,* which means "to divide," was a calendar term used during the time of Caesar.

2. How might you add descriptive details to sentence 2 by using an adjective clause?

A. The term dates back to the earliest Roman calendar, which organized months around the three days of Kalends, Nones, and Ides.

B. The term dates back to the earliest Roman calendar, developed sometime in the 700s B.C.

C. The earliest Roman calendar was introduced by Romulus and included references to the ides.

D. The term dates back to the earliest Roman calendar, organized around the three days of Kalends, Nones, and Ides.

3. How might you add descriptive details to sentence 3 by using an adjective clause?

A. The ides fell on the 15th day in March, May, July, and October, and it fell on the 13th day in the other months.

B. The ides marked a time when the moon was full, falling on the 15th day in March, May, July, and October and on the 13th day in the other months.

C. The ides fell on the 15th day in March, May, July, and October and on the 13th day in the other months of the year.

D. The ides signified a full moon and fell on the 15th day in March, May, July, and October and on the 13th day in the other months.

4. How might you add descriptive details to sentence 4 by using an adjective clause?

A. The ides' significance grew upon the death of Caesar, who was murdered on March 15, 44 B.C.

B. The significance of the ides was forever altered upon the death of Caesar.

C. The ides became even more significant upon the death of Caesar.

D. Caesar's untimely death changed how the ides was perceived.

UNIT 11
Great Reads

Ideas for Independent Reading

Satisfy your curiosity about the real Julius Caesar and other topics related to Shakespeare's play by reading the following works.

Antony and Cleopatra
by William Shakespeare

This is another tragedy based on historical events in ancient Rome. After Julius Caesar's assassination, Mark Antony, Octavius Caesar, and Lepidus jointly rule the Roman Empire. Antony has fallen in love with Julius Caesar's former mistress, Cleopatra, the queen of Egypt. He lives with her in Alexandria, neglecting his duties in Rome. Gradually, the ruling alliance falls apart, and Antony finds himself at war with Octavius Caesar. Has Antony's love for Cleopatra ruined him as a military leader?

Hamlet
by William Shakespeare

Like Brutus in Julius Caesar, the main character in this play also considers murdering his country's ruler. One night Hamlet, the prince of Denmark, is visited by the ghost of his father. The ghost claims that he has been murdered by Hamlet's uncle Claudius, who now is king and is married to Hamlet's mother. Should Hamlet trust the vision he has seen and kill the king in revenge? The decision undoes him, until he thinks of a clever plan to test his uncle's guilt. Hamlet finds out what he wants to know, but it is not the end of his troubles.

Plutarch's Lives, Vol. II
by Plutarch

The ancient Roman historian Plutarch wrote many biographies of famous Greeks and Romans, including Julius Caesar, Brutus, and Mark Antony. Shakespeare used an English translation of *Plutarch's Lives* as his source for the historical events in *Julius Caesar* and *Antony and Cleopatra*. Read the life stories of Caesar and Brutus in this volume to see how faithful Shakespeare was to his source.

The Ides of March
by Thornton Wilder

Author Thornton Wilder, who also wrote the play *Our Town*, describes this work as "a fantasia on certain events and persons in the last days of the Roman Republic." It is an epistolary novel, composed entirely of fictional letters, journal entries, and other documents relating to the reign and assassination of Julius Caesar. Wilder imagines an idealistic Caesar who knew of the plot against him and hoped he would be killed by someone interested only in the welfare of Rome.

The October Horse
by Colleen McCullough

This is the sixth and final volume in McCullough's acclaimed Masters of Rome series. As it opens, Julius Caesar is the busy ruler of Rome, wondering how he can ever get anything done if all his actions must be favorably foretold. The novel goes on to describe his romance with the Egyptian queen Cleopatra and the plots against him by his enemies, who, surprisingly, include Mark Antony. The story builds to Caesar's assassination and its aftermath.

Assassinations: History's Most Shocking Moments of Murder, Betrayal, and Madness
by R. G. Grant

This oversize book contains more than 100 accounts of notorious assassinations and is illustrated with paintings, photographs, diagrams, maps, and timelines. It covers the assassinations of Julius Caesar, Abraham Lincoln, Mahatma Gandhi, and John F. Kennedy. The backgrounds and motives of the assassins are described, and so are the repercussions of the acts.

The Power of Research

BOWERS RECORDING STUDIO

EQUIPMENT | STAFF | RATES & SERVICES | CONTACT US

Make your demo at our studio!
Our expert engineers will give you a dynamic, high-quality sound.

CLICK TO CONTINUE

RESEARCH WORKSHOPS

- Research Strategies
- Writing Research Papers

Why do RESEARCH?

When you read the classified ads to find a summer job, gather information to write a research paper, or call the local multiplex to find out what time a certain movie is playing, you are doing research. Answers to your questions are out there. You just need to know how to find them. This unit will point you in the right direction.

ACTIVITY Make a list of questions concerning topics that you have always wanted to know more about. Next to each question, write two or three possible sources of information on the topic. Here are some questions to get you started:

- How can I find out which jobs and careers best match my skills and interests?

- What was my city, town, or neighborhood like a hundred years ago?

- What kind of diet will allow a person to live to be 100?

- I "freeze up" whenever I take a test. How can I stay relaxed and improve my memory?

OHIO STANDARDS

Preview Unit Goals

DEVELOPING RESEARCH SKILLS
- Plan research
- Develop research questions
- Use library and media center resources
- Distinguish between primary and secondary sources
- Evaluate information and sources, including nonfiction books, periodicals, and Web sites
- Collect your own data

WRITING
- Write a research paper
- Narrow your research topic
- Locate and evaluate sources
- Take notes
- Make source cards
- Summarize and paraphrase
- Quote directly and avoid plagiarism
- Document sources
- Prepare a Works Cited list
- Format your paper

SPEAKING, LISTENING, AND VIEWING
- Create a Web site

ACADEMIC VOCABULARY
- research topic
- research paper
- resources
- sources
- source cards
- plagiarism
- documentation
- Works Cited list
- Web site

Where is the INFORMATION I need?

OHIO STANDARDS

RESEARCH STANDARD
8.2 Identify appropriate sources and gather relevant information

KEY IDEA Knowing how to find accurate **information** quickly can help you whether you are choosing elective classes, researching a purchase, or making plans for your future.

QUICKWRITE Imagine that you have enjoyed playing music by yourself and with friends since you were a child and have started wondering whether a career in music might be right for you. What are some ways to find out what kinds of jobs are available and what qualifications are required? With a group, brainstorm possible answers. Then list places where more information might be available.

Ways to Find
Music-Related Jobs
1. Go to the Internet

Beginning Your Research

Where Do I Start? It's easy to be overwhelmed by all the information sources out there. How can you refine and focus your search?

Making a Smart Start

To avoid wasting time and getting frustrated, take a few minutes to think about what you want to accomplish.

SET A GOAL FOR YOURSELF

Putting your ideas on paper can help you clarify your thoughts.

> **GENERAL GOAL:** Find out about jobs that have to do with music.
>
> **WAYS TO ACCOMPLISH IT:**
>
> - Talk to performers and to people who work behind the scenes. How did they get started? What is a typical day on the job like?
> - Look in the careers section at the library.
> - See what I can find on the Internet.
>
> **SPECIFIC GOAL:** I want to do research and conduct interviews to find out about entry-level jobs and careers in the music industry.

GET AN OVERVIEW OF YOUR SUBJECT

Here are four ways to get an overview of your subject. You could use anywhere from one to all four to help you focus on what it is you're looking for.

- **Talk to people.** Friends and relatives might be able to provide answers themselves or might guide you to someone who can.

- **Use Internet search engines.** Think of words and phrases that are related to your subject. For instance, you might use the phrase *recording studio* and the name of your city or town. Plug the words into search engines and look at relevant Web sites.

- **Head for your school's media center or the local public library.** A research librarian might suggest reference works, books, magazines, or online sources.

- **Be creative.** Flip through the telephone book to see if there are local businesses or organizations that you might call for information. If you know someone who has a job that interests you, consider asking permission to "shadow" him or her—in other words, to spend a few hours or an entire day on the job with that person.

As you find out more about your subject, you might change the focus of your research. For example, spending a day with a local musician may make you want to investigate schools and colleges that offer degree programs in music.

RESEARCH TOOLS
For research tools and strategies, visit the **Research Center** at **ClassZone.com**.

Focusing and Organizing

Once you have specific goals, it's time to decide how you will narrow the focus of your research and how you will organize the information you find.

CREATE RESEARCH QUESTIONS

Write down at least two or three specific questions to help you search more efficiently and accurately. You may think of more key terms, for example.

> • What careers are there in the music industry?
>
> • Could I make a living as a professional songwriter or musician? Would having a college degree from a music school help?
>
> • What entry-level jobs related to music are available, and what qualifications do I need to get one?

DECIDE ON A NOTE-TAKING METHOD

To avoid being overwhelmed by facts, figures, and details, record the information you find in a way that matches your purpose. Here are some examples:

- If you are writing a research paper, you should probably use **note cards.** See page 1244 to learn more about this method.

- A **category chart** is another useful way to organize information.

Music-Related Jobs and Internships		
Name and Location	**Job Description**	**Pay**
McNulty Audio Recording, 1622 Davis	production assistant (duplicating CDs, data entry)	minimum wage
WLCT Radio, 780 Skyline Dr.	intern (data entry, filing, phone calls)	none
Fort Square Church, 155 Lakeside Ave.	guitarist at Sunday evening worship services	$15 per service

- If you are trying to choose between two options, consider a **pro/con chart.**

Interning at WLCT	
Advantages	**Disadvantages**
• can learn about careers in radio • can get there in about 20 minutes	• no pay • minimum 10 hrs/week
Working at McNulty Audio Recording	
Advantages	**Disadvantages**
• a paying job • can learn about audio recording	• takes almost an hour to get there • have to work every Saturday

Using the Internet

Where Do I Find Trustworthy Online Sources? So much information is [on]
the Internet. How can you find accurate, up-to-date information quick[ly?]

Finding and Selecting Web-Based Sources

The World Wide Web is accessible through the Internet, a vast system [of]
computers. The Web includes hundreds of millions of Web sites and li[nks]
billions of Web pages.

Each Web address, or URL, ends with an abbreviation. Knowing wha[t the]
abbreviations mean can help you understand the purpose of each Web [site]
you visit.

Boolean Searches A Bool[ean]
search are related.
• Using the word[s]
both words
front of
• The

• keyword search
• Boolean search
• hyperlink
• menu
• icon

WEB ABBREVIATIONS AND MEANINGS

.COM   commercial—product information and sales; personal sites; some combinations of products and information, such as World Book Online

.EDU   education—information about schools, courses, campus life, and research projects; students' and teachers' personal sites

.GOV   United States government—official sites of the White House, NASA, the FBI, and other government agencies

.MIL   United States military—official sites of the Army, Navy, Air Force, and Marines, as well as the Department of Defense and related agencies

.NET   network—product information and sales

.ORG   organization—charities, libraries, and other nonprofits; political parties

DO A WEB SEARCH

Keyword Searches Begin with a **search engine,** a Web site that lets you look for information using a phrase or term related to your subject. This is called a **keyword search.** Keep these tips in mind while searching:

TIP Use a metasearch engine, such as Metacrawler or Dogpile, to scan many search engines at once.

• Be specific. Instead of *music,* try *music careers.* Look at your research questions for ideas.

• Try putting exact phrases in quotation marks. For instance, *"recording studio"* will give you sites that include those words in that order.

• Some search engines let you replace the end of a word with an asterisk. For example, the keyword *music** leads to sites that contain *music, musician,* and *musicianship.*

...ean search lets you specify how the keywords in your

AND tells the search engine to find all documents that contain ... (*internship* AND *radio*). Some search engines use a plus sign in ... the word instead (*+internship +radio*).

...word OR broadens the search to include all documents that contain either ...word (*job* OR *career*).

- The word NOT—or, for some search engines, a minus sign—excludes unwanted terms from the search (*songwriting* NOT *commercials*).

CHOOSE THE MOST RELEVANT SITES

Your search will result in a list of sites sorted either by date or by relevance. Most search engines base relevance on how often your search terms appear on a particular page and on whether any or all of your search terms appear in the page's URL. However, just because a site is at the top of the list doesn't mean that it is the best or most relevant for you. Read the descriptions of listed items, looking for words that are related to your goals and needs.

TRY IT OUT! *Look at Search Engine Results*

Which of these search results would you choose to explore?

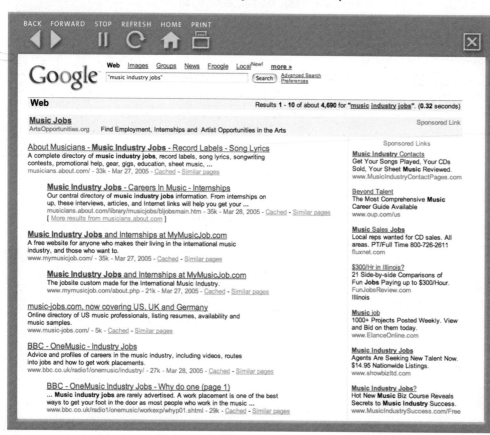

TIP Look for a "Search Tips" or "Advanced Search" hyperlink on each search engine you use. Click on it to find out whether that search engine allows Boolean searches.

INTERACTIVE PRACTICE
For interactive practice of Try It Out! activities, go to the **Research Center** at **ClassZone.com**.

Close Read

1. What keywords did this student use? What makes them an effective combination?

2. What was the total number of sites found? How could this search be made more specific?

3. The results labeled "Sponsored Links" are paid advertisements. Would you be more or less likely to click on a sponsored link? Why?

NAVIGATE EACH SITE

After selecting a few sites, you will need to know how to read them and use the special features they contain. Most Web pages include features that aren't used in books.

TIP To evaluate the usefulness and accuracy of the information on a Web site, use the evaluation guidelines on page 1226.

- Underlined or highlighted words are called **hyperlinks** or links. Clicking on these words leads you to related information on another page on the site or to a different site.

- **Icons** are small pictures or symbols that work the same way as hyperlinks.

- Most Web pages include at least one **menu,** or list of choices. These are often on one side of the page, at the top, or at the bottom.

- Look for a "last updated" reference (often at the bottom of the page) to determine if the Web page you are reading is up-to-date.

TRY IT OUT! *Examine a Web Site*

Take a close look at this site. What information can you find?

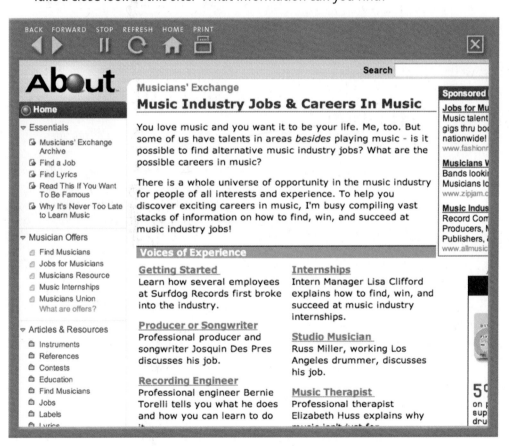

Close Read

1. Is this site appropriate for someone looking for information about entry-level jobs in the music industry? Give reasons for your answer.

2. Which three menu items would you click on to learn more about paid positions in the music industry?

3. Who is Lisa Clifford? Which hyperlink would you click on to learn more about her opinions?

You will use these
terms when doing
research in the library
or media center:

- catalog
- microfilm
- microfiche
- abstract
- primary source
- secondary source
- database
- bibliography
- index
- glossary

Exploring the Library or Media Center

Why Should I Visit the Library? How can the people, materials, and technologies at your local library or media center help you find information?

Using Today's Library or Media Center

Libraries and media centers are treasure troves of information. Your school's media center or your local public library will probably have most or all of these departments.

LIBRARY AND MEDIA-CENTER RESOURCES

BOOKS

Nonfiction books are arranged by subject. See "Library Detective" on page 1232 to learn about the two systems for classifying nonfiction books.

Fiction books are shelved alphabetically by the author's last name.

NEWSPAPERS AND PERIODICALS

Periodicals include magazines, newsletters, and scholarly journals.

Microforms are newspapers, periodicals, and reports stored on film (microfilm) or cards (microfiche) and viewable on special machines.

REFERENCE WORKS

Reference books include encyclopedias, atlases, almanacs, and dictionaries. These usually cannot be checked out of the library.

Search tools include databases, directories, indexes, and the library's catalog. One search tool that can save you time is an index of abstracts. An **abstract** is a short summary of a journal article. By looking at abstracts, you can determine which articles are most closely related to your topic.

ELECTRONIC RESOURCES

DVDs and videos of documentaries and other films and television programs are available at most libraries for free or for a small fee.

E-books are books available in electronic form. They are readable on a personal computer or on various hand-held electronic devices.

Audio resources include books, music, and speeches on CD or MP3.

CD-ROMs of encyclopedias, maps, and other resources are available at many libraries.

OTHER RESOURCES

Your library may have a careers section, a college search section, maps, music scores, genealogy resources to help you trace your family tree, or one-of-a-kind resources to help you learn about local history.

Developing a Search Strategy

Where should you start your library search? Ask a librarian, or consult the library's online resources.

THE RESEARCH LIBRARIAN

Librarians are information detectives. These experts can help you

- determine what you need to know
- choose the most useful print, electronic, and audiovisual sources
- operate equipment, such as microfilm readers
- use interlibrary catalogs to expand your research to other libraries

THE LIBRARY'S CATALOG

The catalog is your road map through the library's resources. Here are four ways to search for a source:

- author
- title
- subject
- keyword

In addition to the source's author, title, and publication date, the catalog entry will include a brief summary of its content, the subject categories it addresses, where it is shelved, and whether it is available.

TRY IT OUT! *Search an Online Library Catalog*

This catalog entry shows information about a specific book.

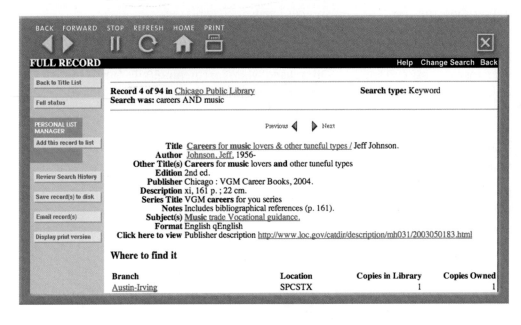

Close Read

1. What two search terms did this student use? Why is it important to include both terms instead of just one?

2. When was this book published? Why is a recent copyright date important when searching for information on careers?

Selecting the Right Sources

You have looked at the library's online catalog, and you're overwhelmed by the amount of information available on your subject. How can you choose the right sources for your needs?

PRIMARY AND SECONDARY SOURCES

One of the first steps in choosing a source is to determine whether it is a primary or a secondary source. This chart explains the differences.

PRIMARY SOURCES	SECONDARY SOURCES
Definition: materials written or created by people who were present at events, either as participants or observers	**Definition:** records of events; created after the events occurred; created by people who were not directly involved in those events
▼	▼
Advantages: firsthand information; can help the researcher understand the attitudes and beliefs of a particular time and place; may contain very specific details	**Advantages:** sometimes include excerpts from many primary sources; often have a broad perspective and many viewpoints; good for getting an overview of a topic
▼	▼
Disadvantages: limited perspective; may need interpretation; may be biased	**Disadvantages:** only as reliable as the sources used; may be biased
▼	▼
Often used when researching: current events, biographical information	**Often used when researching:** complex or technical subjects, ancient history
▼	▼
Examples: autobiographies, letters, interviews, e-mails, diaries, speeches, travelogues, photographs, public documents such as census reports, first-person newspaper and magazine articles	**Examples:** biographies, textbooks, encyclopedias, third-person newspaper and magazine articles

REFERENCE WORKS

A good way to find primary and secondary sources is to [...] reference collection. Use reference works to narrow you[...] questions. Many reference materials are available on CD[...]

DATABASES
What Are Database[...]
arranged so th[...]
Movie Data[...]
but you[...]
data[...]

REFERENCE SOURCES	EXAMPLES
ENCYCLOPEDIAS **General:** Detailed articles on many subjects **Specialized:** Articles on a specific field, such as music, science, or history	Encyclopedia.co[...] *Britannica* *The Billboard Illus[...]* *of Music*
DICTIONARIES **General:** Word meanings, origins, spellings, pronunciations, and usage **Specialized:** Words and terms used in a specific field, such as medicine or music	*The American Heritage Dictionary* *The Harvard Dictionary of Music*
ALMANACS AND YEARBOOKS Statistics and other facts	*The World Almanac and Book of Facts*
THESAURI Synonyms and antonyms	*The American Heritage Thesaurus for Learners of English*
BIOGRAPHICAL REFERENCES Information on the lives of noteworthy people	*The Riverside Dictionary of Biography*
ATLASES Maps and other geographic information	*National Geographic Atlas of the World*
DIRECTORIES Names, addresses, and phone numbers of people and organizations	Telephone books; lists of business organizations, agencies, and publications
INDEXES Alphabetical lists of information	*The Readers' Guide to Periodical Literature*

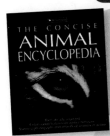

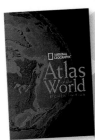

s? A database is a collection of information that has been ... it is easy to search. Some online databases, such as the Internet ... ase and the Web Music Database, are free. Others charge a fee, ... local library may have access to them. For instance, ancestry.com is a ... base of census records, immigration records, and other resources to help people learn more about their family history. Noticias is a database of Spanish-language articles.

What Makes Them Useful? Database searches are more targeted than Web searches because most databases filter out advertisements. Also, most databases are collections of only one type of material—only newspaper articles, only scientific papers, and so on.

When Should I Use Them? Databases are especially helpful when you have narrowed your topic and have a good idea of what information you are seeking. To find out which databases would be most useful for you, ask a librarian.

TRY IT OUT! *Examine a Database*

Books in Print, a database of book titles and descriptions, gives this information about careers in music.

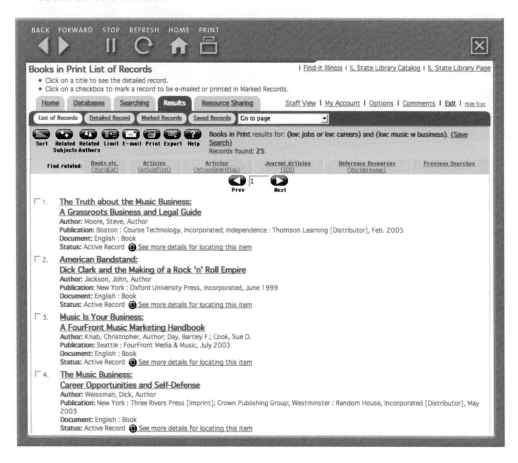

Close Read

1. This student did a Boolean search for "jobs OR careers AND 'music business.'" What keywords might you use to search for your topic on a database like this one?

2. Of the four entries shown, which would be good sources for someone looking for information on jobs that are available in the music industry? Give reasons for your answers.

NONFICTION BOOKS

As you search databases and library shelves, you may find many books that address your topic. How can you quickly determine which ones are right for you?

- Read the book's **title** (and the **subtitle,** if there is one) to get an idea of the general subject matter. Also skim **chapter titles** and **headings.**

- Look for the date of publication on the **copyright page,** which is usually located right after the title page. If you need up-to-the-minute information, don't depend on a book that is several years old.

- Read the **table of contents** at the front of the book, and skim the **index** at the back for terms related to your subject.

- Some books have a **bibliography** or a **recommended readings** section. Either of these can give you ideas for other sources to consult.

- If the book contains difficult technical terms, look for a **glossary** at the back. A glossary lists specialized terms along with their definitions.

TRY IT OUT! *Examine the Parts of a Book*

Use what you have learned about the parts of a book as you look at this example.

BREAKING INTO THE MUSIC INDUSTRY

Your Guide to Jobs and Careers

Raquel Seldera, Ed.D.

SCHNARR PUBLISHING
Danbury, Connecticut

© 2008 by Raquel L. Seldera

All rights reserved. This book may not be duplicated in any form without the written permission of the publisher, except in the form of brief excerpts or quotations for the purpose of review.

First Edition
Printed in the United States

Contents

Bibliography

Crouch, Tanja L. *100 Careers in the Music Business.* New York: Barron's, 2001.

Field, Shelly. *Career Opportunities in the Music Industry.* 4th ed. New York: Facts on File, 2000.

Goldberg, Jan. *Great Jobs for Music Majors.* Chicago: NTC/Contemporary, 2001.

Hatschek, Keith. *How to Get a Job in the Music and Recording Industry.* Boston: Berklee, 2001.

Tieger, Paul D., and Barbara Barron-Tieger. *Do What You Are: Discover the Perfect Career for You Through the Secrets of Personality Type.* 3rd ed. New York: Little, Brown, 2001.

Index

Close Read

1. In your own words, what is the subject of this book?

2. When was this book published? Is it recent enough to be useful?

3. What are some of the careers this book discusses? Where did you find this information?

4. Which page would you consult to find more books on this topic?

NEWSPAPERS AND PERIODICALS

Newspapers, magazines, and academic journals provide concise information on specific topics.

TYPES OF PUBLICATIONS	EXAMPLES
MAGAZINES **General: For most readers** **Specialized: Articles on specific topics**	*Newsweek, Time, Life* *Musician, Rolling Stone* 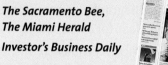
NEWSPAPERS **General: For most readers in a specific geographic area** **Specialized: For readers interested in a certain subject, such as investing**	*The Sacramento Bee,* *The Miami Herald* *Investor's Business Daily*
JOURNALS Journals provide highly specialized information. They are designed for experts. Journals have fewer advertisements than magazines and usually have a more formal writing style.	*Journal of Music Theory* *International Journal of Music Education* 

Use these tips to help you find an article on your topic:

- Ask a research librarian. He or she may know of specialized magazines or journals on your topic.
- Use databases of articles, such as InfoTrac or America's Newspapers, to help you find information on your subject in many sources.

DOCUMENTARIES AND OTHER FILMS

Some of the sources you find may be on DVD or videotape. To quickly assess whether these sources are worth watching, ask yourself these questions:

- Is this a **fiction** or **nonfiction** source? To identify a nonfiction film, read the library's online catalog description. Look for the words *documentary* or *interview.* A fictional film probably does not have enough factual information to serve as a reliable source.
- How recent is the **copyright date?** The online description or the back cover should tell you. Recent documentaries are usually based on updated research.
- What kind of **information** does the film contain? Read the online catalog description and the front and back covers of the DVD or videocassette case. Does the film include **primary sources,** such as speeches or interviews? Did the filmmakers shoot their own footage, or are they using archival materials?

REFERENCE WORKS

A good way to find primary and secondary sources is to examine the library's reference collection. Use reference works to narrow your topic and create research questions. Many reference materials are available on CD-ROMs and online.

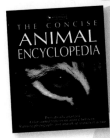

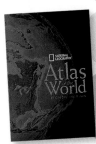

REFERENCE SOURCES	EXAMPLES
ENCYCLOPEDIAS **General:** Detailed articles on many subjects **Specialized:** Articles on a specific field, such as music, science, or history	Encyclopedia.com, *Encyclopaedia Britannica* *The Billboard Illustrated Encyclopedia of Music*
DICTIONARIES **General:** Word meanings, origins, spellings, pronunciations, and usage **Specialized:** Words and terms used in a specific field, such as medicine or music	*The American Heritage Dictionary* *The Harvard Dictionary of Music*
ALMANACS AND YEARBOOKS Statistics and other facts	*The World Almanac and Book of Facts*
THESAURI Synonyms and antonyms	*The American Heritage Thesaurus for Learners of English*
BIOGRAPHICAL REFERENCES Information on the lives of noteworthy people	*The Riverside Dictionary of Biography*
ATLASES Maps and other geographic information	*National Geographic Atlas of the World*
DIRECTORIES Names, addresses, and phone numbers of people and organizations	Telephone books; lists of business organizations, agencies, and publications
INDEXES Alphabetical lists of information	*The Readers' Guide to Periodical Literature*

DATABASES

What Are Databases? A database is a collection of information that has been arranged so that it is easy to search. Some online databases, such as the Internet Movie Database and the Web Music Database, are free. Others charge a fee, but your local library may have access to them. For instance, ancestry.com is a database of census records, immigration records, and other resources to help people learn more about their family history. Noticias is a database of Spanish-language articles.

What Makes Them Useful? Database searches are more targeted than Web searches because most databases filter out advertisements. Also, most databases are collections of only one type of material—only newspaper articles, only scientific papers, and so on.

When Should I Use Them? Databases are especially helpful when you have narrowed your topic and have a good idea of what information you are seeking. To find out which databases would be most useful for you, ask a librarian.

TRY IT OUT! *Examine a Database*

Books in Print, a database of book titles and descriptions, gives this information about careers in music.

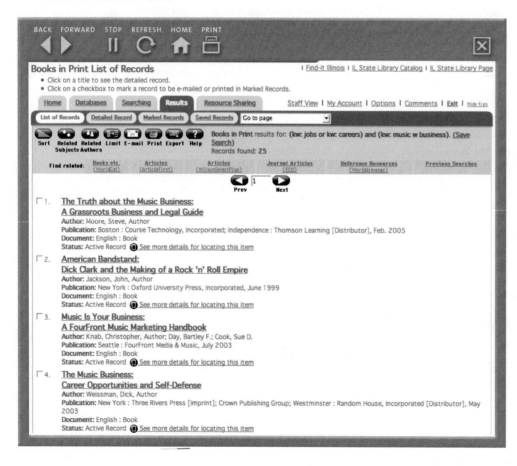

Close Read

1. This student did a Boolean search for "jobs OR careers AND 'music business.'" What keywords might you use to search for your topic on a database like this one?

2. Of the four entries shown, which would be good sources for someone looking for information on jobs that are available in the music industry? Give reasons for your answers.

NONFICTION BOOKS

As you search databases and library shelves, you may find many books that address your topic. How can you quickly determine which ones are right for you?

- Read the book's **title** (and the **subtitle,** if there is one) to get an idea of the general subject matter. Also skim **chapter titles** and **headings.**

- Look for the date of publication on the **copyright page,** which is usually located right after the title page. If you need up-to-the-minute information, don't depend on a book that is several years old.

- Read the **table of contents** at the front of the book, and skim the **index** at the back for terms related to your subject.

- Some books have a **bibliography** or a **recommended readings** section. Either of these can give you ideas for other sources to consult.

- If the book contains difficult technical terms, look for a **glossary** at the back. A glossary lists specialized terms along with their definitions.

TRY IT OUT! *Examine the Parts of a Book*

Use what you have learned about the parts of a book as you look at this example.

BREAKING INTO THE MUSIC INDUSTRY

Your Guide to Jobs and Careers

Raquel Seldera, Ed.D.

SCHNARR PUBLISHING
Danbury, Connecticut

© 2008 by Raquel L. Seldera

All rights reserved. This book may not be duplicated in any form without the written permission of the publisher, except in the form of brief excerpts or quotations for the purpose of review.

First Edition
Printed in the United States

Contents

Bibliography

Crouch, Tanja L. *100 Careers in the Music Business.* New York: Barron's, 2001.

Field, Shelly. *Career Opportunities in the Music Industry.* 4th ed. New York: Facts on File, 2000.

Goldberg, Jan. *Great Jobs for Music Majors.* Chicago: NTC/Contemporary, 2001.

Hatschek, Keith. *How to Get a Job in the Music and Recording Industry.* Boston: Berklee, 2001.

Tieger, Paul D., and Barbara Barron-Tieger. *Do What You Are: Discover the Perfect Career for You Through the Secrets of Personality Type.* 3rd ed. New York: Little, Brown, 2001.

Index

Close Read

1. In your own words, what is the subject of this book?

2. When was this book published? Is it recent enough to be useful?

3. What are some of the careers this book discusses? Where did you find this information?

4. Which page would you consult to find more books on this topic?

NEWSPAPERS AND PERIODICALS

Newspapers, magazines, and academic journals provide concise information on specific topics.

TYPES OF PUBLICATIONS	EXAMPLES
MAGAZINES **General:** For most readers **Specialized:** Articles on specific topics	*Newsweek, Time, Life* *Musician, Rolling Stone* 
NEWSPAPERS **General:** For most readers in a specific geographic area **Specialized:** For readers interested in a certain subject, such as investing	*The Sacramento Bee,* *The Miami Herald* *Investor's Business Daily* 
JOURNALS Journals provide highly specialized information. They are designed for experts. Journals have fewer advertisements than magazines and usually have a more formal writing style.	*Journal of Music Theory* *International Journal of Music Education* 

Use these tips to help you find an article on your topic:

- Ask a research librarian. He or she may know of specialized magazines or journals on your topic.

- Use databases of articles, such as InfoTrac or America's Newspapers, to help you find information on your subject in many sources.

DOCUMENTARIES AND OTHER FILMS

Some of the sources you find may be on DVD or videotape. To quickly assess whether these sources are worth watching, ask yourself these questions:

- Is this a **fiction** or **nonfiction** source? To identify a nonfiction film, read the library's online catalog description. Look for the words *documentary* or *interview.* A fictional film probably does not have enough factual information to serve as a reliable source.

- How recent is the **copyright date?** The online description or the back cover should tell you. Recent documentaries are usually based on updated research.

- What kind of **information** does the film contain? Read the online catalog description and the front and back covers of the DVD or videocassette case. Does the film include **primary sources,** such as speeches or interviews? Did the filmmakers shoot their own footage, or are they using archival materials?

Evaluating Sources

How Do I Find Trustworthy Information? Once you have found several sources, you need to figure out which ones are credible and reliable.

Applying General Evaluation Guidelines

Use the questions in this chart to help you look critically at each source—in print or online—and decide whether you can trust the information in it.

EVALUATING SOURCES

Is the information up-to-date?	Check the copyright page or look for a "last updated" reference. Topics in science, medicine, or sports often require recently updated information. Older publications can be helpful for historical topics.
Is the information accurate?	Can the facts be verified by more than one source? Most print and online encyclopedias, dictionaries, directories, and almanacs are considered reliable because they are updated regularly and go through a rigorous review process.
What is the author's background?	Does the author have a job that qualifies him or her as an expert on the topic? Has he or she written other materials on this topic?
What kinds of materials does the publisher produce?	Magazines that publish trendy articles and gossip are not as reliable as university presses, newsmagazines, or science magazines.
Is there evidence of bias in the source?	Why does the source exist? Does the author list goals in the foreword, preface, or introduction? Is the source designed to inform, persuade, entertain, or some combination of these? Does the author use loaded language, such as "It should be clear to every intelligent person that this plan will be a disaster"?
How much information does the source cover?	Does the source give general or specific information? Does it support other information you have read, or does it add new information? Start by looking at the table of contents, the index, or the menu.
Is the source relevant and appropriate?	Does the source cover aspects of the topic that interest you? Is it written at a level that you can understand?

Evaluating Individual Sources

These tips, questions, and exercises will give you practice in evaluating specific types of sources.

EVALUATE WEB SITES

Web sites are easy to access but difficult to evaluate. They are often a mix of helpful information and attempts to promote a point of view or to sell something.

Commercial Web Sites As you learned on page 1215, URLs ending in *.com* or *.net* are sometimes for-profit sites. When you look at a commercial site, ask yourself these questions:

- **Who created the site?** Look for a link called "About This Site" or "Contact Us."
- **Why was it created?** If the site is designed to sell you something, the site's creators may leave out negative information.

TIP Knowing who created a site can help you figure out why the site exists and whether it will help you in your research.

Organization (.org) Web Sites Many *.org* sites are nonprofit organizations, such as the United Way. Political parties also have URLs with *.org* in them. Think about whether the site you are evaluating is promoting a particular point of view.

- **Who created the site, and when was it last updated?** Look for a link titled "About Us" or "Mission Statement." If there is no way to find the creator of the site, then you should be cautious about the content.
- **What supporting evidence does the site offer?** Look for links to supporting evidence in respected institutions or publications.

Personal Web Sites Anyone can post anything on the World Wide Web, so millions of personal Web sites exist. Some have misleading URLs. For example, students and faculty can post personal Web sites on their university's server, and their Web addresses will contain a university URL. However, these sites might not be reviewed, evaluated, or in any way sanctioned by the institution.

TIP Not all personal Web sites are unreliable, but be cautious.

- **How can I tell if a site is personal even though the address includes the name of an institution?** Look for a forward slash and tilde (/~) and a name or initials following *.edu* in the URL.
- **What does the lack of an official institution logo tell me?** Don't expect the information to be reviewed or approved by the institution.
- **What if most of the links on the site don't work or connect to other items by the same author?** The author may be careless, or he or she may lack outside support.

TRY IT OUT! *Examine Web Sites*

Examine these Web sites. What do they offer to visitors?

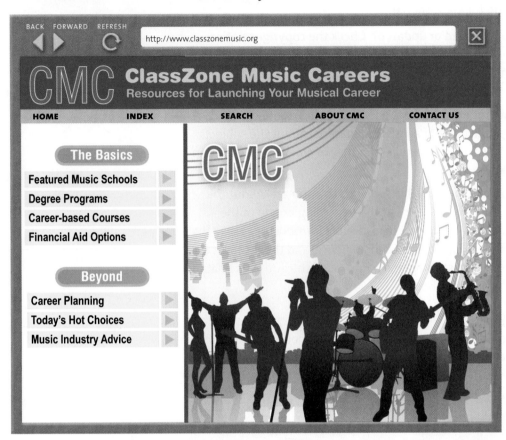

Close Read

1. Which link would you click on to find out more about the sponsoring organization?

2. Why was this site created?

3. Who is the intended audience?

4. Is this is a nonprofit site? How do you know?

5. Links to further information appear at the left of the page. Which link would you click on to find out more about scholarships to music school?

TIP To figure out how a particular Web site is organized, look for a link titled "Site Map" or "Home."

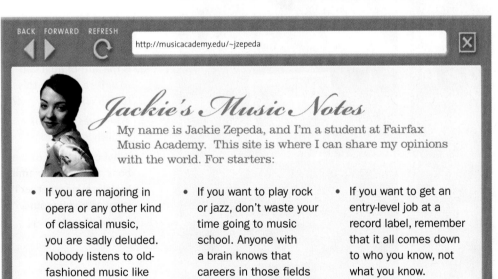

Close Read

1. Who created this site?

2. Why was this site created?

3. Is this an educational site or a personal site? How do you know?

4. What supporting evidence is included?

EVALUATE NONFICTION BOOKS

Nonfiction books can give you detailed information on your topic. Asking these questions will help you find the right sources:

- **When was the book copyrighted or updated?** Check the **copyright notice,** which is usually right after the title page. Look for terms such as *revised and updated edition* on the copyright page or the cover. If a book has gone through many updates and printings, it is likely to be reliable.

- **What sources did the writer use?** Look for a **bibliography.** Some books also include an **appendix**—a collection of additional material about the subject. Notes within the book, such as footnotes, end notes, or cross-references, can also give you clues about sources.

- **What makes the author an expert on this subject?** Look for an "About the Author" description on the book jacket or at the beginning or end of the book. The author may have written a **preface,** a short introductory essay that explains the purpose of the book, its intended audience, and the research on which it is based. If the source is a biography, find out if the author is related to the person he or she is writing about.

TRY IT OUT! *Examine a Nonfiction Book*

Using what you have learned about nonfiction books and about the parts of a book (page 1223), decide whether this book is a relevant source for someone interested in a music career.

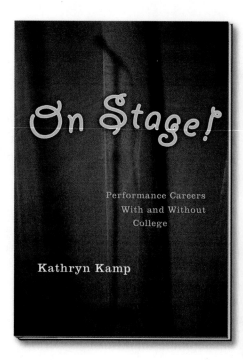

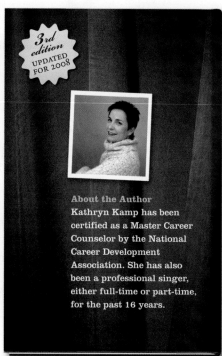

3rd edition UPDATED FOR 2008

About the Author
Kathryn Kamp has been certified as a Master Career Counselor by the National Career Development Association. She has also been a professional singer, either full-time or part-time, for the past 16 years.

Close Read

1. What is the subject of this book? How do you know?

2. Is the author qualified to write a book on this topic? Why or why not?

3. When was this book published?

4. What other parts of the book should you examine to determine whether it is a worthwhile source? (Hint: See page 1223.)

EVALUATE NEWSPAPERS AND PERIODICALS

Newspapers, magazines, and journals are available in the form of printed paper copies, online, or on microfilm or microfiche. Evaluating articles can be challenging because you need to assess the publication itself, the author of the specific article, and the content. Here are some basic questions to ask:

- **Is the publication well-known and respected?** Most large-circulation newspapers and national magazines are reliable sources. Beware of sensationalist publications, such as the *National Enquirer,* however.

- **When was the article published?** Old is not always bad. Out-of-date newspaper and magazine articles can be excellent sources about historical events.

- **Who wrote the article?** You can usually assume that articles by the staff writers or contributing editors are as reliable as the periodical they're published in.

- **Was the article originally published in another source?** If so, make sure the original source is reliable, such as *Scientific American* or a news service such as AP (Associated Press).

- **Can the facts in the article be verified?** Consult other sources, either on paper, online, or in person.

TRY IT OUT! *Examine a Newspaper Article*

Use what you have learned about evaluating sources as you examine this article.

---

from **The Charlotte Observer**

Girlfriend Led Him to Music—Tuba Kept Him There

BY STEVEN BROWN, STAFF WRITER

When Neptune takes flight across the waters in Ottorino Respighi's "The Fountains of Rome," the orchestra's tuba helps pour out the big tune that escorts him on his way. In the Charlotte Symphony's concerts Friday and Saturday, David Mills will be Neptune's bass-clef companion. Mills has been in the orchestra since 1976.

Hometown: Albemarle.

In the beginning was the ulterior motive: "I joined the band," Mills recalled, "so I could sit next to my then-girlfriend. About two weeks later, she quit." That was in the fifth grade. Obviously, Mills—who played the trumpet at the time—stuck with music.

"Once I got started doing it," Mills said, "I loved it. It was the one activity in middle school and high school that I really was crazy about."

Working his way down: To get himself into the marching band, Mills

See TUBA, *page* A17

Close Read

1. In your own words, what is this article about?

2. Knowing that Charlotte is a large city in North Carolina and that the *Observer* is its major newspaper, would you expect this article to be a reliable information source?

3. At the end of the article, there is an e-mail address that allows readers to contact the reporter who wrote the article. Why is this important?

Collecting Original Data

What if I Need to Gather Information Firsthand? Sometimes it isn't possible to find the answers to your questions in a library or on a Web site. How can you collect your own data?

Using People as Primary Sources

For some topics, your own observations and data are your best source of information. Use these techniques to become your own search engine.

INDEPENDENT OBSERVATION AND FIELD RESEARCH

Doing **field research** means going somewhere and making focused, purposeful observations. For instance, you might visit a recording studio to learn more about a career as a recording engineer. Be sure to call ahead, ask permission, and make an appointment. Take notes while you are visiting.

Notes on Visit to McNulty Audio Recording, 5/2/2008

- *4 full-time employees plus 5 to 6 part-time production assistants*
- *some analog equipment, but the studio is mostly digital*
- *studio records some singers and bands but mostly does commercial audio (radio, TV, Internet)*
- *2 to 3 part-time interns; Jenna Tinucci trains interns, coordinates scheduling*
- *Ms. Tinucci says that Dave Zinn, a recording engineer at McNulty, might agree to an interview.*

For some topics, you may want to set up a **field study** in which you do multiple observations and collect specific types of data. For other topics, you might be able to attend a **lecture** at your school, at a public library, or at a nearby community center.

INTERVIEWS WITH EXPERTS

Try tapping the knowledge of people who have experience with your topic. For example, to research careers in music, you might interview musicians, music teachers, or students who have completed music-related internships. You might interview someone in person, over the telephone, or by e-mail. Ask if the person is willing to talk with you, and set a date and time for the interview. Prepare a list of clear, open-ended questions that must be answered with specific information, not just yes or no. Also, take thorough notes. Take a look at these sample interview questions.

Questions for Dave Zinn

1. *What is a typical day like at your job?*

2. *To get a job like yours, does it make more sense to have a college degree or on-the-job experience?*

3. *How much of your job is technical and how much is creative?*

4. *What are the best and worst parts of your job?*

See pages R81–R82: Interview

If you are able to identify an expert, you may wish to send a polite and specific question by e-mail or letter. You can gain an inside track to a group of experts by joining a relevant Internet discussion group, called a list server. For instance, ProAudio is a discussion group for professionals in the recording industry.

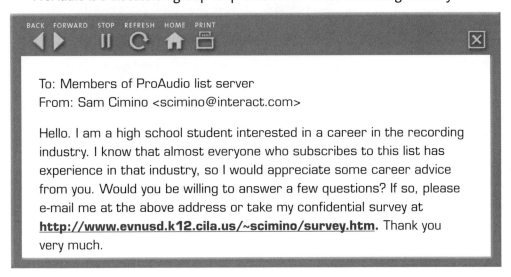

To: Members of ProAudio list server
From: Sam Cimino <scimino@interact.com>

Hello. I am a high school student interested in a career in the recording industry. I know that almost everyone who subscribes to this list has experience in that industry, so I would appreciate some career advice from you. Would you be willing to answer a few questions? If so, please e-mail me at the above address or take my confidential survey at **http://www.evnusd.k12.cila.us/~scimino/survey.htm.** Thank you very much.

QUESTIONNAIRES AND SURVEYS

You can collect questionnaire and survey information by e-mail, by mail, by telephone, through a Web site, or in person. Keep the names of participants confidential to protect their privacy.

TIP For safety reasons, give only an e-mail address to survey participants. Don't post or give out your home address or your telephone number.

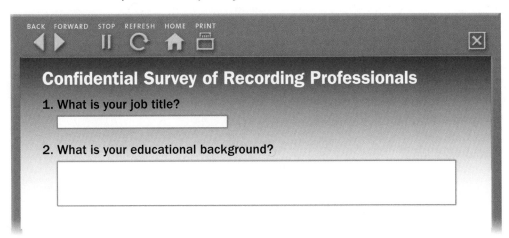

Confidential Survey of Recording Professionals

1. **What is your job title?**

2. **What is your educational background?**

Research Tips and Strategies

Web Tools

Knowing what search tools to use is your first strategy in finding information on the World Wide Web.

Search Engines

Each search engine has its own method of searching and differs in speed, size of database, and other variables. Never use only one search engine.

- Alltheweb
- AltaVista
- Go.com
- Google
- HotBot

Metasearch Tools

A metasearch tool can save you time by searching multiple search engines simultaneously.

- Dogpile
- SurfWax
- Metacrawler

Directories

Directories are useful when you are researching a general topic because they arrange Internet resources into subject categories.

- Lycos
- Galaxy
- About.com
- Yahoo!

Virtual Libraries

At a virtual library, you can look up information in encyclopedias, directories, and indexes. You can even e-mail a question to a librarian.

- Internet Public Library
- Librarians' Index to the Internet

Other Web Resources

Library catalogs: Library of Congress
Encyclopedias: Grolier Online
Newspaper archives: America's Newspapers
News associations: Associated Press, AFP
Specialized databases: ProAudio, Medline

Library Detective

Two basic systems are used to classify nonfiction books. Most high school and public libraries use the Dewey decimal system. University and research libraries generally use the Library of Congress system.

DEWEY DECIMAL SYSTEM

000–099	General works
100–199	Philosophy and psychology
200–299	Religion
300–399	Social science
400–499	Language
500–599	Natural sciences and mathematics
600–699	Technology (applied sciences)
700–799	Arts and recreation
800–899	Literature and rhetoric
900–999	Geography and history

LIBRARY OF CONGRESS SYSTEM

A	General works
B	Philosophy, psychology, religion
C	History
D	General history and history of Europe
E–F	American history
G	Geography, anthropology, recreation
H	Social sciences
J	Political science
K	Law
L	Education
M	Music
N	Fine arts
P	Language and literature
Q	Science
R	Medicine
S	Agriculture
T	Technology
U	Military science
V	Naval science
Z	Bibliography and library science

Checklist for Evaluating Sources

The information . . .

☑ is relevant to the topic you are researching

☑ is up-to-date (This point is especially important when researching time-sensitive topics in areas such as science, medicine, and sports.)

☑ is from an author who is qualified to write about the topic

☑ is from a trusted source that is updated or reviewed regularly

☑ makes the author's or institution's purpose for writing clear

☑ is written at the right level for your needs. (For example, a children's book is probably too simplistic, while a scientific paper may be too complex.)

☑ has the level of detail you need—neither too general nor too specific

☑ can be verified in more than one source

Sharing Your Research

At last you have established your research goals, located sources of information, evaluated the materials, and taken notes on what you learned. Now you have a chance to share the results with people in your world—and even beyond. Here are some options:

• Give a speech to your classmates or to people in your community.

• Create a power presentation using presentation software and share it with classmates, friends, or family members.

• Describe your research findings on your own Web site.

• Summarize the information in a newsletter or brochure.

• Share the results of your research in a formal research paper. **See the following pages.** ▶

See pages 1255–1257 for more information about publishing with technology.

Writing Workshop

Research Paper

In this unit, you have learned many different research strategies. Now it's time to put your knowledge to work by writing a research paper. You might explore a topic in history, science, art, or music, or some aspect of an enduring work of literature.

WRITER'S ROAD MAP

Research Paper

WRITING PROMPT 1

Writing from Literature Formulate a question about *The Tragedy of Julius Caesar* or another work of literature that you would like to explore in detail. Write a research paper that includes information from at least five sources and concludes with a list of works cited.

Questions Related to *Julius Caesar*

- What was Roman society like in Caesar's time?
- How do historical accounts of the assassination compare with Shakespeare's account?
- How do historians' depictions of Mark Antony compare with Shakespeare's depiction?

WRITING PROMPT 2

Writing from the Real World Write a research paper that explores a question that interests you. Your paper should present your own ideas and interpretations as well as factual information. Include information from at least five sources as well as a list of works cited.

Questions to Investigate

- Should human beings continue to explore space?
- What will cars and trucks be like 50 years from now?
- What is the best diet for an athlete to follow?

 RESEARCH TOOLS
For research tools and citation guidelines, go to the **Research Center** at ClassZone.com.

KEY TRAITS

1. IDEAS

- Presents a **thesis statement** that identifies the controlling idea of the entire paper
- Supports the thesis with **evidence**
- Synthesizes information from **multiple sources,** correctly **quoting** or **paraphrasing** authors
- Includes the **writer's own ideas and interpretations**

2. ORGANIZATION

- Has a focused **introduction**
- Is sensibly **organized,** with **transitional words and phrases**
- Comes to an interesting and well-thought-out **conclusion**

3. VOICE

- Maintains an **appropriate tone** for the topic, intended audience, and purpose

4. WORD CHOICE

- Conveys ideas clearly by using **precise language**

5. SENTENCE FLUENCY

- Varies **sentence lengths and structures**

6. CONVENTIONS

- Employs **correct grammar and usage**
- **Credits sources**
- Uses **correct formats and style**

Part 1: Analyze a Student Model

W
6.4
rep

Ferguson 1

Kevin Ferguson
Ms. Lin
English 10
20 May 2008

Capturing Julius Caesar

   Julius Caesar is one of the most recognized figures of any historical
era. His exploits in war, his rise to become dictator of the Roman
Empire, and his brutal assassination in the Senate at the hands of
conspirators—including his great friend Brutus—are legendary. Declared
5 a god by the Senate after his death, Caesar was further immortalized
in William Shakespeare's drama <u>The Tragedy of Julius Caesar</u>. In fact,
much of what most people know about Caesar the man comes from
Shakespeare's play. As the Caesar scholar Suzanne Cross points out, "It is
difficult, now, to separate the most famous Roman of them all from the
10 most famous author of them all" ("Bestriding"). Still, modern readers
wonder if Shakespeare's interpretation of Caesar is accurate. A close look
at the writings of Caesar's era suggests that Julius Caesar was a much
more complex man than the arrogant, aloof, and superstitious tyrant who
appears so briefly in Shakespeare's play.

15 **Caesar's Life**

   Gaius Julius Caesar was born in Rome, most likely in 100 B.C. His
family, the Julii, were patricians, the original Roman aristocracy. Not
only were they aristocrats, the Julii claimed that they were descendants
of the goddess Venus ("Caesar, Julius").
20   In 84 B.C., Caesar married the daughter of a Roman noble and
revolutionary who wanted to end the rule of the dictator Sulla and
restore the Roman republic. Caesar's marriage made him one of the

KEY TRAITS IN ACTION

Concise, interesting
introduction refreshes the
reader's memory about
what Caesar accomplished.

Thesis statement presents
the idea the paper will
investigate.

A variety of **sentence
lengths and structures**
helps maintain the
reader's interest.

revolutionaries. When Sulla crushed the revolution, Caesar feared for his life. He fled Rome and joined the military in Asia. Returning to
25 Rome six years later, he started on a path that led to a political career (Suetonius 61; "Caesar, Julius").

For the next 30 years, Caesar became more powerful both politically and militarily. In 49 B.C., after a lengthy and complicated political dispute with the authorities in Rome, Caesar led his army across the Rubicon
30 River, invading Italy and starting a civil war. Caesar's forces won, and three years later he returned to Rome, where he celebrated by giving five lavish "triumphs," or victory parades. The Senate made Caesar dictator for ten years (Suetonius 66–67; "Caesar, Julius").

> The paper smoothly combines information **from multiple sources.**

The three years of Caesar's reign were marked by military
35 campaigns in Africa and Spain and by his attempts to organize the affairs of the far-flung Roman Empire. In 44 B.C., a band of 60 conspirators dedicated to ending the dictatorship plotted to murder Caesar. On March 15, the ides of March, Caesar was attacked in the Senate and stabbed to death ("Caesar, Julius").

40 **Shakespeare's Portrait of Caesar**

> Subheads help show how the paper is **organized.**

Shakespeare based his play on the writings of the Greek author Plutarch, who was born just two years after Caesar's assassination. In Plutarch's collection of biographies, <u>Parallel Lives</u>, he profiled Caesar, Brutus, and Mark Antony. These biographies contributed to both the
45 plot of Shakespeare's play and the personalities of its principal characters (Schanzer 46; Vernon).

Shakespeare's Caesar is a proud and arrogant man, superstitious and lacking humor (Cross, "Bestriding"; Garber). On the day of Caesar's assassination, Cassius warns his co-conspirators about Caesar's
50 growing superstitious nature:

Ferguson 3

> But it is doubtful yet
> Whether Caesar will come forth today or no;
> For he is superstitious grown of late,
> Quite from the main opinion he held once. . . . (2.1. 193-196)

55 Caesar's arrogance is apparent in his vain boasting about his own invincibility. Before he leaves for the Senate on the day of his death, Caesar tells his fearful wife Calpurnia, "Danger knows full well / That Caesar is more dangerous than he" (2.2. 44-45).

On the other hand, some scholars fault Shakespeare for his narrow 60 characterization of the Roman dictator. Suzanne Cross maintains that Shakespeare failed to offer a full picture of the man:

> There is no hint of the personal charm, wit and magnetism
> for which he was notorious; . . . of the teenage rebel
> refusing to do the bidding of the killer-dictator, Sulla; of the
65 > intellectual second only to Cicero as a speaker and writer. The
> man himself was infinitely more complex and interesting than
> Shakespeare's version. ("Bestriding")

In Shakespeare's defense, it is important to remember that Caesar appears in only three scenes during the play. Caesar isn't on stage 70 often enough or long enough for a well-rounded portrait to emerge. Historians of Caesar's era, however, offer many fascinating glimpses into his character.

A Look at the Historical Record

In his biographical text <u>The Lives of the Caesars</u>, the Roman 75 historian Suetonius describes Caesar's appearance. The description hints at Caesar's pride:

Long **quotation** is correctly **formatted,** with indents and parenthetical documentation.

Short **quotation** is correctly **formatted** and **credited.**

Throughout the paper, **transitions** help the reader understand how ideas are related.

Includes the **writer's own interpretation** of one aspect of the subject.

He is said to have been tall of stature, with a fair complexion,
shapely limbs, a somewhat full face, and keen black eyes. . . .
He was somewhat overnice in the care of his person, being . . .

80   carefully trimmed and shaved. . . . They say, too, that he was
fantastic in his dress. . . . (63)

Suetonius goes on to describe a man who was ruthless, cunning,
and driven to succeed at all costs. At the same time, Suetonius notes,
Caesar could be kind, forgiving, and witty (Cross, "Private").

85   Caesar exhibited a ruthless streak at an early age. In 74 B.C., he was
traveling to Rhodes to study with Apollonius Molo, a famous orator.
Pirates captured Caesar and held him for 38 days, until a ransom was
paid. As soon as he was set free, Caesar raised a fleet, caught the fleeing
pirates, and, fulfilling a promise he had made to his captors while he was

90   their prisoner, had them all crucified (Cross, "Private"; Suetonius 7).

Yet even while putting his captors to death, Caesar demonstrated
a strange kind of mercy. Not wanting the pirates to endure the slow,
agonizing death that was crucifixion, Caesar ordered that their throats
be slit before they were hoisted onto their crosses (Suetonius 95).

95   Caesar was also known for his kindness and loyalty. He often
appointed friends, even those of low birth, to high positions. When he
was criticized for this practice, Caesar "flatly declared that if he had been
helped in defending his honor by brigands [thieves] and cut-throats,
he would have requited [rewarded] even such men in the same way"

100   (Suetonius 93).

Supports the main idea (that Caesar was a complex person) with specific **evidence** that is **paraphrased** from and properly **credited** to the source.

Uses **correct formats** for parenthetical documentation.

Ferguson 5

The ancient historians who chronicled Caesar's life did so with a mixture of admiration and disapproval. The Roman statesman and scholar Marcus Tullius Cicero disapproved strongly of Caesar's dictatorship. Yet he praised Caesar's intellectual abilities. Cicero
105 supposedly wrote, "Do you know any man who . . . can speak better than Caesar? Or anyone who makes so many witty remarks? Or whose vocabulary is so varied and yet so exact?" (qtd. in Cross, "Private").

As with most tragic figures, Caesar's undoing was his pride, which blinded him to everything but his own ambition. Plutarch maintains
110 that Caesar had "an insatiable desire to reign" and says in his biography of Caesar that "the chiefest cause that made him mortally hated was the covetous desire he had to be called king" (qtd. in Schanzer 12). As further evidence of Caesar's pride and ambition, consider this: Caesar's image appeared on Roman coins during his own lifetime. Until Caesar,
115 only the dead had been so honored (Vernon).

Julius Caesar was so complex a character that William Shakespeare was able just to scratch the surface of his personality. Still, the Elizabethan playwright managed to portray the characteristics of one who truly did "bestride the narrow world / Like a Colossus" (1.2.
120 135-136). When Shakespeare's portrait is combined with biographical anecdotes from Caesar's contemporaries, the picture comes into sharper focus, providing a more complete measure of the man who ruled Rome and changed the history of the Western world.

An interesting **quotation** from a source supports a major idea in the paper (that even Caesar's critics admired some of his qualities).

Formal **tone** is appropriate for the intended audience (teacher and classmates) and purpose (to inform).

A thoughtful **conclusion** summarizes the paper.

Works Cited

"Caesar, Julius." <u>Encyclopaedia Britannica Online</u>. 2004. Encyclopaedia
  Britannica. 15 May 2008 <http://search.eb.com/eb/article-
  9108314>.

Cross, Suzanne. "Bestriding the World." <u>Julius Caesar: The Last
  Dictator.</u> 2004. 30 Apr. 2008 <http://heraklia.fws1.com/
  introduction/index.html>.

---. "The Private Man." <u>Julius Caesar: The Last Dictator</u>. 2004. 30 Apr.
  2008 <http://heraklia.fws1.com/private_man/index.html>.

Garber, Marjorie B. "Dream and Interpretation: <u>Julius Caesar.</u>" <u>Dream
  in Shakespeare: From Metaphor to Metamorphosis</u>. New Haven:
  Yale UP, 1974. Rpt. in <u>William Shakespeare's</u> Julius Caesar. Ed.
  Harold Bloom. Modern Critical Interpretations. New York:
  Chelsea, 1988. 43-52.

Schanzer, Ernest. <u>The Problem Plays of Shakespeare</u>. New York:
  Schocken, 1965.

Shakespeare, William. <u>The Tragedy of Julius Caesar</u>. <u>McDougal Littell
  Literature</u>. Evanston, IL: McDougal, 2008. 1097-1182.

Suetonius. <u>The Lives of the Caesars</u>. Trans. J. C. Rolfe. Suetonius.
  Vol. 1. Loeb Classical Library. Cambridge: Harvard UP, 1997.

Vernon, Jennifer. "Ides of March Marked Murder of Julius Caesar."
  <u>National Geographic News</u>. 12 Mar. 2004. Natl. Geographic
  Soc. 18 May 2008 <http://news.nationalgeographic.com/
  news/2004/03/0311_040311_idesmarch.html>.

Online sources

Source by the same author cited in the preceding entry

One essay from a book of essays reprinted in a second source

Book with one author

Primary source

Online periodical

Part 2: Apply the Writing Process

WRITING STANDARD
5.3 Establish and develop a clear thesis statement for informational writing

PREWRITING

What Should I Do?

1. Analyze the prompt.
Look back at the prompts on page 1234 and choose the one that interests you. (Circle) the words that tell you what type of writing you will be doing. <u>Underline</u> the important details about the assignment.

2. Explore a variety of topics; then decide on a focus.
Create a graphic organizer to investigate different topics that interest you. Select one that you can write about in detail in a research paper.

TIP Check online catalogs at your school and local libraries as well as databases such as InfoTrac. If there's very little information about your topic, expand your focus. If there's quite a lot, consider narrowing your topic.

3. Develop research questions.
What key questions do you want your paper to answer? Make a list of these questions and keep them in mind as you research your topic.

What Does It Look Like?

▶ **WRITING PROMPT 1** Formulate a <u>question about *The Tragedy of Julius Caesar* or another work of literature</u> that you would like to explore in detail. Write a (research paper) that <u>includes information from at least five sources</u> and <u>concludes with a list of works cited.</u>

I have to do research and then write a paper about a piece of literature. The paper has to have material from at least five different sources, and I have to list those sources at the end.

▶ *What are some famous assassinations in history?*
Too broad

What was the real Julius Caesar like?

Julius Caesar

Why was Brutus so angry?

How did the real-life conspiracy form?

Were soothsayers popular in Shakespeare's time?
Too narrow

▶ *Research Questions*
1. How much of Julius Caesar is based on historical fact?
2. How does Shakespeare portray Caesar?
3. How did historians of Caesar's time describe him?
4. How does Shakespeare's Caesar compare with the actual historical figure?

What Should I Do?

1. Investigate possible sources.
Start gathering relevant information about your topic. Search the Internet as well as your school and community libraries.

Make a list of the sources that look promising. Your list should include the name of the source (including the author, if that information is available) and a note on where you found it. Also, include comments that will remind you why you believe the source is useful.

2. Evaluate your sources.
Thoroughly examine each source on your list and evaluate it. You want to know if the information is reliable, if it specifically addresses your topic, and if it is the right level for your audience. Reject any source that doesn't meet all these requirements.

TIP To evaluate a source, ask yourself: Is this a primary or a secondary source? Is the author qualified to write about the topic? What biases might the author have? Is the information up-to-date? Who is the intended audience? For information on evaluating sources, see pages 1225–1229.

What Does It Look Like?

Sources	Comments
World Wide Web (bookmarked)	
"Julius Caesar." Wikipedia[1]	lots of links
"Bestriding the World." _Julius Caesar: The Last Dictator_	quotations from many primary sources
"Gaius Julius Caesar." Found through Search.com[2]	lots of info
"Julius Caesar." _Encyclopaedia Britannica Online_	solid biography
School Media Center	
Julius Caesar by Rupert Matthews (xBiog CaesaJ MatthR)[3]	fun to read
Cleopatra by Dorothy Hoobler (xBiog Cleopat Hoobl.D)	interesting info
Public Library	
Materialist Shakespeare: a History by Ivo Kamps (822.331)[4]	very complicated
"Power Play: 'Friends, Generals and Captains of Industry, Lend Me Your Ears.'" Bruce Weber. _New York Times_	more about business than Shakespeare

Reasons for Rejecting a Source

1. Disclaimer says there's no guarantee of validity.

2. Lots of information, but no author or sponsor given. Information may be unreliable.

3. Children's book—too basic for my audience.

4. Very scholarly. Too complicated for my readers.

RESEARCHING

What Should I Do?

3. Create source cards.

Use index cards to record information about each source that you plan to use. Number the cards sequentially in the upper right corner. Include the following information:

World Wide Web
- author (if given)
- title of the Web page or article
- publication information for any print version of the information
- date created or posted
- name of person, institution, or organization responsible for the site
- date accessed
- URL (Web address)

Book
- author or editor
- translator (if applicable)
- title
- location and publisher
- year of publication
- library call number

Encyclopedia
- author (if given)
- title of entry
- name and year of encyclopedia
- location and publisher (if CD-ROM)

Periodical
- author (if given)
- title of article
- name and date of periodical
- page numbers of the article

What Does It Look Like?

World Wide Web

> ③
>
> Cross, Suzanne. "Bestriding the World."
> Julius Caesar: The Last Dictator. 2004.
> 30 Apr. 2008 <http://heraklia.fwsl.com/
> introduction/index.html>

Book

> ⑥
>
> Schanzer, Ernest. The Problem Plays of
> Shakespeare. New York: Schocken, 1965.
> 822.3 SjZs

Encyclopedia

> ⑦
>
> "Antony, Mark." Britannica Student
> Encyclopedia. 2004 ed. CD-ROM. Chicago:
> Encyclopaedia Britannica, 2004.

Periodical

> ⑨
>
> Weber, Bruce. "Power Play: 'Friends,
> Generals and Captains of Industry, Lend Me
> Your Ears.'" New York Times 31 Jan. 2005: B1+.

What Should I Do?

4. Take notes as you read.

Look for information that answers the research questions you prepared. Also, look for new facts and expert opinions. Record each piece of useful information on a separate index card. When you're ready to draft your paper, you can shuffle the cards to try out different ways of organizing and presenting information. Each card should include the following:

- the main idea
- the number of the source (from its source card)
- where the information is located—for example, a page number or a section title

TIP As you record information, note whether it is puzzling or whether it supports or contradicts what you already know.

Restatements

If you are not quoting directly, word for word, from a source, restate the information in your own words. You can either paraphrase the information or summarize it.

Paraphrase—restates all the ideas of the original and is about the same length

Summary—restates the main idea of the original, including key facts and statistics, but is shorter because it omits unnecessary details

What Does It Look Like?

▶ **Original source**

By the time of Caesar, Rome had a long-established republican government headed by two consuls with joint powers. Praetors were one step below consuls in the power chain and handled judicial matters. A body of citizens forming the Senate proposed legislation, which general people's assemblies then approved by vote. A special temporary office, that of dictator, was established for use only during times of extreme civil unrest.

Vernon, Jennifer. "Ides of March Marked Murder of Julius Caesar." National Geographic News

Paraphrase

Roman government	

During Caesar's time, Rome was a republic. Two consuls who had equal authority were the leaders. Just below the consuls were praetors, who dealt with legal issues. Members of the Senate suggested laws, and general assemblies voted on whether to approve the suggestions. The position of dictator was used only when there were serious outbreaks of lawlessness.

Summary

Roman government	

Rome's republican government was made up of consuls, praetors, a senate, and people's assemblies. The position of dictator was temporary and used only during emergencies.

RESEARCHING

| **What Should I Do?** | **What Does It Look Like?** |

5. Quote well-stated ideas directly.
Copy the material exactly as it appears in the original and enclose it in quotation marks.

TIP If you leave out words from a quotation, use ellipses (. . .) in place of the omitted material. If you add a word or phrase to make an idea clearer, enclose it in brackets ([ ]).

▶

The problems with Shakespeare's Caesar ③

"There is no hint of the personal charm, wit and magnetism for which he was notorious; . . . [He] was infinitely more complex . . . than Shakespeare's version" (online, no page number).

6. Never plagiarize.
Plagiarism, the uncredited use of others' words or ideas, is dishonest. Avoid plagiarism by carefully documenting the source of any ideas that aren't common knowledge. Do this whether you are paraphrasing, summarizing, or quoting directly.

TIP If you copy sentences word for word from a source without crediting the source, that's plagiarism. The same is true if you use specific phrases from a source without giving credit. For example, if your source uses the terms "invariable kindness and consideration" and "flatly declared," and you use one of those phrases without citing the source, you are plagiarizing.

▶

Original source

His friends he treated with invariable kindness and consideration. . . . He advanced some of his friends to the highest positions, even though they were of the humblest origin, and when taken to task for it, flatly declared that if he had been helped in defending his honor by brigands and cut-throats, he would have requited even such men in the same way.

Suetonius. *The Lives of the Caesars.* Trans. J. C. Rolfe

Plagiarized

Caesar treated his friends with invariable kindness and consideration. When he was criticized for appointing his friends to high positions, he flatly declared that if pirates and cut-throats had helped him, he would have rewarded them in the same way.

Correctly documented

Caesar often appointed friends, even those of low birth, to high positions. When he was criticized for this practice, Caesar "flatly declared that if he had been helped in defending his honor by brigands [thieves] and cut-throats, he would have requited [rewarded] even such men in the same way" (Suetonius 93).

What Should I Do?

7. Develop a working thesis statement.
A thesis statement describes the main idea of your research paper. A "working" thesis statement is just that—a "work in progress." As you refine, organize, and begin drafting your paper, you may want to reword or refocus the thesis statement so that it is neither too broad nor too narrow.

TIP All information in your paper should be related to your thesis. If you find an interesting new angle as you do research, you should revise your thesis to include it.

8. Organize your research and create an outline.
First, read through your note cards. Group cards that address the same major ideas. Then arrange the major ideas in the order you want to present them. Your arrangement should show the relationship between ideas and reflect their logical development.

When you're ready to create an outline, make each major idea a section of the outline, marked by a Roman numeral. Then use your note cards as a guide as you create subsections under each major idea. As you draft your paper, the entries in the outline will become topic sentences and supporting details.

TIP Other ways to outline your material include using a graphic organizer, such as a flow chart, or rewriting the material as a series of questions and answers.

What Does It Look Like?

Working thesis statement:

The Tragedy of Julius Caesar raises many questions. How accurate is Shakespeare's description of the great leader? ~~What did Brutus think of Caesar's character? Why did Cassius hate Caesar?~~ A close look at the writings of historians who lived at the time of Caesar shows that he was complicated.

My paper is about Caesar, not Brutus or Cassius.

Capturing Julius Caesar

I. Comparing play and history
   A. Shakespeare
   B. Historians and scholars
II. Caesar's life
   A. Early years, joins military
   B. Named dictator
   C. Assassinated
III. Shakespeare's portrayal
   A. Vain, arrogant, superstitious, lacking in humor
   B. Some scholars disagree (Cross)
      1. Charm, wit, magnetism
      2. Intellectual and complex man
IV. The historical record
   A. Proud, ruthless, cunning, driven to succeed; but also kind, loyal, merciful (Suetonius)
   B. An intellectual (Cicero)
   C. Driven by pride, ambition (Plutarch)
V. Conclusion
   A. Complex man
   B. Shakespeare plus historical record lead to balanced view

DRAFTING

What Should I Do?	What Does It Look Like?

What Should I Do?

1. **Create your introduction.**
   Read over your working thesis statement. What does it say about the focus of your paper? Think about ways to lead up to that focus. Remember, this is just the start of the drafting process. You'll have opportunities to refine your introduction as you continue writing.

What Does It Look Like?

> Julius Caesar was a very important person. His accomplishments in war, his political power, and his brutal assassination are still discussed today. Declared a god by the Senate after his death, Caesar was also immortalized in William Shakespeare's play *The Tragedy of Julius Caesar.* In fact, much of what most people know about Caesar the man comes from that play. Modern readers wonder if Shakespeare's interpretation of Caesar is accurate. A close look at the writings of historians who lived at the time of Caesar shows that he was complicated.

What Should I Do?

2. **Continue your first draft.**
   Incorporate the information on your note cards into a draft of your paper. Use the outline you created as a guide to organizing that information. As you draft, remember to mention where you found the information. Include the author and the page number if this information is available. If you are unable to find the author's name, include the title of the work instead. For instructions on how to do this, see "Document your sources" on the next page.

   TIP Avoid plopping quotations into your paper without an explanation of where they came from or what they mean. Instead, weave in each quotation by using a phrase or sentence to introduce it, as this writer has done.

What Does It Look Like?

Note card

> **Caesar and Shakespeare** ③
> Ever since Shakespeare wrote *The Tragedy of Julius Caesar,* most people have believed that the real Caesar was like the character in the play. "It is difficult, now, to separate the most famous Roman of them all from the most famous author of them all" (online, no page number).

Draft

> Caesar was also immortalized in William Shakespeare's play *The Tragedy of Julius Caesar.* In fact, much of what most people know about Caesar the man comes from that play. As the Caesar scholar Suzanne Cross points out, "It is difficult, now, to separate the most famous Roman of them all from the most famous author of them all" ("Bestriding"). Modern readers wonder if Shakespeare's interpretation of Caesar is accurate.

What Should I Do?	**What Does It Look Like?**

3. **Share original ideas and interpretations.**
Much of your paper will consist of presenting the information you located during your research. Nevertheless, your ideas are important, too. Use the facts, examples, and other evidence you found to support your ideas and interpretations.

▶ In Shakespeare's defense, it is important to remember that Caesar appears in only three scenes during the play. Caesar isn't on stage often enough or long enough for a well-rounded portrait to emerge.

4. **Document your sources.**
Include the source of each piece of information in parentheses at the end of the sentence or sentences where the information appears. This enables readers to find the sources you used. In general, documentation should include the author's **last name** and the **page number** (Suetonius 63). Following are some special cases:

- **Author already mentioned in sentence—** use only page number (63)

- **Author unknown—**use shortened title of work ("Character of Caesar")

- **Multiple authors—**use last names for up to three authors (Roberts and Smith 127–28). For more than three authors, use the first author's last name followed by *et al.* (Kensington et al. 57).

- **More than one work by an author—**include shortened name of work (Cross, "Private"; De Mateo, Interpretations 84).

- **More than one source—**information for each source separated by semicolons (Garber 45; Schanzer 234)

TIP Use a highlighter to mark each parenthetical documentation. Later on, this will help you compile the list of works cited.

▶ Not wanting the pirates to endure the slow, agonizing death that was crucifixion, Caesar ordered that their throats be slit before they were hoisted onto their crosses (Suetonius 95).

Basic documentation: author and page number

As soon as he was set free, Caesar raised a fleet, caught the fleeing pirates, and, fulfilling a promise he had made to his captors while he was their prisoner, had them all crucified (Cross, "Private"; Suetonius 7).

Evidence from two sources

Caesar's image appeared on Roman coins during his own lifetime. Until Caesar, only the dead had been so honored (Vernon).

Page number unknown

DRAFTING

What Should I Do?	**What Does It Look Like?**

5. Use sources wisely.

As you draft, present information from various sources clearly and logically. If appropriate, compare and contrast information from different sources. Don't forget to include your own interpretations, observations, and conclusions.

> Shakespeare based his play on the writings of the Greek author Plutarch, who was born just two years after Caesar's assassination. In Plutarch's collection of biographies, <u>Parallel Lives</u>, he profiled Caesar, Brutus, and Mark Antony. These biographies contributed to both the plot of Shakespeare's play and the personalities of its principal characters (Schanzer 46; Vernon).

Synthesizes information from multiple sources

6. Write a memorable conclusion.

An effective conclusion should restate your main idea and summarize critical supporting details. It should also offer an interesting reflection on the paper, such as the importance of the topic or suggestions for further research.

TIP Consider finishing with a powerful quotation, a thought-provoking question, or a relevant anecdote.

> Julius Caesar was so complex a character that William Shakespeare was able just to scratch the surface of his personality. Still, the Elizabethan playwright managed to portray the characteristics of one who truly did "bestride the narrow world / Like a Colossus" (12. 135-136). When Shakespeare's portrait is combined with biographical anecdotes from Caesar's contemporaries, the picture comes into sharper focus, providing a more complete measure of the man who ruled Rome and changed the history of the Western world.

7. Create a Works Cited list.

After you have finished drafting your paper, look through it for the parenthetical documentations you highlighted. Locate the source card for each one. Alphabetize the cards by author's last name (or by title of the work if the author's name is unknown). Then, copy the information on the cards onto a list. For instructions on preparing and formatting a Works Cited list, see pages 1252–1253.

> **Works Cited**
>
> Cross, Suzanne. "Bestriding the World." <u>Julius Caesar: The Last Dictator</u>. 2004. 30 Apr. 2008 <http://heraklia.fws1.com/introduction/index.html>.
>
> Schanzer, Ernest. <u>The Problem Plays of Shakespeare</u>. New York: Schocken, 1965.

What Should I Do?	What Does It Look Like?

1. Craft an attention-getting introduction.

- Highlight the first one or two sentences of your introduction.
- Ask yourself if this introduction is memorable.
- Consider including a question, a quotation, or a vivid description.

▶ ~~Julius Caesar was a very important person.~~ Julius Caesar is one of the most recognized figures of any historical era. His exploits in war, his rise to become dictator of the Roman Empire, and his brutal assassination in the Senate at the hands of conspirators—including his great friend Brutus—are legendary.

2. Sharpen your thesis statement.

- Underline your thesis statement.
- Fine-tune the statement so that it clearly and completely explains the focus of your paper.

▶ _Caesar's era_
A close look at the writings of ~~historians who lived at the time of Caesar~~ suggests that ~~he was complicated.~~ Julius Caesar was a much more complex man than the arrogant, aloof, and superstitious tyrant who appears so briefly in Shakespeare's play.

3. Connect ideas clearly.

- Ask a peer reader to draw a box around any sentences or paragraphs whose logical connection is unclear.
- Add information or transitional words or phrases to show how the ideas are related.

See page 1254: Ask a Peer Reader

▶ _In 84 B.C.,_
Caesar married the daughter of a Roman noble and revolutionary who wanted to end the rule of the dictator Sulla and restore the Roman republic. When Sulla crushed the revolution, Caesar feared for his life.
Caesar's marriage made him one of the revolutionaries.

4. Add effective supporting details.

- Read your paper one paragraph at a time. For each paragraph, ask yourself: Have I included enough evidence to support the paragraph's topic sentence?
- Add quotations, paraphrases, or your own ideas and interpretations as needed.

▶ As with most tragic figures, Caesar's undoing was his pride, which blinded him to everything but his own ambition. Plutarch maintains that Caesar had "an insatiable desire to reign" and says in his biography of Caesar that "the chiefest cause that made him mortally hated was the covetous desire he had to be called king" (qtd. in Schanzer 12).

REVISING AND EDITING

What Should I Do?	*What Does It Look Like?*

5. Credit others' words and ideas.

- (Circle) any ideas or quotations from your sources that you haven't properly documented.

- Follow guidelines for parenthetical documentation.

▶

> When he was criticized for this practice, Caesar "flatly declared that if he had been helped in defending his honor by brigands [thieves] and cut-throats, he would have requited [rewarded] even such men in the same way" (Suetonius 93).

6. Get to the point.

- Ask a peer reader to draw a wavy line under passages that seem wordy or irrelevant.

- Revise or eliminate unnecessary words and sentences.

See page 1254: Ask a Peer Reader

▶

> crushed the revolution,
> When Sulla, ~~triumphed over the revolutionaries who wanted to end his reign,~~ Caesar feared for his life. ~~that Sulla would have him killed.~~ He fled ~~ran far away from~~ Rome and joined the military in ~~the far east on the continent of~~ Asia.

7. Maintain a consistent tone.

- Draw [brackets] around any words, phrases, or sentences that are too slangy or casual for a research paper.

- Substitute words and phrases that are objective and serious but not stuffy or overly formal.

▶

> ~~[You have to remember that Caesar shows up in just three scenes. He isn't on stage often enough or long enough for anyone to figure him out.]~~
>
> In Shakespeare's defense, it is important to remember that Caesar appears in only three scenes during the play. Caesar isn't on stage often enough or long enough for a well-rounded portrait to emerge.

8. Proofread your parenthetical documentation.

- Identify each instance of parenthetical documentation in your paper.

- Proofread each reference to make sure it follows the proper format for parenthetical documentation.

▶

Incorrect: (Caesar, Julius, Vernon)
Correct: ("Caesar, Julius"; Vernon).

Incorrect: (Cross; "Private": Suetonius.)
Correct: (Cross, "Private"; Suetonius 7).

MLA Citation Guidelines

Here are some basic Modern Language Association formats for citing sources. Use these formats on your source cards and in the Works Cited list at the end of your paper.

BOOKS

One author

Schanzer, Ernest. The Problem Plays of Shakespeare. New York: Schocken, 1965.

Two authors or editors

McIver, Bruce, and Ruth Stevenson, eds. Teaching with Shakespeare: Critics in the Classroom.
    Newark: U of Delaware Press, 1994.

Three authors or editors

Bennett, Josephine W., Oscar Cargill, and Vernon Hall, Jr., eds. Studies in the English
    Renaissance Drama. New York: New York UP, 1959.

Four or more authors or editors

The abbreviation et al. *means "and others." Use* et al. *instead of listing all the authors.*

Wells, Stanley, et al. The Complete Works of William Shakespeare. New York: Oxford UP, 1986.

No author given

Elizabethan Literature. New York: Capital, 1957.

An author and a translator

Suetonius. Lives of the Caesars. Trans. Catherine Edwards. New York: Oxford UP, 2000.

An author, a translator, and an editor

Moretti, Salvatore. Essays on Julius Caesar. Trans. Jonathan Walsh. Ed. Louis Kind. New York:
    Devonshire, 1962.

PARTS OF BOOKS

An introduction, a preface, a foreword, or an afterword written by someone other than the author(s) of a work

Heminge, John, and Henry Condell. Preface. Dramatic Works of Shakespeare. Edinburgh:
    William Peterson, 1883.

A poem, a short story, an essay, or a chapter in a collection of works

Roe, John. " 'Character' in Plutarch and Shakespeare: Brutus, Julius Caesar, and Mark Antony."
    Shakespeare and the Classics. Ed. Charles Martindale and A. B. Taylor. New York:
    Cambridge, 2004.

A novel or a play in an anthology

Shakespeare, William. <u>The Tragedy of Julius Caesar</u>. Ed. John Jowett. <u>Willia</u>
   <u>The Complete Works</u>. Ed. Stanley Wells and Gary Taylor. Compact ed.
   Clarendon, 1988. 599-626.

MAGAZINES, NEWSPAPERS, AND ENCYCLOPEDIAS

An article in a newspaper

Weber, Bruce. "Power Play: 'Friends, Generals and Captains of Industry, Lend Me Your Ears.'"
   <u>New York Times</u> 31 Jan. 2005: B1+.

An article in a magazine

Tynan, William. "Cleopatra." <u>Time</u> 24 May 1999: 37-38.

An article in an encyclopedia

"Julius Caesar." <u>Encyclopaedia Britannica</u>. 2004 ed.

MISCELLANEOUS PRINT AND NONPRINT SOURCES

An interview

Covington, Nigel. Personal Interview. 1 Feb. 2008.

A film

<u>Julius Caesar</u>. Dir. Stuart Burge. Perf. Charlton Heston, Jason Robards, Richard Chamberlain,
   and Robert Vaughn. Republic, 1970. DVD. Lions Gate, 2000.

ELECTRONIC PUBLICATIONS

A CD–ROM

"Antony, Mark." <u>Britannica Student Encyclopedia</u>. 2004 ed. CD-ROM. Chicago: Encyclopaedia
   Britannica, 2004.

A document from an Internet site

Entries for online sources should contain as much of the information shown as available.

Author or compiler   Title or description of document

Vernon, Jennifer. "Ides of March Marked Murder of Julius Caesar."

Title of Internet site   Date of Internet site   Site sponsor   Date of access

National Geographic News. 12 Mar. 2004. Natl. Geographic Soc. 18 May 2008

Complete URL enclosed in angle brackets. Break for a new line only after a slash.

<http://news.nationalgeographic.com/news/2004/03/0311_040311_idesmarch.html>.

Apply the Rubric

A strong research paper . . .

☑ has a focused introduction

☑ explains the governing idea of the paper in a clear, interesting thesis statement

☑ develops the thesis with evidence from multiple sources

☑ quotes or paraphrases reliable sources

☑ credits sources completely and correctly

☑ uses a logical organizational pattern and transitions

☑ presents the writer's original ideas and interpretations

☑ has an appropriate tone

☑ uses precise language and a variety of sentence lengths and structures

☑ has a thoughtful conclusion

Ask a Peer Reader

• What did you learn from my paper?

• Do any parts of my paper seem unclear or disorganized?

• Are any parts too wordy?

• If you could add something to my paper, what would it be? Why?

Format Your Paper

Follow these guidelines as you prepare the final draft of your paper:

• Leave one-inch margins at the top, bottom, and sides of each page (except for page numbers).

• Double-space all text, including quotations and the Works Cited list.

• At the top left of the first page, on separate lines, type your name, your teacher's name, the class, and the date.

• On the rest of the pages, in the upper-right corner, half an inch from the top of the page, type your last name and the page number.

• Indent each paragraph one-half inch (or five spaces) from the left margin.

• Indent set-off quotations one inch (or ten spaces) from the left margin.

• Begin the Works Cited list on a separate page. If a citation is more than one line long, indent each subsequent line half an inch (or five spaces). End each citation with a period.

See the *MLA Handbook for Writers of Research Papers* for additional formatting guidelines.

Writing Online

PUBLISHING OPTIONS
For publishing options, visit the **Writing Center** at **ClassZone.com**.

ASSESSMENT PREPARATION
For writing and grammar assessment practice, go to the **Assessment Center** at **ClassZone.com**.

RESEARCH STANDARD
8.7 Use a variety of communication
techniques to present information

PUBLISHING WITH TECHNOLOGY

Creating a Web Site

Now that you have learned a great deal about your subject, why not share your expertise with others? A Web site is the perfect medium for presenting your paper to the world.

Planning the Web Site

1. **Choose a topic.** Select a subject that you will enjoy researching and that could include audio, video, still pictures, or illustrations. For instance, a site on the subject of Julius Caesar could offer artists' illustrations of Caesar and of ancient Rome. The site could also offer excerpts of historians' writings about Caesar and audio and video clips of Shakespeare's play about him.

2. **Consider your audience and purpose.** Who will likely be drawn to your site—students, teachers, people unfamiliar with your subject? What is the main purpose of your site—informing, persuading, entertaining, or some combination of these purposes?

3. **Research your topic thoroughly.** Use search engines and metasearch tools (see page 1232) as well as library resources. Look for maps, illustrations, animation, music, video, photographs—anything that will make your site a special destination for Web users.

Organizing the Web Site

1. **Map the site.** Create a flow chart to help you organize your site. The chart will help you determine how many pages you will need and where to create links to other parts of your site or to other sites. Here is how one student organized a site.

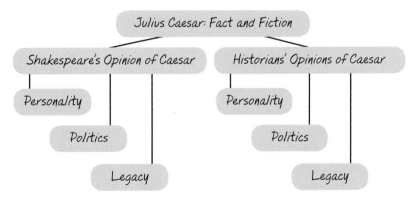

2. **Create a storyboard for each page.** Make sketches showing how you want the pages to look. Be sure to include the placement of text, images, buttons, and links.

TIP Don't distract visitors to your site with blinking images or music that can't be turned off. Stay focused on the purpose of your site.

Caesar's Personality: Shakespeare's View

Picture of Caesar goes here

- **Physically weak:** Brutus and Casca say that Caesar has "the falling sickness"—probably epilepsy (Act One, Scene 2).
- **Easily flattered:** Decius says about Caesar: "...when I tell him he hates flatterers, / He says he does, being then most flattered" (Act Two, Scene 1).
- **Arrogant:** Caesar tells his wife, "Danger knows full well / That Caesar is more dangerous than he" (Act Two, Scene 2).
- **Obstinate:** Caesar tells someone who asks for mercy, "I could be well moved, if I were as you.... But I am constant as the Northern Star" (Act Three, Scene 1).

Read about historians' opinions of Caesar
See a video clip from Act Two, Scene 2
Hear an audio version of the entire play

(Home)   (Politics)   (Personality)   (Legacy)

---

3. **Write the text.** Keep it brief and to the point, using charts and bulleted lists where possible instead of long descriptions. Write captions for photographs and illustrations.
4. **Make it multimedia.** The Web is a multimedia environment. Use images to convey ideas and to add color and punch to your site. Video and audio will enhance the experience for your visitors. Animations help grab viewers' attention.

Producing the Web Site

1. **Prepare the features of your site.** Ask your school's computer specialist for help scanning graphics and saving CD-ROM elements to your project file.

Note: Be careful when using elements from sources like the Internet, books, magazines, and CD-ROMs. These sources often contain copyrighted material that must be cited on a Works Cited page. (See page 1249.) Some materials require permission from the person or organization that holds the copyright. Some Web sites have "terms and conditions" statements for media elements. These statements may specify that students are allowed to use media elements in school projects.

2. **Select an authoring program.** Authoring programs take much of the complexity out of building a Web site. Your school may have an authoring program already. If not, ask the technology administrator for permission to download one from the Internet. Follow the program's instructions for importing media elements. Choose colors, fonts, buttons, and a layout based on the storyboards you prepared earlier. As you build your site, keep these guidelines in mind:

   - Text must be large and clear enough to be read easily. Use a font size of 12 points or larger, and choose contrasting colors for the text and the background.
   - Buttons with the same function should have the same design.
   - Brief titles for each page of your site will help visitors understand what information they will find there.

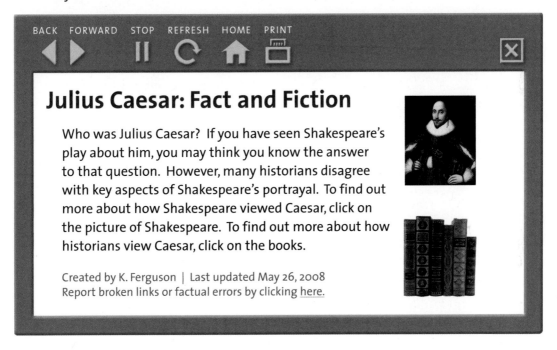

Julius Caesar: Fact and Fiction

Who was Julius Caesar? If you have seen Shakespeare's play about him, you may think you know the answer to that question. However, many historians disagree with key aspects of Shakespeare's portrayal. To find out more about how Shakespeare viewed Caesar, click on the picture of Shakespeare. To find out more about how historians view Caesar, click on the books.

Created by K. Ferguson | Last updated May 26, 2008
Report broken links or factual errors by clicking here.

3. **Test and revise the site.** Carefully proofread each page of your site. Check to make sure that all links are functioning properly. Ask yourself and your peers the following questions:

   - Where is the navigation confusing?
   - Which parts of the site really grabbed your attention?
   - Which visual or audio elements add value to the site? Which are just distracting?

   Use the feedback to revise and improve your site.

4. **Upload your site.** Launch your site on your school's internal server or on the Web. Ask your school's technology administrator for permission first.

Student Resource Bank

Reading any text—short story, poem, magazine article, newspaper, Web page— requires the use of special strategies. For example, you might plot events in a short story on a diagram, while you may use text features to spot main ideas in a magazine article. You also need to identify patterns of organization in the text. Using such strategies can help you read different texts with ease and also help you understand what you're reading.

1 Reading Literary Texts

Literary texts include short stories, novels, poems, and dramas. Literary texts can also be biographies, autobiographies, and essays. To appreciate and analyze literary texts, you will need to understand the characteristics of each type of text.

1.1 READING A SHORT STORY
Strategies for Reading

- Read the title. As you read the story, you may notice that the title has a special meaning.

- Keep track of events as they happen. Plot the events on a diagram like this one.

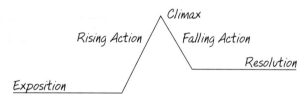

- From the details the writer provides, **visualize** the characters. **Predict** what they might do next.

- Look for specific adjectives that help you visualize the **setting**—the time and place in which events occur.

1.2 READING A POEM
Strategies for Reading

- Notice the **form** of the poem, or the number of its lines and their arrangement on the page.

- Read the poem aloud a few times. Listen for **rhymes** and **rhythms.**

- **Visualize** the images and comparisons.

- **Connect** with the poem by asking yourself what message the poet is trying to send.

- Create a word web or another **graphic organizer** to record your reactions and questions.

1.3 READING A PLAY
Strategies for Reading

- Read the stage directions to help you **visualize** the setting and characters.

- **Question** what the title means and why the playwright chose it.

- Identify the main conflict (struggle or problem) in the play. To **clarify** the conflict, make a chart that shows what the conflict is and how it is resolved.

- **Evaluate** the characters. What do they want? How do they change during the play? You may want to make a chart that lists each character's name, appearance, and traits.

1.4 READING LITERARY NONFICTION
Strategies for Reading

- If you are reading a biography, an autobiography, or another type of biographical writing, such as a diary or memoir, use a family tree or word web to keep track of the people mentioned.

- When reading an essay, **evaluate** the writer's ideas and reasoning. Does the writer present a thesis statement? identify the main points? support opinions with facts?

2 Reading Informational Texts: Text Features

An **informational text** is writing that provides factual information. Informational materials, such as chapters in textbooks and articles in magazines, encyclopedias, and newspapers, usually contain elements that help the reader recognize their purposes, organizations, and key ideas. These elements are known as **text features.**

2.1 UNDERSTANDING TEXT FEATURES

Text features are design elements of a text that indicate its organizational structure or otherwise make its key ideas and information understandable. Text features include titles, headings, subheadings, boldface type, bulleted and numbered lists, and graphic aids, such as charts, graphs, illustrations, and photographs. Notice how the text features help you find key information on the textbook page shown.

Ⓐ The **title** identifies the topic.

Ⓑ A **subheading** indicates the start of a new topic or section and identifies the focus of that section.

Ⓒ **Boldface type** is used to make key terms obvious.

Ⓓ A **bulleted list** shows items of equal importance.

Ⓔ **Graphic aids,** such as illustrations, photographs, charts, graphs, diagrams, maps, and timelines, often clarify ideas in the text.

PRACTICE AND APPLY

1. What are the subheadings on the textbook page shown?

2. What are the key terms on the page? How do you know?

3. What does the graph tell you about a snow line? Can you find this information elsewhere on the page?

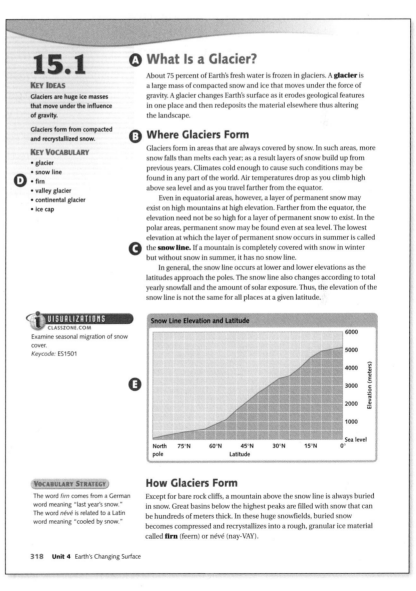

15.1

KEY IDEAS

Glaciers are huge ice masses that move under the influence of gravity.

Glaciers form from compacted and recrystallized snow.

KEY VOCABULARY

Ⓓ
- glacier
- snow line
- firn
- valley glacier
- continental glacier
- ice cap

VISUALIZATIONS
CLASSZONE.COM
Examine seasonal migration of snow cover.
Keycode: ES1501

VOCABULARY STRATEGY

The word *firn* comes from a German word meaning "last year's snow." The word *névé* is related to a Latin word meaning "cooled by snow."

Ⓐ **What Is a Glacier?**

About 75 percent of Earth's fresh water is frozen in glaciers. A **glacier** is a large mass of compacted snow and ice that moves under the force of gravity. A glacier changes Earth's surface as it erodes geological features in one place and then redeposits the material elsewhere thus altering the landscape.

Ⓑ **Where Glaciers Form**

Glaciers form in areas that are always covered by snow. In such areas, more snow falls than melts each year; as a result layers of snow build up from previous years. Climates cold enough to cause such conditions may be found in any part of the world. Air temperatures drop as you climb high above sea level and as you travel farther from the equator.

Even in equatorial areas, however, a layer of permanent snow may exist on high mountains at high elevation. Farther from the equator, the elevation need not be so high for a layer of permanent snow to exist. In the polar areas, permanent snow may be found even at sea level. The lowest elevation at which the layer of permanent snow occurs in summer is called Ⓒ the **snow line.** If a mountain is completely covered with snow in winter but without snow in summer, it has no snow line.

In general, the snow line occurs at lower and lower elevations as the latitudes approach the poles. The snow line also changes according to total yearly snowfall and the amount of solar exposure. Thus, the elevation of the snow line is not the same for all places at a given latitude.

Snow Line Elevation and Latitude

Ⓔ

How Glaciers Form

Except for bare rock cliffs, a mountain above the snow line is always buried in snow. Great basins below the highest peaks are filled with snow that can be hundreds of meters thick. In these huge snowfields, buried snow becomes compressed and recrystallizes into a rough, granular ice material called **firn** (feern) or névé (nay-VAY).

318 **Unit 4** Earth's Changing Surface

2.2 USING TEXT FEATURES

You can use text features to locate information, to help you understand it, and to categorize it. Just use the following strategies when you encounter informational text.

Strategies for Reading

- Scan the title, headings, and subheadings to get an idea of the main concepts and the way the text is organized.

- Before you begin reading the text more thoroughly, read any questions that appear at the end of a lesson or chapter. Doing this will help you set a purpose for your reading.

- Turn subheadings into questions. Then use the text below the subheadings to answer the questions. Your answers will be a summary of the text.

- Take notes by turning headings and subheadings into main ideas. You might use a chart like the following.

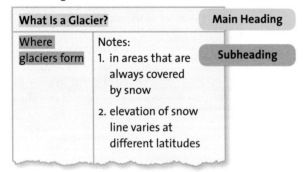

2.3 TURNING TEXT HEADINGS INTO OUTLINE ENTRIES

You can also use text features to take notes in outline form. The following outline shows how one student used text headings from the sample page on page R3. Study the outline and use the strategies that follow to create an outline based on text features.

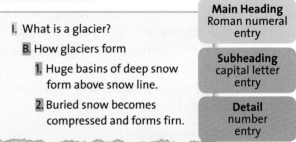

Strategies for Using Text Headings

- Preview the headings and subheadings in the text to get an idea of what different kinds there are and what their positions might be in an outline.

- Be consistent. Note that subheadings that are the same size and color should be used consistently in Roman-numeral or capital-letter entries in the outline. If you decide that a chapter heading should appear with a Roman numeral, then that's the level at which all other chapter headings should appear.

- Write the headings and subheadings that you will use as your Roman-numeral and capital-letter entries first. As you read, fill in numbered details from the text under the headings and subheadings in your outline.

PRACTICE AND APPLY

Reread "Simply Grand: Generational Ties Matter," pages 231–234. Use text features in the selection to take notes in outline form.

Preview the subheadings in the text to get an idea of the different kinds. Write the headings and subheadings you are using as your Roman-numeral and capital-letter entries first. Then fill in the details.

2.4 GRAPHIC AIDS

Information is communicated not only with words but also with graphic aids. **Graphic aids** are visual representations of verbal statements. They can be charts, webs, diagrams, graphs, photographs, or other visual representations of information. Graphic aids usually make complex information easier to understand. For that reason, graphic aids are often used to organize, simplify, and summarize information for easy reference.

Graphs

Graphs are used to illustrate statistical information. A **graph** is a drawing that shows the relative values of numerical quantities. Different kinds of graphs are used to show different numerical relationships.

Strategies for Reading

Ⓐ Read the title.

Ⓑ Find out what is being represented or measured.

Ⓒ In a circle graph, compare the sizes of the parts.

Ⓓ In a line graph, study the slant of the line. The steeper the line, the faster the rate of change.

Ⓔ In a bar graph, compare the lengths of the bars.

A **circle graph,** or **pie graph,** shows the relationships of parts to a whole. The entire circle equals 100 percent. The parts of the circle represent percentages of the whole.

MODEL: CIRCLE GRAPH

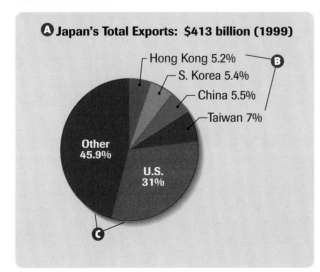

Ⓐ Japan's Total Exports: $413 billion (1999)

- Hong Kong 5.2% **Ⓑ**
- S. Korea 5.4%
- China 5.5%
- Taiwan 7%
- Other 45.9%
- U.S. 31%

Ⓒ

Line graphs show changes in numerical quantities over time and are effective in presenting trends such as global average temperatures over 120 years. A line graph is made on a grid. Here, the vertical axis indicates degrees of temperature, and the horizontal axis shows years. Points on the graph indicate data. The line that connects the points highlights a trend or pattern.

MODEL: LINE GRAPH

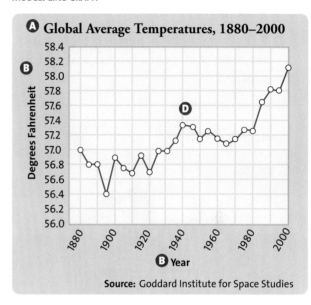

Ⓐ Global Average Temperatures, 1880–2000

Ⓑ Degrees Fahrenheit — 56.0 to 58.4

Ⓓ

Ⓑ Year — 1880, 1900, 1920, 1940, 1960, 1980, 2000

Source: Goddard Institute for Space Studies

In a **bar graph,** vertical or horizontal bars are used to show or compare categories of information, such as the length of major world rivers. The lengths of the bars indicate the quantities.

MODEL: BAR GRAPH

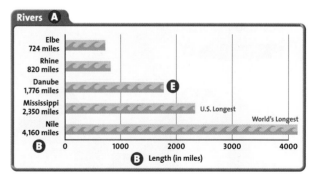

Rivers Ⓐ

- Elbe 724 miles
- Rhine 820 miles
- Danube 1,776 miles **Ⓔ**
- Mississippi 2,350 miles — U.S. Longest
- Nile 4,160 miles — World's Longest

Ⓑ 0 1000 2000 3000 4000

Ⓑ Length (in miles)

WATCH OUT! Evaluate carefully the information presented in graphs. For example, circle graphs show major factors and differences well but tend to minimize smaller factors and differences.

Diagrams

A **diagram** is a drawing that shows how something works or how its parts relate to one another.

A **picture diagram** is a picture or drawing of the subject being discussed.

Strategies for Reading

Ⓐ Read the title.

Ⓑ Read each label and look at the part it identifies.

Ⓒ Follow any arrows or numbers that show the order of steps in a process, and read any captions.

MODEL: PICTURE DIAGRAM

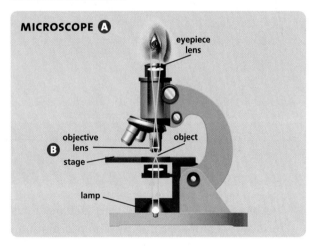

In a **schematic diagram,** lines, symbols, and words are used to help readers visualize processes or objects they wouldn't normally be able to see.

MODEL: SCHEMATIC DIAGRAM

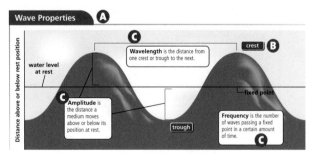

Charts and Tables

A **chart** presents information, shows a process, or makes comparisons, usually in rows or columns. A **table** is a specific type of chart that presents a collection of facts in rows and columns and shows how the facts relate to one another.

Strategies for Reading

Ⓐ Read the title to learn what information the chart or table covers.

Ⓑ Study column headings and row labels to determine the categories of information presented.

Ⓒ Look down columns and across rows to find specific information.

MODEL: CHART

Adult Literacy Rates in South Asia by Gender, 2003 estimates Ⓐ

Country	Male	Female	Total
Bangladesh	53.9%	31%	43%
Bhutan	56%	28%	42% Ⓒ
India	70%	48%	59%
Maldives	97%	97%	97%
Nepal	62%	27%	45%
Sri Lanka	94%	90%	92%
Pakistan	61%	35%	48%

Source: CIA, *The World Fact Book*

MODEL: TABLE

Amendments to the U. S. Constitution After the Bill of Rights Ⓐ

Amendment	Year Proposed by Congress	Year Adopted	What It Does Ⓑ
11	1794	1798	Gives states immunity from certain legal actions Ⓒ
12	1803	1804	Changes the selection of president and vice-president through the electoral college
13	1865	1865	Abolishes slavery
14	1866	1868	Defines citizenship and citizen rights; provides due process and equal protection of the laws
15	1869	1870	Extends the right to vote to all African Americans, including former slaves
16	1909	1913	Gives power to impose income tax

Maps

A **map** visually represents a geographic region, such as a state or country. It provides information about areas through lines, colors, shapes, and symbols. There are different kinds of maps.

- **Political maps** show political features, such as national borders.
- **Physical maps** show the landforms in areas.
- **Road or travel maps** show roads and highways.
- **Thematic maps** show information on a specific topic, such as climate, weather, or natural resources.

Strategies for Reading

Ⓐ Read the title to find out what kind of map it is.

Ⓑ Read the labels to get an overall sense of what the map shows.

Ⓒ Look at the **key** or **legend** to find out what the symbols and colors on the map stand for.

MODEL: THEMATIC MAP

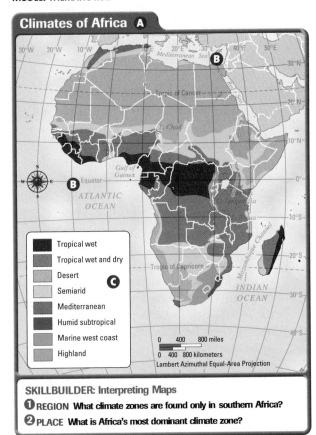

Climates of Africa Ⓐ

Tropical wet
Tropical wet and dry
Desert
Semiarid
Mediterranean
Humid subtropical
Marine west coast
Highland

0   400   800 miles
0 400 800 kilometers
Lambert Azimuthal Equal-Area Projection

SKILLBUILDER: Interpreting Maps

❶ REGION What climate zones are found only in southern Africa?

❷ PLACE What is Africa's most dominant climate zone?

MODEL: PHYSICAL MAP

Map of Egypt Ⓐ

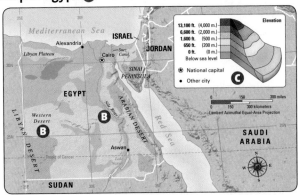

13,100 ft. (4,000 m.)
6,600 ft. (2,000 m.)
1,600 ft. (500 m.)
650 ft. (200 m.)
0 ft. (0 m.)
Below sea level
Elevation

⊛ National capital
• Other city

0   150   300 miles
0   150   300 kilometers
Lambert Azimuthal Equal-Area Projection

PRACTICE AND APPLY

Use the graphic aids shown on pages R5–R7 to answer the following questions:

1. According to the circle graph, did Japan export more to South Korea or to Taiwan in 1999?

2. According to the line graph, in what year were global average temperatures at their lowest?

3. Is the Nile River approximately four or five times longer than the Rhine River, according to the bar graph?

4. How many lenses does a microscope have?

5. Use the information in the schematic diagram to write a definition of a wavelength.

6. In general, according to the chart, were literacy rates in 2003 in South Asia higher for males or for females?

7. In what year was the right to vote guaranteed to African Americans, according to the table?

8. What is one major feature of the natural landscape shown on the physical map of Egypt?

9. Using the key on the climate map of Africa, identify the general area of Africa that is the wettest.

❸ Reading Informational Texts: Patterns of Organization

Reading any type of writing is easier once you recognize how it is organized. Writers usually arrange ideas and information in ways that best help readers see how they are related. There are several common patterns of organization:

- order of importance
- chronological order
- cause-effect organization
- compare-and-contrast organization

3.1 ORDER OF IMPORTANCE

Order of importance is a pattern of organization in which information is arranged by its degree of importance. The information is often arranged in one of two ways: from **most important to least important** or from **least important to most important.** In the first way, the most important quality, characteristic, or fact is presented at the beginning of the text, and the remaining details are presented in an order ending with the least significant. The second pattern is the reverse: the text builds from the less important elements to the most important one at the conclusion. Order of importance is frequently used in persuasive writing.

Strategies for Reading

- To identify order of importance in a piece of writing, skim the text to see if it moves from items of greater importance to items of lesser importance, or the reverse.

- Next, read the text carefully. Look for words and phrases such as *first, second, mainly, more important, less important, least important* and *most important* to indicate the relative importance of the ideas and information.

- Identify the topic of the text and what aspect of it is being discussed—its complexity, size, effectiveness, varieties, and so on. Note what the most important fact or idea seems to be.

- If you are having difficulty understanding the topic, try asking *who, what, when, where, why,* and *how* about the ideas or events.

Notice how the ideas move from the most important to the least in the following model.

Subject	Words showing order of importance

MODEL

If you spend any time outdoors in the summer, at some point you probably will find yourself covered with mosquito bites. The word *mosquito* means "little fly" in Spanish, but the impact these pesky insects have on people is anything but small.

The most important thing to know about mosquitoes is that they can transmit serious diseases such as yellow fever, malaria, and encephalitis. These diseases are not limited to developing countries, either. Outbreaks of West Nile virus, which is related to viruses that can cause encephalitis, have occurred recently in the United States. The symptoms of all these mosquito-borne illnesses include high fever and headaches.

Luckily, not all mosquitoes carry serious diseases. While the bites of these "safe" mosquitoes may not seem as important because they're less life-threatening, they can be extremely annoying. Just thinking about those raised red bumps that itch like crazy is enough to make anyone start scratching frantically.

Although exactly what happens when you get bitten by a mosquito is less important than the bite itself, the mechanism is surprising. First, only female mosquitoes "bite." Second, since the insects lack jaws, they don't actually bite at all. Instead, the mosquito punctures the victim's skin with sharp stylets on the proboscis used for piercing and injects her saliva into the wound. The saliva keeps the victim's blood from clotting, so the mosquito can drink her fill—sometimes up to 150 times her weight.

The saliva sets off an allergic reaction in the victim. Ironically, though, if the person lets the mosquito finish eating, there will be less saliva left in the skin. Therefore, the swelling and itching won't be as severe. Nice to know, but easier said than done.

The best ways to prevent mosquito bites or to lessen the effect if you do get bitten are to stay inside when mosquitoes are out—from dusk to dawn; to use mosquito repellant at all times; and, if you do get bitten, to refrain from scratching!

Read the following passage, and then do the following:

1. Identify whether the order is from most important to least important or from least important to most important.

2. Identify one phrase that helped you figure out the order.

Of the four acknowledged heroes of the event, three are able to account for their behavior. Donald Usher and Eugene Windsor, a park police helicopter team, risked their lives every time they dipped the skids into the water to pick up survivors. On television, side by side in bright blue jumpsuits, they described their courage as all in the line of duty. Lenny Skutnik, a twenty-eight-year-old employee of the Congressional Budget Office, said: "It's something I never thought I would do"— referring to his jumping into the water to drag an injured woman to shore. Skutnik added that "somebody had to go in the water," delivering every hero's line that is no less admirable for its repetitions. In fact, nobody had to go into the water. That somebody actually did so is part of the reason this particular tragedy sticks in the mind.

But the person most responsible for the emotional impact of the disaster is the one known at first simply as "the man in the water." (Balding, probably in his fifties, an extravagant mustache.) He was seen clinging with five other survivors to the tail section of the airplane. This man was described by Usher and Windsor as appearing alert and in control. Every time they lowered a lifeline and flotation ring to him, he passed it on to another of the passengers.

—Roger Rosenblatt, "The Man in the Water"

3.2 CHRONOLOGICAL ORDER

Chronological order is the arrangement of events in their order of occurrence. This type of organization is used in fictional narratives, historical writing, biographies, and autobiographies. To indicate the order of events, writers use words such as *before, after, next,* and *later* and words and phrases that identify specific times of day, days of the week, and dates, such as *the next morning, Tuesday,* and *on July 4, 1776.*

Strategies for Reading

- Look in the text for headings and subheadings that may indicate a chronological pattern of organization.

- Look for words and phrases that identify times, such as *in a year, three hours earlier, in 1871,* and *the next day.*

- Look for words that signal order, such as *first, afterward, then, during,* and *finally,* to see how events or steps are related.

- Note that a paragraph or passage in which ideas and information are arranged chronologically will have several words or phrases that indicate time order, not just one.

- Ask yourself: Are the events in the paragraph or passage presented in time order?

Notice the words and phrases that signal time order in the first three paragraphs of the following model.

MODEL

The Career of Alexander Graham Bell

In 1871, Alexander Graham Bell came to Boston for a few weeks to lecture on his father's system for teaching speech to the deaf. What he didn't know was that this brief trip would have a dramatic impact on his life. Bell's lectures amazed audiences, prompting other Bostonians to extend similar invitations to him. Within the year, the Scottish-born teacher and scientist found himself living in Boston—although he had moved with his parents from London, England, to Ontario, Canada, just a year before.

Time words and phrases

Events

Order words and phrases

By 1872, Bell had opened a school in Boston for training teachers of the deaf. In 1873, he accepted a teaching position at Boston University as professor of vocal physiology.

During this period, Bell also met Thomas Watson, a young repair mechanic and model maker. Watson teamed up with Bell in early 1875. For over two years the men worked together to create an apparatus for transmitting sound by electricity. Then, on April 6, 1875, Bell acquired a patent for a multiple telegraph. A little less than a year later, on the heels of their first success, the two created the first telephone.

The first transmission of human speech took place on March 10, 1876. On that day, Bell called to his assistant over a new transmitter he was trying out, "Mr. Watson! Come here! I want you!" and Mr. Watson heard him.

There was more work to do before others would have actual telephone service, of course. By 1915, however, coast-to-coast telephone communication was a reality.

By then, the two had also succeeded in inventing many other useful devices. In fact, although Bell is best known for inventing the telephone, he was also the father of many other equally amazing devices and scientific advancements.

PRACTICE AND APPLY

Refer to the preceding model to do the following:

1. List at least five words in the last three paragraphs that indicate time or order.

2. Draw a timeline beginning with Bell's arrival in Ontario, Canada, in 1870 and ending with the availability of coast-to-coast phone service in 1915. Chart on the timeline each major event described in the model.

3. A writer may use more than one pattern of organization in a text. In the last paragraph of the model, what pattern of organization does the writer use? How does this pattern contribute to your understanding of the passage?

3.3 CAUSE-EFFECT ORGANIZATION

Cause-effect organization is a pattern of organization that expresses causal relationships between events, ideas, and trends. Cause-effect relationships may be directly stated or merely implied by the order in which the information is presented. Writers often use the cause-effect pattern in historical and scientific writing. Cause-effect relationships may take several forms.

One cause with one effect

One cause with multiple effects

Multiple causes with a single effect

A chain of causes and effects

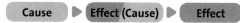

Strategies for Reading

- Look for headings and subheadings that indicate a cause-effect pattern of organization, such as "Effects of Population Density."

- To find the effect or effects, read to answer the question, What happened?

- To find the cause or causes, read to answer the question, Why did it happen?

- Look for words and phrases that help you identify specific relationships between events, such as *because, since, so, had the effect of, led to, as a result, resulted in, for that reason, due to, therefore, if . . . then,* and *consequently.*

- Evaluate each cause-effect relationship. Do not assume that because one event happened before another, the first event caused the second event.

- Use graphic organizers like the diagrams shown to record cause-effect relationships as you read.

Notice the words that signal causes and effects in the following model.

MODEL

The Creation of National Parks

In 1870 and 1871, two expeditions were led through Montana. These men were awestruck by the deep canyons, dense pine forests, and refreshing rivers and waterfalls of Yellowstone, Montana. They were so moved by the area's natural wonders, in fact, that they immediately wanted to protect them. So they trooped off to Washington, D.C., to demand that Yellowstone lands be set aside for public use. There, before Congress, with the help of breathtaking paintings and photographs by artists who had ventured to Yellowstone with government land surveyors, these passionate preservationists presented their case. Dazzled, Congress responded to their pleas by creating the first national park, Yellowstone National Park.

> **Causes**

> **Effect that in turn becomes a cause**

> **Signal words and phrases**

The next several national parks owe their establishment primarily to the enthusiasm and persuasive abilities of one nature lover, John Muir. Muir took influential friends such as Ralph Waldo Emerson and Theodore Roosevelt on spectacular hikes through the Sierras. While on these hikes, he expressed his love of nature in passionate arguments for its preservation. In 1890, largely as a result of Muir's efforts, Yosemite, Sequoia, and General Grant national parks were established.

Interestingly, however, some of today's national parks owe their preservation to looters—or rather, to a Congress roused into action by looters. In 1906, because Congress was concerned that widespread plundering of precious Southwestern archaeological sites was destroying important artifacts, it enacted a law to prevent such plundering. This law, called the Antiquities Act, authorized the president to set aside as national monuments extremely precious or threatened lands. Consequently, by calling on the powers granted to him under this law, President Theodore Roosevelt was able to put under government protection many sites that might otherwise have been destroyed. These sites would eventually earn national-park status.

PRACTICE AND APPLY

Refer to the preceding model to do the following:

1. Use the pattern of multiple causes with a single effect illustrated on page R10 to make a graphic organizer showing the causes described in the text and the effect of those causes.

2. List two words that the writer uses to signal cause and effect in the last paragraph.

3.4 COMPARE-AND-CONTRAST ORGANIZATION

Compare-and-contrast organization is a pattern of organization that serves as a framework for examining similarities and differences in two or more subjects. A writer may use this pattern of organization to analyze two or more subjects, such as characters or movies, in terms of their important points or characteristics. These points or characteristics are called points of comparison. The compare-and-contrast pattern of organization may be developed in either of two ways:

Point-by-point organization—The writer discusses one point of comparison for both subjects, then goes on to the next point.

Subject-by-subject organization—The writer covers all points of comparison for one subject and then all points of comparison for the next subject.

Strategies for Reading

• Look in the text for headings, subheadings, and sentences that may suggest a compare-and-contrast pattern of organization, such as "Plants Share Many Characteristics." These will help you identify where similarities and differences are addressed.

- To find similarities, look for words and phrases such as *like, similarly, both, also,* and *in the same way.*

- To find differences, look for words and phrases such as *unlike, but, on the other hand, in contrast,* and *however.*

- Use a graphic organizer, such as a Venn diagram or a compare-and-contrast chart, to record points of comparison and similarities and differences.

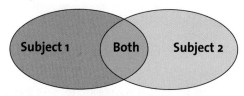

	Subject 1	Subject 2
Point 1		
Point 2		
Point 3		

Read the following models. As you read, use the signal words and phrases to identify the similarities and differences between the subjects and how the details are organized in each text.

MODEL 1

Two Favorite Chips

Tortilla and potato chips are top snack choices among Americans of all ages. Some snackers are happy munching on anything salty that crunches. Others are devoted fans of one chip or the other. Here's a look at some facts about these popular snacks.

While tortilla chips are made from corn, potato chips are made from—you guessed it, potatoes. Both chips are traditionally prepared by frying in vegetable oil with lots of salt, although baked versions are also available. Surprisingly, tortilla chips are lighter than potato chips. A one-ounce serving includes about 24 tortilla chips as opposed to 20 potato chips—about 17 percent more.

Subjects

Contrast words and phrases

Comparison words

Neither snack is featured in weight-loss diets, though, and for good reason. Each is loaded with calories and fat—between 140 and 150 calories per serving, 70–90 of which come from fat. Although both chips are salty, tortilla chips are relatively less so.

As for nutrition, a serving of either tortilla or potato chips contains 2 grams of protein. That's not much, considering that the same amount of dry cereal offers about 300 percent more. It's probably a good thing, in that case, that people choose chips for their taste and texture, not for their food value.

Both chips come in numerous flavors. Tortilla-chip lovers can choose chips made from yellow or blue corn seasoned with salsa, nacho spices, ranch dressing, or guacamole. Similarly, potato chips are made from white or sweet potatoes and are available with barbecue, cheese, sour-cream-and-onion, dill pickle, and salt-and-vinegar flavors, to name just some options.

So choose your chip—just make sure that your snack is only part of a nutritious, well-balanced diet.

MODEL 2

Two Traditions

Almost every culture has a ceremony to mark the passage of young people from childhood to adulthood. In the Latin culture, this rite of passage for girls is *la quinceañera.* For American girls, it is the sweet 16 birthday party.

[**Subjects**]

Quinceañera means "15th birthday," and the occasion is celebrated when a girl reaches that age. The origin of *la quinceañera* is uncertain, although it may have roots in the Aztec, Maya, or Toltec culture. It generally involves celebration of a thanksgiving mass followed by a lavish party for the extended family and friends.

The *quinceañera* arrays herself to look as adult as possible, usually in a long, frilly dress in white or pastel colors. Her ensemble is topped by a hat or headdress. A highlight of the celebration is a waltz that she dances with her father and other male relatives. In Mexico, the celebrant may give her guests a memento taken from a handmade *quinceañera* doll.

The sweet 16 party, in contrast, takes place when a girl is a year older than the *quinceañera.* Unlike the Latin occasion, the sweet 16 celebration does not include a religious component and is designed more for the girl's friends than for the family. Like *la quinceañera,* the sweet 16 party often takes place in a hotel or reception hall. The guests at both celebrations are often treated to a live band, plentiful food, and a many-tiered birthday cake.

[**Contrast words and phrases**]

[**Comparison words**]

Similar to their Latin counterparts, sweet 16s dress to reflect their new adult status, many also choosing white or pastel gowns. On the other hand, sweet 16 attire can run the gamut from frothy and frilly to sleek and sophisticated, depending on the girl's personality.

Whether a girl celebrates *la quinceañera* or her sweet 16, however, the message from the world is the same—"Welcome to adulthood!"

PRACTICE AND APPLY

Refer to the preceding models to answer the following questions:

1. Which model is organized by subject? Which model is organized by points of comparison?

2. Identify two words or phrases in each model that signal a compare-and-contrast pattern of organization. Do not choose words or phrases that have already been highlighted.

3. List at least three points that the writer of each model compares and contrasts.

4. Use a Venn diagram or a compare-and-contrast chart to identify at least two points of comparison and the similarities and differences in model 2.

④ Reading Informational Texts: Forms

Magazines, newspapers, Web pages, and consumer, public, and workplace documents are all examples of informational materials. To understand and analyze informational texts, pay attention to text features and patterns of organization.

4.1 READING A MAGAZINE ARTICLE

Because people often skim magazines, magazine publishers use devices to attract attention to articles.

Strategies for Reading

Ⓐ Notice whether **graphic aids** or **quotations** attract your attention. Sometimes a publisher pulls a quotation out of the text and displays it to get your attention. Such quotations are called **pull quotes.**

Ⓑ Once you decide that you're interested in the article, read the title and other headings to find out more about its topic and organization.

Ⓒ Notice whether the article has a **byline,** a line naming the author.

Ⓓ Sometimes an article will be accompanied by a **sidebar,** a short article that presents additional information. This sidebar also has a **title.** Is your understanding of the main article enhanced by the information in the sidebar?

PRACTICE AND APPLY

1. What is the effect of using a question for the title?

2. From what part of the article is the pull quote taken?

3. What is the relationship of the information in the sidebar to the article?

Ⓑ Shouldn't We Know Who Invented the Windshield Wiper?

Ⓒ by James T. Terry

We know the famous ones—the Thomas Edisons and the Alexander Graham Bells—but what about the less famous inventors? What about the people who invented the traffic light and the windshield wiper? Shouldn't we know who they are?

Joan McLean thinks so. In fact, McLean, a professor of physics at Mountain University in Range, Colorado, feels so strongly about this matter that she's developed a course on the topic. In addition to learning "who" invented "what," however, McLean also likes her students to learn the answers to the "why" and "how" questions. According to McLean, "When students learn the answers to these questions, they are better prepared to recognize opportunities for inventing and more motivated to give inventing a try."

Her students agree. One young man with a patent pending for an unbreakable umbrella is walking proof of McLean's statement. "If I had not heard the story of the windshield wiper's invention," said Tommy Lee, a senior physics major, "I never would have dreamed of turning my frustration during a rainstorm into something so constructive." Lee is currently negotiating to sell his patent to an umbrella manufacturer once it is approved.

So, just what is the story behind the windshield wiper? Well, Mary Anderson came up with the idea in 1902 after a visit to New York City. The day was cold and blus-

Ⓐ "When students learn the answers to these questions, they are better prepared to recognize opportunities for inventing...."

tery, but Anderson still wanted to see the sights, so she hopped aboard a streetcar. Noticing that the driver was struggling to see through the sleet and snow covering the windshield, she found herself wondering why there couldn't be a built-in device for cleaning the window. Still wondering about this when she returned home to Birmingham, Alabama, Anderson started sketching out solutions. One of her ideas, a lever on the inside of a vehicle that would control an arm on the outside, became the first windshield wiper.

Today we benefit from countless inventions and innovations. It's hard to imagine getting by without Garrett A. Morgan's traffic light. It's equally impossible to picture a world without Katherine J. Blodgett's innovation that makes glass invisible. Can you picture life without transparent windows and eyeglasses?

As I think about stories like these, I am convinced that they will help untold numbers of inventors. So, only one question nags: how did we ever manage to give rise to so many inventors before McLean invented this class?

Ⓓ

Someone Also Invented . . .

Dishwashers.................. Josephine Cochran
Disposable Diapers....... Marion Donovan
Fire Escapes .... Anna Connelly
Peanut Butter............... George Washington Carver

4.2 READING A TEXTBOOK

Each textbook that you use has its own system of organization based on the content in the book. Often an introductory unit will explain the book's organization and special features. If your textbook has such a unit, read it first.

Strategies for Reading

Ⓐ Before you begin reading the lesson or chapter, read any **questions** that appear at the end of it. Then use the questions to set your purpose for reading.

Ⓑ **Read slowly and carefully** to better understand and remember the ideas presented in the text. When you come to an unfamiliar word, first try to figure out its meaning from **context clues.** If necessary, find the meaning of the word in a **glossary** in the textbook or in a dictionary. Avoid interrupting your reading by constantly looking up words in a dictionary.

Ⓒ Use the book's graphic aids, such as illustrations, diagrams, and captions, to clarify your understanding of the text.

Ⓓ Take notes as you read. Use text features such as **subheadings** and boldfaced terms to help you organize your notes. Use graphic organizers, such as cause-effect charts, to help you clarify relationships among ideas.

PRACTICE AND APPLY

1. How would you find the definition of *equatorial?*

2. Where on the page can you find out the names of different types of glaciers?

3. Use the text on this page and on page R3 to answer the second question in the Section Review.

Firn resembles the ice of a packed snowball. It is not fluffy, such as new-fallen snow, nor is it as hard as solid ice. The granules of firn start out no larger than grains of sand. As the layer of firn thickens, the firn's crystals may grow as large as kernels of corn. Within a layer of firn, the weight of the material at the top compresses the firn below, turning that firn into solid ice. Under the weight of the overlying snow and firn, the ice begins to flow downward or outward. This moving mass of snow and ice is a glacier.

Types of Glaciers **Ⓓ**

There are two main types of glaciers, valley glaciers and continental glaciers. A **valley glacier** is a glacier that moves within valley walls. A **continental glacier** is a glacier that covers a large part of a continent.

Valley Glaciers **Ⓓ**

Many mountain ranges in the world have peaks and valleys high enough so that snowfall there exceeds snowmelt. The snow builds up and changes to ice as it accumulates in the valleys of such mountain ranges. The ice stays within valley walls, forming a large river of ice and snow, which moves slowly downhill under the influence of gravity. This long, slow-moving, wedge-shaped stream of ice is a valley glacier. Valley glaciers are also known as alpine glaciers, after the Alps in south-central Europe.

Ⓑ Valley glaciers form in regions where mountains are high enough to be in the colder part of Earth's atmosphere. Valley glaciers even form in equatorial regions where mountains are located at high elevations. Valley glaciers exist on all continents except Australia.

Valley glaciers vary in size. Small valley glaciers may be less than 2-kilometers long. Large valley glaciers may be over 100 kilometers long and hundreds of meters thick. Some of the world's largest valley glaciers are in southern Alaska. The world's tallest mountains, the Himalayas, also have very large valley glaciers.

DENALI NATIONAL PARK Muldrow Glacier, a valley glacier in Alaska, is about 56 kilometers long.

Ⓒ

Section Review **Ⓐ**

- What is the snow line?
- Describe how a glacier forms.
- **Critical Thinking** The graph on page 318 shows how snow-line elevations change north of the equator. Predict how snow-line elevations change as latitude increases south of the equator.

4.3 READING A CONSUMER DOCUMENT

Consumer documents are materials that accompany products and services. They usually provide information about the use, care, operation, or assembly of the products they accompany. Some common consumer documents are contracts, warranties, manuals, instructions, schedules, and Web pages. Two examples of consumer documents follow.

Strategies for Reading

Ⓐ Read the **title** to identify the purpose of the document.

Ⓑ Read the general directions to get started.

Ⓒ Look for **numbers** or **letters** that indicate the order in which the steps should be followed. If you do not find letters or numbers, look for signal words such as *first, next, then,* and *finally* to see the order in which the steps should be followed.

Ⓓ Look at the **visuals** that accompany the numbered instructions. Follow the steps in order.

Ⓔ Look for **verbs that describe actions** you should take, such as *press, select,* and *click.*

INSTRUCTIONS FOR CREATING A HOME PAGE

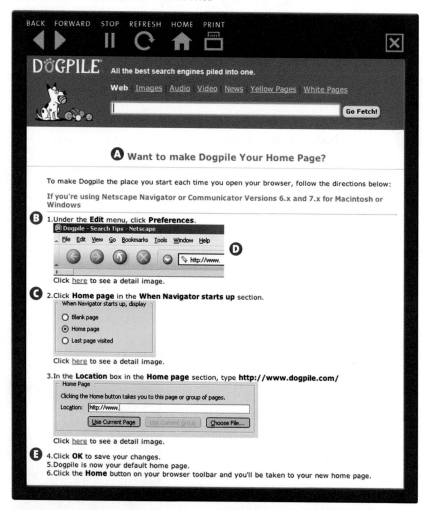

PRACTICE AND APPLY

Reread the Web page telling how to create a home page, and then answer the following questions:

1. Once you have input your preferences for your home page, what must you do to save your changes?

2. After you have saved your changes, how do you get taken straight to your new home page?

The instructions on this page are from a manual for operating a graphing calculator.

Strategies for Reading

Ⓐ Read the **heading** to learn the kind of operation this section of the manual explains.

Ⓑ Look for **numbers** that indicate the order in which the steps should be followed.

Ⓒ Look for **verbs that describe actions** you should take, such as *open, move, press, position,* and *select.*

Ⓓ Examine **graphic aids** that illustrate steps. If you have trouble completing the process, the graphic aids can help you pinpoint what you are doing wrong.

INSTRUCTIONS FOR OPERATING A GRAPHING CALCULATOR

Ⓐ Drawing a Triangle

Ⓑ 1. Open the F2 menu, move the pointer to **Triangle**, and press ENTER. The tool icon at the top left of the screen indicates that the Triangle tool is active. The pointer shape changes to a pen to indicate that you can draw a new point by pressing ENTER at that position.

 Ⓒ

2. Move the pointer to a convenient location for the first vertex of the triangle, and then press ENTER.

3. Move the pointer and then press ENTER to fix the second vertex and continue the same way for the last vertex.

Ⓓ

Changing the Shape of the Triangle

1. Press CLEAR to quit the Triangle tool.

2. Move the pointer close to one of the vertices that you drew. The pointer changes to a hollow arrow and the object that can be selected (the vertex) blinks.

PRACTICE AND APPLY

Reread the page from the manual and then answer the following questions:

1. What does this page explain how to do?

2. What key do you press to begin?

3. What tells you that you can begin drawing a new point?

4. How do you quit the Triangle tool?

Refer to the documents on pages R16–R17 to answer the following question:

5. Compare the document on page R16 with the document on this page. In terms of text features and organization, are they more alike or more different? Support your answer.

4.4 READING A PUBLIC DOCUMENT

Public documents are documents that are written for the public to provide information that is of public interest or concern. These documents are often free. They can be federal, state, or local government documents. They can be speeches or historical documents. They may even be laws, posted warnings, signs, or rules and regulations. The following is one type of public document.

Strategies for Reading

Ⓐ Look at the **title** on the page to discover what the text is about.

Ⓑ Read any lists of **bulleted items** carefully. The bulleted points are usually the essential pieces of information.

Ⓒ Be sure to read the text that immediately precedes a visual. This **lead-in text** can help you understand what the visual is intended to show.

Ⓓ Pay attention to **captions** with pictures or drawings. These will help you interpret what you are seeing.

Ⓔ Study **graphic aids** and **illustrations** closely. These will help you interpret what you are reading and may even provide information not covered in the text.

PAGE FROM A DRIVER EDUCATION MANUAL

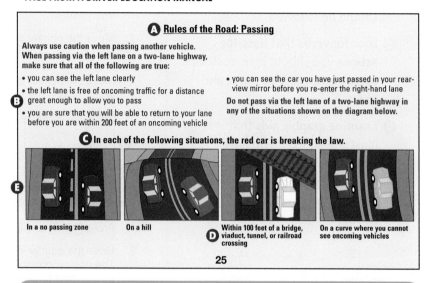

Ⓐ **Rules of the Road: Passing**

Always use caution when passing another vehicle. When passing via the left lane on a two-lane highway, make sure that all of the following are true:

- you can see the left lane clearly
- the left lane is free of oncoming traffic for a distance
Ⓑ great enough to allow you to pass
- you are sure that you will be able to return to your lane before you are within 200 feet of an oncoming vehicle

- you can see the car you have just passed in your rear-view mirror before you re-enter the right-hand lane

Do not pass via the left lane of a two-lane highway in any of the situations shown on the diagram below.

Ⓒ In each of the following situations, the red car is breaking the law.

Ⓔ

In a no passing zone   On a hill   Ⓓ Within 100 feet of a bridge, viaduct, tunnel, or railroad crossing   On a curve where you cannot see oncoming vehicles

25

PRACTICE AND APPLY

Reread the page from the driving-instruction manual and then answer the following questions:

1. What essential piece of information does the lead-in text provide about the illustrations on this page?

2. What are the four driving situations described in which a driver should not pass another vehicle?

3. What do all of the bulleted items concern?

4. What information about lane markings can you gain from the visual that you do not learn from the text on this page?

For more information, see **Reading Informational Texts: Text Features**, pages R3–R7.

4.5 READING A WORKPLACE DOCUMENT

Workplace documents are materials that are produced or used within a workplace, usually to aid in the functioning of a business. These may be documents generated by a business to monitor itself, such as minutes of a meeting or a sales report. These documents may also explain company policies, organizational structures, and operating procedures. Workplace documents include memos, business letters, job applications, and résumés.

Strategies for Reading

A Read a workplace document slowly and carefully, as it may contain **details** that should not be overlooked.

B Notice how to contact the creator of the document. You will need this information to clear up anything that you don't understand.

C **Take notes** to help you remember times, dates, deadlines, and actions required. In particular, note whether you are expected to respond to the document, whether there is a deadline for your response, and to whom you should address your reply.

PRACTICE AND APPLY

Refer to both workplace documents to answer the following questions:

1. Why might the letter from Benjamin Blake be classified as a workplace document?

2. According to the details in Blake's letter, what actions should Ms. Ramirez take?

3. How does Ms. Ramirez use text features, such as graphics and headings, to get her message across clearly and quickly?

4. What actions is Ms. Keene expected to take?

LETTER

B **Benjamin Blake,
Guidance Counselor**
West High School
100 Oak Lane
Timber Creek, NJ 00000
(000) 000-0000
benj80@blake.com

August 8, 2006 **A**

Ramona Ramirez, Vice-President
Packer Press
200 Maple Lane
Timber Creek, NJ 00000

Dear Ms. Ramirez:

C In a recent conversation with your assistant, Kathy Keene, I learned of the list of workplace skills that you give to your employees. Would it **A** be possible for me to have a copy of this document to use with my students this fall? I would, of course, give full credit to your company. **C** Thank you for your consideration of my request.

Sincerely,
Benjamin Blake

MEMO

To:　Kathy Keene
B **From:** Ramona Ramirez
Re:　Teacher Request
Date: August 9, 2006

C Kathy, we can give permission to Mr. Blake to use our skills document. Please send him a copy of the following list to see if these categories will fit his needs:

· Resources
· Interpersonal skills
· Systems
· Technology

A Also, please tell him that we will need a signed agreement from him when we make the arrangements. Thanks.

4.6 READING ELECTRONIC TEXT

Electronic text is any text that is in a form that a computer can store and display on a screen. Electronic text can be part of Web pages, CD-ROMs, search engines, and documents that you create with your computer software. Like books, Web pages often provide aids for finding information. However, each Web page is designed differently, and information is not in the same location on each page. It is important to know the functions of different parts of a Web page so that you can easily find the information you want.

Strategies for Reading

Ⓐ Look at the **title** of a page to determine what topics it covers.

Ⓑ For an online source, such as a Web page or search engine, note the **Web address,** known as a **URL** (Universal Resource Locator). You may want to make a note of it if you need to return to that page.

Ⓒ Look for a **menu bar** along the top, bottom, or side of a Web page. Clicking on an item in a menu bar will take you to another part of the Web site.

Ⓓ Notice any hyperlinks to related pages. **Hyperlinks** are often underlined or highlighted in a contrasting color. You can click on a hyperlink to get to another page—one that may or may not have been created by the same person or organization.

Ⓔ For information that you want to keep for future reference, save documents on your computer or print them. For online sources, you can pull down the **Favorites** or **Bookmarks** menu and bookmark pages so that you can easily return to them or print the information you need. Printing the pages will allow you to highlight key ideas on a hard copy.

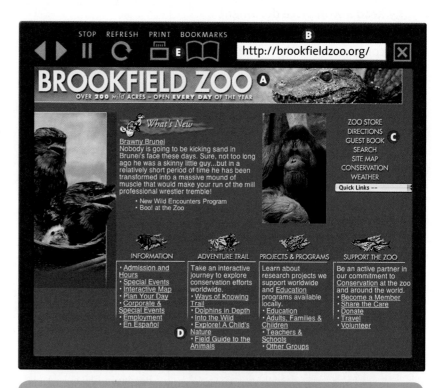

PRACTICE AND APPLY

1. What is the URL of the Web page shown?

2. How do you know that this Web site is regularly updated?

3. What would you do to get the text in Spanish?

5 Reading Persuasive Texts

5.1 ANALYZING AN ARGUMENT

An **argument** expresses a position on an issue or problem and supports it with reasons and evidence. Being able to analyze and evaluate arguments will help you distinguish between claims you should accept and those you should not. A sound argument should appeal strictly to reason. However, arguments are often used in texts that also contain other types of persuasive devices. An argument includes the following elements:

- A **claim** is the writer's position on an issue or problem.

- **Support** is any material that serves to prove a claim. In an argument, support usually consists of reasons and evidence.

- **Reasons** are declarations made to justify an action, a decision, or a belief—for example, "My reason for thinking we will be late is that we can't make it to the appointment in five minutes."

- **Evidence** is the specific references, quotations, facts, examples, and opinions that support a claim. Evidence may also consist of statistics, reports of personal experience, or the views of experts.

- A **counterargument** is an argument made to oppose another argument. A good argument anticipates the opposition's objections and provides counterarguments to disprove or answer them.

Claim	I should be allowed to work a part-time job on weekends.
Reason	Expenses connected with school and activities exceed what I can earn by doing chores.
Evidence	Field trips, uniforms, and transportation cost about $150 a month. I earn about $80 a month now.
Counterargument	I know you think my schoolwork will suffer, but I've always done my homework, and I want stay on the honor roll.

PRACTICE AND APPLY

Read the following editorial and use a chart like the one shown to identify the claim, reason, evidence, and counterargument.

Extracurricular Sports Should Satisfy State Physical Education Requirement

Track, football, soccer, baseball, basketball, and other sports attract dedicated student athletes who often practice every day after school and then participate in weekend games. Should these students be forced to give up an elective class period to take a required physical education class? In order to meet the state's physical education (P.E.) course requirements, that is exactly what Whitman High School asks them to do. I believe that this policy doesn't make any sense. Instead, the [Montgomery County public schools] should exempt student athletes from taking P.E. classes.

First of all, participating in an extracurricular sport meets the objectives of the state's course requirements. Those objectives are to promote fitness and improve athletic skill, according to the Whitman course catalog. Involvement in either a varsity or a club sport for one season already makes a student fit and athletically skilled.

A second reason to change the policy is that the physical education requirement forces students to give up an elective class period. High school students can generally choose only eight elective courses from dozens of class offerings. By eliminating the P.E. requirement for student athletes, the county would give students more freedom in selecting their courses.

Finally, exposing students to different sports is one goal of the P.E. requirement, but this objective alone is not important enough to require students to take P.E. class. Students seldom take P.E. class as seriously as they would an extracurricular sport, so students do not always appreciate sports they sample in P.E. class.

Varsity and club sports require a great deal of time and effort from athletes. The county should recognize that team sports encourage physical activity more effectively than P.E. class. It is more important for student athletes to become well-rounded academically by taking electives than to take P.E. class.

5.2 RECOGNIZING PERSUASIVE TECHNIQUES

Persuasive texts typically rely on more than just the logical appeal of an argument to be convincing. They also depend on **persuasive techniques**—devices that can sway you to adopt a position or take an action.

The chart shown here explains several ways a writer may attempt to sway you to adopt his or her position. Learn to recognize these techniques, and you are less likely to be influenced by them.

Persuasive Technique	Example
Appeals by Association	
Bandwagon appeal Suggests that a person should believe or do something because "everyone else" does	Be where it's at—shop the Magnificent Mall.
Testimonial Relies on endorsements from well-known people or satisfied customers	Links Lorimer, winner of the Wide World Open, uses Gofar golf balls. Shouldn't you?
Snob appeal Taps into people's desire to be special or part of an elite group	Dine at the elite Plaza Inn, where you will be treated like royalty.
Transfer Connnects a product, candidate, or cause with a positive emotion or idea	One spray of Northwoods air freshener and you'll find inner peace.
Appeal to loyalty Relies on people's affiliation with a particular group	Show your support for the Tidewater Tigers by wearing the new Win-Team windbreaker.
Emotional Appeals	
Appeals to pity, fear, or vanity Use strong feelings, rather than facts, to persuade	Don't these abandoned animals deserve a chance? Adopt a pet today.
Word Choice	
Glittering generality Makes a generalization that includes a word or phrase with positive connotations, such as *freedom* and *honor*, to promote a product or idea.	Hop on a Swiftee moped and experience pure freedom.

Identify the persuasive techniques used in this model.

The True Holiday Spirit

The holiday season is almost upon us, and caring people everywhere are opening their hearts and wallets to those who are less fortunate. Charity and community service show democracy in action, and Mayor Adam Miner's actions are setting a good example for village residents. For the last three years, he has volunteered once a week at the local Meals for the Many program. Busing tables, serving soup, and helping wash dishes has made him aware of how fortunate he is and how important it is to share that good fortune. In his Thanksgiving address last week, he urged citizens, "Make this holiday—and all the days that follow—a time of true giving. Join your friends and neighbors in serving others today."

5.3 ANALYZING LOGIC AND REASONING

When you evaluate an argument, you need to look closely at the writer's logic and reasoning. To do this, it is helpful to identify the type of reasoning the writer is using.

The Inductive Mode of Reasoning

When a writer leads from specific evidence to a general principle or generalization, that writer is using **inductive reasoning.** Here is an example of inductive reasoning.

SPECIFIC FACTS

Fact 1 Fewer than 100 Arizona agave century plants remain in existence.

Fact 2 Over the last three generations, there has been a 50 percent reduction in the number of African elephants.

Fact 3 Only 50 Hawaiian crows are left in the world.

GENERALIZATION

Extinction is a problem facing many classes of living things.

Strategies for Determining the Soundness of Inductive Arguments

Ask yourself the following questions to evaluate an inductive argument:

- **Is the evidence valid and sufficient support for the conclusion?** Inaccurate facts lead to inaccurate conclusions.

- **Does the conclusion follow logically from the evidence?** From the facts listed in the previous example, the conclusion that extinction is a problem facing *all* living things would be too broad a generalization.

- **Is the evidence drawn from a large enough sample?** Even though there are only three facts listed above, the sample is large enough to support the claim. If you wanted to support the conclusion that extinction is a problem facing all classes of living things, the sample would not be large enough.

The Deductive Mode of Reasoning

When a writer arrives at a conclusion by applying a general principle to a specific situation, the writer is using **deductive reasoning.** Here's an example.

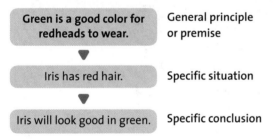

Green is a good color for redheads to wear.	General principle or premise
Iris has red hair.	Specific situation
Iris will look good in green.	Specific conclusion

Strategies for Determining the Soundness of Deductive Arguments

Ask yourself the following questions to evaluate a deductive argument:

- **Is the general principle stated, or is it implied?** Note that writers often use deductive reasoning in an argument without stating the general principle. They just assume that readers will recognize and agree with the principle. You may want to identify the general principle for yourself.

- **Is the general principle sound?** Don't just assume the general principle is sound. Ask yourself whether it is really true.

- **Is the conclusion valid?** To be valid, a conclusion in a deductive argument must follow logically from the general principle and the specific situation.

The following chart shows two conclusions drawn from the same general principle.

All government offices were closed last Monday.	
Accurate Deduction	**Inaccurate Deduction**
West Post Office is a government office; therefore, West Post Office was closed last Monday.	Soon-Lin's Spa was closed last Monday; therefore, Soon-Lin's Spa is a government office.

Soon-Lin might have closed her spa because there would be fewer customers in town when government offices were closed—or for another reason entirely.

PRACTICE AND APPLY

Identify the mode of reasoning used in the following paragraph.

> About a year ago, Dave Champlin and his two roommates lived in what their friends at the University of Missouri called the House of Fat. . . . By sticking to the low-carb, high-protein diet, Champlin lost about 45 pounds, and his roommates each lost about 50 to 60 pounds. Despite being pleased with the results, all three were off the diet by this past summer and have gained back some of the weight.
>
> A study by NPD Group, an independent marketing information company, found that the percentage of American adults on any low-carb diet in 2004 peaked at 9.1 percent in February and dropped to 4.9 percent by early November. Further, it said only one of four people surveyed was significantly cutting carbs and "virtually none" were reducing carbs as much as the diets recommended.
>
> That means many companies that rode the low-carb wave are either out of business or refocusing their strategies.
>
> —Margaret Stafford, *Associated Press*

Identifying Faulty Reasoning

Sometimes an argument at first appears to make sense but isn't valid because it is based on a fallacy. A **fallacy** is an error in logic. Learn to recognize these common fallacies.

TYPE OF FALLACY	DEFINITION	EXAMPLE
Circular reasoning	Supporting a statement by simply repeating it in different words	Wearing a bicycle helmet should be required because **cyclists should use protective headgear.**
Either/or fallacy	A statement that suggests that there are only two choices available in a situation that really offers more than two options	**Either** you eat a balanced diet, **or** you'll die before you're 50.
Oversimplification	An explanation of a complex situation or problem as if it were much simpler than it is	Shared interests lead to a **successful relationship.**
Overgeneralization	A generalization that is too broad. You can often recognize overgeneralizations by the use of words such as *all, everyone, every time, anything, no one,* and *none.*	**Everyone** wants to go to college.
Stereotyping	A dangerous type of overgeneralization. Stereotypes are broad statements about people on the basis of their gender, ethnicity, race, or political, social, professional, or religious group.	**Men** just don't know how to express their emotions.
Attacking the person or name-calling	An attempt to discredit an idea by attacking the person or group associated with it. Candidates often engage in name-calling during political campaigns.	**Mr. Edmonds drives a beat-up car and never mows his lawn,** so you shouldn't take music lessons from him.
Evading the issue	Refuting an objection with arguments and evidence that do not address its central point	I know I didn't clean up my room, **but that gave me more time to study and improve my grades.**
Non sequitur	A statement that uses irrelevant "proof" to support a claim. A non sequitur is sometimes used to win an argument by diverting the reader's attention to proof that can't be challenged.	I'll probably flunk the driving test. **I was late for school today.**
False cause	The mistake of assuming that because one event occurred after another event in time, the first event caused the second one to occur	Marc wore his new goggles in the swim meet and **as a result won with his best time ever.**
False analogy	A comparison that doesn't hold up because of a critical difference between the two subjects	I bet my little brother will be a great skier when he grows up **because he loves playing on the slide.**
Hasty generalization	A conclusion drawn from too little evidence or from evidence that is biased	**I got sick after eating at the pizzeria,** so Italian food must be bad for me.

Look for examples of logical fallacies in the following argument. Identify each one and explain why you identified it as such.

> Everyone agrees that running is the best form of exercise. All you need is a good pair of shoes and you're ready to hit the road. I've run a mile twice this week, so I should know. As a result, I've slept better and my tone on the clarinet has improved. When you run, your heart beats faster because your pulse rate increases. That means that your cells get more oxygen, which is the second most common gas in the earth's atmosphere. You also get to enjoy the beauty of the world around you as you build up your stamina. So if you don't want to be a hopeless couch potato, get going and run for your life!

5.4 EVALUATING PERSUASIVE TEXTS

Learning how to evaluate persuasive texts and identify bias will help you become more selective when doing research and also help you improve your own reasoning and arguing skills. **Bias** is an inclination for or against a particular opinion or viewpoint. A writer may reveal a strongly positive or negative opinion on an issue by presenting only one way of looking at it or by heavily weighting the evidence on one side of the argument. Additionally, the presence of either of the following is often a sign of bias:

Loaded language consists of words with strongly positive or negative connotations that are intended to influence a reader's attitude.

EXAMPLE: *People who mistreat animals are subhuman and deserve to be locked up for life.* (*Subhuman* and *locked up* have very negative connotations.)

Propaganda is any form of communication that is so distorted that it conveys false or misleading information. Some politicians create and distribute propaganda. Many logical fallacies, such as name-calling, the either/or fallacy, and

false causes, are often used in propaganda. The following example shows an oversimplification. The writer uses one fact to support a particular point of view but does not reveal another fact that does not support that viewpoint.

EXAMPLE: *Since we moved to the city, our gas and electric bills have gone down.* (The writer does not include the fact that the move occurred in the spring, when the demand for heat or air conditioning is low anyway.)

*For more information, see **Identifying Faulty Reasoning**, page R24.*

Strategies for Evaluating Evidence

It is important to have a set of standards by which you can evaluate persuasive texts. Use the questions below to help you critically assess facts and opinions that are presented as evidence.

- **Are the facts presented verifiable?** Facts can be proved by eyewitness accounts, authoritative sources such as encyclopedias and almanacs, experts, or research.

- **Are the opinions presented well informed?** Any opinions offered should be supported by facts, be based on research or eyewitness accounts, or be the opinions of experts on the topic.

- **Is the evidence thorough?** Thorough evidence leaves no reasonable questions unanswered. If a choice is offered, background for making the choice should be provided. If taking a side is called for, all sides of the issue should be presented.

- **Is the evidence biased?** Be alert to evidence that contains loaded language and other signs of bias.

- **Is the evidence authoritative?** The people, groups, or organizations that provided the evidence should have credentials that verify their credibility.

- **Is it important that the evidence be current?** Where timeliness is crucial, as in the areas of medicine and technology, the evidence should reflect the latest developments in the areas.

Read the argument below. Identify the facts, opinion, and elements of bias.

Are you tired of listening to people talking on their cell phones? I think those disgusting machines should be banned. Using the dumb things while driving or riding a bicycle distracts the user and creates a serious hazard. The phones also give off energy frequencies that can cause cancer. Cell phone users in a German study, for example, were three times more likely to develop eye cancer than controls. Another study done in Sweden showed that people who used cell phones for ten years or more increased their risk of brain cancer by 77 percent. Although other researchers found no connection between cell phones and cancer, those studies stink. People should wise up and stop harming themselves and bothering everybody else.

Strategies for Determining a Strong Argument

Make sure that all or most of the following statements are true:

- The argument presents a claim or thesis.

- The claim is connected to its support by a general principle that most readers would readily agree with. Valid general principle: *It is the job of a school to provide a well-rounded physical education program.* Invalid general principle: *It is the job of a school to produce healthy, physically fit people.*

- The reasons make sense.

- The reasons are presented in a logical and effective order.

- The claim and all reasons are adequately supported by sound evidence.

- The evidence is adequate, accurate, and appropriate.

- The logic is sound. There are no instances of faulty reasoning.

- The argument adequately anticipates and addresses reader concerns and counterclaims with counterarguments.

Use the preceding criteria to evaluate the strength of the following editorial.

This school needs a swimming pool. Swimming is the most important skill there is, and I believe it is the responsibility of the school to provide this essential part of students' education.

Everybody knows that the school's mission is to educate the whole person—mind and body—and to prepare students to be productive citizens. In addition to our academic subjects, we are taught how to eat right, budget our money, and drive a car. But since the school doesn't teach us water safety skills, it not only isn't preparing us for life, but it could actually be responsible for our deaths someday.

The community and school board are irresponsible idiots, because they repeatedly have refused to fund the building of a pool. They think that the school has more important needs. As one board member put it, "Students can take swimming lessons at the local health club. A high school isn't a recreation center."

That reason is crazy because it just doesn't make sense. Most students can't afford lessons at the health club; and those who have the money don't have the time. After completing homework, taking part in school activities, and working at weekend jobs, we're lucky to get enough sleep to just keep going.

Students' fitness will improve if we have a pool because swimming keeps you in shape. Even if knowing how to swim never saves your life, it can improve its quality. So either this school gets a pool or the education it offers us will be worthless.

6 Adjusting Reading Rate to Purpose

You may need to change the way you read certain texts in order to understand what you read. To properly adjust the way you read, you need to be aware of what you want to get out of what you are reading. Once you know your purpose for reading, you can adjust the speed at which you read in response to your purpose and the difficulty of the material.

Determine Your Purpose for Reading

You read different types of materials for different purposes. You may read a novel for enjoyment. You may read a textbook unit to learn a new concept or to master the content for a test. When you read for enjoyment, you naturally read at a pace that is comfortable for you. When you read for information, you need to read material more slowly and thoroughly. When you are being tested on material, you may think you have to read fast, especially if the test is being timed. However, you can actually increase your understanding of the material if you slow down.

Determine Your Reading Rate

The rate at which you read most comfortably is called your **independent reading level.** It is the rate that you use to read materials that you enjoy. To learn to adjust your reading rate to read materials for other purposes, you need to be aware of your independent reading level. You can figure out your reading level by following these steps:

1. Select a passage from a book or story you enjoy.
2. Have a friend or classmate time you as you begin reading the passage silently.
3. Read at the rate that is most comfortable for you.
4. Stop when your friend or classmate tells you one minute has passed.
5. Determine the number of words you read in that minute and write down the number.
6. Repeat the process at least two more times, using different passages.
7. Add the numbers and divide the sum by the number of times your friend timed you.

Reading Techniques for Informational Material

Use the following techniques to adapt your reading for informational texts, to prepare for tests, and to better understand what you read:

- **Skimming** is reading quickly to get the general idea of a text. To skim, read only the title, headings, graphic aids, highlighted words, and first sentence of each paragraph. In addition, read any introduction, conclusion, or summary. Skimming can be especially useful when taking a test. Before reading a passage, you can skim questions that follow it in order to find out what is expected and better focus on the important ideas in the text.

  When researching a topic, skimming can help you determine whether a source has information that is pertinent to your topic.

- **Scanning** is reading quickly to find a specific piece of information, such as a fact or a definition. When you scan, your eyes sweep across a page, looking for key words that may lead you to the information you want. Use scanning to review for tests and to find answers to questions.

- **Changing pace** is speeding up or slowing down the rate at which you read parts of a particular text. When you come across familiar concepts, you might be able to speed up without misunderstanding them. When you encounter unfamiliar concepts or material presented in an unpredictable way, however, you may need to slow down to process and absorb the information better.

WATCH OUT! Reading too slowly can affect your ability to comprehend what you read. Make sure you aren't just reading one word at a time.

PRACTICE AND APPLY

Find an article in a magazine or textbook. Skim the article. Then answer the following questions:

1. What did you notice about the organization of the article from skimming it?

2. What is the main idea of the article?

Writing is a process, a journey of discovery in which you can explore your thoughts, experiment with ideas, and search for connections. Through writing, you can explore and record your thoughts, feelings, and ideas for yourself alone or you can communicate them to an audience.

WRITING TOOLS
Go to the **Writing Center** at **ClassZone.com** for interactive models, publishing ideas, and other support.

1 The Writing Process

The writing process consists of the following stages: prewriting, drafting, revising and editing, proofreading, and publishing. These are not stages that you must complete in a set order. Rather, you may return to an earlier stage at any time to improve your writing.

1.1 PREWRITING

In the prewriting stage, you explore what you want to write about, what your purpose for writing is, whom you are writing for, and what form you will use to express your ideas. Ask yourself the following questions to get started.

Topic	• Is my topic assigned, or can I choose it? • What am I interested in writing about?
Purpose	• Am I writing to entertain, to inform, or to persuade—or for some combination of these purposes? • What effect do I want to have on my readers?
Audience	• Who is the audience? • What might the audience members already know about my topic? • What about the topic might interest them?
Format	• Which format will work best? Essay? Poem? Speech? Short story? Article? Research paper?

Find Ideas for Writing
- Browse through magazines, newspapers, and Web sites.
- Start a file of articles you want to save for future reference.
- With a group, brainstorm as many ideas as you can. Compile your ideas into a list.
- Interview someone who is an expert on a particular topic.

- Write down anything that comes into your head.
- Use a cluster map to explore subordinate ideas that relate to a general topic.

Organize Ideas
Once you've chosen a topic, you will need to compile and organize your ideas. If you are writing a description, you may need to gather sensory details. For an essay or a research paper, you may need to record information from different sources. To record notes from sources you read or view, use any or all of these methods:

- **Summarize:** Briefly retell the main ideas of a piece of writing in your own words.
- **Paraphrase:** Restate all or almost all of the information in your own words.
- **Quote:** Record the author's exact words.

Depending on what form your writing takes, you may also need to arrange your ideas in a certain pattern.

*For more information, see the **Writing Handbook**, pages R34–R41.*

1.2 DRAFTING

In the drafting stage, you put your ideas on paper and allow them to develop and change as you write. You don't need to worry about correct grammar and spelling at this stage. There are two ways that you can draft:

Discovery drafting is a good approach when you are not quite sure what you think about your subject. You just start writing and let your feelings and ideas lead you in developing the topic.

Planned drafting may work better if you know that your ideas have to be arranged in a certain way, as in a research paper. Try making a writing plan or an informal outline before you begin drafting.

1.3 REVISING AND EDITING

The revising and editing stage allows you to polish your draft and make changes in its content, organization, and style. Use the questions that follow to assess problems and determine what changes would improve your work.

- Does my writing have a **main idea** or central focus? Is my **thesis** clear?

- Have I used **precise** nouns, verbs, and modifiers?

- Have I incorporated **adequate detail** and **evidence?** Where might I include a telling detail, a revealing statistic, or a vivid example?

- Is my writing **unified?** Do all ideas and supporting details pertain to my main idea or advance my thesis?

- Is my writing clear and **coherent?** Is the flow of sentences and paragraphs smooth and logical?

- Have I used a consistent **point of view?**

- Do I need to add **transitional words, phrases,** or **sentences** to clarify relationships among ideas?

- Have I used a **variety of sentence types?** Are the sentences well constructed? Which ones might I combine to improve the rhythm of my writing?

- Have I used a **tone** appropriate for my audience and purpose?

1.4 PROOFREADING

When you are satisfied with your revision, proofread your paper for mistakes in grammar, usage, and mechanics. You may want to do this several times, looking for a different type of mistake each time. Use the following questions to help you correct errors:

- Have I corrected any errors in **subject-verb agreement** and **pronoun-antecedent agreement?**

- Have I double-checked for errors in **confusing word pairs,** such as *it's/its, than/then,* and *too/to?*

- Have I corrected any **run-on sentences** and **sentence fragments?**

- Have I followed rules for **correct capitalization?**

- Have I used **punctuation marks** correctly?

- Have I checked the **spellings of all unfamiliar words** in the dictionary?

TIP If possible, don't begin proofreading just after you've finished writing. Put your work away for at least a few hours. When you return to it, identifying and correcting mistakes will seem easier.

*For more information, see the **Grammar Handbook** and the **Vocabulary and Spelling Handbook,** pages R46–R75.*

Use the proofreading symbols in the chart to mark changes on your draft.

1.5

Proofreading Symbols	
⋀ Add letters or words.	/ Make a capital letter lowercase.
⊙ Add a period.	⌗ Begin a new paragraph.
≡ Capitalize a letter.	⌫ Delete letters or words.
⊃ Close up space.	∿ Switch the positions of letters or words.
⋀ Add a comma.	

PUBLISHING AND REFLECTING

Always consider sharing your finished writing with a wider audience. Reflecting on your writing is another good way to finish a project.

Publishing Ideas

- Post your writing on a Weblog.

- Create a multimedia presentation and share it with classmates.

- Publish your writing in a school newspaper, local newspaper, or literary magazine.

- Present your work orally in a report, speech, reading, or dramatic performance.

Reflecting on Your Writing

Think about your writing process and whether you would like to add what you have written to your writing portfolio. You might attach a note in which you answer questions like these:

- Which parts of the process did I find easiest? Which parts were more difficult?

- What was the biggest problem I faced during the writing process? How did I solve the problem?

- What changes have occurred in my writing style?

- Have I noticed any features in the writing of

published authors or my peers that I can apply to my own work?

1.6 PEER RESPONSE

Peer response consists of the suggestions and comments you make about the writing of your peers and also the comments and suggestions they make about your writing. You can ask a peer reader for help at any time in the writing process.

Using Peer Response as a Writer

- Indicate whether you are more interested in feedback about your ideas or about your presentation of them.

- Ask questions that will help you get specific information about your writing. Open-ended questions that require more than yes-or-no answers are more likely to give you information you can use as you revise.

- Encourage your readers to be honest.

Being a Peer Reader

- Respect the writer's feelings.

- Offer positive reactions first.

- Make sure you understand what kind of feedback the writer is looking for, and then respond accordingly.

For more information on the writing process, see the **Introductory Unit,** *pages 18–21.*

2 Building Blocks of Good Writing

Whatever your purpose in writing, you need to capture your reader's interest and organize your thoughts clearly.

2.1 INTRODUCTIONS

An introduction should present a thesis statement and capture your reader's attention.

Kinds of Introductions

There are a number of ways to write an introduction. The one you choose depends on who the audience is and on your purpose for writing.

Make a Surprising Statement Beginning with a startling statement or an interesting fact can arouse your reader's curiosity about a subject, as in the following model.

> **MODEL**
>
> September should be the seventh month, and October should be the eighth. Any Latin student knows that the root *septem* is "seven" and *octo* is "eight." Where did the calendar makers go wrong? The truth is that when the months acquired their names, during Roman times, the year started in March.

Provide a Description A vivid description sets a mood and brings a scene to life for your reader.

Here, details about a lion observing possible prey set the tone for an essay on survival in the wild.

> **MODEL**
>
> Cool and cunning eyes followed the impala herd from a sturdy low-slung tree branch. The young female lion watched hungrily to see whether any of the impalas might be sickly or slower than the others. She kept every muscle quiet, though tense and ready to spring if an opportunity arose.

Pose a Question Beginning with a question can make your reader want to read on to find out the answer. The following introduction asks questions about the incredible persistence of racial segregation.

> **MODEL**
>
> How is it possible that as late as the mid-20th century in the United States of America, "the land of the free," riders on public buses were segregated by race? How is it possible that even today there are segregated social events, schools, and towns, no longer segregated by law but with effects just as real and damaging?

Relate an Anecdote Beginning with an anecdote, or brief story, can hook your reader and help you make a point in a dramatic way. The following anecdote introduces an essay about the downside of self-closing shoe straps.

MODEL

My five-year-old nephew, Ali, has never tied a shoelace. All of his shoes have self-closing straps. He is developing his large muscles by throwing and climbing, but I wonder if he will ever have the dexterity to handle bows on packages or ties that he wears with his suits.

Address the Reader Speaking directly to your reader establishes a friendly, informal tone and involves the reader in your topic.

MODEL

If you've ever wondered how to avoid using pesticides in your garden, you can find answers from Natural Gardens, Inc. It's easy to protect the environment and have pest-free plants.

Begin with a Thesis Statement A thesis statement expressing a main idea may be woven into both the beginning and the end of a piece of nonfiction writing. The following is a thesis statement that introduces an essay on the relationship between caring for pets and caring for children.

MODEL

Pet owners who are casual about their pet's health and safety are likely to be the same ones who are casual about the health and safety of their children.

TIP To write the best introduction for your paper, you may want to try more than one of the methods and then decide which is the most effective for your purpose and audience.

2.2 PARAGRAPHS

A paragraph is made up of sentences that work together to develop an idea or accomplish a purpose. Whether or not it contains a topic sentence stating the main idea, a good paragraph must have unity and coherence.

Unity

A paragraph has unity when all the sentences support and develop one stated or implied idea. Use the following techniques to create unity in your paragraphs:

Write a Topic Sentence A topic sentence states the main idea of the paragraph; all other sentences in the paragraph provide supporting details. A topic sentence is often the first sentence in a paragraph. However, it may also appear later in a paragraph or at the end, to summarize or reinforce the main idea, as shown in the model that follows.

MODEL

Plastic that does not rust, rot, or shatter is useful, of course, but does add to the ever-increasing problems of waste disposal. It is possible to add chemicals to plastic that make it dissolvable by other chemicals. There are plastics that slowly disintegrate in sunlight. Biodegradable plastic is available and should be preferred over non-biodegradable plastic.

Relate All Sentences to an Implied Main Idea A paragraph can be unified without a topic sentence as long as every sentence supports an implied, or unstated, main idea. In the example, all the sentences work together to create a unified impression of a swim meet.

MODEL

The swimmers lined up along the edge of the pool. Toes curled over the edge, arms swung back in the ready position, and bodies leaned forward. The swimmers' eyes looked straight ahead. Their ears were alert for the starting signal.

Coherence

A paragraph is coherent when all its sentences are related to one another and each flows logically to the next. The following techniques will help you achieve coherence in paragraphs:

- Present your ideas in the most logical order.
- Use pronouns, synonyms, and repeated words to connect ideas.
- Use transitional devices to show relationships among ideas.

In the model shown here, the writer used some of these techniques to create a unified paragraph.

MODEL

As we experience day and night repeatedly, it is hard to imagine the enormous significance of that change. We have day and night because our planet rotates on its axis. We have seasons because Earth revolves around our solar system's star, the sun. Our solar system, along with many others, rotates with the Milky Way Galaxy. The universe is a gigantic structure of which our daily experiences of day and night, summer and winter are tiny parts.

2.3 TRANSITIONS

Transitions are words and phrases that show connections between details. Clear transitions help show how your ideas relate to one another.

Kinds of Transitions

The types of transitions you choose depend on the ideas you want to convey.

Time or Sequence Some transitions help to clarify the sequence of events over time. When you are telling a story or describing a process, you can connect ideas with such transitional words as *first, second, always, then, next, later, soon, before, finally, after, earlier, afterward,* and *tomorrow.*

MODEL

Teaching a puppy to come when called takes patience from the owner and the puppy. First, tie a lightweight rope to the dog's collar and go to a large play area. Play with the pup a while and then call to it. At the same time, pull gently on the rope. Always praise the puppy for coming when called. Next, allow the puppy to play again. Carry out this exercise several times a day.

Spatial Relationships Transitional words and phrases such as *in front, behind, next to, along, nearest, lowest, above, below, underneath, on the left,* and *in the middle* can help your reader visualize a scene.

MODEL

On the porch, wicker chairs stand in casual disorder along the red wall of the house. Next to the red-and-white porch railing, orange day lilies nod in the breeze. Overhead, a flycatcher perches on a bare branch, alert for her next meal. Beyond the lawn, a small stream flows from beneath an arched stone bridge.

Degree of Importance Transitional words such as *mainly, strongest, weakest, first, second, most important, least important, worst,* and *best* may be used to rank ideas or to show degrees of importance.

MODEL

The Repertory Theater performed six plays last year. All the plays were exciting, but the most outstanding one was *Master Class.*

Compare and Contrast Words and phrases such as *similarly, likewise, also, like, as, neither . . . nor,* and *either . . . or* show similarity between details. *However, by contrast, yet, but, unlike, instead, whereas,* and *while* show difference. Note the use of both types of transitions in the model.

MODEL

Dr. Herriot was a successful veterinarian. Mrs. Donovan also took care of sick animals. He cured his patients with medical treatments and laboratory medications. Mrs. Donovan, by contrast, used home remedies and constant affection.

TIP Both *but* and *however* can be used to join two independent clauses. When *but* is used as a coordinating conjunction, it is preceded by a comma. When *however* is used as a conjunctive adverb, it is preceded by a semicolon and followed by a comma.

Cause and Effect When you are writing about a cause-effect relationship, use transitional words and phrases such as *since, because, thus, therefore, so, due to, for this reason,* and *as a result* to help clarify that relationship and make your writing coherent.

> **MODEL**
>
> Because we never feed our dog from the table, she doesn't beg for food while we are eating. We are happy to take credit for her one good habit.

2.4 CONCLUSIONS

A conclusion should leave readers with a strong final impression.

Kinds of Conclusions

Good conclusions sum up ideas in a variety of ways. Here are some techniques you might try:

Restate Your Thesis A good way to conclude an essay is by restating your thesis, or main idea, in different words. The following conclusion restates the thesis introduced on page R31.

> **MODEL**
>
> Although each pet has a personality of its own just as each child does, there are many ways of encouraging the best behavior in each. Love, persistence, patience, and consistency make all the difference in training pets as well as in raising children.

Ask a Question Try asking a question that sums up what you have said and gives your reader something new to think about. The following question concludes an appeal to support a local politician.

> **MODEL**
>
> Have you noticed that the roads are in better repair and that there are more safe playgrounds and parks since Mayor Ballwin has been in office?

Make a Recommendation When you are persuading your audience to take a position on an issue, you can conclude by recommending a specific course of action.

> **MODEL**
>
> You can make your research work much easier by taking advantage of the Internet. Develop a list of key words that will help you narrow your search of the Internet.

Make a Prediction Readers are concerned about matters that may affect them and therefore are moved by a conclusion that predicts the future.

> **MODEL**
>
> If the government continues to spend money from Social Security taxes for current operations, we will create a disastrous burden of debt for future generations.

Summarize Your Information Summarizing reinforces your main idea, leaving a strong, lasting impression. The model concludes with a statement that summarizes a film review.

> **MODEL**
>
> The movie *The Postman* shows the tremendous influence of the Chilean poet Pablo Neruda on a young Italian man—not only in his love life but also in his acquired self-confidence and his dedication to a cause.

2.5 ELABORATION

Elaboration is the process of developing an idea by providing specific supporting details that are relevant and appropriate to the purpose and form of your writing.

Facts and Statistics A fact is a statement that can be verified, and a statistic is a fact expressed as a number. Make sure the facts and statistics you supply are from reliable, up-to-date sources.

MODEL

Our entire solar system speeds through the Milky Way Galaxy at a speed of 180 miles a second. One could worry about the ability of any of us to stay in place with our feet on the ground. Or one could marvel at the magnificence of a universe that keeps everything whirling with such constancy.

Sensory Details Details that show how something looks, sounds, tastes, smells, or feels can enliven a description, making readers feel they are actually experiencing what you are describing.

MODEL

The campers hardly dared to breathe inside their tent as they considered the power of the massive beast they'd glimpsed through the tent flap. Snuffling and crackling brought news that the black bear had found something delectable inside the garbage can.

Incidents From our earliest years, we are interested in hearing stories. One way to illustrate a point powerfully is to relate an incident or tell a story, as shown in the example.

MODEL

January 24, 1848, began one of the most colorful periods of United States history. On that day James Marshall found gold at Sutter's Mill in California. That discovery brought on massive immigration from around the world. It also brought many new images and words—*gold rush, gold miners,* and *forty-niners,* to name a few.

Examples An example can help make an abstract idea concrete or can serve to clarify a complex point for your reader.

MODEL

The mere mention of the names of some writers causes distinct reactions, even from those who have not read the writers' works. For example, the mention of William Shakespeare causes many people to take in a sharp breath of admiration and others to think of something long and tedious.

Quotations Choose quotations that clearly support your points, and be sure that you copy each quotation word for word. Remember always to credit the source.

MODEL

In her book *How to Talk to Your Cat,* Patricia Moyes replies to certain authorities who claim that cats cannot smile: "I can only presume that these people have never owned a cat in the true sense of the word." She describes the cat's smile as a "relaxed upward tilting of the corners of the mouth."

3 Descriptive Writing

Descriptive writing allows you to paint word pictures about anything, from events of global importance to the most personal feelings. It is an essential part of almost every piece of writing.

> **RUBRIC: Standards for Writing**
>
> **Successful descriptive writing should**
> - have a clear focus and sense of purpose
> - use sensory details and precise words to create a vivid image, establish a mood, or express emotion
> - present details in a logical order

3.1 KEY TECHNIQUES

Consider Your Goals What do you want to accomplish with your description? Do you want to show why something is important to you? Do you want to make a person or scene more memorable? Do you want to explain an event?

Identify Your Audience Who will read your description? How familiar are they with your subject? What background information will they need? Which details will they find most interesting?

Think Figuratively What figures of speech might help make your description vivid and interesting? What simile or metaphor comes to mind? What imaginative comparisons can you make? What living thing does an inanimate object remind you of?

Gather Sensory Details Which sights, smells, tastes, sounds, and textures make your subject come alive? Which details stick in your mind when you observe or recall your subject? Which senses does it most strongly affect?

You might want to use a chart like the one shown here to collect sensory details about your subject.

Sights	Sounds	Textures	Smells	Tastes

Create a Mood What feelings do you want to evoke in your readers? Do you want to soothe them with comforting images? Do you want to build tension with ominous details? Do you want to evoke sadness or joy?

3.2 OPTIONS FOR ORGANIZATION

Option 1: Spatial Order Choose one of these options to show the spatial order of elements in a scene you are describing.

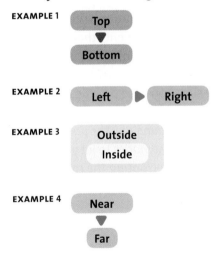

EXAMPLE 1

Top ▼ Bottom

EXAMPLE 2

Left ▶ Right

EXAMPLE 3

Outside / Inside

EXAMPLE 4

Near ▼ Far

MODEL

Thunder's nostrils quivered as he was led into the barn. How would this be as a place to spend nights from now on? In the stall to the left, the straw smelled fresh. Beyond that stall, a saddle hung from rough boards. To the right of his stall was another, from which a mare looked at him curiously.

Option 2: Order of Impression Order of impression is the order in which you notice details.

What first catches your attention ▼ What you notice next ▼ What you see after that ▼ What you focus on last

MODEL

As her foot slipped on the pebbles, her first thought was of whether she would sprain an ankle sliding into the surf. Her heart began a dangerous thumping, but soon the soft sand provided a comfortable seat so that her body responded by calming down. She realized that the water was shallow and warm. Her hat would shade her eyes and prevent sunburn.

TIP Use transitions that help readers understand the order of the impressions you are describing. Some useful transitions are *after, next, during, first, before, finally,* and *then.*

Option 3: Order of Importance You can use order of importance as the organizing structure for a description.

Least important ▼ More important ▼ Most important

MODEL

I checked my backpack for the comforting essentials. Book? Yes. Journal and pencil? Yes. Water bottle? Yes. Tissues? Yes. Then I checked for the required essentials. Passport? Yes. Airline ticket? Yes. Map? Yes. Last of all, I checked the most important possessions for this trip—a light heart and a sense of adventure. I was beginning my first real vacation.

*For more information, see **Transitions,** page R32.*

❹ Narrative Writing

Narrative writing tells a story. If you write a story from your imagination, it is a fictional narrative. A true story is a nonfictional narrative. Narrative writing can be found in short stories, novels, news articles, personal narratives, and biographies.

> **RUBRIC: Standards for Writing**
>
> **A successful narrative should**
>
> - hook the reader's attention with a strong introduction
> - include descriptive details and dialogue to develop the characters, setting, and plot
> - have a clear beginning, middle, and end
> - have a logical organization, with clues and transitions that help the reader understand the order of events
> - maintain a consistent tone and point of view
> - use language that is appropriate to the audience
> - demonstrate the significance of events or ideas

For more information, see **Writing Workshop: Autobiographical Narrative,** *pages 264–271, and* **Writing Workshop: Short Story,** *pages 368–375.*

4.1 KEY TECHNIQUES

Identify the Main Events What are the most important events in your narrative? Is each event needed to tell the story?

Describe the Setting When do the events occur? Where do they take place? How can you use setting to create mood and to set the stage for the characters and their actions?

Depict Characters Vividly What do your characters look like? What do they think and say? How do they act? What details can show what they are like?

> **TIP** Dialogue is an effective means of developing characters in a narrative. As you write dialogue, choose words that express your characters' personalities and that show how the characters feel about one another and about the events in the plot.

4.2 OPTIONS FOR ORGANIZATION

Option 1: Chronological Order One way to organize a piece of narrative writing is to arrange the events in chronological order, as shown in the following example.

EXAMPLE

It is the middle of March in Rome. It is also the first time that young Marius has been able to go into the city.

> **Introduction**
> *Characters and setting*

A crowd gathers to watch the senators arrive. Marius hurries toward the front of the crowd.

> **Event 1**

Marius sees that the emperor has arrived. There is great commotion, with shouts and screams.

> **Event 2**

Marius witnesses the assassination of Julius Caesar. He then goes home with a premonition that there are bad times ahead for Rome.

> **End**
> *Perhaps showing the significance of the events*

Option 2: Flashback In narrative writing, it is also possible to introduce events that happened sometime before the beginning of the story. You can use a flashback to show how past events led up to the present situation or to provide background about a character or event. Use clue words such as *last summer, as a young girl, the previous school year,* and *his earliest memories* to let your reader know that you are interrupting the main action to describe earlier events.

Notice how the flashback interrupts the action in the model.

MODEL

Greg and his friends rejoiced at being the first in line to buy the coveted concert tickets. Greg remembered when his favorite band came to town two years ago. Then, when he and his friends approached the ticket office, the line was five blocks long.

Option 3: Focus on Conflict When a fictional narrative focuses on a central conflict, the story's plot may be organized as shown in the following example.

EXAMPLE

A railroad porter notices a woman boarding the train and pulling along a young child.

> **Describe main characters and setting.**

The porter senses that the child is frightened, so he finds several excuses to appear at their compartment door. When he hears the child crying, he goes to the compartment and sees the glint of gunmetal inside a partially open market basket.

> **Present conflict.**

The porter begins to plan how to identify the woman and child and to separate the child from the woman.

- The porter finds out from a radio news report that a child has been kidnapped.
- He befriends the pair and offers to play with the child while the woman visits the dining car.
- He alerts the police, who then wait at an unscheduled stop.

> **Relate events that make conflict complex and cause characters to change.**

When the train stops, the woman becomes suspicious and begins to search the train for the child. She spots the porter with the child and fires her gun in his direction. Though wounded, the porter manages to throw the child from the train into the arms of a federal agent.

> **Present resolution or outcome of conflict.**

5 Expository Writing

Expository writing informs and explains. You can use it to evaluate the effects of a new law, to compare two movies, to analyze a piece of literature, or to examine the problem of greenhouse gases in the atmosphere. There are many types of expository writing. Think about your topic and select the type that presents the information most clearly.

5.1 COMPARISON AND CONTRAST

Compare-and-contrast writing examines the similarities and differences between two or more subjects. You might, for example, compare and contrast two short stories, the main characters in a novel, or two movies.

> **RUBRIC: Standards for Writing**
>
> **Successful compare-and-contrast writing should**
>
> - hook the reader's attention with a strong introduction
> - clearly identify the subjects that are being compared and contrasted
> - include specific, relevant details
> - follow a clear plan of organization
> - use language and details appropriate to the audience
> - use transitional words and phrases to clarify similarities and differences

Options for Organization

Compare-and-contrast writing can be organized in different ways. The examples that follow demonstrate point-by-point organization and subject-by-subject organization.

Option 1: Point-by-Point Organization

EXAMPLE

I. How true smiles and false smiles are alike   **Point 1**

    Subject A. True smiles; show pleasure; corners of mouth curve up

    Subject B. False smiles; show pleasure; corners of mouth curve up

II. How true smiles and false smiles are different   **Point 2**

    Subject A. True smiles; cheeks move up; no furrow between eyebrows; crow's-feet form

    Subject B. False smiles; cheeks may move up; furrow between eyebrows; no crow's-feet

Option 2: Subject-by-Subject Organization

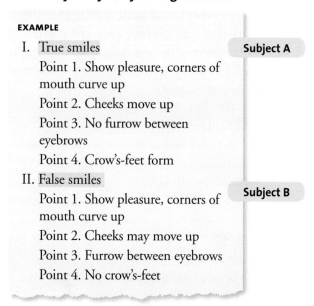

EXAMPLE

I. True smiles — **Subject A**
 Point 1. Show pleasure, corners of mouth curve up
 Point 2. Cheeks move up
 Point 3. No furrow between eyebrows
 Point 4. Crow's-feet form

II. False smiles — **Subject B**
 Point 1. Show pleasure, corners of mouth curve up
 Point 2. Cheeks may move up
 Point 3. Furrow between eyebrows
 Point 4. No crow's-feet

For more information, see **Writing Workshop: Interpretive Essay,** *pages 142–149,* **Writing Workshop: Comparison-Contrast Essay,** *pages 464–471,* **Cause-and-Effect Essay,** *pages 554–561,* **Informative Essay and Interview,** *pages 940–947, and* **Comparing a Play and a Film,** *pages 1194–1201.*

5.2 CAUSE AND EFFECT

Cause-effect writing explains why something happened, why certain conditions exist, or what resulted from an action or a condition. You might use cause-effect writing to explain a character's actions, the progress of a disease, or the outcome of a war.

RUBRIC: Standards for Writing

Successful cause-effect writing should

- hook the reader's attention with a strong introduction
- clearly state the cause-and-effect relationship
- show clear connections between causes and effects
- present causes and effects in a logical order and use transitions effectively
- use facts, examples, and other details to illustrate each cause and effect
- use language and details appropriate to the audience

Options for Organization

Your organization will depend on your topic and your purpose for writing.

Option 1: Effect-to-Cause Organization If you want to explain the causes of an event, such as the closing of a factory, you might first state the effect and then examine its causes.

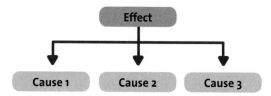

Option 2: Cause-to-Effect Organization If your focus is on explaining the effects of an event, such as the passage of a law, you might first state the cause and then explain the effects.

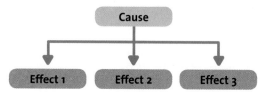

Option 3: Cause-Effect Chain Organization Sometimes you'll want to describe a chain of cause-effect relationships to explore a topic, such as the disappearance of tropical rain forests or the development of home computers.

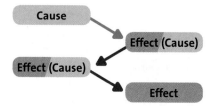

For an example of cause-effect writing, see page R11.

TIP Don't assume that a cause-effect relationship exists just because one event follows another. Look for evidence that the later event could not have happened if the first event had not caused it.

5.3 PROBLEM-SOLUTION

Problem-solution writing clearly states a problem, analyzes the problem, and proposes a solution to the problem. It can be used to identify and solve a conflict between characters, investigate global warming, or tell why the home team keeps losing.

RUBRIC: Standards for Writing

Successful problem-solution writing should

- hook the reader's attention with a strong introduction
- identify the problem and help the reader understand the issues involved
- analyze the causes and effects of the problem
- include quotations, facts, and statistics
- explore possible solutions to the problem and recommend the best one(s)
- use language, details, and a tone appropriate to the audience

Options for Organization

Your organization will depend on the goal of your problem-solution piece, your intended audience, and the specific problem you have chosen to address. The organizational methods that follow are effective for different kinds of problem-solution writing.

Option 1: Simple Problem-Solution

Description of problem and why it needs to be solved

▼

Recommended solution

▼

Explanation of solution

▼

Conclusion

Option 2: Deciding Between Solutions

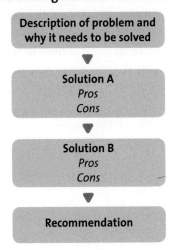

Description of problem and why it needs to be solved

▼

Solution A
Pros
Cons

▼

Solution B
Pros
Cons

▼

Recommendation

5.4 ANALYSIS

In writing an analysis, you explain how something works, how it is defined, or what its parts are.

RUBRIC: Standards for Writing

A successful analysis should

- hook the reader's attention with a strong introduction
- clearly define the subject and its parts
- use a specific organizing structure to provide a logical flow of information
- show connections among facts and ideas through transitional words and phrases
- use language and details appropriate for the audience

Options for Organization

Organize your details in a logical order appropriate to the kind of analysis you're writing. Use one of the following options:

Option 1: Process Analysis A process analysis is usually organized chronologically, with steps or stages in the order they occur. You might use a process analysis to explain how to bake a pie or prepare for a test, or to explain how Arthurian legends have been reinterpreted.

EXAMPLE

Arthurian legends reinterpreted

British ruler in 500s

Step 1: Around 1469, *Le Morte d'Arthur* is compiled.

Step 2: Between 1842 and 1885, *Idylls of the King* is published.

Step 3: In 1960, the musical *Camelot* opens.

> Introduce process.
>
> Give background.
>
> Explain steps.

Option 2: Definition Analysis You can organize the details of a definition analysis in order of importance or impression. Use a definition analysis to explain a quality (such as honor or loyalty), the distinguishing features of a sonnet, or the parts of the brain.

EXAMPLE

Honor

Honor defined as integrity, dignity, and pride.

Quality 1: Integrity

Quality 2: Dignity

Quality 3: Pride

> Introduce term and definition.
>
> Explain features.

Option 3: Parts Analysis The following parts analysis explores three elements of a medieval knight's code of chivalry.

EXAMPLE

Code of chivalry

Part 1: Uphold to Christianity

Part 2: Protect the defenseless

Part 3: Fight injustices, never surrender

> Introduce subject.
>
> Explain parts.

*For more information, see **Writing Workshop: Critical Review,** pages 828–835.*

6 Persuasive Writing

Persuasive writing allows you to use the power of language to inform and influence others. It includes speeches, persuasive essays, newspaper editorials, advertisements, and critical reviews.

> **RUBRIC: Standards for Writing**
>
> **Successful persuasive writing should**
>
> - hook the reader's attention with a strong introduction
> - state the issue and the writer's position
> - give opinions and support them with facts or reasons
> - have a reasonable and respectful tone
> - answer opposing views
> - use sound logic and effective language
> - conclude by summing up reasons or calling for action

*For more information, see **Writing Workshop: Editorial,** pages 670–677, and **Writing Workshop: Persuasive Essay,** pages 1064–1071.*

6.1 KEY TECHNIQUES

Clarify Your Position What do you believe about the issue? How can you express your opinion most clearly?

Know Your Audience Who will read your writing? What do they already know and believe about the issue? What objections to your position might they have? What additional information might they need? What tone and approach would be most effective?

Support Your Opinion Why do you feel the way you do about the issue? What facts, statistics, examples, quotations, anecdotes, or expert opinions support your view? What reasons will convince your readers? What evidence can answer their objections?

Support for Your Argument	
Statistics	facts that are stated in numbers
Examples	specific instances that explain points
Observations	events or situations you yourself have seen
Anecdotes	brief stories that illustrate points
Quotations	direct statements from authorities

For more information, see **Identifying Faulty Reasoning,** *page R24.*

Begin and End with a Bang How can you hook your readers and make a lasting impression? What memorable quotation, anecdote, or statistic will catch their attention at the beginning or stick in their minds at the end? What strong summary or call to action can you conclude with?

MODEL

Beginning

A recent research report finds there is more rain on weekends than during the week. Scientists attribute this to the extra work week pollution that builds throughout the week.

End

We need to plan for more carpooling, efficient heating and cooling, and consolidation of some bus schedules to improve our air quality—and provide better weekend weather.

6.2 OPTIONS FOR ORGANIZATION

In a two-sided persuasive essay, you want to show the weaknesses of the other opinion as you explain the strengths of your own.

Option 1: Reasons for Your Opinion

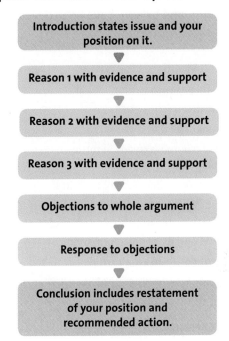

Option 2: Point-by-Point Basis

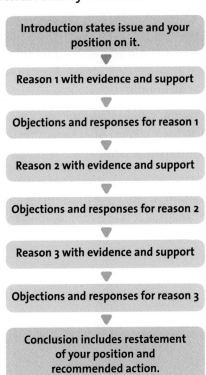

7 Workplace and Technical Writing

Business writing is writing done in a workplace to support the work of a company or business. Several types of formats, such as memos, letters, e-mails, applications, and bylaws, have been developed to make business communication easier.

> **RUBRIC: Standards for Writing**
>
> **Successful business writing should**
>
> - be courteous
> - use language that is geared to its audience
> - state the purpose clearly in the opening sentences or paragraph
> - have a formal tone and not contain slang, contractions, or sentence fragments
> - use precise words
> - present only essential information
> - present details in a logical order
> - conclude with a summary of important points

7.1 KEY TECHNIQUES

Think About Your Purpose Why are you doing this writing? Do you want to promote yourself to a college admissions committee or a job interviewer? Do you want to order or complain about a product? Do you want to set up a meeting or respond to someone's ideas? Are you writing bylaws for an organization?

Identify Your Audience Who will read your writing? What background information will they need? What tone or language is appropriate?

Use a Pattern of Organization That Is Appropriate to the Content If you have to compare and contrast two products in a memo, you can use the same compare-and-contrast organization that you would use in an essay.

Support Your Points What specific details might clarify your ideas? What reasons do you have for your statements?

Finish Strongly How can you best sum up your statements? What is your main point? What action do you want the recipients to take?

Revise and Proofread Your Writing Just as you are graded on the quality of an essay you write for a class, you will be judged on the quality of your writing in the workplace.

7.2 MATCHING THE FORMAT TO THE OCCASION

E-mail messages, memos, and letters have similar purposes but are used in different situations. The chart shows how each format can be used.

Format	Occasion
Memo	Use to send correspondence **inside** the workplace only.
E-mail message	Use to send correspondence **inside or outside** the company.
Letter	Use to send correspondence **outside** the company.

TIP Memos are often sent as e-mail messages in the workplace. Remember that both require formal language and standard spelling, capitalization, and punctuation.

PRACTICE AND APPLY

Refer to the documents on page R43 to complete the following:

1. Draft a response to the letter. Then revise your letter as necessary according to the rubric at the beginning of this section. Make sure you have included the necessary information and have written in an appropriate tone. Proofread your letter for grammatical errors and spelling mistakes. Follow the format of the model and use appropriate spacing between elements.

2. Write a memo in response to the memo. Tell the recipient what actions you have taken. Follow the format of the model.

7.3 FORMATS

Business letters usually have a formal tone and a specific format as shown below. The key to writing a business letter is to get to the point as quickly as possible and to present your information clearly.

MODEL: BUSINESS LETTER

#1 Andover Lane
Sunnydale, CA 93933
July 16, 2010

Customer Service Representative
Bionic Bikes, Inc.
12558 Industrial Drive
Schaumburg, IL 60193
Dear Customer Service Representative:

 I was really pleased to get a Bionic Bike for my birthday in March. I've ridden it every day—to school, to the rec center, and everywhere.

 The bike is great, but the handlebars are not comfortable. I think you should raise the angle of the hand grips about two inches so that riders can hold them comfortably while looking straight ahead.

 Thank you for considering my suggestion.

Sincerely yours,
Marisa LaPorta
Marisa LaPorta

Heading
Where the letter comes from and when

Inside address
To whom the letter is being sent

Salutation
Greeting

Body
Text of the message

Closing

Memos are often used in workplaces as a way of conveying information in a direct and concise manner. They can be used to announce or summarize meetings and to request actions or specific information.

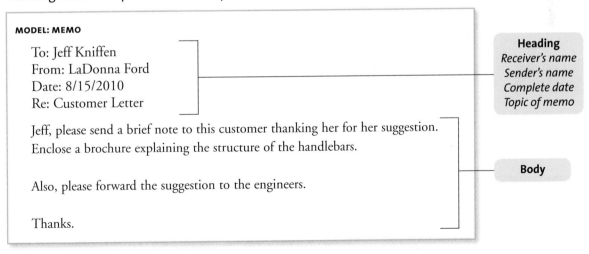

MODEL: MEMO

To: Jeff Kniffen
From: LaDonna Ford
Date: 8/15/2010
Re: Customer Letter

Jeff, please send a brief note to this customer thanking her for her suggestion. Enclose a brochure explaining the structure of the handlebars.

Also, please forward the suggestion to the engineers.

Thanks.

Heading
Receiver's name
Sender's name
Complete date
Topic of memo

Body

TIP Don't forget to write the topic of your memo in the subject line. This will help the receiver determine the importance of your memo.

When you apply for a job, you may be asked to fill out an application form. Application forms vary, but most of them ask for similar kinds of information. If you are mailing your application, you may want to include a brief letter.

EMPLOYMENT APPLICATION

PERSONAL INFORMATION

LAST NAME *Kohl*	FIRST NAME *Rachel*	MIDDLE NAME *Elaine*	IF UNDER 18. AGE *16*
STREET ADDRESS *3240 Maple Dr.*	CITY *St. Augustine*	STATE *FL*	ZIP *32080*

IF EMPLOYED, AND YOU ARE UNDER 16, CAN YOU FURNISH A WORK PERMIT? YES / NO   *YES*

TELEPHONE NUMBER *904/555-1234*	SOCIAL SECURITY NUMBER *525-88-0723*

POSITIONS APPLIED FOR: FULL TIME _____   PART TIME *X*   TEMPORARY _____

EDUCATION

	NAME OF SCHOOL AND ADDRESS	GRADUATED? YES / NO	NUMBER OF YEARS COMPLETED
HIGH SCHOOL	*Riverside High School*	*No*	*2*
COLLEGE			

AVAILIBILITY: PLEASE LIST ALL TIMES AVAILABLE TO WORK

SUN	MON	TUES	WED	THURS	FRI	SAT
9a.m.–5p.m.					*5p.m.–9p.m.*	*9a.m.–5p.m.*

REFERENCES

NAME	OCCUPATION	COMPANY	TELEPHONE NUMBER
Monica Lewis	*Teacher*	*Riverside High*	*904/555-6789*

PRACTICE AND APPLY

Refer to the documents on pages R44 and R45 to complete the following:

1. Visit a business and request an employment application for a job you would like to have. Make sure you understand what each question is asking before you begin to write. Fill out the application as neatly and completely as possible.

2. Write a set of bylaws for an organization that you already belong to or one that you would like to form. Follow the format of the document on page R45.

Sometimes you may have to write technical documents, such as a list of procedures for conducting a meeting, a manual on rules of behavior, or the minutes of a meeting. These documents contain written descriptions of rules, regulations, and meetings and enable organizations and businesses to run smoothly.

These bylaws for an astronomy club include a description of the organization and detailed information about how the club operates. The writer began each section with a heading so that readers could easily find information. The writer was also very specific so that readers would not misunderstand the rules.

MODEL: BYLAWS DOCUMENT

North High School Astronomy Club Bylaws

PURPOSE

1. To understand astronomy
2. To make science enjoyable
3. To inform the school and the community about astronomy

MEMBERSHIP REQUIREMENTS

To qualify for membership, a candidate must

1. be a student at North High School
2. participate in all club fundraisers
3. assist in the production of the newsletter

MEETINGS AND RULES OF ORDER

1. Meetings will be held once a month on a day designated by the vote of the regular membership.
2. Meetings will be held in the Science Lab.
3. All meetings will be conducted according to Robert's Rules of Order.
4. A quorum of seven members must be present for discussion of business items and voting.
5. All officers are voting members of the astronomy club; however, the President votes only when there is a tie.

OFFICERS AND THEIR DUTIES

1. The astronomy club will be governed by a panel of officers elected at the start of each school year.
2. Elected officers will consist of President, Vice-President, Secretary, and Treasurer.
3. Officers will meet twice a month.
4. An officers' meeting requires the attendance of either the President or the Vice-President and the Secretary and Treasurer.
5. Officers may appoint heads to any committee.
6. The President will preside over regular and special meetings.
7. The Vice-President will guide activities of appointed committees.
8. The Secretary will record and distribute meeting minutes.
9. The Treasurer will be responsible for all money collected by the club.

Writing that has a lot of mistakes can confuse or even annoy a reader. A business letter with a punctuation error might lead to a miscommunication and delay a reply. Or a sentence fragment might lower your grade on an essay. Paying attention to grammar, punctuation, and capitalization rules can make your writing clearer and easier to read.

Quick Reference: Parts of Speech

PART OF SPEECH	FUNCTION	EXAMPLES
Noun	names a person, a place, a thing, an idea, a quality, or an action	
Common	serves as a general name, or a name common to an entire group	boat, anchor, water, sky
Proper	names a specific, one-of-a-kind person, place, or thing	Nile River, Acapulco, Swahili
Singular	refers to a single person, place, thing, or idea	map, berry, deer, mouse
Plural	refers to more than one person, place, thing, or idea	maps, berries, deer, mice
Concrete	names something that can be perceived by the senses	stone, crate, wall, knife
Abstract	names something that cannot be perceived by the senses	courage, caution, tyranny, importance
Compound	expresses a single idea through a combination of two or more words	toothbrush, sister-in-law, South Carolina
Collective	refers to a group of people or things	herd, family, team, staff
Possessive	shows who or what owns something	Kenya's, Les's, women's, waitresses'
Pronoun	takes the place of a noun or another pronoun	
Personal	refers to the person making a statement, the person(s) being addressed, or the person(s) or thing(s) the statement is about	I, me, my, mine, we, us, our, ours, you, your, yours, she, he, it, her, him, hers, his, its, they, them, their, theirs
Reflexive	follows a verb or preposition and refers to a preceding noun or pronoun	myself, yourself, herself, himself, itself, ourselves, yourselves, themselves
Intensive	emphasizes a noun or another pronoun	(same as reflexives)
Demonstrative	points to one or more specific persons or things	this, that, these, those
Interrogative	signals a question	who, whom, whose, which, what
Indefinite	refers to one or more persons or things not specifically mentioned	both, all, most, many, anyone, everybody, several, none, some
Relative	introduces an adjective clause by relating it to a word in the clause	who, whom, whose, which, that

PART OF SPEECH	FUNCTION	EXAMPLES
Verb	expresses an action, a condition, or a state of being	
Action	tells what the subject does or did, physically or mentally	run, reaches, listened, consider, decides, dreamed
Linking	connects the subject to something that identifies or describes it	am, is, are, was, were, sound, taste, appear, feel, become, remain, seem
Auxiliary	precedes the main verb in a verb phrase	be, have, do, can, could, will, would, may, might
Transitive	directs the action toward someone or something; always has an object	Mom **broke** the plate.
Intransitive	does not direct the action toward someone or something; does not have an object	The plate **broke.**
Adjective	modifies a noun or pronoun	**frightened** man, **two** epics, **enough** time
Adverb	modifies a verb, an adjective, or another adverb	walked **out, really** funny, **far** away
Preposition	relates one word to another word	at, by, for, from, in, of, on, to, with
Conjunction	joins words or word groups	
Coordinating	joins words or word groups used the same way	and, but, or, for, so, yet, nor
Correlative	used as a pair to join words or word groups used the same way	both . . . and, either . . . or, neither . . . nor
Subordinating	introduces a clause that cannot stand by itself as a complete sentence	although, after, as, before, because, when, if, unless
Interjection	expresses emotion	whew, yikes, uh-oh

Quick Reference: The Sentence and Its Parts

The diagrams that follow will give you a brief review of the essentials of a sentence and some of its parts.

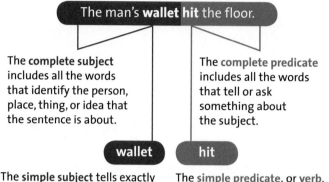

The man's wallet hit the floor.

The **complete subject** includes all the words that identify the person, place, thing, or idea that the sentence is about.

The **complete predicate** includes all the words that tell or ask something about the subject.

wallet

hit

The **simple subject** tells exactly whom or what the sentence is about. It may be one word or a group of words, but it does not include modifiers.

The **simple predicate**, or **verb**, tells what the subject does or is. It may be one word or several, but it does not include modifiers.

Every word in a sentence is part of a complete subject or a complete predicate.

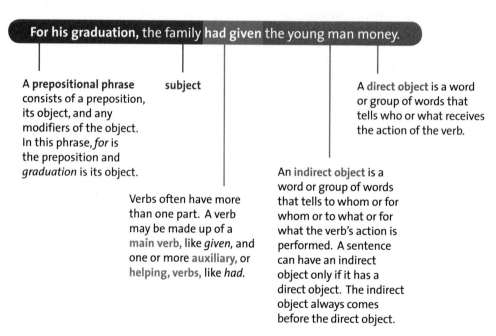

For his graduation, the family had given the young man money.

A **prepositional phrase** consists of a preposition, its object, and any modifiers of the object. In this phrase, *for* is the preposition and *graduation* is its object.

subject

A **direct object** is a word or group of words that tells who or what receives the action of the verb.

Verbs often have more than one part. A verb may be made up of a **main verb**, like *given*, and one or more **auxiliary**, or **helping**, **verbs**, like *had*.

An **indirect object** is a word or group of words that tells to whom or for whom or to what or for what the verb's action is performed. A sentence can have an indirect object only if it has a direct object. The indirect object always comes before the direct object.

Quick Reference: Punctuation

MARK	FUNCTION	EXAMPLES
End Marks period, question mark, exclamation point	ends a sentence	The games begin today. Who is your favorite contestant? What a play Jamie made!
period	follows an initial or abbreviation **Exception:** postal abbreviations of states	Prof. Ted Bakerman, D. H. Lawrence, Houghton Mifflin Co., P.M., A.D., oz., ft., Blvd., St. NE (Nebraska), NV (Nevada)
period	follows a number or letter in an outline	I. Volcanoes A. Central-vent 1. Shield
Comma	separates parts of a compound sentence	I have never disliked poetry, but now I really love it.
	separates items in a series	She is brave, loyal, and kind.
	separates adjectives of equal rank that modify the same noun	The slow, easy route is best.
	sets off a term of address	O Wind, if winter comes . . . Come to the front, children.
	sets off a parenthetical expression	Hard workers, as you know, don't quit. I'm not a quitter, believe me.
	sets off an introductory word, phrase, or dependent clause	Yes, I forgot my key. At the beginning of the day, I feel fresh. While she was out, I was here. Having finished my chores, I went out.
	sets off a nonessential phrase or clause	Ed Pawn, the captain of the chess team, won. Ed Pawn, who is the captain, won. The two leading runners, sprinting toward the finish line, finished in a tie.
	sets off parts of dates and addresses	Send it by August 18, 2010, to Cherry Jubilee, Inc., 21 Vernona St., Oakland, Minnesota.
	follows the salutation and closing of a letter	Dear Jim, Sincerely yours,
	separates words to avoid confusion	By noon, time had run out. What the minister does, does matter. While cooking, Jim burned his hand.
Semicolon	separates items that contain commas in a series	We invited my sister, Jan; her boyfriend, Don; my uncle Jack; and Mary Dodd.
	separates parts of a compound sentence that are not joined by a coordinating conjunction	The last shall be first; the first shall be last. I read the Bible; however, I have not memorized it.
	separates parts of a compound sentence when the parts contain commas	After I ran out of money, I called my parents; but only my sister was home, unfortunately.

MARK	FUNCTION	EXAMPLES
Colon	introduces a list	Those we wrote were the following: Dana, John, and Will.
	introduces a long quotation	Susan B. Anthony said: "Woman must not depend upon the protection of man...."
	follows the salutation of a business letter	To Whom It May Concern: Dear Ms. Costa:
	separates certain numbers	1:28 P.M., Genesis 2:5
Dash	indicates an abrupt break in thought	I was thinking of my mother—who is arriving tomorrow—just as you walked in.
Parentheses	enclose less important material	Throughout her life (though some might think otherwise), she worked hard. The temperature on this July day (would you believe it?) is 65 degrees!
Hyphen	joins parts of a compound adjective before a noun	She lives in a first-floor apartment.
	joins part of a compound with *all-*, *ex-*, *self-*, or *-elect*	The president-elect is a well respected.
	joins part of a compound number (to ninety-nine)	Today I turn twenty-one.
	joins part of a fraction	My cup is one-third full.
	joins a prefix to a word beginning with a capital letter	Is this a pre-Bronze Age artifact? Caesar had a bad day in mid-March.
	indicates that a word is divided at the end of a line	Finding the right title has been a chal-lenge for the committee.
Apostrophe	used with *s* to form the possessive of a noun or an indefinite pronoun	my friend's book, my friends' books, anyone's guess, somebody else's problem
	replaces one or more omitted letters in a contraction or numbers in a date	don't (omitted *o*), he'd (omitted *woul*), the class of '99 (omitted *19*)
	used with *s* to form the plural of a letter	I had two A's on my report card.
Quotation Marks	set off a speaker's exact words	Sara said, "I'm finally ready." "I'm ready," Sara said, "finally." Did Sara say, "I'm ready"? Sara said, "I'm ready!"
	set off the title of a story, an article, a short poem, an essay, a song, or a chapter	We read Hansberry's "On Summer" and Alvarez's "Exile." My eyes watered when I heard "The Star-Spangled Banner."
Ellipses	replace material omitted from a quotation	"Neither slavery nor involuntary servitude ... shall exist within the United States...."
Italics	indicate the title of a book, a play, a magazine, a long poem, an opera, a film, or a TV series, or the name of a ship	*The Mists of Avalon, Julius Caesar, Newsweek, Paradise Lost, La Bohème, ET, The West Wing,* USS *John F. Kennedy*

Quick Reference: Capitalization

CATEGORY	EXAMPLES
People and Titles	
Names and initials of people	Alice Walker, E. B. White
Titles used before or in place of names	Professor Holmes, Senator Long
Deities and members of religious groups	Jesus, Allah, Buddha, Zeus, Baptists, Roman Catholics
Names of ethnic and national groups	Hispanics, Jews, African Americans
Geographical Names	
Cities, states, countries, continents	Charleston, Nevada, France, Asia
Regions, bodies of water, mountains	the Midwest, Lake Michigan, Mount Everest
Geographic features, parks	Continental Divide, Everglades, Yellowstone
Streets and roads, planets	361 South Twenty-third Street, Miller Avenue, Jupiter, Saturn
Organizations, Events, Etc.	
Companies, organizations, teams	Monsanto, the Elks, Chicago Bulls
Buildings, bridges, monuments	the Alamo, Golden Gate Bridge, Lincoln Memorial
Documents, awards	the Constitution, World Cup
Special named events	Super Bowl, World Series
Government bodies, historical periods and events	the Supreme Court, Congress, the Middle Ages, Boston Tea Party
Days and months, holidays	Tuesday, October, Thanksgiving, Valentine's Day
Specific cars, boats, trains, planes	Cadillac, Titanic, Orient Express
Proper Adjectives	
Adjectives formed from proper nouns	Doppler effect, Mexican music, Elizabethan age, Midwestern town
First Words and the Pronoun I	
First word in a sentence or quotation	This is it. He said, "Let's go."
First word of sentence in parentheses that is not within another sentence	The spelling rules are covered in another section. (Consult that section for more information.)
First words in the salutation and closing of a letter	Dear Madam, Very truly yours,
First word in each line of most poetry Personal pronoun *I*	Then am I A happy fly If I live Or if I die.
First word, last word, and all important words in a title	*A Tale of Two Cities,* "The World Is Too Much with Us"

1 Nouns

A **noun** is a word used to name a person, a place, a thing, an idea, a quality, or an action. Nouns can be classified in several ways.

*For more information on different types of nouns, see **Quick Reference: Parts of Speech**, page R46.*

1.1 COMMON NOUNS

Common nouns are general names, common to entire groups.

1.2 PROPER NOUNS

Proper nouns name specific, one-of-a-kind things.

Common	Proper
motor, tree, time, children	Bradbury, Eastern Standard Time, Maine

*For more information, see **Quick Reference: Capitalization**, page R51.*

1.3 SINGULAR AND PLURAL NOUNS

A noun may take a singular or a plural form, depending on whether it names a single person, place, thing, or idea or more than one. Make sure you use appropriate spellings when forming plurals.

Singular	Plural
rocket, sky, life	rockets, skies, lives

*For more information, see **Forming Plural Nouns**, page R74.*

1.4 POSSESSIVE NOUNS

A **possessive noun** shows who or what owns something.

*For more information, see **Forming Possessives**, page R74.*

2 Pronouns

A **pronoun** is a word that is used in place of a noun or another pronoun. The word or word group to which the pronoun refers is called its **antecedent**.

2.1 PERSONAL PRONOUNS

Personal pronouns change their form to express person, number, gender, and case. The forms of these pronouns are shown in the following chart.

	Nominative	Objective	Possessive
Singular			
First person	I	me	my, mine
Second person	you	you	your, yours
Third person	she, he, it	her, him, it	her, hers, his, its
Plural			
First person	we	us	our, ours
Second person	you	you	your, yours
Third person	they	them	their, theirs

2.2 AGREEMENT WITH ANTECEDENT

Pronouns should agree with their antecedents in number, gender, and person.

If an antecedent is singular, use a singular pronoun.

> **EXAMPLE:** *Malcolm waved as he boarded the bus to the airport.*

If an antecedent is plural, use a plural pronoun.

> **EXAMPLES:**
> *Malcolm and Hal shared a sandwich as they waited to board the plane.*
> *Delores and Arnetta rode their bikes to the park.*

The gender of a pronoun must be the same as the gender of its antecedent.

> **EXAMPLES:**
> *William will give his final performance tonight.*
> *Marla played her trumpet.*

The person of the pronoun must be the same as the person of its antecedent. As the chart in Section 2.1 shows, a pronoun can be in first-, second-, or third-person form.

> **EXAMPLE:** *You classical music fans still have time to buy your tickets.*

Rewrite each sentence so that the underlined pronoun agrees with its antecedent.

1. "The Possibility of Evil" tells about a woman in a small town and <u>its</u> strange ideas.

2. Adela thinks the town is hers because her grandfather built <u>them</u>.

3. Adela writes anonymous letters to people in the town and hurts <u>its</u> feelings.

4. Helena Crane worried about her baby; she thought <u>it</u> might be slow.

5. A boy delivers the letter to Don Crane and <u>they</u> take revenge by destroying her roses.

2.3 PRONOUN CASE

Personal pronouns change form to show how they function in sentences. Different functions are shown by different **cases**. The three cases are **nominative, objective,** and **possessive**. For examples of these pronouns, see the chart in Section 2.1.

A **nominative pronoun** is used as a subject or a predicate nominative in a sentence.

An **objective pronoun** is used as a direct object, an indirect object, or the object of a preposition.

SUBJECT	OBJECT	OBJECT OF PREPOSITION
↓	↓	↙

She brought him to us.

A **possessive pronoun** shows ownership. The pronouns *mine, yours, hers, his, its, ours,* and *theirs* can be used in place of nouns.

EXAMPLE: *This book is mine.*

The pronouns *my, your, her, his, its, our,* and *their* are used before nouns.

EXAMPLE: *This is my book.*

WATCH OUT! Many spelling errors can be avoided if you watch out for *its* and *their*. Don't confuse the possessive pronoun *its* with the contraction *it's*, meaning "it is" or "it has." The homonyms *they're* (a contraction of *they are*) and *there* ("in that place") are often mistakenly used for *their*.

TIP To decide which pronoun to use in a comparison, such as "He tells better tales than (I *or* me)," fill in the missing word(s): *He tells better tales than I tell.*

Replace the underlined words in each sentence with an appropriate pronoun and identify the pronoun as a nominative, an objective, or a possessive pronoun.

1. <u>Sophocles</u> was a famous playwright in ancient Greece.

2. *Antigone* is one of <u>Sophocles'</u> most important dramas.

3. <u>Antigone and Ismene</u> are two of the main characters.

4. Creon condemns <u>Antigone and Ismene</u>.

5. <u>The Greek chorus</u> represents the ordinary citizens.

2.4 REFLEXIVE AND INTENSIVE PRONOUNS

These pronouns are formed by adding *-self* or *-selves* to certain personal pronouns. Their forms are the same, and they differ only in how they are used.

A **reflexive pronoun** follows a verb or preposition and reflects back on an earlier noun or pronoun.

EXAMPLES:

He likes himself too much.

Kiyoko treated herself to dessert.

Intensive pronouns intensify or emphasize the nouns or pronouns to which they refer.

EXAMPLES:

The merchants themselves enjoyed sampling the foods.

You did it yourself.

WATCH OUT! Avoid using *hisself* or *theirselves*. Standard English does not include these forms.

NONSTANDARD: *The children sang theirselves to sleep.*

STANDARD: *The children sang themselves to sleep.*

2.5 DEMONSTRATIVE PRONOUNS

Demonstrative pronouns point out things and persons near and far.

	Singular	Plural
Near	this	these
Far	that	those

2.6 INDEFINITE PRONOUNS

Indefinite pronouns do not refer to specific persons or things and usually have no antecedents. The chart shows some commonly used indefinite pronouns.

Singular	Plural	Singular or Plural	
another	both	all	none
anybody	few	any	some
no one	many	more	most
neither	several		

TIP Indefinite pronouns that end in *one*, *body*, or *thing* are always singular.

> **INCORRECT:** *Everyone brought their clarinet.*

> **CORRECT:** *Everyone brought his or her clarinet.*

If the indefinite pronoun might refer to either a male or a female, *his* or *her* may be used to refer to it, or the sentence may be rewritten.

> **EXAMPLES:** *Did everybody play his or her part well?*
> *Did all the students play their parts well?*

2.7 INTERROGATIVE PRONOUNS

An **interrogative pronoun** tells a reader or listener that a question is coming. The interrogative pronouns are *who, whom, whose, which,* and *what.*

> **EXAMPLES:** *Who wrote that song?*
> *From whom did you get the answer?*

TIP *Who* is used as a subject, *whom* as an object. To find out which pronoun you need to use in a question, change the question to a statement.

> **QUESTION:** *(Who/Whom) are you speaking to?*
> **STATEMENT:** *You are speaking to (?).*

Since the verb has a subject (*you*), the needed word must be the object form, *whom.*

> **EXAMPLE:** *Whom are you speaking to?*

WATCH OUT! A special problem arises when you use an interrupter, such as *do you think,* within a question.

> **EXAMPLE:** *(Who/Whom) do you think is the better singer?*

If you eliminate the interrupter, it is clear that the word you need is *who.*

2.8 RELATIVE PRONOUNS

Relative pronouns relate, or connect, adjective clauses to the words they modify in sentences. The noun or pronoun that a relative clause modifies is the antecedent of the relative pronoun. Here are the relative pronouns and their uses.

Replaces	Subject	Object	Possessive
Person	who	whom	whose
Thing	which	which	whose
Thing/Person	that	that	whose

Often short sentences with related ideas can be combined by using a relative pronoun to create a more effective sentence.

> **SHORT SENTENCE:** *Joan Aiken decided to become a writer at an early age.*

> **RELATED SENTENCE:** *Joan Aiken's father was a poet.*

> **COMBINED SENTENCE:** *Joan Aiken, whose father was a poet, decided to become a writer at an early age.*

GRAMMAR PRACTICE

Write the correct form of each incorrect pronoun.

1. Whom has read "By the Waters of Babylon"?

2. Stephen Vincent Benét, which is a famous American author, wrote the story.

3. In "By the Waters of Babylon," him who touches the metal in the Dead Places must be a priest or son of a priest.

4. The narrator's father hisself questioned him.

5. When John saw a heap of broken stones, he cautiously approached them stones.

2.9 PRONOUN REFERENCE PROBLEMS

The referent of a pronoun should always be clear. Avoid problems by rewriting sentences.

An **indefinite reference** occurs when the pronoun *it, you,* or *they* does not clearly refer to a specific antecedent.

> UNCLEAR: *In the article, it claims that the new Pink Blur CD is terrific.*
>
> CLEAR: *The article claims that the new Pink Blur CD is terrific.*

A **general reference** occurs when the pronoun *it, this, that, which,* or *such* is used to refer to a general idea rather than a specific antecedent.

> UNCLEAR: *Trudy practices the guitar every day. This has improved her playing.*
>
> CLEAR: *Trudy practices the guitar every day. Practicing has improved her playing.*

Ambiguous means "having more than one possible meaning." An **ambiguous reference** occurs when a pronoun could refer to two or more antecedents.

> UNCLEAR: *Jeb talked to Max while he listened to music.*
>
> CLEAR: *While Jeb listened to music, he talked to Max.*

GRAMMAR PRACTICE

Rewrite the following sentences to correct indefinite, ambiguous, and general pronoun references.

1. In the story "To Build A Fire," it tells about a man trying to survive in extremely cold conditions.
2. The man almost stepped in a trap. This made him use the dog to test the trail.
3. An old-timer told the miner that running would make his feet freeze faster.
4. Snow from a tree fell and put out the man's fire. This made him panic.

3 Verbs

A **verb** is a word that expresses an action, a condition, or a state of being.

For more information, see **Quick Reference: Parts of Speech,** *page R47.*

3.1 ACTION VERBS

Action verbs express mental or physical activity.

> EXAMPLE: *You hit the target.*

3.2 LINKING VERBS

Linking verbs join subjects with words or phrases that rename or describe them.

> EXAMPLE: *She is our queen.*

3.3 PRINCIPAL PARTS

Action and linking verbs typically have four principal parts, which are used to form verb tenses. The principal parts are the **present,** the **present participle,** the **past,** and the **past participle.**

Action verbs and some linking verbs also fall into two categories: regular and irregular. A **regular verb** is a verb that forms its past and past participle by adding *-ed* or *-d* to the present form.

Present	Present Participle	Past	Past Participle
perform	(is) performing	performed	(has) performed
hope	(is) hoping	hoped	(has) hoped
stop	(is) stopping	stopped	(has) stopped
marry	(is) marrying	married	(has) married

An **irregular verb** is a verb that forms its past and past participle in some other way than by adding *-ed* or *-d* to the present form.

Present	Present Participle	Past	Past Participle
bring	(is) bringing	brought	(has) brought
swim	(is) swimming	swam	(has) swum
steal	(is) stealing	stole	(has) stolen
grow	(is) growing	grew	(has) grown

3.4 VERB TENSE

The **tense** of a verb indicates the time of the action or state of being. An action or a state of being can occur in the present, the past, or the future. There are six tenses, each expressing a different range of time.

The **present tense** expresses an action or a state that is happening at the present time, occurs regularly, or is constant or generally true. Use the present part.

> NOW: *This soup tastes delicious.*
> REGULAR: *I make vegetable soup often.*
> GENERAL: *Crops require sun, rain, and rich soil.*

The **past tense** expresses an action that began and ended in the past. Use the past part.

> EXAMPLE: *The diver bought a shark cage.*

The **future tense** expresses an action or a state that will occur. Use *shall* or *will* with the present part.

> EXAMPLE: *The shark will destroy this cage.*

The **present perfect tense** expresses an action or a state that (1) was completed at an indefinite time in the past or (2) began in the past and continues into the present. Use *have* or *has* with the past participle.

> EXAMPLE: *The diver has used shark cages before.*

The **past perfect tense** expresses an action in the past that came before another action in the past. Use *had* with the past participle.

> EXAMPLE: *He had looked everywhere for a cage.*

The **future perfect tense** expresses an action in the future that will be completed before another action in the future. Use *shall have* or *will have* with the past participle.

> EXAMPLE: *Before the day ends, the shark will have destroyed three cages.*

TIP A past-tense form of an irregular verb is not used with an auxiliary verb, but a past-participle main irregular verb is always used with an auxiliary verb.

> INCORRECT: *I have saw her somewhere before.*
> CORRECT: *I have seen her somewhere before.*
> INCORRECT: *I seen her somewhere before.*

3.5 PROGRESSIVE FORMS

The progressive forms of the six tenses show ongoing actions. Use forms of *be* with the present participles of verbs.

PRESENT PROGRESSIVE: *We are dancing.*
PAST PROGRESSIVE: *We were dancing.*
FUTURE PROGRESSIVE: *We will be dancing.*
PRESENT PERFECT PROGRESSIVE: *We have been dancing.*
PAST PERFECT PROGRESSIVE: *We had been dancing.*
FUTURE PERFECT PROGRESSIVE: *We will have been dancing.*

WATCH OUT! Do not shift from tense to tense needlessly. Watch out for these special cases:

- In most compound sentences and in sentences with compound predicates, keep the tenses the same.

> INCORRECT: *I keyed in the password, but I get an error message.*
> CORRECT: *I keyed in the password, but I got an error message.*

- If one past action happened before another, do shift tenses.

> INCORRECT: *They wished they started earlier.*
> CORRECT: *They wished they had started earlier.*

GRAMMAR PRACTICE

Rewrite each sentence, using a form of the verb in parentheses. Identify each form that you use.

1. In her stories, Alice Walker (show) the dignity of people who are her subjects.

2. Alice Walker (write) "Everyday Use."

3. The mother in the story (know) both her daughters well.

4. The mother (sweep) the yard.

5. Their other house (burn) down.

6. The story (show) how the mother respects the everyday use of the quilts.

Rewrite each sentence to correct an error in tense.

7. Maggie wants the quilts and appreciated their value.

8. Dee wants the quilt and she wanted to display them.

9. Maggie and her mother had knew the quilts could be used as bedcovers.

10. Dee have argued with her family.

3.6 ACTIVE AND PASSIVE VOICE

The voice of a verb tells whether its subject performs or receives the action expressed by the verb. When the subject performs the action, the verb is in the **active voice.** When the subject is the receiver of the action, the verb is in the **passive voice.**

Compare these two sentences:

ACTIVE: *Her sunglasses hid her face.*

PASSIVE: *Her face was hidden by her sunglasses.*

To form the passive voice, use a form of *be* with the past participle of the verb.

WATCH OUT! Use the passive voice sparingly. It can make writing awkward and less direct.

AWKWARD: *She was given the handmade quilts by her mother.*

BETTER: *Her mother gave her the handmade quilts.*

There are occasions when you will choose to use the passive voice because

- you want to emphasize the receiver: *The king was shot.*
- the doer is unknown: *My books were stolen.*
- the doer is unimportant: *French is spoken here.*

4 Modifiers

Modifiers are words or groups of words that change or limit the meanings of other words. Adjectives and adverbs are common modifiers.

4.1 ADJECTIVES

Adjectives modify nouns and pronouns by telling which one, what kind, how many, or how much.

WHICH ONE: *this, that, these, those*
EXAMPLE: *These tomatoes have grown quickly.*

WHAT KIND: *tiny, impressive, bold, rotten*
EXAMPLE: *The bold officer stood in front of the crowd.*

HOW MANY: *some, few, ten, none, both, each*
EXAMPLE: *Some diners had sweet potatoes.*

HOW MUCH: *more, less, enough, fast*
EXAMPLE: *There was enough chicken to serve everyone.*

4.2 PREDICATE ADJECTIVES

Most adjectives come before the nouns they modify, as in the preceding examples. A **predicate adjective,** however, follows a linking verb and describes the subject.

EXAMPLE: *My friends are very intelligent.*

Be especially careful to use adjectives (not adverbs) after such linking verbs as *look, feel, grow, taste,* and *smell.*

EXAMPLE: *The weather grows cold.*

4.3 ADVERBS

Adverbs modify verbs, adjectives, and other adverbs by telling where, when, how, or to what extent.

WHERE: *The children played outside.*
WHEN: *The author spoke yesterday.*
HOW: *We walked slowly behind the leader.*
TO WHAT EXTENT: *He worked very hard.*

Adverbs may occur in many places in sentences, both before and after the words they modify.

EXAMPLES: *Suddenly the wind shifted.*

The wind suddenly shifted.

The wind shifted suddenly.

4.4 ADJECTIVE OR ADVERB?

Many adverbs are formed by adding *-ly* to adjectives.

EXAMPLES: *sweet, sweetly; gentle, gently*

However, *-ly* added to a noun will usually yield an adjective.

EXAMPLES: *friend, friendly; woman, womanly*

4.5 COMPARISON OF MODIFIERS

Modifiers can be used to compare two or more things. The form of a modifier shows the degree of comparison. Both adjectives and adverbs have **comparative** and **superlative** forms.

The **comparative form** is used to compare two things, groups, or actions.

EXAMPLES:

His emperor's chariots are faster than mine.
Brutus' speech was more effective than Cassius' speech.

The **superlative form** is used to compare more than two things, groups, or actions.

EXAMPLES:

The emperor's chariots are the fastest.

Antony's speech was the most effective of all.

4.6 REGULAR COMPARISONS

Most one-syllable and some two-syllable adjectives and adverbs have comparatives and superlatives formed by adding *-er* and *-est*. All three-syllable and most two-syllable modifiers have comparatives and superlatives formed with *more* or *most*.

Modifier	Comparative	Superlative
tall	taller	tallest
kind	kinder	kindest
droopy	droopier	droopiest
expensive	more expensive	most expensive
wasteful	more wasteful	most wasteful

WATCH OUT! Note that spelling changes must sometimes be made to form the comparatives and superlatives of modifiers.

EXAMPLES:

friendly, friendlier (Change *y* to *i* and add the ending.)

sad, sadder (Double the final consonant and add the ending.)

4.7 IRREGULAR COMPARISONS

Some commonly used modifiers have irregular comparative and superlative forms. They are listed in the following chart.

Modifier	Comparative	Superlative
good	better	best
bad	worse	worst
far	farther *or* further	farthest *or* furthest
little	less *or* lesser	least
many	more	most
well	better	best
much	more	most

4.8 PROBLEMS WITH MODIFIERS

Study the tips that follow to avoid common mistakes:

Farther and Further Use *farther* for distances; use *further* for everything else.

Double Comparisons Make a comparison by using *-er/-est* or by using *more/most*. Using *-er* with *more* or using *-est* with *most* is incorrect.

INCORRECT: *I like her more better than she likes me.*

CORRECT: *I like her better than she likes me.*

Illogical Comparisons An illogical or confusing comparison results when two unrelated things are compared or when something is compared with itself. The word *other* or the word *else* should be used in a comparison of an individual member to the rest of a group.

ILLOGICAL: *The narrator was more curious about the war than any student in his class.* (implies that the narrator isn't a student in the class)

LOGICAL: *The narrator was more curious about the war than any other student in his class.* (identifies that the narrator is a student)

Bad vs. Badly *Bad*, always an adjective, is used before a noun or after a linking verb. *Badly*, always an adverb, never modifies a noun. Be sure to use the right form after a linking verb.

INCORRECT: *Ed felt badly after his team lost.*

CORRECT: *Ed felt bad after his team lost.*

Good vs. Well *Good* is always an adjective. It is used before a noun or after a linking verb. *Well* is often an adverb meaning "expertly" or "properly." *Well* can also be used as an adjective after a linking verb when it means "in good health."

INCORRECT: *Helen writes very good.*

CORRECT: *Helen writes very well.*

CORRECT: *Yesterday I felt bad; today I feel well.*

Double Negatives If you add a negative word to a sentence that is already negative, the result will be an error known as a double negative. When using *not* or *-n't* with a verb, use *any-* words, such as *anybody* or *anything*, rather than *no-* words, such as *nobody* or *nothing*, later in the sentence.

INCORRECT: *I don't have no money.*

CORRECT: *I don't have any money.*

Using *hardly, barely,* or *scarcely* after a negative word is also incorrect.

INCORRECT: *They couldn't barely see two feet ahead.*

CORRECT: *They could barely see two feet ahead.*

Misplaced Modifiers Sometimes a modifier is placed so far away from the word it modifies that the intended meaning of the sentence is unclear. Prepositional phrases and participial phrases are often misplaced. Place modifiers as close as possible to the words they modify.

MISPLACED: *The ranger explained how to find ducks in her office.* (The ducks were not in the ranger's office.)

CLEARER: *In her office, the ranger explained how to find ducks.*

Dangling Modifiers Sometimes a modifier doesn't appear to modify any word in a sentence. Most dangling modifiers are participial phrases or infinitive phrases.

DANGLING: *Coming home with groceries, our parrot said, "Hello!"*

CLEARER: *Coming home with groceries, we heard our parrot say, "Hello!"*

GRAMMAR PRACTICE

Choose the correct word or words from each pair in parentheses.

1. The play *Julius Caesar* is about the death of the (powerfulest, most powerful) emperor of Roman times.

2. The emperor didn't pay (no, any) attention to the soothsayer who warned him about the ides of March.

3. Caesar (could, couldn't) hardly know what lay in store for him.

4. He thought Brutus loved him (well, good).

GRAMMAR PRACTICE

Rewrite each sentence that contains a misplaced or dangling modifier. Write "correct" if the sentence is written correctly.

1. Ballerinas were on the television screen with weights.

2. Looking at the television, a buzzer sounded in George's head.

3. White and trembling, tears were in his eyes.

4. Being above average was not allowed in the story "Harrison Bergeron," making people like everyone else.

5 The Sentence and Its Parts

A **sentence** is a group of words used to express a complete thought. A complete sentence has a subject and a predicate.

*For more information, see **Quick Reference: The Sentence and Its Parts,** page R48.*

5.1 KINDS OF SENTENCES

There are four basic types of sentences.

Type	Definition	Example
Declarative	states a fact, a wish, an intent, or a feeling	I read White's essay last night.
Interrogative	asks a question	Did you like the essay?
Imperative	gives a command or direction	Read this paragraph aloud.
Exclamatory	expresses strong feeling or excitement	I wish I had thought of that!

5.2 COMPOUND SUBJECTS AND PREDICATES

A compound subject consists of two or more subjects that share the same verb. They are typically joined by the coordinating conjunction *and* or *or.*

EXAMPLE: *Ray and Joe write about families.*

A compound predicate consists of two or more predicates that share the same subject. They too are typically joined by a coordinating conjunction, usually *and, but,* or *or.*

EXAMPLE: *The father in "Those Winter Sundays" got up early and dressed in the dark.*

5.3 COMPLEMENTS

A **complement** is a word or group of words that completes the meaning of the sentence. Some sentences contain only a subject and a verb. Most sentences, however, require additional words placed after the verb to complete the meaning of the sentence. There are three kinds of complements: direct objects, indirect objects, and subject complements.

Direct objects are words or word groups that receive the action of action verbs. A direct object answers the question *what* or *whom.*

> **EXAMPLES:**
>
> *The students asked many questions.* (Asked what?)
>
> *The teacher quickly answered the students.* (Answered whom?)

Indirect objects tell to whom or what or for whom or what the actions of verbs are performed. Indirect objects come before direct objects. In the examples that follow, the indirect objects are highlighted.

> **EXAMPLES:**
>
> *My sister usually gave her friends good advice.* (Gave to whom?)
>
> *Her brother sent the store a heavy package.* (Sent to what?)

Subject complements come after linking verbs and identify or describe the subjects. A subject complement that names or identifies a subject is called a **predicate nominative.** Predicate nominatives include **predicate nouns** and **predicate pronouns.**

> **EXAMPLES:**
>
> *My friends are very hard workers.*
>
> *The best writer in the class is she.*

A subject complement that describes a subject is called a **predicate adjective.**

> **EXAMPLE:** *The pianist appeared very energetic.*

6 Phrases

A **phrase** is a group of related words that does not contain a subject and a predicate but functions in a sentence as a single part of speech.

6.1 PREPOSITIONAL PHRASES

A **prepositional phrase** is a phrase that consists of a preposition, its object, and any modifiers of the object. Prepositional phrases that modify nouns or pronouns are called **adjective phrases.** Prepositional phrases that modify verbs, adjectives, or adverbs are **adverb phrases.**

> **ADJECTIVE PHRASE:** *The central character of the story is a villain.*
>
> **ADVERB PHRASE:** *He reveals his nature in the first scene.*

6.2 APPOSITIVES AND APPOSITIVE PHRASES

An **appositive** is a noun or pronoun that identifies or renames another noun or pronoun. An **appositive phrase** includes an appositive and modifiers of it.

An appositive can be either **essential** or **nonessential.** An **essential appositive** provides information that is needed to identify what is referred to by the preceding noun or pronoun.

> **EXAMPLE:** *This poem was written by author Walt Whitman.*

A **nonessential appositive** adds extra information about a noun or pronoun whose meaning is already clear. Nonessential appositives and appositive phrases are set off with commas.

> **EXAMPLE:** *He wrote this poem, a sad remembrance of war, about an artilleryman.*

7 Verbals and Verbal Phrases

A **verbal** is a verb form that is used as a noun, an adjective, or an adverb. A **verbal phrase** consists of a verbal along with its modifiers and complements. There are three kinds of verbals: **infinitives, participles,** and **gerunds.**

7.1 INFINITIVES AND INFINITIVE PHRASES

An **infinitive** is a verb form that usually begins with *to* and functions as a noun, an adjective, or an adverb. An **infinitive phrase** consists of an infinitive plus its modifiers and complements. The examples that follow show several uses of infinitive phrases.

> NOUN: *To know her is my only desire.* (subject)
> *I'm planning to walk with you.* (direct object)
> *Her goal was to promote women's rights.* (predicate nominative)
> ADJECTIVE: *We saw his need to be loved.* (adjective modifying *need*)
> ADVERB: *She wrote to voice her opinions.* (adverb modifying *wrote*)

Because *to,* the sign of the infinitive, precedes infinitives, it is usually easy to recognize them. However, sometimes *to* may be omitted.

> EXAMPLE: *Let no one dare [to] enter this shrine.*

7.2 PARTICIPLES AND PARTICIPIAL PHRASES

A **participle** is a verb form that functions as an adjective. Like adjectives, participles modify nouns and pronouns. Most participles are present-participle forms, ending in *-ing,* or past-participle forms ending in *-ed* or *-en.* In the examples that follow, the participles are highlighted.

> MODIFYING A NOUN: *The smiling man ate another fried chicken wing.*
> MODIFYING A PRONOUN: *Ignored, she slipped out of the room unnoticed.*

Participial phrases are participles with all their modifiers and complements.

> MODIFYING A NOUN: *Visiting gardens, butterflies flit among the flowers.*
> MODIFYING A PRONOUN: *Driven by instinct, they use the flowers as meal stops.*

7.3 DANGLING AND MISPLACED PARTICIPLES

A participle or participial phrase should be placed as close as possible to the word that it modifies. Otherwise the meaning of the sentence may not be clear.

> MISPLACED: *The boys were looking for squirrels searching the trees.*
> CLEARER: *The boys searching the trees were looking for squirrels.*

A participle or participial phrase that does not clearly modify anything in a sentence is called a **dangling participle.** A dangling participle causes confusion because it appears to modify a word that it cannot sensibly modify. Correct a dangling participle by providing a word for the participle to modify.

> DANGLING: *Running like the wind, my hat fell off.* (The hat wasn't running.)
> CLEARER: *Running like the wind, I lost my hat.*

7.4 GERUNDS AND GERUND PHRASES

A **gerund** is a verb form ending in *-ing* that functions as a noun. Gerunds may perform any function nouns perform.

> SUBJECT: *Running is my favorite pastime.*
> DIRECT OBJECT: *I truly love running.*
> INDIRECT OBJECT: *You should give running a try.*
> SUBJECT COMPLEMENT: *My deepest passion is running.*
> OBJECT OF PREPOSITION: *Her love of running keeps her strong.*

Gerund phrases are gerunds with all their modifiers and complements.

> SUBJECT: *Wishing on a star never got me far.*
> OBJECT OF PREPOSITION: *I will finish before leaving the office.*
> APPOSITIVE: *Her avocation, flying airplanes, finally led to full-time employment.*

Rewrite each sentence, adding the type of phrase shown in parentheses.

1. Tolstoy was orphaned by age nine. (participial phrase)

2. *War and Peace* was published in 1869. (appositive phrase)

3. Ivan tried to convince his wife. (infinitive phrase)

4. Ivan was happy. (gerund phrase)

5. Ivan gradually lost interest in Varenka. (appositive phrase)

8 Clauses

A **clause** is a group of words that contains a subject and a verb. There are two kinds of clauses: independent clauses and subordinate clauses.

8.1 INDEPENDENT AND SUBORDINATE CLAUSES

An **independent clause** can stand alone as a sentence, as the word *independent* suggests.

> INDEPENDENT CLAUSE: *Emily Dickinson did not wish her poems to be published.*

A sentence may contain more than one independent clause.

> EXAMPLE: *Emily Dickinson did not wish her poems to be published, but seven were published during her lifetime.*

In the preceding example, the coordinating conjunction *but* joins two independent clauses.

*For more information, see **Coordinating Conjunction**, page R47.*

A **subordinate clause** cannot stand alone as a sentence. It is subordinate to, or dependent on, an independent clause.

> EXAMPLE: *Emily Dickinson did not wish her poems to be published, although she shared them with friends.*

The highlighted clause cannot stand by itself.

8.2 ADJECTIVE CLAUSES

An **adjective clause** is a subordinate clause used as an adjective. It usually follows the noun or pronoun it modifies.

> EXAMPLE: *Robert Frost wrote about birch tree branches that boys swing on.*

Adjective clauses are typically introduced by the relative pronoun *who, whom, whose, which,* or *that*.

*For more information, see **Relative Pronouns**, page R54.*

> EXAMPLES:
>
> *One song that we like became our theme song.*
>
> *Emily Dickinson, whose poems have touched many, lived a very quiet life.*

An adjective clause can be either essential or nonessential. An **essential adjective clause** provides information that is necessary to identify the preceding noun or pronoun.

> EXAMPLE: *The candidate whom we selected promised to serve us well.*

A **nonessential adjective clause** adds additional information about a noun or pronoun whose meaning is already clear. Nonessential clauses are set off with commas.

> EXAMPLE: *Brookhaven National Laboratory, which employs Mr. Davis, is in Upton, New York.*

> **TIP** The relative pronouns *whom, which,* and *that* may sometimes be omitted when they are objects in adjective clauses.

> EXAMPLE: *Frost is a writer [whom] millions enjoy.*

8.3 ADVERB CLAUSES

An **adverb clause** is a subordinate clause that is used to modify a verb, an adjective, or an adverb. It is introduced by a subordinating conjunction.

*For examples of subordinating conjunctions, see **Noun Clauses**, page R63.*

Adverb clauses typically occur at the beginning or end of sentences.

> MODIFYING A VERB: *When we need you, we will call.*

> MODIFYING AN ADVERB: *I'll stay here where there is shelter from the rain.*

> MODIFYING AN ADJECTIVE: *Roman felt as good as he had ever felt.*

8.4 NOUN CLAUSES

A **noun clause** is a subordinate clause that is used as a noun. A noun clause may be used as a subject, a direct object, an indirect object, a predicate nominative, or an object of a preposition. Noun clauses are introduced either by pronouns, such as *that, what, who, whoever, which,* and *whose,* or by subordinating conjunctions, such as *how, when, where, why,* and *whether.*

For more subordinating conjunctions, see **Quick Reference: Parts of Speech,** *page R47.*

TIP Because the same words may introduce adjective and noun clauses, you need to consider how a clause functions within its sentence. To determine if a clause is a noun clause, try substituting *something* or *someone* for the clause. If you can do it, it is probably a noun clause.

EXAMPLES: *I know whose woods these are.* ("I know *something.*" The clause is a noun clause, direct object of the verb *know.*)

Give a copy to whoever wants one. ("Give a copy to *someone.*" The clause is a noun clause, object of the preposition *to.*)

GRAMMAR PRACTICE

Add descriptive details to each sentence by writing the type of clause indicated in parentheses.

1. Mr. Davis is a scientist. (adjective clause)
2. He has invented many things. (adjective clause)
3. He works. (adverb clause)
4. He does his best thinking at night. (adverb clause)
5. He should invent a better backpack. (adjective clause)

9 The Structure of Sentences

When classified by their structure, there are four kinds of sentences: simple, compound, complex, and compound-complex.

9.1 SIMPLE SENTENCES

A **simple sentence** is a sentence that has one independent clause and no subordinate clauses.

The fact that such a sentence is called simple does not mean that it is uncomplicated. Various parts of simple sentences may be compound, and simple sentences may contain grammatical structures such as appositive and verbal phrases.

EXAMPLES:

Mark Twain, an unsuccessful gold miner, wrote many successful satires and tall tales. (appositive and compound direct object)

Pablo Neruda, drawn to writing poetry at an early age, won celebrity at age 20. (participial and gerund phrases)

9.2 COMPOUND SENTENCES

A **compound sentence** consists of two or more independent clauses. The clauses in compound sentences are joined with commas and coordinating conjunctions (*and, but, or, nor, yet, for, so*) or with semicolons. Like simple sentences, compound sentences do not contain any subordinate clauses.

EXAMPLES:

I enjoyed Bradbury's story "The Utterly Perfect Murder," and I want to read more of his stories.

Amy Lowell's poem "The Taxi" has powerful images; however, it does not use the word taxi *anywhere in it.*

WATCH OUT! Do not confuse compound sentences with simple sentences that have compound parts.

EXAMPLE: *A subcommittee drafted a document and immediately presented it to the entire group.* (Here *and* joins parts of a compound predicate, not a compound sentence.)

9.3 COMPLEX SENTENCES

A **complex sentence** consists of one independent clause and one or more subordinate clauses. Each subordinate clause can be used as a noun or as a modifier. If it is used as a modifier, a subordinate clause usually modifies a word in the independent clause, and the independent clause can stand alone. However, when a subordinate clause is a noun clause, it is a part of the independent clause; the two cannot be separated.

MODIFIER: *One should not complain unless one has a better solution.*

NOUN CLAUSE: *We sketched pictures of whomever we wished.* (The noun clause is the object of the preposition *of* and cannot be separated from the rest of the sentence.)

9.4 COMPOUND-COMPLEX SENTENCES

A **compound-complex sentence** contains two or more independent clauses and one or more subordinate clauses. Compound-complex sentences are, simply, both compound and complex. If you start with a compound sentence, all you need to do to form a compound-complex sentence is add a subordinate clause.

COMPOUND: *All the students knew the answer, yet they were too shy to volunteer.*

COMPOUND-COMPLEX: *All the students knew the answer that their teacher expected, yet they were too shy to volunteer.*

9.5 PARALLEL STRUCTURE

When you write sentences, make sure that coordinate parts are equivalent, or **parallel,** in structure.

NOT PARALLEL: *Erin loved basketball and to play hockey.* (*Basketball* is a noun; *to play hockey* is a phrase.)

PARALLEL: *Erin loved basketball and hockey.* (*Basketball* and *hockey* are both nouns.)

NOT PARALLEL: *He wanted to rent an apartment, a new car, and traveling around the country.* (*To rent* is an infinitive, *car* is a noun, and *traveling* is a gerund.)

PARALLEL: *He wanted to rent an apartment, to drive a new car, and to travel around the country.* (*To rent, to drive,* and *to travel* are all infinitives.)

🔟 Writing Complete Sentences

Remember, a sentence is a group of words that expresses a complete thought. In formal writing, try to avoid both sentence fragments and run-on sentences.

10.1 CORRECTING FRAGMENTS

A **sentence fragment** is a group of words that is only part of a sentence. It does not express a complete thought and may be confusing to a reader or listener. A sentence fragment may be lacking a subject, a predicate, or both.

FRAGMENT: *Waited for the boat to arrive.* (no subject)

CORRECTED: *We waited for the boat to arrive.*

FRAGMENT: *People of various races, ages, and creeds.* (no predicate)

CORRECTED: *People of various races, ages, and creeds gathered together.*

FRAGMENT: *Near the old cottage.* (neither subject nor predicate)

CORRECTED: *The burial ground is near the old cottage.*

In your writing, fragments may be a result of haste or incorrect punctuation. Sometimes fixing a fragment will be a matter of attaching it to a preceding or following sentence.

FRAGMENT: *We saw the two girls. Waiting for the bus to arrive.*

CORRECTED: *We saw the two girls waiting for the bus to arrive.*

10.2 CORRECTING RUN-ON SENTENCES

A **run-on sentence** is made up of two or more sentences written as though they were one. Some run-ons have no punctuation within them. Others may have only commas where conjunctions or stronger punctuation marks are necessary. Use your judgment in correcting run-on sentences, as you have choices. You can make a run-on two sentences if the thoughts are not closely connected. If the thoughts are closely related, you can keep the run-on as one sentence by adding a semicolon or a conjunction.

RUN-ON: *We found a place for the picnic by a small pond it was three miles from the village.*

MAKE TWO SENTENCES: *We found a place for the picnic by a small pond. It was three miles from the village.*

RUN-ON: *We found a place for the picnic by a small pond it was perfect.*

USE A SEMICOLON: *We found a place for the picnic by a small pond; it was perfect.*

ADD A CONJUNCTION: *We found a place for the picnic by a small pond, and it was perfect.*

WATCH OUT! When you form compound sentences, make sure you use appropriate punctuation: a comma before a coordinating conjunction, a semicolon when there is no coordinating conjunction. A very common mistake is to use a comma alone instead of a comma and a conjunction. This error is called a **comma splice.**

INCORRECT: *He finished the apprenticeship, he left the village.*

CORRECT: *He finished the apprenticeship, and he left the village.*

11 Subject-Verb Agreement

The subject and verb in a clause must agree in number. Agreement means that if the subject is singular, the verb is also singular, and if the subject is plural, the verb is also plural.

11.1 BASIC AGREEMENT

Fortunately, agreement between subjects and verbs in English is simple. Most verbs show the difference between singular and plural only in the third person of the present tense. In the present tense, the third-person singular form ends in *-s.*

Present-Tense Verb Forms	
Singular	**Plural**
I jog	we jog
you jog	you jog
she, he, it jogs	they jog

11.2 AGREEMENT WITH *BE*

The verb *be* presents special problems in agreement, because this verb does not follow the usual verb patterns.

Forms of *Be*			
Present Tense		**Past Tense**	
Singular	**Plural**	**Singular**	**Plural**
I am	we are	I was	we were
you are	you are	you were	you were
she, he, it is	they are	she, he, it was	they were

11.3 WORDS BETWEEN SUBJECT AND VERB

A verb agrees only with its subject. When words come between a subject and a verb, ignore them when considering proper agreement. Identify the subject, and make sure the verb agrees with it.

EXAMPLES:

A story in the newspapers tells about the 1890s.
Dad as well as Mom reads the paper daily.

11.4 AGREEMENT WITH COMPOUND SUBJECTS

Use plural verbs with most compound subjects joined by the word *and.*

EXAMPLE: *My father and his friends play chess every day.*

To confirm that you need a plural verb, you could substitute the plural pronoun *they* for *my father and his friends.*

If a compound subject is thought of as a unit, use a singular verb. Test this by substituting the singular pronoun *it.*

EXAMPLE: *Peanut butter and jelly [it] is my brother's favorite sandwich.*

Use a singular verb with a compound subject that is preceded by *each, every,* or *many a.*

EXAMPLE: *Each novel and short story seems grounded in personal experience.*

When the parts of a compound subject are joined by *or, nor,* or the correlative conjunctions *either . . . or* or *neither . . . nor,* make the verb agree with the noun or pronoun nearest the verb.

EXAMPLES:

Cookies or ice cream is my favorite dessert.
Either Cheryl or her friends are being invited.
Neither ice storms nor snow is predicted today.

11.5 PERSONAL PRONOUNS AS SUBJECTS

When using a personal pronoun as a subject, make sure to match it with the correct form of the verb *be*. (See the chart in Section 11.2.) Note especially that the pronoun *you* takes the forms *are* and *were*, regardless of whether it is singular or plural.

WATCH OUT! *You is* and *you was* are nonstandard forms and should be avoided in writing and speaking. *We was* and *they was* are also forms to be avoided.

INCORRECT: *You was helping me.*

CORRECT: *You were helping me.*

INCORRECT: *They was hoping for this.*

CORRECT: *They were hoping for this.*

11.6 INDEFINITE PRONOUNS AS SUBJECTS

Some indefinite pronouns are always singular; some are always plural.

Singular Indefinite Pronouns			
another	either	neither	one
anybody	everybody	nobody	somebody
anyone	everyone	no one	someone
anything	everything	nothing	something
each	much		

EXAMPLES:

Each of the writers was given an award.

Somebody in the room upstairs is sleeping.

Plural Indefinite Pronouns			
both	few	many	several

EXAMPLES:

Many of the books in our library are not in circulation.

Few have been returned recently.

Still other indefinite pronouns may be either singular or plural.

Singular or Plural Indefinite Pronouns		
all	more	none
any	most	some

The number of the indefinite pronoun *any* or *none* often depends on the intended meaning.

EXAMPLES:

Any of these topics has potential for a good article. (any one topic)

Any of these topics have potential for good articles. (all of the many topics)

The indefinite pronouns *all, some, more, most,* and *none* are singular when they refer to quantities or parts of things. They are plural when they refer to numbers of individual things. Context will usually give a clue.

EXAMPLES:

All of the flour is gone. (referring to a quantity)

All of the flowers are gone. (referring to individual items)

11.7 INVERTED SENTENCES

Problems in agreement often occur in inverted sentences beginning with *here* or *there;* in questions beginning with *how, when, why, where,* or *what;* and in inverted sentences beginning with phrases. Identify the subject—wherever it is—before deciding on the verb.

EXAMPLES:

There clearly are far too many cooks in this kitchen.

What is the correct ingredient for this stew?

Far from the embroiled cooks stands the master chef.

GRAMMAR PRACTICE

1. Most scholars (think, thinks) the author of *Le Morte d'Arthur* is Sir Thomas Malory.

2. (Is, Are) the author Syr Thomas Maleore, knight, the same as Sir Thomas Malory?

3. Sir Thomas himself, who lived during the Middle Ages, (was, were) a knight.

4. There (is, are) many knights and ladies in the tales of King Arthur.

5. One of the greatest prose works in the English language, *Le Morte d'Arthur* (was, were) based on French versions that were told earlier.

6. Many legends of King Arthur (was, were) also preserved in Wales.

7. Nearly everyone reading these tales (enjoy, enjoys) the adventures of the knights and ladies.

8. Several times Malory (was, were) put in prison.

9. He spent the last three years of his life in prison; he wrote *Le Morte d'Arthur* while he (was, were) there.

10. These tales featuring King Arthur (was, were) published after Malory's death.

11.8 SENTENCES WITH PREDICATE NOMINATIVES

When a predicate nominative serves as a complement in a sentence, use a verb that agrees with the subject, not the complement.

EXAMPLES:

The tales of King Arthur are a great work of literature. (*Tales* is the subject and it takes the plural verb *are.*)

A great work of literature is the tales of King Arthur. (The subject is the singular noun *work.*)

11.9 *DON'T* AND *DOESN'T* AS AUXILIARY VERBS

The auxiliary verb *doesn't* is used with singular subjects and with the personal pronouns *she, he,* and *it.* The auxiliary verb *don't* is used with plural subjects and with the personal pronouns *I, we, you,* and *they.*

SINGULAR: *She doesn't want to be without her cane. Doesn't the school provide help?*

PLURAL: *They don't know what it's like to be hungry. Bees don't like these flowers by the door.*

11.10 COLLECTIVE NOUNS AS SUBJECTS

Collective nouns are singular nouns that name groups of persons or things. *Team,* for example, is the collective name of a group of individuals. A collective noun takes a singular verb when the group acts as a single unit. It takes a plural verb when the members of the group act separately.

EXAMPLES:

Our team usually wins. (The team as a whole wins.)

Our team vote differently on most issues. (The individual members vote.)

11.11 RELATIVE PRONOUNS AS SUBJECTS

When the relative pronoun *who, which,* or *that* is used as a subject in an adjective clause, the verb in the clause must agree in number with the antecedent of the pronoun.

SINGULAR: *Have you selected **one** of the poems that **is** meaningful to you?*

The antecedent of the relative pronoun *that* is the singular *one;* therefore, *that* is singular and must take the singular verb *is.*

PLURAL: *The younger **redwoods,** which grow in a circle around an older tree, **are** also very tall.*

The antecedent of the relative pronoun *which* is the plural *redwoods.* Therefore, *which* is plural, and it takes the plural verb *grow.*

The key to becoming an independent reader is to develop a toolkit of vocabulary strategies. By learning and practicing the strategies, you'll know what to do when you encounter unfamiliar words while reading. You'll also know how to refine the words you use for different situations—personal, school, and work.

Being a good speller is important when communicating your ideas in writing. Learning basic spelling rules and checking your spelling in a dictionary will help you spell words that you may not use frequently.

VOCABULARY PRACTICE

For more practice, go to the **Vocabulary Center** at **ClassZone.com.**

1 Using Context Clues

The context of a word is made up of the punctuation marks, words, sentences, and paragraphs that surround the word. A word's context can give you important clues about its meaning.

1.1 GENERAL CONTEXT

Sometimes you need to infer the meaning of an unfamiliar word by reading all the information in a passage.

On extremely hot days, Mariah languidly tends her garden. First she moseys to the yard to water her plants. Then she sits under a shady tree.

You can figure out from the context that *languidly* means "very slowly."

1.2 SPECIFIC CONTEXT CLUES

Sometimes writers help you understand the meanings of words by providing specific clues of the kinds shown in the chart.

1.3 IDIOMS, SLANG, AND FIGURATIVE LANGUAGE

An **idiom** is an expression whose overall meaning is different from the meaning of the individual words. **Slang** is informal language in which made-up words and ordinary words are used to mean something different from their meanings in formal English. **Figurative language** is language that communicates meaning beyond the literal meaning of words. Use context clues to figure out the meanings of idioms, slang, and figurative language.

Trying to find the ring was like looking for a needle in a haystack. (idiom; conveys idea of "difficulty")

When Brenda couldn't find her ring right away, she went ballistic. (slang; means "became angry")

Mr. Gray has had the same car for over 20 years. Now it is just a rusty tin can. (figurative language; rusty tin can symbolizes the age and condition of the car)

Specific Context Clues		
Type of Clue	**Key Words/ Phrases**	**Example**
Definition or restatement of the meaning of the word	or, which is, that is, in other words, also known as, also called	A lichen is an example of *symbiosis*, **a relationship in which two living things live closely together and at least one benefits.**
Example following an unfamiliar word	such as, like, as if, for example, especially, including	*Prokaryotes,* which **include bacteria and blue-green algae,** are among the oldest forms of animal life.
Comparison with a more familiar word or concept	as, like, also, similar to, in the same way, likewise	He was as much a *prankster* **as** his brother was a **practical joker.**
Contrast with a familiar word or experience	unlike, but, however, although, on the other hand, on the contrary	Most organisms **need oxygen to survive, but** many types of bacteria are *anaerobic.*
Cause-and-effect relationship in which one term is familiar	because, since, when, consequently, as a result, therefore	**Because** they have a system of *membranes*, fish can use their **skin and gill tissue to** adjust to different salt levels in the water.

For more information, see **Vocabulary Strategy: Metaphors and Similes,** *pages 502, 664, 790, and 1062.*

2 Analyzing Word Structure

Many words can be broken into smaller parts. These word parts include base words, roots, prefixes, and suffixes.

2.1 BASE WORDS

A **base word** is a word part that by itself is also a word. Other words or word parts can be added to base words to form new words.

2.2 ROOTS

A **root** is a word part that contains the core meaning of the word. Many English words contain roots that come from older languages such as Greek, Latin, Old English (Anglo-Saxon), and Norse. Knowing the meaning of the word's root can help you determine the word's meaning.

Root	Meaning	Example
anthrop (Greek)	human being	anthropology
hydr (Greek)	water	dehydrate
quer, quest (Latin)	ask, seek	question
pend, pens (Latin)	hang	pendulum
hēadfod (Old English)	head, top	headfirst

*For more information, see **Vocabulary Strategy: Word Roots**, pages 42, 220, 258, 315, 350, 358, and 541.*

2.3 PREFIXES

A **prefix** is a word part attached to the beginning of a word. Most prefixes come from Greek, Latin, or Old English.

Prefix	Meaning	Example
anti-	opposed to	**anti**social
de-	down, away from	**de**grade
sub-	under	**sub**marine

*For more information, see **Vocabulary Strategy: Prefixes**, pages 58, 72, 440, and 878.*

2.4 SUFFIXES

A **suffix** is a word part that appears at the end of a root or base word to form a new word. Some suffixes do not change word meaning. These suffixes are

- added to nouns to change the number of persons or objects
- added to verbs to change the tense
- added to modifiers to change the degree of comparison

Suffixes	Meaning	Examples
-s, -es	to change the number of a noun	trunk + s = trunks
-d, -ed, -ing	to change verb tense	sprinkle + d = sprinkled
-er, -est	to change the degree of comparison in modifiers	cold + er = colder icy + est = iciest

Other suffixes can be added to a root or base to change the word's meaning. These suffixes can also determine a word's part of speech.

Suffix	Meaning	Example
-ic	characterized by	sarcastic
-ion	process of	capitalization
-ness	condition of	uneasiness

*For more information, see **Vocabulary Strategy: Suffix -ion**, page 891.*

Strategies for Understanding Unfamiliar Words

- Look for any prefixes or suffixes. Remove them to isolate the base word or the root.
- See if you recognize any elements—prefix, suffix, root, or base—of the word. You may be able to guess its meaning by analyzing one or two elements.
- Consider the way the word is used in the sentence. Use the context and the word parts to make a logical guess about the word's meaning.
- Consult a dictionary to see whether you are correct.

3 Understanding Word Origins

3.1 ETYMOLOGIES

Etymologies show the origin and historical development of a word. When you study a word's history and origin, you can find out when, where, and how the word came to be.

> **co•ma**[1] (kō′mə) *n., pl.* **–mas** A state of deep, often prolonged unconsciousness, usually the result of injury, disease, or poison, in which an individual is incapable of sensing or responding to external stimuli and internal needs. [Greek *kōma*, deep sleep.]

> **gar•lic** (gär′lĭk) *n.* **1.** An onionlike plant of southern Europe having a bulb that breaks into separate cloves with a strong distinctive odor and flavor. **2.** The bulb of this plant. [Middle English, from Old English *gārlēac* : *gār*, spear + *lēac*, leek.]

> **vin•dic•tive** (vĭn-dĭk′tĭv) *adj.* **1.** Disposed to seek revenge; revengeful. **2.** Marked by or resulting from a desire to hurt; spiteful. (From Latin *vindicta*, vengeance, from *vindex, vindic-,* surety, avenger.]

*For more information, see **Vocabulary Strategy: Etymology,** pages 584, 823, and 1008.*

3.2 WORD FAMILIES

Words that have the same root make up a word family and have related meanings. The chart shows a common Greek and a common Latin root. Notice how the meanings of the example words are related to the meanings of their roots.

Latin Root	*spect:* "see"
English	**inspect** look at carefully
	respect look at with esteem
	spectator someone who watches an event
Greek Root	*phil:* "love"
English	**philharmonic** devoted to music
	philosophy love and pursuit of wisdom
	philanthropy love of humankind

*For more information, see **Vocabulary Strategy: The Kosmos Word Family,** page 905.*

3.3 WORDS FROM CLASSICAL MYTHOLOGY

The English language includes many words from classical mythology. You can use your knowledge of Greek, Roman, and Norse myths to understand the origins and meanings of these words. For example, *herculean task* refers to the strongman Hercules. Thus *herculean task* probably means "a job that is large or difficult." The chart shows a few common words from mythology.

Greek	Roman	Norse
nemesis	insomnia	Thursday
atlas	fury	berserk
adonis	Saturday	rune
mentor	January	valkyrie

PRACTICE AND APPLY

Look up the etymology of each word in the chart and locate the myth associated with it. Use the information from the myth to explain the origin and meaning of each word.

3.4 FOREIGN WORDS

The English language includes words from diverse languages such as French, Dutch, Spanish, Italian, and Chinese. Many words stayed the way they were in their original language.

French	Dutch	Spanish	Italian
mirage	cookie	tornado	studio
vague	snoop	bronco	ravioli
beau	hook	salsa	opera

4 Synonyms and Antonyms

4.1 SYNONYMS

A **synonym** is a word with a meaning similar to that of another word. You can find synonyms in a thesaurus or a dictionary. In a dictionary, synonyms are often given as part of the definition of a word. The following word pairs are synonyms:

dry/arid   enthralled/fascinated   gaunt/thin

4.2 ANTONYMS

An **antonym** is a word with a meaning opposite that of another word. The following word pairs are antonyms:

friend/enemy	absurd/logical
courteous/rude	languid/energetic

5 Denotation and Connotation

5.1 DENOTATION

A word's dictionary meaning is called its **denotation.** For example, the denotation of the word *rascal* is "an unethical, dishonest person."

5.2 CONNOTATION

The images or feelings you connect to a word add a finer shade of meaning, called **connotation.** The connation of a word goes beyond its basic dictionary definition. Writers use connotations of words to communicate positive or negative feelings.

Positive	Neutral	Negative
save	store	hoard
fragrance	smell	stench
display	show	flaunt

Make sure you understand the denotation and connotation of a word when you read it or use it in your writing.

*For more information, see **Vocabulary Strategy: Connotation and Denotation,** pages 93, 200, 626, and 1042.*

6 Analogies

An **analogy** is a comparison between two things that are similar in some way but are otherwise dissimilar. Analogies are sometimes used in writing when unfamiliar subjects or ideas are explained in terms of familiar ones. Analogies often appear on tests as well, usually in a format like this:

TERRIER : DOG ::   A) rat : fish
                   B) kitten : cat
                   C) trout : fish
                   D) fish : trout
                   E) poodle : collie

Follow these steps to determine the correct answer:

- Read the part in capital letters as "terrier is to dog as...."
- Read the answer choices as "rat is to fish," "kitten is to cat," and so on.
- Ask yourself how the words *terrier* and *dog* are related. (A terrier is a type of dog.)
- Ask yourself which of the choices shows the same relationship. (A kitten is a kind of cat, but not in the same way that a terrier is a kind of dog. Therefore, the answer is C.)

*For more information, see **Vocabulary Strategy: Analogies** pages 418, 522, 616, and 1029.*

7 Homonyms and Homophones

7.1 HOMONYMS

Homonyms are words that have the same spelling and sound but have different origins and meanings.

> *I don't want to bore you with a story about how I had to bore through the living room wall.*

Bore can mean "cause a person to lose interest," but an identically spelled word means "to drill a hole."

> *My dog likes to bark while it scratches the bark on the tree in the backyard.*

Bark can mean "the sound made by a dog." However, another identically spelled word means "the outer covering of a tree." Each word has a different meaning and its own dictionary entry.

Sometimes only one of the meanings of a homonym may be familiar to you. Use context clues to help you figure out the meaning of an unfamiliar word.

7.2 HOMOPHONES

Homophones are words that sound alike but have different meanings and spellings. The following homophones are frequently misused:

it's/its	they're/their/there
to/too/two	stationary/stationery

Many misused homophones are pronouns and contractions. Whenever you are unsure whether to write *your* or *you're* and *who's* or *whose*, ask yourself if you mean *you are* and *who is/has*. If you do, write the contraction. For other homophones, such as *scent* and *sent,* use the meaning of the word to help you decide which one to use.

8 Words with Multiple Meanings

Over time, some words have acquired additional meanings that are based on the original meaning.

> EXAMPLES: *I was in a hurry, so I jammed my clothes into the suitcase. Unfortunately, I jammed my finger in the process.*

These two uses of *jam* have different meanings, but both of them have the same origin. You will find all the meanings of this word listed in one entry in the dictionary.

9 Specialized Vocabulary

Specialized vocabulary is special terms suited to a particular field of study or work. For example, science, mathematics, and history all have their own technical or specialized vocabularies. To figure out specialized terms, you can use context clues and reference sources, such as dictionaries on specific subjects, atlases, or manuals.

*For more information, see **Vocabulary Strategy: Specialized Vocabulary,** pages 128 and 601.*

10 Using Reference Sources

10.1 DICTIONARIES

A **general dictionary** will tell you not only a word's definitions but also its pronunciation, parts of speech, and history and origin. A **specialized dictionary** focuses on terms related to a particular field of study or work. Use a dictionary to check the spelling of any word you are unsure of in your English class and other classes as well.

*For more information, see **Vocabulary Strategy: Using a Dictionary,** page 928.*

10.2 THESAURI

A **thesaurus** (plural, *thesauri*) is a dictionary of synonyms. A thesaurus can be especially helpful when you find yourself using the same modifiers over and over again.

*For more information, see **Vocabulary Strategy: Using a Thesaurus,** page 642.*

10.3 SYNONYM FINDERS

A **synonym finder** is often included in word-processing software. It enables you to highlight a word and be shown a display of its synonyms.

10.4 GLOSSARIES

A **glossary** is a list of specialized terms and their definitions. It is often found in the back of a book and sometimes includes pronunciations. Many textbooks contain glossaries. In fact, this textbook has three glossaries: the **Glossary of Literary Terms,** the **Glossary of Reading & Informational Terms,** and the **Glossary of Vocabulary in English & Spanish.** Use these glossaries to help you understand how terms are used in this textbook.

11 Spelling Rules

11.1 WORDS ENDING IN A SILENT *E*

Before adding a suffix beginning with a vowel or *y* to a word ending in a silent *e,* drop the *e* (with some exceptions).

> **amaze + -ing = amazing**
> **love + -able = lovable**
> **create + -ed = created**
> **nerve + -ous = nervous**

Exceptions: *change + -able = changeable; courage + -ous = courageous*

When adding a suffix beginning with a consonant to a word ending in a silent *e,* keep the *e* (with some exceptions).

> **late + -ly = lately**
> **spite + -ful = spiteful**
> **noise + -less = noiseless**
> **state + -ment = statement**

Exceptions: *truly, argument, ninth, wholly, awful, and others.*

When a suffix beginning with *a* or *o* is added to a word with a final silent *e*, the final *e* is usually retained if it is preceded by a soft *c* or a soft *g*.

bridge + -able = bridgeable
peace + -able = peaceable
outrage + -ous = outrageous
advantage + -ous = advantageous

When a suffix beginning with a vowel is added to words ending in *ee* or *oe*, the final, silent *e* is retained.

agree + -ing = agreeing   **free + -ing = freeing**
hoe + -ing = hoeing   **see + -ing = seeing**

11.2 WORDS ENDING IN Y

Before adding most suffixes to a word that ends in *y* preceded by a consonant, change the *y* to *i*.

easy + -est = easiest
crazy + -est = craziest
silly + -ness = silliness
marry + -age = marriage
Exceptions: *dryness, shyness,* and *slyness.*

However, when you add *-ing,* the *y* does not change.

empty + -ed = emptied   but
empty + -ing = emptying

When you add a suffix to a word that ends in *y* preceded by a vowel, the *y* usually does not change.

play + -er = player
employ + -ed = employed
coy + -ness = coyness
pay + -able = payable

11.3 WORDS ENDING IN A CONSONANT

In one-syllable words that end in one consonant preceded by one short vowel, double the final consonant before adding a suffix beginning with a vowel, such as *-ed* or *-ing.* These are sometimes called 1+1+1 words.

dip + -ed = dipped   **set + -ing = setting**
slim + -est = slimmest   **fit + -er = fitter**

The rule does not apply to words of one syllable that end in a consonant preceded by two vowels.

feel + -ing = feeling   **peel + -ed = peeled**
reap + -ed = reaped   **loot + -ed = looted**

In words of more than one syllable, double the final consonant when accent is on the last syllable and remains there once the suffix is added, as in the following examples:

be•gin´ + -ing = be•gin´ ning = beginning
per•mit´ + -ed = per•mit´ ted = permitted

However, do not double the final consonant when the accent is on the final consonant but does not remain there when the suffix is added.

tra´vel + er = tra´vel•er = traveler
mar´ket + er = mar´ket•er = marketer

Do not double the final consonant when the accent is on the first syllable, as in the following examples:

re•fer´ + -ence = ref´er•ence = reference
con•fer´ + -ence = con´fer•ence = conference

11.4 PREFIXES AND SUFFIXES

When adding a prefix to a word, do not change the spelling of the base word. When a prefix creates a double letter, keep both letters.

dis- + approve = disapprove
re- + build = rebuild
ir- + regular = irregular
mis- + spell = misspell
anti- + trust = antitrust
il- + logical = illogical

When adding *-ly* to a word ending in *l,* keep both *l*'s. When adding *-ness* to a word ending in *n,* keep both *n*'s.

careful + -ly = carefully
sudden + -ness = suddenness
final + -ly = finally
thin + -ness = thinness

11.5 FORMING PLURAL NOUNS

To form the plural of most nouns, just add -s.

prizes   dreams   circles   stations

For most singular nouns ending in *o,* add -s.

solos   halos   studios   photos   pianos

For a few nouns ending in *o,* add -es.

heroes   tomatoes   potatoes   echoes

When the singular noun ends in *s, sh, ch, x,* or *z,* add -es.

waitresses   brushes   ditches
axes   buzzes

When a singular noun ends in *y* with a consonant before it, change the *y* to *i* and add -es.

army—armies   candy—candies
baby—babies   diary—diaries
ferry—ferries   conspiracy—conspiracies

When a vowel (*a, e, i, o, u*) comes before the *y,* just add -s.

boy—boys   way—ways
array—arrays   alloy—alloys
weekday—weekdays   jockey—jockeys

For most nouns ending in *f* or *fe,* change the *f* to *v* and add -es or -s.

life—lives   calf—calves   knife—knives
thief—thieves   shelf—shelves loaf—loaves

For some nouns ending in *f,* add -s to make the plural.

roofs   chiefs   reefs   beliefs

Some nouns have the same form for both singular and plural.

deer   sheep   moose   salmon   trout

For some nouns, the plural is formed in a special way.

man—men   goose—geese
ox—oxen   woman—women
mouse—mice   child—children

For a compound noun written as one word, form the plural by changing the last word in the compound to its plural form.

stepchild—stepchildren   firefly—fireflies

If a compound noun is written as a hyphenated word or as two separate words, change the most important word to the plural form.

brother-in-law—brothers-in-law
life jacket—life jackets

11.6 FORMING POSSESSIVES

If a noun is singular, add 's.

mother—my mother's car   Ross—Ross's desk

Exception: The *s* after the apostrophe is dropped after *Jesus', Moses',* and certain names in classical mythology (*Zeus'*). These possessive forms can thus be pronounced easily.

If a noun is plural and ends with *s,* just add an apostrophe.

parents—my parents' car
the Santinis—the Santinis' house

If a noun is plural but does not end in *s,* add 's.

people—the people's choice
women—the women's coats

11.7 SPECIAL SPELLING PROBLEMS

Only one English word ends in -sede: *supersede.* Three words end in -ceed: *exceed, proceed,* and *succeed.* All other verbs ending in the sound "seed" are spelled with -cede.

concede   precede   recede   secede

In words with **ie** or **ei,** when the sound is long *e* (as in *she*), the word is spelled *ie* except after *c* (with some exceptions).

i before *e*	thief	relieve	field
	piece	grieve	pier
except after *c*	conceit	perceive	ceiling
	receive	receipt	
Exceptions:	either	neither	weird
	leisure	seize	

12 Commonly Confused Words

WORDS	DEFINITIONS	EXAMPLES
accept/except	The verb *accept* means "to receive or believe"; *except* is usually a preposition meaning "excluding."	**Except** for some of the more extraordinary events, I can **accept** that the *Odyssey* recounts a real journey.
advice/advise	*Advise* is a verb; *advice* is a noun naming that which an *adviser* gives.	I **advise** you to take that job. Whom should I ask for **advice?**
affect/effect	As a verb, *affect* means "to influence." *Effect* as a verb means "to cause." If you want a noun, you will almost always want *effect.*	Did Circe's wine **affect** Odysseus' mind? It did **effect** a change in Odysseus' men. In fact, it had an **effect** on everyone else who drank it.
all ready/already	*All ready* is an adjective meaning "fully ready." *Already* is an adverb meaning "before or by this time."	He was **all ready** to go at noon. I have **already** seen that movie.
allusion/illusion	An allusion is an indirect reference to something. An illusion is a false picture or idea.	There are many **allusions** to the works of Homer in English literature. The world's apparent flatness is an **illusion.**
among/between	*Between* is used when you are speaking of only two things. *Among* is used for three or more.	**Between** *Hamlet* and *King Lear*, I prefer the latter. Emily Dickinson is **among** my favorite poets.
bring/take	*Bring* is used to denote motion toward a speaker or place. *Take* is used to denote motion away from a person or place.	**Bring** the books over here, and I will **take** them to the library.
fewer/less	*Fewer* refers to the number of separate, countable units. *Less* refers to bulk quantity.	We have **less** literature and **fewer** selections in this year's curriculum.
leave/let	*Leave* means "to allow something to remain behind." *Let* means "to permit."	The librarian will **leave** some books on display but will not **let** us borrow any.
lie/lay	*Lie* means "to rest or recline." It does not take an object. *Lay* always takes an object.	Rover loves to **lie** in the sun. We always **lay** some bones next to him.
loose/lose	*Loose* (lo͞os) means "free, not restrained"; *lose* (lo͞oz) means "to misplace or fail to find."	Who turned the horses **loose?** I hope we won't **lose** any of them.
precede/proceed	*Precede* means "to go or come before." Use *proceed* for other meanings.	Emily Dickinson's poetry **precedes** that of Alice Walker. You may **proceed** to the next section of the test.
than/then	Use *than* in making comparisons; use *then* on all other occasions.	Who can say whether Amy Lowell is a better poet **than** Denise Levertov? I will read Lowell first, and **then** I will read Levertov.
two/too/to	*Two* is the number. *Too* is an adverb meaning "also" or "very." Use *to* before a verb or as a preposition.	Meg had **to** go **to** town, **too.** We had **too** much reading **to** do. **Two** chapters is **too** many.
their/there/they're	*Their* means "belonging to them." *There* means "in that place." *They're* is the contraction for "they are."	**There** is a movie playing at 9 P.M. **They're** going to see it with me. Sakara and Jessica drove away in **their** car after the movie.

Effective oral communication occurs when the audience understands a message the way the speaker intends it. Good speakers and listeners do more than just talk and hear. They use specific techniques to present their ideas effectively, and they are attentive and critical listeners.

1 Speech

In school, in business, and in community life, a speech is one of the most effective means of communicating.

1.1 AUDIENCE, PURPOSE, AND OCCASION

When developing and delivering a speech, your goal is to deliver a focused, coherent presentation that conveys your ideas clearly and relates to the background of your audience. By understanding your audience, you can tailor your speech to them appropriately and effectively.

- **Know Your Audience** What kind of group are you presenting to? Fellow classmates? A group of teachers? What are their interests and backgrounds? Understanding their different points of view can help you organize the information so that they understand and are interested in it.

- **Understand Your Purpose** Keep in mind your purpose for speaking. Are you trying to persuade the audience to do something? Perhaps you simply want to entertain them by sharing a story or experience. Your reason for giving the speech will guide you in organizing your thoughts and deciding on how to deliver it.

- **Know the Occasion** Are you speaking at a special event? Is it formal? Will others be giving speeches besides you? Knowing what the occasion is will help you tailor the language and the length for the event.

1.2 PREPARING YOUR SPEECH

There are several approaches to preparing a speech. Your teacher may tell you which one to use.

Manuscript	Prepare a complete script of the speech in advance and use it to deliver the speech. Use for formal occasions, such as graduation speeches and political addresses, and to present technical or complicated information.
Memory	Prepare a written text in advance and then memorize it in order to deliver the speech word for word. Use for short speeches, as when introducing another speaker or accepting an award.
Extemporaneous	Prepare the speech and deliver it using an outline or notes. Use for informal situations, for persuasive messages, and to make a more personal connection with the audience.

1.3 DRAFTING YOUR SPEECH

If you are writing your speech beforehand, rather than working from notes, use the following guidelines to help you:

- **Create a Unified Speech** Do this first by organizing your speech into paragraphs, each of which develops a single main idea. Then make sure that just as all the sentences in a paragraph support the main idea of the paragraph, all the paragraphs in your speech support the main idea of the speech.

- **Use Appropriate Language** The subject of your speech—and the way you choose to present it—should match your audience, your purpose, and the occasion. You can use informal language, such as slang, to share a story with your classmates. For a persuasive speech in front of a school assembly, use formal, standard American English. If you are giving an informative presentation, be sure to explain any terms that the audience may not be familiar with.

- **Provide Evidence** Include relevant facts, statistics, and incidents; quote experts to support your ideas and opinions. Elaborate—provide specific details, perhaps with visual or media displays—to clarify what you are saying.

- **Emphasize Important Points** To help your audience follow the main ideas and concepts of your speech, be sure to draw attention to important points. You can use rhyme, repetition, and other rhetorical devices.

- **Use Precise Language** Use precise language to convey your ideas, and vary the structure and length of your sentences. You can keep the audience's attention with a word that elicits strong emotion. You can use a question or interjection to make a personal connection with the audience.

- **Start Strong, Finish Strong** As you begin your speech, consider using a "hook"—an interesting question or statement meant to capture your audience's attention. At the end of the speech, restate your main ideas simply and clearly. Perhaps conclude with a powerful example or anecdote to reinforce your message.

- **Revise Your Speech** After you write your speech, revise, edit, and proofread it as you would a written report. Use a variety of sentence structures to achieve a natural rhythm. Check for correct subject-verb agreement and consistent verb tense. Correct run-on sentences and sentence fragments. Use parallel structure to emphasize ideas. Make sure you use complete sentences and correct punctuation and capitalization, even if no one else will see it. Your written speech should be clear and error-free. If you notice an error in your notes during the speech, you may not remember what you actually wanted to say.

1.4 DELIVERING YOUR SPEECH

Confidence is the key to a successful presentation. Use these techniques to help you prepare and present your speech:

Prepare

- **Review Your Information** Reread your notes and review any background research. You'll feel more confident during your speech.

- **Organize Your Notes** Some people prefer to include only key points. Others prefer the entire script. Write each main point, or each paragraph, of your speech on a separate numbered index card. Be sure to include your most important evidence and examples.

- **Plan Your Visual Aids** If you are planning on using visual aids, such as slides, posters, charts, graphs, video clips, overhead transparencies, or computer projections, now is the time to design them and decide how to work them into your speech.

Practice

- **Rehearse** Rehearse your speech several times, possibly in front of a practice audience. Maintain good posture by standing with your shoulders back and your head up. If you are using visual aids, practice handling them. Adapt your rate of speaking, pitch, and tone of voice to your audience and setting. Glance at your notes to refresh your memory, but avoid reading them word for word. Your style of performance should express the purpose of your speech. Use the following chart to help you.

Purpose	Pace	Pitch	Tone
To persuade	fast but clear	even	urgent
To inform	using plenty of pauses	even	authoritative
To entertain	usually building to a "punch"	varied to create characters or drama	funny or dramatic

- **Use Audience Feedback** If you had a practice audience, ask them specific questions about your delivery: Did I use enough eye contact? Was my voice at the right volume? Did I stand straight, or did I slouch? Use the audience's comments to evaluate the effectiveness of your delivery and to set goals for future rehearsals.

- **Evaluate Your Performance** When you have finished each rehearsal, evaluate your performance. Did you pause to let an important point sink in or use gestures for emphasis? Make a list of the aspects of your presentation that you will try to improve for your next rehearsal.

Present

- **Begin Your Speech** Try to look relaxed and smile.

- **Make Eye Contact** Try to make eye contact with as many audience members as possible. This will establish personal contact and help you determine if the audience understands your speech.

- **Remember to Pause** A slight pause after important points will provide emphasis and give your audience time to think about what you're saying.

- **Speak Clearly** Speak loud enough to be heard clearly, but not so loud that your voice is overwhelming. Use a conversational tone.

- **Maintain Good Posture** Stand up straight and avoid nervous movements that may distract the audience's attention from what you are saying.

- **Use Expressive Body Language** Use facial expressions to show your feelings toward your topic. Lean forward when you make an important point; move your hands and arms for emphasis. Use your body language to show your own style and reflect your personality.

- **Watch the Audience for Responses** If they start fidgeting or yawning, speak a little louder or get to your conclusion a little sooner. Use what you learn to evaluate the effectiveness of your speech and to decide what areas need improvement for future presentations.

- **Close your speech by thanking your audience.**

Respond to Questions

Depending on the content of your speech, your audience may have questions. Follow these steps to make sure that you answer questions in an appropriate manner:

- Think about what your audience may ask and prepare answers before your speech.

- Tell your audience at the beginning of your speech that you will take questions at the end. This helps prevent audience interruptions, which could make your speech hard to follow.

- Call on audience members in the order in which they raise their hands.

- Repeat each question before you answer it to ensure that everyone has heard it. This step also gives you time to prepare your answer.

❷ Different Types of Oral Presentations

2.1 INFORMATIVE SPEECH

When you deliver an informative speech, you give the audience new information, provide a better understanding of information, or enable the audience to use the information in a new way. An informative speech is presented in an objective way.

Use the following questions to evaluate the presentation of a peer or a public figure, or your own presentation.

Evaluate an Informative Speech
- Did the speaker have a specific, clearly focused topic?
- Did the speaker take the audience's previous knowledge into consideration?
- Did the speaker cite sources for the information?
- Did the speaker communicate the information objectively?
- Did the speaker explain technical terms?
- Did the speaker use visual aids effectively?
- Did the speaker anticipate and address any audience concerns or misunderstandings?

*For more information, see **Speaking and Listening: Delivering an Informative Speech**, page 561.*

2.2 PERSUASIVE SPEECH

When you deliver a persuasive speech, you offer a thesis or clear statement on a subject, you provide relevant evidence to support your position, and you attempt to convince the audience to accept your point of view.

Use the following questions to evaluate the presentation of a peer or a public figure, or your own presentation.

Evaluate a Persuasive Speech

- Did the speaker present a clear thesis or argument?
- Did the speaker anticipate and address audience concerns, biases, and counterarguments?
- Did the speaker use sound logic and reasoning in developing the argument?
- Did the speaker support the argument with valid evidence, examples, facts, expert opinions, and quotations?
- Did the speaker use rhetorical devices, such as emotional appeals, to support assertions?
- Did the speaker hold the audience's interest with an effective voice, facial expressions, and gestures?
- Is your reaction to the speech similar to other audience members'?

2.3 DEBATE AN ISSUE

A debate is a balanced argument covering both sides of an issue. In a debate, two teams compete to win the support of the audience. In a formal debate, two teams, each with two members, present their arguments on a given proposition or policy statement. One team argues for the proposition or statement and the other argues against it. Each debater must consider the proposition closely and must research both sides of it. To argue persuasively either for or against a proposition, a debater must be familiar with both sides of the issue.

For more information, see **Speaking and Listening: Debating an Issue,** *page 1071.*

Use the following guidelines to evaluate a debate.

Evaluate a Team in a Debate

- Did the team prove that a significant problem does or does not exist? How thorough was the team's analysis of the problem?
- How did the team convince you that the proposition is or is not the best solution to the problem?
- How effectively did the team present reasons and evidence supporting the case?
- How effectively did the team refute and rebut arguments made by the opposing team?
- Did the speakers maintain eye contact and speak at an appropriate rate and volume?
- Did the speakers observe proper debate etiquette?

PRACTICE AND APPLY

View a political debate for a local, state, or national election. Use the preceding criteria to evaluate it.

2.4 NARRATIVE SPEECH

When you deliver a narrative speech, you tell a story or present a subject using a story-type format. A good narrative keeps an audience informed and entertained. It also allows you to deliver a message in a creative way.

Use the following questions to evaluate a speaker or your own presentation.

Evaluate a Narrative Speech

- Did the speaker choose a context that makes sense and contributes to a believable narrative?
- Did the speaker locate scenes and incidents in specific places?
- Does the plot flow well?
- Did the speaker use words that convey the appropriate mood and tone?
- Did the speaker use sensory details that allow the audience to experience the sights, sounds, and smells of a scene and the specific actions, gestures, and thoughts of the characters?
- Did the speaker use a range of narrative devices to keep the audience interested?
- Is your reaction to the presentation similar to other audience members'?

2.5 DESCRIPTIVE SPEECH

Description is part of most presentations. In a descriptive speech, you describe a subject that you are personally involved with. A good description will enable your listeners to tell how you feel toward your subject through the images you provide.

Use the following questions to evaluate a speaker or your own presentation.

Evaluate a Descriptive Speech

- Did the speaker make clear his or her point of view toward the subject being described?
- Did the speaker use sensory details, figurative language, and factual details?
- Did the speaker use tone and pitch to emphasize important details?
- Did the speaker use facial expressions to emphasize his or her feelings toward the subject?
- Did the speaker change vantage points to help the audience see the subject from another position?
- Did the speaker change perspectives to show how someone else might feel toward the subject or place?

2.6 ORAL INTERPRETATION

When you perform an oral reading, you use appropriate vocal intonations, facial expressions, and gestures to bring a literature selection to life.

*For more information, see **Speaking and Listening: Delivering an Oral Interpretation,** page 753, and **Delivering a Dramatic Reading,** page 1201.*

Use the following questions to evaluate an artistic performance by a peer or a public presenter, a media presentation, or your own performance.

Evaluate an Oral Interpretation

- Did the speaker speak clearly, enunciating each word carefully?
- Did the speaker maintain eye contact with the audience?
- Did the speaker control his or her volume, projecting without shouting?
- Did the speaker vary the rate of speech appropriately to express emotion, mood, and action?
- Did the speaker use a different voice for the character(s)?
- Did the speaker stress important words or phrases?
- Did the speaker use voice, tone, and gestures to enhance meaning?
- Did the speaker's presentation allow you to identify and appreciate elements of the text such as character development, rhyme, imagery, and language?

PRACTICE AND APPLY

Listen to an oral reading by a classmate or view a dramatic performance in a theater or on television. Use the preceding criteria to evaluate it.

2.7 ORAL RESPONSE TO LITERATURE

An oral response to literature is a personal analytic interpretation of a writer's story, novel, poem, or drama. It demonstrates to an audience a solid and comprehensive understanding of what that piece means to you.

*For more information, see **Speaking and Listening: Presenting an Oral Response to Literature,** page 149.*

Use the following questions to evaluate a speaker or your own presentation.

Evaluate an Oral Response to Literature

- Did the speaker choose an interesting piece that he or she understands and feels strongly about?
- Did the speaker make a judgment that shows an understanding of significant ideas from the text?
- Did the speaker direct the audience to specific parts of the piece that support his or her idea?
- Did the speaker identify and analyze the use of artistic elements such as imagery, figurative language, and character development?
- Did the speaker demonstrate an appreciation of the author's style?
- Did the speaker discuss any ambiguous or difficult passages and the impact of those passages on the audience?

PRACTICE AND APPLY

Listen as a classmate delivers an oral response to a selection you have read. Use the preceding criteria to evaluate the presentation.

3 Other Types of Communication

3.1 CONVERSATION

Conversations are informal, but they are important means of communicating. When two or more people exchange messages, it is equally important that each person contribute and actively listen.

3.2 GROUP DISCUSSION

Successful groups assign a role to each member. These roles distribute responsibility among the members and help keep discussions focused.

Leader or Chairperson

- Introduces topic
- Explains goal or purpose
- Participates in discussion and keeps it on track
- Helps resolve conflicts
- Helps group reach goal

Recorder

- Takes notes on discussion
- Reports on suggestions and decisions

- Organizes and writes up notes
- Participates in discussion

Participants

- Contribute relevant facts or ideas to discussion
- Respond constructively to one another's ideas
- Reach agreement or vote on final decision

Guidelines for Discussion

- Be informed about the topic.
- Participate in the discussion.
- Ask questions and respond appropriately to questions.
- Don't talk while someone else is talking.
- Support statements and opinions with facts and examples.
- Listen attentively; be courteous and respectful of others' viewpoints.
- Work toward the goal; avoid getting sidetracked by unrelated topics.

*For more information, see **Speaking and Listening: Participating in a Group Discussion**, page 471.*

3.3 INTERVIEW

An **interview** is a formal type of conversation with a definite purpose and goal. To conduct a successful interview, use the following guidelines:

Prepare for the Interview

- Select your interviewee carefully. Identify who has the kind of knowledge and experience you are looking for.
- Set a time, a date, and a place. Ask permission to tape-record the interview.
- Learn all you can about the person you will interview or the topic you want information on.
- Prepare a list of questions. Create questions that encourage detailed responses instead of yes-or-no answers. Arrange your questions in order from most important to least important.
- Arrive on time with everything you need.

Conduct the Interview

- Ask your questions clearly and listen to the responses carefully. Give the person whom you are interviewing plenty of time to answer.

- Be flexible; follow up on any responses you find interesting.

- Avoid arguments; be tactful and polite.

- Even if you tape an interview, take notes on important points.

- Thank the person for the interview, and ask if you can call with any follow-up questions.

Follow Up on the Interview

- Summarize your notes or make a written copy of the tape recording as soon as possible.

- If any points are unclear or if information is missing, call and ask more questions while the person is still available.

- Select the most appropriate quotations to support your ideas.

- If possible, have the person you interviewed review your work to make sure you haven't misrepresented what he or she said.

- Send a thank-you note to the person in appreciation of his or her time and effort.

*For more information, see **Speaking and Listening: Presenting an Oral History**, page 271.*

Evaluate an Interview

You can determine how effective your interview was by asking yourself these questions:

- Did you get the type of information you were looking for?

- Were your most important questions answered to your satisfaction?

- Were you able to keep the interviewee focused on the subject?

---

4 Active Listening

Active listening is the process of receiving, interpreting, evaluating, and responding to a message. Whether you listen to a class discussion or a formal speech, use the following strategies to get as much as you can from the message.

Listening with a Purpose		
Situation	**Reason for Listening**	**How to Listen**
A friend tells a story.	enjoyment	Maintain eye contact; visualize images and events.
A friend tells you a problem.	concern for your friend's well-being	Imagine the person's feelings; don't feel that you have to solve the problem.

Before Listening

- Learn what the topic is beforehand. You may need to read background information about the topic or learn technical terms in order to interpret the speaker's message.

- Think about what you know or want to know about the topic.

- Have a pen and paper or a laptop computer to take notes.

- Establish a purpose for listening.

While Listening

- Focus your attention on the speaker. Your facial expressions and body language should demonstrate your interest in hearing the topic. Ignore barriers such as temperature and noise.

- Listen for the speaker's purpose (usually stated at the beginning), which alerts you to main ideas.

- To help you interpret the speaker's message, listen for words or phrases that signal important points, such as *to begin with, in addition, most important, finally,* and *in conclusion.*

- Listen carefully for explanations of technical terms. Use these terms to help you understand the speaker's message.

- Listen for ideas that are repeated for emphasis.

- Take notes. Write down only the most important points.

- If possible, use an outline or list format to organize main ideas and supporting points.

- Note comparisons and contrasts, causes and effects, or problems and solutions.

- As you take notes, use phrases, abbreviations, and symbols to keep up with the speaker.

- To aid your comprehension, note how the speaker uses word choice, voice pitch, posture, and gestures to convey meaning.

After Listening

- Ask relevant questions to clarify anything that was unclear or confusing.

- Review your notes right away to make sure you understand what was said.

- Summarize and paraphrase the speaker's ideas.

- If you like, compare your interpretation of the speech with the interpretations of others who listened to it.

4.1 CRITICAL LISTENING

Critical listening involves interpreting and analyzing a spoken message to judge its accuracy and reliability. You can use the following strategies as you listen to messages from advertisers, politicians, lecturers, and others:

- **Determine the Speaker's Purpose** Think about the background, viewpoint, and possible motives of the speaker. Separate facts from opinions. Listen carefully to details and evidence that a speaker uses to support the message.

- **Listen for the Main Idea** Figure out the speaker's main message before allowing yourself to be distracted by seemingly convincing facts and details.

- **Recognize the Use of Persuasive Techniques** Pay attention to a speaker's choice of words. Speakers may slant information to persuade you to buy a product or accept an idea. Persuasive devices such as inaccurate generalizations, either/or reasoning, and bandwagon or snob appeal may represent faulty reasoning and provide misleading information.

*For more information, see **Persuasive Techniques**, pages 574 and R22.*

- **Observe Nonverbal Messages** A speaker's gestures, facial expressions, and tone of voice should reinforce the message. If they don't, you should doubt the speaker's sincerity and his or her message's reliability.

- **Give Appropriate Feedback** An effective speaker looks for verbal and nonverbal cues from you, the listener, to gauge how the message is being received. If you understand or agree with the message, you might nod your head. If possible, during or after a presentation, ask questions to clarify understanding.

4.2 VERBAL FEEDBACK

At times you will be asked to give direct feedback to a speaker. You may be asked to evaluate the way the speaker delivered the presentation as well as the content of the presentation.

Evaluate Delivery

- Did the speaker articulate words clearly and distinctly?
- Did the speaker pronounce words correctly?
- Did the speaker vary his or her rate?
- Did the speaker's voice sound natural and not strained?
- Was the speaker's voice loud enough?

Evaluate Content

Here's how to give constructive suggestions for improvement:

Be Specific Don't make statements like "Your charts need work." Offer concrete suggestions, such as "Please make the type bigger so we can read the poster from the back of the room."

Discuss Only the Most Important Points Don't overload the speaker with too much feedback about too many details. Focus on important points, such as:

- Is the topic too advanced for the audience?
- Are the supporting details well organized?
- Is the conclusion weak?

Give Balanced Feedback Tell the speaker not only what didn't work but also what did work: "Consider dropping the last two slides, since you covered those points earlier. The first two slides got my attention."

Every day you are exposed to hundreds of images and messages from television, radio, movies, newspapers, and the Internet. What is the effect of all this media? What do you need to know to be a smart media consumer? Being media literate means that you have the ability to think critically about media messages. It means that you are able to analyze and evaluate media messages and how they influence you and your world. To become media literate, you'll need the tools to study media messages.

MEDIA TOOLS

For more information, visit the **Media Center** at **ClassZone.com.**

1 Five Core Concepts in Media Literacy

from The Center for Media Literacy

The five core concepts of media literacy provide you with the basic ideas you can consider when examining media messages.

All media messages are "constructed." All media messages are made by someone. In fact, they are carefully thought out and researched and have attitudes and values built into them. Much of the information that you use to make sense of the world comes from the media. Therefore, it is important to know how media are put together so you can better understand the messages they convey.

Media messages are constructed using a creative language with its own rules. Each means of communication—whether it be film, television, newspapers, magazines, radio, or the Internet—has its own language and design. Therefore, a message must use the language and design of the medium that conveys the message. Thus, the medium actually shapes the message. For example, a horror film may use music to heighten suspense, or a newspaper may use a big headline to signal the significance of a story. Understanding the language of each medium can increase your enjoyment of it as well as alert you to obvious and subtle influences.

Different people experience the same media messages differently. Personal factors such as age, education, and experience will affect the way a person responds to a media message. How many times has your interpretation of a film or book differed from that of a friend? Everyone interprets media messages through his or her own personal lens.

Media have embedded values and points of view. Media messages carry underlying values, which are purposely built into them by the creators of the message. For example, a commercial's main purpose may be to persuade you to buy something, but it also conveys the value of a particular lifestyle. Understanding not only the core message but also the embedded points of view will help you decide whether to accept or reject the message.

Most media messages are constructed to gain profit and/or power. The creators of media messages often provide a commodity, such as information or entertainment, in order to make money. The bigger the audience, the more the media outlet can charge for advertising. Consequently, media outlets want to build large audiences in order to bring in more revenue from advertising. For example, a television network creates programming that appeals to the largest audience possible, and then uses the viewer ratings to attract more advertising dollars.

2 Media Basics

2.1 MESSAGE

When a film or TV show is created, it becomes a media product. Each media product is created to send a **message,** or an expression of belief or opinion, that serves a specific purpose. In order to understand the message, you will need to deconstruct it.

Deconstruction of a media presentation is the process of analyzing it. To analyze a media presentation you will need to look at its content, its purpose, the audience it's aimed at, and the techniques and elements that are used to create certain effects.

2.2 AUDIENCE

A **target audience** is a specific group of people that a product or presentation is aimed at. The members of a target audience usually share certain characteristics, such as age, gender, ethnic background, values, or lifestyle. For example, a target audience may be adults ages 40 to 60 who want to exercise and eat healthful foods.

Demographics are the characteristics of populations, including age, gender, profession, income, education, ethnicity, and geographical location. Media decision makers use demographics to shape their content to suit the needs and tastes of a target audience.

Nielsen ratings are the system used to track TV audiences and their viewing preferences. Nielsen Media Research, the company that provides this system, monitors TV viewing in a random sample of 5,000 U.S. households.

2.3 PURPOSE

The **purpose,** or intent, of a media presentation is the reason it was made. Most media offerings have more than one purpose. However, every media message has a **core purpose.** To discover that purpose, think about why its creator paid for and produced the message. For example, an ad might entertain you with humor, but its core purpose is to persuade you to buy something.

2.4 TYPES AND GENRES OF MEDIA

The term *media* refers to television, newspapers, magazines, radio, movies, and the Internet. Each is a **medium,** or means for carrying information, entertainment, and advertisements to a large audience.

Each type of medium has different characteristics, strengths, and weaknesses. Understanding how different types of media work and the role they play will help you become more informed about the choices you make in response to the media.

For more information, see **Types of Media,** *page 10.*

2.5 PRODUCERS AND CREATORS

People who control the media are known as **gatekeepers.** Gatekeepers decide what information to share with the public and the ways it will be presented. The following diagram gives some examples.

Who Controls the Media?

Media Owners
TV networks
Recording companies
Publishing companies

Media Products
Television
Radio
Magazines
Movies
Newspapers
Internet

Media Creators
Actors
Writers
Directors
Webmasters

Media Sponsors
Clothing manufacturers
Fast-food restaurants
Department stores

Some forms of media are independently owned, while others are part of a corporate family. Some corporate families might own several different kinds of media. For example, a company may own three radio stations, five newspapers, a publishing company, and a small television station. Often a corporate "parent" decides the content for all of its holdings.

2.6 LAWS GOVERNING MEDIA

Four main laws and policies affect the content, delivery, and use of mass media.

The First Amendment to the Constitution forbids Congress to limit speech or the press.

Copyright law protects the rights of authors and other media creators against the unauthorized publishing, reproduction, and selling of their works.

Laws prohibit **censorship,** any attempt to suppress or control people's access to media messages.

Laws prohibit **libel,** the publication of false statements that damage a person's reputation.

2.7 INFLUENCE OF MEDIA

By sheer volume alone, media influences our very existence, values, opinions, and beliefs. Our environment is saturated with media messages from television, billboards, radio, newspapers, magazines, video games, and so on. Each of these media products is selling one message and conveying another—a message about values—in the subtext. For example, a car ad is meant to sell a car, but if you look closer, you will see that it is using a set of values, such as a luxurious lifestyle, to make the car attractive to the target audience. One message of the ad is that if you buy the car, you'll have the luxurious lifestyle. The other message is that the luxurious lifestyle is good and desirable. TV shows, movies, and news programs also convey subtexts of values and beliefs.

Media can also shape your opinions about the world. For example, news about crime shapes our understanding about how much and what type of crime is prevalent in the world around us. TV news items, talk show interviews, and commercials may shape our perception of a political candidate, a celebrity, an ethnic group, a country, or a regional area. As a consequence, our knowledge of someone or someplace may be completely based on the information we receive from the television.

3 Film and TV

Films and television programs come in a variety of types. Films include comedies, dramas, documentaries, and animated features. Televison programs cover an even wider array, including dramas, sitcoms, talk shows, reality shows, newscasts, and so on. Producers of films and producers of television programs rely on many of the same elements to convey their messages. Among these elements are scripts, visual and sound elements, special effects, and editing.

3.1 SCRIPT AND WRITTEN ELEMENTS

The writer and editor craft a story for television or film using a script and storyboard. A **script** is the text or words of a film or television show. A **storyboard** is a device often used to plan the shooting of a film and to help the director envision and convey what the finished product will look like. It consists of a sequence of sketches showing what will appear in the film's shots, often with explanatory notes and dialogue written beside or underneath them, as shown in the example.

For more information, see **Media Study: Produce Your Own Media,** *page 133.*

3.2 VISUAL ELEMENTS

Visual elements in film and television include camera shots, angles, and movements, as well as film components such as mise en scène, set design, props, and visual special effects.

A **camera shot** is a single, continuous view taken by a camera. **Camera angle** is the angle at which the camera is positioned during the recording of a shot or image. Each angle is carefully planned to create an effect. The chart shows what different shots are used for.

Camera Shot/Angle	Effect
Establishing shot introduces viewers to the location of a scene, usually by presenting a wide view of an area	establishes the setting of a film
Close-up shot shows a detailed view of a person or an object	helps to create emotion and make viewers feel as if they know the character
Medium shot shows a view wider than a close-up but narrower than an establishing or a long shot	shows part of an object or a character from the knees or waist up
Long shot is a wide view of a scene, showing the full figure(s) of a person or group and the surroundings	allows the viewer to see the "big picture" and shows the relationship between characters and the environment
Reaction shot shows someone reacting to something that occurred in a previous shot	allows the viewer to see how the subject feels in order to create empathy in the viewer
Low-angle shot looks up at an object or a person	makes a character, an object, or a scene appear more important or threatening
High-angle shot looks down on an object or a person	makes a character, an object, or a scene seem vulnerable or insignificant
Point-of-view (POV) shot shows a part of the story through a character's eyes	helps viewers identify with that character

Camera movement can create energy, reveal information, or establish a mood. The following chart shows some of the ways filmmakers move the camera to create an effect.

Camera Movement	Effect
Pan is a shot in which the camera scans a location from right to left or left to right	reveals information by showing a sweeping view of an area
Tracking shot is a shot in which the camera moves with the subject	establishes tension or creates a sense of drama
Zoom is the movement of the camera as it closes in on or moves farther away from the subject	captures action or draws the viewer's attention to detail

Mise en scène is a French term that refers to the arrangement of actors, props, and action on a film set. It is used to describe everything that can be seen in a frame, including the setting, lighting, visual composition, costumes, and action.

Framing is capturing people and objects within the "frame" of a screen or image. Framing is what the camera sees.

Composition is the arrangement of objects, characters, shapes, and colors within a frame and the relationship of the objects to one another.

3.3 SOUND ELEMENTS

Sound elements in film and television include music, voice-over, and sound effects.

Music may be used to set the mood and atmosphere in a scene. Music can have a powerful effect on the way viewers feel about a story. For example, fast-paced music helps viewers feel excited during an action scene.

Voice-over is the voice of the unseen commentator or narrator of a film, TV program, or commercial.

Sound effects are the sounds added to films, TV programs, and commercials during the editing process. Sound effects, such as laugh tracks or the sounds of punches in a fight scene, can create humor, emphasize a point, or contribute to the mood.

3.4 SPECIAL EFFECTS

Special effects include computer-generated animation, manipulated video images, and fast- or slow-motion sequences in films, TV programs, and commercials.

Animation on film involves the frame-by-frame photography of a series of drawings or objects. When these frames are projected—at a rate of 24 per second—the illusion of movement is achieved.

A **split screen** is a special-effects shot in which two or more separate images are shown in the same frame. One example is when two people, actually a distance apart, are shown talking to each other.

3.5 EDITING

Editing is the process of selecting and arranging shots in a sequence. The editor decides which scenes or shots to use, as well as the length of each shot, the number of shots, and their sequence. Editing establishes pace, mood, and a coherent story.

Cut is the transition from one shot to another. To create excitement, editors often use quick cuts, which are a series of short shots strung together.

Dissolve is a transitional device in which one scene fades into another.

Fade-in is a transitional device in which a white or black shot fades in to reveal the beginning of a new scene.

Fade-out is a transitional device in which a shot fades to darkness to end a scene.

Jump cut is an abrupt and jarring change from one shot to another. A jump cut shows a break in time or continuity.

Pace is the length of time each shot stays on the screen and the rhythm that is created by the transitions between shots. Short, quick cuts create a fast pace in a story. Long cuts slow down a story.

Parallel editing is a technique that cuts from one shot to another so as to suggest simultaneous action—often in different locations.

4 News

The **news** is information on events, people, and places in your community, your region, the nation, and the world. The news can be categorized by type, as shown in the chart.

Type	Description	Examples
Hard news	fact-based accounts of current events	local newspapers, newscasts, online wire services
Soft news	human-interest stories and other accounts that are less current or urgent than hard news	magazines and tabloid TV shows such as *Sports Illustrated, Access Hollywood*
News features	stories that elaborate on news reports	documentaries such as history reports on PBS
Commentary and opinion	essays and perspectives by experts, professionals, and media personalities	editorial pages, personal Web pages

4.1 CHOOSING THE NEWS

Newsworthiness is the significance of an event or action that makes it worthy of media reporting. Journalists and their editors usually weigh the following criteria in determining which stories should make the news:

Timeliness is the quality of being very current. Timely events usually take priority over previously reported events. For example, a car accident with fatalities will be timely on the day it occurs. Because of its timeliness it may be on the front page of a newspaper or may be the lead story on a newscast.

Impact measures the importance of an event and the number of people it could affect. The more widespread the impact of an event, the more likely it is to be newsworthy.

Proximity gauges the nearness of an event to a particular city, region, or country. People tend to be more interested in stories that take place locally and affect them directly.

Human interest is a quality of stories that cause readers or listeners to feel emotions such as happiness, anger, or sadness. People are interested in reading stories about other people.

Uniqueness belongs to uncommon events or circumstances that are likely to be interesting to an audience.

Compelling video and **photographs** grab people's attention and stay in their minds.

4.2 REPORTING THE NEWS

While developing a news story, a journalist makes a variety of decisions about how to construct the story, such as what information to include and how to organize it. The following elements are commonly used in news stories:

5 *W*'s and *H* are the six questions reporters answer when writing news stories—*who, what, when, where, why,* and *how*. It is a journalist's job to answer these questions in any type of news report. These questions also serve as a structure for writing and editing a story.

Inverted pyramid is the means of organizing information according to importance. In the inverted pyramid diagram below, the most important information (the answers to the 5 *W*'s and *H*) appears at the top of the pyramid. The less important details appear at the bottom. Not all stories are reported using the inverted pyramid form. The style remains popular, however, because it enables a reader to get the essential information without reading the entire story. Notice the following example.

> Men known as swan uppers have protected swans on the River Thames in London for more than eight centuries.
>
> Every July, the men, dressed in dark red or blue jackets, row three or more boats up the middle of the river to up, or check on the condition of, the swans.
>
> The term *upping* is believed to mean simply "going up the river."

Angle or slant is the point of view from which a story is written. Even an objective report must have an angle.

Consider these two headlines that describe a library program.

Patrons Should Return Books to Help Dwindling Collection

Library Offers Amnesty for Overdue Books

The first headline focuses on an opinion of library patrons and has a negative slant. The second headline focuses on facts about a program the library is offering.

Standards for News Reporting

The ideal of journalism is to present news in a way that is objective, accurate, and thorough. The best news stories thus contain the following elements:

- **Objectivity** The story takes a balanced point of view on the issues; it is not biased, nor does it reflect a specific attitude or opinion.

- **Accuracy** The story presents factual information that can be verified.

- **Thoroughness** The story presents all sides of an issue; it includes background information, telling *who, what, when, where, why,* and *how*.

Balanced Versus Biased Reporting

Objectivity in news reporting can be measured by how balanced or biased the story is.

Balanced reporting represents all sides of an issue equally and fairly.

A balanced news story

- represents people and subjects in a neutral light

- treats all sides of an issue equally

- does not include inappropriate questions, such as "Will you seek counseling after this terrible tragedy?"

- does not show stereotypes or prejudice toward people of a particular race, gender, age, religion, or other group
- does not leave out important background information that is needed to establish a context or perspective

Biased reporting is reporting in which one side is favored over another or in which the subject is unfairly represented. Biased reporting may show an overly negative view of a subject, or it may encourage racial, gender, or other stereotypes and prejudices. Sometimes biased reporting is apparent in the journalist's choice of sources.

Sources are the people interviewed for the news report and also any written materials and documents the journalist used for background information. From each source, the journalist gets a different point of view. To decide whether news reporting is balanced or biased, you will need to pay attention to the sources. For a news story on a new medicinal drug, for instance, if the journalist's only source is a representative from the company that made the drug, the report may be biased. But if the journalist also includes the perspective of someone neutral, such as a scientist who is objectively studying the effects of drugs, the report may be more balanced. It is important to evaluate the **credibility,** or the believability and trustworthiness, of both a source and the report itself. The following chart shows which sources are credible.

Sources for News Stories	
Credible Sources	**Weak Sources**
• experts in a field • people directly affected by the reported event (eyewitnesses) • published reports that are specifically mentioned or shown	• unnamed or anonymous sources • people who are not involved in the reported event (for example, people who heard about a story from a friend) • research, data, or reports that are not specifically named or are referred to only in vague terms (for example, "Research shows that . . .")

5 Advertising

Advertising is a sponsor's paid use of various media to promote products, services, or ideas. Some common forms of advertising are shown in the chart.

Type of Ad	Characteristic
Billboard	a large outdoor advertising sign
Print ad	typically appears in magazines and newspapers; uses eye-catching graphics and persuasive copy
Flyer	a print ad that is circulated by hand or mail
Infomercial	an extended ad on TV that usually includes detailed product information, demonstrations, and testimonials
Public service announcement	a message aired on radio or TV to promote ideas that are considered to be in the public interest
Political ad	broadcast on radio or TV to promote political candidates
Trailer	a short film promoting an upcoming movie, TV show, or video game

Marketing is the process of transferring products and services from producer to consumer. It involves determining the packaging and pricing of a product, how it will be promoted and advertised, and where it will be sold. One way companies market their product is by becoming media sponsors.

Sponsors pay for their products to be advertised. These companies hire advertising agencies to create and produce specific campaigns for their products. They then buy television or radio airtime or magazine, newspaper, or billboard space to feature ads where the target audience is sure to see them. Because selling time and space to advertisers generates much of the income the media need to function, the media need advertisers just as much as advertisers need the media.

Product placement is the intentional and identifiable featuring of brand-name products in movies, television shows, video games, and other media. The intention is to have viewers feel positive about a product because they see a favorite character using it. Another purpose may be to promote product recognition.

5.1 PERSUASIVE TECHNIQUES

Persuasive techniques are the methods used to convince an audience to buy a product or adopt an idea. Advertisers use a combination of visuals, sound, special effects, and words to persuade their target audience. Recognizing the following techniques can help you evaluate persuasive media messages and identify misleading information:

Emotional appeals use strong feelings rather than factual evidence to persuade consumers. An example of an emotional appeal is "Is your home safe? ProAlarm Systems will make sure it is."

Bandwagon appeals use the argument that a person should believe or do something because "everyone else" does. These appeals take advantage of people's desire to be socially accepted by other people. Purchasing a popular product seems less risky to those concerned about making a mistake. An example of a bandwagon appeal is "More and more people are making the switch to Discountline long-distance service."

Slogans are memorable phrases used in advertising campaigns. Slogans substitute catchy phrases for factual information.

Logical appeals rely on logic and facts, appealing to a consumer's reason and his or her respect for authority. Two examples of logical appeals are expert opinions and product comparison.

Celebrity ads use one of the following two categories of spokesperson:

- **Celebrity authorities** are experts in a particular field. Advertisers hope that audiences will transfer the respect or admiration they have for the person to the product. For example, a famous chef may endorse a particular brand of cookware. The manufacturers of the cookware want you to think that it is a good product because a cooking expert wouldn't endorse pots and pans that didn't perform well.

- **Celebrity spokespeople** are famous people who endorse a product. Advertisers hope that audiences will associate the product with the celebrity.

Product comparison is comparing between a product and its competition. Often mentioned by name, the competing product is portrayed as inferior. The intended effect is for people to question the quality of the competing product and to believe the featured product is superior.

❻ Elements of Design

The design of a media message is just as important as the words are in conveying the message. Like words, visuals are used to persuade, inform, and entertain.

Graphics and images, such as charts, diagrams, maps, timelines, photographs, illustrations, cartoons, and symbols, present information that can be quickly and easily understood. The following basic elements are used to give meaning to visuals:

Color can be used to highlight important elements such as headlines and subheads. It can also create mood, because many colors have strong emotional or psychological impacts on the reader or viewer. For example, warm colors more readily draw the eye and are often associated with happiness and comfort. Cool colors are often associated with feelings of peace and contentment or sometimes sadness.

Lines—strokes or marks—can be thick or thin, long or short, and smooth or jagged. They can focus attention and create a feeling of depth. They can frame an object. They can also direct a viewer's eye or create a sense of motion.

Texture is the surface quality or appearance of an object. For example, an object's texture can be glossy, rough, wet, or shiny. Texture can be used to create contrast. It can also be used to make an object look "real." For example, a pattern on wrapping paper can create a feeling of depth even though the texture is only visual and cannot be felt.

Shape is the external outline of an object. Shapes can be used to symbolize living things or geometric objects. They can emphasize visual elements and add interest. Shapes can symbolize ideas.

Notice how this movie poster uses design elements.

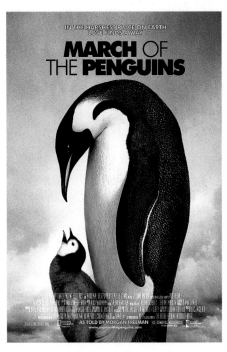

- **Texture** Texture is used to show the contrast of the baby penguin's downy feathers to the adult penguin's smoother feathers.
- **Shape** The shape of the adult penguin's body and the downward slope of its head emphasize the bird's parental nature.
- **Color** Grayish blues and whites suggest the arctic environment that the penguins live in.

7 Evaluating Media Messages

Being able to respond critically to media images and messages will help you evaluate the reliability of the content and make informed decisions. Here are six questions to ask about any media message:

Who made—and who sponsored—this message, and for what purpose? The source of the message is a clue to its purpose. If the source of the message is a private company, that company may be trying to sell you a product. If the source is a government agency, that agency may be trying to promote a program or philosophy. To discover the purpose, think about why its creator paid for and produced the message.

Who is the target audience and how is the message specifically tailored to it? Think about the age group, ethnic group, gender, and/or profession the message is targeting. Decide how it relates to you.

What are the different techniques used to inform, persuade, entertain, and attract attention? Analyze the elements, such as humor, music, special effects, and graphics, that have been used to create the message. Think about how visual and sound effects, such as symbols, color, photographs, words, and music, support the purpose behind the message.

What messages are communicated (and/or implied) about certain people, places, events, behaviors, lifestyles, and so forth? The media try to influence who we are, what we believe, how we view things, and what values we hold. Look or listen closely to determine whether certain types of behavior are being depicted and if judgments or values are communicated through those behaviors. What are the biases in the message?

How current, accurate, and credible is the information in this message? Think about the reputation of the source. Note the broadcast or publication date of the message and whether the message might change quickly. If a report or account is not supported by facts, authoritative sources, or eyewitness accounts, you should question the credibility of the message.

What is left out of this message that might be important to know? Think about what the message is asking you to believe. Also think about what questions come to mind as you watch, read, or listen to the message.

Strategies and Practice for the SAT, ACT, and Other Standardized Tests

The test items in this section are modeled after test formats that are used on the SAT. The strategies presented here will help you prepare for that test and others. This section offers general test-taking strategies and tips for answering multiple-choice items, as well as short-response and extended-response questions in critical reading and writing. It also includes guidelines and samples for impromptu writing and essay writing. For each test, read the tips in the margin. Then apply the tips to the practice items. You can also apply the tips to Assessment Practice Tests in this book.

1 General Test-Taking Strategies

- Arrive on time and be prepared. Be sure to bring either sharpened pencils with erasers or pens—whichever you are told to bring.

- If you have any questions, ask them before the test begins. Make sure you understand the test procedures, the timing, and the rules.

- Read the test directions carefully. Look at the passages and questions to get an overview of what is expected.

- Tackle the questions one at a time rather than thinking about the whole test.

- Refer back to the reading selections as needed. For example, if a question asks about an author's attitude, you might have to reread a passage for clues.

- If you are not sure of your answer, make a logical guess. You can often arrive at the correct answer by reasoning and eliminating wrong answers.

- As you fill in answers on your answer sheet, make sure you match the number of each test item to the numbered space on the answer sheet.

- Don't look for patterns in the positions of correct choices.

- Only change an answer if you are sure your original choice is incorrect. If you do change an answer, erase your original choice neatly and thoroughly.

- Look for main ideas as you read passages. They are often stated at the beginning or the end of a paragraph. Sometimes the main idea is implied.

- Check your answers and reread your essay.

❷ Critical Reading

Most tests contain a critical reading section that measures your ability to read, understand, and interpret passages. The passages may be either fiction or nonfiction, and they can be 100 words or 500 to 800 words. They are drawn from literature, the humanities, social studies, and the natural sciences.

> **Directions:** Read the following passage. Base your answers to questions 1 and 2 on what is stated or implied in the passage.

PASSAGE

Every four years, Greek statesmen and peasants, merchants and philosophers traveled the roads and waterways leading to Olympia. . . . A festival atmosphere prevailed as hawkers peddled their wares, old friends reunited, orators expounded their ideas, and men consumed vast quantities of food and drink. It was noisy, hot, and crowded. Nevertheless, thousands returned time and time again because Olympia offered something unique: the best athletes in the Greek world fighting for supremacy in its most prestigious contest—the Olympic Games. . . .

. . . The competitions celebrated the godlike qualities inherent in man. Victory brought great fame and glory both to the athletes and to their families and hometown. A fifth century B.C. Olympic winner named Diagoras fathered two sons who in turn won Olympic crowns at the 448 B.C. games. The devoted sons placed their wreaths on Diagoras's head and carried him about the stadium on their shoulders. A friend called out as they passed, saying in essence: "Die now, Diagoras, for you have nothing but the heights of Olympus left to scale."

—What Life Was Like at the Dawn of Democracy, *Time-Life Books*

❶ stem

1. The (outcome) of the Olympic Games brought ❷

   ❸ choices

   (A) shame to the hometowns of the losers
   (B) fame and glory to the hometowns of the victors
   (C) fame and fortune to the merchants of Olympia
   (D) war to the towns of the competing athletes ❹
   (E) money to the parents of victorious athletes

2. Which statement most likely explains the remark "Die now, Diagoras"? ❺

   (A) Diagoras's sons shamed him by losing.
   (B) The friend was challenging Diagoras to a duel.
   (C) Diagoras already had achieved great honors.
   (D) Diagoras would die climbing Mount Olympus.
   (E) The friend was from a different city-state.

Tips: Multiple Choice

A multiple-choice question consists of a stem and a set of choices. The stem is usually in the form of a question or an incomplete sentence. One of the choices correctly answers the question or completes the sentence.

❶ Read the stem carefully and try to answer the question without looking at the choices.

❷ Pay attention to key words in the stem. They may direct you to the correct answer.

❸ Read all of the choices before determining the correct answer.

❹ After reading all of the choices, eliminate any that you know are incorrect. In question 1, you can immediately eliminate choice (D), because the passage does not mention this idea.

❺ Some questions ask you to interpret a statement or figure of speech. In question 2, Diagoras's friend is not ordering him to die. The friend means that no matter how long Diagoras lives, he will never surpass the honors he and his sons earned at the Olympic Games.

Answers: 1 (B), 2 (C)

Directions: Following are two passages from a true story of a black youth's life under South Africa's policy of racial discrimination during the 1970s. Base your answers to questions 1 and 2 on these passages.

PASSAGE 1

I don't believe in schools, woman," my father said emphatically. "Just look at all those so-called educated people. What has education done for them? They pick garbage, wash cars, work as garden boys and delivery boys." . . .

One of his strong points whenever he argued with my mother about the pros and cons of schooling was that blacks, before the coming of the white man to Africa, had always taught their offspring ways of being useful and productive in the villages while they were still in the cradle, and that by the time boys and girls were five, six, seven, and eight years old they were already making meaningful contributions to tribal society.

—Mark Mathabane, *Kaffir Boy*

PASSAGE 2

"I want you to go to school because I believe that an education is the key you need to open up a new world and a new life for yourself, a world and life different from that of either your father's or mine. It is the only key that can do that, and only those who seek it earnestly and perseveringly will get anywhere in the white man's world. Education will open doors where none seem to exist."

—Mark Mathabane, *Kaffir Boy*

1. Which statement best describes the two speakers' attitudes toward education?

(A) The speaker in passage 1 thinks that a white person's education is a waste of time for black people. The speaker in passage 2 thinks that education is the key to success in life.

(B) The speaker in passage 1 thinks that education should be free. The speaker in passage 2 thinks that education is worth any price.

(C) The speaker in passage 1 thinks that people should not be overeducated. The speaker in passage 2 thinks that education is only for those who want it.

(D) The speaker in passage 1 thinks that blacks and whites should be educated differently. The speaker in passage 2 thinks that both races should receive an equal education.

(E) The speaker in passage 1 thinks that there are no jobs for black South Africans. The speaker in passage 2 thinks that you can't get ahead in the black world without an education.

2. What does the speaker in passage 2 mean by "Education will open doors where none seem to exist"?

(A) Education is a one-time opportunity.

(B) Education presents its own obstacles.

(C) Education will open imaginary doors.

(D) People will open the door for educated people.

(E) Education will provide new opportunities.

Tips: Two Passages

Questions are sometimes based on a pair of related passages. The passages might express completely different points of view, or they might explore different aspects of the same subject.

❶ Before reading the passages, skim the questions to see what information you will need. The questions here ask about attitudes toward education. Knowing this, you can focus on the key parts of the passages.

❷ Sometimes, it helps to know the historical context of a passage. The directions may provide that information.

❸ Look for a topic sentence in each passage and ask yourself whether the body of the passage supports or refutes that statement.

❹ Analyze the attitudes that are expressed in the readings. When the speaker in passage 1 calls black people who have gone to school "so-called educated people," he conveys his contempt for the white educational system.

❺ Analyze any figures of speech in the readings. How do the images advance the point of view? The speaker in passage 2 compares education to a key that will open doors.

Answers: 1 (A), 2 (E)

Directions: Read the following passage. Base your answers to questions 1 through 4 on what is stated or implied in the passage.

PASSAGE

Now the winter was come upon them. In the forests all summer long, the branches of the trees do battle for light, and some of them lose and die; and then come the raging blasts, and the storms of snow and hail, and strew the ground with these weaker branches. Just so it was in Packingtown; the
5 whole district braced itself for the struggle that was an agony, and those whose time was come died off in hordes. All the year round they had been serving as cogs in the great packing machine; and now was the time for the renovating of it, and the replacing of damaged parts. There came pneumonia and grippe, stalking among them, seeking for weakened constitutions; there
10 was the annual harvest of those whom tuberculosis had been dragging down. There came cruel, cold, and biting winds, and blizzards of snow, all testing relentlessly for failing muscles and impoverished blood. Sooner or later came the day when the unfit one did not report for work; and then, with no time lost in waiting, and no inquiries or regrets, there was a chance for a new
15 hand.

The new hands were here by the thousands. All day long the gates of the packing houses were besieged by starving and penniless men; they came, literally, by the thousands every single morning, fighting with each other for a chance for life. Blizzards and cold made no difference to them, they
20 were always on hand; they were on hand two hours before the sun rose, an hour before the work began. Sometimes their faces froze, sometimes their feet and their hands; sometimes they froze all together—but still they came, for they had no other place to go. One day Durham advertised in the paper for two hundred men to cut ice; and all that day the homeless and starving
25 of the city came trudging through the snow from all over its two hundred square miles. That night forty score of them crowded into the station house of the stockyards district—they filled the rooms, sleeping in each other's laps, toboggan fashion, and they piled on top of each other in the corridors, till the police shut the doors and left some to freeze outside. On the morrow, before
30 daybreak, there were three thousand at Durham's and the police reserves had to be sent for to quell the riot. Then Durham's bosses picked out twenty of the biggest; the "two hundred" proved to have been a printer's error.

—Upton Sinclair, *The Jungle*

Tips: Reading Text

❶ Sometimes, test questions will ask you to interpret an image or comparison. Note how the author uses the first three sentences in the opening paragraph to set up the comparison of trees in the forest to the work situation in Packingtown.

❷ Use words in the passage to help you visualize the people, places, and events as you read. The "cruel wind," "blizzards of snow," and "impoverished blood" depict the harshness of the packinghouse workers' lives.

❸ Analyze the tone of a piece. The author notes that when an unfit worker did not report to work, "there was a chance for a new hand." The stark language conveys the cold reality of survival of the fittest.

❹ Look beyond a literal interpretation. The author writes that the number 200 was a printer's error, but you might consider the possibility that the company had asked for 200 men so that it would have a large pool of applicants from which to pick its 20 men.

Answers: 1 (D), 2 (C), 3 (C), 4 (E)

1. In lines 1–4, the author compares the fallen branches of trees to
    (A) damaged machine parts
    (B) failing muscles
    (C) weak blood
    (D) dying packinghouse workers
    (E) biting winds

2. In line 19, the phrase "a chance for life" refers to
    (A) the decision in a boxing match
    (B) a place out of the cold
    (C) a job in the stockyard district
    (D) recovery from a disease such as tuberculosis
    (E) a life sentence for rioting

3. In line 7, comparing the workers to "cogs in the great packing machine" suggests that they are
    (A) lazy
    (B) well-trained
    (C) replaceable
    (D) unskilled
    (E) mechanized

4. The main idea of this passage is that
    (A) packinghouse workers got sick because they didn't take care of themselves
    (B) unemployed workers were ungrateful for an opportunity to work
    (C) winter was especially cold that year, so many workers were fired
    (D) the great packinghouse machine had many broken parts
    (E) packinghouse owners took advantage of the surplus supply of workers

The critical reading section may feature sentence completion questions that test your knowledge of vocabulary. They may also measure your ability to figure out how different parts of a sentence logically fit together.

Directions: Choose the word or set of words that, when inserted, best fits the meaning of each of the following sentences.

1. *A Christmas Carol* by Charles Dickens illustrates the literary _____ of a man who is driven by _____ greed. ❶
    (A) conflicts . . illicit
    (B) motif . . voracious
    (C) metaphor . . intermittent
    (D) stratagem . . abject
    (E) sophistry . . overweening ❷

2. The Beatles' _____ style of music reflects sounds as _____ as the American blues guitar and the Indian sitar. ❸
    (A) esoteric . . innate
    (B) ephemeral . . ebullient
    (C) incendiary . . potent
    (D) obscure . . ubiquitous
    (E) eclectic . . disparate ❸

3. Because they need to be kept _____ , golf courses in arid regions like the American Southwest can _____ water shortages. ❹
    (A) verdant . . exacerbate
    (B) utopian . . presage
    (C) torrid . . ameliorate
    (D) brackish . . effect
    (E) fallow . . instigate

4. Nelson Mandela _____ the movement against apartheid in South Africa.
    (A) gleaned
    (B) permeated
    (C) proscribed
    (D) galvanized ❺
    (E) pillaged

Tips: Sentence Completion

❶ When you are completing sentences with two words missing, look at both blanks and think about what kinds of words will fill them.

❷ If one of the words in an answer choice is wrong, you can eliminate that set of words. In sentence 1, the word *overweening* is an appropriate description of Scrooge's greed, but *sophistry*, a philosophical term, doesn't fit here.

❸ If you don't know the exact meaning of a word, look for clues in the sentence. In sentence 2, the instruments from different cultures are a clue. The prefix *dis-* in the word *disparate* means "apart."

❹ Look for words or phrases that link the ideas in a sentence. The word *because* in sentence 3 indicates a cause-and-effect relationship between golf courses and water shortages.

❺ You might recognize some words from a completely different context. *Galvanize* means "to subject to the action of applying an electric current." Nelson Mandela energized the anti-apartheid movement.

Answers: 1 (B), 2 (E), 3 (A), 4 (D)

❸ Writing

To measure your ability to express ideas clearly and correctly, tests ask you to identify errors in grammar and usage and to improve sentences and paragraphs.

Directions: Select the one underlined part that must be changed to make the following sentence correct. There is no more than one error in the sentence. If the sentence is correct as written, select answer choice E.

1. When we look at the seven continents today, <u>it's</u> difficult <u>for you</u> to imagine
   (A)❷   (B)❸

   that at one point in the earth's geologic history, they were a <u>contiguous</u> land mass
                                                                        (C)❹

   <u>that</u> was connected by an area called Pangaea. <u>No error</u> ❶
   (D)   (E)

Directions: Determine if the underlined part of the following sentence needs improvement and select the best change presented in the five choices.

2. The national forest system in the United States stretches over 191 million acres, <u>which is including</u> temperate rainforests of the Northwest, the hardwood forests of the Southeast, and high-desert pines of the Great Basin.
   (A) which is including ❺
   (B) which include
   (C) that includes
   (D) including both
   (E) and including

Directions: Read the following passage and answer the question.

> (1) One of New Hampshire's most recognizable residents was the Old Man of the Mountain, a natural rock formation. (2) The profile of the craggy-faced man appears on the reverse of the New Hampshire state quarter, making it America's first two-headed coin. (3) It's a good piece to use in a coin toss. (4) If you call heads, you're sure to win!

3. What is the *best* way to combine sentences 3 and 4? ❻
   (A) It's a good piece to use in a coin toss, because if you call heads you're sure to win.
   (B) It's a good piece to use in a coin toss, if you call heads you're sure to win.
   (C) It's a good piece to use in a coin toss if you call heads; you're sure to win.
   (D) If you call heads you're sure to win because this is a good piece to use in a coin toss.
   (E) Knowing that if you call heads you're sure to win makes it a good piece to use in a coin toss.

Tips: Grammar and Style

❶ Read the entire sentence or passage to grasp its overall meaning. Pay particular attention to any underlined portions.

❷ Misuse of the apostrophe in *its* and *it's* is a common grammatical error. The usage is correct in sentence 1.

❸ A good sentence maintains a consistent point of view. If the subject of one clause is *we*, it should be carried through in the next clause.

❹ Use prefixes to aid your reading comprehension. You may not know what *contiguous* means in sentence 1, but if you know that the prefix *con*- means "together," you can figure out that the land masses were joined in some way.

❺ In choosing a revision, read through all of the choices before you decide which one is best. Choose answer (A) only if the sentence is correct as it appears originally.

❻ To combine sentences, determine how ideas are related. Are they contrasting ideas? Do they express a cause-and-effect relationship? Are they chronological?

Answers: 1 (B), 2 (B), 3 (A)

Some tests may measure your understanding of a passage by asking you to write a response.

Directions: Read the passage. Then follow the directions.

Back then, boys could learn by working on their cars without expensive tools, computers, and complex training, and any who discovered their mechanical talents followed their fathers happily into the factories, where they found financial security, a sense of professionalism, and a pathway up. Michael Summers was young, but he had a sense of that history, and he missed it. "Kids today do not have the ability to work on mechanical things," he said. "We're in a throwaway society where the lawn mower breaks, you don't tear apart this little two-cycle engine. You throw it out and you get another one. . . . [We have a] shortage of tool and dye makers and fluid power mechanics, the guys who are basically screwing things together and building systems. People who are good at that are good because they like it, they have an aptitude for it, and they've had exposure to it. There are a lot of kids who would be good at it, but they have no clue that they have mechanical interest."

—David Shipler, *The Working Poor*

SHORT RESPONSE

Give a short definition of a throwaway society.

SAMPLE SHORT RESPONSE

A throwaway society is one in which things are used just a few times and then thrown away. A good example is the disposable DVD, which automatically erases so that you can't view it again. ❶

EXTENDED RESPONSE

In the passage, Michael Summers argues that kids today never get the chance to discover whether they have an aptitude for fixing things. Explain in one or two paragraphs why you agree or disagree with him. ❷

SAMPLE EXTENDED RESPONSE

I agree that young people today are not learning traditional manual skills, but we do have opportunities to figure out how things work. Today we use different tools. ❸

With computers, we can learn about anything we are interested in and even get hands-on experience. ❸ Last year I searched the Internet to find out how windmills produce electricity. With that information I designed a model windmill that I entered into a science fair. A friend of mine in the school orchestra downloaded an inexpensive computer program for composing music. ❹ He was able to compose a sonata for violin.

Computers can give you experience in figuring things out. With experience comes confidence in your own abilities.

Tips: Responding to Writing Prompts

❶ Short-response prompts are often fact based rather than interpretive. Get to the point in your answer, and stick to the facts.

❷ Make sure you write about the assigned topic. If you are asked to agree or disagree with a passage, don't just restate the author's arguments. Develop your own point of view and support it with examples.

❸ When you are writing an extended response, build your paragraphs around clear topic sentences that will pull your ideas together.

❹ Don't try to cover the entire subject in your response. Focus on one or two main points.

❺ Proofread your response for errors in capitalization, punctuation, spelling, and grammar.

❹ Essay

To determine how well you can develop and support your thoughts, many tests ask you to write an essay in response to an assignment, or prompt. The essay will represent a first draft and will be scored based on the following:

- **Focus** Establish a point of view in the opening paragraph.
- **Organization** Maintain a logical progression of ideas.
- **Support for Ideas** Use details and examples to develop an argument.
- **Style/Word Choice** Use words accurately and vary sentences.
- **Grammar** Use standard English and proofread for errors.

Think carefully about the issue presented in these quotations and the assignment that follows.

> The fact is there is a responsible case to be made for driving SUVs. It can be summed up in three words: "This is America."
>
> —Reg Henry, *Pittsburgh Post-Gazette*
>
> If you buy an SUV, you're buying your safety at the expense of another's. Hit someone and you'll kill them.
>
> —Randy Cohen, *New York Times*

Assignment: What is your view on the idea that sport utility vehicles (SUVs) are being driven on city streets and highways?

SAMPLE ESSAY

Today, light trucks and sport utility vehicles (SUVs) account for nearly half of all new vehicle sales. Although there are some legitimate uses for these oversized vehicles, they are generally unnecessary for today's city and suburban lifestyle. ❶

Sport utility vehicles are designed for off-road travel. That means dirt roads and other rugged terrain. The elevated chassis, four-wheel drive, and heavier body are wasted on the paved streets and highways that we use to get to work or to the shopping malls. Even when we travel across the country, we ride on a system of well-maintained highways. ❷

Some people say SUVs are safer because of their size and weight. That's true only if you are in the SUV. In fact, the bigger vehicles pose a serious risk to the dwindling number of people who still drive compact cars. In a side impact crash, the driver of an SUV might not even be scratched, but the people in the sedan will be severely injured or killed. ❸

The strongest argument against SUVs is environmental. The law allows SUVs to have far worse fuel economy than regular-size cars, and they do. Many popular SUVs get only 12 to 15 miles per gallon of gas. The law also allows SUVs to emit higher levels of toxic pollution.

SUVs have their place, but many of them are not being used appropriately. If we can't convince people not to buy big vehicles they don't need, we can certainly improve the SUVs' fuel economy and emissions. ❹

Tips: Writing an Essay

The SAT allows only 25 minutes for you to write an essay. So before you begin writing, take a few minutes to gather your thoughts. Write down the main points you want to make. Allow time to reread your essay before you hand it in. Make sure your handwriting is legible.

❶ When you're writing a persuasive essay, state your point of view in the introduction.

❷ Concrete examples make your writing come to life, no matter what the topic is. Use examples in the body of your essay to clarify your points and strengthen your arguments. The writer of this essay uses facts and personal observations to bolster the arguments.

❸ Take the opposing point of view into consideration and respond to it.

❹ Make sure your essay has a conclusion, even if it's just a single sentence. A conclusion pulls your ideas together and lets the reader know you have finished.

❺ Allow enough time to reread what you have written. If you have to make a correction, do so neatly and legibly.

Act An act is a major division within a play, similar to a chapter in a book. Each act may be further divided into smaller sections, called scenes. Plays can have as many as five acts, as in Shakespeare's *Julius Caesar*. Anton Chekhov's *A Marriage Proposal* is a one-act play.

Allegory An allegory is a work with two levels of meaning—a literal one and a symbolic one. In such a work, most of the characters, objects, settings, and events represent abstract qualities. Personification is often used in traditional allegories. As in a fable or a parable, the purpose of an allegory may be to convey truths about life, to teach religious or moral lessons, or to criticize social institutions.

Alliteration Alliteration is the repetition of consonant sounds at the beginning of words. Note the repetition of the *h* and *s* sounds in these lines.

> Mother whose heart hung humble as a button
> On the bright splendid shroud of your son,
> —Stephen Crane,
> "Do not weep, maiden, for war is kind"

See pages 444, 690.
See also **Consonance.**

Allusion An allusion is an indirect reference to a famous person, place, event, or literary work. The title of Stephen Vincent Benét's "By the Waters of Babylon" is an allusion to the beginning of Psalm 137 in the Bible: "By the rivers of Babylon, there we sat down, yea, we wept, when we remembered Zion."
See page 290.

Analogy An analogy is a point-by-point comparison between two things that are alike in some respect. Often, writers use analogies in nonfiction to explain unfamiliar subjects or ideas in terms of familiar ones.
See also **Extended Metaphor; Metaphor; Simile.**

Antagonist An antagonist is a principal character or force in opposition to a **protagonist,** or main character. The antagonist is usually another character but sometimes can be a force of nature, a set of circumstances, some aspect of society, or a force within the protagonist. In Guy de Maupassant's "Two Friends," the German officer who encounters the fishermen is the main antagonist. In Isabel Allende's "And of Clay Are We Created," the destructive force unleashed by the volcano may be considered an antagonist.
See pages 75, 406, 528.

Archetype An archetype is a pattern in literature that is found in a variety of works from different cultures throughout the ages. An archetype can be a plot, a character, an image, or a setting. For example, the association of death and rebirth with winter and spring is an archetype common to many cultures.

Aside In drama, an aside is a short speech directed to the audience, or another character, that is not heard by the other characters on stage. In the following example from *Julius Caesar*, the aside reveals Trebonius' murderous intentions after Caesar has asked him to stand near him in the Forum:

> Trebonius. Caesar, I will. [*aside*] And so near will I be
> That your best friends shall wish I had been further.
> —William Shakespeare, *Julius Caesar*

See pages 243, 1094.
See also **Soliloquy.**

Assonance Assonance is the repetition of vowel sounds within nonrhyming words. An example of assonance is the repetition of the short *u* sound in the following line.

> He hung a grunting weight,
> —Elizabeth Bishop, "The Fish"

Author's Perspective An author's perspective is a unique combination of ideas, values, feelings, and beliefs that influences the way the writer looks at a topic. **Tone,** or attitude, often reveals an author's perspective. In "A Chip of Glass Ruby," Nadine Gordimer writes from a perspective that reflects her experiences as a South African.
See pages 223, 257, 482, 529, 630.
See also **Author's Purpose; Tone.**

Author's Purpose A writer usually writes for one or more of these purposes: to express thoughts or feelings, to inform or explain, to persuade, or to entertain. For example, David McCullough's purpose for writing *The Johnstown Flood* is to inform readers of a natural phenomenon that made history.
See also **Author's Perspective.**

Autobiography An autobiography is a writer's account of his or her own life. In almost every case, it is told from the first-person point of view. Generally, an autobiography focuses on the most significant events and people in the writer's life over a period of time. Shorter autobiographical narratives include **journals, diaries,** and letters. An **autobiographical essay,** another type of short autobiographical work, focuses on a single person or event in the writer's life. Examples of autobiographical writing include Jeanne Wakatsuki Houston's *Farewell to Manzanar* and Coretta Scott King's *Montgomery Boycott*.

See pages 864, 880.

See also **Memoir.**

Ballad A ballad is a type of narrative poem that tells a story and was originally meant to be sung or recited. Because it tells a story, a ballad has a setting, a plot, and characters. **Traditional ballads** are written in four-line stanzas with regular rhythm and rhyme. **Folk ballads** were composed orally and handed down by word of mouth. These ballads usually tell about ordinary people who have unusual adventures or perform daring deeds. A **literary ballad** is a poem written by a poet in imitation of the form and content of a folk ballad. "Lord Randall" is an example of a traditional ballad.

Biography A biography is the true account of a person's life, written by another person. As such, a biography is usually told from a third-person point of view. The writer of a biography usually researches his or her subject in order to present accurate information. The best biographers strive for honesty and balance in their accounts of their subjects' lives.

Blank Verse Blank verse is unrhymed poetry written in **iambic pentameter.** That is, each line of blank verse has five pairs of syllables. In most pairs, an unstressed syllable is followed by a stressed syllable. The most versatile of poetic forms, blank verse imitates the natural rhythms of English speech.

Much of Shakespeare's drama is in blank verse. The following lines, spoken by the conspirator Casca, describe one of the wonders Casca observed during the storm on the night before Caesar's assassination. Note the iambic pentameter and the lack of end rhyme.

> Ă commŏn slăve—yŏu knŏw hĭm wĕll bў sĭght—
> Hĕld ŭp hĭs lĕft hănd, whĭch dĭd flăme ănd bŭrn
> —William Shakespeare, *Julius Caesar*

See also **Iambic Pentameter.**

Cast of Characters In the script of a play, a cast of characters is a list of all the characters in the play, usually in order of appearance. It may include a brief description of each character.

Character Characters are the individuals who participate in the action of a literary work. Like real people, characters display certain qualities, or **character traits;** they develop and change over time; and they usually have **motivations,** or reasons, for their behaviors.

Main characters: Main characters are the most important characters in literary works. Generally, the plot of a short story focuses on one main character, but a novel may have several main characters.

Minor characters: The less prominent characters in a literary work are known as minor characters. Minor characters support the plot. The story is not centered on them, but they help carry out the action of the story and help the reader learn more about the main character.

Dynamic character: A dynamic character is one who undergoes important changes as a plot unfolds. The changes occur because of his or her actions and experiences in the story. The change is usually internal and may be good or bad. Main characters are usually, though not always, dynamic.

Static character: A static character is one who remains the same throughout a story. The character may experience events and have interactions with other characters, but he or she is not changed because of them.

Round character: A round character is one who is complex and highly developed and has a variety of traits and different sides to his or her personality. Some of the traits may create conflict in the character. Round characters tend to display strengths, weaknesses, and a full range of emotions. The writer provides enough detail for the reader to understand their feelings and emotions.

Flat character: A flat character is one who is not highly developed. A flat character is a one-sided character: he or she usually has one outstanding trait, characteristic, or role. Flat characters exist mainly to advance the plot, and they display only the traits needed for their limited roles. Minor characters are usually flat characters.

See page 158.

See also **Characterization.**

Characterization The way a writer creates and develops characters' personalities is known as characterization. There are four basic methods of characterization:

- The writer may make direct comments about a character's personality or nature through the voice of the narrator.
- The writer may describe the character's physical appearance.

- The writer may present the character's own thoughts, speech, and actions.
- The writer may present pertinent thoughts, speech, and actions of other characters.

See pages 160, 211.
See also **Character.**

Chorus In the theater of ancient Greece, the chorus was a group of actors who commented on the action of the play. Between scenes the chorus sang and danced to musical accompaniment in the orchestra—the circular floor between the stage and the audience—giving insights into the message of the play. The chorus is often considered a kind of ideal spectator, representing the response of ordinary citizens to the tragic events that unfold. In Sophocles' *Antigone*, the chorus represents the leading citizens of Thebes.

See pages 958, 959, 964, 973.
See also **Drama.**

Climax In a plot, the climax is the point of maximum interest or tension. Usually the climax is a turning point in the story, after the reader has understood the **conflict** and become emotionally involved with the characters. The climax sometimes, but not always, points to the **resolution** of the conflict.

Example: In Stephen Vincent Benét's "By the Waters of Babylon," John's discovery of the dead "god" can be considered the climax of the story. As a result of his discovery, John realizes the truth about the past.

See pages 26, 57, 290.
See also **Plot.**

Comedy A comedy is a dramatic work that is light and often humorous in tone, usually ending happily with a peaceful resolution of the main conflict. A comedy differs from a farce by having a more believable plot, more realistic characters, and less boisterous behavior.

Comic Relief Comic relief consists of humorous scenes, incidents, or speeches that are included in a serious drama to provide a reduction in emotional intensity. Because it breaks the tension, comic relief allows an audience to prepare emotionally for events to come. In many of Shakespeare's plays, comic relief is provided by a fool or through scenes with servants or common folk.

Complication A complication is an additional factor or problem introduced into the rising action of a story to make the conflict more difficult. Often, a plot complication makes it seem as though the main character is getting farther away from the thing he or she wants.

Conflict A conflict is a struggle between opposing forces. Almost every story has a main conflict—a conflict that is the story's focus. An **external conflict** involves a character pitted against an outside force, such as nature, a physical obstacle, or another character. An **internal conflict** is one that occurs within a character.

Examples: In "To Build a Fire," the man and the dog are in conflict with the external environment. At the same time, the man experiences internal conflict as he tries to think of ways he might be able to survive this extreme setting. In some stories, such as Chinua Achebe's "Marriage Is a Private Affair," the source of the conflict is cultural; that is, it arises from differences in beliefs and values.

See pages 26, 33, 76, 183, 896.
See also **Plot.**

Connotation A connotation is an attitude or a feeling associated with a word, in contrast to the word's **denotation,** which is its literal, or dictionary, meaning. The connotations of a word may be positive or negative. For example, *enthusiastic* has positive associations, while *rowdy* has negative ones. Connotations of words can have an important influence on style and meaning and are particularly important in poetry.

Consonance Consonance is the repetition of consonant sounds within and at the end of words, as in "lonely afternoon." Consonance is unlike rhyme in that the vowel sounds preceding or following the repeated consonant sounds differ. Consonance is often used together with **alliteration, assonance,** and **rhyme** to create a musical quality, to emphasize certain words, or to unify a poem.
See also **Alliteration.**

Couplet A couplet is a rhymed pair of lines. A couplet may be written in any rhythmic pattern.

> So long as men can breathe, or eyes can see,
> So long lives this, and this gives life to thee.
> —William Shakespeare, "Sonnet 18"

See also **Stanza.**

Critical Essay *See* **Essay.**

Denotation *See* **Connotation.**

Dénouement *See* **Falling Action.**

Dialect A dialect is a form of language that is spoken in a particular geographic area or by a particular social or ethnic group. A group's dialect is reflected in its pronunciations, vocabulary, expressions, and grammatical structures. Writers use dialects to capture the flavors of locales and to bring characters to life, re-creating the way they actually speak.

Dialogue Dialogue is written conversation between two or more characters. Writers use dialogue to bring characters to life and to give readers insights into the characters' qualities, traits, and reactions to other characters. Realistic, well-paced dialogue also advances the plot of a narrative. In fiction, dialogue is usually set off with quotation marks. In drama, stories are told primarily through dialogue. Playwrights use stage directions to indicate how they intend the dialogue to be interpreted by actors.

Diary A diary is a daily record of a writer's thoughts, experiences, and feelings. As such, it is a type of autobiographical writing. The terms *diary* and *journal* are often used synonymously.

Diction A writer's or speaker's choice of words and way of arranging the words in sentences is called diction. Diction can be broadly characterized as formal or informal. It can also be described as technical or common, abstract or concrete, and literal or figurative. A writer for *Scientific American* would use a more formal, technical, and possibly abstract diction than would a writer for the science section of a local newspaper.
See pages 489, 766.
See also **Style.**

Drama Drama is literature in which plots and characters are developed through dialogue and action; in other words, it is literature in play form. Drama is meant to be performed. Stage plays, radio plays, movies, and television programs are types of drama. Most plays are divided into acts, with each act having an emotional peak, or climax. Certain modern plays, such as *A Marriage Proposal*, have only one act. Most plays contain stage directions, which describe settings, lighting, sound effects, the movements and emotions of actors, and the ways in which dialogue should be spoken.

Dramatic Irony *See* **Irony.**

Dramatic Monologue A dramatic monologue is a lyric poem in which a speaker addresses a silent or absent listener in a moment of high intensity or deep emotion, as if engaged in private conversation. The speaker proceeds without interruption or argument, and the effect on the reader is that of hearing just one side of a conversation. This technique allows the poet to focus on the feelings, personality, and motivations of the speaker. "Exile" by Julia Alvarez is a dramatic monologue.
See page 136.
See also **Lyric Poetry; Soliloquy.**

Dynamic Character *See* **Character.**

Elegy An elegy is an extended meditative poem in which the speaker reflects on death—often in tribute to a person who has died recently—or on an equally serious subject. Most elegies are written in formal, dignified language and are serious in tone.

Epic An epic is a long narrative poem on a serious subject, presented in an elevated or formal style. It traces the adventures of a great hero whose actions reflect the ideals and values of a nation or race. Epics address universal concerns, such as good and evil, life and death, and sin and redemption. Homer's *Iliad* and *Odyssey* are famous epics in the Western tradition. The *Ramayana* is a great epic of India.

Epic Hero An epic hero is a larger-than-life figure who embodies the ideals of a nation or race. Epic heroes take part in dangerous adventures and accomplish great deeds. Many undertake long, difficult journeys and display great courage and superhuman strength.

Essay An essay is a short work of nonfiction that deals with a single subject. Some essays are **formal**—that is, tightly structured and written in an impersonal style. Others are **informal,** with a looser structure and a more personal style. Generally, an **expository essay** presents or explains information and ideas. A **personal essay** is typically an informal essay in which the writer expresses his or her thoughts and feelings about a subject, focusing on the meaning of events and issues in his or her own life. In a **reflective essay,** the author makes a connection between a personal observation or experience and a universal idea, such as love, courage, or freedom. A **critical essay** evaluates a situation, a course of action, or a work of art. In a **persuasive essay,** the author attempts to convince readers to adopt a certain viewpoint or to take a particular stand.
Examples: E. M. Forster's essay "Tolerance" seeks to persuade its audience to adopt a different attitude toward people around the world. In "The Man in the Water," Roger Rosenblatt reflects on current events and therefore combines qualities of both the reflective and expository essays.
See pages 352, 448.

Exposition Exposition is the first stage of a typical story plot. The exposition provides important background information and introduces the setting and the important characters. The conflict the characters face may also be introduced in the exposition, or it may be introduced later, in the rising action.
See pages 26, 27.
See also **Plot.**

Expository Essay *See* **Essay.**

Extended Metaphor An extended metaphor is a figure of speech that compares two essentially unlike things at some length and in several ways. It does not contain the word *like* or *as.* For example, Shakespeare makes a comparison between ambition and a ladder in this extended metaphor:

> That lowliness is young ambition's ladder,
> Whereto the climber-upward turns his face;
> But when he once attains the upmost round,
> He then unto the ladder turns his back,
> Looks in the clouds, scorning the base degrees
> By which he did ascend.
> —William Shakespeare, *Julius Caesar*

See also **Metaphor.**

External Conflict *See* **Conflict.**

Fable A fable is a brief tale told to illustrate a moral or teach a lesson. Often the moral of a fable appears in a distinct and memorable statement near the tale's beginning or end.

Falling Action In a plot, the falling action follows the climax and shows the results of the important decision or action that happened at the climax. Tension eases as the falling action begins; however, the final outcome of the story is not yet fully worked out at this stage. Events in the falling action lead to the **resolution, or dénouement,** of the plot.

Example: In Stephen Vincent Benét's "By the Waters of Babylon," the falling action occurs after the main character has discovered the dead "god." During the falling action, John realizes the truth about the past and the destruction of a way of life.

See pages 26, 290.
See also **Climax; Plot.**

Fantasy Fantasy is a type of fiction that is highly imaginative and portrays events, settings, or characters that are unrealistic. The setting might be a nonexistent world, the plot might involve magic or the supernatural, and the characters might employ superhuman powers.

Farce Farce is a type of exaggerated comedy that features an absurd plot, ridiculous situations, and humorous dialogue. The main purpose of a farce is to keep an audience laughing. The characters are usually stereotypes, or simplified examples of individual traits or qualities. Comic devices typically used in farces include mistaken identity, deception, physical comedy, wordplay—such as puns and double meanings—and exaggeration. Anton Chekhov's *A Marriage Proposal* is an example of a farce.

Fiction Fiction is prose writing that consists of imaginary elements. Although fiction can be inspired by actual events and real people, it usually springs from writers' imaginations. The basic elements of fiction are plot, character, setting, and theme. The novel and the short story are forms of fiction.

See also **Character; Novel; Plot; Setting; Short Story; Theme.**

Figure of Speech *See* **Figurative Language; Hyperbole; Metaphor; Personification; Simile; Understatement.**

Figurative Language Figurative language is language that communicates meanings beyond the literal meanings of the words. In figurative language, words are often used to symbolize ideas and concepts they would not otherwise be associated with. Writers use figurative language to create effects, to emphasize ideas, and to evoke emotions. Simile, metaphor, extended metaphor, hyperbole, and personification are examples of figurative language.

Example: The narrator in Alice Walker's "Everyday Use" says of Dee's hair, "It stands straight up like the wool on a sheep. It is black as night and around the edges are two long pigtails that rope around like small lizards disappearing behind her ears." Obviously, Dee's pigtails do not literally move like lizards, but the passage vividly suggests the look of Dee's hair.

See pages 46, 135, 136, 314, 461, 692, 705, 790, 791.
See also **Hyperbole; Metaphor; Onomatopoeia; Personification; Simile.**

First-Person Point of View *See* **Point of View.**

Flashback A flashback is an account of a conversation, an episode, or an event that happened before the beginning of a story. Often a flashback interrupts the chronological flow of a story to give the reader information needed for the understanding of a character's present situation. Haruki Marakami's "The Seventh Man" is told almost exclusively through flashback.

Foil A foil is a character who provides a striking contrast to another character. By using a foil, a writer can call attention to certain traits possessed by a main character or simply enhance a character by contrast.

Foreshadowing Foreshadowing is a writer's use of hints or clues to suggest events that will occur later in a story. The hints and clues might be included in a character's dialogue or behavior, or they might be included in details of description. Foreshadowing creates suspense and makes readers eager to find out what will happen.

Form *Form* refers to the principles of arrangement in a poem—the ways in which lines are organized. Form in poetry includes the following elements: the length of lines, the placement of lines, and the grouping of lines into stanzas.
See also **Stanza.**

Frame Story A frame story exists when a story is told within a narrative setting, or "frame"; it creates a story within a story. This storytelling technique has been used for over one thousand years and was employed in famous works such as *One Thousand and One Arabian Nights* and Geoffrey Chaucer's *The Canterbury Tales.*

Free Verse Free verse is poetry that does not contain regular patterns of rhythm or rhyme. The lines in free verse often flow more naturally than do rhymed, metrical lines and thus achieve a rhythm more like that of everyday speech. Although free verse lacks conventional meter, it may contain various rhythmic and sound effects, such as repetitions of syllables or words. Free verse can be used for a variety of subjects. Elizabeth Bishop's poem "The Fish" is one of several examples of free verse included in this book.
See pages 689, 713, 793.
See also **Meter; Rhyme.**

Genre The term *genre* refers to a category in which a work of literature is classified. The major genres in literature are fiction, nonfiction, poetry, and drama.

Haiku Haiku is a form of Japanese poetry in which 17 syllables are arranged in three lines of 5, 7, and 5 syllables. The rules of haiku are strict. In addition to the syllabic count, the poet must create a clear picture that will evoke a strong emotional response in the reader. Nature is a particularly important source of inspiration for Japanese haiku poets, and details from nature are often the subjects of their poems.

Hero A hero is a main character or protagonist in a story. In older literary works, heroes tend to be better than ordinary humans. They are typically courageous, strong, honorable, and intelligent. They are protectors of society who hold back the forces of evil and fight to make the world a better place.

The term **tragic hero,** first used by the Greek philosopher Aristotle, refers to a central character in a drama who is dignified or noble. According to Aristotle, a tragic hero possesses a defect, or **tragic flaw,** that brings about or contributes to his or her downfall. This flaw may be poor judgment, pride, weakness, or an excess of an admirable quality. The tragic hero, noted Aristotle, recognizes his or her own flaw and its consequences, but only after it is too late to change the course of events. Brutus is often considered the tragic hero of *Julius Caesar.*

The term **cultural hero** refers to a hero who represents the values of his or her culture. King Arthur, for example, represents the physical courage, moral leadership, and loyalty that were valued in Anglo-Saxon society. Antigone can also be considered a cultural hero because her sense of duty to family and the gods, as well as her courage, reflects the values of ancient Greece.
See pages 958, 960, 964, 1007, 1046.
See also **Tragedy.**

Historical Fiction A short story or novel can be classified as historical fiction when the settings and details of the plot include real places and real events of historical importance. Historical figures may appear as major or minor characters, as Napoleon does in Leo Tolstoy's classic novel *War and Peace.* In historical fiction, the setting generally influences the plot in important ways.

Horror Fiction Horror fiction contains strange, mysterious, violent, and often supernatural events that create suspense and terror in the reader. Edgar Allan Poe is an author famous for his horror fiction.

Humor In literature, there are three basic types of humor, all of which may involve exaggeration or irony. **Humor of situation** arises out of the plot of a work. It usually involves exaggerated events or situational irony, which arises when something happens that is different from what was expected. **Humor of character** is often based on exaggerated personalities or on characters' failure to recognize their own flaws, a form of dramatic irony. **Humor of language** may include sarcasm, exaggeration, puns, or verbal irony, in which what is said is not what is meant.
See page 487.
See also **Irony.**

Hyperbole Hyperbole is a figure of speech in which the truth is exaggerated for emphasis or humorous effect. The expression "I'm so hungry I could eat a horse" is an example of hyperbole.

Iambic Pentameter Iambic pentameter is a metrical pattern of five feet, or units, each of which is made up of two syllables, the first unstressed and the second stressed. Iambic pentameter is the most common meter used in English poetry; it is the meter used in blank verse and in the sonnet. The following lines are examples of iambic pentameter.

> Thís wás ăn ĭll bĕgínnĭng ŏf thĕ níght!
> —William Shakespeare, *Julius Caesar*

See pages 729, 1088.
See also **Blank Verse; Sonnet.**

Idiom An idiom is a common figure of speech whose meaning is different from the literal meaning of its words. For example, the phrase "raining cats and dogs" does not literally mean that cats and dogs are falling from the sky; the expression means "raining heavily."

Imagery Imagery consists of descriptive words and phrases that re-create sensory experiences for the reader. Imagery usually appeals to one or more of the five senses— sight, hearing, smell, taste, and touch—to help the reader imagine exactly what is being described. In D. H. Lawrence's "Piano," the phrase "the boom of the tingling strings" appeals to the sense of hearing and touch.
See pages 237, 495, 692, 720, 766.

Internal Conflict See **Conflict.**

Interview An interview is a conversation conducted by a writer or a reporter, in which facts or statements are elicited from another person, recorded, and then broadcast or published. "Jhumpa Lahiri: Pulitzer Prize Winner" is an example of an interview.
See page 438.

Irony Irony is a special kind of contrast between appearance and reality—usually one in which reality is the opposite of what it seems. One type of irony is **situational irony,** a contrast between what a reader or character expects and what actually exists or happens. Another type of irony is **dramatic irony,** where the reader or viewer knows something that a character does not know. **Verbal irony** exists when someone knowingly exaggerates or says one thing and means another.
Examples: In Guy de Maupassant's "Two Friends," the reader expects the Frenchmen to eat the fish they have caught. However, it is the German officer who eats the fish, after he executes the men (**situational irony**). Julius Caesar goes to the Senate on the Ides of March in the belief that he may receive the crown. The audience knows, however, that the conspirators are planning his assassination (**dramatic irony**). The speaker in Stephen Crane's famous war poem "Do not

weep, maiden . . ." continually repeats that "war is kind" while presenting images that suggest quite the opposite (**verbal irony**).
See pages 406, 443, 967.

Journal See **Diary.**

Legend A legend is a story handed down from the past, especially one that is popularly believed to be based on historical events. Though legends often incorporate supernatural or magical elements, they claim to be the story of a real human being and are often set in a particular time and place. These characteristics separate a legend from a myth. The story of the rise and fall of King Arthur is a famous example of a legend.
See page 965.
See also **Myth.**

Limited Point of View See **Point of View.**

Line The line is the core unit of a poem. In poetry, line length is an essential element of the poem's meaning and rhythm. **Line breaks,** where a line of poetry ends, may coincide with grammatical units. However, a line break may also occur in the middle of a grammatical or syntactical unit, creating a meaningful pause or emphasis. Poets use a variety of line breaks to play with sense, grammar, and syntax and thereby create a wide range of effects.

Literary Criticism Literary criticism is a form of writing in which works of literature are compared, analyzed, interpreted, or evaluated. Two common forms of literary criticism are book reviews and critical essays.

Literary Nonfiction Literary nonfiction is nonfiction that is recognized as being of artistic value or that is about literature. Autobiographies, biographies, essays, and eloquent speeches typically fall into this category.

Lyric Poetry A lyric poem is a short poem in which a single speaker expresses personal thoughts and feelings. Most poems other than dramatic and narrative poems are lyric poems. In ancient Greece, lyric poetry was meant to be sung. Modern lyrics are usually not intended for singing, but they are characterized by strong melodic rhythms. Lyric poetry has a variety of forms and covers many subjects, from love and death to everyday experiences.

Magical Realism Magical realism is a literary genre that combines fantastic or magical events with realistic occurrences in a matter-of-fact way to delight or surprise the reader. A famous example of magical realism is Gabriel García Márquez's novel *One Hundred Years of Solitude.*

Memoir A memoir is a form of autobiographical writing in which a writer shares his or her personal experiences and observations of significant events or people. Often informal or even intimate in tone, memoirs usually give readers insight into the impact of historical events on people's lives. Coretta Scott King's "Montgomery Boycott" is an example of a memoir.

See pages 853, 880.

See also **Autobiography.**

Metaphor A metaphor is a figure of speech that makes a comparison between two things that are basically unlike but have something in common. Unlike similes, metaphors do not contain the word *like* or *as*. In "By the Waters of Babylon" by Stephen Vincent Benét, the narrator uses the metaphor "Truth is a hard deer to hunt" to convey his difficulty in finding out what really happened in the Place of the Gods.

See also **Extended Metaphor; Figurative Language; Simile.**

Meter Meter is a regular pattern of stressed and unstressed syllables in a poem. The meter of a poem emphasizes the musical quality of the language. Each unit of meter, known as a **foot,** consists of one stressed syllable and one or two unstressed syllables. In representations of meter, a stressed syllable is indicated by the symbol ´; an unstressed syllable, by the symbol ˘. The four basic types of metrical feet are the **iamb,** an unstressed syllable followed by a stressed syllable (˘´); the **trochee,** a stressed syllable followed by an unstressed syllable (´˘); the **anapest,** two unstressed syllables followed by a stressed syllable (˘˘´); and the **dactyl,** a stressed syllable followed by two unstressed syllables (´˘˘).

See pages 690, 729, 1088, 1106.

See also **Rhythm.**

Mise en Scène *Mise en scène* is a term from the French that refers to the various physical aspects of a dramatic presentation, such as lighting, costumes, scenery, makeup, and props.

Mood In a literary work, mood is the feeling or atmosphere that a writer creates for the reader. Descriptive words, imagery, and figurative language contribute to the mood of a work, as do the sound and rhythm of the language used. In "The Pit and the Pendulum," Edgar Allan Poe creates a mood of dread and horror.

See pages 24, 61, 101, 770.

See also **Tone.**

Motivation *See* **Character.**

Myth A myth is a traditional story, usually concerning some superhuman being or unlikely event, that was once widely believed to be true. Frequently, myths were attempts to explain natural phenomena, such as solar and lunar eclipses or the cycle of the seasons. For some peoples, myths were both a kind of science and a religion. In addition, myths served as literature and entertainment, just as they do for modern-day audiences.

Many classical Greek dramas were based on myths that would have been familiar to audiences in ancient Greece. The origins of *Antigone,* for example, can be traced to myths about the family of King Oedipus.

Narrative Nonfiction Narrative nonfiction is writing that reads much like fiction, except that the characters, setting, and plot are real rather than imaginary. Its purpose is usually to entertain or to express opinions or feelings. Narrative nonfiction includes, but is not limited to, autobiographies, biographies, memoirs, diaries, and journals.

Narrative Poetry Narrative poetry tells a story or recounts events. Like a short story or a novel, a narrative poem has the following elements: plot, characters, setting, and theme. Joy Harjo's poem "Crossing the Border" is a narrative poem.

Narrator The narrator of a story is the character or voice that relates the story's events to the reader.

See also **Persona; Point of View.**

Nonfiction Nonfiction is writing that tells about real people, places, and events. Unlike fiction, nonfiction is mainly written to convey factual information, although writers of nonfiction shape information in accordance with their own purposes and attitudes. Nonfiction can be a good source of information, but readers frequently have to examine it carefully in order to detect biases, notice gaps in the information provided, and identify errors in logic. Nonfiction includes a diverse range of writing—newspaper articles, letters, essays, biographies, movie reviews, speeches, true-life adventure stories, advertising, and more.

Novel A novel is an extended work of fiction. Like a short story, a novel is essentially the product of a writer's imagination. Because a novel is considerably longer than a short story, a novelist can develop a wider range of characters and a more complex plot. George Orwell's *Animal Farm* is an example of a novel.

Novella A novella is a work of fiction that is longer than a short story but shorter than a novel. A novella differs from a novel in that it concentrates on a limited cast of characters, a relatively short time span, and a single chain of events. The novella is an attempt to combine the compression of the short story with the development of the novel.

Ode An ode is a complex lyric poem that develops a serious and dignified theme. Odes appeal to both the imagination and the intellect, and many commemorate events or praise people or elements of nature.

Omniscient Point of View *See* **Point of View.**

Onomatopoeia Onomatopoeia is the use of words whose sounds echo their meanings, such as *buzz, whisper, gargle,* and *murmur.* Onomatopoeia as a literary technique goes beyond the use of simple echoic words, however. Skilled writers, especially poets, choose words whose sounds intensify images and suggest meanings. In "The Sound of Night," for example, Maxine Kumin makes use of words such as *skitter* and *prink* to add sensory richness to the natural scene she describes.

Oxymoron An oxymoron is a special kind of concise paradox that brings together two contradictory terms, such as "venomous love" or "sweet bitterness."

Paradox A paradox is a seemingly contradictory or absurd statement that may nonetheless suggest an important truth.

Parallelism Parallelism is the use of similar grammatical constructions to express ideas that are related or equal in importance.

> Love is not all: it is not meat nor drink
> Nor slumber nor a roof against the rain;
> Nor yet a floating spare to men that sink
> —Edna St. Vincent Millay, "Sonnet XXX"

Parallel Plot A parallel plot is a particular type of plot in which two stories of equal importance are told simultaneously. The story moves back and forth between the two plots.

Parody A parody is an imitation of another work, a type of literature, or a writer's style, usually for the purpose of poking fun. It may serve as an element of a larger work or be a complete work in itself. The purpose of parody may be to ridicule through broad humor, deploying such techniques as exaggeration or the use of inappropriate subject matter. Such techniques may even provide insights into the original work.

Pastoral A pastoral is a poem presenting shepherds in rural settings, usually in an idealized manner. The language and form of a pastoral tends to be formal. English Renaissance poets were drawn to the pastoral as a means of conveying their own emotions and ideas, particularly about love.

Persona A persona is a voice that a writer assumes in a particular work. A persona is like a mask worn by the writer, separating his or her identity from that of the speaker or the narrator. It is the persona's voice—not the writer's voice— that narrates a story or speaks in a poem.
See also **Narrator; Speaker.**

Personal Essay *See* **Essay.**

Personification Personification is a figure of speech in which human qualities are given to an object, animal, or idea. Notice the use of personification in this excerpt of poetry:

> In moving-slow he has no Peer.
> You ask him something in his Ear,
> He thinks about it for a Year;
> —Theodore Roethke, "The Sloth"

See pages 314, 692, 718.
See also **Figurative Language.**

Persuasive Essay *See* **Essay.**

Play *See* **Drama.**

Plot The sequence of events in a story is called the plot. A plot focuses on a central **conflict** or problem faced by the main character. The actions that the characters take to resolve the conflict build toward a climax. In general, it is not long after this point that the conflict is resolved and the story ends. A plot typically develops in five stages: exposition, rising action, climax, falling action, and resolution.
See pages 26, 30, 31, 33, 45, 203, 1143.
See also **Climax; Exposition; Falling Action; Rising Action.**

Poetry Poetry is a type of literature in which words are carefully chosen and arranged to create certain effects. Poets use a variety of sound devices, imagery, and figurative language to express emotions and ideas.
See also **Alliteration; Assonance; Ballad; Free Verse; Imagery; Meter; Rhyme; Rhythm; Stanza.**

Point of View *Point of view* refers to the method of narration used in a short story, novel, narrative poem, or work of nonfiction. In a work told from a **first-person** point

of view, the narrator is a character in the story, as in "The Pit and the Pendulum" by Edgar Allan Poe. In a work told from a **third-person** point of view, the narrative voice is outside the action, not one of the characters. If a story is told from a **third-person omniscient,** or all-knowing, point of view, as in "The Doll's House" by Katherine Mansfield, the narrator sees into the minds of all the characters. If events are related from a **third-person limited** point of view, as in Hwang Sunwŏn's "Cranes," the narrator tells what only one character thinks, feels, and observes.
See pages 282, 289, 321, 353, 770.
See also **Narrator.**

Prologue A prologue is an introductory scene in a drama. Some Elizabethan plays include prologues that comment on the theme or moral point that will be revealed in the play. The prologue is a feature of all Greek drama.

Prop The word *prop,* originally an abbreviation of the word *property,* refers to any physical object that is used in a drama.

Prose Generally, *prose* refers to all forms of written or spoken expression that are not in verse. The term, therefore, may be used to describe very different forms of writing— short stories as well as essays, for example.

Protagonist A protagonist is the main character in a work of literature, who is involved in the central conflict of the story. Usually, the protagonist changes after the central conflict reaches a climax. He or she may be a hero and is usually the one with whom the audience tends to identify. In R. K. Narayan's "Like the Sun," the protagonist is Sekhar, a man who encounters problems while seeking to tell the truth.

Quatrain A quatrain is a four-line stanza, or group of lines, in poetry. The most common stanza in English poetry, the quatrain can have a variety of meters and rhyme schemes.

Realistic Fiction Realistic fiction is fiction that is a truthful imitation of ordinary life. "On the Rainy River" by Tim O'Brien and "Shoofly Pie" by Naomi Shihab Nye are examples of realistic fiction.

Recurring Theme *See* **Theme.**

Reflective Essay *See* **Essay.**

Refrain A refrain is one or more lines repeated in each stanza of a poem.
See also **Stanza.**

Repetition Repetition is a technique in which a sound, word, phrase, or line is repeated for emphasis or unity. Repetition often helps to reinforce meaning and create

an appealing rhythm. The term includes specific devices associated with both prose and poetry, such as alliteration and parallelism.
See pages 690, 721.
See also **Alliteration; Parallelism; Sound Devices.**

Resolution *See* **Falling Action.**

Rhetorical Devices Rhetorical devices are techniques writers use to enhance their arguments and communicate more effectively. Rhetorical devices include **analogy, parallelism, rhetorical questions,** and **repetition.**
See also **Analogy; Repetition.**

Rhyme Rhyme is the occurrence of similar or identical sounds at the end of two or more words, such as *suite, heat,* and *complete.* Rhyme that occurs within a single line of poetry is **internal rhyme.** Rhyme that occurs at the ends of lines of poetry is called **end rhyme.** End rhyme that is not exact but approximate is called **slant rhyme,** or **off rhyme.** Notice the following example of slant rhyme involving the words *low* and *prow.*

> The gray sea and the long black land;
> And the yellow half-moon large and <u>low</u>;
> And the startled little waves that leap
> In the fiery ringlets from their sleep,
> As I gain the cove with the pushing <u>prow</u>,
> And quench its speed i' the slushy sand.
> —Robert Browning, "Meeting at Night"

See pages 690, 691, 697, 698, 700, 729, 735.

Rhyme Scheme A rhyme scheme is a pattern of end rhymes in a poem. A rhyme scheme is noted by assigning a letter of the alphabet, beginning with *a,* to each line. Lines that rhyme are given the same letter. Notice the rhyme scheme of the first four lines of this poem.

> There will come soft rains and the smell of the ground, *a*
> And swallows circling with their shimmering sound; *a*
> And frogs in the pools singing at night, *b*
> And wild plum-trees in tremulous white; *b*
> —Sara Teasdale, "There Will Come Soft Rains"

See pages 690, 696.

Rhythm Rhythm is a pattern of stressed and unstressed syllables in a line of poetry. Poets use rhythm to bring out the musical quality of language, to emphasize ideas, to create moods, to unify works, and to heighten emotional responses. Devices such as alliteration, rhyme, assonance, consonance, and parallelism often contribute to creating rhythm.

See pages 690, 691, 711, 713.
See also **Meter.**

Rising Action Rising action is the stage of a plot in which the conflict develops and story events build toward a climax. During this stage, complications arise that make the conflict more intense. Tension grows as the characters struggle to resolve the conflict.

See page 26.
See also **Plot.**

Romance A romance refers to any imaginative story concerned with noble heroes, chivalric codes of honor, passionate love, daring deeds, and supernatural events. Writers of romances tend to idealize their heroes as well as the eras in which the heroes live. Medieval romances, such as Malory's *Le Morte d'Arthur*, include stories of kings, knights, and ladies who are motivated by love, religious faith, or simply a desire for adventure.

See pages 960, 1010.

Satire Satire is a literary technique in which ideas, customs, behaviors, or institutions are ridiculed for the purpose of improving society. Satire may be gently witty, mildly abrasive, or bitterly critical, and it often involves the use of irony and exaggeration to force readers to see something in a critical light.

Scansion Scansion is the notation of stressed and unstressed syllables in poetry. A stressed syllable is often indicated by the symbol ´; an unstressed syllable, by the symbol ˘. Using scansion can help you determine the rhythm and meter of a poem.

See page 690.
See also **Meter.**

Scene In drama, the action is often divided into acts and scenes. Each scene presents an episode of the play's plot and typically occurs at a single place and time.

See also **Act.**

Scenery Scenery is a painted backdrop or other structures used to create the setting for a play.

Science Fiction Science fiction is fiction in which a writer explores unexpected possibilities of the past or the future, using known scientific data and theories as well as his or her creative imagination. Most science fiction writers create

believable worlds, although some create fantasy worlds that have familiar elements. Ray Bradbury, the author of the story "There Will Come Soft Rains," is famous for his science fiction.

See also **Fantasy.**

Screenplay A screenplay is a play written for film.

Script The text of a play, film, or broadcast is called a script.

Sensory Details Sensory details are words and phrases that appeal to the reader's senses of sight, hearing, touch, smell, and taste. For example, the sensory detail "a fine film of rain" appeals to the senses of sight and touch. Sensory details stimulate the reader to create images in his or her mind.

See also **Imagery.**

Setting Setting is the time and place of the action of a short story, drama, novel, narrative poem, or narrative nonfiction work. In addition to time and place, setting sometimes includes the larger historical and cultural contexts that form the background for a narrative. Setting is one of the main elements in fiction and often plays an important role in what happens and why.

See pages 24, 25, 61, 75, 388, 395.
See also **Fiction.**

Short Story A short story is a work of fiction that centers on a single idea and can be read in one sitting. Generally, a short story has one main conflict that involves the characters, keeps the story moving, and stimulates readers' interest.

See also **Fiction.**

Simile A simile is a figure of speech that makes a comparison between two unlike things using the word *like* or *as*.

> His brown skin hung in strips
> like ancient wallpaper,
> —Elizabeth Bishop, "The Fish"

See page 714.
See also **Epic Simile; Figurative Language; Metaphor.**

Situational Irony See **Irony.**

Soliloquy In drama, a soliloquy is a speech in which a character speaks his or her thoughts aloud. Generally, the character is on the stage alone, not speaking to other characters and perhaps not even consciously addressing an audience. *Julius Caesar* has several soliloquies. For example,

Casca begins plotting how to win over Brutus in a soliloquy that begins with these lines.

> Well, Brutus, thou art noble; yet I see
> Thy honorable mettle may be wrought
> From that it is disposed.
> —William Shakespeare, *Julius Caesar*

See also **Aside; Dramatic Monologue.**

Sonnet A sonnet is a lyric poem of 14 lines, commonly written in **iambic pentameter.** Sonnets are often classified as Petrarchan or Shakespearean. The Shakespearean, or Elizabethan, sonnet consists of three quatrains, or four-line units, and a final couplet. The typical rhyme scheme is *abab cdcd efef gg.*
See also **Iambic Pentameter; Rhyme Scheme.**

Sound Devices Sound devices, or uses of words for their auditory effect, can convey meaning and mood or unify a work. Some common sound devices are **alliteration, assonance, consonance, meter, onomatopoeia, repetition, rhyme,** and **rhythm.** The following lines contain alliteration, repetition, assonance, consonance, rhyme, and rhythm, all of which combine to help convey both meaning and mood.
See page 690.
See also **Alliteration; Assonance; Consonance; Meter; Onomatopoeia; Repetition; Rhyme; Rhythm.**

Speaker In poetry the speaker is the voice that "talks" to the reader, similar to the narrator in fiction. The speaker is not necessarily the poet. For example, in Rita Dove's "Lady Freedom Among Us," the experiences related may or may not have happened to the poet.
See pages 551, 689.
See also **Persona.**

Speech A speech is a talk or public address. The purpose of a speech may be to entertain, to explain, to persuade, to inspire, or any combination of these aims. "On Nuclear Disarmament" by Carl Sagan was written and delivered in order to persuade an audience.
See page 592.

Stage Directions A play typically includes instructions called stage directions, which are usually printed in italic type. They serve as a guide to directors, set and lighting designers, performers, and readers. When stage directions appear within passages of dialogue, parentheses are usually used to set them off from the words spoken by characters.
See pages 7, 243, 244, 968, 1057, 1059, 1095.

Stanza A stanza is a group of two or more lines that form a unit in a poem. A stanza is comparable to a paragraph in prose. Each stanza may have the same number of lines, or the number of lines may vary.
See also **Couplet; Form; Poetry; Quatrain.**

Static Character *See* **Character.**

Stereotype In literature, a simplified or stock character who conforms to a fixed pattern or is defined by a single trait is known as a stereotype. Such a character does not usually demonstrate the complexities of a real person. Familiar stereotypes in popular literature include the absent-minded professor and the busybody.

Stream of Consciousness Stream of consciousness is a literary technique developed by modern writers, in which thoughts, feelings, moods, perceptions, and memories are presented as they randomly flow through a character's mind.

Structure Structure is the way in which the parts of a work of literature are put together. In poetry, structure involves the arrangement of words and lines to produce a desired effect. A common structural unit in poetry is the stanza, of which there are numerous types. In prose, structure is the arrangement of larger units or parts of a work. Paragraphs, for example, are basic units in prose, as are chapters in novels and acts in plays. The structure of a poem, short story, novel, play, or nonfictional work usually emphasizes certain important aspects of content.
See also **Act; Stanza.**

Style *Style* refers to the particular way in which a work of literature is written—not *what* is said but *how* it is said. It is the writer's unique way of communicating ideas. Many elements contribute to style, including word choice, sentence structure and length, tone, figurative language, and point of view. A literary style may be described in a variety of ways, such as formal, informal, journalistic, conversational, wordy, ornate, poetic, or dynamic.

Surprise Ending A surprise ending is an unexpected plot twist at the end of a story. The surprise may be a sudden turn in the action or a piece of information that gives a different perspective to the entire story. Saki is famous for using this device, as exemplified in his story "The Interlopers."
See page 394.

Suspense Suspense is the excitement or tension that readers feel as they wait to find out how a story ends or a conflict is resolved. Writers create suspense by raising questions in readers' minds about what might happen next.

The use of **foreshadowing** is one way in which writers create suspense.

See pages 107, 113, 295, 338, 775, 1111.

See also **Foreshadowing.**

Symbol A symbol is a person, a place, an object, or an activity that stands for something beyond itself. For example, a flag is a colored piece of cloth that stands for a country. A white dove is a bird that represents peace.

Example: In "Cranes" by Hwang Sunwŏn, the birds represent the childhood friendship of the two main characters, as well as peace and tranquility.

See pages 386, 389, 407.

Tall Tale A tall tale is a humorously exaggerated story about impossible events, often involving the supernatural abilities of the main character. Stories about folk heroes such as Pecos Bill and Paul Bunyan are typical tall tales.

Theme A theme is an underlying message about life or human nature that a writer wants the reader to understand. It is a perception about life or human nature that the writer shares with the reader. In most cases, themes are not stated directly but must be inferred. A theme may imply how a person should live but should not be confused with a **moral.**

Example: Kurt Vonnegut Jr., in "Harrison Bergeron," never directly states his criticism of society and government. The reader must put details and events together in order to identify Vonnegut's theme about the damage that can be done when people go to extremes in the service of equality.

  Recurring themes are themes found in a variety of works. For example, authors from varying backgrounds might convey similar themes having to do with the importance of family values. **Universal themes** are themes that are found throughout the literature of all time periods.

See pages 34, 41, 330, 386, 388, 395, 421, 443, 983, 990, 1006.

See also **Moral.**

Third-Person Point of View *See* **Point of View.**

Tone Tone is the attitude a writer takes takes toward a subject. Unlike mood, which is intended to shape the reader's emotional response, tone reflects the feelings of the writer. A writer communicates tone through choice of words and details. Tone may often be described by a single word, such as *serious, humorous, formal, informal, somber, sarcastic, playful, ironic, bitter,* or *objective.* For example, the tone of the essay "The Man in the Water" by Roger Rosenblatt might be described as somber and reflective, whereas John Updike's poem "Ex-Basketball Player" has an ironic, somewhat humorous tone.

See pages 489, 694, 766.

See also **Author's Perspective; Mood.**

Tragedy A tragedy is a dramatic work that presents the downfall of a dignified character (**tragic hero**) or characters who are involved in historically or socially significant events. The events in a tragic plot are set in motion by a decision that is often an error in judgment (**tragic flaw**) on the part of the hero. Succeeding events are linked in a cause-and-effect relationship and lead inevitably to a disastrous conclusion, usually death. Shakespeare's *Julius Caesar* is a tragedy.

Tragic Flaw *See* **Hero; Tragedy.**

Tragic Hero *See* **Hero; Tragedy.**

Traits *See* **Character.**

Turning Point *See* **Climax.**

Understatement Understatement is a technique of creating emphasis by saying less than is actually or literally true. It is the opposite of **hyperbole,** or exaggeration. One of the primary devices of irony, understatement can be used to develop a humorous effect, to create satire, or to achieve a restrained tone.

See also **Hyperbole; Irony.**

Universal Theme *See* **Theme.**

Verbal Irony *See* **Irony.**

Voice Voice is a writer's unique use of language that allows a reader to "hear" a human personality in the writer's work. Elements of style that contribute to a writer's voice include sentence structure, **diction,** and **tone.** Voice can reveal much about the author's personality, beliefs, and attitudes.

See pages 776, 915.

Word Choice *See* **Diction.**

Glossary of Reading & Informational Terms

Almanac *See* **Reference Works.**

Analogy *See Glossary of Literary Terms, page R102.*

Argument An argument is speech or writing that expresses a position on an issue or problem and supports it with reasons and evidence. An argument often takes into account other points of view, anticipating and answering objections that opponents of the position might raise.
See also **Claim; Counterargument; Evidence.**

Assumption An assumption is an opinion or belief that is taken for granted. It can be about a specific situation, a person, or the world in general. Assumptions are often unstated.

Author's Message An author's message is the main idea or theme of a particular work.
See also **Main Idea; Theme,** *Glossary of Literary Terms, page R114.*

Author's Perspective *See Glossary of Literary Terms, page R102.*

Author's Position An author's position is his or her opinion on an issue or topic.
See also **Claim.**

Author's Purpose *See Glossary of Literary Terms, page R102.*

Autobiography *See Glossary of Literary Terms, page R102.*

Bias Bias is an inclination toward a particular judgment on a topic or issue. A writer often reveals a strongly positive or strongly negative opinion by presenting only one way of looking at an issue or by heavily weighting the evidence. Words with intensely positive or negative connotations are often a signal of a writer's bias.

Bibliography A bibliography is a list of books and other materials related to the topic of a text. Bibliographies can be good sources of works for further study on a subject.
See also **Works Consulted.**

Biography *See Glossary of Literary Terms, page R103.*

Business Correspondence Business correspondence includes all written business communications, such as business letters, e-mails, and memos. In general, business correspondence is brief, to the point, clear, courteous, and professional.

Cause and Effect A **cause** is an event or action that directly results in another event or action. An **effect** is the direct or logical outcome of an event or action. Basic **cause-and-effect relationships** include a single cause with a single effect, one cause with multiple effects, multiple causes with a single effect, and a chain of causes and effects. The concept of cause and effect also provides a way of organizing a piece of writing. It helps a writer show the relationships between events or ideas.
See also **False Cause,** *Reading Handbook, page R24.*

Chronological Order Chronological order is the arrangement of events in their order of occurrence. This type of organization is used in both fictional narratives and in historical writing, biography, and autobiography.

Claim In an argument, a claim is the writer's position on an issue or problem. Although an argument focuses on supporting one claim, a writer may make more than one claim in a work.

Clarify Clarifying is a reading strategy that helps a reader to understand or make clear what he or she is reading. Readers usually clarify by rereading, reading aloud, or discussing.

Classification Classification is a pattern of organization in which objects, ideas, or information is presented in groups, or classes, based on common characteristics.

Cliché A cliché is an overused expression. "Better late than never" and "hard as nails" are common examples. Good writers generally avoid clichés unless they are using them in dialogue to indicate something about characters' personalities.

Compare and Contrast To compare and contrast is to identify similarities and differences in two or more subjects. Compare-and-contrast organization can be used to structure a piece of writing, serving as a framework for examining the similarities and differences in two or more subjects.

Conclusion A conclusion is a statement of belief based on evidence, experience, and reasoning. A **valid conclusion** is a conclusion that logically follows from the facts or statements upon which it is based. A **deductive conclusion** is one that follows from a particular generalization or premise. An **inductive conclusion** is a broad conclusion or generalization that is reached by arguing from specific facts and examples.

Connect Connecting is a reader's process of relating the content of a text to his or her own knowledge and experience.

Consumer Documents Consumer documents are printed materials that accompany products and services. They are intended for the buyers or users of the products or services and usually provide information about use, care, operation, or assembly. Some common consumer documents are applications, contracts, warranties, manuals, instructions, package inserts, labels, brochures, and schedules.

Context Clues When you encounter an unfamiliar word, you can often use context clues as aids for understanding. Context clues are the words and phrases surrounding the word that provide hints about the word's meaning.

Counterargument A counterargument is an argument made to oppose another argument. A good argument anticipates opposing viewpoints and provides counterarguments to refute (disprove) or answer them.

Credibility *Credibility* refers to the believability or trustworthiness of a source and the information it contains.

Critical Review A critical review is an evaluation or critique by a reviewer or critic. Different types of reviews include film reviews, book reviews, music reviews, and art-show reviews.

Database A database is a collection of information that can be quickly and easily accessed and searched and from which information can be easily retrieved. It is frequently presented in an electronic format.

Debate A debate is basically an argument—but a very structured one that requires a good deal of preparation. In academic settings, *debate* usually refers to a formal argumentation contest in which two opposing teams defend and attack a proposition.
See also **Argument.**

Deductive Reasoning Deductive reasoning is a way of thinking that begins with a generalization, presents a specific situation, and then advances with facts and evidence to a logical conclusion. The following passage has a deductive argument imbedded in it: "All students in the drama class must attend the play on Thursday. Since Ava is in the class, she had better show up." This deductive argument can be broken down as follows: generalization—all students in the drama class must attend the play on Thursday; specific situation—Ava is a student in the drama class; conclusion—Ava must attend the play.
See also **Analyzing Logic and Reasoning,** *Reading Handbook, pages R22–R23.*

Dictionary *See* **Reference Works.**

Draw Conclusions To draw a conclusion is to make a judgment or arrive at a belief based on evidence, experience, and reasoning.

Editorial An editorial is an opinion piece that usually appears on the editorial page of a newspaper or as part of a news broadcast. The editorial section of a newspaper presents opinions rather than objective news reports.
See also **Op-Ed Piece.**

Either/Or Fallacy An either/or fallacy is a statement that suggests that there are only two possible ways to view a situation or only two options to choose from. In other words, it is a statement that falsely frames a dilemma, giving the impression that no options exist but the two presented—for example, "Either we stop the construction of a new airport, or the surrounding suburbs will become ghost towns."
See also **Identifying Faulty Reasoning,** *Reading Handbook, page R24.*

Emotional Appeals Emotional appeals are messages that evoke strong feelings—such as fear, pity, or vanity—in order to persuade instead of using facts and evidence to make a point. An **appeal to fear** is a message that taps into people's fear of losing their safety or security. An **appeal to pity** is a message that taps into people's sympathy and compassion for others to build support for an idea, a cause, or a proposed action. An **appeal to vanity** is a message that attempts to persuade by tapping into people's desire to feel good about themselves.
See also **Recognizing Persuasive Techniques,** *Reading Handbook, pages R21–R22.*

Encyclopedia *See* **Reference Works.**

Essay *See Glossary of Literary Terms, page R105.*

Evaluate To evaluate is to examine something carefully and judge its value or worth. Evaluating is an important skill for gaining insight into what you read. A reader can evaluate the actions of a particular character, for example, or can form an opinion about the value of an entire work.

Evidence Evidence is the specific pieces of information that support a claim. Evidence can take the form of facts, quotations, examples, statistics, or personal experiences, among others.

Expository Essay *See* **Essay,** *Glossary of Literary Terms, page R105.*

Fact versus Opinion A **fact** is a statement that can be proved or verified. An **opinion,** on the other hand, is a statement that cannot be proved because it expresses a person's beliefs, feelings, or thoughts.

See also **Inference; Generalization.**

Fallacy A fallacy is an error in reasoning. Typically, a fallacy is based on an incorrect inference or a misuse of evidence. Some common logical fallacies are **circular reasoning, either/or fallacy, oversimplification, overgeneralization,** and **stereotyping.**

See also **Either/Or Fallacy, Logical Appeal, Overgeneralization; Identifying Faulty Reasoning,** *Reading Handbook, page R24.*

Faulty Reasoning *See* **Fallacy.**

Feature Article A feature article is a main article in a newspaper or a cover story in a magazine. A feature article is focused more on entertaining than informing. Features are lighter or more general than hard news and tend to be about human interest or lifestyles.

Functional Documents *See* **Consumer Documents; Workplace Documents.**

Generalization A generalization is a broad statement about a class or category of people, ideas, or things, based on a study of only some of its members.

See also **Overgeneralization.**

Government Publications Government publications are documents produced by government organizations. Pamphlets, brochures, and reports are just some of the many forms these publications may take. Government publications can be good resources for a wide variety of topics.

Graphic Aid A graphic aid is a visual tool that is printed, handwritten, or drawn. Charts, diagrams, graphs, photographs, and maps can all be graphic aids.

See also **Graphic Aids,** *Reading Handbook, pages R5–R7.*

Graphic Organizer A graphic organizer is a "word picture"—that is, a visual illustration of a verbal statement—that helps a reader understand a text. Charts, tables, webs, and diagrams can all be graphic organizers. Graphic organizers and graphic aids can look the same. For example, a table in a science article will not be constructed differently from a table that is a graphic organizer. However, graphic organizers and graphic aids do differ in how they are used. Graphic aids are the visual representations that people encounter when they read informational texts. Graphic organizers are visuals that people construct to help them understand texts or organize information.

Historical Documents Historical documents are writings that have played a significant role in human events or are themselves records of such events. The Declaration of Independence, for example, is a historical document.

How-To Book A how-to book is a book that is written to explain how to do something—usually an activity, a sport, or a household project.

Implied Main Idea *See* **Main Idea.**

Index The index of a book is an alphabetized list of important topics and details covered in the book and the page numbers on which they can be found. An index can be used to quickly find specific information about a topic.

Inductive Reasoning Inductive reasoning is the process of logical reasoning from observations, examples, and facts to a general conclusion or principle.

See also **Analyzing Logic and Reasoning,** *Reading Handbook, pages R22–R23.*

Inference An inference is a logical assumption that is based on observed facts and one's own knowledge and experience.

Informational Nonfiction Informational nonfiction is writing that provides factual information. It often explains ideas or teaches processes. Examples include news reports, science textbooks, software instructions, and lab reports.

Internet The Internet is a global, interconnected system of computer networks that allows for communication through e-mail, listservers, and the World Wide Web. The Internet connects computers and computer users throughout the world.

Journal A journal is a periodical publication issued by a legal, medical, or other professional organization. Alternatively, the term may be used to refer to a diary or daily record.

Loaded Language Loaded language consists of words with strongly positive or negative connotations intended to influence a reader's or listener's attitude.

Logical Appeal A logical appeal relies on logic and facts, appealing to people's reasoning or intellect rather than to their values or emotions. Flawed logical appeals—that is, errors in reasoning—are considered logical fallacies.

See also **Fallacy.**

Logical Argument A logical argument is an argument in which the logical relationship between the support and the claim is sound.

Main Idea A main idea is the central or most important idea about a topic that a writer or speaker conveys. It can be the central idea of an entire work or of just a paragraph. Often, the main idea of a paragraph is expressed in a topic sentence. However, a main idea may just be implied, or suggested, by details. A main idea and supporting details can serve as a basic pattern of organization in a piece of writing, with the central idea about a topic being supported by details.

Make Inferences *See* **Inference.**

Monitor Monitoring is the strategy of checking your comprehension as you are reading and modifying the strategies you are using to suit your needs. Monitoring may include some or all of the following strategies: **questioning, clarifying, visualizing, predicting, connecting,** and **rereading.**

Narrative Nonfiction *See Glossary of Literary Terms, page R109.*

News Article A news article is a piece of writing that reports on a recent event. In newspapers, news articles are usually written in a concise manner to report the latest news, presenting the most important facts first and then more detailed information. In magazines, news articles are usually more elaborate than those in newspapers because they are written to provide both information and analysis. Also, news articles in magazines do not necessarily present the most important facts first.

Nonfiction *See Glossary of Literary Terms, page R109.*

Op-Ed Piece An op-ed piece is an opinion piece that usually appears opposite ("op") the editorial page of a newspaper. Unlike editorials, op-ed pieces are written and submitted by named writers.

Organization *See* **Pattern of Organization.**

Overgeneralization An overgeneralization is a generalization that is too broad. You can often recognize overgeneralizations by the appearance of words and phrases such as *all, everyone, every time, any, anything, no one,* and *none.* Consider, for example, this statement: "None of the sanitation workers in our city really care about keeping the environment clean." In all probability, there are many exceptions. The writer can't possibly know the feelings of every sanitation worker in the city.
See also **Identifying Faulty Reasoning,** *Reading Handbook, page R24.*

Overview An overview is a short summary of a story, a speech, or an essay. It orients the reader by providing a preview of the text to come.

Paraphrase Paraphrasing is the restating of information in one's own words.
See also **Summarize.**

Pattern of Organization A pattern of organization is a particular arrangement of ideas and information. Such a pattern may be used to organize an entire composition or a single paragraph within a longer work. The following are the most common patterns of organization: **cause-and-effect, chronological order, compare-and-contrast, classification, deductive, inductive, order of importance, problem-solution, sequential,** and **spatial.**
See also **Cause and Effect; Chronological Order; Classification; Compare and Contrast; Problem-Solution Order; Sequential Order; Analyzing Patterns of Organization,** *Reading Handbook, pages R14–R20.*

Periodical A periodical is a publication that is issued at regular intervals of more than one day. For example, a periodical may be a weekly, monthly, or quarterly journal or magazine. Newspapers and other daily publications generally are not classified as periodicals.

Personal Essay *See* **Essay,** *Glossary of Literary Terms, page R105.*

Persuasion Persuasion is the art of swaying others' feelings, beliefs, or actions. Persuasion normally appeals to both the intellect and the emotions of readers. **Persuasive techniques** are the methods used to influence others to adopt certain opinions or beliefs or to act in certain ways. Types of persuasive techniques include emotional appeals, logical appeals, and loaded language. When used properly, persuasive techniques can add depth to writing that's meant to persuade. Persuasive techniques can, however, be misused to cloud factual information, disguise poor reasoning, or unfairly exploit people's emotions in order to shape their opinions.
See also **Emotional Appeals; Loaded Language; Logical Appeal; Recognizing Persuasive Techniques,** *Reading Handbook, pages R21–R22.*

Predict Predicting is a reading strategy that involves using text clues to make a reasonable guess about what will happen next in a story.

Primary Source *See* **Sources.**

Prior Knowledge Prior knowledge is the knowledge a reader already possesses about a topic. This information might come from personal experiences, expert accounts, books, films, or other sources.

Problem-Solution Order Problem-solution order is a pattern of organization in which a problem is stated and analyzed and then one or more solutions are proposed and examined. Writers use words and phrases such as *propose, conclude, reason for, problem, answer,* and *solution* to connect ideas and details when writing about problems and solutions.

Propaganda Propaganda is a form of communication that may use distorted, false, or misleading information. It usually refers to manipulative political discourse.

Public Documents Public documents are documents that were written for the public to provide information that is of public interest or concern. They include government documents, speeches, signs, and rules and regulations. *See also* **Government Publications.**

Reference Works General reference works are sources that contain facts and background information on a wide range of subjects. More specific reference works contain in-depth information on a single subject. Most reference works are good sources of reliable information because they have been reviewed by experts. The following are some common reference works: **encyclopedias, dictionaries, thesauri, almanacs, atlases, chronologies, biographical dictionaries,** and **directories.**

Review *See* **Critical Review.**

Rhetorical Devices *See Glossary of Literary Terms, page R111.*

Rhetorical Questions Rhetorical questions are those that do not require a reply. Writers use them to suggest that their arguments make the answer obvious or self-evident.

Scanning Scanning is the process of searching through writing for a particular fact or piece of information. When you scan, your eyes sweep across a page, looking for key words that may lead you to the information you want.

Secondary Source *See* **Sources.**

Sequential Order A pattern of organization that shows the order in which events or actions occur is called sequential order. Writers typically use this pattern of organization to explain steps or stages in a process.

Setting a Purpose The process of establishing specific reasons for reading a text is called setting a purpose.

Sidebar A sidebar is additional information set in a box alongside or within a news or feature article. Popular magazines often make use of sidebar information.

Signal Words Signal words are words and phrases that indicate what is to come in a text. Readers can use signal words to discover a text's pattern of organization and to analyze the relationships among the ideas in the text.

Sources A source is anything that supplies information. **Primary sources** are materials written by people who were present at events, either as participants or as observers. Letters, diaries, autobiographies, speeches, and photographs are primary sources. **Secondary sources** are records of events that were created sometime after the events occurred; the writers were not directly involved or were not present when the events took place. Encyclopedias, textbooks, biographies, most newspaper and magazine articles, and books and articles that interpret or review research are secondary sources.

Spatial Order Spatial order is a pattern of organization that highlights the physical positions or relationships of details or objects. This pattern of organization is typically found in descriptive writing. Writers use words and phrases such as *on the left, to the right, here, over there, above, below, beyond, nearby,* and *in the distance* to indicate the arrangement of details.

Speech *See Glossary of Literary Terms, page R113.*

Stereotyping Stereotyping is a dangerous type of overgeneralization. Stereotypes are broad statements made about people on the basis of their gender, ethnicity, race, or political, social, professional, or religious group.

Summarize To summarize is to briefly retell, or encapsulate, the main ideas of a piece of writing in one's own words. *See also* **Paraphrase.**

Support Support is any material that serves to prove a claim. In an argument, support typically consists of reasons and evidence. In persuasive texts and speeches, however, support may include appeals to the needs and values of the audience.

Supporting Detail *See* **Main Idea.**

Synthesize To synthesize information is to take individual pieces of information and combine them with other pieces of information and with prior knowledge or experience to gain a better understanding of a subject or to create a new product or idea.

Text Features Text features are design elements that indicate the organizational structure of a text and help make the key ideas and the supporting information understandable. Text features include headings, boldface type, italic type, bulleted or numbered lists, sidebars, and graphic aids such as charts, tables, timelines, illustrations, and photographs.

Thesaurus *See* **Reference Works.**

Thesis Statement In an argument, a thesis statement is an expression of the claim that the writer or speaker is trying to support. In an essay, a thesis statement is an expression, in one or two sentences, of the main idea or purpose of the piece of writing.

Topic Sentence The topic sentence of a paragraph states the paragraph's main idea. All other sentences in the paragraph provide supporting details.

Visualize Visualizing is the process of forming a mental picture based on written or spoken information.

Web Site A Web site is a collection of "pages" on the World Wide Web that is usually devoted to one specific subject. Pages are linked together and are accessed by clicking hyperlinks or menus, which send the user from page to page within the site. Web sites are created by companies, organizations, educational institutions, branches of the government, the military, and individuals.

Workplace Documents Workplace documents are materials that are produced or used within a work setting, usually to aid in the functioning of the workplace. They include job applications, office memos, training manuals, job descriptions, and sales reports.

Works Cited A list of works cited lists names of all the works a writer has referred to in his or her text. This list often includes not only books and articles but also nonprint sources.

Works Consulted A list of works consulted names all the works a writer consulted in order to create his or her text. It is not limited just to those works cited in the text.
See also **Bibliography.**

Glossary of Vocabulary in English & Spanish

abash (ə-băsh´) v. to make ashamed or embarrass
   avergonzar v. mortificar o humillar

acquiesce (ăk´wē-ĕs´) v. to agree or give in to
   consentir v. aceptar o ceder

acquiescence (ăk´wē-ĕs´əns) n. passive agreement; acceptance without protest
   conformidad s. aceptación pasiva; consentimiento

adaptation (ăd´ăp-tā´shən) n. the process of adjusting to suit one's surroundings
   adaptación s. proceso de acostumbrarse a lo que nos rodea

adversary (ăd´vər-sĕr´ē) n. an opponent; enemy
   adversario s. opositor; enemigo

affable (ăf´ə-bəl) adj. warm and friendly
   afable adj. cálido y amistoso

afford (ə-fôrd´) v. to provide or offer
   proveer v. dar u ofrecer

alleviate (ə-lē´vē-āt´) v. to make easier or provide relief
   aliviar v. facilitar o calmar

anarchist (ăn´ər-kĭst) n. a person favoring the overthrow of government
   anarquista s. persona a favor del derrocamiento del gobierno

annihilate (ə-nī´ə-lāt´) v. to destroy completely
   aniquilar v. destruir por completo

anthology (ăn-thŏl´ə-jē) n. a collection of written works—such as poems, short stories, or plays—in a single book or set
   antología s. colección de obras escritas —poemas, cuentos u obras de teatro— encuadernadas en un libro o una colección

apprehension (ăp´rĭ-hĕn´shən) n. fear and worry for the future
   aprensión s. temor y preocupación por el futuro

ascertain (ăs´ər-tān´) v. to discover with certainty
   determinar v. establecer con certeza

assail (ə-sāl´) v. to attack or deliver a blow
   atacar v. asaltar o agredir

atrocity (ə-trŏs´ĭ-tē) n. a very cruel or brutal act
   atrocidad s. acto muy cruel o brutal

auspicious (ô-spĭsh´əs) adj. promising success; favorable
   propicio adj. que promete éxito; favorable

autonomy (ô-tŏn´ə-mē) n. freedom; independence
   autonomía s. libertad; independencia

avidly (ăv´ĭd-lē) adv. with great eagerness and enthusiasm
   ávidamente adv. con mucho entusiasmo

boisterous (boi´stər-əs) adj. noisy and lacking in restraint or discipline
   escandaloso adj. alborotado y sin control o disciplina

boycott (boi´kŏt´) n. a form of protest in which a group stops using a specific service or product in order to force a change
   boicot s. forma de protesta en que un grupo deja de usar un servicio o un producto a fin de buscar un cambio

burnish (bûr´nĭsh) v. to polish
   bruñir v. sacar brillo

capricious (kə-prĭsh´əs) adj. impulsive, unpredictable
   caprichoso adj. impulsivo, inestable

carnage (kär´nĭj) n. massive slaughter
   matanza s. gran mortandad

catalyst (kăt´l-ĭst) n. something or someone that brings about change
   catalizador s. algo o alguien que causa un cambio o acción

cavalcade (kăv´əl-kād´) n. a procession of people on horseback
   cabalgata s. procesión de gente a caballo

censure (sĕn´shər) n. harsh criticism or disapproval
   censura s. crítica o desaprobación fuerte

chaotic (kā-ŏt´ĭk) adj. extremely confused or disordered
   caótico adj. extremadamente confuso o desordenado

coercion (kō-ûr´zhən) n. the act of compelling by force or authority
   coerción s. uso de poder o amenazas para obligar a actuar

collaborative (kə-lăb´ə-rə´tĭv) adj. done in cooperation with others
   en colaboración adj. hecho en cooperación

commiserate (kə-mĭz´ə-rāt´) v. to express sorrow or pity for another's troubles
   conmiserarse v. expresar dolor o piedad por los problemas de otro

compassionate (kəm-păsh'ə-nĭt) *adj.* feeling or sharing the suffering of others
  compasivo *adj.* que comparte el sufrimiento ajeno

compatriot (kəm-pā'trē-ət) *n.* a person from one's own country
  compatriota *s.* persona del mismo país que uno

complicity (kəm-plĭs'ĭ-tē) *n.* association or partnership in a crime or offense
  complicidad *adj.* participación en un delito u ofensa

concede (kən-sēd') *v.* to admit or acknowledge, often reluctantly
  reconocer *v.* admitir o aceptar

conceivably (kən-sēv'ə-blē) *adv.* possibly
  concebible *adj.* posible

condolence (kən-dō'ləns) *n.* an expression of sympathy
  condolencia *s.* pésame

conflagration (kŏn'flə-grā'shən) *n.* a large, destructive fire
  conflagración *s.* incendio destructivo

confound (kən-found') *v.* to confuse or astonish
  confundir *v.* desconcertar o sorprender

conjectural (kən-jĕk'chər-əl) *adj.* involving guesswork
  conjetural *adj.* basado en suposiciones

conspire (kən-spīr') *v.* to plan or plot secretly
  conspirar *v.* complotar en secreto

consternation (kŏn'stər-nā'shən) *n.* confused amazement or fear
  consternación *s.* abatimiento o disgusto

contempt (kən-tĕmpt') *n.* an attitude of regarding someone or something as worthless or inferior
  desdén *s.* actitud de desprecio

contemptuous (kən-tĕmp'chōō-əs) *adj.* scornful or disrespectful
  desdeñoso *adj.* despectivo o irrespetuoso

contending (kən-tĕn'dĭng) *adj.* struggling in rivalry
contend *v.*
  contendiente *adj.* rival, contrario contender *v.*

contingent (kən-tĭn'jənt) *n.* a gathering of people representative of a larger group
  contingente *s.* reunión de representantes de un grupo mayor

contrary (kŏn'trĕr'ē) *adj.* stubbornly uncooperative or contradictory
  contrario *adj.* opuesto o adverso

cosmopolitan (kŏz'mə-pŏl'ĭ-tn) *adj.* containing elements from all over the world; sophisticated
  cosmopolita *adj.* que tiene elementos de muchos países; sofisticado

cower (kou'ər) *v.* to crouch down in fear
  encogerse *v.* doblarse con miedo

deference (dĕf'ər-əns) *n.* polite respect; submission to someone else's wishes
  deferencia *s.* respeto cortés; sumisión a los deseos ajenos

deficit (dĕf'ĭ-sĭt) *n.* a shortfall or deficiency
  déficit *s.* cantidad que falta para llegar al nivel necesario

defile (dĭ-fīl') *v.* to make dirty, unclean, or impure
  profanar *v.* ensuciar o deshonrar; quitarle la pureza

deflect (dĭ-flĕkt') *v.* to fend off or avert the direction of something
  desviar *v.* evitar o cambiar la dirección

degraded (dĭ-grā'dĭd) *adj.* corrupted, depraved
  degradado *adj.* corrupto, depravado

degrading (dĭ-grā'dĭng) *adj.* tending or intended to cause dishonor or disgrace
  degradante *adj.* que busca quitar dignidad u honor

dejectedly (dĭ-jĕk'tĭd-lē) *adv.* in a disheartened, depressed way
  abatido *adj.* desalentado, con el ánimo por los suelos

delirium (dĭ-lîr'ē-əm) *n.* a temporary state of mental confusion usually resulting from high fever or shock
  delirio *s.* estado pasajero de confusión mental por fiebre o shock

destiny (dĕs'tə-nē) *n.* the determinded fate of a particular person or thing; lot in life
  destino *s.* suerte o función de determinada persona o cosa; sino

din (dĭn) *n.* a deafening noise
  estruendo *s.* mezcla de ruidos fuertes

disarm (dĭs-ärm') *v.* to win over; to make less hostile
  desarmar *v.* reducir sospecha u hostilidad

discord (dĭs'kôrd') *n.* disagreement; lack of harmony
discordia *s.* desacuerdo; falta de armonía

disengage (dĭs'ĕn-gāj') *v.* to detach or remove oneself
desconectarse *v.* soltarse o retirarse

disparage (dĭ-spăr'ĭj) *v.* to speak of in a negative or insulting way
menospreciar *v.* tratar de modo negativo o insultante

disparagement (dĭ-spăr'ĭj-mənt) *n.* belittlement
menosprecio *s.* desprecio

dissuasion (dĭ-swā'zhən) *n.* an attempt to deter a person from a course of action
disuasión *s.* utilización de razones para cambiar la opinión o el propósito de alguien

doctrine (dŏk'trĭn) *n.* a set of rules, beliefs, or values held by a group
doctrina *s.* conjunto de principios o reglas de un grupo

draft (drăft) *n.* a gulp or swallow
sorbo *s.* trago

eccentric (ĭk-sĕn'trĭk) *adj.* strange; peculiar
excéntrico *adj.* extraño; peculiar

edict (ē'dĭkt') *n.* a command issued by an authority
edicto *s.* orden de una persona de autoridad

eloquent (ĕl'ə-kwənt) *adj.* vividly expressive
elocuente *adj.* que se expresa con emoción

emaciated (ĭ-mā'shē-ā'tĭd) *adj.* excessively thin as a result of starvation **emaciate** *v.*
emaciado *adj.* en los huesos; muy delgado por pasar hambre **emaciarse** *v.*

emblemized (ĕm'blə-mīzd') *adj.* represented; symbolized **emblemize** *v.*
emblemático *adj.* simbolizado **emblematizar** *v.*

embody (ĕm-bŏd'ē) *v.* to give shape to or visibly represent
encarnar *v.* dar forma concreta o representar

emphatically (ĕm-făt'ĭk-lē) *adv.* with strong emphasis
enfáticamente *adv.* con énfasis; con fuerza

enmity (ĕn'mĭ-tē) *n.* hostility and ill will
enemistad *s.* hostilidad y odio

exalt (ĭg-zôlt') *v.* to glorify, praise, or honor
exaltar *v.* glorificar, alabar u honrar

fanatical (fə-năt'ĭ-kəl) *adj.* extremely enthusiastic
fanático *adj.* extremadamente entusiasta

fictitious (fĭk-tĭsh'əs) *adj.* fabricated; created by the imagination
ficticio *adj.* inventado; creado por la imaginación

fidelity (fĭ-dĕl'ĭ-tē) *n.* faithfulness to duties; loyalty and devotion
fidelidad *s.* responsabilidad hacia obligaciones; dedicación y lealtad

flailing (flā'lĭng) *adj.* waving vigorously **flail** *v.*
agitar *v.* sacudir, ondear

forbear (fôr-bâr') *v.* to refrain from; resist
abstenerse *v.* restringirse

fortitude (fôr'tĭ-tōōd') *n.* strength of mind; courage
fortaleza *s.* fuerza emocional; valor

furtive (fûr'tĭv) *adj.* sneaky, secretive
furtivo *adj.* solapado; que tiene un motivo o propósito oculto

glutton (glŭt'n) *n.* a person who eats too much
glotón *s.* persona que come mucho

haggard (hăg'ərd) *adj.* appearing worn and exhausted
ojeroso *adj.* de aspecto cansado y exhausto

hapless (hăp'lĭs) *adj.* pitiful; unfortunate
desafortunado *adj.* desventurado; lastimoso

heritage (hĕr'ĭ-tĭj) *n.* something passed down through generations, such as tradition, values, property
herencia *s.* tradiciones, valores o propiedades transmitidas de generación en generación

hiatus (hī-ā'təs) *n.* a gap or break in continuity
pausa *s.* interrupción momentánea

ignominiously (ĭg'nə-mĭn'ē-əs-lē) *adv.* shamefully
ignominiosamente *adv.* vergonzosamente

impassively (ĭm-păs'ĭv-lē) *adv.* in a way that shows no emotion or feeling
impasivamente *adv.* sin emoción

impeccably (ĭm-pĕk'ə-blē) *adv.* perfectly; flawlessly
impecablemente *adv.* sin falla; perfectamente

impede (ĭm-pēd') *v.* to obstruct or hinder
impedir *v.* obstruir o dificultar

imperative (ĭm-pĕr′ə-tĭv) *adj.* urgently necessary
　imperativo adj. urgentemente necesario

imperceptible (ĭm′pər-sĕp′tə-bəl) *adj.* impossible or difficult to notice
　imperceptible adj. imposible o difícil de captar

implacable (ĭm-plăk′ə-bəl) *adj.* impossible to calm or satisfy; relentless
　implacable adj. imposible de apaciguar o satisfacer; despiadado

incongruous (ĭn-kŏng′grōō-əs) *adj.* unsuitable; incompatible
　inapropiado adj. fuera de lugar; incompatible

indeterminate (ĭn′dĭ-tûr′mə-nĭt) *adj.* not precisely known or determined
　indeterminado adj. que no se conoce con precisión

indomitable (ĭn-dŏm′ĭ-tə-bəl) *adj.* not easily discouraged or defeated
　indomable adj. que no se deja desalentar, derrotar o someter

inevitable (ĭn-ĕv′ĭ-tə-bəl) *adj.* unavoidable
　inevitable adj. que no se puede evitar

infatuated (ĭn-făch′ōō-ā′tĭd) *adj.* intensely fond
　encaprichado adj. enamorado

innovative (ĭn′ə-vā′tĭv) *adj.* able to create new, original ideas
　innovador adj. que tiene ideas nuevas y originales

insolence (ĭn′sə-ləns) *n.* rudeness and disrespect
　insolencia s. grosería y falta de respeto

insuperable (ĭn-sōō′pər-ə-bəl) *adj.* impossible to overcome
　insuperable adj. imposible de vencer

intangible (ĭn-tăn′jə-bəl) *adj.* unable to be perceived with the senses
　intangible adj. que no se puede percibir con los sentidos

intemperate (ĭn-tĕm′pər-ĭt) *adj.* extreme
　inmoderado adj. extremado; desmedido

interloper (ĭn′tər-lō′pər) *n.* one that intrudes in a place, a situation, or an activity
　intruso s. el que se mete en un lugar, situación o actividad

interminable (ĭn-tûr′mə-nə-bəl) *adj.* having no limit or end
　interminable adj. que no tiene final

irrational (ĭ-răsh′ə-nəl) *adj.* not possessed with reason or understanding
　irracional adj. que no se guía por la razón

isolated (ī′sə-lā′tĭd) *adj.* separated from others
　aislado adj. separado

lamentation (lăm′ən-tā′shən) *n.* an expression of grief
　lamentación s. expresión de dolor

languor (lăng′gər) *n.* a lack of feeling or energy
　languidez s. abatimiento físico o emocional

laudable (lô′də-bəl) *adj.* worthy of high praise
　loable adj. digno de alabanza

lethargy (lĕth′ər-jē) *n.* prolonged sluggishness; unconsciousness
　letargo s. sopor; inconsciencia

lucid (lōō′sĭd) *adj.* clear; mentally sound
　lúcido adj. que comprende claramente

malice (măl′ĭs) *n.* a desire to harm others
　malicia s. deseo de hacer daño

mandate (măn′dāt′) *n.* a command or instruction
　mandato s. orden u instrucción

manipulate (mə-nĭp′yə-lāt′) *v.* to move, operate, or handle
　manipular v. mover, manejar

marauder (mə-rôd′ər) *n.* one who raids and loots
　maleante s. persona que roba y saquea

meditate (mĕd′ĭ-tāt′) *v.* to consider for a long time
　meditar s. considerar por largo tiempo

mentor (mĕn′tôr′) *n.* a wise and trusted counselor or teacher
　mentor s. maestro sabio y de confianza

militant (mĭl′ĭ-tənt) *adj.* aggressive or combative
　militante adj. de espíritu de lucha o combativo

morose (mə-rōs′) *adj.* gloomy; sullen
　moroso adj. lento; triste

naive (nī-ēv′) *adj.* unsophisticated, lacking worldly experience
　ingenuo adj. sin malicia ni experiencia

negotiable (nĭ-gō′shə-bəl) *adj.* able to be bargained with
　negociable adj. que se puede cambiar o rebajar

neutralize (nōō′trə-līz′) *v.* to counteract or cancel out the effect of
neutralizar *v.* contrarrestar o cancelar un efecto

nostalgia (nŏ-stăl′jə) *n.* a wistful longing for the past or the familiar
nostalgia *s.* recuerdo triste del pasado o de lo conocido

oblivious (ə-blĭv′ē-əs) *adj.* paying no attention, completely unaware
distraído *adj.* que no pone atención, ajeno a lo que sucede

ominous (ŏm′ə-nəs) *adj.* menacing; threatening
ominoso *adj.* amenazante

pandemonium (păn′də-mō′nē-əm) *n.* a wild uproar or noise
pandemonio *s.* alboroto o escándalo incontrolable

paranoia (păr′ə-noi′ə) *n.* an irrational fear of danger or misfortune
paranoia *s.* temor irracional

patronize (pā′trə-nīz′) *v.* to behave in a manner that shows feelings of superiority
condescender *v.* actuar con superioridad

pensive (pĕn′sĭv) *adj.* thoughtful in a wistful, sad way
pensativo *adj.* meditabundo; triste o preocupado

peremptorily (pə-rĕmp′tə-rə-lē) *adv.* in a commanding way that does not allow for refusal or contradiction
perentorio *adj.* autoritario; que no permite contradicción

permeate (pûr′mē-āt′) *v.* to spread or flow throughout
impregnar *v.* calar, penetrar

perpetuation (pər-pĕch′ōō-ā′shən) *n.* the act of continuing or prolonging something
perpetuación *s.* continuación a largo plazo

persevere (pûr′sə-vîr′) *v.* to persist in an action or belief despite difficulty
perseverar *v.* persistir; seguir adelante a pesar de dificultades

pertinacity (pûr′tn-ăs′ĭ-tē) *n.* unyielding persistence or adherence
pertinacia *s.* terquedad; persistencia

pervade (pər-vād′) *v.* to spread throughout
dominar *v.* invadir; impregnar

perverse (pər-vûrs′) *adj.* willfully determined to go against what is expected or desired
perverso *adj.* que contraría con intención

pestilential (pĕs′tə-lĕn′shəl) *adj.* likely to spread and cause disease
pestilente *adj.* que contagia; de mal olor

pinioned (pĭn′yənd) *adj.* restrained or immobilized
pinion *v.*
inmovilizado *adj.* restringido inmovilizar *v.*

precipitous (prĭ-sĭp′ĭ-təs) *adj.* extremely steep
escarpado *adj.* muy inclinado

precursor (prĭ-kûr′sər) *n.* something that comes before and signals or prepares the way for what will follow
precursor *s.* algo que precede o prepara el camino para lo que sigue

predisposed (prē′dĭ-spōzd′) *v.* inclined to something in advance
predispuesto *v.* inclinado de antemano a hacer algo

premonition (prē′mə-nĭsh′ən) *n.* a hunch or feeling about the future; a foreboding
premonición *s.* corazonada o presentimiento del futuro

preoccupied (prē-ŏk′yə-pīd′) *adj.* absorbed in one's thoughts; distracted
preocupado *adj.* absorto en sus pensamientos; distraído

prestigious (prĕ-stē′jəs) *adj.* having a great reputation; highly respected
prestigioso *adj.* de muy buena reputación; altamente respetado

presumption (prĭ-zŭmp′shən) *n.* behavior or language that is boldly arrogant or offensive
presunción *s.* conducta o lenguaje arrogante u ofensivo

proponent (prə-pō′nənt) *n.* a person who pleads for or supports a cause
defensor *s.* persona que apoya una causa

prostrate (prŏs′trāt′) *adj.* lying in a flat, horizontal position
postrado *adj.* en posición horizontal

prowess (prou′ĭs) *n.* superior skill, strength, or courage, especially in battle
valor *s.* gran fuerza, valentía y arrojo, especialmente en la batalla

rapt (răpt) *adj.* fully absorbed; entranced
   embelesado *adj.* totalmente absorto

recompense (rĕk′əm-pĕns′) *n.* amends for damage or payment for service
   recompensa *s.* pago como premio o a cambio de un servicio

recompose (rē′kəm-pōz′) *v.* to restore to calm, to settle again
   serenar *v.* recobrar la calma, poner en orden

reconcile (rĕk′ən-sīl′) *v.* to restore friendly relations
   reconciliarse *v.* volver a las amistades

reconciliation (rĕk′ən-sĭl′ē-ā′shən) *n.* the act of settling or resolving
   reconciliación *s.* acto de arreglar o resolver

reiterate (rē-ĭt′ə-rāt′) *v.* to repeat
   reiterar *v.* repetir

rejuvenated (rĭ-jōō′və-nā′tĭd) *adj.* made new or young again **rejuvenate** *v.*
   rejuvenecido *adj.* que ha recuperado la juventud **rejuvenecer** *v.*

replenish (rĭ-plĕn′ĭsh) *v.* to fill again
   reponer *v.* volver a llenar

reprehensible (rĕp′rĭ-hĕn′sə-bəl) *adj.* deserving blame and criticism
   reprensible *adj.* que merece culpa y crítica

reprisal (rĭ-prī′zəl) *n.* retaliation in the form of harm or injury similar to that received
   represalia *s.* venganza con daños o heridas similares a los recibidos

repute (rĭ-pyōōt′) *n.* reputation; fame
   renombre *s.* reputación; fama

resignation (rĕz′ĭg-nā′shən) *n.* passive acceptance of something; submission
   resignación *s.* aceptación pasiva; sumisión

respite (rĕs′pĭt) *n.* a period of rest or relief
   respiro *s.* período breve de descanso o alivio

resurrect (rĕz′ə-rĕkt′) *v.* to bring back to life
   resucitar *v.* traer de vuelta a la vida

reticence (rĕt′ĭ-səns) *n.* the quality of keeping silent or reserved
   reticencia *s.* reserva; prudencia y discreción

retrospect (rĕt′rə-spĕkt′) *n.* a view or contemplation of something past
   retrospectiva *s.* contemplación del pasado

reverence (rĕv′ər-əns) *n.* awe and respect
   reverencia *s.* admiración y respeto

rhetoric (rĕt′ər-ĭk) *n.* grand but empty talk
   retórica *s.* discurso grandilocuente y vacío

rigorous (rĭg′ər-əs) *adj.* strict, uncompromising
   riguroso *adj.* estricto, intransigente

robustly (rō-bŭst′lē) *adv.* in a strong, powerful way
   enérgicamente *adv.* con fuerza y vigor

rudimentary (rōō′də-mĕn′tə-rē) *adj.* very basic, in the beginning stages
   rudimentario *adj.* básico, en las etapas iniciales

sate (sāt) *v.* to satisfy fully
   saciar *v.* satisfacer por completo

savagery (săv′ĭj-rē) *n.* extreme violence or cruelty
   salvajismo *s.* violencia o crueldad extremas

savoring (sā′vər-ĭng) *n.* a full appreciation and enjoyment **savor** *v.*
   sabor *s.* aprecio y gusto **saborear** *v.*

sententiously (sĕn-tĕn′shəs-lē) *adv.* in a pompous, moralizing manner
   sentenciosamente *adv.* en tono pomposo y regañón

sentiment (sĕn′tə-mənt) *n.* feeling or emotion
   sentimiento *s.* emoción

silhouette (sĭl′ōō-ĕt′) *n.* an outline that appears dark against a light background
   silueta *s.* perfil que se destaca sobre un fondo claro

sinister (sĭn′ĭ-stər) *adj.* threatening or foreshadowing evil
   siniestro *adj.* que amenaza un mal

smite (smīt) *v.* to inflict a heavy blow on; *past tense*—smote (smōt)
   golpear *v.* dar un fuerte golpe

sovereignty (sŏv′ər-ĭn-tē) *n.* complete independence and self-governance
  soberanía *s.* independencia completa y autogobierno

speculative (spĕk′yə-lə-tĭv) *adj.* based on guesses and theories rather than fact
  especulativo *adj.* basado en suposiciones y no en hechos

stark (stärk) *adj.* harsh or grim
  crudo *adj.* duro o agreste

stature (stăch′ər) *n.* the height of a person, animal, or object in an upright position
  estatura *s.* altura de una persona, animal u objeto en posición vertical

stealth (stĕlth) *n.* a concealed manner of acting
  secreto *s.* conducta callada u oculta

stratagem (străt′ə-jəm) *n.* a clever trick or device for obtaining an advantage
  estratagema *s.* truco o maquinación para conseguir ventaja

stridently (strīd′nt-lē) *adv.* harshly; conspicuously
  estridentemente *adj.* con dureza y escándalo

stupor (stoo′pər) *n.* a state of mental numbness, as from shock
  estupor *s.* pasmo; profundo asombro

sublime (sə-blīm′) *adj.* supreme, splendid
  sublime *adj.* supremo, espléndido

subordinate (sə-bôr′dn-āt′) *v.* to lower in rank or importance
  subordinar *v.* bajar de rango o importancia

succession (sək-sĕsh′ən) *n.* the sequence in which one person after another acquires a title, dignity, or estate
  sucesión *s.* secuencia en que se transmiten títulos, rango o propiedades de una persona a otra

succor (sŭk′ər) *n.* help in a difficult situation
  socorro *s.* ayuda en una situación difícil

supposition (sŭp′ə-zĭsh′ən) *n.* something supposed; an assumption
  suposición *s.* conjetura; creencia

synchronize (sĭng′krə-nīz′) *v.* to match the timing of
  sincronizar *v.* hacer que dos cosas ocurran al mismo tiempo

tact (tăkt) *n.* an understanding of the proper thing to do or say around others
  tacto *s.* sensibilidad para tratar a otras personas con delicadeza

tactic (tăk′tĭk) *n.* a planned action or maneuver to reach a certain goal
  táctica *s.* acción o maniobra planeada para alcanzar una meta

tenacity (tə-năs′ĭ-tē) *n.* the quality of holding persistently to something; firm determination
  tenacidad *s.* tesón y constancia; obstinación

trajectory (trə-jĕk′tə-rē) *n.* the path of a moving body through space
  trayectoria *s.* camino que sigue un objeto en movimiento en el espacio

transgress (trăns-grĕs′) *v.* to violate or break (a law, command, or moral code)
  transgredir *v.* violar una ley, una orden o un código moral

translucent (trăns-loo′sənt) *adj.* allowing light to shine through
  translúcido *adj.* que deja pasar la luz

trauma (trô′mə) *n.* severe physical or emotional distress
  trauma *s.* daño físico o emocional fuerte

tremulous (trĕm′yə-ləs) *adj.* trembling, unsteady
  trémulo *adj.* tembloroso

tribulation (trĭb′yə-lā′shən) *n.* great distress or suffering
  tribulación *s.* gran sufrimiento o preocupación

unavailing (ŭn′ə-vā′lĭng) *adj.* useless, ineffective
  inservible *adj.* inútil, ineficaz

unperturbed (ŭn′pər-tûrbd′) *adj.* calm and serene; untroubled
  impasible *adj.* calmo y sereno; impertérrito

usurper (yoo-sûrp′ər) *n.* someone who wrongfully takes possession of something
  usurpador *s.* el que toma posesión de algo que no le corresponde

vagrant (vā′grənt) *adj.* wandering
  vagabundo *adj.* que va de un lado al otro sin rumbo fijo

vehemently (vē′ə-mənt-lē) *adv.* in a fierce, intense manner
  vehementemente *adv.* con intensidad

vigilance (vĭj′ə-ləns) *n.* alert attention, watchfulness
   vigilancia *s.* atención alerta, cuidado

vindicate (vĭn′dĭ-kāt′) *v.* to clear of suspicion, doubt, or blame
   vindicar *v.* exculpar de sospecha o duda

voluble (vŏl′yə-bəl) *adj.* especially talkative, fluent with words
   locuaz *adj.* hablador, charlatán

voracity (vô-răs′ĭ-tē) *n.* greed for food
   voracidad *s.* apetito ansioso

wince (wĭns) *v.* to shrink or flinch involuntarily, especially in pain
   estremecerse *v.* encogerse o contraerse involuntariamente por dolor

wizened (wīz′ənd) *adj.* withered and dry
   arrugado *adj.* seco y marchito

Pronunciation Key

Symbol	Examples	Symbol	Examples	Symbol	Examples
ă	**a**t, g**a**s	m	**m**an, see**m**	v	**v**an, sa**ve**
ā	**a**pe, d**ay**	n	**n**ight, mitte**n**	w	**w**eb, t**w**ice
ä	f**a**ther, b**a**rn	ng	si**ng**, ha**ng**er	y	**y**ard, law**y**er
âr	f**air**, d**are**	ŏ	**o**dd, n**o**t	z	**z**oo, rea**s**on
b	**b**ell, ta**b**le	ō	**o**pen, r**oa**d, gr**ow**	zh	trea**s**ure, gara**ge**
ch	**ch**in, lun**ch**	ô	**aw**ful, b**ough**t, h**o**rse	ə	**a**wake, ev**e**n, penc**i**l,
d	**d**ig, bore**d**	oi	c**oi**n, b**oy**		pil**o**t, foc**u**s
ě	**e**gg, t**e**n	ŏŏ	l**oo**k, f**u**ll	ər	p**er**form, lett**er**
ē	**e**vil, s**ee**, m**ea**l	ōō	r**oo**t, gl**ue**, thr**ough**		
f	**f**all, lau**gh**, **ph**rase	ou	**ou**t, c**ow**	**Sounds in Foreign Words**	
g	**g**old, bi**g**	p	**p**ig, ca**p**	KH	*German* i**ch**, au**ch**;
h	**h**it, in**h**ale	r	**r**ose, sta**r**		*Scottish* lo**ch**
hw	**wh**ite, every**wh**ere	s	**s**it, fa**c**e	N	*French* e**n**tre, bo**n**, fi**n**
ĭ	**i**nch, f**i**t	sh	**sh**e, ma**sh**	œ	*French* f**eu**, c**œu**r;
ī	**i**dle, m**y**, tr**ie**d	t	**t**ap, hopp**ed**		*German* sch**ö**n
îr	d**ear**, h**ere**	th	**th**ing, wi**th**	ü	*French* **u**tile, r**ue**;
j	**j**ar, **g**em, ba**dge**	th	**th**en, o**th**er		*German* gr**ü**n
k	**k**eep, **c**at, lu**ck**	ŭ	**u**p, n**u**t		
l	**l**oad, ratt**le**	ûr	f**ur**, **ear**n, b**ir**d, w**or**m		

Stress Marks

ʹ This mark indicates that the preceding syllable receives the primary stress. For example, in the word *language*, the first syllable is stressed: lăngʹgwĭj.

ʹ This mark is used only in words in which more than one syllable is stressed. It indicates that the preceding syllable is stressed, but somewhat more weakly than the syllable receiving the primary stress. In the word *literature*, for example, the first syllable receives the primary stress, and the last syllable receives a weaker stress: lĭtʹər-ə-chŏŏrʹ.

Adapted from *The American Heritage Dictionary of the English Language,* fourth edition. Copyright © 2000 by Houghton Mifflin Company. Used with the permission of Houghton Mifflin Company.

INDEX OF FINE ART

Index of Skills

A

Abbreviations
    in note taking, R83
    postal, R49
    punctuating, R49
    web, 1215
Academic journals, 1224
Academic vocabulary, 5, 6, 7, 10, 23, 159, 281, 385, 481, 571, 687, 763, 845, 957, 1081, 1211, 1215, 1218. *See also* Specialized vocabulary.
Act (in a play), 7, R102
Active listening, R82–R83
Active reading, 12
Active voice. *See* Voice, of verbs.
Adjective clauses and phrases, 1145, 1185, 1202, R54, R60, R62*
Adjectives, R47, R57
    versus adverbs, R57
    commas and, R49
    comparative, 1200, R57
    personification and, 790
    precise, 39, 43
    predicate, R57, R60
    proper, R51
    sensory, 179, 184, 277
    superlative, 1200, R57
Adverb clauses and phrases, 517, 523, 562, R60, R62
Adverbs, 426, 441, 472, R47, R57
    versus adjectives, R57
    comparative, 1200, R57
    conjunctive, 560
    descriptive, 426, 441
    relative, 1185
    superlative, 1200, R57
Advertising, 10, 666–669, R90–R91
    marketing, R90
    persuasive techniques in, 667–669, R91
    political ad, 666–669, R90
    types of, 667, R90
Aesthetics and literary criticism. *See* Literary criticism.
Affixes. *See* Prefixes; Suffixes; Word parts.
Agreement
    pronoun-antecedent, R52
    subject-verb, R65–R67
Allegory, R102
Alliteration, 690, 697–698, 702, 756, 789, R102
Allusion, 289, 302, 965, R102
Almanacs, 1218, 1221, R25, R119. *See also* References.

Ambiguous pronoun references, R55
Analogies, 418, 522, 616, 1029, R71, R102. *See also* Rhetorical devices.
    false, R24
Analysis, writing
    definition, R40
    parts, R40
    process, R40
Anecdotes, 230, 456, 557, 764, R30–R31, R41
Anglo-Saxon. *See* Old English (Anglo-Saxon) word parts.
Animation, 1255, R88
Antagonist, 75, 92, 974, R102
Antecedent-pronoun agreement, R52
Antonyms, 15, 93, 220, 358, 418, 522, 541, 601, 616, 790, 862, 905, 1029, R71
Apostrophes, R50
Appeals, 574–575. *See also* Persuasive techniques.
    by association, 574–575
    authority, R91
    bandwagon, 574, R22, R83, R91
    emotional, 574–575, 605–615, 667–669, R22, R91, R116
    ethical, 574
    loaded language in, 574–575, 1225, R25, R117
    logical, 449, R91, R118. *See also* Arguments.
    to loyalty, R22
    to pity, fear, or vanity, 574–575, R22, R116
    "plain folks," 574, 667
    to values, 574
Appendix, 1228
Applications, job, R19, R44, R120
Appositives, and appositive phrases, 355, 359, 376, R60
Approaches to literature. *See* Literary criticism.
Archetypes, R102
Arguments, 572–573, 579–583, R115. *See also* Appeals; Persuasive techniques.
    analysis of, 259, 572–573, 579–583, 617, 678, R21, R26
    claim, 572–573, 670, 671, R21, R23, R24–R26, R115
    counterarguments, 572–573, 591, 619–625, 670, 671, R21, R116
    deductive, 587–591, R23, R115, R116
    evaluating, 572, 583, 591, 600, 676, 1070

    evidence in, 449–453, 572, 587–591, 625, 827, R21
    faulty, 675, 676, 1071, R24, R117
    inductive, 593–600, R22–R23, R115, R117
    logical, 449, 587–591, 593–600, R22–R23, R91, R116, R117, R118
    reasons in, 449–453, 625, R21, R41
    strategies for reading, R21
    support, 572–573, 583, 615, 625, 670, 672, 1249, R21, R119
    tone in, 91, 670, 672
Art. *See* Visuals.
Articles (parts of speech), 834, 1035
Articles (written). *See* Feature articles; Journal articles; Magazine articles; News articles; Newspapers, articles in.
Articulation. *See* Speaking strategies.
Artistic effects. *See* Media presentation.
Aside, 7, 243, 248, 1081, 1095, R102
Assessment practice
    reading comprehension, 150–153, 272–275, 376–379, 472–475, 562–565, 678–681, 754–757, 836–839, 948–951, 1072–1075, 1202–1205
    vocabulary, 154, 276, 380, 476, 566, 682, 840, 952, 1076, 1206
    writing and grammar, 155, 277, 381, 477, 567, 665, 683, 841, 953, 1077, 1207
Assonance, 690, 721, R102, R110
Assumptions, 591, R23, R115
Atlases, 1218, 1221. *See also* References.
Attitudes, comparing, 540
Audience
    media, 84, 667, 668, R85
    speaking and listening, R76, R78, R83
    target, 667, 668, R28, R85
    writing for, 142, 264, 368, 424, 427, 554, 670, 746, 828, 940, 1064, 1194, 1234, R28, R34, R41, R42
Authority. *See* Sources.
Author's background, 33, 45, 61, 75, 101, 113, 135, 167, 187, 203, 211, 223, 243, 289, 305, 321, 333, 353, 361, 395, 407, 421, 443, 449, 455, 489, 495, 509, 529, 547, 579, 587, 593, 605, 629, 645, 697, 705, 713, 721, 729, 735, 771, 793, 801, 809, 815, 853, 865, 881, 897, 909, 931, 949–950, 1011, 1031, 1045, 1225
    influence of, 846–847, 850–851,
Author's intent. *See* Author's purpose.

Extemporaneous speeches, R76. *See also* Oral presentations.
Extended metaphors, 706, 710, R106
External conflict, 26, 368, 421, R104
Eye contact, while speaking, 149, 471, 753, 1071, 1201, R78–R80

F

Fable, R106, R121
Facial expression in speeches, 753, 1071, R78–R80, R82–R83
Facts, R116–R117. *See also* Evidence; Supporting statements.
   in elaboration, R33
   media credibility and, 525, 667
   versus opinion, 579–583, 678, 881–890, R83, R116–R117
   synthesizing, 316
   verifying, R25
Fallacy, 676, 1070, R24, R116, R117
Falling action, 26, 71, R2, R106. *See also* Plot.
False analogy, R24
False cause, R24, R25
Fantasy, R106
Farce, 4, 242, R106
   characters in, 243–257
Faulty reasoning, R24
Fear, appeals to, 574, R22, R116
Feature articles, 4, 8, 316, 483–485, 573, 824, R117
Feedback. *See* Peer response.
Fiction, strategies for reading, 5, 11–15, R2. *See also* Reading skills and strategies.
Fiction, types of, 4, 5
   fantasy, R106
   historical, 5, R107
   horror, R107
   novellas, 4, 5, R109
   novels, 4, 5, R109
   realistic, R111
   science fiction, 5, 304, R112
   short stories, 4, 5, R112
Field research, 1230
Figurative language, 6, 135, 455, 692, 693, 705–710, 790, 1031, R68, R106
   extended metaphors, 706, 710, R106
   hyperbole, 692, 1061, R106, R107, R114
   metaphors, 502, 562, 664, 692, 705, 706, 710, 733, 790, 1062, R106, R109
   onomatopoeia, 697, 701, 793–799, R110
   paradox, R110
   personification, 314, 363, 692–693, 705, 708, 710, 718, 780, 791, 836, R110
   similes, 351, 376, 502, 562, 664, 692–693, 705, 790, 801, 1031, 1062, R112

Figures of speech. *See* Figurative language.
Film reviews, 18, R33, R109, R116
Films, 130, 260, 1190, R86–R88. *See also* Camera shots in film and video; Editing, of films and video; Media elements and techniques.
   characterization in, 260–263, 1191
   comparing with drama, 1195–2000
   documentaries, 947, 1218, 1224
   editing of, 947, R88
   feature, 10, 130, 260, 1190
   and product placement, 10, R91
   as research source, 1218, 1224
   script and written elements, 947, R86
   setting in, 130–133, 1191
   sound in, 131, 947, R87
   special effects in, R88
   storyboards, 133, 947, R86
   visual elements in, 131–133, 261, 937–939, R87–R88
Firsthand and expressive writing. *See* Narrative writing.
First-person narrators. *See* Narrators.
First-person point of view. *See* Point of view.
Flashbacks, 268, 284–285, 287, 314, 333–349, 371, 376, 538, R36, R106
Flat characters, 160–161, 333, R103
Flow chart, 371, 385, 1255
Fluency in writing, 18, 142, 264, 368, 464, 554, 670, 746, 828, 940, 1064, 1194, 1234
Foils (character), 183, 1061, R106, R107
Folk ballads, 735, R103
Folk tales. *See* Oral tradition.
Foreign words in English, R70, R129
Foreshadowing, 75, 284, 333–349, 1090
   to create suspense, R107, R113
Formal language, 297, 303, 617, 624, 627, 863, 1031, R42, R76
Formatting
   quotations, 752, 1237, R50
   research paper, 1254
   workplace documents, R42–R44
   works cited, 1252–1253
Form in poetry, 103, 688–689, 705, 713–719, 754, 729, 733, 735, 754, 793, R107
Forms of writing. *See* Writing skills and strategies.
Fragments. *See* Sentence fragments.
Frame (on screen), 261, 947, 1191, R87, R88
Frame story, R107
Free verse, 688–689, 713–719, 809–813, R107
Freewriting, 19, 145, 793, 809. *See also* Quickwriting.

Functional documents, 8. *See also* Consumer documents; Workplace documents.
Functional reading, R3–R20

G

Generalizations, R117
   in deductive reasoning, 587–591, R23, R115, R116
   hasty, 572, R24
   in inductive reasoning, 593–600, R22–R23, R115, R117
   making, 235, 272
   overgeneralization, 593, 1070, R24, R118. *See also* Stereotyping.
General pronoun reference, R55
Genre, 4, 770, 815, 1045, R107. *See also* Drama; Fiction; Informational texts; Nonfiction; Poetic forms.
   argument and persuasion across, 569, 645–663
   author's message across, 455–462
   comparing across, 383, 455–462, 645–663, 1045–1061
   parody across, 1045–1061
Gerunds and gerund phrases, 900, 906, 948, R60, R61
Gestures, while speaking, 753, R78
Glittering generality, 667, R22
Glossary, R72, R102, R115, R121
Government publications, R117
Grammar, R46–R65. *See also specific grammar concepts.*
   checking, 148, 270, 374, 470, 560, 676, 752, 834, 946, 1070, 1200
   style and, 18, 43, 59, 73, 110, 129, 184, 201, 221, 259, 303, 351, 359, 405, 419, 441, 503, 523, 585, 602, 617, 627, 643, 703, 711, 791, 807, 863, 879, 906, 929, 1009, 1043, 1185, R99
Graphic aids, 504–507, R5–R7, R14
   captions, 504, 542, 543, 677, R3, R6, R14, R15, R17, R18
   charts, R6
   in consumer documents, R17
   cutaway diagrams, 506
   diagrams, 505, 506, R6
   graphs, R5
   interpreting, 504–507
   maps, R7
   photographs, 505, 543
   pie graphs, R5
   in public documents, R6
   schematic diagrams, 505
   strategies for reading, R15, R17, R18, R27
   tables, R6

Italics, R50. *See also* Formatting.
author's style and, 781

J

Job applications, R44, R116, R120
Journal articles, 726, 1218
Journalists and journalism, 482, 525, 528, 552, 576, 764, R89–90
Journals, 1218, 1224, R117. *See also* Diary; Narrative nonfiction; Periodicals; References.
evaluating, 1229
personal, 11, 19, 763
Judgments, making, 33, 127, 199, 305, 421, 583, 591, 625, 629, 641, 663

K

Key traits of effective writing, 18, 142, 264, 368, 464, 554, 670, 746, 828, 940, 1064, 1194, 1234
Keyword searches
Boolean, 1216
database, 1222
Internet, 1215
library catalog, 1219

L

Language. *See also* Diction; Literary elements; Word choice.
figurative, 6, 135, 455, 608, 617, 692, 705, 710, 727, 752, 780, 790, 791, R34, R68, R106
formal, 297, 303, 617, 624, 627, 863, 1031, R42, R76
informal, 617, 627, 863, R68, R76. *See also* Slang.
loaded, 574–575, 1225, R25, R117
persuasive, 670, 671, 675
powerful, 449
precise, 43, 469, 642, 664, 671, 703, R77
sensory, 501, 692, 766, 793, 801, 931, R34, R112
Shakespearean, 1088–1089, 1090
tone and, 608, 617, 863
using appropriate, in speech, R76
using appropriate, in writing, 303, 464, 1194
Latin word parts, 584, R69. *See also* Word parts.
affixes, 58, 72, 440, 878
word roots, 220, 258, 272, 314, 350, 358, 376, 541, 1008
Layout. *See* Formatting.
Legend (graphic aid), 504
Legends, R108. *See* Oral tradition.

Letters
business, R19, R42–R43, R115
personal, 798
as primary sources, 1220
writing, 627
Librarian, research, 1219, 1232
Library
catalog, 1219
classification systems in, 1232
media resources, 1218
research in, 1219, 1220–1229
searching in, 1219
selecting sources in, 1220–1224
virtual, 1232
web resources, 1232
Library of Congress classification system, 1232
Line breaks, in poetry, 721–727
end-stopped, 721
enjambed, 721, 723
in quotations, 752
Line graphs, R5
Lines, in poetry, 4, R2. *See also* Line breaks; *specific poetic forms.*
Listening skills, R82–R83. *See also* Speaking.
List servers, 1231, R117
Literary analysis, 1–11, 33, 45, 75, 101, 113, 135, 167, 187, 203, 211, 223, 237, 243, 289, 305, 321, 333, 353, 361, 395, 407, 421, 443, 455, 529, 547, 629, 645, 697, 705, 713, 721, 771, 793, 801, 809, 815, 853, 865, 881, 897, 909, 931, 967, 1031, 1045, 1095
Literary criticism
author's style, 71, 183, 219, 314, 439, 764
biographical context, 229, 417, 540, 806, 935, 1007
critical interpretation, 41, 57, 109, 209, 241, 257, 331, 349, 357, 403, 641, 702, 710, 719, 787, 890, 904, 1153, 1169, 1184
cultural context, 848, 849, 904, R112
different perspectives, 861
historical context, 302, 447, 799, 813, 877, 1028, 1113, 1115
philosophical context, 92
social context, 199, 367, 553, 822, 927, 1041
Literary elements and devices, 801, R105, R107. *See also* Characters; Conflict; Plot; Point of view; Settings; Theme.
allegories, R102
allusions, 289, 302, 965, R75, R102
archetypes, R102
assonance, 690, 721, R102
author's message, 455–462

author's perspective, 223–229, 257, 482–483, 529–540, 909–927
author's purpose, 482–483, 495–501, 547–553
blank verse, 806, 1088, 1115, R103
character foils, 183, 1061, R106, R107
characterization, 160, 211–219, 243, 261, 263, 529–540, 1031, 1041, R103–R104
character motivation, 162–165, 187–199, 257, 272, 388, 1132
characters, 45, 135, 160–165, 203–209, 237–241, 289, 302, 314, 331, 421–439, 897, 1011, R37, R103, R111
character traits, 160–161, 167–183, 221, 223–229, 230, 272, 641, 1045, 1061
comic relief, R104
conflict, 26–31, 33–41, 45–57, 75–92, 150, 203, 421, 962, R37, R104
consonance, R104
cultural symbols, 667
dialect, 735, R104
dialogue, 7, 135, 261, 735, 801, 964, 1031, 1045, 1088, 1186, R105
diction, 489, 495, 766, R105
dramatic irony, 965, 967, 1086, R108
epic hero, R105
extended metaphors, 706, 710, R106
figurative language, 6, 135, 455, 692, 705, 790, 1031, R68, R106
flashbacks, 268, 284–287, 333–349, 376, R106, R136
foreshadowing, 75, 284, 333, 349, 1090, R107, R113
humor, 96, 243, 488, 937, 1045
hyperbole, 692, R107
imagery, 6, 237, 495, 547–553, 690, 692, 713, 720, 771–789, 809, R108
irony, 257, 403, 417, 443–447, 663, 801, 965, 967, 1007, 1086, R108
metaphors, 502, 664, 692, 705, 790, 1062, R106, R109
meter, 690, 713, 729, 735, 793, 931, 1008, R103, R107, R109
mood, 24–25, 61–71, 101–109, 404, 462, 690, 1042, R30, R35, R36, R87, R88, R109, R118
narrative devices, 282–287
personification, 314, 363, 718, R110
plot, 26–31, 33–41, 105, 135, 160, 203–209, 268, 333, 338, 1086, R110
point of view, 8, 282–283, 289–302, 321–331, 361–367, 376, 771–789, 853, 1220, R103, R110
repetition, 443, 576, 593, 602, 690, 697, 721, 793, 892–895, 1088, R77, R102, R111

Metaphors, 502, 562, 664, 692, 705, 706, 710, 790, 1062, R109
  extended, 733, R106
Metasearch engines, 1215, 1232, 1255
Meter, 690, 713, 729–733, 735, 793, 931, R109
  anapest, R109
  dactyl, R109
  foot, 729
  iamb, 729, R109
  iambic pentameter, 729, 1008, R103, R107
  pentameter, 729
  trochee, R109
Microfiche, 1218, 1229, 1194
Microfilm, 1218, 1219, 1229
Minor characters, 160, 282, 977, 982, 1001, 1007, R103
Mise en scène, 1191–1192, R87, R109
MLA citation guidelines, 1252–1253
Modes of reasoning. See Reasoning.
Modifiers, 272, R48, R57. See also Adjectives; Adverbs; Commonly confused words.
  clauses, R62–R63
  comparative and superlative forms, 1200, R57–R58
  comparison of, 1200, R57–R58
  dangling, R59
  effective use of, 193, 201
  essential adjective clauses, R62
  irregular comparison of, R58
  misplaced, R59
  nonessential adjective clauses, R62
  phrases, R60–R61
  problems with, R58–R59
  regular comparison of, 1200, R58
Monitoring, 12, 61–71, 333–349, 395–403, 529–540, 619–625, 865, R118
Monologue
  dramatic, 243, 247, R105
  interior, 268
Mood, 24–25, 61–71, 150, R109
  analysis of, 24, 101–109
  connotation in creating, 404, 1042
  in descriptive writing, R30
  setting and, 24–25, 61–71, R36
Motivation
  author's, 846
  of characters, 162–165, 187–199, 257, 388, 967, 1115, 1153, 1191, R103
  description to show, 1045
  dialogue to show, 372
  and dramatic conventions, 1045, 1086
  listening skills to determine, R83
  making judgments about, 100
  reading skills to determine, 33
  theme and, 388
Motives. See Motivation.

Movies. See Films.
Multimedia presentations. See Media presentations and products; Oral presentations.
Multiple-choice questions, R94
Multiple-meaning words, R72
Multiple-step instructions. See Instructions.
Musical, 1044, 1056
Mythology, words from classical, R70
Myths, 965, 997, R108, R109

N

Name-calling, reasoning and, 675, 676, R24
Narrative and expressive writing, 142–148, 264–270, 368–374, R36–R37
  autobiographical narrative, 264–270
  interpretive essay, 142–148
  key techniques in, R36
  letters, R36–R37, R42–R43
  motives, R83
  options for organization, R36–R37
  rubric for, 148, 270, 374, R36
  short stories, 368–374
Narrative elements. See Character; Conflict; Plot; Point of view; Setting; Theme.
Narrative essays. See Essays.
Narrative map, 268
Narrative nonfiction, 100, 112, 508, R36–R37, R109. See also Literary nonfiction.
  analysis of, 509–521
Narrative poetry, 135–141, R109
Narrative speeches, R79. See also Oral presentations.
Narrators, 282–283, 289. See also Point of view.
  and credibility of text, 282–283, 289–302, 321
  effect of, 282–283, 289, 295, 331
  first-person, 282–283
  naïve, 289, 302
  point of view of, 302
  third-person, 282–283, 302, 314, 321–331
  third-person limited, 282
  third-person omniscient, 282–283, 302, 321–331
Negatives, double, R58–R59
News, 524–527, R88–R90. See also Media genres and types.
  angle, R89
  balance in reporting, R89
  bias in reporting, R90
  choosing, R88
  commentary and opinion, R88
  credibility, 525–526
  editorial, R116

evaluating, 527
five W's and H, R89
human interest, R88
interviews, 525
inverted pyramid, R89
newscast, 524–525
newsworthiness, R88
proximity, R88
purpose of, 525
reporting, R88–R90
slant, R89
sources for, 525–527, R90
standards for reporting, R89
timeliness, R88
widespread impact, R88
News articles, 4, 8, 185, 316, 542, 825, R36, R116, R118.
  analysis of, 542–545
  captions in, 542, 543
  graphic aids in, 544, 545
  headlines, 542
  lead, 542, 543
  writing, 110
News formats, 524–527, R88–R90, R118
Newspapers, 8, 10, 316, 1218, 1220, 1224, 1232, R3
  articles in, 185, 316, 542, 825, R116, R118
  columns in, 824–827, R40, R88, R118
  evaluating, 1229, R14, R84
  MLA citation guidelines, 1253
News reports, 524–527, 542–543, R88–R90
Nominative pronoun case, R52
Nonfiction, 4, 8, 1223, 1232, R2, R108, R109, R117
  argument in, 449, 579–583. See also Informational texts; Persuasive techniques.
  author's purpose, 495–501
  characterization in, 211–219, 223
  diction, 489–493
  evaluating, 509–521, 1228
  persuasive. See Persuasive techniques.
  suspense in, 113–127
  text features in, 484–486, R3–R4, R14, R16, R117, R118, R119, R120
  tone, 489–493
Nonfiction, strategies for reading, 8–10, 12, 15, R2
Nonfiction, types of, R88
  autobiographies, R102–R103. See also memoirs, below.
  biographies, R103
  critical reviews, 828–835
  diaries, 848, R105
  editorials, R40, R88
  encyclopedia articles, 881, 1220, 1232

INDEX OF TITLES & AUTHORS

Page numbers that appear in italics refer to biographical information.

ACKNOWLEDGMENTS

UNIT 1

University of Pittsburgh Press: "The Bass, the River, and Sheila Mant," from *The Man Who Loved Levittown* by W. D. Wetherell. Copyright © 1985, W. D. Wetherell. Used by permission of the University of Pittsburgh Press.

Dell Publishing: "Harrison Bergeron," from *Welcome to the Monkey House* by Kurt Vonnegut, Jr. Copyright © 1961 by Kurt Vonnegut, Jr. Used by permission of Dell Publishing, a division of Random House, Inc.

Harcourt: "Everyday Use," from *In Love & Trouble: Stories of Black Women* by Alice Walker. Copyright © 1973 by Alice Walker. Reprinted by permission of Harcourt, Inc. This material may not be reproduced in any form or by any means without prior written permission of the publisher.

Rutledge Hill Press: "Alice Walker on Quilting" by Alice Walker, from *A Communion of the Spirits* by Roland L. Freeman. Published by Rutledge Hill Press. Reprinted by permission of Rutledge Hill Press, Nashville, Tennessee.

Brandt & Hochman Literary Agents: "Searching for Summer," from *The Green Flash* by Joan Aiken. Copyright © 1969 by Joan Aiken. Reprinted by permission of Brandt & Hochman Literary Agents, Inc.

W. W. Norton & Company: Excerpts from *Deep Survival: Who Lives, Who Dies, and Why* by Laurence Gonzales. Copyright © 2003 by Laurence Gonzales. Used by permission of W. W. Norton & Company, Inc.

Simon & Schuster Adult Publishing Group: Excerpt from *The Johnstown Flood* by David G. McCullough. Copyright © 1968 by David G. McCullough. Copyright renewed. Reprinted with permission of Simon & Schuster Adult Publishing Group.

People Weekly: Excerpt from "Nine-Year-Old Amber Colvin Rides Out a Killer Flood in Ohio" by Michael Neill and Ken Myers, *People Weekly,* 2 July 1990. Copyright © 1990 Time Inc. All rights reserved. Reprinted by permission.

Times Books: Excerpt from *Leadership Moment* by Michael Useem. Copyright © 1998 by Michael Useem. Used by permission of Times Books, a division of Random House, Inc.

Susan Bergholz Literary Services: "Exile," from *The Other Side/ El Otro Lado* by Julia Alvarez. Copyright © 1995 by Julia Alvarez. Published by Plume/Penguin, a division of Penguin Group (USA). Reprinted by permission of Susan Bergholz Literary Services, New York. All rights reserved.

Joy Harjo: "Crossing the Border," from *How We Became Human: New and Selected Poems* by Joy Harjo. Copyright © 2002 by Joy Harjo. Reprinted by permission of the author.

Viking Penguin: Excerpt from *The Grapes of Wrath* by John Steinbeck. Copyright 1939, renewed © 1967 by John Steinbeck. Used by permission of Viking Penguin, a division of Penguin Group (USA) Inc.

UNIT 2

Academy Chicago Publishers: Excerpt from "The Opportunity," from *Thirteen Uncollected Stories* by John Cheever. Copyright © 1994 Academy Chicago Publishers. Used by permission of Academy Chicago Publishers.

Coffee House Press: Excerpt from *A Place Where the Sea Remembers* by Sandra Benítez. Copyright © 1993 by Sandra Benítez. Reprinted with the permission of Coffee House Press, Minneapolis, Minnesota.

HarperCollins Publishers and Faber & Faber: Two brief excerpts from pp. 286 & 293 "Initiation," used as a literary model, from *Johnny Panic and the Bible of Dreams* by Sylvia Plath. Copyright 1952, 1953, 1954, 1955, 1956, 1957, 1960, 1961, 1962, 1963 by Sylvia Plath. Copyright © 1977, 1979 by Ted Hughes. Used by permission of HarperCollins Publishers.

Elizabeth Walsh Peavoy: Excerpt from "Brigid," from *Collected Stories* by Mary Lavin, published by Houghton Mifflin Co. (1971). Originally published in *Long Ago and Other Stories,* Little, Brown and Company. Copyright © 1971 by Mary Lavin. Reprinted by permission of Elizabeth Walsh Peavoy.

Naomi Shihab Nye: "Shoofly Pie" by Naomi Shihab Nye. Copyright © 2001 by Naomi Shihab Nye. First published in *The Color of Absence: 12 Stories About Loss and Hope,* edited by James Howe (Simon & Schuster). By permission of the author, Naomi Shihab Nye.

The New York Times: Excerpt from "A Mexican Feast for Bodies and Souls" by Dave Roos, the *New York Times,* 27 October 2004. Copyright © 2004 by the New York Times Co. Reprinted with permission.

Bantam Books: "The Possibility of Evil," from *Just an Ordinary Day: The Uncollected Stories* by Shirley Jackson. Used by permission of Bantam Books, a division of Random House, Inc.

Viking Penguin: "Like the Sun," from *Under the Banyan Tree* by R. K. Narayan. Copyright © 1985 by R. K. Narayan. Used by permission of Viking Penguin, a division of Penguin Group (USA) Inc.

Harvard University Press: "Tell all the Truth but tell it slant—" by Emily Dickinson. Reprinted by permission of the publishers and the Trustees of Amherst College from *The Poems of Emily Dickinson,* Thomas H. Johnson, ed., Cambridge, Mass.: The Belknap Press of Harvard University Press, Copyright © 1951, 1955, 1979 by the President and Fellows of Harvard College.

Nicholas Gage: "The Teacher Who Changed My Life" by Nicholas Gage, *Parade,* 17 December 1989. Copyright © 1989 by Nicholas Gage. Reprinted by permission of the author.

Susan Bergholz Literary Services: Excerpt from "A Celebration of Grandfathers" by Rudolfo Anaya. Copyright © 1983 by Rudolfo Anaya. First published in *New Mexico Magazine,* March 1983. Reprinted by permission of Susan Bergholz Literary Services, New York. All rights reserved.

Time: "Simply Grand: Generational Ties Matter, and Grandparents Are Finding New Ways to Play Starring Roles in the Lives of Their Grandchildren" by Megan Rutherford, *Time,* Online Edition,

11 October 1999. Copyright © 2004 by Time Inc. Reprinted by permission.

BOA Editions: "The Gift," from *Rose* by Li-Young Lee. Copyright © 1986 by Li-Young Lee. Reprinted by permission of BOA Editions, Ltd.

Liveright Publishing Corporation: "Those Winter Sundays," from *Collected Poems of Robert Hayden* by Robert Hayden. Copyright © 1966 by Robert Hayden. Reprinted by permission of Liveright Publishing Corporation.

Arte Público Press: Excerpt from "Tío Nano" by Lionel G. García is reprinted with permission from the publisher of *I Can Hear the Cowbells Ring* (Houston: Arte Público Press–University of Houston, 1994).

Random House and Phoebe Larmore: Excerpt from "Uncles," from *Wilderness Tips* by Margaret Atwood. Copyright © 1991 by O.W. Toad Limited. Used by permission of Doubleday, a division of Random House, Inc., and Phoebe Larmore.

UNIT 3

Felicity Bryan Literary Agency: Excerpt from "Lalla" by Rosamunde Pilcher. Copyright © Rosamunde Pilcher. Reproduced by permission of Felicity Bryan Literary Agency and the author.

Scholastic: Excerpt from "Catch the Moon," from *An Island Like You: Stories of the Barrio* by Judith Ortiz Cofer. Copyright © 1995 by Judith Ortiz Cofer. Reprinted by permission of Scholastic Inc.

Houghton Mifflin Company: Excerpt from *The Namesake* by Jhumpa Lahiri. Copyright © 2003 by Jhumpa Lahiri. Reprinted by permission of Houghton Mifflin Company. All rights reserved.

Curtis Brown: Excerpt from *A Separate Peace* by John Knowles. Copyright © 1959 by John Knowles, renewed. Reprinted by permission of Curtis Brown, Ltd.

Brandt and Hochman Literary Agents: "By the Waters of Babylon" by Stephen Vincent Benét, from *Selected Works of Stephen Vincent Benét,* published by Holt, Rinehart & Winston, Inc. Copyright © 1937 by Stephen Vincent Benét. Copyright renewed © 1955 by Rosemary Carr Benét. Reprinted by permission of Brandt and Hochman Literary Agents, Inc.

Don Congdon Associates: "There Will Come Soft Rains" by Ray Bradbury. First published in *Collier's National Newsweekly Magazine,* 6 May 1950. Copyright © 1950 by Crowell-Collier Publishing Company, renewed 1977 by Ray Bradbury. Reprinted by permission of Don Congdon Associates, Inc.

Dow Jones & Company: "Inside the Home of the Future" by Kelly Greene. Wall Street Journal Online. Copyright © 2004 by Dow Jones & Company Inc. Reproduced with permission of Dow Jones & Company Inc. in the format Textbook via Copyright Clearance Center.

Alfred A. Knopf: "The Doll's House," from *The Short Stories of Katherine Mansfield* by Katherine Mansfield. Copyright © 1923 by Alfred A. Knopf, a division of Random House, Inc., and renewed 1951 by John Middleton Murry. Used by permission of Alfred A. Knopf, a division of Random House, Inc.

International Creative Management: "The Seventh Man" by Haruki Murakami. Copyright © 1998 by Haruki Murakami. Reprinted by permission of International Creative Management, Inc.

Review of Contemporary Fiction: Excerpt from "An Interview with Haruki Murakami" by Sinda Gregory, Toshifumi Miyawaki, and Larry McCaffery. Previously published in *Review of Contemporary Fiction* (Summer 2002). Copyright © 2002 Review of Contemporary Fiction. Reproduced with permission.

Time Inc.: "The Man in the Water" by Roger Rosenblatt, *Time,* 25 January 1982. Copyright © 1982 Time Inc. Reprinted by permission.

Joanne Hyppolite: "Dyaspora" by Joanne Hyppolite. Copyright © 2001 by Joanne Hyppolite. Reprinted by permission of the author.

Lisa Fugard: Excerpt from "Night Calls" by Lisa Fugard, *Outside Magazine,* May 1995. Copyright © 1995 by Lisa Fugard. Reprinted by permission of the author.

Alfred A. Knopf: Excerpt from *The Snow Goose* by Paul Gallico. Copyright 1940 by the Curtis Publishing Company. Copyright renewed 1968 by Paul Gallico. Used by permission of Alfred A. Knopf, a division of Random House, Inc.

UNIT 4

Peter H. Lee: "Cranes" by Hwang Sunwŏn, translated by Peter H. Lee, from *Flowers of Fire: Twentieth-Century Korean Stories,* edited by Peter H. Lee. Reprinted by permission of Peter H. Lee.

Arnold Kellett: "Two Friends" by Guy de Maupassant, from *The Dark Side of Guy de Maupassant,* translated by Arnold Kellett. Copyright © 1972, 1976, 1989 by Arnold Kellett. Reprinted by permission of Arnold Kellett.

Houghton Mifflin Company: "When Mr. Pirzada Came to Dine," from *Interpreter of Maladies* by Jhumpa Lahiri. Copyright © 1999 by Jhumpa Lahiri. Reprinted by permission of Houghton Mifflin Company. All rights reserved.

MacNeil-Lehrer Productions: Excerpt from "Interview with Jhumpa Lahiri," from *The NewsHour with Jim Lehrer,* 12 April 2000. Copyright © 2000 MacNeil-Lehrer Productions. Reprinted by permission.

Brooks Permissions: "the sonnet-ballad," from *Blacks* by Gwendolyn Brooks (Chicago: Third World Press, 1991). Copyright © 1991 by Gwendolyn Brooks. Reprinted by consent of Brooks Permissions.

Harcourt, the Provost and Scholars of King's College, Cambridge, and the Society of Authors: Excerpt from "Tolerance," from *Two Cheers for Democracy* by E. M. Forster. Copyright © 1951 by E. M. Forster and renewed 1979 by Donald Parry. Reprinted by permission of Harcourt, Inc., the Provost and Scholars of King's College, Cambridge, and the Society of Authors as the Literary Representatives of the E. M. Forster Estate.

Andrew Lam: "Letter to a Young Refugee from Another" by Andrew Lam. Copyright © 1999 by Andrew Lam. Reprinted by permission of the author.

Columbia University Press: "Song of P'eng-ya" by Tu Fu, from *The Columbia Book of Chinese Poetry,* translated and edited by Burton

Watson. Copyright © 1984 Columbia University Press. Reprinted with the permission of the publisher.

UNIT 5

Skiing: Excerpt from "Go Faster, Turn Easier" by Chris Anthony, *Skiing,* January 2004. Copyright © 2004 Time4 Media, Inc. All rights reserved. Reprinted with permission.

Tribune Media Services: Excerpt from "Snow Immobile" by Dave Barry, the *Washington Post,* 12 February 1995. Copyright © 1995 the Washington Post Company. Reprinted by permission of Tribune Media Services.

Outside: Excerpt from "At Home in the Discomfort Zone" by Kevin Foley, *Outside,* April 2002. Copyright © 2002 Mariah Media, Inc. All rights reserved. Reprinted by permission.

New York Times: "Observer: The Plot Against People" by Russell Baker, the *New York Times,* 18 June 1968. Copyright © 1968 by the New York Times Co. Reprinted with permission.

Random House: "Why the Leaves Turn Color in the Fall," from *A Natural History of the Senses* by Diane Ackerman. Copyright © 1990 by Diane Ackerman. Used by permission of Random House, Inc.

W. W. Norton & Company: Excerpts from "Blowup: What Went Wrong at Storm King Mountain," from *Fire* by Sebastian Junger. Copyright © 2001 by Sebastian Junger. Used by permission of W. W. Norton & Company, Inc.

Scribner: "And of Clay Are We Created," from *The Stories of Eva Luna* by Isabel Allende, translated from the Spanish by Margaret Sayers Peden. Copyright © 1989 by Isabel Allende. English Translation Copyright © 1991 by Macmillan Publishing Company. Reprinted with the permission of Scribner, an imprint of Simon & Schuster Adult Publishing Group.

Boston Globe: "Girl, Trapped in Water for 55 Hours, Dies Despite Rescue Efforts" by Julia Preston, the *Boston Globe,* 17 November 1985. Reprinted courtesy of the *Boston Globe* in the format Textbook via Copyright Clearance Center.

Arte Público Press: "Peruvian Child," from *My Own True Name: New and Selected Poems for Young Adults* by Pat Mora (Houston: Arte Público Press–University of Houston, 2000). Text copyright © 2000 by Pat Mora. Reprinted with permission from the publisher.

Rita Dove: "Lady Freedom Among Us," from *On the Bus with Rosa Parks* by Rita Dove, W. W. Norton & Company. Copyright © 1999 by Rita Dove. Reprinted by permission of the author.

Doubleday: Excerpts from "Interview with Rita Dove" by Bill Moyers, from *The Language of Life: A Festival of Poets* by Bill Moyers. Copyright © 1995 by Public Affairs Television, Inc., and David Grubin Productions, Inc. Used by permission of Doubleday, a division of Random House, Inc.

Discovery Books: Excerpt from Discovery *Channel: Insects & Spiders.* Copyright © Discovery Communications, Inc. Reprinted by permission of Discovery Books, a division of Random House, Inc.

Viking Penguin: Excerpt from "How to Write a Letter," from *We Are Still Married: Stories & Letters* by Garrison Keillor. Copyright © 1989 by Garrison Keillor. Used by permission of Viking Penguin, a division of Penguin Group (USA) Inc.

UNIT 6

The Advertising Council: Excerpts from "Youth Civic Engagement/Voter Participation," from the Advertising Council Website (http:www.adcouncil.org/issues/voting). Copyright © 2005 the Advertising Council. All rights reserved. Reprinted by permission of the Advertising Council.

International Creative Management: Excerpt from "Mount Holyoke Commencement Speech" by Anna Quindlen. Copyright © 1999 by Anna Quindlen. Reprinted by permission of International Creative Management, Inc.

"Doing Nothing Is Something" by Anna Quindlen. Copyright © 2002 by Anna Quindlen. Reprinted by permission of International Creative Management, Inc.

Business Week: "Abolishing the Penny Makes Good Sense" by Alan S. Blinder, *Business Week,* 12 January 1987. Copyright © 1987 by the McGraw-Hill Companies, Inc. Reprinted by special permission.

The Estate of Carl Sagan and Ann Druyan: "On Nuclear Disarmament" by Carl Sagan and Ann Druyan. Copyright © 1998 by the Estate of Carl Sagan and Ann Druyan. Reprinted with permission from the Estate of Carl Sagan and Ann Druyan.

Sterling Lord Literistic: "I Acknowledge Mine" by Jane Goodall, from *Visions of Caliban* by Dale Peterson and Jane Goodall. Copyright © 1993 by Dale Peterson and Jane Goodall. Reprinted by permission of Sll/Sterling Lord Literistic, Inc.

American Medical Association: Excerpt from "Use of Animals in Biomedical Research." Copyright © 1989 American Medical Association. Reprinted by permission of the American Medical Association.

Viking Penguin: "A Chip of Glass Ruby," from *Selected Stories* by Nadine Gordimer. Copyright © 1961 by Nadine Gordimer. Used by permission of Viking Penguin, a division of Penguin Group (USA) Inc.

National Council of the Churches of Christ in the United States of America: Excerpt from "1 Timothy 5," from the *New Revised Standard Version Bible.* Copyright © 1989, Division of Christian Education of the National Council of the Churches of Christ in the United States of America. Used by permission. All right reserved.

Time: "Why Go Back to the Moon?" by Michael D. Lemonick, *Time* magazine, 26 January 2004. Copyright © 2004 Time Inc. Reprinted by permission.

Matt Silver: Excerpts from "In Defense of Space Exploration" by Matt Silver, *The Tech,* Volume 123, Number 66, 28 January 2004. Copyright © 2004 by Matt Silver. Reprinted by permission of the author.

UNIT 7

Angela de Hoyos: Excerpt from "Look Not to Memories" by Angela de Hoyos is reprinted with permission from the author and with permission from the publisher

BOA Editions: "i am not done yet," from *Good Woman: Poems and a Memoir, 1969–1980* by Lucille Clifton. Copyright © 1987 by Lucille Clifton. All rights reserved. Reprinted by permission of BOA Editions, Ltd.

Brooks Permissions: "We Real Cool," from *Blacks* by Gwendolyn Brooks. Copyright © 1945, 1949, 1953, 1960, 1963, 1968, 1970, 1971, 1975, 1981, 1987 by Gwendolyn Brooks Blakely. Reprinted by consent of Brooks Permissions.

Wesleyan University Press: "The Base Stealer," from *The Orb Weaver* by Robert Francis. Copyright © 1960 by Robert Francis. Reprinted by permission of Wesleyan University Press.

"Slam, Dunk, & Hook," from *Pleasure Dome* by Yusef Komunyakaa (Wesleyan University Press, 2001). Copyright © 2001 by Yusef Komunyakaa. Reprinted by permission of Wesleyan University Press.

The University of Georgia Press: Excerpt from "Memory," from *This Is My Century: New and Collected Poems* by Margaret Walker. Copyright © 1989 by Margaret Walker Alexander. Reprinted by permission of the University of Georgia Press.

Sylvia Winner: Excerpt from "Elegy for My Father," from *The Sanity of Earth and Grass: Complete Poems* by Robert Winner. Copyright © 1979, 1983 by Robert Winner. Copyright © 1994 by Sylvia Winner. Reprinted by permission of Sylvia Winner.

W. W. Norton & Company: Excerpt from "Wind Chill," from *Carnival Evening: New and Selected Poems, 1968–1998* by Linda Pastan. Copyright © 1998 by Linda Pastan. Used by permission of W. W. Norton & Company, Inc.

Farrar, Straus & Giroux: "Midsummer, Tobago," from *Collected Poems: 1948–1984* by Derek Walcott. Copyright © 1986 by Derek Walcott. Reprinted by permission of Farrar, Straus & Giroux, LLC.

Agencia Literaria Carmen Balcells and The Grove Press: Excerpt from "Horses," from *Pablo Neruda: A New Decade* by Pablo Neruda, translated by Alastair Reid. Copyright © Fundacion Pablo Neruda. Reprinted by permission of Agencia Literaria Carmen Balcells, S.A. and The Grove Press.

Alfred A. Knopf: Excerpt from "Departure," from *The Collected Poems* by Sylvia Plath. Copyright © 1960, 1965, 1971, 1981 by the Estate of Sylvia Plath. Reprinted by permission of Alfred A. Knopf, a division of Random House, Inc.

"Ex-Basketball Player," from *Collected Poems: 1953–1993* by John Updike. Copyright © 1993 by John Updike. Used by permission of Alfred A. Knopf, a division of Random House, Inc.

Anderson Literary Agency: "The Sound of Night" by Maxine Kumin, from *Halfway*, Holt, Rinehart & Winston. Copyright © 1961 by Maxine Kumin. Reprinted by permission of the Anderson Literary Agency, Inc.

Harvard University Press: "I dwell in Possibility–" by Emily Dickinson. Reprinted by permission of the publishers and the Trustees of Amherst College, from *The Complete Poems of Emily Dickinson*, Thomas H. Johnson, ed., Cambridge, Mass.: The Belknap Press of Harvard University Press. Copyright © 1951, 1955, 1979 by the President and Fellows of Harvard College.

New Directions: "Variation on a Theme by Rilke," from *Breathing the Water* by Denise Levertov. Copyright © 1987 by Denise Levertov. Reprinted by permission of New Directions Publishing Corp.

BOA Editions: "blessing the boats," from *Quilting: Poems 1987–1990* by Lucille Clifton. Copyright © 1991 by Lucille Clifton. Reprinted by permission of BOA Editions, Ltd.

Farrar, Straus & Giroux: "The Fish," from *The Complete Poems 1927–1979* by Elizabeth Bishop. Copyright © 1979, 1983 by Alice Helen Methfessel. Reprinted by permission of Farrar, Straus & Giroux, LLC.

Random House: "Christmas Sparrow," from *Nine Horses* by Billy Collins. Copyright © 2002 by Billy Collins. Used by permission of Random House, Inc.

Doubleday: "The Sloth," from *The Collected Poems of Theodore Roethke* by Theodore Roethke. Copyright 1950 by Theodore Roethke. Used by permission of Doubleday, a division of Random House, Inc.

Viking Penguin: "Piano" by D. H. Lawrence, from *The Complete Poems of D. H. Lawrence,* edited by V. de Sola Pinto & F. W. Roberts. Copyright © 1964, 1971 by Angelo Ravagli and C. M. Weekley, Executors of the Estate of Frieda Lawrence Ravagli. Used by permission of Viking Penguin, a division of Penguin Group (USA) Inc.

Graywolf Press: "Fifteen," from *The Way It Is: New & Selected Poems* by William Stafford. Copyright © 1966, 1998 by the Estate of William Stafford. Reprinted with the permission of Graywolf Press, Saint Paul, Minnesota.

Agencia Literaria Carmen Balcells and Random House UK: Original "Poema 20" from the work *Veinte Poemas de Amor y Una Canción Desesperada* by Pablo Neruda. © Fundación Pablo Neruda, 1924. Used by permission of Agencia Literaria Carmen Balcells, S. A. "Puedo Escribir Los Versos . . ."/"Tonight I Can Write. . . ," from *Selected Poems* by Pablo Neruda, translated by W. S. Merwin, edited by Nathaniel Tarn and published by Jonathan Cape. Used by permission of the Random House Group Limited.

Elizabeth Barnett, Literary Executor: Sonnet XXX of *Fatal Interview* by Edna St. Vincent Millay. From *Collected Poems*, HarperCollins. Copyright 1931, 1958 by Edna St. Vincent Millay and Norma Millay Ellis. All rights reserved. Reprinted by permission of Elizabeth Barnett, literary executor.

Writers House: "Ballad"/"Balada," from *Selected Poems: A Bilingual Edition* by Gabriela Mistral, translated by Doris Dana (Baltimore: the Johns Hopkins University Press, 1971). Copyright © 1961, 1964, 1970, 1971 by Doris Dana. Reprinted with the permission of Writers House, LLC, New York, on behalf of the proprietors.

Alfred A. Knopf: "Midwinter Blues," from *The Collected Poems of Langston Hughes* by Langston Hughes. Copyright © 1994 by the Estate of Langston Hughes. Used by permission of Alfred A. Knopf, a division of Random House, Inc.

Everyman's Library: From *Blues Poems,* edited by Kevin Young. Copyright © 2003 by Everyman's Library. Used by permission of Everyman's Library, a division of Random House, Inc.

Little, Brown and Company: "Reprise," from *Versus* by Ogden Nash. Copyright © 1950 by Odgen Nash. By permission of Little, Brown and Company.

UNIT 8

Scribner: Excerpt from "Big Two-Hearted River," from *The Nick Adams Stories* by Ernest Hemingway. Copyright © 1972 The Ernest Hemingway Foundation. Reprinted with permission of Scribner, a division of Simon & Schuster Adult Publishing Group.

Farrar, Straus & Giroux: Excerpt from "A Walk to the Jetty," from *Annie John* by Jamaica Kincaid. Copyright © 1985 by Jamaica Kincaid. Reprinted by permission of Farrar, Straus & Giroux, LLC.

Henry Holt and Company: "Birches" and "Mending Wall" by Robert Frost, from *The Poetry of Robert Frost*, edited by Edward Connery Lathem. Copyright © 1967 by Lesley Ballantine Frost. Copyright © 1944, 1958 by Robert Frost. Copyright 1916, 1930, © 1969 by Henry Holt and Company. Reprinted by permission of Henry Holt and Company, LLC.

Harcourt: "Fourth of July Night," from *Wind Song* by Carl Sandburg. Copyright © 1960 by Carl Sandburg and renewed 1988 by Margaret Sandburg, Janet Sandburg, and Helga Sandburg Crile. Reprinted by permission of Harcourt, Inc. This material may not be reproduced in any form or by any means without prior written permission of the publisher.

New Directions: "The Red Wheelbarrow," from *Collected Poems: 1909–1930, Volume I* by William Carlos Williams. Copyright © 1938 by New Directions Publishing Corp. Reprinted by permission of New Directions Publishing Corp.

Susan Bergholz Literary Services: "Only Daughter" by Sandra Cisneros. Copyright © 1990 by Sandra Cisneros. First published in *Glamour*, Volume 88, November 1990. Reprinted by permission of Susan Bergholz Literary Services, New York. All rights reserved.

From *Caramelo* by Sandra Cisneros. Copyright © 2002 by Sandra Cisneros. Published by Vintage Books in paperback in 2003 and originally in hardcover by Alfred A. Knopf, Inc. Reprinted by permission of Susan Bergholz Literary Services, New York. All rights reserved.

Fairyland Music: Excerpt from the song lyric "Moon Men Mambo," words and music by Paul Parnes. Copyright © by Fairyland Music (ASCAP). All rights reserved. Reprinted by permission of Fairyland Music.

The Orange County Register: "Author brings back memories of not so long ago" by Yvette Cabrera, *The Orange County Register*, 15 April 2002. Copyright © 2002 by The Orange County Register. Reprinted by permission.

Scribner: "Old Man at the Bridge," from *The Short Stories of Ernest Hemingway* by Ernest Hemingway. Copyright 1938 by Ernest Hemingway, renewal copyright © 1966 by Mary Hemingway. Reprinted with the permission of Scribner, an imprint of Simon & Schuster Adult Publishing Group.

UNIT 9

Faith Childs Literary Agency and The Feminist Press: Excerpt from "To Da-duh, in Memoriam," from *Reena and Other Stories* by Paule Marshall. Copyright © 1983 by The Feminist Press. All rights reserved. Reprinted by permission of The Feminist Press.

Harcourt and the Wendy Weil Agency: "Women," from *Revolutionary Petunias & Other Poems* by Alice Walker. Copyright © 1970 and renewed 1998 by Alice Walker. This material may not be reproduced in any form or by any means without prior written permission of the publisher. Reprinted by permission of Harcourt, Inc. and the Wendy Weil Agency.

Viking Penguin: Excerpt from *The Grapes of Wrath* by John Steinbeck. Copyright 1939 by John Steinbeck. Copyright renewed 1967 by John Steinbeck. Used by permission of Viking Penguin, a division of Penguin Group (USA) Inc.

Zhang Jie: Excerpt from "Love Must Not Be Forgotten" by Zhang Jie. Copyright © Zhang Jie. Reprinted by permission of the author.

Hill and Wang: Excerpt from *Night* by Elie Wiesel, translated by Stella Rodway. Copyright © 1960 by MacGibbon & Kee. Copyright renewed 1988 by the Collins Publishing Group. Reprinted by permission of Hill and Wang, a division of Farrar, Straus and Giroux, LLC.

Nobel Foundation: Excerpt from Nobel Prize acceptance speech by Elie Wiesel. Copyright © 1986 the Nobel Foundation. Reprinted by permission of the Nobel Foundation.

Houghton Mifflin Company: Excerpt from *Farewell to Manzanar* by James D. Houston and Jeanne Wakatsuki Houston. Copyright © 1973 by James D. Houston. Reprinted by permission of Houghton Mifflin Company. All rights reserved.

Henry Holt and Company: Excerpt from *My Life with Martin Luther King, Jr.* by Coretta Scott King. Copyright © 1969 by Coretta Scott King. Revised edition copyright © 1993 by Coretta Scott King. Reprinted by permission of Henry Holt and Company, LLC.

Doubleday and Harold Ober Associates: "Marriage Is a Private Affair," from *Girls At War and Other Stories* by Chinua Achebe. Copyright © 1972, 1973 by Chinua Achebe. Used by permission of Doubleday, a division of Random House, Inc., and Harold Ober Associates Incorporated.

Fawcett Books: Excerpt from *Mixed Matches* by Joel Crohn, PhD. Copyright © 1995 by Joel Crohn, PhD. Used by permission of Fawcett Books, a division of Random House, Inc.

Houghton Mifflin Company/Seymour Lawrence: "On the Rainy River," from *The Things They Carried* by Tim O'Brien. Copyright © 1990 by Tim O'Brien. Reprinted by permission of Houghton Mifflin Company/Seymour Lawrence. All rights reserved.

Cathy Song: "Who Makes the Journey" by Cathy Song, from *Breaking Silence: An Anthology of Contemporary Asian American Poets*, edited by Joseph Bruchac. Reprinted by permission of the author.

Farrar, Straus & Giroux: "Freedom to Breathe," and "The Bonfire and the Ants," from *Stories and Prose Poems* by Alexander Solzhenitsyn, translated by Michael Glenny. Copyright © 1975 by Alexander Solzhenitsyn. Translation copyright © 1975 by Farrar, Straus & Giroux, LLC. Reprinted by permission of Farrar, Straus & Giroux, LLC.

UNIT 10

Viking Penguin: Excerpt from "Oedipus the King," by Sophocles, from *Three Theban Plays* by Sophocles, translated by Robert Fagles. Copyright © 1982 by Robert Fagles. Used by permission of Viking Penguin, a division of Penguin Group (USA) Inc.

Constance Hieatt: Excerpt from *Sir Gawain and the Green Knight*, retold by Constance Hieatt. Copyright © 1967 by Constance Hieatt. Reprinted by permission of the author.

Harcourt: Excerpts from *Antigone*, from *Sophocles: The Oedipus Cycle, An English Version* by Dudley Fitts and Robert Fitzgerald.

Dutton Signet: Excerpts from "The Tale of King Arthur," from *Le Morte d'Arthur* by Sir Thomas Malory, translated by Keith Baines. Copyright © 1962 by Keith Baines, renewed © 1990 by Francesca Evans. Used by permission of Dutton Signet, a division of Penguin Group (USA) Inc.

Harcourt: *Antigone*, from *Sophocles: The Oedipus Cycle, An English Version* by Dudley Fitts and Robert Fitzgerald. Copyright 1939 by Harcourt, Inc., and renewed © 1967 by Dudley Fitts and Robert Fitzgerald. Reprinted by permission of the publisher. This material may not be reproduced in any form or by any means without the prior written permission of the publisher. CAUTION: All rights, including professional, amateur, motion picture, recitation, lecturing, performance, public reading, radio broadcasting, and television, are strictly reserved. Inquiries on all rights should be addressed to Harcourt, Inc., Permissions Department, Orlando, FL 32887-6777.

Dutton Signet: Excerpt from "The Tale of King Arthur," and "The Tale of Sir Launcelot du Lake," from *Le Morte d'Arthur* by Sir Thomas Malory, translated by Keith Baines. Copyright © 1962 by Keith Baines, renewed © 1990 by Francesca Evans. Used by permission of Dutton Signet, a division of Penguin Group (USA) Inc.

Alfred A. Knopf: Excerpt from *A Distant Mirror: The Calamitous 14th Century* by Barbara W. Tuchman. Copyright © 1978 by Barbara W. Tuchman. Used by permission of Alfred A. Knopf, a division of Random House, Inc.

Farrar, Straus and Giroux: Excerpt from "Sir Lancelot of the Lake," from *The Acts of King Arthur and His Noble Knights* by John Steinbeck. Copyright © 1976 by Elaine Steinbeck. Reprinted by permission of Farrar, Straus and Giroux, LLC.

Viking Penguin: Excerpt from *Don Quixote* by Miguel de Cervantes Saavedra, translated by Samuel Putnam. Copyright 1949 by the Viking Press, Inc. Used by permission of Viking Penguin, a division of Penguin Group (USA) Inc.

Random House and Alan S. Honig: Excerpt from *Man of La Mancha* by Dale Wasserman, lyrics by Joe Darion, and music by Mitch Leigh. Copyright © 1966 by Dale Wasserman. Copyright © 1965 by Helena Music Corp. and Andrew Scott, Inc. Used by permission of Random House, Inc., and Alan S. Honig, administrator for the Estate of Joe Darion.

UNIT 11

The Nation: Excerpt from "Review of Julius Caesar" by Thomas M. Disch. Reprinted with permission from the April 23, 1998, issue of the *Nation*. For subscription information, call 1-800-333-8536. Portions of each week's *Nation* magazine can be accessed at http://www.thenation.com.

Diane Goldsmith: "Hail, Caesar!" by Edith Oliver. Originally published in the *New Yorker,* 28 March 1988. Copyright © 1988 Edith Oliver. Reprinted by permission of Diane Goldsmith on behalf of the Estate of Edith Oliver.

UNIT 12

The Charlotte Observer: Excerpt from "Girlfriend Led Him to Music – Tuba Kept Him There" by Steven Brown, the *Charlotte Observer,* 8 May 2005. Copyright © 2005 the Charlotte Observer. Reprinted by permission of the Charlotte Observer.

STUDENT RESOURCE BANK

Time: Excerpt from "The Man in the Water" by Roger Rosenblatt, *Time,* 25 January 1982. Copyright © 1982 Time Inc. Reprinted by permission.

Time Life Books: Excerpt from "Winning Glory at the Games," from *What Life Was Like at the Dawn of Democracy.* Copyright 1997 Time Life Inc. All rights reserved. Reprinted by permission of Time Life Books.

Texas Instruments: "How to Draw a Triangle," from TI-84 Plus Cabri® Jr. Application Web page (http://education.ti.com/US/products/apps/cabrijr.html). Copyright © 1995–2005 Texas Instruments Incorporated. Used with permission of copyright owner, Texas Instruments.

Alfred A. Knopf: Excerpt from "The Daunting Workplace," from *The Working Poor* by David Shipler. Copyright © 2004 by David K Shipler. Reprinted by permission of Alfred A. Knopf, a division of Random House, Inc.

Associated Press: Excerpt from "Low-carb dieters losing interest" by Margaret Stafford, *Associated Press,* 20 December 2004. Copyright © 2004 Associated Press. Reprinted by permission of the Associated Press.

CONSULTANTS

Title page © Getty images; Photo © Duane McCubrey; Photo © Mark Schmidt; Photo © Bruce Forrester; Photo © McDougal Littell; Photo © Howard Gollub; Photo © Tamra Stallings; Photo © Mark Schmidt; Photo © Robert J. Marzano; Photo © McDougal Littell; Photo © Dawson & Associates Photography; Photo © Gitchell's Studio; Photo © Michael Romeo; Photo © Monica Ani; Photo © William McBride; Photo © Bill Caldwell; Photo © Gabriel Pauluzzi; Photo © Steven Scheffler.

TABLE OF CONTENTS

Contents in Brief verso *top, Apple Picking* (1878), Winslow Homer. Watercolor and gouache on paper, laid down on board. 7″ × 8³/₈″. Terra Foundation for American Art, Daniel J. Terra Collection 1992.7. Photograph courtesy of Terra Foundation for American Art, Chicago; *bottom* © Sarah Doehring; **recto** *top* © Evan Sklar/Getty Images; *bottom* Copyright © Donald Cooper/Photostage; **Unit 1 verso** *left* © Gavin Hellier/Getty Images; *right, Utopie* (1999), Bob Lescaux. Oil on canvas, 81 cm × 65 cm. Private collection. Photo © Bridgeman Art Library; **recto** © PunchStock; **Unit 2 verso** *left* © Illustration Works/Getty Images; *right* Courtesy of Nicholas Gage; **recto** © PunchStock; **Unit 3 verso** *left* © Michael S. Yamashita/Corbis; *right, Sudden Shower over Shin-Ohashi Bridge and Atake* (1800s), Ando Hiroshige or Utagawa. Plate 58 from *One Hundred Famous Views of Edo.* Woodblock color print. © Brooklyn Museum of Art, Brooklyn, New York/Bridgeman Art Library; **recto** © PunchStock; **Unit 4 verso** *left, Lamentation: Memorial for Ernst Barlach* (1940), Käthe Kollwitz. Bronze.© SuperStock, Inc. © 2008 Artists Rights Society (ARS), New York/VG Bild-Kunst, Bonn; *right, Civilization is a method of living, an attitude of equal respect for all men* from the series, *Great Ideas of Western Men* (1955), George Giusti. India ink and goache on paper, 24⁷/₈″ × 18⁵/₁₆″. Gift of the Container Corporation of America. Smithsonian American Art Museum, Washington, D.C. Photo © Smithsonian American Art Museum, Washington, D.C./Art Resource, New York; **recto** © PunchStock; **Unit 5 verso** *left* © Bob Rowan; Progressive Image/Corbis; *right, Path Through the Forest* (1914), Suzanne Valadon. Oil on canvas. Musée Fabre, Montpelier, France © Superstock, Inc./SuperStock © 2008 Artists Rights Society (ARS), New York/ADAGP, Paris; **recto** © PunchStock; **Unit 6 verso** *left, The Merry Jesters* (1906), Henri Rousseau. © Philadelphia Museum of Art/Corbis; *right* © Michael Nichols/Getty Images; **recto** © PunchStock; **Unit 7 verso** *right, Trees at Night,* Thomas Meteyard. Berry Hill Gallery, New York. Photo © Edward Owen/Art Resource, New York; *left* © Brooks Walker/Getty Images; **recto** © PunchStock; **Unit 8 verso** *left* © Peter Casolino/Corbis; *right* © Firefly Productions/Corbis; **recto** © PunchStock; **Unit 9 verso** *left* © Bettmann/Corbis; *right* © Scott Braut; **recto** © PunchStock; **Unit 10 verso** *left, Queen Guinevere's Maying,* John Collier. Bradford Art Galleries and Museums, West Yorkshire, United Kingdom. Photo © Bridgeman Art Library; *right* © Donald Cooper/Photostage; **recto** © PunchStock; **Unit 11 verso** *left* © Archivo Iconografico, S.A./Corbis; *right* © Andrea Pistolesi/Getty Images; **recto** © PunchStock; **Unit 12** © Michael Newman/PhotoEdit.

INTRODUCTORY UNIT

1 *left* © Historical Picture Archive/Corbis; *top right* © Firefly Productions/Corbis; *bottom right* © Peter Casolino/Corbis; **2** *left,* Detail of *Melancholy,* Edvard Munch. National Gallery, Oslo, Norway. Photo © Scala/Art Resource, New York © 2007 The Munch Museum/The Munch-Ellingsen Group/Artists Rights Society (ARS), New York; *right* © Flip Schulke/Corbis; **3** *left, Sosteniendo el Tiempo* (1998), Satenik Tekyan. Mixed media, 95 cm × 80 cm. www.artesur.com/satenik; *right* © The Royal Shakespeare Company, London; **8** *top* © Bettmann/Corbis; *center* AP/Wide World Photos; *bottom* Rex USA; **10** *top to bottom* © 1995 Universal City Studios, Inc./Courtesy of Universal Studios Licensing LLLP; © Getty Images; © J. Silver/SuperStock; Photograph by Sharon Hoogstraten; NASA; **14** © Jo-Ann Richards/Veer; **16** *left* © Sonny T. Senser/Age Fotostock America, Inc.; *center* © Herb Watson/Corbis; *right* © Time & Life Pictures/Getty Images; **17** *left* © PhotoDisc; *right* © Flying Colours Ltd./Getty Images; **18** © Jason Ernst/Age Fotostock America, Inc.; **19** *left* © Stock4B/Getty Images; *center* © John Henley/Corbis; *right* © Flying Colours, Ltd./Getty Images.

UNIT 1

21 *left, Utopie* (1999), Bob Lescaux. Oil on canvas, 81 cm × 65 cm. Private Collection. Photo © Bridgeman Art Library; *right* © Gavin Hellier/Getty Images; **22** *left* © MGM/The Kobal Collection; *right* © Dreamworks/Warner Bros./Andrew Cooper/The Kobal Collection; **24** *left* © Don Farrall/Getty Images; *center left* © Herman Agopian/Getty Images; *center right* © Anthony Nagelmann/Getty Images; *right* © Tim Thompson/Corbis; **32** © Nick White/Getty Images; **33** © Marko Shark/Corbis; **44** © Ted Streshinsky/Corbis; **45** © Frank Capri/Hulton Archive/Getty Images; **47** *Home Chores* (1945), Jacob Lawrence. Gouache and graphite on paper. 29 1/2″ × 21 1/16″. Anonymous gift. The Nelson-Atkins Museum of Art, Kansas City, Missouri. F69-6. Photo by Jamison Miller © 2008 The Jacob and Gwendolyn Lawrence Foundation, Seattle/Artists Rights Society (ARS), New York; **56** *top* © 1992 Roland L. Freeman; *bottom, Crazy patchwork quilt* (1875), unknown artist. © Smithsonian Institution, Washington, D.C./Bridgeman Art Library; **60** © Japack Company/Corbis; **61** © Beth Gwinn; **74** © Chase Swift/Corbis; **75** © Underwood & Underwood/Corbis; **77** © Jeff Vanuga/Corbis; **79** © Gordon Wiltsie/Getty Images; *inset* © Ted Wood/Getty Images; **82** © Tim Thompson/Corbis; *inset* © Don Farrall/Getty Images; **87** © Ragnar Sigurdsson/Getty Images; *inset* © Herman Agopian/Getty Images; **91** © Anthony Nagelmann/Getty Images; *inset* © James Martin/Getty Images; **94** © Jeff Vanuga/Corbis; **95** © Ted Streshinsky/Corbis; **96** © Photo by Ric Potter; **100** © David W. Hamilton/Getty Images; **101** AP/Wide World Photos; **103** © Corbis; **106** © Bettmann/Corbis; **108** © Corbis; **111** © 1990 Michael A. Smith/People Weekly; **112** © Bettmann/Corbis; **113** Wharton Communication, University of Pennsylvania; **115** NASA; **117** © Bettmann/Corbis; **118, 123, 125** NASA; **126** © Bettmann/Corbis; **130** NASA; **131** © 1995 Universal City Studios/Courtesy of Universal Studios Licensing LLLP; **132** *top left, bottom left* © 1995 Universal City Studios, Inc./Courtesy of Universal Studios Licensing LLLP; *background* © Richard Wahlstrom/Getty Images; **134** © Erin Patrice O'Brien/Getty Images; **135** *top* AP/Wide World Photos; *bottom* Christopher Felver/Corbis; **142, 148** © Craig Aurness/Corbis; **149** © Charles Gupton/Corbis; **156** © Siede Preis/Photodisc/Getty Images.

UNIT 2

157 *left* © Illustration Works/Getty Images; *right* © Benno de Wilde/ Imageshop-Zefa Visual Media, UK, Ltd./Alamy Images; 158 *left* Cover of *Robin Hood* illustrated by N.C. Wyeth. Public Domain; 158–159 © Phil Schermeister/Corbis; 162 *top left* © Volker Möhrke/Corbis; *top right* © Don Johnston/Stone/Getty Images; *bottom* © Alberto Incrocci/ The Image Bank/Getty Images; 164 © Getty Images; 166 © Steve Taylor/Getty Images; 167 Photo by Madison Nye; 169 © Ray Laskowitz/ Lonely Planet Images; 172 © Getty Images; 176 © Helen King/Corbis; 178 © Steve Lovegrove/Picture Tasmania Photo Library; 182 © Gary Conner/Index Stock/PictureQuest/Jupiterimages Corporation; 185 © Foodpix/Jupiterimages Corporation; 186 © The Image Bank/Getty Images; 187 AP/Wide World Photos; 189 © Illustration Works/Getty Images; 191, 196 © Images.com/Corbis; 198 © Photodisc Green/ Getty Images; 202 © Vaide Dambrauskaite/istockphoto.com; © Vaide Seskauskie/Shutterstock; 203 © Marilyn Silverstone/Magnum Photos; 208 © Delphoto/PictureQuest/Jupiterimages Corporation; 210 © Duomo/ Corbis; 211 AP/Wide World Photos; 213 © Eddie Adams; 214, 215, 217 © Courtesy of Nicholas Gage; 222 © Buzz Bailey/Getty Images; 223 Courtesy of Mimi; 224 *Campesino* (1938), Diego Rivera. © 2008 Banco de México Diego Rivera & Frida Kahlo Museums Trust. Av. Cinco de Mayo No. 2, Col. Centro, Del. Cuauhtémoc 06059, Mexico, D.F. 231 © Leland Bobbé/Corbis; 226 *Peasants*, Diego Rivera. © 2008 Banco de México Diego Rivera & Frida Kahlo Museums Trust. Av. Cinco de Mayo No. 2, Col. Centro, Del. Cuauhtémoc 06059, Mexico, D.F. ; 230 *Campesino* (1938), Diego Rivera. Watercolor with black ink on rice paper, 38.7 cm × 27.7 cm. Private collection. Photo © The Bridgeman Art Library © 2008 Banco de México Diego Rivera & Frida Kahlo Museums Trust. Av. Cinco de Mayo No. 2, Col. Centro, Del. Cuauhtémoc 06059, Mexico, D.F. 236 © Tom Stewart/Corbis; 237 *top* © 2002 Margaretta K. Mitchell; *bottom* © Schomburg Center/Art Resource, New York; 239 © Images.com/Corbis; 242 © Chris Collins/Corbis; 243 © Hulton Archive/Getty Images; 245 *The Promenade* (1917), Marc Chagall. Oil on canvas. Photo © Scala/ Art Resource, New York. © 2008 Artists Rights Society (ARS), New York/ADAGP, Paris; 246 *The Window at the Country House* (1915), Marc Chagall. Photo © Scala/Art Resource, New York; 249 *Woman Reaping* (before 1930), Marc Chagall. National Gallery, Prague, Czech Republic. Photo © Nimatallah/Art Resource, New York © 2008 Artists Rights Society (ARS), New York/ADAGP, Paris; 250 *The Harvest*, Natalia Goncharova. Russian State Museum, St. Petersburg, Russia. Photo © Scala/Art Resource, New York © 2008 Artists Rights Society (ARS), New York/ADAGP, Paris; 261 *left, right, Finding Forrester.* Courtesy of Columbia Pictures; 262 *background* Photo by Sharon Hoogstraten; *top left, bottom left, Finding Forrester.* Courtesy of Columbia Pictures; 263 *left* © Andersen Ross/Photodisc Green/Getty Images; *right* © David Young-Wolff/Getty Images; 264, 270 © Joseph Sohm; ChromoSohm Inc./Corbis; 271 © Mark Richards/PhotoEdit; 278 © Siede Preis/Photodisc/Getty Images.

UNIT 3

279 *left, Sudden Shower over Shin-Ohashi Bridge and Atake* (1800s), Ando Hiroshige or Utagawa. Plate 58 from *One Hundred Famous Views of Edo.* Woodblock color print. © Brooklyn Museum of Art, Brooklyn, New York/ Bridgeman Art Library; *right* © Michael S. Yamashita/Corbis; 280 Photo by Gordon Lewis; 284 *top, left to right* © Erik Simonsen/Getty Images; © Royalty-Free/Corbis; © Firefly Productions/Corbis; © Photofest; *bottom, left to right* © Photofest; © Jon Deshler/Corbis; © Michael Keller/Corbis; © Jon Deshler/Corbis; 288 © Kathleen Finlay/Masterfile; 289 National Archives; 304 © www.CartoonStock.com; 305 © Bassouls Sophie/Corbis Sygma; 307, 309, 311, 312, 316, 317 © PhotoDisc; 320 © Philip Gould/ Corbis; 321 The Granger Collection, New York; 323, 330 Illustration by Dave Henderson/Mendola Ltd.; 332 © Paul Conklin/PhotoEdit; 333 © Rune Hellestad/Corbis; 348 © PhotoDisc; 352 AP/Wide World Photos; 353 © Mario Ruiz/Time Life Pictures/Getty Images; 355 AP/Wide World Photos; 360 © A. Ramey/PhotoEdit; 361 © Patrick Sylvain; 368, 374 © Daryl Benson/Masterfile; 375 © Sonny T. Senser/Age Fotostock America, Inc.; 382 © Siede Preis/Photodisc/Getty Images.

UNIT 4

383 *left, Civilization is a method of living, an attitude of equal respect for all men* from the series, *Great Ideas of Western Men* (1955), George Giusti. India ink and goache on paper, 24⁷/₈″ × 18⁵/₁₆″. Gift of the Container Corporation of America. Smithsonian American Art Museum, Washington, D.C. Photo © Smithsonian American Art Museum, Washington, D.C./Art Resource, New York; *right* AP/Wide World Photos; 384–385 AP/Wide World Photos; 386 *left* © British Library, London/akg-images, London; *center, Venus, hunting, appears to Aeneas*, Pietro da Cortona. Louvre, Paris. © Erich Lessing/Art Resource, New York; *right* TM & © 2005 Marvel Characters, Inc. Used with permission; 394 © Matthew Antrobus/Getty Images; 395 The Granger Collection, New York; 397 © Johner/Getty Images; 399 © Brad Wilson/Getty Images; 402 © Chase Swift/Corbis; 406 © Digital Vision/Getty Images; 407 © Chris Hellier/Corbis; 420 © Olson Scott/Corbis Sygma; *background* © Artbeats; 421 © Mark Mainz/ Getty Images; 423 © David Papazian Photography, Inc./Getty Images; 427 Photo by Sharon Hoogstraten; 428 *top center* AP/Wide World Photos; *curtain/wall/chair/TV* © PhotoDisc; Photo by Sharon Hoogstraten; 430, 433 Photo by Sharon Hoogstraten; 436 *top center* AP/Wide World Photos; *TV* PhotoDisc; Photo by Sharon Hoogstraten; 438 *left* © MacNeil-Lehrer Productions. Reprinted by permission; © PhotoDisc; *right* © MacNeil-Lehrer Productions. Reprinted by permission; 442 © Philip James Corwin/ Corbis; 443 *top* The Granger Collection, New York; *bottom* Photo © Nancy E. Crampton; 446 *Lamentation: Memorial for Ernst Barlach* (1940), Käthe Kollwitz. Bronze.© SuperStock, Inc.; 448 © Jeff Greenberg/PhotoEdit; 449 The Granger Collection, New York; 454 © Peter Turnley/Corbis; 455 *top* Courtesy of the author; *bottom* China Stock Photography; 457 © Reuters/Corbis; 461 © Corbis; 464, 470 © Richard Sisk/Jupiterimages Corporation; 471 © Spencer Grant/ PhotoEdit; 478 © Siede Preis/Photodisc/Getty Images.

UNIT 5

479 *left* © Bob Rowan; Progressive Image/Corbis; *right, Path Through the Forest* (1914), Suzanne Valadon. Oil on canvas. Musée Fabre, Montpelier, France. © Superstock, Inc./SuperStock © 2007 Artists Rights Society (ARS), New York/ADAGP, Paris; **480–481** © David McLain/Getty Images; **482** © Ross Anania/Getty Images; **486** © Larry Brownstein/Getty Images; **488** © Rob Casey/Getty Images; **489** AP/Wide World Photos; **494** © Wayne Bennett/Corbis; **495** © Nancy E. Crampton; **497** © Charles Krebs/Corbis; **498** © Kennan Ward/Corbis; **500** © Getty Images; **504** © Charles Krebs/Corbis; **505** *top center* © Biophoto Associates/Photo Researchers, Inc.; *bottom* © Keith Kasnot; **506** *top left* © Photodisc/Getty Images; *center left* Illustration by Debbie Maizels; *right* © Donna Disario/Corbis; **508** AP/Wide World Photos; **509** © David Katzenstein/Corbis; **511, 516** © Sarah Doehring; **519** © Wayne Williams/Smokejumper Center/USDA Forest Service; **520** AP/Wide World Photos; **524** © W. Perry Conway/Corbis; **525** *top* © Getty Images; *center left, center right* © NBC News Archives; *bottom left* © Comstock Images/Punchstock; *bottom right* © Getty Images; **526** *background* © Sam Barricklow/Workbookstock.com/Jupiterimages Corporation; *top left* © NBC News Archives; **528** © Phil Hunt/Getty Images; **529** AP/Wide World Photos; **542** *Niña* (1943), Julia Diaz. Oil on canvas. 30 cm x 35 cm. Courtesy of the Julia Diaz Foundation; **543, 544** *top* Rex USA; **544** *bottom* GeoNova, LLC; **546** AP/Wide World Photos; **547** *top* Courtesy Pat Mora/Photo by Cheron Bayna; *bottom* © Photograph of Rita Dove by Fred Viebahn; **549** © Galen Rowell/Corbis; **551** *left, right* The Architect of the Capitol, Office of the Curator, March 2001; **552** PBS ® and the PBS logo are registered trademarks of the Public Broadcasting Service and are used with permission. All rights reserved.; **554, 560** © Daryl Benson/Masterfile; **561** *left* © Mary Kate Denny/PhotoEdit; *right* © Tom Prettyman/PhotoEdit; **568** © Siede Preis/Photodisc/Getty Images.

UNIT 6

569 *left, The Merry Jesters* (1906), Henri Rousseau. © Philadelphia Museum of Art/Corbis; *right* © Michael Nichols/Getty Images; **570–571** © Getty Images; **575** *left* © Jon Riley/Getty Images; *right* © Robin Nelson/PhotoEdit; **577** © ThinkStock/SuperStock; **578** © Ron Fehling/Masterfile; **579** © Bernard Gotfryd/Hulton Archive/Getty Images; **580** © Tom Stewart/Corbis; **586** © Francisco Cruz/SuperStock; **587** © Time Life Pictures/Getty Images; **588** © Corbis; **590** © Charles O'Rear/Corbis; **592** © Craig Aurness/Corbis; **593** AP/Wide World Photos; **595** © Corbis; **596** © Lester Lefkowitz/Corbis; **599** © Kevin Fleming/Corbis; **604** © Alan Schein Photography/Corbis; **605** AP/Wide World Photos; **607** © Michael Nichols/Getty Images; **609** © Tom Brakefield/Corbis; **610** Photo © Susan Farley; **613** © Martin Harvey; Gallo Images/Corbis; **618** © Charles E. Rotkin/Corbis; **620** © LWA-Paul Chmielowiec/Corbis; **623** © Bettmann/Corbis; **628, 629** AP/Wide World Photos; **644** © Michael Keller/Corbis; **645** © Michael Nicholson/Corbis; **656** *frame* © Getty Images; **666** © Richard Levine/Alamy Images; **667** *top right, center right* Courtesy of Ronald Reagan Presidential Library; *bottom right* Democratic National Committee; **668** *top left* Courtesy of Ronald Reagan Presidential Library; *background, bottom left* Democratic National Committee; **669** © Paul Barton/Corbis; **670, 676** © J. David Andrews/Masterfile; **677** © Dynamic Graphics Group/Creatas/Alamy Images; **680** *background* © David Jeffrey/Getty Images; *foreground* © Joson/zefa/Corbis; **684** © Siede Preis/Photodisc/Getty Images.

UNIT 7

685 *left, Graffiti Divas* (2003), Jen Thario. Spray paint on paper, 22″ × 22″. © Jen Thario; *right* © Galen Rowell/Corbis; **686** © Massimo Mastrorillo/Corbis; **690** © Paul Edmondson/Getty Images/Jupiterimages Corporation; **696** © David W. Hamilton/Getty Images/Jupiterimages Corporation; **697** *top* © Getty Images; *center* The Granger Collection, New York; *bottom* AP/Wide World Photos; **699** *Spring Landscape* (1909), Constant Permeke. Constant Permeke Museum, Jabbeke, Belgium. Photo © Dagli Orti/The Art Archive; **704** © oote boe/Alamy Images; **705** *top* The Granger Collection. New York; *center* © Christopher Felver/Corbis; *bottom* © Michael Glaser/St. Mary's College of Maryland; **707** *Cape Cod Morning* (1950), Edward Hopper. Photo © Smithsonian American Art Museum, Washington, D.C./Art Resource, New York; **708** © Brooks Walker/Getty Images; **709** © James Marshall/Corbis; **712** © Corbis; **713** *top* © Bettmann/Corbis; *center* © Christopher Felver/Corbis; *bottom* © Bettmann/Corbis; **714–715** © Davies & Starr/Getty Images; **717** © Getty Images; **718** © Tom Brakefield/Corbis; **720** © Brooklyn Productions/Getty Images; **721** *top* The Granger Collection, New York; *center* AP/Wide World Photos; *bottom* © Sam Falk/New York Times Company/Getty Images; **723** © Robert Houser/Index Stock Imagery; **726** © The Nobel Foundation; **728** © Universal Press Syndicate; **729** *top* The Granger Collection, New York; *bottom* © Bettmann/Corbis; **734** © Peter Mason/Getty Images; **735** *top* © Bettmann/Corbis; *bottom* © Corbis; **739** *Melancholy*, Edvard Munch. National Gallery, Oslo, Norway. Photo © Scala/Art Resource, New York/Artists Rights Society (ARS), New York; **742** *The Vitriol Thrower* (1894), Eugene Grasset. Lithograph. Cecil Higgins Art Gallery, Bedford, Bedfordshire, United Kingdom. Photo © Bridgeman Art Library; **743** © Manuela Hoefer/Getty Images; **746, 752** © Jason Ernst/Age Fotostock America, Inc.; **753** © Ryan McVay/Getty Images; **760** © Siede Preis/Photodisc/Getty Images.

UNIT 8

761 *left, Sunflowers,* Vincent van Gogh © Philadelphia Museum of Art/Corbis; *right* © Evan Sklar/Getty Images/Jupiterimages Corporation; **762–763** © Thomas Hoepker/Magnum Photos; **764** *left* © Hulton-Deutsch Collection/Corbis; *right* © PhotoDisc; **766** *left, Nathaniel Hawthorne* (1840), Charles Osgood. Oil on canvas. © Peabody Essex Museum, Salem, Massachusetts /Bridgeman Art Library; *right* © Getty Images; **770** © Tomek Sikora/Getty Images; **771** © Bettmann/Corbis; **773–785** Illustration © Cliff Nielson; **792** © Albert Normandin/Masterfile; **793** National Archives; **795** © Peter Casolino/Corbis; **796–797** © Kevin Fleming/Corbis; **798** © Time Life Pictures/Getty Images; **800** © Michael DeYoung/Corbis; **801** National Archives; **808** © Getty Images; **809** *top, center* © Bettmann/Corbis; *bottom* National Archives; **810** © Farrell Grehan/Corbis; **811** © Firefly Productions/Corbis; **812** © Evan Sklar/Getty Images/Jupiterimages Corporation; **814** *left* © Banana Stock/Age Fotostock America, Inc.; *right* © Scott Tysick/Masterfile; **815** © Gene Blevins/Corbis; **824** *Sandra Cisneros* (2000), Raquel Valle Senties. Oil, 20 " × 20". www.soycomosoyyque.com; **825** © Gene Blevins/Corbis; **828, 834** © Alain Choisnet/Getty Images; **835** *left* © Getty Images; *right* © CD Library; **842** © Siede Preis/Photodisc/Getty Images.

UNIT 9

843 *left, Miss Liberty* (1987), Malcah Zeldis. Oil on corrugated cardboard. Smithsonian American Art Museum, Washington, D.C. Photo © Smithsonian American Art Museum, Washington, D.C./Art Resource, New York; *right* © Bettmann/Corbis; 844–845 © Scott Braut; 846 AP/Wide World Photos; 847 © Photodisc Green/Getty Images; 848 © Bettmann/Corbis; 850 © Sophie Bassouls/Corbis Sygma; 852 © Eric Bouvet/Corbis Sygma; 853 © Owen Franken/Corbis; 860 AP/Wide World Photos; 864 © John Florea/Time Life Pictures/Getty Images; 865 © Photo by Howard Ikemoto; 867 © Bettmann/Corbis; 869, 870 © Corbis; 873 © Dorothea Lange/Wra/National Archives/Time Life Pictures/Getty Images; 874 © Bettmann/Corbis; 880 © Joseph Sohm; ChromoSohm Inc./Corbis; 881 © William Coupon/Corbis; 883 © Flip Schulke/Corbis; 884 Library of Congress, Prints and Photographs Division/AP/Wide World Photos; 887 © Don Cravens/Time Life Pictures/Getty Images; 889 Photo © Dan Weiner/Courtesy Sandra Weiner; 892 © Flip Schulke/Corbis; 894 © Bettmann/Corbis; 896 © Corbis; 897 Photo Courtesy of Chinua Achebe; 907 Photo by Sharon Hoogstraten; 908 © Keith Neale/Masterfile; 909 © Marilyn Knapp Litt; 911 © Getty Images; 912–913 © Randy Faris/Corbis; 912, 913 © David J. and Janice L. Frent Collection/Corbis; 917 © Reg Charity/Corbis; *background* © American Map Corporation; 918 © Chris M. Rogers/Getty Images; *background* © American Map Corporation; 921 © Layne Kennedy/Corbis; *background* © American Map Corporation; 923 © Getty Images; *background* © American Map Corporation; 924 © Thinkstock/Getty Images; *background* © American Map Corporation; 930 © Gary Houlder/Corbis; 931 *top* The Granger Collection, New York; *bottom* © John Eddy/University of Pittsburgh Press; 932 © Bettmann/Corbis; 934 © Alinari Archives/Corbis; 936 *left* © David Arky/Corbis; *center* © Ian McKinnell/Getty Images; *right* © Jim Wehtje/Getty Images; 937 *top* © The New Yorker Collection. © 2001 Mike Twohy from cartoonbank.com. All Rights Reserved.; *center, 9-11–The World's Finest Comic Book Writers & Artists Tell Stories to Remember* © 2003 DC Comics. All rights reserved. Used with permission; *bottom, background* © age-fotostock/SuperStock; *bottom-inset* © Anser Institute for Homeland Security; 938 *left, 9-11–The World's Finest Comic Book Writers & Artists Tell Stories to Remember* © 2003 DC Comics. All rights reserved. Used with permission; *bottom* © Scott Braut; 940, 946 © Sam Barricklow/Jupiterimages Corporation; 947 © Rachel Epstein/PhotoEdit; 950 © Bill Sanders/Kentucky Library and Museum, Western Kentucky University; 954 © Siede Preis/Photodisc/Getty Images.

UNIT 10

955 *left* © Bridgeman Art Library/Getty Images; *right* © 1999 TNT, Inc. A Time Warner Company/Photofest; 956–957 NASA Johnson Space Center; 958 *The Three Fates,* Pietro della Vecchia. Galleria Estense, Modena, Italy. Photo © Alinari/Art Resource, New York; 960 *Combat between Lancelot and Gawain* (1400s) from the *Cycle de Lancelot.* MS Fr 120, f.590 v.107a. Bibliotheque Nationale de France, Paris. Photo © Bibliotheque Nationale de France, Paris; 964 *top* © Donald Cooper/Photostage; *bottom* © Archivo Iconografico, S.A./Corbis; 966 © Bettmann/Corbis; 967 The Granger Collection, New York; 969, 971, 975, 981, 984–985, 989, Photo © 1989 Martha Swope; 995 Photo © 1987 Martha Swope; 999 Photo © 1989 Martha Swope; 1010 © Kelly-Mooney Photography/Corbis; 1030 © Toby Melville/Reuters/Corbis; 1031 © Bettmann/Corbis; 1044 © Bettmann/Corbis; 1045 *top, Miguel de Cervantes* (1800s). Stipple engraving. The Granger Collection, New York; *bottom* © Martha Nelly Garza/Dale Wasserman; 1047, 1051, 1053 © 1999 TNT, Inc. A Time Warner Company/Photofest; 1056 © Joan Marcus; 1064, 1070 © Jupiterimages Corporation © PictureQuest; 1071 © Michelle D. Bridwell/PhotoEdit; 1078 © Siede Preis/Photodisc/Getty Images.

UNIT 11

1079 *left* © Christie's Images/SuperStock; *right* © International Shakespeare Globe Centre, Ltd.; **1082** *top* © G. P. Bowater/Alamy Images; *left* © Archivo Iconografico, S.A./Corbis; *right* © Bettmann/Corbis; **1083** © Andrea Pistolesi/Getty Images; **1084** © Nik Wheeler/Corbis; **1085** *left* © Paramount/The Kobal Collection; *right* © Bob Basha /Miramax/ Dimensional Films/The Kobal Collection; **1086** *Brutus,* Michelangelo. Museo Nazionale del Bargello, Florence. Marble. Inv. 97. © Erich Lessing/ Art Resource, New York; **1094** © Bob Daemmrich/Stock Boston; **1095** © Bettmann/Corbis; **1096–1097** © Nik Wheeler/Corbis; **1099** © International Shakespeare Globe Centre, Ltd.; **1109** *top* © Getty Images; *center* The cast of The Shakespeare Theatre's 1993–1994 production of William Shakespeare's *Julius Caesar.* Directed by Joe Dowling. Photo by Richard Anderson; *bottom* © Joan Marcus/ArenaPal/Topham/The Image Works, Inc.; **1117** © Pete Jones/ArenaPal/Topham/The Image Works, Inc.; **1125** *top* Helen Carey as Portia and Robert Stattel as Marcus Brutus in The Shakespeare Theatre's 1993–1994 production of *Julius Caesar.* Directed by Joe Dowling. Photo by Richard Anderson; *center* © 1988 Martha Swope/ Time Inc.; *bottom* Photo © Pete Jones/ArenaPal/Topham/The Image Works; **1135** © International Shakespeare Globe Centre, Ltd.; **1138** *top* Photo by Manuel Harlan. © The Royal Shakespeare Company, London; *center* Photo © Clive Barda/ArenaPal/Topham/The ImageWorks; *bottom* © The Royal Shakespeare Company, London; **1155** © Colin Willoughby/ ArenaPal/Topham/The Image Works, Inc.; **1159** *top* © The Royal Shakespeare Company; *center* Photo by Martha Swope © Time Inc.; *bottom* Robert Stattel as Marcus Brutus and Philip Goodwin as Caius Cassius in The Shakespeare Theatre's 1993–1994 production of William Shakespeare's *Julius Caesar.* Directed by Joe Dowling. Photo by Richard Anderson; **1163, 1171, 1174** © International Shakespeare Globe Centre, Ltd.; **1183** *left* © 2005 Eddie Guy; *center* © Teacher's Discovery, Auburn Hills, Michigan; *right* © Michael Diamond/ArenaPal/Topham/The Image Works, Inc.; **1186** © Nik Wheeler/Corbis; **1190** *Mark Antony's Oration,* George Edward Robertson. Oil on canvas. © Hartlepool Museum Service, Cleveland, United Kingdom. Photo © Bridgeman Art Library; **1191, 1192** *left top, center* Clip from *Julius Caesar.* Courtesy of Paramount Pictures.; *background* © M. Angelo/Corbis; **1194** © Neil Emmerson/Getty Images; **1201** © Ryan McVay/Getty Images; **1206** © Neil Emmerson/Getty Images; **1207** © Comstock Images /Getty Images; **1208** © Siede Preis/Photodisc/Getty Images.

UNIT 12

1209 © Michael Newman/PhotoEdit; **1210–1211** © William Whitehurst/ Corbis; **1212** © Michael Newman/PhotoEdit; **1216** © Google; **1217** © About.com; **1219** © Chicago Public Library, Chicago, Illinois; **1220** *background* © 1994 Artbeats; *left* © CMCD, Inc.; *right* © Bryan Mullennix/Photodisc Green/Getty Images; **1221** *top* Cover of *The Concise Animal Encyclopedia* by David Burnie. Cover design by Jo Brown. © Kingfisher Publications Plc 2003 a Houghton Mifflin Company imprint; *bottom* Cover of *National Geographic Atlas of the World, Eighth Edition* © 2004. Published by permission of the National Geographic Society, Washington, D.C., Cover image Public Domain; **1222** The WorldCat screen shot is used with OCLC's permission. WorldCat™is a registered trademark of OCLC Online Computer Library Center, Inc; **1224** *top* © Time Life Pictures/Getty Images; *center* © Crain's Chicago Business; *bottom* Cover of *The Instrumentalist Magazine.* Photo © University of Illinois, Champaign, Illinois; **1227** *muscians* © Nicholas Monu/ iStockphoto.com; *notes and waves* © Paola Condreas/iStockphoto.com; *bottom* © PhotoDisc; **1228** © PhotoDisc; **1229** *top* © The Charlotte Observer. Reprinted by permission of The Charlotte Observer; *bottom* © Digital Vision/Getty Images; **1233** © Antonello Tuchetti/Photodisc Red/ Getty Images; **1234, 1254** © Claver Carroll/Jupiter Images; **1255** *top left* © Archivo Iconografico, S.A./Corbis; *bottom left* © PhotoDisc; *right* © Spencer Grant/PhotoEdit; **1257** *top* © Archivo Iconografico, S.A./Corbis; *bottom* © PhotoDisc.

STUDENT RESOURCE BANK

R6 Illustration by Dan Stuckenschneider; **R7** GeoNova, LLC; **R14** © Corbis; **R15** © E.R. Degginger/Color-Pic, Inc.; **R16** © 2005 Infospace, Inc. All rights reserved. Reprinted with permission of Infospace, Inc.; **R20** © Brookfield Zoo, Brookfield, Illinois; **R84** © Digital Vision/Getty Images; **R92** © Photofest.

BACK COVER

© Getty Images.

OHIO ACADEMIC CONTENT STANDARDS FOR ENGLISH LANGUAGE ARTS GRADE 10

1 Acquisition of Vocabulary

Contextual Understanding

1.1 Define unknown words through context clues and the author's use of comparison, contrast and cause and effect.

Conceptual Understanding

1.2 Analyze the relationships of pairs of words in analogical statements (e.g., synonyms and antonyms, connotation and denotation) and infer word meanings from these relationships.

1.3 Infer the literal and figurative meaning of words and phrases and discuss the function of figurative language, including metaphors, similes, idioms and puns.

1.4 Analyze the ways that historical events influenced the English language.

Structural Understanding

1.5 Use knowledge of Greek, Latin and Anglo-Saxon roots, prefixes and suffixes to understand complex words and new subject-area vocabulary (e.g., unknown words in science, mathematics and social studies).

Tools and Resources

1.6 Determine the meanings and pronunciations of unknown words by using dictionaries, glossaries, technology and textual features, such as definitional footnotes or sidebars.

2 Reading Process: Concepts of Print, Comprehension Strategies and Self-Monitoring Strategies

Comprehension Strategies

2.1 Apply reading comprehension strategies, including making predictions, comparing and contrasting, recalling and summarizing and making inferences and drawing conclusions.

2.2 Answer literal, inferential, evaluative and synthesizing questions to demonstrate comprehension of grade-appropriate print texts and electronic and visual media.

Self-Monitoring Strategies

2.3 Monitor own comprehension by adjusting speed to fit the purpose, or by skimming, scanning, reading on, looking back, note taking or summarizing what has been read so far in text.

Independent Reading

2.4 Use criteria to choose independent reading materials (e.g., personal interest, knowledge of authors and genres or recommendations from others).

2.5 Independently read books for various purposes (e.g., for enjoyment, for literary experience, to gain information or to perform a task).

3 Reading Applications: Informational, Technical and Persuasive Text

3.1 Identify and understand organizational patterns (e.g., cause-effect, problem-solution) and techniques, including repetition of ideas, syntax and word choice, that authors use to accomplish their purpose and reach their intended audience.

3.2 Critique the treatment, scope and organization of ideas from multiple sources on the same topic.

3.3 Evaluate the effectiveness of information found in maps, charts, tables, graphs, diagrams, cutaways and overlays.

3.4 Assess the adequacy, accuracy and appropriateness of an author's details, identifying persuasive techniques (e.g., transfer, glittering generalities, bait and switch) and examples of propaganda, bias and stereotyping.

3.5 Analyze an author's implicit and explicit argument, perspective or viewpoint in text.

3.6 Identify appeals to authority, reason and emotion.

3.7 Analyze the effectiveness of the features (e.g., format, graphics, sequence, headers) used in various consumer documents (e.g., warranties, product information, instructional materials), functional or workplace documents (e.g., job-related materials, memoranda, instructions) and public documents (e.g., speeches or newspaper editorials).

3.8 Describe the features of rhetorical devices used in common types of public documents, including newspaper editorials and speeches.

4 Reading Applications: Literary Text

4.1 Compare and contrast an author's use of direct and indirect characterization, and ways in which characters reveal traits about themselves, including dialect, dramatic monologues and soliloquies.

4.2 Analyze the features of setting and their importance in a literary text.

4.3 Distinguish how conflicts, parallel plots and subplots affect the pacing of action in literary text.

4.4 Interpret universal themes across different works by the same author or by different authors.

4.5 Analyze how an author's choice of genre affects the expression of a theme or topic.

4.6 Explain how literary techniques, including foreshadowing and flashback, are used to shape the plot of a literary text.

4.7 Recognize how irony is used in a literary text.

4.8 Analyze the author's use of point of view, mood and tone.

4.9 Explain how authors use symbols to create broader meanings.

4.10 Describe the effect of using sound devices in literary texts (e.g., to create rhythm, to appeal to the senses or to establish mood).

4.11 Explain ways in which an author develops a point of view and style (e.g., figurative language, sentence structure and tone), and cite specific examples from the text.

5 Writing Processes

Prewriting

5.1 Generate writing ideas through discussions with others and from printed material, and keep a list of writing ideas.

5.2 Determine the usefulness of and apply appropriate pre-writing tasks (e.g., background reading, interviews or surveys).

5.3 Establish and develop a clear thesis statement for informational writing or a clear plan or outline for narrative writing.

5.4 Determine a purpose and audience and plan strategies (e.g., adapting focus, content structure, and point of view) to address purpose and audience.

5.5 Use organizational strategies (e.g., notes, outlines) to plan writing.

Drafting, Revising and Editing

5.6 Organize writing to create a coherent whole with an effective and engaging introduction, body and conclusion, and a closing sentence that summarizes, extends or elaborates on points or ideas in the writing.

5.7 Use a variety of sentence structures and lengths (e.g., simple, compound and complex sentences; parallel or repetitive sentence structure).

5.8 Use paragraph form in writing, including topic sentences that arrange paragraphs in a logical sequence, using effective transitions and closing sentences and maintaining coherence across the whole through the use of parallel structures.

5.9 Use language, including precise language, action verbs, sensory details and colorful modifiers, and style as appropriate to audience and purpose, and use techniques to convey a personal style and voice.

5.10 Use available technology to compose text.

5.11 Reread and analyze clarity of writing, consistency of point of view and effectiveness of organizational structure.

5.12 Add and delete information and details to better elaborate on stated central idea and more effectively accomplish purpose.

5.13 Rearrange words, sentences and paragraphs and add transitional words and phrases to clarify meaning and maintain consistent style, tone and voice.

5.14 Use resources and reference materials (e.g., dictionaries and thesauruses) to select effective and precise vocabulary that maintains consistent style, tone and voice.

5.15 Proofread writing, edit to improve conventions (e.g., grammar, spelling, punctuation and capitalization), identify and correct fragments and run-ons and eliminate inappropriate slang or informal language.

5.16 Apply tools (e.g., rubric, checklist and feedback) to judge the quality of writing.

Publishing

5.17 Prepare for publication (e.g., for display or for sharing with others) writing that follows a manuscript form appropriate for the purpose, which could include such techniques as electronic resources, principles of design (e.g., margins, tabs, spacing and columns) and graphics (e.g., drawings, charts and graphs) to enhance the final product.

6 Writing Applications

6.1 Write narratives that:

   6.1.a sustain reader interest by pacing action and developing an engaging plot (e.g., tension and suspense);

   6.1.b use a range of strategies and literary devices including figurative language and specific narration;

   6.1.c include an organized, well-developed structure.

6.2 Write responses to literature that organize an insightful interpretation around several clear ideas, premises or images and support judgments with specific references to the original text, to other texts, authors and to prior knowledge.

6.3 Write business letters, letters to the editor and job applications that:

6.3.a address audience needs, stated purpose and context in a clear and efficient manner;

6.3.b follow the conventional style appropriate to the text using proper technical terms;

6.3.c include appropriate facts and details;

6.3.d exclude extraneous details and inconsistencies;

6.3.e provide a sense of closure to the writing.

6.4 Write informational essays or reports, including research that:

6.4.a pose relevant and tightly drawn questions that engage the reader;

6.4.b provide a clear and accurate perspective on the subject;

6.4.c create an organizing structure appropriate to the purpose, audience and context;

6.4.d support the main ideas with facts, details, examples and explanations from sources;

6.4.e document sources and include bibliographies.

6.5 Write persuasive compositions that:

6.5.a support arguments with detailed evidence;

6.5.b exclude irrelevant information;

6.5.c cite sources of information.

6.6 Produce informal writings (e.g., journals, notes and poems) for various purposes.

7 Writing Conventions

Spelling

7.1 Use correct spelling conventions.

Punctuation and Capitalization

7.2 Use correct capitalization and punctuation.

Grammar and Usage

7.3 Use clauses (e.g., main, subordinate) and phrases (e.g., gerund, infinitive, participial).

7.4 Use parallel structure to present items in a series and items juxtaposed for emphasis.

7.5 Use proper placement of modifiers.

8 Research

8.1 Compose open-ended questions for research, assigned or personal interest, and modify questions as necessary during inquiry and investigation to narrow the focus or extend the investigation.

8.2 Identify appropriate sources and gather relevant information from multiple sources (e.g., school library catalogs, online databases, electronic resources and Internet-based resources).

8.3 Determine the accuracy of sources and the credibility of the author by analyzing the sources' validity (e.g., authority, accuracy, objectivity, publication date and coverage, etc.).

8.4 Evaluate and systematically organize important information, and select appropriate sources to support central ideas, concepts and themes.

8.5 Integrate quotations and citations into written text to maintain a flow of ideas.

8.6 Use style guides to produce oral and written reports that give proper credit for sources, and include an acceptable format for source acknowledgement.

8.7 Use a variety of communication techniques, including oral, visual, written or multimedia reports, to present information that supports a clear position about the topic or research question and to maintain an appropriate balance between researched information and original ideas.

9 Communication: Oral and Visual

Listening and Viewing

9.1 Apply active listening strategies (e.g., monitoring message for clarity, selecting and organizing essential information, noting cues such as changes in pace) in a variety of settings.

9.2 Interpret types of arguments used by the speaker such as authority and appeals to audience.

9.3 Evaluate the credibility of the speaker (e.g., hidden agendas, slanted or biased material) and recognize fallacies of reasoning used in presentations and media messages.

9.4 Identify how language choice and delivery styles (e.g., repetition, appeal to emotion, eye contact) contribute to meaning.

Speaking Skills and Strategies

9.5 Demonstrate an understanding of the rules of the English language and select language appropriate to purpose and audience.

9.6 Adjust volume, phrasing, enunciation, voice modulation and inflection to stress important ideas and impact audience response.

9.7 Vary language choices as appropriate to the context of the speech.

Speaking Applications

9.8 Deliver informational presentations (e.g., expository, research) that:

9.8.a demonstrate an understanding of the topic and present events or ideas in a logical sequence;

9.8.b support the controlling idea or thesis with well-chosen and relevant facts, details, examples, quotations, statistics, stories and anecdotes;

9.8.c include an effective introduction and conclusion and use a consistent organizational structure (e.g., cause-effect, compare-contrast, problem-solution);

9.8.d use appropriate visual materials (e.g., diagrams, charts, illustrations) and available technology to enhance presentation;

9.8.e draw from multiple sources, including both primary and secondary sources, and identify sources used.

9.9 Deliver formal and informal descriptive presentations that convey relevant information and descriptive details.

9.10 Deliver persuasive presentations that:

9.10.a establish and develop a logical and controlled argument;

9.10.b include relevant evidence, differentiating between evidence and opinion, to support a position and to address counter-arguments or listener bias;

9.10.c use persuasive strategies, such as rhetorical devices, anecdotes and appeals to emotion, authority and reason;

9.10.d consistently use common organizational structures as appropriate (e.g., cause-effect, compare-contrast, problem-solution);

9.10.e use speaking techniques (e.g., reasoning, emotional appeal, case studies or analogies).

Holistic Rubric for the Ohio Graduation Test in Writing

6 This is a superior piece of writing. The prompt is directly addressed, and the response is effectively adapted to audience and purpose. It is exceptionally developed, containing compelling ideas, examples, and details. The response, using a clearly evident organizational plan, actively engages the reader with a unified and coherent sequence and structure of ideas. The response consistently uses a variety of sentence structures, effective word choices and an engaging style.

5 This is an excellent piece of writing. The prompt is directly addressed and the response is clearly adapted to audience and purpose. It is very well developed, containing strong ideas, examples, and details. The response, using a clearly evident organizational plan, engages the reader with a unified and coherent sequence and structure of ideas. The response typically uses a variety of sentence structures, effective word choices and an engaging style.

4 This is an effective piece of writing. While the prompt is addressed and the response adapts to audience and purpose, there are occasional inconsistencies in the response's overall plan. The response is well developed, containing effective ideas, examples and details. The response, using a good organizational plan, presents the reader with a generally unified and coherent sequence and structure of ideas. The response often uses a variety of sentence structures, appropriate word choices and an effective style.

3 This is an adequate piece of writing. While the prompt is generally addressed and the response shows an awareness of audience and purpose, there are inconsistencies in the response's overall plan. Although the response contains ideas, examples and details, they are repetitive, unevenly developed and occasionally inappropriate. The response, using an acceptable organizational plan, presents the reader with a generally unified and coherent sequence and structure of ideas. The response occasionally uses a variety of sentence structures, appropriate word choices and an effective style.

2 This is a marginal piece of writing. While an attempt is made to address the prompt, the response shows at best an inconsistent awareness of audience and purpose. When ideas, examples and details are present, they are frequently repetitive, unevenly developed and occasionally inappropriate. The response, using a limited organizational plan, does not present the reader with a generally unified and coherent sequence and structure of ideas. The response is exemplified by noticeable lapses in sentence structure, use of appropriate word choices and a clear, readable style.

1 This is an inadequate piece of writing. There is a weak attempt made to address the prompt. The response shows little or no awareness of audience and purpose. There is little or no development of ideas, or the response is limited to paraphrasing the prompt. There is little or no evidence of organizational structure. The response is exemplified by severe lapses in sentence structure, use of appropriate word choices and a clear, readable style.

0 The following are categories of papers that cannot be scored: off task, completely illegible, in a language other than English, or no response.

Conventions Rubric for the Ohio Graduation Test in Writing

3 The written response is free from errors that impair a reader's understanding and comprehension. Few errors, if any, are present in capitalization, punctuation and spelling. The writing displays a consistent understanding of grammatical conventions.

2 Occasional errors may impair a reader's understanding of the written response. Some capitalization, punctuation and spelling errors are present. The writing displays some understanding of grammatical conventions.

1 Errors are frequent and impair a reader's understanding of the written response. Numerous errors in capitalization, punctuation and spelling are present. The writing displays a minimal understanding of grammatical conventions.

0 The following are categories of papers that cannot be scored: off task, completely illegible, in a language other than English, or no response.
OR
The length and complexity of the response are insufficient to demonstrate the writer has control over standard English conventions.